DATE DUE

			PRINTED IN U.S.A.

CLASSICAL AND MEDIEVAL LITERATURE CRITICISM

Guide to Gale Literary Criticism Series

When you need to review criticism of literary works, these are the Gale series to use:

If the author's death date is:	You should turn to:

After Dec. 31, 1959 (or author is still living)

Contemporary Literary Criticism

for example: Jorge Luis Borges, Anthony Burgess, William Faulkner, Mary Gordon, Ernest Hemingway, Iris Murdoch

1900 through 1959

Twentieth-Century Literary Criticism

for example: Willa Cather, F. Scott Fitzgerald, Henry James, Mark Twain, Virginia Woolf

1800 through 1899

Nineteenth-Century Literature Criticism

for example: Fedor Dostoevski, Nathaniel Hawthorne, George Sand, William Wordsworth

1400 through 1799

Literature Criticism From 1400 to 1800 (*excluding Shakespeare*)

for example: Anne Bradstreet, Daniel Defoe, Alexander Pope, François Rabelais, Jonathan Swift, Phillis Wheatley

Shakespearean Criticism

Shakespeare's plays and poetry

Antiquity through 1399

Classical and Medieval Literature Criticism

for example: Dante, Homer, Plato, Sophocles, Vergil, the Beowulf Poet

Gale also publishes related criticism series:

Black Literature Criticism

This three-volume series presents criticisms of works by major black writers of the past two hundred years.

Children's Literature Review

This series covers authors of all eras who have written for the preschool through high school audience.

Short Story Criticism

This series covers the major short fiction writers of all nationalities and periods of literary history.

Poetry Criticism

This series covers poets of all nationalities and periods of literary history.

Drama Criticism

This series covers dramatists of all nationalities and periods of literary history.

ISSN 0896-0011

Volume 10

CLASSICAL AND MEDIEVAL LITERATURE CRITICISM

Excerpts from Criticism of the Works of World
Authors from Classical Antiquity through the
Fourteenth Century, from the First Appraisals
to Current Evaluations

Jelena O. Krstović
Editor

Tina Grant
Alan Hedblad
Michael W. Jones
James E. Person, Jr.
Associate Editors

Gale Research Inc. · *DETROIT* · *WASHINGTON, D.C.* · *LONDON*

STAFF

Jelena O. Krstović, *Editor*

edblad, Michael W. Jones, James E. Person, Jr., *Associate Editors*

James A. Edwards, Meggin M. Greaves, Eric Priehs, Brian J. St. Germain, Debby Wells, *Assistant Editors*

Jeanne A. Gough, *Permissions & Production Manager*

Linda M. Pugliese, *Production Supervisor*

Paul Lewon, Maureen Puhl,
Camille Robinson, Jennifer VanSickle, *Editorial Associates*

Donna Craft, Rosita D'Souza, Sheila Walencewicz, *Editorial Assistants*

Sandra C. Davis, *Permissions Supervisor (Text)*

Maria L. Franklin, Josephine M. Keene, Michele M. Lonoconus, Denise M. Singleton,
Kimberly F. Smilay, *Permissions Associates*

Brandy Johnson, Shalice Shah,
Permissions Assistants

Margaret A. Chamberlain, *Permissions Supervisor (Pictures)*

Pamela A. Hayes, *Permissions Associate*

Karla Kulkis, Keith Reed, Nancy Rattenbury, *Permissions Assistants*

Victoria B. Cariappa, *Research Manager*

Maureen Richards, *Research Supervisor*

Robert Lazich, Mary Beth McElmeel, Tamara C. Nott, *Editorial Associates*

Andrea B. Ghorai, Daniel J. Jankowski, Julie Karmazin, *Editorial Assistants*

MaryBeth Trimper, *Production Director*

Catherine Kemp, Mary Winterhalter, *Production Assistants*

Cynthia Baldwin, *Art Director*

Nicholas Jakubiak, C. J. Jonik, Yolanda Y. Latham, *Keyliners*

Since this page cannot legibly accommodate all the copyright notices, the Appendix constitutes an extension of the copyright notice.

While every effort has been made to ensure the reliability of the information presented in this publication, Gale Research Inc. does not guarantee the accuracy of the data contained herein. Gale accepts no payment for listing; and inclusion in the publication of any organization, agency, institution, publication, service, or individual does not imply endorsement of the editors or publisher. Errors brought to the attention of the publisher and verified to the satisfaction of the publisher will be corrected in future editions.

The paper used in this publication meets the minimum requirements of
American National Standard for Information Sciences—Permanence Paper
for Printed Library Materials, ANSI Z39.48-1984.

Copyright © 1993 by
Gale Research Inc.
835 Penobscot Building
Detroit, MI 48226

All rights reserved including the right of reproduction in whole or in part in any form.

Library of Congress Catalog Card Number 88-658021
ISBN 0-8103-7956-2
ISSN 0896-0011

Printed in the United States of America

Published simultaneously in the United Kingdom by Gale Research International Limited
(An affiliated company of Gale Research Inc.)

Contents

Preface   vii

Acknowledgments   xi

Preface

Since its inception in 1988, *Classical and Medieval Literature Criticism* has been a valuable resource for students and librarians seeking critical commentary on the writers and works of these periods in world history. Major reviewing sources have assessed *CMLC* as "useful" and "extremely convenient," noting that it "adds to our understanding of that rich legacy left by the ancient period and the Middle Ages," and praising its "general excellence in the presentation of an inherently interesting subject." No other single reference source has surveyed the critical reaction to classical and medieval literature as thoroughly as *CMLC*.

Scope of the Series

CMLC is designed to serve as an introduction for students and advanced readers of the works and authors of antiquity through the fourteenth century. The great poets, prose writers, dramatists, and philosophers of this period form the basis of most humanities curricula, so that virtually every student will encounter many of these works during the course of a high school and college education. By organizing and reprinting an enormous amount of commentary written on classical and medieval authors and works, *CMLC* helps students develop valuable insight into literary history, promotes a better understanding of the texts, and sparks ideas for papers and assignments. Each entry in *CMLC* presents a comprehensive survey of an author's career, an individual work of literature, or a literary topic, and provides the user with a multiplicity of interpretations and assessments. Such variety allows students to pursue their own interests; furthermore, it fosters an awareness that literature is dynamic and responsive to many different opinions.

CMLC continues the survey of criticism of world literature begun by Gale's *Contemporary Literary Criticism (CLC), Twentieth-Century Literary Criticism (TCLC), Nineteenth-Century Literature Criticism (NCLC), Literature Criticism from 1400 to 1800 (LC)* and *Shakespearean Criticism (SC)*. For additional information about these and Gale's other criticism series, users should consult the Guide to Gale Literary Criticism Series preceding the title page in this volume.

Coverage

Each volume of *CMLC* is carefully compiled to present:

- criticism of authors and works who represent a variety of genres, time periods, and nationalities

- both major and lesser-known writers and works of the period (such as non-Western authors and literature increasingly read by today's students)

- 4 - 6 authors or works per volume

- individual entries that survey the critical response to each author or work, including early criticism, later criticism to represent any rise or decline in the author's reputation, and current retrospective analyses. The length of each author or work entry also indicates relative importance, reflecting the amount of critical attention the author or work has received from critics writing in English, and from foreign criticism in translation.

An author may appear more than once in the series if his or her writings have been the subject of a substantial amount of criticism; in these instances, specific works or groups of works by the author will be covered in separate entries. For example, Homer will be represented by three entries, one devoted to the *Iliad,* one to the *Odyssey,* and one to the Homeric Hymns.

Starting with Volume 10, *CMLC* will also occasionally include entries devoted to literary topics. For example, *CMLC*-10 focuses on Arthurian Legend and includes general criticism on that subject as well as individual entries on writers or works central to that topic—Chrétien de Troyes, Gottfried von Strassburg, Layamon, and the Alliterative *Morte Arthure.*

Organization of the Book

An author entry consists of the following elements: author heading, biographical and critical introduction, principal English translations or editions, excerpts of criticism (each preceded by an annotation and followed by a bibliographic citation), and a bibliography of further reading.

- The **author heading** consists of the author's most commonly used name, followed by birth and death dates. If the entry is devoted to a work, the heading will consist of the complete title, followed by the most common form of the title in English translation (if applicable), and the date of the original composition. Located at the beginning of the introduction are any name or title variations.

- A **portrait** of the author is included when available. Many entries also feature illustrations of materials pertinent to the author or work, including manuscript pages, book illustrations, and representations of people, places, and events important to a study of the author or work.

- The **biographical and critical introduction** contains background information that introduces the reader to an author or work and to the critical debate surrounding that author or work. When applicable, biographical and critical introductions are followed by references to additional entries on the author in other literary reference series published by Gale, including *Short Story Criticism, Dictionary of Literary Biography, Children's Literature Review,* and *Something about the Author.*

- The list of **principal English translations** or **editions** is chronological by date of first publication and is included as an aid to the student seeking translated versions or editions of these works for study. The list will focus primarily on twentieth-century translations, selecting those works most commonly considered the best by critics.

- **Criticism** is arranged chronologically in each entry to provide a useful perspective on changes in critical evaluation over the years. All titles by the author featured in the critical entry are printed in boldface type to enable the user to ascertain without difficulty the works being discussed. Also for purposes of easier identification, the critic's name and the publication date of the essay are given at the beginning of each piece of criticism. Anonymous criticism is preceded by the title of the journal in which it appeared. Publication information (such as publisher names and book prices) and parenthetical numerical references (such as footnotes or page and line references to specific editions of works) have been deleted at the editors' discretion to provide smoother reading of the text. Many critical entries in *CMLC* also contain translations to aid the users.

- Critical excerpts are prefaced by **annotations** providing the reader with information about both the critic and the criticism that follows. Included are the critic's reputation, his or her approach to literary criticism, the scope of the excerpt, and the growth of critical controversy or changes in critical trends regarding an author or work. In some cases, these notes include cross-references to excerpts by critics who discuss each other's commentary. Dates in parentheses within the annotation refer to a book publication date when they follow a book title, and to an essay date when they follow a critic's name.

- A complete **bibliographic citation** designed to facilitate the location of the original essay or book follows each piece of criticism.

- An annotated bibliography of **further reading** appears at the end of each entry and lists additional secondary sources on the author or work. In some cases it includes essays for which the editors could not obtain reprint rights.

Topic entries are subdivided into several thematic rubrics in which criticism appears in order of descending scope.

Cumulative Indexes

Each volume of *CMLC* includes a cumulative index listing all authors who have appeared in *Contemporary Literary Criticism, Twentieth-Century Literary Criticism, Nineteenth-Century Literature Criticism, Literature Criticism from 1400 to 1800, Classical and Medieval Literature Criticism,* and *Short Story Criticism,* along with cross-references to the Gale series *Children's Literature Review, Authors in the News, Contemporary Authors, Contemporary Authors Autobiography Series, Dictionary of Literary Biography, Concise Dictionary of American Literary Biography, Something about the Author, Something about the Author Autobiography Series,* and *Yesterday's Authors of Books for Children.* Useful for locating an author within the various series, this index is particularly valuable for those authors who are identified with a certain period but who, because of their death dates, are placed in another, or for those authors whose careers span two periods. For example, Geoffrey Chaucer, who is usually considered a medieval author, is found in *Literature Criticism from 1400 to 1800* because he died after 1399.

Beginning with the tenth volume, *CMLC* includes a cumulative index listing all topic entries that have appeared in the Gale Literary Criticism Series *Classical and Medieval Literature Criticism, Contemporary Literary Criticism, Literature Criticism from 1400 to 1800, Nineteenth-Century Literature Criticism,* and *Twentieth-Century Literary Criticism.*

Beginning with the second volume, *CMLC* also includes a cumulative nationality index. Authors and/or works are grouped by nationality, and the volume in which criticism on them may be found is indicated.

Title Index

Each volume of *CMLC* also includes an index listing the titles of all literary works discussed in the series. Foreign language titles that have been translated are followed by the titles of the translations—for example, *Slovo o polku Igorove (The Song of Igor's Campaign).* Page numbers following these translated titles refer to all pages on which any form of the title, either foreign language or translated, appears. Titles of novels, dramas, nonfiction books, and poetry, short story, or essay collections are printed in italics, while all individual poems, short stories, and essays are printed in roman type within quotation marks. In cases where the same title is used by different authors, the author's name or surname is given in parentheses after the title, e.g. *Collected Poems* (Horace) and *Collected Poems* (Sappho).

Critic Index

An index to critics, which cumulates with the second volume, is another useful feature of *CMLC.* Under each critic's name are listed the authors and/or works on whom the critic has written and the volume and page number where criticism may be found.

A Note to the Reader

When writing papers, students who quote directly from any volume in the Literary Criticism Series may use the following general forms to footnote reprinted criticism. The first example pertains to material drawn from a periodical, the second to material reprinted from books.

Rollo May, "The Therapist and the Journey into Hell," *Michigan Quarterly Review,* XXV, No. 4 (Fall 1986), 629-41; excerpted and reprinted in *Classical and Medieval Literature Criticism,* Vol. 3, ed. Jelena O. Krstovic (Detroit: Gale Research, 1989), pp. 154-58.

Dana Ferrin Sutton, *Self and Society in Aristophanes* (University Press of America, 1980); excerpted and reprinted in *Classical and Medieval Literature Criticism,* Vol. 4, ed. Jelena O. Krstovic (Detroit: Gale Research, 1990), pp. 162-69.

Suggestions Are Welcome

Readers who wish to suggest authors to appear in future volumes, or who have other comments regarding the series, are cordially invited to write or call the editors.

ACKNOWLEDGMENTS

The editors wish to thank the copyright holders of the excerpted criticism included in this volume, the permissions managers of many book and magazine publishing companies for assisting us in securing reprint rights, and Anthony Bogucki for assistance with copyright research. We are also grateful to the staffs of the Detroit Public Library, Wayne State University Purdy/Kresge Library Complex, and the University of Michigan Libraries for making their resources available to us. Following is a list of the copyright holders who have granted us permission to reprint material in this volume of *CMLC*. Every effort has been made to trace copyright, but if omissions have been made, please let us know.

COPYRIGHTED EXCERPTS IN *CMLC*, VOLUME 10, WERE REPRINTED FROM THE FOLLOWING PERIODICALS:

ACTA, v. XI, 1986. Copyright © 1986 by The Center for Medieval and Early Renaissance Studies. Reprinted by permission of the publisher.—*Euphorion,* v. 67, 1973. Reprinted by permission of the publisher.—*Forum for Modern Language Studies,* v. VI, January, 1970 for "Profanity and Its Purpose in Chrétien's *Cligés* and *Lancelot*" by D. D. R. Owen; v. XV, July, 1979 for "The Prison of the Senses: 'Fin' Amor' as a Confining Force in the Arthurian Romances of Chrétien de Troyes," by Raymond H. Thompson. Copyright © 1970, 1970 by *Forum for Modern Language Studies* and the authors. Both reprinted by permission of the publisher and the respective authors.— *History Today,* v. 37, November, 1987. © History Today Limited 1987. Reprinted by permission of the publisher.— *L'Esprit Créateur,* v. V, Winter, 1965. Copyright © 1965 by *L'Esprit Créateur.* Reprinted by permission of the publisher.—*The Modern Language Review,* v. LIX, October, 1964 for "Gottfried's *Tristan*: The Coherence of Prologue and Narrative" by H. B. Willson. © Modern Humanities Association 1964. Reprinted by permission of the publisher.—*Modern Philology,* v. 87, August, 1989, for "The Fictional Margin: The Merlin of the *Brut*" by Jeff Rider. © 1989 by The University of Chicago. Reprinted by permission of the University of Chicago Press and the author/ v. 71, November, 1973. © by The University of Chicago. Reprinted by permission of the University of Chicago Press.—*Nottingham Mediaeval Studies,* v. III, September, 1964. Reprinted by permission of the publisher.—*Papers on Language & Literature,* v. 22, Spring, 1986. Copyright © 1986 by the Board of Trustees, Southern Illinois University of Edwardsville. Reprinted by permission of the publisher.—*Philological Quarterly,* v. 56, Summer, 1977 for "Narrative Design in the Alliterative *Morte Arthure*" by James L. Boren. Copyright 1977 by The University of Iowa. Reprinted by permission of the publisher and the author.—*PMLA,* V. 85, October, 1970. Copyright © 1970 by the Modern Language Association of America. Reprinted by permission of the Modern Language Association of America.—*Romance Notes,* v. XII, Autumn, 1970; v. XXI, Spring, 1981. Both reprinted by permission of the publisher.—*Studia Neophilologica,* v. XLII, 1970. Reprinted by permission of the publisher.—*Tennessee Studies in Literature,* v. XI, 1966. Copyright © 1966, by The University of Tennessee Press. Reprinted by permission of The University of Tennessee Press.—*Transactions of the American Philosophical Society,* v. 78, 1988. Copyright © by The American Philosophical Society. Reprinted by permission of the publisher.

COPYRIGHTED EXCERPTS IN *CMLC*, VOLUME 10, WERE REPRINTED FROM THE FOLLOWING BOOKS:

Ashe, Geoffrey. From "The Arthurian Fact," in *The Quest for Arthur's Britain.* By Geoffrey Ashe and others. Frederick A. Praeger Publishers, 1968. © 1968 by Geoffrey Ashe. All rights reserved. Reprinted by permission of Henry Holt and Company, Inc.—Barron, W. R. J. and S. C. Weinberg. From an introduction to *The Arthurian Section of Layamon's "Brut" (Lines 9229—14297).* Edited and translated by W. R. J. Barron and S. C. Weinberg. Longman, 1989. All rights reserved. Reprinted by permission of the publisher.—Batts, Michael S. From *Gottfried von Strassburg.* Twayne, 1971. Copyright © 1971 by Twayne Publishers, Inc. All rights reserved. Reprinted with the permission of Twayne Publishers, an imprint of Macmillan Publishing Company.—Borges, Jorge Luis. From *Other Inquisitions: 1937-1952.* Translated by Ruth L. C. Simms. University of Texas Press. Reprinted by permission of the publisher.—Bromwich, Rachel. From "Celtic Elements in Arthurian Romance: A General Survey," in *The Legend of Arthur in the Middle Ages.* Edited by P. B. Grout and others. D. S. Brewer, 1983. © Rachel Bromwich. Reprinted by permission of the publisher.—Bryant, Nigel. From an introduction in *Perceval: The Story of the Grail.* By Chrétien de Troyes, translated by Nigel Bryant. D. S. Brewer, 1982. Translation © Nigel Bryant 1982. Reprinted by permission of the publisher.—Cline, Ruth Harwood. From an introduction to *Yvain: or, The Knight with the Lion.* By Chrétien de Troyes, translated by Ruth Harwood Cline. University of Georgia Press, 1975. Copyright © 1975 by Ruth Harwood Cline. All rights reserved. Reprinted by permission of the publisher.—Dean, Christopher.

Arthurian Legend

INTRODUCTION

Arthurian legend refers to a corpus of medieval literature whose principal subject is the exploits of Arthur, a sixth-century British king who fought to protect Britain from fierce Germanic tribes attempting to subjugate the island after the western Roman Empire collapsed. Originally concerned with the history of Arthur and the "Matter of Britain," the legend developed into a more literary than purely historical form during the Middle Ages, incorporating elements of Celtic myth and medieval chivalry. Further, by the twelfth century Arthurian legend had become established in the literatures of France, Germany, Italy and other countries, resulting in a great diversity of Arthurian characters, themes, and motifs. The appearance of Thomas Malory's *Le Morte Darthur* (1485) initiated yet a new phase in the development of the legend that continued during the Renaissance, followed by a notable decline in the seventeenth and eighteenth centuries. Apart from an extraordinary revival in the Victorian age, the literature surrounding the legend has received less attention in modern times. Nonetheless, scholars agree that the study of Arthurian literature is indispensable to an informed understanding of medieval culture and society.

Scholars typically divide Arthurian legend into two broadly overlapping domains, the "pseudo-historical Arthur" and Arthurian romance. The historical aspect of Arthurian legend developed chiefly in the British Isles. There Arthur's name is mentioned in conjunction with a number of battles in chronicles and poems beginning in the sixth century; but the most significant depiction of Arthur in the early histories is found in Nennius's *Historia Brittonum* (c. ninth century), which describes Arthur's twelve battles against the Saxons. The *Annales Cambriae* of the mid tenth century, the Welsh triads, and William of Malmesbury's *Gesta Regum Anglorum* (1125) further elaborate on the theme of Arthur as an heroic warrior king. Geoffrey of Monmouth's *Historia Regum Britanniae* (c. 1136), drawing on Bede, Nennius, and Welsh histories, contributes immeasurably to Arthurian legend. Geoffrey's glorified portrayal of Arthur transgresses historical fact, but in so doing introduces new motifs such as the Isle of Avalon, the figure of Merlin, and Arthur's sword, Excalibur. Robert Wace translated Geoffrey's *Historia* into French in his *Roman de Brut* (1155), introducing the theme of the Round Table and elements from French chivalric romances in his depiction of Arthur's court at the Isle of Avalon. Layamon's twelfth-century *Brut* further embellishes the mythical and martial aspects of Wace's history, and also enhances its purely supernatural elements, most notably in the figure of Merlin.

While in its early phase Arthurian legend was essentially confined to England, the real flowering of Arthurian romance occured in France during the late twelfth century. Chrétien de Troyes is considered undoubtedly the greatest contributor to that genre. His numerous verse romances

German sculpture of King Arthur, possibly from a group of the Nine Worthies, 13th c.

consolidate many of the legend's best known features: the romance of Lancelot and Guinevere, Sir Gawain as a model of noble conduct, and the quest for the mysterious "graal," or Holy Grail. Further, Chrétien shifted attention away from Arthur and toward his illustrious consort of knights, who henceforward became a primary leitmotif of the legend. Among Chrétien's numerous imitators were Robert de Boron, whose *Joseph d'Arimathie* (1191-1202?) lends a specifically Christian interpretation to the Grail legend, while his *Merlin* (c. 1200) is significant for introducing the motif of the sword in the stone. The "Matter of France" was the principal subject for two important anonymous works that appeared shortly afterwards, *Perlesvaus* (1225-50) and the Didot-*Perceval* (1200). The vogue for Arthurian romance also spread to Germany, where it was vigorously developed by Gottfried von

Strassburg in his *Tristan und Isolde* (c. 1210) and by Wolfram von Eschenbach in *Parzival* (1220?). These works were instrumental in establishing a specifically German mythological version of the legend, known as the "Matter of Germany." By the late thirteenth century Arthurian legend was firmly entrenched in the literatures of France, Spain, Italy, Scandinavia, the Low Countries, and even the Near East. Of these, the French Vulgate cycle (circa thirteenth century), a collection of five courtly romances by various authors, is considered the most important development in Arthurian legend at that time because it shifts treatment of the material from verse to prose.

Arthurian legend continued to evolve after the fourteenth century, most importantly in England. Among the best known works of the period are the alliterative *Morte Arthure* (c. 1375), influenced by French narrative poetry as well as the English chronicle tradition; *Sir Gawain and the Green Knight* (circa fourteenth century), the standard Middle English Arthurian romance; and the stanzaic *Le Morte Arthur* (c. 1460-80), an historical account of Arthur's reign based on French sources. Malory's markedly eclectic *Le Morte Darthur* distills prior Arthurian material into a unified cycle, thus completing the medieval phase of the legend. *Le Morte Darthur* is highly esteemed on several counts. It is a mirror of medieval culture, a seminal work of English prose, and an entertaining narrative of enduring value. William Caxton's printed edition codified Malory's text and achieved a wider circulation than any of the legend's predecessors.

During the English Renaissance, Arthurian legend was not forgotten. Edmund Spenser's epic poem *The Faerie Queene* (1590) resurrected Arthur both as a model for noble conduct and as an heroic complement to the work's protagonist, Gloriana, the Faerie Queen, an allegorical representation of Elizabeth I. Later, in the seventeenth and eighteenth centuries, the classical norms governing European literature practically excluded such medieval matters as Arthurian legend. An entirely new trend developed in the nineteenth century as poets and artists introduced a romanticized view of the Middle Ages into European literature. This was particularly true in England, where the Pre-Raphaelite Brotherhood, a group of artists and writers, advocated a new aesthetic that incorporated medieval elements and emphasized the depiction of Arthurian characters and scenes. As the century progressed, the revival of Arthuriana in literature become even more pronounced. Sir Walter Scott's *The Bridal of Triermain; or, The Vale of St. John* (1813), William Morris's *The Defence of Guenevere, and Other Poems* (1858), and Algernon Charles Swinburne's *Tristram of Lyonesse, and Other Poems* (1882) exemplify the prominent place the legend occupied in the poetry and fiction of the day. However, critics regard Alfred, Lord Tennyson's epic *Idylls of the King* (1859-85) as the central work in the Arthurian revival. In the *Idylls,* Tennyson examines the rise and fall of an ideal society, represented by Arthur's court, focusing on his concern about modern culture's growing tendency toward hedonism and its attendant rejection of spiritual values.

With the advent of Modernism in the early twentieth century, the formal literary development of Arthurian legend ended. Nonetheless, the legend continues to be reinterpreted in the realm of popular fiction and other media. Further, the early historical sources of the legend still attract the attention of archaeologists, and critics and scholars continue to study the vast domain of Arthurian literature in order to clarify the stylistic and thematic provenance of its numerous branches. Arthurian legend itself continues to resonate within Western culture, representing adventure, tragedy, and the idealism embodied by the code of chivalry.

The essays included in this entry focus on the origins of the Arthurian legend and its development to 1400. Additional coverage of the nineteenth-century Arthurian revival is contained in the following source published by Gale Research:*Nineteenth-Century Literature Criticism*, Vol. 36.

HISTORICAL CONTEXT AND LITERARY BEGINNINGS

Geoffrey Ashe

[Ashe is an English scholar and lecturer who has written extensively on the historical and literary aspects of Arthurian legend and has been involved with archaeological excavations in search of Camelot. In the following excerpt, Ashe reviews the historical context of the Arthurian legend and also documents the early written sources of the legend.]

From a strange medley of clues, patiently pieced together in the last forty or fifty years, one certainty at least emerges. The Arthurian Legend, however wide-ranging its vagaries, is rooted in an Arthurian Fact. As the legend is unique, so the fact is unique. In essence, it is this. Britain, alone among the lands of the Roman Empire, achieved independence before the northern barbarians poured in, and put up a fight against them—a very long, and at one stage a successful, fight. Between Roman Britain and Anglo-Saxon England there is an interregnum, which is not a chaos as historians once imagined, but a creative epoch with a character of its own. This rally of a Celtic people in some degree Romanised and Christianised is the reality of Arthur's Britain. It occurs in a dark age, the mysterious gap in British history. The modern investigator's problem is to bring light into the darkness—where it may, possibly, reveal the features of Arthur himself.

The story begins farther back, in the middle of the fourth century AD. 'Britannia', divided into four provinces, stretched from the Channel up to Hadrian's Wall, with a debatable zone beyond. The people were Celts, related to the Gauls and the Irish. But at the higher social levels there was no longer a sharp distinction between ruling 'Romans' and subject 'Britons'. Only in Wales was Roman rule predominantly an affair of alien garrisons. Elsewhere, the civil servants and army officers came from various countries, and some were British by birth or adoption. All free men were citizens of the Empire, and the better-off intermarried, spoke Latin and gave their children a classical education. While Caesar's word was law, Britons enjoyed a growing autonomy in local government and defence; London was a fairly important trading centre. The landowners, merchants and magistrates assembled on regional councils. The peasants supplied recruits for the army.

For some decades, a quiet reassertion of Celtic life-patterns had been going on within the imperial scheme. Towns—the conquerors' special institution—were less important than they had been. Celtic preference for the country expressed itself in the adoption of the Roman villa. Especially in the south-east and in what is now Gloucestershire, luxurious houses disposed round courts dotted the landscape. Here, with central heating and every comfort, lived many of the wealthier Britons as well as officials from other lands. Their households were large. Their dozens of slaves grew food and supplied basic needs. Britain was nearer to self-sufficiency than in previous centuries, though exporting as much: grain, iron, coal, hides, hunting-dogs (which were famous) and slave labour.

Christianity, rescued from persecution by the protection of the Emperor Constantine, was now the ascendant faith of the Roman world. It had been practised in Britain for many years. Its strength came from the educated class and their dependants. The peasants in the villages remained pagan. Britain had given four martyrs to the calendar, the best-known being St. Alban of Verulamium. In the fourth century, British bishops went overseas to the Church's councils, and British pilgrims made the long trip to the Holy Land, where priests exclaimed at their energy.

The island, indeed, deserved a share of the credit for the Church's prosperity. The reason lay in a sequence of events which proved that Britain was no mere backwater, no inert subject territory, but a place where things could happen. Within the memory of the oldest inhabitants, Britain had been the centre of an imperial crisis. An admiral named Marcus Aurelius Carausius, equipped with a fleet to drive off Saxon pirates, had set himself up as ruler of Britain *c.* 286 and declared his independence. The Emperor Constantius at last recaptured Britain, striking a medallion portraying London at his feet, with the motto 'Restorer of the Eternal Light'. Constantius remained in the country for some time, rebuilding the economy and protecting the coast with a chain of forts. The greater Constantine was his son, and in 306, at York, the army of Britain proclaimed Constantine emperor. He overthrew all his rivals, made Christianity the state religion and gave the Empire a peace marked in London by coins imprinted *Beata Tranquillitas*. At mid-century, that phrase was still not wholly ironic.

For Britons, the imperial system began to dissolve in 367. The island was suddenly attacked by three barbaric nations together. From across the North Sea, after a long lull, came Saxons—fierce, tricky Teutonic warriors in crazy boats, carrying short-swords, bows, lances and round wooden shields. Their ancestral home was in Schleswig-Holstein, but they had been advancing along

the German coast. In the north, parties of Picts scrambled past the garrisons and over the Wall—bearded, tattooed and armed with slings. In the west, the shores were harassed by Irish tribes whom the Romans called Scots, after one of their chief groups which had not yet settled in Caledonia. They sailed in hide-covered curraghs and blew terrifying blasts on enormous curled war-horns.

Raids had occurred before, but never in such force and never in concert. The defences collapsed. For months the invaders controlled the countryside, strengthened by runaway slaves and peasant malcontents. Towns were cut off. Roman authority was not fully restored till 369, and the social order did not recover even then. Too many villas had been wrecked, too many slaves had gone. Henceforth the Britons, in their exposed position far from the imperial centre, were more inclined to look to themselves. New temples were built to their old gods, in pursuance of a lead given about the time of the disaster, at Lydney in the Forest of Dean. Maiden Castle, the Dorset hill-fort, was the site of another such temple. Rustics camped in deserted villas and lit their cooking fires on the splendid mosaics.

But most of the Britons who had a voice in public affairs still saw themselves as members of the imperial world. They shared its civilisation with the citizens of other provinces, all the way to Mesopotamia. They had no wish to give up this heritage and merge totally into outer darkness. The question was whether they could survive. During the next hundred years, by a strange, zigzag process, Britain was to achieve her unparalleled status as a Roman land detached from Rome, holding out against the barbarians.

Unluckily, our chief witness to this process, and almost our only native one, is an irritating monk named Gildas. Somewhere about 545, he wrote a diatribe against the rulers of Britain in his day. This includes a survey of recent history, and is described very frankly as a *liber querulus* or Complaining Book. It is rhetorical, cryptic and sometimes plainly wrong. In retrospect Gildas exaggerates the Britons' tendency to be restless and unassimilable under Roman rule. But he gives us glimpses of the transition through the eyes of a literate cleric of Roman sympathies.

Gildas dates the essential break as far back as 383, when the army in Britain repeated the York coup of 306 by proclaiming its own emperor. Maximus was Spanish; but he probably had a British wife, and the revolt was largely a movement of Britons in protest against the government's corruption and its weakness in the face of continuing barbarian threats. Maximus asserted his claim throughout Western Europe. He captured Rome with a force which included Britons, many of them, it would seem, rashly withdrawn from the Wall. Unlike Constantine, he failed to progress beyond Italy. In 388, he was defeated and killed by the Emperor of the East, Theodosius. But his impact on the country which had enthroned him was permanent. It is said that the British settlement in Armorica, the future Brittany, was begun under his auspices. He lives on in the traditions of later ages as Prince Macsen, a hero of Welsh and Cornish folklore. Because of his adventure, the British sense of identity grew stronger.

However, it was a deeply troubled identity. After Maximus, Roman power was never completely re-established. Administration devolved on the regional councils or *civitates,* which soon had to cope with fresh assaults from three sides. In 395, the High King of Ireland, Niall-of-the-Nine-Hostages, led a pirate invasion that sacked Chester and Caerleon. Some of the Irish seized bits of territory in Wales and stayed on. Gildas—correct in his main drift, though sometimes wildly astray in his details—describes a series of British appeals for help. It may have been in response to the first of these that the imperial general Stilicho, himself partly German, came to Britain about 399 with reinforcements. He drove back the barbarians and tried to create an autonomous defensive system, entrusting the highlands and borderlands to native magnates under whom Celtic tribalism began to revive. Most of his troops left, but in 405 the Britons won a sea victory, killing Niall and much reducing the menace from Ireland.

The following year a Teutonic inroad into Gaul cut Britain off. After several internal coups, the remnant of the army again proclaimed its own emperor, a soldier who assumed the title of Constantine III. This is the Constantine who figures in Geoffrey of Monmouth. He also figures in Welsh legend as Bendigeit Custennin, Blessed Constantine, perhaps because he had close ties with the Church. Hopes that he would stay in Britain were dashed. Afraid to wait in case the real Emperor Honorius organised his removal, Constantine took the last legionaries overseas in 407 and traversed Gaul. His second-in-command was a Briton, Gerontius or Geraint. Becoming disillusioned, Gerontius undermined his leader's authority in the rear. Whether the Briton had what would now be called nationalistic motives, it is impossible to tell. But after another Saxon attack on Britain in 410, the regional councils, in effect, declared British independence. They wrote to Honorius saying they were still in the Empire, but not as subjects. He replied with a vague message telling them to look to their own safety, and leaving the question of sovereignty in the air. Constantine and Gerontius both perished in the continental turmoil, and the island stood alone.

The network of local dignitaries that now governed Britannia took measures for defence. Again there seemed to be a respite, again it did not last. The Picts, aided by Scottish settlers, continued to raid southward. Meanwhile, the Saxons were multiplying and spreading. They were planting themselves along the opposite coast, and they were overrunning Frisia, the modern Holland. Frisia could never satisfy them. The natives lived miserably on earth mounds, in constant fear of inundation, eating fish, drinking rain-water, burning peat and building up their mounds with rubbish and dung. The Saxons mingled with the mound-dwellers and found footholds in the silt. However, as their numbers increased, the prospect of colonisation in nearby Britain looked more and more alluring. A few perhaps were already living there, with or without official connivance, but not nearly enough to ease the pressure.

With the growth of danger, there may have been a British appeal to Rome to return. Gildas speaks of a second military rescue like Stilicho's. A strange source, the *Anglo-Saxon Chronicle,* records a Roman expedition to Britain in 418. Scanty clues suggest that these hints may be right, and that by some agreement with the regional councils, an imperial force did come back. If it did, the reoccupation was spectral. By 425 at latest, British independence was an accomplished fact. But the spiritual ties were not broken. Towards the middle of the fifth century, Prosper, a Gaulish chronicler, still contrasts the 'Roman' island of Britain with the 'barbarian' island of Ireland.

Over wide areas, the last of the urban and villa people remained in control for several decades. They kept up a shaky version of the old administrative system, and stayed in touch, through trade and otherwise, with the Mediterranean. They spoke a somewhat debased Latin, wrote the language in a fashion that aspired to be classical, and were mostly Catholic Christians, although a sense of established proprieties perhaps counted for more than conviction. The first Briton to affect the intellectual life of Europe was the heretic Pelagius, who taught in Rome and elsewhere from 405 onward. His writings are the earliest specimens of British literature. A waterer-down of Christian doctrine, he clashed with St Augustine and was condemned by the pope. But his ideas were brought back to his native country by a preacher named Agricola.

The peasants spoke only the Celtic British language, the ancestor of Welsh and Breton. They were still largely pagan, though Christianity was doubtless beginning to gain ground, as it had been gaining in Gaul since the missions of St Martin of Tours in the 370s. Apart from one or two technical innovations, their life was what it had been for centuries. But they were quietly rising in importance. The end of Roman rule had stopped the compulsory export of British grain, and the rural population was eating better and bringing new land under cultivation. In Verulamium the Roman theatre was a ruin, but not disused, because the traders in a neighbouring and flourishing vegetable market used it as a rubbish-dump.

Meanwhile, in the higher and wilder country, and especially in Wales, forces were astir which seemed likely to quicken the reversion to rural ways. Here tribalism was fast returning, and regional despots, who were already in effect tribal chiefs, had entrenched themselves. They claimed to be legitimate successors of Rome. The main basis of this claim was the frontier policy of which Stilicho had been the major exponent. British tribes had been planted north of the Wall to subdue the Picts, and dispositions of the same sort had been made in the west against the Irish. At some point, Cunedda, a northern chieftain, migrated to Wales, where he wiped out Irish buccaneer colonies and his sons founded local dynasties. But, besides deriving a title from such real or asserted measures of security, several British kinglets apparently claimed kinship with the pretender Maximus.

These new leaders appear in Welsh genealogies and legends with the title *gwledig*. The first *gwledig* is Maximus himself, Prince Macsen, the Briton-by-marriage. Those who come after him (with one exception to be noted) are manifestly men who stood for the Celtic way of life rather than the imperial. As their influence grew—promoted in lowland Britain, perhaps, by the exploitation of peasant grievances against Romanised landlords—the ancient

Celtic culture revived further. After centuries of eclipse, craftsmen were again making delicately embellished bowls and experimenting with designs in linear tracery. These craftsmen were to be found not only in Wales but in the south-east also.

The old religion, though doomed as such, also acquired a brief vigour that enabled it to live on in another form. At Lydney, the god Nodens inhabited a temple which was still fairly new. As Britain drifted into her age of transition, kindred Celtic figures emerged from the shadows into mythology, if not worship. It was a strange, confused, haunting mythology which passed later into Welsh folklore and the Arthurian Legend itself. Arthur, in one of his weirder guises, is a Wild Huntsman who rides through the clouds snatching the spirits of the dead; and his companion is Gwyn-ap-Nudd, Gwyn the son of Nodens. Gwyn is King of the Fairies and the underworld. Another transmuted god was Maponus, who became the hero Mabon. Another was Belinus, who became Beli son of Manogan, king of Britain and brother-in-law of the Virgin Mary. Among his relations was Bran the Blessed, who made an enchanted voyage across the Atlantic, and whose head, buried on Tower Hill, protected Britain against invasion. Both Beli and Bran occur in the pedigrees of several Welsh families. British consciousness, in fact, was flung by independence into a kaleidoscope of motifs and images. One of the results was the slow formation of the legends of Glastonbury, where Christian hermits were possibly already living. Gwyn-ap-Nudd was eventually said to have an unseen palace on Glastonbury Tor, and Bran reappeared as Brons, a keeper of the Holy Grail.

It would be wrong to picture a sharp early conflict between Romanised citizens and Celtic masses reverting to tribalism. Indeed, the key to Arthur lies in the fact that some Britons occupied intermediate ground, and that these included the best and most creative figures the island produced. Such were St Ninian, who went northward to Galloway as a missionary among the Picts, and St Patrick, who was the true founder of the Church in Ireland, though not the first Christian who ministered there. Patrick came from a western coastal district and his Latin was rustic. But his name was Roman—Patricius—and he regarded his Irish converts as Romans, Christianity being, for him, the religion of the imperial civilisation.

When a real cleavage divided British society, it happened because there were too few Britons like Patrick to hold it together. This was clearly a time of questioning and heartsearching. With the rise of a chieftain known as Vortigern, the trend away from Rome seems to have reached a point where it would not be absurd to speak of Celtic nationalism. Vortigern's home was probably in central Wales. He began to extend his influence about 425. His party favoured the Pelagian heresy as a native version of Christianity. This policy brought an envoy from Rome: not political but ecclesiastical Rome. Pope Celestine I sent over Germanus, bishop of Auxerre, a versatile cleric who is said to have practised as a lawyer and served as governor and commander in Armorica. Germanus sailed from Boulogne in 429 and threw all his abilities into the problems of Britain. He toured the decaying towns, meeting civic

dignitaries and opposing the heretics in public debate. Also he led a British force to repel a combined host of Pictish and Saxon raiders. The victory was bloodless. Coached by Germanus, the British soldiers roared 'Alleluia!' and the invaders fled in panic. For the moment, his efforts were fruitful. The Pelagians were not yet politically strong enough to hinder the mission. There is reason to think that a British bishop named Faustus, who had a brilliant career in Gaul, was a son of Vortigern whom Germanus detached from his heretical father.

Then the Saxons returned and grew steadily more menacing. By the 440s, their unrefuted boasts that they had things all their own way in Britain created an impression abroad that they had conquered the island. This was not so. Whatever Saxon settlements existed were not yet extensive. The raids, however, were severe, and the Britons had little military capacity left. According to Gildas, the councils sent a last appeal for imperial help, addressing it to the great general Aëtius in or about 446. No help was forthcoming, and the discredited Romanised element succumbed to the nationalists. Vortigern rose to ascendancy over much of Britain. The bishops, fearing a Pelagian revival under his aegis, had already asked Germanus to come over again. But the preachers of heresy were not numerous. Germanus founded schools for the better training of priests, and secured sentences of banishment against the active Pelagians: sentences in which Vortigern seems to have been driven to acquiesce.

The theological faction was no longer of use to Vortigern. He was in a strong position, and a flash of economic recovery gave him confidence. His resources, however, were unequal to the double challenge of Pict and Teuton. Though a seceder from the Empire, he adopted an imperial strategy: allowing one set of barbarians to live in the country as auxiliaries (*foederati*) and paying them to fight another set of barbarians. Somewhere about the middle of the fifth century, heathen warriors from across the North Sea began entering Britain as permitted colonists instead of as raiders and squatters. Three types could be distinguished: Saxons, Angles and Jutes, though the old term 'Saxon' tended to be used to cover them all. They came from various parts of the continental littoral. The record of their first and subsequent settlement is confused. But, roughly speaking, the Saxons made their way into Britain via Hampshire, Sussex and Essex; the Angles, across the east coast; and the Jutes, chiefly (though not solely) through Kent.

Their first authorised colonies did not stretch so far. The oldest accounts represent Vortigern and his council as inviting the Jutish brothers Hengist and Horsa to make their homes in Kent—the Isle of Thanet is mentioned—with three shiploads of mercenaries. More warriors and their families then arrived, and were stationed at various points on the east coast. Vortigern's plan succeeded in its immediate aim. His allies marched north and repulsed the Picts for good. But, lacking the Empire's treasury, he could not keep the policy up as the emperors had done. A dispute arose over the payments in kind which he had contracted to give. Negotiations broke down. The reinforced Jutes pushed forward to the Medway. The *Anglo-Saxon Chroni-*

cle notes a battle at Aylesford in 455, and the English monk Bede, a much better historian than the chronicler or Gildas, says that about the same time the Angles joined forces with the Picts whom they had just defeated. Legends of this crisis, which were used but not invented by Geoffrey of Monmouth, describe a fresh treaty and a marriage of Vortigern to Hengist's daughter. But if any peace was patched up, it did not last. The *Anglo-Saxon Chronicle* claims that in 457 the Britons were overwhelmed at Crayford and fled to London, abandoning Kent.

For a while the collapse was total. Massacre and pillage spread to the western sea, and refugees streamed away to the mountains, across to Armorica, and even to Spain. These Teutons who invaded Britain were not like those who invaded Gaul and Italy. The latter were Christians, although of the Arian heresy, and open to civilisation. The bandit swarms that swept Vortigern's regime into ruin were neither. They were more terrible; but also, in the end, they inspired a stronger will to resist.

After their first onslaught subsided and they were back at their bases, the question was not whether Britain could recover its former condition, but how much could be saved at all. Most towns were deserted, the semblance of political unity was gone. The local rulers were squabbling despots who could no longer produce even a genuine coinage. The Church, which had still been in touch with Gaul before the rout, was almost cut off.

Yet the discreditable failure of Vortigern had a surprising result. Over an area large enough to matter, the remnant of the Romanised and Catholic party came to the fore again. Its leader was Ambrosius Aurelianus, who was destined to join Vortigern and the pretender Constantine III as a character in Geoffrey of Monmouth's *History*. Reasons exist for connecting him with Gloucestershire, where the villa society reached an apogee. In Welsh tradition, Ambrosius is the *gwledig* Emrys, a borderland chief like other borderland chiefs, established in a citadel in northern Wales bestowed on him by Vortigern. But even the legends portray him as leading a rival party, and he clearly stood for a different culture and conviction. According to Gildas, his family had 'worn the purple'. Whichever emperor or pretender that phrase points to, Ambrosius raised his own standard, and the people who still called themselves 'citizens'—subjects of the Empire—flocked to it.

By the late 460s, a shrunken but not negligible Britannia was moving toward re-entry into the imperial scheme. Ambrosius is said to have built a navy. Certainly Britons could cross the Channel in large organised bands, despite the Saxon fleets, and the departure of fighting men did not lead to new Saxon inroads at home. In 470, a seaborne British force joined the Armorican settlers to fight for the Emperor Anthemius, who was trying to restore Roman authority in Gaul. The campaign failed and the final crumbling of Rome in the West halted this initiative. But it did occur. Ambrosius's Britons were the last nation north of the Alps to show any active loyalty to a Western emperor.

Within Britain, the Roman revival can hardly have been spectacular. It gave a last spell of popularity to the custom of calling children by Roman names: for example, Tacitus (which became Tegid), Constantine (Custennin), Paternus (Padarn), and—curiously—Tribune (Triphun). A dragon emblem, borne by the later emperors, was perhaps adopted at this time, whence ultimately the Red Dragon of Wales. 'Dragon' became a royal title. Gildas applies it to Maelgwn, the most important Welsh king of the sixth century, and in Arthurian legend Uther is called Pendragon, the Head Dragon.

Besides these details, the British Church became confirmed in its Catholicity, in its communion with the see of Rome and the orthodoxy of its teachings, although it was bound to diverge in its practices and very soon did. The wealthier Britons of the west imported oil, wine and other luxuries from the Mediterranean. A biographer of Germanus, writing fairly soon after Ambrosius's rise, felt able to speak of Britain as prosperous. Yet none of these developments would have carried much weight if Britain had been passively waiting for the next Saxon offensive. What gave Ambrosius his place both in history and legend was the fact of his taking the offensive himself.

The fortunes of the British counter-attack are obscure. Gildas makes nothing plain, except that it went on through victories and defeats for many years—probably about forty—and culminated in a British triumph at the 'siege of Mons Badonicus'. This battle brought a generation of peace and relative order, marred only by British feuds, not by heathen harassment. An early Welsh source, the *Annales Cambriae,* dates the 'battle of Badon' with a slight ambiguity in 516 or 518. The *Anglo-Saxon Chronicle,* while it ignores the Anglo-Saxons' defeats, sheds a little light by the petering-out of their victories. We get a dim impression of Hengist's Kentish kingdom being driven back into consolidation; of fresh Saxon landings along the south coast, followed by containment; and of a near-cessation of advance in mainland Britain from 514 to 547. Archaeology is consistent with a major Saxon retreat early in the sixth century, after a disaster in the region between Reading and Gloucester.

Interest centres on Mount Badon. This victory undoubtedly happened, and such things do not happen without leadership. But it comes too late for Ambrosius Aurelianus. The obvious question is the identity of the general who completed the work Ambrosius began. Gildas, while stressing the battle and its results, does not name this general. His only allusion is doubtful and oblique. But Gildas has an annoying habit of seldom naming anybody, and in this case he may have had a personal motive. Welsh tradition gives the commander's name with complete unanimity. It was Arthur; and the phase of British ascendancy after Badon was what Geoffrey made out to be Arthur's reign.

In assessing the value of this tradition, the first query is whether 'Arthur', as the name of a Celt born somewhere about the 470s, is credible. The answer is that it fits very well. It belongs to the same class as Tegid and Custennin, being a Celticised Roman name, in this case Artorius. A third-century officer called Artorius Justus held a command in Britain and may have left descendants. But the history of the name gives a more positive support to tradition than mere credibility. Before the sixth century, none of the known Artorii are natives of Britain. After 550, we have records of several such, including a prince in Argyll. The inference is that all these Arthurs were named after a British hero of slightly earlier date.

Another theory—that Arthur was a Celtic god, the centre of a pagan patriotic revival—will not bear looking into. Admittedly, the Arthur of legend has mythical attributes. He rides through the sky, he slays giants, he takes the form of a raven. But a Celtic deity with a Roman name seems unlikely. The extant records of Celtic religion show no trace of him. Also, we have Gildas's testimony. He denounces the sixth-century Britons for every wickedness under the sun . . . except apostasy. Their nominal Christianity is never in question. If a pagan revival had occurred, the vitriolic monk would have mentioned it.

Arthur, then, was a human being if he was anything. His status as a leader with an intelligible career rests mainly on one chapter in a Welsh *History of the Britons*. This chaotic work was compiled early in the ninth century by Nennius, a Bangor cleric striving to reassert national dignity after a long eclipse. His most valuable matter dates from a time not too hopelessly remote from Arthur's. The strongest point in Nennius's favour is, paradoxically, his sheer badness as a writer and scholar. On his own showing, he has simply 'made a heap of all he has found' in rummaging among ancient parchments and translating Welsh stories into his clumsy Latin. The result is not a literary fraud like Geoffrey of Monmouth's book, because Nennius is plainly not equal to that. The ingredients of his heap are authentic, whatever weight we give to them.

Nennius (or rather the document he transcribes when writing of the British war effort around 500) introduces Arthur as a man without dynastic rank. There were 'many more noble than he'. Then comes a sketch of his campaigns.

> Arthur fought against the Saxons alongside the kings of the Britons, but he himself was the leader in the battles [*dux bellorum*]. The first battle was at the mouth of the river which is called Glein. The next four were on the banks of another river, which is called Dubglas and is in the region Linnuis. The sixth was upon the river which is called Bassas. The seventh was in the wood of Celidon; that is, Cat Coit Celidon. The eighth was by Castle Guinnion, in which Arthur carried on his shoulders an image of St Mary Ever-Virgin, and there was a great slaughter of them, through the strength of Our Lord Jesus Christ and of the holy Mary his maiden-mother. The ninth was in the City of the Legion. The tenth was on the bank of the river which is called Tribruit. The eleventh was on the hill called Agned. The twelfth was on Mount Badon, in which—on that one day—there fell in one onslaught of Arthur's, nine hundred and sixty men; and none slew them but he alone, and in all his battles he remained victor.

In an appendix Nennius adds some bits of folklore. These connect 'Arthur the soldier' with places in Brecknockshire and Herefordshire, and refer to a son, Anir, whom Arthur

himself killed and buried. They do not look like history. The passage about the battles does. Precisely because the names are obscure, they are likely to be genuine. A literary contriver would have given us a comprehensible war fought on well-known sites. Arthur's lone exploit at Mount Badon has been invoked to dismiss the whole paragraph as fabulous. But the deeds of the great do get exaggerated. A similar tale is told of the Emperor Constantine. It is more to the point to ask where the places are, and whether Nennius is correct in ascribing so many victories to the same leader.

To begin with, the battles seem to be widespread. Various attempts to locate them all in one area are unconvincing and tend to cancel each other.

For three of the sites—Bassas, Guinnion and Agned—no cogent identification exists at all. The City of the Legion is Chester or Caerleon. The river Glein could be the Lincolnshire or the Northumberland Glen. Linnuis is probably the Lindsey district of Lincolnshire, bordered on the north by the Humber. The wood of Celidon figures in Welsh legend, and must be sought around the head-waters of the Tweed and Clyde, Celidon being Caledonia. Tribruit belongs to the same part of the Scottish Lowlands. This battle is mentioned in a Welsh poem which includes Bedwyr—the original Bedevere—among the warriors.

Glein and Linnuis could represent action against the Angles, encroaching up the Wash and the Humber. Celidon and Tribruit take Arthur to a turbulent region where the Picts were still strong, and where the British chieftains, to judge from a letter of St Patrick and other clues, were free-booters liable to strike out at anybody. Some foray into this lawless area might have produced a conflict that found its way into the list. The City of the Legion is frankly awkward. As for Badon, Gildas's Mons Badonicus, historical considerations confine it to the south. A good candidate (not the only one) is Liddington Castle, a hill-fort near Swindon, which has a village called Badbury at its foot. 'Badbury' is Saxon—Baddan-byrig—but the first part of this name could be derived from a Celtic 'Badon'. Britons of Arthur's time might have reoccupied the imposing earthworks.

This is probably the best that can be done with the map at present. How much further do we get with Arthur himself?

To Nennius, he is clearly a commander-in-chief rather than a king. In the *Annales Cambriae* he is likewise uncrowned. Under the year 516, or 518, we find the following:

> The battle of Badon in which Arthur carried the cross of Our Lord Jesus Christ, for three days and three nights, on his shoulders, and the Britons were victorious.

And twenty-one years later:

> The battle of Camlaun in which Arthur and Medraut were slain; and there was death in England and Ireland.

Here are Medraut, otherwise Modred the traitor, and the 'last weird dim battle'. Camlaun could be Camboglanna,

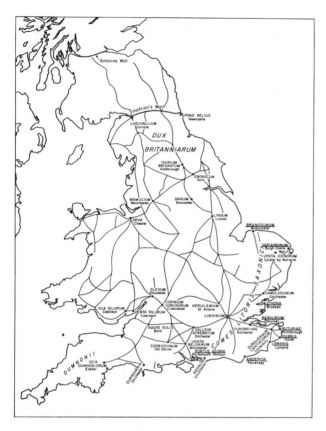

Map of Roman Britain around the end of the fourth century.

a fort on Hadrian's Wall, at Birdoswald in Cumberland. But the river Cam in Somerset, and the Camel in Cornwall, cannot be ruled out.

Records of a strictly historical kind yield no more. They disclose a British leader who almost certainly did command at Badon, because the immense credit of that triumph was never claimed for anyone else; and who fell at Camlaun. Even the two dates cannot be relied on, though the error is not likely to be great. To assess Nennius's grandiose picture, with its national captaincy, we must study Arthur as he appears in other contexts.

First, in Welsh poetry. This began with a school of bards in what is now Cumberland but was then the British kingdom of Rheged, toward the close of the sixth century. They and their successors know Arthur as a war-leader of proverbial glory, and take it for granted that their audiences do, never pausing to explain who he was. About the year 600, Aneirin composed a long poem, *Gododdin,* lamenting over a corps of nobles who died fighting the Angles at Catraeth (*i.e.,* Catterick). He says of one of them that, 'although he was no Arthur', his valour was great. That, unfortunately, is all. Arthur's presence in a poem about northerners does not imply that he was one of them. Aneirin knows southerners as well: a certain Gereint, for instance.

An early poem in a collection called the *Black Book of Carmarthen* gives a list of Arthur's followers. Among them are Kei and Bedwyr, *i.e.,* Kay and Bedevere. The same volume contains poems alluding to Arthur's son Llacheu and to a West Country force apparently known as Arthur's Men. None of these poems refers to Arthur as a king, but the last refers to him as *amherawdyr,* the Latin *imperator* or emperor. That title recurs in a medieval Welsh tale, *The Dream of Rhonabwy.*

Further poems speak of Arthur's horse, his kinsfolk, his bards, but only briefly. The most interesting are *The Spoils of Annwn* and *The Song of the Graves.* The former is the one that describes a quest for a magic cauldron, and looks like a tenth-century version of the Grail legend. The latter is a list of renowned warriors and their alleged places of burial. Arthur is the exception. His grave is said to be a mystery. Perhaps the poet implies only that the Britons tried to conceal his death from the Saxons, or to protect his grave from desecration. But the line may be the germ of the prophecy about his return.

In Welsh legend, as distinct from poetry, the search leads to results equally tantalising. Most of the actual stories are lost. With a few precious exceptions, the best of them in the *Mabinogion,* all that has come down is a jumbled mass of 'triads'. These are mnemonics. Story-tellers grouped their favourite themes in linked sets of three: the *Three Great Treacheries,* the *Three Exalted Prisoners,* and so on. Each triad was a summary of three stories, located in a glorified 'Island of Britain' before the Anglo-Saxon conquest.

Most of the triads that mention Arthur or companions of his are medieval, influenced by French romance, and devoid of any historical interest. Some, however, give glimpses of him in more primitive and barbaric guises. He is one of the *Three Red Ravagers* and one of the *Three Frivolous Bards.* He is guilty of one of the *Three Wicked Uncoverings:* digging up the head of Bran, Britain's talisman against foreign invasion, on the ground that Britain should not rely on magic. Several triads introduce Medraut and Arthur's wife Gwenhwyvaer. Arthur is stated, most surprisingly, to have had three wives all so named. One of these ladies was assaulted by Medraut in a raid on Arthur's fortress at Kelliwic in Cornwall. Medraut made a treacherous treaty with the Saxons which caused the fatal battle of Camlaun, a sort of Bosworth where many combatants changed sides.

Meagre as the triads are, they convey at least one crucial fact: Arthur's uniqueness. No other hero is so frequently mentioned. He is the only person so important that triads are enlarged into tetrads to fit him in. An instance is the triad about the *Three Exalted Prisoners.* After saying who they were, it adds that there was another more famous even than they, and this was Arthur. His imprisonments, as sketched in the triad, have a mythical air. Yet the fact that he was thought of as a prisoner at all should not be overlooked. The oldest traditions do not make him a serene, triumphant monarch. He sounds more like an adventurer with a background of guerrilla war and plain feuding. The strangest of all the triads is the *Three Powerful Swineherds.* It ends:

> The third was Trystan son of Tallwch, who guarded the swine of March son of Meirchion while the swineherd had gone on a message to

Essyllt to bid her appoint a meeting with Trystan. Now Arthur and Marchell and Cai and Bedwyr undertook to go and make an attempt on him, but they proved unable to get possession of as much as one porker either as a gift or as a purchase, whether by fraud, by force, or by theft.

These few sentences supply six familiar names—Tristram, Mark, Iseult, Arthur, Kay, Bedevere—and the Tristram-Iseult motif. Yet the whole assemblage is concerned with nothing grander than an inglorious attempt at pig-stealing.

Out of the shipwreck of Welsh legend, the *Mabinogion* has saved one Arthurian story intact from the pre-Geoffrey era. This is *Culhwch and Olwen.* It tells how the gallant youth Culhwch (pronounced Kil-hooch, with the *ch* as in 'loch') enlists Arthur's aid in performing a fantastic series of tasks, which he must do to win Olwen as his bride. The verve and savagery of the tale, its fierce humour, exuberant richness and occasional beauty, belong to a wholly pre-romantic world. It testifies, just as the triads do, to Arthur's special position in folk memory. The author makes Culhwch go to him for help because, in this way, a vast medley of ready-made Arthurian saga matter can be brought in. There is a list of over two hundred of Arthur's followers. Many take part in the adventures. Some are fairy-tale figures: men who can drink up seas, hear ants fifty miles away, and so forth. But among them are Bedwyr, Cei (another variant of the name which reaches the romances as Kay) and also Gwalchmei, who eventually becomes Gawain.

One further source, while extremely suspect, supplies hints that have a certain value; partly in themselves, partly because of the way they interlock with the other data. Medieval Wales and Brittany produced a mass of Saints' Lives. As the Celts bestowed the title of 'saint' most generously, hordes of dark-age priests from the West British regions are embalmed in this form. To anybody who cares for sound history the Lives are depressing, with their childish miracles, anachronisms and would-be edification. However, though few of them can be trusted singly, the effect of taking many together is more impressive. They shed light on each other; they give cross-references and a vague time-scheme; they reveal attitudes. And several bring in Arthur. The Welsh ones are associated with the abbey of Llancarfan. Their authors seem to be drawing on a body of tradition current in southern Wales.

> **Arthur's Britain, however divided and ruinous, did stand for such civilisation as it remembered, and gave this, through the Church, a fresh vigour in all the part of the British Isles which its victories protected.**
>
> **—Geoffrey Ashe**

The *Life of St Cadoc,* composed by Lifris about 1100, has a preface on the marriage of the saint's parents. Gwynnlyw, king of Glamorgan, eloped with a Brecknock princess named Gwladys and took her into his own domain with her father in pursuit. Fleeing over a hill, they found Arthur playing at dice with Cei and Bedwyr. Arthur took an unwelcome interest in Gwladys, but the two warriors (with a curious anticipation of the romances) reminded him that it was their custom to help those in distress. He confronted the pursuing father and made him go home. The lovers married at once—perhaps as a precautionary measure—and in due course Cadoc was born.

Long afterwards, we are told, when he was abbot of Llancarfan, Cadoc gave sanctuary for seven years to a man who had killed three of Arthur's soldiers. This length of time was doubtfully legal. The ageing chieftain finally ran the fugitive to earth, and came to the Usk to argue with Cadoc and the monks. They stayed on the other bank. An arbitrator awarded Arthur a herd of cattle as compensation. He demanded that all the cattle should be part red, part white. The monks got them, with divine aid, and drove them across a ford. But when Arthur's soldiers took charge, the cows changed into bundles of fern. Arthur was understandably daunted and recognised Cadoc's right to give sanctuary for seven years, seven months and seven days.

However baseless these incidents may be, at least two points of interest emerge. First, the Welsh monastic tradition would seem to have been unfriendly to Arthur. Even when he is well-established as a national hero, Lifris portrays him in a way that presupposes this minority view. Secondly, though Arthur pays homage to Christian duty, he appears as a hard-bargaining warrior chief out for what he can get. Does the second fact explain the first? Did the monks dislike him because he harassed them and tried to extort goods from them?

The plausibility of such an idea is strengthened by the portrayal of Arthur in other Saints' Lives. That of St Carannog describes the holy man as launching a floating altar on the Bristol Channel, and vowing to preach wherever it landed. He traced it to the neighbourhood of Dindraethou—Dunster, in Somerset—where Arthur reigned as junior colleague of a prince named Cadwy. When Carannog reached the spot, the altar was nowhere to be seen. Arthur, however, was near by, looking for a huge serpent which was annoying the people of Carrum (Carhampton). Carannog asked where the altar was. Arthur promised to tell him if he would help in disposing of the serpent. Carannog banished it in the same manner as St Patrick, and then Arthur produced the altar. He had commandeered it himself and used it as a table, but everything he put on it fell off. In gratitude he allowed Carannog to settle at Carrum.

The *Life of St Padarn* was written in the twelfth century, when a respectful tone toward the hero could be expected unless the monks' adverse tradition was very stubborn. Yet it speaks contemptuously of 'a certain *tyrannus* by the name of Arthur'. *Tyrannus* is the word used by Gildas for Vortigern, implying power without legitimacy. Arthur, it seems, burst into Padarn's cell and demanded that he hand over a tunic given him by the patriarch of Jerusalem. When the saint refused, Arthur persisted. Thereupon the earth opened and he sank in up to his neck. He had to apologise before he escaped.

Both these legends give the same impression as *Cadoc.* Arthur is a military despot who tries to plunder the monks. Historically it is a fair deduction that he requisitioned church property to maintain his troops. A parallel case is Charles Martel, who did this in the eighth century to finance his defence of France against the Arabs. Although he saved western Christendom, ecclesiastical authors treat him as a villain.

We may, indeed, have an explanation here for Gildas's curious unwillingness to discuss the Badon campaign in detail, or to name its leader: clerical rancour. Arthur was unmentionable, a deliverer whom he could not attack yet would not praise. The Welsh *Life of St Gildas,* by Caradoc of Llancarfan, at least hints at strained relations. According to this, Gildas was a northern Briton, one of the many sons of Caw, who lived near the Clyde. Most of them were driven by Pictish raids to migrate to Wales. The eldest, however, named Hueil, stayed in the north. The brothers fought against Arthur—described as a *tyrannus* and a *rex rebellus* claiming to rule all Britain—until Hueil was captured and put to death. Gildas was the family spokesman in demanding compensation, and Arthur had to pay. Later they met again. Gildas was now at Glastonbury. Melwas, the king of Somerset, kidnapped Arthur's wife 'Guennuvar' and kept her in Glastonbury, which was protected by the river and marshes. Arthur arrived with levies from Devon and Cornwall. Battle was imminent, but Gildas and the abbot negotiated a treaty by which the lady was restored.

The abduction of Guennuvar, or Guinevere, is an episode that turns up again in the romances. As to the indications of Arthur's power in the West Country, and Glastonbury's role as a stronghold, their value depends on corroboration (if any) from other sources. But the story of Caw's sons has a feature of genuine interest. It brings Arthur into conflict with lawless elements in Pictland and northern Wales. The war with Caw's sons could account for the battles of Celidon and Tribruit, even for the City of the Legion, if this is Chester. We may not be getting facts, but we may be getting glimpses of whatever saga has gone into Nennius. There are more hints in *Culhwch and Olwen,* where Arthur's fight with Hueil is mentioned, and he and the other sons of Caw, presumably subdued, are at Arthur's court.

Outside Wales there is one very strange Saint's Life, that of the Breton Goeznovius. Its preface recalls the flight of Britons to Armorica during the Saxon invasion. The tide was stemmed, it continues, by Arthur, 'the great king of the Britons', who won victories in Britain and Gaul. After he was 'summoned from human activity', the Saxons advanced again and the flight to Armorica was resumed. Here we have Arthur crowned, making war overseas, and not dying. The monastic writer has drawn on a tradition quite unlike the Welsh. To judge from this, it was chiefly in Brittany that imagination began transforming the soldier into the immortal King Arthur, whose myth the

French priests collided with at Bodmin in 1113. From there, as well as from western Britain, Geoffrey of Monmouth and the romancers must have drawn the themes which they worked up into literature.

Historically speaking, the Arthurian Fact is far clearer than Arthur himself. Some time before 500, the Britons rallied against the invader. Their leaders clung to the Roman and Christian heritage, and their struggle had a staunch conviction that was not found in other imperial provinces. As the years passed, Celtic resurgence doubtless reduced *Romanitas* to a hazy mystique with little meaning outside religion. But the rally went on, and the triumph at Badon brought a spell of peace and good order which even Gildas admits. Not until the middle of the sixth century did the heathen begin to bite again into mainland Britain.

Arthur became the symbol of the rally and, in tradition, the winner of all the victories after Ambrosius's death or retirement. Some such person existed. Or at any rate, it is much easier to suppose that he did than that he did not. To deny his reality would solve no problems. It would merely mean postulating another British leader to fill the same role—or, at all events, to win the decisive battle of Badon—and then explaining why he was totally forgotten. Arthur, however, was not king of Britain, or even a local king, except in the petty Irish sense. We may picture him as a rustic noble, born in the 470s or thereabouts, of still dimly-Romanised stock. Hence his name, Artorius. His youth was spent in raiding and feuding. By an unusual flair for leadership he attracted a following. His personal corps—the 'knights', if we care to use the word—aided British kings against Anglo-Saxon encroachments. He made himself indispensable over the whole zone of his operations, becoming Ambrosius's successor and, in a crude way, a statesman. But, despite victory, his standing was never quite secure. Quarrels with the monks, probably over levies in kind, deprived him of proper recognition in the writings of the only people who wrote. He met his end fighting an enemy to whom there is no reason not to give the name Modred.

As far as it goes, this is a credible career. No one need assume that the later growth of mythology casts any doubt on it. Even in recent times, tall stories have gathered round American folk-heroes such as Davy Crockett (a man perhaps not unlike Arthur). Yet some at least of those folk-heroes were real people. With the faintly outlined Briton, for whom we cannot hope to find so much evidence, the amount of filling-in that can ever be done is open to debate. However, there are three questions which can be asked with some prospect of getting answers.

First: Where was Arthur's home territory? Here, all tradition converges. The problem is whether tradition can be trusted. It makes him a West-Countryman. Even such nebulous clues as place-names and local legends point that way. They cover, indeed, a vast stretch of Britain (nobody else is commemorated so widely, except the Devil); and, as Tennyson said, Arthur's name streams over the land like a cloud. But the cloud has shape as well as extent. In all its length, from the Isles of Scilly to Perth, only the West Country supplies Arthur with dwelling-places. His

Cornish home is Kelliwic, probably a hill-fort in the parish of Egloshayle near Padstow. Cadbury Castle in Somerset, which is close to Queen Camel (formerly plain Camel), has been identified with Camelot from time immemorial. The oldest triads locate Arthur in Cornwall. The *Life of St Carannog* connects him with Dunster. The *Life of St Gildas* portrays him summoning the troops of Cornwall and Devon. If Kelliwic, Dunster and Cadbury are all authentic, he must have moved as his power increased. But the vital point is that no comparable places exist outside the West Country. The courts at Caerleon and Winchester are found only in medieval literature. Geoffrey of Monmouth himself gives the same testimony. His story of the birth at Tintagel is not evidence as to history, but it shows that Arthur was supposed, even in Wales, to have come from that quarter. Likewise, even the Welsh bard who spoke to Henry II indicated that Somerset, not Wales, was thought of as the right place for his burial.

Many investigators today are disposed to accept the area in general if not the legends in detail. Those who disagree point out that Arthur looms large in the north also, and very early. Aneirin's *Gododdin* proves that he was already proverbial there before the close of the sixth century, and Prince Arthur of Argyll was the first and most notable of the men named after him. Nor are these the only considerations.

Whatever inference we shall draw from this aspect of his fame is bound up with a second question. Was he a local resistance leader afterwards inflated by legend and credited with exploits in places he never saw; or could he have been mobile—a national figure, so far as the term had meaning then, who really did leave his home territory and go everywhere?

The former view of him looks more likely, yet it leads to trouble. We cannot confine him either to the southwestern or to the northern zone without perplexity over his status in the other. Not only the shape of the tradition, but historical and archaeological arguments, point to the south-west. Yet on purely literary grounds the case for the north may well be stronger. If we look at the saga alone, or what little is left of this, it is far easier to believe that it began in the north and was carried southward rather than the reverse. A north-south movement can be documented in other cases, a south-north one cannot. The more romantic alternative view turns out, in fact, to cover the data somewhat better. A wide-ranging Arthur could have lived where tradition says, and gone out to fight where Nennius says: Glein and Linnuis representing a Lincolnshire campaign against Angles, Celidon, and Tribuit taking him to quell Picts or dissident Britons, and Badon bringing him south again, with a reputation left behind everywhere, but exploited first in poetry by the northern bards.

The case against this tempting idea is that it may suggest more cohesion among the Britons, and better communications, than they would actually have had. That objection leads in turn to a third question. What sort of leader was Arthur? What were his official rank and his mode of warfare?

Two epithets in Welsh literature look like titles: the *imperator* of the poem, and the *dux bellorum* of Nennius. *Imperator* may have its primary Latin meaning of commander-in-chief. Or it may echo some last tremor of imperial politics, such as an attempt by the British soldiers to proclaim Arthur emperor, as their predecessors proclaimed Constantine and Maximus. Both interpretations are guesswork. Yet however we take the word, if it implies anything at all, it implies a big rather than a small leader.

Dux bellorum raises more serious issues. Though not a recognised title, it certainly seems to hint at some military office. In 1891, Sir John Rhys ventured the theory that Arthur held, or revived, a specific Roman command set up toward the end of the Western Empire. Generals in charge of provincial defence had the ranks of *dux* and *comes,* the original forms of the words 'duke' and 'count'. Britain, early in the fifth century, was allotted a *Comes Britanniarum*—Count of the British Provinces—with a roving commission from the Channel to Caledonia. His command was never effectively organised. But Rhys thought Arthur might have restored it in his own person, or been appointed to it by an alliance of British kings.

Rhys's conjecture was pursued further by R. G. Collingwood in the first volume of the *Oxford History of England.* He fastened on the likelihood that the tide of warfare was turned by a change in methods. This raised the topic of cavalry. The Anglo-Saxons fought on foot and had very little horsemanship for even civilian purposes. Procopius, the Emperor Justinian's court historian, notes that when some Anglian envoys came to Constantinople, they were laughed at for their failure to ride properly in a parade. Before the fifth century, on the other hand, Rome had developed mailed horsemen called *cataphractarii* and *clibanarii.* The latter—whose arms and tactics were imitated from Persia—wore helmets and carried spears, and horse as well as rider was protected by mail. While the frontiers were manned by peasant militia, mounted forces could move swiftly behind them to threatened areas. The technique came too late to save the West, and was probably less effective than some historians have assumed, but it was a factor in the long endurance of Constantinople.

The *Comes Britanniarum* was assigned six cavalry units. Perhaps they only existed on paper. However, the Britons may have seen mounted soldiers in 418. Although Gildas does not mention any as taking part in the first rescue of Britain by Stilicho, he does mention 'unexpected bands of cavalry' in the second rescue, which happened about 418 if it happened at all. Collingwood argued that Arthur, as *Comes,* recreated a mounted force to which the enemy had no answer.

This theory, as stated by Collingwood, is open to grave criticism. It implies a fuller survival of Roman Britain than the rest of the evidence attests. By Arthur's time, even the Romanising effect of Ambrosius must have largely worn off. But he might have adopted a remembered title and organised cavalry of a sort: do-it-yourself *clibanarii,* so to speak. Aneirin's poetry shows that British nobles were riding to battle quite soon after Arthur's time. Whether they, or for that matter the horsemen of the Empire, charged and fought in the saddle like medieval knights is an unresolved question. It is uncertain whether the stirrup, or any comparable device, was known in Europe so early, and how much a man on horseback could do without it. But even 'mounted commandos' (the phrase is suggested by Robert Graves) would have given Arthur's Britons two advantages: moral effect and mobility. As to the first, mounted men undoubtedly could strike panic into superstitious barbarian mobs. Constantine the Great is said to have routed an army with only twelve, a feat hardly less amazing than Arthur's alleged onslaught at Mount Badon. Tactical mobility, the capacity for swift movement and surprise, might also have made a decisive difference under a bold leader.

If Arthur had cavalry, whatever meaning we attach to that term, the view of him as ubiquitous rather than local acquires further plausibility. Long marches can, of course, be made on foot, even in rough country. But the only account we actually have of sixth-century British warriors traversing a great distance is in Aneirin's *Gododdin,* and they do go on horseback.

Assertions are sometimes made about Arthur's cavalry as if there were direct proof of it. There is none. Nennius and the poets leave us in the dark about his methods of war. Still, the theory remains an attractive way of fitting the evidence together. And archaeological support is not beyond hoping for.

Just as the Arthurian Fact—the British rally which Arthur stands for—is better outlined than the hero himself, so its ramifications are easier to feel sure of than his human associates. Which of the famous characters are, in fact, real people? A defensible answer would be: Kay, Bedevere, Modred, Tristram. Probably, Guinevere. Possibly, Mark, Gawain and Iseult. They are the medieval guises of British Celts who appear earlier as Cei, Bedwyr, Medraut, Trystan, Gwenhwyvaer, March, Gwalchmei and Essyllt. The first two are always Arthur's lieutenants, and continue so in Geoffrey and Wace, though they yield the limelight afterwards to undocumented knights, such as Lancelot. Medraut is normally hostile and never friendly. Trystan is a puzzling nobleman connected with Cornwall, whose name was originally spelt Drustans and looks Pictish. Of Arthur's wife we can say very little. Gwalchmei is scarcely more than mentioned, but at least he is mentioned before Geoffrey of Monmouth wrote.

A further word is needed about Merlin. Although he was invented by Geoffrey, the invention was not quite devoid of factual basis. There was a northern British bard named Myrddin, whose name Geoffrey used, changing it a little to avoid an unfortunate French pun. Myrddin flourished around the year 573, when he was involved in a battle near Carlisle. If he met Arthur at all, he can only have done so as a boy in the commander's advanced years. Even apart from magic, his legendary role is impossible.

All these variously shadowy figures have a feature in common. They would never have been immortalised for their own sake. It was the British rally that gave their names an imperishable setting. Yet since the rally finally failed, why did it leave so deep a mark?

Partly because of poetry, and the stubborn pride of Wales

and Cornwall. But the poetry and the pride had unique matter to feed upon. For fully thirty years the rally preserved what was, in effect, the last remnant of the Western Empire. Throughout the imperial world, moreover, Arthur was the only fighter against Teutonic invaders who drove any substantial number out again after conquest. Once in Gaul, the barbarians stayed. In Britain, most of them stayed likewise, but some did not. Some became discouraged and looked elsewhere. For this retreat we have two witnesses. Neither is conclusive alone, together they confirm each other.

Procopius, writing in Constantinople toward the middle of the sixth century, describes Britain as inhabited by Britons, Angles and Frisians, the last being evidently Saxons named from their previous home. All three races multiply fast, he says, and the surplus population goes over to the continent, where the Frankish rulers permit settlement. Procopius's information seems to have come from some northern Angles who were at Constantinople with a Frankish embassy between 534 and 548. His British emigration is the movement out of the West Country that was now turning Armorica into Brittany. But the Angles and Saxons never took to the sea without solid reasons. They must have gone out of Britain because the way to further land-seizure was barred.

A ninth-century chronicler at the German monastery of Fulda gives another aspect of the same story. Speaking of 'Saxons' living north of the Unstrut, he explains that they are descended from Angles forced out of Britain by the need for new land. They joined the Frankish king Theuderich in a war fought in 531 and he gave them a conquered area to live in. The area which the monk has in mind is still known as Engilin.

Faintly, but satisfactorily, a picture emerges. The Teutonic advance in Britain was disputed by Ambrosius and turned back by Arthur. A rough demarcation line wandered southward from Yorkshire. West of it, Britain could take breath and recover. In one respect at least, this Indian summer of the Celts brought a renaissance which, like the rest of their achievement, had no counterpart abroad. Behind the barrier raised by the soldiers, the Church burst into flower. St Patrick's lonely eminence ended, and he began to have successors.

The reborn Christianity of the Celts was now cut off from the Church on the European continent, and different in system and atmosphere, though not in doctrine. Its centres were rural monasteries instead of city sees, and its heads were abbots instead of bishops. Celtic community life was less binding on the individual than the Rule of St Benedict. Each monk had his separate cell. All ate together and assembled for worship in a chapel, but they enjoyed some freedom of movement. They were not only priests and missionaries but teachers, doctors, farmers and builders. Britain's religious renewal was primarily an upsurge of energy in Wales, and the work of one remarkable man, St Illtud.

Illtud may have attended one of the schools set up by Germanus, and it is said, though on no very safe authority, that he served as a soldier under Arthur. After some years as a hermit, he founded the monastery of Llantwit Major in Glamorgan. His monks reclaimed land and pioneered an improved method of ploughing. Illtud became, in the words of Gildas (who, however, does not name him, any more than he names Arthur), 'the polished teacher of almost the whole of Britain'. His disciples—Gildas himself, St Sampson, St Paul Aurelian, Prince Maelgwn who became king of Gwynedd—made their mark outside Wales. Sampson and his own disciples virtually created the Breton Church. Meanwhile, independently of Illtud, St Cadoc founded Llancarfan, and travelled north to Pictland and south to Cornwall.

The success of these tireless clerics was a direct result of military triumph and British security. Thence also came the preservation of the work of St Patrick. Going westward across the sea, and welcoming Irish pupils in their own schools, the monks of Britain regenerated the faltering Church of Ireland. The blaze of Celtic genius which made the smaller island a beacon to dark-age Europe was possible because Arthur had kept the heathen at arm's length.

The effects of the Arthurian Fact were profound; and they were lasting. When the conquest finally came, it was slow and piecemeal. Devon held out till 710, Cornwall till 825. Wales and parts of northwest England never succumbed to the Anglo-Saxons at all. Moreover, the Anglo-Saxons who did eventually conquer were no longer the savages of the fifth century. Christian missions from Rome in the south, and from Celtic Iona in the north, had opened up their little states to civilising influences. The England which took shape under Alfred, and the United Kingdom which grew round that, were fusions of many elements— the Celtic included.

When Geoffrey of Monmouth took up that Celtic element, and evoked Arthur's Britain in medieval guise, how far was he falsifying? Of course, he depicted a better organised realm than can possibly have existed, with an unreal monarch, a glamourised Christian knighthood, an absurd empire. Yet he did not desert the truth altogether. Arthur led warriors, who may well have been mounted; he beat the Saxons; he and his men were Christian, at least in name. Arthur's Britain, however divided and ruinous, did stand for such civilisation as it remembered, and gave this, through the Church, a fresh vigour in all the part of the British Isles which its victories protected. (pp. 41-74)

Geoffrey Ashe, "The Arthurian Fact," in The Quest for Arthur's Britain, by Geoffrey Ashe and others, Frederick A. Praeger Publishers, 1968, pp. 41-74.

Beram Saklatvala

[*In the following excerpt, Saklatvala chronicles the military history of Arthur's reign, utilizing key primary sources such as Nennius's* Historia Brittonum *(c. ninth century).*]

The earliest witness to mention Arthur is Nennius, in his *History of the Britons*. According to R. W. Chambers, it was written down not later than AD 800-830 and not be-

fore AD 680, that is to say not less than 160 and not more than 300 years after the time of Arthur. Certain passages seem to draw upon earlier sources. Its general tone is reliable and scholarly; it it entitled to be given all the weight of a work into which older traditions have been incorporated, which is close to the period it describes, and which has been written or edited by a sober and careful hand.

After describing the death of Vortigern, and after a digression on the activities of St Germanus, Nennius writes:

> In that time the Saxons increased in numbers and their strength grew in Britain.
>
> When Hengist was dead, Octha his son crossed from the left hand side of Britain into the kingdom of the Cantii, and from him descended the Kings of the Cantii.
>
> Then Arthur fought against those people in those days with the Kings of the Britons, but he himself was the *Dux Bellorum* or General in these battles.
>
> The first battle was on the mouth of the river which is called Glein. The second, and the third, and the fourth, and the fifth upon another river, which is called Dubglass, and is in the kingdom Linnus. The sixth battle was upon the river which is called Bassas.
>
> The seventh was the battle in the wood of Celidon, that is Cat Coit Celidon, (which is 'The Battle of the Wood of Celidon' in the old British tongue).
>
> The eighth was the battle in the stronghold of Guinnion, in which Arthur carried upon his shoulders an image of the Blessed Mary, the Eternal Virgin. And the pagans were turned to flight on that day, and great was the slaughter brought upon them through the virtue of our Lord, Jesus Christ, and through the virtue of the Blessed Virgin Mary, His Mother.
>
> The ninth battle was fought in the City of the Legion. He fought the tenth battle on the shore of the river which is called Tribruit. The eleventh battle was waged in the mountain which is called Agned.
>
> The twelfth battle was on Mount Badon where in one day nine hundred and sixty men fell in one charge of Arthur's. And no one laid them low but himself alone.
>
> And in all these battles he stood out as victor.

The names given of the places where Arthur's battles were fought cannot now be certainly identified. This very difficulty argues the age and reliability of the passage, suggesting that Nennius was using old material in which British place names, now submerged under the new names given by the English, had been used. He does not attempt to make them comprehensible, but is content to repeat the older information. This is very different from Malory, Geoffrey of Monmouth and others, who write of Arthur's adventures in Winchester, Canterbury and other places whose names, in those English forms, did not exist in Arthur's day. Moreover, in the case of the seventh battle, after giving the Latin form *in silva celidonis,* he adds *id est cat coit Celidon,* giving the old British phrase for 'The Battle of the Wood of Celidon'. This supports the view that he is drawing from an older sources in which a language contemporary with the events was being used.

Nennius's report that after the death of Hengist his son and successor withdrew into Kent hints at a retreat by the English after Hengist's death which again suggests that his death was associated with a military reverse—supporting the story of his defeat and death at the hand of Ambrosius.

Next, Nennius makes it clear that Arthur was not himself a king. He fought together with the kings of the various States of Britain but (and the word 'but' adds emphasis to the distinction) he himself had the designation *Dux Bellorum,* or leader of the battles. Arthur's method of organising the British resistance to the invaders is now clear: he was continuing the revival of the Roman system begun by Ambrosius. Nennius could mean that Arthur consciously revived the title of Duke of Britain, or used some adaptation of it. It has been suggested that the title he revived was that of Count of Britain; but the counts were commanders of mobile expeditionary forces sent to the provinces by the central government. Arthur knew that any hope of a force from the Continent was now remote and that his sole hope lay in the army in Britain. The Duke of Britain had always been supreme commander of the garrisons and army groups in the island and the title would have been a reminder of past successes and a symbol that unity had been achieved, that the old military skills were again to be used, and that a well-organised and ably-commanded force was available. There is no need to reject or modify Nennius's words. Arthur, Duke of Britain, reviver of Roman forms and unifier of Britain, is a credible figure.

Nennius next lists the twelve battles which Arthur fought against the English. The first six are fought upon rivers, and no fewer than four upon a single river. These seem to be defensive rather than aggressive engagements. Presumably Arthur was trying to prevent the English from crossing into new territory, and the struggles for the crossings were renewed more than once. Although Arthur, according to Nennius, won all his battles, it is clear that at this stage he inflicted no defeat on his enemies sufficiently overwhelming to prevent them from making fresh attempts. We are reminded of the bitterly contested battle of Aylesford, forty or fifty years before, when the English had tried to cross their first river barrier, the Medway.

No one now knows where these battles took place. The British names which Nennius used have vanished. For the first, the battle of the River Glein, there have been many conjectures: there is a river Glen in Lincolnshire; there is a river Glen in Northumberland; and the Lun in Westmorland and the Leven in Cumberland have also been suggested. But we should look in the area where both strategically and tactically a battle was most likely to have taken place. Geoffrey Ashe (*Caesar to Arthur*) suggests that the Glen should be taken as being near the Wash, and there is much to support this.

As already seen the English made at least one sortie to the

A fourth-century floor mosaic from a Roman villa at Hinton St. Mary, Dorset, England.

North, and one of the main tasks of the army of Britain would have been to prevent the English in the South East from joining forces with their hereditary northern allies, the Picts. If the first phase of Arthur's campaigns was aimed at pinning down the English within the southeastern corner of the island, preventing any further movement north, then his first major battles would have been on the northern boundary of the area occupied by the English, somewhere along their line of communication with the Picts. This line was the Roman road from London to York, and it is somewhere along its southern stretch, at a point where it might easily be defended, that the first battle might have taken place.

From London the road ran slightly east of north, following the line of the river Lee. Thence, with only minor changes of direction, it ran to the important city of Lindum Colonia, the modern Lincoln, a walled city of great military importance. Forty miles south of Lincoln is the modern town of Bourne. Hereabouts, because of the great bay of the Wash, the road is only some twenty miles from the coast. To attempt to hold the road south of this point would be difficult. An enemy approaching from the south would have the width of Norfolk for manœuvre, and could easily work his way behind the defender's left flank. But at Bourne, the sweeping coastline approached the road. The Britons' left flank would have rested secure on the marshlands, and an enemy could make only a frontal attack.

Moreover about ten miles north of Bourne rises a small river, the Glen; it runs parallel with the road and to the west of it. As it turns eastward to the Wash, the road crosses it. Here, strategically and tactically, is a place where a battle might well have been fought—on a river Glen. Somewhere here perhaps, with his right flank protected by the river and his left flank resting on the marshlands, Arthur fought his first major independent engagement. If this was the northern frontier of the English and if Arthur succeeded at this battle in establishing the Wash as the northernmost point of the Anglo-Saxon advance, the county name of Norfolk becomes significant. Here, for some years, lived the most northern folk of the English. Though later they took all the land up to the Wall, they were held here long enough to give to this area the name (whose meaning is now lost in the map of modern England) of the home of the North Folk.

To picture Arthur at this Battle of the River Glen we may turn to the portraits of other men of this period on the later Roman coins. We see him, probably still a young man, wearing an ornamented and embossed cuirass, and a close-fitting helmet with protecting cheekpieces. He carries a slender horseman's spear and probably a round shield. Remembering the traditions and successes of the past, he had reformed the cavalry units whose effectiveness against the barbarians had so often been proved. Each troop was led by an officer whose essential qualities had to be both military skill and loyalty to the commander. These officers were not merely his subordinates but his companions, as in former days the counts had been the companions of the Emperors.

Perhaps at this battle there was a final charge down the wide paved road when the heavy armoured horsemen moved with levelled lances towards the bridge. The compact body of horsemen would gather speed until not even the obstinate bravery of the English could stand against them, though many riders would fall against the stubborn line of barbarians standing grimly behind their shield wall. For the English, there was no retreat. To retreat and flee was to be ridden down; to stand was at least to have the chance, in the grim war play, of killing before being killed.

After the charge, and after the trumpets had recalled the more impetuous horsemen from the chase, swords would be wiped and lances held at rest in hands weary from the fight. Amid the bitter smell of horse and leather and the sweetish smell of new blood, the men would gather the scattered arms and strip the dead of their armour. Swords, shields and helmets were of inestimable worth, and their harvesting was one of the fruits of victory. Later, over the silent field the ravens would gather and the wolves intrude.

The bridge was cleared and the leaders gathered to discuss the battle, and the points where it had gone well or ill. For the prisoners there was slavery; for the dead, the callous unarming and swift burial; for the defeated, the weary march south, and the resolution of revenge; and for Arthur and his companions, excited talk late into the night; the planning of the next move, the projecting of new units, and the everlasting hope of ultimate victory.

A northern frontier having been imposed upon the English, it was now necessary to check them in the West. By now the English had doubtless spread westwards from Kent, particularly along the southern coast, where in 490 the Roman fort at Pevensey had been taken. If the Romanised West, within which further armies could be raised and trained for the final victory, was to be preserved, the enemy's left flank had now to be engaged, and the English had to be held as firmly there as they had been to the north. This must have been Arthur's next preoccupation. After the victory at the River Glen, he would have left there one or more of his companions, with an army strong enough to stop any renewed attack up the road to York. But he himself, with the main body, turned southward.

The river Dublass of Nennius has been variously identified, for example as the river Duglas in Leicestershire. It is sensible however to seek a river whose modern name is a translation of the old British one. *Du* or *dhu* meant 'black' in the British tongue, and there are several rivers called Blackwater. One such is in Hampshire, forming part of the boundary with Sussex. Here Arthur's strategy might well have brought him and this might well be the Dubglass of the battle.

The road from London to the West crossed the Thames at Staines, and thence ran to Calleva Atrebatum, near Reading. South-west of Ascot the old road, now known as the Nine Mile Drive and further west as the Devil's Highway, still runs straight and true between stretches of dark forest. South, and at right angles, flows the river Blackwater. With Calleva Atrebatum (Silchester) as his base, and with the Icknield Way as a link with his forces north-east of the Saxons, this would have been a logical place for Arthur to have begun his holding action to the west of the English. The river Blackwater (still a county boundary) would have provided a natural frontier behind which the English might be contained. Behind him lay Chichester on the coast, and inland the walled cities of Calleva Atrebatum and Venta (Winchester). These were now the heartland of Roman Britain, to be defended at all costs.

On Blackwater he met a more resolute enemy than had confronted him at Bourne. No one battle, no single charge of his horsemen, could achieve victory. For on this river were fought no fewer than four important battles. The intervals at which these were fought are unknown; the word Nennius uses is *bellum,* which means a war as well as a battle. So each may have been the climax of a campaign and the four wars on the river Dubglass may have covered a span of four years or more, with the English doggedly renewing their attacks each summer, and with Arthur as doggedly defeating them.

Although Nennius tells us that Arthur emerged victorious from all his battles, obviously here he had a hard-fought struggle, with final victory long in doubt. At this time there was in fact an opponent in the area who could have had the strength and persistence. This was Cerdic, leader of the West Saxons, who had landed in the island in 495.

The next battle is also on a river, the Bassas, the identification of which is lost. The suggestion that Basingstoke marks the site is feasible; it presupposes that after the engagements on the Dubglass, Arthur had withdrawn some few miles to the northwest. The name Basingstoke, considered to be of Saxon origin, not British, means the village built by the followers of a Saxon leader named Basa. But this leader may have given his name to a local river and the new name may have been current in Nennius's day. Geographically this site is not impossible, for here was Cerdic's country, the infant kingdom of the West Saxons.

The site of the seventh battle, the wood of Celidon, was probably north of the Wall, for the wood of Celidon is the wood of Caledonia. Since the English had not penetrated into these northern regions, Arthur was apparently faced by two entirely separate groups of opponents. To the south-east lay the English and their allies whom, by his successful campaigns, he had held firmly within a limited area. But in the North were the hereditary enemies of Roman Britain, the Picts. Although Arthur's successful battle on the river Glen had prevented the English from joining hands with the Picts, the latter were no doubt conscious of their opportunity. We know from the end of Arthur's story (for he was to die on the Wall in a civil war) that some northern Britons themselves were hostile to him, and the Picts may have found unexpected allies among these. So Arthur was forced to march northwards to put down a rising in southern Scotland. Again the stubborn line of the enemy, this time a mixed force of Picts and dissident Britons, would have received charge after charge of Arthur's heavy cavalry; again the victorious horsemen rode with poised spears at the broken enemy, overrunning their positions and destroying the last desperate resistance with downward thrusts of their bloody lances.

The eighth battle, at the Castle of Guinnion, might have taken place at Winchester, which in the Breton poem of Chrétien de Troyes is spelt 'Guincestre', or even at Windsor, which in the same text is spelt 'Guinesores'. Neither is geographically impossible, one being at the southern, the other at the northern extremity of Arthur's defensive line which held the Saxons from breaking out to the West.

It is likely that on his return from his northern wars, Arthur found the Saxons active in the South again, and that a campaign near the sites of his early battles became necessary. According to Nennius it was at this battle that Arthur bore the image of the Virgin Mary as his standard. The *Imaginifer,* a standard-bearer who carried the image of the Emperor, was a normal officer in the Roman army. Identifying the cause of Britain with the Christian cause, rather than with that of Imperial Rome, yet anxious to perpetuate the forms and practices of the past, Arthur substituted a Christian standard for the old Imperial ensign. But his particular choice is significant. With the Constantinian tradition so strong in Britain, and with Arthur's firm reliance upon the magic of things past, he might logically have revived Constantine's standard, the sacred

monogram of Christ. He must have had very strong and positive motives for chosing another.

The Old Church at Glastonbury was dedicated to the Virgin Mary, and traditionally this dedication dated from apostolic times. If Arthur had been brought up in the Romanised western kingdom of Ambrosius, and if he had been a follower of the Marian cult of Glastonbury, his use of Mary's image as his standard becomes credible and reasonable. Nennius's statement points not only to the important part which Christianity played in the leadership and motives of Arthur, but also to the probability of a link between him and the Old Church of Glastonbury.

The ninth battle was at the 'City of the Legion', almost certainly Chester. This too was probably part of the campaign against the rebellious Britons of the North West. After the successful battle in the wood of Celidon, he might be expected to go on to reduce other points of resistance in the area. His own successes, which had lessened the dangers in the South East, were causing the urgent sense of a need for unity in the island to fade from men's minds. Not for the last time a man who had united a nation in the face of danger found that unity fading when his own effort began to defeat the external peril.

The tenth battle, the Battle of Tribruit, is documented in other sources than Nennius. The *Black Book of Carmarthen,* a medieval book of Welsh poetry, tells of one of Arthur's companions who came back with a broken shield from 'Tryvrwd'. To lose one's shield in battle had always been taken by the Romans as a sign of defeat and disgrace. (The poet Horace wryly admits to having left his behind at the battle of Philippi.) So this story conveys that the victory was barely won, and that defeat had been narrowly avoided. The same poem tells us that the casualties were heavy: that one of Arthur's men killed his enemies three at a time, and another a hundred at a time. It also refers to 'the shores of Tryvwyd'. So Tribruit was a river and again this was a battle for a crossing. It cannot now be identified but it has been placed in the North, and may have been a resumption of the campaign that opened with the battle of Celidon. If so, then Arthur's opponents were again not the English but Picts and such of his own fellow countrymen as rejected his leadership.

The Britons in the North and North West could not see the Saxon danger as vividly as those in the South: the independence of their own kingdoms was of more immediate importance than the safety of the island. They could see no urgent reason, divided as they were by long distances of hills and forests from the turbulent South East, for accepting Arthur as supreme commander of Britain. So the battle of Tribruit, like that of Celidon, may have been a battle fought by Arthur to establish his position as Duke of Britain. The kings in the North seemed content to recognise that the Saxons had come to stay permanently in the island. They saw Arthur as a greater danger to themselves and to their independence than the remote settlers south of the Wash and east of Winchester. On the shores of Tribruit, Arthur established his ascendancy, and made good his claim as military leader of the island. The *Black Book of Carmarthen* mentions one opponent by name, Eidyn, who may have been king of one of the northern states in Britain. The fact that this battle was fought between men of the same faith and country may account for its bitterness and the narrowness of the victory.

Malory is perhaps repeating the fact that Arthur was not accepted in the North but only south of the river Trent when he tells us 'that there should no man of war ride nor go in no country on this side Trent Water, but if he had a token from King Arthur.' In Malory's story one of Arthur's first battles is fought against a confederation of knights and kings from the North Country: 'Now shall we see,' says one of Arthur's allies with grim irony, 'how these northern Britons can bear the arms.'

Another possible reason for the battle of Tribruit emerges when the story of Excalibur is examined (Chapter XII). Arthur may have fought to defend the iron workings in Northamptonshire, near the modern steel town of Corby. With Continental supplies of arms no longer available, he would have reacted violently to any threat to his own iron industries. This too could explain the bitterness and fame of the battle.

The eleventh battle was fought on the hill called Agned. According to a marginal note in some of the manuscripts, this is in Somerset. If this is so, it would appear that while Arthur's main army was engaged in the North, the English had broken through in the South, and marched deep into the West Country.

This theory is borne out by the twelfth and most important of Arthur's battles, the battle of Mount Badon. Geoffrey Ashe places this at Badbury in Wiltshire, just south of Liddington. 'Badbury', as he points out, could be derived from 'Badon-Byrig', the fort of Badon. There is however another possibility. A few miles to the south-west is the small village of Baydon, standing on the old Roman road from Calleva Atrebatum northwards to Corinium, the modern Cirencester. North of the village rises the steep hill of Baydon, on the slopes of which can be still seen scars and ditches that may well be the vestiges of an old fortification. The first part of the name seems to be Saxon. The earliest recorded spelling of it (in AD 1146) is 'Beidona', and it is suggested that it was originally 'Beg-dun', the dun (or fort) where berries grow. But the Saxon word 'Beg' is merely deduced from the later spelling. On the other hand, the second half of the name is definitely British, revealing that there was a dun or fort here before the English came. So the mixed form of Beg-dun may never have existed, and the name may in fact indicate the Badon of Arthur's famous battle.

To the west, the ground falls steeply away. Here is the last high ground between the eastern part of the island and the plains of Wiltshire. Beyond it lay the rich city of Bath, and all the western States of Britain. We can imagine an English advance, while Arthur's army was in the North Country, over the disputed Blackwater and along the Nine Mile Drive and the Devil's Highway to Calleva Atrebatum. Without pausing to reduce that formidable city, with its virtually impregnable walls, the English host struck north-west, along the road to Newbury. Encouraged by news of growing disunity among the Britons, and knowing that Arthur's main forces were scattered between North

and South and weakened by his struggles in the North, the English moved forward towards Corinium. They were not to be successful. Indeed the *Anglo-Saxon Chronicle* reports that they did not seize the three prizes of the west, Gloucester, Cirencester and Bath, until 577—some sixty years later.

Gloucester was a legionary fortress and had been founded as a *colonia*. In this place, with its long military traditions, and with its barracks and store-rooms, no doubt part of the army of Britain lay. And perhaps it rode out along the straight road to Cirencester and beyond to meet the English host. Arthur fought alone this day, with his own personal army, and with none of the kings of the States of Britain. For Nennius says that the 960 casualties on the other side were caused by 'one charge of Arthur's. And no one laid them low but himself alone.' If the enemy had penetrated so deeply, Arthur's position was desperate, and all his earlier victories would have been meaningless had he been defeated so far to the west. He may have thought bitterly of the kings of Britain, who had failed to help at this crisis. During the days when the Saxons conquered, the States of Britain had been glad to follow him. But each king was now looking to his own kingdom. Some he had quelled by force; others held to him uneasily and suspiciously, jealous of their own local authority, and mindless of the island's total danger.

Perhaps, by penetrating so far to the West, the English were unwittingly helping his cause. Surely no British leader, whatever the outcome of this day's fighting, would ever again reject the need for a unified command. So might Arthur have mused, as he led his men up the long incline of the road, with the land falling steeply to his right, and the Saxon army somewhere in the high ground to his front.

The English it seems took refuge in the old hillside fortifications, for this battle has also been described by Gildas as a siege. To assault a hill fort is no task for cavalry. The steep slopes would slow down the charge, and the old ramparts stood between the attackers and their quarry. Arthur settled down to invest the fort in proper form. Deploying his men round the foot of the hill, out of bowshot but close enough to form an unbroken ring, he waited for thirst or hunger, or the exasperation that comes to fighting men cooped up defensively, to incite the Saxons to leave the safety of the fort. The siege lasted for three days. Then the English came out, to fight on open ground. At last Arthur's horsemen had room to charge; the slaughter of the Saxons was immense and Arthur's victory complete. The threat to the West was ended and no Saxon army ever fought a pitched battle against Arthur again.

The States of Britain for some years remembered the lesson of Badon, that the English peril was a continuing one and that in spite of Arthur's early victories there was always the danger of a sudden and unexpected thrust by the Saxons. The network of roads, an asset when the island was fully garrisoned, had now become a liability, giving opportunities of sudden mobility to the enemy. The need for a Duke of Britain, to watch over the whole island and to ensure the safety of what was left of the province, was clear. It was a paramount need that surpassed the local ambition of kings and regions. So for many years, while men remembered, there was peace and the victory of Badon appeared to be final. (pp. 95-109)

Beram Saklatvala, in his Arthur: Roman Britain's Last Champion, *David & Charles, 1967, 221 p.*

An excerpt from Geoffrey's *Historia Regum Britanniae* (c. 1136):

Whenever I have chanced to think about the history of the kings of Britain, on those occasions when I have been turning over a great many such matters in my mind, it has seemed a remarkable thing to me that, apart from such mention of them as Gildas and Bede had each made in a brilliant book on the subject, I have not been able to discover anything at all on the kings who lived here before the Incarnation of Christ, or indeed about Arthur and all the others who followed on after the Incarnation. Yet the deeds of these men were such that they deserve to be praised for all time. What is more, these deeds were handed joyfully down in oral tradition, just as if they had been committed to writing, by many peoples who had only their memory to rely on.

At a time when I was giving a good deal of attention to such matters, Walter, Archdeacon of Oxford, a man skilled in the art of public speaking and well-informed about the history of foreign countries, presented me with a certain very ancient book written in the British language. This book, attractively composed to form a consecutive and orderly narrative, set out all the deeds of these men, from Brutus, the first King of the Britons, down to Cadwallader, the son of Cadwallo. At Walter's request I have taken the trouble to translate the book into Latin, although, indeed, I have been content with my own expressions and my own homely style and I have gathered no gaudy flowers of speech in other men's gardens. If I had adorned my page with high-flown rhetorical figures, I should have bored my readers, for they would have been forced to spend more time in discovering the meaning of my words than in following the story.

Geoffrey of Monmouth, in his The History of the Kings of Britain, *translated by Lewis Thorpe, Penguin, 1966.*

Thomas Jones

[*In the following essay Jones assesses the textual sources of Arthurian legend up to the appearance of Geoffrey of Monmouth's* Historia Regum Britanniae (c. 1136), *observing that "this heroic figure [Arthur] . . . attracted to himself more and more sagas and popular legends, which were originally independent of him."*]

The object of this article is a reconsideration of those references to Arthur which are fairly certainly earlier than 1136, in which year Geoffrey of Monmouth published his *Historia Regum Britanniae.* I shall try to show the evolution which can be traced in the story of Arthur in the period before the great developments which can be seen in the work of Geoffrey of Monmouth, Chrétien de Troyes, and the host of romancers who followed them. I wish to stress

that it is the pre-Geoffrey "legend of Arthur" which concerns me, not the ramifications of the later "Arthurian legend" in all its complexity.

The evidence for the existence of traditions and stories about Arthur in the period before 1136 is restricted to Welsh texts, and to a few Latin texts which are for the most part the work of Welshmen. There are also two or three other texts in Irish and Latin which mention historical figures named Arthur, and these must be considered when we ask who exactly was the Arthur who became the central figure in so many stories. The evidence itself has not increased much in quantity for many years, but there have been many and various attempts to interpret it.

It is difficult to say anything precise about the Arthur of history. The idea that he was a mythological figure is no longer acceptable. It seems to me that there is no reason to reject entirely the entries in the *Annales Cambriae* in MS. Harley 3859 (*c.* 1100) which refer to Arthur, and which are discussed below. This means that I accept the idea that there was a historical person of the name of Arthur early in the sixth century, who may have been one of the leaders of the Britons against their enemies, whoever they were, the Picts or Scots or Saxons, or any combination thereof. The name 'Arthur' seems to be a borrowing from the Latin *Artorius.* Our knowledge of Britain about the end of the fifth century and the beginning of the sixth suggests that he came of a family with Roman connexions, and that he played some part in the task of defending and reorganizing the island in the troubled period when Britain had lost the protection of the Roman legions, and when it was both divided internally and suffering attacks from foreign enemies. I do not see that the evidence allows us to suggest more than that, but from time to time many theories have been proposed which have been argued so skilfully that there is a danger that we may forget that they are only theories.

It is natural to ask whether we have a single contemporary reference to Arthur. Gildas wrote his *De Excidio Britanniae* before the death of Maelgwn Gwynedd, and according to the *Annales Cambriae,* Maelgwn died about 547. Gildas says that the Saxons came to Britain first as mercenaries, at the invitation of a "proud tyrant" (*superbo tyranno;* probably Vortigern was meant), to help him in his struggle against the Picts and Scots. The hired soldiers turned against their hirers and plundered the island, but at last they were defeated in battle by Ambrosius Aurelianus, the *Emrys Wledig* of Welsh tradition. After that, says Gildas, sometimes the Britons would be victorious and sometimes the Saxons, over a period of time the close of which is noted in words which are rather ambiguous in their context and may be interpreted in more than one way:

> . . . usque ad annum obsessionis Badonici montis novissimaeque ferme de furciferis non minimae stragis, quique quadragesimus quartus, ut novi, orditur annus, mense iam uno emenso, qui et meae nativitatis est.

Of the different interpretations of these words which have been put forward, it seems to me that the most convincing one is the following: " . . . until the year of the siege of

Mount Badon and almost the last great massacre of the gallows-birds, and this year (i.e. the year in which Gildas is writing) begins the forty-fourth year (after that) and one month has already come after, as I know, since that year is also the year of my birth.''

It is frequently said that Gildas refers to Arthur, but that is not true. It is possible, however, that Arthur was the British leader in the victory of Mount Badon, just as Ambrosius Aurelianus (who was of Roman stock, *Romanae gentis,* says Gildas), was the leader in the earlier victory over the Saxons recorded in *De Excidio Britanniae.* This possibility depends on whether or not the battle or siege of Mount Badon (obsessio Badonici montis) is the same as the battle of Badon (Bellum Badonis) recorded in the *Annales Cambriae.* Because of the difficulties of dating we cannot be sure that they are the same. Since we do not know for certain the actual date of the 'first year' in the *Annales Cambriae,* it is difficult to determine the dates of its entries. Maelgwn Gwynedd died in 547 or 549. Supposing that Gildas was writing in 549, the date of the battle of Mount Badon would be 506. Yet the date of *Bellum Badonis* in the *Annales Cambriae* is 516 or 518. A common mistake in copying annals is to leave out or to add an 'x' in giving the dates. It is not unreasonable to suggest that *Bellum Badonis* has been dated ten years too late in the *Annales Cambriae.* At least, this suggestion would account for the discrepancy between Gildas's date and the date in the *Annales Cambriae;* taking for granted, though it cannot be proved, that they are the same battle, and that the entry in the *Annales Cambriae* is authentic and independent of other texts.

Here is the complete entry in the *Annales Cambriae:*

> Bellum badonis inquo arthur portauit crucem domini nostri ihu xp'i. tribus diebus & tribus noctibus inhumeros suos & brittones uictores fuerunt.

In one way this entry is very unlike the other early entries in the *Annales Cambriae.* Without exception the other entries are short and factual, and free of miraculous and fictional elements. The reference to Arthur carrying Christ's Cross on his shoulders in battle savours of a religious legend. Judging by the nature of the other early entries in the *Annales Cambriae* it may be suggested that the original form of the entry in the earliest source (if the whole thing is not an insertion under the influence of the reference to the battle of Badon in the *Historia Brittonum*), read as follows:

> Bellum badonis & (*or* in quo) brittones uictores fuerunt.

The date of MS. B. M. Harley 3859 is *c.* 1100. Despite the internal evidence in favour of supposing that the *Annales Cambriae* was compiled about 955, it is not safe to conclude, as has been done much too readily, that the reference to Arthur carrying Christ's Cross on his shoulders is necessarily an early element. The picture of Arthur fighting with the Cross on his shoulders is not convincing either in a historical record or a legend. In some of the early entries in the *Annales Cambriae* there are signs of translation from Welsh and it was suggested as early as the

days of Thomas Price (Carnhuanawc, 1787-1848) that *in humeros suos* (on his shoulders) was the result of a confusion between Old Welsh *scuit* 'shield' and Old Welsh *scuid* 'shoulder.' It would be easier to accept the idea, historical or legendary, that the picture of Christ's Cross was engraved on Arthur's shield. One important point must be noted, however: if the clause *in quo arthur . . . inhumeros suos* is deleted as being an interpolation made between *c.* 955 and *c.* 1100, then there is no mention at all of Arthur in the remnant of the entry, and all we have is a reference to the battle of Badon and the British victory. That is all that Gildas himself tells us about Mount Badon. Perhaps the insertion derived from a slightly variant form of the legendary element connected with the battle of *Castle Guinnion* in the *Historia Brittonum* (see below). However, in the entry as it stands in the *Annales Cambriae,* we can see the Arthur of history beginning to turn into a figure of legend.

The second Arthurian entry in the *Annales Cambriae* is that which mentions the battle of Camlan:

> (537 or 539) Gueith cam lann inqua arthur & medraut corruerunt.

Perhaps this entry is the most authentic historical reference to Arthur which remains to us, and if we could locate Camlan definitely we might learn something more of the background of the battle, and decide to which area Arthur belongs. The best attempt, at least at first sight, is to understand Camlan as a later form of *Camboglanna,* the name of a fort on Hadrian's Wall, near where Birdoswald is now. However, we cannot accept this unhesitatingly: the form in the *Annales Cambriae* is *Camlann,* but from *Camboglanna* the form we should expect in Old Welsh is *Camglann,* cf. *Annales Cambriae, s.a.* 796, *Rudglann, s.a.* 807, *Arthgen.* We cannot infer anything from the entry about the relationship between Arthur and Medrod, and there is no suggestion of the treachery of Medrod described in Geoffrey of Monmouth's *Historia.* Since the majority of

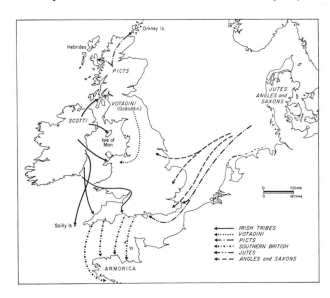

Map showing the Barbarian invasions and migrations into Britain from the fourth to the sixth centuries.

19

early entries in the *Annales Cambriae* refer to events in the north of the island, and Camlan may have been in the north too if the above derivation is correct, it is fair to infer that Arthur belongs to the "men of the North," like Urien, Rhydderch Hael, Llywarch Hen, and a host of historical figures of the early period about whom heroic traditions grew up in Wales. It is not irrelevant to connect with this the fact that it is in the poetry connected with the Britons of the North that we get one of the earliest references, perhaps the very first, to Arthur in Welsh poetry, the reference in the *Gododdin* (see below).

Let us now turn to another question. Have there been preserved any early references in other historical documents to men called Arthur who could have fought in the battle of Badon, whether its true date be 506, 516, or 518, and in the battle of Camlan in 537 or 539?

In the *Vita Columbae,* written by Adamnán before 704, and in the *Annals of Tigernach* there are references to Arthur son of Aidán mac Gabráin, who belongs in a North British context. According to the *Annals of Ulster* and the *Annals of Tigernach,* Aidán mac Gabráin died in 606, and according to the *Annals of Tigernach* his son Arthur was slain in battle in 594, nearly sixty years later than the date of the battle of Camlan given in the *Annales Cambriae.*

In another Irish text, *Tairired na nDéssi* (The Wanderings of the Déssi) or *Indarba inna nDési* (The Exile of the Déssi) attributed to the eighth century, and in the genealogies of MS. B. M. Harley 3859, there are references to another Arthur, a great-great-grandson of Gwerthefyr son of Aergol, and therefore a man of Dyfed. This Arthur, like Arthur son of Aidán, is much too late to have fought at Camlan; but the use of the name by a man of Dyfed and by Aidán's son in the North perhaps reflects the fame of an earlier historical Arthur.

We have seen that the only definite record of Arthur in the *Annales Cambriae* is that he fell with Medrod in the battle of Camlan, and that there is doubt as to the genuineness of the relative clause, mentioning Arthur's name, which is found in the entry about the battle of Badon. There is nothing dependable from other historical sources to add to this evidence. This brings us to what is said about Arthur in the *Historia Brittonum* as revised by Nennius, who refers to himself as a pupil of Elfoddw. According to the *Annales Cambriae* and to *Brut y Tywysogion,* Elfoddw died about 809. It is certain that Nennius was not the author of the whole of the *Historia Brittonum,* although what he says in his foreword shows that he wrote parts of it. It must be stressed again, as Sir Ifor Williams has done in showing that the story of Vortigern and the "Treachery of the Long Knives" is based on a Welsh legend, that Nennius himself says that one of his sources is the "tradition of our ancestors." This must be remembered in trying to analyse what he says about Arthur in chapter 56:

> In illo tempore Saxones invalescebant in multi-
> tudine et crescebant in Brittannia. Mortuo
> autem Hengisto, Octha filius eius, transivit de
> sinistrali parte Britanniae ad regnum Cantorum
> et de ipso orti sunt reges Cantorum. Tunc Ar-
> thur pugnabat contra illos in illis diebus cum re-
> gibus Brittonum, sed ipse dux erat bellorum.

> Primum bellum fuit in ostium fluminis quod di-
> citur Glein. Secundum et tertium et quartum et
> quintum super aliud flumen quod dicitur Dub-
> glas et est in regione Linnuis. Sextum bellum
> super flumen quod vocatur Bassas. Septimum
> fuit bellum in silva Celidonis, id est *Cat Coit
> Celidon.* Octavum fuit bellum in castello Guinn-
> ion, in quo Arthur portavit imaginem sanctae
> Mariae perpetuae virginis super humeros suos et
> pagani versi sunt in fugam in illo die et caedes
> magna fuit super illos per virtutem domini nostri
> Iesu Christi et per virtutem sanctae Mariae vir-
> ginis genetricis eius. Nonum bellum gestum est
> in urbe Legionis. Decimum gessit bellum in li-
> tore fluminis quod vocatur Tribruit. Undeci-
> mum factum est bellum in monte qui dicitur
> Agned. Duodecimum fuit bellum in monte Ba-
> donis, in quo corruerunt in uno die nongenti sex-
> aginta viri de uno impetu Arthur, et nemo
> prostravit eos nisi ipse solus. Et in omnibus bellis
> victor extitit.

Various points in the above quotation are worth noticing. This is the first time we are definitely told that Arthur fought the Saxons. There is no mention of the battle of Camlan. Why? Perhaps Nennius (or whoever wrote chapter 56), did not know any version of the early entries which were later included in the *Annales Cambriae.* Perhaps also the belief that Arthur had not died had already been developed, so that Nennius deliberately refrained from mentioning the battle of Camlan, even if he knew of a record similar to that in the *Annales Cambriae.* Was he, in the section on Arthur, giving preference to 'the tradition of our ancestors' about Arthur's victories, and keeping quiet about the battle where he was killed? These possibilities are at least worth mentioning.

Of the names of the places where the twelve battles were fought, only two can be identified with any confidence: Caerlleon is Chester, and Coed Celyddon must be somewhere in the south of Scotland. Possibly *Linnuis* is Lindsey. The locations of the others are not known with any certainty, though *Tryfrwyd* could be in Scotland, and Mount Badon somewhere in the mid-South of England. The geographical distribution of these five place-names (two certain and three uncertain), suggests that it is most unlikely that the historical Arthur fought in every one of the battles; and anyway, according to what we know, it is hard to believe that the Britons were fighting as far west as Chester and as far north as Southern Scotland in the last part of the fifth century and the beginning of the sixth. This suggests the most important thing of all which ought to be mentioned in connection with Nennius's list of battles, namely that it should not be looked on as a list of battles in all of which the historical Arthur fought, even if he did so in one or several of them. This means that no theories about the historical Arthur can be based on the locations of these battles. We will return to this point later.

The battle of Mount Badon is named twelfth and last in the list, which recalls Gildas's description of the battle of *Mons Badonicus* as "almost the last great massacre of the gallows-birds." Perhaps this is only a coincidence, but perhaps also the cleric, Nennius or another, who wrote chapter 56, put the battle of Mount Badon last in the list as an

> It is difficult to say anything precise about the Arthur of history. The idea that he was a mythological figure is no longer acceptable.
>
> —*Thomas Jones*

echo of Gildas's words. The *Historia Brittonum* calls the battle *in monte Badonis* which suggests the influence of the *De Excidio Britanniae.* Again, according to Nennius, it was in the battle of *Guinnion* and not in the battle of Badon (as in *Annales Cambriae*) that Arthur carried the image of the Virgin Mary (not the Cross of Christ as in the *Annales Cambriae*) on his shoulders. F. Lot suggested that it was the influence of Bede's description of the victory of Oswald over Cadwallon in the battle of Cant Ysgawl (= Hexham), through the help of the Virgin Mary, which is responsible for the mention of carrying Mary's image. Whatever the truth of this suggestion, and whatever the details of the connexion between the mention of Christ's Cross in the *Annales Cambriae* and the mention of the image of Mary in the *Historia Brittonum,* it is obviously a legendary element of ecclesiastical origin.

Where did Nennius get his list of twelve battles? A. G. Brodeur conceived the idea that chapter 56 in the *Historia Brittonum* is based on a Latin poem, and he sought to show that there are traces of Commodian Latin hexameters in the piece. In my opinion Brodeur failed to prove his case. However, it may be asked whether the list was based on an early Welsh poem which contained a list of famous battles attributed to Arthur, but in all of which he did not necessarily fight. In early Welsh poetry there are examples of this kind of list, and the earliest is the short list of battles in the poem to Cynan Garwyn fab Brochfael Ysgithrog of Powys, whose son Selyf ap Cynan was killed in the battle of Chester in 613. It is a praise-poem, and part of the eulogy is the reference to Cynan's battles on the Wye, in Anglesey, in South-West Wales and in Brycheiniog:

> Kynan kat diffret . . .
> kat ar wy kyrchet . . .
> kat ymon mawrdec . . .
> kat yg cruc dymet . . .
> kat ygwlat brachan . . .

In another poem the battles of Ulph and Urien Rheged are listed, but it appears from the internal evidence that part of the poem is later than Urien's time:

> kat yn ryt alclut kat ymynuer
> kat gellawr brewyn kat hireurur
> kat ymprysc katleu kat yn aber ioed . . .
> kat glutuein gweith pen coit.

Similarly in a poem which is difficult to date, but which is later than the time of Owain ab Urien, there is a list of battles in which Owain is said to have fought. The first line looks like a variant of the first line of the previous quotation:

> kat yn ryt alchut. kat yn ygwen
> kat yg gossulwyt abann udun.
> kat rac rodawys eiwyn drych . . .
> kat tuman llachar derlyw derlin . . .

It is significant that neither the second nor the third of the above quotations mentions the battle of Argoed Llwyfain, at which both Urien and his son Owain fought, according to a poem which does seem to be a genuine work of Taliesin, nor is there mention of the battle of Gwen Ystrad. Listing a chief's victorious battles was a fairly common feature of Welsh poems of praise from the earliest poets onwards. It was adopted by the vaticinatory poets in referring to the expected victories of the Prophesied Hero. There are traces of translation from Welsh in parts of the *Historia Brittonum,* and one should not overlook the possibility that a Welsh poem is at the root of the list of battles in chapter 56. We can even ask, hesitantly, if the names Dubglas / Bassas, and Celidon / Guinnion / Legion / Bregion / Badon reflect part of the original rhyme-scheme.

Some other details in chapter 56 must be considered. The phrase *tywyssawc cat* occurs in the early poetry, and its original meaning was probably 'leader of a host or army.' In this poetry, however, *cat* can mean 'battle' as well as 'host,' 'army.' Perhaps the phrase *dux bellorum* as a description of Arthur in the *Historia Brittonum* is a literal translation of *tywyssawc cadeu,* with *cadeu* understood as 'battles' rather than 'hosts, armies'; but before accepting this possibility, it should be remembered that the phrases *dux praelii* and *dux agminis* are used by Bede in describing the 'Hallelujah Victory.'

It is asserted in the *Historia Brittonum* that Arthur himself (*ipse solus*) slew 960 men in the battle of Mount Badon, a strange assertion in a prose text, but there are many examples of this kind of exaggeration in the Welsh eulogies and elegies. In the *Gododdin* it is said of Hyfaidd the Tall that 'five fifties' fell before his sword:

> kwydei *bym pymwnt* rac y lafnawr
> o wyr Deiuyr a Bryneich dychiawr
> ugein kant eu diuant en un awr.

Compare this with what is said about the son of Nwython in the same poem:

> em ladaut lu maur
> iguert i adraut
> ladaut map Nuithon
> o eur dorchogyon
> cant o deyrnet.

In a legendary poem, *Kat Godeu* ('The Battle of the Trees') Taliesin boasts that he has killed nine hundred men, *neu gorwyf gwaetlan. ar naw kant kynran,* 'I have made a massacre of nine hundred warriors.' Possibly it is some statement of this kind in a eulogy, not necessarily sung to the living Arthur, which is behind the assertion in the *Historia Brittonum* that Arthur slew 960 men. I do not wish to lay too much stress on the number 960 but it is worth noting that the corresponding form of the number in Welsh would be 'three three-hundreds and three-twenties,' a phrase which has affinities with the language and craftsmanship of the early poetry.

The evidence of the *Annales Cambriae* and the *Historia Brittonum* so far discussed shows that in the tenth century there were traditions of Arthur as a leader and winner of victories against the Saxons. It is very doubtful whether any of these traditions, apart from that of the battle of Camlan, can be accepted as real history. Reference in other texts added to the *Historia Brittonum* in MS. B. M. Harley 3859 show that non-heroic stories had begun to gather round the heroic tradition of Arthur by the tenth century. In the *Mirabilia* attached to the *Historia* the following story occurs:

> Est aliud mirabile in regione quae dicitur Buelt: est ibi cumulus lapidum et unus lapis superpositus super congestum cum vestigio canis in eo; quando venatus est porcum Troynt impressit Cabal, qui erat canis Arthuri militis, vestigium in lapide et Arthur postea congregavit congestum lapidum sub lapide in quo erat vestigium canis sui, et vocatur *Carn Cabal*. Et veniunt homines et tollunt lapidem in manibus suis per spatium diei et noctis et in crastino die invenitur super congestum suum.

The stone which always returns to its own place no matter where it is carried is a recognized motif in folk-tales, and that is the nucleus of the above story; but it has been turned into an onomastic story to give a fictitious explanation of the place-name Carn Cafall near Rhaeadr in Radnorshire (*Corn Cafallt* on modern maps). Nennius or someone else may have blundered in speaking of Cafall as a dog's name. *Carn* is not the usual word for a dog's paw; it means the hoof of a horse. As an onomastic story purporting to explain the name Carn Cafall, it would be much more effective if *Cafall* had been given as the name of Arthur's horse, and not that of his hound. The word *cafall* may be derived from Latin *caballus*, or may be cognate with it, if *caballus* is a Latin borrowing from Celtic as has been suggested. In *Canu Aneirin* lines 1202-3, *cauall* occurs as a word for 'horse': *Oid girth oed cuall / ar geuin e gauall* ('He was strong, he was swift / on his horse's back'). In the part of *Kulhwch and Olwen* which describes the hunting of Twrch Trwyth, Cafall is the name of Arthur's hound, but Cafall also occurs as the name of a horse. Altogether, it is fairly certain that originally Cafall was the name of a horse.

The second passage of Arthurian interest in the *Mirabilia* is the following:

> Est aliud miraculum in regione quae vocatur Ercing: habetur ibi supulcrum iuxta fontem qui cognominatur *Licat Anir;* et viri nomen qui sepultus est in tumulo sic vocabatur Anir: filius Arthuri militis erat et ipse occidit eum ibidem et sepelivit. Et veniunt homines ad mensurandum tumulum in longitudine aliquando sex pedes, aliquando novem, aliquando duodecim, aliquando quindecim; in qua mensura metieris eum in ista vice, iterum non invenies eum in una mensura, et ego solus probavi.

Llygad Amr (*al.* amir, anir) is the same as Gamber Head in Herefordshire today, cf. the *Book of Llandav*, ed. J. G. Evans and John Rhŷs, 1893, *usque ad amyr flumen,* p. 174: *super ripam amyr,* p. 200: *bet blain nant merthir. id*

est, amir, p. 226. This is another onomastic story with a common folk-motif, that a grave (or some other object) varies in its measurements. Both stories in the *Mirabilia* show that the name of 'Arthur the soldier' was known in the tenth century in south-east Wales, and that it was attracting to it non-heroic stories. In one we see the name of a cairn turn into the name of his dog (or horse) and in the other the name of a stream becomes the name of his son. Possibly the same process of the accumulation of popular stories round the name of Arthur was going on elsewhere too, but there is no evidence outside Buellt and Ergyng.

So much for the records of the *Annales Cambriae* and the *Historia Brittonum,* Latin texts from Welsh sources, in connexion with the story of Arthur. Let us now turn to early Welsh poetry. It is frequently said that the first reference to Arthur in Welsh goes back to the sixth century. This reference comes in the following lines in the *Gododdin:*—

> godolei o heit meirch e gayaf
> gochore brein du ar uur
> caer ceni bei ef Arthur.

If we take *gochore* as a copyist's mistake for *gochone,* the meaning of the two last lines seems to be: 'He glutted black ravens on the fortress wall, although he (i.e. Gwawrddur, the hero celebrated in the stanza) was not Arthur,' the poet's way of saying that Gwawrddur was a good fighter. This reference presupposes that Arthur was a recognized model of courage when these lines were written. It cannot, however, be proved that this was a part of the original *Gododdin* and therefore as old as the end of the sixth century or the beginning of the seventh. The text of the *Gododdin,* as we have it in a manuscript copied about 1250, contains some stanzas which cannot possibly be part of the original poem. However, the orthography of the stanza in which the above lines occur suggests that the stanza existed in a written form in the ninth century; we cannot say positively that it is older than that.

All that can be said is that this reference to Arthur is as early as the ninth century, and *could* be as early as the year 600, if it is part of the original *Gododdin.* Whatever its date, the reference confirms the historicity of Arthur, because there are no references in early Welsh heroic poetry to legendary or unhistorical figures. The stanza definitely belongs to the poetry of the old North, and this offers some support for the belief that Arthur was a chieftain from the North.

This reference, and chapter 56 of Nennius, reflect the heroic tradition of Arthur as a valiant leader. There is no sign in them, as there is in the *Mirabilia,* of the accumulation of popular non-heroic stories around his name. We can, however, find evidence of this sort of development in a number of early poems. The great common difficulty with these poems is to date them, but their orthography, language, rhyme and technique show that they are earlier than 1100. For some of these poems, this date is supported by the opinion of Sir Ifor Williams.

By now it has been established that some of the poems in the *Book of Taliesin* (*c.* 1275) are monologues and dialogues belonging to two early forms *of* the 'Story of Taliesin.' *Preiddeu Annwfn* ('The Spoils of the Underworld') is a poem of this kind (*The Book of Taliesin,* pp. 54-6), and Sir Ifor Williams gives his opinion that it is definitely pre-Norman. It can be argued that it is a monologue spoken by Taliesin in one of the early forms of the story which gathered round his name. The speaker says in a series of stanzas that he went with Arthur in his ship *Prydwen* to various castles (*caer* = fortress, castle): Caer Siddi, Caer Feddwid, Caer Rigor (or Rygor), Caer Goludd, Caer Fandwy and Caer Ochren. At the end of each stanza is a kind of refrain, naming Arthur and his ship *Prydwen:*

Tri lloneit *Prytwen* yd aetham ni idi.
nam seith ny dyrreith o Gaer Sidi. (*Book of Taliesin,* p. 54, lines 23-4).

A phan aetham ni gan *Arthur* trafferth lechrit
namyn seith ny dyrreith o Gaer Vedwit.   (*ibid.,* 55, 6-8).

Tri lloneit *Prytwen* yd aetham ni ar vor.
namyn seith ny dyrreith o Gaer Rigor.   (*ibid.,* 55, 11-3).

Tri lloneit *Prytwen* yd aeth gan *Arthur*
namyn seith ny dyrreith o Gaer Golud.   (*ibid.,* 55, 17-8).

A phan aetham ni gan *Arthur* auyrdwl gofwy.
namyn seith ny dyrreith o Gaer Vandwy. (*ibid.,* 55, 23-5).

Pan aetham ni gan *Arthur* afyrdwl gynhen.

namyn seith ny dyrreith o Gaer Ochren.   (*ibid.,* 56, 2-4).

["Three shiploads of Prydwen we went to it,
save seven, none returned from Caer Siddi . . .
And when we went with Arthur, (?) famed was the disaster,
save seven, none returned from Caer Feddwid . . .
Three shiploads of Prydwen we went on the sea.
save seven, none returned from Caer Rigor . . .
Thre shiploads of Prydwen went with Arthur,
save seven, none returned from Caer Goludd . . .
And when we went with Arthur, calamitous the visitation,
save seven, none returned from Caer Fandwy . . .
When we went with Arthur, calamitous the contest,
save seven, none returned from Caer Ochren."]

There is also a reference to *Caer Wydr* ('the fortress of glass') beyond which 'they had not seen Arthur's valour,' and to *Caer Bedryfan* ('the four-cornered or four-peaked castle'). From Arthur's expedition or expeditions only seven returned, says the poem, and these presumably include the poet himself. It looks like something more than a coincidence that Taliesin's name appears in *Branwen Ferch Lyr* as one of the seven men who escaped back to the Island of the Mighty after the great massacre of the Irish and Welsh in Ireland. Possibly the story of Bendigeidfran's expedition to Ireland, told in *Branwen,* is

a rationalized form of an earlier story, told, though not in full, in *Preiddeu Annwfn.*

Significantly, the poem has a reference to the imprisonment of Gweir in Caer Siddi "according to the tale of Pwyll and Pryderi," a tale of which we have one form in the first and third branches of the "Four Branches of the Mabinogi." The poem also refers to the cauldron of the Chieftain of the Underworld (*Pen Annwfn*) and it will be remembered that the first branch of the Mabinogi says that Pwyll's title 'Prince of Dyfed' (*Pendefig Dyfed*) was changed to 'Chieftain of the Underworld' (*Pen Annwfn*) because of the hero's sojourn in the Underworld. Arthur plays no part in the Four Branches as such, but this poem shows that at least part of their basic material was connected with Arthur in an early form of the 'Story of Taliesin.' In other words, the heroic tradition of Arthur was becoming mixed with early legends and folk-lore. This process is taken a step further in *Preiddeu Annwfn,* though it cannot be traced in every detail, and it seems that many traditions of every kind, heroic and legendary, accumulated round his name.

Two other poems which appear to belong in the first place to the Taliesin-story are *Kat Goddeu* ('The Battle of the Trees,' *Book of Taliesin,* pp. 23-9) and *Cadeir Teyrnon* ('The Seat of Teyrnon,' *ibid.,* 34-5). Arthur is named in both of these:

derwydon doethur darogenwch y *Arthur.* (*ibid.,* 27, lines 8-9).

treded dofyn doethur y vendigaw *Arthur*
Arthur vendigat (MS vendigan) ar gerd gyfaenat.   (*ibid.,* 34, 21-3).

["Wise prophets, you prophesy of Arthur"
"One of three deeply (?) wise to bless Arthur,
Arthur blessed (?) in harmonious song."]

A poem with a similar background is the *Marwnat Uthyr Pen* ('The Death-song of Uthyr the Chief,' *ibid.,* p. 71), where Arthur is named once again:

Neu vi a rannwys vy echlessur
nawuetran yg *gwrhyt Arthur.* (*ibid.,* 71, lines 15-6).

["I have shared my refuge,
A ninth share in the *valour of Arthur.*"]

In the *Black Book of Carmarthen* (ed. J. Gwenogvryn Evans, 1910), there is material which is much more closely connected with elements which occur in later Arthurian stories. The manuscript belongs to the end of the twelfth century or the beginning of the thirteenth, but much of the contents is earlier than that. The *englynion* on pp. 71-3 form a soliloquy about Geraint ab Erbin, hero of the Welsh Arthurian romance *Geraint and Enid,* who corresponds to Erec in Chrétien de Troyes's poem *Erec et Enide.* In three *englynion,* each beginning *Rac Gereint* ('Before Geraint'), Geraint is praised as a brave warrior against his enemies. Then come nine *englynion,* each beginning *En Llogborth,* and then six *englynion* beginning *Oet re rereint* (read *reteint* = redeint), and concluding:

Ban aned Gereint oet agored
pirth new. rotei Crist a arched

prid mirein Prydein wogoned.

["When Geraint was born, Heaven's gates were
    opened; Christ granted what was asked, a fair
    countenance, the glory of Britain."]

The heroic tradition of Geraint is connected with Devon,
and it would seem that the Llongborth which is named in
the poem is an old form of the name Langport on the bank
of the Parret in Somerset. The reference to Arthur in the
following stanza shows that whatever story of Geraint had
been preserved, it had already come in contact with the
story of Arthur:

En Llogborth y gueleise y Arthur
guir deur kymynint a dur
ameraudur llywiaudir llawur.

["At Llongborth I saw Arthur—brave men
    hewed with steel—emperor, battle-ruler."]

The poem is part of an early form of a Geraint-legend. It
is difficult to date exactly, but it is certainly earlier than
1100, and could be as early as the ninth or tenth century.
It shows the heroic tradition of Devon already connected
with Arthur before the days of Geoffrey of Monmouth and
Chrétien.

Another poem in the *Black Book of Carmarthen* (pp.
94-6), which must be discussed is the dialogue between
Arthur and the Porter, Glewlwyd Gafaelfawr (lit. 'Brave-
grey mighty-grasp'). It can be inferred from the dialogue
that Arthur and his men are outside the house of which
Glewlwyd Gafaelfawr is the porter:

A.   Pa gur yv y porthaur?
G.   Gleuluid Gauaeluaur.
        Pa gur ae gouin?
A.   Arthur a Chei Guin.
G.   Pa imda genhid?
A.   Guir gorev im bid.
G.   Ym ty ny doi
        onys guaredi.
A.   Mi ae guaredi
        a thi ae gueli.

[A.   What man is porter?
G.   Glewlwyd Mighty-grasp.
A.   What man asks it?
A.   Arthur and Cei Wyn.
G.   What company have you?
A.   The best men in the world.
G.   Into my house thou shalt not come
        Unless thou disclose them.
A.   I will disclose them,
        and thou shalt see them.]

Then Arthur names his followers; Cei, Mabon fab Modron ('Uther Pendragon's servant'), Cysteint fab Banon,
Gwyn Godyfrion, Manawydan ap Llŷr ('profound was his
counsel'), Mabon fab Mellt, Anwas the Winged, Llwch
Llawynnawg, and others. Cei's feats are praised beyond
those of anyone else, and mention is made of Llacheu, who
elsewhere (see below) is called Arthur's son:

Kei Guin a Llacheu
digonint we kadeu
kin gloes glas vereu.

["Kei Wyn and Llacheu waged battles before the
    pang of blue spears."]

It will be remembered that the *Historia Brittonum* mentioned the seventh battle of Arthur as: *in litore fluminis
quod vocatur Tribruit* (MS. H); *quod nos vocamus Trath
Treuroit* (MS. M). *Tribruit* represents Tryfrwyd and *Trath
Treuroit* represents Traeth ('shore, strand') Tryfrwyd. In
the poem under consideration there are two references to
Tryfrwyd by Arthur when relating the feats of his men:

Neus tuc Manauid
eis tull o Trywruid. . . .

Pop cant id cuitin
id cvitin pop cant
rac Beduir Bedrydant
ar traethev Trywruid
in amvin (a) Garwluid.

["Manawyd brought a broken shield from Tryfr-
    wyd. . . . By the hundred they fell, they fell by
    the hundred, before Bedwyr Bedrydant, on the
    shores of Tryfrwyd, defending (?) Garwlwyd."]

There is also mentioned a fight with a hag in 'Afarnach's
Hall,' which reminds us of Arthur's attack on the White
Witch, daughter of the Black Witch, in the story of *Kulhwch and Olwen*. Certainly the reference to the porter
Glewlwyd (though it is not said that he is Arthur's porter),
the list of Arthur's followers and the citations of their abilities and feats connect the poem closely with *Kulhwch and
Olwen,* a story which is older than Geoffrey of Monmouth.
If only we knew more of the story which is the background
of the dialogue! One suggestion may be made: if the meaning of *gwared* in the beginning of the dialogue is 'disclose,
discover' as I think it is, it suggests that Arthur's followers, and perhaps Arthur himself, had become invisible for
a time; and since Arthur promises to reveal them, perhaps
one of his 'endowments' or magical gifts in the background story was the power to make men invisible, as does
Menw fab Teirgwaedd in *Kulhwch and Olwen* (*White
Book Mabinogion,* col. 472), and as does Arthur's own
cloak in *Breudwyt Ronabwy* (*ibid.,* col. 212).

Also in the *Black Book of Carmarthen* are two *englynion*
of Arthurian interest, referring to the graves of heroes.
One of them comes in a series of *englynion* (*loc. cit.,* pp.
99-100), which form a monologue in which someone says,
as part of a story, that he has been in the places where
early heroes were slain, such as Gwenddolau ap Ceidiaw,
Brân ab Iwerydd, Meurig ap Careian, and Llacheu son of
Arthur:

Mi a wum lle llas Llachev
mab Arthur uthir ig kertev
ban ryre[e]int brein ar crev.

["I have been where Llacheu son of Arthur was
    slain, marvellous (?) in songs (or crafts), when
    ravens croaked over blood."]

Here is another reference to Llacheu son of Arthur, mentioned above in the dialogue "What man is porter?" All
that the two references suggest is that he was a brave soldier killed in battle, and that he was known as a legendary
figure rather than as a historical one.

The second *englyn* comes in the series *Englynion y Beddau* ('The Stanzas of the Graves'; *loc. cit.,* p. 67, lines 12-3):

> Bet y March. bet y Guythur.
> bet y Gugaun Cletyfrut.
> anoeth bid bet y Arthur.

The first two lines simply mean: 'there is a grave for March, a grave for Gwythur, a grave for Gwgawn of the Red Sword.' The third line is a crux; taken as it stands it can mean 'a wonder of the world is Arthur's grave.' Sir Ifor Williams has suggested that the word *braut* ('judgment') originally stood after *bid,* giving the meaning: 'A wonder till Judgment (Day) a grave for Arthur.' This makes the line too long, however, unless we delete the *y* before *Arthur,* and since it already stands before the names March, Gwythur and Gwgawn, I believe the line should be left as it stands. The stanza as it is, is a regular *englyn milwr,* with seven syllables in each line. Since the word *anoethau,* plural of *anoeth,* is used in *Kulhwch and Olwen* for the difficult objects which Kulhwch must find before he may win Olwen as his wife, the word *anoeth* in this *englyn* may be taken as meaning 'something difficult to find,' with *bid* ('world') strengthening the meaning that nowhere can it be found.

I think it can be concluded from this that Arthur had attracted to himself the folk-motif of the Vanished Undying Hero. Other Welsh examples of this motif are Hiriell of Gwynedd, Owain Lawgoch and Owain Glyndŵr. Other references in the 'Stanzas of the Graves' reflect the existence of other stories about heroic and legendary characters who had become, in legend, followers of Arthur. It is significant that in the above *englyn* Arthur is mentioned together with March (Mark), the king in the Tristan-Esyllt legend, and with Gwythur (? son of Greidawl) and Gwgawn Red-Sword, who all figured in heroic tradition, so far as we can tell from the broken fragments which remain to us.

The existence of a host of stories which were being brought more and more into contact with Arthur is strongly suggested by the evidence of the earliest Triads. Apart from the 'Triads of the Horses' in the *Black Book of Carmarthen* (pp. 27-8) which do not refer to Arthur at all, the oldest collection of the 'Historical Triads' is the one in Peniarth MS. 16. The manuscript belongs to the thirteenth century, but the Triads in it are almost wholly free of the influence of the Norman romances, and they refer to stories which are much older than the date of the manuscript. In some of them Arthur himself is named, as well as other characters connected with him, e.g.:

> Three Well-Endowed (?) Men of the Isle of Britain: Gwalchmei fab Gwyar and Llacheu fab Arthur and Rhiwallawn Broom-Hair.
>
> Three Frivolous Bards (*overveird*) of the Isle of Britain: Arthur and Cadwallawn fab Cadfan and Rahaut *eil* (son of) Morgan.
>
> Three Red Ravagers (*ruduoawc*) of the Isle of Britain: Arthur and Rhun fab Beli and Morgan Mwynfawr.
>
> Three Mighty Swineherds (*gwrdveichyat*) of the Isle of Britain: Tristan son of Tallwch, who kept

the swine of March son of Meirchiawn while the swineherd went to ask Esyllt to come to speak with him. And Arthur sought one pig of them, either by deceit or force, (but) he did not get it . . .

When the evidence of the early poetry, the Triads and the *Mirabilia* is combined, we can see fairly clearly the process of connecting with Arthur folk-stories and heroic sagas which had once been independent of him. The process had begun in Wales at least as early as the ninth century, long before the days of Geoffrey of Monmouth and before any possible influence by Continental romance-writers. Those stories and sagas were recited orally, and only very few were written down.

The one Arthurian story in Welsh which is definitely earlier than Geoffrey of Monmouth's *Historia* is *Kulhwch and Olwen,* and in it we see how the Arthurian legendary cycle was increasing steadily. In the surviving fragments of the saga of Heledd daughter of Cyndrwyn, believed to have been composed about 850, there is a reference to Kulhwch as a brave hero:

> Kyndylan, *Gulhwch* gynnifiat llew,
> Bleid dilin disgynnyat
> Nyt atuer twrch tref y dat.

There is no way of knowing whether Kulhwch's story had already been connected with Arthur when the Heledd-saga was composed, but certainly by the time of Nennius another independent story, that of the hunting of Twrch Trwyth, had become part of the Arthurian legend, as we have already seen. In *Kulhwch and Olwen* the stories of Kulhwch, of Goreu son of Custennin, of the hunting of Twrch Trwyth, of Mabon son of Modron, of the Oldest Animals, and a host of other originally independent tales have been joined together.

There is a list of Arthur's warriors, reminiscent of the shorter list in the poem 'What man is porter?' in the *Black Book.* The list has developed in the process of bringing more and more figures who originally belonged to other Welsh and Irish sagas, to history, to legend and folk-lore, into the orbit of Arthur. Nennius' *dux bellorum,* the 'leader of battles' who fought with the Kings of Britain against the Saxons, has become the 'Chief of the Princes of this Island,' and has fought in Greater and Lesser India, in Africa, in Corsica, and in Greece. He has his wife *Gwenhwyfar,* 'chief of the Ladies of this Island,' his ship *Prydwen* (as in *Preiddeu Annwfn*), his cloak (called *Gwen* in *Rhonabwy's Dream*), his spear *Rhongomyniad* (as in Geoffrey's *Historia*), his shield *Wyneb Gwrthucher,* his sword *Caledfwlch,* his knife *Carnwennan,* his dog *Cafall,* his mare *Llamrei,* his hall *Ehangwen* which was built by his carpenter, and his bishop *Bedwini* to bless his food and drink. The magnanimous words of Arthur to his porter contain at least the seed of the courtly dignity of the Christian Emperor depicted in Geoffrey's *Historia* and the chivalrous society of the Round Table:

> A shameful thing it is to leave in wind and rain a man such as you speak of. . . . We are noble men so long as we are resorted to. The greater the bounty we show, the greater will be our nobility and our fame and our glory.

Some of the warriors of Arthur's court who help Kulhwch in his quest for Olwen are Cei, Bedwyr, Cynddylig the Guide, who was as good a leader in a strange land as in his own country, Gwrhyr Interpreter of Tongues, who knew every language, including those of the birds and beasts, Gwalchmei son of Gwyar, who never returned home without accomplishing the mission on which he had departed, and Menw son of Teirgwaedd, the magician who cast a spell on men, so that they were not seen, but could themselves see everyone. All this, taken together, shows that Arthur had attracted to himself a wealth of stories, in which he remained the central figure.

The Arthurian legend was not confined to Wales. According to Hermann of Tournai in his *De Miraculis S. Mariae Laudunensis* (1146), some canons of Laon, who were journeying from Exeter to Bodmin in 1113, were shown 'the throne and oven of that King Arthur who is famed in the stories of the Britons (*Britannorum*).' According to the same author, there was a squabble in Bodmin between the servants of one of the canons and a Cornishman who insisted that Arthur still lived, 'just,' says Hermann, 'as the Bretons (*Britones*) quarrel with the French about King Arthur.' In 1113, therefore, the Cornish as well as the Welsh knew popular tales about Arthur connected with special places, and the Cornish and the Bretons believed that the hero was not dead. The line *Anoeth bid bet y Arthur* in the *englyn* from the *Black Book* already discussed shows that this last belief was held among the Welsh. William of Malmesbury knew about the belief among the Bretons; in his *Gesta Regum* (1125) he says that 'vain stories of the Bretons (*nugae Britonum*) prate to this day' about Arthur, and that 'Arthur's grave is nowhere to be seen, with the result that old songs (*antiquitas naeniarum*) say that he will come again.'

Geoffrey of Monmouth was a contemporary of William of Malmesbury, and it is likely that they were acquainted. Since Geoffrey was of Breton descent and had been brought up in Wales, it is a fair supposition that he knew some of the stories told of Arthur by the Welsh, Bretons and Cornish. In his *Prophetia Merlini,* written in 1134-5 and published separately before being included in the *Historia* (1136), Merlin refers to Arthur as 'the boar of Cornwall,' prophesies his victories, and says that 'his end will be uncertain,' that 'his praises will be sung on the lips of the people,' and that 'his deeds will be food for story-tellers.' It is an entirely reasonable conclusion that the last phrase means that the deeds of Arthur were already 'food for story-tellers' when Geoffrey was writing the *Prophetia Merlini,* i.e. that oral tales about Arthur were being narrated by story-tellers.

I believe that the evidence dealt with so far shows, at least partly, how a historical figure, perhaps from North Britain, belonging to the late fifth or early sixth century, grew into a figure of heroic tradition, as did Llywarch Hen, Urien and his son Owain, and many another historical figure from the same period and place. This heroic figure, for some reason which may never be exactly explained, attracted to himself more and more sagas and popular legends, which were originally independent of him. The zenith of this development before Geoffrey's *Historia,* as far as the written evidence is concerned, is *Kulhwch and Olwen.* In discussing the evidence, I have not dealt with the Saints' lives; deliberately, since so little critical analysis of them has been done so far. They too show the existence of stories about Arthur, principally in the *Life of Cadog* (c. 1090) by Lifris of Llancarfan, the *Life of Carannog* (c. 1100?), the *Life of Illtud* (c. 1100?), and the *Life of Padarn* (c. 1120), and if we remember the ethical purpose which

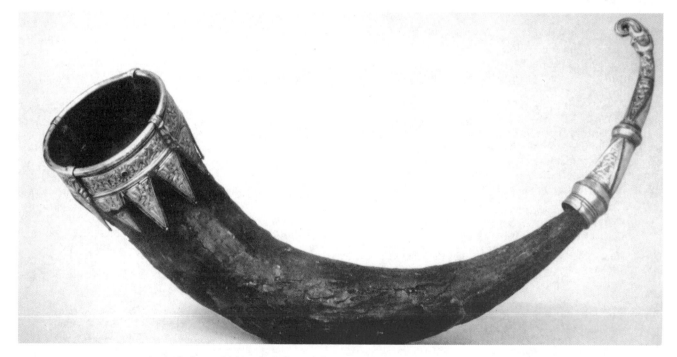

An Anglo-Saxon drinking horn discovered in a burial-mound at Taplow, Buckinghamshire.

motivated their composition, they support and strengthen the development we have described.

In my opinion, Geoffrey's *Historia* is not much indebted for its material to oral tales about Arthur, nor did the French romances grow from Geoffrey's book. The *Historia* and the Romances represent two further steps, each separate from the other, in the development of the stories about Arthur, but it is no part of my purpose to discuss those steps here. (pp. 3-21)

> *Thomas Jones, "The Early Evolution of the Legend of Arthur," in* Nottingham Mediaeval Studies, *Vol. VIII, 1964, pp. 3-21.*

DEVELOPMENT OF THE LEGEND THROUGH MALORY

William Caxton

[Caxton is revered as the first English printer. In 1475, while living in Bruges, he set up and published The Recuyell of the Historyes of Troye, *the first book printed in English. One year later he established a press in Westminster, where, during the next decade and a half, he produced over 80 separate works. Caxton was a gifted editor, translator, and author in his own right. He often wrote prefaces to the works he published, supplying information (when available) about authorship, textual history, genre, intended audience, narrative structure, and other critical and aesthetic matters. His most famous publications include Geoffrey Chaucer's* Canterbury Tales *(1478 and 1484), John Gower's* Confessio amantis *(1483), a translation of* The Golden Legend *(1483), and Malory's* Noble and Joyous book entytled le morte Darthur *(1485). In the following excerpt from the preface of the last-named work, Caxton argues that Arthur's reputation is chiefly literary. He outlines the historicity of Arthur's story and briefly traces the steps that led to his publishing Malory's* Morte.]

After that I had accomplysshed and fynysshed dyvers hystoryes as wel of contemplacyon as of other hystoryal and worldly actes of grete conquerours and prynces, and also certeyn bookes of ensaumples and doctryne, many noble and dyvers gentylmen of thys royame of Englond camen and demaunded me many and oftymes wherfore that I have not do made and enprynte the noble hystorye of the Saynt Greal and of the moost renomed Crysten kyng, fyrst and chyef of the thre best Crysten, and worthy, kyng Arthur, whyche ought moost to be remembred emonge us Englysshemen tofore al other Crysten kynges.

For it is notoyrly knowen thorugh the unyversal world that there been nine worthy and the best that ever were, that is to wete, thre Paynyms, thre Jewes, and thre Crysten men. As for the Paynyms, they were tofore the Incarnacyon of Cryst whiche were named, the fyrst Hector of Troye, of whome th'ystorye is comen bothe in balade and in prose, the second Alysaunder the Grete, and the thyrd,

Julyus Cezar, Emperour of Rome, of whome th'ystoryes ben wel knowen and had. And as for the thre Jewes whyche also were tofore th'Yncarnacyon of our Lord, of whome the fyrst was Duc Josué whyche brought the chyldren of Israhel into the londe of byheste, the second Davyd, kyng of Jerusalem, and the thyrd Judas Machabeus, of these thre the Bybliie rehercheth al theyr noble hystoryes and actes. And sythe the sayd Incarnacyon have ben thre noble Crysten men stalled and admytted thorugh the unyversal world into the nombre of the nine beste and worthy, of whome was fyrst the noble Arthur, whos noble actes I purpose to wryte thys present book here folowyng. The second was Charlemayn, or Charles the Grete, of whome th'ystorye is had in many places, bothe in Frensshe and Englysshe; and the thyrd and last was Godefray of Boloyn, of whos actes and lyf I made a book unto th'excellent prynce and kyng of noble memorye, kyng Edward the Fourth.

The sayd noble jentylmen instantly requyred me t'emprynte th'ystorye of the sayd noble kyng and conquerour kyng Arthur and of his knyghtes, wyth th'ystorye of the Saynt Greal and of the deth and endyng of the sayd Arthur, affermyng that I ought rather t'enprynte his actes and noble feates than of Godefroye of Boloyne or ony of the other eyght, consyderyng that he was a man borne wythin this royame and kyng and emperour of the same, and that there ben in Frensshe dyvers and many noble volumes of his actes, and also of his knyghtes.

To whome I answerd that dyvers men holde oppynyon that there was no suche Arthur and that alle suche bookes as been maad of hym ben but fayned and fables, bycause that somme cronycles make of hym no mencyon ne remembre hym noothynge, ne of his knyghtes.

Whereto they answerd, and one in specyal sayd, that in hym that shold say or thynke that there was never suche a kyng callyd Arthur myght wel be aretted grete folye and blyndenesse, for he sayd that there were many evydences of the contrarye. Fyrst, ye may see his sepulture in the monasterye of Glastyngburye; and also in Polycronycon, in the fifth book, the syxte chappytre, and in the seventh book, the twenty-thyrd chappytre, where his body was buryed, and after founden and translated into the sayd monasterye. Ye shal se also in th'ystorye of Bochas, in his book DE CASU PRINCIPUM, parte of his noble actes, and also of his falle. Also Galfrydus, in his Brutysshe book, recounteth his lyf. And in dyvers places of Englond many remembraunces ben yet of hym and shall remayne perpetuelly, and also of his knyghtes: fyrst, in the abbey of Westmestre, at Saynt Edwardes shryne, remayneth the prynte of his seal in reed waxe, closed in beryll, in whych is wryton PATRICIUS ARTHURUS BRITANNIE GALLIE GERMANIE DACIE IMPERATOR; item, in the castel of Dover ye may see Gauwayns skulle and Cradoks mantel; at Wynchester, the Rounde Table; in other places Launcelottes swerde and many other thynges.

Thenne, al these thynges consydered, there can no man resonably gaynsaye but there was a kyng of thys lande named Arthur. For in al places, Crysten and hethen, he is reputed and taken for one of the nine worthy, and the fyrst of the thre Crysten men. And also he is more spoken of beyonde the see, moo bookes made of his noble actes, than there be in Englond; as wel in Duche, Ytalyen, Spaynysshe, and Grekysshe, as in Frensshe. And yet of record remayne in wytnesse of hym in Wales, in the toune of Camelot, the grete stones and mervayllous werkys of yron lyeng under the grounde, and ryal vautes, which dyvers now lyvyng hath seen. Wherfor it is a mervayl why he is no more renomed in his owne contreye, sauf onelye it accordeth to the word of God, whyche sayth that no man is accept for a prophete in his owne contreye.

Thenne, al these thynges forsayd aledged, I coude not wel denye but that there was suche a noble kyng named Arthur, and reputed one of the nine worthy, and fyrst and chyef of the Cristen men. And many noble volumes be made of hym and of his noble knyghtes in Frensshe, which I have seen and redde beyonde the see, which been not had in our maternal tongue. But in Walsshe ben many, and also in Frensshe, and somme in Englysshe, but nowher nygh alle. Wherfore, suche as have late ben drawen oute bryefly into Englysshe, I have, after the symple connynge that God hath sente to me, under the favour and correctyon of al noble lordes and gentylmen, enprysed to enprynte a book of the noble hystoryes of the sayd kynge Arthur and of certeyn of his knyghtes [The Noble and Joyous Book Entytled Le Morte Darthur], after a copye unto me delyverd, whyche copye syr Thomas Malorye dyd take oute of certeyn bookes of Frensshe and reduced it into Englysshe. (pp. cxi-cxiii)

> *William Caxton, in a preface to* The Works of
> Sir Thomas Malory, Vol. 1, *edited by Eugène
> Vinaver, Oxford at the Clarendon Press, 1947,
> pp. cxi-cxv.*

Jessie L. Weston

[*Weston was a noted Arthurian scholar. In the following excerpt, she considers the historical genesis of Arthurian legend and reviews the principal genres of Arthurian romance.*]

King Arthur and his knights! Was there ever a time when to English ears these words were not an "open sesame" to the gates of a Fairy-land, the more charming in that we believed it to be partly, at least, real? Even in the stern Puritan days when romance was a thing to be abhorred of the "saints" Milton could have dreams of devoting an epic to the glory of the British hero. (We wonder what the poet of the *Paradise Lost* would have made of that fascinating and tangled web of Celtic-French fact and fancy!) And yet how little, how very little, we know about them. Let any of us take any twelve of our friends, of those whom we know to be above the average in intelligence and culture, and ask them one by one, what they can tell us of King Arthur, and how we can gain information as to his life and doings, and what shall we be told? Certainly we should be referred to Malory and Tennyson—and there for ten out of the twelve the matter would end. Perhaps, only perhaps, the other two might be able to tell us that there was a history by a certain Geoffrey of Monmouth, out of which a certain Walter Map drew materials to invent the legend of Arthur and the Grail, and it might be, that if exception-

---

An excerpt from *Sir Gawain and the Green Knight* (c. fourteenth century):

When the last assault had been delivered, and the siege of Troy was over, and the city was destroyed by fire and laid in ashes, Prince Aeneas sailed away with his noble kindred, and they conquered new realms and made themselves lords of well-nigh all the riches of the Western Isles. Romulus made his way swiftly to Rome, and built that city splendidly, and called it after himself by the name which it still bears. Ticius went to Tuscany and built dwellings there, and Langobard did the like in Lombardy. And far over the French flood Felix Brutus, with joy in his heart, founded a broad realm on the hills of Britain. In that kingdom there have been many wars and tumults and wonders, with shifts of good fortune and of ill.

And when Britain had been founded by this noble Prince, a bold race of men was bred there, lovers of battle, who wrought much strife as the years passed. And more marvels befell in that land than are told of in any other. But of all that dwelt here as Kings of Britain, King Arthur, they tell us, was the noblest. And so I mean to tell of an adventure, which some men hold a marvel; among all the tales about Arthur it is one of the strangest.

> Sir Gawain and the Green Knight, *in* Medieval Romances, *edited by Roger Sherman Loomis and Laura Hibbard Loomis, Random House, 1957.*

---

ally well informed, our last friend might contradict this statement and say, "No, it was not Map who invented the Grail story at all, but a French poet, called Chrétien."

And, indeed, if we get as much information as that, we shall be fortunate! It is no exaggeration to say the few names just mentioned represent all that is known, and that at second or third hand, by even highly educated people, of this great body of literature. A few years ago a *History of English Poetry* was published, and received with acclamation, in which the writer practically attributed the whole body of Arthurian Romance, so far as he considered it worthy of notice, to Walter Map. Only the other day, in one of our leading journals, there appeared a long article from the pen of a popular writer, who poses as a person of exceptional culture and literary discernment, wherein Wagner's *Parsifal* was severely criticised as a "wide departure from Malory!" So much do even our would-be teachers know of the matter.

There are certainly reasons which might be urged in excuse for this widespread ignorance of a legend which we have every right to claim as national; the greater portion of Arthurian literature is in a foreign tongue, and it is only in comparatively recent years that a systematic attempt has been made to arrive at a clear idea of the date, authorship, and mutual relation of the romances composing the cycle. For long even professed scholars were content with the most meagre, confused, and superficial knowledge on a subject which touches us so nearly.

But have we any right to look on King Arthur as a national hero? It has been objected that since Arthur was a *British* chieftain we are entirely wrong in treating him as an *English* hero. This is surely a pedantic accuracy which over-shoots its own mark; we might as reasonably contend that the French have no right to glory in the *Matière de France,* since Charlemagne was certainly no Frenchman! The truth appears to be that absolute racial identity between hero and hero-worshippers is a factor of minor importance in the case of peoples, who, like the English and the French, are compounded of various racial elements. What *is* essential to a national hero is that he shall have successfully maintained the honour of the *land*. Arthur represented the honour of Britain, Charlemagne that of *"la douce France,"* the feeling which glorified both was patriotism in the most exact and accurate sense of the word.

The evolution of Arthur as a national hero, indeed, is a very curious and striking example of the unconquerable vitality and power of impressing itself characteristic of the Celtic genius. We reject, and very reasonably, the tradition which represents the British King as carrying his arms triumphantly through France and Italy, and vanquishing even the power of Rome; but what the *historical* Arthur did not do, the *legendary* Arthur assuredly achieved. Not only did the English people (representative of the Saxon, Danish, and Norman invaders of British soil) take him to their heart, and as they became welded into one folk accept him as the traditionary embodiment of the spirit of their land, but he took captive the imagination alike of France and of Italy. He is immortalised in French verse and in Italian architecture; Sicily claims to be his resting-place; and there is no European literature of any importance which does not contribute its quota to the great mass of Arthurian romance.

Yet a comparatively small proportion only of this literature is in the English tongue. When the Arthurian legend was at the height of its popularity the dominant language was French, and it was in the form of French romance that the *literary* legend became popularised in this land.

Nevertheless it is, I believe, a mistaken view which ascribes this popularity entirely to court influence, and the charm of Chrétien's verse: the legend had not been entirely forgotten in its own land, and re-introduced from without; nor is there any reason to suppose, as some scholars have done, that the knowledge of it was confined exclusively to the survivors of the original inhabitants of the Island. Too much has, I think, been made of the racial animosity existing between Briton and Saxon. We know for instance, that for a period extending over two centuries at least the two nationalities lived side by side in the city of Exeter. Even to-day archæologists will point out where the line of demarcation between the two towns (for such they practically were) ran, nor were the Britons treated as a subjugated folk. William of Malmesbury distinctly says that they enjoyed equal rights with the English. This state of matters lasted well into the tenth century; are we to believe that during all these years the memory of bye-gone strife was kept alive to such an extent that Saxon and Briton never came into friendly contact with each other, held no intercommunion, never inter-married, never made common

cause against their common foe the Danes? They ask a great deal who ask us to believe this! Evidence points the other way; in Cornwall, the refuge of the surviving British population we find to-day families bearing a name of such purely *Saxon* origin as Eddy (Æddi) and yet claiming to be of pure Cornish descent; in East Anglia, a Saxon stronghold, we find in the seventh century the British name of Cadwallon. Surely it is more reasonable to suppose that by the transmission of oral legend the name and fame of the British chief had become thoroughly familiar to the Saxon population long before the "literary" stage of evolution had been reached.

Every folk must have its national hero, and it is worthy of note that the Saxon or Tentonic heroic legends never took real root in this land. That they were introduced we know. Have we not the poem of *Beowulf?* But Beowulf and his fight with Grendel and the dragon, were less popular than the record of how Arthur slew the giant of Mont S. Michel, and conquered the Demon Cat. The great *Siegfried* legend certainly came to these shores, and we find traces of its influence in Celtic romance; but the only Teutonic hero who seems to have gained firm footing on English ground was *Wieland,* who as *Wayland Smith* still survives in popular tradition.

Whatever the reasons may have been, the fact remains that as the various nationalities in this island slowly welded themselves into one people, and Briton, Saxon, Dane and Norman became *English,* the hero adopted as their national hero was the chief of the conquered, not of the conquering races. Thus when Geoffrey of Monmouth, drawing upon a work probably compiled by a continental Breton, gave to the world his *"Historia Britonum"* in which the pseudo-historical deeds of Arthur were solemnly related, the book was received with avidity, and Norman and Angevin Kings, without a drop of British blood in their veins, gloried in the renown of their predecessor. His history was bound up with the history of Great Britain, and the inhabitants of that land, recognising this, hailed him as their own.

But, as I said before, in its literary form the Arthurian legend came to us mainly in a foreign tongue. With the scanty materials at our disposal it is difficult to say what was the date, and what the extent, of the original Welsh Arthurian literature. At one time it probably formed a considerable body of romance, but by the twelfth century, from which period the real popularity of the Arthurian legend may be dated, Welsh was, as its very name indicates, an unknown tongue alike to the English-speaking majority of the nation and to the Norman conquerors, and as such had no power of competing with French, the language of the court and the nobility. The survival of the legend as a living force, both here and on the continent, was doubtless due to Celtic influence; its immense popularity as a Romantic literary cycle was due to French genius.

Thus the main body of Arthurian literature is French, some of the finest poems are German, little, very little is English. Previous to Malory English Arthurian literature consisted of scattered ballads and metrical romances, and these, save for scholars, are practically unreadable. If any student desires to get a clear idea of the slow growth of the

English language, and the time it took for the various elements composing it to be welded into a national tongue, I can suggest nothing more illuminating than for him to take three Arthurian romances, say a poem of Chrétien de Troyes with its contemporary German translation, and our *Sir Gawayne and the Grene Knyghte* (the best of our English Arthurian romances) and compare them. If he has any real knowledge of French and German he will not find the two first over-difficult; there are, of course, obsolete words and obsolete forms of spelling, but read them aloud, and they are quite intelligible. At the close of the twelfth century France and Germany had, each of them, a language and a literature. But the English poem, two centuries later in date and nearer our day than the others, is practically in "an unknown tongue," so little relation does it bear to the modern form of our language. To read it at all is a task which demands great patience—and an excellent glossary!

Previous to the compilation of Sir Thomas Malory, which is almost entirely a translation and abridgment of the later French prose romances, we have no English Arthurian literature accessible, or intelligible, to the general reader.

This naturally accounts, in a large measure, for the ignorance of the Arthurian legend common in England; it has also unhappily affected the work of those scholars who have seriously set themselves to study the subject. The *legend* certainly belongs to us, but the *literature* belongs elsewhere, and this fact was at first not sufficiently recognised. Comparatively speaking it is only in our own day that the value of romantic literature has been realised, and its study systematically attempted; for long such subjects were deemed unworthy the attention of a serious scholar. A lifetime might be spent over the elucidation of some obscure Greek or Latin writer (who had, perhaps, left only half a poem behind him), but to attempt to understand the tales in which our forefathers had delighted, on which the childhood of the nation had been fed, was quite beneath the dignity of a learned man. We know better now; we know that if we would understand a folk we must study its tales, and that important evidence of the inter-relation of peoples, the spread of culture from one land to another, the influence of one race on another, is to be gathered from their popular literature. The study of romance means also the study of history, and in the subject we are now considering any student of Arthurian literature will readily admit that historical considerations play no unimportant part.

At first interest in the question naturally shewed itself in printing and making accessible to the public the principal texts. To such writers as Southey, who edited the *Morte d'Arthur;* Ritson, who published several volumes of *Ancient English Metrical Romances;* Dunlop, who wrote a *History of Fiction,* and Sir Frederick Madden, who published a selection of poems dealing with *Sir Gawain,* we owe a debt of gratitude none the less deep because the progress of study has necessitated most of their work being done over again.

Early labourers in this field contented themselves with the reproduction of a MS. Interesting as the work was they hardly held it of sufficient importance to undertake the labour involved in reconstructing the original text by means of careful and critical comparison of all the available MSS. Nor were the materials for such a task at their disposal to the same extent as they are at ours. Much, very much, still remains to be done, but every year facilitates the task; new editions of the various romances are published; critical editions, already in our hands, revised and improved; here and there a search-light is thrown on some special point of interest by means of studies and monographs from the pen of scholars of known repute. But in all this labour it is regretfully to be acknowledged that we, in this land, still lag behind. Of late years the study of romance literature in general and of the Arthurian cycle in particular has made immense strides on the Continent, but any one interested in the matter cannot fail to be struck by the paucity of English works of solid value as compared with the mass of French and German critical literature. To a monograph on the Grail legend, published by a German scholar last year, was appended a list of books dealing with the Arthurian legend; out of two hundred and thirty-six works noted, only *fifteen* bore English names, and of those fifteen not more than seven, at the outside, would be of any solid value for critical purposes.

In a brief study like this it would, of course, be impossible fully to discuss this great body of romance, or to give more than such a sketch of its general character as may serve to guide the reading of any one desirous to make acquaintance, at first hand, with the works of which it is composed. As we shall see, these works are not only many in number but also very diverse in character. We class under the general title of *the Arthurian cycle* a large body of literature, dating for the most part from the latter half of the twelfth and first quarter of the thirteenth centuries, some of which deals only indirectly with the British King. Indeed we are accustomed to include under this heading certain romances, such as the early *Tristan* poems, which have absolutely no connection whatever with Arthur. The fame of the hero-king caused him to become a convenient centre round which to group a circle of recitals of miscellaneous character. Arthur's Court and Arthur's Round Table, had they ever existed in the form familiar to us, would certainly have drawn to themselves, as to a point of attraction, the most valiant spirits of the land and time; from a literary point of view they operated in precisely the same way—the legend drew to itself and absorbed, more or less completely, other legends, some of older, many of clearly independent origin.

This literature divides itself naturally into two sections, poetry and prose. Which of the two was the earlier has been a much debated question; the view now generally accepted is that the poetical romances preceded the prose. M. Gaston Paris very happily demonstrated this in a study on Chrétien de Troyes' *Chevalier de la Charette,* showing that the poetical version had been transferred, almost literally, to the prose *Lancelot.* It does not, of course, follow that a prose romance was *never* versified; for instance, there exists a mediæval Dutch verse rendering of the *Queste,* the only such version known; here, scholars are unanimously of opinion that the prose contained in all the other MSS. represents the original form.

As a rule the poems, especially the earlier ones, such as the works of Chrétien de Troyes and his German contemporaries, are much more simple and straightforward than the prose versions. There is only one hero, or at most two as in the *Perceval* poems, and the main interest of the story is kept clear, and not confused by side issues. Later on more characters are introduced: we follow the fortunes now of one knight now of another; their adventures (generally with a strong family likeness to each other) cross and recross; the titular hero disappears, often for several consecutive sections of the romance, till in the tangle the reader becomes doubtful as to which knight the compiler designed specially to honour. This tendency to diffuseness is a special characteristic of the prose romances in their later and extended form.

Another characteristic of the two sections is that in the earlier, the poetical versions, the rôle assigned to Arthur is of comparatively small importance. As M. Gaston Paris has pointed out, his court is simply the point of arrival and departure for the knights in quest of adventures, little or none of the action takes place there. In the later, or prose, romances, on the contrary, Arthur plays a much more important part, much of the action passes at the court, and the loves of Lancelot and Guinevere become the central point of interest.

It must not be concluded from the above remarks that the romances, even the prose versons, are as a rule wearisome to read; on the contrary they are charmingly written. The style is simple, direct, and marked by a certain graceful humour which is very attractive. I incline myself to the opinion that the later Grail romances, the *Grand S. Graal* and the *Queste,* with their love of far-fetched allegory, pronounced tendency to sermonising, and false conception of the relation between the sexes, are decidedly the least interesting. The earlier poets, Chrétien de Troyes, Raoul de Houdene, Hartmann von Aue, Wolfram von Eschenbach, and Gottfried von Strassburg are each and all delightful, and will well repay study.

Perhaps one might again sub-divide the versions dealing more especially with Arthur into two classes, the historical (or pseudo-historical) and the romantic. That a certain historical basis for his legend exists may be freely admitted; how far it extends is doubtful. *Certainly* he fought against the Saxons, *perhaps* he was betrayed alike by his wife and by his nephew; we can scarcely look upon anything further in his story as based upon fact.

The adventures ascribed to the king are not, as a rule, of a purely chivalric character. He is a valiant soldier and successful general; he slays monsters, the Boar *Twrch Trwyth,* the Demon Cat of Losanne, the Giant of Mont S. Michel, but he does not, as a rule, rescue maidens, assail magic castles, or ride on the Grail Quest. For adventures of this type we must turn to the stories of the various knights, not to those which deal with the king.

In the following pages I propose to group, under the names of Arthur and his leading knights, the romances dealing more directly with each; by this means we shall succeed in classifying the main body of Arthurian romance. Of course certain romances will not fall under any of these headings, as not all the Arthurian heroes immortalised in prose or verse can boast of being the centre of a cycle; other romances, again, may have to be mentioned more than once, as being of importance for the study of more than one branch of the legend; but I shall endeavour to omit no work of solid literary or critical worth. . . . (pp. 1-15)

To begin with KING ARTHUR himself, the historical basis of the whole legend is to be found in Nennius' *Historia Britonum,* compiled towards the end of the eighth century. This furnished materials for the more famous *Historia* of Geoffrey of Monmouth, written about 1136. In both of these we have an account of Arthur's struggle with the Saxon invaders, but the meagre historical element is largely intermingled with fables, *e.g.* the account of the adventures of Brutus, and the founding of the kingdom of Britain. It is to Geoffrey that we owe the introduction to the general public of the picturesque figure of the enchanter *Merlin;* a full and adequate account of the source and development of the *Merlin* legend has not yet been published. The popularity of Geoffrey's "history" was immense; it was translated into French by Wace (who added details not to be found in his source) under the title of *Li Romans de Brut,* and Wace, again, was translated into Anglo-Saxon by Layamon.

Following the same lines, but having no claim to be considered other than pure romance, is the prose *Merlin.* This gives an account of Arthur's predecessors, of his election to the kingdom, his wars with the Saxons, and early reign, carrying on the history to the birth of Lancelot. In this, its latest form, it was evidently intended to be an introduction to the prose *Lancelot.*

The first part of the romance, that dealing more especially with MERLIN himself, is the work of Robert de Borron, to whom other romances of the cycle are attributed; we do not know who concluded it. Two forms of the *Merlin* exist: the vulgate or ordinary *Merlin,* of which there are several MSS.; and another ending, known as the *Suite de Merlin,* which is found in one MS. alone, and of which the first four books of Malory's *Morte d'Arthur* offer an abridged translation. The "Ordinary" *Merlin* is much superior to the *Suite,* which, though it has some features of especial interest, *e.g.* it is the only authority for the fine story of Balaan and Balaain—is very diffuse and contradictory in its statements, and is, moreover, unfortunately incomplete. Both versions have been edited, and are accessible.

The latter part of Arthur's reign, and his death, are related in the French romance of *Le morte Arthur,* or *La Mort au roi Artus* (this must not be confounded with Malory's compilation, of which it forms only a small part). *Le Morte Arthur* is now generally found incorporated with the prose *Lancelot.* The *Lancelot* as a whole, though dealing more with Arthur's knights than with Arthur himself, yet contains a good deal directly relating to the monarch (*e.g.* his deception by the false Guinevere), and is, as noted above, closely connected with the *"Merlin"* in its latest and most extended form.

An entirely different version of the events of the later part of Arthur's reign is presented by the prose *Perceval li Gallois.* The author of this romance, in common with the author of the German *Diu Krône,* was in possession of a tradition which represented the British king in a very unflattering light, as a slothful, self-indulgent *roi fainéant.*

To sum up, the tradition of which Arthur is the real hero is contained in the chronicles above mentioned, the *Merlin,* and the great compilation known as the prose *Lancelot.*

One of the earliest knights connected with King Arthur is SIR GAWAIN. He was, probably, the centre of an independent, and it may be earlier, cycle of adventures. He is certainly the hero of a larger body of episodic romance than belongs to any other knight (he is the hero of most of our middle English Arthurian literature), and it would be difficult to name any leading work of the cycle in which he does not play a part, generally an important part. At the same time he is not the hero of any long biographical romance such as are dedicated to Lancelot and Tristan.

The most important poems in which Sir Gawain figures are the *Conte del Graal* or *Perceval* of Chrétien de Troyes, and its German counterpart, the *Parzival* of Wolfram von Eschenbach; a good half of these poems is devoted to Gawain, rather than to the titular hero, Perceval. He is also the hero of *Diu Krône* by Heinrich von dem Türlin—a long, rambling poem with many interesting and archaic features. Here, Gawain is the achiever of the Grail quest, in which Perceval has failed. Gawain also plays an important rôle in the *Chevalier de la Charrette,* and the *Chevalier au Lion,* both by Chrétien de Troyes (though the former was completed by another hand); and under his Welsh name of *Gwalchmei* he is a leading figure in the *Mabinogion,* and in the fragments of Arthurian tradition contained in the *Triads.*

A number of English metrical romances connected with this hero have been collected and printed by Sir Frederick Madden, under the title of *Syr Gawayne.* The chief of these, *Syr Gawayne and the Grene Knyghte,* has more than once been published separately.

In vol. xxx. of *Histoire Littéraire de la France* M. Gaston Paris has given summaries of episodic romances of which Gawain is the hero; some of them have never been printed, some are included in the Dutch verse translation of the *Lancelot* and are found nowhere else. In the earlier stages of the Arthurian legend Gawain is represented as the *beau-idéal* of chivalrous valour and courtesy, and no other knight ever gained so firm a hold on English imagination; in our vernacular metrical romances he is decidedly a more important figure than even Arthur. He was also the "adventurous hero" *par excellence* of the cycle, and the feats ascribed to him are often of a fantastic, and even purely mythical, character. He is certainly one of the most elusive, and at the same time one of the most picturesque and charming figures of the whole legend.

SIR PERCEVAL. Next to Gawain, the most important of the early Arthurian knights is Perceval, but his connection with the king is far less close than is the case with the first-named hero. Gawain is always and everywhere Arthur's nephew; this relationship is once attributed to Perceval

Map of Britain around the early sixth century showing the approximate areas of Teutonic settlement (shaded areas) and the British kingdoms.

(Metrical Romance of *Sir Percyvelle*), once to Lancelot (*Lanzelet*), and once to Caradoc (*Li Conte del Graal*). Save in quite the latest forms of his story, such as the *Queste,* Perceval is but a passing guest at Arthur's Court, only appearing there at long intervals; he is never an *habitué* as is Gawain.

It is generally agreed that the earliest form of his story now extant is that contained in the *Conte del Graal* or *Perceval* of Chrétien, and the *Parzival* of Wolfram von Eschenbach. The relation between these two poems has been much debated; at one time the German poem was held to be a mere translation from the French, but of late years the opinion has gained ground that the two, though ultimately going back to the same source, are only indirectly connected with each other. Both are very fine poems; the French is superior in literary style, but the German is the more poetical in conception, and richer in human interest and pathos. The Arthurian cycle has no more fascinating figure than that of the lonely boy, brought up in the wilderness by his widowed mother, coming to Arthur's Court, an uncouth, untutored lad, to demand knighthood, and gradually, by the discipline of life, and loyal fulfilment of natural duties, developing into a "very perfect, gentle knight"; *A brave man, but slowly wise.* The later Perceval, the knight of the *Queste* and prose versions, is not a very interesting figure; his virtues are too self-conscious and proselytising; but the early Perceval is so simple, natural, and human, that I find it difficult to believe that his legend has not a basis in fact.

Chrétien's *Perceval* is unfortunately extremely difficult to obtain; but the *Parzival,* either in its original form, in modern German, or in an English translation, is within the reach of all. The fact that Wagner's beautiful drama, *Parsifal,* is based upon this poem has of late years given an additional stimulus to its study.

Perceval is also the hero of a romance by Robert de Borron, which we only possess in a prose form; of the Middle-English metrical romance of *Sir Percyvelle of Galles;* and of the prose *Perceval li Gallois.* He is also identical with the hero of the Welsh Mabinogi, *Peredur ap Evrawc.* It is with the legend of the Holy Grail that Perceval is most closely connected. He is, beyond a doubt, the *original* hero of the Quest, though in the later romances, familiar to us by Malory's translation, he plays a rôle secondary to that of Galahad.

Into the question of the Grail romances I do not propose to enter here; they form of themselves an important section of Arthurian literature and will be treated separately, and fully, by a more skilful hand. For information on the legend of Perceval as Grail hero the student should consult Mr. Alfred Nutt's *Studies on the Legend of the Holy Grail,* but from whichever point of view he be regarded, whether as representative of a prehistoric Aryan hero, or as achiever of the mystical quest, he is a deeply interesting figure, and the literature connected with him includes some of the most fascinating romances of the cycle.

SIR LANCELOT. It will, doubtless, be a surprise to readers whose idea of the Arthurian cycle has been founded upon Malory and Tennyson, to learn that this knight, so important a figure in the story as we know it, really plays a very insignificant rôle in Arthurian literature. Apart from the great prose compilation bearing his name (of which the adventures of other knights form no inconsiderable portion), Lancelot has very little literature connected with him. He is the hero of the *Lanzelet* of Ulrich von Zatzikhoven (which appears to contain the earliest version of his story now extant), and of Chrétien de Troyes' *Chevalier de la Charrette.* Chrétien's other poems barely mention his name, in the *Perceval* he is not once referred to, and the only adventure to which the most famous of Arthurian poets alludes is that which he himself relates in the *Charrette* poem. It seems very doubtful whether even this adventure, the rescue of Guinevere from Meleagaunt, did not originally belong to some other knight.

Lancelot plays a rôle in *Diu Krône,* and in a few of the smaller episodic poems, such as *Rigomer* and *Lancelot et le cerf au pied blanc,* though again in this latter case M. Gaston Paris thinks he was not the original hero of the tale, but the literature connected with him is far less varied in character, and far less important in its relation to traditional sources, than that of which either Gawain or Perceval is the hero.

It is to the popularity of Lancelot as the lover of Guinevere that the commanding position occupied by him in later Arthurian romance is due, and in this character he appears first in the *Chevalier de la Charrette.* Whether the story of the loves of Lancelot and Guinevere is thus to be placed to the credit of the French poet; whether it be based on a previous legend of which some other knight was the hero; or whether it be but a late and poor imitation of the *Tristan* story, authorities are at present divided. Probably the truth lies between the last two theories. I do not myself think the story due either to an invention or a mistake on the part of Chrétien.

However the story arose, the fact remains that the prose Arthurian romance in its present form has been worked over and re-modelled in conformity with this, the central point of interest. The prose *Merlin* has been extended and amplified to serve as introduction to the *Lancelot* proper (a process specially noticeable in the *Suite de Merlin*), and the later Grail romances, such as the *Grand S. Graal* and the *Queste,* if not, as seems most probable, originally composed under the same influence, have been submitted to a similar process and practically incorporated with the Lancelot legend.

As it now exists the prose *Lancelot* is a great rambling romance, practically dividing itself into six sections, of the first three of which, alone, Lancelot is the undisputed hero. Of the remaining three sections, the *Agravain* is quite as much devoted to the deeds of other knights of the Round Table; the *Queste* has Galahad and Perceval for its heroes; and the *Morte d'Arthur,* though ranking Lancelot as the first of Arthur's knights, is concerned more especially with the fortunes of the king. Unfortunately this important romance has not been edited, and is not easily accessible. M. Paulin Paris published an abridged and modernised version of the first three sections in his *Romans de la Table Ronde* (Vols. III., IV., & V.), to which is appended an abstract of the concluding portions. A Dutch verse translation of the last three books exists, and has been edited by M. Jonckbloet. It is of great value, as, judging from the version it gives of the *Queste,* it represents an older MS. than any we now possess; it also includes a number of minor episodic romances, some of which are not known in any other form.

Who was the author of the *Lancelot* is uncertain, for long popular tradition ascribed the whole vast compilation to Walter Map and even to-day uncritical writers are apt to make the assertion, but students of Arthurian literature are now generally agreed that it is extremely doubtful whether Map ever had any hand in the matter at all. Certainly the same author did not compose the *Lancelot* and the *Queste;* the style of the two sections is entirely different, and the characters ascribed to the leading knights contradictory of each other. The *Lancelot* and the *Morte d'Arthur* are more consistent; but even in the earlier part of the romance we know that one entire section, that dealing with the *Charrette* adventure, was really the work of Chrétien de Troyes, and simply taken over bodily into the prose romance; so that the more reasonable point of view seems to be that which regards the *Lancelot* simply as a compilation drawn from various sources on which at various times many hands have worked, and for which no one writer can be held responsible. It is no more homogeneous than is the *Conte del Graal* in its extended form, and *that* is the work of at least five writers.

SIR TRISTAN. It is only in the later forms of his story that this hero can be considered as in any way belonging to the circle of Arthur's knights; even then his connection with the court is, like Perceval's, intermittent, not close and continuous as in the case of Gawain and Lancelot. In the best version of the tale Arthur is but referred to as a poetical simile, and Mark is King, not merely of Cornwall, but of England also.

As a consistent and connected story, the *Tristan* legend probably took shape earlier than the Arthurian romances proper. Though it has undergone considerable development, the central *motif,* the love of Tristan for Iseult his uncle's wife, has known no change. There is no moment in the Tristan, as in the Lancelot, legend to which you can point as being anterior to the introduction of the love element. Whether the Lancelot-Guinevere story be but an imitation of the Tristan-Iseult legend or not, the two love tales have manifestly come into contact with and affected each other, and of the two there can be no reasonable doubt which is at once the older and the finer.

The legend of Tristan was apparently at first enshrined in detached *lais,* which, at some period not to be definitely determined, in the course of the twelfth century were woven into connected poems, probably first by *French* minstrels. These poems only exist in fragments. The most important form parts of a poem by a certain Béroul, and of one by an Anglo-Norman, Thomas of Brittany. Both were rendered into German, and these translations still exist. Béroul's version is preserved in the work of Eilhart von Oberge; Thomas's in that of Gottfried von Strassburg. Chrétien de Troyes wrote a *Tristan* which is lost, but which some scholars incline to think lies at the root of the prose *Tristan.* This latter belongs to the same stage of Arthurian tradition as the *Lancelot;* like it, it is a long rambling composition, differing greatly from the version of the story contained in the poems, and containing, like the *Lancelot,* a *Queste* which differs in many details from the better known *Lancelot* version.

Of all the *Tristan* romances the finest is undoubtedly the poem of Gottfried von Strassburg; from a *literary* point of view it is probably the best romance of the entire Arthurian cycle, though *ethically* it is inferior to Wolfram's *Parvival.* Indeed the German romances as a whole form a most important and interesting section of this literature; where not direct translations from the French, a French original lies at the root of each, but in every case the German poet has treated his source with so much spirit and independence, and with so deep an insight into human nature, that the works have a character and an interest all their own. Gottfried is certainly, in grace of style, the equal even of the much vaunted Chrétien, while Wolfram is far his superior in depth of thought.

Of the *Tristan* romances the most generally popular appears to have been the prose version. Dr. Sommer remarks that it was printed more often than any other of the cycle, but unfortunately, like the *Lancelot,* it has not, so far, found an editor. Gottfried's poem, on the contrary, has been printed more than once, and can easily be obtained.

From the prose *Tristan* Malory drew largely for his compilation, which indeed represents very fairly the three great prose branches of the cycle, the *Merlin,* the *Lancelot* (including the *Queste*), and the *Tristan.* For the *Morte d'Arthur* proper, Malory seems to have used an English translation, not the French of the *Lancelot* version. Inasmuch as these prose versions represent in each case a later and complicated form of the stories with which they deal, we must not go to Malory with the idea that he will give us the original story of Arthur and his knights. The style is admirable, and the work must always remain a classic of the English language, but the picture it presents of such heroes as Gawain, Perceval, or Tristan, is very far from doing any one of them justice.

Of other knights whose names are well known, none beyond the four first mentioned possess much literary importance. GALAHAD, for example, only appears in the latest versions of the Grail story, the greater portion of the Arthurian literature knows nothing about him. KAY, who is certainly one of the oldest characters of the legend, probably had, at one time, romances directly connected with him. Now we only have fragmentary allusions in Welsh tradition (some of which appear to be of very ancient date) a romance *Gawain and Kay* included in the Dutch *Lancelot,* and certain poems such as *The Avowynge of Arthur* in which he plays a secondary rôle.

An important little group of poems connected with the cycle, is that of which the hero is generally termed *The Fair Unknown;* but who in the majority of instances is Guinglain or Gyngalyn, Gawain's son. These are *Sir Libeaus Desconus* (English), *Le Bel Inconnu* (French), *Wigalois* (German), and *Carduino* (Italian). Malory's seventh Book, for which no direct source has yet been discovered, probably represents a variant of this group. Inasmuch as these poems are of importance for the study of the Gawain legend, they might perhaps be classed with the literature belonging to that hero.

Of isolated Arthurian poems, we may mention *Sir Launfal,* translated and amplified from the *lai* of that name by Marie de France. Originally the story of Launfal or Lanval had, as we see from the *lai* of *Graalent* (which the English translator also used) nothing to do with Arthur; the King at whose Court the adventure takes place was anonymous, and the theme, as Dr. Schofield has shown, is a very old one. It is a good illustration of the manner in which earlier and independent stories were adapted to the requirements of an age which found its most popular theme in the Arthurian legend.

Other good examples of isolated Arthurian poems are the *Cligés* of Chrétien de Troyes, and the *Méraugis de Portlesguez* of Raoul de Houdenc, but the best of this class are certainly the *Erec* and *Yvain* (*le Chevalier au Lion*) of the first-named poet. Both these works were rendered, and finely rendered, into German by Hartmann von Aue (the *Yvain* being also translated into English under the title of *Yvain and Gawain*), and of both we possess Welsh prose versions. Erec is identical with Geraint, the hero of the Mabinogi of *Geraint ap Erbyn,* while Yvain, or Owain, is the hero of the *Lady of the Fountain* just as Perceval is, as noted above, identical with *Peredur.*

What is the exact relationship between these three poems of Chrétien and the three corresponding *Mabinogion*, scholars have found it difficult to decide. At one time the view was very generally entertained that, in spite of the marked difference of manner and matter, the Welsh stories were only free translations from the French poems. This was certainly an easy way of settling the question, but there were many who felt that the variance in matters of detail, and the very archaic character of the Welsh tales did not lend themselves easily to such a solution. That the *origin* of the stories is Welsh is very generally admitted. Of late years the opinion has gained ground that the *Mabinogion* really represent the *insular* version as preserved among the Celts of Britain, while Chrétien's poems represent the *Continental* version as told by the Celts of Brittany. This seems the truer solution and the one which accounts the best alike for the points of contact and of divergence. If the emigrants remembered their national tales it seems rather absurd to suppose that their brethren who remained in their own land should have utterly forgotten them. At the same time, in view of the popularity of Chrétien's fine versions (which we know, from the translation of *Yvain,* came to this land), it is, of course, possible that the final form of the Welsh stories, as we know them, has been affected by French influence.

Be that as it may, the relative part played by Celtic tradition and French genius in the formation and transmission of the Arthurian legend is a subject which will afford matter of debate for many a year to come; whether the question can ever be definitely settled is doubtful. Large as is the body of extant Arthurian literature, it is certain that it only represents a part, probably but a small part, of the original whole. Every romance that we possess postulates a previous version of the tale it tells; in no one instance would any critical scholar with a due care for his reputation venture to assert that we possess "the original story, whole and incorrupt, as it was first told."

It is not easy work to reconstruct a chain of which the primary and most important links are lacking, and those of us who undertake a share in the task must be prepared for many a disappointment. Are not the old tales parables for us? Too often we build a tower four square, and fair to look upon, only to find, like Vortigern, that there is a fatal flaw in the foundation which must needs ruin our structure. Or like the knights themselves, wandering in the enchanted forests, we find a fair-seeming road which leads us only to an impenetrable thicket, so that we must perforce retrace our steps.

But, after all, the fascination of the work itself is its own best reward, and if any one to whom this subject has been so far an unfamiliar one has a desire to try his, or her, luck on enchanted ground, it may be that these few pages will aid them in determining how and where they will begin their labours; it is only fair to warn them that they need never hope to *end* them. (pp. 15-33)

Jessie L. Weston, "King Arthur and His Knights: A Brief Introduction to the Study of Arthurian Literature," in her King Arthur and His Knights: A Survey of Arthurian Ro-

mance, *1899. Reprint by AMS Press, 1972, pp. 1-33.*

James Douglas Merriman

[*In the following excerpt, Merriman describes the genesis of the Arthurian legend from the Dark Ages to the early Renaissance, purporting that "the* Morte Darthur, *taken as a whole, remains incomparably the greatest of the earlier English treatments of the central story of Arthur and his knights." He also compares Sir Thomas Malory's* Morte *with medieval versions of Arthur's story.*]

MYTHIC ORIGINS

The beginnings of Arthurian story are lost in the dim prehistory of the peoples of Western Europe. Yet by piecing together scattered bits of evidence, scholars have been able to suggest that its first traces are to be found in the mythologies of the eastern Mediterranean peoples, which over a period of hundreds, perhaps even thousands, of years were carried to Southern Ireland. Here the stories and rituals slowly mingled with native Irish mythology and, as this growing body of legend moved into Wales, with various Brythonic and Romano-British religious elements. Whatever the processes of this diffusion and accretion were, it

Merlin and the Child Arthur, *an illustration by Gustave Doré in Tennyson's* Idylls of the King, *1868.*

seems clear that long before the conversion of the Celtic peoples to Christianity (and therefore long before the existence of the historical Arthur, if he existed at all), there had developed among them an extensive literature of gods and heroes among whom nearly all of the chief figures around Arthur had their first recognizable forms. Such mythic origins were recognized even in the Middle Ages, as occasional references make clear, but it was not until the nineteenth century that these origins became the object of serious study. Matthew Arnold was quick to note of the characters of the *Mabinogion*:

> These are no mediaeval personages; they belong to an older, pagan, mythological world. The very first thing that strikes one . . . is how evidently the mediaeval story-teller is pillaging an antiquity of which he does not fully possess the secret; he is like a peasant building his hut on the site of Helicarnassus or Ephesus; he builds, but what he builds is full of materials of which he knows not the history, or knows by a glimmering tradition merely;—stones "not of this building," but of an older architecture, greater, cunninger, more majestical.

Later studies show clearly that in many of the characters and incidents of medieval Arthurian romance and "history" we have survivals of ancient solar and lunar myths, seasonal and vegetation myths, fertility cults, and initiation rites. The Gawain of later story whose strength waxes before noon and wanes afterward, the Guenevere whose abduction is related to the changing seasons, the Grail King whose wounded "thighs" leave his land sterile and waste—these are not arbitrary creations of individual imaginations.

While the antiquity of these knights and ladies of the Round Table is thus clear, Arthur himself presents, curiously enough, a very different problem. His name, unlike those of his companions, cannot properly be derived from any of the Celtic deities. Instead it appears to have the Roman proper name *Artorius* as its source. And when we first meet him in the early ninth-century *Historia Brittonum* of Nennius, he is not a god, but a man, a *dux bellorum* or "battle chief" who is said to have led the Britons successfully in twelve battles against the Saxons at a time some three hundred years previously—that is, around the end of the fifth and beginning of the sixth centuries. At the same time, obviously fabulous elements were already gathering around the name and figure of Arthur. In one of the twelve battles, he is said to have slain 960 men singlehanded, and in the *Mirabilia* attached to the *Historia,* we learn of marvels associated with the tomb of Arthur's son, Amir, and with a footprint left by Arthur's hound, Cabal, during the great chase of the boar Troynt. But Arthur is also clearly a Christian hero; in at least one of his battles he bore the image of the Virgin on his shoulders, an act which appears to have assisted his routing of the pagans.

Arthur's success against the pagan warriors was evidently matched by his victories over the pagan deities, and here too the symbol of the new religion no doubt played its part. A variety of evidence shows clearly that in the eleventh century, the legendary king was already the center to which were drawn a number of originally independent heroes. Arthur and tales about him are mentioned frequently in the Welsh triads, and Cei (Kay) and Bedwyr (Bedivere) are among the first gods to be demoted to subordinates of the new king. In the *Spoils of Annwfn* Arthur and his men engage in what is clearly an expedition to the Celtic Other World, obtaining there a magical cauldron that will not cook for a coward. This cauldron, as well as the chase of the fabulous monster boar, Twrch Trwyth, alluded to in the Nennian *Mirabilia,* makes another appearance in the Welsh tale of Culhwch and Olwen in which Arthur and a numerous body of his knights are active in many adventures of a fabulous sort, some of them involving the execution of various agricultural tasks. Mere battle chief no more, Arthur has become a king ruling over an extensive area and a band of wondrous heroes, many of whom are clearly mythological figures. Together they accomplish marvelous feats of land cleansing and such culture activities as plowing and bringing back to their people the advantages of the Other World. How much of the tragic ending of Arthur's story had developed by this time is unclear; possibly his mortal wounding at the hands of his treacherous nephew was already known, and certainly his mystic survival either in Avalon or some other place was widely believed in from an early time.

The much belabored question of whether Arthur ever "really" existed is of no great consequence here; after all, it is not as an actual ruler, but as a king of romance that Arthur made a realm and ruled in literature. But it is of the greatest consequence that there was a *belief,* very likely widespread, in the historical existence of such a hero. It was just this belief, including as it did Arthur's championing of the cause of Christ against the pagan, that permitted the survival in the Christian society of the Middle Ages of elements that would otherwise have been all too clearly recognizable as pagan. Like the Celtic cross with its Christian cross superimposed on the elder solar circle, Arthur was an acceptable fusion of antithetical elements: Christian and pagan, cryptohistorical and mythological. And just as the early Church had grown in strength by absorbing the energies of the old religions, the extraordinary vitality of Arthurian story may in part result from its progressive synthesis of these elements.

GEOFFREY'S HISTORIA

The vitality of the story of Arthur is already clear in the first really impressive treatment of the legend by an Englishman. Geoffrey of Monmouth's *Historia Regum Britanniae* (*ca.* 1136) purports, as its title indicates, to be a comprehensive history. But for Geoffrey's readers in the twelfth century as well as for those in the twentieth, the story of Arthur was certainly the most impressive part of the book, and it seems likely that Geoffrey intended it to be so received. In the shaping heat of his imagination, history and tradition fused into a continuous narrative of tragic dignity and significance. Begotten on Igrayne by Uther Pendragon through Merlin's magic ruse, Arthur succeeds to the throne despite his clouded title, drives the Saxons from his realm, and takes Ganhumara as his queen. Abroad he extends his conquests, and at home maintains a court to which come the greatest knights of the world to live in gallantry and honor under his liberal reign. On his last great campaign against Lucius of Rome, he is triumphant until he learns that his nephew Modred, to whom he had entrusted his queen and realm, has gathered together an army of rebels, usurped the throne, and taken Ganhumara as his wife. Arthur returns, fights Modred's forces, kills Modred in a last great battle, is mortally wounded himself, and carried to Avalon to be healed.

The underlying motifs of much of this story were, as we have seen, already present in the core of the legend, but there are also important additions: the mysterious circumstances surrounding Arthur's parentage, conception, and birth; his marriage to the fatally attractive Ganhumara; and his betrayal and the consequent destruction of his realm and life through the treachery of his nephew Modred. If these motifs, so clearly mythological in origin as they are, cannot be credited to Geoffrey's originality, a very significant shift in atmosphere and emphasis can be. In the *Historia,* the vague culture hero of Celtic tradition has become an actualized Christian king, a champion of women, and a righter of wrongs. His court has become at the same time an idealized gathering place for the noblest knights and ladies of his time—a time which is neither that of sixth-century Britain nor that of twelfth-century Norman England, but rather the time of heroic legend and romance, which is never a definite past and never the present, but always "long, long ago." It is this strange combination of actualized characters with romantic or heroic time and place that is Geoffrey's signal contribution to Arthurian story.

The importance of Geoffrey in the evolution of Arthurian story is, however, difficult to assess. The two-hundred-odd extant manuscripts along with various translations and abridgements and the denunciations of subsequent historians attest to the popularity of his work. There can be no doubt at all that he is the source and originator of the long line of chronicles that for centuries maintained Arthur's place in what passed for serious and exact history. Through them or directly, his influence from the Renaissance on into the eighteenth century was to be, as we shall see, enormous. Nor is there any reason to doubt that his presentation of Arthur as a historical figure produced a more serious attitude toward the legend and thereby assisted at least indirectly the success of imaginative Arthurian literature. But his direct influence on early romances on the Continent appears to be very doubtful.

ARTHUR AMONG THE ROMANCERS

It is to the Breton *conteurs* or professional storytellers, as Loomis has noted, that we must assign "the preponderant share . . . in popularizing the Arthurian legend in the courts and baronial halls of France and England during the twelfth century." From such oral sources a vast body of metrical and prose romances proliferated in the following centuries, spreading over all of Western Europe, and in the process profoundly affecting the nature of the story itself. The taste of the age lay in the direction of the fantastic, and accordingly the stories became an endless and frequently tedious succession of meaningless marvels, extravagant and unmotivated incidents. Since "Arthur's warlike exploits and his achievements on a large public scale naturally did not furnish the medieval romancers with such at-

tractive material as the private adventures of love and knight-errantry which his followers undertook," the emphasis tended to shift from Arthur himself to the exploits of his knights—Gawain, Tristram, Lancelot, and others— or to adventures such as the Quest of the Grail in which he had little if any part. But if Arthur was reduced in the metrical versions to a mere nucleus about which the biographical romances of his heroes accreted, in the later prose romances his fame, at least as the faultless king of the romantic historians, was blackened by the addition of the mythological motif of an unwitting incestuous relationship with his half-sister from which sprang the instrument of his fate, Modred. MacCallum's contention that Arthur was thus made "the author of his own ruin," may explain the intentions, dimly realized if at all, of the romancers, but it ignores the fact that such an accidental, essentially unwilled sin, no matter how satisfactory it might be for classical tragedy (e.g., *Oedipus*), was radically inadequate for a Christian society. That some of the romancers themselves perceived its inadequacy may be gathered from their steady emphasis on another of their additions, the adultery between Lancelot and Guinevere, a sin of the will which has as its consequences the deterioration of the Round Table and the destruction of Arthur and his realm. This emphasis on adultery was, of course, a reaction to more than abstract theological or moral requirements; it was a reflection of the intellectual and emotional tensions generated by the doctrines of courtly love, which pervaded the secular thought of the Middle Ages and not a little of its religious speculation. It is in this responsiveness, this adaptability of Arthurian story to the tastes and imaginative needs of the age that one clue to its popularity is to be found.

THE VOGUE OF ARTHURIAN ROMANCE

The enormous popularity of Arthurian story is clearly such as to justify the epithet "miraculous." In the rapidity of its diffusion through Western Europe and even as far as Iceland and Jerusalem, in its ascendancy over the earlier matters even to the extent of markedly influencing them, and in its absorption of many of the greatest imaginative talents of the Middle Ages, Arthurian story obviously dominated medieval romance. The reasons for this vogue are not, however, so obvious. The view that a "perfect explanation for the miraculous spread of the Arthurian legend" is to be found in the Breton *conteurs'* recounting of these tales "with such verve that they were able to fascinate counts and kings," while it may explain *how* the story became popular, is, as far as explaining *why,* little more than a perpetuation of one of the more ubiquitous latter day Celtic myths: the supernatural storytelling abilities of the Celtic people. Nor is the solution materially advanced by such explanations of "the chief causes" as this:

> The search for the strange and exotic which found satisfaction in the marvels of the Alexander legend took delight also in the wonders which had once abounded in the land of Logres, the Out Isles, and the fay-haunted forest of Broceliande—turning castles, testing horns, enchanted springs. . . . So, too, the new interest in the various manifestations of love, which was first exploited by the authors of *Enéas* and the

Roman de Troie, found larger scope in the amorous adventures of Gawain, the tragic fate of Tristan and Isolt, the imperious whims and the jealousy of Guenevere, and the agonies of Lancelot. The Grail quest, so tantalizing in its contradictions and obscurity, led to ponderings on the mysteries of religion, while profound lessons of morality could be extracted from the history of Parzival.

But surely this is to say little more than that when one puts rabbits in a hat one may draw out rabbits. After all, the "amorous adventures" of Gawain were what the medieval authors added to the original solar god; the Christian symbolism and moral truths of the Grail story were what they had grafted onto the stock of a Celtic fertility myth. The problem, in short, is why was this particular hat chosen? why did the matter of Arthur rather than that of, say Charlemagne or Alexander, become one of the most comprehensive expressions of medieval sensibility?

In a very general way, these questions are to be answered, as MacCallum suggested, "by supposing that the new matter was exceptionally suitable to the spirit of the time. It must have met a deep-felt want, and shown itself capable of receiving the stamp of the medieval spirit and expressing the medieval modes of life and thought more perfectly, than any previous theme." If we are to understand this "deep-felt want," we must consider the situation from which it arose. The efforts of historical reconstructionists have been so far successful that we tend to overlook the fact that in the medieval governing and military classes among which romance found its natural audience, barbarism, primitive violence, and unbridled passions survived well into the later Middle Ages. Earlier these savage energies had been well employed in fighting off the incursions of heathen invaders, but by the end of the first Christian millennium this work had been done, and the feudal knights had become what Hearnshaw has called "dangerously unemployed anachronisms," hated by king, clergy, and people alike for their greediness and defiance of civil and religious authority. Out of the various attempts to convert their energies into socially useful, religiously acceptable activities grew, at least in part, the institution of Christian chivalry. There were, to be sure, other factors that contributed to the rise of chivalry as an institution. On the part of the lesser knightly class itself, chivalry was an attempt to justify through a code of high aspiration its climb from a mere horse soldiery to a position of social eminence in the increasingly prosperous and civilized courts of later feudal society. Again, as Huizinga has suggested, chivalry, along with all the rigid formality and ceremony of medieval upper-class society, represents an effort of an emotionally primitive and savage military caste to control its violence and pride. As the Middle Ages wore on, the attendant ritual of chivalry increasingly became, it is true, a mere device by which a strong but progressively less important noble class would evade the facts of political and social reality. But in its origin, chivalry was above all a serious attempt to effect "a kind of compromise between the ascetic theology of the medieval church and the unsanctified life of the world which the church rejected as wholly bad."

Romano-Celtic stone relief from France, depicting a Triple Goddess, perhaps the mythical precursor of Guinevere.

The chivalric code that was thus evolved, though it nowhere reaches any fixed or formal uniformity, demanded of its adherents virtues essentially Christian, but with emphasis on those which were particularly proper for the fighting man: "To defend the church, attack unbelief, venerate the priesthood, protect the poor from injury, keep peace in the state, pour out their blood for their brothers," as John of Salisbury defined its duties. From such general obligations there developed an elaborate and minutely particularized code governing every aspect of the ideal knight's life. In its very beginnings the oath of the chivalric knight had enjoined along with martial service of church and king, the protection of women, and chivalry thus easily absorbed into its blend of war and religion the theories of courtly love, which from the end of the eleventh century had begun to take the ascendant in medieval erotic thought. While the knightly code that thus evolved inevitably permitted a concentration on essentially anti-Christian ideals of personal honor and glory and the passionate service of woman rather than God, nevertheless, even as late as the fifteenth century, "chivalry was still, after religion, the strongest of all the ethical conceptions which dominated the mind and the heart." And like other widely held theories of conduct, chivalry doubtless early created a very large demand for artistic expression, which in all times and places has been the layman's philosophy.

That the Arthurian story was hit upon for that expression is no doubt partly due to the simple coincidence that the new story material was becoming available on the Continent at almost the same moment in time in which the new chivalric ideal was arising. But a more compelling explanation is to be seen in the fact that the other great matters available to the poets were radically unsuitable as embodiments of chivalry. The matter of Charlemagne leaned too far in the direction of ecclesiastical heroism; the matter of

Alexander and other heroes of classical tradition obviously could not be bent far enough in the direction of Christianity. And, as MacCallum puts it, "In each case the hero . . . had a character too obstinately representative of another age and another code of life, thoroughly to submit to a change that would make him merely a chivalrous knight, neither more nor less." Arthur, on the other hand, suffered from none of these disabilities. From the beginning, as we have seen, he had been a fusion of Christian warrior and purely secular hero. Nor had he any of the recalcitrance of genuine historical figures to artistic manipulation in terms of manners or the atmosphere in which he moved. And finally, by right of the band of heroes already grouped about him from early times, his story was capable of expressing the whole gamut of variations which develop in any widely held theory of social and spiritual relationships. Added to these qualifications were the Arthurian legend's inherent tragic dignity and its richness in the marvels so dear to the medieval mind. The combination, then, so well suited to the interests of the age, awaited only the touch of genius to flower into a great expression of that age and its ideals. On the Continent it received that touch from Chrétien de Troyes, Gottfried von Strassburg, Robert de Boron, to mention only a few. In time the ensuing multiplication of individual romances resulted in a huge and appallingly heterogeneous mass of stories. The duplications, contradictions, and discrepancies between the various versions must early have attracted attention, and from the late thirteenth century on, more or less ambitious compilations involving varying degrees of systematization begin to make their appearance.

MALORY AND LE MORTE DARTHUR

The popularity of various *rifacimenti* of Arthurian story doubtless played its part in William Caxton's decision to "enprynte a book of the noble hystoryes of the sayd kynge Arthur and of certeyn of his knyghtes, after a copye unto me delyverd, whyche copye syr Thomas Malorye dyd take oute of certeyn bookes of Frensshe and reduced it into Englysshe." The importance of Malory's *Le Morte Darthur,* as Caxton refers to it in his colophon, would be difficult to exaggerate. Appearing in 1485 at the very end of the Middle Ages and culminating the medieval Arthurian tradition, "thys noble and Ioyous book" has been the seminal source of nearly every worthwhile subsequent artistic treatment of the legend in English. Nevertheless, it is peculiarly difficult to arrive at a just estimate of the work. Influenced by the alterations, additions, representations, and implications supplied by the "symple connynge" of Caxton, readers and critics for four-and-a-half centuries took the book to be intended as a single, continuous whole and praised and blamed it accordingly. Lang noted that the adventures in Malory are, "unlike the Homeric adventures, without an end or aim," but Strachey was led to assert that "the plan of the book is properly epic," and that it has an "epic unity and harmony, 'a beginning, a middle, and an end.' " And Saintsbury, with customary orotundity, declared: "What is certain is that [Malory], and he only in any language, makes of this vast assemblage of stories one story, and one book." Yet the discovery in 1934 and subsequent editing of the Winchester manuscript, the only known manuscript of Malory, led Eugène Vinaver to as-

sert that "one book" is just what Malory had neither attempted nor produced. On the contrary, Vinaver, in his significantly titled edition of the manuscript, *The Works of Sir Thomas Malory,* declared that the work, which the "knight-prisoner" completed in 1469, was a series or set of eight distinct and quite separate romances, individually more or less consistent, but exhibiting noticeable contradictions from one to another.

The question of unity in the *Morte Darthur* thus raised by Vinaver has all but dominated Malory studies for more than two decades. One group of scholars has argued with considerable ingenuity—and some heat—that Malory produced a single book manifesting a very high degree of unity—both "critical" and "historical" (i.e., intentional). Nor has Vinaver's hypothesis had any very active support among scholars. Nevertheless, the claims of his opponents have often struck more detached observers as excessive and their arguments as overly ingenious and occasionally even willful.

The fact that the question of unity could arise at all and that it could be argued so plausibly or, at any rate, so extensively, and, finally, so inconclusively, suggests that the question has not always been properly posed. To begin with, it has been put in terms, C. S. Lewis points out, that Malory, as a medieval writer, would not have understood:

> I do not for a moment believe that Malory had any intention either of writing a single "work" or of writing many "works" as we should understand the expressions. He was telling us about Arthur and the knights. Of course his matter was one—the same king, the same court. Of course his matter was many—they had had many adventures.
>
> The choice we try to force upon Malory is really a choice for us. It is our imagination, not his, that makes the work one or eight or fifty. We can read it either way. We can read it now one way, now another. We partly make what we read.

Moreover, insofar as *unity* is regarded as an absolute feature of a literary work rather than as what it always is in practice—a feature present to some degree in any work, the use of the term has predictably confused the issue. And finally, the claims for an *intentional* unity raise questions that probably need not be resolved and in any event certainly cannot be resolved by the methods adopted.

Perhaps the right way, then, to put the question of Malory's unity is in other terms. What kind of unity is it probable for Malory to have had in mind? What degree of unity did he achieve? Clearly he could not have intended the kind of detailed integration and scrupulous economy that is the aim of much modern novelistic technique; he could not for the simple reason that neither the novel form nor Jamesian theories about it existed in Malory's time. Nor is it likely that he even intended, as Helaine Newstead points out, a "tightly unified structure, like the *Divine Comedy.*" Dante's work was a conscious, autonomous fiction in a way that Malory's could not be. Malory and other medieval writers engaged in handing on a traditional matter, C. S. Lewis reminds us, "proceed as if they were more or less historians; unscholarly, decorating, and emotional historians to be sure, like Livy or Plutarch, but (by and large) historians still." Thus some material that a modern novelist would surely have eliminated or drastically curtailed had to be included at inconvenient length simply because it was part of the matter. Nevertheless, the *Morte Darthur* could have—and it does have—the unity of its subject matter. If the subject is a great one—and Malory's is—then it will go a long way toward generating a sense of significant unity by itself, no matter how unfortunate this may be for the more delicate aesthetic speculations of our day. Moreover, it was possible within the framework of the more or less familiar, traditional material to achieve a certain kind of "connectedness" or "cohesion," to use the terms advocated by D. S. Brewer. Various kinds of links, references to what was to come or what had already taken place, some degree of consistency of characterization, even (though less clearly and surely) some degree of consistency in thematic emphasis and attitude—all these contribute toward our feeling that the *Morte Darthur* is more one thing than it is eight separate things, that its sections or parts or tales are to be read in a "particular order," and that so read they have a "cumulative effect."

What the older critics referred to as Malory's "failure" to unify completely his materials may very well have been due to his artistic tact. To talk, as MacCallum does, of a need for gathering "the loose threads . . . together" and assigning "each of the adventures . . . its proper place in one grand scheme," is to fall into the trap of confusing fiction with history, and is to suggest not "a task that might engross the best powers of the loftiest genius," but rather an undertaking as absurdly impossible as, say, attempting to assign a chronological place in Lincoln's biography to all the anecdotes he is supposed to have told. Nevertheless, Malory's accomplishments in the direction of simplification were not inconsiderable. The narrative method of the various English and French romances in verse and prose on which he drew was excessively complicated; no matter how consciously chosen the method by which "each episode appeared to be a digression from the previous one and at the same time a sequel to some earlier unfinished story," it has generally struck modern readers, as it did Southey, as highly "inartificial":

> Adventure produces adventure in infinite series; not like a tree, whose boughs and branches bearing a necessary relation and due proportion to each other, combine into one beautiful form, but resembling such plants as the prickly pear, where one joint grows upon another, all equal in size and alike in shape, and the whole making a formless and misshaped mass. Even this clumsy mode of transition is often disregarded, and the author passes from adventure to adventure without the slightest connection, introducing you without prologue or prelude of any kind to a new scene, and bringing forward a new set of personages.

Malory must have felt a similar dissatisfaction with the older method; at any rate, he clearly labors in all of his work to disentangle the various stories and by a variety of alterations including condensation, combination, and rearrangement to achieve a simplified, single line of narration. He thus anticipated modern fictional structure. The resultant gain in unity of effect might well have been sufficient in itself to have guaranteed the survival of Malory's version of the Arthurian cycle.

That survival also owes a great deal to other remarkable qualities of the work and the man. Malory's prose style is, to use the conventional adjectives, concise, vigorous, and straightforward. It would probably be more precise to speak of styles, for Malory is master of many tones from the most matter-of-fact narrative summary to the most impassioned rhetoric. He is, in short, nearly always capable of suiting the words to the action. And here too, in his directness and lucidity, he anticipates modern notions of narrative writing. The same can also be said for his achievement, considerably more limited, in shifting his emphasis from mere action to character with its attendant interests of emotion, conscience, and motivation. While some of the earlier romances contain a great deal of overt psychological analysis, Malory's presentation of character is consistently dramatic. This objective approach to character is but one aspect of a pervasive matter-of-factness in his treatment of the stories. Generally skeptical of the nonmaterial and the nonrational, Malory characteristically deemphasizes not only the more fanciful extremes of chivalry and *amour courtois,* but also the supernatural elements and doctrinal elucidations which had come to bulk so large in many of the Continental romances. The same sturdy, commonsense bias seems to mark Malory's moral sensibility insofar as it is to be detected in a book that is remarkably free of moralizing. "Malory is," as Andrew Lang puts it, "throughout strong on the side of goodness." In such alterations of emphasis from mannered artificiality to vigorous simplicity, from subjectivity to objectivity, from doctrinal subtlety to practical ethics may well lie a large share of Malory's greatness. For it was by these alterations that the great story of the British hero was reacclimated to the land of its origin.

Recognition of Malory's achievement ought not, however, to obscure the fact that the work has many faults, many failures of consistency:

> variations in political or religious or narrative emphasis in the different tales; differences in proportions, selectiveness, technique, and even style; the belated mention of vital episodes which are not even narrated; inconsistencies in the biographical and historical timing; the institution of motifs and the apparent forgetting of them for great stretches; the extraordinary differences in the character of some knights between one tale and another; the many episodes that seem to have no more connection with the rest than that they take place in Arthur's realm.

For all his compression and combination, there remains in Malory a plethora of foolish and meaningless incidents, successions of monotonously similar tournaments and adventures. Knights errant encounter, challenge, and tilt at each other like so many brainless automata without a hint of motivation. The dearest friends, even brothers, are incapable of recognizing each other except by name, and this information they regularly refuse to supply. Hermits appear with relentless regularity to offer interpretations only a trifle more incomprehensible than the dreams or events they profess to explain. Despite Malory's efforts at simplification, the narrative line splits and resplits in a way that sometimes defies comprehension. These faults are particularly obvious in his treatment of the Tristram story and the legend of the Grail Quest. In the former he not only unhappily chose the inferior version in which Tristram meets his death at Mark's hands, but at the same time failed to complete the story, leaving that death to be reported later by a mere casual allusion. In the Grail adventures, Malory himself appears to have been as thoroughly mystified as his reader. Contradiction and inconsequence give the effect of dreamlike unreality and, at times, insupportable tedium to the narrative.

Nevertheless, the *Morte Darthur,* taken as a whole, remains incomparably the greatest of the earlier English treatments of the central story of Arthur and his knights; to it indeed, as Vinaver says, "Arthurian romance owes its survival in the English-speaking world." There is no exaggeration even in saying that interest in Arthurian matter closely parallels interest in Malory. The century and a half between Caxton's first publication and Stansby's edition (1634), which saw the appearance of Spenser's *Faerie Queene* and the evolution in young John Milton's mind of a plan for an epic treatment of Arthurian story, also saw the publication of six separate editions of Malory. In the succeeding period of nearly two centuries there was not a single edition of the *Morte Darthur,* and artistic interest in Arthurian story correspondingly reached its nadir. Then, in a matter of only two years (1816-1817) three competing editions came into the market in quick succession just before the second great flowering of the legend began.

THE ESSENTIAL ARTHURIAN STORY

The unmistakable correlation between the fortunes of Malory's book and the fortunes of the Arthurian legend itself suggests that the *Morte Darthur* contains within itself virtually all that is truly significant in Arthurian story as story. Such long popularity and such influence on later poets are not wholly explained by merely formal literary excellences—"noble prose," "limpid narrative," "vivid characterization"—even if Malory had actually manifested these qualities to the degree claimed by his editors. Nor does his importance rest on invention. Translator, abridger, adapter, rearranger, condenser—Malory was all of these, but it is unlikely that he added a single important narrative element to the Arthurian story. Quite the contrary; his real triumph—a partial one, to be sure—lay in the fact that beneath all the tangled accretions, he discerned, consciously or unconsciously, the indispensable elements in the legend. This is not to say, of course, either that he isolated these essential elements and ignored the rest, or that he achieved a completely successful artistic subordination of the multifarious episodes of the adventures of Arthur's other knights to the story of the king's tragic career. The former course would have been repugnant to his uninhibited enthusiasm for the whole range of Arthurian romance; the latter would doubtless have been far beyond his shaping powers. Nevertheless, as he proceeded in his work, he clearly emphasized more and more and at the same time purified of irrelevant elements that

core or central story. It is this essential story, its events and its spirit, that abides and even strengthens in the reader's mind long after he has closed the book, long after he has forgotten the book's other virtues and, for that matter, its *longueurs.* And it is this story that accounts for much of the sense of unity that critics have felt in the book.

The essential Arthurian story or, in Platonic terms, the ideal story, as it manifests itself in Malory combines a number of elements which go back to Nennius and Geoffrey with a variety of additions which entered the story during its centuries of popularity on the Continent. Through Merlin's magic, Uther Pendragon begets Arthur on Igrayne, Duchess of Cornwall, during the very night that the Duke, as it happens, is killed. At his birth, in accord with a promise exacted of Uther by Merlin, Arthur is handed to the mage, who secretly gives him to Sir Ector to rear. Years later, after Uther's death and when the land is being ravaged by civil discord, Arthur unwittingly reveals his right to the kingship by removing a sword from a stone, and hence is crowned by the people. But many struggles with petty kings must be gone through before his throne is secure. In one of these wars he succours Lodegreaunce, father of Gwenyvere. Despite Merlin's prediction of tragic consequences, he marries her and founds his Round Table of many knights. With them he cleanses his land, rights old wrongs, and conquers an empire. But at the same time that the strength of his realm increases, so also the sinful love of Gwenyvere and Lancelot, Arthur's greatest knight and dearest friend, grows steadily stronger. The Grail makes a temporary appearance among his knights and leads them all to vow its quest, a quest which, as Arthur foresees, weakens the Round Table and from which many fail to return. Of those who go, only three, Bors, Percival, and Galahad, are successful; Lancelot, held back by his sin, is only partially successful. The court becomes increasingly filled with dissension over the adulterous couple, and finally when he kills Gawain's brothers in his attempts to protect Gwenyvere, Lancelot is forced to flee, and the unity and fellowship of Arthur's Round Table are irrevocably destroyed. While Arthur is abroad besieging Lancelot, his nephew Mordred treacherously seizes the kingdom. Arthur, returning without the help of Lancelot and his knights, is mortally wounded and nearly all his knights are killed in a great battle with the dissident factions under Mordred. His final end is not certainly known, whether he is buried or goes to Avalon to heal himself of his wounds. Gwenyvere and Lancelot, separated from each other, die afterwards in bitterest remorse and contrition. Such, with one omission, is the outline of the central story in Malory.

That omission is the sequence of events before Arthur's marriage to Gwenyvere in which Arthur, unaware that Margawze is his half-sister, incestuously begets upon her Mordred, who is thus both his son and his nephew. In an effort to avert the dire consequences of this offense, Arthur unsuccessfully tries to kill Mordred by having all the children born on May Day set adrift. Yet despite the prominence given to this episode by some of the critics, especially in the nineteenth century, it seems clear that the incest motif is not essential to the story. It does not appear in the earlier versions, e.g., Geoffrey's, but is instead a later romance addition, and its relevance to the central conflict is so slight that even Malory, who follows the Continental versions in including it, puts little emphasis on it. After the barest recital of the events and a few allusions to Mordred's incestuous begetting in the first two books, Malory appears to forget the matter altogether. Though Mordred is mentioned a number of times in the next seventeen books he is regularly identified only as Gawain's brother and never as Arthur's son; a weak, mean-spirited, evil-tongued knight, he is of little importance until he begins to work against Lancelot, mostly through the latter's adulterous relationship with Gwenyvere. Not until late in the twentieth book after Arthur goes to make war against Lancelot and leaves Mordred in charge of the kingdom, is Mordred again identified as Arthur's son, and even here Malory makes nothing but the most noncommital allusions to the relation. Whether from a lack of interest in the motif or from a consciousness of the danger of diverting attention from the tragic conflict involved in the adultery motif, Malory makes no attempt to develop the pathos so imminent in the father-son relationship. Mordred is nowhere presented as embittered by or even concerned with his origins, and Arthur's reaction to his treason is not the grief of a father at a child's betrayal but the anger of a king at the threat to his throne. The incest motif, clearly, remained a mere attachment to the story, never assimilated into its spirit or emotional structure.

The essential conflict on which that emotional structure is based is the adulterous love of Gwenyvere and Lancelot. From this tragic betrayal of the king springs all the pathos of the story, and, significantly, it is for this betrayal that Arthur grieves. Out of this unsanctified love comes the breakup of the Round Table and the destruction of Arthur's weakened forces in the last great battle. The fatal attractiveness of the queen may be traced back to the earliest Celtic versions of Arthurian story, and is doubtless, in her remarkable susceptibility to abduction, ultimately related to ancient culture myths of a solar or vegetation goddess being carried off by the powers of darkness. So persistent in the later versions is the motif of Guinevere's adultery, either freely chosen or forced, that, as Miss Bensel has put it, "whether Arthur is the brave world-conqueror of the chronicles, the courteous, affable king of romance, or the world-reformer of later times, the queen's infidelity marks the fatal end of his glorious career and entails the final destruction of his kingdom." What in pagan times had been a symbolization of primitive man's conception of natural processes became increasingly in a Christian society a matter of moral concern and a question of sexual ethics. Even in Geoffrey's *Historia,* untouched by erotic speculation, that concern was already felt; as a result of Arthur's governance of his court, Geoffrey tells us, the women "became more chaste and better, and the knights for love of them more brave." But the erotic problem did not receive suitable narrative formulation until Continental romancers, impelled to find artistic expression for the doctrines of courtly love and seizing on hints in the tales recited by the Breton *conteurs,* elevated Lancelot, a figure scarcely mentioned before Chrétien's *Le Chevalier de la Charrette,* to a position of paramount importance. By the first quarter of the thirteenth century, Lancelot's love for Guinevere had become, as Professor App says, "the pivotal point of the whole story."

The danger in this rapid elevation of Lancelot was, of course, that the queen's lover might come to overshadow the queen's husband, the king. And indeed that is just what often happened in the French romances. Arthur's court became only "the conventional starting point of knightly quests and Arthur himself a fantastic character, a king of Fairyland." Malory must have perceived that such a weakening of the third side of the triangle inevitably weakened the tension of the conflict. If Arthur was a mere *roi fainéant,* a complaisant cuckold, where was the tragedy? Thus Malory labored to restore Arthur's grandeur, and, as Professor Vinaver points out, he makes his Arthur in the early books "the true embodiment of heroic chivalry," not "a mere abstract centre of the fellowship of the Round Table, but . . . a political and military leader, conscious of his responsibility for the welfare and prestige of his kingdom," a brave and generous leader. Not only in his actions, but also in his moral rectitude, he is an influence for the better on his knights. Only on such an exalted foundation could the sin of Lancelot and Guinevere attain dignity and significance. Only on such a foundation could Malory have built the tragedy with which his story closes, a tragedy in which "the clash of loyalties, the exuberance of the noble passions that once made Arthurian chivalry great, causes the downfall of Arthur's kingdom."

In his restoration of heroic dignity to the figure of Arthur and in his emphasis on the adultery motif, Malory shows something beyond an awareness of the indispensable events or actions of the essential Arthurian story. He reveals a profound sensitivity to that story's spirit or inherent nature of which the events are but the concrete form. While that spirit is as necessary as the form, it is obviously less easy to describe. Yet if we are to understand the later history of the Arthurian legend, we shall have to understand its essential nature.

To begin with, the story of Arthur is not historical. As we have seen, the historical Arthur, if he existed at all, was no more than the grain of sand about which a pre-existing body of mythic materials accreted and thereby survived into Christian times. What little we may guess about the Arthur of history is almost wholly lacking in poetic interest or significance; the mere chieftain of battles lacks the royal éclat of a king. His story has no details outside the battles and no dramatic conflict—in short, it is not a story at all. The writers of the Middle Ages, untroubled by any notions of exact history, rejected the *dux bellorum* as, for that matter, the folk and the *conteurs* had already done. The Arthurian story that counts—the story found in the romances—is not even a result of the magnification of the achievements of such a petty warlord. Nor is it to be comprehended simply as an ordinary fiction or folktale.

On the contrary, the Arthurian legend is distinguished from the other *matières* by a mysteriousness that is not a simple matter of the "magical elements of folklore." And it is further distinguished by the enduring fascination that it has exercised over men's minds. Both that mysteriousness and that persistency derive from the fact that its basic materials had been evolved, as has been noted, out of the mythopoeic impulses of primitive peoples. The essential Arthurian story is no arbitrary, excogitated creation of individual imagination; instead it is, in the fullest anthropological and literary sense of the word, a myth. In the mysterious circumstances of Arthur's begetting, the concealment of his parentage, his rearing by comparatively humble persons, and the revelation of his royal origins by a magical feat, the similarities to the myths of the births of such heroes as Oedipus and Perseus are obvious. The parallels in the later careers, betrayals, and final ends of Arthur and a wide variety of mythic heroes are equally conspicuous. In earlier times these myths were probably closely related to the religious activities of the community; it is likely, even, that they grew directly out of primitive religious rituals. The attachment of the myths to natural phenomena such as solar, lunar, or vegetative cycles was perhaps an early response to man's desire to "understand" his universe, or perhaps a reflection of his anxiety to conceal from himself the psychic content of the myths. But when men ceased to believe that fertility could be restored to the land only by a ritual mating of the king with a goddess, or that the disappearance of the sun was to be "explained" by a story of a god killed in a great battle in the west, the myths should, logically speaking, have withered away. The fact is that they did not.

That such mythic elements persisted in the stories of Arthur and his knights and survived into the Christian Middle Ages, that they remained perceptible here and there beneath the romancers' occasional and more or less perfunctory attempts at rationalization, suggests that we are dealing with a legend capable of exercising a lasting and all but universal fascination. At its heart lay some of the deepest intuitions of the race. Whether or not we accept Jung's explanation of the mechanism by which these "archetypal patterns" exert their influence on the human mind is of little significance here. What is important to see is that such a legend is from the beginning relatively fixed both in form and spirit. Growing out of the unconscious or nonrational mind, its configuration will reject any significant alteration in events. And it is equally resistant to any change in its spirit.

That spirit in the central story of Arthur is profoundly tragic. That is to say, the story's significance, whether we think of Arthur as a culture hero or as a heroic rebel against elder authority, is intimately bound up with its tragic outcome. It can no more have a "happy ending" than could the stories of Oedipus or Orestes or Hamlet. Merely to state the matter is to make apparent the ridiculousness of such an alteration—the tragedy *is* the story. Nor can the early "happy" parts of the central story when Arthur and his Round Table are still increasing in glory be used successfully apart from the tragic denouement. They are as insignificant by themselves as would be, let us say, a play dealing with Hamlet's student days in Wittenberg.

But if the Arthurian legend is, as are other myths, relatively fixed in form and spirit, it is at the same time—again like other myths—remarkably responsive to changes in its symbolic content. It is this flexibility that Ernest Rhys referred to when he wrote: "The power of romance is that it fits itself anew to every period. Each one takes up again the undying legend of Arthur, and more or less deludes itself with the notion that its latest version is the truest. But every century must still read its own emotion and its own colours into the past." From the beginning the story's characters and events had carried concealed meanings, had expressed in symbolic terms the fears, aspirations, and intuitions of men. Arthur especially "has always figures as an ideal king," Miss Bensel observes; "he is not representative of his age, strictly speaking, but far better and nobler than the best people of that time. Hence he embodies their strongly idealized morals and social views."

In its absorption of the social views of the Christian Middle Ages, Arthurian legend underwent—without any violation of its essential form or spirit—an alteration that almost amounts to a qualitative change. This change distinguishes the legend sharply from classical myth, and consequently, as we shall see, from classical epic or tragedy. Like other myths, the Arthurian story in its earlier forms depends for its interest almost wholly on the actions and fate of a single hero. But unlike the classical myths, Arthurian legend in its serious artistic handlings was deeply influenced by a secular ideal—that is, the chivalric ideal— that was markedly social rather than individual in it simplications. In absorbing this ideal, the story became no longer an individual tragedy, but instead the tragedy of a society. The result was a number of slight adjustments necessary to give full expression to the new ideal or content.

The most important of these adjustments was, as we have seen, the increasingly heavy emphasis laid on the socially significant sin of the betrayal of trust involved in the adulterous relationship of Lancelot and Guinevere. In this sin the romancers saw the conflict of the story, the moral evil that brought on the collapse of the society founded by Arthur. It is no accident that in the conflict between Lancelot's duty to his king as defind by the chivalric ideal and his duty to the queen as defined by the doctrines of courtly love lay the point of extreme contradiction in the social ideal that the myth had been made to symbolize. The sin also represents symbolically the highest tension between the calls of the flesh and the spirit. The paradox of chivalry was, of course, only a shadow of the basically paradoxical nature of Christianity itself with its impossible and still categorical commands. Out of the need to give expression in the story to this absolute ideal grew a further adjustment of the legend—the development of the Grail story. Only from this quest could the society receive its final test and reveal its failure in terms of a comparison with absolute standards.

Both of these elements, the adultery motif and the Grail Quest, had been built up on foundations, or at least suggestions, already present in the body of stories that had gathered around Arthur in the dim times before the cycle was carried to the Continent. It was also in these stories with their extensive cast of characters that the romancers found the other element necessary to give full expression to the social ideal. As we have already noted, the fact that the cycle contained many heroes rather than a single one allowed the presentation of the whole range of variations of which the chivalric ideal was capable. But from an artistic standpoint it is more important that the essentially social chivalric ideal could thus find expressive form in the growth, flowering, decay, and destruction not of an individual, but of a society. In this assimilation of the various knights of the early stories, the conflict and fall are not merely the tragedy of Arthur, an individual, but they are rather the tragedy of the whole Round Table, a society.

Endowed thus with such significance, Arthur's knights were no longer mere supernumeraries, but integral parts of the whole. If that whole does not manifest the special variety of unity of classical epic or tragedy, it has nevertheless the only kind of unity that really counts—the unity of theme and form. And that unity, it may be observed, is no less sophisticated than the classical unity. Indeed, if anything it is more sophisticated. Like the architecture whose growth paralleled the legend's development, Arthurian story's triumph was the unification of almost unbelievable diversity, the harmonization of the demands of matter with the aspiration of the spirit. If its unity is thus not geometrical, it is clearly organic; not imposed by canon, it rises out of the vital spirit of the feudal society whose aspirations it expressed.

And also, just as French Gothic architecture, after passing through a series of great changes, quickly reached a perfected and comparatively unchanging type, the essential story structure of Arthur's reign also attained, though less rapidly, a formal and expressive completeness. To summarize its essential narrative elements is, as it should be, to summarize its spiritual and moral dialectic: In a land racked by evil, a hero of mysterious though kingly birth makes his way to his throne, cleanses the land, and founds an ideal form of life, a society of glorious heroes. That society is tested in the material world by the fleshly passions of wife and friend, and in the world of spiritual absolutes by a mysterious quest. Found false to its ideal, the society is destroyed in a tragic denouement in which both its good and evil meet their end.

It is this exact correspondence of content and form, as well as the mythic evolution of the legend that explains the relatively fixed nature of the story, its obstinate rejection of significant alteration, and hence the failure of every later attempt at arbitrary addition or subtraction. There is "something impertinent," MacCallum observes, about the procedure of wholesale change adopted by many of the later authors who took up the story; "it rouses the same kind of recalcitrance that is felt when well-known historic characters are distorted in novel or drama." And well it might, for such manipulations are in both cases tamperings with truth—with the truth of fact on the one hand and with the truth of imagination or poetry on the other hand. In the failure to appreciate the fixed nature of the essential Arthurian story, then, lies the explanation for the relative unsuccess of efforts to rouse Arthur from his long sleep in Avalon during most of the next three-and-a-half centuries. (pp. 9-29)

> *James Douglas Merriman, in his* The Flower of Kings: A Study of the Arthurian Legend in England between 1485 and 1835, *The University Press of Kansas, 1973, 307 p.*

An excerpt from Malory's *Le Morte Darthur* (1485):

'Yea,' said King Arthur, 'I love Guenever the King's daughter Leodegrance, of the land of Camelerd, the which holdeth in his house the Table Round that ye told he had of my father Uther. And this damosel is the most valiant and fairest lady that I know living, or yet that ever I could find.'

'Sir,' said Merlin, 'as of her beauty and fairness she is one of the fairest alive, but and ye loved her not so well as ye do, I should find you a damosel of beauty and of goodness that should like you and please you, and your heart were not set; but there as a man's heart is set, he will be loth to return.'

'That is truth,' said King Arthur.

But Merlin warned the king covertly that Guenever was not wholesome for him to take to wife, for he warned him that Launcelot should love her, and she him again; and so he turned his tale to the adventures of Sangrail. Then Merlin desired of the king for to have men with him that should enquire of Guenever, and so the king granted him, and Merlin went forth unto King Leodegrance of Camelerd, and told him of the desire of the king that he would have unto his wife Guenever his daughter.

'That is to me,' said King Leodegrance, 'the best tidings that ever I heard, that so worthy a king of prowess and noblesse will wed my daughter. And as for my lands, I will give him, wist I it might please him, but he hath lands enow, him needeth none, but I shall send him a gift shall please him much more, for I shall give him the Talbe Round, the which Uther Pendragon gave me, and when it is full complete, there is an hundred knights and fifty. And as for an hundred good knights I have myself, but I fault fifty, for so many have been slain in my days.'

And so Leodegrance delivered his daughter Guenever unto Merlin, and the Table Round with the hundred knights, and so they rode freshly, with great royalty, what by water and what by land, till that they came nigh unto London.

> *Sir Thomas Malory,* Le Morte D'Arthur, *Vol. 1, edited by Janet Cowen, Penguin Books, 1969.*

Margaret J. C. Reid

[*In the following excerpt, Reid provides a critical overview of the literary sources of Arthurian legend from Nennius to Malory.*]

The Arthurian legend, which later had so many branches, had its main roots in the story of King Arthur, told in the pseudo-histories of Nennius, Geoffrey of Monmouth, Wace and Layamon. Later in the romances, the adventures of the Knights of the Round Table obscured those of the King, and he became a mere figure-head, and his court a centre from which knights sallied out on their various quests and returned with their trophies.

The two strands, interwoven in the stories which have Arthur as a hero, are the two which are found in most legends, the mythical and the historical or pseudo-historical, treating Arthur as a human being, though of heroic stature.

The twelfth-century historians, of course, had little idea of history as a relation of fact; they wove together probable incidents and quite improbable ones, many of the latter being derived from oral legends. The mythical element is also strongly represented in the *Mabinogion,* translated by Lady Charlotte Guest from a fourteenth-century manuscript, the "Red Book of Hergest." These tales are, however, considerably older than the manuscript and the two oldest which contain Arthurian matter, "Kilhwch and Olwen" and the "Dream of Rhonabwy" show no traces, as the later stories do, of the Normanised world of Geoffrey of Monmouth. They show Arthur as a kind of superman, towering above his underlings in a world of magic. This magic communicated itself to all which Arthur possesses. The importance of Geoffrey of Monmouth in the history and development of Arthurian legend can hardly be exaggerated. What were his sources, the authenticity of the "liber" of which he makes mention, how much or how little he took from his sources, in what manner he adapted, transformed and added to them, what legends were current in his own day—all these questions over which scholars have laboured are of interest. But from the wider point of view of Arthurian literature, and English literature in particular, there is one chief fact to be emphasised and remembered. This is that Geoffrey was the first to give in eloquent and rhetorical Latin a detailed account of Arthur, his barons and knights, an account which, written as history, appealed to the imagination of the future poets and prose writers who were to elaborate still further the various incidents.

The researches of scholars have brought to notice certain passages in the contemporary and Pre-Galfridian chronicles which go to prove that Arthur held a certain place as a character in history (or pseudo-history) round which legendary stories had begun to gather. The first mention of him is in an entry in the ninth-century Chronicle of Nennius. Arthur in this entry is mentioned as fighting against the Saxons as "dux bellorum." Twelve battles are here given, including the twelfth, Mount Badon, when Arthur "alone in one day killed nine hundred and sixty men" and in which he was victor. In the eighth battle at the fortress Guinnion, it is stated that he "bore the image of the Virgin Mary on his shoulders (*super humeros suos*)." As regards his rank, the Vatican manuscript adds "although many were nobler by birth (*nobliores*) than he."

This description speaks for itself, but it is interesting to note that Arthur has already been made a Christian warrior. The tenth-century "Annales Cambriæ" gives two entries relating that Arthur, in the Battle of Badon, carried the cross of our Lord Jesus Christ for three days and three nights on his shoulders. The chronicle also mentions the battle of "Camlann" in which Arthur and Medraut fell.

Of especial interest in regard to the legendary Arthur, are the passages in the Appendix to the *Historia* of Nennius, the Mirabilia which relate marvels of the South Country.

"In the region of Buelt is a heap of stones and on the top is one stone bearing the print of a dog's foot." This mark was made by Cabal—so the document goes on to relate—and he was the dog of Arthur the warrior when he hunted the boar Troynt. The cairn was called Carn Cabal.

Another passage tells of the wonders of the tomb Anir in the region of Ercing (Hereford), who was the son of Arthur (Arthur *militis*) and killed by him and buried here.

The story of the hunting of the boar Troynt is of especial interest as it appears again in the story of "Kilhwch and Olwen."

There is, before Geoffrey, still another important witness to the fame of Arthur, namely, William of Malmesbury, a contemporary of Geoffrey and a historian of considerable critical discernment for his times, and a worthy follower of Bede. In his *Gesta Anglorum,* of which the first version was finished about 1125, he makes an important statement concerning Arthur: "This is that Arthur of whom the trifling of the Britons talks such nonsense even to-day; a man clearly worthy not to be dreamed of in fallacious fables, but to be proclaimed in veracious histories, as one who long sustained his tottering country, and gave the shattered minds of his fellow-citizens an edge for war."

From the above excerpts it will be seen that there is enough written evidence from the Chronicles to show that Arthur was already known as a successful British chief and that legends were collecting round his name.

Besides this, the students of comparative mythology have examined Geoffrey's characters and names and have in many instances attempted to trace the origin of these to mythological sources. Even although there is much disagreement concerning these, nevertheless there is a general consensus of opinion that there is in his *History* a considerable foundation of legend. Among the figures concerning whom there was probably a more or less established tradition, are Kei and Bedwyr, known in the *Mabinogion* and the "Triads" and in the *Vita of Cadoc.*

Geoffrey has created them great lords and followers of Arthur. Bedevere the butler is made Duke of Normandy, and Kay the Seneschal, Duke of Anjou. In the final battle against Mordred, both were killed and Arthur had them embalmed and buried. Bedevere the butler was carried into Bayeux and Kay buried near Chinon.

Arthur's weapons, his shield Pridwen, his sword Caliburnus and his lance Ron, are mentioned in the tale of "Kilhwch and Olwen," although Prydwen (so spelt) is a ship, not a shield. The lance Ron has, in the Welsh tale, the form Rhongomyant, and the sword Caledvwlch; the latter has been equated with the Irish Caladbolg, the fairy sword of the hero Cuchulain and the Excalibur of the romances. The ship Prydwen is also mentioned in a Taliessin poem "Preiddeu Annwfn," the Harryings of Hades, which may belong to an earlier nucleus of Welsh tales than "Kilhwch and Olwen."

The main interest in Geoffrey's picture of Arthur up to and including the eighteenth century was a patriotic one. Geoffrey was regarded as a skilful portrait-painter and the likeness to his original was not too closely examined. The later chroniclers, poets and romancers, only elaborated the detail. To them Arthur was the type of a successful British king whose conquests reached far and wide.

In the ninth book of the *History* there is a magnificent and eloquent description of Arthur's crowning at "Urbs Legionum" (Caerleon) on the Usk, at Whitsuntide. He had had a previous ceremony at York. A long list is given of the vassals who were invited to attend the court at Caerleon, including four kings of Scotland. The scene is one of great pomp and grandeur, such as would have accompanied the crowning of a great Norman king, like William the Conqueror. Geoffrey relates that after Arthur had been invested with the "ensigns of the kingship" he went in procession to the "Church of the Metropolitan See." He was supported on either side by two archbishops, and four kings of Albany, Cornwall, North and South Wales, marched before him bearing four golden swords, while marvellously sweet music was being chanted by the clerics. The Queen also went in royal state to the "Church of the Virgins dedicate" and was attended likewise by four queens, bearing four white doves. The whole day was given up to national celebration and the streets were thronged by the populace. After the divine service the courtiers entered the palace and the meats and the drinks were served to them by a thousand youths and pages in livery. The master of the food ceremonies was Kay the Seneschal, clothed in a "doublet, furred of ermines." He is a very different figure from the Kei in "Kilhwch and Olwen" reproved by Arthur for discourtesy, and possessing many mythological characteristics. Bedevere the butler presided over the drinks. Meanwhile the women feasted in another palace. Then after the banquet, both men and women adjourned to view the tournament and sports which lasted for three days. On the fourth day, Arthur, as a great feudal lord, dispersed honours and offices, "unto each was made grant of the honour of the office he held, in possession, earldom, to wit, of city or castle, archbishopric, bishopric, abbacy, or whatsoever else it might be."

There are one or two details not Norman, such as the separation of the men and women, and, at the sports, the game of flinging heavy stones seems native in origin. But in the main, the account is that of a great Norman king or great feudal lord with his court.

Among the many translations and adaptations of Geoffrey, two stand out and may be classed as original works. The first of these is Wace's *Brut,* a French metrical romance, and the second, Layamon's *Brut.* Wace's *Brut* was finished in 1155 and the *Brut* of Layamon is approximately dated at the end of the twelfth century.

Little is known of Wace's life except a few facts which, however, are significant. He was born in the Island of Jersey, educated in part in Paris and lived at Caen in Normandy, holding a regular position at the court. Layamon mentions that a dedication of Wace's *Brut* was addressed to Queen Eleanor, wife of Henry II, but it is lacking in the extant manuscripts.

Although Wace's poem is, in general, a translation of Geoffrey, yet it is distinctive and vivid in style and shows the influence of the French chivalric ideals then permeating the mediæval court. Probably, too, Wace was acquainted with some of the actual French romances. In the portrait, for example, which he draws of Gawain, he introduces the romance conception of this hero. He makes him praise peace even in the Council of War, and say that the pleasures of love are good and that for the sake of his *amie* a young man performs feats of chivalry. Geoffrey gives no account of a speech of Gawain. Again, Wace, all through his work, minimises the details of barbarity and cruelty which he found in his source to suit the more civilised conception of his audience. The conception of Arthur as the centre of a court of knight-errantry, instead of a world-conquering hero, is beginning to appear in his poetic chronicle. The circumstances of his own age of feudalism are portrayed: fortresses become feudal castles; senators, barons; and consuls, contes. And not only in his matter, but in his manner and style Wace has, for the most part, the characteristics of the romantic poet, conscious of his audience and taking the delight of an artist in dwelling on picturesque details.

Layamon, in his epic the *Brut,* gives a stirring account of Arthur's deeds and paints a different portrait of the heroic and warlike king from that of Wace. In Wace, Arthur is a chivalric hero of romance with his mediæval court, but in Layamon's poem, which partakes of the nature of a saga, he is more of an actual English monarch winning victories over his enemies. True, his exploits and qualities are magnified and represent Layamon's own idea of what an English king should be—brave beyond dispute, stern to his followers, unbending and often cruel and revengeful towards his foes. Thus Layamon gives in greater detail than Wace the number of his hostages, and evidently delights in portraying the submission of the conquerors, Gillomar and others. This exultant patriotic feeling probably causes the poet to expand such a triumphant scene as Arthur's elevation to the throne.

Layamon is not a mere dull chronicler, he is the poetic successor of the unknown author or authors of *Beowulf,* and in action and description his ringing words and phrases seem to have been hammered out in the glowing forge of his own exultant feeling.

Detail of a mosaic floor in Otranto Cathedral c.1160, depicting an equestrian Arthur.

In one or two passages in which he breaks away from his chief source, he demonstrates his own dramatic power. For example, he gives a more detailed account than Wace of the circumstances in which Arthur received the evil tidings of the betrayal of Modred. A young knight had come one evening to the court of Arthur. He had been deputed to bear the news of the rebellion of Arthur's nephew Modred and his abduction of Arthur's wife Guinevere (Wenhaver). Arthur welcomed him as a messenger of good news and he did not dare to tell the king the real truth. So the king went to bed in ignorance. During the night he was haunted by distressing dreams. He thought that he was in his hall and that Wenhaver and his knights were pulling down the roof and the pillars about his ears and that all was going to destruction. On awaking, he felt ill and calling for the messenger related his terrifying dream. When he finished, the knight turned and said "Lord, if it had happened, and may God forbid, that Modred had taken thy Queen and thy land, yet thou mightest avenge thee and stay all thine enemies."

Arthur replied that he never supposed that Modred and Wenhaver would betray him and then, at this dramatic point, the knight stated the facts bluntly.

One of the most important elaborations is the account of the making the Round Table, mentioned also by Wace. There is a most realistic description of the preliminary brawl which arose at the Yuletide feast where seven kings with seven hundred knights began to quarrel about precedence. The fight raged hotter and hotter to the shedding of blood until Arthur arrived and quelled it in an equally savage manner. After this, Layamon relates, the King went to Cornwall, where a carpenter informed him that he could make a table where sixteen hundred men and more could sit without one being more exalted in place than the other. This convenient table Arthur could carry wherever he went. Timber was bought and the work completed in four weeks.

Celticists maintain that the table is of fairy and Celtic origin. Whether this be so or not, other original passages show that Layamon, in spite of his realistic Anglo-Saxon outlook, used legendary material in this poetic chronicle. For example, he describes how Arthur armed himself with burnie, shield and sword. The burnie, the poet informs us, was the work of Wygar, an elfish smith, his spear, of the smith Griffin. This seems to have reference to the Wayland legend. His shield "Pridwen" and his sword "Ron" is also mentioned, and a special name "Goswhit" is given to his helm, which may be British or from Teutonic saga.

Layamon also gives a graphic account of the fight with the monster at Mont St Michel, with details of his own.

The most famous of his descriptions is that of Arthur's death and the coming of Argante, the Courteous, who with another woman, wondrously fair, bore him in a small boat to Avalon to be healed of his wounds. This incident, the poet remarks in a former passage, was foreseen by Arthur himself and his own return prophesied.

The *Morte Arthure,* a northern alliterative poem named from the scrivener Thornton, calls for attention both for its subject-matter and its fine literary qualities. The author is unknown, though it has been ascribed to Huchown of the Awle Ryale. It gives a vivid and detailed account of Arthur's campaign against Rome, after the spurning of Lucius the Roman ambassador, and the submission of Rome. Written about the middle or end of the fourteenth century, the writer handles the subject-matter in a way to glorify the English people. Many of the details are evidently taken from the campaigns and accountrements of the warlike Edward III and his soldiers who fought in France.

Underneath the portrait of Arthur, the conquering British king, can be discovered an earlier representation of a more mythical Arthur, the slayer of the monster of St Michel's Mount who "sups on seven children of the commons, chopped up on a charger of pure white silver with pickles and finely ground spices and wines of Portugal mixed with honey." This monster also has a mantle made of the beards of kings and demands the beard of Arthur. This trait has been copied from the King Ritho of Welsh legend.

But the writer's chief interest and enthusiasm is for the heroic and chivalrous Arthur. He waxes eloquent in describing the glittering armour and trappings of warfare, showing a technical knowledge of heraldic symbols. He takes a delight in colour wherever displayed, either in the moving mass of warriors and steeds or in the details of the ladies' dresses. And what is more remarkable in a mediæval poem of battle, is the writer's appreciation of the sweet sounds and peaceful scenes of Nature:

> Thane they roode by θat ryver, θat rynnyd so swythe,
> θare θe ryndez overrechez with realle bowghez;
> The roo and the rayne-dere reklesse thare rounene,
> In ranez and in rosers to ryotte thame selvene;
> The frithez ware floreschte with flourez fulle many,
> With fawcouns and fesantez of ferlyche hewez;
> All θe feulez thare fleschez, that flyex with wengez,
> ffore thare galede the gowke one grevez fulle lowde,
> Wyth alkyne gladchpe θay gladdene theme selvene;
> Of θe nyghtgale notez θe noisez was swette,
> They threpide wyth the throstills thre-hundreth at ones.
> θat whate swowynge of watyr, and syngnynge of byrdez,
> It myghte salve hyme of sore, that sounde was nevere!

[Then they rode by that river that runneth so swift where the trees overstretch with fair boughs, the roe and the reindeer run recklessly there in thickets and rose-gardens to feast themselves. The thickets were in blossom with mayflowers, with falcons and pheasants of fair hues—all the birds there which fly with wings, for there sang the cuckoo full loud on the bushes, with all birds of merriment they gladden themselves; the voice of the nightingale's note was sweet, they strove with the throstles three hundred at once, that this murmur of water and singing of birds might cure him of ill who never was whole.]

This narrative partakes of the qualities of the chronicle and the romance and has borrowed from both. The substance of the story of Arthur's wars against Lucius, the author takes from Geoffrey of Monmouth's *Chronicle*, but his work shows the influence of Layamon's *Brut* and he must also have known one or more of the Romances. On the other hand, the chief *motif* is that of a Chanson de Geste rather than a Romance, for it is the virile one of the glory of wars and victories, nor does the writer spare his audience the realistic details of carnage. The fights are not, as so often in Malory, mere tournaments for the sake of prowess, but often life-and-death duels, as in the case of Sir Priamus and Sir Gawain, or fierce struggles between the hosts of Arthur and the Roman barons and knights or between Arthur's men and Modred's. Again the tragedy of the final act is not that of conflict between passionate love and loyalty as in the "Stanzaic Morte" and Malory. The treachery of Lancelot whose "honour rooted in dishonour stood" is not a theme of the "Thornton Morte." It is Modred, not Lancelot, who is the betrayer of Arthur and who carries Gaynor off, evidently considered only as part of the booty. The tragedy mourned is one of costly victory in battle with its consequent slaying of the finest flower of Arthur's knights. One of the most poignant and eloquent of speeches is that of Arthur's lament over the fallen Gawain, the noblest of friends and the bravest and most chivalrous of foes.

This heroic poem reaches its highest level when the disastrous end is sighted. It is foreshadowed, in true mediæval fashion, by a dream of Arthur's in which he beholds fickle Dame Fortune spinning her wheel. In the vision he is shown six kings of the earth, including Alexander the Great and Julius Cæsar, who have mounted to its highest rung and been ignominiously hurled down. Arthur himself is placed on the wheel and whirled under until all parts of his body are smashed to pices. He awakes trembling, and on demanding from his magician the interpretation of the dream, learns that it is his turn to be cast down to the lowest rung, he who has ascended so high as a brave conqueror of the world!

Almost immediately Sir Cradock arrives in breathless haste as the bearer of evil tidings. In the King's absence Modred has seized the kingdom and his wife Gaynor, made common cause with the Danes, and awaits him at Southampton. King Arthur must summon his followers and embark for England. The naval battle is described in a stirring fashion with details evidently taken from contemporary fighting. Arthur is to the foremost; as in the Chronicles, his chief banner "bears a 'chalk-white maiden with a Child in her arms' who is Lord of Heaven": and the chief hero is the good Gawain. The grappling together of the ships, the inrush of the men on to the vessels, the falling of the masts, the fierce hand-to-hand fighting on board until the hatches are filled with dead Danish men (allies of Modred), the swift and sure havoc of the famous archers of England—all are described in vigorous phraseology. These convey to the mind the mortal conflict, the deadly blows, the noise and confusion of a great struggle in a small space. Even the few lines quoted below give some idea of the effect of the packed style:—

> Thane was hede-rapys hewene θat helde upe θe mastes:
> Thare was conteke fulle kene, and crachynge of chippys!
> Grett cogges of kampe crasseches in sondyre!
> Mony kabane clevede, cabilles destroyede!
> Knyghtes and kene men killide the braynes!
> Kidd castelles were corvene with alle theire kene wapene,
> Castelles fulle comliche that coloured ware faire!

> · · · · ·

> Thus they dalte that daye thire dubbide knyghtes,
> Tille alle θe Danes ware dede, and in θe depe throwene.

> [Then were the stays hewn down that hold up the masts: there was a furious collision and the cracking of ships could be heard: great battle-ships burst asunder, many a cabin was broken and the cables destroyed; knights and keen men killed the enemy—fine castles were cleft asunder with their keen weapons—full fair castles that were beautifully coloured.

> · · · · ·

> Thus they dealt blows that day, these dubbed knights, till all the Danes were dead and thrown into the deep.]

The narrative now moves on with dramatic swiftness. Genuine and heart-stirring is Arthur's grief on losing his battle-lords, especially Gawain, who is buried with all the honours of war. Modred is finally slain in a hand-to-hand encounter with the King, but in his death-struggle he inflicts a mortal wound on his foe, who is conveyed to a manor of the Isle of Aveloyne (Avalon). Here Arthur dies, bequeathing his kingdom to Constantine. The royal monarch is buried at Glastonbury according to this chronicler, who gives a dignified account of his end.

The "Stanzaic Morte" has not the same descriptive excellence as the "Thornton Morte Arthure." At the best, it has a certain naïve sincerity and pathos which make up for its unpolished form. Its subject-matter is, however, of great interest, as the poem contains a version of the story of the Maid of Ascolat and of Arthur's death. The question of the sources of the poem and its relation to Malory's *Morte Darthur*, Books XVIII, XX and XXI, have been the subject of keen controversy. Suffice it to say here that it is agreed that this *Morte* and Malory have for common source a lost redaction or redactions of the French prose Lancelot. Thus it is clear that the relation between the *Morte* and Malory is a close one. For example, in the now famous story in which King Arthur commands Bedivere to throw his sword into the lake, which command the knight does not obey till the third time, there is great similarity in incident and in phraseology.

Scholars have established the following facts concerning the "Stanzaic Morte." It is contained in a unique MS. written in two hands. Its dialect is Midland, although whether East or North-West Midland is disputed. Linguishts show evidence that it belongs to the latter half of the fourteenth century. The author, probably belonging to the minstrel class, is unknown. Recurring phrases such as "bright as blossom on brere," "hende and free," its crude form (stanzas in eight lines of four accents, with alternate rhymes) as well as its plain unvarnished story, place it in the category of the ballad.

Even if Malory had not, with his more sophisticated art, immortalised the romantic story, this ballad-poem would have been worthy of note. There is a certain directness about the simple and human emotions which impress the reader. The true love which Lancelot's fellow-knights show towards him, their delight in his prowess, and grief at his absence, make a sincere appeal. The pathos of the story of the maid who dies for love of Lancelot has been finely transmitted in Malory's rendering. And surely never has a fight been more sorrowfully waged than that of the unwilling Lancelot with Gawain, revengeful of his brother's death! Full of poignancy is Arthur's lament for his fallen comrades. The passionate attachment of Lancelot and Guinevere and the havoc it threatens to bring about is succinctly summed up by the bishop, the ambassador for peace, in his appeal to Lancelot, "Wemen are frele of hyr entayle. Syr lettes not ynglande go to noght."

In the chronicles of Wace, Layamon and the two "Mortes," there has been an interpenetration and development of the romantic outlook. The "Alliterative" or "Thornton Morte" which has been shown by scholars to be a near parallel to Book V of Malory's *Morte Darthur* forms thus a link between the chronicle and the romance in English literature. The other sources of the first four books of Malory have been found to be the "Ordinary" or "Vulgate" Merlin, the "Continuation" and the "Huth" Merlin. The first four books of Malory tell of the doings of Arthur and Merlin, including the story of Arthur's birth, and the incident of the sword fast embedded in the stone at Westminster, which would only yield to the fore-ordained hero, Arthur. There are other legendary and pseudohistorical narrations. Book V shows Arthur to be the heroking of England waging war both against giants and against Rome.

Drawn from so many sources, the picture of Arthur in Malory is not altogether unified. At one time he is king in a fairy land, over which Merlin presides as the king's helper, overcoming all difficulties by means of his magic wiles. At another, he is a truly English king with his loyal followers Gawain and Lancelot, all concerned in bringing England glory with their swords, and refusing to submit even to that great world-conqueror, Rome. In the later books, the king is somewhat overshadowed by his knights, but comes to his own again in the poignant narrative of his death.

The sources from which the picture of Arthur is drawn in English literature in the next four or five centuries, are Geoffrey of Monmouth's *Chronicle* and Malory's *Morte Darthur*. The more prosaic eighteenth century, in depicting the historical Arthur, drew mainly from the *Chronicle,* and Spenser and the romantic poets of the nineteenth and twentieth centures from Malory.

The five editions of Malory, published from 1485 to 1634, show his popularity. Indeed, Roger Ascham would not have condemned the *Morte Darthur* so thoroughly, if it had not had such a wide influence and been such a favourite in the sixteenth century. (pp. 14-29)

> *Margaret J. C. Reid, "Arthur in the Chronicles and Malory," in her* The Arthurian Legend: Comparison of Treatment in Modern and Mediæval Literature, a Study in the Literary Value of Myth and Legend, *Oliver and Boyd, 1938. pp. 14-29.*

Rachel Bromwich

[*In the following excerpt, Bromwich traces the influence of Celtic literary sources on the later development of continental Arthurian romance.*]

The nature of the indebtedness of continental Arthurian romance to antecedent Celtic sources, together with that of the likely channels by which Celtic material reached the continent, has been a matter of hot debate for the best part of a century. In the light of the advances which have been made in Celtic scholarship during the same period, however, I hope that it may now be possible to establish certain basic principles concerning this transmission which will prove acceptable to Romance scholars and to Celticists alike—that is, acceptable both to those whose main concern is with the early indigenous literature of the Celts in Wales, Cornwall, and Brittany, and to those who look back from the high noon of Arthurian romance as this is reflected in the later prose and verse masterpieces in French, English, and German, but who nevertheless retain some interest in the question of 'origins'.

I begin by setting forth four basic propositions which I shall elaborate in the course of this paper. These are:

i) that the personal nomenclature of French Arthurian romance, in so far as it is of Celtic derivation, is derived from the names of characters who played a part in antecedent Welsh, Cornish, and Breton tradition, and who are frequently identifiable in Welsh sources which are too early to have been subjected to continental influences;

ii) that the development of Arthur as the centre of a cycle, drawing into his orbit the names of a number of independent figures belonging to this native tradition, is an indigenous development which took place in Celtic countries at too early a date to have been influenced from without;

iii) that the Brittonic names which entered French romance in this way did not necessarily do so in combination with any narrative elements previously attached to those who bore them in the native records, but that Celtic names and Celtic story-themes for the most part penetrated continental romance independently of each other;

iv) that the question of Arthur's rise to fame in western literature is essentially a Welsh literary problem, and that the scanty references to Arthur in early sources can only be interpreted in the light of a full understanding of the character and development of the literature to which they belong.

Firstly, then, the question of Arthurian names. The name 'Arturus' appears first in the Latin of the Welshman who redacted the *Historia Brittonum* some time in the early ninth century, and as 'Arthur' in several Welsh poems which are believed to go back approximately to the same date—one of them indeed, the famous reference to Arthur in the *Gododdin,* may even be considerably earlier. Arthur's two most frequent companions in a number of early sources are Cai and Bedwyr (*Keu* and *Bedoier,* Kay and Bedivere), and these appear as his companions already in one of the poems to which I refer, *Pa gur* (= *Pa wr*) 'What man is the gatekeeper?', of which I offer a tentative translation below. The names of both Arthur and Cai (*Caius*) are generally believed to be of Latin derivation, but this, if it be accepted, need prove no obstacle, for names derived from Latin are by no means rare among the names in the early Welsh genealogies, for men who were born approximately between the dates AD 300 and 450: they become less common after that date. (The name of St Patrick, from *Patricius,* is an example). Arthur's queen Gwenhwyfar (*Guenievre*) 'fair enchantress', though not attested quite so early as these latter names, does seem to belong to the early native tradition, if we are to believe the Triads, and Geoffrey of Monmouth latinizes her name as *Guanhumara,* a form which he must have derived from a written source in Old Welsh. The names of a number of independent heroes who at varying dates became absorbed into the Arthurian complex or 'brought to Arthur's court' may also be here referred to—examples are Gwalchmai, Peredur, Drystan. Loose approximations were made in French in the cases of the first two when they became *Gauvain* and *Perceval,* while the last was borrowed in the written form in which it is early attested in Old Welsh as *Tristan.* This name is attested, quite independently of the romance hero, as the name of a witness to a charter in the *Book of Llan Dâv* (early 12th century, but based on older sources), and this appears to be a unique instance in which this name is recorded in Welsh for a character other than the Tristan of the romances. 'Gauvain' and 'Perceval' are loose approximations to the antecedent Welsh forms, but they are no looser than is 'Merlin' (Geoffrey's *Merlinus*) derived from the name of the Welsh prophetic poet Myrddin. 'Perceval' is an instance in which a French name has taken the place of a Brittonic name which sounded somewhat similar; a parallel instance is 'Isolt' from Welsh and Cornish Esyllt, Eselt. The very looseness of such borrowings as these is an indication that they derive from oral rather than from written sources—it would be only too easy for the French narrator of a tale transposed from Welsh or Cornish or Breton to reproduce such names incorrectly, or to conflate them with existing names of a kind more familiar to him. On the other hand it is certain that some names, such as that of Tristan, were borrowed through *written* sources, because they were pronounced quite differently in the two languages. *Yvain* from Welsh Owein, Ywein or Ewein (from Latin *Eugenius*) is another instance, like that of 'Tristan', in which the obscure vowel represented by *i* or *y, o,* or *e* in Welsh was given an entirely different sound in French. The transposition of 'Owein fab Urien' into *Yvain li fiz Uriens* is also particularly interesting from another point of view: it is one of only three examples in which a personal name, together with its patro-

nymic, are seen to have been borrowed together from Welsh into French. The other two instances of this are for quite minor characters—*Ider* or *Yder fiz Nut* from 'Ede(y)rn fab Nut (Nudd)' who is listed in *Culhwch and Olwen,* and *Giflet fiz Do* from 'Gilfaethwy fab Don' in *Mabinogi Math.* Another quite exceptional occurrence is for a name to be transferred together with its Welsh epithet: 'Uthyr Pendragon' (U. 'head of Dragons', i.e. 'leader of warriors') of the poem *Pa gur,* preserved in almost identical form in the chronicles and in the poems of Chrétien, is one such example. The transposition of 'Caradawc Freichfras (Old Welsh *Brecbras*) into *Caradues Brie(f)bras* is a fascinating instance, in which the original epithet meaning 'strong arm' was misinterpreted in French as 'short arm', giving rise to a new story, found in the First Continuation of the *Conte del Graal,* to account for the manner in which Caradawc lost his arm. According to Piette this name must have entered French through a written borrowing from a source in Middle Breton rather than in Welsh, since the Breton endings *-oc* and *-uc* (corresponding to Middle Welsh *-awc*) were rendered in French as *-ue(s).* The case of *Tristan* is somewhat similar, for here a misinterpretation of the name as containing the French adjective *triste* gave rise to the story of the hero's 'sad' birth.

The names borrowed from antecedent stories which have not survived in Welsh included even the names of animals. The most famous of these is Kein Caled, or the 'hard-backed', the horse of Gwalchmai who is listed in the Triads of Horses, and who gave in French the name of Gauvain's horse *le Guingalet,* the English *Gryngolet* in *Sir Gawain and the Green Knight.* Another is the Cath Palug, the cat-monster of Anglesey, who became in French *le Chapalu,* a new story being evolved which described Arthur's fight in a bog with a monstrous cat—the same kind of ingenious misinterpretation of a Brittonic name (Fch. *palus* 'marsh, fen') as though it were French that we get in the cases of *Caradues Briebras* and *Tristan;* in all of these instances new stories were evolved in order to give intelligible explanations of these names for French audiences. Another horse, Lluagor, the 'host-splitter', the steed of Caradawc Freichfras according to the Triads of Horses, supplied the name of the foal *Lorzagor,* the congenital animal companion born at one birth with *Caradues Briebras,* according to the *Livre de Carados.* Similarly the ferocious boar known from *Culhwch and Olwen* as the Twrch Trwyth, appears as the boar *Tortain* in the same source. It is therefore an established fact that a number of personal names of Brittonic derivation—whether Welsh, Cornish, or Breton—have passed into twelfth-century French romance. The animal-names even retain their animal identity after the transference. Such name-borrowings are particularly rich in the poems of Chrétien, although the large number of obscure names found in his works and in those of his contemporaries and continuators leaves room for a considerable margin of doubt concerning some of the particular derivations which have been proposed, since many of these names have come down in so corrupt a form as to be unrecognisable in any language, and some of the Celtic derivations which have been advocated are far from satisfactory, indeed quite unacceptable. I would certainly not go so far, for instance, as to claim any Celtic antecedent for the name and character of Lancelot—still less for that of his son Galahad. These are French creations, and they originated entirely in the post-Celtic development of the romances. Although a proportion of the names in Chrétien correspond with names in the existing Welsh poems and triads and native tales, the large number of names in the French romances which cannot be explained, and which have obviously been borrowed in forms which are corrupt, favours the belief that oral transmission was by far the more frequent and widespread means for the transference of Celtic names and stories into French; though we must allow always for several significant instances of written borrowings. This is indeed what one would expect to find, in view of the essentially oral nature of the Celtic tradition right down through the Middle Ages and beyond—so that what actually became preserved in writing in early Welsh sources is, so to speak, the mere tip of an iceberg. This, coupled with the fact that the medieval oral literature of Cornwall and Brittany is almost entirely lost, is the reason that the *disjecta membra* of Brittonic names and stories which have come down in the French romances are so interesting and present so challenging a problem to the Celticist, even though the attempts to interpret them have so often led merely to a wild surmise. It follows also that strict philological rules do not apply to such borrowings, but that a number of very loose approximations were made: classic examples are *Merlin* (*Merlinus*) from Welsh Myrddin, *Perceval* from Welsh Peredur, and *Gauvain* from Welsh Gwalchmai. And further, as Piette has emphasized, very little headway can be made on purely linguistic criteria in distinguishing borrowings from Welsh as distinct from Cornish or Breton, since these languages were so close until as late as the twelfth century. As it is, Welsh literature is almost exclusively our source for detecting such borrowings.

The next point that I wish to emphasize is that early Welsh literature provides abundant evidence in poetry, triads and tales, for the fact that Arthur was already becoming the centre of a cycle of stories at a date too early for there to be any question of back-influence from continental sources. The earliest evidence for this cyclic development of Arthurian material in Wales is the dialogue poem *Pa gur* in the Black Book of Carmarthen, to which I have already referred, and which may be dated to before 1100—perhaps more than a century earlier. This poem begins with a verbal interchange between Arthur and a certain Glewlwyd Gafaelfawr ('G. Mighty Grasp'), who is the gatekeeper of a hostile fortress to which Arthur is seeking to gain admittance for himself and his men. He lists a number of the names of these, and refers to their wonderful feats in slaying monsters and witches. The conclusion of the poem is absent, owing to the loss of a leaf from the manuscript, but in spite of this, and in spite of some obscurities which I cannot here discuss in detail, it is on the whole straightforward, if in places disjointed, and the following translation will serve to give its substance. (I have used italics for the lines and half-lines presumably spoken by Glewlwyd; it will be seen that the poem rapidly develops into a monologue spoken by Arthur).

What man is the gate-keeper? *Glewlwyd Might Grasp.*

What man asks it? Arthur and fair Cai.
What (company) goes with you? The best men in the world.
Into my house thou shalt not come unless thou disclose(?) them.
I will disclose(?) them, and thou wilt see them.
Wyth(n)eint, Eléi, and Ssiwyon (?) all three,
Mabon son of Mydron, the servant of Uthyr Pendragon,
and Gwyn Godyfrion. My servants were harsh in defending (or 'fighting for') their rights:
Manawydan son of Llŷr, profound was his counsel.
Indeed Manawyd brought shattered shields from Tryfrwyd;
and Mabon son of Mellt, he spotted the grass with blood;
and Anwas the Winged, and Llwch of the Striking Hand,
they were defending Eidyn on the border.
A lord would satisfy them where(?) he would recompense (them).
Cai entreated them as he hewed them down by threes.
When Celli was lost men endured savagery.
Cai mocked them as he cut them down,
Arthur, though he laughed, the blood was flowing,
in the hall of Afarnach, fighting with a hag.
He smote the 'Cudgel-head' in the settlements of Dissethach,
on the mountain of Eidyn he fought with the 'Dog-heads'.
They fell by the hundred, by the hundred they fell
before Bedwyr Perfect of Sinew;
on the banks of Tryfrwyd fighting with a 'Rough Grey',
furious was his nature, with shield and sword,
A host was futile compared with Cai in battle;
he was a sword in battle, to his hand was given a pledge.
They were steadfast leaders of an army for the benefit of their country,
Bedwyr and Brydlaw. Nine hundred to listen,
six hundred to scatter, his onslaught would be worth.
I used to have servants—it was better when they were alive.
Before the lords of Emrys I saw Cai in haste.
He carried away booty, the 'long man' was hostile(?);
heavy was his vengeance, fierce was his anger.
When he drank from a buffalo-horn he drank for four,
when he came into battle he slew for a hundred.
Unless it were God who caused it, Cai's death were impossible.
Fair Cai and Llachau, they made slaughter before the pang (ie. 'death') from blue spears;
on the uplands of Ystafngwn Cai killed nine witches.
Fair Cai went to Môn to destroy lions(?);
his shield was a fragment against Palug's Cat.
When people ask 'Who killed Palug's Cat?'
nine score warriors would fall as her food,
nine score champions . . .

The narrative background of the poem is obviously similar

to that of a part of *Culhwch and Olwen.* Obvious parallels exist in the episode in which Cai seeks to gain admittance to the fortress of the giant Wrnach Gawr, and that in which Glewlwyd Gafaelfawr acts as Arthur's own gate-keeper and demands Culhwch's credentials before admitting him to Arthur's court. Another suggested parallel is to be found in the scene depicted on the Modena archivolt, in which Arthur and Cai discourse with a porter who guards the fortress where Winlogee (Guinevere?) is imprisoned. There is also an early and significant mythological parallel in Irish, in the *Battle of Moytura* in which the god Lugh (Lleu) enumerates his qualifications before gaining admittance to the fortress of Tara. The priority which the poem gives to the feats of Cai (and in a lesser degree to those of his companion Bedwyr) is significant in view of the deterioration of Cai's character in later sources. Others of the characters named in the poem are commemorated in the Triads or in the tale of *Culhwch* (*circa* 1080), where the wonderful and incredible list of heroes assembled at Arthur's court includes many who had no original connection with Arthur at all—even *Gwilenhin brenin Ffrainc* ('William king of France', i.e. William the Conqueror) and the protagonists of the Irish Ulster Cycle. In the Triads the 'Arthur's Court' framework is similarly used on occasion as an umbrella formula for bringing together a number of independent and unrelated heroes such as Llywarch Hen, a dramatic figure in the Powys englyn cycle. All these things provide clear evidence for the cyclic development of the Arthurian legend at an early date in Wales.

After this rapid survey of the extent of the name-borrowings made into Arthurian romance from Brittonic sources, I pass on now to consider the nature of the traditions which were introduced into Europe from the Celtic world. How much of this material was historical or semi-historical, how much mythology, how much deliberate fiction? It is certain that these borrowings were not all from Celtic mythology, as has sometimes been too readily assumed. Early heroic narrative concerning prominent Brittonic heroes also formed a very important ingredient. Probably the most outstanding example of this is the case of Owain fab Urien who became in French *Yvain li fiz Uriens,* the famous son of an early historical ruler in southern Scotland, known as Urien of Rheged. Both father and son are the subject of eulogies and an elegy by the poet Taliesin, and these poems are authoritatively believed to have been originally composed as early as the end of the sixth century. We do not know at what stage Owain first became associated with Arthur, since there is no evidence for this earlier than the romance of *Owain* (Chrétien's *Yvain*). Geoffrey of Monmouth presents Urien as Arthur's contemporary, but makes it clear that he regarded his son Owain as belonging to a later generation. A similar case could be made for Gwalchmai and Peredur, who are both independent legendary—and possibly historical—heroes who belonged to the 'Old North', the early British kingdoms which were situated in southern Scotland and northern England. There is also Chrétien's Erec (*Guerec*), whose name originates in that of the legendary founder of the Breton kingdom of Vannes (*Guerocus*). But I would feel much less certainty in advocating the historicity of Arthur's two early companions Cai and Bedwyr, of whom

the earliest mention is found in the poem *Pa gur,* where they appear in company with such obviously mythological figures as Mabon, who is the Celtic god *Maponos* (though described in the poem as 'servant of Uthyr Pendragon') and Manawydan, originally also a deity known to both the Irish and the Welsh. Mythical elements undoubtedly formed a large part in the Arthurian tradition from an early date—witness the 'Marvels' attached to Arthur's name in the *Historia Brittonum*—and it is indeed often difficult, if not impossible to draw a clear distinction between the elements of heroic legend, myth, and fiction. The widespread notion that all early Celtic literature is 'Celtic myth' has, however, often formed the basis for a belief that Arthur himself was no more than a 'myth.' But to recognize the degree to which the *dramatis personae* of Arthurian romance are indebted, not only to mythology, but also to 'saga' concerning legendary Brittonic heroes of whom some, such as Urien and Owain, certainly had a historical existence, is in itself a strong plea for Arthur's own historicity. This plea gains additional support from the very early allusion to Arthur in the *Gododdin* poem.

A related question, about which there is room for speculation and debate, is the extent to which the body of narrative attached to the heroic, legendary, and mythical figures I have mentioned formed part of a common inheritance of traditional lore and belief which was shared by *all* the Brittonic-speaking Celts, from the 'Old North' down through the whole length of Wales to Devon and Cornwall, and across the sea to the colony in Brittany. For instance, there is evidence to believe that the cult of Arthur as a returning hero or promised deliverer was more firmly entrenched in the south-west and in Brittany than it was in Wales. But as Piette emphasized, this cult must have been imported *from* Britain as the result of the common cultural tradition shared between Wales, Cornwall, and Brittany down to at least the ninth century; it is most unlikely to have originated as far back as the age of the sixth-century Breton migrations, which were too close to Arthur's own time; and a certain time-lapse must be allowed for between the date of a hero's death and the evolution of a legend concerning him. As evidence for the community of culture shared between Bretons and Welsh during the second half of the ninth century we have a significant statement found in the Book of Llan Dâv concerning a certain Welsh nobleman called Guidnerth who was sent to do penance for the crime of fratricide in the cathedral church of Dol in Brittany, and the text explains that he and the Britons of that diocese were *unius linguae et unius nationis:* they spoke the same language and belonged to the same nation, although divided by the sea, so that to go to Brittany was not for Guidnerth like undertaking to do penance in a distant and alien country. Although at the end of the ninth century the Scandinavian invasions threatened the communications between Britain and Brittany, it is significant that Giraldus Cambrensis, writing in the late twelfth century, states that the Cornish and the Bretons speak a language similar to Welsh and for the most part easily understood by Welsh people, though it is interesting that he offers the opinion that the speech of the former 'approaches more nearly to the ancient British idiom.'

Medieval representation of the sword in the stone legend, from a Flemish manuscript illustration, c. 1290.

It has been rightly emphasized (most recently by J. R. F. Piette) that the absence of any appreciable amount of early literature from either Cornwall or Brittany is no argument that such did not once exist. The Celtic cultural tradition was essentially an oral one, as has been previously emphasized, and it is of the nature of an oral tradition that an immeasurable amount is liable to be lost through failure to be recorded. There is a small but significant amount of evidence that the Breton poets once practised techniques similar to those practised in Wales. Fifteenth-century verse in the Breton language preserves traces of a rudimentary from of *cynghanedd lusg* (i.e. rhyme of the penultimate syllable in a line with a preceding syllable), and also of something like the device known as *cyrch gymeriad,* in which the rhyme is carried on from the final of one stanza into the beginning of the next: a fact which offers eloquent testimony for the survival of a learned order of professional poets for a considerable period after the migration. As in Wales also, it was no doubt these professional poets who were the primary custodians of the Breton dynastic genealogies which have come down in the cartularies and in the saints' Lives, sometimes in forms which correspond closely with those from Wales, and which show interestingly archaic linguistic features. Evidently the Bretons re-

garded themselves in the ninth century, and to an appreciable, though gradually decreasing extent for some centuries afterwards, as being of the same nation as the insular Britons. They shared with them the memory of a great hero called Arthur, and this belief implied far more than the mere fact itself, for it meant that they were partners in a body of tradition about their national past which linked the two peoples closely together, including also the western Britons of Devon and Cornwall. The Bretons had their own origin legends about the foundation of the kingdoms which formed their emigrant colony, and these follow a pattern which is pan-Celtic, being recognisable in both medieval Welsh and Irish literature. Traces of this have come down in such of the so-called 'Breton lays' (in French) as relate to the traditional founders of these kingdoms, as well as in Chrétien's poem about *Erec* or *Gueroc,* the traditional founder of the Breton kingdom of Vannes, for whom the Welsh version substitutes the Devon hero Gereint. The substitution in Wales of Gereint for *Erec* is indeed a symptomatic indication of a significant fact: for although it would seem that the Bretons clung tenaciously to the national traditions which they inherited from insular Britain, the same did not happen in reverse, since the legends of the founders of the Breton kingdoms made no impact upon the general corpus of native Welsh traditions, which tell us nothing of such heroes as *Gradlon Mor* (the founder of Breton Cornouailles) or *Guingamor* (a name borne by successive Counts of Léon) any more than they do of *Gueroc* the founder of Vannes. The only minor exception to this that I have noted is the appearance in Welsh sources of that indeterminate figure 'Emyr Llydaw,' whose name means merely 'an emperor (ruler) of Brittany' and his son Howel, a figure borrowed from Geoffrey of Monmouth. The Bretons preserved their own version of the story of the settlement of their country by Maximus's soldiers, a story which existed already in Brittany in the tenth century, in a version evidently used by Geoffrey of Monmouth, and one which is independent from the narration of the same events in the Welsh tale of the 'Dream of Maxen.' And the Bretons appear to have contributed no small measure to the story of the romance-hero Tristan, in the final form in which his story reached the French, contributing to it both a birth-tale, and the final episode of Tristan's marriage and death, in the theme of the second Isolt. Although it is apparent from the analogy of the Gaelic world that community of culture can, and does, over-ride political divisions, and can even survive a dividing sea, it is nevertheless a striking fact that traditions of the legendary Breton heroes were not apparently re-absorbed into Wales by a process similar to that which saw the re-localization in medieval Wales of the stories of the prominent heroes of the 'Old North', such as Owain ab Urien, Gwalchmai, Peredur, and others—some but not all of whom became subjected to the further transference from Wales into continental Arthurian romance.

Irish personal names in Arthurian romance are virtually non-existent. A striking and wholly exceptional instance in that of *le Morholt* in the *Tristan* romances. It is impossible to reject some ultimate connection between this name and that of the Irish mythical monsters known as the *Fomóire,* who levied a human tribute from Ireland and from the western islands of Scotland, just as did *le Morholt* from Cornwall. Their exaction of a human tribute from the Hebridean islands is recounted in the story of the Pictish hero Drust mac Seirb, who is the ultimate original of Tristan. R. S. Loomis advocated an original in the Irish common noun *bachlach* ('churl, rustic') for the 'Green Knight' in *Sir Gawain and the Green Knight,* but any Celtic derivation for this name is no longer convincing in view of the most recent opinion that the manuscript reading of the name (which only occurs once) is *Bertilak* and not *Bercilak.* But when we turn from personal names to the story-themes of Arthurian romance, the evidence is entirely different. Owing to the fact that a considerable number of parallels undoubtedly to exist between these themes and themes which occur in early Irish tales, there has been a widespread view held among Arthurianists that the majority of such themes are of Irish origin, and that they passed over from Ireland into Britain, to be transferred again by the Welsh and Cornish to the Normans and French. But this is extremely improbable, as Kenneth Jackson and others have frequently reiterated. While it is evident from a study of the *Mabinogi* that Irish story-themes certainly *did* enter Wales in the early Middle Ages—and we actually have in *Culhwch and Olwen* the names of a group of Irish heroes who are presented as

members of the court of Arthur—the views which have frequently been expressed on this matter have been not a little distorted by the fact that so much more early Irish literature has been preserved than has come down in Welsh: perhaps, as Proinsias Mac Cana has recently suggested, because the learned and literary classes in Ireland concerned themselves with committing their oral literature to writing at a much earlier date than did the corresponding classes in Britain. But here again we must remind ourselves of the essentially oral character of the Celtic tradition wherever it existed, and of the numerous pointers which are to be found, in the Triads and elsewhere, to the richness and 'density' of the oral tradition in Wales. The explanation is simply that Welsh stories failed to be committed to writing in anything like the abundance enjoyed by the early Irish tales. This is an accepted fact among Celticists: the debate is now no longer whether or not it was so, but concerns rather the speculation as to why it was that Irish stories received so much fuller a documentation than did Welsh. Whatever the reason may have been, there can be no doubt of the great value for comparative purposes of early Irish literature, no less than that of Welsh, for the Arthurianist.

Coming now to my third proposition, I have always regarded it as a general maxim that we should look primarily to Welsh sources for the personal nomenclature of Arthurian romance, but to Irish for parallels to the narrative themes. Just as names may be freely transferred right out of their original narrative context, so it can be shown that story-motives moved about freely *within* the field of Celtic literature, passing from one character to another, in the same way as they did subsequently after their transference into continental Arthurian romance. An example of such a 'movable' theme within the Celtic field is that of the 'Boyhood Deeds' of a hero, leading to his arrival as an awkward initiate at the court of the supreme ruler, whether this be King Conchobar mac Nessa or King Arthur: this theme is associated with the Irish heroes Cú Chulainn and Finn, and in Wales with Peredur, the prototype of Chrétien's Perceval; and there are indications also of its association with Tristan, though it can hardly be proved that these belonged to the Celtic vernacular tradition of Brittany. Another theme which required the publicity of a royal court for its proper presentation is that of the 'Beheading Game', associated with Cú Chulainn at the court of Ulster in *Bricriu's Feast,* but with Gawain and Arthur's court in *Sir Gawain and the Green Knight,* (following various intermediary versions). Yet another 'movable' theme is the dynastic myth of the 'Sovereignty', which is found attached to the names of the founders of dynasties in Ireland, Wales, and Brittany, in one or both of two forms— the 'Chase of the White Hart' and that of the 'Transformed Hag.' There are, of course, a few outstanding exceptions in which particular story-themes attached to particular characters have survived the transference from a Celtic source into Arthurian romance. Examples of this are the variant forms of the rape or elopements of Guinevere; and another very striking instance is the theme of the Fisher King with his disabling wound through the thighs, which appears to go back to the prestigious figure of Brân Fendigaid in the *Mabinogi* who, in the words of the story, was 'wounded in the foot with a poisoned spear.' The Perseus-Andromeda-like theme of the Dragon Fight, first attested in western Europe in the story of the Pictish *Drust,* the likely prototype of Tristan, has clung tenaciously to his successor in the romances, being repeated no less than three times in the different versions based upon the poem of Thomas. These are, however, the exceptional examples which traditionally go to prove the rule. It is now becoming generally and increasingly recognized that we should think far more in the terms of a common fund of narrative themes which were once shared among *all* the Celtic peoples and moved about freely among them, to be appropriated to different heroes as local and national interests dictated—to King Conchobar mac Nessa, Cú Chulainn, and Finn mac Cumhaill and the heroes who surrounded them in Ireland, but to Arthur and to his attendant warriors in Britain.

There are certain themes later transferred into Arthurian romance which make their earliest appearance in association with figures in the Welsh *Mabinogi:* the 'Waste Land', which is very clearly delineated in the enchantment which descended upon the land of Dyfed, leaving it completely barren and waste, in the tale of *Manawydan,* and often repeated introduction to Arthurian adventures, by which the Arthurian court is holding high feast at Pentecost or some other festival, and the king refuses to eat until some marvel appears before him. This theme is anticipated in the First Branch of the *Mabinogi* when the hero Pwyll goes up to the mound of Arberth—a centre for magical happenings—between the first and second courses of his meal, in the hopes of seeing some marvel, and this marvel presently occurs when his magical wife Rhiannon appears. These two themes are what I would call 'Arthurian commonplaces.' But the latter, the court scene, is a simple narrative device which served again and again as the send-off for an Arthurian quest, while the former, the 'Waste Land' theme, is obviously loaded with mythological import, however difficult it is for us to recover its full significance today. There are a number of other 'Arthurian commonplaces' which are significantly paralleled in antecedent sources in Welsh or Irish. It is somewhat perilous to embark upon even a preliminary list, since no doubt analogies for each one of them can be cited from elsewhere, but here are some: magic fountains and magic mists, frequent transformations of humans into birds or animals, quests—often involving Otherworld visits—for a magic animal or a magic talisman (e.g. the Grail), cauldrons of plenty or re-birth, sword-bridges and revolving castles, dismembered heads on stakes. These may be called 'commonplaces' in the sense that they are continually repeated in the romances, so that any original mythological meaning they may once have held has long since become obliterated and forgotten. Nevertheless, it is in relation to such themes as these that the term 'Celtic myth' may with some appropriateness be employed, because what we have in them is the débris of an imperfectly understood mythology. This mythology, based upon pagan Celtic religious belief, formed the substratum upon which much of the elaborate Arthurian superstructure became erected, and it was a possession which belonged in common to the whole of the Celtic world—to ancient Gaul, as far as our evidence goes—no less than to Britain and Ireland. We can deduce from the evidence available that pagan Celtic religion recognized a multiplicity of gods and goddesses who were tribal and local rather than representative of specific functions; and it is indeed the consequent strongly localized character of early Celtic religion which lies at the basis of the great importance attached to place-name lore (the Irish *dindshenchas*) in all medieval Celtic literature. These concepts, inherited from primitive mythology and handed down almost exclusively by oral tradition, gave to the storytellers in Celtic countries the immense repository of imaginative, colourful, and even fantastic story-themes on which their high reputation was based, and which proved to have such a rare attraction for foreign audiences. The great difference between Ireland and Wales lay in the different legendary and geographical backgrounds to which the traditional concepts became related, each country realizing similar ideas in terms of its own native heroes. As the Arthurian tradition crystallized in Wales, there is no doubt that the remembered heroes of the lost kingdoms in the 'Old North' formed a significant part: I have already instanced the cases of Urien Rheged, and his son Owain, together with Gwalchmai and Peredur. There were of course heroes from Wales as well, such as Caradawg Friechfras, who seems from the earliest sources to have once held a greater prominence than came to be his lot in the extant romances, and Gereint son of Erbin, a hero who belonged to Devon and Cornwall but who was also known to tradition in south-eastern Wales. It was the names of these and other Brittonic heroes, some of them belonging to quite independent stories, which became grouped around the central figure of Arthur in Welsh sources, and which eventually came, with Arthur himself, to form the names of the leading heroes of continental romance. No doubt some of these names and stories may have been transferred to the French through oral sources in Brittany, since the Bretons continued for long to remember the heroes who were celebrated in Britain itself, even though their own heroes failed to win any comparable recognition, and made hardly any impact upon the traditions of Britain as a whole. In the twelfth century it can be accepted that there was in circulation among all the Brittonic peoples a body of stories, derived from heroic saga, Celtic and international folk-tale motives and pan-Celtic mythology, representing a corpus of tradition which was their common property, and to which all had made a contribution of one kind or another.

My fourth and final proposition concerns Arthur himself. The cyclic development of the Arthurian material may be presumed to have taken place in Britain and Brittany by successive stages between the ninth and eleventh centuries, unaffected by any external influences from the continent of Europe. We find that as early as the ninth century, in the Arthurian *Mirabilia* attached to the *Historia Brittonum,* Arthur appears as a folk-hero whose deeds are associated with the mountain-top of Corn Gafallt (*recte Carn Cafall*) in Radnorshire, where his dog's footprint was to be seen, and to a grave-mound at Gamber Head in Herefordshire, said to be that of his son *Amr* or *Anir* (unknown from any other source). Similarly stories of a folk-tale type, dispersed widely over Wales and the south-west, are to be found in Welsh saints' Lives redacted in the eleventh and twelfth centuries. It is however from Cornwall, in the early twelfth century, that we first hear of Arthur as a messianic hero who will return and lead his people to victory. A similar concept, though under a slightly different form, reappears in different places all over Britain (but particularly in the Celtic areas and places adjacent to them) where the legend is localized that Arthur is sleeping in a cave, surrounded by his warriors, awaiting the final trumpet-call to action in the hour of his country's greatest need. This portrayal of Arthur as the hoped-for deliverer, a *defender* of his people against all kinds of enemies including giants, witches, and monsters, seems to characterize the indigenous popular traditions concerning him and to have survived both in Welsh folk-tradition and in the early sources we have been considering—a plausible memory, perhaps, of a great leader who in the remote past had once led a British force against an enemy of foreign invaders.

There are a number of indications that Geoffrey of Monmouth came into contact with an Arthurian tradition localized in the south-west of Britain, since he seems to have known a curiously circumstantial story about Arthur's birth which involved a Cornish duke Gorlois and his fortresses at Tintagel and Damelioc (identified with Domellick, near St Denis) and a tradition which localized his last battle on the river Camel in Cornwall. There is also the significant fact that both the Triads and the tale of *Culhwch and Olwen* claim that Arthur's chief court was at 'Celli Wig in Cornwall': a place whose identification is not certain, but which with a certain amount of probability has been identified with Killibury or Kelly Rounds, in the parish of Egloshayle near the north coast. It is impossible to know how old may be the name of Celli Wig for Arthur's court in Cornwall, but we have seen above that there is a possible allusion to it in the line relating to *Celli* in the poem *Pa gur.* If this were the only evidence concerning the sphere of activity of an early hero named Arthur, it would constitute a substantial case for the belief that the birthplace of the Arthurian tradition lay in the south-west of Britain.

But to conclude thus would not be a fair presentation of the evidence for the sphere of Arthur's original activities. We have yet to consider the evidence which associates Arthur with the 'Old North'—the Brittonic kingdoms north of the Border which extended southwards into Cumbria, Yorkshire and Lancashire. What may well be the oldest of all the references to Arthur is the one which is found in the early Welsh poem known as the *Gododdin,* a series of elegies on the British warriors who had come down from their tribal territory situated around Edinburgh to present a fruitless opposition to the invading Angles at a great battle at Catterick in Yorkshire, about the year 600. Of one of these warriors it is said that he performed great deeds of valour *ceni bei ef Arthur* 'though he was not Arthur.' This reference comes from the earlier of the two texts of the poem: it may go back to the ninth century, it may even be older and date from the original redaction of the poem, whether in oral or written form, in the seventh century. No evidence exists on which this can be decisively proved, either positively or negatively. Whatever the date, the importance of the allusion consists in two facts—its north-British provenance, and the evidence it provides for Arthur's historicity. Some years ago Professor Thomas

Jones pointed out that in the context of a heroic poem such as the *Gododdin* no name would be cited for eulogistic comparison in this way unless it belonged to a hero who was believed to have really existed—no fictional or mythological figure would have served for such a purpose. The fleeting unexpanded allusion strongly suggests that the poet who made it placed full reliance on his hearers' cognizance of all the circumstances of Arthur's career, and recognized his name as a famous name to be conjured with in the society to which his listeners belonged—the name of a hero who, like the Gododdin warriors, had fought against the English invaders in an earlier generation.

There are two other important sources of information about Arthur which may be credibly supposed to antedate the ninth-century documents in which they first appear. One is the account of Arthur's twelve victorious battles in the *Historia Brittonum;* the other comprises the two allusions in the *Annales Cambriae* to Arthur's victory at Mt Badon, and to the battle of Camlann at which he and Medraut both fell. There is much to be said concerning the significance of both sets of passages: the battle-list is now generally believed to derive from a battle-listing poem of a kind for which there are several analogies in early Welsh. It is unlikely that all the named battles could have been fought by Arthur himself, or that they were indeed all fought against the English, rather than against the Picts, Scots, or rival British factions. It has been suggested with some plausibility that the battle of Mt Badon or *Mons Badonicus* may have been quite wrongly associated with Arthur and was not necessarily fought by him at all. My present concern, however, is with the likely source of these entries, rather than with their historical import.

We are indebted to Kenneth Jackson for stressing the high significance of the British kingdom of Strathclyde, which preserved its independence for several hundred years after the neighbouring kingdoms of the Gododdin and of Rheged had in the course of the seventh century fallen to the invaders. The capital of Strathclyde was at Dumbarton—the 'Fortress of the Britons'—and its ecclesiastical centre was at Glasgow. There is some evidence which suggests that it was here, at Glasgow itself, that the vernacular records of the 'Men of the North' were conserved and developed and at least partially committed to writing between the seventh and the ninth centuries. It was from this latter date onwards that many of them became transferred to Wales: we have evidence for the general movement of much of the poetic remains, chronicle material, genealogies and oral traditions of the northern Britons, including those relating to such figures as Myrddin, Urien Rheged and Owain, Rhydderch Hael, Llywarch Hen, probably also Tristan, Peredur and Gwalchmai—some but not all of whom were to reappear later in continental Arthurian romance in the role of the most prominent of Arthur's 'knights.' All, however, were important figures in early Welsh literature before this transference took place. The movement southwards and fresh localization in Wales of much heroic tradition which stemmed originally from the 'Old North' is therefore a fact of seminal importance for any discussion of the genesis of the legend of Arthur. Historical and archaeological speculation concerning Arthur's possible identity, together with the proper interpretation of the early documentary references to him, must therefore take full account of this movement as one of the basic facts of Welsh literature. It cannot be too strongly stressed that the problem of Arthur is first and foremost a Welsh literary problem. (pp. 41-55)

> Rachel Bromwich, "Celtic Elements in Arthurian Romance: A General Survey," in The Legend of Arthur in the Middle Ages, *edited by P. B. Grout and others, D. S. Brewer, 1983, pp. 41-55.*

Roger Sherman Loomis

[*Loomis was an American educator and scholar of Arthurian legend and medieval literature whose principal publications include* Celtic Myth and Arthurian Romance *(1927);* Arthurian Tradition and Chrétien de Troyes *(1949); and* Arthurian Literature in the Middle Ages *(1959), which he edited. In the following excerpt, Loomis evaluates the popular diffusion of the "Matter of Britain" throughout Europe during the eleventh and twelfth centuries.*]

When we direct our attention to the vast literature which began to appear on the European continent in the twelfth century and of which likewise Arthur was the most conspicuous personage, we are faced with a puzzling, an amazing phenomenon.

Why this exaltation of an alien king and court by the most sophisticated men of letters of Western Europe, men who, so far as one can tell, had not the slightest incentive to popularize a figure of so remote a time and people? How did poets who knew no Celtic language come into possession of a fund of story, full of Welsh and Breton names, localized at Caerleon, Caerwent, Cardigan, Tintagel, Edinburgh, and the city of Snowdon (Caer Seint near Carnarvon), and embodying numerous Irish and Welsh motifs and story patterns? The influence of Geoffrey of Monmouth and Wace affords no explanation, for these authors supply only a small fraction of the Celtic elements in the early romances. Surely this knowledge was not acquired by continental poets through a visit to Great Britain. Only rarely can one feel sure that a French author had seen the places he describes, as when the author of *Fergus* shows an intimacy with southern Scotland. Knowledge of Celtic tradition cannot be due, then, to travel in Celtic lands; it cannot be due to the export of Celtic manuscripts since they would have been unreadable outside of Brittany; it cannot be due to books in other languages written by natives of Wales, for even the most influential of these books, Geoffrey of Monmouth's works, made little impression on the verse romances. What, then, could have been the transmitting agency?

The diffusion of the Matter of Britain is a subject of the greatest importance, for without some clear understanding of how it took place, much will be incomprehensible or will be wrongly interpreted. Some recent writers have ignored the problem, and even among those who recognize a considerable Celtic element in the Matter of Britain one finds either a certain vagueness or a marked divergence of opinion. The latter are divided into two principal camps, one battling to prove that the Celtic stories passed directly from the Welsh to the Anglo-Normans and through them to the French, the other contending that it was the bilingual Bretons who were mainly responsible for developing and transmitting to the Anglo-Normans and the French the tales which centred about their racial hero. Here we witness a most unusual spectacle in controversy, for the scholars who have most vigorously opposed the claims of the Bretons are their French compatriots, Ferdinand Lot, Joseph Loth, and Jean Marx, while among those who have conceded the claims of the Bretons have been two great Welsh literary historians, Thomas Stephens and W. J. Gruffydd. The evidence, consisting of the testimony of contemporaries, name forms, and literary affinities, has been most formidably presented by the Germans, Zimmer and Brugger, and, for the Tristan legend, by Bédier. In spite of some errors, they have made a case which establishes the preponderant share of the Bretons in popularizing the Arthurian legend in the courts and baronial halls of France and England during the twelfth century. On their work most of what follows is based.

First, let us observe that Wales was not the only Celtic territory which possessed a tradition about Arthur. Like the Welsh, the people of Cornwall were descended from the Britons, and though the Saxon victory of Dyrham in 577 and the conquest of Devon in the next century drove a wedge between the Cornish and their kinsmen of Wales, there can be no doubt that relations were maintained across the Bristol Channel. Several Welsh writers who mention Arthur's court at Kelliwic in Cornwall seem to be reflecting a local tradition; Caradoc of Lancarvan, telling (*c.* 1130) how Arthur set out to recover his queen from the possession of Melvas (Chrétien's Meleagant), represents him as gathering the forces of Cornwall and Devon to besiege Glastonbury. A Frenchman, Herman of Laon, reports that nine canons of that city were shown in 1113 on their journey from Exeter in Devon to Bodmin in Cornwall the chair and the oven 'of that King Arthur, famed in the fables of the *Britanni*'. Herman also records a fracas between one of the canons' servants and a Cornishman, who declared that Arthur was still alive. Just so, he says, 'the Bretons quarrel with the French': 'Britones solent iurgari cum Francis pro rege Arturo.' Herman's careful distinction between *Britanni* and *Britones* makes it clear that the former were insular Britons, the people of Cornwall and Wales, and the latter were their cousins across the Channel, neighbours of the French. The 'fabulae Britannorum' which the canons heard on their tour may be represented in part by Geoffrey of Monmouth's account of Arthur's birth and passing, since he not only localizes these events in Cornwall but consistently uses Cornish place and personal names: Tintagol, Ridcaradoch, Dimilioc, Gorlois, Modredus. Possibly, of course, he may have obtained these famous tales from Cornish reciters, and, if so, these would be the only clear evidence of their circulation outside Celtic territory. But Geoffrey may have heard them in Cornwall or read them in a book.

Herman's remarks about the Bretons are corroborated by the statement, wrongly ascribed to Alanus de Insulis, that anyone who proclaimed in Armorica that Arthur was dead like other men would be lucky to escape being crushed by the stones of his hearers. And the more one studies the spread of Arthur's fame, the more it becomes clear that it was to these ardent Bretons that this prodigious phenomenon was due.

No early Breton literature concerned with Arthur has reached us, with the exception of two saints' lives in Latin. The *Life of Goeznovius,* which mentions Arthur's victories, has been shown by Faral and Tatlock to be dependent on Geoffrey of Monmouth, in spite of the spurious dating in 1019. The *Life of St. Efflam* is surely independent of Geoffrey and may well go back to the twelfth century, to which a very crude sculpture in the church at Perros can be assigned. It represents a figure with a crozier, presumably Efflam; a prostrate figure with a shield, possibly Arthur, exhausted by a battle with a dragon, the coils of which seems to be indicated by a pile of lumpish objects; a mysterious figure with exaggerated *membrum virile.* Here, as with Welsh hagiographers, Arthur's prowess is contrasted with the miraculous power of the saint; but this attitude hardly proves that Arthur was not a hero for the laity, and nothing is more significant for the problem of diffusion than the consistency with which the facts point to the Bretons as the most active propagandists for their racial hero.

The Norman Wace has a reference in his *Brut* (1155) to the Round Table, 'of which Bretons tell many stories'. Thirty years earlier the Anglo-Norman chronicler, William of Malmesbury, had written in his *Historia Regum Anglorum:* 'He is that Arthur about whom the trifles of the Bretons (*nugae Britonum*) rave even today, a man worthy not to be dreamed about in false fables but proclaimed in veracious histories, for he long upheld his sinking fatherland and quickened the failing spirits of his countrymen to war.' Giraldus Cambrensis, the ardent Welsh patriot, writing about 1216, likewise attributes to the 'fabulosi Britones' the story of Arthur's transportation by a certain imaginary goddess, named Morganis, to the island of Avalon (*Avalloniam*) for the healing of his wounds.

The crucial word in both passages is *Britones.* When referring to Arthur's time the word, of course, meant the insular Britons, but by the twelfth century, as applied to contemporaries, it always meant the emigrants to Armorica and their descendants, the Bretons. Thus in a thirteenth-century poem we have the *Britones* carefully distinguished from their kinsmen the *Cambrenses* (Welsh) and *Cornubienses* (Cornish). We have seen above how clearly Herman of Laon differentiated the *Britones* from the *Britanni,* or insular Britons, and indicated that the former were neighbours of the French. We have the testimony of both Geoffrey of Monmouth and Giraldus that the word *Britones* was no longer applied to Welshmen. Giraldus, moreover, in the passage cited above used the name-forms *Morganis* and *Avalloniam,* for which the Welsh equivalents were Modron and Avallach. The natural inference is that he had heard this tradition, not from his fellow-countrymen but from the Bretons. Thus the Norman Wace, the Anglo-Norman William of Malmesbury, and the Welshman Giraldus agree in attributing to the Bretons circulation of stories about Arthur, his Round Table, and his passing to Avalon.

Ferdinand Lot objected that it would be very odd if William of Malmesbury, living at no great distance from the Welsh border, should have the distant Bretons in mind when speaking of the *nugae Britonum* about Arthur. It is much more strange that a historian like Lot should have been unaware that England had attracted many Bretons after 1066. Zimmer, as early as 1890, pointed out the significance of this fact, and was followed by Ahlström and Warnke. Bédier in 1905 declared that after the battle of Hastings 'toute la civilisation normande se trouva brusquement transplantée telle quelle dans les châteaux d'Outre-Manche, et les jongleurs armoricains y suivirent leurs patrons: jongleurs armoricains, mais plus qu'à demi romanisés, mais vivant au service de seigneurs français, et contant pour leur plaire'. Lot's objection has, therefore, no validity; William could easily have heard the fantastic tales of the Bretons not only in the hall of some transplanted Breton lord but also in Anglo-Norman households.

The testimony of William is in harmony with the facts; it is in accord with that of Wace and Giraldus Cambrensis; it is also supported by the internal evidence of the romances themselves, where we find a sprinkling of Breton names. Bédier discovered five of them in the Tristan romances; to which may be added Roald and Morholt. Chrétien de Troyes's earliest extant romance assigns to the hero the Breton name Erec, and contains seven other names of the same origin—Brien, Gandeluz, Rinduran, Guerehes, Graillemer, Guigamor, Guivret. Yvain is the Breton Ivan, recorded in the eleventh century and substituted for Welsh Owain, and Lancelot has been recognized by Zimmer, Lot, and Bruce as influenced by the name Lancelin, recorded in Brittany in the same century.

Further confirmation of Breton transmission of Arthurian matter to the French and Anglo-Normans is supplied by the marked resemblance between certain romances and the Breton lais. There is an intimate connexion between the episode of the testing horn in the *Livre de Caradoc* and Biket's *Lai du Cor,* between Chrétien's *Yvain* and *Desiré,* between the hunt of the white stag in the Second Continuation of Chrétien's *Perceval* and the same theme in *Tyolet.*

Again, there is a marked affinity between episodes in the romances and certain modern Breton folk-tales. A variant of Béroul's story of King Mark's equine ears was told in Finistère in 1794; the falsehood about the black and white sails, which led to Tristan's death, was also the theme of tales current on the islands of Ouessant and Molène fifty years ago. The Provençal romance of *Faufré,* the Italian *Pulzella Gaia,* and *Perlesvaus* contain incidents which bear so precise a likeness to Breton folk-tales of the nineteenth century that chance alone cannot be responsible.

To all this accumulation of evidence, external and internal, in favour of Breton transmission of Welsh and Cornish lore to the French-speaking world only one objection of consequence has been offered, namely, that the Bretons of the twelfth century did not possess the talent to make so momentous a contribution to culture. But how is such an estimate to be reconciled with the fact that two of the greatest geniuses of the period, Abelard and Adam of St. Victor, were Bretons? So, too, were Bernard of Chartres, 'the most abounding spring of letters in Gaul' in his day,

Medieval respresentation of a procession centering on the Holy Grail.

his brother Thierry, Peter of Blois, and, in the opinion of some authorities, Geoffrey of Monmouth, who called himself 'Brito'. Otto of Freising testified that Brittany produced in abundance clerics of genius, devoted to liberal arts. It seems safe, therefore, to make the generalization that it was Bretons of a quite different species of talent, the *conteurs,* who successfully adapted their heritage of romantic tales to French taste and acquired such a reputation as entertainers that even in England they had little competition from the Welsh and Cornish.

Still, the possibility of exceptions is not ruled out, and it is an astonishing and misleading fact that the one reciter of Arthurian tales whose fame is attested from several sources was a Welshman, Bleheris. He is mentioned by Giraldus Cambrensis as a 'fabulator famosus'; by Thomas, the author of *Tristan,* as one who knew the history of all the counts and all the kings of Britain; by the second continuator of *Perceval* as one who had been born and brought up in Wales and who had told a tale of Gauvain and a dwarf knight to the Count of Poitiers (either William VII or VIII), who liked it better than any other. The same person is cited in the *Elucidation,* prefixed to *Perceval,* under the corrupt form Blihis, as an authority on the secrets of the Grail, and under the disguise of the saintly name Blaise as an omniscient source for the early history of Arthur and Merlin. These various independent testimonies to the reputation of Bleheris seem to prove that he was a story-teller of pre-eminent artistry and power. Certainly there was no more discriminating literary centre in Western Europe than that of the counts of Poitou in the time of the troubadour William VII and of his son William

VIII, who died in 1137. Now, though Bleheris was a Welshman born and bred, he must have been fluent in French, and the internal evidence of such romances as profess, rightly or wrongly, to have been derived from his repertoire shows no closer relation to Welsh tradition than that of other romances in French, and in the Tristan and Grail poems one finds significantly Breton names. Apparently his stories were not derived from his native inheritance but were polished and stirring versions of Breton tales, and there is no hint anywhere that any other Welshman crossed over into England or France to exploit his wares in a wider market. Despite the one exception of Bleheris, the evidence goes to show that the disseminators of the Matter of Britain outside Celtic territory in the eleventh and twelfth centuries were Bretons.

The records, moreover, agree in representing these early reciters not as amateurs but as professionals, and the stories themselves not as old wives' tales or tavern-haunters' yarns but as the stock-in-trade of a class of entertainers who appealed to the highest society. In this respect Bleheris at the court of Poitou was typical. Geoffrey of Monmouth ascribed to Merlin the prophecy that the deeds of Arthur would be *cibus narrantibus,* 'food to story-tellers', in the sense that telling Arthur's deeds of prowess would provide them with their bread and butter. Wace reported that the story-tellers had so embellished their narratives that they had made everything seem to be fictitious (*fables*). Chrétien referred to Erec as the hero of tales which those who wished to make a livelihood by telling stories, 'cil qui de conter vivre vuelent', were wont to mangle and spoil in the presence of kings and counts, and he declared that his *Perceval* was the best tale ever told in a royal court.

Most significant is a passage in the Second Continuation of that poem which expresses the haughty attitude of the literary man to these itinerant entertainers.

> Now there are many vassals going from court to court telling tales, who distort the good stories, stretch them out, and add so many lies that the tales are entirely spoiled and thus throw discredit on the good books. Those who listen and hear do not know what good stories are worth, but they say, when these minstrels spend a night in their lodging and are made to tell a little of an adventure without rime, that they have heard the whole authentic history, which they will never hear in the course of their lives. Thus they are led to believe falsehood and are told spurious history and lies are spread.

It is amusing to find the poet attacking the veracity of these wandering minstrels in view of the doubtful historicity of his own narrative. But he does give us a glimpse into their lives and he bears witness that (unlike the *jongleurs* who chanted the *chansons de geste* and unlike the Anglo-Saxon *scops* who used alliterative verse) these minstrels related the adventures of Arthur and his knights in prose. This fact would accord, as Zimmer has shown, with the general practice of the Celts.

Without doubt the *conteurs* must have possessed histrionic talents or they would have had no audiences. The word *histriones,* in fact, is applied to them, both by the Scottish author of a *Life of St. Kentigern,* dated 1147-64, in speaking of Ewen the son of Urien, and by Peter of Blois in a memorable passage: 'the *histriones* tell certain stories about Arthur, Gawain, and Tristan by which the hearts of the listeners are smitten with compassion and pricked even to tears'. Another witness to the emotional effect of these tales is Ailred of Rievaulx in Yorkshire, who, writing his *Speculum Caritatis* in 1141-2, quotes a novice as confessing with shame that, though he could not squeeze out a tear at a pious reading or discourse, he had often in his former life wept over fables which were commonly composed about an unknown Arthur.

The array of facts supplied by these scattered references furnishes a perfect explanation for the miraculous spread of the Arthurian legend throughout Western Europe—a people passionately devoted to the memory of Arthur and believing him to be still alive, linked to the Welsh by blood and by continuing intercourse, but speaking a language which was current among the nobility from the Firth of Forth to the Jordan; a class of strolling minstrels who took advantage of this fact to make a livelihood by telling their tales, of which Arthur was the centre, with such verve that they were able to fascinate counts and kings who had not the slightest racial or political tie with the British hero.

The evidence thus far presented also shows that the *conteurs* were known to authors living in Scotland and Yorkshire, at Oxford and Malmesbury—regions where Breton and Norman lords were ready enough to hear the tales, not only because of their intrinsic interest but for local and historic reasons. Did not some of these magnates possess the very lands where Arthur had supposedly ruled and where strange adventures had taken place? But the casual references of the troubadours and Chrétien prove that the *conteurs* must have ranged far outside the Anglo-Norman sphere of influence, and it is an astonishing but demonstrable fact that they must have established a vogue in the Po valley about 1100. Rajna discovered in a document of 1114 an Artusius, brother of Count Ugo of Padua; another Artusius signed his name in 1122, and I discovered a third who was a benefactor of Modena Cathedral in 1125. In 1136 and after, the name Walwanus appears with several variations in Paduan charters. Artusius is the regular Italian Latinization of the name Arthur when the source is French, and Walwanus is identical in form with the name of Gawain in one of the best manuscripts of Geoffrey's *Historia.* Evidently nobles were christening their sons by the names of the British king and his nephew before and shortly after 1100.

It is also startling that the earliest appearance of Arthur and his knights in art is found on an archivolt over the north doorway of Modena Cathedral. The art historians of Italy, Germany, England, and the United States are almost unanimous in dating this sculpture between 1099 and 1120. The cathedral documents which reveal that the edifice was consecrated in 1106 and that some fine sculptures had already been completed, the costume and armour, and the name-forms incised above the figures are reconcilable with this date; the development of sculptural style in Lombardy proves it. The scene represented is the deliverance of a woman, Winlogee, by Artus, Isdernus, Galvaginus, and Che from a moated fortress occupied by a trio of unpleasant characters, Burmaltus, Mardoc, and Carado. There is good reason to suppose that the incident is a variant of the rescue of Guenievre as described in *Durmart le Gallois,* and is related to the rescue of Gauvain from Carado of the Dolorous Tower in the *Vulgate Lancelot,* as Foerster and Mâle recognized. The name Winlogee applied to Arthur's queen is a transitional form between Breton Winlowen and French Guinloie. It follows that the *conteur* who provided these names was a Breton. Possibly he came down into Italy with the Breton contingent to the First Crusade under their Duke. They were at Bari during the winter of 1096–7, and the sculpture and architecture of Modena Cathedral, as Kingsley Porter showed, were strongly influenced by work recently executed at Bari.

A mosaic pavement laid down in the cathedral of Otranto, near Bari, in 1165 still depicts 'Arturus Rex' bearing a sceptre and riding a goat. No passage in literature assigns to the king so strange and so humble a mount. The only plausible explanation is found in the fact that the immortal Arthur was identified in the twelfth century with various supernatural potentates, such as the ruler of a subterranean realm, and that Walter Map about 1190 narrates a tale in which the king of a subterranean realm rode a large goat.

Gervase of Tilbury, who visited Sicily about 1190, reported that the British king had been seen, still alive, in the subterranean depths of Mount Etna. Caesarius of Heisterbach gives a variant of the same story, and dates the event at the time of the conquest of the island by the Emperor

Henry (*c.* 1194). There is no hint in these Sicilian legends that they were imported by Bretons, but from 1072 to 1189 Sicily was ruled by a Norman dynasty, and Zimmer quoted a chronicler to the effect that spirited young Norman or Breton knights sought Italy for adventure at various times after 1017. At the siege of Taormina in 1079 the life of Count Roger was saved by his nephew, 'natione Brito'. At any rate, by the end of the twelfth century Arthur was at home in Sicily.

It is a matter of high significance that these early examples of Arthurian tradition in Italy—the sculpture at Modena, the mosaic at Otranto, the local legend of Etna—were not derived from any known literary source, and there is a strong presumption that they were transmitted orally by adventurous Bretons, seeking patronage wherever French was understood, as it was in northern Italy, Apulia, and Sicily, and creating as elsewhere a great sensation by their novel and fantastic fictions.

The most eloquent testimony to the permeation of Latin Christendom by the renown of the British hero is to be found in the work formerly attributed in error to Alanus de Insulis and now dated by De Lage 1167-74. Commenting on the passage in Geoffrey of Monmouth's *Prophetiae Merlini,* 'In the mouth of peoples he [Arthur] will be celebrated', the author declared:

> Whither has not flying fame spread and familiarized the name of Arthur the Briton, even as far as the empire of Christendom extends? Who, I say, does not speak of Arthur the Briton, since he is almost better known to the peoples of Asia than to the *Britanni* [the Welsh and Cornish], as our palmers returning from the East inform us? The Eastern peoples speak of him, as do the Western, though separated by the width of the whole earth. . . . Rome, queen of cities, sings his deeds, nor are Arthur's wars unknown to her former rival Carthage. Antioch, Armenia, Palestine celebrate his acts.

If one realizes how much of Asia Minor and Syria was at this time colonized by peoples of French blood or speech, one will not reject this affirmation as sheer balderdash. The writer was patently amazed by the phenomenon. That Geoffrey of Monmouth and Wace were being read in clerical and courtly circles throughout Christendom by 1175 may be readily acknowledged, but unless the evidence assembled in this chapter has been totally misleading, we may safely assign the major part in the spread of the Matter of Britain as far as the Latin states of the East to the activities of the Breton *conteurs.* Direct testimony is lacking; but when in instance after instance the signs point to oral rather than literary circulation, it is a logical inference that these same story-tellers accompanied or followed the Frankish hosts who conquered the lands of the eastern Mediterranean.

When we approach the question, how long did the reciters of such tales continue to be welcome in the courts of Europe? we find no definite answer. Béroul mentions them in his *Tristan,* vs. 1265; the author of *Perlesvaus* in l. 7277; and that brings us well into the thirteenth century. A poem of the same century represents two *bourdeurs ribauds* boasting their knowledge of romances, which was badly muddled, for the first knew about 'the evil speech of Gauvain and the good knight Queu [Kay], about Perceval le Blois and Pertenoble le Gallois'! The latest reference known to me is in the Provençal *Flamenca,* which possibly postdates 1272. During the wedding festivities of Flamenca at Bourbon, the *jongleurs* are described as reciting tales, among which the five Arthurian poems of Chrétien are recognizable, as well as other themes from the same cycle. If this means that the *jongleurs* memorized Chrétien's lines and repeated them, the fact is significant. The old, less polished prose tales had gone out of fashion; the purely oral tradition had come to an end, and probably the Bretons had long since ceased to monopolize the exploitation of the Matter of Britain. Italian *cantastorie,* however, and English minstrels composed and sang *cantari* and verse romances from the fourteenth to the end of the fifteenth century. . . . (pp. 52-63)

Several characteristic features of oral recitation are to be detected in the Arthurian texts preserved to us. The wide variations in the handling of a given theme can sometimes be explained only as the result of a long preliterary development, when every reciter made his modifications. Certain proper names have been adapted to the speech-

---

An excerpt from Spenser's *The Faerie Queene* (1590) describing Arthur's magic shield

> His warlike shield all closely covered was,
> Ne might of mortal eye be ever seen.
> Not made of steel nor of enduring brass—
> Such earthly metals soon consumèd been—
> But all of diamond perfect pure and clean
> It framèd was, one massy entire mold,
> Hewn out of adamant rock with engines keen,
> That point of spear it never piercen could,
> Ne dint of direful sword divide the substance
>   would. . . . No magic arts hereof had any
>   might,
> Nor bloody words of bold enchanter's call,
> But all that was not such as seemed in sight
> Before that shield did fade and sudden fall.
> And when him list the rascal routs appall,
> Men into stones therewith he could transmew,
> And stones to dust, and dust to nought at all;
> And when him list the prouder looks subdue,
> He would them gazing blind, or turn to other
>   hue.
> Ne let it seem that credence this exceeds,
> For he that made the same was known right well
> To have done much more admirable deeds.
> It Merlin was, which whilom did excel
> All living wights in might of magic spell.
> Both shield and sword and armor, all, he
>   wrought
> For this young prince when first to arms he fell;
> But when he died, the Faery Queen it brought
> To Faeryland, where yet it may be seen if
>   sought.

Edmund Spenser, in Books I and II of The Faerie Queene, *edited by Robert Kellogg and Oliver Steele, The Odyssey Press, 1965.*

patterns of different peoples; thus the Welsh epithet *Gwallt-advwyn,* meaning 'Bright Hair', became successively Galvagin, Galvain, Gauvain, Gawain. Nowhere are the earmarks of minstrel composition more plainly discernible than in the short form of the First Continuation of Chrétien's *Perceval.* It is a collection of originally independent tales. It contains an appeal to the authority of Bleheris, who is identified in the Second Continuation as a *conteur.* There are frequent addresses to members of the audience as 'Signeur', and at one point they are asked to repeat a paternoster for the dead and to give the reciter a drink of wine before he proceeds. Thus internal evidence amply corroborates the external testimony to the oral diffusion of the Matter of Britain before, and even after, it came into favour with poets and prose romancers. (p. 63)

> *Roger Sherman Loomis, "The Oral Diffusion of the Arthurian Legend," in* Arthurian Literature in the Middle Ages: A Collaborative History, *edited by Roger Sherman Loomis, Oxford at the Clarendon Press, 1959, pp. 52-63.*

Margaret J. C. Reid

[*In the following excerpt, Reid investigates the literary sources of the myth of the Holy Grail, focusing on the anonymous twelfth-century* Queste *and Wolfram's* Parzival.]

The origins and early texts of the Holy Grail have been the subject of study, conjecture, and controversy, of many eminent scholars, English, German and French, of late years. A knowledge of these texts and their relationship and of the main discussions concerning these, is of course of value to those studying modern Arthurian poets. But for the present argument, it is sufficient to emphasise the general nature of these origins, and to confine our particular study of texts to two, which are later and which have determined in the main the traditions which modern poets have accepted.

At this stage, it will be sufficient merely to mention them. One of these is the anonymous twelfth-century *Queste* (the actual manuscript of which is lost) which Malory transcribed and abbreviated in his thirteenth to seventeenth books of the *Morte Darthur.* It is an exceedingly fruitful exercise to read these together and note the differences and the reasons for change or abbreviation. It makes the reader realise as nothing else does, how, especially in these books, Malory is chiefly an abbreviator and transcriber. His real originality is in the magic of his style.

The second text, which Dr Weston has given us in a most vigorous translation, in stanzas, is that of Wolfram von Aeschenbach's *Parzival* (thirteenth century). It is one of the finest poems of the Middle Ages. Though lengthy and very detailed (it contains the adventures of Gawain as well as Parzival), it is, on the whole, a unified, purposeful tale, and moves on steadily to its end and climax. It has considerable literary merit. Wagner followed, in the main, the events in this poem for his drama, the *Parsifal,* and thus its story has become familiar throughout Europe, associated with the heart-stirring Grail music. Wolfram von

Aeschenbach himself proclaims that he took the story from a certain "Kiot." Some have doubted this declaration and scholars suspect this source does not exist. But as this statement of Wolfram's has not exactly been disproved, others have taken it as it stands, as Dr Weston does in the notes of her translation of the *Parzival.*

In regard to the general origins of the Grail, scholars mainly agree that the foundation of the story lies in the far-off region of pagan myth. Dr Weston considers that "close parallels exist between the characters and incidents of the Grail story and a certain well-marked group of popular beliefs and observances, now very generally recognised as fragments of a once widespread Nature-cult."

This Nature-cult, she tells us, was connected with sex-rites and fertility and the coming of Spring (as in the "Adonis" rites in Greece). Thus the feast of the Grail was, according to this theory, a celebration of the awakening powers of Nature and the cup and lance, male and female phallic symbols. The special servants of the Grail were those "initiated" into the hidden powers of life and they had to go through certain rites. This theory also attempts to explain the central incident of the suffering Grail-king, who was wounded in the thighs and who could only be healed by the asking of a certain question. The disability was connected with the reproductive faculties and in this misfortune the "wailing land" shares. The question, of course, is one of those magic formulæ like the "Open Sesame" with which we have been familiar from our childhood. When the hero rode up the second time to recite the formula, *i.e.* ask the required question, the land rejoiced. It had been freed from the curse.

The whole legend became in course of time rationalised into a hero-story, Christianised and moralised.

In the earlier texts the primitive element is not altogether absent. We trace it here and there, jutting out like the peaks of high rocks in the ocean, which the tide has not altogether submerged. In Chrétien de Troies, for example, his mention of the "wailing of the land" and the "wailing of the women" (also mentioned in the "Adonis" legend) seems to demand an explanation not given in the actual events of the tale. Chrétien did not finish his poem so we do not know how he would have treated the Grail, but from indications in his poem, probably he regarded it only as a wonder-working talisman, worthy of reverence. The process of rationalisation is far advanced in this poet. Chrétien explains Perceval's first failure to achieve the sick king's healing as a punishment for his having caused his mother's death through heedless folly.

In its later form in the continuators of Chrétien, and especially in the Robert de Borron texts (or those ascribed to the latter), the Grail legend has come into contact with the Joseph of Arimathea legend and the process of Christianising has been taking place. The cup in which Joseph of Arimathea catches the drops of Christ's blood has been identified with the cup of the Last Supper. Joseph of Arimathea had taken it with him over to England to Christianise that land and it had performed many miracles, such as feeding him and his followers in prison. Then it disappeared, only to reappear to certain favoured ones.

In the *Queste* and in Malory, this food-producing vessel and life-giving feast is identified with the Mass and Eucharist. All manner of meat and drink is still provided, when it first appears to King Arthur's knights sitting at meat. But one of the chief qualities it possesses is the producing of a kind of spiritual ecstasy. "Then I shall tell you," said Galahad, "the other day when we saw a part of the adventures of the Sangreal I was in such a joy of heart, that I trow never man was that was earthly." It can only be seen by the pure in heart, which implies strict celibacy. The sight of the Grail for its own sake thus becomes the goal of the seekers rather than the healing of the sick king. True, Galahad does touch the maimed king with the blood of the sacred spear and heal him, but this is not made the central incident. To care so much for one's own spiritual satisfaction seems to the modern mind a selfish aim, even though disguised under the symbol of holy things.

In Wolfram of Aeschenbach the conception of the Grail is far otherwise. The central incident is the healing of the sick king and the whole theme of the poem the perfecting of the hero Parzival for this end. It is important to notice, however, that the Grail is not connected with Our Lord's Passion, though it is with Christianity. It is a magic stone which produces food and restores youth. Borne in procession by the Grail-maidens, it evidently has some moral implication, as those maidens must be chaste and pure of life. The power of the stone is renewed every Good Friday by a dove bearing a wafer, so it shows Christian influence. No unbaptized heathen such as the chivalrous Feirefis can view it. Its surroundings are magical rather than mystical in the more spiritual sense, "Unawares must they chance upon it for I wot in no otherwise." The conception of the Grail is also influenced by the Crusades and there exists a military knighthood at Monsalvasch, who guard it, which descends from father to son. The Grail keeper can marry but not his attendants, unless they go to foreign lands.

Though Wagner has shown in his opera, *Parsifal,* the dramatic possibilities of the story of Perceval and the Holy Grail, this version was not followed in English literature. There was, however, an early Welsh rendering of the story, of extreme importance in the history of origins in "Peredur" in the *Mabinogion.* It had some incidents in common with Wolfram von Aeschenbach—the description of Peredur's early life and upbringing, his appearance in the hall of the wounded king, who inhabited with his courtiers the "wailing land." There is also a strange admonition to the hero *not* to ask any questions, which seem to point originally to some form of taboo. It is evidently some tale of revenge; there is mention of the bloody spear, the gory head in a charger carried by two maidens but of no Holy Grail as such; nor has this story any religious atmosphere. Peredur has also many adventures of the usual chivalrous kind, such as rescuing distressed maidens.

The other source, the *Queste,* which Malory used and abbreviated and which commended itself to Tennyson and other English poets, is of a very different nature. It is of great interest to the student of religious life in the Middle Ages and has a moral, spiritual and some literary value. But it has not the living interest of Wolfram.

Pauphilet, in his able study on the *Queste,* points out that it is a *tableau* of Christian life probably written and adapted by a Cistercian monk. It is of the most ascetic character and makes reference to means of spiritual grace adopted in the monastery, such as fasting, confession and Mass with its attendant doctrines. For example, in Mass the presence of the "real body" is assumed, that is, the doctrine of Transubstantiation as held by the Catholic Church at that time. In Book XVII, chapter 20, of Malory, it is written how Galahad and his fellows were fed of the Holy Sangreal and how Our Lord appeared to them. "And then the bishop made semblant as though he would have gone to the sacring of the mass. And then he took an Ubblye (a wafer) which was made in likeness of bread. And at the lifting up there came a figure in likeness of a child, and the visage was as red and as bright as any fire, and smote himself into the bread, so that they all saw it that the bread was formed of a fleshly man."

The order of the moral virtues is altogether different from that assumed in the chivalric code adopted elsewhere by Malory. The chief virtues are humility and sexual purity in its most severe form. One of the sins most severely censored is *la luxure* in which marriage as well as irregular love is condemned. Next comes pride, especially the pride which is aroused by successful combats. Lancelot is therefore one of the chief transgressors, though, to the modern reader, he is the most interesting character in the *Queste,* which is not strong in character-drawing. He has to repent of his irregular love of Queen Guinevere, if he is to have any hope of seeing the Holy Grail. Again, he is reproved for putting his trust in his sword rather than in God. Malory, translating closely from the *Queste,* gives it thus: "The dwarf smote him and said 'Oh man of evil faith and poor belief, wherefore trowest thou more on thy harness, than in thy Maker.' " There are combats in this world but they are waged against spiritual enemies with spiritual armour. Galahad's chief weapon is trust in God.

In order to provide a hero to fit into these lofty but intangible ideals, a man had to be found of mysterious origin, without family ties. He is named Galahad, and like Parzival is the one promised aforetime. It is prophesied that he will sit in the perilous seat, enter the magic ship, fit together the broken sword and behold the Grail. Having beheld the Grail, he seems too lofty and pure for this mortal and sinful life and is translated to the Heavenly Kingdom. Perceval (the form in the *Queste* of the name) is also one of the questers and has retained his ingenuity and air of candour and, most important of all in this monastic treatise, has retained his virginity. In the earlier forms of the *Queste,* as Dr Weston has pointed out in her series of studies, Gawain was the original hero. In these earlier romances he is depicted as courteous, chivalrous and a loyal companion, ready for all adventures. But, alas! he has many loves, probably because as a favourite English hero, many stories of love and adventure, which did not originally belong to him, became attached to his name. At any rate, he did not suit the monkish writer of the *Queste.* To him, as to Thomas à Kempis, earthly graces were very different from heavenly ones. So Gawain becomes in this treatise the example of a worldling, light and frivolous, and is condemned by its severe standards. In the *Queste* the incidents related are far removed from the possibilities of real life. They form a contrast to Wolfram's story, which, in spite of its mediæval chivalrous setting, has yet an air of reality about it, not far removed from that of Froissart's *Chronicle* of his own times. But the incidents in the *Queste* are more intangible and impossible than the most romantic incidents of Malory in his other books. They tell us of phantom ships, neophytes who subsist for long periods on the grace of God alone, and of the champions of impossible feats. The writer loves the elaborate allegories and long moralisings in which the Middle Ages indulged.

One of the most elaborate, interesting and obscure allegories is that of the miraculous ship, described thus by the modern poet William Morris:

> There shall you find the wondrous ship wherein
> The spindles of King Solomon are laid,
> And the sword that no man draweth without sin,
> But if he be most pure.

In the course of their adventures, Galahad, Perceval and Sir Bors enter a strange and empty ship, borne over the waters miraculously and silently. In it they find a bed with magnificent silk coverings, and at its foot a sword hanging, whom no one but the chosen Galahad can dislodge from its sheath.

The story is a curious mixture of Celtic magic, Bible lore and moralising allegory. This sword with the strange girdle "espee as estranges renges" is a sword whose first girdle was of hemp which contrasted strongly with the magnificence of its scabbard of serpent's skin and its scaly handle, made from the scales of beasts that possessed magic properties, so that he who handled it should never feel weary. It has been prophesied that a new girdle would be made by a king's daughter and she must be a maiden. This virgin is, of course, Perceval's sister, who makes a girdle of her own hair bound with gold and set with precious stones.

The tale of the building of the ship is connected with Solomon and his wife and goes still further back to the beginning of things in the Garden of Eden. The three wooden spindles, from which the sword hangs, are made of three different kinds of wood, white, green and red, from the Tree in the Garden of Eden. The Tree was white at the time of our parents' innocence, it became green when Cain was conceived and red when Abel was murdered.

The story, with its numerous allusions to mediæval legends and beliefs, is difficult to understand without commentary, and Malory, in abbreviating it, makes it even more so (Book XVII). But Malory's style, like the sauce of a good cook, makes this strange mixture palatable, and the passage describing the ship and the fair bed (chapter 3) has a charm for the ear if not for the rational sense.

From this short summary of the contents it can be seen that the aims, ideals and subject-matter of the *Queste* are very different to those in Malory's other books, where it is the idealised love of woman, usually another man's wife, which is the chief motive of action, especially of fighting and adventures. Lancelot, the noblest and most chivalrous of them all, fits in uneasily to the new régime. All his for-

mer glories and attainments are counted to him as sins. He has to repent them utterly. In the original *Queste,* Lancelot remarks that the new (spiritual) life pleased him a hundred times better than the old. But Malory, purposely or otherwise, omits this saying in his rendering!

Thus, though Malory's adaptation of the *Queste* is of value in itself, it does not add to the unity of purpose of the *Morte Darthur* as a whole. So when Malory returns to his last books, leading to the destruction of the Round Table and the death of Arthur, through the treachery of Modred, we read that the court made glad when Sir Lancelot "began to resort unto Queen Guenever again, and forgat the promise and the perfection that he made in the quest." (pp. 128-35)

Margaret J. C. Reid, "The Holy Grail: Earlier Versions," in her The Arthurian Legend: Comparison of Treatment in Modern and Mediæval Literature, a Study in the Literary Value of Myth and Legend, *Oliver and Boyd, 1938, pp. 128-35.*

An excerpt from Arthur's deathbed speech in Tennyson's *Morte D'Arthur* (c. 1835)

> "The sequel of today unsolders all
> The goodliest fellowship of famous knights
> Whereof this world holds record. Such a sleep
> They sleep—the men I loved. I think that we
> Shall never more, at any future time,
> Delight our souls with talk of knightly deeds,
> Walking about the gardens and the halls
> Of Camelot, as in the days that were.—
> I perish by this people which I made—
> Though Merlin sware that I should come again
> To rule once more—but let what will be be,
> I am so deeply smitten through the helm
> That without help I cannot last till morn.
> Thou therefore take my brand Excalibur,
> Which was my pride; for thou rememberest how
> In those old days, one summer noon, an arm
> Rose up from out the bosom of the lake,
> Clothed in white samite, mystic, wonderful,
> Holding the sword—and how I rowed across
> And took it, and have worn it, like a king;
> And, wheresoever I am sung or told
> In aftertime, this also shall be known.
> But now delay not; take Excalibur,
> And fling him far into the middle mere;
> Watch what thou seest, and lightly bring me
>   word."

Alfred, Lord Tennyson, in his Morte D'Arthur, *in* Poetry of the Victorian Period, *Third Edition, edited by Jerome Hamilton Buckley and George Benjamin Woods, Scott, Foresman and Company, 1965.*

DEVELOPMENT OF THE LEGEND FROM MALORY TO THE VICTORIAN AGE

Christopher Dean

[*In the following excerpt, Dean reviews the stylistic and thematic transformations in Arthurian literature of the Renaissance.*]

Malory's *Morte d'Arthur,* published by Caxton in 1485, brought to an end the period in which genuine Arthurian literature was created. Throughout the Middle Ages the Arthurian theme had been a major subject for literary treatment, so much so that even in the first decade of the thirteenth century Jean Bodel, writing in France, had already classified the 'Matter of Britain' as one of the three main romance topics. From the twelfth to the fifteenth centuries, first in verse and then in prose, Arthurian themes and the romance genre had gone hand in hand. After 1500, however, the situation changed. Arthurian subjects were no longer looked upon favourably by major writers, so that with the exception of Spenser's *The Faerie Queene* no Renaissance work of the first rank even indirectly derived its inspiration from Arthurian material. At the same time, the material also lost its dominant hold on a single genre. Although in the sixteenth and seventeenth centuries works with Arthurian themes appear infrequently in most of the genres that make up Renaissance literature, they are never a major constituent of any one of them. Arthur as a subject for literary works is pushed more and more into the background. He never entirely disappears in the Renaissance period but he ceases to be important.

Arthur's appeal came under attack for many reasons after 1500, and it is ironic that one of them was the newly aroused interest in him as a historical figure, which came about through his being used to bolster the claims of the reigning Tudor monarchs to the throne. As Merriman points out, this concern for him as a historic figure actually made him less suitable as a character in works of fiction, since all authors, not just those interested in establishing his place in British history, tended to avoid the romantic and supernatural elements in his story. Arthur's mysterious birth and final passing, the achievements of his knights, his betrayal by his wife and nephew, and the quest for the grail were all discarded as superstitious or fantastical. They were seen as events that cast doubt on the crucially important 'facts' of Arthur's existence. Stripped of his mysterious origins, of his fellowship of knights, and of his fatally attractive queen, Arthur emerged from the heated controversies of the historians lacking much of his poetic appeal and significance.

Arthur also suffered from the general attack directed against all chivalric romances by the humanistic writers of the sixteenth and seventeenth centuries. They objected to such romances for a variety of reasons. Erasmus and More, for example, disliked tyrants and tyranny in all their forms and were opposed to war and the glamour that was associated with it. They attacked romances because they saw them holding up for admiration antisocial ideals of a hero with superhuman qualities as well as giving false

ideas about honour, glory, and the greatness of man. The influence of Erasmus, who held an overwhelming position in the minds of the educated people in the early sixteenth century, was particularly significant in this Renaissance criticism of the romance genre.

Other writers opposed medieval chivalric romances because they judged them to be immoral. Roger Ascham's denunciation of Malory's *Morte d'Arthur* has already been cited [in an unexcerpted portion of this text], but though his remarks are perhaps the best-known they are no different in nature from the comments of at least a dozen other critics of the time. In 1523 Juan Luis Vives, who became Latin tutor to Princess Mary, wrote a Latin treatise on the education of women called *De Institutione feminae christianae.* A contemporary translation into English says: 'Therfore hit were conuenient by a comune lawe to put away foule rebaudy songes / out of the peoples mouthes: which be so vsed / as though nothyng ought to be songen in the cite / but foule and fylthy songes / that no good man can here without shame / nor no wyse man without displeasure.' Nathaniel Baxter in 'The Epistle Dedicatorye' to *The Lectures or Daily Sermons, of that Reuerend Diuine, D. Iohn Caluine* (1578) also deplores contemporary reading tastes: 'We see some men bestowe their time in writing, some in printing, and mo men in reading of vile & blasphemous, or at lest of prophan & friuolous bokes, such as are that infamous legend of K Arthur (which with shame inough I heare to be newly imprinted) with the horrible actes of those whoremasters, Launcelot du Lake, Tristram de Liones, Gareth of Orkney, Merlin, the lady of the Lake, with the vile and stinking story of the Sangreal, of king Peleus, etc.' Last, we can quote John Florio, reader in Italian to Queen Anne and a groom of the privy chamber, who translated Montaigne's *Essays* in 1603: 'For of King *Arthur,* of *Lancelot du Lake,* of *Amadis,* of *Huon of Burdeaux* and such idle time consuming and witbesotting trash of bookes wherein youth doth commonly amuse itself, I was not so much as acquainted with their names.'

The last objections to romances by humanist writers at this time were not so much based on general principles as on the consequences of contemporary circumstances. Romances were condemned for being propagators of false popish doctrine, something especially reprehensible in a country newly converted to Protestantism. In *The Anatomie of Absurditie* Nashe calls them 'the fantasticall dreames of those exiled Abbie-lubbers,' and in *Toxophilus* Ascham says that they 'were made the moste part in Abbayes and Monasteries, a very lickely and fit fruite for suche an ydle and blynde kinde of Iyvyng.' Other writers somewhat snobbishly rejected the older romances because they were judged to be crude in style and valueless in content beside works of classical origin.

Not all the writers of this period, however, automatically rejected the possibilities offered by the Arthurian story. Ben Jonson is supposed to have said to William Drummond in 1619 that the story of King Arthur could provide suitable material for 'a Heroik poeme,' while from the same source we learn that Sidney at one time at least intended to transform all his *Arcadia* into a selection of Arthurian stories. While not from the pen of a major writer, Lord Berners' translation of a fourteenth-century French romance, *Artus de la Petite Bretagne,* published about 1555 under the title of *Arthur of Little Britain,* points to an ongoing enjoyment of Arthurian-type marvels and adventures. We can only call the adventures of this story 'Arthurian-type,' for none derives from the subject matter of the authentic Arthurian cycle. Berners' romance is a fairy-tale in which Arthur first sees his beloved in a dream and then seeks for her human counterpart. This is an interesting anticipation of the situation that Spenser was to use later in *The Faerie Queene.*

George Puttenham, in his *The Arte of English Poesie* (1589), even defends romances, including those with Arthur as their subject. In Book I, Chapter 10, he lists the subject-matter that poetry can properly use and includes in his enumeration, 'the worthy gests of noble Princes, the memoriall and registry of all great fortunes, the praise of vertue & reproofe of vice.' He justifies his statement by reference to his own work: 'And we our selues who complied this treatise haue written for pleasure a litle brief *Romance* of historicall ditty in the English tong, of the Isle of great *Britaine,* in short and long meetres . . . where the compa-

King Arthur shown standing above the crowns of thirty kingdoms in an illustration from the Chronical *of Peter of Langtoft, c. 1300.*

ny shalbe desirous to heare of old aduentures & valiaunces of noble knights in times past, as are those of king *Arthur* and his knights of the round Table, Sir *Beuys* of *Southampton, Guy* of *Warwicke,* and others like.' (II 43-4)

Whatever the learned critics had to say about romances, it seems to have made little difference to the reading habits of the general public in the sixteenth and seventeenth centuries. They went on reading romances avidly. A few people still knew them in their manuscript form, such as that of *Merlin,* inserted into a Latin chronicle of the kings of Britain in the *Liber Rubeus Bathoniae,* or the fragments of *Of Arthour and Merlin* incorporated as late as 1560 into the MS Harley 6223 of the British Museum in a prose chronicle. A manuscript copy of the metrical *Morte Arthur* was owned by Robert Farrers in 1570. Most people, however, read romances in printed form in the volumes put out by William Copland, John Kynge, Thomas Marsh, John Alde, Wynkyn de Worde, and the like. We have already seen how popular Malory's *Morte d'Arthur* was throughout this period, but other romance texts were equally so. Crane identifies four editions of *Guy of Warwick* between 1500 and 1569; Ellison tells us that there were fourteen reissues of *Huon of Bordeaux* in the sixteenth century and nine Tudor editions of *Bevis of Hampton.* Wynkyn de Worde reissued three of Caxton's romances in addition to the *Morte d'Arthur,* before going on to print romances of his own choosing, while Copland, according to Bennett, printed a dozen or more romances between 1548 and 1557.

All of the works cited so far are old works; the first half of the sixteenth century saw no new chivalric romances created in England. By the third quarter of the century a desire for something new began to emerge. The public turned away from works inherited from the Middle Ages in favour of foreign romances from Spain and Portugal. The vogue of Spanish and Portuguese romances began about 1578 with the publication of Margaret Tyler's translation from Ortunez of the first part of *The Mirrour of Princely deedes and Knighthood,* and soon romances with such exotic titles as *Palmerin d'Oliva, Bellianis, Palladine of England, The Adventures of Brusanus, Prince of Hungarie,* and *Primaleon of Greece* became available to satisfy a reading public demanding novelty.

The romance remained popular right up to the early years of the seventeenth century, but at that time a major change in its reception took place. At the beginning of the Renaissance period the romance was still the favourite type of fiction for all classes of readers, and to some extent the love for French Arthurian texts that we noticed among the nobility in the medieval period still continued. Towards the end of the sixteenth century, however, the romance had largely become the reading material of the middle and lower classes. Robert Laneham's *Letter,* written in 1575 to his friend Humphrey Martin, describes the library of a prosperous mason of Coventry, a certain Captain Cox, and Laneham's account probably indicates rather accurately the taste of the English middle class in Elizabethan times. The library had nearly two hundred books, of which Laneham gives the titles of 72. Four of these, a fairly high proportion, are Arthurian: *King Arthurz book,* either a copy of Malory or an abstract of the various French prose romances; *Syr Lamwell,* a version of *Sir Launfal; Syr Gawyn,* which is *The Jeaste of Sir Gawaine;* and *The Seaven Wise Masters,* a collection of tales, in one of which Merlin is a character. By 1600, the taste for romances had degenerated even further, as they became almost exclusively the fare of the lower classes, though, as Wright notes, they always remained popular with women of all ranks of society. *The Complaynt of Scotlande* suggests the kind of literature that was popular with the lower classes. Its author wanders into the countryside where he meets some shepherds. The chief shepherd speaks at length, praising the pastoral life, until his wife rudely interrupts him and tells him to stop his 'tideus melancolic orison.' The shepherds then turn to tale-telling. There follows a wonderful mix of romances, classical legend, fairytales, and history, including some Arthurian titles: *the prophysie of merlyne, the tayle of syr euan, arthours knycht, gauen and gollogras, Lancelot du lac, Arthour knycht he raid on nycht vitht gyltin spur and candil lycht.*

Tom o Lincoln is one of the two new Arthurian romances written during this period. The work of Richard Johnson (1573-1659?), a freeman of London and a writer of elegies, ballads, pamphlets, and an antiquarian tract, as well as romances, its first part was entered in the Stationers' Register in 1599 and its second part in 1607. Although no edition has survived earlier than the sixth, which is dated 1631, there is no reason to assume that five editions had not preceded it. Certainly it was popular, for later editions appeared in 1635, 1655, 1668, 1682, and 1704.

Critical assessments of *Tom o Lincoln* vary. Barber says of it merely that the story is 'completely invented and of little merit,' but Baker much more bluntly condemns the book as 'trash' and 'a vulgarization, in high-flown language, of the romantic figures, [and] the chivalric ideals.' More neutral, Davis calls it a romance of the most fantastic kind but at least allows that it has a theme, that of the low-born hero rising to become a member of the nobility. Only Hirsch, its recent editor, has suggested *Tom o Lincoln* has merit, claiming that it is a moral work that at first makes us admire the hero, then, when we see him justly punished for his misdeeds, makes us feel guilty for having admired him, and thus brings us eventually to a new sense of what is truly admirable.

We may wonder, however, if Johnson has any intention other than to present a series of exaggerated adventures of the most fantastic kind. He employs all kinds of stock situations in the most mechanical way, and his romance is particularly noteworthy for its melodramatic use of the sensational and macabre. Angellica, for example, dies in a room 'hung all about with blacke' after seven servers, each carrying a dish as if at a banquet and each suggesting a different manner of violent death, have come to her and compelled her to choose how she will die. Equally exaggerated is the style, which is ornate, rhetorical, and bombastic, and so close at times to the absurd that one might be forgiven for thinking that Johnson is writing a parody. In such a context, King Arthur, who comes to woo Angellica, is reduced to the level of a foppish simpleton: 'Faire of all faires, . . . deuine and beautious Paragon, faire

Flower of London, know that since my aboad in thy Fathers house, thy beauty hath so conquered my affections, and so bereaued me of my liberty, that vnlesse thou vouchsafe to coole my ardent desires with a willing graunt of thy loue, I am like to dye a languishing death, and this Countrey England of force must loose him, that hath filde her boundes with many triumphant Victories'.

The Arthurian framework of the romance adds nothing of thematic value to the work, nor does it significantly contribute a chivalric atmosphere or mood. It does, however, have some limited value for the plot since Lancelot, Tristram, and Triamore, three of Arthur's knights, can legitimately appear, but of these only Lancelot has a real role. He accompanies the Red Rose Knight to Fayerie-land and then goes to the city of Prester John, where he advises the Red Rose Knight not to fight a dragon. Lancelot, thus, plays the part in *Tom o Lincoln* that famous knights often played in medieval romances: he refuses, as a renowned champion, to do something that the hero of the work then proceeds to do. By contrast, the hero's bravery now seems much greater than if he had simply done the deed on his own. Arthur's court, too, has a traditional role in *Tom o Lincoln,* as a suitable place from which the hero can leave to seek adventure and to which he can later return in triumph to receive a princely welcome.

A noticeable feature of *Tom o Lincoln* is the way Arthur and Guenevere are drawn as evil and immoral characters. Lowering the reputation of the king is not unusual in romances; we have already seen the process widely used in the medieval works of earlier centuries. What is unusual is the degree to which *Tom o Lincoln* blackens the royal couple. Arthur is an adulterer, pursuing Angellica in a most besotted manner, and then, much worse, scandalously maintaining his liaison with her after she becomes a nun. At the point of death, he reveals the whole affair but in doing so shows that he has poorly judged the characters to whom he confesses, for his mistress is quickly murdered at the command of his vindictive queen and the Red Rose Knight's marriage is ruined because Anglitora is not willing to have the king's bastard son for her husband.

Johnson's hero is low-born and his rise to fame and fortune is part of the dream of the lower classes to whom this romance is addressed, but there is another side to this consciousness of social rank: that is, the desire of the lower classes to mock irreverently the institutions and standards of those who are socially above them. Consequently, for Tom to join the nobility of the land is cause for empathetic celebration in the heart of every Tudor apprentice lad who reads the tale, but also, to laugh and jeer at those who in real life stand far above the apprentice is also cause for satisfaction. In part, therefore, Lancelot and Arthur are figures of fun in this romance and are made to look foolish by their actions and by the way they are described, such as when Lancelot is seen at the end as 'so old and lame that through his bruises in chiualry, hee seemed rather an impotent creature, then a Knight at Armes'. It is a clear sign of how little Arthur was revered among the lower classes in the sixteenth century that Johnson can freely take such scurrilous liberties with the king's character.

The other new Renaissance Arthurian romance is Christopher Middleton's *The History of Chinon of England.* While it has the same zest for exaggerated adventure that we saw in *Tom o Lincoln,* it has none of its macabre atmosphere. Its world is that of splendid chivalry, and all the characters, pagans excepted, are admirable. In theme, however, it closely resembles *Tom o Lincoln,* in that it shows an unlikely character rising to fame. But Chinon is not of low birth like Tom. Rather he is the son of Cador, earl of Cornwall, but he has other handicaps. He is 'in his minde more than a maimed man, wanting that portion of sensible capacity which commonly doth accompany euen the meanest seruillitie.' He proves himself a valiant knight, however, and wins Cassiopeia, the daughter of the chief counsellor of the king of Egypt, as his bride.

Arthur in *Chinon of England* is no more than a background figure, the head of a court of renowned chivalric knights. He is: 'Monarch of this little worlde, with his attendant Knights, whose valorous exploits, euery where acted for theyr Countries honour, hath eternized their euerliuing names, euen in the farthest coasts of the barbarous Pagans'. A few of his knights have small roles. Tristrem and Lancelot go to France and take part in a tournament. In addition, in a newly invented love affair, Lancelot falls passionately in love with Laura, Chinon's sister. The main purpose served by these two knights in the story is to evoke the appropriate atmosphere of chivalry and to act as foils for the hero. They fail where he succeeds and so by contrast enhance his prowess. Neither *Tom o Lincoln* nor *Chinon of England* can properly be called Arthurian stories; at best they can only be described as having an Arthurian flavour. Nevertheless, that both authors would attach their stories to the name of Arthur and to his court is certainly a sign of the popularity of Arthur, at least as a fictional character, among the lower classes in England at this period.

We know of nine Arthurian ballads from the Renaissance period. For the two earliest, we have only entries in the Stationers' Register, since their actual texts have not survived. One was entitled 'a pleasaunte history of an adventurus knyghte of kynges Arthurs Couurte' and was licensed to Richard Jones between July 1565 and July 1566; the other, a 'ballade of the lewde life of Vortiger kinge of Bryttaine and of the firste commynge of Hingeste and the Saxons into this Lande,' was entered on 10 May, 1589. The earliest ballad for which we have a text is Thomas Deloney's *The Noble Actes of Arthur of the Round Table,* which appears as poem number 8 in part 1 of *The Garland of Good Will,* published in 1631. Lawlis has suggested that an entry by Thomas Pavier dated 1 March, 1602 may refer to Deloney's ballad collection, but he would put the actual period of composition back even farther to between 1586 and 1598, dates that match closely Howarth's suggestion that the poem was composed about 1593. *King Arthur and King Cornwall, The Legend of King Arthur, King Arthur's Death, The Boy and the Mantle, The Marriage of Sir Gawain,* and *Sir Lancelot du Lake* are the other Arthurian ballads, and all of them appear in the badly damaged Percy Folio MS, a paper manuscript of the seventeenth century.

King Arthur and King Cornwall, and *The Marriage of Sir*

Gawain survive only as fragments, so that their plots have to be put together by comparison with other works. *King Arthur and King Cornwall* is a version of *Le Pèlerinage de Charlemagne,* an Old French romance that was widely known in Britain. *The Legend of King Arthur* is based on Richard Lloyd's *A Briefe Discourse . . . of . . . the Nine worthies,* or it may even have been composed by Lloyd himself. *King Arthur's Death* is a continuation of the *Legend* and owes some debts to Malory. Although Child cites numerous parallels for it, *The Boy and the Mantle* can be traced to no specific source. *The Marriage of Sir Gawain* also has no known source, but medieval parallels are widespread. *Sir Lancelot du Lake* seems to be a fragment from a longer ballad. Probably based on Malory, it relates the victory of Lancelot over Sir Tarquin in single combat. Although it does not mention Arthur, the ballad is important because it shows the continuing late interest in Arthur's knights, especially when their stories can be reduced to simple action-filled adventures that pit a hero against an evil opponent.

The ballads vary considerably in the way they treat King Arthur. Only *The Legend* considers the king an authentic historical figure, and for the most part this ballad is nothing but an impersonal summary of the facts found in the chronicles. But the note of grim satisfaction in Arthur's account of the ending of Lucius, 'Whose carkasse I did send to Roome, / Cladd poorlye on a beere,' brings the king to life for us. *King Arthur's Death, King Arthur and King Cornwall,* and *The Marriage of Sir Gawain* are basically romance narratives recast in ballad style. *The Boy and the Mantle,* which in the manner of a folk-tale describes a trial of the fidelity of the wives at Arthur's court, stands apart from the other ballads in that it alone has virtually no plot. Its appeal lies in the account of the cynically humorous situation that of all the ladies only Craddok's wife is virtuous.

If, as Gerould claims, the nature of ballads in general is to stress situation rather than story, then most of the Renaissance Arthurian ballads are not typical of their genre. They read more like cut-down simplified versions of the medieval romances from which they ultimately derive. No doubt this is that they were intended to be. As the romances moved lower and lower on the social scale to be read by less and less well-educated readers, we can assume that eventually they became either too long or too difficult for easy reading and so had to give way to something shorter and simpler. Retelling the stories or parts of them in ballad form solved the problem. After 1600, there was still an audience for authentic Arthurian stories, but it needed tales that had been stripped to the bare bones as with *The Marriage of Gawain,* or reduced to single episodes as in Deloney's *The Noble Acts of Arthur.*

Turning now to the drama, the genre in which the greatest literature of this period was written, we are interested in two kinds of plays, both well represented on the Elizabethan stage. One is the romance drama; the other is the chronicle play. Neither made much use of Arthurian themes.

There may have been romance plays associated with fairs, marriages, and village wakes in medieval times, but if so no records of them have survived. The earliest examples we know are two mid-fifteenth-century plays, 'at seint albons the last of Juyn a play of Eglemour and Degrebelle' and 'a play at Bermonsey of a knight cleped fflorence.' By the late sixteenth century, however, such plays are common, so much so that of the fifty-two plays presented before Elizabeth between 1570 and 1585, twenty-four seem to be romances and the majority of these were apparently derived from medieval romances of chivalry.

Arthur and his knights rarely appear on the post-medieval stage and there are no more than two references that even doubtfully suggest the existence of Arthurian romance plays. Listing the dramas presented at court in the 1570s, Wilson names one as *The Irish Knight* and suggests that this may have been a play about Marhalt of Ireland from the Arthurian cycle. The other piece of evidence, slight and not entirely trustworthy because its author mentions every important source of romantic material except the Spanish pastoral, is Stephen Gosson's comment about the plays current in London in his day. In his *Playes Confuted in Fiue Actions* (1582), he says: 'I may boldely say it because I haue seene it, that the Palace of pleasure, the Golden Asse, the Aethiopian historie, Amadis of Fraunce, the Rounde table, baudie Comedies in Latine, French, Italian, and Spanish, haue beene throughly ransackt to furnish the Playe houses in London.' The reference to 'the Rounde table' certainly suggests a play or plays with Arthurian themes but if one ever existed it has not survived.

The chronicle play is more productive of Arthurian topics or topics related to them. To the Elizabethan sense that history was entertaining, instructive, and useful was added towards the end of the sixteenth century a feeling for national unity, patriotism, and England's glorification, which revived in a very specific way an interest in the country's past and in its heroes. This led to the rapid proliferation of chronicle plays, though it was a bubble that soon burst. According to Schelling, between 1590 and 1600 almost eighty chronicle plays were performed, but after 1610 subjects drawn from English history and myth are rare, and the choice of such subjects at this time could be regarded as virtually accidental.

The story of Brutus and the long line of British kings was a rich source of material for dramatists in the Elizabethan and Jacobean ages; *Gorboduc, Locrine, King Lear,* and *Cymbeline* are a few of the plays that utilize this subject-matter. Even so, plays actually set in the time of Arthur or close to it are not common. We have the texts of four. The first is *The Misfortunes of Arthur* by Thomas Hughes, presented for the entertainment of Queen Elizabeth at Gray's Inn on 28 February 1588. The second is Ben Jonson's *The Speeches at Prince Henries Barriers* (1610), though it is a masque not a play. The third is *Hengist,* also called *The Mayor of Queenborough,* by Thomas Middleton. Although not published until 1661, it may well have been written as early as 1619 or 1620. The last play is *The Birth of Merlin,* published in 1662 but again written much earlier, possibly soon after 1620.

Hengist and *The Birth of Merlin* have much in common. Each deals with the same events, the invasion of the British Isles by the Saxons and the wars between them and the

British. The main plot of each play quickly takes up the theme of treachery and division among the British, and attributes these sins to the infatuation of a British king with a Saxon princess. The main plot of each is sensational and melodramatic, and makes no serious attempt to present history. Probably the subplots held the main appeal of both plays to contemporary audiences. In *Hengist* this subplot is farcical, and it was clearly popular since it eventually supplied the title by which the play is now best-known. Needless to say, the subplot has nothing to do with British history. Its characters are contemporary London citizens guilty of the sins of vanity, pride, and desire for power, and it provides comedy by exposing the London dignitaries to ridicule. *The Birth of Merlin* also has low-class people as subplot characters. This subplot is vigorous, coarse, and bawdy in spirit, but it jars too much with the main plot for the two to combine in a unified play.

Neither *Hengist* nor *The Birth of Merlin* depends in any significant way upon the Arthurian cycle or upon British legendary history. To all intents and purposes they are what we today would call 'costume-plays' set ostensibly in the past; if the characters had had Italian names and the setting had been changed to Venice or Padua, the themes of the plays—lust, murder, and intrigue, relieved by low comedy—would have made the two 'Arthurian' plays indistinguishable from scores of other plays staged at this time.

Jonson's intentions in *The Speeches at Prince Henries Barriers* are no more than to praise England by reciting the glories of some of her more recent kings and to pay compliments to James I and his son, but the work is at least genuinely Arthurian in that the king appears as one of the characters. The Arthurian legend is used first to create an atmosphere of chivalry and then to allow the appearance of Merlin in the role of prophet and teacher. After Arthur has appeared and told us, 'I, thy ARTHVR, am / Translated to a starre . . . / ARCTVRVS, once thy king, and now thy starre' (65-6, 70), he goes on to promise that Henry will restore chivalry to England: 'Let him be famous, as was TRISTRAM, TOR, / LAVNC'LOT, and all our List of knight-hood' (86-7). Then Merlin praises the kings of England for their great deeds, beginning with Richard I and ending with James, the greatest of all. He foretells what lies in store for Henry:

> Not the deedes
> Of antique knights, to catch their fellowes
> 　steedes,
> Or ladies palfreyes rescue from the force
> Of a fell gyant, or some score to vn-horse.
> These were bold stories of our ARTHVRS age;
> But here are other acts; another *stage*
> And *scene* appeares; it is not since as then:
> No gyants, dwarfes, or monsters here, but men.
> His arts must be to gouerne, and giue lawes
> To peace no lesse then armes.

In doing so he indicates very clearly that the Arthurian world and the romantic chivalric qualities it reputedly stood for have gone. Jonson's is a new world with values and preoccupations that have significantly changed.

The one Renaissance dramatic work that attempts to

make a play with a serious theme out of the Arthurian legend is *The Misfortunes of Arthur,* written by Thomas Hughes and others. Dated 1587, it was devised for the entertainment of Queen Elizabeth and played before her in 1588. It is modelled on *Thyestes,* 'the most popular and the most gruesome of Seneca's tragedies,' with many of its lines being direct translations. Three of the themes in the play—a royal family that must expiate its sins, a discussion of good and bad conduct carried on in dialogue between major characters and wise subordinates, and views expressed on Fortune, worldly goods, and death—are all traditionally Senecan. In the same way the play's style and structure, with its formal five acts, its use of blank verse, its stichomythia, its soliloquies of self-analysis, and its moralizing choruses bringing each act to an end, all derive from the same classical source.

Hughes, however, did more than just copy Seneca. He modified his material freely and his changes are as important as his borrowings, because they indicate the purposes to which he intended to put his play. The main non-Senecan feature of *The Misfortunes of Arthur* is that the royal family's evil is more than just domestic in its effect; Hughes shows it plunging the whole state into treason and civil war. The hero is also altered. Instead of making Arthur merely a member of a tainted dynasty, Hughes presents him much more as a virtuous man. Guenevere is changed from a guilty Senecan adulteress to a loyal repentant subject. Even Gorlois' ghost is not just the vengeful spirit that occasions the destruction of Arthur's kingdom, as his Senecan counterpart would have been; instead he talks of treason and civil war and contemplates their effects on the nation in a manner typical of a character in a chronicle play. Finally, because Elizabeth is portrayed as a 'braunch of *Brute*' (v.ii.19), the family cannot be 'razed out' (v.ii.10) in typical Senecan manner as Gorlois has wished.

The Arthurian legend is much more central to the story than in any of the other plays so far discussed. Arthur is the principal character, and the plot deals with some of the more dramatic episodes of his history, his return to England to deal with Guenevere's infidelity, Mordred's defiant rebellion, and the catastrophe that results, including his own death. Hughes, however, is no historian or romanticist interested in the story for its own sake, powerful though it is. He treats it as a vehicle to carry a political message of contemporary relevance.

In general terms, the play emphasizes the need for loyalty to the crown and dwells on the horrors of rebellion and civil war. Usurpation of the throne is recognized as an impious crime that God will punish, and as the Chorus makes clear in act IV, such punishment will be extended to all those who accept the illegal rule of the usurper. Most critics, however, go beyond such generalities and see in the play a reference to the plots of Mary, Queen of Scots, to overthrow Elizabeth and to Elizabeth's unwillingness to put Mary to death for her actions. Mordred thus becomes a symbol for Mary and Arthur for Elizabeth. In an attempt to get around some of the problems posed by the equation of Elizabeth and Arthur, Waller makes a different equation, identifying Mordred as the younger Both-

well and Guenevere as Mary. Arthur, who can be taken as a man who is superstitious, prone to philosophize rather than act, and reluctant to punish traitors, now stands for James VI of Scotland. In Waller's view, Elizabeth is not any one character but the sum of all those who give good advice to Arthur. Lindabury is alone in seeing an entirely different message in the play. Noting that Elizabethan drama on the whole favours war because it brought honour and glory to men, he thinks that *The Misfortunes of Arthur* is one of the few plays that takes a contrary view by consistently portraying Arthur as the champion of peace.

The merits of *The Misfortunes of Arthur* are few. Its characters, for example, are not credible but a more serious drawback is structural, the play's failure to connect the later action with the opening. At the beginning of the play, Gorlois demands justice against a sinful tyrant, but at the end pathos dominates when we see a good king crushed by events he cannot control. The significance of *The Misfortunes of Arthur* for our study is that Hughes saw in the Arthurian story a plot that suited his political needs. That he could take such liberties with Arthur's character and the tragedy of his death shows that by the early seventeenth century Arthur was no longer tied to medieval tradition. Arthur was not a historical figure for Hughes but one of legend, and consequently, the king's story could be manipulated freely to suit the author's ends. But even so, Arthur was still considered a serious enough character that he did not seem out of place in tragedy.

Some other writers in the early seventeenth century, however, still took Arthur's reign as historical fact. Robert Chester, for example, still seemed to accept Arthur as an authentic part of the country's past. He published his *Love's Martyr* in 1601, though some of the parts may have been composed a great deal earlier. The work is one of the many allegorical poems designed to praise Elizabeth. In the course of the narrative, Nature and the Phoenix fly from Arabia to Paphos. On the way they cross Britain, which prompts Nature to expound on the country's history. Passing Windsor Castle, she says that it was built by Aviragus and finished by King Arthur, whose life she then proceeds to narrate. Chester is clearly advocating the historicity of Arthur. He says bluntly that some writers declare that the British king never lived, that others have 'let slip the truth of this Monarch,' and that to the country's shame he is better remembered in French, Roman, Scottish, Italian, and Greek histories than in English. Singing Arthur's praises, Chester calls the king 'famous Arthur,' 'noble Arthur,' 'great Arthur,' and 'renowned Arthur.'

Chester follows the chronicle tradition closely, but the emphases he places in the story are his own. For no obvious reason he tells the story of Uther and the begetting of Arthur at unusually great length, but the prominence he gives to the speeches of Cador, Howell, and Angusel when they reply to the Roman demand for tribute may derive from his patriotic spirit as he depicts foreign foes stoutly defied by native speakers. The romance elements of the story apparently do not appeal to him. Lancelot is absent; there is no reference to the grail; Guenevere plays no part in Arthur's downfall. On the Roman campaign Arthur does not fight a giant nor does he have prophetic dreams. Writing as he is in the chronicle vein and playing down the romantic elements, Chester surprises us, however, when he departs from the traditional material at one point to set out a lengthy pedigree for Arthur that proves he descended from Joseph of Arimathea.

Another work that still expresses a belief in Arthur as a real king is Thomas Heywood's *Troia Britanica,* published in 1609. Called by Bush the 'last of the "historical" leviathans,' it is a long poem on the history of Troy, and woven into its fabric are many interesting digressions on contemporary Elizabethan figures and affairs. The last two cantos tell the story of the arrival of Brutus in England, allowing Heywood the chance to chronicle all the British kings right down to James himself. The manner of treatment and the context of genuine kings into which Arthur is placed suggest that Heywood took him seriously as a historical personage. Heywood had space for only a single stanza about each king, so his account of Arthur is brief and straightforward:

> *Arthur* the worthy, next the State ascended,
> Fought twelue set battailes, and the order made
> Of the Round Table, whose renowne extended
> Through all the world, whilst *Arthur* doth inuade
> Forraine Dominions, and Christs Faith defended,
> *Mordred* at home, his Crowne and Queene betrayde:
> Twixt whom, at *Arthurs* backe returne againe,
> War was commenst, in which both Kings were slain.

He was more enthusiastic about Arthur a little earlier in the poem, however, when he broke off his narrative in canto 2 to ask,

> How many an English Knight hath borne his head
> As hie as those, whom *Troy* or *Greece* hath bread?

Then, answering his own question, he lists some famous English warriors, including:

> Renowned *Arthur* famous in his age,
> In his round Table, and his thirteene Crownes,
> Hie *Romes* Imperious Senate felt his rage,
> and paid him homage in their purple Gownes,
> His Came'lot Knights their hardiments ingage,
> Through all the world to purchase their renownes.

Quite different is another lengthy poem, Michael Drayton's *Poly-Olbion.* Drayton, who loved all things British, early steeped himself in the country's medieval legends. His poem celebrates on a vast scale every aspect of 'Merry England' as he knew it. He planned the work as early as 1598 and entered the first part in the Stationers' Register in 1612. The second part was published before 1618. According to his principal biographer, Drayton intended the *Poly-Olbion* to be the great achievement of his life and it was a bitter disappointment to him that it was received with such coldness and neglect. He was an antiquarian

speaking about a kind of past that few people seemed to care about anymore.

Drayton enthusiastically supported King Arthur saying, in Song VIII:

> Out of whose ancient race [Troy's], that warlike
> *Arthur* sprong:
> Whose most renowned Acts shall sounded be as
> long
> As *Britains* name is known: which spred themselves so wide,
> As scarcely hath for fame left any roomth beside.

He organizes his work geographically, recalling the legends associated with each place in Britain he mentions. He writes of the Arthurian associations with the River Camel (Arthur's death), Glastonbury (Arthur's tomb), Camelot (the place of the Round Table), and Caerleon (Arthur's weapons and coronation).

Drayton's friend, John Selden, illustrated and explained the poem's text in lengthy notes, but Selden's temperament is quite different from the poet's and represents the more modern contemporary attitude that was beginning to prevail towards early British history. Selden believes no accounts of any time before Caesar but says, 'to explaine the Author, carrying himselfe in this part, an *Historicall,* as in the other, a *Chorographicall* Poet, I insert oft, out of the *British* story, what I importune you not to credit.' He faithfully illustrates Drayton's references, and so in connection with the passage on the Camel he tells the story of Arthur's magically aided conception, but he cannot resist the cynical remark afterwards: 'Here have you a *Jupiter,* an *Alcmena,* an *Amphitryo,* a *Sosias,* and a *Mercury;* nor wants there scarce anything, but that truth-passing reports of Poeticall Bards have made the birth an *Hercules*' (Song 1, 19-20).

A work that openly sets out to put history to use is the *Mirror for Magistrates.* Following the pattern of Lydgate's *Fall of Princes,* it has as its purpose the teaching of political lessons by means of historical examples. In a series of imaginary dialogues, ghosts of figures from the past come forward to relate their unfortunate ends, the message being always the same—that the tragic hero has been marked out for God's vengeance because of his sin. The *Mirror* went through a series of revisions in editions from 1559 to 1610, each longer than the last as extra tragedies were added to the existing corpus. In 1574, John Higgins published tragedies dealing with British history from Brutus to the Christian era, but it was not until 1578, when Thomas Blenerhasset added a second series from Caesar to William the Conqueror, that the Arthurian cycle entered the work. In this series we find the story of Vortiger, with his lust for Hengist's daughter as its principal theme, and the account of Vter Pendragon, who also pays a price for illicit love. Finally, in the 1610 edition, Richard Niccols includes Arthur. According to Brinkley, 'The ghost of Arthur is called up to tell his own story, which is given in great detail, following Geoffrey's account with extreme closeness except that all suspicion of Arthur's bastardy is refuted.' Nearing suggests that in the 1610 edition Niccols chose figures more for their dramatic appeal than for their didactic value, but what he saw in the case of Arthur was not a warning to the readers as the nature of the *Mirror* would lead them to expect, but an inspiration for them by virtue of his praiseworthy deeds.

Only one writer of the first rank attempted an Arthurian work in the Renaissance period. Epic in proportion and allegorical in signification, Edmund Spenser's *The Fairie Queene* at the narrative level is pure chivalric romance. Its ingredients are the staple ones of knights and ladies, castles and bowers, giants and fairies, forests, caves, and endless plains over which characters ceaselessly travel in pursuit of adventures. If the subject matter is a little old-fashioned for serious literature at the end of the sixteenth century, the language is also of the past with its archaic words and obsolete syntax. The names of some of the characters, such as 'two wicked Hags' one called *'Impotence'* and the other *'Impatience'* (11.xi.23), or 'a gentle Husher, *Vanitie* by name' (1.iv.13), or *Braggadochio,* or *Kirkrapine,* or *Sansfoy,* clearly indicate that the poem has an allegorical nature, but the battles these characters fight with the different heroes are straightforward matters of lance and sword in the standard medieval manner. On the surface, therefore, *The Fairie Queene* tells a story of the kind met with in many medieval romances of chivalry. When we read the poem at this simple narrative level, however, we are left with a real sense of dissatisfaction, because the matter is not at all resolved into any coherent design. Stories are left with their ends ungathered, and the virtues that the poem proclaims are not wrought into any explicitly defined relationship with each other.

When we turn to Arthur, the ostensible hero of the poem, our puzzlement increases. We realize at once, of course, that Spenser's Arthur is a new creation and that his adventures have been put into that conveniently empty period that the chronicles and romances do not deal with, the period between his reaching maturity and his becoming king. As Parker says: 'By placing the events in the time before Arthur was king, Spenser has with one stroke eliminated the Round Table, the Holy Grail, Morgan le Fay, the Lady of the Lake, Lancelot, Guinevere, Gawaine, Kay. His horse is Spumadore, his sword Mortdure, his squire Timias, his foster-father Timon.' Even if Spenser had gone on to finish his story with Arthur finding Gloriana, one suspects that none of the essential elements of the medieval story and nothing of its tragic spirit would have appeared.

We can see why, in a negative way, Spenser was forced to drop so much of the Arthurian tradition. As soon as he decided to make his knights the representatives of the twelve moral virtues, Spenser saw that none of the traditional knights of the Round Table qualified for these parts. Lancelot, Kay, and Gawain had to yield to the likes of Guyon, Artegall, and Calidore. Equally important, when Spenser made Gloriana the mistress of an Order of Maidenhead, there was no longer a place in the poem for an Order of the Round Table with Arthur as its head. On the positive side, Arthur's traditional adventures disappear because Spenser's conception of Arthur is different. No longer the head of a chivalric court, Arthur becomes instead the allegorical figure of Magnificence, and the tasks

Depiction of Lancelot relating his adventures, from a French manuscript illustration c. 1316.

he must perform to support his role have to be as new and different as the value that Spenser newly ascribes to him.

The obvious place at which to start an investigation of Arthur's character and role in *The Faerie Queene* is the letter Spenser wrote to Sir Walter Raleigh on the publication of the first three books of the poem. In it, he proposes to discover 'the general intention and meaning' of the work by making the statement that Arthur is depicted in 'the image of a braue knight, perfected in the twelue priuate morall vertues' and that he represents 'magnificence in particular, which vertue . . . is the perfection of all the rest.' Despite Spenser's words, however, many critics have read other qualities into Arthur, such as that he stands for the kingdom of England or the Christ of the *Book of Revelations,* that he is 'the good and perfect gift which comes down from the Father of Light,' or that he is a chivalric version of the mythological Hercules. Bennett gets around Spenser's equation of Arthur with Magnificence by claiming that the letter to Raleigh is a late rationalization on the author's part to explain the final shape of a poem that may have changed course many times in the process of composition.

Let us assume, however, that Spenser meant what he said and that he needed as his principal character and hero a figure who would stand for the quality of Magnificence, a virtue that would somehow embrace and sum up all the other virtues. We would expect Spenser, therefore, to have followed the practice he had established with the individual heroes of each book and to have invented a character called Sir Magnificence or some other suitably identifying name. The poem's structure, however, may have demanded rather more than this. This character was intended to surpass all the other knights in the poem, and so perhaps a higher rank than a simple knight was called for. Furthermore, it was likely that Spenser intended to end the poem with some form of union, though not necessarily marriage, between his hero and Gloriana. Therefore, it was necessary for Magnificence to be of royal rank, a prince at least if not a king. The question we must ask in this study, then, is not what Spenser's main character stands for—we can assume Magnificence, however that is defined—but rather why Spenser chose to equate this character with King Arthur, for in doing so he certainly created problems for himself, problems that he could have avoided by using an entirely fictitious allegorical character.

We have already noted that though *The Fairie Queene* has an allegorical significance it is in form a medieval chivalric romance. Arthur was the greatest chivalric figure that Renaissance authors inherited from their medieval past and for this reason alone was the obvious choice for Spenser's hero. Furthermore, by using Arthur's name, Spenser could put to use all kinds of ready-to-hand concepts of courtly chivalry, of knightly splendour, and of noble ideals. In addition, Arthur was a figure from antiquity, and by setting his poem thus in Arthur's days, especially in those even vaguer days of Arthur's youth for which no records of any kind existed, Spenser removed his work from his own day into a more uncertain time when allegory might have a freer rein to play its part. The setting in the vague past also allowed him to conceal more discreetly any contemporary allusions that he did not wish to make too embarrassingly obvious. Yet another reason for choosing Arthur as his hero was that Spenser, by then linking him with Gloriana, could compliment Queen Elizabeth, whom Gloriana stood for, by such an association. it also reminded people of the historical title to Elizabeth's throne, which she along with all the Tudor monarchs claimed. Finally, of course, the story of Arthur was popular among a segment of English society in the late part of the sixteenth century, and Spenser may have seen advantage for himself in addressing his poem to those people who enjoyed British history or British legends.

Spenser, therefore, took a figure who was for many a national symbol and tried to remodel him in an entirely different way. But the odds were clearly too great for him to succeed. Arthur's story was too well known for an author to take such great liberties and hope to get away with them in a serious work. The established story resisted excessive manipulation and augmentation, and reader expectations were too rigid to allow the new perspectives to drive out the old.

Cummings, in *Spenser: The Critical Heritage,* quotes some 161 pages of contemporary criticism written between 1579 and 1660, and it is enlightening to note in them that no one talks of *The Fairie Queene* as an Arthurian work that continued a tradition inherited from the Middle Ages, or thinks of it as developing a new tradition about Arthur. Spenser's poem seems to have been well received by the poets of his own day, but it never enjoyed wide fame among the reading public at large. Cummings suggests in fact that many of the early readers may have been 'overwhelmed and confused' by the work. If Cummings is right

in this idea, part of the reason for their confusion may well have been the manner in which Arthur was treated.

Indeed, there were probably two quite different categories of reader for this work. Some, among whom Cummings includes John Milton and Henry More, took the poem as a moral allegory, but others clearly regarded it as a romance 'with the Stories of the Knights, and Giants, and Monsters, and brave Houses.' This latter group must have had particular trouble with Spenser's view of King Arthur. Judged as a work built on a story with Arthur as its central figure, *The Fairie Queene* must be seen as deficient. Yet the very fact that Spenser found it so difficult to create a convincing Arthur with new values and new deeds is in itself important testimony that there was still enough life and vitality in the old traditions for them to resist Spenser's new directions.

To sum up the treatment of Arthur in the literature of the Renaissance period, we see that after 1500 the attitudes ceased to be those that had prevailed in the Middle Ages. In the first place, despite the official Tudor interest in Arthur, there was increasing scepticism about the historical figure of the medieval chronicles. Consequently, he was kept alive chiefly for political ends or from a love of things antiquarian. Out of the small core of facts that were still accepted, there was little material that readily lent itself to literary adaptation. In the works of Chester, Drayton, and Heywood, we sense an atmosphere more of antiquarian curiosity than of literary vitality.

The humanist attacks upon the medieval romances had severely reduced the audience that still found the old tales of chivalry rewarding, but even so some interest in the story of Arthur and his knights remained if only as fiction, as the production of fresh editions of Malory clearly indicate. However, any desire that Elizabethan and Jacobean writers expressed to retell the story did not result in new versions of the legend. The idea of an Arthurian work seems still to have had an appeal, but in practice no major writer took it up except Spenser, and he changed the traditional material so radically that really only the name of Arthur was preserved.

What creativity there was in treatments of the traditional narrative in the sixteenth and seventeenth centuries existed only at the unsophisticated level of the ballad. A few writers did attempt to capitalize on the appeal of Arthur's name by attaching new stories to it, either in prose romance (*Tom o Lincoln* and *Chinon of England*) or in drama (*Hengist* and *The Birth of Merlin*). In such cases the Arthurian world still provided a convenient background setting, but its value was little more than this. These new works gave their readers fabulous heroes and fantastic adventures. In addition they satisfied the social attitudes of their lower-class audiences either by burlesquing and parodying the values of the upper classes or by showing that lower-class figures could rise in the world and emulate people of higher birth.

The Misfortunes of Arthur and *The Fairie Queene* alone in the Renaissance period attempt in a serious way to adapt Arthurian material to new uses. Though very different in literary method and achievement, both were ultimately unproductive in establishing new treatments of the cycle. In particular Spenser's use of Arthur as an allegorical figure inspired no writer of the period in emulation. Both works proved to be once-only ventures and no similar works succeeded them. After them, the literary inspiration provided by the Arthurian legends virtually ceased until it appeared again revitalized in the nineteenth and twentieth centuries. (pp. 107-27)

> Christopher Dean, "Arthurian Literature in the Renaissance Period," in his Arthur of England: English Attitudes to King Arthur and the Knights of the Round Table in the Middle Ages and the Renaissance, *University of Toronto Press, 1987, pp. 107-27.*

Beverly Taylor

[*Taylor is an American educator and critic and the author of several works on Victorian literature. In the following excerpt, she explores the reasons behind the Victorian resurrection of the Arthurian legend, concluding that the "stories of King Arthur and the Round Table appealed to Victorian poets because, for all their remoteness and quaintness, they deal with ethical, moral, and emotional problems that transcend custom, place, or time."*]

In the final pages of Sir Thomas Malory's late fifteenth-century *Morte Darthur,* King Arthur bids farewell to Sir Bedivere—and to English medieval romance—as he is carried from the battlefield to a barge destined for Avalon, where he may be healed of his wounds. Although Malory records that the king died and was buried at Glastonbury, he also narrates the alternative legend that Arthur survived and awaits return—the once and future king. After three centuries of banishment from literature truly Arthurian in focus and inspiration, Arthur reappeared in England early in the nineteenth century, and he must certainly have felt himself to have chosen an unlikely time and place for his second coming. Industrialisation, urbanisation, utilitarianism, democratisation, along with modern science and rational skepticism, seemed to be extirpating all traces of the world familiar to Arthur or to the writers who celebrated him throughout the Middle Ages. The environmental change is succinctly sketched in Gerard Manley Hopkins' description of the once gracefully medieval Oxford, wearing in the nineteenth century 'a base and brickish skirt' ('Duns Scotus's Oxford', 1879). Long before Hopkins' observation, brickish factories dominated landscapes, and man found himself inhabiting not only a different physical world, but a new and frequently bewildering spiritual realm as well. Hence Matthew Arnold compared modern man to an inexperienced child, shorn of the secure religious faith represented by the Middle Ages, yet lingering fearfully in the shade of the medieval monastery in which he could no longer dwell ('Stanzas from the Grande Chartreuse', 1855).

Despite an external and internal landscape apparently hostile to romance, Arthur returned to English literature after more than three hundred years with an intensity remarkable for both the quality and the quantity of works produced. Even those who avoided specifically Arthurian

subjects—Robert Browning, for example—were influenced by Arthurian concepts such as the quest and the chivalric code. From Alfred Tennyson's early Arthurian poems published in the 1830s and 1840s, through William Morris' *Defence of Guenevere* volume published after mid-century, to Algernon Charles Swinburne's *Tristram of Lyonesse* and *The Tale of Balen* appearing in the last two decades of the century, Arthurian materials fascinated important writers throughout the Victorian era. The major literary work achieved by Arthur's return, Tennyson's *Idylls of the King* (1859-85), occupied the poet for more than fifty years and came closer than any other work of the age to being an epic and a national poem.

This Victorian enthusiasm, contrasting sharply with the preceding century's general lack of interest in the Middle Ages (Voltaire acerbically judged the life of medieval men to be of no greater interest than the activities of bears and wolves), vividly signalled Arthur's second coming. Although between Malory's romance, printed in 1485, and Tennyson's publication in 1832, Arthurian works had appeared in England in an inconstant but unbroken flow, these works generally had little connection with medieval tradition other than names or occasional episodes familiar from the Middle Ages. By and large these Renaissance and Enlightenment works, such as Spenser's epic *Faerie Queene,* Dryden's dramatic opera *King Arthur,* or Fielding's play *Tom Thumb,* simply wove Arthur or his famous knights into a tapestry of situations and events remote from Arthurian stories and concerns. Malory's romance, the major collection of Arthurian legends available in English, having appeared frequently between Caxton's edition in 1485 and Stansby's corrupt version of Caxton in 1634, thereafter remained unpublished and was mainly known only to antiquarians until the nineteenth century.

The resurrection of Malory, and of Arthurian legend in general, may be largely credited to the work of such antiquarians as Richard Hurd, Thomas Percy, Thomas Warton, George Ellis, Sir Walter Scott, and the more scholarly Joseph Ritson. Their painstaking labours recovered medieval romance from obscurity and brought it to a large body of cultured readers. While their editing and other studies may be said to have stimulated the first serious historical and linguistic interest in the literary documents of the Middle Ages, they also focused attention on medieval romance as distinguished literature which had influenced the giants—Chaucer, Shakespeare, Milton, and Spenser. Moreover, the eighteenth-century antiquarians made modern writers aware of models other than the classics, thereby expanding the subject matter and stimulating the inventiveness of contemporary literature. Renewed interest in Malory, specifically, may be traced to Thomas Warton's *Observations on the Faerie Queene* (1754, revised 1762), which described Spenser's indebtedness to the *Morte Darthur,* among other medieval romances, for much of the imaginative richness of his epic.

As a result of the antiquarian zeal of the eighteenth century, Malory was rediscovered with such enthusiasm that the *Morte Darthur* appeared in two separate editions in 1816, another in 1817, and a fourth in 1858. Though the printing of 1817, introduced by Robert Southey, was rather expensive, the editions of 1816 were relatively inexpensive and aimed at a popular audience. The effect of these publications was to take Malory beyond the domain of antiquarians, into the hands of poets such as Tennyson and Morris, thus effectively transporting Arthur back from Avalon and restoring him to prominence in English letters.

This revival of interest in Arthur was in Britain the most concentrated literary aspect of the pervasive phenomenon of nineteenth-century medievalism, which registered in the work of linguists and editors, historians, architects, painters, and writers throughout Europe, and to a lesser extent even in America. While the efforts to retrieve the past through studying folklore and literature and emulating medieval plastic arts may be seen as a self-conscious historicism—and even, in the case of Germany, as an attempt to recreate a nationalistic heritage—the broad medievalism of the Romantic period began as varied reactions against neo-classical symmetry, decorum, and order. Ironically, although eighteenth-century novelists, for example, had used medieval (or pseudo-medieval) machinery to intrigue their readers with the exotic or unfamiliar—stimulating terror with dungeons, ancient curses, and haunted castles—aspects of the Middle Ages became increasingly popular and meaningful to the nineteenth-century as they became more familiar, as the influence of medieval architecture visibly testified. Beginning in such eccentricity as Horace Walpole's Strawberry Hill—a plain Georgian house fantastically remodelled after 1750 with battlements, twisted chimneys, and quatrefoil windows—nineteenth-century architectural medievalism soon domesticated the strange Gothic-style banks and railway stations. (pp. 15-17)

[Scott's] immensely popular metrical romances and 'medieval' novels (more than a half dozen, from *Ivanhoe* in 1819 to his last work, *Castle Dangerous* in 1832), may in part be credited with stimulating the medieval interests of the century, but they must also be seen as his shrewd efforts to tap currents originating elsewhere. To a great extent the popularity of Scott's medieval works grew out of nostalgia—both his and his readers'—a desire to freeze, if only in literature, an essentially familiar way of life which was rapidly changing in the face of shifts from rural to urban dwelling, from agriculture and cottage crafts to mechanised industry, from secure religious faith to profoundly unsettling skepticism, from government centred in the hands of aristocracy and gentry to democracy. Scott's medieval novels memorialise a relatively static society with a defined set of values, which if imperfect, was also a known quantity attractive to nervous skeptics of change because it had survived for centuries. Admittedly, Scott's version of the Middle Ages offered fancy and local colour more than history. As A. O. J. Cockshut has observed [in his *The Achievement of Walter Scott,* 1969], Scott 'was writing for a public ready to be entertained and bewitched by an unreal middle age, a public that had emancipated itself from the stock Augustan prejudices about medieval barbarism, and was now ready to adopt different misconceptions, and to be deceived in new ways.'

Yet Scott's depictions, regardless of historical misrepresentations, were not escapist literature. While some of his characters represent ideals of chivalry—a concept which Scott defined for his age in the *Encyclopedia Britannica* (1818) as an individual's altruistic devotion to his society and religion—others criticised the excesses and misapplications of the chivalric code, as, for example, when Rose in *The Betrothed* questions a knight's automatically claiming marriage to a damsel he has saved. In *Count Robert of Paris* Scott shows the decay of chivalric idealism into jaded pretension. In such a work as *The Antiquary,* where he focuses on a relatively modern period, he criticises his contemporaries' superficial and warped view of the past (by showing, for instance, the discrepancy between Oldbuck's daydreams and actuality), suggesting simultaneously that in some ways the past was superior to the present and that man can probably never fully understand former ages. His depictions of changing society also show the foolish vulnerability of characters (like Arthur Philipson and his father in *Anne of Geierstein*) who fail to adapt to changes or to understand contemporary man and moment. But at the same time, Scott suggests that the past age is in many ways more engaging than the present, not only more picturesque but more noble. In his medieval world, ideals of chivalry and honour thrive, though only in rare individuals. While his romanticised past scarcely reflects the brutal actualities of life in the Middle Ages, it focuses on ideals which from the distance of centuries

Morgan le Fay and Tristan, illustrated by Aubrey Beardsley in Malory's Le Morte d'Arthur, *1893-94.*

could be distilled from the adulterating mass of petty details of daily living.

Besides representing the ideals popularised by Scott—chivalrous individual behaviour and a comfortably traditional society—the Middle Ages for other nineteenth-century writers illustrated an ideal social, economic, and political order. Although the actualities of feudalism would scarcely have suited a society which increasingly recognised the evils of slavery and the worth of democracy, the medieval relationship between lord and vassal was easily sentimentalised as a familial bond. The worker who fulfilled his obligations with dignity was in turn succoured by a paternal lord. This envisioned relationship surely contrasted attractively with the contemporary chasm between rapacious captains of industry and exploited workers. In addition to offering the idealised notion of society organised in a secure, hierarchical economic family, the Middle Ages for such figures as John Ruskin and William Morris represented an economy desirably built upon individual craftsmanship and accomplishment rather than on mechanised uniformity, and also built upon the fellowship of trade guilds rather than on cut-throat competition. All of these economic and social notions appealed to Thomas Carlyle, who in *Past and Present* (1842) cites the medieval monastic society of Bury St. Edmunds as an instructive contrast to his age. In his view the monastic order reflected vigorous spirituality and a communal co-operation sacrificed by his own materialistic, competitive society. At the same time, the heroic leadership of the medieval Bishop Samson illustrated the merit of organising a hierarchy behind a strong, enlightened leader. Thus Carlyle's work illustrates the nineteenth-century sense that the Middle Ages could not only represent noble ideals but also offer practical lessons and patterns for modern economic and social organisation.

Many of Carlyle's contemporaries, on the other hand, saw that medieval life was not always noble, practical, or organised. At least one nineteenth-century poet described the Middle Ages not as a more civilised time, but as an age of violence. If order existed, it grew from conflicts between individual desires and visions of right. William Morris's poems based on Froissart's *Chronicle* focus on militaristic values and bloodshed. In 'The Judgment of God' (1858), for example, a knight recalls his father's instructions to slash at his foe's head 'When you catch his eyes through the helmet-slit / . . . And the Lord God give you joy of it!' To cite but one other instance, in 'The Haystack in the Floods' (1858) a damsel watches her jealous lord slay her lover: 'Right backward the knight Robert fell, / And moan'd as dogs do, being half dead, / . . . so then / Godmar turn'd grinning to his men, / Who ran, some five or six, and beat / His head to pieces at their feet.' By portraying such scenes so graphically, Morris in one sense refrained from idealising the Middle Ages. But in another sense, the very coarseness of his portrait idealised the vitality of medieval man. In contrast to Englishmen of the present age—when, Arnold declared, 'The kings of modern thought are dumb; / . . . . They have the grief men had of yore, / But they contend and cry no more' ('Stanzas from the Grande Chartreuse')—the warriors of Morris' Middle Ages acted—fiercely, violently, but more impor-

tant, dynamically. And even in this vibrant, brutal world, Morris portrayed subtle psychological and emotional states.

Other writers eschewed a sentimental view of the Middle Ages for purposes of satire. Peacock, for example, was one of many who satirised the medieval enthusiasms of his age. *Nightmare Abbey* (1818), like Jane Austen's *Northanger Abbey* (1817), mocks Gothic architecture and the conventions of the Gothic novel; it also mocks the taste of Romantic writers for remote ages and quaint, exotic customs. Far more frequently, however, the medieval period served as a vehicle for satirising the present. Peacock himself seriously studied Welsh language and lore and in his novels translated or emulated medieval ballads and romances to provide aesthetic contrasts to the modern emphasis on fact and figures. In *Crochet Castle* (1831), although Peacock satirises his protagonist's excessively sentimental enthusiasm for the weapons, dress, and customs of the Middle Ages, he also allows this Mr. Chainmail (who may be seen as a parody of Scott) to condemn the commercialism of the modern world by praising the earlier era. In a central episode, characters debate whether the present state of society is inferior or superior to that of the twelfth century. Ultimately the novel resolves this issue by showing modern perspectives, whether pragmatic or transcendental, to be inadequate equipment for coping with growing materialism. Whereas contemporary currents—derisively termed 'the march of the mind'—promote greed, corruption, and loveless marriages, the medieval values of Mr Chainmail underlie his affectionate, familial relationship with his domestics and allow him to achieve genuine love and even a measure of valour.

Mr Chainmail's delight in battle-axes, coats of mail, and other physical trappings of medieval custom, though comic in its excess, suggests another level on which the Middle Ages appealed to the nineteenth century. In the midst of increasingly sombre surroundings, the quaint, remote world of the Middle Ages offered colour, elegance, ritual, and pageantry. While such ritual doubtless appealed to man's desire for order and stability, it also satisfied purely aesthetic hungers. Medieval stained glass windows and illuminated manuscripts could hardly fail to attract artists like Dante Gabriel Rossetti who painted under skies being darkened by industry. The extreme example of the Eglinton Tournament suggests the delight in pageantry and colour afforded by medieval practices. When the coronation of Queen Victoria was modernised and divested of much of its medieval pomp, the disappointed Earl of Eglinton sponsored a chivalric extravaganza complete with a formal procession, medieval costumes, jousting, a Queen of Beauty, and thousands of participants. The event was not just a frolic for the idle rich, for it attracted a crowd of spectators numbering between sixty and eighty thousand, and press coverage—which ranged from mockery to measured admiration—by its volume alone suggests the cultural significance of the tournament. For an age of mass production, urban dwelling, and the consequent blighting of nature's brightness and of human individuality—likewise an age of utilitarianism and sober social customs which prescribed the frock coat and iron corset—the flamboyance of prancing chargers and glint-

ing armour, fluttering pennons and colourful pavilions exerted great attraction. The notion of English gentlemen in
1839 reviving the lapsed customs of the tourney is on one
level ludicrous. Trollope satirised such a plan in *Bar-
chester Towers* (1857), where one gentleman eschews tilt-
ing at a flour sack to preserve his clothing, while another
trips his horse with the unwieldy twelve-foot lance. Yet
the very fact that so many participants lavished so much
money on accoutrements and so much time in preparing,
to be watched by so many spectators who could share the
experience only vicariously, testifies that the Eglinton
tournament addressed significant needs arising from what
Matthew Arnold later termed the deficiency of the 'poetical' in 'the age and all one's surroundings.' To him nineteenth-century England was 'not unprofound, not ung-
rand, not unmoving:—but *unpoetical*' [from *The Letters
of Matthew Arnold to Arthur Hugh Clough,* 1932]. (pp. 18-
21)

While the Middle Ages might awaken the imagination and
supply pleasing colours and tones, artists clearly had to
face modern technical matters related to their media. In
literature this issue received extensive attention from critics who insisted that poets address timely concerns in
modern forms and language. In her verse novel *Aurora
Leigh* (1857), which dealt with current issues such as materialism, illegitimacy, and prostitution, Elizabeth Barrett
Browning stated the argument for contemporaneity. Medieval works tended to exaggerate events and figures of the
past, and more important, to diminish awareness of the
grandeur of one's own age:

> All actual heroes are essential men,
> And all men possible heroes; every age,
> Heroic in proportion . . .
> . . . Ay but every age
> Appears to souls who live in't (ask Carlyle)
> Most unheroic. . . .
> . . . That's wrong thinking, to my mind,
> And wrong thoughts make poor poems . . .
> Nay if there's room for poets in the world . . .
> Their sole work is to represent the age,
> Their age, not Charlemagne's . . .
> [That] spends more passion, more heroic heat,
> Betwixt the mirrors of its drawing rooms,
> Than Roland with his knights at Roncesvalles
> . . . King Arthur's self
> Was commonplace to Lady Guenever,
> And Camelot to minstrels seemed as flat
> As Fleet Street to our poets.

Similarly, Robert Browning's 'Tray' (1879) disparaged
modern celebrations of knights written in the archaic style
of medieval romances. Such tedious, artificial poems,
'Tray' implies, are decidedly inferior to a realistic story
about a heroic dog (concluding with a topical protest
against vivisection) recounted in contemporary language.

In a critical climate encouraging modernity and 'relevance', Tennyson's Arthurian poems drew fire for being
irrelevant and artifical, in both style and subject matter.
As one critic admonished, 'The old epics will probably
never be surpassed, any more than the old coats of mail;
and for the same reason; nobody wants the article; . . .
they are become mere curiosities' [William J. Fox, *Westminster Review,* 14 (January 1831)]. Even Ruskin, who

was so much attracted to the creative economic example
of the Middle Ages, felt that the 'treasures of wisdom' and
incomparable 'word-painting' of Tennyson's *Idylls of the
King* were squandered: 'it seems to me that so great power
ought not to be spent on visions of things past but on the
living present. For one hearer capable of feeling the depth
of this poem I believe ten would feel a depth quite as great
if the stream flowed through things nearer the hearer'
[quoted in *Alfred Lord Tennyson: A Memoir,* 1897]. Although most critics celebrated Tennyson's felicitous language and imagery, they generally concurred that 'to be-
witch us with our own daily realities, and not with their
unreal opposites, is a still higher task' [John Sterling,
Quarterly Review, 70 (September, 1843)]. In part such objections arose from critics' sense that modern treatments
of the Middle Ages distorted actuality. Sentimental views
of the past obscured not only distant history, but also the
relative merits of the present. Yet many critics conversely
recognised that creative distortion of fact could illuminate
essential truth. [Walter Bagehot, in *National Review,* 9
(October 1859)] argued, for example, that 'the events of
the chivalric legend are better adapted to sustained and
prolonged poetry than the events of . . . the present
day . . . because they abound much less in dangerous
detail, . . . give us a sort of large-hand copy of life which
it is comparatively easy to understand.' Unfettered by
petty facts, literature based on medieval matter could reflect universal concerns.

Other critics defended works set in the Middle Ages on
grounds that they allowed aesthetic pleasure and free play
of the imagination. Despite his own argument for contemporary relevance, Ruskin also recognised an aesthetic appeal inherent in the medieval world but not in his own:
'On the whole, these are much *sadder* ages than the early
ones; not sadder in a noble and deep way, but in a dim
wearied way,—the way of ennui, and jaded intellect. . . .
The Middle Ages had their wars and agonies, but also intense delights. Their gold was dashed with blood; but ours
is sprinkled with dust' [*The Works of John Ruskin,* V, edited by E. T. Cook and Alexander Wedderburn, 1904]. Arnold echoed these sentiments when he declared [quoted in
James Knowles, "Aspects of Tennyson, II: A Personal
Reminiscence," *The Nineteenth Century,* 33 (1893)] that
although the Middle Ages were marked by 'a strong sense
of . . . irrationality', they exerted a 'peculiar charm and
aroma', 'poetically the greatest charm and refreshment
possible for me.'

Though such critics recognised the value of aesthetic escape from pressing contemporary issues and a comparatively drab environment, the important Arthurian works
of the nineteenth century do not merely afford temporary
diversion or aesthetic relief. While Tennyson, for example,
acknowledged the romantic value of remoteness—'it is the
distance that charms me in the landscape, the picture and
the past, and not the immediate to-day in which I move'
[in a letter to Frances Arnold dated 17 December 1860]—
he also insisted that his was not escapist art; it was essentially didactic and aimed at modern problems. He adopted
medieval setting and story in part because he felt that men
would accept lessons couched in myth and romance.

Ironically, Tennyson, who was criticised for writing about the past rather than the present, was also criticised for not being sufficiently medieval. Reviewers argued that he had merely depicted Victorian characters and concerns in the garb of the early era. Thus Gerard Manley Hopkins [in a letter to Richard Watson Dixon dated 27 February 1879] termed the *Idylls* 'Charades from the Middle Ages' in which picturesque effects—like 'real lace and good silks and real jewelry' used in a blatantly artificial tableau—never disguised the Victorian presence.

The pressure of this critical debate over setting poetry in the Middle Ages probably prompted Tennyson to frame his early medieval narratives within contemporary scenes. In *The Princess* (1847), for example, a modern episode introduces the timely issue of higher education for women. The subject then develops in a romance vaguely set in the medieval period. This rather daring blend of old and new struck many readers as merely absurd. When Browning heard of the scheme—a female university to be described in a 'fairy-tale'—he declared [in a letter to Elizabeth Barrett dated 31 January 1846] such anachronistic treatment to be unsuitable for a world in which 'locomotives . . . must keep the very ghosts of [fairies] away.' Although some critics echoed Browning's judgement and held that the medieval ambience and the contemporary concerns blurred each other, Tennyson by pursuing what he termed a 'strange diagonal' between romance and realism, medieval and modern, succeeded in treating the controversial 'woman question' with humour, sensitivity, and detachment. Approaching the contemporary issue through medieval fiction allowed him to convey a complex attitude, to champion the cause of university training for women and to oppose male domination, while simultaneously defending the values of traditional female roles rejected by his educationally ambitious heroine, Princess Ida. In addition, throughout the medieval tale he subtly employed references to modern scientific thought in order to suggest that traditional attitudes must adapt to a new sense of mankind and the world.

Tennyson similarly used a modern frame for the earliest published portion of his Arthurian *Idylls,* embedding the narrative of Arthur's death within 'The Epic' (1842), and English idyl which illustrates customs among the nineteenth-century gentry. The modern frame raises the topic of prevailing critical debate—the value of old literary forms and subject matter for the present century. In the introduction, the host of a Christmas party reads the salvaged fragment of an Arthurian epic which its author had years before cast into the fireplace. The poet had destroyed most of the work because he decided that 'truth / Looks freshest in the fashion of the day' and that the epic form is outmoded—'why should any man / Remodel models?' Moreover, the subject matter—the Round Table society—is extinct, and 'nature brings not back the Mastodon, / Nor we those [heroic] times.' Yet the rescued poetic fragment proves to be no mastodon of verse, for it affects the listeners, particularly the narrator. Stirred by the reading, he dreams of Arthur's returning to nineteenth-century England, freshly dressed—like truth—in the fashion of the day, as 'a modern gentleman / Of stateliest port.' When the narrator awakens to the sound of Christmas

bells memorialising another ideal figure who promised a second coming, we fully see the applications of the medieval tale to the modern world described in the frame. This contemporary world has been characterised by one speaker, Parson Holmes, as a declining society: 'all the old honour had from Christmas gone'; schism, geology, and debates over church procedure have rendered a 'general decay of faith / Right through the world.' This modern complaint is echoed in the medieval narrative by Sir Bedivere, who laments Arthur's defeat and the failure of the Round Table order: 'For now I see the true old times are dead, / When every morning brought a noble chance, / And every chance brought out a noble knight.' Bedivere himself links the early promise of Camelot to the birth of Christ: 'Such times have been not since the light that led / The holy Elders with the gift of myrrh.' Thus the culmination of the modern coda, linking the envisioned reappearance of Arthur in the modern world with the tolling of Christmas bells, signals an opportunity for the ideals of Christianity and of medieval chivalry to be restored to the world Parson Holmes has declared moribund. In effect we see that, as King Arthur comments, 'The old order changeth, yielding place to new, / And God fulfills Himself in many ways, / Lest one good custom should corrupt the world.' Each day—even in the nineteenth century—brings a noble chance, and each chance can bring forth a noble knight—although chance, knight, and nobility can be clothed (like Arthur in the narrator's dream) in the fashion of the new order and the new day.

In 'The Epic' Tennyson joins the medieval narrative and its modern frame to suggest two important principles about nineteenth-century medieval works. The first arises from a cyclical concept of history and implies that man may learn from the examples of the past. After suggesting that the Arthurian order recaptured the ideals of early Christianity, the conclusion, which depicts a symbolic second coming of Arthur and memorialises the birth of Christ, implies that the modern world can, despite Parson Holmes' harangue, recapitulate the ideals common to Christian and Arthurian society. As the Round Table order attempted to remodel the model of Christ, the Victorian world may profit from the patterns of the past. The second important principle suggested by the combined modern frame and the framed medieval narrative is that for the contemporary world, literature will provide the enlightened leadership supplied in earlier periods by messiahs and kings, or in more recent times by ministers. In declaring that there is 'no anchor, none, / To hold by,' the Parson in effect betrays his responsibility to represent just such an anchor. The modern parallel to King Arthur—or to the Parson—as a spiritual leader of men is the diffident poet Everard Hall, whose epic fragment inspires the narrator to dream of Arthur and the ideals of Camelot restored to the present age. Whereas Tennyson's combining medieval and modern elements in *The Princess* distances a volatile contemporary issue and permits him simultaneously to commend and to caution against feminist attitudes, the similar combination in 'The Epic' and the 'Morte d'Arthur' establishes the contemporaneity of a superficially remote Arthurian narrative. Throughout the century poets used medieval materials both to focus on modern concerns through the objectifying distance permitted by a medieval setting or myth and to discern in traditional tales emblems meaningful, even instructive, to the present. (pp. 22-6)

What is most significant about readers' and writers' increasing awareness of multiple versions of Arthurian legend is that nineteenth-century Arthurian poets recognised that they were writing in a tradition, that they were selecting tales from various versions and were consciously deleting, adding, and rearranging details, motifs, and themes. They were consciously crafting new expressions in an already rich and manifold body of literature. This awareness contrasts markedly with the approaches of writers between Malory and Tennyson, who by and large appropriated characters and motifs to works which otherwise had little kinship to Arthurian tradition. In many instances, the nineteenth-century writer measured his own innovations against medieval treatments to emphasise his contribution and either his fidelity to tradition or the independence of his vision. While Tennyson, for example, cited suggestions in Joseph of Exeter, Albéric des Trois-Fontaines, and the *Brut ab Arthur* to justify his portrait of Arthur, he also liked to emphasise the individuality of his Lancelot, his 'own great imaginative knight' [*The Poems of Tennyson,* 1969]. Tennyson specifically proposed to modernise the tales and to show their special relevance to his age. As Hallam Tennyson explained about his father's treatment of Arthurian legends, he 'infused into them a spirit of modern thought and an ethical significance, . . . as indeed otherwise these archaic stories would not have appealed to the modern world at large' [*Alfred Lord Tennyson: A Memoir,* 1897]. When Tennyson read the suggestion that his Grail narrative echoed medieval treatments, he demurred: 'I can't conceive how the Grail . . . can well be treated by a poet of the 13th century from a similar point of view to mine, who write in the 19th, but, if so, I am rather sorry for it, as I rather piqued myself on my originality of treatment." Although medieval literature provided the fabric from which the *Idylls* were fashioned, the cut and style were to Tennyson's mind his own.

But while Tennyson intended to do something new and contemporary, he also aimed to partake of the rich literary heritage. He based his *Idylls* primarily on Malory's *Morte Darthur* and the *Mabinogion.* Justly noted for the quantity and eclecticism of his reading, however, he also informed his sense of the Middle Ages by investigating not only medieval romance and songs, but also studies of medieval literature, history, and folklore—and some of the material he probably read in Welsh. Swinburne likewise conducted 'research' of sorts for his Arthurian poetry. Before reshaping the Tristram legend, he read all available extant medieval versions of the story, including Malory, Scott's edition of *Sir Tristrem,* and Francisque Michel's *Tristan: Recueil de ce qui reste des poèmes relatifs à ses aventures, composés en français, en anglo-normand, et en grec dans les XII. et XIII. siècles* (1835-39), which includes Béroul and Thomas.

Swinburne may have known Wagner's opera *Tristan und Isolde* (based on Gottfried von Strassburg), the libretto for which was begun in 1857 and finished in 1859, although the opera was not actually performed until 1865. This point raises the issue of Wagner's possible influence on Victorian Arthurians. Tennyson expressed little interest in Wagner's operatic treatment of Arthurian legend. When one enthusiast recommended the subject of his opera on the son of Perceval, the Swan Knight Lohengrin, for a poem, the Laureate brushed the suggestion aside by noting 'what a remarkably sharp nose you've got' [as quoted in Charles Tennyson's *Alfred Tennyson,* 1949]. Arnold, who found Wagner's Tristram story interesting although the music was not, felt his own version of the legend, which antedated the opera, to be superior. Swinburne seems to have been alone among Victorian Arthurians in his enthusiasm for the German composer. Discussing his projected *Tristram of Lyonesse,* he wrote [in a letter to Edward Burne–Jones dated 4 November 1869] that 'Wagner's music ought to abash but does stimulate me.' Although Wagner's operatic reshaping of the Tristram legend represented, in effect, the overwhelming love tragedy of the age, it does not seem to have affected English poets as it did German audiences. Wagner's other Arthurian opera, *Parsifal,* based largely on the *Parzival* of Wolfram von Eschenbach, was his last opera, not performed until 1882 although the liberetto was apparently written by 1877, eight years after Tennyson completed the major nineteenth-century version of the Grail story in English.

Swinburne purposefully consulted medieval versions of the Tristram story because he intended to work within established tradition, to create a new poem 'acceptable for its orthodoxy and fidelity to the dear old story'. Although he could not include 'a tithe of the various incidents given in the different old versions', he meant to include 'everything *pretty* that is of any importance, and is in keeping with the tone and spirit of the story'. He also planned to portray the legend more authentically than his contemporaries had: Arnold had 'transformed and recast the old legend, and Tennyson—as usual, if I may be permitted to say so—has degraded and debased it' [in a letter to R. H. Horne dated 15 February 1882]. We need not agree with Swinburne that Tennyson's 'Morte d'Albert' dressed Victorians in medieval costume and actually represented the modern 'divorce-court' more than a courtly past ('Under the Microscope') in order to recognise that such debate marked a serious interest among Victorian poets in the place of their works in Arthurian tradition.

Clearly not all nineteenth-century writers were so much concerned with literary antecedents. After Arnold read the Tristram story in the *Revue de Paris,* he turned to Malory but found that his own poem 'was in the main formed, and I could not well disturb it' [in a letter to Herbert Hill dated 5 November 1852]. Except for echoing the summary of the thirteenth-century French Vulgate *Ystoire de Merlin* which prefaces Southey's edition of Malory, and echoing the *Morte Darthur* in the haunting last line, Arnold's *Tristam and Iseult* distinctly resists many traditional elements of the legend. Also countering the general concern with tradition were writers like William Morris, who may be said to have subscribed unconsciously to Scott's theory that 'tradition, generally speaking, is a sort of perverted alchemy which converts gold into lead' [Sir Walter Scott, *Quarterly Review,* 1 (1809)]. Far from rehashing events in

The Round Table in the hall of Winchester Castle, probably made in the 13th c. and decorated in Henry VII's reign. The Tudor rose in the center and the twenty-four alternating spokes in white and green demonstrate the Tudor claim to descent from Arthur.

earlier works, Morris, once inspired by Malory, freely invented details and formulated radically independent conceptions of characters.

Yet even the poems of Arnold and Morris fall well within Arthurian tradition. Romancers of the Middle Ages, who used basic legends again and again, frequently altered plot, recombining narrative details and familiar motifs to create many different versions of a single legend. Variety in plot, literary form, and style have always marked Arthurian literature, as versions of the Tristram legend ranging from Béroul's twelfth-century poem to Malory's late fifteenth-century prose attest. Whether a writer—like Gottfried and Swinburne—linked Tristram's death to the classical motif of the black and white sails; or—like Malory and Tennyson—described Mark's ignoble stroke; or—like Arnold—adapted no medieval version, the legend allowed a variety of archetypal and symbolic effects. What Arnold, Morris, Tennyson, and Swinburne shared with medieval writers, whether or not they followed narrative details, was recognition of the expressive, didactic, and symbolic potential of Arthurian legends. Even the earliest medieval versions are set in the distant past or the long-ago of fairy tale and myth. That they may initially have derived from historical events and actual customs notwithstanding, the tales became in medieval romances meaningful emblems rather than slices of life. The most encompassing symbolic potential lies in the idea of Camelot as an ideal order. The concept of the Round Table inextricably combines social, political, ethical, and religious ideals in a society which flourished yet ultimately failed. Thus Arthurian story provided for nineteenth-century writers a broad canvas and crowded palette with which to delineate significant contemporary concerns and to paint either brightly optimistic pictures of human potential or darker possibilities.

As the key which unlocked the treasury of Arthurian legend for the nineteenth century, Malory's *Morte Darthur* can scarcely be emphasised sufficiently. His style—curiously diffuse for modern readers—was not always admired. Scott, celebrating the 'high tone of chivalry', nevertheless described the work as 'extracted at hazard, and without much art or combination' (preface to *Sir Tristrem*). Tennyson thought the *Morte Darthur* 'much the best' of chivalric romances. Even though it contained 'very fine things', however, they were 'all strung together without Art' [*Alfred Lord Tennyson: A Memoir*, 1897]. Yet in these 'very fine things' distilled from Malory's voluptuous presentation, Tennyson found the heady essence for his own greatest work. This essence, curiously, is conflict. The *Morte Darthur* depicts a world of conflict ranging from the physical encounters of international battles and civil wars, tournaments, and the almost incessant jousting of individual knights; to the emotional clashes of illicit love, adultery, and jealousy; to the spiritual conflict of religious faith belied by action, the hope of eternal salvation jeopardised by awareness of immediate sin. Stories of King Arthur and the Round Table appealed to Victorian poets because, for all their remoteness and quaintness, they deal with ethical, moral, and emotional problems that transcend custom, place, or time. (pp. 30-3)

Beverly Taylor, "The Return of Arthur: Nineteenth-Century British Medievalism and Ar-thurian Tradition," in The Return of King Arthur: British and American Arthurian Literature Since 1800 *by Beverly Taylor and Elisabeth Brewer, D. S. Brewer, 1983, pp. 15-33.*

An excerpt from William Morris's *Defence of Guenevere* (1858)

But, knowing now that they would have her speak,
She threw her wet hair backward from her brow,
Her hand close to her mouth touching her cheek,

As though she had had there a shameful blow,
And feeling it shameful to feel aught but shame
All through her heart, yet felt her cheek burned so,

She must a little touch it; like one lame
She walked away from Gauwaine, with her head
Still lifted up; and on her cheek of flame

The tears dried quick; she stopped at last and said:
"O knights and lords, it seems but little skill
To talk of well-known things past now and dead.

God wot I ought to say, I have done ill,
And pray you all forgiveness heartily!
Because you must be right, such great lords; still

Listen—suppose your time were come to die,
And you were quite alone and very weak. . . . ."

William Morris, in his Defence of Guenevere, *in* Portrait of the Victorian Period, *Third Edition, edited by Jerome Hamilton Buckley and George Benjamin Woods, Scott, Foresman and Company, 1965.*

THEMES AND MOTIFS

Eugène Vinaver

[*Vinaver was a Russian-born educator and author who served as editor of the journal* Arthuriana *and as president of the Society for the Study of Medieval Language and Literature from 1939 to 1948. In the following excerpt, Vinaver investigates themes of chivalry and courtly romance in Arthurian literature from Chrétien to Malory, affirming that "Malory's work is in fact a complete negation of the two principles upon which the French prose romances were based."*]

If I were to choose a motto for this paper I would suggest the famous lines from the last act of Richard II:

No thought is contented.
The better sort, as thoughts of things divine,

> Are intermix'd with scruples and do set
> The word itself against the word (v.v.11-14)

These lines were written four and a half centuries after the first appearance of courtly romance on the European literary scene, and yet they seem to sum up the very essence of the genre that in the hands of poets like Chrétien de Troyes revolutionized the literary life of medieval France and subsequently of the whole of Western Europe.

Thoughts intermixed with scruples were not in themselves a novelty; they had played a prominent part in the composition of some of the great epic poems that antedated the birth of courtly romance by half a century or more. There is perhaps no better example of ambiguity in early narrative poetry than the unresolved conflict between Roland and Oliver, for the poet never tells us which of them was right: "Rolant est proz e Oliver est sage" [Roland is bold, Olivier is wise], he writes, and because by the standards of feudal chivalry, prowess and wisdom are virtues of equal value. He says in the very next line that both Roland and Oliver are men of outstanding valor: "Ambedui unt merveillus vasselage" [And both of them are marvelously brave].

To juxtapose two contrasting ideas or images was by no means an uncommon procedure at a time when no one preached the classical doctrine of unity. What romance added to this practice was the insistence on the elucidation of the theme, the urge to make the problems of human behavior more manifest and the conflicts more articulate, more meaningful. Along with Abelard's device of *sic et non,* romance writers transferred into the secular sphere the scholastic *manifestatio* which helped to make the problems less soluble and the controversies more acute.

The term *courtly love* is, of course, not authentically medieval. We all know that it owes its existence to the nineteenth-century scholar Gaston Paris and that it has been under attack in recent years. But it does represent something for which no more convenient name has been found. What it stands for, so far as twelfth-century poets are concerned, particularly poets like Chrétien de Troyes and his contemporaries, is not a coherent systematic doctrine, not a fixed set of rules of behavior, but rather the means of discovering fascinating and insoluble problems concerning the psychology and ethics of love, problems that are all the more fascinating because they are insoluble. Courtly love in the twelfth century is primarily a matter of controversy, a rich source of dilemma which it is the poet's task to explore, to elucidate and to discuss often from two opposite points of view without necessarily committing himself to either. One major issue which is central to all courtly literature is that of love versus honor. It dominates Chrétien's most famous romance *The Story of the Cart* or *The Romance of Lancelot;* and because modern critics, unlike medieval poets, are more interested in seeking solutions than in understanding problems, hardly a year goes by without some solution being found, some new meaning being forced upon that particular work.

The story is that of a rescue which is essentially a chivalric quest and which has two distinct aims: that of delivering Guinevere from her captor Meleagant and that of giving Lancelot the opportunity of exhibiting his valor and his devotion to his lady, the opportunity of proving that he is worthy of her love. The most striking example of Lancelot's commitment to this second purpose of the quest—which might be described as its spiritual purpose—occurs very early in the story, in the scene in which for the first time we see the mysterious figure of a knight walking, followed by his wounded horse, in what he thinks is the direction taken by the abductor of the queen. It is then that he meets a dwarf driving a cart. The cart was in those days the equivalent of the pillory; it was an ignominious vehicle used for carrying prisoners to the place of punishment. Lancelot asks the dwarf if he has seen the queen, and the dwarf offers to take him to the place where he would have early news of her.

Only a momentary hesitation precedes Lancelot's acceptance of this offer, but this momentary hesitation is perhaps the essence of the whole work. What Lancelot has to decide is whether, in order to accelerate the rescue of the Queen, he can legitimately degrade himself by riding in the cart, whether he can sacrifice his honor as a knight for the sake of his duty as a lover. The hesitation here takes the form of a dialogue in Lancelot's mind between two allegorical figures, Reason and Love. It is Reason that counsels Lancelot to refrain from degrading himself, but Reason, the poet tells us, dwells only on the knight's lips, not in his heart: in his heart dwells Love. The dialogue between Reason and Love is symmetrically arranged with six lines devoted to each, and each group of six lines corresponds to one of Lancelot's steps. This crucial dialogue can be described as the scene of Lancelot's two steps, perhaps the most important two steps in the history of literature.

We are not told whether the choice he makes is the right one, but the sequel is not devoid of a certain element of dramatic surprise. When Lancelot, after innumerable trials and adventures and after having defeated Guinevere's captor Meleagant in a fierce battle, is at last admitted to her presence, she receives him coldly and refuses to speak to him. And so he goes away in despair, convinced that it was his acceptance of the dwarf's offer that caused his lady's displeasure and that she is unable to forgive him the loss of chivalric honor which he accepted so readily. He will soon learn that the reason for Guinevere's anger is the reverse: she found fault with his conduct not because he rode in the cart but because he hesitated for two steps before getting into it. The dictates of love, according to her, should not be a matter of debate for a knight-lover: there should not be even a moment's hesitation between the contrasting ideals that were responsible for Lancelot's two steps. Love and Reason. Reason must yield to Love without question, without creating in the lover's mind anything that could be described as a moral dilemma. Not many people in the story, apart from Guinevere herself and ultimately Lancelot, hold this view. Most of those who see Lancelot in the cart think he has disgraced himself and some of them despise him for it. And so we are left to wonder what it is that Lancelot ought to have done. Was it right or was it wrong for him to hesitate? We don't really know.

And here I must pause to consider the aesthetic implications of this state of affairs. We see nothing abnormal or even unusual in modes of thinking which allow contradictions to remain unresolved—we are quite prepared to listen to an argument developed on the lines of *Sic et non.* But when it comes to a serious work of fiction we regard any unanswered question as an artistic imperfection. Why? Simply because we have been brought up to believe that each work must have one central meaning. And so we cannot rest until we have decided which side Chrétien was on: on the side of chivalry or on the side of courtly love conceived as total dedication to the service of the beloved no matter what sacrifices such a service may involve. And because Chrétien's supreme artistry enables us to make a perfect case for either interpretation, critics since the turn of the century have been having a glorious time pulling now in one direction, now in the other—fighting as they so often do over a nonexistent issue. If only they had paid attention to the fact that ambivalence figures prominently in medieval lyric poetry and fiction as a source of inspiration and of pleasurable emotion, they would have realized the irrelevance of their approach and we would all have been spared many tiresome controversies. Like all writers of courtly romance, Chrétien aims at an explicit presentation of the central problem of his work—so explicit, in fact, that it appears insoluble. Lancelot may have hesitated for only two steps before getting into the cart, but in the reader's mind the hesitation is meant to go on indefinitely, and the romance itself will not answer the question of what the right thing was for Lancelot to do.

There is one type of work in which a modern reader admits this kind of situation and that is tragedy, in which the tragic dilemma itself can become a unifying factor and can act as an emotional and conceptual center. Nothing of the kind happens in Chrétien's *Lancelot;* there is nothing there that could be called tragic. Lancelot may experience great distress after having been rebuked by Guinevere, but he is soon comforted when he discovers the real reason for her coldness and when at last he realizes how he was at fault from her point of view. What we have to accept is an aesthetic situation in which an insoluble problem instead of being a source of tragedy becomes one of intellectual enjoyment. And once we have accepted this we shall understand why, while going through many trials and tribulations, Arthurian characters in the early romances never cast a dark shadow on the smiling landscape in which they move.

Half a century elapsed before Lancelot appeared again in a work of fiction, this time in the spacious *Roman de Lancelot du Lac,* a prose romance that formed the central and by far the most ambitious part of the great Arthurian prose cycle produced between the years 1220 and 1225. The landscape continues to be bright and smiling but no longer for the same reasons: Lancelot and Guinevere seem to have left their courtly dialectics far behind. They now live in a world in which it seldom occurs to anyone to contrast reason and love.

A perfectly consistent philosophy of love and honor takes the place of unresolved controversies—a process that bears some resemblance to contemporary developments in the field of theological thinking. A story such as the epi-

sode of the cart could find little justification in a work that makes every effort to show within the considerably widened boundaries of Arthur's realm how love and honor can serve to exalt one another. At the same time, however, the episode was too much a part of the known story of Lancelot to be left out. So the prose writer reproduced it accurately but gave it a new motivation. Lancelot hesitates to get into the cart because he does not know whether he can trust the dwarf. In this way the initial dilemma is avoided. The degrading nature of the vehicle is deliberately played down, Lancelot is not concerned about his loss of honor, and the entire episode is transferred from the original spiritual level of the quest to its adventurous or narrative level.

But what of Guinevere's displeasure, which is also part of the episodic content of the romance? It too is there, but again the motivation is altered. She is angry with Lancelot for two hitherto unknown reasons: he left the court without asking her permission; and, as a result of Morgan le Fay's extraordinary machinations involving the use of the supernatural, he has parted with Guinevere's ring. The queen thinks that she has reason to be jealous, but the misunderstanding is soon cleared up and all ends well.

Not that the cultivation of controversy as an intellectual pastime and an artistic device had suddenly ceased. On the contrary, it continued, sometimes even in more acute form than ever before, but the problems that attracted the attention of thirteenth-century writers were not the same as earlier. They were if anything of wider significance, and the practice of leaving them unresolved had considerably more serious consequences for all concerned. The antinomy of love and honor which had proved to be an inexhaustible source of lively argument in courtly lyric and early romance gives way to a harmonious view of chivalric life—a change that fully accounts for the new version of the cart episode. But as one antinomy goes, another takes its place, another category of "thoughts intermix'd with scruples." There is in the French Arthurian cycle a fundamental dichotomy fully developed in the last branches: the divine chivalry of the Grail on the one hand and the earthly chivalry of the Round Table. Corbenic, and Camelot on the other. So far any attempt made to reduce the Grail theme and the Arthurian theme proper to a harmonious synthesis has proved futile.

What is characteristic of the work as a whole is the deliberate sharpening of the contrast, setting the two worlds—that of the Grail and that of Arthur—against one another. Divine grace symbolized by the Grail is accorded to the pure knight Galahad and to a lesser extent to his two close companions, Perceval and Bors, but is withheld from the greatest of all Arthurian heroes, Lancelot. No one can tell which of the two ideals should dominate the other, with the result that it was possible for Paolo and Francesca to be the victims of the enchanting prose of the Lancelot romance in the famous scene describing the first kiss of Lancelot and Guinevere and "to read that day no more" (*Inf.*, v.138), just as it is possible for some modern readers to interpret the entire cycle in terms of the Grail theme alone. No one can claim to have understood its meaning who fails to see simultaneously the two facets of the work and to derive from their juxtaposition the kind of enjoyment that a true artistic experience can provide. And if the work has remained virtually unknown in modern times it is not simply because of its length and complexity but because it presupposes in the reader the ability to savor a contrast without seeking to reconcile the two sides, the readiness to contemplate two boldly juxtaposed ideals.

Nor is there any tragic sense about their juxtaposition, any more than there is in the earlier forms of romance. The author uses multiple motivation, so that each important event is accounted for in a variety of ways—an arrangement which rules out the tragic concept of a single determining cause.

The remarkable thing is, however, that the ideological cleavage does not interfere in any way with the careful planning and scrupulously coherent structure of the narrative. It is in fact one of the most fully integrated compositions of its kind. It is an elaborate and a wonderfully well thought-out *Summa* of various, often heterogeneous themes which the twelfth century had bequeathed to the writers of the new age, a work inspired by a consistent desire to establish connections where none had existed before and to show how any given tradition could acquire added interest by being linked with others. It was in this work that the Grail became part of the Lancelot romance, for the Grail hero here is not Perceval, but Galahad, Lancelot's son. This is only one of a great number of material links between the courtly world of Lancelot and the spiritual world of the Grail. The movement toward greater cohesion, so typical of late medieval fiction, was nowhere more manifest than in the narrative technique of the Arthurian prose cycle.

And yet this urge to establish coherent relationships at the narrative level coexists with an equally strong tendency to accentuate contrasts on the ideological level—a significant discrepancy between the treatment of the *matter* and the *meaning,* the coherence of the former and the deliberate ambiguity of the latter—an ambiguity that most of us still find difficult to accept. When Ferdinand Lot published his book on the prose *Lancelot* and established the pattern of its narrative texture, many of us felt that this was a challenge to find a corresponding degree of coordination at the ideological level—to discover the common spiritual denominator for the major themes of the work. Myrrha Lot-Borodine and many others after her displayed great ingenuity in trying to reconcile the two, but all to no purpose. Galahad and Lancelot to this day resist any attempt to treat them as facets of a single spiritual entity. No such entity exists except in the minds of people who are incapable of seeing the validity of two contrasting philosophies, a regrettable and typically modern limitation imposed upon us by our outmoded literary conventions.

It was in this complex and highly sophisticated form that Arthurian romance reached Sir Thomas Malory, the last and the greatest of medieval Arthurian writers, while he was composing his *Book of Sir Lancelot and Queen Guinevere,* which was to be followed by the greatest of all his books, *The Tale of the Death of King Arthur.* On a superficial level he merely dramatized the traditional stories and gave them a more realistic coloring. Lancelot meets a cart

driven by two woodcutters who have been sent by Meleagant to the forest to fetch wood. It is clearly not the cart used to carry prisoners to the place of punishment. Neither Guinevere nor Lancelot is concerned about its possible significance. Far from hesitating to get into it Lancelot orders the two men to let him ride in it, and upon their refusal he strikes one of them with his mailed gauntlet and kills him. The other woodcutter, seeing what has happened and fearing for his own life, offers to take Lancelot wherever he wants to go. And as Lancelot triumphantly jumps into the cart the long history of the episode is concluded in a way which would have surprised its original inventor.

It is a far cry from the allegorical debate between Reason and Love to the brutal killing of the woodcutter, but we must remove once and for all from our minds any notion of Malory's direct connection with the original form of Arthurian romance and particularly with Chrétien de Troyes. Like his contemporaries Malory was a reader of prose romances not of the Arthurian verse romances of the twelfth century. The transition from the latter to the former had been a spectacular change from fantasy to tangible reality. So that when Malory came to his high theme, what he had before him was not an allegorical vision of chivalric rescue but a whole world of complex human relationships, of conflicts and conquests, passions and friendships, great deeds and heroic sacrifices. And as I have just said, in that vast composition embodying the whole history of Arthurian fellowship from its foundation to its downfall as well as a variety of other themes and motifs old and new, the remarkably skillful coordination of disparate episodes and characters at the narrative level went hand in hand with the unresolved antinomy of earthly and divine chivalry. This is precisely what is so alien to the modern mind and indeed to Malory's temperament as a storyteller.

Malory's work, in spite of its outward resemblance to the earlier forms of Arthurian fiction, is in fact a complete negation of the two principles upon which the French prose romances were based. At the narrative level he makes little attempt to imitate, let alone reproduce, the system of cross links, references, echoes, and anticipations which forms the sophisticated fabric of his French models, while at the ideological level he fails to see how one can glorify both Lancelot and Galahad and at the same time recognize the spiritual cleavage between them. He can see no essential difference between the chivalry of Lancelot and that of his son Galahad. He even thinks that the sword that Merlin left for Lancelot, the sword of fratricide, could be used equally well by Galahad. The result is a work from which one can deduce a simple and coherent philosophy of chivalric behavior but no consistent design linking the various episodes with one another, a work consisting of many noble tasks, unified much more by their spirit than by their matter.

Thus the two most characteristic features of medieval romantic fiction vanish from the Arthurian scene; but in their place something new and vital arises which confers true greatness upon Malory's work: an awareness of the tragic potential inherent in human passions and loyalties.

The discovery and the fulfillment of this potential occurs in Malory's last book, *The Most Piteous Tale of the Morte Arthur sauns guerdon,* and the transformation of romance into a tragic prose tale is achieved by the seemingly simple process of isolating one vital theme from a number of concomitant themes. What Malory does is to place in the center of things the one single cause of what Caxton calls so startlingly the "dolorous deth and departyng out of thys world of them al" (III.1260n.), namely Lancelot's inability to choose between the two loyalties by which he is equally bound; loyalties not to abstract ideals of honor and love but to real people: Guinevere, Arthur, Gawain and the whole Fellowship of the Round Table. Hence the fatal contrast between Lancelot and Gawain, the irony of Gawain's death caused by a wound received from Lancelot, and finally the downfall of Arthur's kingdom. As in ancient Greek theater, tragedy is born here out of the concentration of the resources of language and thought upon an individual fate torn out of its original epic or cosmic content, a destiny that in virtue of its isolation can no longer be dissolved in an all embracing harmony of a vast mythical universe.

This was not William Caxton's idea of the book that he published in 1485—"thys noble and loyous book entytled le morte Darthur." He hoped that his readers would find in it enough variety of incident and character to see the story of the death of Arthur in a wide perspective in which joy and sadness would be balanced against each other. In so doing he distorted Malory's tragic vision and impressed upon the English-speaking world an image of Arthurian chivalry in which the "dolorous death and departing" is merely one incident among many. It is perhaps time that we began to see the work of a great prose writer in its true light and the history of Arthurian romance as an example of how the alchemy of art can change the pageantry of chivalric life with its decor of ever green woods and meadows into the human reality of Malory's most piteous *Tale* by the magic of simplification of structure and language.

Malory is probably the first writer to have brought the language of romance so close to ordinary speech and one of the few to realize that in order to speak to us convincingly, tragedy needs only the simple words of everyday life. Witness, for example, the relentless power of unadorned statement such as the brief remark that concludes the description of Lancelot's grief over the deaths of Arthur and Guinevere: "and there was no comfort that the Bysshop, nor syr Bors, nor none of his felowes coude make hym, it avaylled not" (III.1257).

Such is the last and perhaps the finest landmark in the long history of Arthurian romance, obscured by later adapters and even more by commentators, few of whom have noticed the changing panorama of the medieval literary scene. The great event brought about by the artistry of the last medieval Arthurian writers was the emergence of a new artistic vision from the old. To understand the full significance of this event and to experience it we have to see the work both in its aesthetic immediacy and as part of a complex historical process: two approaches which correspond to the two dimensions of any artistic achievement—two powerful sources of light thanks to which the

Tale of the Death of King Arthur appears in sharp relief as the conclusion of one great tradition and the first step toward another. (pp. 17-31)

> *Eugène Vinaver, "Landmarks in Arthurian Romance," in* The Expansion and Transformations of Courtly Literature, *edited by Nathaniel B. Smith and Joseph T. Snow, The University of Georgia Press, 1980, pp. 17-31.*

Brian Stone

[*Stone is a British educator who is well regarded for his numerous translations of medieval English literature, including* Sir Gawain and the Green Knight *(1959). In the following essay, Stone investigates aspects of kingship, chivalry, and courtly love in Arthurian literature from 1300 to 1500.*]

'Though ye be our king in that degree, ye are but a knight as we are, and ye are sworn unto knighthood as well as we.' Thus Sir Mador (*Malory*) to King Arthur. The circumstance was that Mador's cousin Sir Patrise had been poisoned by an apple handed to him in innocence by Queen Guinevere, but intended by the poisoner for Sir Gawaine; and Mador, requiring justice from Arthur, found it slow in coming. Significantly, in the French source, *La Mort le Roi Artu,* Arthur at first entertains the idea that Guinevere may be guilty, but neither Malory nor the poet of the *SMA* [the stanzaic *Le Morte Arthur*], both Englishmen, so tarnish the image of England's mythical hero king. As a super-knight among knights, but nevertheless himself 'but a knight', he should appear doubly just: he should not only set in motion the formal processes of the law, but also be motivated by an inward feeling for natural justice.

Malory generally insists on Arthur's perfection as a chivalric justicer and, like a good medieval preacher, he also gives prominence to exemplars of Arthur's opposite, like King Mark of the Tristram episodes. On one occasion, disguised in black, Mark attacks two of his guests from Arthur's court who are out on a night ride, and is beaten. His adversary, Sir Gaheris, having found out who he is, answers his plea for mercy with: 'Thou art a king anointed with chrism, and therefore thou shouldest hold with all men of worship; and therefore thou art worthy to die' (*Malory*). As Lamorak says to Tristram, in contrasting Mark and Arthur, 'The honour of both courts be not alike'.

The anointing with chrism and the obligation to hold with all men of worship were the two conerstones of the ideal of kingship in both the literature and the society of the time. Each carried a wealth of conceptions and assumptions, not all of which sort well together, though most of them bear on each other. The moral and spiritual obligations of accepting chrism on the one hand, and the attaining and holding of worship (=honour) on the other, were bound to be in frequent conflict. Such essential qualifications for knighthood as noble blood, wealth and murderous courage in conflict—to leave aside for the moment Christian devotion, loyalty and generosity, and the obligations to be humble, courteous and kind to women—are

Portrait of the Nine Worthies from a 14th c. French manuscript illustration. Arthur stands with his personal emblem third from right.

against the spirit of the Beatitudes. The two special knightly qualities of prowess, which means courage and all the skills of fighting including leadership, and of largesse, which means spiritual as well as practical generosity, underpin all other qualities, because prowess derives from rank and conquest, and the exercise of largesse depends on the ability to give. What was true of knights was even more true of kings.

Edward III, who set up the Order of the Garter in 1348, was the second of the many medieval European kings and princes to found a secular order of knighthood. Like his formidable warrior grandfather, Edward I, he was an Arthurian enthusiast, who took King Arthur and his Round Table as patterns of chivalry. Not surprisingly, Maurice Keen writes: 'Fifteenth-century chivalric literature is a little more true to life than is sometimes recognised'.

Edward III died in 1377, and the other warrior king of England of the period was Henry V (1413-22); a reading public of their or immediately subsequent times would expect some verisimilitude in the literary treatment of matters they knew about in real life, such as government, wars and jousting.

The three literary works upon which I shall mainly draw in discussing kingship are the stanzaic *Le Morte Arthur* (*circa* 1350), the alliterative *Morte Arthure* (*circa* 1400) and Malory's prose epic *Le Morte D'Arthur* (*circa* 1470, printed 1485 by Caxton). All are infused with English fourteenth- and fifteenth-century ideas and detail, and the *AMA* [the alliterative *Morte Arthure*] in particular is full of topical reference, while the magical and folkloristic matter of the twelfth- and thirteenth-century sources—Geoffrey of Monmouth, Wace, Layamon and so on—is severely curtailed. King Arthur's fight with the Giant of Mont St Michel, and Sir Gawain's fight against Sir Pria-

mus, whose sword caused unstaunchable wounds wherever it struck, are the only important magical episodes in the *AMA* which occur to me. Both are also treated by Malory, who bases his accounts mainly on the alliterative poem. I do not refer to the best of the English Arthurian romances, *Sir Gawain and the Green Knight,* because in it Arthur's rôle is largely formal, as the holder of the chivalric ring within which Gawain tackles his moral and religious problem.

As the nonpareil in armed combat, the remote national king from whose pseudo-history Edward I and Edward III sought to derive their ritual strength as heroic monarchs was an equivocal figure. In French Arthurian literature he appears often weak and indecisive, as if he were turning a blind eye to his queen's adultery with Lancelot, perhaps because he sets uniquely high value on the chivalric support he received from the adulterer—an outstanding example of the way in which the literature of male-oriented societies, from earliest times until at least the eighteenth century, sets honour between man and man above honour between man and woman. In actual combat, whether in war or tourney, this king tends to be closely supported by knights, whose help he requires after defeating two or three adversaries. But in some of the earliest versions and in several English romances, he is a warrior excelled not even by Lancelot, who can kill twenty—the standard number—or more of the enemy in a single sally. 'And Arthur was so bloody, that by his shield there might no man know him, for all was blood and brains on his sword' (*Malory*). In this kind of manifestation, Arthur sometimes exhibits the kind of grim humour which is found in Icelandic saga and Anglo-Saxon epic. In the great battle against the Roman Empire which forms the centre-piece of the *AMA,* Arthur:

Got close to Golopas, who had done greatest
  harm,
And cut him in two clean through the knees.
'Come down!' said the King, 'And account for
  it to your fellows!
You are too high by half, I have to tell you.
You'll be even hansomer soon, with Our Lord's
  help!'
And with his steely sword he struck off his head.

(AMA)

As a general, Arthur often holds his own force in reserve while he watches those of his loyal knights or allies conduct the opening exchanges. At the siege of Metz, though he reconnoitres the position personally, exposing himself carelessly to shots from the walls, Arthur notes that his French allies are fighting so feebly that he has to send a foraging force to find meat for them to eat, and he takes no part in the routing of the Duke of Lorraine's army outside the walls, before conducting the siege himself. The same principle of holding his own force in reserve, in order to complete a victory, was followed at Crécy, where Edward III divided his army in three, and led the reserve third himself.

At Crécy the chivalrous spirit of the French knights led them to disaster; approaching the English position with the evening sun in their faces, they decided to attack at once instead of waiting to attack the following morning with the rising sun behind them, as they had been advised. In comparable chivalric spirit, the blind King of Bohemia rode with them, and was killed. In the *AMA,* Arthur shows the same kind of tactical sense as Edward; when not prepared for a particular attack from the Romans:

. . . our wily King was wary and watched for
  this force,
And wisely withdrew his warriors from the
  woods,
But had the fires fed so that they flamed up high
As they trussed up their trappings and stole
  away.

(AMA)

Another resort of England's ideal king in this poem is the *chevauchée,* the medieval equivalent of scorching the earth. The king refrains from this raping, looting and burning while fighting in the French territories that he regards as his own, but uses it from Lorraine to Italy, being particularly severe on Tuscany. Lucius conducts a *chevauchée* through France, on his way to do battle with Arthur, and in the *SMA* Arthur conducts one in Lancelot's French dominions when prosecuting both Gawain's feud with Lancelot and his own revenge for the famous adultery. The *chevauchée* was a frequent resort of Edward's armies in France: his sweep from the Cotentin peninsula to Calais, fighting Crécy on the way, is well known, and the Black Prince similarly ravaged the vineyard region in the southwest during the campaign the main battle of which was at Poitiers (1346). There John II of France was captured, after which he languished as a prisoner in England until his ransom was paid. But then the hostages who replaced him escaped, and he felt in honour bound to return to London, where he died in 1364.

That was the kind of punctilio Arthur generally observes in medieval romance. He is scrupulous about ransom, but usually tries to rescue those of his knights who have been captured, before the battle ends. On the other hand, when the situation is particularly difficult, or the enemy has behaved atrociously, as Mordred did before and during the last battle, then Arthur orders that no quarter be given. However, when he takes an enemy city, such as Metz or Como, he responds to pleas from noble female citizens, and forbids his men to rape or kill them, or to attack or despoil children or holy men and women. It seems that Edward tried without success to prevent his men looting and raping in Caen during his Crécy campaign, and with some reluctance responded to the pleas of the burghers of Calais. To show mercy after a successful siege was to blunt a main aim of medieval warfare, which was the acquisition of loot.

Other ideals reflecting actual practice may be noted in the fictional Arthur's battle repertoire. He displays his own true banner and shield, unlike Mordred, who 'Because of his cowardice cast off his own device' (*AMA*). In contrast, Arthur exhorts his men:

Neither attend nor protect me, nor take account
  of me,
But be busy about my banners with your bright
  weapons,
Ensuring that strong knights sternly defend
  them,
And hold them nobly high for our army to see.

(AMA)

Arthur's battlefield orations, vows and encomiums over the dead in this poem are perhaps the best expression of heroic medieval spirit to be found anywhere, and they constantly remind the reader of their Anglo-Saxon precursors in *Beowulf* and the *Anglo-Saxon Chronicle.* The description of the king's grief over the dead Gawain, his expressions of lamentation and his vow to avenge his cousin make that passage one of the most moving in medieval literature. And his speeches in the face of his own imminent death after killing Mordred, unlike those containing the mystical concerns of the dying Arthur in the *SMA* and Malory, which are memorably caught by Tennyson, express the fundamental responsibilities of royal leadership: recognition of mutual service between king and lieger, recognition of achievement, provision for the succession and for his own burial, forgiveness to Guinevere, thanks to God and a final '*In manus*'. Here are the first six lines:

O King rightly crowned, in care I am left!
All my lordship is laid low to the ground.
Those who gave me gifts through the grace of
  God,
Maintained my majesty by their might in battle
And set me up in honour as Earth's master,
In a terrible time this trouble has come to
  them . . .

(AMA)

This matter of speech, whether it is made by or to the model of kingship, is important because through it the relation between king and subject is made explicit, in both meaning and tone, on the chief issues which affect them jointly: such issues as government policy, allegiance, alliances, personal and social justice, promotions and rewards, dynastic arrangements. The orations are found in all the Arthurian works so far mentioned, but are almost always more detailed, and more in accordance with the ideal practice in the real world, in the *AMA*. After a generous courtly feast, policy is decided in council, with the king opening the subject (such as replying to the demand that Arthur pay tribute and yield sovereignty to Rome). Members of the assembly speak in turn, in order of rank. On the occasion cited, the heir to the throne, Cador, speaks first, followed by the kings of Scotland, Brittany and Wales. When Lancelot's turn comes, he stresses that he is one of the 'lesser men'. Each of the six speakers recommends war on Rome, and all except Cador specify the number and kind of troops they will contribute to the campaign, and vows to perform a particular deed of prowess or revenge for past indignities. Though most vows in the romances call on divine personages, here each subject of Arthur's swears by Saint Veronica, patron saint of pilgrimage, which is ironically appropriate for soldiers who have Rome as their campaign target. (On other occasions kings and knights may swear by their own names, or by their lands, as King Mark does (*Malory*).)

Each of the vowed feats is achieved during the subsequent battles against Rome, hundreds of lines later, which shows that the making and fulfilling of vows in royal presence is structural in this kind of literature. A similar debate, though without the detail, appears in the *SMA*, the true hero of which is Lancelot, when he is exercising his kingship in his French province of Benwick (Bayonne? or in Brittany?). The subject there is whether Lancelot should continue his passive resistance to the forces of Arthur and Gawain which are laying waste his lands, or issue from his stronghold and defeat them. When Lancelot eventually yields to the necessity of doing battle against the king who originally knighted him, his response to the unhorsing of Arthur in the ensuing conflict is chivalrous in the highest imaginable degree:

> 'Alas,' said Lancelot, 'What woe
>   That ever I should see
> Unhorsed before my very eyes
>   The King who knighted me!'
> And then, dismounting from his steed
>   —So generous was he!—
> He horsed the King on it, telling him
>   Out of harm's way to flee.
>
>   (*SMA*)

One further element in the speech-making and council-holding processes must be mentioned. When faced with the enemy, the ideal king does not commit his forces to battle before offering a final parley, in order to establish the justice of his cause and to confirm the inveterate hostility of his foe.

Most battles, and some individual tourneys, begin and end with religious grace notes. The vow of the resolve, with allowance for the will of God, begins the context, and when the dust settles, God is given the credit. When the people of Brittany praise Arthur for killing the Giant of Mont St Michel, who raped their duchess and slit her to the navel in killing her, Arthur gives the credit to God alone before organising the distribution of treasure from the giant's lair, and goes even further in religious celebration of the

event, by setting up a monastery 'In memory of that martyr in her mountain resting-place' (*AMA*). Similarly, in Malory, after slaughtering 30,000 in the Battle of the Humber, Arthur 'kneeled down and thanked God meekly', and founded the Abbey of La Beale Adventure on the spot (*Malory*).

Yet in the romances as in real life there is constant tension between the Christian advocacy of peace and the heroic warrior's insistence on the resort of war. Just as throughout Edward's campaigns in France papal nuncios were always trying to prevent battles, so in the *SMA* a papal messenger visits Arthur in Carlisle to stop the war he and Gawain are waging:

> He read the letter of the Pope
>   For everyone to hear:
> The King must agree with Lancelot
>   And take back Guinevere;
> Their peace must be a lasting one
>   Or else, through their despite,
> All England shall be interdicted
>   And fall in evil plight.'
>
>   (*SMA*)

The wills of Arthur and Lancelot to accept this ruling are frustrated by Gawain, who is intent on avenging the deaths of his brothers during Lancelot's rescue of Guinevere from the bale-fire.

As can be seen, the bonds of piety formally seal every event and activity for the ideal king. A king was secularly installed but ecclesiastically crowned. The difference between a coronation and a knightly dubbing was that a knight was dubbed by a king or a noble of prowess, not a priest, though the ceremony of initiation into knighthood included a night vigil in church and other rituals. Maurice Keen notes that occasions appropriate for dubbing were when court was being held, when a crusade was being launched, and before battle. In the *AMA*, Arthur's dubbings usually take place in connection with a battle; before it starts, or during a lull. The emphasis is on the effect on morale, because a newly dubbed knight fights harder in order to express his pride and allegiance. In Malory, whose general process of narrative is geared more to tourney and individual joust than to warfare by armies, dubbings may take place at any time, and the emphasis is on the maturation process and the enlarging of nobility that dubbing achieves.

While ostensibly conducting wars for the greater glory of the Christian religion and increasing the stock of knightly men devoted to upholding the Cross—the late form of Arthur's arms included two crosses *argent,* with a Virgin and Child *or* in each—the ideal king of romance fulfilled several religious functions. In Malory's version of the Priamus episode already referred to, King Arthur gives Gawain permission to have Priamus christened before the final attack on Metz. Arthur's piety in battle is demonstrated when he deals with the dead, giving friend and foe equal rites of sanctity and honour, and doing his best to see that their bodies are returned to their birthplaces. It is true that in returning the bodies of Lucius and his nobles to Rome, he with grim humour presents the coffins as the tribute Rome demanded of him in the first place; but:

They laid out and oiled those honoured bodies,
Lapping them in sixty layers of linen
And enclosing them in lead lest they
    decompose . . .
With their banners above and their badges
    below.

(AMA)

Since Arthurian romance of our period was composed against the background of the Crusades, the idea of Jerusalem as a goal and an opportunity for killing or converting pagans is often shown to be in the mind of the ideal king and his knights. So special emphasis is given to the heathen identity of enemies in both the main works cited here; in the *AMA* in particular, great play is made with the hordes of oriental pagans and warlocks recruited into the Emperor's forces, and on Arthur's return to England to deal with his usurping cousin Mordred (in Malory, he is the incestuous son), England is depicted as overrun by Scandinavian and other Northern European heathens whom Mordred has rewarded with lands and titles.

That largesse of Mordred's was illegal because he gave away what was not his; but Arthur's largesse, as a prime quality of an anointed king, is everywhere stressed. What he gives is his own, and it is given as reward for meritorious service. A conspicuous reward is the one he confers on the herald who brings him news of Gawain's victory outside Metz:

'High-spirited herald,' said Arthur, 'by Christ
You have healed my heart, I would have you
    know:
A hundred-pound holding in Hampton I freely
    give you!'

In Malory, after the fall of Metz, Arthur 'made dukes and earls, and made every man rich'; conferring titles on the deserving, as well as enriching them, is supreme largesse. In the matter of lavish entertaining and carelessness in the distribution of cash favours, the Roman ambassador reports back to Rome of Arthur:

Speak of him as a spender who despises silver,
Gives gold no more regard than great boulders,
Rates wine as water that wells from the ground,
And worships no wealth in this world but glory.

(AMA)

That value of the ideal king may be understood in the light of May McKisack's judgement on Edward III. He:

. . . may fairly be charged with vanity, ostentation, and extravagance, if it is remembered that Edward's subjects called these things by different names and thought them proper to a king.

Concerning the attitude of the ideal king to womankind, there is nothing in the *AMA* except Mordred's treason in stealing Guinevere and getting her with child, and the resultant damage to Arthur's state, together with his instant and swiftly prosecuted resolve to take revenge. Guinevere's acceptance of Mordred is treated simply as treason. But in the *SMA* and in Malory, Guinevere resists Mordred by a trick, feigning a wish to buy clothes for the wedding in London, and shutting herself up in the Tower when she gets there, with a strong defence.

Throughout French and English medieval romance, queens are like other women, that is to say, chattels with few formal rights in the dynastic and power structures of men, though they exist there on pedestals. Volition they have, particularly to fall in love and seduce men; and it is mostly women who exercise magical arts. But the context is usually one of male business, such as the offence to knightly chastity of a man who breaks a vow or a loyalty by making love outside the rules. The special queenly characteristic is to plead for the oppressed, as the ladies of Metz do, and as Chaucer's Hippolyta does in the *Knight's Tale.*

A paramount duty of a knight, and of that super-knight, a king, was to honour and defend women. It may be noted that Edward III took his wife Philippa and the many ladies of her court on shipboard into the dangerous naval battle of Sluys (1340), where he humiliated the French and so freed England's south coast from sea-borne raids for many years. He assigned Philippa as guard, 300 men-at-arms (that is, dismounted knights) and 500 archers. I find no such solicitous provision for queens in the Arthurian romances that I have read.

The allocation of women in marriage is usually conducted by men—prospective husbands and fathers-in-law—the brides-to-be being scarcely consulted. It is illuminating that when the Arthurian stories reached Scandinavia, women are often consulted, and there are conspicuous cases of knights refusing to pursue their proposals because the women turn them down, and of the fathers accepting their daughters' refusals. That does not happen in English literature until after Shakespeare, except untypically, or when such a powerful duke of comedy as Theseus in *A Midsummer Night's Dream* craftily thwarts a testy and possessive father.

The ideal king, at least in early sources which Malory used, may express royal virility outside marriage; that is the privilege, like the occasional act of tyranny, which popular imagination accords a national hero. Arthur lusts for 'Lionors, a passing fair damosel' and 'had ado with her, and gat on her a child', and he fatally begets Mordred on Margawse, the wife of the Orkney king, Lot. At the time Arthur does not know she is his half-sister, being the daughter of his mother Igraine and her husband the Duke of Cornwall. He is just lusting after a mother of four who happens to be visiting his court. But both those episodes took place before Arthur married Guinevere, and in their marriage it is she, through her long adulterous connection with Lancelot, who breaks the rule of chastity in royal marriage. In so doing, she poses the king the problem, when she is caught *in flagrante delicto,* of whether she should be burnt, the standard sentence for that kind of treason. Arthur does not waver in either Malory or the *SMA,* though it grieves him to follow his own laws in the case. But of course Lancelot, in rescuing Guinevere from the bale-fire, saves the king from the consequences of his altruistic behaviour. Even so, it should be emphasised that Arthur seems to express not jealousy, but only hurt at the treason of his wife and best knight. The poet of the *SMA* annotates the moment briefly, but with due regard for the proprieties of justice, which include consultation between the king and his knights:

> It was no time to take their ease:
>   Arthur in anguish drew
> His knights to him in conference
>   To deem what they must do.
> They all were keen to doom the Queen
>   The fate that she had earned;
> That very day, without delay,
>   They said she must be burned.
>
> <div align="right">(<i>SMA</i>)</div>

Malory's judgement on Guinevere is contained in the extraordinary short chapter entitled 'How true love is likened to summer', which concludes Book XVIII: '. . . while she lived she was a true lover, and therefore she had a good end'. Her guilt and penitence, and her acknowledgement that her sin brought ruin to the Round Table, are wonderfully expressed in the stanzaic poem.

It remains to consider briefly the factors of the imaginary which in all ages tend to collect round the idealised figure of majesty. In Arthurian romance they tend to exploit simple exaggeration of observed reality and the magical, whether derived from pagan or Christian cultures. Their features are developments of what is found in contemporary reality, though formalised and harmonised into the art that is literature.

Arthur's begetting was magical: his father Uther Pendragon, through the magic of Merlin, made love to Igraine in the guise of her husband, the Duke of Cornwall. Then, in the *AMA* and elsewhere, Arthur's heroic and fierce countenance terrifies ambassadors and enemies:

> . . . and he looked like a lion, on his lips biting.
> The Romans in rank terror cringed on the
>   ground
> Through fear of his face as if fated to die.
>
> <div align="right">(<i>AMA</i>)</div>

Something of that idea comes through in the accompanying illustration. In battle, Arthur survives disabling wounds and recovers miraculously to full strength, as indeed does Lancelot times without number; he slaughters on an impossible scale when making sallies into huge hostile hordes; his strength is such that in the shock of a mounted charge, it is the horse which yields, not the man. In the *AMA,* he twice rises to his knees while dying.

Especially in his most destructive war actions, Nature conspires, beautifying the legitimately gory process with blossoms, flowering trees and pleasant waters which shimmer as they flow. The magical facility which puts the Arthurian hero-king in touch with cosmic supernature in the workings of fate and its ineluctable morality is the capacity to experience prophetic dreams. Very many such dreams are dreamed by fictional Arthurs. The two main dreams of the *AMA*, which are structural in the poem, giving form and meaning to its first and last events, I regard as unrivalled for their force and the poetic quality of their narration. In the first (*AMA*), in his cabin when embarked for France, Arthur dreams of a mighty combat in the sky won by a dragon against a bear, which is interpreted to him as prophetic of his coming victories against the Romans. He dreams the second dream (*AMA*) when at the

height of his fortunes and about to march on Rome; in it he meets the goddess Fortune, who first pampers him with ravishing delights and then whirls him downwards on her wheel. It is prophetic of his fall.

This medieval model king, with his savagery, his pride and his primitive apprehension operating under an umbrella of profound social loving kindness and pious humility, presents an instructive paradox in the historical development of the human spirit. (pp. 32-8)

Brian Stone, "Models of Kingship," in History Today, *Vol. 37, November, 1987, pp. 32-8.*

An excerpt from Percivale's speech in Tennyson's *The Holy Grail* (1869)

> "Then on a summer night it came to pass,
> While the great banquet lay along the hall,
> That Galahad would sit down in Merlin's chair.
>
> And all at once, as there we sat, we heard
> A cracking and a riving of the roofs,
> And rendering, and a blast, and overhead
> Thunder, and in the thunder was a cry.
> And in the blast there smote along the hall
> A beam of light seven times more clear than day;
> And down the long beam stole the Holy Grail
> All over covered with a luminous cloud,
> And none might see who bare it, and it passed.
> But every knight beheld his fellow's face
> As in a glory, and all the knights arose,
> And, staring each at other like dumb men,
> Stood, till I found a voice and sware a vow.
>
> I sware a vow before them all, that I,
> Because I had not seen the Grail, would ride
> A twelvemonth and a day in quest of it,
> Until I found and saw it, as the nun
> My sister saw it; and Galahad sware the vow,
> And good Sir Bors, our Lancelot's cousin,
>   sware,
> And Lancelot sware, and many among the
>   knights,
> And Gawain sware, and louder than the rest."

Alfred Lord Tennyson, in his The Holy Grail, *in* Poetry of the Victorian Period, *Third Edition, edited by Jerome Hamilton Buckley and George Benjamin Woods, Scott, Foresman and Company, 1965.*

Roger Sherman Loomis

[*In the following excerpt, Loomis identifies the early mythological and ritualistic elements of the legend of the Grail.*]

One after another of the features of the Grail legend becomes comprehensible in the light of the theory that it is essentially a seasonal myth containing the following elements: the testing of the young god by the old god; the display of certain talismans representing sometimes the lightning and the fecundity of the earth; the entry of the young god into possession of these talismans, and his marriage to the vegetation goddess. This interpretation harmonizes not only with the details of the various Grail romances but also with that mythologic background . . . behind the whole Arthurian cycle.

But it does not explain two vital points. It does not explain why the spear should bleed into the Grail, nor why the failure to ask a question concerning the meaning of Spear and Grail should be particularly emphasized as the source of disaster. Here is the riddle which not only fascinates the layman today but also has baffled the erudite.

As early as 1855 Heinrich noted that what Perceval experienced was "less a series of adventures than a series of initiations." But it remained for Nitze and above all Miss Weston with her article on *The Grail and the Rites of Adonis,* published in 1907, to give this earlier suggestion the weight and fulness of a serious theory. She has followed up her first article in her later books, *The Legend of Sir Perceval, The Quest of the Holy Grail,* and *From Ritual to Romance.* Her theory has been attacked on the ground that she based it on the questionable testimony of members of occult orders. She has been able to counter by quoting in its favor some of the most eminent authorities on anthropology and classical myth and ritual. Her book entitled *From Ritual to Romance* Marett has characterized as "scholarly, scientific work through and through." Hartland declared that it "has solved what had been a problem for 700 years." Miss Jane Harrison wrote: "The more I read it, the more conviction grows." Cornford went so far as to say that "the argument is self-evident, once stated." In this last opinion I concur. And luckily the evidence is so palpable that one need not be either an initiate or a specialist in primitive religion to feel its force. One may not find so convincing Miss Weston's views on the transmission and later history of the material, but her main thesis, as developed in her books, is amply supported. Here let me merely sum up her reasons for seeing in the question test the survival of an initiation ritual into a fertility cult.

First, several texts inform us that connected with the Grail are secret doctrines. The *Elucidation* prefixed to the *Conte del Graal* speaks of the mysteries of the Grail which, if Master Blihis lie not, none may reveal. In Wauchier's continuation the damsel of the white mule when asked what the Grail is replies: "Sir, this may not be, for I ought not to tell you thereof more. If you were a hundred times my lord, I could not tell more, for this is a matter so sacred, that it may not be uttered by dame, damsel, maid, or virgin, nor by any man who is not an ordained priest or a man of holy life." In the Christianized forms of the legend we meet the same assertion. Here, of course, the idea is related to the esoteric doctrines of the mass. Robert de Boron says in his *Joseph:* "I dare not nor could not tell this unless I had the great book wherein the histories are written by the great clerks; therein the great secrets are written that are called the Graal." Later in the book an angel declares that Bron "is to keep the vessel after Joseph, who must instruct him properly, especially concerning the holy words which God spoke to Joseph in the prison, which are properly called the secrets of the Graal." In the *Didot Perceval* the voice of the Holy Spirit says to Bron: "Our Lord com-

mands thee to teach to Perceval those secret words which he taught Joseph in prison when he delivered the Grail to thee." The tradition of secrecy permeates the cycle.

Secondly, according to Crestien, *Diu Krone,* and certain MSS. of Pseudo-Wauchier, the Grail is carried by a woman, the spear by a youth or youths.

Thirdly, in the question test the sword does not enter at all, but all the emphasis is on the Spear and Vessel, and the way in which one bleeds into the other is distinctly suggestive of a sexual symbolism.

Fourthly, the language of the question itself as found in Pseudo-Wauchier and *Didot Perceval* lends itself perfectly to a sex initiation. Perceval asked wherefore the Lance bled on its shaft; he failed to ask *for what* the Grail served.

Fifthly, we have already noted that the Maimed King is frequently said to be wounded in or between the thighs. Joseph of Arimathea, according to *Sone de Nansai* as a punishment for marrying a heathen, was wounded by God "in the reins and below." Wolfram's Klinschor is lord of the Chateau Merveil, which we have equated in Chapter XVII with the Grail Castle. Klinschor, then, is a sinister development of the Grail King, and indeed of the Maimed King. For we discover that he has been mutilated by a jealous husband to prevent his enjoying longer the pleasures of love. Anfortas, Wolfram's Grail King, has also been visited by God with a malady because he had taken up arms in the cause of unlawful love: he was smitten with a poisoned spear in the groin. The wound was presumably as appropriate as in the cases of Joseph and Klinschor. Though hidden under the recurrent euphemism of a wound in or between the thighs, the affliction of the Maimed King which had such a powerful sterilizing effect upon land and folk must have been the loss of his reproductive power.

Sixthly, success in the quest, involving the cure of the Maimed King, and his displacement by the youthful hero, brings about not only fertility to the earth but also to birds, beasts, and people. *Sone de Nansai,* which in spite of its Christianization has preserved so many pagan features, not only makes clear the sexual nature of the Grail King's malady, but also tells us, "no child was born of man, no maiden had husband, . . . no bird or beast had young, so sore was the king maimed."

In the presence of these facts, does it require any assurances from adepts or occultists to convince us that the question form of the test is a sexual initiation ceremony? Or that the Bleeding Spear and the Grail stand for the male and female principles? Or that the secrets of the Grail were in all probability a solemn doctrine regarding the universal mystery of reproduction and its human application? Perhaps the virginity of the Grail hero, so stressed by late Christian redactors, may be a reminiscence of the virgin state of the initiate in the pagan ceremonial.

Several difficulties remain, but none that cannot be adequately met. How, it may be asked, does it come about that the gods are the actors in what after all is essentially a human ritual? Is it not absurd to conceive of the young god as requiring such instruction or as failing to ask the momentous question? On the contrary, nothing is more familiar to the modern student of religion than the primitive habit of assigning to the god the primacy in those human activities which seem most vital. The modern school of classical mythologists recognizes a tendency not only to make the gods participators in human work and ceremony, but also to invent gods for just such purposes. As Miss Jane Harrison puts it: "We know now that social institutions tend to 'project' mythological figures. Though their aspect as culture heroes was of great importance, the central function of the Kouretes remained that of husbands and potential fathers. On the symbolic performance in ritual of this function depended the fertility and, in general, the luck or fate of the whole community. Primitive ritual is always magical in character: i.e., the worshipper does what he wants done, his rites are those of magical induction: he marries that the land may be fertile, he tends symbolically a holy child that his own children may be nurtured. Then as the religious instinct develops, he projects a daemon leader—a Greatest Kouros, to whom he hands over the functions which he himself performed." In some such way, we may believe that the young god Pry eri or Gwri became the first initiate, the first to undergo a ritual test on which was supposed to depend the fatness of the crops, the abundance of fish, the number and vigor of the children yet to be born,—all that meant most to the prosperity and the power of the tribe.

How such a mythical ceremony might become the theme of professional story-tellers is well explained in two passages of Van Gennep's *Rites of Passage.* Speaking of the Eleusinian Mysteries he says: "One knows at least that the initiation included: (a) a journey across a hall divided into dark compartments, each representing a region of Hades: the ascent of a stairway; the arrival in regions brilliantly lighted and the entry into the *megaron* with the exhibition of the sacred objects: (b) a dramatic representation of the abduction of Kore (Persephone), with certain elements unknown to the profane." Testimony exists that among the objects venerated at Eleusis were symbols of both sexes. Later, referring to the *Purgatory of St. Patrick,* Van Gennep says: "These myths and legends may be, in certain cases, only the oral remains of rites of initiation, for it must not be forgotten that, particularly in ceremonies of initiation, the old men, instructors, chiefs of ceremonies, and so forth, recount that which the other members of the social group execute." In fact, it has been urged that not only the legends connected with Lough Derg in Donegal, the site of the *Purgatory of St. Patrick,* but even the Christian ceremonies still observed there contain traces of pagan initiations. One of the legends, *Qwain Miles,* relates how a warrior of King Stephen's by the name of Owain resolved as a penance to undergo the terrifying ordeal of Lough Derg. He was locked in the cave, descended into the darkness, found in a twilit hall fifteen men in white with a clerical appearance, who instructed him regarding his journey. After visiting purgatory, he crossed by a sharp bridge, to the Terrestrial Paradise, where Adam and Eve once dwelt. After eating food there he had no desire to return to earth. But being admonished, he started back, passed the fifteen men in white, was told by them what his future was to be, reached the door safely, and when morn-

ing came was taken out. In this legend not only does the Earthly Paradise savor of the pagan Other World, but also the whole adventure with its locking up of a solitary man over night in a cave, the instructions of the reverend men in white, the release in the morning seem to hark back to a pagan initiation. In the actual practice of early Christian times, pilgrims who persisted in spite of the warnings of bishop and prior, might descend into the cave after receiving benediction. The door was made fast till the next morning. If the penitent were there, he was taken out. If not, it was understood that he had perished in purgatory, and he was never mentioned again. Christianized stories of the initiation rites of Lough Derg did penetrate into French literature as the legends of St. Patrick's Purgatory. It is not unlikely, therefore, that stories of similar pagan rituals should at an earlier period have reached the Breton *conteurs,* inheritors of the druidic lore of Dummonia, Wales, and Ireland. For the druids of Gaul we know instructed the youth in secret doctrines, which they themselves received from Britain, and whatever else they taught, they doubtless did not omit certain esoteric matter regarding the cosmic processes of reproduction and the human mystery of generation and birth.

But here I shall be challenged: where is the specific evidence that the sexual aspects of this cycle of legend came from the druids or from any source in the British Isles? The evidence, I grant, is meager, but in the absence of any other immediate source, I think it sufficient. In the first place, we have some hints that in the British Isles worship with a sexual tinge existed. There is the ithyphallic giant cut in the chalk at Cerne Abbas, of unknown date but quite possibly as old as the British period. In the *Life of St. Sampson* we read of Cornishmen worshipping at a certain shrine after the custom of bacchantes by means of a certain play in honor of an abominable image, who declared that thus they were keeping the festival of their ancestors. More precise information as to what the custom of their ancestors probably was we gain from another Celtic territory. At Inverkeithing across the Firth from Edinburgh in Holy Week of the year 1282 a priest compelled the girls of the village to form choral dances, bore phallic emblems on a pole before them, and by lewd gestures and words excited the orgiastic spirit. Highly significant is the fact that he was allowed to keep his benefice after his performance on the plea that it was the established custom of the country. In other words, it was not a chance outcropping of the licentious spirit, but a survival of pagan spring festivals. In Ireland Patrick testifies that the pagans worshipped idols and foul things (*immunda*). Fergus mac Roich, a predecessor of Conchobar in the kingship of Ireland and foster-father of Cuchulinn, presumably therefore semi-divine, had together with other gigantic features enormous sexual organs. Sexual imagery entered into the myth and ritual of many lands where the sun was adored. The Thracians, when reproached by the Church fathers for their cult of the phallus, replied that it was an emblem of the sun, of the vitalizing influence of the heavenly light on all Nature. Probably the peoples of the British Isles likewise associated their worship of the sun with a reverence for the vital mysteries of reproduction.

In the second place, Macalister has already noted that for

Arthur as one of the Nine Worthies, detail from a tapestry dated c. 1400.

the Irish the prosperity of the land depended on the generative function of the divine king. "It is extremely important to notice indications that, in the case of the King of Temair [Tara], the marriage of the king was essential to secure the boon which he was supposed to bring his people. This is probably the reason why the nobles of Erin refused to countenance the unwedded king Eochu Airem and boycotted his assembly; and in the story edited by Mr. Best, under the title of *The Adventures of Art Son of Conn,* the men of Ireland enjoy three harvests of corn annually so long as Conn is wedded to his fitting spouse Eithne Taebfota; but when she dies and he marries in her stead the disreputable Becuma, there 'is neither corn nor milk in Ireland.' The exercise by the king of his martial functions acts sympathetically on the fertility of the land and of the cattle." In other words, there can be little doubt that the Irish would regard the emasculation of their kings as certain to have the same dire effects as the wounding of Joseph of Arimathea or Pellean, and his healing or replacement by a young king as equally certain to restore "the Waste Land."

In the third place, one of the greatest of ancient Irish festivals, the Lugnasad at Teltown was supposed to celebrate the marriage of the sun-god Lug to the land of Erin. Westropp pointed out: "Oengus after the so-called 'first battle of Magh Tured' made the Lugnasad feast for the marriage of Lug to (the kingdom of) Eriu, when Lug was made king after Nuada. . . . Now Erin was in some tales a daughter of Umor, and Tailltiu was daughter of Mae Umoir. The solar god Mac Greine, too, had married a goddess (the same or bearing the same name) Eriu." Westropp further shows that the union of the sun-god with the goddess of Erin was deemed an auspicious occasion for human matings not always of a dignified or permanent nature. Teltown marriages were more or less notorious right down into the nineteenth century. Thus we see that one of the great festivals of Ireland centered about the union of Lug with the earth-goddess and the fecundating influence it was presumed to exert.

But the most striking evidence of a phallic element in Irish tradition bears precisely on the point at issue. The spear of Lug itself and the Luin of Celtehar which Brown has equated with it seem upon examination to be a compound of lightning weapon and phallic symbol. The constant elements in the descriptions of these legendary lances are two: first, their fiery destructiveness; second, their periodic assuaging in a caldron of blood or other dark liquid. The latter characteristic is entirely inappropriate in a lightning weapon, but commends itself to me and to others whose attention has been called to it as apt enough in a phallic symbol. There seems to have taken place on Irish soil precisely that confusion of lightning spear and phallic spear which did not take place in Arthurian romance till much later. The significant point for us is that the ancient Irish attached a sexual symbolism to lance and caldron.

If this interpretation be correct, the development of the Grail and Lance may be traced as follows. By chance there existed in Irish sacred tradition two spears and two caldrons. There were the mythical spear and caldron of the gods, the first a symbol of the lightning, the second a symbol of the fertility of the earth, akin to the various caldrons and horns of plenty in Celtic and classical mythology. These, together with two other divine talismans, a sword and a stone, were in the possession of the Tuatha De Danann. The stone at least served as a test for the semi-divine kings of Ireland. But none of the talismans were carried in ritual procession, nor were they the subject of a question test. A caldron like that of the Dagda, and a spear which had to be dipped in a caldron, like that of Lug, existed in the palace of Da Derga, but we read of no such use of them as of the talismans in the Grail Castle. The visit of Cormae to Manannan's palace and his receiving the Cup of Truth, prototype of the Grail, are described but there is no testing of Cormac by its means. Likewise the visit of Conn to Lug's palace and his receipt of the Cup of Sovereignty provides no analogy to the Grail test. When Cuchulinn passes the night in Curoi's castle, where the caldron of Blathnat is, the talisman is not even mentioned, and though the young god is tested, it is through no ritual question. Neither is there in any of these stories a wounded god. These facts go to show that the Treasures of the Tuatha De did not belong with the question test or the Maimed King.

But originally distinct from the feeding caldron and lightning spear of the gods were a spear and a caldron which had their origin in a pagan initiation rite, and represented the male and female organs of generation. These tended to take on a sacred character; they became associated with the ritual resuscitation of the maimed or slain representative of the god; they gradually came to be thought of as his possessions. These talismans were presumably borne in ritual procession before the initiate, and on his question concerning their use was supposed to depend the health of the god and prosperity of the tribe.

Both sets of talismans were thus sacred, the possessions of the gods. The spear and vessel of the initiation rite served from the first as a test, and bore a sympathetic relation to the vitality of nature. The Treasures of the Tuatha De, also, so far as we can infer, acquired in the Welsh and Dumnonian stages this function of testers and this connection with the seasons. The caldron will not boil the food of a coward. The sword can be drawn or re-welded only by the young god. To re-weld the sword brings the return of verdure. To sit unworthy in the Siege Perilous is to bring desolation upon the land. To lose the vessel of plenty is the cause of languishment.

Now once both sets of talismans had become divine possessions, which served to test the young hero and which were related mythologically or ritually to the abundance of grain, fruit, milk, and fish, then it was only a matter of time before the inevitable contamination should take place. The scenes in the Grail Castle are a mystifying compound of mythological tests of the power of the young god and ritual tests of a human initiate into a fertility cult.

It is an intriguing task to disentangle the ritual from the mythical elements and to reconstruct the ancient initiation ceremony. We may presume that the youth was of noble blood, a natural successor to the chieftainship, a virgin from whom the functions of sex had been hitherto kept rigorously secret. He was introduced at night to an island sanctuary or a strange palace hall. On a sumptuous couch lay an aged man, groaning with pain. About him women wailed asking how long his agony would endure. Presently, they departed and in complete silence a maiden entered bearing a caldron. After her paced a youth bearing a bleeding lance which he held over the caldron. They stood expectant but silent. If the initiate asked the question: "For what do these things serve?" at once there arose from an invisible audience a great shout of joy. The aged king stepped down from his couch, declaring that his infirmity was healed, that the fertility of the land was assured, and that all the folk owed their welfare to the youth. Thereupon perhaps the aged man revealed the mysteries of nature in the process of reproduction. It was now incumbent upon the youth as chief of the tribe to exercise his generative energies, and there followed a ritual marriage with the damsel of the caldron. It was a ceremony somewhat like this which coalesced with the visits of heroes and Kings to the palaces of Curoi, Lug, and Manannan, with their talismans of plenty and mythical weapons, to form the typical visit to the Grail Castle.

On this interpretation, both mythological and ritual elements have their immediate origin in the British Isles. . . . It must be admitted that there is no trace of such a ritual in Irish or Welsh literature. Yet the very nature of the material precluded its publication until its meaning had been lost. To the Christian the whole performance was an abomination of the heathen: to the pagan it was a *secretum secretorum,* a tradition which was passed on orally, to be sure, but was never regarded as fit for any but the most privileged members of the cult. It would be preposterous to expect that the arcana of a secret and discredited order should be written down until the stories had passed into the hands of men who did not realize their true import. The tradition of high significance and extraordinary mystery persisted, and Christian redactors of the Grail legend interpreted it as referring to the hidden meanings of the mass. It has remained for modern scholars, especially Miss Weston and Nitze, to demonstrate that we have here the relics of pagan mysteries. (pp. 260-70)

> Roger Sherman Loomis, "The Mysteries of the Grail," in his Celtic Myth and Arthurian Romance, *Columbia University Press, 1927, pp. 260-70.*

PRINCIPAL CHARACTERS

Rosemary Morris

[*In the following excerpt, Morris attempts to define "the 'essential' Arthur, the common property and creation of all the individual authors."*]

The 'biographer' of Arthur, unlike an ordinary biographer, does not have the comforting assurance that behind the sources, however scanty or misleading they may be, dwells a real person. There may be as many Arthurs as there are authors to write about him. However, the writers themselves *were* convinced that they were handling a genuine historical character. They respected their sources, and, while not shirking alteration, did not deliberately reject the 'truth'. If a large part of the resulting character *was* invented, is this not true also of many modern biographies?

It is therefore not wholly vain to seek for a basically consistent character of Arthur. Not all consistent traits will be moral: outward trappings like possessions may contribute largely to the portrayal. We go, then, in search not of the 'real' Arthur but of the 'essential' Arthur, the common property and creation of all the medieval authors.

The 'novelistic' analysis and development of character was little practised in the Middle Ages. Arthur exemplifies this, especially as it is hard to discern the man through the parade of typical regal virtues and vices. Nowhere is there a portrait of Arthur to match that of Claudas in LP [*Lancelot en Prose*]. The strings of clichés, such as 'dous et deboneres', 'preus et courtois', express judgment on his character but do the opposite of individualising it. He does have a 'true' character, but it is built up from scattered hints and comments: 'Arthur wes wunsum þer he hafde his iwillen' (Layamon 1.11235); 'nus ne savoit si bien atraire gent a sa volenté comme il savoit' (Micha III. 111). Sometimes the 'real' man seems to emerge in spite of the author; it is then that he is most convincing.

Arthur emerges most often through relationships. As we have seen, authors mould him ruthlessly to fit the status of the current protagonist; nevertheless consistent traits emerge. He is affectionate, open-hearted, trusting, considerate and generous. When he does treat people harshly—the true Guinevere, Yder, the young Gawain, the Cote Maltaille—this strikes an experienced reader as exceptional. Either the author has an axe to grind, or he is trying to refresh an outworn motif. On the negative side, Arthur tends to be over-emotional and malleable, and to have favourites, some unworthy. The net result is a humanly attractive figure who normally retains sympathy. On the kingly level he is sometimes weak; but in medieval eyes a generous, trusting king was preferable to a cold-hearted, suspicious tyrant. It is not surprising that the age of Machiavelli had no brief for Arthur, who even in Layamon distinctly lacks self-interested calculation.

A corollary of Arthur's affectionateness is forgiveness. Only in Layamon and the Huail story is he cruel or vindictive—and neither attained widespread circulation. He may thirst for some opponents' blood—Angrés, the *Suite* Morgain, Mordred—but in such cases justice, and outraged affection, are on his side. When he hates, he hates in hot blood, but more deeply 'characteristic' is the recurring scene of Arthur pardoning a defeated enemy and seating him at the Table. Vindictiveness is not one of his borrowings from the medieval Alexander.

A further feature of Arthur's relationships is consistency, for he repeatedly expresses refusal to go back on his pledged word. This normally laudable kingly characteristic can turn to ill, as in *Erec* or, more tragically, in the Vulgate *Mort.* It is not invariable: the LP *preudom* (II. 217), the *Suite* barons and the Scottish chroniclers accuse Arthur of faithbreaking. The accusations are justified in context, but are definitely exceptional. Like most trusting people, Arthur is trustworthy.

We may now pass to consideration of Arthur's 'moral' character. Medieval characterisation often involves moral, as against kingly, knightly or courtly norms; their nuancing helps to build up individuality. In Arthur's case, the moral dimension is particularly important. As the Grail theme increases its importance in the Arthurian mainstream, there is a growing tendency to judge the characters on a spiritual and religious, as well as a chivalrous, plane. Those who fail on this plane are debarred from realising their highest human potentialities; and on this plane the great king may fail utterly.

For convenience's sake I shall group my preliminary moral discussion around the Seven Deadly Sins—a system of character analysis well known and subtly used in the Middle Ages. Let us see how much of a general picture emerges.

We may be quick to accuse Arthur of Lust and Pride. Lust, however, is confined to a few areas. The lustful Arthur of the *Life of Cadog* is exposed for a saintly rebuke—which by a twist of narrative is administered by a layman. In LP, Arthur lusts for Camille; but although he is accused of lust also vis-à-vis the False Guinevere, the confusion of wives is scarcely his fault. The salacious *Livre d'Artus* appears to consider lust indispensable to a knight-errant. In the Boron *Merlin* his incest with Loth's wife is totally damnable—but for its incestuousness, not its lust. The affair with Lisanor, which Merlin sanctions, can pass for the natural indulgence of a wifeless youth. In verse romances, the English, the Vulgate *Mort,* the chronicles, Arthur is a faithful husband. He never becomes an exemplum of lust. He cannot attain the rigid austerity of the Quest, or the adulterous fidelity of Lancelot or (usually) Tristan; but, then, he is never expected to. As for the 'daughter' sins of lust—blindness of mind, hardness of heart, inconstancy, cruelty—they are on the whole uncharacteristic of Arthur. Lust occasionally tempts, but does not govern him.

Pride is the defect of a kingly virtue, and all princes are prone to it. In Arthur it exists only in the chronicle and Middle English texts which present him as a conqueror, and even there is not always condemned. Geoffrey's and Layamon's Arthurs are splendid in their pride, and it is not blamed for their downfall; indeed, where pride is blamed, the blame comes in a package with the figure of Fortune, and Arthur is unnaturally forced into a commonplace mould dear to the classifying mind of the late medieval moralist. Never is Arthur's pride nourished on the lies of flatterers, for like Alexander's it is based on solid success. It is never closely analysed, either in relation to Arthur's spiritual health or as an exemplum, save briefly in the alliterative *Morte.* LP analyses the sin of pride—but in relation to its new hero, the great conqueror Galehaut, not to Arthur.

The romance Arthur, indeed, more often evinces a becoming humility, which is none the less genuine for being forced on him by literary circumstances. It mitigates to some extent the humiliation of Arthur's dominance by his knights, for Arthur, being free from jealous resentment, almost invariably accepts his knights' triumphs as his own. It is they, indeed, who are more likely to suffer from vainglory.

'Daughters' of pride are presumption, hypocrisy, obstinacy, quarrelsomeness and disobedience. All, save perhaps obstinacy, are uncharacteristic of Arthur—and obstinacy may be an intensification of the virtue of consistency. In fact, Pride never roots deeply enough in Arthur to shape his whole character.

Closely allied to Pride is Covetousness. Again it is only as conqueror that Arthur exhibits it. He is never greedy of money or goods—quite the reverse. The only exceptions to this are the *Lives* of Cadog, Carannog and Padern, and they are alien to the mainstream even in Wales. As for covetousness of land, there is a direct accusation only in *Auntyrs.* The connection with pride is strong: *Auntyrs* sees it as the root of all evil. The alliterative *Morte,* which probably inspired *Auntyrs,* implies condemnation of Arthur's covetousness, as do texts like *Sagramor,* which castigate a greed for others' lands that involves neglect of one's own. We may conclude that Arthur's conquering career exposes him to the charge of covetousness, but that only a few morally-minded writers press it. Others expressly defend him, such as the author of *Golagros,* and, even more notably, that of *Palamède,* in which Arthur indignantly rejects the idea of attacking Pharamond: ' . . . et il fust . . . assiés plus miens hanemis qu'il n'est, ge lui donroie avant de ma terre que ge ne li taudroie de la soie' (Lathuillière). This voluntary restraint is a relief from the normal prose-romance scepticism about Arthur's conquering abilities.

Arthur may, perhaps, suffer from the 'daughter' sins of covetousness, 'fear of loss' and 'worldly sorrow'. These are marks of an excessive preoccupation with earthly, unspiritual concerns, and point us forward to our consideration of Arthur's theological limitations.

Envy is totally uncharacteristic, and not the most hostile or moral author insinuates otherwise. When he is supreme in his world, he has none to envy. When he is not, he either takes prompt steps to make himself so, or generously recognises the other's superiority.

Sloth will strike some as very characteristic of Arthur. But, as we have sought to show, sloth does not equal *fainéantise.* It is when Arthur also neglects his *fainéant* duty of maintaining courtly *joie* that he can be accused of sloth. This occurs memorably in the first branch of *Perlesvaus,* but there the *volentez deslaianz* is imposed on Arthur from without, and is not a 'characteristic'. Real sloth occurs in the First Continuation, but still would not imply a characteristic were it not for Arthur's tendency, curiously recurrent in the verse romances and LP, towards fits of abstraction. These build up a picture of a man very prone to fits of spiritual paralysis or *tristitia* from which he is powerless to emerge unaided, a man very prone, in fact, to the sin of sloth. This characteristic of Arthur's does not appear to be borrowed from any real king, though it faintly recalls Saul's possession, from which David roused him. There is no need, however, even for that inspiration, since the melancholy is always induced by concern for a missing knight, and that is universally typical of Arthur. The abstraction is not progressive, nor unique to Arthur; it is his personal manifestation of the cliché 'tristes et pensis'. Successive imitation creates the impression of an individual quirk, such as a novelist might use to give a character life.

The daughter sins of sloth are relevant to Arthur: hatred of spiritual things, weakness in prayer, *accidia,* moral cowardice, despair. This again hints at the spiritual limitations which are so important to many authors.

Gluttony we may dismiss. We seldom hear details of the lavish fare provided in Arthur's hall, and Arthur's custom of delaying the start of a feast argues a degree of self-control which many authors (and characters!) find excessive. The *Livre d'Artus* hints at over-indulgence in wine by young Arthur. But drunkenness in high places appears to be a pet hate of this author. The Scots, as often, reverse normal Arthurian trends to accuse Arthur of gluttony as yet another symptom of British degeneracy. Love of ease, a 'daughter' of gluttony, might attach to the *fainéant* Arthur, but his eagerness to perform, or at least hear of, adventure militates against this.

Anger, too, is uncharacteristic of Arthur: indeed his lack of it sometimes irritates the reader. His famous attack of royal rage in the alliterative *Morte* clearly delights the author, but belongs to genre, not to Arthur. Malory, realising this, tones it down to almost nothing. Even in the *Morte* the anger is controlled, almost theatrical; not the 'deadly' anger which perverts will and judgment. Arthur exhibits that sort of anger only in the Vulgate *Mort,* against Mordred. Anger's daughter-sins are the vices of a tyrant: the TP [*Tristan en Prose*] Mark has them all, a fact which highlights his opposite number's general lack of them.

Through this survey Arthur emerges as a far from perfect character, but more white than black. He is spiritually limited, but can cut a deservedly good figure before the world. Except in some chronicles he is not conspicuously 'great'; rather is he disarmingly ordinary beneath his kingship. He is, as it were, humanised by long familiarity.

Let us now pass to the spiritual plane. A general survey of the material will convince us that Arthur seldom fails in conventional piety. As early as *Culhwch* he is the favoured of God. The pious correctness of Geoffrey's Arthur, with the influence of the Glastonbury legends, ensures his wide acceptance as a Christian hero. Throughout the romance material he is meticulous in attendance at Mass, and he is fertile in good works: founding monasteries, reconstructing churches, distributing holy objects, sponsoring a crusade. Some texts, mainly chronicles, mention a special devotion to the Virgin. In most contexts, Arthur is on good terms with the Church, and when he is not—as in the Welsh saints' lives, the Galehaut war or the Vulgate *Mort*—it is not deliberate provocation on his part. All in all, Arthur has just the right degree of public piety which is required of a king. But in the mainstream literature, this is judged to be insufficient for perfection in both the king and the man.

Once again, we may look at Chrétien as the initiator of this trend. As he moves from romance to romance, he takes an ever severer view of Arthur's spiritual limitations. Even in *Erec* his clumsy handling of the *Fier Baiser* custom provokes criticism. In *Cligès* he lacks Christian mercifulness, and on the occasion of Cligès' visit to England, Arthur presides over a court wholly devoted to rather pointless frivolity. In *Lancelot* Arthur has no spiritual resources to deal with the Méléagant crisis. The first scene of *Yvain* shows, as is often remarked, a slothful court with crumbling morale; and Yvain's later sojourn there, instead of glorifying him as it does Cligès, proves disastrous. Yvain has to grow spiritually *away* from his high renown at court before he becomes a 'complete' man. *Perceval* crowns this trend and takes it much further. Criticism of the chivalric and military code is felt from the beginning, and Perceval first sees Arthur in a most inglorious state. Perceval's own ambitions are rapidly directed away from Arthur, though neither the hero nor his instructors yet openly condemn the Arthurian ideal. But Gawain—already on the downgrade in *Lancelot*—exhibits in *Perceval* the limitations and absurdities of Arthurian success. His position at the end shows how the court's attitudes lead it up a spiritual blind alley.

The severity of *Perceval*'s judgement is mitigated by some of Chrétien's successors: worldly Arthurianism still has a long, glittering future. The *Perceval* continuations celebrate that future, but as they progress, Perceval becomes more and more distant from the court, so that Arthur remains totally cut off from the Grail world. In *Perlesvaus,* Arthur triumphantly overcomes one spiritual limitation, his 'volontez delainz', represents Christianity against the Old Law, and is even permitted himself to experience the Grail; but still only Perlesvaus, the new Messiah, can in his mystic isolation attain to the highest spiritual experiences.

The *Lancelot-Graal,* however, continues Chrétien's trend. In Part One of LP, Arthur is still considered the favoured of God. But Arthur's defeat by Galehaut, followed by the long castigation of the *preudom,* reminds us that that favour must be earned—and Arthur has not done so. Far from attaining spiritual excellence, he is not even equipped for the ordinary duties of a king. So harshly is he judged that he must undergo the penance which, in real life, was deemed adequate for Henry II's implication in the murder of a saintly archbishop! Even after a full reform, he is still unable to overcome Galehaut, who would seem at this stage to have God's immanent approval. In Part One, Arthur, Claudas and Galehaut are all shown to be spiritually lacking. The author is saying that even kings are subject to God's laws—all the more so, indeed, for their position exposes them to greater temptations.

The author of Part One may not have the Grail theme in mind when he castigates Arthur. But his criticisms tie in very well with Chrétien's: both accuse the whole Arthurian system of spiritual sterility. Part One of LP thus points the way to the *Queste,* which takes Chrétien's view to the uttermost extremes. Arthur, his knights and their whole way of life are here *irrelevant* to the Grail, even if they are not blind to its importance. Far from being hallowed by the Grail, Arthur's kingdom only appears more evil for its presence. The logical working out of this theory appears, of course, in the Vulgate *Mort,* where the evils which the presence of the Grail, and the desire for it, have restrained break loose in total calamity. The *Mort* author is particularly conscious of Arthur's own spiritual limitations. Whereas Lancelot, Guinevere and even Gawain succeed before they die in attaining a personal understanding and love of God, Arthur continues to take refuge in conventional piety, cannot understand why this does not work, and dies in spiritually equivocal circumstances.

Not all later authors judge Arthur, as a Christian, so severely; few accept the *Queste*'s scorn for the worldly chivalry which he admittedly represents. But the centrality of the Grail theme to the developing legend established a tragic equivocation at the centre of Arthur's story: his whole reign aspires towards a goal whose achievement will invalidate and destroy all he stands for. Arthur falls because of his spiritual inadequacy.

The contributions of many authors to Arthur's characterisation produce a remarkably self-consistent picture. Arthur is loyal and trusting; easily-led and affectionate; not piercingly intelligent, but capable of kingly tact and discretion; given to violent emotion and subject to depression; brave, proud in conquest, but somewhat lacking in moral fibre; pious, but lacking an entire spiritual dimension. This composite, cumulative portrait is convincing, as the rare and cliché-ridden direct descriptions of Arthur cannot be. It is not the 'real' Arthur, but it is an Arthur in whose historical reality it is possible to believe—and an Arthur whose character is his fate.

Most heroes are individualised partly by personal possessions. This is very true of Arthur, who is incomplete without his Round Table, his Excalibur, Camelot or (in Welsh) Celliwig and the hound Cabal. All authors acknowledge their importance; some authors make startlingly original use of them.

The Round Table is a case in point. Generally it is thought to seat all Arthur's knights; that its roundness equalises them all; that Arthur sat at it; that it was unique and made especially for him. In fact, all these ideas are seriously challenged in the material. Only in Layamon does the Table seat all the knights; elsewhere the number fluctuates enormously. Normally it is for the select few. Seven authors consider all its occupants equal: Wace (though he contradicts himself elsewhere), Layamon, Thomas Gray, Vasconcellos, and the authors of *L'Atre périlleux, Arthur* and *The Grene Knight.* Each of these could have conceived this highly sensible notion independently of the others. It is not part of the mainstream tradition, which abounds with squabbles over the relative merits of the knights and eventually sorts them out as neatly as a football league.

As for Arthur, he usually sits at the *maistres dois* like any medieval baron. Only the *Suite* and the enthusiastic Hardyng seat him at the Table. Illustrators—including medieval ones—who put him there make an assumption unwarranted by most texts, and probably based on pictures of the Last Supper. Never is Arthur a Christ-figure, although the occupant of the Siege Perilous certainly is. Arthur is both greater and lesser than the members of the Table, over whom he presides although they outstrip him in prowess.

As for the Table being made especially for Arthur, this is so only in the Wace tradition. Others deny it, for various reasons. For Boron, the Table's roots are in a remote, mystical past, more significant than the petty squabbles of the Arthurian court. In LP, Arthur is belittled by the suggestion that his most familiar synechdochic possession is not really his at all, and that the best knights in the world go with the Table, not with Arthur. In *Perlesvaus,* Madaglan's demand for the return of the Table is a bombshell, part of the general disintegration of Arthurian organisation towards the end of the romance. Nevertheless the verse romancers and chronicles continue to champion Arthur's rights in the Table, and even the late prose romances—TP and *Palamède*—assent to them. Nevertheless, his right to the Table is another belief held in the teeth of much Arthurian evidence.

The Table's uniqueness depends on its symbolic meaning. In the earlier material, that meaning depends on Arthur and his knights themselves, whose unique glory gives uniqueness to the Table. It is not The *Round* Table, it is *The* Round Table, Arthur's table. The religious symbolism developed by Boron militates against the Table's uniqueness, though the Three Tables echo and enrich one another's significance. Other texts, which do not have Boron's enriching symbolism, also mention more than one Table. In the *Tavola Ritonda,* Arthur's Table is a mere copy of Uther's; in *Sagramor* Sagremor's is a copy of Arthur's. Both inventions destroy the concept of the uniqueness of Arthur's whole reign and civilisation, as well as of his Table. In the ballad of *King Cornwall,* excellent round tables seem to abound, to the ultimate loss of any meaning in Arthur's. It is really the Vulgate *Mort* and the post-Vulgate, with their fostering of the Ban faction, which shatter the concept of uniqueness, as the excellence of Ban and his followers cuts sheer across that of the Round Table fellowship, and the strife between factions finally obliterates the idea—never very strong—that the Tablers form an apostolic fellowship.

The Table does have a few interesting peculiarities. Chief of them is the Siege Perilous with its adaptable *sen.* Also interesting, however, is the post-Vulgate notion that each seat is labelled by God. This may rob Arthur of freedom of choice, but it also gives divine sanction to the fellowship—even if the divinity is little felt in the action, and is hard to reconcile with the presence of Agravain or Mordred. It produces a very interesting evolution. When a knight dies, his name fades. Therefore, the seats keep a check from afar on the knights' fortunes. The notion is thus assimilated to the common folktale motif of the sympathetic object which changes according to its owner's fortunes. Most likely the author had heard such tables, and (perhaps subconsciously) altered his motif, inherited from the Vulgate, to conform to them. Here is an unusual demonstration of folklore's power to influence written literature.

Such peculiarities, however, are confined to a few texts. Overall the chief appeal of the Table lies in the excellence of the knights who adorn it. To Arthurian imitators, a *table ronde* meant not an artefact but a tourney, in fact an imitation of Arthur's paladins. The Table is the concrete expression of Arthur's knight-centredness.

I have little to add to previous studies of Arthur's sword. We must note, however, that the way in which the French Excalibur shuttles between Arthur and Gawain weakens its individualising significance for Arthur and throws its symbolism into confusion. Most absurd is VM [*Vulgate Merlin*], which, in order to justify Gawain's possession of Excalibur in LP, makes Arthur gradually lose interest in what, after Boron, ought to be hallowed as the divine instrument of his kingship. In the post-Vulgate, degradation of Gawain justifies Arthur's retention of the sword—which in turn justifies his lamentations over it at the end, largely invalidated in the Vulgate *Mort* by the fact that it has for years not been his sword. The post-Vulgate author also eliminates much Vulgate incoherence with its new, parallel hand-in-the-lake scene. But this invention produces a fresh complication. If Excalibur comes from the Lake, it cannot be the God-given sword in the stone. Therefore the latter must be eliminated. The author's method is even more untrue to the Boron *sen* than VM's. He castigates the sword's inferiority as a weapon, which quickly causes it to break. Thus all Boron's imagery is destroyed, while the new Excalibur has little significance, being indeed inferior to its own scabbard. As so often, the post-Vulgate author fails to think through what is basically a good idea.

In sum, Excalibur is often considered to be significant, though only Boron is sure of its meaning. It is not unique

Depiction of the legendary battle between Arthur and Mordred at Camlann, from a 15th c. English manuscript illustration.

to Arthur, a fact which produces much confusion. It is nowhere vividly described; in the legend as a whole it takes a forlorn second place to the satisfyingly mysterious and ubiquitous Sword with the Strange Hangings. These negative findings comport a paradox. In the popular imagination, Excalibur is as famous a sword as Durendal. What makes it so is precisely that connection with Arthur which so many authors challenge. Once again, we find that general Arthurian beliefs are held in the teeth of much of the evidence.

No other possessions of Arthur's attain such general fame as the Sword and the Table. Others are occasionally mentioned, and may represent abortive attempts to individualise Arthur further. An example is the list of weapons in *Culhwch,* but these do not appear to have featured largely even in Welsh lore. Each has an obvious descriptive name: the sword 'Hard-notch', the spear 'Hewer-spear', the knife 'Pearl-handle'(?), the shield 'Face of the Evening'. None is obviously magical, and it is Arthur who individualises the weapons as much as vice versa. Geoffrey's ignorance of all save Ron and possibly Caledfwlch consigns them to a rapid oblivion. All evidence principally the Welsh passion for names and clarifications.

In an age when detailed enthusiasm for weapons might be expected in many readers, it is rather surprising to find so little general interest in Arthur's. Only Layamon extends Geoffrey's largely conventional Arming of the Hero. There is one exception to this lack: Arthur's shield. This recurs almost as often as the Sword, though it did not so catch the popular imagination. The *Culhwch* name, Wynebgorucher, occurs nowhere else, but it may be significant that Geoffrey's Pridwen (a name better suited to a shield than to the ship which bears it in Welsh) has a similar meaning, 'fair face'. Both names may allude to the possibly ancient idea that Arthur bore a portrait of the Virgin on his shield, a 'fair face' indeed.

Early sources are much confused as to the nature of the image which Arthur bore on his shield. Wace and Giraldus take Geoffrey to mean that Arthur bore a portrait of the Virgin *inside* his shield as an object of private devotion, not outside as a blazon. This is the more likely as Geoffrey's allusion is apparently the first mention of a religious device being painted on a shield. However, as interest in personal heraldic devices developed, from the late twelfth century onwards, it became possible to consider Arthur's Virgin badge as such a device. William of Rennes seems to see it as such. At the least, if openly displayed it proclaims the wearer's allegiance to Christianity, and usefully identifies him in battle against the pagans.

However, after William's time a concatenation of circumstances prevented the general recognition of Arthur's Virgin badge. The verse romancers take little interest in the nascent heraldic art, and the prose romancers, who adopt it with ever-increasing enthusiasm, gain by a process whose nature can only be guessed the conviction that Arthur's device was three (or more) crowns. This device never receives an explanation such as the prose romancers normally give, but it wholly ousts the HRB [*Historia Regum Britanniae*]/Wace conception. Thus Arthur's Virgin shield, and with it the particularising—even spiritualising—notion of a special devotion to the Virgin, are thrust out of the mainstream development. It lingers, however, in byways, maintained by the quiet persistence of the chronicle tradition. Two 'explanations' of it exist. One is in the thirteenth-century Vatican Nennius, which sees it as a momento of Arthur's visit to Jerusalem. Such mementos are so common that the story does not denote any special piety in Arthur. John of Glastonbury's explanation, whereby the device commemorates Arthur's Glastonbury vision, connotes a more genuinely intense religious experience, through which the *sen* of shield and vision enrich one another. John has some interest in 'spiritualising' Arthur, as his record of his ancestry shows; but he is too late and obscure to influence the mainstream conception.

The Virgin device survives into the late Middle English, despite general acceptance of the Three Crowns, but in a rather different form. Hardyng, the alliterative *Morte* and Boece all transfer it to Arthur's banner, indicating that it is no longer personal insignia, but a focus for allegiance, belonging to Arthur only insofar as he represents England, and proclaiming the whole nation's devotion to the Christian cause. This enlargement of meaning epitomises Arthur's transformation from Dark Age tribal warrior to fifteenth-century monarch.

Whatever its exact significance, the Three Crowns heraldry clearly celebrates Arthur's worldly kingship, and does more honour to it than the French prose romancers might wish; the English might see in it the emblem of dominion over England, Scotland and Wales. It figures in all representations of Arthur among the Nine Worthies, which assures its popular acceptance; but it vanquishes the Virgin device by repetition, not by superior *sen*.

Neither Virgin nor Crowns are hereditary devices, but Arthur may have one such: the dragon which Geoffrey puts on his helmet and VM transfers to his banner. Geoffrey continually associates the dragon with the House of Constantine, and seems to see it as a true, hereditary heraldic device. VM, however, makes the *sen* of the dragon-banner uniquely and intensely personal to Arthur (see II. 264). Here, by a splendid piece of symbolic irony, Arthur unknowingly carries his fate and his nation's about with him wherever he goes. Moreover, in order to communicate the *sen,* the author has to describe the banner in considerable detail. It is a pity that this memorable device should be adopted only by VM's faithful follower, the *Livre d'Artus.* Battle-standards had great symbolic and practical importance in medieval warfare, and Arthurian war ought not to lack them. Also largely lacking is that other means of identification in the field, the war-cry. Charlemagne's 'Munjoie!' roused echoes in the breast of every Frenchman, while the Spaniards thrilled to El Cid's 'Santiago!'. What has Arthur to offer? Wace suggests 'Dius aie, Sainte Marie' (I. 8057). This excellently combines the Anglo-Norman traditional cry with Arthur's special devotion, but unfortunately it does not catch on. LP substitutes the uninspiring 'Clarence!', which may be a pale imitation of 'Monjoie!' since both are place-names, but which certainly does not thrill us as does Charlemagne's cry. Only VM and the *Livre d'Artus* take up—in duty bound—LP's sug-

gestion. Unintentionally they make it even more distasteful by the confusion induced by constant mention of the real place, Clarence. The cry particularises Arthur, but does him little honour. More inspiriting is the alliterative *Morte,* where Arthur's faithful followers simply cry his name.

Where Arthur's battle-accoutrements are concerned, many good opportunities are missed or rejected by the authors. Overall, however, he does little worse than other characters in the material. From this viewpoint, the authors would perhaps have done well to look *more* closely at real-life details.

The same could be said in connection with Arthur's residences and general peacetime possessions. Scattered descriptions of houses, council-rooms and tents fail on the whole either to individualise Arthur or to draw him fully into the burgeoning world of medieval civilisation. The material generally is not lacking in descriptions of magnificent residence, but I do not think that the general vagueness over Arthur's residences is intended to insult him. It is simply assumed that he always has all of the best:

> Li plus bas jours de la semaine,
> quant plus priveement estoit,
> Pasques d'un autre roi sambloit.
>
> (*Deus espees* 34-6)

The reader is invited to imagine the most luxurious lifestyle he can conceive—whether it features 'hot peppered chops' or the tapestried magnificence of a fifteenth-century castle—intensify it ten times, and take it as a description of Arthur's lifestyle. He is particularised by superlatives rather than by distinct details.

Arthur's non-possession of magical objects generally is disappointing, but it has compensations. All the wonders and luxuries of the Arthurian universe belong to Arthur as the centre of that universe. The knights' tales, to which he so avidly listens, offer to him in homage all the strangeness of his realm. Paraphrasing K. H. Göller, we may say of Arthur: 'Seine Welt ist seine Persönlichkeit'. Everything which happens in the Arthurian world individualises Arthur: that is why his very name carries such magic. (pp. 119-29)

> *Rosemary Morris, "Personal Attributes," in her* The Character of King Arthur in Medieval Literature, *D. S. Brewer, 1982, pp. 119-29.*

Norma Lorre Goodrich

[*Goodrich is a noted scholar of medieval history and literature. In the following excerpt, she examines the legend of Guinevere.*]

Queen Guinevere died in Scotland, before the dawn of history there. She did not long survive King Arthur's passing, around 542, and she had been his wife for thirty or forty years. Neither his nor her death ended that relationship. The mystery of their lives has only deepened as the Dark Ages try to slide down the ramp of time, deeper and deeper, into total obscurity.

But this primary human mystery, even today, is clearer than the other black envelope that shuts her and her champion Lancelot into their secret, star-crossed love affair. Somewhere in that dark north land their phantoms must still stretch out a helping hand to the beloved.

By name and fame, by stature and ill-repute, Queen Guinevere may well be the world's most glamorous woman. She reportedly walked in queenliness and incomparable beauty. Her beloved, the forever youthful Lancelot, stood by her side, swore she was innocent of all charges against her, laid down his tartan, drew his naked sword, and offered to die for her if he could not kill all her accusers. He killed them all, and swore to her again a deathless love.

Was it her beauty or her majesty that raised her posthumously to such heights of glamour? Or was it her crimes, and especially this adulterous liaison with Lancelot?

This queen's black-hearted adultery, it is still falsely charged, was what caused the collapse of King Arthur's golden kingdom. Thus wretchedly ended his gallant life and paradisal rule. Tar with a full brush, says the adage, and slap it on her; some calumny will stick, no matter how many times the queen protested and how fiercely Lancelot denied it. Not even judicial trials by combat could stop the slanderers' mouths. They said she caused King Arthur's final, deathly battle at a place called Camlan, which was very probably the Camboglanna Roman fort on Hadrian's Wall. There on high land north of the deep river bend King Arthur met his last young nephew Modred in a terrible battle. The two died, or slew each other. What tragedy!

Despite the deaths of Arthur and Modred there at Camlan, wildly untrue and unreconciled rumors remain: Queen Guinevere had remarried Modred; Modred had escorted her to safety in the Highlands. Queen Guinevere was drawn and quartered by horses; she escorted King Arthur to the Grail Castle where he died. She caused his kingdom to collapse; she died of grief in England. She entered a monastery, where King Arthur visited her and forgave her. The queen was Lancelot's unrepentant lover in the triangular relationship: Arthur, Lancelot, and Guinevere. Queen Guinevere was barren. Her grave is in Meigle, Scotland; her grave is in Glastonbury, England. She had three fathers; she was a twin (or a triplet); King Arthur had three wives, all three named Guinevere.

None of these false charges and countercharges, scandalous rumors and accusations, has been subjected either to evidence or to the corroboration of reason. With a cool head, in an American place, safe from the special pleadings of impassioned British nationalism, religious prejudice, and racial rancor, a foreign historian now offers to reexamine the Guinevere question.

In the old days an old notion of woman prevailed. Nobody has as yet argued in Guinevere's case that she seems to have been a warrior queen. Would that not throw a different light on her character and personality? Nobody has as yet argued that she was King Arthur's archivist in a land where neither he nor any other warrior except Merlin the Archbishop was literate. Does not her higher education throw a more flattering light on this illustrious queen? Why did it not occur to the chroniclers, who mention her

only as an adjunct to Arthur, Gawain, Merlin, and Lancelot, that she may have been a native and, therefore, a foreign princess caught in cross fire between invading Irish Scots on the west coast of Britain and conquering Anglo-Saxons on the east coast?

Nowadays scholars in Scotland particularly have taken to walking the terrain to measure the land, to search for landmarks described in Arthurian manuscripts, and to argue time and distance. They have also succeeded in locating ancient sites, cities (*civitates*), and hill forts. They are currently sifting with spoons Arthur's old battlefields. Wars have passed over these northern parts of Great Britain between the Roman walls, Hadrianic and Antonine, and been settled at these same fords, these same reconstructed strongholds, these same pleasant meadows; across the very same bogs, waterways, and mosses. Today as a result we locate Salisbury in Edinburgh rather than in England, Arthur's Camelot number one as Carlisle near the Solway Firth, and Guinevere's birthplace even farther north where lived Pictish natives, who were to be absorbed by Scots, Angles, and English. Guinevere was probably one such foreigner—a native Pict.

Today again we may wish to approach the problem of love, which was Guinevere's and Lancelot's private relationship, with more caution than has as yet been exercised. Early in our century such famous authors as Simone de Beauvoir in France and Denis de Rougemont, whose English editor was T. S. Eliot, in Switzerland launched long attacks against the notion of passionate love synonymous, they said, with the longing for death first developed by medieval authors of Arthurian texts. However that may be, we should be willing to look hard at those Arthurian manuscripts, which supposedly propose adulterous love, a madly passionate love (*fin amor*) as the relationship of Lancelot and the queen. What if only one text so represented the situation—and by error in translation? Was Guinevere being caluminated or was the French lady commissioner of the text, by way of Guinevere, being tarred?

Truly one cannot find in Denis de Rougemont (Paris, 1939), who blamed the Guinevere-Arthur-Lancelot triangle of adultery, and/or in the Isolde-Isolde-Tristan triangle any evidence of deep scholarship in medieval texts. Idem, for Simone de Beauvoir. Either readily accepts inherited translation and received opinion. Thus, an attempt at an investigative biography of Queen Guinevere must be undertaken. We are in our century, observed the Parisian barrister, Madame Nathalie Sarraute (Paris, 1956), entered on an Age of Suspicion. Today we ask for evidence and proof. We would prefer a record set straighter.

Guinevere's story and her life descend to us in bits and pieces from the Dark Ages, which was a period of invasion and unparalleled demolition of homes, fortresses, and hill forts with an attendant destruction of most written records. In such cataclysms, under repeated floods of invaders on all coasts from all northern seas, does it seem likely on the face of it that Guinevere and Lancelot indulged in love games decade in and decade out? Planned defense, personal courage, excellent physical training, eloquence in oratory, daring escapes would have served—and did serve—Guinevere, Arthur, and Lancelot better in the

Dark Ages. Parlor games, divorce, and betrayal more became the eighteenth century with its powdered wigs, lice, bare bosoms, and monstrous palaces without plumbing or running water. Guinevere's home lay beside a bank of the Forth River in eastern Scotland. She could go boating and get washed at least.

Guinevere's biography will not be endebted either to Denis de Rougemont or Simone de Beauvoir, much less to any so-called medieval cult of deathly, passionate love, but rather to Arthurian writers and scholars from every country of the Western world, chiefly from America to Scotland and Germany via Ireland and France. Her story will draw on history, archives, ancient voices, and such modern authors versed in mythology as Heinrich Zimmer and his editor Joseph Campbell. Eschewed will be all soap operas, especially the Victorian, where Tennyson's queen grovels wickedly at Arthur's feet, rolls her eyes, and cries out her remorse. To us in the twentieth century she did no such thing, for in Guinevere's day, as we know, adultery was immediately punished by death. Neither appeal nor rank would have saved Guinevere for one minute. Hers would have been the bonfire if Lancelot ever failed to prove her innocence. He could not fail, he said, because *she was innocent.*

If heroical epics had ever been written about women heroines, or if epics had ever even portrayed a heroic woman, then that sort of biography would have suited Queen Guinevere. But alas, epic heroes are always male sacrificial victims expendable for the good of the community. That was far from Guinevere's case. Gawain died in combat. So did Lancelot. Modred, who was Arthur's heir, died in combat either beside or against his Uncle Arthur. Perceval, Galahad, and Lohengrin disappeared, or went as pilgrims to Jerusalem. Guinevere was the sole survivor of them all. But she seems much more an epic figure than a sob sister in some Victorian hole-and-closet romance. Much less suited is she to the stock opinion: that Lancelot jumped on her bed, made love to Arthur's queen, and caused her sheets to be bloody. How distasteful are dirty books of any century.

Nor will tragedy suit Guinevere's story, for even if she were put to death by being torn apart by horses, that would make her only a wretched figure, but not a grandly tragic heroine defiant to the end but bowed in disgrace *through no fault of her own.* So she fits no literary genre, and the same is true for Lancelot. Both he and Gawain die in battle and according to the fortunes of war. Both had in peacetime gone guarantee for Guinevere whom both cherished as their true and lawful sovereign.

Lancelot was certainly Guinevere's love. It is far from certain that he ever became her lover. And yet ladies the world over adore him before Arthur. Why is that? What is there about Lancelot that sends the heart to beating, which caused young ladies in his days to diet madly for weeks before he was to appear before them and they before him?

In 1948 the German scholar Heinrich Zimmer put his finger on Lancelot. Zimmer's editor Joseph Campbell recorded this new interpretation of the Guinevere-Lancelot

love affair not as adultery but as love-to-the-death between liege and sovereign, perhaps something like Benjamin Disraeli's reverence for and adoration of Queen Victoria. Lancelot was no epic hero either, decided Zimmer. No less a tragic hero fallen like Oedipus from a great estate to ignominy:

> Lancelot is an incarnation of the ideal for manhood that exists, not in the world of masculine social action, but in the hopes and fancies of the feminine imagination.

Reflecting upon Zimmer's conclusion, one must ask another obvious question: Whose feminine imagination did he think created Lancelot? We know that Arthurian manuscripts originated like the German *Lanzelet* in Carlisle, as in Melrose (both then in Scotland). Then who besides Merlin could have been the recorder of Lancelot's deeds? Several texts specify in so many words that when Lancelot returned from time to time to Arthur's Court, he had his adventures written. By whom? By what "feminine imagination," if not that of Queen Guinevere? Merlin employed his own full-time scribe, or bard, named Blaise. Guinevere was Arthur's full-time scribe, or bard; and Ireland boasted many such who were royal women and also fine poets.

The vast Arthurian corpus, or literature—which is, in fact, the largest in the world—did not accumulate around an uninspired nucleus. It required over the centuries patient and talented recorders who were trained writers and probably also avid readers themselves. While impossible to prove today, because *Northern Annals* are still missing, one may at least ponder Zimmer's original suggestion and extend it to a logical corollary that Guinevere herself, like Queen Elizabeth I after her and like the probably royal Arthurian poet Marie de France, was this Lancelot's original author. In fact, her wedding contract so stipulated that the new queen would act as court recorder. Thus this hero Lancelot who over succeeding ages has so appealed to women, young and elderly alike, may have been a projection of Queen Guinevere's ideal man. He was, if so, truly her beloved. No Arthurian text has missed that last point, which is their relationship.

The French writers of the Middle Ages have always claimed Lancelot as a native son, thought him native French because of his elegance and his French-sounding name, its three syllables easily pronounceable in Old or in modern French. Only recently was the etymology discerned, making *Lancelot* merely a translation into French of the Latin name *Anguselus.* Therefore Lancelot was not a native of continental France, but a royal clan chieftain of the Gael, or Celts, whose name in modern English would be "the Angus" (i.e., Latin, *Anguselus;* Old French, *L'Ancelot*).

This Lancelot, who was held to be of both royal and saintly lineage, was a revered son of two dead, departed kings also named Lancelot. Their gravestones he guarded and moved to safer repositories as Arthur's wars appeared to be worsening. Lancelot was clearly portrayed as a gorgeous hero and a royal prince before whose passage maidens and ladies queued up, before whom everybody bowed and gasped in adulation, doubtless with streaming eyes.

The charge of adultery was not leveled at Lancelot by the Oxford don Geoffrey of Monmouth nor, in fact, by any clergyman in Britain. That allegation, which also comprised all the nastier details of bloodied bedding, came from eastern France circa 1172. It took only some thirty-five years for the immense popularity of Geoffrey's *History of the Kings of Britain* (1136) to inspire an Old French work centered entirely about the personage of this royal Lancelot.

The paid continental author Chrétien de Troyes, from Troyes in Champagne, who wrote the *Lancelot* of 1172, has never been referred to as less than a genius in bloom. France has a tradition centuries older than England's, and older than the English language itself, of respecting authors who like Geoffrey and Chrétien were literary men of genius. Chrétien is always granted the benefit of the doubt, unqualified praise, despite the fact that his Arthurian texts cannot compare, either in historical stature, in lofty impartiality, or in sheer beauty of language to Geoffrey's much more popular and successful *History of the Kings of Britain* (composed originally in Latin).

After Chrétien's *Lancelot,* Queen Guinevere is suddenly and widely branded an adulteress whose supposed crime supposedly distanced Lancelot from his military duties to King Arthur. Some later authors go so far as to make Lancelot leave Britain altogether and desert Arthur's side and Guinevere's. Such treatments have not gone unprotested by historians of Scotland, for both Scotland and England claim Lancelot and Guinevere. Geography cannot allow the latter, however. The Scots must now be heard. They have other explanations for Lancelot and Guinevere, which understandings surface in the massive Old French volumes of the *Prose Lancelot* (written in 1220-1230). They come in French, of course, from Scotland and the days when the French were still governing Britain.

Guinevere and Lancelot today, then, still stand at the apex of controversy, the late English texts blaming them, the earliest Latin text of Geoffrey at Oxford, England, exonerating them. Paradoxically, the earliest French text of Chrétien rises to world fame by dwelling on the immorality of these royal British personages and the inevitable catastrophes that ensued: no less than the expulsion from Paradise of the loathsome female Guinevere before the dissolution of the paradise that had been King Arthur's peaceful reign of some long years, or even decades.

Possibly none of this alleged adultery may have been taken seriously, until modern critics such as Geoffrey Ashe commenced considering these royal personages as historical. While Guinevere sobs out her guilt at a convent in Amesbury, England, as per Sir Thomas Malory's *Le Morte d'Arthur* of the fifteenth century and Alfred, Lord Tennyson's *Idylls of the King* in the nineteenth century, readers may nod complacently at her. Adulterous women are no longer burned at the stake or stoned to death in England or France. Adultery nowadays is perhaps even condoned. Guinevere foresaw her terrible reputation, Tennyson wrote, and dreamed that she would ever be maligned. It came to her in an "awful dream," or was she perhaps a priestess?

But when we confront the possibility that after all these fifteen hundred years since Arthur's death circa 542 our characters in Malory's exquisite prose and Tennyson's unforgettable poetry may have been historical, then we must look deeper into the allegations. History does not condone adultery, and certainly not in queens. Nor was Guinevere guilty.

This attempt at a biography of Guinevere amounts to a second look at her situation in history and Lancelot's. Principally, who was this Guinevere? Where did she hail from? Why her great reputation for grace and beauty? What was her military expertise, which even Sir Thomas Malory accepted? Through what testings did she earn her homage for extraordinary courage and heroism in mortal peril? What was this powerful woman who brought home to Carlisle (Camelot) two wounded warriors by leading their horse, on which she had loaded them, through the perilous forest? How to explain her longevity when all about her had died? If she was escorted to safety in Scotland, then where in Scotland did she go? Where in Scotland was she sheltered, and why? And why Guinevere? Can anyone seriously believe Scots ever sheltered an adulterous queen of Britain?

The Scot historian Boethius in the sixteenth century, studying history then at the University of Paris, proclaimed Guinevere's honorable interment in Scotland. Not only that, he personally *had seen her funeral monument inside Scotland,* which was not only a tall gravestone but also a marvel of the sculptor's chisel, a work of art. According to historians of Scotland, Modred was no traitor and no abductor of Queen Guinevere, but a prince of Scotland and King Arthur's duly named heir. Quite clearly, Guinevere's case needs a second look and much more study.

The mysteries dancing attendance on Queen Guinevere are those that shroud every human personality and particularly women's because women are taught to be closed and secretive. Perhaps the lady Guinevere belongs royally and rightfully, by birth, by marriage, and by longevity to the most royal of sovereigns like the queens Elizabeth, Victoria, and Boudicca of the ancient Iceni in England. Because of her notoriety, Guinevere belongs perhaps also with Cleopatra and Catherine the Great. But her case is still more special than even Malory or Tennyson guessed when they rose to the supreme heights of literature in their holy treatments of dear Arthur's coming and passing from this world.

The mystery of Guinevere thus depends on several vexed questions. The most important points remain to be solved. Her most profound secrets all demand to be unveiled, for she is still so unhappily shrouded. Everything about this ancient queen, whose history in the *Prose Lancelot* fills page after page, volume after volume, must be reevaluated.

While the world remains moonstruck before her, as it were, and totally absorbed in puzzling over her adultery, it lets the queen slide peripherally away from our vision. Obsessed with sex and her lack of morality, the modern world has ceased to note the more perplexing problems her situation raises. Meanwhile we have neglected another reading of the kindly, much more voluminous sources such as the *Prose Lancelot.* These later texts pay closer attention to facts and details such as her marriage contract, her betrothal ceremony, her wedding night, her twin sister or double, and her reactions whenever she stood in danger of her life during more than one emergency. These later authors are not infatuated with sex, or with the various ancient queens of Britain as Geoffrey of Monmouth was infatuated. These *Prose Lancelot* authors have rid themselves of the stringencies of poetry; they write cool prose, the prime purpose of which is to share information. They write loftily, above any bee in the bonnet concerning sin, like noble clergymen well aware of the human condition and how to deal even with heinous lapses. In their wake we, too, have a less-passionate view of ancient royalty.

In any event, given the nature of the human personality, Guinevere will never allow us to lose our sense of mystery before her or our desire to know her better. Even if we journey again and again to Scotland and lay our hand on her gravestone there, which towers over us, and even if we then have tears in our eyes, they will not be tears of sorrow for Queen Guinevere, but tears of gratitude that so much of our commonly shared ancient past is recoverable. All we shall ever know comes from experience, all of which lies in the past. It is worth weeping over, by the long road into the Highlands.

In touching her rosy and beautiful gravestone, which ever since Boethius wrote about it in Paris five hundred years ago many have journeyed to Scotland to see and touch, we actually do lay our hands on Guinevere, as on her past. Her case is much unlike Arthur's, for whom, say the *Annals of Wales,* recently edited by Rachel Bromwich at Cardiff University, there never was a grave. It is true that the late Nora Chadwick (also of Cardiff University in Wales) pointed to a site twenty miles from Carlisle (Camelot) at a parish named Arthuret as a site peculiarly connected to King Arthur because it was named after him: "Arthuret." But it is only a one parish church and overgrown, ancient *graveyard.* It may be Arthur's grave, however.

In Guinevere's case we do have her real grave, beside a village church, in an isolated area of Scotland. Nowadays her gravestone has been moved. It now stands inside a Woman's Museum to which admission is open and free if one can find the caretaker. Furthermore, distinguished visitors have over the last few centuries visited this site and given us the benefit of their expertise and experience. (It was one of them who looked at her sculptured stone memorial and concluded falsely that Guinevere was evil in life, that she was drawn and quartered by horses—and richly deserved it, for the crime of adultery.)

If asked for an opinion, a modern reader of Arthurian texts from the High Middle Ages would have to reply that Queen Guinevere strangely resembled several of her contemporaries. Because of her extraordinary courage and presence of mind, she resembles the Geneviève who became the patron saint of Paris (Luxembourg Gardens). When from the city wall she saw the army of Huns approaching, Geneviève advised her fellow countrymen to hide in perfect silence behind the ramparts. Believing the city looted and abandoned, Attila and his army withdrew. The ancient Guinevere also much resembles the brave Mary of the Gael who set a new standard for women worldwide when she chose virginity and joined the Church, eventually meriting the honor of being interred beside Saint Patrick, not in Glastonbury, England, but in Ireland at Downpatrick. The evidence that Queen Guinevere still wore the antique green of a holy Druidess raised and educated on the Isle of Man, Irish Sea, comes as the most stunning of surprises.

Queen Guinevere will not be what we expected to find. She and Lancelot alone knew the way at low tide to the Grail Castle, on Saint Patrick's islet, facing Ireland. After he survived a painful initiation, Lancelot termed the place paradise: "Isle of Joy." The queen also, but earlier than Lancelot, was educated on that same Isle of Maidens (priestesses) where commissions were being received for King Arthur's sculptured sarcophagus and where Lancelot actually raised the lid on the tomb where all too soon he, too, would lie ceremoniously in death.

Because Merlin was then High-Priest in Britain, he must have known Guinevere while she was still a pupil of Merlin's chosen lady teacher for Lancelot and his cousin Bors. The Lady of the Lake may also have superintended Guinevere's formal instruction, for it had included not only the symbols used in Pictish sculptures such as standing Celtic crosses but also the calligraphy used on parchment (manuscripts), or handwritten texts. It was the Lady of the Lake Niniane/Vivian, her name reading one way in Scotland and another in Wales.

The German Wolfram, author of *Parzival,* which belongs among the earliest of Arthurian texts, claimed that "Grail Maidens" educated by the Lady of the Lake were sent "out," or home, at the end of their school days so that they could wed equally royal youths. Such were Guinevere and Arthur: royal Roman by birth, because born in the Roman Empire.

Of course, we are to recall that Britain, even including parts of what is now Scotland, had been ruled by Rome for five hundred years before Arthur and Guinevere were born. This Roman world with its Roman structures they saw every day of their lives. By the time of Merlin's archiepiscopal rule, and King Arthur's assumption of royal sovereignty, these isles had been Christianized. Saint Patrick had led the way, having become the first Christian Bishop of Man and the southern isles some three decades before Merlin was born. Without her long training by royal and Christian teachers, Queen Guinevere could never have become King Arthur's archivist.

Finally, any biography of Guinevere depends almost wholly on ancient sources as rewritten in the Middle Ages. It is necessary to translate proper names from Old French back into Celtic. Familiar personal names will be let stand during the following narratives, which will eventually allow final corrections into some original form, such as:

English	*Latin*
Merlin	Dubricius (*Sanctus*)
Arthur	Arturus (*Rex*)
Lancelot	Anguselus (*Ille*)

Depiction of Merlin confronting King Vortigern, indicating two fighting dragons that portend Britain's future. From an English manuscript illustration, 15th c.

Guinevere   Guanhumara (*Regina*)

(*Sanctus,* "saint"; *Rex,* "king"; *Ille,* "the famous"; *Regina,* "queen")

The kind of biography Guinevere will acquire in these following pages depends on Old French, Welsh, and Old German original translations of lost sources from Britain, which France was governing in the Middle Ages. It may be assumed that all our authors, even those prominent scholars who wrote the *Prose Lancelot* and preferred dignified anonymity, almost certainly knew each other and most certainly collaborated. One can only imagine with what naked greed these medieval writers searched for manuscripts and haggled over borrowing and lending just as do our Inter-Library Loan Offices in American universities today.

Even Geoffrey of Monmouth probably had read and also had met his follower and alter ego, Chrétien de Troyes, according to Eugene J. Weinraub. . . . If that is so, and it truly seems so, then Chrétien would also have had professional and perhaps also political reasons for contradicting Geoffrey with pleasure and for chuckling over the result. The measure of Chrétien's success as an author rests today

directly proportionate to Geoffrey's early and late abysmal disgrace.

Nobody must fall off the chair at the likelihood that Queen Guinevere and Lady Macbeth shared a common heritage, birthright, and somewhat similar first names. Any slight understanding of Pictish real estate law opens the door to realizing why Guinevere was personally so sought after as bride and persecuted to the point of being kidnapped after marriage. How be sure the pretender to her body had her and not her double if the real heiress was not tattooed? The location of Guinevere's dowry would alone have dictated her supreme position in Merlin's eyes, in Arthur's, in Gawain's, in Galehaut's—but probably not in Lancelot's.

Only Lancelot had learned as a child to love Guinevere, according to German writers. She had been an older sister, Wolfram von Eschenbach believed, to Lancelot when he was a baby forlorn, alone, cold, orphaned, motherless, half-drowned, and pulled out of the lake barely in time to save his life. That childhood danger alone would make Guinevere's anguish clear as years later and in daily danger of her own execution she saw Lancelot again at his maturity. The ties that bound these two far surpassed the hidden pleasures of any passing sex.

A woman reading the scene of their first meeting as adults feels Guinevere's repressed emotion at the sight of the child Lancelot grown into a splendid man. It was the never-forgotten love of the small girl for the even smaller boy (cousin?) playmate. As a woman Guinevere certainly never forgot this special, tender, protective love of the older girl for the younger male child who is more vulnerable, who must be watched over and helped through his tests. For all the while she knows that he is alive only for a day. His birth requires him to die young in battle on some foreign field that will in all likelihood be her own property. And she herself will live to learn of it, perhaps will have to view the site where he fell on the bloody ground.

Even after the Lancelot-Guinevere relationship is viewed thus alternately, a far greater mystery remains. Something characteristic of Guinevere is still missing. Who was she really? Was she only an heiress-become-queen at Arthur's Court? It would appear that so far our sources have failed to alert us plainly to Queen Guinevere's prime functions. Money alone and property, immense though her real holdings doubtless were, would guarantee not much more than her marriage. After that day everything she owned would be administered by King Arthur, before whom she too constituted mere personal property. Rather than sink gracefully into second place, Guinevere continued to rise and still rises or looms, veiled probably, green clad certainly, bejeweled and bedecked in another majesty, superior by far.

So we must turn to those whom we consider superior authors from the Middle Ages and for long moments shunt both Geoffrey of Monmouth and Chrétien de Troyes onto an unused siding. Authors on the main line will have to be newly interrogated, for they claim certain advantages such as anonymity, distance, open-mindedness, lack of bias, worldliness, stature, sympathy, high birth, leisure, and superior knowledge. The essential ancient material they had to have at hand was twofold: *bardic paeons* of praise, and a clear understanding of symbols.

The Bards of Arthur's day had been prepared over long years to celebrate fittingly the lives and great deeds of their royals. Consequently, they wrote set pieces appropriate to each great occasion. For this reason we are able to see Guinevere first as she acted publicly: her reception of visitors, her betrothal, her wedding, her coronation, her testings at Arthur's Court, her trials, her presence at judicial combats, her leadership at ceremonies, and her stops along journeys. Aside from such occasions, we have some knowledge of her background, her contracts, her functions, and her feelings.

What we must unfortunately learn for ourselves, each one of us separately, is the meaning of those symbols that more than any other body of information, even more than language, reveal the hidden Guinevere to us. It is generally understood today that certain symbols occur as our common property in four areas: folklore, tales, art, and religion. Fortunately for the world, each area contributes im-

mediately to our understanding of Guinevere: art precisely through the Pictish carvings in eastern Scotland and, specifically in her case, the sculptured standing stone that is her rose-colored memorial. She is also a heroine of folklore because of the colors she wears, because of her jewels, because of that particular metal that surrounds her on special occasions, because of her human conditions of fiancée, confederate, bride, wife, sister, and queen among others. We note that both tales and folklore, her written and ancient material that is the basis of history, come from literature itself. Every symbol mentioned thus far is also the property of myth, ergo of religion. All ancient myths were once in some way and to some degree liturgy.

Let us prepare by looking in paraphrase now at certain of the lesser symbols that characterize Guinevere: crown, dove, pillar(s), fountain, and blood.

In Guinevere's case her two crowns symbolized her aura, an aureole, plus a token of majesty and royal authority, which resembled and brought vaguely to mind the bridal crown of Venus, for example, or a godly crown in which the Holy Grail gleamed like a fiery ruby, some crown of Wisdom, a crown of Christian love, a crown of the spring flowers of Flora, and the red heart encircled by Christ's Crown of Thorns. Ultimately free association leads each allusion back to religion, both to Satan and to Christ.

The four doves carried before Guinevere at her coronation are recognizable as descending from heaven at the baptism of Jesus, or as the Holy Ghost. Only Perceval, who was to be crowned last king at the Grail Castle, and Guinevere herself are allowed white doves as cognizance. Flocks of doves also attended olden priestesses in Asian oracular shrines. Ancient tombs were, therefore, called "dovecotes" in honor of priestesses of the dead. The dove also brings to mind the superior elevation of the priestess's soul (*anima, psyche, alma*). Guinevere's *four* doves resemble the four nails of Christ, the four rivers of Paradise, and the four-leafed clover, which is prophylactic. Because of Noah's dove, hers also become tokens of the sea, suggesting Guinevere herself was a foreigner from across the sea; the Irish would have called her "Fomorian."

When Lancelot lurched unexpectedly toward a goddess figure inside a domed, gilded temple, he saw Guinevere standing between two gemstone pillars. That day he must have recognized her. It was, indeed, Guinevere, but clad in ceremonial vestments. All ancient temples were entered, like Solomon's Temple in Jerusalem, by passing between twin pillars. Freemasonry knows this, and the twin pillars could have suggested those that upheld the poles. Women were called "pillars" of the early Christian churches. There were two solid gold pillars at Tyre. Guinevere also was a twin.

Guinevere's adventures grow more and more arcane from her halt at the (Irish) fountain such as the one where Gawain received the gift of eternal youth. Nearby or subsequent to the fountain of spring water the heroine herself performed the Celtic cauldron-regeneration ceremony, which must have come down from the pagan god Fons of the Fountain. Close by it loomed the black entrance to

Purgatory where everyone brave enough descended to be purged and made pure.

The most fearsome of elemental symbols associated with her is blood (water) because it belongs with flesh (earth), breath (air), and fire (heat), all curative powers. Because blood is a powerful healing agent, the hero Lancelot will become a donor by means of a phlebotomy. From her cauldron or cup or Grail the priestess will let Lancelot drink before he descends into hell and the Irish Land-below-the-Waves. Then we sense that he is fated to die within the year, which knowledge freed his mind by releasing it from fear. Blinded as he arose by the red gem surmounting the Holy Grail, he prepared to kill Guinevere's enemy Meleagant next day.

A blood ceremony is called in Christian teaching the doctrine of transubstantiation.

Other similar symbols are also called "things composed of two." They are said, as here in Guinevere's case, to light the way to eternity, to foreshadow the future, to link past to present, to confront the reader with the unknown, and to deepen awareness of the universe.

The Irish priestess sings:

> There is a distant isle,
> Around which sea-horses glisten:
> A fair course against the white-swelling surge—
> Four pedestals uphold it.
>
> . . . . .
>
> Colours of every shade glisten
> Throughout the gentle-voiced plains:
> Joy is known, ranked around music,
> In Silver-cloud Plain to the southward.

Symbols preceded all written language. Considered as profound as any other kind of instant communication, symbols picture for us hitherto unsuspected reality midway between ignorance and understanding, day and night, the human and the divine. They alone reveal Guinevere during her journey to Purgatory and Paradise. There she stands clad in her true qualifications, performing at the Grail Castle rites thought to have been celebrated before her time by Christ and the Virgin Mary.

Such symbols light the way to eternity. The Romans knew this was a holy ceremony performed by the Celts. They called it "journey to Paradise": *iter ad paradisum*. The Romans well knew from experience that when they fought Celts, they warred until the bitter end—all the way to death. The Celts, said the Romans, go gladly to war after this particular pardon ceremony. They fight fearlessly, said the Romans, who were defeated at least twice in northeastern and Pictish Scotland, under the dreadful flying Red Dragon of Death. Merlin Pendragon? King Arthur Pendragon? Guinevere Pendragon?

Guinevere was a queen of the death-defying Celts. Her life story starts in the middest. The Romans called it *in medias res*. (pp. 1-18)

> *Norma Lorre Goodrich, in her* Guinevere, *HarperCollins Publishers, 1991, 273 p.*

Major Media Adaptations: Motion Pictures and Television

Parsifal (1904)

Lancelot and Elaine (1909)

Parsifal (1912)

Tristan et Yseut (1920)

A Connecticut Yankee at King Arthur's Court (1921)

A Connecticut Yankee (1931)

King Arthur Was a Gentleman (1942)

L'Éternal Retour (1943)

The Adventures of Sir Galahad [15-part serial] (1949)

A Connecticut Yankee in King Arthur's Court (1949)

Knights of the Round Table (1953)

The Black Knight (1954)

Prince Valiant (1954)

The Siege of the Saxons/ King Arthur and the Siege of the Saxons (1963)

The Sword in the Stone (1963)

The Sword of Lancelot/ Lancelot and Guinevere (1963)

Camelot (1967)

Tristan et Iseult (1972)

Gawain and the Green Knight (1973)

Lancelot du Lac (1974)

King Arthur, the Young Warlord (1975)

Monty Python and the Holy Grail (1975)

Mark Twain's A Connecticut Yankee in King Arthur's Court (1978)

Perceval le Gallois (1978)

The Legend of King Arthur (1979)

Tristan and Isolt/ Lovespell (1979)

The Unidentified Flying Oddball/ King Arthur and the Spaceman (1979)

Parzival (1980)

Excalibur (1981)

Feuer und Schwert/ Tristan und Isolde (1981)

Knightriders (1981)

Arthur the King (1982-1985)

Parsifal (1982)

Sword of the Valiant/ The Legend of Gawain and the Green Knight (1983)

The Morte D'Arthur (1984)

Norma Lorre Goodrich

[*In the following excerpt, Goodrich examines the histori-cal development of the legend of Merlin, emphasizing the importance of primary sources, particularly the* Prophecy.]

Strangely enough, despite centuries of writings, Merlin, the man, is an enigma. His name is known as that of a wiser, older man who counseled King Arthur. It is be-lieved that, in fact as in legend, he arranged for Arthur to be born. He is purported to have reared Arthur expressly to defend Britain from foreign invasion. However, com-peting claims, nationalistic prejudices, superstition, and even ignorance have muddled his history.

Both Merlin and Arthur, who was probably his junior by twenty-five years, undertook a defense of Britain in the fifth century. Rome had been sacked in 410. At this time of dire calamity and wholesale massacre of civilians, Rome had been obliged to withdraw from its Roman prov-ince of Britain the four Roman legions stationed as an army of occupation for the past five hundred years.

Large numbers of Romano-Britons had decided to remain in Britain on their landed estates. The line of the "Roman" commanders-in-chief,—Maximus—Constantine—Ambrosius—Uther Pendragon—Arthur, stepped in to de-fend the formerly Roman forts along the two walls of de-fense: the Antonine to the north (Glasgow-Edinburgh line) and Hadrian's Wall to the south (Carlisle on the west to the North Sea on the east). These east-west lines of de-fense separated what is now England from what is now Scotland, the northern line erecting a barrier between the lowlands and the highlands, where the northern Picts dwelled, a still largely unknown people. (The modern area between these two walls is still called Borders). These lands constituted Merlin's and Arthur's battlegrounds.

At this time the Scots from Ireland were still emigrating into what is now Wales, Cornwall, and the western Isles, and establishing their new kingdoms. But the Anglo-Saxons from across the Baltic and North seas had, by the time Arthur reached the command age of fifteen, already taken eastern Britain and were holding east of the line Southampton to Edinburgh. The situation was not only grave for the resident peoples, but desperate.

For Merlin to be so fondly remembered in Scotland today, far and near, high and low, he must have been a very exalt-ed personage—indeed, even someone more exalted than King Arthur himself. Then who was Merlin? What was his profession? What was his title?

These are questions that have been argued back and forth by scholars for some time now: Were there not two Mer-lins? Or was there only one? The archives of Wales claim that, in fact, there were two Merlins and give the two gene-alogies. The older one *is* King Arthur's Merlin. He was born probably about 450 and died in 536.

The theory of only one Merlin even now seems to stumble on the fact of dating, by extending his life span too long—by several decades. One Merlin could not have been the victorious contemporary of King Arthur, who died in 542, in the first half of the sixth century, and also a defeated

contemporary of a British chieftain of the Old North called Gwenddolau, slain at the battle of Arthuret (Arf-derydd), Scotland, in 573.

One must now commence a new search through the pri-mary documents to discover who the mysterious Merlin was and how he was related to Arthur, what his profession was, and what his accomplishments were while he lived. Such an investigation will also answer questions about Morgan "le Fay," the Lady of the Lake, and about the big-gest mystery: Who killed Merlin?

The first person in question was a warrior and supporter of King Arthur, and he was named Merlin. The second person in question, one who survived the battle of Arthu-ret—because of which he went insane—was named Myrd-din. He lived on for many years after 573 as a wild man in the "Caledonian" forests of Scotland.

Both candidates for the prestige and rank of Merlin were authors, Merlin of orations and the world-famous *Prophe-cy.* The latter, Myrddin, wrote, probably, a body of ob-scure verse in Old British, which was a language similar to modern Welsh, and this verse is stored in Wales. It has unfortunately been much rewritten over the centuries.

The former, Merlin, was interred on the seashore of west-ern Scotland in the year 536. The latter, Myrddin, was still alive between 573 and 600, for at some time in those years he conversed with and was blessed by Saint Kentigern (Mungo), the older patron saint of Scotland. Myrddin was probably interred in the border uplands of Scotland.

Merlin was called Merlinus in Latin, Merlin in French and in English, in which three languages his major ex-ploits as a counselor to four British kings (Vortigern, Am-brosius, Uther, and Arthur) are told. His death, while King Arthur was still living, is also recounted in several texts. In none is he ever called Myrddin, which is a Welsh name. Neither his Latin name (Merlinus) nor his French and English name (Merlin), occurs in Welsh or in a Welsh dictionary.

King Arthur was always known as a Romano-Briton, Roman on his father's side and British on his mother's side, both families being warriors or commanders of the line. Merlin was at least twenty-five years older than Ar-thur and *probably* a near relative. Freeborn Romans and Celts customarily bore three names, and sometimes four. The Romans were given:

1. a *praenomen,* or first name,

2. a *cognomen,* family or last name,

3. a *nomen,* or middle name indicating his *gens* (clan), and sometimes, if a man was very dis-tinguished,

4. an *agnomen,* which was a surname often be-stowed as a title of honor, or fondly as a nickname.

In Britain any noble Celt such as Merlin would also have had three personal names, as we see now in Welsh, his *en-nwau personau: cyfenw* (a surname), *enw bedydd* (a baptis-mal name), *llwyth* (a tribal name), or *tylwyth* (a family name, ancestral name), or *brychan* (his plaid, or tartan name). Without a clan name, both Briton and Roman would been scorned as a nobody (*sine gente*).

A premonition suggests that "Merlin" was an agnomen. It urges a search through those languages primarily connected to King Arthur's Merlin: English, Latin, French, and Scottish. The personal name "Merlin," one remembers at once, is also spelled "merlin" as a common noun. This suggests that "Merlin" was the man's familiar name, fondly bestowed, his affectionate nickname. More than any man alive, King Arthur's Merlin would have merited a title of honor, an affectionate tribute, for meritorious service well beyond the call of duty. He was, like Arthur, a father to his country.

Doubtless, Merlin and Myrddin have long since merged into one personage held in equal affectionate remembrance by one and all, one man in the public mind. But it seems imperative now, in the name of justice, to separate them into the Arthurian hero and battle leader, adviser to the four British kings, scholar and mysterious, great, but still unrevealed noble personage, and the pitiful, suffering poet Myrddin, who went mad, ate apples, wandered for decades, naked, cold, and starving through the forests. Myrddin was forgiven and blessed by Saint Kentigern about 600, and was even seen centuries later by Saint Waldhave while recuperating from a serious illness.

Even during his lifetime Merlin was largely ahistorical and unrevealed. He is even unrevealed in the manuscripts that recount his life story. He was always largely unknown to the greater public, except as "Merlin." When he was summoned by the kings or needed desperately to recruit other noble allies, he came silently, disguised as a poor shepherd, as a woodcutter, or as a peasant. Even the sovereigns failed to recognize him under his various disguises. He practiced this concealment habitually and for a long period of time. It would be useful to examine the written texts to see if this practice can be explained.

Who in Arthur's day would have been obliged to disguise himself as he passed through the battle lines into Arthur's command post? But more significantly, how was Merlin occupied when he was away, neither advising Arthur nor leading Arthur's battle line ahead of the king?

Merlin played many roles, it would seem, since he wore many costumes. Yet, contrary to King Arthur, Merlin's physical appearance is so meticulously detailed as to make him instantly recognizable in any street of Carlisle, Peel, Glasgow, or Edinburgh.

There is the story of Merlin's birth and the story of his childhood as a prodigy. He was a rare case in history. Having satisfied ourselves as to his name, it is possible to follow him as a child, as a youth, and as a prodigy. In Scotland he is still hailed as "Marvelous Merlin" because he worked such wonders for Arthur that he has come down as the very prototype of the shaman, or wizard, or magician. And yet these words do not sit well upon Merlin's august shoulders. He is too venerable even for them, too imposing.

Although it may be impossible to persuade the modern reader of this fact, Merlin's chief glory rests not in any magical performance but in his famous *Prophecy*. This great work of art, *which has changed history down through the centuries* in Europe, overshadows even his exploits as standard-bearer and foremost warrior of Celtic Britain, which is saying a good deal.

His principal attraction for poets and readers throughout the centuries has been his physical attraction to women. He must have been a beautiful man. Morgan "le Fay," who was the Queen of Ireland and the Out-Isles and a mother to at least one of the clans of present Scotland, was said to have been romantically involved with Merlin. She was also romantically involved with Lancelot and with Accolon, to name only two of her other lovers or luckless suitors. Merlin's greatest romantic attachment was to the Lady of the Lake. That Lady Niniane, or Vivian, for her names are double at least, has always been said to have seduced Merlin, which seems to have been every woman's wish in those days. As the gossip goes, after having seduced him, the Lady persuaded him to teach her his most difficult magic tricks. Such stories supply us with the larger part of Merlin's legend. Its end is sad enough to please all lovers and to shock others, for the Lady then killed Merlin. What were her reasons for murder?

Even murder could not silence Merlin. It continued his legend with a new breath of wind. He was then afforded a voice from beyond the grave where the cruel beauty had shut him in his cold, stone sarcophagus. As he lay so treacherously entombed, Merlin cried out messages for posterity. He did not die at once but lingered on as long as he had breath and words to transmit. One must have another look at these stories, judge their merits, fathom their secrets, discover how Merlin died and where, and reach some satisfactory truth behind the legend.

Yet Merlin's claim to immortality during the Middle Ages rested upon his Christianity and upon his authorship of the *Prophecy*. That text was eagerly seized by the leading churchmen of northern France in the twelfth century since it came from the pen of Geoffrey of Monmouth. Geoffrey first translated it from Old British into Latin, which was then the universal language of all churchmen. Fragments of this prophecy or of others still circulate in Scotland. However, and here is the bitterest controversy among scholars and theologians today: they do not accept as truth the words of Geoffrey of Monmouth. They also reject Merlin's authorship. Too many scholars still believe that Geoffrey of Monmouth forged the Merlin *Prophecy*, that Geoffrey wrote it, and that the *Prophecy* refers to twelfth-century politics at the court of King Henry II. Thus, the famous Merlin *Prophecy*, for centuries the wonder of world literature, has fallen into modern disrepute. . . . Merlin's major work, then, was a *Prophecy* in the manner of the ancient prophets of Israel and Judah whom in life and dress Merlin imitated. We know of King Arthur's dedication to the Virgin, and that he and Merlin re-Christianized the Grail Castle on its western isle adjacent to the Isle of Man.

The *Prophecy* may still be what the Middle Ages considered it in those later days of faith, as imaginative literature from a great mind that had allowed memory to wander among openended symbols back to the frenzy of combat:

naked warriors covered in blood; black whips flailing naked flesh like the sting of vipers; animals tearing, clawing, rending, raging in uncontrolled savagery. The battle frenzy of the archaic Celtic warrior explodes before us like a cornered, bristling boar charging from the thicket. Over the battlefields of this war for one's home territory soars like some ancient dragon Merlin's flaming red banner, a dragon sometimes called gargoyle, called sphinx, an image of death and fire that the Saxon hero must fight and extinguish.

When Merlin himself was not more than one year old, his future symbols were already revered among the Franks in Gaul. The Frankish King Meroveus, who is said to have killed Attila the Hun, dreamed he had been fathered by just such a dragon, a dragon-king, or some coiled serpent-king. Another Merovingian sovereign dreamed of a horrible three-headed monster and was informed that his dream summarized history: the way France was ravaged by three successive conquerors—a lion (the Celts), an eagle (the Romans), and a venomous toad (the Franks). Here is Merlin's animal symbolism of the *Prophecy* already made. Another Frankish noble who became a saint also dreamed that the eagle (Rome) was destroyed by a lion (the Celts) and then by a serpent (the Welsh); this was not a dream but a nightmare. Similarly, Britain was lashed by the Saxon chieftain Hengist, a German worm, said the Celts, that swam underwater like wolves or like Beowulf. They were wolves of the ocean, says Merlin.

Then Merlin's *Prophecy* takes off to float freely onto another association: the Lion of Scotland, the Pictish Boar from the Highlands, the Red Dragon of Wales. Altogether his archaic symbols shift so often that they become incomprehensible to us. They are so ancient in the history of man, so much older than our books, that they are really relics of a truly forgotten prehistoric past.

Merlin's use of symbols in lieu of history, conveys to us some lost past of the human race where we merely glimpse in the mind's eye the olden Germanic kings and also their preferred insignia: beasts that represented each heathen monarch. The British Celts, who had been converted to Christianity directly from Jerusalem, it is still believed, gasped in horror.

But among the ancient Celts of Gaul, who did not even remember them, birds and animals once symbolized rivers, forests, and even mountains. The animal drawings of the Picts still impress us with their vivid beauty. In Merlin the three limbs of the tree seem in one flash to symbolize the three tribes of the British Celts. Such seemingly accidental associations in the Merlin *Prophecy* convey spontaneously and better than a thousand words Merlin's hopes and fears for his time. His masterful use of animal symbolism, especially when compared to the Pictish glyphs, puts his modern readers not before Merlin, but beside him, looking out with his eyes at wild hogs, at white giants of iniquity in the mountains of Wales, at bear cubs born to a lioness, at the oracular heron, harbinger of the storm, who flew like a druid, or like the soul of Hercules, who was also Merlin's Arthur, up into an oak tree.

In one passage of the *Prophecy* Merlin almost falls into a

coherent narrative. In that passage he tells how the heron gave birth to a king of Scotland. Her firstborn offspring was a fox who devoured its dam, wore an ass's head, bit a boar, became a wolf, devoured the boar, became a boar, and slew the wolf. Afterward he was kinged, that is, he metamorphosed himself into a royal, rampant lion. Every now and then, despite himself, Merlin corroborates our knowledge, such as that those ancient sub-kings wore gold torques instead of crowns. He always stimulates recollections of the modern history books, with his symbols that persist in reminding his reader of Maximus, Constantine, Ambrosius, Uther Pendragon, and Arthur. Even the ubiquitous, evil King Vortigern seems almost to float to the surface. These evocations remain only that, however, as they slip from our grasp and float off into freer air. We are left with Merlin's view.

Thus, in Merlin's *Prophecy,* the lion, the wolf, and the fox have not yet been confined to their set roles, as in the medieval fable (or beast-epic). This later medieval form was political and attacked the monarchy. The ancient Merlin has no comic relief and no homely, barnyard domesticity. Merlin is like a biblical prophet. He never veers away from his given task, which is to present war in its unrelieved horror. His is a fierce, crude portrayal of ancient warfare at its worst. Nor does he confuse his terrible images of a bloody history with the consecrated symbols of his Christianity.

The *Prophecy,* which long ago slipped from the pens of Merlin and Geoffrey, escaped alone into the world where like all great literature it still lives a life of its own, as public property. Thus, we shall all be free to decide finally if it seems truly to be an eyewitness account of the Dark Ages. If so, it is doubly precious, for such firsthand accounts are very rare indeed. The Celts were not trained in history, which is a modern discipline. (pp. 5-14)

Norma Lorre Goodrich, in her Merlin, *Franklin Watts, 1987, 386 p.*

Roger Sherman Loomis

[*In the following excerpt, Loomis sketches the development of the Merlin tradition in Arthurian literature during the Middle Ages, proposing that the legend's original sources were undoubtedly of Celtic provenance.*]

The metamorphoses of Curoi are matched in Arthurian romance by the well-known transformations of Merlin. Curoi vaunts his arts, and Merlin his "crafts." Curoi, under the name of Terror Son of Great Fear, used to form himself into whatever shape he pleased, and the same was true of Merlin. Among the shapes . . . Curoi assume[s] are those of a Giant Herdsman and of a Man of the Wood; the earliest accounts of Merlin show him in the same guises. However, an influential group of scholars have asserted that there was practically no independent Celtic tradition about the name of Merlin, and that it was merely the caprice of Geoffrey of Monmouth in foisting upon this insignificant figure certain Oriental tales of remarkable prophecies which had already been fastened by the Welsh to the name of a certain Lailoken, that started Merlin upon his career.

Now Gaster has shown conclusively that as Merlin is first clearly represented under his own name in Geoffrey of Monmouth's *History,* his story is based upon Talmudic legends regarding Solomon and Asmodeus, which are already attached in Nennius to a marvelous youth called Ambrosius. Gaster concludes:

> Given the practice of assimilating old legends to new surroundings and spelling the past in the letters and ideas of the present, of substituting better known names for less known ones and making a romance out of the ancient tales of Greece and Palestine, then this legend can only be the reflex of the oriental tales and motives, not even skilfully worked up. One can easily detect the seams in the coat. The latter part of the Merlin legend entirely belies the first. There is absolutely no connection between the later adventures of Merlin at the courts of Vortigern, Uter, and his son, and the incidents at the beginning of the tale.

Let us grant everything Gaster has claimed; but let us also note the admissions he has incidentally made. First, that before Geoffrey adopted him, Merlin's name was already well known, and therefore the centre of a tradition. Second, that even in Geoffrey's *History* Merlin's career is a composite. Thirdly, that Talmudic and apocryphal legends explain only a part of that composite. As Miss Weston at once showed, Layamon gives a more primitive account of Merlin's birth. "The story discussed by Dr. Gaster only touches a very small part of the Merlin legend and offers no parallel to the shape-shifting which was so marked a feature of his career, nor to his 'wood-abiding' madness and his prophecies." Parry has pointed out a remarkable parallel to the *Vita Merlini* in the Irish *Frenzy of Suibhne,* and Sullivan long since pointed out an Irish parallel to the story of Vortigern's tower.

We may agree, then, that there was a Merlin and that he was famous before Geoffrey exploited him. Who or what he was originally I do not pretend to know. The Welsh poems in which he figures are to me too obscure to shed any light, and since their date is most uncertain there is little profit in discussing them. They prove, however, that there was a Welsh tradition independent of Geoffrey of Monmouth. It is possible that he was a historic bard of the sixth century who, like Arthur, took on supernatural traits. It is also possible that the process was reversed and that we have in Myrddin a degraded god whose special domain was poetry and prophecy. But from the first when he appears in the full blaze of Geoffrey's *History* he is far more than human.

As has been long recognized, Geoffrey took the story of Merlin's birth from Nennius' account of the birth of one who is never called Merlin. In the well-known story, Vortigern, being told by his magi that a certain tower may never be built unless he sprinkle the earth with the blood of a fatherless child, has brought before him a boy whose mother swore that he had no father, for she had never had intercourse with any man. The boy reveals supernatural knowledge, and the king asks his name. He replies, "I am called Ambrosius," that is, the Immortal. So far the story is quite consistent. But a new and really incongruous element enters at this point, for the boy's declaration that he is Ambrosius is followed by the gloss: "That is, he meant that he was Embreis the Chief or Emperor." And presently the story is utterly confused by the boy's assertion that his father is a Roman consul. This narrative Liebermann characterizes as "a nauseous farrago attached, not without self-contradiction and impossible miracles" to the historical leader of the Britons, Ambrosius Aurelianus, celebrated by Gildas. Liebermann adds, "I venture to charge Nennius with blending the half-druidical boy of miraculous origin with the historical prince." But is this blending without meaning or motive? Does it not seem probable that some stupid person has taken the ambiguous remark, "I am called Ambrosius," without a glimmer of its double meaning and quite prosaically proceeded to equate the wonder child with the historic hero of Gildas, Ambrosius Aurelianus, the general of Roman descent who successfully fought the Saxons? Hence the absurdity, and hence the curious combination of sage and ruler which both Ambrosius and Geoffrey's Merlin, who was modeled on Ambrosius, present.

But it may well be asked, what right, besides that of making sense of the story, has one to interpret the name Ambrosius as the Immortal One? First, there is the almost universal habit of supernatural beings to give cryptic answers regarding their identity. We have noted it particularly in the case of Custennin in *Kilhwch* and of the Fer Caille in *Da Derga's Hostel,* both shapes which we shall presently see Merlin assuming. Secondly, the story of the wonder child's birth as it developed in the case of Merlin presents clearer and clearer affinities to the stories of divine birth. In Geoffrey's *History* Merlin's mother declares:

> One appeared unto me in the shape of a right comely youth and embracing me full straitly in his arms did kiss me, and after that he had abided with me some little time did as suddenly evanish away so that nought more did I see of him. Natheless, many a time and oft did he speak unto me when that I was sitting alone, albeit that never once did I catch sight of him. But after that he had thus haunted me of a long time I did conceive and bear a child.

Geoffrey offers the explanation that the supernatural visitor was an incubus. But Layamon, who was using a version of Wace expanded from Breton tradition, makes the divine paternity even clearer. The child's mother relates: "When I was in bed in slumber, with my soft sleep, then came before me the fairest thing that ever was born, as if it were a tall knight, arrayed all of gold. This I saw in dream each night in sleep. This thing glided before me, and glistened of gold: oft it kissed me and oft it embraced me; oft it approached me and oft it came to me very nigh." Now whether this had any relation to the original birth story of Myrddin or whether the wonder-child of Nennius was Myrddin, no one can tell. But at any rate the story of Ambrosius' birth was recognized as that of a divine child and was developed accordingly. That cannot be gainsaid, even though the more orthodox clerics who got hold of the story had to interpret the divine father as an incubus or a devil.

Even more striking is the fact that Merlin, the inheritor

of Ambrosius' story is without exception the most clearly deathless figure in Arthurian romance. Native Welsh legends say that he departed with nine bards into the sea in a Glass House, and that nothing was heard of him since; or that he dwells in a Glass House in the Isle of Bardsey. In 1810 a Breton tradition is recorded, which said that Merlin was inclosed by his mistress in a tree on the Ile de Sein. In the French romances we have the practically uniform story of the beguiling of Merlin by his love and his eternal imprisonment. In the *Vulgate Merlin* Niniane confines him in the Forest of Broccliande in walls of air, which to others present only a thick mist but to him is the fairest tower in the world. In the *Vulgate Lancelot* she seals him asleep in a cave. In the *Prophecies* the Lady of the Lake imprisons him in a tomb where his body wastes away but his soul lives on for all who come. In Malory we learn that the Damsel of the Lake, Nyneue, made Merlin go under a stone and wrought so that he came never out for all the craft he could do. The *Didot Perceval* closes with stating that Merlin retired to an *esplumeor* or cabin, and that no one had seen him since. Only the *Huth Merlin* makes his imprisonment in the tomb by Niniane end in death. But in so doing it violates what is practically a uniform tradition of Merlin's immortality. I do not believe, therefore, that Geoffrey's identification of Merlin with Ambrosius was wholly arbitrary. Whoever the wonderchild was who called himself Ambrosius, he shared with Merlin the trait of immortality. There is every reason, then, to believe that the ambiguity of the statement, "Ambrosius vocor," led to the confusion of the Immortal One with Ambrosius Aurelianus.

Merlin reappears in Geoffrey's *Vita Merlini,* but the figure is so different from that in the *History* that it can hardly be the fabrication of Geoffrey, who would certainly have attempted some sort of harmony between the accounts. As a matter of fact we hear nothing of the marvelous birth, of Vortigern and Uter, and very little of Arthur. The only feature which the Merlin of the *Vita* has in common with the Merlin of the *History of the Kings of Britain* is the prophetic power. I think the conclusion is hardly avoidable that Geoffrey is following two separate traditions. This difference is responsible for Giraldus Cambrensis' conclusion that there were two Merlins: Merlin Ambrosius and Merlin Silvester (of the wood) or Celidonius.

In the really charming *Vita,* Merlin, overcome with sorrow at the death of his three brothers in battle, flees to the forest, where he appears in the rôles already shown to be characteristic of Curoi—wild man of the woods and ruler of wild animals. Let me translate: "He enters the forest and delights in hiding beneath the mountain ash-trees. He gazes on the wild beasts feeding in the glade. He eats the fruit of herbs, he eats herbs, he eats the fruit of trees and the berries of the bramble-bush. He becomes a man of the woods (*silvester homo*) as if he had been born among them." "There was a spring on the topmost peak of the mountain, surrounded on all sides by hazel trees and dense thickets. There Merlin took his seat; from it he gazed on all the woods, the courses and games of the wild beasts. The messenger [of his sister Ganieda] ascends to this point, and with soft step he goes up the hill seeking the

Figure of Galahad (center) from a French manuscript illustration, 15th c.

man. Finally he espies the spring and Merlin seated behind it on the grass."

Merlin is enticed by the messenger back to the court of his brother-in-law Rodarchus. But arrived there, he declares that "To these things he prefers the forest and the spreading oaks of Calidon, the high mountains and the green meadows below." The king has him chained, but Merlin after startling him with his soothsaying, returns to the forest, and there for years he spends his life with the wild herds and from a mountain top watches the courses of the stars. One night he discovers in the heavens signs that his wife Guendoloena is unfaithful. "He passes through all the woods and glades, collecting all the herds of stags into a host, together with fallow deer and roe-deer. He sat on a stag, and driving the host before him he hastens at dawn to the place where Guendoloena is being wed." He calls Guendoloena to look out at the gifts he has brought her, and she wonders at the sight of him riding the stag, at the animal's tameness, and at the multitude he alone is driving before him "as a herdsman is wont to lead his sheep to pasture." Guendoloena's new spouse laughs at him, and Merlin in anger tears the antlers from the stag, hurls them, and kills him.

As "wood man" and as "herdsman" Merlin corresponds to Curoi as the Fer Caille and *bachlach*. Further evidence that the tradition of the *Vita* has ultimate connections with the Irish is the fact that at one point Merlin instructs his sister to make a secluded house in the forest with seventy doors and seventy windows, in order that he might observe the stars. In the *Imram Snedgusa* of the 9th or 10th century, one of the Otherworld islands contains a royal dwelling with a hundred doors. And as already stated, Parry has shown the remarkable parallel to the whole *Vita* supplied by the *Frenzy of Suibhne*.

It is, of course, true that the stories of Curoi and Geoffrey's stories of Merlin show so far no correspondences in detail. Only the divine birth and the rôle of man of the forest and giant herdsman suggest an equation. But it must be remembered that Geoffrey by explaining Merlin's mysterious father as an incubus, by reducing his prophetic powers to that of a merely human astrologer, and by his use of stories culled from Eastern legends shows that the version he followed was by no means the pure Celtic tradition. The question of Merlin's true nature and of his connection with Curoi can be solved by observing whether in the later Arthurian romances he possesses the distinctive traits assigned him by Geoffrey or those which are associated with the mythical figure of the Giant Herdsman. That the Merlin of Geoffrey's *History* has greatly influenced later romances is clear, but the real issue is round the Merlin of the *Vita*. Do we detect Merlin in the French romances as an astrologer, as a madman, as related to Rodarchus, Ganieda, and Guendoloena? If not, if we find instead that his identify with the mythical Giant Herdsman and his shape-shifting are developed, then it is clear that the *Vita* did not initiate the conception of Merlin Silvester or Celidonius, but rather that the mythical conception is independent and naturally earlier. It is Arthurian romance which has preserved the tales of the Bretons more clearly than Geoffrey or any other source. And there Merlin seems quite clearly to have inherited the nature of the old sun-god.

In the *Vulgate Merlin* he comes to the messengers of Uther Pendragon "like a wood-cutter, a big ax at his neck, wearing big shoes, a short coat all torn. His hair was bristly, his beard large, and he looked much like a wild man of the woods." He bids the messengers tell Uther to come to the forest of Northumberland the next day, and there he will meet Merlin. Sure enough one of the king's followers discovers "a great multitude of beasts and a very ugly man in disguise who was tending these beasts." After appearing successively as a comely man, well arrayed, and as a beautiful boy, Merlin finally visits the king in his own semblance and admits that it was he who was transformed into the man of the woods and the herdsman.

Again Merlin approaches the lodges of Arthur by the river in the guise of a earl shooting wild fowl. "He wore great cow-hide boots, a coat and surcoat of coarse wool and a hood, and was girded with a knotted thong of sheep-skin. He was big and tall and black and bristly, and seemed right cruel and fierce."

Again Merlin "took on an aged aspect, and was again in an old coat of coarse wool all torn and rent, and though

he had before been tall and stout, now he was short and hump-backed and old, and his head was a composite, and his beard was long. He held a club beside his neck and drove a very great multitude of beasts before him."

But Merlin's power of metamorphosis and his predilection for the shape of a wild man or churl comes out more clearly in the Grisandole story in the same *Vulgate Merlin*. Miss Paton has studied this story and concluded that it is based not on Geoffrey but on an independent Celtic tradition. Instead of riding on a stag as in the *Vita*, Merlin actually assumes the form of a huge stag of five branches, with a white fore-foot. Again he comes on the scene as a black man, shaggy, barefoot, wearing a torn coat, and allows himself to be captured. Before leaving the emperor's court, he writes on the wall in Hebrew letters that the wild man and the stag were Merlin. All through the *Vulgate Merlin*, then, we have evidence of a powerful tradition which made far more of Merlin's penchant for shape-shifting than Geoffrey does, and also stresses his peculiar fondness for the rôle of the Giant Herdsman or churl.

It is in the *Livre d'Artus*, however, that he is most clearly presented in this character. Let me translate the passage in full.

> It came to his (Merlin's) mind to go and divert himself in the forest of Broceliande and to do something for which he should be spoken of forever. So on the day when the three messengers departed from Calogrenant, he transformed himself into such a shape as no man ever saw or heard of before. He became a herdsman, a great club in his hand, clad in a great hide, the fur of which was longer than the breadth of the largest hand known, and it was neither black nor white but smoked and browned and seemed to be a wolf-skin. He took his place in a great clearing on the border of a ditch, right over the bank, leaning on an old mossy oak, and held his club down to the bottom of the ditch and bent over it. He was large, bent, black, lean, hairy, old with a great age, shod without in marvelous leggings that reached his girdle. He was transformed so that his ears hung down to his waist, wide as a winnowing fan. He had eyes in his head as large and black as a—, and a head as big as a buffalo's, and hair so long that it brushed his girdle, all bristly, stiff, and black as ink. His mouth was as large and wide as a dragon's, and gaped up to the ears; his teeth were white; and his thick lips were always open so that the teeth showed all around. He had a hump behind on his spine, as big as a mortar. His two feet were where the heels ought to be in an earthly man, and the palms of the hands where the backs should be. He was so hideous and ugly to see that no man living would not be seized with great dread, unless he were brave and valiant. He was so tall when he stood up that a rod of eighteen feet would not reach him, and in proportion to his height he had the breadth of a thin man. His voice was so loud when he spoke that it seemed like a trumpet when he spoke a little loud. When Merlin had turned himself into this shape and placed himself on the road by which Calogrenant was traveling, he caused by his art stags, hinds, bucks,

and all manner of wild beasts to come and graze around him; and there were such a multitude that no one could tell the number. He ruled them so that when he scolded one roughly, it did not dare to eat or drink till he commanded.

When Calogrenant saw the "hom sauvage" he set himself in a posture for defense, but turned toward him to ask the way. To his question, what man he was, the herdsman replied: "Vassal, what would you do? I am such as you see, for I am never anyone else, and I watch over the beasts of these woods and the forest, of which I am wholly lord. For there is no beast so bold that when I have chidden or rebuked it will dare to eat or drink until I bid. They go to drink in a fountain of mine near by, which a friend of mine guards." Then follows a description of the storm-making fountain and its defender, Brun sans Pitié. "Now tell me," said Calogrenant, "on what you live. Have you a manor in the neighborhood where you sleep or a retreat where you take your meat and whatsoever you need to live?" He answered that he ate nothing but herbs and roots of the wood just like these other beasts; "for I do not care for other food, and these are all my arts, and I have no desire to have an abode but only a rough oak where I may rest at night, and when it is cold and stormy, to be clad as you see. If it is cold and I need to warm myself, I have a fire as long as I like; and if I wish to eat meat I always have as much as I want." "Truly," said Calogrenant, "you are a lord when you thus have your desires." The "hom sauvage" then directs Calogrenant to a hermitage, where he is well entertained before going on to the fountain.

Now anyone familiar with Calogrenant's meeting with the Giant Herdsman as he relates it in Crestien's *Ivain* will detect at once a close resemblance to the account we have just quoted from the *Livre d'Artus*. Besides the name of the hero and the location in the forest of Broceliande and the general similarity in the situations, there are the following correspondences in detail: the clearing, the stump, the club, the herdsman's blackness, huge head, large hanging ears, wide mouth, hump back, hide covering, and his height of seventeen or eighteen feet. In *Ivain* the dialog at times is almost identical with that in the *Livre d'Artes*. In the former Calogrenant asks: "What man art thou?" "Such as thou seest. I am never anyone else." "What dost thou do here?" "I was watching over these beasts throughout this wood." And after describing the method by which he tamed their fierceness, the Herdsman says, "Thus I am lord of my beasts." It seems therefore highly probable that the author of the *Livre d'Artus* used *Ivain* or, since we know that Crestien stuck close to his source, the source of *Ivain*. But Miss Paton, Freymond, Zenker have contended that the *Livre d'Artus* embodies in its picture of the Giant Herdsman certain authentic features from tradition not supplied by Crestien. The bulls that constitute in *Ivain* the forest herd are replaced in the *Livre d'Artus* by stags, hinds, and bucks. Now in *Owain* the Giant Herdsman summons the animals by striking a stag; in the *Vita* Merlin rides upon a stag, and in the *Frenzy of Suibhne* the mad prophet sings, "Thou stag, . . . pleasant is the place for seats on the top of thy antler points." Again *Ivain* does not mention the Herdsman's diet of roots and herbs; but the *Vita* expressly says that Merlin eats the fruit of herbs,

herbs, the fruit of trees, and the berries of the bramble-bush. Since, however, the *Livre d'Artus* shows no other signs of connection with the *Vita,* I believe it must have derived these two traits from the Merlin tradition, not from that book. It is furthermore worthy of note that whereas the normal development in Arthurian romance is continually to minimize the supernatural element, the Merlin of the *Livre d'Artus,* unlike the Merlin of the *Vita,* has no fear of the elements, but boasts his supernatural powers as coolly as in *Ivain* or *Owain.*

The conclusion of it all is that Merlin the Shapeshifter manifests a predilection for precisely the same forms as Curoi,—the churl, the Giant Herdsman, the Man of the Woods,—and that this predilection was not an arbitrary invention of Geoffrey's, but was an established tradition into which Geoffrey or his source introduced some Oriental stories of prophetic power. And accordingly it seems that when the legends of Curoi swept over Wales and certain story-tellers were passing them on as stories of Gwri, Gwrnach, Gwrvan, Gware, and so forth, other story-tellers, recognizing the similarity of Curoi to their own Myrddin, attached some of these stories to him. It is exactly the same process as occurred when the Romans attached the Greek legends of Aphrodite to Venus, of Hera to Minerva, of Hermes to Mercury, of Kronos to Saturn. In much the same sense, then, as we say that Vulcan is Hephaistos or Diana is Artemis, we may say that Merlin is Curoi.

Other clues lead us to the same destination. We have already noted that Merlin on one occasion transformed himself into a stag with a white fore-foot. In the lai of *Tyolet* and in the Dutch *Lancelot* we find a story in which the stag and his white foot seem to play a part analogous to that of the mule and his bridle, which we have already studied. A damsel appears at Arthur's court and promises either her own hand or that of her queen to the knight who shall bring her the stag's foot. Kay sets out but turns back in fright. The hero, however, successfully encounters seven lions which guard the stag, cuts off the white foot, whereupon a knight immediately appears, who deals him a treacherous blow. Here the False Claimant motif is interwoven, but in the *Tyolet* version the story ends properly with the marriage of the hero to the damsel for whom he had procured the stag's white foot. Miss Weston perceived that the stag was "the enchanted relative of the princess who sought the hero's aid," and I have little doubt that, like the mule, he is the old god transformed, and that his white foot is his external soul, or at least the seat of his power. Irish gods who took on the stag's shape were Donn and Mongan. And in view of the recognized phenomenon that Irish saints absorbed characteristics of pagan deities, it is not without significance that Patrick transformed himself into a stag. Miss Weston also notes the fact that Merlin transforms himself into a stag with a white fore-foot, and that in the *Queste del Saint Graal* a stag guarded by four lions actually turns into Christ with the four Evangelists. In identifying the stag, certainly a metamorphosed god, with Christ, the author of the *Queste* has done exactly what we saw had taken place in the modern Irish folktale, where the part of Curoi is played by the Hung-up Naked Man. The author makes a like substitution when he implies that the mysterious voice which is constantly heard threatening or commanding, is that of God, while a similar voice in the *Didot Perceval* is said to be that of Merlin.

Another of Merlin's protean changes brings us to the same conclusion. In the well-known story of the begetting of Arthur as we have it in Geoffrey of Monmouth Merlin transforms himself and Uter in order to gain access to Igerna. Miss Schoepperle demonstrated that the part of Uter is due to a misinterpretation of the phrase applied to Arthur, *mab uter,* meaning either "terrible (or wonderful) youth," or "son of Uter." Gruffydd has advanced the theory that according to one tradition at least the father of Arthur was really Merlin. This view gains support from a statement in the *Livre d'Artus* that Merlin carried Arthur's mother away to the Chastel de la Merveille. Now oddly enough, in *Diu Krone* the enchanter who carries Arthur's mother to the same castle is Gansguoter, and Gansguoter, we have seen, is manifestly Curoi. So once more we are forced to recognize a tradition which equated Merlin with Curoi.

Merlin's extraordinary interest in the fortunes of Arthur thus becomes clearly motivated. To be sure, in the *Didot Perceval* he displays equal solicitude for the hero, who is son of Alain le Gros, and in the *Huth Merlin* he watches over Balaain, the son of the King of Northumberland. One must grant that in these heroes Merlin's interest is not paternal. Nevertheless in all three cases Merlin, the old god, seems to act as a sort of omniscient and omnipotent arranger of tests and master of ceremonies, with all good will conducting the heroes through the trials and struggles which fall to their lot. (pp. 124-36)

Merlin . . . exemplifies in his attitude toward Arthur, Perceval, and Balaain that curous mingling of the kindly helper and contriver of perilous tests for the young god which we have found so characteristic a tradition of Celtic and Arthurian romance. It is also fortunate that in Merlin at last we have a god who can produce explicit evidence of his divinity. Doubtless some readers have thought that while the various figures considered did possess supernatural traits, it was rash to call them divine. But of Merlin [and] of Morgan le Fay, the Grail Bearer, and the original of the Fisher King, the word god or goddess is actually used. Not only does a Welsh triad call Britain Merlin's Close, not only does *Claris and Laris* refer to Merlin as he "who knows all, does all, and sees all." But also the *Vulgate Lancelot* states that he "knew all the wisdom that can descend from the devils, and therefore he was so feared of the Britons and so honored that all called him the holy prophet and all the lesser folk their god." (p. 136)

> *Roger Sherman Loomis, "Merlin the Shapeshifter," in his* Celtic Myth and Arthurian Romance, *Columbia University Press, 1927, pp. 124-36.*

Howard Maynadier

[*In the following excerpt, Maynadier discusses the complex literary associations of the Lancelot legend, focusing on the twelfth-century texts of Chrétien and Marie de France.*]

Though the Lancelot story was not at first so closely connected with the Arthur hero-legend as the Merlin story, it influenced it in the end far more. In the principal English versions of the legend—Malory's *Morte Darthur* and Tennyson's *Idylls of the King*—the guilty love of Lancelot and Guinevere has become the centre of interest.

The first literary mention of Lancelot is in Chrétien's *Érec,* where the poet tells us that Lancelot was the third best knight of the Round Table—surpassed only by Gawain, who was the first, and Erec, who was the second. This is equivalent to saying that Lancelot was the second, if not the first; for Gawain's supremacy does not militate against Lancelot's; Gawain was always the first knight in Chrétien's time; and always next to him was the hero of the particular romance in which Gawain had been introduced. We should expect Gawain and Erec, therefore, both to be classed ahead of Lancelot in *Érec et Énide;* his position just after them is as high as could be expected. Lancelot is mentioned again in Chrétien's *Cligès,* where it is recounted that he was overthrown by the hero of the romance. This, again, is not at all to Lancelot's discredit, for Chrétien's heroes regularly overthrow every one but Gawain, with whom the fight is generally undecided; and in this very *Cligès,* Perceval met a fate similar to Lancelot's. Thus Chrétien's two preliminary mentions of Lancelot show that he was a warrior worthy of becoming himself the central character of a story, as Chrétien made him in his *Conte de la Charrette* or *Chevalier de la Charrette,* frequently called the *Lancelot.*

Though this is the earliest Lancelot romance extant, a version of the story anterior to it is preserved in the *Lanzelet* of Ulrich von Zatzikhoven, a Swiss poet. Ulrich, who like so many other Arthurian poets, wrote in the last years of the twelfth century, translated into his own tongue a book which, he says, was brought to Germany by Hugh de Morville—one of the seven English gentlemen who were hostages for Richard I when he was released from captivity by the German emperor, Henry VI. As Morville went to Germany in 1194, his book, which contained the Lancelot story, must have been written earlier, very likely before Chrétien's *Charrette.*

According to Ulrich's rough and confused poem, Lancelot, when still a baby, was carried away from his mother, widow of the king of Benwick, by a fairy, who took him to her land in the midst of a lake. Her purpose was to train him that in time he might kill a giant, the arch-enemy of her son. When Lancelot was fifteen years old, the fairy, thinking him ready to become versed in knightly deeds of arms, sent him into the world in search of adventure. Like Perceval, in Chrétien's later Grail romance, Lancelot went out a raw, ignorant youth; and like Perceval, he found a kind baron who instructed him in knighthood. Then he entered on a course of strange adventures, in which he was married at least twice, to say nothing of one or two amours besides. He killed, moreover, two giants,—one of them the enemy of the fairy's son,—achievements which in each case immediately won him the love of the victim's daughter; for in this romance, killing a father was one way to a daughter's heart.

It was much against his will that Lancelot fought with his

second giant; for Mabuz, the son of the fairy, had a castle, like so many others in mediæval romance, with a strange "custom." Every knight, no matter how valorous, became cowardly the instant he entered the castle gate. Accordingly, Lancelot, who had hitherto shown remarkable bravery, submitted to all sorts of indignities from the inmates of the castle; and when the giant presented himself before the gate, refused to go out to fight him. Mabuz, therefore, had Lancelot armed and set on his horse forcibly, and fairly dragged outside. Then Lancelot, now himself again, killed the giant, whose daughter Iblis speedily became Lancelot's wife; and so she remained throughout the poem.

Soon after this adventure, the Lady of the Lake, the water-fay who had abducted Lancelot, sent word to him that he should go to Arthur's court, for his mother was Arthur's sister; moreover, he was destined in time to recover his own realm of Benwick. Scarcely had Lancelot, following the fairy's behest, introduced himself as a nephew to King Arthur, who made him a knight of the Round Table, when news came that there was a queen of Pluris whom no hero might marry unless he overthrew the hundred knights who guarded her. Lancelot, though married, and apparently happily, decided to try the adventure for the honor of it. He came near getting more honor than he desired, for when, after defeating the knights, he wished to return to his wife, he found that the queen insisted that he should take the promised reward of her hand and heart. On his refusal, she threw him into a prison, whence he made his escape only when the Lady of the Lake sent four of Arthur's knights to Lancelot's rescue.

The next adventure which Lancelot undertook he was urged to by his wife, Iblis. She told him of a serpent that had attracted considerable attention in the neighborhood while he had been away. It was a terrible creature, that demanded a kiss from every knight it met, which no one yet had been brave enough to give. Lancelot immediately went to the forest and complied with the monster's strange request, whereupon there stood before him a fair woman. She was a princess of Thule, who had been enchanted and doomed to retain her foul shape till some knight should be bold enough to kiss her.

So his adventures continued, till in time Lancelot went back to Benwick, to the great joy of his mother, who had long thought him dead. In his own land he was crowned in the presence of Arthur and many of his court, who went to honor the coronation. And there Lancelot and Iblis both lived to a good old age, and there finally both died on the same day.

Of all the adventures in this loosely constructed romance, the one most important in the subsequent development of the Arthurian legend remains to be mentioned. This was Lancelot's assisting Arthur in the rescue of Guinevere from a king who abducted her. The king was named Valerin; and at the time when Lancelot first came to Arthur's court, before he had revealed himself as the great king's nephew, Valerin was making a claim that Guinevere was rightly his, on the ground that her hand had been promised to him before it was given to Arthur. Valerin agreed, however, to waive his pretensions to the queen, if

he was defeated in single combat. Lancelot offered himself as Guinevere's champion, and by defeating Valerin, seemed to render her position at the court secure. Valerin, however, was not true to his word. While Lancelot was off on the adventure of the queen of Pluris, Valerin appeared again, and this time carried off Guinevere while a hunting party engaged the attention of most of Arthur's court. Having taken her to a remote place, encircled by a thick wood full of terrible serpents, he there threw her into a magic slumber. Then Arthur set out to rescue the queen, accompanied by a few of his best knights, among whom was Lancelot. Though a magician, Malduc, was of most service in rescuing Guinevere, for it took his spells to disperse the serpents, Lancelot played a fairly important part.

In this story of Ulrich's, it will be seen there is no hint that Lancelot was the lover of Guinevere. Such a relation appears first in Chrétien's *Conte de la Charrette*. According to this, on Ascension Day, when Arthur was holding court at Camelot, most romantic of all capitals of Arthur, because more than any other difficult to take out of the nowhere of poetry and locate definitely in this working-day world,—on Ascension Day, there came before Arthur a knight in full armor, by name Meleaguant, boasting that in the land of his father, King Bademaguz, certain knights and ladies of Arthur's court were held captive. He promised to free them, if one of Arthur's knights could overcome him in single combat. But if he himself was victorious, he was to lead away captive another lady, greater than any held in his father's land, the Queen herself.

Now Arthur had recently granted his seneschal, Sir Kay, a boon without any knowledge of its terms—an act of folly which experience never taught Arthur to desist from, though boons with conditions not stated were forever getting him into trouble. Kay, on hearing Meleaguant's challenge, decided that his boon should be nothing less than the privilege of defending Guinevere. He accordingly offered himself as her champion, much to the regret of the court, for Kay, a churlish, unloved knight, was notoriously a bad fighter. He was defeated, as every one expected he would be, and Meleaguant departed for his own land with Kay and Guinevere both.

At this juncture Gawain set out to rescue his sovereign lady. He had gone but a little way when he met a knight, with visor down, whom he did not recognise, though it was Lancelot, who seems to have been away from the court on Meleaguant's arrival, just as he was in Ulrich's poem, when Valerin carried off the queen. Lancelot, having borrowed a horse from Gawain, for his own was spent, spurred off furiously in pursuit of Guinevere and her captor. Gawain, following on, presently found Lancelot's horse killed, apparently in a fight between his rider and the men of Meleaguant, and Lancelot himself going on foot. Soon the two knights met an ill-favored dwarf driving a cart or tumbril, such as that in which criminals were carried to execution. Lancelot directly asked the dwarf if he knew anything of the Queen. The dwarf replied that he would give news of her if Lancelot would get into the cart and ride with him. For a brief moment Lancelot hesitated to do so, thinking it unknightly to proceed even a short distance in such a base conveyance. Love for the Queen, however, speedily prevailed; he got up beside the dwarf, who said that Meleaguant and his captives had gone the very way they were going. So they went on, Lancelot in the tumbril with the dwarf and Gawain riding, till all three came to a castle—Lancelot, the while, jeered at by knights and ladies whom he met, who called him mockingly "The Knight of the Cart," whence the name of the poem.

When Lancelot and Gawain departed from the castle the next morning, they learned from a damsel that the Queen had been carried to the land from which no man returns. It lay beyond a deep river, which could be crossed only by two bridges—one a keen-edged sword two lances in length, the other through the waves, with as much water above as below. The two knights set out to reach the apparently inaccessible land, and both succeeded in getting over the river—Gawain by the bridge under the waves, from which he came out almost half drowned, and some time earlier Lancelot, who crawled over the sword bridge. Though his hands and feet were terribly cut, he had no hesitation in engaging the next morning in combat with Meleaguant, whom he defeated.

After this, at the command of Meleaguant's father, Bademaguz, who is represented as a kindly old king, Lancelot presented himself to the Queen to tell her that she was free. To his surprise, she received him coldly, and Lancelot, like a dutiful lover, was in despair; but the next time he met her, there was a reconciliation. She let him know that her coldness was occasioned by his hesitating even for a moment to mount the cart, though how she knew of his hesitation is by no means clear. He had no business, she urged, to consider his own reputation in the least when it was a question of rendering service to her. However, as a token of her forgiveness, she appointed a meeting for that night. At the time set, Lancelot climbed up on a ladder to Guinevere's window, which was guarded by iron bars. These he tore away from the masonry, and so passed the night with her.

There were traces of blood in her chamber which came from his hands, that were cut as he tore away the bars; and so Meleaguant, when he visited the Queen the next morning, made charges against her, which both she and Lancelot could honestly declare untrue, for Meleaguant suspected the wounded Kay of passing the night with Guinevere. Lancelot thereupon offered himself as the Queen's champion, declaring that the question of her virtue should be settled in single combat between him and Meleaguant. As in their former fight, Lancelot was victor. Still, Meleaguant insisted on another single combat, to be fought later at Arthur's court. In the mean time, he tried to prevent Lancelot from presenting himself on the appointed day; but Lancelot overcame Meleaguant's plots, and defeated and slew the treacherous prince.

Such, roughly, is Chrétien's *Lancelot.* Of most of this, there was probably nothing in the original Lancelot story, which, we may surmise, concerned itself with Lancelot's abduction by a fairy and his performance of some great adventure for her, in the course of which he won the love of a damsel, whom he married, and with whom he lived happily. To this simple tale were added the other adventures

which made up the rambling, disconnected *Lanzelet* of Ulrich von Zatzikhoven.

Among these added adventures, the most important in its subsequent influence was that which Lancelot shared with Arthur, when they went to bring back Guinevere from her abductor. Almost every account of the Queen which is anything like comprehensive has her carried off by somebody; and in this persistent story of her abduction is one of the most likely traces, in the whole mass of Arthurian romance, of Celtic mythology. According to Chrétien, Meleaguant is son to the king of that land from which no man returns, that is, a god from the other world. In the nineteenth book of Malory's *Morte Darthur* the same prince carries Guinevere off while she is maying, an abduction suggestive of the rape by Pluto, god of the other world, of Proserpina when she was picking flowers in Sicily. Probably Guinevere's husband originally got her back unaided, as Orpheus regained his lost Eurydice—though only to lose her again. A trace of this earlier form of the story seems to persist in a Welsh tradition incorporated in the *Life of Gildas* (*Vita Gildae*), which has been ascribed to Geoffrey of Monmouth's contemporary, Caradoc of Lancarvon; though, according to Gaston Paris, it is doubtful if the work is really so old. Whatever its age, it serves to preserve an ancient Welsh legend, which makes out that Guinevere was carried away by a certain king, Melwas, to Glastonbury, whence she was restored to her husband without bloodshed through the mediation of St. Gildas. This seems to be a variant of the story told by Chrétien in his *Lancelot.* Paris takes Melwas to be a name from the same root as the French Meleaguant, and Glastonbury to be synonymous with Avalon, with which in local traditions the place was associated; for in the twelfth century the Saxon meaning of the name "town of Glaestings" was generally forgotten, and by false etymology Glastonbury was understood to be "town of glass." This is one reason why it became confused with the Welsh Ynys Witryn, translated into French as Ile de Verre, one of the names given to the Celtic Island of the Blessed. The situation of Glastonbury, a pleasant group of hills rising from flat marsh land, which even now in winter is sometimes covered a foot or two deep by water, no doubt made the confusion easier.

This old Welsh tradition, then, seems to show in fairly primitive form an instance of Guinevere's abduction by a god from the other world. Doubtless some such legend of a great queen, or perhaps a goddess, stolen from her husband, was current among the Celts in the earliest times. Probably a variant of the legend caused an early teller of the Tristram story to make an Irish warrior carry Iseult off from Mark's court, and to have her rescued by Tristram before she was taken beyond the sea; for by the British Celts, Ireland, a mysterious land of the West, separated by a great water, was sometimes looked on as the other world. Probably a Gaelic variant of the same legend is the Irish story, in the *Book of the Dun Cow,* of the abduction of Etain, wife of the mortal king Airem, by the fairy king Mider. And so Gaston Paris was justified in saying that the story of Guinevere's abduction may have been sung in Britain and Gaul, though with other names than those of

Arthur and Guinevere, long before Cæsar had marched his legions beyond the boundaries of the Roman province.

All this gets us far enough away from Lancelot as Guinevere's lover. How, now, did he come to stand in this relation? We may surmise as follows: Some early teller of the episodic Lancelot story, wishing to enhance the fame of his hero by the introduction of some new adventure, made him, as he appears in Ulrich's *Lanzelet,* an assistant in rescuing Guinevere from her other-world abductor. In time he became her sole deliverer because, as the hero of the whole poem, he was made the hero of every incident. But always he went to her rescue, we may presume, from the same motive as Gawain in Chrétien's *Conte de la Charrette,* that is, out of the purest loyalty to the queen of his sovereign lord.

Perhaps at this stage in the development of the story, the incident of the cart was introduced for a different purpose from that which Chrétien assigns. As Malory tells the adventure, Lancelot, after his horse was killed, got tired from walking in his heavy armor; and so, when the cart came along, he mounted it through fatigue, but with more or less attendant disgrace from faring in a vehicle which often carried criminals. As Chrétien tells it, we have seen that the fatigue disappeared, though the disgrace remained. Thus the dwarf made his invitation to Lancelot to get into the cart virtually a test of the knight's love.

There are various reasons why this love might have come into the Lancelot legend. In the early Arthurian stories there are two conflicting views of Guinevere's character. All Chrétien's romances but his *Charrette,* and those of a good many other poets, represent Guinevere as an ideal queen, a gracious, dignified consort to Arthur, and a sweet womanly wife. There can be little doubt, however, that the old mythological story of Guinevere's abduction gave wide currency to a tradition of her faithlessness. That this was independent of her amour with Lancelot is proved by the fact that in some parts of Wales, to call a girl Guinevere has been as much as to say that she was no better than she should be; and yet Welsh romance has never known anything of the Queen's love for Lancelot. Many early accounts of Guinevere, therefore, make her fickle if not unfaithful. In Geoffrey and the other chroniclers, she is more than semi-acquiescent in her adultery with Mordred. In Marie's *Lanval,* Arthur's queen—here nameless, to be sure, but probably by many readers unconsciously identified with Guinevere—is unblushingly faithless. And so it would not have been difficult for Chrétien, or any other romancer, to give Guinevere a lover, if he saw fit.

Two reasons may have determined him to do so. One was the great popularity of the Tristram story, the essence of which was the love of a queen for the best knight of her husband's court. Why not introduce a similar element of interest into the Lancelot story? A yet weightier reason was the peculiar nature of fashionable love in northern France in the second half of the twelfth century.

Fashionable or courtly love—*l'amour courtois,* the French called it—seems to have come from the Provençal poets, who represented love as something conventional, governed by so many rules that spontaneous passion was hid-

den under an artificial system. The troubadour lyrics, which express this system, became popular in the North at the time of Chrétien's literary fame; and Chrétien, Gaston Paris thinks, was one of the first, perhaps the very first, who imitated in the "langue d'oïl," or northern French, the lyric poetry of the "langue d'oc." Three extant songs of his are thoroughly in the spirit of the Provençal love lyrics. "No one," he says in one of the songs, "can know the first principle of love, who is not himself courtly and well informed:"—

> Nuls, s'il n'est cortois et sages,
> Ne puet riens d'amors aprendre.

These lines set forth the essence of the Provençal theory of love which became *l'amour courtois* of northern France, that only a polished man of the world could be an ideal lover. He must know how to conduct himself in the presence of his lady according to rules of etiquette as definite as those for a courtier in the presence of his sovereign. He was also to be the unquestioning servant of his lady. Whatever she bade him do, he did. Whatever sacrifice she called for, he made without hesitation.

Such a conception of love naturally appealed to that talented, imperious, and rather amorous queen, Eleanor of Aquitaine, who on her marriage to Louis VII of France sought to make popular at the French court the love system of her native South. In all the intricacies of the system Eleanor instructed the Princess Marie, her daughter by Louis VII. This princess, on her marriage with Henry, Count of Champagne, became Chrétien's sovereign lady. By that time she had become likewise one of the first leaders of fashion in northern France, having succeeded in a way to the position her mother had held; for Marie inherited both the worldly and the literary tastes of her mother, with whom she probably remained in as close communication as the times would permit, even after Eleanor, divorced from Louis, had taken for a second husband Henry II of England, a youth eleven years younger than herself. More than any one else Marie de Champagne, Chrétien's liege lady, seems to have made fashionable in the North that system of courtly love which had been familiar to her mother, Queen Eleanor, from the time that she could first read.

Proof both of the artificiality of the system and of Marie's importance as an authority on it is found in a book written early in the thirteenth century by André le Chapelain, entitled *Flos Amoris,* or *De Arte Honeste Amandi,* which might be translated *The Art of Loving "à la Mode."* It contains many rules for the conduct of a lover, such as: On account of marriage no one is excused from being in love. Every lover has always before his eyes, even in absence, his loved one. He is inclined to be suspicious and jealous. He is always in a state of fearful uncertainty. He sleeps and eats less than other people. At the sight of his lady he turns pale. If he beholds her suddenly, his heart palpitates; he almost faints.

Besides setting forth these rules and others for unquestioning obedience in a lover, the *Flos Amoris* explains the system of courtly love by considering disputed questions. In one place it recounts a fictitious interview between a knight and a lady whose love he sought. She was inclined

Representation of Arthur in Avalon based on Malory's Morte Darthur: Le Morte d'Arthur *by James Archer, c.1861.*

to reject the knight's suit on the ground that, loving an excellent husband and being loved by him, she could love no one else. The knight, after maintaining stoutly that the love she bore her husband was not true love, persuaded the lady to refer the question to the Countess Marie de Champagne. The Countess decided for the knight, declaring that true love between husband and wife was impossible; there was no credit in love to which people were bound by marriage vows, though there was credit in love which, if detected, would cause danger and disgrace; nor was there uncertainty in the fixed condition of marriage, and uncertainty and jealousy were both necessary to true love. Her opinion, the Countess said, was given after mature reflection, and was confirmed by the advice of several well-informed ladies to whom she had submitted the matter.

The same book records other judgments of disputed love questions. Three are given by the Countess of Narbonne, three by the Countess of Flanders, three by the Queen of France, who was Marie's sister-in-law, four by the Queen of England, Marie's mother, and seven by Marie de Champagne herself. On courtly love she was thus presumably the greatest authority.

This brings us to the question, had Marie, steeped in such a system of love, a considerable part in introducing into the Arthurian legends the love affair of Lancelot and Guinevere? That she would have approved it there can be no doubt, for Lancelot's love in the *Conte de la Charrette* is quite fashionable love. When he and Gawain, for instance, looking from a castle window, caught an unexpected glimpse of the Queen as she was led captive by Meleaguant, Lancelot nearly fell to the ground, and trembled so that Gawain thought his companion would faint. Again, in his journey to the land whence no man returns, Lancelot came to a spring by which lay a golden comb with a few hairs in it, so radiantly golden that gold a hundred thousand times refined were to them as dark night to the most brilliant day in a whole summer. The damsel who accompanied him told him that the hairs were from the head of Guinevere, who had recently used the comb. At this Lancelot, who had got down from his horse at the damsel's request to pick up the comb for her, felt such weakness that he had to catch hold of the pommel of his saddle to keep from falling. He turned pale, and could not speak. The damsel, in fear for him, quickly got off her horse, and went to the knight's aid. Somewhat ashamed then of the emotion he had shown, he asked the damsel roughly why she had dismounted. To take the comb from him, she said tactfully, because her eagerness to possess it was so great that she could not wait for him to give it to her. He accordingly gave her the comb, but removed the golden hairs, which he kissed over and over again and pressed against his face and finally placed in his bosom, where he would have kept them, even had any one offered him in exchange a cartload of emeralds and carbuncles and other precious stones. Lancelot could not have acted more in accord with the strict etiquette of courtly love, had he committed to memory, "Omnis consuevit amans in coamantis aspectu pallescere," "In repentina coamantis visione cor tremescit amantis," and all the other rules of the *Flos Amoris*.

These two instances are enough to show that Lancelot in the *Conte de la Charrette* is an ideal courtly lover. Now the Countess Marie, according to Chrétien's own account, gave him the material and the spirit (*matiere et san*) of his story. Gaston Paris has concluded, therefore, that Chrétien, in telling an old tale of Lancelot's rescue of Guinevere, in which the knight did his duty in Platonic fashion as the loyal servant of the queen, deliberately changed their relations, and at the suggestion of Marie de Champagne made Lancelot Guinevere's lover.

An objection to this theory is that Chrétien nowhere hints that he is telling a new story; he seems to take knowledge of the love affair for granted. This Paris explains by saying that Chrétien's desire was to mystify his readers as much as possible, as he shows by concealing the name of the Chevalier de la Charrette till line 3676 of the poem. In the meantime the fact that the love of the unrevealed knight for the Queen was mentioned as a well-known affair would pique the curiosity of readers still further.

To many of us the Arthur legend is more interesting because more human, if we think that the love of the Queen and her knight owes something to the desire of a royal princess of long ago to see in verse, if nowhere else, the devoted love which she and other great ladies of her time longed for but found not in their exalted life. There is no reason why those who like the fancy should not indulge it. At the same time, it cannot be said that Gaston Paris has proved the origin of Lancelot's love to be what he himself, like so many of us, was pleased to imagine it. Nevertheless, the fact remains that no mention of Lancelot's guilty passion has been found earlier than Chrétien's *Conte de la Charrette*. And further, even if it had got into the Arthurian stories before, it had probably not taken on fashionable, courtly form. This peculiarity of Lancelot's love is due, almost undoubtedly, to Chrétien, acting at the command of his liege lord's wife, and so indirectly to the Countess Marie herself. Because courtly love at the time was so much the fashion, it became immensely popular in the Lancelot story. Once introduced there, it could not be forgotten; and so it bound the Lancelot story inseparably to the greater Arthur story. The more this grew, the more important Lancelot's passion became; till in time some writer, feeling called on to recount at length the first meeting of Lancelot and Guinevere, invented that episode of Galehault's introducing the knight to the Queen, after they had long looked on each other with eyes of love. In the presence of his lady, the knight, true to the traditions of the courtly lover, was so timid that finally the Queen

herself had to make the first advance, and taking him by the chin, she gave him the first kiss.

The German *Lanzelet* shows that other stories than Chrétien's concerning Lancelot were current in the twelfth century. Early in the thirteenth, some unknown writer gathered various of these into a prose romance combined with parts of the Perceval story. This enlarged *Lancelot* was further developed by the addition of more extraneous matter. Many manuscripts still existing, not only in French, but in most languages of western Europe, testify to the popularity of these later versions of the romance. Probably it was some form of this enlarged *Lancelot* which, coming into the hands of Dante, led him to make the story of Lancelot's first meeting with Guinevere that which Paolo and Francesca were reading when they confessed their love for each other. And so the influence of Chrétien, and through him, that of Marie de Champagne—dreaming of such devotion as no woman ever had, or if any had, she would find cloying—reached to Dante, as it has reached since to Malory and Tennyson. (pp. 84-104)

> *Howard Maynadier, "Lancelot," in his* The Arthur of the English Poets, *Houghton, Mifflin and Company, 1907, pp. 84-105.*

James Douglas Bruce

[*Bruce was a major early twentieth-century contributor to Arthurian scholarship. In the following excerpt, he explicates the legend of Tristan and Iseult, distinguishing its original Celtic formation from later French medieval versions.*]

The following succinct outline . . . [represents] in essentials, with virtual certainty, the content of the lost French romance [*Tristan*]:

Tristan was the son of Rivalen, King of Loenois (in some versions, Armonie or Parmanie) in Great Britain and of Blanchefleur, sister of Marc, King of Cornwall. Blanchefleur dies in the act of giving birth to Tristan, whose name was suggested by the affliction that accompanies his birth. A knight, named Gorvenal, instructed the young Tristan in the accomplishments of knighthood, and when his charge was fifteen years old, they set out for Cornwall and arrive at Marc's court. Although Tristan does not disclose his identity, he becomes a favorite at court. In the course of time an opportunity arises which enables him to show his prowess. A great knight called Morholt, brother-in-law of the Irish king, comes from Ireland to exact the tribute of every third child of fifteen years old, but he was ready to settle the matter with any suitable Cornish champion. The Cornish knights hold back, but Tristan undertakes the combat, after having first had himself knighted. The duel takes place on the isle of Saint-Samson and only the combatants are present. Morholt is mortally wounded, but escapes to his boat with a fragment of Tristan's sword in his head. He expired before he could reach Ireland; nevertheless, his niece, Iseult, daughter of the Irish king, kept the fragment of Tristan's sword.

Tristan, too, had been wounded in the combat and his condition grows constantly worse. In despair, he finally has himself put in a boat which is pushed out to sea. He carries his harp with him. The boat drifts to the Irish coast, and the king, hearing Tristan playing on his harp, takes him ashore, and Iseult, who is skilled in the healing art, cures him. He calls himself Tantris, and so eludes identification. He then returns to Cornwall.

King Marc had always refused to marry, but one day a swallow brings to his hall some strands of a woman's hair as beautiful as gold. The king thought that he could rid himself of the importunities of his courtiers by declaring that he was willing to marry the woman to whom this hair belonged, but no one else. Tristan goes forth to discover the unknown beauty and is borne by chance to Ireland. The king's officer is sent to slay him, but Tristan pretends that he is a merchant and secures a delay. A dragon was then devastating Ireland and the king promises his daughter's hand to any man that would kill the monster. Tristan accomplishes this and cuts out the dragon's tongue as a token of his victory. He falls afterwards into a swoon and the king's seneschal, stealing the dragon's tongue, represents himself as the victor. Iseult knows, however, that the seneschal is a coward, suspects some deceit, goes forth with her mother to look into the matter and finds Tristan. Aided by her mother, she heals him, but Tristan, perceiving her golden hair, sees that she is the woman for whom he is looking. She, however, observes that the fragment taken from the dead Morholt's head fits exactly a gap in Tristan's sword. She would have informed on him, despite his prayers, but she knew that she would then be compelled to marry the treacherous seneschal. The deceit of this man is disclosed and the Irish king pardons Tristan, who asks for Iseult's hand on behalf of his uncle. Iseult is sent to Marc under the charge of Tristan. Then follows the incident of the fatal love-potion. Iseult's mother had prepared it, to render perpetual the love of her daughter and Marc, but, through an accident on the voyage, Bringvain (Brangien), Iseult's female attendant, gives it to Tristan and Iseult, so that they are united in an undying passion. Accordingly, on Iseult's wedding night, Bringvain takes her place with Marc and she remains with her lover.

Fearing that Bringvain would betray the deception practised on Marc, Iseult engages two men to murder her. By a clever allegory the girl touches the hearts of these men and they spare her. They report to Iseult that they have executed their commission, but she exhibits such remorse that they tell her the truth.

One day an Irish harper plays at court on condition that Marc will grant anything he wishes. It turns out that he wishes Iseult, and Marc, though reluctant, is constrained to comply with his promise. The Irishman takes the queen to his ship, but Tristan returns at this moment from the forest and goes to seek Iseult. He tells her captor that he can quiet her distress with his rote. He gains time in this way, wins the Irishman's confidence, and finally manages to carry off Iseult, flinging back the taunt, as he goes, that the Irishman has won her with his harp, but that he has won her back with his rote.

The lovers now continue their intrigue, but Audret (Andret), another nephew of Marc's, who hates Tristan, spies on the pair, and, assisted by a wicked dwarf, endeavors to

The boy Arthur draws the sword from the stone in Walt Disney's film of T. H. White's book The Sword in the Stone.

ruin them. Tristan communicates with his mistress by sending inscribed pieces of wood down a stream which flows through Iseult's chamber. They have all sorts of escapes. Once Marc is hidden in a tree above them, listening to them, but they observe his shadow in a spring and give their conversation such a turn that he is deceived. They are, however, finally detected. Tristan is sleeping in the same chamber with the king and queen. The king by design leaves the chamber and Tristan wishes to join Iseult. The dwarf has strewn the floor between them with meal, so that Tristan's tracks may be shown, but, seeing the snare, Tristan springs over to Iseult's bed. He had lately been wounded, however, and the exertion broke his wound. The blood accordingly stained both his bed and Iseult's and their guilt was divulged. Tristan escapes, but Marc, who at first had determined to burn his wife, later decides to give her up to a band of lepers. Her lover, however, rescues her from this fate and they fly to the forest and spend two years there in the enjoyment of each other's love. One day Marc, in hunting, came upon them asleep in their hut, but Tristan's sword lay between them, which convinced him of their innocence. On awakening, the lovers observe signs that Marc had been there (his sword and his glove) and fly deeper into the forest.

The forest-life, however, becomes no longer bearable, and Tristan and Iseult agree to part. Tristan threw a letter into Marc's chamber, inquiring whether he would take her back. By another letter Marc signified his willingness to do so, provided Tristan left the kingdom.

Tristan now goes to Arthur's court, but with Gawain's help has another meeting with his mistress. Arthur hunts near Tintagel and Marc has to receive him and his followers, including Tristan. To guard Iseult from Tristan, he has sharp blades set near her bed. Tristan is wounded by them, but, in order to protect him, his companions feign a fight, get wounded with the same blades, and so it is impossible the next day to convict him. The king now compels Iseult to make a public declaration of her innocence. To confirm her veracity, she will have to endure the test of holding a red-hot iron in her hand. On the way to the place where the test is to be made Iseult is borne across a ford by Tristan disguised as a beggar. She swears afterwards that no one but the king and this man had touched her. The people do not see into the real significance of this oath, but it enables the queen to go through the test unharmed.

Tristan next goes to Brittany and helps Duke Hoel of Carhaix in his war with a rival. The latter has a daughter named Iseult (Iseult of the White Hands she is called) and she is wedded to Tristan, but the marriage remains merely nominal, the husband's mind still dwelling on Iseult of Cornwall. The wife lets her brother Kaherdin know this. Tristan tells this brother of the love of Iseult of Cornwall for him and they go then to Cornwall together, where Tristan has a secret meeting with Iseult. Afterwards, however, through a misunderstanding, Iseult is out of humor with him because of a supposed act of cowardice on his part. Disguised as a leper, he seeks an interview with her to explain, but although she recognizes him, she has him beaten away. He returns, therefore, to Brittany and becomes really the husband of the other Iseult. Iseult of Cornwall now feels remorseful in regard to her lover and even puts on haircloth. On hearing the news of this, Tristan again comes from Brittany—meets her in secret—the next day bears off the prize in some sports, but is detected by accident and escapes. At a later time, however, having been much altered in appearance because of his sufferings from a wound which he had received in war, he goes back to Cornwall, disguised as a madman, and carries on his clandestine *amours* with Iseult, until he is finally detected and returns to Brittany.

Kaherdin carries on an intrigue with the wife of Bedenis. In the fight that follows on account of this affair he is killed and Tristan severely wounded. Tristan sends to Iseult of Cornwall to come and cure him. It is agreed that the ship on its return shall hoist a white sail, if it brings her—otherwise a black sail. She comes, but Tristan's wife is jealous and reports that the sail is black. At this the hero dies, and when Iseult of Cornwall arrives, she too expires upon his body. Marc at last learns how the lovers were bound together by the fatal potion and has them buried side by side. Rose-bushes spring up out of the two graves and intertwine their branches.

Now, the investigations of Miss Gertrude Schoepperle [Later Mrs. R. S. Loomis] have made it virtually certain that the starting-point of this long and romantic narrative is a Celtic *Aithed* (elopement story), similar to the Old Irish story of *Diarmaid and Grainne*. In this Irish story, too, the hero (Diarmaid), under the influence of passion, violates the obligations of friendship and loyalty and flies with the wife of his uncle and king to the forest. They are pursued from place to place and have to endure all sorts

of hardships. *Diarmaid and Grainne* is preserved only in such varying fragmentary and corrupt versions that it is difficult to compare the story with that of Tristan in detail, and the difficulty is still further enhanced by the fact that these versions are so largely lyrical. The central *motif,* however, is the same in the two stories, so that the derivation of the latter from the former or some similar *Aithed* seems to be an acceptable conclusion. It is, doubtless, due to this origin that the Tristan of the Old French poems still differs so greatly from the conventional hero of the French romances of chivalry—Gawain, for example, whose main function is to exemplify the knightly virtues of prowess and courtesy in their highest manifestations. Tristan's nimbleness of hand and foot, his forest cunning, his skill in elementary feats of strength (leaping, putting the stone) are all surviving traits of a more primitive type. Apart, however, from the numerous accretions to the central theme and the coloring of French chivalrous society which the whole story has received, it must be acknowledged that the Celtic tale, even in respect to this central theme, has undergone a transformation in the hands of the French romancers, who developed it into what is, perhaps, the greatest love-story in literature. The transformation, indeed, is so great that some scholars have been disposed to deny any Celtic influence at all in the shaping of the love-story. In particular, it has been objected that the conflict of passion and law which constitutes the tragedy of the lovers in the romance could not have been of Celtic origin, since the dissolution of the marriage tie was easy among the Celts and the idea of womanly modesty and virtue had little force among the Celtic populations in the period with which we are concerned. There is a measure of truth in the first of these objections, for the moral reprobation of adultery is not emphasized in these Celtic tales, which reflect a more primitive condition of society than the French romances, but the parallelism with *Diarmaid and Grainne,* or even with the more celebrated story of the love of Naisi and Deirdre, wife of Conchobar, is too striking to be accidental. All three of these tales, with their forest setting to a drama of adultery, in which the principal actors are a hero, his uncle (a king), and the latter's wife, bear unmistakably, it would seem, the stamp of the same mint. A recognition of this fact, however, does not conflict with the view that, after all, the tragedy of Tristan and Iseult, which, through the romances, has impressed itself on the imagination of the modern world so deeply, owes its strength, mainly, to the changes which the French poets wrought in the Celtic tradition. Leaving aside the addition of the story of Iseult of Brittany to the original *Aithed* and other accretions that heighten, in a variety of ways, the interest of the legend, one may note among these changes the discardal of the bizarre paganism of the Old Irish tale with its duplicate *motifs* of the hero's lovespot and the heroine's *geis*—both based on forms of superstition that are too primitive to win the interest or sympathy of modern society—and the substitution in the romances of the incident of the love-drink, shared by the two lovers, which has the double advantage of a unified *motif* and of the hallowed familiarity of classical associations. But, above all, the power of the story in the French romances is due to the initial scene of Tristan and Iseult's love-story (the scene of the love-potion), with its definite symbolism that dominates the rest of the narrative—the symbolism of a passion against which no human convention can stand—to the elaboration of the forest scenes, to the true and vivid picture of the passion that constantly draws the hero back to the heroine, contrary to the obligations of kinship and personal loyalty, and, despite every variety of obstacle, not permitting him to forget her even in the embraces of another woman. The Celtic texts, such as *The Reproach of Diarmaid* and *Death of Diarmaid,* have a beauty of their own that testifies to a more intimate contact with the life of nature, but the French romances are manifestly the products of a higher civilization and a more strongly sustained narrative art.

Granting, now, the Celtic origin of this famous love-story of Tristan and Iseult of Cornwall, it remains to fix as far as possible, the history of its growth before it reached the French romancers and the share which the different regions, inhabited by the Celts, had in this process. The task is one which has long enlisted the energies of the ablest students of the *matière de Bretagne.*

As is customary in cases where the records are so scanty, scholars have turned to the nomenclature of the story in the search for light regarding the question just mentioned. In his well-known studies of Arthurian names, the late Professor Zimmer endeavored to establish the Pictish origin of the hero's name, and that scholar's identification was all but universally accepted, even by those who had been engaged in the bitterest controversies with him. In the Irish chronicles of the Picts we have in the eighth century a *Talorcan filius Drostan* and a *Drest filius Talorcan.* Now, Celtic scholars are agreed that *Drostan* is the same as *Drest (Drust)*, with a common Celtic suffix added, and that *Tristan* is derived from *Drostan*. It has been shown, however, that *Drust (Drest* and its derivatives) is not confined to the Picts, as Zimmer maintained, but belongs to the general nomenclature of the Brythonic Celts, although commonest among the Picts. As far, then, as the name alone is concerned, we could not infer anything positively as to the ultimate origin of the story. It might have belonged to any branch of the Brythonic Celts. Nevertheless, there are sufficient reasons, I believe, for regarding Tristan as, in the first instance, a Pict. First of all, the name, although not confined to the Picts, is much commoner among them than among the other Celts. Furthermore, all the chief versions of the story represent the hero's father as ruling *Loonois (Loenois)* and the region in which he and Iseult lead their forest-life as *Morois.* Now, despite mistaken identifications in the romances, themselves, it seems most probable that *Loonois* is the Scottish *Lothian* and *Morois (Morrois)* the Scottish *Murray*—so two districts that were undeniably inhabited by the Picts.

The fame of Tristan began, then, as we may assume, with the Picts, probably merely as a character in heroic saga, with no love-story attached; but did it pass through Wales and, perhaps, Cornwall on its way to the French, and, if so, what accretions did it receive in those regions? The principal evidence bearing on the Welsh side of the question is that which is offered by the Triads. In one of these (Loth's *Mabinogion,* II, 231) Tristan is called one of the three chief diadem-wearers of Britain; in another (*ibid,* p.

238) he is one of the three machine-masters of Britain; in still another, (*ibid,* p. 260), he is one of the three lovers of Britain. Lastly, in a fourth triad (*ibid,* pp. 247f.), he is one of the three great swine-herds of Britain, but he is, at the same time, the lover of Marc's wife, apparently. He keeps Marc's swine, whilst the regular swine-herd goes on a message to Essyllt, as she is here called; Arthur, Marc, Kay and Bedivere could not get a single hog from him, whether by ruse, violence, or theft. Furthermore, in the *Dream of Rhonabwy,* a prose tale of the *Mabinogion* collection, he appears (*Drystan mab Tallwch*) among Arthur's counsellors. This tale is certainly not earlier than the middle of the twelfth century and it may have been influenced by the French poems. The triads, enumerated above, are found only in a MS. of the fourteenth century, when the French romances had spread the fame of Tristan throughout Europe, and if we were dependent entirely on them, it would be impossible to say whether, in representing the hero as a lover of Marc's wife, they were really reflecting native tradition. After he became known through the French romances, it would be only natural that native writers should weave still other stories about him and his famous mistress. This seems certainly the origin of the pretty tale in which Arthur is called on to judge between Marc and Tristan as to the possession of Iseult. It includes a metrical dialogue of mutual compliment between Tristan and Gawain (Gwalchmai), the latter's object being to induce his friend to meet Arthur.

The following considerations, however, seem to show that the conception of Tristan as the lover of Iseult originated either in Wales or, more probably, in Cornwall. The mistress of Tristan is in all versions represented as the wife of Marc (Mark), King of Cornwall. Now *Mark* is common as a Germanic name, but it is also given as the name of a king of Cornwall in the sixth century in the life of the saint, Paulus Aurelianus. It is said of this saint in his Latin biography, which was written by Wrmonoc, a monk of Landevennec (in Brittany) in 884, that his fame reached the ears of King Marc—"otherwise Quonomorius". Quonomorius, it may be observed, is a Celtic name occurring elsewhere. On the other hand, *Marc* means *horse* in the Celtic languages. In the *Tristan* poem by Béroul, King Marc is represented as having the ears of a horse, which he tries to conceal, and we have here, doubtless, a trait of Cornish tradition which came to Béroul through the primitive *Tristan.* Moreover, Marc's seneschal, Dinas of Lidan, bears a name of Welsh or Cornish origin, which, to be sure, as it appears in the French poems, rests on a misunderstanding, since *Dinas Lidan* in these languages means "large fortress." In the poem the proper name (perhaps, *Dinan*) or title, which must have stood in the original Celtic source, has dropped out. This character, it should be remembered, has an intimate connection with the legend and his name is, therefore, significant of the origin of the romance, or, at least, of the episodes in which he plays a part.

As regards the name of the heroine, Iseult, this has been usually regarded as of Germanic origin, and, accordingly, seemed to conflict with the theory of the Welsh or Cornish, or, indeed, Celtic origin of the love-story. *Iswalda, Ishild* (parallel to *Brunehild, Richild*) have been suggested as Germanic equivalents. Zimmer disputed the Celtic character of the name, *Essylt,* which is given to Marc's wife in the Welsh triads, and derived it from the Anglo-Saxon *Ethylda.* This accorded with his view that the triads about Tristan and Essylt do not reflect a native tradition. The Cornish place-name, *Ryt-Eselt* ("Eselt's ford"), which is found in an Anglo-Saxon charter of the year 967, proves, however, that this name could be Cornish as well as Welsh. The matter is too technical for a layman to pass judgment on, but, on the whole, the argument in favor of the Celtic origin of the name appears to carry with it the weight of probability, and it seems, furthermore, mere pedantry to lay stress on the fact that the French *Iselt* (*Iseut*) is not quite exact in its phonetic correspondence to Welsh *Essylt* or Cornish *Eselt.* Foreign names are seldom caught correctly and the difference, after all, is very slight. This difficulty seems, then, to offer no serious obstacle to the acceptance of the Welsh or Cornish origin of the love-saga.

As between Wales and Cornwall, the evidence would seem to point rather to the latter as the region in which the great love-story of Tristan and Iseult first took shape. Indeed, but for the rôle of an intermediary between Pictland and Cornwall—regions far apart—which we are compelled to assume, there would be no reason to attribute to Wales any part at all in the development of the legend. The wronged husband, as we have seen, bore a Cornish name, and was very likely an actual Cornish king. As Loth has pointed out, his Lancien was identical with the *Lantien* (*Lantyan*) of our own day, a village on the river Fowey, and the parish in which this village is situated is still called Saint Sampson's—that is to say, still bears the same name as the church where, according to Béroul (l. 2977), Marc and Iseult performed their devotions. In the neighborhood there is a place of the name of *Kilmarth,* a corruption for *Kilmarch* ("Marc's retreat"). Taking into consideration the evidence of these place-names, to say nothing of some others, suggested by Loth, which are more open to question, and the fact that the *Tristan* poems distinctly locate the story in Cornwall, there can be no doubt that Cornwall had a main share in the formation of the legend. It would appear that the fame of a character, originally Pictish, had spread through Wales and Cornwall, and that in the latter, owing to circumstances over which time has drawn an impenetrable veil, that character became the hero of this crowning love-story of the Middle Ages.

Apart from the Pictish, Welsh and Cornish elements already noted, an analysis of the Tristan tradition reveals still further Breton and French names, which point to the conclusion that both of these people likewise had a hand in the final shaping of the story, before it reached the author of the lost romance which was the common source of the extant Tristan poems. For instance, the names of Rivalin, Tristan's father, and Hoel, his father-in-law, are unmistakably Breton, whereas Blanchefleur, the name of his mother, and Petiteru, that of his marvellous dog, are evidently French. It is plain, then, that the Bretons acted as intermediaries in the transmission of the story from Great Britain to the French. The fact that one of the hero's parents bears a French name, the other a Breton name, is especially significant. The inventor of this part of the leg-

Merlin and Vivien *by Sir Edward Burne-Jones.*

end must have been familiar with both languages and he was, doubtless, a Breton from the bi-lingual zone. According to Bédier, it was the Breton jongleurs who were drawn to Great Britain by the Norman occupation that brought the story of the lovers home with him across the channel, but since the researches of Loth have shown that there was certainly, to say the least of it, an early localization of this story in Cornwall, it would seem likely that it was transmitted directly from Cornwall to Brittany by the ordinary processes of oral tradition.

Accepting, in general, the theory that the essential feature of the Tristan legend—the love-motif—was Celtic, and that it reached the French poets in the manner that has been described, I will conclude with an examination of those elements in the story which we may regard as later accretions.

It has always been recognized that the various stratagems by which the lovers elude the vigilance of King Marc were not characteristically Celtic and were probably brought into the story at a comparatively late stage. Thus the incident of the blades by which Tristan is wounded, with the subsequent trick to deceive the husband, has been shown to be a modification of a story as old as Herodatus—the tale of the thief who robs a king's treasury. Iseult's oath that no one has touched her save Marc and the beggar (really the disguised Tristan) is likewise a wide-spread folk-lore *motif.* For instance there is a close parallel to the incident in the Icelandic Grettissaga (end of thirteenth century). Take also the episode in which Marc, concealed in a tree, listens to the lovers, who, becoming aware of his presence, change their conversation so as to deceive him. This was manifestly suggested by the pear-tree story, so well known to folklorists and immortalized by Chaucer in the "Merchant's Tale". The *motifs,* to be sure, are not the same, for in the pear-tree tale the lovers persuade the husband that the disgraceful scene which he has witnessed was the result of optical illusion. Nevertheless, the situation is so similar—the husband hidden in the tree and the lovers beneath—that we may safely accept the *Tristan* episode as a mild adaptation of that story.

More important than these matters is the question of the origin of the opening and concluding divisions of the romance—Tristan's birth and childhood, on the one hand, and the story of Iseult of Brittany, on the other. There is no indication of these features of the romance in the scanty Welsh tradition, and there can be hardly a doubt that both episodes are later developments in the story—doubtless, inventions of the author of the lost primitive French *Tristan.* In the *chansons de geste,* nearly all the great heroes had *enfances,* including occasionally some romantic narrative concerning their parents, so that when the legend of Tristan passed into the hands of a poet familiar with French epical tradition, Tristan, too, was provided with a set of youthful adventures. The name, for which the hero's tragical fate suggested a connection with French *triste,* set the poet's imagination to work, and we have as a result the sorrowful birth of the character. Then for the last division of the romance—the elements here also seem plain. The man loved by two wives was one of the common themes of mediaeval romance, *Eliduc,* the lay by Marie de France, being perhaps the most famous example of it. Combine with this, now, the classical legend of *Oenone,* the jealous wife of Paris, who is skilled in the healing art, but refuses to save her wounded husband, from jealousy of her rival Helen, and we have the essentials of the concluding episode in our romance, beginning with the expulsion of Tristan after his second detection with Iseult.

To be sure, Iseult of Cornwall retains the knowledge of the healing art which she had evidently possessed already in the Celtic legend, so in this respect the conditions required that she, rather than her rival, should resemble the mymph of the classical legend, but the general situation is obviously the same, and I see no reason for rejecting Golther's identification of the stories. On the other hand, with equal confidence we may accept the *motif* of the white and black sails as derived from the legend of Theseus, in which the hero's father, Aegeus, perished in consequence of his son's forgetfulness in regard to this same signal. Servius's commentary on the *Aeneid,* doubtless, made this incident the common property of the Middle Ages.

It will be observed that even the central theme of the primitive French *Tristan,* as outlined above, is a much more complex affair than the Irish *Aitheda* (*Diarmaid und

Grainne etc.), from which we have derived it. We have, in addition to the *motifs* of the *Aitheda,* the combat with Morholt, the two voyages to Ireland, the first of which involves the hero's healing at the hands of an enemy and the second his quest for the princess of the beautiful hair, the part played by Bringvain, besides the series of incidents, in which the lovers evade detection. Now, the combat with the Irish champion, Morholt, and the voyage for healing manifestly belong together, and, inasmuch as the name of this strange champion seems Celtic, we may accept both combat and voyage as of Celtic origin, although the idea of a wound which can be healed only by an enemy is by no means confined to the Celts. It has been suggested that this episode reflects early historical conditions, when the Pictish population of Scotland were being subjugated by Irish invaders. This would seem to be a plausible conjecture, and if Tristan was, indeed, in the beginning, a Pictish hero, no incident is so likely to have belonged to him in the character as that of this combat and its sequel. The second voyage in which Tristan goes forth on his indeterminate search for the unknown golden-haired princess, owes its suggestion, too, no doubt, to a favorite class of Celtic tales—the *Inrama* (tales of fantastic voyages), one of which in its Christianized form, the legend of St. Brendan, enjoyed a wide-spread popularity in the Middle Ages throughout Western Europe. In the episode of the *Tristan* under consideration, however, the object of the voyage has no parallel in these Celtic tales, and the *imram motif* seems plainly combined with that of a hero's quest of a bride for a king, and in a specific form which is apparently unknown to the Celts—the search for the girl, the strands of whose hair have been brought to the king by a bird. A distinguished scholar, indeed, once regarded this adaptation of the well-known fairy-tale of the Fair Maid with the Golden Locks as the fundamental theme of the Tristan legend, but the fairy tale in question, beautiful as it is, is too gossamerlike ever to have suggested the most passionate love-story in literature, and, since the publication of Miss Schoepperle's researches, we may safely regard this adaptation as merely a later embellishment—introduced, no doubt, by a French poet—of what is, in itself, a secondary element in the legend, the second voyage to Ireland. (pp. 165-91)

James Douglas Bruce, "Traditions, Chronicles, Lays, and Romances: Tristan," in his The Evolution of Arthurian Romance from the Beginnings Down to the Year 1300, Vol. I, *second edition, Dandenhoed & Ruprecht, 1928, pp. 152-91.*

FURTHER READING

Adams, Alison; Diverres, Armel H.; Stern, Karen; and Varty, Kenneth, eds. *The Changing Face of Arthurian Romance: Essays on Arthurian Prose Romances in Memory of Cedric E. Pickford.* Cambridge, England: Boydell Press, 1986, 168 p.

Essay collection focusing on the general theme of "the development of the Arthurian prose romance, from soon after the death of Chrétien de Troyes up to the end of the medieval period."

Alcock, Leslie. *Arthur's Britain: History and Archaeology, AD 367-634.* New York: St. Martin's Press, 1971, 415 p.
Historical and archeological study of Britain during the transitional phase between the Roman *imperium* and Anglo-Saxon domination.

Ashe, Geoffrey. *King Arthur: The Dream of a Golden Age.* London: Thames and Hudson, 1990, 96 p.
Profusely illustrated popular introduction to Arthurian legend.

Barber, Richard. *Arthur of Albion: An Introduction to the Arthurian Literature and Legends of England.* New York: Barnes and Noble, 1961, 216 p.
Discussion of Arthurian legend tracing "Arthur's progress from his place in history to his appearances in modern poetry."

————. *King Arthur: Hero and Legend.* New York: St. Martin's Press, 1961, 209 p.
Study of the personage and legend of King Arthur encompassing British and European versions of the legend.

————. *The Figure of Arthur.* London: Longman, 1972, 160 p.
Probes the historical and political dimensions of the figure of Arthur.

Baswell, Christopher, and Sharpe, William, eds. *The Passing of Arthur: New Essays in Arthurian Tradition.* New York: Garland, 1988, 316 p.
Essay collection addressing a range of Arthurian subjects from medieval France to Victorian England.

Billings, Anna Hunt. *A Guide to the Middle English Metrical Romances Dealing with English and Germanic Legends, and with the Cycles of Charlemagne and of Arthur.* Yale Studies in English, edited by Albert S. Cook. New York: Henry Holt and Company, 1901, 232 p.
Encyclopedic compendium of the principal myths and legends of Arthurian literature.

Bogdanow, Fanni. *The Romance of the Grail: A Study of the Structure and Genesis of a Thirteenth-Century Arthurian Prose Romance.* Manchester, England: Manchester University Press, 1966, 308 p.
Reviews the major classifications of thirteenth-century Arthurian romance.

————. "Morgain's Role in the Thirteenth-Century French Prose Romances of the Arthurian Cycle." *Medium Aevum* XXXVIII, No. 2 (1969): 123-31.
Argues that "[Morgain's] character, like most of the features of the prose romances, would . . . seem to be the product of an organic growth, motivated from within, and requiring no explanation beyond the logic and the method of the mediaeval prose writers themselves."

Braswell, Mary Flowers, and Bugge, John, eds. *The Arthurian Tradition: Essays in Convergence.* Tuscaloosa: University of Alabama Press, 1988, 258 p.
Diverse compilation of essays "directed toward both the specialist and the informed generalist."

Bruce, James Douglas. *The Evolution of Arthurian Romance: From the Beginnings down to the Year 1300.* 2 vols. Gottingen, Germany: Vandenhoed and Ruprecht, 1923.
Surveys Arthurian Romance in Europe from the sixth century to 1300.

Cavendish, Richard. *King Arthur and the Grail: The Arthurian Legends and Their Meaning.* London: Weidenfeld and Nicolson, 1978, 229 p.
Interpretive study of Arthurian legend and iconography.

Cosman, Medeleine Pelner. *The Education of the Hero in Arthurian Romance.* Chapel Hill: University of North Carolina Press, 1965, 239 p.
Study of leading protagonists in Arthurian literature affirming that "appreciation of the formation, the development, and the utilization of the *enfance* and the education of the Arthurian hero provides fresh insights into the medieval romancer's style, intention, and art."

Cross, Tom Peete, and Nitze, William Albert. *Lancelot and Guenevere: A Study on the Origins of Courtly Love.* Chicago: University of Chicago Press, 1930, 104 p.
Study of the Lancelot legend that aims "to outline the romance by Chrétien, to trace it back to its origins, and, lastly, to set forth in detail the evolution that the theme underwent at the hands of the French poet."

Fletcher, Robert Huntington. *The Arthurian Material in the Chronicles, Especially Those of Great Britain and France,* Second edition. New York: Burt Franklin, 1966, 335 p.
Considers "what Arthurian material is contained in the European chronicles . . . from the middle of the sixth to the end of the sixteenth century."

Knight, Stephen. *Arthurian Literature and Society.* New York: St. Martin's Press, 1983, 229 p.
Survey of Arthurian literature that "restricts its discussion to texts that seem of major importance and relevance to the English-speaking world."

Korrel, Peter. *An Arthurian Triangle: A Study of the Origin, Development and Characterization of Arthur, Guinevere and Mordred.* Leiden, Netherlands: E. J. Brill, 1984, 301 p.
Detailed textual analysis of three of the leading figures of Arthurian legend.

Lagorio, Valerie M., and Day, Mildred Leake, eds. *King Arthur Through the Ages.* 2 vols. New York: Garland, 1990.
Essay compilation addressing a wide range of historical topics as well as contemporary issues in Arthurian scholarship.

Loomis, Roger Sherman. *The Development of Arthurian Romance.* London: Hutchinson University Library, 1963, 199 p.
Review of Arthurian Romances in the Middle Ages based on a "careful and thorough investigation of sources and analogues."

————. *Studies in Medieval Literature: A Memorial Collection of Essays.* New York: Burt Franklin, 1970, 338 p.
Representative collection that "makes available essays which originally appeared in widely scattered books and journals often difficult to come by except in the largest libraries."

————, ed. *Arthurian Literature in the Middle Ages: A Collaborative History.* Oxford: Clarendon Press, 1959, 574 p.

Highly regarded selection of scholarly articles addressing all aspects of Arthurian legend.

Moorman, Charles. *A Knyght There Was: The Evolution of the Knight in Literature.* Lexington: University of Kentucky Press, 1967, 170 p.

Traces "the changing concept of the character of the knight through the really important literary works of the Middle Ages and Renaissance."

———. "King Arthur and the English National Character." *New York Folklore Quarterly* XXIV, No. 2 (June 1968): 102-12.

Argues that "the Arthur legend . . . continues as a living force in both English literature and English life."

Morris, John. *The Age of Arthur: A History of the British Isles from 350 to 650.* New York: Charles Scribner's Sons, 1973, 665 p.

Surveys "the history of the British Isles between the end of Roman Britain and the birth of England and Wales."

Owen, D. D. R. *Arthurian Romance: Seven Essays.* New York: Barnes and Noble, 1971, 102 p.

Seven essays addressing a wide range of topics in Arthurian literature.

Pochoda, Elizabeth T. *Arthurian Propaganda:* Le Morte Darthur *as an Historical Ideal of Life.* Chapel Hill: University of North Carolina Press, 1971, 185 p.

Explores the political ramifications of Arthurian legend, offering that "much of Arthurian literature might be said to be a kind of social propaganda."

Utley, Francis Lee. "Arthurian Romance and Folklore Method." *Romance Philology* XVII, No. 3 (February 1964): 596-607.

Purports that "folklore science offers warnings to the Arthurian against hasty generalization; it affords revelations of cultural transformation, the demonstration of a worldwide matrix, and clues to artistic structure."

Van der Ven-Ten Bensel, Elise Francisca Wilhelmina Maria. *The Character of King Arthur in English Literature.* New York: Haskell House, 1966, 215 p.

Treats Arthurian history, legend, and myth from late antiquity to the nineteenth century.

Wheatley, Henry B. *Merlin or the Early History of King Arthur: A Prose Romance,* Vol. I. 1899. Reprint. New York: Greenwood Press, 1969, 188 p.

Analysis of the Merlin tradition and its literary treatments.

Woodruff, Douglas, ed. *For Hilaire Belloc: Essays in Honor of his Seventy-First Birthday.* 1942. Reprint. New York: Greenwood Press, 1969, 218 p.

General overview of the historical and literary branches of Arthurian legend.

Wyatt, Isabel. *From Round Table to Grail Castle.* Sussex, England: Lanthorn Press, 1979, 264 p.

Twelve studies of Arthurian legend that aim to "penetrate to the spiritual realities behind the happenings in the various versions of the Arthurian and Grail stories, as they are affirmed and illumined by Rudolf Steiner's spiritual-scientific researches."

Chrétien de Troyes

Circa Twelfth Century

(Also referred to as Chrestien, Christian, and Christianus)
French poet.

INTRODUCTION

One of the most important European medieval poets, Chrétien is best known as the originator of the Arthurian romance genre and as the writer who first focused on Arthurian characters and themes, inspiring immense literary activity on the part of other writers. He was also the greatest exponent of the ideals of courtly love and chivalry in the Middle Ages. As a result, Chrétien became much better known for his subject matter than for his poetic craftsmanship and style, despite his mastery of both. His influence on the romance genre was widespread and long lasting, and his works—*Erec et Enide* (*Erec and Enide*), *Cligés, Yvain, Lancelot,* and *Perceval*—were imitated in France and abroad in his own lifetime and for several centuries thereafter. In particular, Chrétien's *Perceval,* the earliest known account of the quest for the Grail, inspired a long tradition of poems and romances on the Grail theme. Chrétien was, as W. T. H. Jackson stated and as most critics would agree, "by far the most prolific and influential writer of French narrative poetry in the twelfth century."

Few details of Chrétien's life are known. The poet identified himself as "Chrétien de Troyes" in his first romance, *Erec and Enide,* implying that he was either born or resided in the city of Troyes, then an important regional center and the seat of the court of Marie de Champagne. The Countess of Champagne and her mother, Eleanor of Aquitaine, were renowned for their encouragement of the arts and sponsorship of writers throughout the twelfth century. Chrétien's career is usually associated with the second half of the twelfth century on the basis of Marie's patronage of his *Lancelot;* in his prologue to the work, he identified Marie as not only the patron of the project, but also as the source of its subject matter. Since her marriage to the Count of Champagne did not take place until 1164, that year is the earliest date possible for Chrétien's composition of *Lancelot.* Most of Chrétien's biography is conjectural, but literary historians concur on this fact and one other: because Philip d'Alsace, Count of Flanders and Chrétien's patron for *Perceval,* departed on the Third Crusade in 1190, Chrétien must have begun the story of the Grail before then. Some scholars also speculate that Chrétien died before completing *Perceval,* since what survives of it appears unfinished. Other details about Chrétien's life, such as his grounding in classical literature and knowledge of Latin and the poetics and rhetoric of the Middle Ages, have been suggested by evidence in his works. Several critics have asserted that, as a result of his

Above: Perceval meets the five knights. Lower left: Perceval arrives at Arthur's court. Lower right: Perceval slays the Red Knight. (Paris. B.N., f. fr. 12576, fol. lr.)

connection with Marie and Eleanor, Chrétien probably traveled in England—a theory that would explain his evident familiarity with British geography and politics in his second poem, *Cligés,* as well as his knowledge of Celtic Arthurian legends.

No original texts of Chrétien's romances survive, and the earliest extant manuscripts date from at least a generation after he composed the works. The large number of copies of Chrétien's works indicates his great popularity in the Middle Ages. However, only two manuscripts contain all five of his romances. In the text labelled Bibliothèque Nationale f. fr. 794 (also named the Guiot manuscript, after its scribe), Chrétien's Arthurian romances appear among other works in the context of a pseudo-factual chronological account of ancient history. They are also inserted in the middle of the Arthurian section of Robert Wace's *Roman de Brut* (1155) in the Bibliothèque Nationale f. fr. 1450 manuscript, presumably to expand more fully upon the Arthurian legends. The earliest and best text of Chrétien's works, the Annonay manuscript, only survives in fragments because it was cut apart to serve as filling for book bindings in the eighteenth century. Several remaining manuscripts contain two or more of the romances in partial or complete form, while some twenty-three others include the text of one of his romances apiece, among works by other authors.

Chrétien's complete works were first edited in 1884-99 by Wendelin Foerster under the title *Christian von Troyes: Sämtliche erhaltene Werke.* Most critics accept this edition as the best and most inclusive modern text of the romances, since Foerster attempted to incorporate every available Chrétien manuscript. Other scholars prefer the Mario de Roques edition, *Les romans de Chrétien de Troyes* (5 vols., 1952-75), which is considered more conservative because it is based only on the Guiot manuscript, the text believed to be closest to Chrétien's original. While the individual romances were edited and translated into English at various times in the nineteenth century and more frequently in the twentieth century, the first extensive translation did not appear until 1914, when W. W. Comfort translated all the romances except *Perceval* in *Chrétien de Troyes: Arthurian Romances.* Complete English translations of the poems have recently been published by David Staines (1990) and William Kibler (1991).

Erec and Enide, the first of Chrétien's romances, was composed around 1169 and recounts the tale of Erec's winning of Enide and his subsequent neglect of his knightly duty in favor of his wife's constant company. To regain his reputation for valor, he undertakes a dangerous quest and forces Enide to accompany him. The journey ends successfully when Erec proves his prowess at arms. With this romance Chrétien established one of his principal themes—the search for balance between love and duty. Scholars believe that *Cligés* was written next, probably about 1176. It presents the adventures of Alexandre of Constantinople and his son, Cligés. Cligés's story resembles the legend of Tristan, the subject of numerous romances, with the youth involved in a love triangle with his uncle Alis and Alis's wife, Fenice. Like Tristan and his lover Isolde, Cligés and Fenice arrange to be together, but Chrétien reworks the Tristan legend in an attempt to avoid the appearance of adultery. Critics still debate whether Chrétien intended to parody the Tristan legend or to dispel the moral stigma of adultery from his story.

The next two romances, *Yvain* and *Lancelot,* were composed either successively or concurrently around 1178 or 1179. In *Yvain,* Chrétien reused the theme of *Erec and Enide,* this time treating it from a different perspective. *Yvain* (sometimes also titled *Le Chevalier au lion, or The Knight with the Lion*) is the story of a knight who neglects his marriage in his pursuit of adventure and prowess. Returning home late from a year of tourneying with Gauvain, Yvain is banished by his wife, Laudine, and goes mad. The remainder of the romance follows Yvain's progression from a vainglorious man to a knight dedicated to the service of others, and his eventual return to Laudine as a worthy husband. Many of Chrétien's typical themes appear in *Yvain,* including the moral development of the hero and the conflict between the individual's desires and society's demands. *Lancelot* (also known as *Le Chevalier de la charrete, or The Knight of the Cart*) reflects the French chivalric themes popular in the court of Marie de Champagne. Critics point out that the conduct of Lance-

lot, especially his submission to his lady love's wishes, exemplifies the code of courtly love as it was understood in the twelfth century. The plot concerns Guenevere's abduction by an evil knight and her rescue by the adoring Lancelot. Shocked when Guenevere shuns him after her successful rescue, Lancelot learns later that she is aggrieved because he hesitated to endure a shameful experience for her sake. Chrétien did not complete *Lancelot,* leaving it to Godefroi de Lagny to finish, with his approval.

Chrétien appears to have left *Perceval* incomplete as well, though some critics believe that the purposely ambiguous ending was intended to tantalize his audience; several later poets continued the story. *Perceval,* also called *Li Conte du graal,* or *The Story of the Grail,* follows the quest for the Grail by Perceval and Gauvain. Perceval is an innocent young man who leaves his mother to become a knight. After many adventures, including a period at Arthur's court, Perceval finds himself at the Grail Castle with the Fisher King, where he witnesses the mystical Grail procession but fails to inquire about its significance. After his departure, he is chastised by a cousin and a "loathly damsel" for his ignorance and failure in the quest, and Perceval sets off again in search of the castle. The story then turns to a similar quest by Gauvain. His adventures center particularly around his attempt to find the bleeding lance featured in the Grail procession, and end at the Castle of Marvels, from which no one can leave. The most supernatural of Chrétien's romances, *Perceval* intrigued its medieval audience, and the Grail story was the most frequently adapted of all his tales.

Besides his five well-known Arthurian romances, Chrétien is also believed to have written *Guillaume d'Angleterre,* a non-Arthurian story based on the legend of St. Eustace, and two lyric poems, *Le Chevalier à l'épée* and *La Mule sans frein.* These attributions are not widely accepted, however. The prologue to *Cligés* lists other works the poet claims to have written as well: a version of the Tristan legend ("King Mark and Iseut the Fair") and translations of portions of Ovid's *Ars Amatoria* (c. 1st century B.C.), including "The Shoulder Bite" and a version of *Philomena,* the story of Philomena's rape and her revenge. *Philomena* is the only one of these disputed works to survive.

Much of the critical work on Chrétien has focused on establishing his place in the history of European literature. Scholars have attempted to identify and analyze his sources and the historical and literary traditions that influenced him in order to determine the extent of his originality and the validity of his claim as the originator of Arthurian romance. On this question, Jean Frappier voiced a prevalent opinion when he insisted that "the virtual borrowing of subjects or themes is much less important than their treatment, and, in fact, in Chrétien's case, his poetics reveal most clearly and most precisely his innovations in romance and his creative talent." Other critics concur, arguing further that because Chrétien's romances were the first of the genre to be recorded and the leading influence on all later Arthurian romance literature, his designation as the originator of the form is well deserved. Before Chrétien's romances, King Arthur had appeared in folk legends as a warrior leader and little more. He became a more courtly character as the tradition evolved, but Chrétien was the first to portray Arthur's court as the pinnacle of chivalric society. In Chrétien's works, Arthur's court is a place of leisure where adventure is sought for its own sake and for the cause of love, not for conquest or war. The codes of courtly love and chivalry guide the conduct of the court's inhabitants, and the court figures merely as a place where prowess is best evaluated and adventure sanctioned and encouraged. Arthur's part in Chrétien's romances is not of primary importance, though he and other members of his court—such as Guenevere, Kay, and Gauvain—play pivotal roles. The central characters are the knights of Arthur's Round Table, with the king's court serving as a backdrop to their adventures.

Chrétien's treatment of his principal theme, love, has invited a great deal of examination. Although most critics maintain that Chrétien's depiction of the ideals of the twelfth-century French court brought the theme of courtly love to its highest point in medieval literature, they consider his version of love in the Arthurian court highly individualistic. The term *amor courteois* ("courtly love") generally refers to a code of conduct for medieval ladies and their lovers in which the lady is dominant and the knightly lover's duty is to please her and obey her commands; these relationships are very often openly presented as adulterous. According to many commentators, Chrétien did not approve of the adulterous love affairs condoned by the code of courtly love but sought instead to place his heroes in married relationships, as he did in *Erec and Enide* and *Yvain*. He also attempted to provide motivation for his characters' feelings and actions beyond the standards of the court. Through the use of monologues and other techniques, Chrétien analyzed the thoughts and emotions of the lovers in his romances, realistically probing the psychological and moral dilemmas faced by lovers. Critics often cite Chrétien's portrayal of Fenice in *Cligés* and of Laudine in *Yvain* as the best examples of his psychologically motivated characters. On the other hand, Lancelot and Guenevere in *Lancelot,* a story on a theme not of Chrétien's choosing, represent an exception to the norm in his romances: they comply least with his personal value system and are presented as conventional courtly lovers. Commentators have noted that Chrétien's use of humor and irony in *Lancelot,* especially in his portrayal of Lancelot's actions, implies subtle ridicule of courtly love and reveals its limitations.

Irony and humor are very important elements in Chrétien's narratives generally, serving as vehicles for his commentary on medieval society and its world view. Scholars believe that Chrétien's realistic depiction of the details of life at court through motifs, characterization, and symbolism cunningly concealed his critical attitude toward them. The interweaving of multiple legends and themes, rich symbolism, and many possible levels of interpretation are considered the hallmarks of Chrétien's style. His masterful description of setting and action, intricate psychological characterization, easy handling of meter and rhyme, as well as his eloquent language all contribute to the technical virtuosity of his work.

Despite his extraordinary significance to medieval literature, little English criticism on Chrétien's work appeared before the twentieth century. Early twentieth-century studies focused primarily on the question of Chrétien's sources and his treatment of courtly love. Although these are still regarded as key issues, in later decades commentators began to attend more closely to the underlying themes of Chrétien's Arthurian romances in order to dispel some of the questions surrounding his work. The mysterious and mystical themes treated by Chrétien serve to promote ambiguity and his narratives often end without being resolved. For example, scholars have suggested numerous theories about the meaning of the Grail theme in *Perceval:* they have related the quest for the Grail to the problem of life and death, and to the medieval campaign to convert the Jews to Christianity, among other theories. Acceptance of these underlying themes in Chrétien's romances and recognition of his extensive symbolism have moved critics to view him as a more complex writer than previously assumed. Assessing the role of Arthur and his court in Chrétien's works, recent commentators have further noted his complex treatment of Arthurian lore, observing that the purported originator of the Arthurian romance tradition used the form for his own evaluation of and commentary on the Arthurian court. In effect, they maintain, Chrétien began the progression away from Arthurian literary conventions even as he invented them.

Critics concur that Chrétien's importance lies not only in his introduction of Arthurian material into the literary sphere and his influence on later generations of European writers, but in the inherent aesthetic quality of his works. His artistic achievement and reputation endure because, as Ruth Harwood Cline asserts, "Chrétien's romances are outstanding in themselves, as poetry, as well-constructed and entertaining tales of love and adventure, as perceptive studies of human psychology and emotion, and as portraits of mankind's struggle to attain the earthly ideals of self-perfection and joy."

PRINCIPAL ENGLISH TRANSLATIONS

Perceval (translated by S. Evans) 1898-1912
King William the Wanderer: An Old British Saga from Old French Versions (Guillaume d'Angleterre) (translated by W. G. Collingwood) 1904
Cligés (translated by L. J. Gardiner) 1912
* *Chrétien de Troyes: Arthurian Romances* (translated by W. W. Comfort) 1914
The Story of the Grail (translated by R. W. Linker) 1952
Chrétien de Troyes's Yvain; or, The Knight with the Lion (translated by Ruth Harwood Cline) 1975
Lancelot; or, The Knight of the Cart (translated by William W. Kibler) 1981
Perceval: The Story of the Grail (translated by Nigel Bryant) 1982
Lancelot, the Knight of the Cart (translated by Deborah Webster Rogers) 1984
The Knight with the Lion; or, Yvain (translated by William W. Kibler) 1985

Erec and Enide (translated by Carleton W. Carroll) 1987

The Complete Romances of Chrétien de Troyes (translated by David Staines) 1990

†*Chrétien de Troyes: Arthurian Romances* (translated by William W. Kibler) 1991

*This edition does not include *Perceval*.

†In this edition *Erec et Enide* was translated by Carleton W. Carroll.

Chrétien de Troyes   (poem date c. 1169)

[*In the following excerpt from his prologue to* Erec and Enide, *Chrétien advocates the pursuit of knowledge, offering his "beautifully ordered composition" as an example of what one may achieve through learning. As no exact composition date can be determined for* Erec and Enide, *the most commonly accepted date has been used to date this excerpt.*]

> The peasant says in his proverb
> that one may hold in contempt something
> that is worth much more than one believes;
> therefore he does well who makes good use of his
>   learning
> according to whatever understanding he has,
> for he who neglects his learning
> may easily keep silent something
> that would later give much pleasure.
> Therefore Chrétien de Troyes says
> that it is reasonable
> that each person think and strive in every way
> to speak well and to teach well,
> and from a tale of adventure he draws
> a beautifully ordered composition,
> whereby one may prove and know
> that he does not act intelligently
> who does not give free rein to his knowledge,
> as long as God gives him the grace to do so.
> This is the tale of Erec, son of Lac,
> which, before kings and before counts,
> those who try to live by storytelling
> customarily mangle and corrupt.
> Now I shall begin the story
> which evermore will be in memory
> for as long as Christendom lasts—
> of this does Chrétien boast.
>
>   (p. 3)

> *Chrétien de Troyes, in his* Erec and Enide, *edited and translated by Carleton W. Carroll, Garland Publishing, Inc., 1987, 349 p.*

Chrétien de Troyes   (poem date c. 1179)

[*In the excerpt below from the prologue to* Lancelot, *Chrétien describes how he began the task of writing the poem and how he received its subject matter. The most commonly accepted composition date has been used to date this excerpt.*]

Since my lady of Champagne wills me to undertake the making of a romance, I shall undertake it with great goodwill, as one so wholly devoted that he will do anything in the world for her without any intention of flattery. But another man might begin this in order to flatter her; he would say, and I could only agree, that she surpasses all living ladies as the south wind blowing in April or May surpasses all winds. On my word, I am not one who would flatter his lady. Shall I say, "The Countess is worth as much in queens as a precious gem is worth in brocades and semiprecious stones?" No indeed, I shall say nothing of this, though it is true despite my silence. I shall say only that her command is more important in this undertaking than any thought or effort I may expend.

Christian is beginning his book of the Knight of the Cart. The Countess presents him with the matter and the meaning, and he undertakes to shape the work, adding little to it except his effort and his careful attention. (p. 170)

> *Chrétien de Troyes, in his* The Complete Romances of Chrétien de Troyes, *translated by David Staines, Indiana University Press, 1990, 542 p.*

W. P. Ker   (essay date 1897)

[*Ker was a noted English scholar of medieval literature and an authority on comparative European literature and the history of literary forms. In the following excerpt from his* Epic Romance, *first published in 1897, he examines Chrétien's representation of sentiment and sensibility in his works, focusing particularly on* Erec and Enide *and* Cligés.]

[The] early romantic schools, though they are generally formal and sentimental, and not dramatic, have here and there the possibilities of a stronger drama and a truer imagination, and seem at times almost to have worked themselves free from their pedantry.

There is sentiment and sentiment: and while the pathos of medieval romance, like some of the effusion of medieval lyric, is often merely formal repetition of phrases, it is sometimes more natural, and sometimes the mechanical fancy seems to quicken into true poetical vision, or at least to make room for a sane appreciation of real life and its incidents. Chrestien of Troyes shows his genius most unmistakably in his occasional surprising intervals of true description and natural feeling, in the middle of his rhetoric; while even his sustained rhetorical dissertations, like those of the *Roman de la Rose* in the next century, are not absolutely untrue, or uncontrolled by observation of actual manners. Often the rhetorical apparatus interferes in the most annoying way with the clear vision. In the ***Chevalier au Lion,*** for example, there is a pretty sketch of a family party—a girl reading a romance to her father in a garden, and her mother coming up and listening to the story—from which there is a sudden and annoying change to the common impertinences of the amatory professional novelist. This is the passage, with the two kinds of literature in abrupt opposition:—

> Messire Yvain goes into the garden, and his people follow; and he sees a goodly gentleman reclining on a cloth of silk and leaning on his

elbow; and a maiden was sitting before him reading out of a romance, I know not whose the story. And to listen to the romance a lady had drawn near; that was her mother, and he was her father, and well might they be glad to look on her and listen to her, for they had no other child. She was not yet sixteen years old, and she was so fair and gentle that the God of Love if he had seen her would have given himself to be her slave, and never would have bestowed the love of her on any other than himself. For her sake, to serve her, he would have made himself man, would have put off his deity, and would have stricken himself with the dart whose wound is never healed, except a disloyal physician tend it. It is not right that any should recover from that wound, unless there be disloyalty in it; and whoever is otherwise healed, he never loved with loyalty. *Of this wound I could talk to you without end,* if it pleased you to listen; but I know that some would say that all my talk was idleness, for the world is fallen away from true love, and men know not any more how to love as they ought, for the very talk of love is a weariness to them! [ll. 5360-5396].

This short passage is representative of Chrestien's work, and indeed of the most successful and influential work of the twelfth-century schools. It is not, like some affected kinds of romance, entirely cut off from reality. But the glimpses of the real world are occasional and short; there is a flash of pure daylight, a breath of fresh air, and then the heavy-laden, enchanted mists of rhetoric and obligatory sentiment come rolling down and shut out the view.

It is possible to trace out in some detail a line of progress in medieval romance, in which there is a victory in the end for the more ingenuous kind of sentiment; in which the rhetorical romantic forms are altered and strengthened to bear the weight of true imagination.

This line of progress is nothing less than the earlier life of all the great modern forms of novel; a part of European history which deserves some study from those who have leisure for it.

The case may be looked at in this way. The romantic schools, following on the earlier heroic literature, generally substituted a more shallow, formal, limited set of characters for the larger and freer portraits of the heroic age, making up for this defect in the personages by extravagance in other respects—in the incidents, the phrasing, the sentimental pathos, the rhetorical conceits. The great advantage of the new school over the old was that it was adapted to modern cosmopolitan civilisation; it left the artist free to choose his subject anywhere, and to deal with it according to the laws of good society, without local or national restrictions. But the earlier work of this modern enlightenment in the Middle Ages was generally very formal, very meagre in imagination. The progress of literature was to fill out the romantic forms, and to gain for the new cosmopolitan schemes of fiction the same sort of substantial contents, the same command of human nature and its variety, as belong (with local or national restrictions) to some at any rate of the earlier epic authors. This being so, one of the interests of the study of medieval romance

must be the discovery of those places in which it departs from its own dominant conventions, and seems to aim at something different from its own nature: at the recovery of the fuller life of epic for the benefit of romance. Epic fulness of life within the limits of romantic form—that might be said to be the ideal which is *not* attained in the Middle Ages, but towards which many medieval writers seem to be making their way.

Chrestien's story of *Geraint and Enid* (Geraint has to take the name of *Erec* in the French) is one of his earlier works, but cannot be called immature in comparison with what he wrote afterwards. In Chrestien's **Enid** there is not a little superfluity of the common sort of adventure. The story of Enid in the *Idylls of the King* (founded upon the Welsh *Geraint,* as given in Lady Charlotte Guest's *Mabinogion*) has been brought within compass, and a number of quite unnecessary adventures have been cut out. Yet the story here is the same as Chrestien's, and the drama of the story is not the pure invention of the English poet. Chrestien has all the principal motives, and the working out of the problem is the same. In one place, indeed, where the Welsh romance, the immediate source of Tennyson's *Enid,* has shortened the scene of reconciliation between the lovers, the Idyll has restored something like the proportions of the original French. Chrestien makes Erec speak to Enid and renounce all his ill-will, after the scene in which "the brute Earl" is killed; the Welsh story, with no less effect, allows the reconciliation to be taken for granted when Geraint, at this point in the history, with no speech of his reported, lifts Enid on his own horse. The Idyll goes back (apparently without any direct knowledge of Chrestien's version) to the method of Chrestien.

The story of Enid in Chrestien is very unlike the other stories of distressed and submissive wives; it has none of the ineradicable falsity of the story of Griselda. How much is due to Chrestien for this can hardly be reckoned, in our ignorance of the materials he used. But taking into account the other passages, like that of the girl reading in the garden, where Chrestien shows a distinct original appreciation of certain aspects of life, it cannot be far wrong to consider Chrestien's picture of Enid as mainly his own; and, in any case, this picture is one of the finest in medieval romance. There is no comparison between Chrestien of Troyes and Homer, but it is not impious to speak of Enid along with Nausicaa, and there are few other ladies of romance who may claim as much as this. The adventure of the Sparrowhawk, one of the finest pieces of pure romance in the poetry of this century, is also one of the finest in the old French, and in many ways very unlike the commonplaces of chivalry, in the simplicity of the household where Enid waits on her father's guest and takes his horse to the stable, in the sincerity and clearness with which Chrestien indicates the gentle breeding and dignity of her father and mother, and the pervading spirit of grace and loyalty in the whole scene.

In the story of Enid, Chrestien has a subject which recommends itself to modern readers. The misunderstanding between Enid and her husband, and the reconciliation, are not peculiarly medieval, though the adventures through which their history is worked out are of the ordinary romantic commonplace.

Indeed the relation of husband and wife in this story is rather exceptionally divergent from the current romantic mode, and from the conventional law that true love between husband and wife was impossible. Afterwards, in his poem of **Lancelot** (**Le Chevalier de la Charrette**), Chrestien took up and worked out this conventional and pedantic theory, and made the love of Lancelot and the Queen into the standard for all courtly lovers. In his **Enid,** however, there is nothing of this. At the same time, the courtly and chivalrous mode gets the better of the central drama in his **Enid,** in so far as he allows himself to be distracted unduly from the pair of lovers by various "hyperboles" of the Romantic School; there are a number of unnecessary jousts and encounters, and a mysterious exploit of Erec in a magic garden, which is quite out of connexion with the rest of the story. The final impression is that Chrestien wanted strength of mind or inclination to concentrate himself on the drama of the two lovers. The story is taken too lightly.

In **Cliges,** his next work, the dramatic situation is much less valuable than in **Enid,** but the workmanship is far more careful and exact, and the result is a story which may claim to be among the earliest of modern novels, if the Greek romances, to which it has a close relation, are not taken into account. The story has very little "machinery"; there are none of the marvels of the Faërie in it. There is a Thessalian witch (the heroine's nurse), who keeps well within the limits of possible witchcraft, and there is the incident of the sleeping-draught (familiar in the ballad of the *Gay Goshawk*), and that is all. The rest is a simple love-story (or rather a double love-story, for there is the history of the hero's father and mother, before his own begins), and the personages are merely true lovers, undistinguished by any such qualities as the sulkiness of Erec or the discretion of Enid. It is all pure sensibility, and as it happens the sensibility is in good keeping—not overdriven into the pedantry of the more quixotic troubadours and minnesingers, and not warped by the conventions against marriage. It is explained at the end that, though Cliges and Fenice are married, they are lovers still:—

> De s'amie a feite sa fame,
> Mais il l'apele amie et dame,
> Que por ce ne pert ele mie
> Que il ne l'aint come s'amie,
> Et ele lui autresi
> Con l'an doit feire son ami:
> Et chascun jor lor amors crut,
> N'onques cil celi ne mescrut,
> Ne querela de nule chose.
>
> [l. 6753]

This poem of Chrestien's is a collection of the finest specimens of medieval rhetoric on the eternal theme. There is little incident, and sensibility has it all its own way, in monologues by the actors and digressions by the author, on the nature of love. It is rather the sentiment than the passion that is here expressed in the "language of the heart"; but, however that may be, there are both delicacy and eloquence in the language. The pensive Fenice, who

debates with herself for nearly two hundred lines in one place (4410-4574), is the ancestress of many later heroines.

> Meis Fenice est sor toz pansive;
> Ele ne trueve fonz ne rive
> El panser dont ele est anplie,
> Tant li abonde et mouteplie.
>
> [l. 4339]

In the later works of Chrestien, in **Yvain, Lancelot,** and **Perceval,** there are new developments of romance, more particularly in the story of Lancelot and Guinevere. But these three later stories, unlike **Cliges,** are full of the British marvels, which no one would wish away, and yet they are encumbrances to what we must regard as the principal virtue of the poet—his skill of analysis in cases of sentiment, and his interest in such cases. **Cliges,** at any rate, however far it may come short of the **Chevalier de la Charrette** and the **Conte du Graal** in variety, is that one of Chrestien's poems, it might be said that one of the twelfth-century French romances, which best corresponds to the later type of novel. It is the most modern of them; and at the same time it does not represent its own age any the worse, because it also to some extent anticipates the fashions of later literature. (pp. 352-59)

> *W. P. Ker, in his "Romance and the Old French Romantic Schools," Epic and Romance: Essays on Medieval Literature, Dover Publications, Inc., 1957, pp. 321-72.*

Jessie L. Weston (essay date 1901)

[*Weston was a noted Medievalist and Arthurian scholar. In the following excerpt, she compares Chrétien's* Lancelot *with the poet's other romances and with other early versions of the legend of Guenevere's rescue.*]

With the poem [*Le Chevalier de la Charrette*] we reach a fresh stage in the Lancelot tradition, and one which, though it has already been the subject of acute and scholarly discussion, still presents many points of difficulty.

The story related in the poem is so well known, and the poem itself so accessible, that it is unnecessary to do more than summarise the leading features. It is, as we all know, the story of Guinevere's abduction by Meleagant, and her rescue by Sir Lancelot.

A knight (Meleagant) appears at Arthur's court, and boasts of the Breton subjects he holds in captivity. Arthur can free them if he will commit Guinevere to the care of a knight who will fight a single combat with him; if he (Meleagant) be defeated, all the prisoners shall be freed; if he be victor, Guinevere, too, is his captive. Kay, by demanding from Arthur a boon, the nature of which is unspecified, and which the king grants before hearing, obtains permission to escort the queen. Gawain follows, meets Kay's horse, riderless and covered with blood, and is then confronted by an unnamed knight (Lancelot), who begs the loan of a steed. Gawain gives him his, and follows on a spare steed as quickly as possible, only to find traces of a sanguinary conflict, and his own horse slain. He overtakes Lancelot, who, meeting a dwarf driving a cart, mounts after a momentary hesitation, and the two continue the pursuit together. Meleagant's land (or rather that of his father Baudemagus) is surrounded by deep water, crossed by two bridges, one of a sword-blade, the other under the water. Lancelot chooses the first, crosses in safety, fights with Meleagant, and frees Guinevere, who, however, receives him coldly, being offended at his momentary hesitation before mounting the cart. Lancelot, in despair, tries to commit suicide; Guinevere, hearing a rumour of his death, is overwhelmed with grief, and on his next appearance receives him with the greatest favour. They pass the night together, Lancelot gaining access to the queen's chamber by means of a heavily barred window, and severely wounding his hands in wrenching asunder the bars. The traces of blood on the bed-clothes cause the queen to be accused of a *liaison* with Kay, who, severely wounded, is sleeping in the ante-chamber. Lancelot undertakes to prove Guinevere's innocence by a combat with Meleagant, which shall take place at Arthur's court; but, having set out to seek Gawain, is treacherously decoyed into prison by his foe. Meleagant, by means of forged letters, persuades the queen that Lancelot has returned to court, whither Guinevere repairs, escorted by Gawain, who has meanwhile arrived on the scene. Lancelot, who has been released on parole by his jailor's wife, to attend a tourney, is subsequently walled up in a tower by Meleagant, from which prison he is released by his rival's sister, and reaching court at the last moment, overcomes and slays Meleagant.

The capital importance of this poem lies in the fact that here, for the first time, so far as our present knowledge goes, we meet with those relations between Lancelot and the queen which form so important a part of the completed Arthurian legend. Are these relations, then, an invention of Chrétien, or were they already familiar to the public for whom he wrote? Here I shall only treat this question incidentally . . . ; the questions which mainly concern us relate rather to the nature (a) of the story itself, (b) of Chrétien's share in its development.

In the introductory lines we learn that the poem was written at the instance of the Countess Marie de Champagne, who supplied 'Matiere et san.' I take this to mean that she only supplied a verbal outline of the story, and left it to Chrétien to fill in details. Thus, as regards source, Chrétien stands in a different position in this poem than in his other romances. In every other instance he had either in *livre* or *conte* (which latter I take to be the recital of a professional story-teller) a fixed source from which he drew his tale.

The internal evidence agrees with these indications: the *Charrette* is far inferior to Chrétien's other work; the construction is feeble in the extreme, and bristles with contradictions and obscurities. Why, for instance, does Meleagant suggest that Guinevere shall be put in charge of a knight and follow him? Why not challenge a single combat at the court, where there would be a public to see that the rules of such combat were observed? It may be that the original scene of abduction was a wood, and this is an awkward attempt to combine a later version, *i.e.* Arthur's court, with a primitive feature; but in any case it starts the story on wrong lines. Gawain (who is also mounted) fol-

lows *directly* on Lancelot's track, but before he comes up with him there has been time for a fierce conflict to take place. These conflicts with a valiant knight do not as a rule terminate so quickly, even though the odds be unequal! Gawain, who of course knows Lancelot well, apparently fails to recognise him, even when he unhelms for supper. The maiden of the castle warns them against sleeping in a certain bed; whoever does so will scarce escape with his life. Lancelot braves the adventure, but the next morning when he is found safe and well, the lady expresses no surprise. We are told that the maiden whom Lancelot frees from the knight at the ford knows him and *is afraid he will know her,* but no explanation of this is vouchsafed, and her identity is not revealed. We are expressly told that the kingdom of Gorres is surrounded by a water which none may pass, but before Lancelot even arrives at the water and bridge he is in the kingdom of Gorres, peopled by captive Bretons. No explanation is given of how Guinevere knew of Lancelot's hesitation to mount the cart; there was no witness but the dwarf, and if he noted so momentary an indecision he must have had a curiously keen appreciation of the rules of *Minne;* and how did he come to see Guinevere? But perhaps it was a case of telepathy. In the same manner Kay becomes mysteriously aware of what has passed between Lancelot and the queen. And these instances might be indefinitely multiplied. Chrétien's **Lancelot** is scarcely less incoherent than Ulrich von Zatzikhoven's; and we begin to wonder if there were not some inherent weakness in the legend itself, which rendered it impossible for any one to give an intelligible account of the hero's proceedings.

I think it is clear that the decided inferiority of the **Charrette** as compared with Chrétien's other poems is due to the deficiencies of his source. He was left in the lurch, and his genius was not of a nature to extricate him from his difficulties. When he had before him a story the form of which was already practically fixed, and which required polishing rather than re-arrangement, Chrétien could put it into charming language, and make a finished and artistic piece of work out of a simple original. I should express the charm of his work as being that he clad the folk-tale in the garments of the court, and taught it to move easily in its foreign trappings. But when his materials were scanty, and he was called upon to supplement them from his own imagination, he was unequal to the task; and he was artist enough to know it, and to leave unfinished a work which did him little credit, while he turned to one the nature of which precisely suited his special talent. It is not, I think, without significance that the best of Chrétien's poems follows immediately on his worst. He had a reputation to retrieve, and he did it gallantly in the **Yvain.**

Nor is Chrétien really successful in depicting lovers as lovers: they are little more than lay figures; they talk at great length, and indulge in analysis of their feelings, expressed in the most graceful and ingenious language; but one

> 'Iseut ma drue, Iseut m'amie,
> En vous ma mort, en vous ma vie!'

is worth all Chrétien ever wrote on the subject; the breath of the god is not in it. Yet, so far as the **Charrette** goes, this is scarcely to be laid to his blame. Nowhere, save perhaps in one chapter of Malory, is there the least ring of reality in the loves of Lancelot and Guinevere. They go through all the prescribed gestures of their rôle with admirable precision. Guinevere is by turns gracious, disdainful, frantically jealous, and repentant of her jealousy; Lancelot is courteous, humble, despairing, hopeful: their relation to each other is all that *Minne dienst* can require between a knight and his lady, but nowhere in the whole wearily drawn-out story does the real, pent-up human feeling break through. We can never imagine these two taking one another by the hand and wandering off into the wilderness, content, and more than content, with each other's presence. The story of Lancelot and Guinevere is artificial, not natural; it demands the setting of the court, not of the woodlands. Only in the passage where Malory describes their parting do they, for a moment, become real; and the effect produced is probably due to the simplicity of the old knight's language, and the virile force of the English tongue.

Nor do I think that these relations are due to Chrétien. He treats them as an already established fact, well known to his readers, and needing no explanation. Certain episodes of the poem, the finding of the comb, the testing of the knight's fidelity to the queen by the lady in whose castle he passes the night, presuppose a state of things generally familiar. Every one knows who Lancelot is; every one will know why he, and no other knight, shall rescue the queen.

That there was a previous story of Guinevere's rescue from imprisonment under analogous circumstances is quite clear: the references found in the Arthurian romance are too numerous, and too archaic in form to be derived from a poem so late in date, so artificial in character, and so restricted in popularity as the *Charrette*. Of this story we have at least three distinct accounts: (*a*) that given by Ulrich von Zatzikhoven, where the 'other-world' character of the imprisonment is strongly marked, but the rescue is the work of an enchanter, and not of Arthur or any of his knights; (*b*) that given in the *Vita Gildæ*, when the abductor is Melwas, king of *Æstiva Regis* (Somerset), the place of imprisonment Glastonbury, and there is again no special rescuer, Arthur marches at the head of his armies to her relief, but it is the intervention of St. Gildas and the Abbot of Glastonbury which brings about the desired result; (*c*) the account given in the poem under discussion.

Of these three variants the version of the *Lanzelet* stands by itself; it represents the 'other-world' under an entirely different, and probably more primitive, aspect, and makes no effort at localisation. The other two variants fall together, Melwas, the king of *Æstiva Regis,* which is admittedly Somerset—Meleágant of Gorres, whose chief city is *Bade*—Bath, also in Somerset. These later versions have been localised, and I think it is clear that the localisation took place on English soil, *i.e.* it is an insular and not a continental variant.

Now, from the very nature of the story it is clear that in its *earliest* forms it would not be attributed to any special locality, and therein the *Lanzelet* version again appears to be the elder; further, the variants must have arisen at a time when it was clearly understood that, however they might apparently differ, Valerîn's thorn-girt dwelling and

Meleagant's water-circled castle meant one and the same thing, *i.e.* that both were recognised methods of describing the 'other-world.' In this connection it is instructive to recall the versions of Brynhild's wooing by Siegfried; her residence is universally admitted to be an 'other-world' dwelling, and we find it depicted under forms closely corresponding with the variants of the Guinevere story; *e.g.* Waberlohe (*Volsunga saga*)=Valerin's hedged magic slumber; Castle surrounded by water (*Thidrek saga*) =Meleagant's stronghold; Glasberg (*Folk-songs*) =Glastonbury. The parallelism is significant.

It is quite clear, I think, that such a story can be in no way ascribed to the invention of a poet living towards the end of the twelfth century, but must be of very much earlier date. Chrétien was dealing with a late variant of a primitive and very widely known theme. But could this variant, which, as seems probable, only reached him through the medium of a tale related by the Countess Marie of Champagne, have come from England, to which country the localisation of Glastonbury, Somersetshire, and Bath point? It is quite possible. We must remember who Marie de Champagne was: she was a princess of France, the daughter of King Louis VII. and Eleanor of Aquitaine, who, on her divorce from the French king, married Henry of Normandy, afterwards Henry II. of England. That is, at the time Chrétien wrote, the mother of his protectress was Queen of England and wedded to a sovereign who took a keen and personal interest in all that concerned King Arthur. The *possibility* of transmission is as clear as daylight; the question of course is, Would Marie be inclined to take advantage of it? The relations between her father and his divorced wife were certainly curious, as Louis made no objection to the marriage of the eldest son of Henry and Eleanor with his daughter by his second marriage, but whether there was intercourse between mother and daughter I have not been able to discover. But the question ought to be easily solved by some historical specialist who has made a study of that period. The point is interesting and important, and it is to be hoped some one will clear it up for us.

A question of secondary interest is whether Chrétien's poem is the source of contemporary and later allusions to the story. Of such allusions, or rather versions, we have two of special importance, that contained in Malory's compilation, and that given by Hartmann von Aue, in his *Iwein*. With regard to the former, I can only say that though I am in a position to offer new and important evidence with regard to the manuscript Malory used, and his method of composition, yet that evidence leaves the *Charrette* question unsolved. Of *direct* evidence there is none; the *indirect* and *inferential* evidence tends to show that Malory's source was *not* the poem of Chrétien de Troyes. The two points on which we can be certain are, (*a*) that Malory did not know the earlier part of the prose *Lancelot* at all, that his manuscript began at a point subsequent to the *Charrette* adventure; and (*b*) that he does not invent adventures, and but rarely details. Dr. Sommer's conclusions, as set forth in his *Study on the Sources of Malory,* are founded on very insufficient premises, and will need to be thoroughly revised to bring them into accordance with our present knowledge. . . . The *Iwein* version is of great importance, and though I have previously referred to it [in the *Legend of Sir Gawain,* chap. viii], yet in the light of Professor Foerster's strongly repeated assertion [in the introduction to his edition of Chrétien's works] that Hartmann knew no other version of the story than that given by Chrétien, I think it is worth while going over the evidence again.

It must be remembered that Hartmann's *Iwein* is a translation of Chrétien's **Chevalier au Lion,** and though rather more diffuse, follows its source closely. In the French poem which, as we have noted above, immediately succeeded the **Charrette,** Chrétien deftly introduces more than one allusion to Guinevere's abduction. He says that Guinevere has been carried off by a knight *d'estrange terre,* who went to the court to demand her; but he would not have succeeded in carrying her off had it not been for Kay, who deceived or deluded (*anbricona*) the king into putting the queen in his charge (ll. 3916-39). In another place, he says that the king, *'Fist que fors del san Quant aprés lui l'an anvoia. Je cuit que keus la convoia Jusqu'au chevalier qui l'an mainne'* (ll. 3706-11). Now, let us suppose that, as Professor Foerster insists, Hartmann had not read the **Charrette** and knew no other version of the story, what would he, who knew French well, and translates without blunders and confusion, understand by this? We must note particularly what Chrétien tells and what he omits. He distinctly says that the knight came to the court and demanded the queen (the real version of the poem is less blunt, as we have seen); that Arthur, deluded, put the queen in Kay's charge to lead her to the knight, and that they followed him. He does *not* say that the whole catastrophe came about through Arthur's granting a boon before he knew in what it consisted; he implies that the folly lay in Arthur's sending the queen after the knight, not in the circumstances which forced him to do so.

Now what does Hartmann say? In his version a knight appeared before Arthur and demanded a boon, the nature of which he refused to specify beforehand. Arthur granted it. It was that he should carry off the queen. This he did. The knights armed and followed. Kay was the first to overtake him, and was struck from his horse with such violence that his helmet caught in a tree and he hung suspended. He was not carried off captive. One after another all the knights are vanquished, and the queen carried off. Gawain is not at court; he returns the next day, and goes in search of the queen. Lancelot is not mentioned throughout; and the inference is that Gawain frees her.

What is specially noticeable in this account is that Hartmann agrees with Chrétien in the very feature which the French poet does *not* specify, *i.e.* the cause of the queen's abduction—a boon rashly granted, though he transfers the asking from Kay to the knight; while he differs from Chrétien in the feature which he *does* specify, *i.e.* that Kay takes Guinevere *after* the knight. Further, he adds details which would clear up some of the inconsistencies in Chrétien's own account: *i.e.* if Gawain were not present at the time, and all the knights followed one after the other and were defeated by Meleagant, we can quite understand that when Gawain returned the next day and followed on the trail, he *would* find traces of the severe and bloody conflict

for which Chrétien's version leaves no room. On the face of it, Hartmann's version is much the more logical and coherent of the two. I have remarked above on the extreme awkwardness of the action at the outset of the story; that Meleagant should carry off Guinevere by a ruse similar to that employed by Gandîn in the *Tristan* poems is far more in accordance with mediæval tradition. If Hartmann's divergence is a mere 'invention,' he not only deserves praise for his sagacious skill in constructing a story, but excites admiration for the acuteness which enabled him to detect the leading *motif* of the adventure to which his source afforded absolutely no clue.

Wolfram von Eschenbach's references to the **Charrette** adventure are curious; at first sight it seems certain that he is referring to Chrétien's poem, but on closer examination the matter is not so clear. Thus he says that Lancelot crossed the sword-bridge, fought with Meljakanz (Meleagant), and freed Guinevere—all of which agree with Chrétien. But, on the other hand, he mentions Kay's suspension on the tree (Hartmann's version), and does not know that Meleagant was slain by Lancelot, or that the captive Bretons were freed by his coming—both Meleagant and the Breton knights are fighting at the tournament of Beaurösch. Indeed, Wolfram appears to know far more of these latter than can be gathered from Chrétien's poem. Of course, we cannot here say whether these references are due to Wolfram or to his source, which, as recent research has clearly shown, was certainly the work of a man of varied and extensive learning. Nor is it at all clear that Wolfram knew Lancelot as Guinevere's lover; he simply says that her imprisonment grieved him *'im was gevancnisse leit, die frou Ginòvêr dolte,'* which might be postulated of any loyal servant of Arthur's. Again when, at the beginning of Book xii., the poet recites Gawain's love-sorrows, he compares his pains first to those suffered by various heroes in the achievement of knightly deeds in general, and then rehearses the parallel cases of sundry lovers. In the first list Lancelot and the sword-bridge appear in company with Iwein and the fountain, and Erec and the *'Schoie de la kurt'* adventure, neither of which were undertaken for the sake of love (why Garel slew the lion and fetched the knife, we do not know), but among the lovers he and Guinevere are not mentioned.

Taking into consideration the fact that the story is, by its very nature, far older than any literary form we possess; that there was certainly in existence one version at least other than Chrétien's (proved by the *Lanzelet*); and that Chrétien's source was avowedly an *informal* one, I do not think it impossible that in the poems of Hartmann and Wolfram we have references to the original form of the story of which Chrétien had only an incomplete knowledge. Hartmann's version is certainly not drawn from the **Charrette;** in Wolfram's case we can only give the verdict *'not proven.'*

In the whole investigation I think we can only consider two points as satisfactorily settled: the original character of the story, and the fact that Lancelot was not at first the hero of the adventure. (pp. 40-53)

Jessie L. Weston, "Le Chevalier de la Charrette," in her The Legend of Sir Lancelot du

Lac: Studies upon Its Origin, Development, and Position in the Arthurian Romantic Cycle, *David Nutt, 1901. Reprint by AMS Press, 1972, pp. 40-53.*

W. W. Comfort   (essay date 1914)

[*In the excerpt below, Comfort appraises the literary significance of Chrétien's romances in the context of Arthurian legend and medieval narrative poetry as a whole.*]

Chrétien de Troyes has had the peculiar fortune of becoming the best known of the old French poets to students of mediæval literature, and of remaining practically unknown to any one else. The acquaintance of students with the work of Chrétien has been made possible in academic circles by the admirable critical editions of his romances undertaken and carried to completion during the past thirty years by Professor Wendelin Foerster of Bonn. At the same time the want of public familiarity with Chrétien's work is due to the almost complete lack of translations of his romances into the modern tongues. The man who, so far as we know, first recounted the romantic adventures of Arthur's knights, Gawain, Yvain, Erec, Lancelot, and Perceval, has been forgotten; whereas posterity has been kinder to his debtors, Wolfram von Eschenbach, Malory, Lord Tennyson, and Richard Wagner. . . . (p. v)

Such extravagant claims for Chrétien's art have been made in some quarters that one feels disinclined to give them even an echo here. The modern reader may form his own estimate of the poet's art, and that estimate will probably not be high. Monotony, lack of proportion, vain repetitions, insufficient motivation, wearisome subtleties, and threatened, if not actual, indelicacy are among the most salient defects which will arrest, and mayhap confound, the reader unfamiliar with mediæval literary craft. No greater service can be performed . . . in such a case than to prepare the reader to overlook these common faults, and to set before him the literary significance of this twelfth-century poet.

Chrétien de Troyes wrote in Champagne during the third quarter of the twelfth century. Of his life we know neither the beginning nor the end, but we know that between 1160 and 1172 he lived, perhaps as herald-at-arms (according to Gaston Paris, based on *Lancelot,* 5591-94), at Troyes, where was the court of his patroness, the Countess Marie de Champagne. She was the daughter of Louis VII. and of that famous Eleanor of Aquitaine, as she is called in English histories, who, coming from the South of France in 1137, first to Paris and later to England, may have had some share in the introduction of those ideals of courtesy and woman-service which were soon to become the cult of European society. The Countess Marie, possessing her royal mother's tastes and gifts, made of her court a social experiment station, where these Provençal ideals of a perfect society were planted afresh in congenial soil. It appears from contemporary testimony that the authority of this celebrated feudal dame was weighty and widely felt. The old city of Troyes, where she held her court, must be set down large in any map of literary history. For it was there that Chrétien was led to write four romances which

together form the most complete expression we possess from a single author of the ideals of French chivalry. These romances, written in eight-syllable rhyming couplets, treat respectively of Erec and Enide, Cligés, Yvain, and Lancelot. Another poem, *Perceval le Gallois,* was composed about 1175 for Philip, Count of Flanders, to whom Chrétien was attached during his last years. . . . It is true the romance of *Lancelot* was not completed by Chrétien, we are told, but the poem is his in such large part that one would be over-scrupulous not to call it his. The other three poems mentioned are his entire. In addition, there are quite generally assigned to the poet two insignificant lyrics, the pious romance of *Guillaume d'Angleterre,* and the elaboration of an episode from Ovid's *Metamorphoses* (vi., 426-674) called *Philomena* by its recent editor (C. de Boer, Paris, 1909). All these are extant and accessible. But since *Guillaume d'Angleterre* and *Philomena* are not universally attributed to Chrétien, and since they have nothing to do with the Arthurian material, it seems reasonable to limit the present enterprise to *Erec and Enide, Cligés, Yvain,* and *Lancelot.*

Professor Foerster, basing his remark upon the best knowledge we possess of an obscure matter, has called *Erec and Enide* the oldest Arthurian romance extant. It is not possible to dispute this significant claim, but let us make it a little more intelligible. Scholarship has shown that from the early Middle Ages popular tradition was rife in Britain and Brittany. The existence of these traditions common to the Brythonic peoples was called to the attention of the literary world by William of Malmesbury (*Gesta regum Anglorum*) and Geoffrey of Monmouth (*Historia regum Britanniæ*) in their Latin histories about 1125 and 1137 respectively, and by the Anglo-Norman poet Wace immediately afterward. Scholars have waged war over the theories of transmission of the so-called Arthurian material during the centuries which elapsed between the time of the fabled chieftain's activity in 500 A.D. and his appearance as a great literary personage in the twelfth century. Documents are lacking for the dark ages of popular tradition before the Norman Conquest, and the theorists may work their will. But Arthur and his knights, as we see them in the earliest French romances, have little in common with their Celtic prototypes, as we dimly catch sight of them in Irish, Welsh, and Breton legend. Chrétien belonged to a generation of French poets who took over a great mass of Celtic folk-lore which they imperfectly understood, and made of it what, of course, it had never been before: the vehicle to carry a rich freight of chivalric customs and ideals. As an ideal of social conduct, the code of chivalry never touched the middle and lower classes, but it was the religion of the aristocracy and of the twelfth-century *honnête homme.* Never was literature in any age closer to the ideals of a social class. So true is this that it is difficult to determine whether social practices called forth the literature, or whether, as in the case of the seventeenth-century pastoral romance in France, it is truer to say that literature suggested to society its ideals. Be that as it may, it is proper to observe that the French romances of adventure portray late mediæval aristocracy as it fain would be. For the glaring inconsistencies between the reality and the ideal, one may turn to the chronicles of the period. Yet, even history tells of many an ugly sin rebuked and of many a gallant deed performed because of the courteous ideals of chivalry. The debt of our own social code to this literature of courtesy and frequent self-sacrifice is perfectly manifest.

What Chrétien's immediate and specific source was for his romances is of deep interest to the student. Unfortunately, he has left us in doubt. He speaks in the vaguest way of the materials he used. There is no evidence that he had any Celtic written source. We are thus thrown back upon Latin or French literary originals which are lost, or upon current continental lore going back to a Celtic source. This very difficult problem is as yet unsolved in the case of Chrétien, as it is in the case of the Anglo-Norman Béroul, who wrote of Tristan about 1150. The material evidently was at hand and Chrétien appropriated it, without much understanding of its primitive spirit, but appreciating it as a setting for the ideal society dreamed of but, not realised in his own day. Add to this literary perspicacity, a good foundation in classic fable, a modicum of ecclesiastical doctrine, a remarkable facility in phrase, figure, and rhyme and we have the foundations for Chrétien's art as we shall find it upon closer examination.

A French narrative poet of the twelfth century had three categories of subject-matter from which to choose: legends connected with the history of France (*matière de France*), legends connected with Arthur and other Celtic heroes (*matière de Bretagne*), and stories culled from the history or mythology of Greece and Rome, current in Latin and French translations (*matière de Rome la grant*). Chrétien tells us in **Cligés** that his first essays as a poet were the translations into French of certain parts of Ovid's most popular works: the *Metamorphoses,* the *Ars Amatoria,* and perhaps the *Remedia Amoris.* But he appears early to have chosen as his special field the stories of Celtic origin dealing with Arthur, the Round Table, and other features of Celtic folk-lore. Not only was he alive to the literary interest of this material when rationalised to suit the taste of French readers; his is further the credit of having given to somewhat crude folk-lore that polish and elegance which is peculiarly French, and which is inseparably associated with the Arthurian legends in all modern literature. Though Béroul, and perhaps other poets, had previously based romantic poems upon individual Celtic heroes like Tristan, nevertheless to Chrétien, so far as we can see, is due the considerable honour of having constituted Arthur's court as a literary centre and rallying-point for an innumerable company of knights and ladies engaged in a never-ending series of amorous adventures and dangerous quests. Rather than unqualifiedly attribute to Chrétien this important literary convention, one should bear in mind that all his poems imply familiarity on the part of his readers with the heroes of the court of which he speaks. One would suppose that other stories, told before his versions, were current. Some critics would go so far as to maintain that Chrétien came toward the close, rather than at the beginning, of a school of French writers of Arthurian romances. But, if so, we do not possess these earlier versions, and for lack of rivals Chrétien may be hailed as an innovator in the current schools of poetry.

And now let us consider the faults which a modern reader will not be slow to detect in Chrétien's style. Most of his salient faults are common to all mediæval narrative literature. They may be ascribed to the extraordinary leisure of the class for whom it was composed—a class which was always ready to read an old story told again, and which would tolerate any description, however detailed. The pastimes of this class of readers were jousting, hunting, and making love. Hence the preponderance of these matters in the literature of its leisure hours. No detail of the joust or hunt was unfamiliar or unwelcome to these readers; no subtle arguments concerning the art of love were too abstruse to delight a generation steeped in amorous casuistry and allegories. And if some scenes seem to us indelicate, yet after comparison with other authors of his times, Chrétien must be let off with a light sentence. It is certain he intended to avoid what was indecent, as did the writers of narrative poetry in general. To appreciate fully the chaste treatment of Chrétien one must know some other forms of mediæval literature, such as the fabliaux, farces, and morality plays, in which courtesy imposed no restraint. For our poet's lack of sense of proportion, and for his carelessness in the proper motivation of many episodes, no apology can be made. He is not always guilty; some episodes betoken poetic mastery. But a poet acquainted, as he was, with some first-class Latin poetry, and who had made a business of his art, ought to have handled his material more intelligently, even in the twelfth century. The emphasis is not always laid with discrimination, nor is his yarn always kept free of tangles in the spinning.

Reference has been made to Chrétien's use of his sources. The tendency of some critics has been to minimise the French poet's originality by pointing out striking analogies in classic and Celtic fable. Attention has been especially directed to the defence of the fountain and the service of a fairy mistress in **Yvain,** to the captivity of Arthur's subjects in the kingdom of Gorre, as narrated in **Lancelot,** reminding one so insistently of the treatment of the kingdom of Death from which some god or hero finally delivers those in durance, and to the feigned death of Fenice in **Cligés,** with its many variants. These episodes are but examples of parallels which will occur to the observant reader. The difficult point to determine, in speaking of conceptions so widespread in classic and mediæval literature, is the immediate source whence these conceptions reached Chrétien. . . . However, such convincing parallels for many of Chrétien's fairy and romantic episodes have been adduced by students of Irish and Welsh legend that one cannot fail to be impressed by the fact that Chrétien was in touch, either by oral or literary tradition, with the populations of Britain and of Brittany, and that we have here his most immediate inspiration. Professor Foerster, stoutly opposing the so-called Anglo-Norman theory which supposes the existence of lost Anglo-Norman romances in French as the sources of Chrétien de Troyes, is, nevertheless, well within the truth when he insists upon what is, so far as we are concerned, the essential originality of the French poet. The general reader will to-day care as little as did the reader of the twelfth century how the poet came upon the motives and episodes of his stories, whether he borrowed them or invented them himself. Any poet should be judged not as a "finder" but as a "user" of the common stock of ideas. The study of sources of mediæval poetry, which is being so doggedly carried on by scholars, may well throw light upon the main currents of literary tradition, but it casts no reflection, favourable or otherwise, upon the personal art of the poet in handling his stuff. On that count he may plead his own cause before the jury.

Chrétien's originality, then, consists in his portrayal of the social ideal of the French aristocracy in the twelfth century. So far as we know he was the first to create in the vulgar tongues a vast court, where men and women lived in conformity with the rules of courtesy, where the truth was told, where generosity was open-handed, where the weak and the innocent were protected by men who dedicated themselves to the cult of honour and to the quest of a spotless reputation. Honour and love combined to engage the attention of this society; these were its religion in a far more real sense than was that of the Church. Perfection was attainable under this code of ethics: Gawain, for example, was a perfect knight. Though the ideals of this court and those of Christianity are in accord at many points, yet courtly love and Christian morality are irreconcilable. This Arthurian material, as used by Chrétien, is fundamentally immoral as judged by Christian standards. Beyond question, the poets and the public alike knew this to be the case, and therein lay its charm for a society in which the actual relations of the sexes were rigidly prescribed by the Church and by feudal practice, rather than by the sentiments of the individuals concerned. The passionate love of Tristan for Iseut, of Lancelot for Guinevere, of Cligés for Fenice, fascinate the conventional Christian society of the twelfth century and of the twentieth century alike but there is only one name among men for such relations as theirs, and neither righteousness nor reason lie that way. Even Tennyson, in spite of all he has done to spiritualise this material, was compelled to portray the inevitable dissolution and ruin of Arthur's court. Chrétien well knew the difference between right and wrong, between reason and passion, as the reader of *Cligés* may learn for himself. Fenice was not Iseut, and she would not have her Cligés to be a Tristan. Infidelity, if you will, but not a *ménage à trois*. Both *Erec* and *Yvain* present a conventional morality. But *Lancelot* isflagrantly immoral, and the poet is careful to state that for this particular romance he is indebted to his patroness Marie de Champagne. He says it was she who furnished him with both the *matière* and the *san,* the material of the story and its method of treatment.

Scholars have sought to fix the chronology of the poet's works, and have been tempted to speculate upon the evolution of his literary and moral ideas. Professor Foerster's chronology is generally accepted, and there is little likelihood of his being in error when he supposes Chrétien's work to have been done as follows: the lost *Tristan* (the existence of which is denied by Gaston Paris in *Journal des Savants,* 1902, pp. 297 *f.*), *Erec and Enide, Cligés, Lancelot, Yvain, Perceval*. The arguments for this chronology, based upon external as well as internal criticism, may be found in the Introductions to Professor Foerster's recent editions. When we speculate upon the development of Chrétien's moral ideas we are not on such sure ground.

As we have seen, his standards vary widely in the different romances. How much of this variation is due to chance circumstance imposed by the nature of his subject or by the taste of his public, and how much to changing conviction? It is easy to see, when we consider some contemporary novelist, how dangerous it is to judge of moral convictions as reflected in literary work. *Lancelot* must be the keystone of any theory constructed concerning the moral evolution of Chrétien. The following supposition is tenable, if the chronology of Foerster is correct. After the works of his youth, consisting of lyric poems and translations embodying the ideals of Ovid and of the school of contemporary troubadour poets, Chrétien took up the Arthurian material and started upon a new course. *Erec* is the oldest Arthurian romance to have survived in any language, but it is almost certainly not the first to have been written. It is a perfectly clean story of love, estrangement, and reconciliation in the persons of Erec and his charming sweetheart Enide. The psychological analysis of Erec's motives in the rude testing of Enide is worthy of attention, and is more subtle than anything previous in French literature with which we are acquainted. The poem is an episodical romance in the biography of an Arthurian hero, with the usual amount of space given to his adventures. *Cligés* apparently connects a Byzantine tale of doubtful origin in an arbitrary fashion with the court of Arthur. It is thought that the story embodies the same motive as the widespread tale of the deception practised upon Solomon by his wife, and that Chrétien's source, as he himself claims, was literary (*cf.* Gaston Paris in *Journal des Savants,* 1902, pp. 641-655). The scene where Fenice feigns death in order to rejoin her lover is a parallel of many others in literary history, and will, of course, suggest the situation in *Romeo and Juliet.* This romance well illustrates the drawing power of Arthur's court as a literary centre, and its use as a rallying-point for courteous knights of whatever extraction. The poem has been termed an "Anti-Tristan," because of its disparaging reference to the love of Tristan and Iseut, which, it is generally supposed, had been narrated by Chrétien in his earlier years. Next may come *Lancelot,* with its significant dedication to the Countess of Champagne. Of all the poet's work, this tale of the rescue of Guinevere by her lover seems to express most closely the ideals of Marie's court—ideals in which devotion and courtesy but thinly disguise free love. *Yvain* is a return to the poet's natural bent, in an episodical romance, while *Perceval* crowns his production with its pure and exalted note, though without a touch of that religious mysticism which later marked Wolfram von Eschenbach's *Parzival*. *Guillaume d'Angleterre* is a pseudo-historical romance of adventure in which the worldly distresses and the final reward of piety are conventionally exposed. It is uninspired, its place is difficult to determine, and its authorship is questioned by some. It is aside from the Arthurian material, and there is no clue to its place in the evolution of Chrétien's art, if indeed it be his work.

A few words must be devoted to Chrétien's place in the history of mediæval narrative poetry. The heroic epic songs of France, devoted either to the conflict of Christendom under the leadership of France against the Saracens, or else to the strife and rivalry of French vassals among themselves, had been current for perhaps a century before our poet began to write. These epic poems, of which some three score have survived, portray a warlike, virile, unsentimental feudal society, whose chief occupation was fighting, and whose dominant ideals were faith in God, loyalty to feudal and family ties, and bravery in battle. Woman's place is comparatively obscure, and of love-making there is little said. It is a poetry of vigorous manhood, of uncompromising morality, and of hard knocks given and taken for God, for Christendom, and the king of France. This poetry is written in ten- or twelve-syllable verses grouped, at first in assonanced, later in rhymed, "tirades" of unequal length. It was intended for a society which was still homogeneous, and to it at the outset doubtless all classes of the population listened with equal interest. As poetry it is monotonous, without sense of proportion, padded to facilitate memorisation by professional reciters, and unadorned by figure, fancy, or imagination. Its pretention to historic accuracy begot prosaicness in its approach to the style of the chronicles. But its inspiration was noble, its conception of human duties was lofty. It gives a realistic portrayal of the age which produced it, the age of the first crusades, and to this day we would choose as our models of citizenship Roland and Oliver rather than Tristan and Lancelot.

The epic poems, dealing with the pseudo-historical characters who had fought in civil and foreign wars under Charlemagne, remained the favourite literary pabulum of the middle classes until the close of the thirteenth century. . . . But the refinement which began to penetrate the ideals of the French aristocracy about the middle of the twelfth century craved a different expression in narrative literature. Greek and Roman mythology and history were seized upon with some effect to satisfy the new demand. The *Roman de Thèbes,* the *Roman d'Alexandre,* the *Roman de Troie,* and its logical continuation, the *Roman d'Enéas,* are all twelfth-century attempts to clothe classic legend in the dress of mediæval chivalry. But better fitted to satisfy the new demand was the discovery by the alert Anglo-Normans perhaps in Brittany, perhaps in the South of England, of a vast body of legendary material which, so far as we know, had never before this century received any elaborate literary treatment. The existence of the literary demand and this discovery of the material for its prompt satisfaction is one of the most remarkable coincidences in literary history. It would seem that the pride of the Celtic populations in a Celtic hero, aided and abetted by Geoffrey of Monmouth, who first showed the romantic possibilities of the material, made of the obscure British chieftain Arthur a world conqueror. Arthur thus became already in Geoffrey's *Historia regum Britanniæ* a conscious protagonist of Charlemagne and his rival in popularity. This grandiose conception of Arthur persisted in England, but this conception of the British chieftain did not interest the French. For Chrétien Arthur had no political significance. He is simply the arbiter of his court in all affairs of justice and courtesy. Charlemagne's very realistic *entourage* of virile and busy barons is replaced by a court of elegant chevaliers and unemployed ladies. Charlemagne's setting is historical and geographical; Arthur's setting is ideal and in the air. In the oldest epic poems we find only God-fearing men and a few self-effacing women; in the Arthurian romances we meet gentlemen and ladies,

more elegant and seductive than any one in the epic poems, but less fortified by faith and sense of duty against vice because breathing an enervating atmosphere of leisure and decadent morality. Though the Church made the attempt in *Parzival,* it could never lay its hands so effectively upon this Celtic material, because it contained too many elements which were root and branch inconsistent with the essential teachings of Christianity. A fleeting comparison of the noble end of Charlemagne's Peers fighting for their God and their King at Ronceval with the futile and dilettante careers of Arthur's knights in joust and hunt, will show better than mere words where the difference lies.

The student of the history of social and moral ideals will find much to interest him in Chrétien's romances. Mediæval references show that he was held by his immediate successors, as he is held to-day when fairly viewed, to have been a master of the art of story-telling. More than any other single narrative poet, he was taken as a model both in France and abroad. . . . Poets in his own land refer to him with reverence, and foreign poets complimented him to a high degree by direct translation and by embroidering upon the themes which he had made popular. The knights made famous by Chrétien soon crossed the frontiers and obtained rights of citizenship in countries so diverse as Germany, England, Scandinavia, Holland, Italy, and to a lesser extent in Spain and Portugal. The inevitable tendency of the fourteenth and fifteenth centuries to reduce poetry to prose affected the Arthurian material; vast prose compilations finally embodied in print the matter formerly expressed in verse, and it was in this form that the stories were known to later generations until revived interest in the Middle Ages brought to light the manuscripts in verse.

Aside from certain episodes of Chrétien's romances, the student will be most interested in the treatment of love as therein portrayed. On this topic we may hear speaking the man of his time. *Cligés* contains the body of Chrétien's doctrine of love, while Lancelot is his most perfect lover. His debt to Ovid has not yet been indicated with sufficient preciseness. An elaborate code to govern sentiment and its expression was independently developed by the troubadours of Provence in the early twelfth century. These Provençal ideals of the courtly life were carried into Northern France partly as the result of a royal marriage in 1137 and of the crusade of 1147, and there by such poets as Chrétien they were gathered up and fused with the Ovidian doctrine into a highly complicated but perfectly definite statement of the ideal relations of the sexes. Nowhere in the vulgar tongues can a better statement of these relations be found than in *Cligés.*

So we leave Chrétien to speak across the ages for himself and his generation. He is to be read as a story-teller rather than as a poet, as a casuist rather than as a philosopher. But when all deductions are made, his significance as a literary artist and as the founder of a precious literary tradition distinguishes him from all other poets of the Latin races between the close of the Empire and the arrival of Dante. (pp. v-xvi)

W. W. Comfort, in an introduction to Arthurian Romances *by Chrétien de Troyes, translat-*

ed by W. W. Comfort, J. M. Dent & Sons Ltd., 1914, pp. v-xvi.

An excerpt from *Perceval*

As they were speaking of one thing and another,
a squire came forth from a chamber
gripping a white lance
by the middle of its shaft;
he passed between the fire
and those seated upon the bed,
and everyone in the hall saw
the white lance with its white point,
from whose tip there oozed
a drop a blood,
and this red drop flowed
down to the squire's hand.
The youth who had come there that night
observed this marvel,
but refrained from asking
how it came about,
for he recalled the admonishment given
by the gentleman who had knighted him,
who taught and instructed him
not to talk too much;
he was afraid that if he asked
they would consider him uncouth,
so he did not ask,

Then two other squires entered
holding in their hands candelabra
of pure gold, worked with enamel inlays.
The young men carrying the candelabra
were extremely handsome.
In each of the candelabra there were
at least ten candles burning.
A maiden accompanying
the two young men was carrying
a grail in her two hands;
she was beautiful, noble, and richly attired.
After she had entered the hall
carrying the grail,
the room was so brightly illuminated
that the candles lost
their brilliance like stars
when the sun rises, or the moon.

Chrétien de Troyes, in his The Story of the Grail (L'Contes del Graal), or Perceval, *translated by William W. Kibler, Garland Publishing, 1990.*

Charles Grimm   (essay date 1925)

[*In the following excerpt, Grimm discusses Chrétien's ironic attitude toward women in his works, concluding that the various stances he takes in portraying female characters suggest a particular chronological order to his romances.*]

During the last four or five years several articles on Chrestien de Troyes have appeared in various scientific journals showing that there is still a very strong interest in this Balzac of the twelfth century, and proving also that the last word about his works, his theories, his psychology is yet far from having been told. Chrestien is generally considered as the best exponent of courtly love as it was understood in the twelfth century and in the early part of the thirteenth; and it is also generally assumed that he was a *convinced* exponent, that he believed in what he was preaching, as does Miss Borodine, when she says [in her *La Femme et l'amour au XIIe siècle d'après les poèmes de Chrétien de Troyes,* 1909]:

> Entraîné par le courant des idées sentimentales qui s'épanouissent autour de lui, le poète champenois compose sa trilogie admirable de l'amour courtois: *Cligès, Lancelot, Yvain.* L'idéal de la gloire, chanté naguère avec enthousiasme [*Erec*], s'efface et pâlit maintenant devant l'éclat de l'astre nouveau.

A certain irony, however, which I think can be seen throughout the works of Chrestien (in varying degrees, to be sure) and a certain matter-of-factness which appears time and again in his treatment of woman, lead me to the opinion that he was not perhaps as firm a believer in the theories which he was expounding as has been thought and said.

When we speak of Chrestien's irony we immediately think of the famous, almost savagely ironical passage in *Yvain* in which Laudine accepts to return the love and to become the wife of the man who a few days before slew her husband, proving to herself through a love casuistry, which must have delighted Chrestien's admirers, that it is perfectly proper to do so, for he really has done her no harm!

> "Va!' fet ele, 'puez tu noiier,
> Que par toi ne soit morz mes sire?'
> 'Ce,' fet il, 'ne puis je desdire,
> Ainz l'otroi bien.'—'Di donc, por quoi?
> Feïs le tu por mal de moi,
> Por haïne ne por despit?'
> 'Ja n'aie je de mort respit,
> S'onques por mal de vos le fis.'
> 'Donc n'as tu rien vers moi mespris,
> Ne vers lui n'eüs tu nul tort;
> Car, s'il poïst, il t'eüst mort.
> Por ce mien esciant cuit gié,
> Que j'ai bien et a droit jugié."
>
> (*Yv.* 1760-72)

And when Yvain is brought before her by Lunete, she has not a single word of reproach, she cannot even be severe, she immediately adopts a bantering tone; and if she does not fall upon his neck as soon as he appears, it is only because she thinks it might be jarring even to him (cf. v. 1975 ff.).

If we considered only this passage, we would say that Chrestien undoubtedly was a woman-hater who could say nothing scathing enough about the weaker sex. But was he? Anyone who has written such a charming tale as *Erec et Enide* can hardly be accused of misogyny. If there is no sarcasm in this novel, there are at least touches of kindly irony here and there, as for instance when our poet tells us that Enide is going to commit suicide because she thinks Erec is dead, and yet makes her delay long enough to enable Count Oringle de Limors to come and rescue her:

L'espee fors del fuerre tret,
Si la comance a regarder.
Deus la fist un po retarder,
Qui plains est de misericorde.

(*E. et E.* v. 4670-3)

Again we find a good deal of gentle irony in *Cligès.* Even if we leave aside the irony which appears in the rather long passages in which Soredamor and Cligès are analyzing their nascent love (v. 475 ff.; 625 ff.; 897 ff.; 998 ff.; etc.)—and which [Foster E. Guyer, in "The Influence of Ovid on Crestien de Troyes," *Romanic Review* XII] shows us not to be peculiar to Chrestien, but to be Ovidian—we have other touches which seem to be more personal, as when, for example, Chrestien states that Soredamor accepts Alexander because she is entirely "au comandemant la reïne" (2338), or when he tells us that after having rescued Fenice from the hands of the Saxon duke, Cligès is taking her back to the Greeks' camp and that, although both would like nothing better than to talk of their love for each other, they are afraid to do so. The poet adds:

Se cele comancier ne l'ose,
N'est mervoille; car sinple chose
Doit estre pucele et coarde.

(*Cl.* 3839-41)

A rather amusing statement for us who know of the love potion she has caused her husband to drink!

If leaving aside irony we will now consider matter-of-factness, we will also find plenty of examples. One of the first things which strikes us in reading Chrestien's works is the slight regard with which woman is so often treated in the serious matters of life. She is at times exalted, almost deified, and the next moment she is treated almost like chattel. This, of course, may be due to the fact that courtly love had become an art, a science of which woman was the high-priestess, whereas in real life she occupied a secondary, dependent legal position. Nevertheless, the two things are hard to reconcile; and it shows, I think, that Chrestien—and he was not alone—did not take very seriously the science of courtly love, and even considered it as foolish.

In *Erec et Enide,* for instance, when Erec comes to the vavassor's house, he thinks nothing of letting Enide, at her father's command, take his horse to the stable, remove its saddle and bridle, currycomb and groom it, and then give it oats and hay (v. 451-58); again when he discovers how pretty and well behaved the girl is, he falls in love with her; but he does not swoon or change color, he merely asks bluntly for her hand:

"Mes je vos promet et otroi,
Se vos d'armes m'aparelliez
Et votre fille me baillez
Demain a l'esprevier conquerre,
Que je l'an manrai an ma terre,
Se Deus la victoire me done."

(*E. et E.* v. 657-63)

The vavassor himself is just as blunt, he does not ask his daughter what she thinks about it, nor does he discuss the question with his wife; he merely takes the girl by the hand and says to Erec: " 'Tenez!' fet il, 'je la vos doing' " (678). Enide herself is perfectly matter-of-fact in all this. She has

absolutely nothing to say on the subject, and seems to be entirely passive. Of course, she loves Erec, but this love was very sudden for she had never seen him before, and probably had never heard of him. Somehow we have a feeling that she would have submitted in very much the same fashion had it been anyone else than Erec.

There is nothing exalted or even refined about Fenice when she is discussing her love for Cligès with her nurse, and in the extremely frank statements she makes about her husband-to-be (cf. v. 3170 ff.). This is almost shocking in a young girl who is not supposed to know much about life! Further on, in the same book, when Cligès has come back from Arthur's court and Fenice one day is telling him of the way her husband was drugged on his wedding-day with the attendant result (v. 5235 ff.), we can see nothing poetical about it. Her matter-of-factness, her cunning and her desire for security in her sin and for avoiding all blame are rather distasteful and show a calculating woman rather than a great lover. She would be much more charming if she abandoned herself in a more natural fashion, without all the careful planning which is used in preparing what becomes deliberate and perfectly conscious adultery. Her manner of telling Cligès that she will not be his until he has found a way of insuring her complete safety and blamelessness seems more like a bargain than a lover's promise (v. 5263 ff.); and Fenice makes us think of a woman who sells herself rather than of one who freely abandons herself to the one she loves.

It would hardly be worth while to discuss at length every passage which shows matter-of-factness. It will be sufficient that such passages be merely mentioned, as those familiar with Chrestien's works will immediately recall the episodes alluded to.

In *Guillaume d'Angleterre* we have the way in which the king takes his misfortune when separated from his wife and newborn sons (v. 748-9; 871 ff.). In the same work, we may mention the marriage venture of Graciene with Gleoläis (v. 1107 ff.). Especially interesting is the passage in which Chrestien shows the moral struggle which takes place in Graciene's mind: she does not want to become the wife of Gleoläis, but on the other hand she would like very much to have his estate, she would like to have the social prestige which would come to her by such a marriage without having to fulfill the obligations which it would entail upon her—in other words she would like to do what the French call "ménager la chèvre et le chou," a most common of human characteristics if not one of the noblest, which shows Chrestien's common sense and understanding of the average man's or woman's psychology (v. 1196 ff.).

In *Lancelot* when the hero is reconciled with Guenevere and he asks her if he could not see her at some other time to talk with her more freely:

"Et la reïne une fenestre
Li mostre a l'uel, non mie an doi,"

(*Lan.* v. 4524-5)

we have a very graphic and matter-of-fact detail, as are also the arrangements which the two make later in the night about Lancelot's coming into the Queen's room.

Finally in *Yvain,* the passage already mentioned at the beginning of this [essay] during which Laudine and Yvain come to terms, and especially the way in which, after having accepted Yvain as her next husband, Laudine adds:

> ". . . De ci nos an irons
> An cele sale, ou mes janz sont,
> Qui loé et conseillié m'ont,
> Por le besoing que il i voient,
> Que mari a prandre m'otroient."
>
> (*Yv.* v. 2040-44)

If I have examined somewhat at length those passages showing either irony or matter-of-factness, it is not because they are very new, but because, to my mind, they show the real Chrestien as contrasted with the literary, artificial Chrestien. Our Champenois was, I think, a well-balanced, sensible person who had too much common sense—and probably he was not devoid of a touch of what we know as "esprit gaulois"—to accept fully and believe genuinely in courtly love. I should even go further and say that he had a real distaste for the art or science of love, and that if he wrote such romances as *Cligès, Lancelot, Yvain* or *Perceval* in which love is sublimated and woman exalted, it is not because he had an exalted idea of either, but because it was the fashion in his day and because, as a court poet, and in order to exist, he was obliged to write to suit the taste of his patrons and admirers. I believe that Chrestien, had he been entirely free, would have preferred to write such stories as *Erec et Enide* or *Guillaume d'Angleterre,* and that these represent his true, natural manner.

This leads me to say a word about the chronology of the earlier works of Chrestien, and especially about the place to which his *Guillaume d'Angleterre* must be assigned. While I agree with Miss Gay when she tells us at the end of ["The Chronology of the Earlier Works of Crestien de Troyes," *Romanic Review* XIV] that her

> examination of the Ovidian material in *Cligès* shows that there is not enough in it that was not already in the literature with which Chrestien was familiar before he wrote *Erec,* to create even a slight probability that before he wrote *Cligès* he had taken a fresh draft from Ovid

I don't think that this is sufficient in itself to reach her conclusion about the accepted chronology: the Ovidiana, the *Tristan* story, *Erec, Cligès.* On the other hand while I am of the same opinion as Mr. Guyer in thinking that *Erec et Enide* is Chrestien's first work, I do not agree with him when he says, speaking of *Guillaume d'Angleterre:*

> The author of such a love episode might have been he who wrote *Erec et Enide* before his interest in Ovidian love had been awakened, but surely not that Chrestien of the latter period who had acquired a new psychology of love.

This might be true if we could assume that when he wrote *Erec et Enide* Chrestien knew nothing about Ovidian love, a thing which Miss Gay has shown conclusively, I think, to be impossible, or if we granted that Chrestien became a thoroughly uncompromising apostle of Ovidian or courtly love, something I hope to have shown improbable. I know it is hard to believe that a man having written

nothing before should for his coup d'essai give such a work as *Erec et Enide,* but we must not forget that geniuses are born, not made.

In an article entitled ["Chrétien de Troyes et le Conte de *Guillaume d'Angleterre,*" *Romania,* 1920], M. Wilmotte comes to the following conclusion concerning the place to be assigned to *Guillaume* among the works of Chrestien:

> Tout au plus serais-je, à titre conjectural, enclin à admettre, comme le début de *Cligès* ignore notre conte et que celui-ci fait trop d'honneur à l'auteur pour qu'il l'ait volontairement omis, qu'il y travaillait en même temps qu'à l'histoire du fils de Soredamor, mais qu'il ne le publia qu'après.

I believe he is right in his last statement, viz., that *Guillaume* was published after *Cligès,* but I doubt whether the two works were written at the same time.

The only thing that remains to be explained is this: How is it that Chrestien should have written two novels which show no Ovidian influence or so little as to amount to nothing when he seems to have been so very much influenced by the Latin poet in his other works; and how is it that those two works which seem to stand apart from the rest should also be apart from one another? I am inclined to explain it thus: Chrestien who was evidently a very gifted youth wrote the story of *Erec et Enide.* This was, of course, noticed by the reading public and probably brought Chrestien to the attention of wealthy patrons who must have told him that he should devote his talent to writing novels which would be more to the liking of such patrons and, especially, patronesses. Someone may even have commissioned him to translate Ovid into French. While thus engaged he might have had the idea of writing a novel of courtly love, or he might have been asked to do so: this novel is *Cligès.* Then, more or less weary of such a romance, weary of writing about something he did not really have at heart, he began to write another story, a novel of adventure in a more natural way, *Guillaume d'Angleterre.* Would it be too rash to suppose that having shown part of this tale to his patroness Marie de Champagne, she might have expressed strong disapproval and might even have ordered Chrestien to write only on themes dealing with courtly love; and that our poet, exasperated at this treatment, in a sort of paroxysm of rage wrote *Lancelot* in which he shows what the results of such love may be, then *Yvain* in which he rebels against the tyranny of woman, and finally *Perceval* which he did not finish, perhaps through lack of sufficient interest. This might also perhaps explain the shortness of *Guillaume* (only 3366 lines) which our poet might have intended to make about as long as his other works, but which, under the circumstances, he would have brought to an end sooner than he had contemplated. To me this does not seem rash or improbable, it even seems likely; and it is why I should be disposed to arrange Chrestien's works in the following order: *Erec et Enide,* the Ovidiana, *Cligès, Guillaume d'Angleterre, Lancelot, Yvain,* and last, of course, the unfinished *Perceval.* (pp. 236-43)

> *Charles Grimm, "Chrestien de Troyes's Attitude Towards Woman," in* The Romanic Re-

view, *Vol. XVI, No. 3, July-September, 1925, pp. 236-43.*

Robert Anacker (essay date 1935)

[*In the following excerpt, Anacker describes Chrétien as the first French psychological novelist, pointing to the motif of conflict between a husband's duty to his vocation and his devotion to his wife in* Erec and Enide *and* Yvain *as his principal and most complex psychological theme.*]

Much has been written and said about Chrétien de Troyes; he is certainly the most universally known of all the mediaeval French authors, and any student of English, German, Italian, Welsh and Icelandic literature is likely to come across a hundred references to him. His name is forever linked with all the problems of the so-called "Matter of Brittany," especially the Arthurian cycle, of chivalry and of courtly love. Even if it were only for his subject matter he would hold his place in the literature of all European nations, having been the first author to treat this matter in elaborate romances, or at least the first one to do it successfully. But it is not this priority which makes Chrétien's work outstanding and quite unique: whereas there are still many controversies as to his possible sources, all scholars agree in stating that the way in which Chrétien treats matter distinguishes him from all other mediæval authors. There are perhaps hundreds of more typical Arthurian romances, but there are no others like those of Chrétien.

It has been pointed out by several scholars that there could hardly be any greater contrast than that between the mental attitude of this 12th century French bourgeois and the mysticism and the wild imagination of the Celtic storytellers who indirectly provided him with his subject matter. In Lanson's *Histoire de la Littérature française* a whole chapter is devoted to the illustration of this contrast: we see how the powerful visions and the deep mysticism of the Celtic myths shrink and vanish as soon as they come in contact with Chrétien's rationalism and positivism. For him, all these mythical elements are nothing but pleasant nonsense, mere conventional ornaments to make a long story more agreeable to his readers, but he is utterly unable to understand and appreciate them as the venerable symbols of very ancient wisdom. On the other hand, if Chrétien does not know the real meaning of his enchanted castles, "from where no one ever returns," he certainly knows very much about the human heart, and if he does not believe in the speaking animals he describes, he is quite familiar with the refined conversation of aristocratic circles. This is why Lanson calls him "a Paul Bourget of the 12th century."

Others have stressed the fact that Chrétien de Troyes liked to display his knowledge of psychology, that while he does not care to motivate any of the various adventures his heroes find, he never fails to motivate their decisions, that he shows why and how they change their mind, that he carefully analyses all their most secret thoughts. To illustrate this no passage is better fitted than the famous episode in *Yvain*, where Laudine, after a long soliloquy and an imaginary conversation with the hero, comes to the conclusion that by slaying her husband he did her no wrong, and finally yields to Lunete's frightfully logical arguments; since Yvain was able to kill this much adored husband he must necessarily be a still better man and there can be no harm in admiring and loving him. This is certainly not the conventional treatment of courtly love. Neither is there any relation with the mystic world of Celtic folklore: it is French positivism, the matter of fact attitude of a French bourgeois. In others of Chrétien's works, however, we find the conventional courtly love carefully analysed: in *Lancelot*, in *Cligés*, where all the casuistry of this unique human madness is displayed.

But the mere fact that there is an unusual amount of psychology in all of Chrétien's romances would not entitle one to call him a psychological novelist. Any poetry, any literature of value is based on psychology. It must be in some way "true to life," rooted in human emotions or human experience. "Knowledge of the human heart" as the French classics put it, is and will always be the first requirement for anyone who wants to write. But this knowledge is obtained by intuition rather than by scientific investigation and is therefore independent—quite fortunately—of what we commonly call progress. There is nothing astonishing in the assumption that a medieval author might have had much more of this psychological instinct than some modern, "successfully psychoanalysed" novelist.

If we call Chrétien de Troyes a psychological novelist we mean to say that like any modern novelist he has a definite theme, that he puts a problem, which he develops and tries to solve. This is what makes him outstanding among the hundreds of good and excellent authors of the 12th century. Yet this remarkable quality has very seldom been pointed out and I never found it mentioned in any of the more popular criticisms of Chrétien's works. Scholars of the rank of Förster or Bédier had of course a great many other things to show and to emphasize, and it is not surprising that they did not stress this particular point.

I should like therefore to dwell a little longer on this aspect of Chrétien's work. What is this psychological theme of Chrétien's "novels?" What is the problem that he develops and tries to solve? Strangely enough, this medieval author is not interested at all in the courtly love he praises and defends, his problem is whether married life is compatible with a man's full devotion to some task or mission. At first this seems to be a very poor and banal theme, but, as usually, the simpler a psychological problem first appears, the more complex it proves to be after careful investigation. I am inclined to believe that by far the most difficult problems are those for which we think we have an answer ready.

The question whether a man can fully give himself to a woman and to his vocation at the same time, is most certainly one of the main sources of conflicts between the sexes. It is a problem as old as mankind, a problem that will never be definitely solved, that will always arise again, one of the fundamental problems in the relations of men and women. It is still and will always be one of the most difficult things for any woman, no matter how intelligent and tolerant and understanding she might be to acknowledge and accept the fact that a man she loves may have something else besides her, something on which to bestow his care, his interest, his vitality. It will always make her feel that he does not love her as much as she does him, that he is withholding something from her which she, in his place, would not withhold. On the other hand, no woman can stand it if a man neglects all other things for her sake, if he cares for nothing but her and is completely and definitely contented with his domestic happiness. In that case, she will get impatient, will try to stimulate him, will push him into active life, will by all means make him do something. All this, no doubt, sounds very old fashioned and may remind one of all sorts of cheap generalizations and conventional prejudices, but there are certain things that are so banal, that is to say so generally human, that they will always remain the invariable basis of all the possible ancient and modern variations of taste, attitude and style. And, as a rule, banalities of that sort are not a bad theme for literature.

Chrétien de Troyes was so fascinated by this psychological theme that he had to treat it again, each time in a different way, wherever the subject of his romance permitted it. To invent a new subject, to create heroes of his own, heroes who would have been perfect representatives of what he wanted to demonstrate, this modern technique was forbidden to him. For nothing would have been worse in the opinion of the 12th century, than to relate a story that had never been told before by somebody else. He had to tell some old story in a new way, and so he wrote the romances of *Erec* and *Yvain.* Yet he was so fond of his psychological

theme that he treated it twice in *Erec* and once more in *Yvain,* and only death prevented him from treating it again in *Perceval.*

Erec, after having married Enide, so fully enjoys his happiness that he does not care for anything else in the world. He completely forgets that being a knight, and even one of king Arthur's knights, he has a mission to fulfill, a task to accomplish. This task, of course, would consist primarily in fighting, in finding adventures and gaining fame, but this is but a symbol for any real call a man may have to follow. But Erec is about to "degenerate in marriage," as Chrétien puts it. He does not pay any attention to what people whisper around him. He seems contented forever, decided to enjoy this peaceful happiness for all the rest of his life. Enide however hears well what people say, and although she is very much in love and very happy, she does not like this gossip and feels ashamed for her husband. Moreover she thinks she is responsible for Erec's indolence and this thought destroys all her happiness. So she finally tells him, and this, of course, is a hard blow for Erec. Had he not sacrificed everything for her, fame and honor and the joy of fighting, had he not changed his habits and deserted his former friends for no other reason than because he loved her so much? And now, instead of being grateful, she reproaches him. He would never pardon her, he would make her suffer for that. He feels bitterly offended, particularly because he must secretly admit that she is right. So he treats her with the utmost cruelty, makes her worse than his slave, never has a friendly word or a smile for her. She has to come with him on his quest for adventures, has to take care of all the horses he wins in

Perceval arrives at the Fisher King's castle. (Paris, B.N., f. fr. 12577, fol. 18v.)

battle. Her patient suffering does not move him, it is only after a long series of fights and adventures that he comes to his senses and sees how much she loves him. But strangely enough, the last of their adventures brings them in contact with two people who have obviously tried to avoid that same psychological conflict. They meet a knight who always stays with his mistress and yet has a fine opportunity to do great deeds and to earn great fame. They live in a magic garden, and whoever intrudes into that garden will have to fight with the knight. Hundreds of brave men have tried in vain and were defeated and had their heads put on stakes. Thus Mabonagrain, the knight of the garden, has become famous all over the world although he never left his lady. But she had saved him from matrimonial degeneration by making her garden so dangerously attractive: if anyone should conquer her knight, his would be the magic "Joy of the Court," a joy so great that no words can describe it.

Thus behind all the incoherent adventures of Erec there is to be found this very plain teaching: it is very difficult for a happily married man to devote himself to his vocation or mission and he will simply have to find some quite personal solution to the problem. If he fails to struggle for this solution he will of necessity destroy his own happiness.

The same theme is developed more clearly in **Yvain.** This knight, after the introductory adventures, marries Laudine, the lady of the Magic Fountain. They are very fond of each other and very happy. So Yvain, too, forgets that he might have something else to do than merely to enjoy his happiness. But he is saved from degeneration by his friend Gawain, who uses all his eloquence to show him how critical the situation already is. If Yvain should tarry too long, he would never be able to become active again, he would become indifferent and, as nothing can last forever, he would even lose the intensity of passion which constitutes his happiness. Yvain realizes the danger and decides to leave his wife for a short time in order to seek fights and adventures. She agrees reluctantly, but he must promise that he will be back at a definite date. He then sets out and lives as it is fitting for a knight to live, but he does it so well and with so much intensity that he quite forgets the date. This is what she will never forgive: since he failed to be back in time there is no use for his coming back at all. She will never see him any more: he has too clearly shown her how little he cared for her. Of course she cannot see that her cruelty drives him mad; for her the situation is clear. If he had loved her as much as she did him he would not have forgotten the date. It is only after a very long time that her love at last triumphs over her resentment, but even then Lunete needs all her shrewdness to make her admit it.

If in **Erec** and **Yvain** Chrétien shows that it might not be impossible to solve the problem, to find some compromise, some combination of peaceful happiness and active life, the fragment of **Perceval** illustrates the suffering of the woman whose lover is driven away from her by some obscure call. Perceval's father is the type of man who just cannot stay at home, the type that Edna Ferber likes to describe, the man who gives up everything that is safe in

exchange for something that is to be conquered. And Perceval himself, much more serious than his father, is unable to stay with his young wife: he obscurely feels that some great things are still to be done, things that only he could do and that he certainly cannot do if he stays with her. He loves her so much that her image haunts him: three drops of blood on the white snow appear to him as her face. He stares at it unconscious of anything else. Unconsciously he defeats and almost kills three of king Arthur's knights, and he would perhaps remain there forever if the spell were not broken by Gawain.

Perceval is but a fragment and it is impossible to tell whether Chrétien would have given us a solution of the problem or not. All the various continuations, imitations and translations, including the unsurpassed masterpiece of Wolfram von Eschenbach, are obviously written in a different spirit.

The only two complete psychological novels by Chrétien are therefore **Erec** and **Yvain.** In both of them the main theme takes little space besides all the thrilling fights and adventures and all the elaborate descriptions of arms and armour, of costumes, festivities and refined conversation. A so-called "roman breton" had to be "vain and pleasant" by definition. But this is exactly what our modern motion pictures attempt to be—they are usually quite successful in regard to the first of these two requirements!: their only aim is to entertain, that is to carefully avoid any mental effort on the part of the spectator. Yet quite a few Hollywood productions treat psychological problems, and one out of every 2,000 might even treat an interesting problem in an interesting way. Chrétien, too, wants first of all to entertain: he gives his readers what they ask him for. If the countess of Champagne orders him to write the story of Lancelot he will gladly do so and will use all his skill to sing the praise of courtly love. He will narrate all the fantastic adventures his readers are so fond of, but he will always cover them, impregnate them with his delightful irony. It will always be quite obvious that he does not believe a word of what he writes, he will never give up his half concealed smile, no matter whether he describes Yvain's lion—first weeping bitter tears and then attempting to commit suicide with his master's sword!—or any of those fights which are so terrible that they are almost comical. But this same Chrétien who never seems to take anything seriously, neither the ideals of chivalry nor those of the Church, is greatly concerned about the real relations between men and women, relations which are the exact opposite of the fashionable game that is called courtly love.

The most difficult task of anyone who wishes to interpret medieval literature will always be strictly to avoid the interference of modern views and ideas we attribute to Chrétien de Troyes. Might there not perhaps be something we simply read into him, ideas and views of our own that would be as strange to him as the conception of wireless telegraphy? Did Chrétien really mean to develop a psychological theme or was it perhaps an intrinsic part of the story he told, a feature that he reproduced without understanding it? Was he conscious of writing psychological novels? If this had not been the case, that is if Chrétien had expressed all these ideas without knowing it, his readers would not have noticed them either: they would have enjoyed his novels just as they did other Arthurian Romances: the "Knight with the two Swords," the "Marvels of Rigomer" and the hundreds of adventure-stories in which there is no psychological theme whatsoever. Yet there cannot be the slightest doubt that at least one of Chrétien's medieval readers clearly understood the psychological theme to be the main thing in *Erec* as well as in *Yvain*. The German poet Hartmann von Aue, who translated these two romances, did all he could to stress and emphasize the underlying problem: especially in Yvain he condensed and cut the various adventures to the absolute minimum, whereas he lengthened and intensified all the parts which could throw light on the main idea. In his version Gawain not merely warns his friend in more or less abstract words: he draws a highly realistic portrait of the kind of a man Yvain would become if he stayed at home any longer. "You would be like those fellows who, when you visit them, can talk of nothing but the weather or of this year's crop and last year's harvest, and who would complain endlessly about all the petty worries of every day life." It is quite obvious that to Hartmann von Aue Chrétien's romances meant exactly what they mean to us.

We do not know of any Arthurian romance previous to Chrétien's *Erec.* There might of course have been a great many of them and there certainly must have been written sources of some kind. Chrétien cannot possibly have been the first French author to write about king Arthur and his knights, he is just the first one who did it so successfully that his works were preserved. His title to fame, however, is not that he was the first but rather that he was the last French author to combine a psychological theme with an Arthurian romance. After him the poets got tired of displaying much conventional, artificial courtly psychology, in Arthurian and later in allegorical romances, but no one ever attempted to write anything we could justly call a psychological novel. (pp. 293-300)

> *Robert Anacker, "Chrétien de Troyes: The First French Psychological Novelist," in* The French Review, *Vol. VIII, No. 4, March, 1935, pp. 293-300.*

C. S. Lewis (essay date 1936)

[*Lewis is considered one of the foremost Christian and mythopoeic authors of the twentieth century. Also a noted academic and scholar, he held posts at Oxford and Cambridge, where he was an acknowledged authority on medieval and Renaissance literature. In the following excerpt from his* The Allegory of Love *he surveys the evolution of Chrétien's portrayal of love from* Erec *and Enide to* Lancelot, *focusing on his use of allegory as a method of representing emotions and moods.*]

Chrétien de Troyes is [the greatest representative of twelfth-century French poetry]. His *Lancelot* is the flower of the courtly tradition in France, as it was in its early maturity. And yet this poet is not wholly the product of the new conceptions: when he began to write he seems scarcely to have accepted them. We must conceive him as a poet

of the same type with Dryden: one of those rare men of genius who can trim their sails to every breeze of novelty without forfeiting their poetic rank. He was among the first to welcome the Arthurian stories; and to him, as much as to any single writer, we owe the colouring with which the 'matter of Britain' has come down to us. He was among the first (in northern France) to choose love as the central theme of a serious poem: such a poem he wrote in his *Erec,* even before he had undergone the influence of the fully developed Provençal formula. And when that influence reached him, he was not only the first, but perhaps the greatest, exponent of it to his fellow countrymen; and, combining this element with the Arthurian legend, he stamped upon men's minds indelibly the conception of Arthur's court as the home *par excellence* of true and noble love. What was theory for his own age had been practice for the knights of Britain. For it is interesting to notice that he places his ideal in the past. For him already 'the age of chivalry is dead' [*Yvain,* vv. 17 and 5394]. It always was: let no one think the worse of it on that account. These phantom periods for which the historian searches in vain—the Rome and Greece that the Middle Ages believed in, the British past of Malory and Spenser, the Middle Age itself as it was conceived by the romantic revival—all these have their place in a history more momentous than that which commonly bears the name.

An appreciation of Chrétien's work as a whole would here be out of place. That he has claims on our attention, far beyond the restricted purpose for which I cite him now, must surely be admitted. It is his fate to appear constantly in literary history as the specimen of a tendency. He has deserved better. And the tragedy of the thing is that he himself was never really subdued to that tendency. It is very doubtful whether he was ever dazzled by the tradition of romantic adultery. There are protests in *Cligés* which seem to come from the heart. He tells us in the opening lines of *Lancelot* that he wrote it at the command of the Countess of Champagne, and that she furnished him with both the story and the treatment. What does this mean? I am probably not the first reader who has seen in the fantastic labours which Lancelot undergoes at the bidding of the Queen, a symbol of the poet's own genius bent to tasks unworthy of it by the whim of a fashionable woman. However this may be, there is assuredly something in Chrétien beyond the reach of all changes of taste. After so many centuries, it needs no historical incantation to bring to life such lines as

> A! wher was so gret beautee maked?
> —God wroughte hir with His hond al naked,
> [*Yvain,* v.1497]

nor to appreciate the superb narrative power in the opening of the *Lancelot.* How irresistible is that cryptic knight who comes and goes we know not whence or whither, and lures the reader to follow as certainly as he lured the Queen and Kay. How nobly the poem of *Yvain* approaches to the romantic ideal of a labyrinthine tale in which the thread is never lost, and multiplicity does no more than illustrate an underlying singleness. For our present purpose, however, we must give Chrétien short shrift. What is of interest to us is that versatility which enables us to trace, in the distance between *Erec* and *Lancelot,* the extent of the emotional revolution which was taking place in his audience.

In *Erec*—almost certainly an early work—the later rules of love and courtesy are outraged at every turn. It is indeed a love story; but it is a story of married love. The hero has married the heroine before the main action of the poem begins. This, in itself, is an irregularity; but the method of his wooing is worse. Erec sees Enide in her father's house, and falls in love with her. There are no passages of love between them: no humility on his part, no cruelty on hers. Indeed it is not clear that they converse at all. When he comes to the house, the maiden, at her father's command, leads his horse to stable and grooms it with her own hands. Later, when they are seated, the father and the guest talk of her in her presence as if she were a child or an animal. Erec asks her in marriage, and the father consents. It does not seem to occur to the lover that the lady's will could be a relevant factor in this arrangement. We are given to understand that she is pleased, but only a passive role is expected of her, or indeed allowed to her. The whole scene, however true it may be to the marriage practices of the time, is strangely archaic compared with the new ideals of love. We are back in a world where women are merely the mute objects of gift or barter, not only in the eyes of their fathers, but even in the eyes of their lovers. When we pass on to the main story, this lack of 'courtesy' is even more striking. The tale of Erec's behaviour to his wife will be familiar to every one from Tennyson's *Geraint and Enid*. Chrétien renders it more credible by following a version in which the plot does not turn wholly on the absurd device of a soliloquy overheard, and in which the husband has subtler and truer motives for his anger than Tennyson can give him. But this does not alter the inherent brutality of the theme. The story belongs to the same general type as that of Griselda—the story of wifely patience triumphing over ordeals imposed by the irresponsible cruelty of a husband—and, as such, it cannot possibly reconcile itself with even the most moderate ideal of courtesy. But Erec does not confine his discourtesy within the limits of the ordeal. Just as he had allowed Enide to groom his horse for him before their marriage, so, in their journeyings, he lets her watch and hold the horse all night, while he himself sleeps at ease beneath the cloak which she has taken from her own back to cover him.

When we turn to the *Lancelot* all this is changed. The Chrétien of *Lancelot* is first and foremost the Chrétien who has translated Ovid's *Art of Love*, and who lives at the court of my lady of Champagne—herself an ultimate authority on all questions of courtly love. As against the married life of Erec and Enide we have the secret love of Lancelot and Guinevere. The story turns mainly on the Queen's captivity in the mysterious land of Gorre, where those that are native can go both in and out but strangers can only go in, and on her rescue thence by Lancelot. It is one of Chrétien's misfortunes that the dark and tremendous suggestions of the Celtic myth that lurks in the background of his story should so far (for a modern reader) overshadow the love and adventure of the foreground. He has, however, no conception of this. We think of the Middle Ages playing with the scattered fragments of classical

antiquity, and failing to understand them, as when, by an intolerable degradation, they make Virgil a magician. But indeed they have dealt as roughly with the fragments of the barbarian past, and understood them as little: they have destroyed more magic than they ever invented. Lancelot sets out to find the Queen and almost at once loses his horse. In this predicament he is met by a dwarf driving a tumbril. To his questions, the dwarf—surly like all his race—replies, 'Get in, and I will bring you where you shall have news of the Queen'. The knight hesitates for a moment before mounting the cart of shame and thus appearing as a common criminal; a moment later he obeys. He is driven through streets where the rabble cry out upon him and ask what he has done and whether he is to be flayed or hanged. He is brought to a castle where he is shown a bed that he must not lie in because he is a knight disgraced. He comes to the bridge that crosses into the land of Gorre—the sword-bridge, made of a single blade of steel—and is warned that the high enterprise of crossing it is not for one so dishonoured as he. 'Remember your ride on the cart', says the keeper of the bridge. Even his friends acknowledge that he will never be rid of the disgrace. When he has crossed the bridge, wounded in hands, knees, and feet, he comes at last into the presence of the Queen. She will not speak to him. An old king, moved with pity, presses on her the merits of his service. Her reply, and the scene that follows, deserve to be quoted in full:

> 'Sire, alle his tyme is spilt for noght,
> For sooth to seyn he hath at me
> No thankes wonnen ne no gree'.
> Lancelot sory chere maketh
> Yet lyk a lovere al he taketh
> In meknesse and seyth humblely,
> 'Dame, I am greved certeinly;
> Yet, for the cause of your chiding,
> I dar nat asken for no thing'
> Greet pleynte tho to make him liste
> If that the Quene wolde hit liste,
> But to encrese his were and wo,
> She yeveth him no wordes mo.
> Into a bour she paceth nouthe,
> And evere as ferforth as he couthe
> This Lancelot with eyen two
> Hir folwed and with herte also.
>   [*Lancelot;* vv. 3975-89]

It is only later that he learns the cause of all this cruelty. The Queen has heard of his momentary hesitation in stepping on to the tumbril, and this lukewarmness in the service of love has been held by her sufficient to annihilate all the merit of his subsequent labours and humiliations. Even when he is forgiven, his trials are not yet at an end. The tournament at the close of the poem gives Guinevere another opportunity of exercising her power. When he has already entered the lists, in disguise, and all, as usual, is going down before him, she sends him a message ordering him to do his poorest. Lancelot obediently lets himself be unhorsed by the next knight that comes against him, and then takes to his heels, feigning terror of every combatant that passes near him. The herald mocks him for a coward and the whole field takes up the laugh against him: the Queen looks on delighted. Next morning the same command is repeated, and he answers, 'My thanks to her, if she will so'. This time, however, the restriction is withdrawn before the fighting actually begins.

The submission which Lancelot shows in his actions is accompanied, on the subjective side, by a feeling that deliberately apes religious devotion. Although his love is by no means supersensual and is indeed carnally rewarded in this very poem, he is represented as treating Guinevere with saintly, if not divine, honours. When he comes before the bed where she lies he kneels and adores her: as Chrétien explicitly tells us, there is no *corseynt* in whom he has greater faith. When he leaves her chamber he makes a genuflexion as if he were before a shrine. The irreligion of the religion of love could hardly go further. Yet Chrétien— whether he is completely unconscious of the paradox, or whether he wishes, clumsily enough, to make some amends for these revolting passages—represents his Lancelot as a pious man and goes out of his way to show him dismounting when he passes a church, and entering to make his prayer; by which, according to Chrétien, he proves both his courtesy and wisdom.

Chrétien de Troyes, judged by modern standards, is on the whole an objective poet. The adventures still occupy the greater part of his stories. By the standard of his own times, on the other hand, he must have appeared strikingly subjective. The space devoted to action that goes forward only in the souls of his characters was probably beyond all medieval precedent. He was one of the first explorers of the human heart, and is therefore rightly to be numbered among the fathers of the novel of sentiment. But these psychological passages have usually one characteristic which throws special light on the subject of this book. Chrétien can hardly turn to the inner world without, at the same time, turning to allegory. No doubt the Provençals here served him as a model; no doubt both the poet and his audience loved the method for its own sake, and found it clever and refined. Yet it would not surprise us if Chrétien found some difficulty in conceiving the inner world on any other terms. It is as if the insensible could not yet knock at the doors of the poetic consciousness without transforming itself into the likeness of the sensible: as if men could not easily grasp the reality of moods and emotions without turning them into shadowy *persons.* Allegory, besides being many other things, is the subjectivism of an objective age. When Lancelot hesitates before mounting the cart, Chrétien represents his indecision as a debate between *Reason* which forbids, and *Love* which urges him on. A later poet would have told us directly—though not, after all, without metaphor—what Lancelot was feeling: an earlier poet would not have attempted such a scene at all. In another place Lancelot is asked by a lady for the head of a knight whom he has just disabled. The knight begs for mercy, and two duties within the chivalrous code are thus brought into collision. The resulting state of Lancelot's mind becomes for Chrétien a debate between Largesse and Pitë. Each fears defeat and between them they hold him a prisoner. Again, in *Yvain,* where Gawain and the hero, who are fast friends, meet without recognition and fight, the contrast between their amicable intentions and their hostile acts is worked up into a very elaborate allegory of Love and Hate—Hate looking from the windows, Hate mounting into the saddle, while Love (here used in its larger sense), who shares the same house, is upbraided for skulking in an inner room and not coming to the rescue. This certainly seems frigid to a modern reader, and does not rise as naturally from the context as those which I have quoted from the *Lancelot.* Yet we should beware of supposing too hastily that the poet is merely being clever. It is quite possible that the house with many rooms where Love can be lost in the background, while Hate holds the hall and the courtyard, may have come to Chrétien as a real revelation of the workings of circumstance to produce such various actions from the emotions of a single heart. We have to worm our way very cautiously into the minds of these old writers: an *a priori* assumption as to what can, and what can not, be the expression of real imaginative experience is the worst possible guide. The allegory of the Body and the Heart—also from *Yvain*—is an interesting example. That Chrétien has borrowed it from Provence does not in the least alter the fact that it is for him an expression—perhaps the only possible expression—of something well and truly imagined. But he has not yet learned the art of dropping such tools when they have done their work. The glitter of the weapon takes his fancy when the thrust has already been given, and here we may feel almost confident that what begins as live allegory dies into mere virtuosity in the course of the next ten lines. The more commonplace, and reiterated, allegory of Death in *Cligés* will recur to the memory of any of its readers.

The figure of Love personified himself is almost equally connected with the subject of the 'love-religion' and with that of allegory. The references to his archery in *Cligés* belong to a familiar type, and might come out of any classical love-poet. The idea of Love as an avenging god, coming to trouble the peace of those who have hitherto scorned his power, belongs also to the Latin tradition, but it is more serious for Chrétien than for Ovid. The repentance of those who had been fancy free, and their self-surrender to a new deity, are touched with a quasi-religious emotion. Alexander, in *Cligés,* after a brief resistance, confesses that love chastens him thus in order to instruct him. 'Let him do with me as he will, for I am his.' Soredamors, in the same poem, acknowledges that Love has humbled her pride by force, and doubts whether such extorted service will find favour. In the same spirit Yvain determines to offer no resistance to his passion: not only to resist love, but even to yield unwillingly, is an act of treason against the god. Those who have thus sinned against him deserve no happiness. In *Lancelot* the same doctrine is carried further. It is only the noblest hearts which Love deigns to enslave, and a man should prize himself the more if he is selected for such service. We find also the conception of lovers as the members of an *order* of Love, modelled upon the orders of religion: of an *art* of Love, as in Ovid; and of a *court* of Love, with solemn customs and usages, modelled upon the feudal courts of the period. (pp. 23-32)

C. S. Lewis, *"Courtly Love,"* in his The Allegory of Love: A Study in Medieval Tradition, *Oxford at the Clarendon Press, 1936, pp. 1-43.*

Urban T. Holmes, Jr.   (essay date 1947)

[*Holmes was an American scholar of French and romance philology whose works include* A History of Old French Literature: From the Origins to 1300 *(1937). In the excerpt below from an essay originally published in 1947, he contends that Chrétien undertook* Perceval *in order to develop "in a popular or romance form the theme of the conversion of the Jewish people to Christianity."*]

The present writer is tremendously aware of the vast amount of material that has been written to explain the symbols and the origin of the Holy Grail. The three principal theories are (1) that the Grail procession and the facts attendant upon it are derived from the Christian Sacrifice of the Mass, perhaps from the Byzantine rite; (2) that the Grail story combines a group of more or less related Celtic tales, with perhaps some additional elements thrown in; (3) that the Grail is reminiscent of a fertility cult, such as that of Adonis or the Eleusinian Mysteries. James Douglas Bruce, Konrad Burdach, and Rose Peebles have made prominent contribution towards the Christian explanation; the late A. C. L. Brown, and more recently, William A. Nitze, and Helen Adolf, have argued strongly for the Celtic; Miss Jessie L. Weston will always be remembered for her critique of the other theories and insistence upon cultist origins. The earlier writings on the Grail are summarized effectively by James Douglas Bruce in his *The Evolution of Arthurian Romance* (Göttingen, 1927, 2nd ed.). Very recently indeed Nitze and Miss Adolf have taken up the problem, once more. Nitze observed in *MLN*, XIX (1944), 567:

> The time is ripe for some Romance scholar to collaborate with a Celticist in a book on Chrétien's last romance.

In *Speculum*, XXI (July, 1946), 303-311, Nitze undertakes to do some of this. He believes that one of the source tales told how Perceval had to recover a fertility cup for his clan (against the Red Knight); still another was concerned with a cauldron of plenty which had some connection with the Fisher King (Irish Nuadu). To elaborate upon this vessel and "place it in the brightest light" it was identified with a *graal,* reminiscent of the Byzantine Mass. The bleeding lance was a Gawain story, but it and the Grail procession are reminiscent of the Byzantine rite. In sum, Chrétien "in true mediaeval fashion . . . modernized antiquity. . . . So he would place Celtic legend (his chief source), Byzantine ritual, the lance of Longinus, Good Friday penitence, Alexander—all on the same evangelical level." His mainstay in this was Philip of Flanders.

Miss Helen Adolf also, in *Modern Language Quarterly,* VIII (March, 1947), 3-19, seeks to carry out Professor Nitze's instructions in much the same way, but she gives different details. For her the Grail (or cup) carried by the fairy equals a fairy. The Fisher King is, as Brown had previously suggested, death-in-life; the bleeding lance stands for a wounded man; and so on. She makes this general statement:

> Our theory, however, would rest on a weak foundation, if it were not supported by the fact that there are plenty of inconsistencies in Chré-

tien's romance. These point to a multiplicity of defective joints and transitions (p. 7).

Personally I am fearful of our creating more inconsistencies than any mediaeval man ever dreamed of by this redoubled effort to explain the *Contes del Graal* of Chrétien as a monstrous combine of Celtic tale, fairy lore, Byzantine Mass, metonymy, and mistakes. I should like to make another effort, following different lines of thought, to seek a more consistent solution. In doing this we will assume that the original meaning of the Grail was not known to the continuators of Chrétien or to those who wrote other Grail works. Thus we will exclude from our investigation the *Perlesvaus,* Robert of Boron, Wolfram von Eschenbach and the prose Vulgate Cycle, which are quite frequently cited by Grail scholars, who thereby give the impression that they think these later writers had some acquaintance with Chrétien's sources. With that we do not agree.

For the reader's benefit we will review very briefly the significant motifs of the Grail Castle and procession as presented by Chrétien in his *Perceval.*

Perceval is seeking a place to lodge and he comes upon a river. He sees a boat with two men fishing, using for bait little fish slightly larger than minnows. One of the men directs him to a castle which he finds with some difficulty. As he gazes upon it he thinks it fairer than anything from there to Beyruth. He enters over the drawbridge; four servitors appear and he is wrapped in a mantle of scarlet. (This need not mean "vermeille," but it usually does.) He finds a series of *loges* leading to a great hall, perfectly square, in which there are columns of copper. An old man is in the center by a fire, clad in black with purple edging. Four hundred men could have been contained in that hall. Perceval sits with the old man upon his couch. A squire enters with a sword, sent by the old man's *nièce, la sore pucele,* to be given to anyone whom he may choose. The sword is handed to Perceval, for whom it has been destined. It is remarked that there are only three of its kind and that there will be no more; furthermore that it will fail its possessor in only one case known to the maker. Next comes the Grail procession. A squire enters with a lance that drops blood on the bearer's hand. Two more squires appear with ten branched candlesticks and then a damsel with a Grail in her hand. There is bright light around the Grail. They are followed by a second damsel with a silver plate. Perceval asks no questions and the procession goes out. An ivory table is brought and placed upon trestles of strange and rare wood. The meat is a venison haunch. The food is served to each upon a "gastel qui fu antiers." At each course the damsel with the Grail returns and passes between the couch and the fire. Perceval puts off all questions until the morrow. That evening he is served many delicious fruits *au couchier.* When the day dawns the Castle appears deserted. Perceval finds his arms and goes forth. The drawbridge pulls up after him. He soon encounters a girl holding the headless trunk of a knight who was recently killed in fight. She asks Perceval whether he had spent the night at the Castle of the "rice roi Pecheor." He says yes. She tells him that the host and the fisher were the same, that the king had been wounded in a battle, in both *hanches,* and that if he had asked concerning the Castle and the procession "Le buen roi qui est maheigniez, Toz eüst ragaeigniez Ses manbres et terre tenist Et si granz bien an avenist" (v. 3587-90). He (Perceval) is in a state of mortal sin, she says, because his mother has died as a result of his having left her. She declares that the sword which he carries will fail him. He asks where it can be mended in such a case and she replies "au lac qui est sor Cotoatre" and that he must entrust it there to the smith who made it; his name is Trebuchet. Perceval begs her to leave the dead and come with him, the living. She refuses to abandon the body until it has been buried. Perceval sets out again. He meets a lady, in very sorry condition now, from whom he had taken a ring and many kisses in the course of his early adventures. He defeats her knight, li Orgueilleus de la Lande, who has been oppressing her because of that first meeting. It was li Orgueilleus who beheaded the slain knight outside the Grail Castle. There follows an extraneous episode in the course of which Perceval once more visits Arthur's court. A hideous damsel appears and denounces Perceval for his Grail failure while announcing other possible adventures which attract Gawain, etc. But Perceval wanders again, this time for five years without any memory of God. His sin has prevailed. On a Good Friday he is induced to visit a hermit and confess. At this point the Grail episode resumes once more. The hermit tells Perceval that in a chamber beyond the one where the Fisher King received his guest was a being who was fed by the Grail bread or *oiste* alone. This being has not left the chamber for a long time (specified differently in the manuscripts, some as fifteen, others as twelve years, and so on). This being is the brother of the hermit and of Perceval's mother. He is the father of the Fisher King. The hermit absolves Perceval from the guilt of his mother's death.

> Einsi Percevaus reconut
> Que Deus au vandredi reçut
> Mort et si fu crocefiiez

(v. 6509-11)

Our predecessors have spent much time sketching in a "romantic" background of sources which could have been drawn upon by a creative imagination such as they attribute to Chrétien de Troyes. Their interpretation draws no pattern of meaning from the literal level. In mediaeval technique the poet began with a fairly coherent story (the *matière*) through which he thought to achieve an expression of *sens* on various other levels: the allegorical, moral and anagogical. In order to prove a consistent pattern in the *sens* the salient details in the *matière* must be consistently accounted for.

The reasoning of those who have discussed the Grail has begun too often with *a priori* conceptions upon which they have later sought to make scattered comparisons which might fit. With the exception of the ritualist cult solutions, which were advanced by Jessie L. Weston, and at one time by W. A. Nitze, the investigators have not begun with a clean slate—listing important details and proceeding from these to a solution. The Christian ritual theory was forced upon us by the next generation after Chrétien which chose the only explanation that could have seemed logical in their day. The Celtic theory for the Grail thrust itself upon us because many of us believe that the motifs of Chrétien's

earlier works are undeniably Celtic. That he might have had a change of theme, with his change of patron, when he left the service of Henri de Champagne for Philippe d'Alsace, is not taken strongly into consideration. The nature cults that have been proposed do offer a freer opportunity for independent judgment, but unfortunately we know almost nothing about the Eleusinian Mysteries and Adonis cult. We have little guarantee that these persisted with any strength during eight hundred years of Christianity in western Europe. The solution found in the Welsh *Peredur* is hardly worthy of consideration.

Details which do not seem to be fortuitous are among the following. There are two men in the boat—not one. The Fisher King is baiting his hook with *fish,* to catch fish. This is a more violent form of fishing which does not agree with what we should expected if the Fisher King were intended to be Christ. I believe that a net would have been the device described, in this case, by Chrétien. The Grail hall is peculiar. What are the *loges* which precede the hall itself? Why is that hall a perfect square? Surely the columns of *arain* or copper are not mentioned because that was a common material for such columns in France or England. The Fisher King himself must have been an individual of great distinction to give point to the Grail episode. If he were just an uncle of Perceval, with no unusual qualities the tale would fall flat as it does in the Welsh *Peredur*. Why are his garments edged with purple? The Grail when it appears is attended by light—hardly a condition surrounding a Celtic cauldron of plenty. It is undeniably a vessel that provides food, however, that satisfies hunger of a bodily kind. It can produce venison and other varieties of physical meats. I should not say that it was merely a source of food for the spirit. It is carried by a feminine figure, and this is indeed a hard enigma for those who prefer the Christian ritual explanation. What is the *taule* or *tailleor,* a sheet or plate of silver which is brought in with equal solemnity? There are just two maidens; the other members of the procession are men. From the lance blood drips upon the hand of the squire who carries it. I have a distinct feeling that no one who was a Christian would treat in this way the Blood of Our Lord. Remember that Joseph of Arimathea used a vessel to receive the Sacred Blood. Giotto in his mural at Assisi has angels collecting the Blood from the Cross. Such a picture of dripping blood as Chrétien gives reminds one more of a sacrifice of a carnal kind. Why was the Fisher King lame? There is no record in Christian authority that Christ was lame after the Resurrection. Who was there in Celtic tradition who fits this description? It is important to know just why a state of mortal sin would keep Perceval from resolving the Grail tragedy, for a tragedy it seems to have been. It is difficult to understand how Perceval could have made the great Dagda any happier by inquiring after his cauldron of plenty and the poisonous spear of Fiacail, or the Luin of Celtchar held vertically over a cauldron of blood. We are told that the solution of the Grail tragedy by Perceval would result in great good. In this the nature cult solution seems more logical, because we assume then that the healing of the Adonis or the ailing king would bring about at least a season of spring. By the Christian interpretation all that can result is an adoration of the Host by Perceval individually. The Celtic themes hold that the land would be thus saved from enchantment. We could multiply such questions as these, but the results will continue to be the same. If the Grail solution does not have greater meaning than has been suggested so far, then the words of the damsel who nurses the headless body of her knight are a meaningless exaggeration.

I believe that the Castle of the Grail was a symbolical representation of the Temple of Solomon in Jerusalem, colored with some of the trappings of mediaeval feudalism. The Grail, the lance, the blood, the silver plate were the vessel of manna, Aaron's rod (which took many forms in the tradition as we shall presently see), the blood of sacrifice made by the High Priest, and the tablet of the Law. These were sacred objects preserved in the Holy of Holies, a large square, or rather cubical, chamber, which the High Priest of the Temple visited once a year. "Into the second [Tabernacle] went the high priest alone once every year, not without blood, which he offered for himself, and for the errors of the people" (Epistle to the Hebrews, 9.7). In the Grail Castle the High Priest was that great father of the Tribes of Israel, Jacob, who was lame as a result of his struggle with the Angel of the Lord. Over the Ark in the Holy of Holies were two "Cherubim obumbrantia propitiatorium," or 'shadowing the mercy seat.' Although these were images in actual fact, for his dramatic effect Chrétien was obliged to have the table of the Law and the vessel of manna borne in by human beings not too removed in popular imagination from Cherubim, and so these are carried in by maidens. The Quest of the Holy Grail, in our opinion, was the conversion of the Jewish Temple to Christianity. That was the great good that would result, which would restore Jacob to his health and to his estates. In the words of St. Paul in the Epistle to the Hebrews, which I have already quoted from above, "the way into the holiest of all was not yet made manifest . . . as the first tabernacle was yet standing . . . which stood only in meats and drinks, and divers washings and carnal ordinances, imposed on them until the time of reformation" (9.8-10). Paul goes on to say that when the Blood of Christ entered into the holy place all this became unnecessary. The blood of the new testament will suffice for the redemption of the transgressions that were under the first testament.

In our belief it was St. Paul's Epistle to the Hebrews which was the inspiration for the Quest of the Grail. In a way it is attested by the text of Chrétien that he had been recently handling this Epistle. Chrétien quotes from the fourth chapter of the First Epistle of John which is only some one or two folios before the Epistle of Paul to the Hebrews [in mediaeval manuscripts of the New Testament], if we can imagine Chrétien having in his hands a MS containing the Pauline and other Epistles of the New Testament. Such a MS would not have been so conveniently supplied with page heading and display titles as we have now come to expect. If Chrétien turned back to the first Epistle of John and thought he was still reading St. Paul it must have been because he had been perusing something of St. Paul's a few minutes previously. This is the passage in the Perceval to which we are referring:

> Deus est charitez, et qui vit
> Au charité, selonc l'escrit,
> Sainz Pos le dit et *je le lui*

Il maint an Deu et Deu an lui

(v. 48-51)

Please note that Chrétien comments that he had read with his own eyes: *je le lui*.

The Epistle to the Hebrews was addressed to Christian Jews who were in danger of falling away from the gospel. It is basically a comparison between Judaism and Christianity stating that Judaism is "only the earthly shadow of the heavenly realities that Jesus Christ came to establish and bring within our reach" [J. R. Dummelow, *The One Volume Bible Commentary,* 1941]. The priesthood of Christ is contrasted with the Levitical priesthood. The heart of the Epistle is in Chapter 9 which, we contend, contains the core of Chrétien's Grail procession. The validity of the New Testament (playing upon the two meanings of the word) is derived from His death. The sacrifice in the Old Testament must be repeated yearly; Christ's sacrifice was for once and all. Christ entered the tabernacle in His own blood after the Crucifixion. This we contend is the doctrine which Chrétien was presenting in the form of his Romance.

In support of our theory that the Grail Castle is a mediaeval dramatization of the issues in Hebrews chapter 9 we will pass in review most of the details contained in the Grail episode and see how they can be explained in terms of the Old Testament and of Jewish oral tradition, notably by the Midrashim. Of inestimable help in this connection are the six volumes compiled by Louis Ginzberg with index in the seventh volume by Booz Cohen, entitled (in English translation) *The Legends of the Jews* and published in English by the Jewish Publication Society of America (1913-1938).

We will take the details in the order in which they occur in Chrétien's story. First there are the Fisher King and his companion in the boat. Ginzberg narrates for us the Midrash tradition about Jacob and his son Zebulon. This son of Jacob is, in my suggestion, the other man who was with the Fisher King in the boat. When Zebulon was one hundred and fourteen years of age, which was two years after the death of Joseph, he summoned his sons and counselled them:

> "When I was in Canaan, catching fish at the shores of the sea for my father Jacob, many were drowned in the waters of the sea, but I came away unharmed. For ye must know that I was the first to build a boat for rowing upon the sea, and I plied along the coasts in it, and caught fish for my father's household, until we went down into Egypt. Out of pity I would share my haul with the poor stranger, and if he was sick or well on in years, I would prepare a savory dish for him, and I gave unto each according to his needs, sympathizing with him in his distress and having pity upon him. Therefore the Lord brought numerous fish to my nets, for he that gives aught to his neighbor, receives it back from the Lord with great increase. For five years I fished in the summer, and in the winter I pastured the flocks with my brethren" (Ginzberg II, 205-6).

Again making use of the Midrashim, as interpreted by

Ginzberg (II, 138), Jacob bestowed this blessing on his grandchildren: "May your names be named on Israel, and like unto fishes may you grow into a multitude in the midst of the earth, and as fishes are protected by the water, so may you be protected by the merits of Joseph." It is meant by this that the children of Joseph (the Ephraimites), who were descendants of Jacob, were likened to a multitude of fish. We have looked further for the motif which is represented by Jacob's baiting his hook, with fish as bait. He was sending little fish to be swallowed by bigger ones. This may be reminiscent of the Haggadah tradition in which the Ten Commandments are equated each with the ten words with which God created the world. To quote Ginzberg: "The Sixth Commandment: 'Thou shalt not kill,' corresponds to the word: 'Let the waters bring forth abundantly the moving creature,' for God said: 'Be not like the fish, among whom the great swallow the small' " (III, 105). For one acquainted with the Haggadah tradition the large fish being caught by means of the small suggests a breaking of the commandment which forbids violence. It is this association of Judaism with killing which is further illustrated in the Grail Castle.

The details of the Grail hall are reminiscent of what we know about the Temple of Solomon. The *loges* through which Perceval enters before he finds himself in the hall are porticoes before the front of the Temple: "porticum vero ante frontem" (2 Paralip. or Chronicles 3.4). Other correspondences are: the copper or brass pillars (3 Kings 7. 15-16); the square-shaped hall (2 Paralip. 3.8); Chrétien's table of ivory set upon trestles of *ebenus* which corresponds to the shewbread table with trestles of setim wood (Exodus 25.28). Concerning the Temple one Bible text says: "And he made ten candlesticks of gold according to their form and set them in the Temple, five on the right hand and five on the left." (2 Paralip. 4.7). These *candelabra aurea decem* surely did not mean ten-branched candelabra in the Temple of Solomon, but a mediaeval reader might be pardoned for interpreting in that way. The golden *urna* or Grail of the Second Tabernacle was filled with the manna of the Lord, the spiritual food of the Old Testament, and the inference would be that this manna fed the table of the Fisher King who, we suppose, is Israel or Jacob, the spiritual father of the Jews. Christ likened Himself to Jacob in John 1.49, while speaking to Nathaniel. "And he said unto him, Verily, verily, I say unto you, Hereafter ye shall see heaven open, and the angels of God ascending and descending upon the Son of man." The light around the Grail does not require much explanation when we know that sacred things were generally assumed to be accompanied by light. It is true, however, that the Tabernacle of the Lord when first erected was surrounded by "the appearance of fire by night" (Numbers 9.16).

Jacob was the father of the Levites or priests. He wore the high priest clothing which was first worn by Adam, the first born man in the world (Ginzberg I, 332; II, 139; V, 284). In this capacity it is perfectly correct for him to be in Chrétien's mind a symbol of the high priesthood, within the Holy of Holies of the Grail Castle. The sable garments which he wears are, to be sure, not those of the high priest; in this case they may denote mourning—sackcloth and ashes. But what of the purple edging? The Law of Moses (Numbers 15.38) required purple fringes upon the garments: "Loquere filiis Israel, et dices ad eos ut faciant sibi fimbrias per angulos palliorum, ponentes in eis vittas hyacinthinas . . . "

With regard to the meal that was served at the Grail feast we can explain the venison haunch which was placed before the King and Perceval. In Genesis 25.28 we learn that Isaac, the father, loved Esau "because he did eat of his venison." The Jewish oral law gives much more detail on this fondness of Isaac for venison. We will quote from Ginzberg (I, 331-7). Rebekah tells Jacob to prepare savory meat for his father that "he may bless thee before his death." She dressed Jacob in the garments of Esau, "the high-priestly raiment in which God had clothed Adam, 'the first-born of the world,' " which had been descended from Adam through Noah, Shem, Abraham, and Isaac, to Esau. Jacob prepares the feast and says to his father, "Arise, I pray thee, sit and eat of my venison" (Ginzberg I, 336). Later when Esau appears Isaac tells him that Jacob's venison had marvellous qualities. Isaac said: "I had only to wish for bread, or fish, or locusts, or flesh of animals . . . it had the taste of any dainty one could wish for."

On the manna which we assume was in the vessel of the Graal the Bible itself is very explicit. This fell and fed the Israelites during their forty years in the wilderness; only when they reached Gilgal and began to partake of grain did the manna cease. Aaron was instructed to gather some in a vessel and lay it before the testimony (Ex. 16.17-35; Josh. 5.10-12). The word *manna* meant "What is it?" (Ex. 16.15), a phrase used by the Israelites when they first saw it. The Rabbinical tradition (Ginzberg III, 44-45) states that the manna had different taste according to the wishes of those who partook of it. When some of it melted it was consumed by beasts in the field and their own flesh was impregnated with the taste. That is the only way that the unfaithful could taste of this spiritual food.

If Perceval were one of the unfaithful it was only through such flesh as venison that he could partake of the manna. Remember that each portion of venison, in Chrétien's story, was placed upon a whole *gastel* and served in that way. What were these *gastels*? I suggest that the *panes propositionis* or shewbread are intended. These were loaves of unleavened bread, changed every Sabbath, which were placed upon the table of setim or shittim wood (Lev. 24.5-6).

If the Grail is not to be taken in this way—as the vessel of manna preserved in the Holy of Holies—if the Christian ritual theory is correct, how then can Perceval partake of it, in sin as he is, and after being fed by the Host how does he remain in this sin?

Critics of this theory may be puzzled by our equating of the bleeding lance with Aaron's budding rod. The Rabbinical tradition has it that God created this rod on the Sixth day of Creation (*Jewish Encyc.*). He gave it to Adam when the latter was driven from Paradise. From Adam it passed through the hands of Shem, Enoch, Abraham, Isaac, and Jacob. Jacob bestowed it upon Joseph. An Egyptian noble

Jethro stole it and planted it in his garden whence it was rescued by Moses who married Jethro's daughter. The manner in which Moses obtained it is of special interest to us. The rod could not be pulled from the ground save by Moses who knew the name of God engraved upon it and uttered this. This motif is similar to that of the sword that cannot be pulled forth except by one hero for whom it is intended. According to the Haggadic modification of this tradition, King Josiah later concealed the rod and the Ark, and their whereabouts would remain unknown until the coming of the Messiah. There is still another legend (Ginzberg VI, 106-107) which identifies the rod of Aaron with the staff of the kings (Judah, David, and the Messiah). According to still another interpretation the rod is symbolic of the Temple to be built by the Messiah (*ibid.*). It was because Aaron's rod alone budded that he and his descendants were designated for the priesthood (Numbers 17.1-8).

The rod, of course, was capable of changing shape of its own accord when thrown upon the ground. It was the holy staff of Israel which early Christians desired in some way to associate with their own traditions. On the Day of Atonement when the High Priest visited the Altar of incense in the Tabernacle he tipped the horns or corners of this altar with sacrificial blood (Ex. 30.10). In the Epistle to the Hebrews we learn that "Moreover he sprinkled with blood both the tabernacle and *all the vessels of the ministry*." A lance was the common variety of rod in use in the Middle Ages. Banners were fastened to it; it was a badge of authority, as was the rod among ancient peoples. I find no difficulty in seeing in the lance from which blood dropped upon the bearer's hand (there is no steady stream of blood suggested in the text) a symbol of the "rod of the Old Testament" with its mark of carnal sacrifice. It is entirely probable that the lance form (for the rod) was used in order to enable Chrétien to continue his allegory further when, at the dissolution of the Grail Castle, the Jewish relics should pass into the most sacred relics of the Passion. Just as Perceval knew his name (*Perce-voile?*) in advance of his achieving his quest to "penetrate the veil" (Leviticus 21.23), even so the lance of the Passion was thus prefigured in the rod of Aaron with its carnal blood of ritual sacrifice. The rod or lance of the Jews, after the accomplishment of the Quest, becomes the Sacred Lance which was stained only with Christ's Blood. This transformation is not figured in exactly the same way but it is suggested by Origen (*In Exodus,* c. 7): "This rod of Moses by which Egypt was subdued is in a figure the Cross of Christ by which the world is conquered."

In a later passage, in the midst of Gawain adventures, the *vavassor* of Guinganbresil advises that Gawain be given a chance to go look for the bleeding lance (v. 6110-17) and he adds:

> E s'est escrit qu'il iert une ore
> Que toz li reaumes de Logres
> Qui ja dis fu la terre as ogres
> Sera destruiz par cele lance.
>
> (v. 6168-71)

We take it that this refers to prophecies of destruction of England (Logres) by the Jews (which Chrétien must have known to be ridiculous). We know from Perceval's conversation with the damsel who held the beheaded knight in her arms that the essence of the Grail question, which would have brought about such good, was "Why is there blood on the lance?" (v. 3552-3):

> "Et demandastes vos por quoi
> Ele seignoit?"

The hideous damsel also chides him:

> Que tu ne poïs demander
> Por qoi cele gote de sanc
> Saut par la pointe del fer blanc.
>
> (v. 4656-8)

The lance and its blood are the central motif of the theme. If we interpret correctly, this meant the carnal sacrifice of the Jews as opposed to the Sacrifice of the Body and Blood of Our Lord. It should not be forgotten that there was a dreadful massacre of the Jews at Blois in 1171, and Blois was associated with Troyes (Marie de Champagne's sister had married Thibaut de Blois), where the Jews were accused of using Christian blood in their sacrifice.

The quest of the lance by Gawain is contrasted with the quest by Perceval, in Chrétien's mind. Gawain will seek to overthrow the lance by violent means. Perceval's quest will be accomplished by persuasion, by asking the Grail question. The motif of the Question which opens the way is a favorite in Jewish tradition. My friend A. H. Schutz informs me that in the Haggadah tradition the Passover ceremony begins with four questions that must be asked by the youngest person (the greatest fool?). The most important is: "Why is this night different from all others?" We are not forcing a comparison between the Passover and the Grail; but the question motif is there.

The gift of the sword which shall fail in only one special condition also offers itself for a solution along similar lines. The *sore pucelle* we will not identify for the moment. She is a descendant (*nièce*) of the King. The smith who made the sword manufactured only three. In the Epistle to Hebrews (chapter 4) St. Paul says: "For the word of God is quick and powerful, and sharper than any two edged sword. . . . " Abelard in his famous Commentary *In Epistolam ad Hebraeos* gave the accepted explanation for the word of God as a sword: "Et hoc est, quia 'sermo,' id est Filius Dei, Christus videlicet" [Arthur Landgraf, *Commentarius Cantabrigiensis in Epistolas Pauli e schola Petri Abaelardi in Epistolam ad Hebraeos,* 1945]. If Christ is as a sword there are two others like it, the Father and the Holy Ghost. Christ (the word of God) was sent to Perceval as a sword that would fail him in only one case. Need we ask what this case would be? There sat Perceval wrapped in the red mantle (of mortal sin), the one case (in the Doctrine of Penance) when Christ cannot avail. If Perceval had not been in mortal sin he could have asked the Grail question and with Christ's help could have freed the King from the Old Testament Covenant, and that meant all the Jews, from the Old Law. Scarlet, as Isaiah said, was the color of sin: "Though your sins be as scarlet . . . " (1.18). This is the one proper designation for a cloak of mortal sin. See also Apocalypse 17.3-4.

Who was the girl with the beheaded knight in her arms? The obvious answer is that this knight was representative of John the Baptist, who lost his head in an endeavor to accomplish a similar quest. I said that I might identify the *sore pucelle,* the *nièce* of Jacob, who sent the sword (the Word of God, Christ). Presumably this is Mary, the Virgin. Beauty of a feminine kind was usually designated in the Twelfth century by reference to blond locks.

What is the lake beside Cotoatre? The name *Cotoatre* suggests . . . [Kattath in Joshua 19.15. . . . Kattath is one of the cities allotted to the children of Zebulon. The lake which is nearby is the Sea of Galilee]. The smith who made the sword, and who alone can mend it is called Trebuchet. One of the meanings of this word is that of 'assaying scales.' Such scales would symbolize the Justice of God. God is Justice (Deut. 32.4). He made the sword. If we are correct in assuming that Perceval will find that it fails him while he is in sin, then Penance alone will repair it. (Perceval subsequently fights with this sword against li Orgueilleus and it does not fail, although the damsel had told him it would be of no use to him. But then li Orgueilleus was a special case. Sagramors and Kay later are unhorsed by lance alone.)

In our resumé above we did not list the motifs which preceded the episode of the Grail Castle. We should like to mention them, giving details as we go. These fit well into our framework. Perceval's mother informed him about Christianity when she explained the Church to him:

> "Une maison bele et saintisme
> Et de cors sainz et de tresors.
> S'i sacrefie l'an le cors
> Jesucrist, la prophete sainte,
> Cui Giu firent honte mainte;
>
> (v. 578-82) . . .
>
> Vos lo gie au mostier aler."
> "Donc irai je mout volantiers
> As iglises et as mostiers,"
> Fet li vaslez, 'd'ore an avant
> Einsi le vos met an covant.'
>
> (v. 594-98)

This is the first real introduction of Perceval to Christianity. He has no baptized name as yet; he is merely *biaus fils.* His father

> Fu parmi les janbes navrez
> Si que il maheigna del cors.
> Sa granz terre, ses granz tresors
> Que il avoit come prodon,
> Ala tot a perdicion.
>
> (v. 436-40)

This father bears strong resemblance to the Fisher King, whom we have so far identified as Jacob, the symbol of Israel. The damsel in the tent, which Perceval mistakes for a church, from whom he takes the emerald ring (emerald represents the stone of the Levites placed in the Holy Ark) is strongly rebuked by her knight, li Orgueilleus de la Lande (Herod?), who accuses her wrongly of lack of chastity with the young Perceval and who says that henceforth she shall be oppressed by him until Perceval is beheaded. We suggest that the damsel is representative of Judaea. It will be recalled by our *resumé* above that Perceval eventually overcomes li Orgueilleus de la Lande and causes the oppression of the lady to be lifted.

To return to the earlier episodes. After leaving this lady in the tent Perceval stops for a brief time in Arthur's court (long enough to have a brush with Kay) and then follows a knight in red who has snatched Arthur's golden cup. He wants the knight's armor. This knight, if we follow out our allegory, must be "worldliness" or something similar. After killing the red knight Perceval takes his arms but refuses to give up entirely the simple garments furnished him by his good mother. This refusal to abandon his simple clothing is emphasized over and over, so that we can be certain it had some meaning for Chrétien. Gornemanz, the *prod'home,* whom he then visits, finally persuades Perceval to leave off completely his mother's clothing and her instructions. We identify this Gornemanz with *Li Sages,* or Ecclesiastes. Gornemanz is continually quoting from Ecclesiastes in his instruction:

> Et li Sages dit et retret;
> Qui trop parole, pechié fet.
> Por ce, biaus frere, vos chasti
> De trop parler . . .
>
> (v. 1653-56)

The general trend of remarks in Ecclesiastes is to reform the "fool."

At this point something must be said about the events that take place in Arthur's Court before the hero sets forth to stop the Red Knight. He is mocked by Kay. His future greatness, however, is proclaimed by the lowest man present—a jester—and by a maid. Kay slaps the girl for this and Perceval vows to avenge the blow, upon Kay. Obviously the characters of Arthur's Court are not to be treated as *personnes à clef.* They were already fixed as types in Chrétien's mind, and in those of most of his hearers. But the motifs of these scenes are strongly reminiscent of passages in the Wisdom books of the Bible. We suggest that Chrétien was here using the Arthurian characters to set the theme of his Grail quest. The Ecclesiastes says: "Better is a poor and wise child than an old and foolish king, who will no more be admonished" (4.13). "Wisdom is better than strength; nevertheless the poor man's wisdom is despised, and his words are not heard" (9.16). In the Song of Solomon the girl who calls out to her beloved says: "I called him . . . The watchmen . . . they smote me" (5.7). The character of Kay is more or less a personification of Pride and Vanity wherever it is met with. Perceval's desire to humble Kay, although a natural one, suggests: "When pride cometh, then cometh shame" (Proverbs 11.1) and also "Pride goeth before destruction and an haughty spirit before a fall" (*ibid.,* 16.18).

Perceval meets with still another influence before he has the adventure of the Grail Castle. He comes to the castle of Blancheflor. She admits that she is a relative of Gornemanz. She is a lovely blond lady dressed in regal purple with vair and sable fur. She is in great distress at the time as she is sore pressed by King Clamadeus and his seneschal Anguingueron. She is chaste, for she lies in bed with Perceval and makes no attack on his virtue. Also she will not send him out of her own volition against the knight of superior force, Anguingueron or (as I would interpret it) Angigneron. For her Perceval overcomes Angigneron, and finally Clamadeus (after a brief siege). The defeat of the latter is made possible because God sends providentially ships with provisions for the castle. (We learn at a later stage, from the lips of the hermit who confesses Perceval that the prayers of Perceval's mother brought this about and thus saved Perceval from imprisonment.) She admits her relation to Gornemanz, who for us is *Li Sages,* but her environment is profoundly Christian. There are two religious houses in the town. The people of Belrepaire commend the hero knight to the Holy Cross as he goes out to fight Anguingueron or Angigneron. The lady remarks that so many good men have died for her; that it is only right she should be discomforted. I have no trouble in identifying this Blancheflor de Belrepaire with Wisdom, Christian Wisdom, as descended from, but opposed to, the Jewish Wisdom of Gornemanz. Although Perceval overcomes for her Angigneron 'deceiver' (*Engignerie* is Old French for 'deceit' or 'trickery') and, with some help from Providence, Clamadeus, who is stronger but whose name certainly means 'accuser of God,' still the knight is not yet a Christian. He prays that God may place his mother, if she is dead, into the Bosom of Abraham:

> Que Deus el sain saint Abraham
> Le mete avuec les pies ames
>
> (v. 2966-7)

and he commends the people of Belrepaire to the king of kings, which has Old Testament flavor. Perceval (as we must continue to call him even before he knows his name) wants very much to return to Belrepaire and promises to do so. He does not have a name until after he leaves the Grail Castle when he unconsciously and vaguely admits that he is Perceval:

> Et cil qui son non ne savoit
> Devine et dit que il avoit
> Percevaus li Galois a non,
> N'il ne set s'il dit voir ou non;
> Mes *il dist voir, et si nel sot*
>
> (v. 3573-77).

It is evident that Chrétien attached special significance to the name. Perceval "divines" his name because of the *sens* which it implies. Perceval suggests *perce voile,* one who is destined to pierce the veil which shuts off the innermost Holy of Holies. It is then after he knows his name, that our protagonist mentions the Savior for the first time (v. 3496) since leaving his mother (v. 172-3).

Belrepaire, the stronghold of Blancheflor, is surrounded by Waste Land. This might be expected when a castle has been besieged for a length of time; but we are reminded here of the words of the Wisdom of Solomon: "*Wisdom* delivered the righteous men who fled from the fire . . . Of whose wickedness even to this day the *waste land* that showeth is an testimony" (10.6-7).

Next comes our most important problem. Who is the being who is within the inner chamber to which the vessel of manna is carried? This manna is a spiritual food which, according to the Jewish tradition is the food of the angels. "Man did eat angel's food; He sent them meat to the full" (Psalm 78.25): This refers to manna. Furthermore when Christ was in the wilderness "angels ministered unto him." These two concepts placed side by side could mean that Christ while fasting in the earthly sense was fed by

angels with spiritual food. I mean that such an idea could have been held in the Middle Ages. The room of the Fisher King was the Holiest of Holies of the first covenant, of the Jewish Temple. "But Christ being come an high priest of good things to come, by a greater and more perfect tabernacle, not made with hands, that is to say, not of this building (Epist. Hebr. 9.11). . . . For Christ is not entered into the holy places made with hands, which are the figures of the true; but into heaven itself . . . nor yet that he should offer himself often, as the high priest entereth into the holy place every year with the blood of others" (*ibid.,* 9.24-25).

In other words, Christ in the new covenant does not make use of the Jewish Holy of Holies but of a far finer tabernacle—which is Heaven in symbol. And Christ is not a high priest after the order of Aaron but after the order of the new covenant (Melchisedec). "If, therefore, perfection were by the Levitical priesthood . . . what further need was there that another priest should rise after the order of Melchisedec and not be called after the order of Aaron? For the priesthood being changed there is made of necessity a change also of the law (Epist. Hebr. 7.11-12). For it is evident that Our Lord sprang out of Judah of which tribe Moses spake nothing concerning priesthood. And it is yet far more evident: for that after the similitude of Melchisedec there arises another priest, Who is made, not after the law of a carnal commandment, but after the power of an endless life (*ibid.,* 7.14-15) . . . For there is verily a disannulling of the commandments going before, the weakness and unprofitableness thereof " (*ibid.,* 7.18).

According to the Christian ritual interpretation of the Grail Quest, the being in this inner room, whoever he is, is served by the Sacred Host, the Corpus Domini, and that alone. (This makes it impossible to identify him with the Holy Ghost.) The *oiste* in the Grail could hardly be a consecrated Host. We identify it with the spiritual food borne by the damsel who personifies one of the Cherubim ministering unto Christ. This manna

> il est si espiritaus
> Qu'a sa vie plus ne convient
> Que l'oiste qui el graal vient.
>
> (v. 6426-28)

We assume, therefore, that Christ the high priest of the new Covenant is symbolically present in the room beyond the Jewish Holy of Holies. It is a vague place, not described. Perceval is not aware of it although he sees the Grail disappear in that direction. It is out of this world. One difficulty seems to remain. It is stated that the inner being has not left that chamber:

> Quinze anz a ja esté einsi
> Que fors de la chambre n'issi
> ou le graal veis antrer.
>
> (v. 6429-31)

The symbolical meaning of the number fifteen may escape us. On the other hand it is possible to interpret it by the Kabbalah. The fifteenth letter of the Hebrew alphabet is Samech which has the value of sixty. If the "quinze anz" is not to be taken literally, and I do not see how any of the Grail story could have been set in exact time, then the *sens* of that number can best be explained by Numerology, the process of *gematria* in the Kabbalah. Sixty, of course, is an indefinite round number (Ginzberg I, 120, 303). Chaucer refers to "sixty bokes olde and newe" that he possessed (*Leg. Good Women* G, 273) which is assumed to be a round, indefinite number. The number of years that had elapsed between the Ascension and the era of Arthur and his knights could not even be guessed at by an intelligent man of the Twelfth century. The copyists of the *Conte del Graal* were not sure of the "quinze anz." Some substituted *douze,* others *vint* in this particular passage.

The hermit says that he and the mother of Perceval are "brother and sister" of the King in the inner chamber. Being Christians they are of one blood with Christ. But the Fisher King is only a child of God, being a Jew. The Grail question, we assume, would have opened up the inner chamber to Jacob and the Jews would have been freed from their sorrows and tribulations. Many lives would be saved, thereby. As it was, Jacob like Perceval partook of the manna only in the form of the venison placed upon the *gastels,* while in the Holy of Holies.

I believe that Philippe d'Alsace, the new protector of Chrétien, whom Chrétien praises enthusiastically for his charity and generosity, gave to Chrétien the task of developing in a popular or romance form the theme of the conversion of the Jewish people to Christianity. Chrétien says:

> Ce est li contest del Graal
> Don li cuens li baille le livre.

> (v. 66-7)

This book may have been a MS of the Epistles of St. Paul, with, in particular, the Epistle addressed to the Hebrews. We know today St. Paul was not actually the author of the Epistle to the Hebrews, but he was thought to be so in Chrétien's time.

If Chrétien were assigned this task of elaborating on the theme of conversion from Judaism to Christianity it is not unlikely that there was a basic reason for his selection. Our assumption is that he himself was a Perceval—a converted Jew who was given the *Crestianus* at the time of his baptism. It has been established beyond much reasonable doubt that *Crestiens li Gois* who signed the *Philomena* was a Jew, and from his name, he was certainly a Christianized one. Raphael Levy will not agree that this *Crestiens li Gois* was our Chrétien [*PMLA*, XLVI, 1931]. On this I disagree strongly. I am in accord with those who think that *Crestiens li Gois* and Chrétien de Troyes were one and the same. To be sure, we are not obliged to assume that our poet was a Jew in order to explain his knowledge of Jewish oral tradition. After all, we know that he was a resident of the town of Troyes in Champagne, and that Troyes had been the seat of rabbinical schools of international importance since the time of Rashi (d. 1105).

For me an *argumentum ex silentio* is that Chrétien never signed as witness any of the many cartularies which were executed for the Count of Champagne. We know that such documents were witnessed by those who happened to be present in the *salle* when they were drawn up, depending upon the social position of those present. Apparently Chrétien did not have much social position. If he were a

converted Jew this would have been the case. Of course, he could have been a common Christian *jongleur.* But such an assumption hardly fits the dignity and learning which the poet of the **Yvain, Lancelot,** etc., displays.

Be it understood that I am not attacking the theory of Celtic origins for the motifs in Chrétien's earlier works. Rather I am even offering a better explanation of how he could have come upon much of this same material. As Troyes was a center of Jewish learning, students came there from Lincoln and other points in Great Britain. Nor am I attacking the obvious fact that Robert of Boron and the Continuators of Chrétien thought of the whole Grail story as a purely Christian one. The only contention which we wish to make is that in the mind of Chrétien, and in that of Phillippe d'Alsace, the Grail story was the conversion of Judaism to Christianity. This original purpose was not clear to later writers on the Grail theme, which includes the compiler of the Welsh *Peredur.* (Incidentally this would make it quite evident that the *Peredur* followed Chrétien's **Perceval** in date of composition.)

This interpretation that we seek to give to the Grail serves Chrétien better than other theories have done. It shows him to have been an artist who could be represented in pale tones beside the greater and far more magnificent figure of Dante. After all, Chrétien would deserve an almost unique place for his romantic representation of a problem and a solution which was a burning one to his contemporaries. And, as one of my kind critics has recently said, there is grandeur in the thought that Chrétien, if he were a converted Jew, was telling on a greater scale his own life story and conversion in this Quest of the Grail. His Quest had an ending, while the Quest of Perceval had none. (pp. 7-31)

Urban T. Holmes, Jr., "A New Interpretation of Chrétien's 'Conte del Graal'," in University of North Carolina Studies in the Romance Languages and Literatures, *No. 8, 1948, pp. 7-31.*

John T. Nothnagle (essay date 1965)

[*In the following essay, Nothnagle discusses Chrétien's realistic depiction of the twelfth century in his works, noting that "with Chrétien, perhaps for the first time in literature, woman has found her identity."*]

As a literary concept realism is a term the critic would do well to avoid. Too often it evokes an expectation of uncompromising fidelity to phenomena, usually of a sordid or tawdry nature. If this observation suggests a trite definition, it nevertheless is faithful to the canons of traditional literary history which has associated realism primarily, sometimes exclusively, with the many writers of the nineteenth and twentieth centuries whose most conspicuous bond has been an almost photographic attention to the details of reality. But such a definition is necessarily too narrow. The function of art has always been to treat reality. Variations, and thus problems for the historian and the critic, arise on recognition that reality is an individual perception, true only to the eye and the heart of the beholder. The medieval world provides the major exception, but that only because the concept of realism at that time corresponded to idealism in ours.

It would be a stimulating task to deal with the romances of Chrétien de Troyes as specimens of realistic art in the twelfth-century sense of the term, and in fact the burden of recent scholarship and criticism devoted to Chrétien has fallen on this aspect of his creation. Such studies have been extremely useful and have drawn attention to what must be considered the major qualities of his work for modern readers: the poetry and the rich symbolism that yield a story told on many levels and illuminate it with the charm of discovery and wisdom. To appreciate this, one has but to compare Chrétien with the ever more dreary productions of his successors from the thirteenth through the sixteenth centuries. Like the French classical tragedy, courtly romance began with masterpieces and fell into consistent decline thereafter. Chrétien was indeed a realist in the medieval sense of the word, and even perhaps in the more tolerant definition the term has acquired today.

And yet, on the basis of close study of Chrétien and of the admittedly limited world for which he wrote, a case might be made to claim him the first realist in the nineteenth-century meaning of the term. To be sure, he portrayed idealized heroes and heroines and set them in an idealized world. Nevertheless, the knight of the twelfth century would have recognized himself in those romances. Clichés and stereotypes of the middle ages make us forget that the "period" comprised a thousand years of growth and progress. The major difference between that age and our own is that change did not proceed so rapidly nor so uniformly. There were long periods of stagnation and even decline. But, in contrast, there were others of extraordinary progress, like the hundred or so years from 1050 to 1150 immediately preceding Chrétien's career. This was a time when practically no aspect of western European life was left untouched by a spurt of amazing progress. Leadership for much of that advance was centered in an area which hitherto had been a backwater of Europe: the Duchy of Normandy and the Norman Kingdom of England. Chrétien, whose life and career were spent on the confines of that territory and under its evident influence, was privileged to write his book in a world which—if it appears idealized or stereotyped to later centuries—was practically brand new to his. The type of castle in stone that Chrétien describes, with its towers, moats, and drawbridges, was new to Europe and only to be found in the sphere of the Normans. Similarly, a new kind of saddle had just made its introduction into Europe from the Arabic world. Its sturdy seat and stirrups made possible a new style of knightly combat, quite different from that described in the *Chanson de Roland* and depicted in the Bayeux tapestry. For the knight still working to master its techniques, Chrétien's descriptions of the new style of fighting would have been a valuable manual. And the new luxuries of courtly life that Chrétien so often and so fondly describes—garments, jewelry, fabrics, ornament—had only recently appeared in western Europe in the wake of secured trade routes and the beginning of a money economy. It is possible, moreover, that the childlike delight with which these products were welcomed was one of the unexpected consequences of the antinomianism inherent in the Gregorian Reform.

Attention to such elements of everyday reality does not constitute the limit of Chrétien's realism, however. Like the novelists of a later age he appreciated and was concerned with the sociological and psychological structure of the world for which he wrote. His oblique treatment of kingship, in this respect, is highly revealing, especially when considered against the historical background of the time. The King Arthur whom Chrétien depicts no more resembles any memorable king of the twelfth century than he does the original Arthur—if such existed—in the fifth. He is rather a projection of the mid- or late twelfth-century knight's conception of what a desirable king should be: an amiable and generous figurehead who is as much subject to the laws and traditions of the realm as are his knights. In fact, the great kings of France, England, and Germany at that time were tough-minded realists. Inspired by the remarkable achievements of William the Conqueror, freed from the bothersome restraints of earlier theocratic notions of monarchy, enlightened by the revival of Roman law, they devoted themselves to the creation of the type of nation-state that we have known to this day. Their efforts were not unresisted. Finding that they exercised real sovereignty only over their own domain, they set about to enlarge this at the expense of the landed aristocracy. Moreover, to assure themselves loyal military service, they gathered companies of landless knights pledged directly to them and not to an intermediary and frequently autonomous duke. Against such a background, Chrétien's Arthur is completely out of place, except to the wishful thinking of the knights and nobles for whom he wrote.

The new status of the knight in the twelfth century accounts for the rise of the chivalric code, or *courtoisie,* that occupies such a large part of Chrétien's narratives. Contact with the more cultivated Arabic world undoubtedly added many refinements and concepts to this code, but it is probable that something analogous would have developed anyway in view of the evolution of early medieval life. The primitive medieval warrior was an anonymous member of a tribe in arms. In the early, and true, feudal period he became a vassal endowed with temporary or hereditary land rights by his suzerain in return for his military service. Conditions in the twelfth century determined a new development, at least in the West. The needs of expanding monarchy, land shortage, and the policy of maintaining and augmenting the royal domain made necessary a new kind of warrior pledged directly to the service of the king and holding no land or hereditary rights. Such knights spent much of their lives at the royal court in the company of their peers in a situation not unlike that of the fictional Round Table. Such knights, unlike their ancestors who had fought for survival or for such tangible rewards as land or booty, had to reconcile themselves to the more abstract compensations of honor. Distinction could be won only by the gratuitous performance of feats. Chrétien's enchanted bower, sword bridge, and magic fountain had their counterpart in the war games where a landless knight could seek distinction, and by distinction the hand of a wealthy widow or the command of a fort. Such was, in fact, the career of the Englishman, William Marshal, whose biography has come down to us. He was a landless knight who exploited his skill in the tournaments of the twelfth century to win appointment as the military tutor in the household of Henry II, the hand of a wealthy heiress, and tenancy of a lucrative earldom. This documented career resembles in many ways the stories of Erec and Yvain in Chrétien's romances who also earned fame, fortune, a wife, and an estate by playing the knightly game.

The fact that in all his romances except *Perceval* and *Lancelot* Chrétien's heroes woo and win a wife attests the central importance of love in his work. It is difficult to determine in what way these love stories correspond to the realities of his time. They seem in any case to violate the conventions of courtly love, and this may be revealing. Except in *Lancelot,* the courtships lead to marriage, and in *Erec et Enide* and *Cligès* even to children. In *Erec et Enide, Cligès* and *Yvain* there is no adultery. Finally, in *Erec et Enide* the lady occupies an inferior social status with respect to her lover. Moreover, in all these stories there is a frank and unabashed sexuality quite foreign to the longing and spiritualized desire of the Provençal lyric.

Again, a consideration of the conditions of the knights of the time may provide an explanation for the originality and distinctiveness of Chrétien's treatment of love. Such a knight, first of all, had no need of a working wife, a companion in household and in arms who would be a second self in the struggle for survival. Such wives are to be found in Norse literature and even some Anglo-Norman romances, but they exist in quite a different world from twelfth-century Champagne. What the knight in Chrétien's world sought was a rich wife whose lands would compensate for his own relative poverty. As long as she existed at the level of dream he could well endow her with all those qualities transmitted to the northern courts by the Provençal lyric: beauty, charm, dignity, even obstacles to inflame his passions. But the ultimate objective is matrimony and the establishment of his fortunes.

What supports this view is not only the plausibility of the situation and the fact that it essentially describes the love intrigue of *Yvain* and, with variations, of *Erec et Enide,* but also the success of Chrétien's feminine portraits. Enide, Soredamor, Laudine are not only beautiful beyond comparison; they are intelligent, self-possessed, dignified, capable of winning the love and the respect of the heroes who court them. They resemble closely neither the heroines of antiquity and of the epics, nor the haughty or distant *dames* of the troubadours. They announce rather the modern woman and the birth of a world in which the role and functions of the sexes have been codified and balanced. With Chrétien, perhaps for the first time in literature, woman has found her identity.

The discovery of the self, which is perhaps only secondary or accidental for the feminine characters of Chrétien, is on the other hand the primary concern of his men. That so modern a theme would occur in the twelfth century is not surprising in view of the nature of the century. The change from a simple agricultural economy and a closed, static social order was in rapid progress. This lesson of history was reflected in the evolution of the hero of literature. The heroes of the earliest medieval works, the warriors of the Carolingian cycle, the saints, even the classical champions as they were adapted for the *romans d'antiquité,* were depicted as symbolic of the values and proof of the validity of the earlier world view. But by the middle of the twelfth century the winds of change were blowing strong, and one of the most vigorous gusts followed what was perhaps the greatest discovery of that creative age: the discovery of personality. Such dissimilar figures as Peter Abelard and John of Salisbury are witness in their own writing of a new awareness of the individual self in its restless quest for identity. At the other end of the social ladder the anonymous masses in the new cities, in their embrace of new forms of piety and millenarian heresies, are proof of the deep restlessness in the middle ages following the disruption of traditional patterns. Chrétien treats the theme in a very limited manner, dealing with only one class to the virtual exclusion of others, and with heroes who have been singularly gifted by nature. Nevertheless, he deals with the subject as evidence again of his concern with the realities of his time. And, despite the limitations he sets for himself, he develops it with remarkable skill.

At the beginning of each romance Chrétien's heroes are virtually unknown. Even the name of Lancelot, who already enjoys a certain fame in *Le Chevalier à la charette,* is kept a secret well into the story. They are moreover young, single, separated from their homes, and—in the manner of youth—quite unconcerned with all that does not directly concern them. As personalities they are no more bound by their past than the plot of the romance is determined by history or legend. In each story the hero and the narrative start out together, the theme of the road matching the linear structure of the novel to make possible the succession of episodes and adventures by which the hero comes to know himself. The romance then becomes his world, and it is he who gives it order and unity. Some of Chrétien's devices to show this growth of order are patently artificial, like his number and animal symbolism. Nevertheless, through the fiction of a free and imagined character moving successively through the adventures of a stylized world, he duplicates the development of personality as it comes to know itself and, by knowing itself, to know and impose order upon the exterior world.

With rare insight Chrétien shows by means of each of his heroes that the supreme challenge for the maturing personality is love. This is not the exterior relationship that leads to marriage and to the establishment of the hero's fortunes, but the interior experience by which the individual transcends the spiritual limits of his being. With sophisticated insight he shows in *Erec et Enide* and in *Yvain* that love, once it has been embraced for the fulfillment of the self, cannot be doubted or betrayed without suffering the gravest of consequences. In these romances the heroes risk total destruction before they are able to reconstruct the fragile edifice of their own personalities. We have but to substitute for Chrétien's love another absolute drawn from religion, or art, or one's own ambition to appreciate his deep understanding of the finitude and contingencies of human nature without that necessary dimension that spirit alone can give.

It would seem then that the works of Chrétien, for all their myth and symbolism, are strongly rooted in the actual reality in which he wrote. His insights into the needs and desires of certain at least of his contemporaries provide a useful addition to our understanding of a remarkable century. But more important, his assessment of human nature and his projection of it to the level of fiction mark a milestone in the development of narrative art. And yet, paradoxically, from our vantage point in this swiftly passing century, when literature in its new directions joins science to shake our faith in our traditional views of reality, of the sovereign and unique personality, as well as our hopes to find meaning in a bewildering universe, these aspects of Chrétien de Troyes may come to seem as naïve as his magic fountain and his enchanted bower. (pp. 202-07)

> *John T. Nothnagle, "Chrétien de Troyes and the Rise of Realism," in* L'Esprit Créateur, *Vol. V, No. 4, Winter, 1965, pp. 202-07.*

An excerpt from *Erec and Enide*

> He slept and she lay awake;
> she remembered what
> many people throughout the land
> were saying about her lord.
> When she began to remember that,
> she could not refrain from weeping;
> she felt such pain and sorrow
> that by mischance it happened
> that she made a remark
> for which she later counted herself a fool,
> but she meant no evil thereby.
> She began to contemplate
> her lord from head to foot;
> she saw his handsome body and fair face,
> and wept so violently
> that, as she wept,
> her tears fell upon his chest.
> "Wretch," said she, "unhappy me!
> Why did I come here from my land?
> The earth should truly swallow me up,
> since the very best of knights,
> the boldest and the bravest,
> the most loyal, the most courtly
> that was ever count or king,
> has, because of me,
> completely abandoned all chivalry.
> Now have I truly shamed him;
> I should not have wished it for anything."
>   Then she said to him: "My friend, how
>   unfortunate for you!"
> Then she fell silent, and said no more.
> But he was not deeply asleep:
> he heard her voice as he slept;
> he awoke upon hearing her words,
> and was greatly astonished
> to see her weeping so bitterly.

> *Chrétien de Troyes, in his* Erec and Enide, *edited and translated by Carleton W. Carroll, Garland Publishing, 1987.*

Jean Frappier   (essay date 1968)

[*In the following excerpt from an essay originally written in French in 1968, Frappier attempts to define the nature of Chrétien's literary significance, particularly focusing on his originality as a writer of Arthurian verse romance and his influence on the traditions of that genre.*]

All the unknowns of twelfth-century literary history and the extensive lacunae in Chrétien's biography blur with uncertainty any serious effort to measure precisely his originality. However enticing the works may be, the shadows (to choose one major problem) surrounding the very genesis of his Arthurian romances remain filled with unanswerables. Even though, due to nearly complete ignorance of his immediate sources, we are prevented from evaluating their influence, we assume that the *matière de Bretagne* existed before him and we suspect that, in spite of his scorn of them, he was indebted in some way to various unknown predecessors. However, the virtual borrowing of subjects or themes is much less important than their treatment, and, in fact, in Chrétien's case, his poetics reveal most clearly and most precisely his innovations in romance and his creative talent. Certain indirect testimony, like the Middle High German *Lanzelet,* the three Welsh romances, *The Lady of the Fountain, Peredur Son of Efrawg,* and *Gereint Son of Erbin,* as well as Chrétien's own pithy declarations regarding *matière, sen,* and *conjointure,* tend to prove that, until his **Erec and Enide,** Arthurian narrative had not risen beyond the level of what Chrétien himself called the "tale of adventure"—by apparent contrast with the more elaborate structure of his romances. Everything within his work points to a lively sense of the craft of fiction and, for a medieval romancer, to an unequaled degree of esthetic awareness. His distinct contribution was to cut classical features into a form yet to be determined, bringing it to perfection through creative imitation and sophisticated invention. Of course, there were other authors at this time who devised and applied artistic principles of composition that might be called *courtly,* but the word *classical* does not seem to suit their endeavors. These rivals, among which the most remarkable is Thomas of England, along with Chrétien, turned a page in French literary history. Yet it seems more appropriate to grant Chrétien primacy over his literary generation.

Indeed, for the second half of the twelfth century, his output is exceptionally rich by comparison with his contemporaries, whom he outproduced in sheer numbers of works. (Assuming that the lesser ones are those not extant, the five romances are preserved in a quite abundant manuscript tradition, a sign of success rather than chance.) But, better still, it is in the choice of subjects that Chrétien manifests most energetically his great artistic vision, from one romance to the next, even when he must work at the behest of a patron. Dovetailing as if fortuitously in a complementary series of alternations and compensations, the diverse themes are joined with a kind of unique dynamic approach to human truths. Thus, the amorous and heroic ardor of **Erec and Enide** contrasts with the slow and precious sentimental analyses and the bashful boldness of sincere hearts in **Cligés;** in succession, the voluntary and mystic disciplines of the courtly lover in the **Lancelot** are followed by the surprises of adventure and love and by worldly bliss lost and regained in the **Yvain.** And, finally, we have the image of chivalry imbued with divine love in the **Conte du Graal.** However concerted this interplay, Chrétien remains throughout a keen observer, one who easily combines ironic and empathetic modes: within the totality of his work, diversity provides the key to harmony. Like a true artist, Chrétien is enabled by his gift to create his own poetic world, a personal one that goes beyond mere ornamentation and pretty expression. Chrétien's deft hand is felt when he delights in viewing and depicting the spectacle of society; his style (his lifestyle, in a way) is to consider the problems of ethics and of action, to *shape* the conduct of his characters, and to make them ideal models of life.

Chrétien's prologues do not really embody what could be called edifying aims: the rhymester tells pleasant stories to divert the audience. Nevertheless, our author remains a moralist, scattering here and there proverbs and maxims, tarrying sometimes with a brief pronouncement on the vices and virtues. Or he will slip in an occasional reflection, a bit of practical advice, or he will let one of his characters speak on his behalf; indeed, certain of his lines sound like moral precepts. In this way, the real meaning and didactic value of a given tale become clearer. The *sen,* his important concept, which is evidence enough of the

moralistic intentions in his works, at once recalls the finite nature of man and his world and excludes the notion of art for art's sake, a remote idea for medieval authors. Even though the proem to **Erec and Enide** (vv. 11-12) may advise unequivocally ". . . . that one ought always to study and strive to speak well and teach the right," Chrétien's lessons usually remain more tacit, more subdued, almost inexpressible; with all possible variations in mind, the *sen* must be deduced, according as the levels differ, to include episodic development and character description. The reader's share is a double measure of ethical solace and unobtrusive food for thought. Perhaps Chrétien was thinking of himself and of the interpretation of his whole work when, in **Yvain,** he entrusts Calogrenant, who is to tell of his earlier misadventure at the marvelous fountain, with the declaration that, in order to grasp his narrative, more important than that of the *ear* is understanding by the *heart* (vv. 149-70). Thus arises already the relationship between the story itself and its moral, a notion not unlike that expressed by Voltaire's proclamation in *The White Bull:* "I choose that a story should be founded on probability, and not always resemble a dream. . . . And I desire above all, that under the appearance of fable there may appear some latent truth, obvious to the discerning eye, though it escape the observation of the vulgar." This is why **Erec and Enide, Yvain, Perceval,** and even **Cligés** or **Lancelot** are moral rather than thesis romances, for in each case, a well-defined psychological problem is resolved and the situation each time is so crisply handled as to lay bare the human heart and set forth an art of living. As always, however, the solutions offered accord with the chivalric courtly ethos of Chrétien's elite audience.

The very aristocracy found a kind of social justification in the flattering Round Table fictions whose rules of good manners and noble sentiments were easily learned. The court of Arthur—the king who makes knights—helped set upper-class lifestyles, but it also appears as a privileged center, a collectivity which arbitrates in matters of prowess and which, through praise, may celebrate a hero's glory. Some of Chrétien's most brilliant episodes highlight this normative function of the Arthurian community, in which the lords and ladies of Champagne and France ideally participated. But only in error would we reduce the moral of Chrétien's works to the mere observance of dogmas pertaining to a single, refined social group. For his prominent heroes act on their own, while Arthur's court and its courteous paragon, Gawain, cannot but reflect a certain conformity. Erec, Yvain, and Perceval each respond to generous instincts or to their own conscience, autonomous in their inner freedom; Fenice endeavors to control her inner destiny; and Lancelot himself, the willing slave of love, obeys the law of his existence to the point of scorning social respect. Somehow, in every romance, Chrétien manages to set apart the true hero from all the others. When the most perilous of strange adventures, the "Joy of the Court," arises, Erec ignores the warnings of friendship and the anguished pity of the crowd: " 'Nothing could restrain me from going to seek the Joy' " (vv. 5424-25). Similarly, as Yvain advances toward the castle of *Pesme Aventure,* he says: " ' . . . my wayward heart leads me on inside, and I shall do what my heart desires' " (vv. 5176-77). As for Perceval, he alone of the

The marriage of Yvain and Laudine. (Garrett MS 125, fol. 52r.)

Round Table resolves, against all hope, to attempt the quest for the Grail, even after the Loathly Damsel's imprecations. Across adventures and trials, by their failures and by their exploits, the exemplary heroes loom large, take on character, and become what they are. The most lofty moral of Chrétien's romances, too often forgotten, lies in fact in this very display of individual dynamism, in this simultaneously subjective and objective development of personality. It is unthinkable, of course, that Chrétien would have us admire strength or prowess for their own sakes; the gigantic and naive Mabonagrain—who would be a gem of a knight were he not so large—the victim of an extravagant love service, the valiant upholder of a barbarous custom, is undone by the hearty Erec. The hero, then, must give his all yet retain a sense of moderation and justice, an equilibrium of audacity in check which corresponds to the optimistic *finales* when all the virtualities are realized and reconciled. For, in the end, heroes like Erec or Yvain persevere, determined not to sacrifice love to glory or glory to love, and attain thereby a more beautiful, more human happiness, won in plenitude.

This confidence in the hero and in his inherent resources seems to be one facet of courtly humanism. Until his *Conte du Graal,* Chrétien's ethos is almost uniformly free of religious concerns, filled with profane meditations on man and his world. God is not ignored, he just remains a distant abstraction, a kind of guarantor synonymous with the right. With one exception, we might even say that chivalry in Chrétien's Arthurian romances is nearly that of a lay civilization: Knights of the Round Table, indifferent to the Crusades, never fight enemies of the faithful. The spiritual role of the clergy is nonexistent; religious ceremonies are reduced to sheer convention, ornaments of social life. Not a single heartfelt religious emotion as such elicits prowess.

The *Conte du Graal* brings a change in spirit. As the hermit says to Perceval: " 'Believe in God, love God, worship God' " (line 6459). Thus charity, human and divine, is now praised as the yeast of the interior life. The notion of sin and repentance, missing from Chrétien's earlier romances or else reserved for the psychology of love, becomes a moral reality; on Good Friday, pious knights and ladies walk shoeless, dressed as penitents, for the salvation of their souls—a significant image setting a new pace for the romance of adventure. After writing his first four poems, perhaps Chrétien's opinions on chivalry changed; perhaps the purely courtly and profane notion of knighthood was felt to be insufficient, or, possibly in line with Philippe of Alsace's views, it needed renovation. Still, the religious inspiration of the *Conte du Graal* does not go as far as asceticism or mysticism; rather it proclaims that a knight must live according to Christian charity, must repent devoutly for his sins, must hear Mass daily and not leave before the end of the service; he must also honor priests and defend widows and orphans. Such are the hermit's accessible, humanly attainable counsel, by which the eager Perceval will abide.

Between the romances of *Lancelot* and of *Yvain* and the *Conte du Graal* the change is quite marked, but is it a fundamental one? To call it an abrupt break would be inaccu-

rate, for it is not so much dramatic as gradual. Nowhere in *The Story of the Grail* does Chrétien recant courtly values, except that for Perceval courtly love—as revealed in two episodes, one at Blancheflor's castle, the other in contemplation of the blood drops on the snow—has new meaning. With Chrétien's last romance, the ethos of his entire work is broadened significantly, though not to the extent of including a theoretical conflict between secular and religious ideals. As we have said, the ethical problems are treated alternatively, as if in a kaleidoscope.

Under these circumstances, how shall we characterize his ethos in a comprehensive way? Its embodiment does not lie in abstractions, like honor, love, and God, which, though distinct, are complementary in his romances rather than mutually exclusive. The ethos of his works is manifested no less harmoniously, but much more in the arena of life and action, by analogous solutions, destined to safeguard at once the reciprocity of social relations and the spontaneity of conscious decisions. On the one hand, Chrétien stresses the art of urbanity, elegant manners, polite language, discrimination in mundane cheer, loyalty, self-control, and liberality, and, of course, disdain for the vulgar or envious—all the qualities of a twelfth-century gentleman. But he also idealizes the difficult, the heroic, the almost superhuman quest for happiness purified by trials of valor. These two aspirations confer an upward movement on Chrétien's ethos and on the structure of his romances, so that values swing from hedonism to abnegation, and always with the subtle interplay of nodal antithesis or of rationally attenuated paradox. Chrétien's conception of love and chivalry encompasses both this hierarchy of values and the blend of the real with the ideal.

In his most accessible way, Chrétien is adverse neither to joie de vivre nor to civilized dilettantism. On his list of diversions enjoyed by Arthur's court in Laudine's castle are flirting, or "amiable regards" (*accointances*) that unite lovers like Gawain and Lunete, and the "love tokens" (*donoi*), by which is traded the small change of sentimental pleasures (*Yvain,* vv. 2441-67). Here indeed is an indulgent passage, even a little ironic, judging from this decrescendo: " . . . [there were ladies] of exalted birth, so the men could agreeably employ themselves in caressing and kissing them, and in talking to them and in gazing at them while they were seated by their side: that much satisfaction they had at least." This atmosphere of courtly sensuality does not put Chrétien off, yet he does not prolong it, but flavors the narrative with a brief comment for the ladies: " . . . such persons may properly be rated as fools for thinking that a lady is in love with them just because she is courteous and speaks to some unfortunate fellow, and makes him happy and caresses him. A fool is made happy by fair words and is very easily taken in." With this brief disquisition the author sets apart courtier's trifles from true love. The amiability of the lady is a mark of noble breeding; and only deluded fools and fops misinterpret the full play of flirting in society.

Chrétien was in no way a puritan. But over and above casual affections and coquetry, beyond the charm of the simple love pledge, he conceives of love as a profound sentiment by which our destinies are engaged and by which, through a kind of reenactment in his romances, happiness is threatened, guarded, then augmented. The situations are always various, the problems are never quite the same from one work to the next (though the **Lancelot** seems to be marginal to his own ethical views). But in general Chrétien tends to rework or add nuance to courtly notions, both as adherent and heretic of *fine amor.* His personal ethos is emphasized when he refuses the fatality of love, rejecting the love philtre drunk by Tristan, and when he insists on the primacy of willful election of the beloved. For him, *fine amor* is a gift enjoyed and a religion practiced by the "members of its order" (**Yvain,** line 16). By contrast, Chrétien does not hold to the principle that love and marriage are incompatible; illegitimate or uncommitted unions of passion are condemned, so that the marriage of love is considered the ideal solution: *"Qui a le coeur, si ait le cors"* ("Who has the heart has the body, too" **Cligés,** line 3163). Thus are reconciled the affections and the reason, love's sovereign privileges and respect for the social code. Chrétien's apology for conjugal love must in fact be seen as quite original and persuasive for a time when marriage was often no more than a feudal contract in which little account was taken of the woman's consent. Chrétien was patently capable, then, of withstanding the clannish prejudices of courtly society. His greatest merits as a moralist are doubtless his depictions of conjugal devotion and his celebrations of total marital mutuality, characterized as a marriage of minds in which rights and duties are shared, in which happiness must be won unselfishly, and in which love and chivalry must correspond.

Like that of love, the chivalric ethos is revitalized in each romance, also moving in an ascending rhythm, gradually unfolding an ever nobler ideal. Unlike the epic hero, the Arthurian hero is above all associated with individual prowess. In Chrétien's works, he fights neither for house, nor king, nor religion. (Alexander, of course, in the beginning of **Cligés,** who defends King Arthur, proves the rule.) Residing in an indeterminate and fabulous Britain, without a formal frame of reference and, in a way, prefiguring the knight-errant, he seems more a champion of civilization in opposition to barbarism. But the Arthurian hero seeks *adventure* first of all to try himself, to increase his worth, and to join the virtual with the real while succumbing to the charm of the marvelous. There is in all this a certain virtuosity beguiled by fame won in tourneys, which Chrétien describes with graphic vitality, especially at the opening of **Yvain,** but which is only a prelude to a still loftier image of knighthood. Expansive because of some inner torments or because they are conscious of missions, his heroes, his knights of the right, will come to defend the weak and deliver the oppressed, an ideal remarkably exalted in Chrétien's last three romances. Erec accomplished only a single act of prowess, namely, the liberation of the pathetic prisoner from two giants. Lancelot, Yvain, and Perceval represent at once a more militant and rueful notion of chivalry, given to self-sacrifice, to a kind of sainthood. This quasi-religious concept in itself will elevate Lancelot and Perceval to the status of predestined heroes, although Chrétien's moral hierarchy abhors asperity, for he prefers multifarious psychological depiction.

Chrétien's artful depiction is not limited to primary char-

acters: surrounding the hero, a number of varied episodic roles sustain and stir the illusion of life. From scene to scene, from one romance to the next, without contrivance and as if by the mere movement of the narrative, the tableau of a whole society is pieced together. While Chrétien's manner is quite unlike that of Balzac, it would not be inaccurate to designate his work as a twelfth-century *Human Comedy,* for, like Balzac's novels, his poems are peopled with characters inseparable from their social conditions, and they are not always condensed from the upper strata. By means of a widening perspective, noticeable especially in **Yvain** and **Perceval,** Chrétien's sights fall on townsmen and peasants and on contemporary political and economic realities. Finally, with the world of Arthurian story, in which the author's imagination seems to move naturally, Chrétien spins a vast, seamless web, a human comedy in which time meets space and whole biographies are elaborated. And it is most curious, to say the least, that Chrétien, in his successive romances, employs well before the "frantic glutton for life" the technique of recurring characters.

His use of it, of course, involves especially the somewhat official representatives of continuity, those of the Round Table, King Arthur, Queen Guenevere, and Kay the seneschal, as well as the king's nephew and counselor, Gawain. Chrétien clearly took particular delight in the last named, whose portrait is limned to completion as each poem unfolds. Less admired in the **Lancelot** or **Perceval** (by whose disconcerting heroes he is eclipsed) than in **Erec** or **Yvain,** Gawain remains throughout the soul of courtesy, elegance, liberality, and bravura. A knight is ranked by jousting with him, for never did he suffer defeat in battle, unless, like Yvain, you could equal him. To him more than to any other belongs the honorific "my lord," a title that soon became his alone, like a mark of distinction. My lord Gawain is also a worldly knight and a ladies' man who, of course, has no thoughts or time for marriage—love's butterfly cares not to alienate his liberty. His code of life, which he gladly expounds to his friend Yvain threatened by *recreantise,* is a mixture of sporty, chivalric energy and epicurean wisdom, an economy of amorous pleasures stimulated by interruptions and kept up by delays: " 'Pleasures grow sweeter through postponement; and a little pleasure, when delayed, is much sweeter to the taste than a great pleasure enjoyed at once. The sweets of a love which develops late are like a fire in a green bush; for the longer one delays in lighting it the greater will be the heat it yields, and the longer will endure its force' " (**Yvain,** vv. 2515-23). The antithesis of the noble, refined, desultory, and sometimes bemocked Gawain is the seneschal Kay, uncourteous, abusive, presumptuous, but zealous and faithful. Thus Chrétien controls and contrasts stress and silence, darkness and light in his undivine comedy.

Even though his artful sense of technique seems pervasive here, and even though the multiplicity of secondary characters is easily diversified and enlivened through fantasy and humor, Chrétien's guide nevertheless at all times is the study of mankind. Perhaps like La Bruyère later at Chantilly, at the court of Champagne he could doubtless sample humanity at will. Can we not assume that he was inspired by living models for his sketches, among many others, of Baudemagus, of Gornemant de Gohort, or Calogrenant? This latter, in fact, Chrétien turns into a discreet model of urbanity, a great knightly gentleman, detached enough to joke about his own misadventures at the fountain of Broceliande; by contrast, in the Welsh story of Owein (*The Lady of the Fountain*), the analogous character, Cynon, stands out rather because of his flashy fury. But to this same Calogrenant, amazed by such ugliness, and curious as to what kind of creature he is, the monstrous churl, busy watching wild bulls, answers in stout simplicity: " 'I am a man' " (line 330). How robust and profound a statement, for immediately it links the cultivated mortal Calogrenant to the teratological oaf, a character behind whose frame lurk the shadows of man's fate. The villein's response would be a fitting epigraph to Chrétien's whole fictional output, in which he ever offers a portrayal of man.

This portrayal is clearly seconded by diverse situations and a graphic handling of attitudes and gestures, but is not limited to a sparkling parade of superficial characters. Even in a quick character sketch, his gift of catching the latent comes through. Undeniable as well is his talent as psychological analyst of love, especially versatile in laying open the mysteries of the female heart. With each, from Enide to Clarissant, the last in his lively procession of heroines, he holds up the mirror to a new facet of love.

Chrétien has been sometimes belittled for his cool, superficial manner, or for his overly witty, jejune style. In a sense, these criticisms are justified; Chrétien is less emotional than intellectual. Though more awkward, Thomas of England's probes of Tristan's amorous anguish are more forceful and penetrating; his empathy with the hero is more intimate. True, Chrétien can engage interest and sympathy for his favorite characters, but almost always, at some point, he turns or steps back, and seems faintly amused by them. Is this necessarily a shortcoming, however? Rather, this hindsight is beneficial for comical and humorous effects, as well as for the study of characters. For this loss of emotional power we are compensated by a gain in lucidity.

Contrary to certain claims, he does not altogether avoid tempestuous passions, yet he prefers to circumvent the storm rather than to cross it: he strikes sail just long enough to describe Lancelot's despair, Guenevere's remorse, or Yvain's folly. He only once represents the pangs of jealousy—in the Proud Knight of the Glade—who believes his mistress unfaithful and is haunted by a real image of betrayal (*Conte du Graal,* vv. 3855-76). Although Ovidian in inspiration (*Ars amatoria,* l: 661-78), Chrétien retouches the theme with originality: as articulated pointedly by the jealous one, the Latin sermon, by variation, acquires dramatic force and the terseness of a watercolor.

Chrétien is at his delightful best in slow-motion scenes of lovers, startled or troubled by thoughts of love, who seek self-understanding. Shades of feeling and deep-seated contradictions Chrétien thus unravels concisely; such depictions are all part of his quest and transcription of human truths. And it is upon these that is predicated his heady penchant for somewhat theoretical debates. A similar tendency reduces psychological analysis to examinations of

inner conflict and cases of conscience, although introspection by a given personage usually concludes with a rational and deliberate decision. For this reason, many critics have recognized in Chrétien a foreshadowing of classical style and expression.

In *Cligés,* for example, even though conventional mannerisms are not avoided, order and clarity temper the speed of monologues and the direction of dialogue, so that the palpable is never hidden by excessive logic or stiffness. But Chrétien's mature experience in matters of life and of technique doubtless enable him to find more buoyant procedures. And he often attains that ethereal moment when his narrative technique disappears completely, when characterization and sentiment are transposed, without artifice, by means of verbal and tonal modulation: then it is that we can not only visualize, but also hear the characters through Chrétien's living words.

Yet another innovation is achieved because of Chrétien's regard for reason and free will; he does not fail to appreciate the importance of affective states or the role of the subconscious. With his deft and pervasive psychological method, he explores or at least alludes to those half-hidden mental states in which free will falters, in which illusions seek shelter, and in which dreams suppress reality. In Alexander's monologue, for example, the excessively subtle, hypertrophic imagery is not just part of some literary game, for, through it, a cause and effect relationship is established between the lover's timidity, the avowal repressed by passion, and his obsessive delirium (*Cligés,* vv. 536-38, 602-8, 627-28, 654-57, 2282-83). Elsewhere appears the phenomenon whereby, once cued, Laudine demonstrates to herself that she does not have the right to hate her husband's slayer, that she could even love him (by a kind of auto-suggestion, ostensibly defined by the witty progression of "the bush which only smokes with the flame beneath, until someone blows it or stirs it up," *Yvain,* 1778-80). Lunete's words are the first spark; then, unknown to Laudine, an inner process causes smoke, in other words, anger, her indignant reaction, as well as the rationalizations hiding the reality of her new feelings; and the flame that dissipates the smoke is her increasingly stronger desire to remarry. With a light but positive touch, Chrétien could depict the hidden harmony between confused affections and the self-deluding intellect. Also related to the handling of subconscious states are the rapturous ecstasies of Lancelot and Perceval, or Lancelot's hallucinatory lions at the end of the sword-bridge. It was truly a stroke of genius to associate such observations with the portrayal of exemplary heroes and with their growing consciousness as part of their personality development.

Chrétien's gifts as moralist and psychologist have not always received their full due, but there is unanimity regarding his admirable imagination and talent as a writer.

He was a born artist no doubt, yet he manifestly enhanced his competence through study and reflection. The pervasive influence of education, of the arts of rhetoric, and of the humanist tradition reminds us that his work cannot be dissociated from a whole literary movement. His poetics of the romance genre are not altogether his own: other courtly authors betray analogous tendencies. With a phrase like *dire en uni* ("to keep to one account," "to collect, gather [material]"), Thomas of England, for instance, expressed in his own way a concern for logic and coherence not unlike Chrétien's *conjointure.* However, by his sense of proportion and equilibrium, Chrétien stands out among contemporary narrators, none of whom combined the internal harmony of *matière, conjointure,* and *sen*—a disparity arising either from the content itself, or from individual excellence, or both. In any case, Chrétien's artful accomplishment alone may be duly compared to the cup given as a reward to Alexander by King Arthur (*Cligés,* vv. 1536-46, 2214-15). Very fine and rich first because it was of gold, it is more esteemed because of the workmanship—the artist's expertise—and, still again, in truth, of most value because of the precious decorative stones set outside it. One might say that through this praise the author wished to enfold within its graduations his conception of romance. Does not the hierarchy of three elements seem to correspond to that of *matière:* one must be able to select a potentially obliging subject; of *form,* without which there is no true creation; and, finally, of *sen,* which illuminates the entire work, like the precious gems that give the trophy its superb dazzle?

In *Erec, Yvain,* and even the *Conte du Graal,* certain parallelisms of plot indicate a deliberate preference for a specific type of structure. The schema, perfected in Chrétien's first Arthurian romance, is characterized by a tripartite composition: a first adventure concludes with the mutual bliss of hero and heroine; then a crisis emerges to link an interior, psychological drama to a moral and social conflict and causes the action to rebound. The third part of the triptych is larger, consisting of a progression of adventures, of which, one most mysterious and marvelous expands the hero's role and ends happily with the reconciliation of the lovers. This methodical pattern is pliant enough to permit variations, but from poem to poem its general features are identifiable. Moreover, in every case thematic or cognate analogies divide the schema, although their order may be altered; examples include the preponderant role of the Arthurian court in the economy of the narrative (the *locus* from which the hero departs or to which he returns, by which he is sought or met); lodging with the hospitable host; battle with a Red Knight, insults avenged; and the passion of a marvelous fairy or of a most beautiful woman. Furthermore, judging from a comparison with the Welsh romances *Gereint Son of Erbin, The Lady of the Fountain,* and *Peredur Son of Efrawg,* it seems likely that Chrétien took the initial framework of his romances from his sources. His innovation was to organize with skill and cogency a yet rough diamond, to cut from it a still latent or virtual form (*conjointure*). With restriction and depth, he augments, like classical writers, the dramatic and psychological interest of the subject; he interrelates convincingly outer behavior and inner motivation, thereby seeking to create an entity in which everything dovetails. Thus he transforms the "tale of adventure" into romance. Chrétien can also implement rhetorical doctrines with great skill. In *Cligés,* he emulates Thomas's *Tristan,* applying studiously the method of "bipartition" recommended by the *artes poeticae* (manuals of poetics and rhetoric): he gives first the story of the parents, Alexander and Soredamors, which takes up almost one-third of the narrative

before the son is introduced. However, in the *Lancelot, Yvain,* and *The Story of the Grail* he ingeniously shifts the principle of dualism to the partial parallelism of the adventures by making of Gawain a "brilliant second" in relation to the main hero. It may be noted that in the manuals of rhetoric, elegant and graceful style—a quality everywhere manifest in Chrétien's works—is praised. But was such a style derived solely from poetic doctrines? Though not worthless, the influence of his pedagogical formation cannot report to us about his personal talents, about the secrets of his craft, or about his charming manner as storyteller and poet.

Chrétien is first of all a master of rapidity. He narrates effortlessly, seemingly without deliberation. From *Cligés* we select one sample among many of his incredibly buoyant methods of introducing characters. As Alexander arrives at King Arthur's court, and the king is ready to sail for Brittany, no mention has yet been made of the heroine. But lines 420-21 tell specifically of Alexander's awesome liberality, so much so " . . . that the king, the queen, and the nobles bear him great affection." In this way, Guenevere enters on stage. After fifteen lines, the maidens of honor appear: " . . . King Arthur set out the next day, accompanied by the queen and her damsels" (vv. 436-37). Eight lines later, Soredamors is presented: "Into the ship in which the king sailed there entered no youth or maiden save only Alexander and Soredamors, whom the Queen brought with her. This maiden was scornful of love . . . " (vv. 441-46). Thus the story slides along with ease, moving toward the depiction of nascent love. With this skillful and agile narration Chrétien means to hold our interest through sustained enigmas and surprises. Long before authors of detective stories used the technique, Chrétien delights in delayed explanations, which entail to some extent the introduction of *suspense*—especially in the *Lancelot* and *Le Conte du Graal*—effected by mingling mystery with mystification. Along these lines, then, is another aspect of his craft, the deliberate narrative tempo, accelerated or slackened at will, like the analyses in free indirect discourse which alternate smoothly and rhythmically with direct narration. Following Calogrenant's retrospective flashback narrating details of his journey to the fountain of Broceliande, we learn of Yvain's impetuous rush to adventure, during which time the same series unfolds, but episode and image are abbreviated according to a precipitous cadence to translate the hero's impatience.

To the diversity of narrative movement must be added Chrétien's even more subtle tonal variegation. The almost imperceptible shift from the serious to the pleasant, or from the tender to the ironic, produces a kind of iridescence not unmindful of the ethereal games of nuance by La Fontaine—whose manner, in fact, in "The Bear and His Two Companions," for instance, seems foreshadowed in form and content by the fablelike scene in *Erec,* in which five thieving knights divide the coveted booty before attacking (vv. 2925-58). Chrétien's tonal changes easily lend themselves to humorous treatment; sometimes while relating high adventure or amorous drama he secretly amuses himself: the witty thought, the pointed trifle, the incisive "I think" or "it seems to me," and some verbal fantasies and puns are all characteristic stylistic signals of his intimate diversion, though the reader's share is balanced by many authorial smiles and winks of complicity. It must be understood that this detached manner and discreet freedom with humor in no way compromises the beauty of the story or the grandeur of the hero; rather, like an intellectual accompaniment, it adds to the narrative flavor and is necessary in fact for ethical distance. Sometimes also a more intense, objective humor emerges from the situations themselves or from characterization. Finally, let us note that in the **Knight with the Lion** and **Perceval,** he betrays a propensity for farce and caricature.

All combined, these diverse effects, controlled surprises, assorted tones, and the blend of tragic and ironic, leave an impression of virtuosity, of a kind of verbal acrobatics inherited perhaps from the study of dialectics. In this way Chrétien is able to perform brilliant, moving, though gratuitous variations on the related themes of feigned death and thwarted suicide. Enide, believing Erec dead and herself guilty for it, is on the verge of suicide until restrained by the count of Limors and his people. The two themes reappear with slight modification in **Cligés** (vv. 6220-84) and **Lancelot** (vv. 4175-440). Derivation from *Piramus et Tisbé* is quite apparent, but Chrétien suppresses the tragic conclusion and never lets his heroes die. This paradoxical pathos, based on error caught in the nick of time, culminates with a fourth variation in **Yvain,** when the personage ostensibly ready for suicide is none other than the lion. One might complain of parody here were it not for Chrétien's real capacity to balance off emotion and humor. Returning by chance to the fountain beneath the pine tree, Yvain swoons in sorrow, mindful of his former happiness. In falling, his sword slips out and pierces his neck. At the sight of blood, the lion " . . . thinks that he sees his master and companion dead." In despair he will kill himself by rushing on the sword which he has taken up in jaws and placed on a fallen log, with the point up, handle steadied against a tree trunk. At the eleventh hour, Yvain recovers and the noble beast restrains his fatal leap (**Yvain,** vv. 3485-525). It is hard to resist a smile here, and yet the lion's conduct echoes that of Enide, the most devoted and most touching of Chrétien's heroines.

As if a cross between something from the bestiaries and from the fairy world, this humanized lion alone proves how much room for articulation our author leaves himself in dealing with the marvelous. But, however aware that a legendary atmosphere fascinates, Chrétien carries off in his romances a poetic impression of spatial and temporal distancing. Doubtless reaching him in a more or less deteriorated state, the fabulous tales, the subjects of which, by adding moral and psychological interest, he created from within, on occasion lose something of their original coherence. But we must not, as others have often done, rush to charge him with absurd and uncontrolled primitive marvels, or with contradictory improbabilities in his narrative. For Chrétien's artful storytelling must include the strange and the unexplained, inasmuch as his audience expected bewilderment, intrigue, and escape. Is it really credible that, imprisoned with her lover, Mabonagrain, the damsel of the enchanted orchard, suddenly turns out to be Enide's cousin? Can we accept without hesitation the fact that Guenevere also had to cross either the sword-bridge or the water bridge—the only access to the kingdom of Gorre? But logic fails next to mysterious otherworld adventures. However Chrétien adapted the mythical to twelfth-century civilization, the inconsistencies of the narrative seem in part deliberate, suggestive again of the imaginary, the poetic, the ambiguous realm beyond. Certain blurs of *chiaroscuro* between the supernatural and some logical explanation are met particularly in **The Knight of the Cart** and **The Story of the Grail.**

As if at play Chrétien marries the extraordinary tale to observations of reality. Concrete details, small facts, or sketches relating to social and material life—castles, furniture, clothing, arms, hunting, feasting, tourneying, and feudal customs—continually inject familiar, human truths into the magical atmosphere. This unartificial union does not jeopardize, but materializes the marvelous. Notable, too, is that as an episode increases in fantasy, realistic traits accumulate proportionately—such as in **The Story of the Grail.**

Such realism is, in fact, habitually graphic and salient. Chrétien's power of description is expressive, exact, and unusually varied. For example, depiction of myriad battles is as integral to romance as to epic (although collective battles are the exception in romances of adventure). Chrétien's accomplishment in the literary order is an act of prowess indeed, so much is he capable, throughout his whole work, of diversity in wielding the ordeals of the joust and clash of arms. Wace had already broken the tradition of conventional schemata in epic descriptions, but Chrétien outdistanced him by direct observation of attitude and movement, though he did not turn altogether from doctrinal precepts regarding *the* brilliant ornament, *descriptio.* In particular, the *artes poeticae* had rhetorical principles for "descriptions of people," whereby, it was taught, one must present in descending order, detail by detail, from head to toe, the physiognomy of characters. For his portrait of Philomena, Chrétien applies these formulas, as well as for the more subtle portrayals of Enide and Cligés. But in truth, beginning with **Erec,** he seems to sense the danger, if not the absurdity, of fashionable descriptive themes, which often become awkward or tedious in narration. He refuses to describe Enide's chamber in King Evrain's dwelling (vv. 5570-79) or to enumerate the food served at Erec's coronation (vv. 6939-43). Similarly, in **Cligés,** he omits a dubbing scene: " . . . now that they are knights I will say no more of them . . . " (line 1209). He refuses to relate in detail the splendrous wedding feast of Alexander and Soredamors (vv. 2358-60) or the celebration for the betrothal of Emperor Alis and Fenice (vv. 3245-47). Elsewhere he boasts of not tarrying over useless specifics (vv. 4636-39, 5137-39). He wittily avoids a minute portrait of Fenice, which he paints by not painting it, confessing in malicious modesty that he finds himself unable to represent such beauty: " . . . for if I should live a thousand years, and if my skill were to double every day, yet should I waste all my time in trying to tell the truth about her" (vv. 2732-41). Such remarks are obviously directed at his rivals, and sometimes at himself—for he too is sometimes guilty of the fault, yet the barbs characterize his quite personal conception and practice in matters of style.

Part of his original manner, in fact, consists of replacing stylized and continuous description with brief, picturesque traits, matching the narrative in a functional way. These light, selective touches are felt at the proper moment by their dramatic and ethical significance. The story thus becomes a moving description, often subjective, because everything appears as if seen through the eyes of the characters. This impressionistic style is noticeable as early as **Erec** and dominates the three last romances. Instead of the usual inventory-portrait, for example, how much human life is everywhere manifest at the funeral of Esclados the Red; how much human truth is apparent in the successive tableaux, the varying attitudes in which Laudine's beauty is reflected in the ever more amorous gaze of Yvain!

During the brief moments of respite from her vehement mourning, the young widow " . . . reads her psalms in her gilt-lettered psalter" (vv. 1414-15). The reader has guessed that the lover is less interested in the book than in the beautiful hands holding it; yet the brilliant, illuminated letters cannot escape his attention. This small detail of light and color simultaneously communicates Yvain's visual impression and awakens the narrative. Chrétien is also a master at setting the descriptive trait, but not only as a miniaturist who reproduces tiny facets of reality or sketches a line, gesture, or movement; he can also mount a whole scene, control lighting or perspective, and give life to an entire fresco (e.g., the tournament of Noauz in **Lancelot,** vv. 5786-844, or the Grail procession, vv. 3190-343). To all this description the role of imagery is no less important. Sometimes the metaphors are a bit contrived, like the three different joys and honors won by Alexander in a single day, the town of Windsor, the best kingdom in Wales, and the hand of Soredamors, " . . . the greatest joy of all was the third—that his sweetheart was queen of the chessboard where he was king" (**Cligés,** vv. 2371-73). Sometimes, less ingenious, a simile may smack of simplicity, like the "nag" that is "as fat and round as an apple" (**Lancelot,** line 2299); or, when Yvain is healed from his folly by a marvelous ointment, he is quite amazed to find himself "as naked as ivory" (**Yvain,** line 3020); to defend the lion the hero attacks the serpent shooting fire from its open throat, "which was larger than a pot" (line 3368). Often a comparison is amplified to take on grandiose epic rhythms, such as in this passage drawn from the single combat between Cligés and the duke of Saxony (**Cligés,** vv. 4070-79):

> *As espees notent un lai*
> *Sor les hiaumes qui retantissent,*
> *Si que lor janz s'an esbaïssent,*
> *Et sanble a ces qui les esgardent,*
> *Que li hiaume espraingnent et ardent.*
> *Et quant les espees resaillent,*
> *Estanceles ardanz an saillent*
> *Ausi come de fer qui fume,*
> *Que li fevres bat sor l'anclume*
> *Quant il le tret de la favarge.*

("Upon their resonant helmets they play such a tune [lai] with their swords that it seems to those who are looking on that the helmets are on fire and send forth sparks. And when the swords rebound in air, gleaming sparks fly off from them

as if from a smoking piece of iron which the smith beats upon his anvil after drawing it from the forge," trans. by W.W. Comfort.)

In all battle descriptions, there was nothing original in the banal evocation of lance shocks upon arms or the clicking of swords. The image of sparks around the helmet is found as early as the *Chanson de Roland* (line 3586; *"Des helmes clers li fous en escarbunet,"* "And fiery sparks come flashing from their helms," trans. by P. Terry). Chrétien artfully rejuvenates these conventions, but first we observe the affectation of assimilating to the tumultuous cadence of swords a *lai*—a word which must be taken here in the sense of "musical composition" executed on the Celtic harp—an excessively subtle metaphor that nevertheless seems to imbue the battle with a lyrical and humorous quality. On the other hand, the comparison between sparks shooting from helmets and red iron struck on the anvil introduces a forceful and familiar realism; and the powerful sonority of the lines emphasizes the descriptive brilliance. No northern poet before Chrétien could match such style.

His literary generation understood the importance of art; more and more consciously they would interrelate poetic creation with language and expression, the instruments of poetry. Cultivated courtly society, more so than the audience of the *chansons de geste,* appreciates now variety and purity in vocabulary, brilliance and clarity in syntax—in a word, elegant style. It is at this time that the idea of "good French" begins to emerge, a formula implying esthetic awareness, doubtless predicated upon the existence of a literary language based, for the most part, on the Ile-de-France dialect (i.e., Parisian). However that may be, Huon de Méri, in the thirteenth century, credited our author with spreading abroad "good French by the handful." Chrétien is without peer for his manipulation of the French language at this period: he exploited to the full its resources of precision, logic, harmony, and plasticity.

Chrétien was a craftsman with words. He displays an extensive vocabulary, filled with the right words and carefully chosen images, chancing sometimes the felicitous but daring expression. Even in syntactic innovations he excels: he was apparently the first to use temporally the conjunction *que que,* "during"—usually "although." One may sympathize with the need he felt to forge new syntactic tools: the octosyllable line carried with difficulty the many temporal locutions of the language (e.g., *dementres que, endementres que, endementiers que, parmi tot ce que,* "while"), quite suited to the epic decasyllable, but cumbersome in the lighter verse of romance and contrary to its vivid style. Similarly, Chrétien expeditiously introduced the usage of *lors que* "while" to bend grammar to artistic needs, and at a time when an able writer could do so without blame. The respective tense values, hardly differentiated in the twelfth century, are particularized in his works, in accord with the various narrative levels and ethical nuances [Tatiana Fotitch, *The Narrative Tenses in Chrétien de Troyes,* 1950]. Chrétien also understood the use of full periods, while marking off subordinate relationships clearly.

His originality is no less manifest in his use of the rhetorical "color" or figure, from the manuals of poetics, called *annominatio:* "It consists of repeating nearly the same word while changing only one or two letters, . . . or again of associating words having the same form but semantically different" [Edmond Faral, *Les Arts poétiques du XII et du XIII siècle,* 1923]. Such reproduction of words and sounds is often no more than verbal artifice, something by which Chrétien himself was fascinated; but three passages in *Cligés* reveal a fruitful use of the figure. As Alexander and his companions enter the ship, about to sail for Britain, their relatives and friends climb a hill near the beach to watch the ship's departure.

> *D'iluec esgardent lor enui*
> *Tant com il le pueent veoir.*
> *Lor enui esgardent por voir;*
> *Que del vaslet mout lor enuie.*
>
> (vv. 264-67)

("From here they sadly gaze, as long as their eyes can follow them. With sorrow indeed, they watch them go, being solicitous for the youths . . . ," trans. by Comfort.)

Mindful of Wace's manner, the *annominatio* is here linked by chiasmus—*esgardent: lor enui: lor enui esgardent*—as if psychologically bound to the parting emotions of sadness, worry, and regret. Elsewhere in *Cligés,* Count Angrés and his knights, surrounded at Windsor, will try a nocturnal sally, hoping to surprise Arthur's army in the shadows. To punish them, God "illuminated the darkness" and caused the moon to rise.

> *Mout lor est la lune nuisanz,*
> *Qui luist sor les escuz luisanz,*
> *Et li hiaume mout lor renuient,*
> *Qui contre la lune reluisent.*
>
> (vv. 1713-16)

("They are much hampered by the moon, as it shines upon their shields, and they are handicapped by their helmets, too, as they glitter in the moonlight," trans. by Comfort.)

Once again, the figure seems to fit the mood of vexation, an impression confirmed by the third passage: Cligés, an exile in Britain, hopes in vain to forget Fenice, but is so preoccupied with memories of her that he decides to return to Greece:

> *Que trop a fet grant consirree*
> *De vëoir la plus desirree*
> *Qu'onques nus poïst desirrer.*
> *Ne s'en voudra plus consirrer.*
>
> (vv. 5077-80)

(" . . . for he has been deprived too long of the sight of the most desired lady who was ever desired by anyone. He will not prolong this privation . . . ," trans. by Comfort.)

The disposition and variation of the rhyme words function here to modulate love's nostalgic obsession.

From the collocation of these three examples, it is quite patent that *Cligés* represents a loosening of *annominatio* from its scholarly matrix; three lines from *Yvain* prove further Chrétien's increasing success in this regard. A damsel, in search of Yvain, is lost in a deep wood on a rainy night; she hastens to find shelter:

> *Et la nuiz et li bois li font*
> *Grant enui, mes plus li enuie*
> *Que li bois ne la nuiz, la pluie.*
>
> (vv. 4844-46)

("The night and the woods cause her great distress, but she is more tormented by the rain than by either the woods or the night," trans. by Comfort.)

Once again, we have a chiasmus: *la nuiz et li bois: li bois ne la nuiz.* But the perfection of this *annominatio* may be ascribed to the exquisite accord of consonants and vowels, suggesting both the dripping rain and damsel's distress: Chrétien the poet elevates rhetoric to music.

A prestigious storyteller, a talented romancer, he charms us also with his supple and brilliant versification. Routinely, he uses the broken couplet, a technique whereby lines connected by rhyme are dissociated from the same sentence both in syntax and in meaning. This rarely found freedom—until Chrétien's exercise of it—avoids the monotonous octosyllabic hum and provides added rhythmical combinations while inaugurating delicate stops in the narrative. Nor will Chrétien hesitate to break the unity of the octosyllable, that tenuous line with no caesura, but upon which he confers rhythm and harmony through expressive placement of words, through frequent and diverse rests and run-on lines, which themselves sometimes speed up or decelerate the cadence. Such graphic little surprises in the verse transmit gestures, intonations, and movements of thought and of the heart. Meshing with the variety of rhythms is his art of attuning rhyme, whereby consonants and vowels are disposed musically. For instance, the reiterated liquids *l* and *r* intensify the freshness and fluidity in the evocative line depicting the spring beneath the pine tree in the forest of Broceliande: *Ombre li fet li plus biaus arbres* ("It is shadowed by the fairest tree . . . ," *Yvain,* line 382). Later, light, sonorous tappings are amplified: *Sonent flaütes et fresteles, Timbre, tabletes et tabor* (" . . . flutes and pipes are played, kettle drums, drums and cymbals . . . ," *Yvain,* vv. 2352-53); or at the entrance of the lodging, the echoing steps: *Le pont et la porte passames* (" . . . we crossed the bridge, and passing through the gate . . . ," *Yvain,* line 210). Elsewhere in *Yvain,* clear vowels harmonize with the calm after the storm: *Et quant je vi l'er cler et pur* "And when I saw the air clear and serene . . . ," line 455). It would not be difficult to augment this list of paintings in sound.

Chrétien is an effortless poet who never sacrifices the meaning or tortures syntax for the sake of homophony. His rapid narrative sometimes permits sufficient, even quite simple rhyme, but he can also, with considerable virtuosity, catch unexpected, rich, yet unforced rhymes. Here and there, dexterity is sprinkled with contrivance, and, like others, Chrétien was also often given to padding, though he seems to excuse himself with good humor. Everything about his style and expression reveals his delight in following the imaginary poetic adventures of his heroes, in immortalizing Yvain, Lancelot, and Perceval.

To measure, insofar as possible, Chrétien's influence would require a long and minute study. Whether he was a leader of a school or not cannot be determined, although his fame appears considerable by the end of the twelfth century and throughout the thirteenth century. His charming stories were appreciated and his stylistic power—even its artifice—admired. Huon de Méri [, in *Le Tornoiemenz Antecrist,* 1888,] lavishes praise not only upon his expertise with "good French"; he adds the commendation that Chrétien de Troyes "was gifted and reputed for his craft" (*qui tant ot de pris de trover*)—that is, he excelled in literary invention. Huon was particularly impressed with the preciosity of *Cligés:* "Chrétien de Troyes wrote most ineffably of the heart transfixed by the arrow of Love shot through the eyes" (*Chrétien de Troyes dit miex Du cuer navré, du dart, des iex, Que je ne vos porroie dire*). But the influence of the author, represented here as an imposing master, was felt especially by numerous imitators, verse romancers who, for some fifty years later, all depended upon him directly or indirectly. They may often be unaware of his artful *conjointure,* but still borrow unsubtly from the elaborate model, myriad characters, situations, motives, and procedures. Whether in romance of adventure, of love, or of morals, or in works mingling, as he did, the marvelous and the real, Chrétien's preponderance is recognizable, even among those, like Jean Renart, phlegmatic toward the *matière de Bretagne.*

However, between *Erec* and *Perceval,* this very matter was so brilliantly ornamented that for two generations Arthurian verse romance flourished. Let us enumerate just a few of the grandiose titles: the *Continuations of the Grail Story, Guinglain* or the *Bel Inconnu, Chevalier aux deux épées, Fergus, Durmart le Gallois, Meraugis de Portlesguez, Vengeance Raguidel,* and *Gliglois.* The vogue continued on up to the fourteenth century, as evidenced by Jean Froissart's *Meliador.* With much banality and few innovations (with the possible exception of Raoul de Houdenc, author of *Meraugis*), this literary tradition follows in Chrétien's footsteps.

Meanwhile, with the Arthurian prose romance, born under a different esthetic star, nurtured around 1220-30, authors will amplify and order the Round Table adventures, progressively, around a central theme—the conflict of the courtly and religious ideals; while it combines within a vast, powerfully original skein the two heterogeneous legends of Lancelot and the Grail, it remains nevertheless largely indebted to Chrétien de Troyes.

The success of the *Prose Lancelot* will soon eclipse the master's reputation, whose work, however, was continuously copied and read in some fifteen manuscripts dating from about 1220 to the 1350s, and later (including four copies of *Erec,* three of *Cligés,* two of *Lancelot,* two of *Yvain,* and eight of *Perceval*). Thereafter, twelfth-century French becomes too difficult to understand, and prose adaptations begin to appear, assuring a momentary revival for *Cligés* and *Erec* (ca. 1454) and for *Perceval* (1530). But after this brief spurt, Chrétien became enshrouded, like so many others, in the so-called gothic shadows. During the sixteenth century, the erudite curiosities of Etienne Pasquier and Claude Fauchet, then the "troubadour"

genre, and later, the popular eighteenth-century romances of chivalry rescued him for a time from neglect. But an enormous critical undertaking was necessary during the second half of the nineteenth century, and it continues today, with the purpose of defining and redefining Chrétien's importance in literary history. And, of course, controversy as to the precise nature of his sources and as to the character of his talent will not end here.

But at a time when romance was only just groping for form, did he not impel this vital genre toward its extraordinary course in modern literature? This particular contribution seems all the more convincing as his work was so soon recognized and imitated beyond the borders of northern France. The *Erec* and *Iwein* of Hartmann von Aue and Wolfram von Eschenbach's *Parzival* comprise indeed the most splendid evidence for the European flowering of the *matière de Bretagne*—as fostered by the French genius, Chrétien de Troyes. (pp. 157-82)

> *Jean Frappier, in his* Chrétien de Troyes: The Man and His Work, *translated by Raymond J. Cormier, Ohio University Press, 1982, 241 p.*

Norris J. Lacy (essay date 1970)

[*Lacy is an American scholar of romance languages and literature whose works include* The Craft of Chrétien de Troyes: An Essay on Narrative Art *(1980) and* The Arthurian Handbook *(1987). In the essay below, he proposes that the lion in* Yvain *primarily serves as a symbol of Yvain's moral evolution, rather than as a symbol of Christ, as previous critics have maintained.*]

In the course of the **Chevalier au lion,** Yvain comes to the aid of a lion, and the animal follows him throughout the remainder of his adventures, serving him faithfully. This story clearly owes much to that of Androcles, but the function of Yvain's lion in the work itself is much less clear. Gaston Paris considered that it served no purpose at all [in *Mélanges de littérature française du Moyen Age,* (1910)], and later critics have seen it as a symbol of *courtoisie* or a representation of all of Yvain's opponents. In his important study on the subject in 1949 ["The Role of the Lion in Chrétien de Troyes' *Yvain,*" *PMLA,* LXIV], Professor Julian Harris advanced the argument that this lion is a symbol of Christ. First of all, that was the common symbolic meaning of the lion in the medieval Bestiaries. Moreover, as Harris points out, Yvain or someone else invokes the aid of God in each of the hero's combats after this episode. The conclusion is that Yvain is at last admitting the inadequacy of his mortal powers and his consequent need for aid from a higher source. We are thus witnessing the transformation of the perfect worldly knight into a highly religious knight, or of a courtly ethic into a religious one.

As provocative as Professor Harris's interpretation is, it nonetheless presents certain problems. For example, Yvain earns the animal's gratitude by saving his life, and we hardly expect to find Christ helping the hero because of a debt of gratitude. In addition, on more than one occasion, Yvain sends the lion aside and even beats him to insure that he will not intrude in the battle. Does Yvain not want or need God's help during these times? On the contrary, Harris explains that " . . . Yvain obviously has such faith that God will come to his aid that he is sure to win, come what may." The conclusion is curious: Yvain has such faith in God's aid that he excludes the symbol of that aid from those situations in which he most needs it.

It cannot be denied that the lion commonly represented Christ for the medieval reader; yet, it seems to me that this religious interpretation is perhaps not the fundamental one. I shall propose an alternate interpretation, which is suggested both by the lion's actions and by the structure and development of the work.

Early in the *roman,* Chrétien takes care to establish in our minds a parallel between Yvain and Gauvain. Yvain is the hero of the work and the knight who can avenge Calogrenant's defeat at the fountain, and Laudine marries him when Lunete convinces her that he who killed her husband must logically be the better man of the two. Gauvain, on the other hand, is presented as the epitome of knighthood, and Chrétien says of him:

> Cil, qui des chevaliers fu sire
> Et qui sor toz fu renomez,
> Doit bien estre solauz clamez.
> Por mon seignor Gauvain le di;
> Que de lui est tot autressi
> Chevalerie anluminee,
> Con li solauz la matinee
> Œvre ses rais et clarté rant
> Par toz les leus, ou il s'espant.
>
> (vss. 2400-08)

The parallel between the two knights is carried to greater length in the scene of the wedding feast; as Yvain has promised himself to Laudine, so Gauvain assures Lunete that he will be her knight, to come to her aid whenever she needs him. Finally, it is Gauvain who persuades his friend to leave with him to look for adventure, telling him that a knight should not cease to exercise his prowess just because he has given his love to a lady. During this entire section of the work, and particularly during the year's leave which Yvain takes from his wife, the two knights represent the same ideals—the exercise of valor and the pursuit of adventure for its own sake.

As long as the two remain together, there is little difference in their character. Soon, however, Yvain begins to distinguish himself from his friend, and Chrétien marks this divergence by separating them physically and recounting henceforth the adventures of Yvain, making only periodic references to Gauvain. Yvain's evolution begins immediately after his *folie.* He is no less valiant after this incident; if anything, his valor is increased. But the significant fact is that his strength and courage are now put to the service of others, and particularly of maidens in distress (vss. 4819-20), whereas Gauvain continues to think only of the thrill that adventure will bring him. The latter is not to be found when he is needed by those to whom he owes allegiance—first Lunete and later his own nephews and niece. In each of these instances Yvain comes to the aid of those in need. He continues to do so and thus develops until he is worthy of Laudine's forgiveness. At this

point he stands in strong contrast to Gauvain. This, then, is Gauvain's role in the work; he is at first morally indistinguishable from Yvain, and, since he undergoes no evolution, he remains for the reader a figure of what Yvain once was—a knight who sought adventure for its own sake, with little consideration of his obligations. Yvain does evolve, of course, and we see the emergence not so much of a religious ideal as of a new ideal of knighthood, the principles of which are responsibility and service.

Shortly after Gauvain leaves the scene the lion appears, and from that point on it is the animal, rather than Gauvain, which we see with Yvain. Thus, the hero simply exchanges one companion for another, and having noted the symbolic relationship between Gauvain and Yvain, we may reasonably seek a relationship of a similar nature between Yvain and the lion.

In any consideration of the animal's role, we should take into account not only the usual beliefs about lions (as Professor Harris has done), but also the characteristics peculiar to this one: his gratitude, devotion, and service to his master. For it is important to keep in mind that we are dealing not simply with a lion, but specifically with a *tamed* lion. This, it seems to me, is the key to the understanding of his basic role. A reader might well associate a lion either with Gauvain or with Yvain, for all three embody certain virtues, principally courage and strength. But if a lion is emblematic of courage and strength, then a *tamed* lion must suggest those traits subdued or, more precisely, put to use in the service of one who needs aid. And once this dimension is added to what we know of the lion, the identification with Gauvain is no longer possible, while that with Yvain is strengthened. For the lion represents not only courage and strength but also the ideals of devotion and service, ideals generally foreign to Gauvain but now actively pursued by the hero.

Like Gauvain, Yvain had first considered adventure a value and an end in itself, whereas he has now come to understand that, instead of leaving others to seek the thrill of adventure, he must undertake adventure precisely in order to serve others. The lion's constancy is evidence that the quest for adventure is not incompatible with devotion to a single person, as Gauvain had led his friend to believe. Yvain must now work to make himself worthy of Laudine's love, and from this point on he cannot pause in his search for a new reputation and identity. That this identity is symbolized by the lion is made evident not only by his literal association with the animal, but also by the very name by which he wishes henceforth to be known—*le Chevalier au lion.* The name is not casually chosen; during the second half of the romance, Yvain puts himself at the service of others, just as the lion at the same time puts himself in Yvain's service. The lion must then be the personification of his master's new purpose and resolve.

Thus, Gauvain and the lion can be seen as symbolic opposites, insofar as the former represents adventure for its own sake, and the latter, responsible adventure, or adventure undertaken in the service of others. As Yvain progresses chronologically through the work, he also progresses from an identification with Gauvain to an identification with the ideal which the lion represents.

As we read descriptions of the lion in the Bestiaries, it is not difficult to understand why it could symbolize Christ, for the King of Beasts quite logically represents the King of Men. It is the strongest, noblest, and most courageous of beasts. These are the features which make it a symbol of Christ; why do they not at the same time make it an apt figure of the knight, who sought to distinguish himself by strength, nobility, and courage? It is difficult to imagine that such as interpretation should not occur to a medieval reader of chivalric romances. But the essential point is that this particular lion corresponds not to what Gauvain was, but to what Yvain has become.

Yvain's evolution is principally a moral rather than religious development, although he quite naturally serves God and the cause of right at the same time as he serves his lady and others in need. There is clearly a religious dimension added to Yvain's character, and it would be altogether possible for a medieval reader to interpret the lion as a religious symbol. Yet, such an interpretation does not impose itself as the sole or basic one, and in my opinion the animal should be seen *first* as a personification of Yvain's ideal—responsibility, devotion, and service—rather than as a symbol of Christ. (pp. 198-202)

Norris J. Lacy, "Yvain's Evolution and the Role of the Lion," in Romance Notes, *Vol. XII, No. 1, Autumn, 1970, pp. 198-202.*

Richard L. Michener   (essay date 1970)

[*In the excerpt below, Michener explores the evolution of Chrétien's treatment of courtly love and its demands in his romances, focusing especially on* Erec and Enide *and* Yvain.]

Nearly all critics of Chrétien de Troyes agree that in his poetry there is a progression from a form mainly comprised of epic elements to a style definitive in the composition of courtly romance. C. S. Lewis claims [in *The Allegory of Love,* 1936] that he is able "to trace, in this distance between *Erec* and *Lancelot,* the extent of the emotional revolution which was taking place in his audience." L. Cazamian goes on to say that Chrétien "in his main works takes the lead toward new motives of interest . . . His scenes of life-like realism make more and more room for marvelous episodes, adding to the excitement of adventure the glamour of fairy tales" [*A History of French Literature,* 1955]. But many critics deplore this increased emphasis on romantic and fanciful motifs. W. P. Ker grudgingly admits that Chrétien's work "is not, like some affected kinds of romance, entirely cut off from reality." He adds, however, that "the glimpses of the real world are occasional and short; there is a flash of pure daylight, a breath of fresh air, and then the heavy-laden enchanted mists come rolling down and shut off the view." [*Epic and Romance,* 1908].

Whatever their individual judgments, critics take for granted that Chrétien's works turn away from courageous action and brutal combat to a self-portrayal of domestic knighthood in its mores and ideals, in which external forms of conduct are examined in leisurely fashion. Yet surprisingly little scholarship has surveyed the specific ways in which the various elements of the code of courtly love come to color and finally to dominate his stories, especially as regards characterization. Therefore, it is worthwhile to scrutinize an unexplored yet crucial aspect of his romances, namely, his use of the "Demande d'Amour," the question of love, "the famous monologues in which the person in love debates with himself or herself the probability or improbability of a return of affection from a loved one." [F. E. Guyer, *Chrétien de Troyes: Inventor of the Modern Novel,* 1957]. Such an approach is particularly relevant because Chrétien's contribution to the genre is the self-analysis of the symptoms and effects of love after Ovid's treatment of it as a disease, warfare or torment inflicted by a domineering man or woman upon a subservient partner.

It is notable, first of all, that the painful problems thrashed out in the various monologues are increasingly the result of a cruel streak in the beloved. In addition, the question is used to point up the characters of the lovers at a critical moment, so that Jessie Crosland states [in *Medieval French Literature,* 1955,] that "we might with justice call Chrétien the great exponent of the 'question dilemmatique'." Eric Auerbach goes so far as to say that "these anti-thetical reasonings over the emotions involved [are] seemingly naive yet of accomplished artistry and grace." [*Mimesis: the Representation of Reality in Western Literature,* 1953]. But Crosland qualifies her praise by noting that this process of introspection is "one of the most artificial sides of Chrétien's writing which must have been one of his concessions to the taste of the times and to his predominately female audience." Thus, the question of love can be used to gauge the nature and the extent of the artistic transformation apparent in his four Arthurian romances: *Erec et Enide, Cligés, Yvain* and *Lancelot.*

Erec et Enide evidences its early composition by its many holdovers from epic material and by its lack of romantic elements found in his later poems. Guyer thinks that "the omission of courtly love from the first romance is evident from the initial meeting of Erec and Enide, who is the daughter of a poor nobleman." Indeed, the story describes neither mental torment nor physical anguish on the part of either spouse regarding love itself. The very marriage of the two is outside the code of courtly romance, although "as far as the refinements of life are concerned—rich and brilliant externals, careful etiquette and polished manners—these are already given prominence . . . " [J. D. Bruce, *The Evolution of Arthurian Romance from the Beginnings to the year 1300,* 1928]. It is apparent that Chrétien was not yet inclined to portray love as the crucial factor in human existence, that he had not yet been touched deeply by the spirit of *amour courtois* that was to occupy him in his later works, particularly under the influence of Marie de Champagne. This deficiency is further illustrated by the low estate of women, the lack of esteem in which they are held, as especially reflected in the series of questions of love. Most of these are concerned with only a single dilemma which, significantly, represents the pain and frustration of the female rather than the male. As a means of testing his wife while undertaking a perilous journey to redeem his reputation as a knight, Erec forbids her to address him, even though she espies many dangers of which her husband should be aware. Probably the best example of this circumstance occurs when Enide notes the rapid approach of five hostile knights and then soliloquizes:

> 'Alas,' said she, 'I know not what to say or do; for my Lord severely threatens me, and says that he will punish me, if I speak a word to him . . . ' Then she softly calls to him, 'Sire!' 'What,' says he, 'what do you want?' 'I want to tell you that five knights have emerged from yonder thicket, of whom I am in mortal fear . . . ' Erec replies: 'You had an evil thought when you transgressed my command . . . , your service has been ill-employed; for it has not awakened my gratitude, but has rather kindled the more my ire.'

Thus, C. S. Lewis seems justified when he remarks on "the inherent brutality of the theme." The plot belongs to the Griselda motif, the story of wifely patience overcoming the irresponsible cruelty of a husband. While it is true that in the *Joie de la Cort* episode near the end of the poem there is an example of a knight's submission to the dictates of his lady, this episode is inserted principally to re-unite the separated cousins and, in any case, no question of love is really uttered therein, nor is the matter of Erec's declining renown after his marriage. What is present, then, in *Erec et Enide* is a clashing of the old epic values with the new concepts of courtly love, that ultimately is resolved in favor of the former, as the two lovers are reconciled in spite of their bickering and resume a happy marriage. This clash is particularly prominent in the the questions of love, which display the antagonism of a warrior's code of valor to the domestic idealization of love as a paramount concern.

Less has been written about *Cligés,* the second of Chrétien's romances, because critics have agreed that it is distinguished neither by plot nor by characterization and is notable only as it reflects the imposition of further elements of the code of courtly love. In sharp contrast to Chrétien's first attempt at romance in which adventures were predominant and even formed a necessary part of lovers' trials, especially the questions of love,

> the kernel of this romance is the love-affair of Cligés and Fenice, including the deceits which it involves to defeat the consummation of the latter's marriage with the uncle of Cligés and to bring about the union of the lovers. All the rest is secondary and, for the most part, as is obvious, merely added to give variety to the poem. [Bruce]

Furthermore, the focus of this poem is on the love-affair itself, the participants in which "are merely true lovers undistinguishable by any such qualities as the sulkiness of Erec or the discretion of Enide" [Ker]. But it is the questions of love which best demonstrate the profound change in temper and tone. The first time that the heroine is confronted with a dilemma, it concerns whether she should address the man she loves. Whereas Enide was ordered silent by her haughty lover, in this case the female is preoccupied with the ritualistic manner in which courtly love is to be conducted:

> She considers how she can address him first and

what the first word is to be—whether she should address him by his name; and thus she takes counsel with herself: 'What shall I say first?' she says, 'shall I address him by his name, or shall I call him friend. Friend? Not I. How then . . . God.'

A pattern is set for future romances in the fact that this preoccupation is ultimately self-defeating, for the queen summons away the lover before a word can be uttered.

At this point it is necessary to acknowledge the influence of Ovid upon the transformation of the poem, for in the work that "first inspired Chrétien, Ovid declares himself the victim of love. He holds out his hands in a sign of complete subjection and asks only to obey. Love is his master and he is Love's slave" [Guyer]. In other words, love becomes the dominant force in life, the prime motivation for action and thought alike, a process which has a debilitating effect upon the tormented partner yet produces as well a pain delightful and never wearied of. In fact, Chrétien uses almost exactly those words to describe Fenice's position. The situation is illustrated by the way in which she questions herself about her relationship with Cligés, after he has left for Britain to prove his mettle as a knight:

> She both opposes and defends her position, and engages in the following argument: 'With what intention should Cligés say I am altogether yours unless it was love that prompted him . . . ? I, who cannot escape its power, will prove by my own case that unless he loved me he would never say that he was mine any more than I could say that I was altogether his unless love had put me in his hands.'

It is notable that the questions of love studied so far have all been soliloquies on the part of women. In *Erec et Enide* it is fitting for Enide to be the one who worries, for her position is subservient and it is she who must be concerned with pleasing her partner. And when it is remembered that *Cligés* is notable for its increased emphasis upon courtly manners and not for any new depth of characterization, it is equally fitting that women, the objects of desire, should be the ones to consider how an affair ought to be conducted. Erec and Cligés may be pained at times because their beloveds are absent, but it is largely due to their individual involvement in matters aside from wooing that they are separated in the first place.

In *Lancelot,* or *Chevalier de la Charrette,* the tables are turned completely, an indication of the influence of Chrétien's patroness Marie de Champagne, whom he confesses in the famous passage beginning the poem as having been the inspiration of its matter and its sense alike. Therefore, *Lancelot* can be regarded as "the first French romance to make use of the theme of courtly love [which] centers about the cult of woman. The lady is always married, and honourable marriage cannot be the goal of her lover. His affection must take the form of a service of a secret and eternal devotion" [Holmes]. In sharp contrast to the initial two of Chrétien's romances, the males now bear the torments of love, because "all the suffering inflicted by the adored object of the courageous lover's affection is after all a sort of test of the male's sincerity" [Guyer]. Perhaps the best example of this test occurs when Lancelot mounts the tumbril, usually used to carry convicted criminals to the gallows, in his hasty pursuit to rescue the queen. After he has endured unbelievable hardships in his service of the queen, he receives from her only a stoney silence that causes him to lament, "God! What could my crime have been? I think she must have known that I mounted upon the cart." Finally Lancelot learns that the queen is piqued because he hesitated "two whole steps" before mounting the cart, to which Lancelot replies, 'May God save me from such a crime again . . . and may God show me no mercy, if you were not quite right!"

It is increasingly apparent that the poet's main concern is no more than pleasing a patroness, a task that seems even to disgust him at several places, so that his artistry "was limited to developing a relationship already established, bringing it into conformity with the doctrines of *amour courtois,* and touching up the given scenes and situations in order to illustrate the behavior of an ideal lover as conceived by Marie de Champagne" [R. S. Loomis, *Arthurian Tradition and Chrétien de Troyes,* 1949]. This procedure is exemplified in the absurd self-questioning that Lancelot undergoes when he happens to see that his hostess is about to be raped by a number of heavily armed men. The action stops because "the knight hesitated at the door and thought: 'God, what can I do? I am engaged in no less an affair than the quest of Queen Guinevere." The pendulum has swung so far that the commands of one's lady love now take precedence over honor itself.

It can be objected that **Lancelot** is atypical of Chrétien's works because its motivation and composition are the result of an outside influence which hardly seems to have pleased him. But when **Yvain** is scrutinized differences between the two poems appear to be those of degree rather than those of kind. **Yvain,** or **Chevalier au lion** is so improved in structure and in characterization that it seems a much more deliberate aesthetic effort on the part of the poet. Yet he continues his commitment to the code of courtly ethics and to the viewpoint that love is the most important concern of a knight. Yvain himself, during a mood of despairing introspection after he learns that he has killed in battle the husband of Laudine, whom he loves, states directly that "whoever does not welcome Love gladly, when he comes to him, commits treason and folly . . . I must live in accordance with Love's desire." Although there is a sort of regression insofar as the story is similar to **Erec et Enide,** the temper and meaning of **Yvain** are completely different. "The central core . . . is the winning of a lady's love at the end of an almost impossible feat of valor in a distant land, a conflict between the claims of honor and valor on the part of a man and those of love, the loss of the lady and the re-winning of her love" [Guyer]. There is a quarrel between man and wife just as in the first poem, with the difference that Chrétien's present manner indicates that he has adopted fully the Ovidian type of love. For example, Enide was a meek and obedient spouse, whereas Laudine is the arrogant woman who demands total acquiescence on the part of the male.

That the lady is truly imperial is shown by the way that she uses the question of love to handle Yvain after he final-ly has been granted an interview with her. Yvain begins by prostrating himself before her and stating:

> 'I will not crave your pardon, lady, but rather thank you for any treatment you may inflict upon me, knowing that no act of yours could ever be distasteful to me.' 'Is that so, sir? And what if I think to kill you now?' 'My lady, if it pleases you, you will never hear me speak otherwise.'

This passage seems at first to indicate that **Yvain** is only a more skillful treatment of the courtly motifs in **Lancelot.** But it must be remembered that the latter poem has been condemned on the grounds that there is little characterization and that events occur at random, unrelated either to matters of adventure or of love. To a certain extent, these factors weaken **Cligés** as well. For this reason, the best way of summation is to compare Chrétien's initial and final attempts at romance.

While **Erec et Enide** boasts relatively consistent personages, it is weakened by the fact that the main action and the courtly elements have little relation to one another. But this deficiency is remedied by the time of **Yvain,** so that the questions of love arise directly from the adventures related earlier, a process most striking in the way that Laudine is able to rationalize the killing of her husband and thereby to accept Yvain as a suitor:

> Come,' she says, 'canst thou deny that my lord was killed by thee?' 'Indeed, I fully admit it.' 'Tell me, then, the reason of thy deed. Didst thou do it to injure me, prompted by hate or by spite?' 'May death not spare me now, if I did it to injure you.' 'In that case, thou hast done me no wrong, nor are thou guilty of aught toward him. For he would have killed thee, if he could. So it seems to me that I have decided well and wisely.'

Now, the reader may be unconvinced by this argument, but it is undeniable that her logic arises out of previous events and provides a foundation for future action. Eric Auerbach explains the situation by postulating that, when **Yvain** was composed, "only two themes were considered worthy of a knight: feats of arms and love." The change from **Erec et Enide** lies primarily in the fact that the daring-do of a knight is prompted by and subordinated to his futile affections for an aloof lady. The transitional period embodying this change is represented in the four Arthurian romances of Chrétien and most especially in his varying usage of the "Demande d'Amour." (pp. 353-60)

> *Richard L. Michener, "Courtly Love in Chrétien de Troyes: The 'Demande d'Amour',"* in Studia Neophilologica, *Vol. XLII, No. 2, 1970, pp. 353-60.*

D. D. R. Owen   (essay date 1970)

[*Owen is an English educator whose works include* The Evolution of the Grail Legend *(1968) and* The Vision of Hell: Informal Journeys in Medieval French Literature *(1970). In the following essay originally published in 1970, he outlines some Christian themes present in*

Cligés *and* Lancelot, *maintaining that Chrétien's seeming irreverence and use of a profane style added a parodic element to his works that served to distance the audience from his characters.*]

The realisation of what Chrétien de Troyes is doing in substantial parts of his **Cligés** and **Lancelot** might move the modern reader to level against him a charge of wilful blasphemy. That no such accusation has, so far as I am aware, been made is due perhaps as much to the common view of Chrétien as an eminently moral, even devout, man as to the circumspection of the critics. His honest reputation may well have played some part in deflecting attention from the remarkable acts of irreverence that he has surreptitiously perpetrated in these two romances—so surreptitiously, indeed, that one might wonder if his contemporary public were always conscious of just what was happening. But when they were, would they have raised the cry of "Blasphemy"?

I cannot here explore the twelfth-century conception of blasphemy or the Church's attitude towards it. It is reasonable, though, to assume that, despite a certain libertinism to be discerned in courtly and literary circles, Chrétien would not deliberately set out to offend either ecclesiastical authority or the public for whom he worked. So it is more prudent to speak of irreverence or even profanity than of blasphemy; and there is abundant evidence that this was condoned by the medieval layman, while among the writers it had almost the status of a recognised literary device. But of course there are degrees of irreverence.

The Church, its ministers, institutions and rites were always vulnerable to ridicule, a fact that was exploited to the full by the poets of the *Roman de Renart,* say, or the fabliaux, who had much gross fun at their expense. There was little harm in this or even, given its humorous context, in Aucassin's fervent desire for Hell provided his sweet Nicolette be there—although the aim might here be thought rather nearer to the heart of the Christian faith. If we raise our eyebrows higher at Gottfried von Strassburg's notorious reference to Christ's pliancy in abetting dishonest acts, this can perhaps be passed off as irony and Gottfried's character remain untarnished.

Courtly love was a theme particularly apt to attract more or less daring embellishment. The romance of *Guillaume de Dole,* for instance, offers a picture of knights and ladies philandering in tents pitched in a smiling countryside:

> Il ne pensent pas a lor ames;
> Si n'i ont cloches ne moustiers
> (Qu'il n'en est mie granz mestiers),
> Ne chapelains fors les oiseaus.

Latin writings were certainly no less reticent than the vernacular texts. However innocent the intention, there is surely more than a touch of irreverence about the delicious "Si linguis angelicis . . . ", with its very earthly love expressed through the phraseology of the liturgy. Take the stanza so transparently modelled on the *Ave Maria:*

> Ave, formosissima gemma preciosa!
> ave decus virginum, virgo gloriosa!
> ave lumen luminum, ave mundi rosa,
> Blanziflôr et Helena, Venus generosa!

But if here a plea for leniency may be advanced, there can be no doubt of the profanity of that outrageous burlesque of Church assemblies, the *Council of Remiremont.* It is convened under the presidency of a female cardinal to debate the relative merits as lovers of knights and clerics. Ovid is read "quasi evangelium"; and the judgment is given that those who henceforth love knights in preference to ecclesiastics will be excommunicated.

Among the Latin writings we must not forget a strange episode in the *De amore* of Andreas Capellanus, Chrétien's contemporary and, one assumes, his acquaintance at Troyes. I mean the description of the company of dead women and their lovers led by the God of Love, and the portrayal of the otherworld where they dwell in greater or lesser bliss according to their amorous deserts. The whole account is clearly patterned on Christian eschatological notions as embodied in texts such as the *Vision of St Paul* (one of the women is even granted respite from her pains at the instance of the narrator); and the enumeration by the God of Love of his twelve commandments merely extends the irreverence. Incidentally, the French *Lai du trot,* which is based on Andreas' story, omits the more obviously parodic sections.

It is a commonplace of troubadour poetry that in the expression of profane love the terminology of divine love often found a home, and vice versa. Could this have played some part in encouraging a parodic element when the love situation is treated in this or that romance? It would be unwise to take the argument of cause and effect too far; but the possibility may be worth considering, particularly in connection with Chrétien's romances. For we know that he practised the courtly lyric himself. And in one of his two surviving poems there is a trace of religious phraseology:

> S'Amors por essaucier sa loi
> viaut ses anemis convertir,
> de sans li vient, si con je croi,
> qu'as suens ne puet ele faillir.

But if there is a link between such a conceit as this and the extreme irreverence I shall point to in his romances, it is frail indeed.

Before considering these romances, we may recall one other French text, the thirteenth-century fabliau *Saint Pierre et le jongleur.* The poor minstrel dies in sin and is carried off to Hell, where even Lucifer's heart is touched by his wretched condition, and he is left in charge of the infernal cauldron and all the damned when the devils leave to pursue their forays on earth. A dignified old gentleman enters the nether realm and induces him, without much difficulty, to stake the souls in a dice game. St Peter, for the intruder was no less a personage, makes coup after coup until he is able to lead the entire company of rejoicing souls back with him to Paradise. Now as I have shown [in "The Element of Parody in *Saint Pierre et le jongleur*", *French Studies* IX (1955)], the basic theme of this tale parodies the popular accounts of Christ's Harrowing of Hell. Even the most solemn moments of the Christian story were not immune in the Middle Ages from such irreverent, parodic treatment.

This is not the kind of thing, however, that we would expect from Chrétien, even if we have little faith in the arguments of those who would make of him a pious allegorist. He was, we are bound to feel, a man of conventionally upright views, stressing in particular the orthodox line on love (no adulterous liaisons for him, whether in the Provençal style or after the fashion of Tristan), and insisting on the religious element in the education of a young man bent on chivalry. Yet at the same time there is a certain disingenuousness about most of his works bred not from malice or deceit but from an ability to stand at a critical distance from his characters and their problems. Chrétien is one of the most coolly intelligent of French writers and endowed moreover with an extremely fine-grained sense of humour. As a result, I believe that most of his work has an ambivalent quality: he is inclined to compose tongue-in-cheek, inviting us to take his story seriously if we wish, but hinting that it would be more fun if we would share the secret joke he is playing on his heroes and heroines.

In an excellent recent study [*Aesthetic Distance in Chrétien de Troyes: Irony and Comedy in "Cligés" and "Perceval"*, 1968], Peter Haidu comes to similar conclusions. He sees in particular an ironical intention informing many of the situations in **Cligés.** This is doubtless so; and in one important instance I think he could have gone a good deal deeper in his examination of the "aesthetic distance" between author and characters or events. I refer to the episode of Fénice's feigned death.

It will be remembered that, despite the mutual love of Cligés and Fénice, the girl has been forced to marry Cligés' uncle, the Emperor of Greece and Constantinople. Her virginity is nevertheless spared through the administration to the Emperor of a potion concocted by her witch of a nurse, Thessala. Cligés proposes an elopement to Brittany; but Fénice fears they would earn the reputation of Tristan and Iseut; and she misquotes St Paul to the effect that those who will not live chaste should act with such caution as to avoid public reproach. Her plan is to feign death, so that Cligés will be able to rescue her from the tomb and carry her off to some hidden retreat. To this end Thessala will prepare another of her potions, whilst Jehan, a serf of Cligés', will construct a sepulchre and place a secret tower of his own at the lovers' disposal. The plan is almost brought to grief by the meddlesome interference of three physicians from Salerno, who suspect a trick and try to revive Fénice by torturing her. But in the end it is carried through, and the lovers find their happiness in Jehan's splendid tower and a delightful adjoining garden.

The case I wish to put is that Chrétien has modelled the whole of this episode of shammed death and revival on the account, probably the scriptural account, of Christ's Passion and Resurrection. To begin with, though he tells us that the maiden's name was Fénice because of the unrivalled beauty of the phoenix, others have pointed out that the bird that rose from its ashes was also used in the Middle Ages as a symbol of resurrection. I would go further and suggest that Chrétien had in mind Christ's own rising from the dead, which is the allegory supplied by the medieval bestiaries. Let us, then, look at the episode in more detail.

At the beginning of Fénice's pretended illness, a curious equation is made between Cligés and God. When the empress says that one alone has the power of life or death over her, the bystanders think she refers to God. But Chrétien makes it plain:

> . . . ele n'antant s'a Cligés non:
> C'est ses Dex qui la puet garir
> Et qui la puet feire morir.   (5644-6)

This sets the tone for what follows.

Significant, I think, are certain indications of time, as when all agree that Fénice cannot go beyond the ninth hour before yielding up the ghost, and it is then that she is given Thessala's potion to drink. (We recall the hour of Christ's death, as well as the vinegar in the sponge.) At once the draught has its effect, and all cry aloud thinking her dead. They lament the loss of "la meillor chose et la plus sainte" (5728); and when the three physicians arrive on the scene, they are told that God had illumined the world with a radiance and light that death has now extinguished, and in one person death has carried off more goodness than it has left behind on earth (5770-80). At this point one reflects that such hyperbole is hardly apt when applied to a woman who is duping her wedded husband, whereas of course it is not only appropriate but commonly used with reference to Christ. In particular, much play is made on the idea of Christ the light of the world in that section of the apocryphal *Gospel of Nicodemus* which relates the Harrowing of Hell and which, as we shall see, was not unknown to Chrétien.

The suspicious physicians get to work. In order to expose Fénice's pretence, they first scourge her savagely with leather thongs (5900-11), but to no effect. Then they boil lead, which they pour onto her hands so that the palms are quite pierced (5924-5). (The parallels with the Crucifixion are too obvious to need comment.) And when we are told that over a thousand women watch Fénice's ordeal through a small opening in the palace door (5934-41), we think of the scriptural account (for instance in *Matthew* XXVII.55) of the many women who beheld the Crucifixion from afar. They see Fénice's *martire*—"torment", or more technically "martyrdom"—and the word is later repeated (5941, 5972).

When the women have defenestrated the physicians, Thessala anoints Félice's wounds with a very precious ointment, and the women wrap the body in a white cloth (5980-9). We are specifically told that they leave the face uncovered; and the point could have been made in deliberate contrast with the use of the napkin in Christ's entombment, as reported both in *John* XX.7 and in the *Gospel of Nicodemus*. That night is spent in lamentations.

Next day Jehan is ordered by the Emperor to construct a tomb. But he says (and of course we are at once reminded of Joseph of Arimathaea) that he has already prepared a finely hewn sepulchre, which he had intended for a holy body or relic; but let the Empress be laid there, for she is "molt sainte chose" (6004-12).

Fénice's body is taken for burial; but its bearers fall in a swoon (6069; cf. *Matthew* XXVII.4), so that Jehan is able to make his final adjustments unseen. He closes and seals

The battle of Yvain and Gawain. (Garrett MS 125, fol. 38r.)

the sepulchre with care, and for no clear reason a guard is set (6074, 6081). Again we recall a verse of *Matthew* (XXVII.66): "Illi autem abeuntes, munierunt sepulcrum, signantes lapidem, cum custodibus."

That night the guards fall asleep (6086-7: they merely report having slept in *Matthew* XXVIII.13); and Cligés comes with Jehan to remove the body. The sepulchre is opened after Cligés has descended from a tree into the cemetery (a reminiscence, perhaps, of the angel's descent to roll back the stone?). And Fénice's body is removed to the tower. There she revives and is restored to health by means of Thessala's ointments and medicaments. And I might add that if one cares to work out the chronology of these events, it appears that the "resurrection" took place during the night preceding the third day. Moreover, Fénice, though not caught up to Heaven, is reunited with her lover (who had earlier been equated with the deity) in a veritable paradise on earth.

All these correspondences cannot be explained away as coincidence. Nor would I care to ascribe them to unwitting, involuntary reminiscence by Chrétien of the well-known scriptural events. I am sure he knew what he was about; and so this amounts to a deliberate and quite me-

thodical use for the elaboration of his story of the account of the Crucifixion and Resurrection—parody certainly, even burlesque? The incongruity of it all is startling. Here is a love-situation of which Chrétien surely disapproved, involving moral if not legal adultery (the non-consummation of Fénice's marriage left a legal loophole), with the wife's deceit of her husband acted out in terms of the central Christian mystery. What could Chrétien's purpose have been?

And what was his purpose in *Lancelot,* composed some time later? This is a romance entirely devoted to the adulterous pursuit by Lancelot of his liege lord's wife; and throughout the central section, Chrétien chooses to incorporate what amounts to a diffuse parody of Christ's Harrowing as set out in the *Gospel of Nicodemus.* Let me summarise the relevant parts of *Nicodemus* from the Latin versions that were well known in Chrétien's day.

After Christ left the tomb, many other sepulchres were found to be empty; and among the resurrected were Simeon's two sons, who made separate depositions about their experience. They had been in Hell with all those who had died from the beginning of the world, when the darkness was dispelled by a great light. The prophets announce that this heralds the coming of the Son of God for their deliverance.

While all the saints rejoice at the news, Satan the prince of Hell bids Inferus prepare to receive Jesus; but Inferus is alarmed, fearing that he has come to deprive Hell of its dead. The devils' dispute is interrupted by a thunderous voice commanding that they remove the gates so that the King of Glory may come in. Inferus orders Satan out to meet the intruder; but after a further summons, the gates and their bars are shattered, and Christ enters in majesty. Inferus and Death and their legions admit defeat. Christ tramples upon Death, delivers Satan into the keeping of Inferus, and draws the exulting souls of the righteous into his glory.

To return now to Chrétien, Lancelot has pursued his search for the abducted Guenevere to the bounds of the mysterious land of Gorre, whence no traveller returns (and in which most scholars recognise some Celtic otherworld in thin disguise). For part of the way he has ridden in a shameful tumbril—a re-enactment of Christ's journey to Calvary? In any case, when he enters a cemetery full of empty tombs, we are surely entitled to recall the happenings after the Crucifixion. The finest tomb bears an inscription referring to the slab that covers it:

> "Cil qui levera
> cele lanme seus par son cors
> gitera ces et celes fors
> qui sont an la terre an prison,
> don n'ist ne clers ne gentix hon
> des l'ore qu'il i est antrez;
> n'ancors n'en est nus retornez:
> les estranges prisons retienent;
> et cil del pais vont et vienent
> et anz et fors a lor pleisir."
>
> (1900-9)

Lancelot raises the slab without effort and pursues his journey.

He has now entered the hostile realm; and some captives he meets tell him that there is no escape from the land (which is envisaged as one vast prison) until such time as one of them manages to leave, when all will be free to go without hindrance. The inhabitants are "gent sarradine / qui peior que Sarrazin sont" (2134-5).

Word of Lancelot's arrival soon spreads among the captives, and an enemy squire reports:

> "Ce dïent an cest païs tuit
> que il les deliverra toz
> et metra les noz au desoz."
>
> (2300-2)

With some companions he is briefly shut in a castle; but coming to a gate, they assault it and break the bar (2356-60) to emerge into a place where the captives are in revolt against their oppressors. Lancelot enters the fray with predictable success, and the captives ask who is this knight. Their joy knows no bounds when they are told:

> "Seignor, ce est cil
> qui nos gitera toz d'essil
> et de la grant maleürté
> ou nos avons lonc tans esté;

> se li devons grant enor feire
> quant, por nos fors de prison treire,
> a tant perilleus leus passez . . . "
>
> (2413-9)

Chrétien now leaves for a time the scheme of the *Gospel of Nicodemus* to describe Lancelot's passage of the sword bridge. It may be that for this feature as for many others in the romance there is a remote Celtic source. But details of Chrétien's account leave us in very little doubt that he had in mind the testing bridge of Hell as described in the *Vision of St Paul, St Patrick's Purgatory,* or some other well-known pious legend. Not only does it span a torrent as grim and black "con se fust li fluns au deable" (3012), but it is razor-sharp and may be crossed only by a true believer. Lancelot has no fear:

> "Mes j'ai tel foi et tel creance
> an Deu qu'il me garra par tot."
>
> (3084-5)

So Chrétien is still thinking in eschatological terms; and in describing Lancelot's painful crossing of the bridge he prepares the way for a fresh injection of *Nicodemus* material. For from this point on, considerable stress is laid on the fact that the heroic deliverer is sorely wounded in his hands and feet.

After his ordeal he comes to the castle of King Bademagu, father of Guenevere's abductor Meleagant. From a window the king and his son have witnessed "le plus grant hardemant / qui onques fust mes nes pansez" (3192-3); and Bademagu is prepared to receive Lancelot into his castle. But his son shows only hostility; and there follows a heated dispute reminiscent of the quarrel between Satan and Inferus at the coming of Christ, though the arguments and motives are made to conform, of course, to the romance situation.

Eventually Bademagu goes out to meet Lancelot, honouring him for the unique courage of his feat: no other such perilous undertaking has ever been or will ever be achieved. He will see to the healing of his wounds, he says. And then, as if to leave no doubt as to the parallel he is drawing, Chrétien puts these very incongruous words into Bademagu's mouth:

> "De l'oignemant as trois Maries
> et de meillor, s'an le trovoit,
> vos donrai ge . . . "
>
> (3358-60)

A duel is arranged between Lancelot and Meleagant; and all the captives flock together to watch it as if they were assembling for church on a feast day. The captive maidens from Arthur's court had fasted and gone barefoot for three days (surely a covert allusion to the three days of Easter)

> por ce que Dex force et vertu
> donast contre son aversaire
> au chevalier, qui devoit faire
> la bataille por les cheitis.
>
> (3528-31)

We notice that although the real matter at issue between these two is the possession of Guenevere, it is the broader concern that is given prominence here, plainly by analogy with the Harrowing. And again we are told that

> Li prison et les prisonieres
> trestuit por lor seignor prioient,
> qu'an Deu et an lui se fioient
> de secors et de delivrance.
>
> (3580-3)

Their prayers are answered, Meleagant is worsted in the duel, and Lancelot thus earns the queen's release. Once more we are reminded that if one goes, all are free to leave. So the captives' joy knows no bounds: they throng round Lancelot, welcoming him as their predestined saviour, each one struggling to touch him; and for those who succeed there is no greater bliss (3906-20). And all do in the end return to Arthur's court.

The case for a parodic treatment of the Christian story seems as incontestable here as in *Cligés.* But in neither instance do I suggest that the parody is in itself humorous. Certainly we have cause to smile as we reflect that Lancelot, who elsewhere in the romance is abject almost to the point of imbecility in his devotion to Guenevere, nevertheless appears to acquire through the parody and his role of predestined saviour an aura of near-divinity. Yet when we consider these elements apart from the burlesque which I take to underlie the rest of the romance, they have nothing of the comic about them. Again, it is rather the incongruity that strikes us.

We find Chrétien once more using an otherworld motif in his unfinished burlesque romance of Gauvain (which is what I hold the second part of the **Conte du Graal** to be). Here too it is associated with the hero's sentimental involvements, since the recurrent theme in his adventures is his fatal weakness for the fair sex. On the other hand, I see no hint of irreverence or Christian parody in the Château des Merveilles episode, which embodies the otherworld material.

Now I believe that Chrétien's **Gauvain** (if I may call it that) inspired at least two other short burlesque romances in which Arthur's nephew plays the chief part. And in one of these we do find the profane and parodic use of pious texts. It is **La Mule sans frein** (also known as the *Demoisella à la mule*); and in the course of a prologue inspired by Chrétien's introduction to his **Erec,** the author names himself as Paien de Maisières. This is evidently a play on the elements of "Chrétien de Troyes"; but while one cannot dismiss the possibility that this is Chrétien himself working under a pseudonym, it is safer for the present to assume that we are dealing with a pupil, perhaps, or at least an admirer of the poet of Troyes. In any case, he was well conversant with Chrétien's work and techniques.

The story tells of how first Kay and then Gauvain set out in search of a bridle mislaid by the damsel of the alternative title. They ride on her mule, which leads them through a forest peopled by wild beasts and then into a deep, dark valley. The fire-breathing serpents and other creatures lurking there are fearsome enough, but even worse is the terrible stench of the place; and a further torment is the bitter, eternal cold as well as the biting winds that blow. The travellers emerge into a fair and flowery meadow, where a clear spring provides refreshment. But beyond this is a rushing, black river spanned by an iron bridge of no more than a hand's breadth. The poet explains that this is "li fluns au deable" (398), and one seems to see nothing but demons in it. The sight is too much for Kay; but when Gauvain comes there, he commends himself to God and rides across the bridge, which sags frighteningly as he goes.

The borrowing from eschatological legend is transparent; and again, as I have said, it is worked into a general burlesque context. The valley belongs to the infernal regions, with its typical features of darkness, vermin, overpowering stench, extreme cold and wind. The meadow and fountain beyond recall accounts of the Earthly Paradise, normally reached by the traveller after Hell is passed; but with the bridge we are back to the places of torment and the testing bridge over the infernal river that we encountered in **Lancelot.** The pleasant region has merely been misplaced. The details are still too commonplace for us to identify a particular source, but the visions of St Paul and Tundal, and the legend of St Patrick's Purgatory spring to mind.

If I am right in my belief that **La Mule sans frein** was a direct source for the Middle English *Sir Gawain and the Green Knight* and that this French account of the infernal valley inspired Gawain's wintry journey on his way to the Green Knight's dwelling, it is interesting to find that the Englishman has stripped away all the eschatological connotations, including the river and its testing bridge. He could scarcely have failed to recognise them for what they are. So it may be that he found more pleasure in the description of nature than of diabolic device. Or perhaps (and this is quite likely) he disapproved the irreverence implicit in the French narrative. Along with the reticence shown, as I remarked, by the author of the *Lai du trot,* this might be construed as showing that not all medieval writers of romance were equally happy to indulge in the profane exploitation of themes from devout writings.

There is another feature of **La Mule sans frein** that I should like to mention. It occurs when Gauvain has achieved his quest, in the course of which he has slain some ferocious beasts that had kept the inhabitants of a castle cowering in cellars and crypts. They joyfully emerge; and Gauvain is told:

> " . . . Or dïent en lor langage:
> Dieus les a par vos delivrez,
> Et de toz biens enluminez
> La gent qui en tenebre estoient.
> Si grant joie ont de ce qu'il voient
> qu'il ne püent graingnor avoir."
>
> (1030-5)

Here we catch echoes of Zacharias' prophecy in *Luke* I.79 that Christ will come to give light to them that sit in darkness; and we think of *Isaiah* IX.2: "Populus, qui ambulabat in tenebris, vidit lucem magnam." But we remember too that such phraseology as this is found in the *Gospel of Nicodemus* and is typical of the accounts of Christ's spoliation of Hell. The pseudo-Paien de Maisières is plainly thinking of Gauvain's somewhat fortuitous salvation of the castle's inhabitants in terms of the Harrowing. He has learnt well from his master.

It seems, then, that after Chrétien the insertion of this kind of profane cross-reference to pious texts in the course of tales of courtly adventure was recognised as a legitimate literary device. Sometimes it appears innocent enough. The use of the testing bridge does not shock in a genre where perilous passages of one kind or another abound; and indeed we find it reappearing in a number of works, including the Second Continuation of the **Perceval,** *Perlesvaus,* the prose *Lancelot,* and the Dutch romance of *Walewein.* Certainly it is much indebted to the infernal bridge of Christian legend, whatever one's views may be on Celtic prototypes; but it would be unfair to brand as impiety the purloining of a purely mechanical contraption so suitable for trying the mettle of venturesome knights.

The parodic treatments of Crucifixion and Harrowing must, though, give real food for thought. And again the question arises as to whether deliberate blasphemy is conceivable. I take it that blasphemy would be present if there were in these texts some intention to bring the Christian story into ridicule by reducing its events to the level of a dubious adventure tale. But this, surely, was never in the authors' minds. In so far as any ridicule was intended, it must have been aimed at the hero (or heroine in the case of Fénice), who is bound to suffer in the comparison that is offered with Christ—unless, of course, one feels that the analogy makes Fénice's endurance seem more admirable and serves to magnify the achievements of Lancelot and Gauvain. In either case, the authors would not be conscious of doing anything to offend the susceptibilities of their public.

So now we have to decide whether there is in fact any intention to ridicule the characters, or whether they were really being paid a rather oblique compliment. This cannot be settled by looking at the particular episodes in isolation: they have each to be seen against the background of the whole romance, and here opinions may well differ. In the case of **Lancelot** and **La Mule sans frein** I would plead for an underlying burlesque intention. Throughout his adventures Lancelot is for me a mock-heroic figure. He stumbles, like Gauvain in Chrétien's last romance, from one embarrassment into another. And most of them stem not from external circumstances but from his own abject passion for the queen, which reduces him to a quite pitiful state. He almost throws himself out of a window, suffers agonies of conscience having agreed to go to bed with a charming hostess, is so rapt in his reveries that he fails to hear a challenge and comes to in the cold waters of a ford; he fights Meleagant with his back turned so as not to take his eyes off Guenevere . . . Need I go on? Aucassin was not more besotted by love than was Lancelot, and the effect is different only in degree. And so, rather than impute to Chrétien an inconsistency in his portrayal, I take the episodes under discussion to have their place in the total burlesque design. The same applies to **La Mule sans frein,** where Gauvain rides to meet his destiny on the eponymous mule, has to make a well-timed leap into a spinning castle, and there undergo a beheading test and fight a stout

tussle with a knight who had previously been run through the body.

The case of **Cligés** is less obvious. But here, as in **Lancelot,** Chrétien is illustrating the exaggerations to which a wrongly based love can lead. He carries the lovers headlong on, but at the same time invites us to withhold our full sympathy. Three times he makes Fénice express her horror of being classed with Iseut; but she goes in the end one better than even Tristan's *amie.* So I would suggest that in the feigned death episode there is at least a touch of burlesque; and our amused disapproval is not lessened by the thought that if this is Fénice's Passion, it is a very private and selfish one, and without any redemptive value beyond herself and Cligés.

If I am right, one might well ask if some of this might not be lost on the public of the day. Indeed it might. But that, I believe, was part of Chrétien's genius. He deliberately composed at least the majority of his romances in such a fashion that his public could take them in one of two ways, as I suggested earlier: either with straight faces, or with a grain or two of his own mocking humour. "Here is my story of Lancelot", he might say. "What a buffoon he is—or what an example to all courtly lovers! And here is Fénice. Just see what deceits she could practise to get by an unwanted husband. Or, if you prefer, how nearly she illustrates Christ's saying that there is no greater love than to lay down one's life for one's friends." Is it too rash to wonder if something of this double vision may not be reflected in his treatment of the loves of Erec, Yvain, even Perceval? Chrétien was a writer of greater subtlety than is always recognised. Moreover, he was composing for a fairly heterogeneous public of both sexes, and we should not assume uniformity in either tastes or intelligence or in the degree to which individuals would associate themselves with his characters.

His displays of irreverence, then, were far from gratuitous. They supplied a purposeful element of incongruity in his romances, designed to advance his burlesque schemes, or at least to set his audience, or those of them who wished, at a critical distance from his characters and their actions. Irreverence, but not blasphemy, was part of his artistic technique, and a very significant part. He may well have invented this particular use of it; at all events it was recognised and taken over by the poet of *La Mule sans frein.* And it is interesting to reflect that already with the father of Arthurian romance we find a concern to probe its weaknesses in this and other ways. But that is another and wider question. Suffice it now to sound a note of praise for a very sophisticated and truly remarkable artistic personality, a man as daring in his techniques as he was enigmatic in his purposes, a man of aristocratic talent but who as often as not applied that talent, I fancy, to the sly pulling of courtly legs. (pp. 37-48)

D. D. R. Owen, "Profanity and Its Purpose in Chrétien's 'Cligés' and 'Lancelot'," in Arthurian Romance: Seven Essays, *edited by D. D. R. Owen. Barnes & Noble Books, 1971, pp. 37-48.*

Eugène Vinaver   (essay date 1971)

[*Vinaver was a Russian-born educator and author who served as editor of the journal* Arthuriana *and as president of the Society for the Study of Medieval Language and Literature from 1939 to 1948. Among his works are* The Love Potion in Primitive Tristan Romance *(1924) and* The Rise of Romance *(1971). In the following excerpt from the latter work, he examines the continuity of meaning and matter in Chrétien's narratives, asserting that Chrétien adapted his subject matter to the meaning he wished to convey.*]

In Roman times Rhetoric was conceived as a means of conveying the speaker's conception of the case, his way of looking at the events and the people concerned; it was also, according to Martianus Capella [in his *De Nuptiís Philologiae et Mercurii*], the means by which the orator could display his talent 'despite the meagreness of the case'. What a speaker trained in the use of Rhetoric felt naturally compelled to do was not simply to elucidate the matter but to adapt it to a given point of view. Carried one stage further this method was bound to result in the remodelling of the matter itself, or at least of those parts of it which were at variance with the thoughts and feelings one wished to convey. Rhetoric could thus lead to a purposeful refashioning of traditional material, and the adaptor could become to all intents and purposes an original author, except that, unlike some authors, he would care above all for the *way* in which he told his stories and measure his achievement in terms of such new significance as he was able to confer upon an existing body of facts.

These distinctions were new in twelfth-century vernacular literature, and Chrétien de Troyes was, so far as we know, the first French writer to formulate them. In the opening lines of his **Conte de la Charrette** he said that he owed both its *matiere* and its *sen,* meaning presumably 'significance' or 'purpose', to his patroness, Marie de Champagne: *matiere et san l'an donne e livre.* The marriage of matter and meaning, of narrative and commentary, was the key to the new kind of narrative poetry—the poetry that assumed in the reader both the ability and the desire to think of an event in terms of what one's mind could build upon it, or descry behind it. One is reminded of Master Léonin, *optimus organista,* an exact contemporary of Chrétien de Troyes and the real founder of the art of polyphony which was essentially an art of building musical commentaries—*organa dupla,* or two-part *organa*—upon traditional chants. The possibility of adding such commentaries was *implied* in every one of these chants, but never *realized* until the idea of a *sen* had crossed the mind of a great musician. What happened then was exactly parallel to what the poets did when they elaborated a traditional tale in a direction which might be thought to have been implied in it from the beginning.

The initiators of this technique in the field of secular narrative were Chrétien's immediate predecessors, the authors of romances based upon classical subjects: *Thebes, Troie,* and *Enéas*—all written probably between 1150 and 1160. Lavinia, having seen Aeneas, tells us in fifty lines (8083-133) how greatly his mere appearance has impressed her, and then suddenly interrupts her speech by asking herself: '*Fole, qu'as tu dit?*' Fifteen lines follow in which her heart and her reason argue the case between them. She knows that she has to marry Turnus—what then will she do with her love for Aeneas? Is she to belong to both? At this point another 'self' intervenes and speaks to her in the first person singular, thus completing the pattern of what was to become in later literature the so-called interior monologue. Aeneas proceeds likewise: he too is, as it were, divided against himself, and his *alter ego* addresses him without much ceremony, telling him to keep quiet and that his love is sheer folly. Earlier on in the poem Dido's complaint was expressed through a dialogue—a conversation with her sister and confidante Anna; and according to one critic [Omer Jodogne, in 'Le caractère des œuvres antiques aux XIIe et XIIIe siècles', in *L'Humanisme médiéval dans les littératures romanes du XIIe au XIVe siècle,* 1964]. this transference of the deliberative function from the dialogue to a monologue corresponds to a transition from the technique of story-telling to that of organized fiction: from being a narrator the author becomes a novelist.

Not that the mere introduction of the interior monologue is sufficient to create this new form of art. In the Old French version of the story of the Trojan War, *Le Roman de Troie* by Benoît de Sainte-Maure, a poem based upon Dares's *De Excidio* and Dictys's *Ephemeris Belli Trojani,* Achilles, in contrast to his silent classical prototype, bursts into a long soliloquy describing the devastating effects of his love for Polyxena, a theme suggested by Dares. Achilles' complaint contributes little to the progress of the action, still less to our knowledge of the human heart, but Benoît de Sainte-Maure clearly regards it as an essential part of the story he is writing; not because the hero's passion is too strong to remain silent, but because as a writer trained in a certain way he cannot conceive of any passion being silent. The term 'gratuitous' clarification applied by Erwin Panofsky to the scholastic *manifestatio* is equally true of this and many other early monologues. Their aesthetic justification came later, when they were already in existence as a recognized form of literary expression. In the five verse romances of Chrétien de Troyes, written between 1165 and 1181, the monologue often serves as the focus of the entire action of the story. The story of Cligès and Fénice is prefaced by that of the hero's parents, Alexandre and Soredamors. Alexandre, the son of the Emperor of Byzantium, drawn by the fame of King Arthur's court, enters King Arthur's service at Winchester and accompanies him across the sea to Brittany. On this journey he meets King Arthur's niece Soredamors who until then had despised love. But she is soon punished for her pride: the moment she sees Alexandre, elegant, handsome, noble in every thought and gesture, their glances meet, love makes them his captives, and they struggle in vain against his power. In a long monologue Soredamors reveals every wavering thought that passes through her mind, drawing her inspiration from Ovid's *Metamorphoses* and freely echoing the monologues of Pomona, Medea, and Thisbe. Alexandre's passionate soliloquy is conceived in a similar fashion. 'I feel', he exclaims, 'that my illness is too grievous to be healed by any medicine or draught, by any herb or root. For some ills there is no remedy, and mine lies so deep that it cannot be treated . . . And yet', he adds, 'I do not know what disease this is which has me in its grip, and I know not whence this pain has come. I do not know? I think I know full well: it is Love that causes me this pain. How is that? Can Love do harm? Is he not gentle and well-bred? I used to think that there was naught but good in Love; *mes je l'ai molt felon trové.*' Finally he resigns himself to his fate:

> Now let Love do what he will with me as with one that belongs to him, for I wish it and it pleases me. Let not this malady leave me; I would rather it always maintained its hold and that health never came to me save from the source that causes the disease.

Gaston Paris [in *Journal des Savants,* 1902]. thought that all this was out of place in the story because Alexandre and Soredamors had no reason to fear any obstacle to their happiness: the son of an emperor and the niece of a king need have no hesitation in declaring their love to each other and to the world at large; admirably matched as they are, they can dispense with heart-searchings and contemplate marriage as a matter of course. The error here is one which is by no means confined to nineteenth-century 'realistic' criticism: it is still being perpetrated almost daily by critics who judge medieval writings by their own standards of *vraisemblance.* Chrétien's object was not to tell us how such things normally happen, but to make a very simple story into one which develops simultaneously on two levels: that of feeling and that of action, one constantly motivating the other, even when by realistic standards no such motivation is required. It is not contemporary morals or proprieties that dictate the structure and composition of the romance, but the feeling that certain ways of presenting even the most straightforward issues are part of the kind of artistry that the reader expects and enjoys.

A later critic, Myrrha Borodine, in her fine analysis of the poem [*La Femme et l'amour au XIIe siècle d'après les poèmes de Chrétien de Troyes,* 1909], suggests that in this case the absence of external obstacles is, on the contrary, part of the psychological situation which Chrétien endeavours to portray: 'The conflict is within the lovers' hearts, not outside them, and Chrétien's art consists in revealing to us a world of duties, scruples and delicate hesitations, which is the essence of courtly love.' This is certainly true in the sense that from Chrétien's point of view there was room for scruples and hesitations in the lovers' minds no matter how favourable the circumstances in which they found themselves; but one should add that the reason why he found room for such things even in the most unlikely situations was not his desire to explore uncommon states of mind, but his determination to make the work structurally complete. The monologues of Alexandre and Soredamors are examples of interpretation accompanying and clothing a seemingly simple incident and thus providing it with a new dimension.

When later on in the same work Chrétien has to describe how the hero comes to take leave of the heroine, Fénice, prior to his departure for the court of King Arthur, Chrétien makes him say: 'It is right that I should ask leave from you to whom I altogether belong', and the poet adds that although many a secret sigh and sob marked the scene, the eyes of none were keen enough, nor the hearing sharp enough, to learn from what they said that there was any love between Cligès and Fénice. This does not prevent Fénice's thoughts from going back to the scene. She 'takes on her tongue', as Chrétien puts it, 'instead of spice, a sweet word which for all Greece she would not wish Cligès to have used in any sense other than that in which she understood it when he first uttered it'. Cligès had said that he was 'altogether hers'. This word 'she takes into her mouth and heart to be all the more sure of it . . . She strives to find and hold some ground on which to stand . . . ' With what intention did Cligès say 'I am altogether yours'? Was it love that prompted him? Fénice is far from certain that this was really so, and the interior monologue—one of the first on record—goes on for well over a hundred lines, disclosing further doubts and hesitations in the heroine's mind.

This is 'interlinear' commentary. Nothing like it is to be found in the literature of medieval Europe before the middle of the twelfth century; but to us, eight hundred years after it was written, it seems so familiar that we can hardly imagine an age when such things were unknown. It is *our* language that Fénice speaks when she embarks upon her minute analysis of the simple words spoken by Cligès. And it is again *our* language that Chrétien speaks when on another occasion, in his most famous romance, **Lancelot,** he analyses his hero's behaviour. The facts of the story are simple. In an attempt to rescue Guinevere from captivity Lancelot loses his horse and has to face the choice between failure and utter disgrace. As he walks in his heavy armour he meets a dwarf driving a cart and cries out: 'Dwarf, tell me if you have seen my lady the queen pass by.' And the dwarf replies: 'If you will get up into the cart you will hear by to-morrow what has happened to the queen.' A cart in those days, Chrétien tells us, was never used except for criminals, and whoever was put in a cart lost all honour and was never afterwards welcomed in any court. So Lancelot hesitated, but only for two steps, before getting in. This is the story, or at least the main part of it. And here is the commentary:

> It was unlucky for him that he shrank from the disgrace and did not jump in at once, for he later regretted the delay. Reason, which is inconsistent with the dictates of love, bids him refrain from getting in, warning him and counselling him not to do or undertake anything for which he may reap shame and dishonour. Yet reason which dares thus speak to him reaches only his lips, not his heart; for love is enclosed within his heart bidding him and urging him to mount at once upon the cart. So he jumps in, since love will have it so, feeling no concern about the shame: he is prompted by love's commands.

Thus an incident which, the poet tells us, did not last more than a second or two—the space of Lancelot's two steps—is made the subject of a disquisition in which the problem of the relative importance of love and honour, of duty to chivalry and duty to the lady, is raised in all its daunting complexity. The subtle balance between the two duties, between the dictates of reason and the dictates of love, is what motivates both the hero's hesitation and his action, just as later on in the story a somewhat different balance between the same conflicting principles of conduct will motivate the scene in which, to Lancelot's distress, Guinevere will rebuke him: not for having disgraced himself, but for having hesitated to do so. The narrative proper will not be devoid of interest; but it will matter little compared to its increasingly more subtle and systematic elucidation, just as in contemporary, or slightly later, polyphony—in the work of Léonin's successor, Perrotin, in the three-part counterpoint or *organum triplum*—the complexity of the upper parts will be matched by the diminishing importance of the *cantus firmus*.

This same work—the 'story of the cart'—can serve as an example of the other—the rhetorical type of elaboration. Lancelot's adventures on the way to the castle where Guinevere is held captive, the exploits he performs on her behalf, her release from captivity, her attitude to Lancelot, and his distress at her displeasure are all related to a particular conception of courtly love, which was perhaps not Chrétien's own, but which he adopted here as a means of showing how these various episodes of the story could be arranged and presented if human behaviour were governed by the extreme form of courtly service. In his attempt to rescue Guinevere Lancelot sacrifices his knightly honour: he humbly submits to being driven in a cart—a symbol of public disgrace. And yet, in spite of this, and in spite of all his feats of bravery, he is rebuked by Guinevere because she knows that before getting into the cart he paused 'for two steps'; even this momentary hesitation between his duty to her and his honour was, she thought, an offence against courtly love. In **Yvain** the courtly theme appears in a less rigid form. Yvain is persuaded to join the company of Arthur's knights and leave his lady, Laudine, who lets him go provided that he will return at the end of the year. He is filled with grief. 'The king can take his body away; but over his heart he has no power, for his heart remains attached to her whom he leaves behind, and no one can remove it from her.' And Yvain goes on to say that a year would be too much: he could never stay away so long. The irony of it is that he does. The excitement of the adventure gets into his blood, and this is precisely what gives point and substance to his monologue on the eve of his departure. What Chrétien wants us to know and to feel is not simply that Yvain forgot his lady, but how it comes about that the deepest feelings in a man's heart are eclipsed for a time under the stress of circumstances: a state of things which in our own century has been called *les intermittences du cœur*. As a recent critic [Julian Harris in 'The Rôle of the Lion in Chrétien de Troyes' *Yvain', Publications of the Modern Language Association of America,* 1949] puts it: 'It is the story of a knight who lost the favour of his *dame* through pride and neglect of his duty, but who won her back by humility, faith in God and the right, and careful attention to his duties as a good knight.' Our attention is constantly directed not so much to the details of Yvain's adventures, nor even to the fact of his apparent disloyalty towards Laudine, but to the motives behind the visible action of the story. The narrative remains continuous on both levels: that of the meaning and that of the matter, and the two 'voices' are heard simultaneously throughout.

All this is not to say that it is permissible for us to classify Chrétien's romances as examples of psychological realism in the modern sense of the term. Chrétien lets the characters enact a line of argument that happens to interest him, no matter what kind of characterization, real or unreal, may emerge as a result. He certainly would not have understood Hugh Walpole's remark to the effect that the character in any novel 'should have existed before the book that reveals it to us began and should continue after the book is closed' [*The Waverley Pageant*]. The world of fiction is to him an essentially literary world, almost as remote from the 'portrayal of people' as the animal ornament of the Romanesque period was from any likeness to real living creatures. This does not exclude occasional touches of realism in the description of the characters' behaviour, any more than the stylized animal ornament excludes an occasional likeness to real animals. But it would be misleading to say that Chrétien's purpose in introducing such characters as Enide, Fénice, Lancelot, or Guinevere was to make them behave like 'real people': everything they do is related to a problem and its elaboration within the work, since it is with problems that courtly poetry is concerned, not with human realities. 'Life', even courtly life, is for Chrétien not a model, but 'a vast mass of potential literary forms' [Northrop Frye, *Anatomy of Criticism*], only a few of which can materialize in the framework of a romance; and the choice is invariably related to the problem raised. The next stage in the development of 'character' brings us no closer to the realm of psychological realism. The habit of seeing in a story an expression of a meaning or theme naturally leads to the creation of personified meanings and themes which may behave as characters, although it is clear that they have no existence of their own. Indeed no good poet, so Dante tells us, would allow such a confusion to arise in the reader's mind, for 'it would be a shameful thing if one should rime under the cloak of a figure of speech or colour of rhetoric and afterwards, being questioned thereof, should be unable to strip one's words of such clothing and reveal their true meaning' [*Vita Nuova,* XXV]. The 'true meaning'—*verace intendimento*—is the sense concealed by the figure of speech, the thought behind what Dante calls 'figura o colore rettorico'—in this instance, Love represented as if it were not only an intelligent substance, but a *sustanzia corporale*. The method used by Chrétien de Troyes thus leads naturally to the allegory of the *Romance of the Rose* and of the *Vita Nuova,* not to the 'story of character' as understood by modern realistic novelists. It is the first example in French literature of a *roman d'analyse* based not on observation but on reflection.

The themes of Chrétien's five romances are strikingly inconsistent with one another: they represent varying attitudes to such important 'doctrinal' issues as the courtly code of behaviour, the duties of a knight towards his lady and towards knight-errantry, and the duties of the lady herself. The only constant feature is the practice of expressing through each story a particular point of view and conveying in this fashion several different facets of courtly feeling. The proper medium for a consistent expression of courtly ideology is lyric and allegorical poetry; romance by its very nature favours variety rather than consistency: ideas are there merely to show how the story could be adapted to them, and it is a merit, not a fault, in a poet like Chrétien to have shifted his ideological ground in passing from one romance to another. Ideologically he remained uncommitted even after he had produced his two *romans à thèse, Cligès* and *Lancelot;* as uncommitted as any artist would be who had no preoccupations outside his art. Claudel once said that he could not really tell what love meant to him as an author except that it was one of the devices ('un des engins') used in the composition of his plays [Paul Claudel, *Mémoires improvisés recueillis par Jean Amrouche,* 1954]. For him as for Chrétien the work was a means of giving shape to amorphous matter and thought—of producing the desired relationship between events and their antecedents. It was a statement not of philosophy, but of an ordered emotion'. The real novelty of romance was precisely this 'ordering' quality: the urge not merely to move and to impress, but to understand. (pp. 22-32)

> *Eugène Vinaver, "The Discovery of Meaning," in his* The Rise of Romance, *Oxford University Press, Inc., 1971, pp. 15-32.*

Robert G. Cook   (essay date 1973)

[*In the excerpt below, Cook offers a comparative analysis of the structures of Chrétien's* Erec and Enide *and* Yvain, *noting that both Erec and Yvain progress through several stages of character and spiritual development.*]

Among students of Chrétien de Troyes there has been an understandable urge to analyze his large and rambling romances in terms of a simplified structure. William S. Woods [in "The Plot Structure in Four Romances of Chrestien de Troyes," *Studies in Philology,* 1953], for example, has drawn our attention to the similar plot structure in the *Guillaume d'Angleterre, Erec et Enide,* the *Chevalier au lion (Yvain),* and the *Conte del Graal:*

> A hero achieves the realization of his worldly ambitions and desires in an introductory passage. He is then made aware of some error or fault or of some less obvious reason which forces him to abandon his lofty pinnacle of happiness. This point in the plot can be likened to the initial impulse of a drama for it serves to motivate the main body of the poem which is a series of adventures concerned with the hero's efforts to recover his former status, presumably through his becoming more deserving of it by the correction of his error or by the expiation of his fault.

Of the four romances treated by Woods, two—*Erec* and *Yvain*—are especially similar in structure, as various critics have noticed. Jean Frappier observes: "there is a striking parallelism in the structure of the two poems [*Erec* and *Yvain*]. Both narratives fall into three parts: both tell how the hero wins a beautiful and worthy bride; both tell how their wedded happiness is seemingly lost for ever; both conclude with a complete reconciliation after a period of trial" ["Chrétien de Troyes," in *Arthurian Literature in the Middle Ages: A Collaborative History,* ed. Roger Sherman Loomis, 1959]. Similarly, T. B. W. Reid comments:

Both these poems comprise (I) by way of exposition, a narrative which, beginning at King Arthur's court, introduces the hero, relates the adventures through which he wins his bride, and is rounded off with an account of Court festivities in such a way that it could almost stand alone as an independent poem; then (II), rather briefly and casually introduced, a crisis in the relations between husband and wife, which creates a conflict and states a moral problem; finally (III) a series of progressively more formidable adventures, leading ultimately to the resolution of the conflict and the reconciliation of the hero and heroine; but the conclusion of the story is postponed by the insertion into the series of adventures of (IV) an elaborate episode, complete in itself, which is not essential to the plot, but serves to display the prowess of the hero and to introduce fantastic or supernatural elements. [Introduction to the French Classics edition of *Yvain,* 1942].

On the assumption that a pattern twice used must have had some importance in the author's mind, this article will trace the structural resemblances between *Erec* and *Yvain* in greater detail than has been done before; the pattern of both of these romances—Chrétien's most original—should be more apparent after such comparison. But first a warning: "structure" will not be applied rigidly here. Though I prefer to see a tripartite structure, where others see two sections or five, I recognize the arbitrariness of such schemes. More important than numbers is the shape and tendency of the narrative. From such long and episodic romances as *Erec* and *Yvain* it is possible to extrapolate structural patterns ad infinitum simply by redefining, recombining, and renumbering episodes. Such analyses are of little value unless they (1) relate to the meaning of the work or (2) demonstrate a convincing numerological design, or both. The *sens* or meaning is what we are groping for, and my hope is that the parallels noticed here will stimulate thinking in that direction.

In both *Erec* and *Yvain* the initial adventure of the hero comes as a result of his having cut himself off in some way from Arthur's wishes for an enterprise involving all his knights. In *Erec,* Arthur decrees, in spite of Gauvain's protest, that on the next day they will all hunt the white stag:

> "Demain matin a grant deduit
> Irons chacier le blanc cerf tuit
> An la forest avantureuse."
>
> [63-65]

[The edition of *Erec* cited is that of Wendelin Foerster, *Kristian von Troyes: Erec und Enide,* 24 ed. (Halle, 1909). References are to lines throughout.] But Erec seems to have disregarded this, for on the next day we see him riding, not with the king and his knights, but with the queen and a *pucele.* They set out after the others (77), and in contrast to the hunters, who carry bow and arrows (76), Erec carries only his sword (103-4). He is clearly not taking part in the hunt, though the reason for this is not given. Similarly, although Arthur vows to see the magic fountain (661 ff.) [References to *Yvain* are to the Wendelin Foerster text as reprinted in T. B. W. Reid's French Classics edition, 1942] and "all the court" (674) wish to accompany him, Yvain decides to set out secretly on his own:

> Mes il ne les atandra mie,
> Qu'il n'a soing de lor conpaignie,
> Eincois ira toz seus son vuel
> Ou a sa joie ou a son duel.
>
> [691-94]

It is also common to both poems that in this opening episode Arthur is deficient—even slightly ridiculous—and inferior to Guinevere. In *Erec* he is advised by Gauvain of the folly of hunting the white stag, the slayer of which must kiss the most beautiful maiden in the court (41-58), but haughtily insists that a king's word must be obeyed, simply because it is a king's word:

> "Ja ne doit estre contredite
> Parole, puis que rois l'a dite."
>
> [61-62]

Later, when Gauvain's warning proves to have been well founded and Arthur seeks advice in a difficult situation (308-10), it is the queen who suggests that he put off the kiss until the third day, on which Erec promised to return (336-39). When Yder presents himself to the king to admit his defeat at the hands of Erec, the queen pointedly reminds Arthur of her advice and how he did well to heed it:

> "Mout vos donai buen consoil ier,
> Quant jel vos loai a atandre.
> Por ce fet il buen, consoil prandre."
>
> [1220-22]

In *Yvain,* Arthur unaccountably rises during the Pentecost festivities at Carlisle and retires to his chamber where he eventually "forgets himself and falls asleep" (52). The queen, on the other hand, remains awake and joins the knights outside the chamber door who are listening to Calogrenant's tale. It is she who effectively rebukes Kai for his rudeness, and it is she who repeats the story of Calogrenant to Arthur, after he has finally roused himself (649-60).

Both Erec and Yvain, then, as a consequence of having separated themselves from a court in which King Arthur himself is seen as weak, enter upon their initial adventures. The adventures have these things in common: each is an unexpected encounter with a strange knight, prefaced by a meeting with an unnatural man (a dwarf in *Erec,* a seventeen-foot herdsman in *Yvain*); each hero also stays with a hospitable *vavassor* prior to the combat, a host who has a surpassingly beautiful daughter. Of course, these parallel elements do not occur in the same order in the two works: In *Erec* the meeting with the dwarf comes before the entertainment by the friendly host; in *Yvain* the hero first spends the night with the hospitable host and then meets the giant herdsman.

In their initial adventures both Erec and Yvain are required to fight with the strange knight as a result of having disturbed him in a matter in which he has a kind of proprietary interest. It was generally understood that Yder would claim the hawk for his lady without opposition, as he had for the two previous years:

> "Par deus anz l'a il ja eü,
> Qu'onques chalangiez ne li fu;
> Mes se il ancore oan l'a,
> A toz jorz desresnié l'avra."
>
> [595-98]

But Erec, an unexpected outsider, comes and takes away what Yder thought of as virtually his own. In *Yvain,* Esclados is the guardian of the fountain which Yvain disturbs. Another similarity is that neither Yder nor Esclados is a tyrant whose defeat is necessary or beneficial (as will be the case with later adventures). Yder's defeat brings forth mixed reactions (cf. 1073-80), and the slaying of Esclados brings great grief to his people. In both poems, then, it is natural that the knight accuse the hero of motiveless provocation. Yder, ignorant that Erec is the same knight whom his dwarf had offended, asks innocently:

> "Ha! jantis chevaliers, merci!
> Por quel forfet ne por quel tort
> Me doiz tu donc haïr de mort?
> Ains mes ne te vi, que je sache,
> N'onques ne fui an ton damache
> Ne ne te fis honte ne let."
>
> [1002-7]

This speech is very similar to Esclados's words to Calogrenant (which we can take as applying to Yvain as well, since he goes through the same series of experiences as did his cousin):

> "Vassaus! mout m'avez fet
> Sanz desfiance honte et let."
>
> [491-92]

But although both Erec and Yvain are accused of gratuitous troublemaking, each has his own sufficient motive: revenge. Erec is avenging the whipping which both he and Guinevere's damsel received from Yder's dwarf, and Yvain is avenging the shame to his cousin. In a word, each is taking vengeance for a *honte:*

> "Mes itant prometre vos vuel
> Que, se je puis, *je vangerai*
> *Ma honte* ou je l'angreignerai."
>
> [*Erec,* 244-46; italics added]

> "Se je vos ai 'fol' apelé,
> Je vos pri qu'il ne vos an poist;
> Car, se je puis et il me loist,
> *J'irai vostre honte vangier.*"
>
> [*Yvain,* 586-89; cf. 747-49; italics added]

At this point, of course, large differences between the two romances will occur to the reader. Each hero wins his combat with the strange knight—Erec by forcing his surrender, Yvain by killing him—but they are in quite different positions after the victory. Erec is proclaimed a hero for having aided Enide (1075-78, 1251-68), if not for having subdued Yder, whereas Yvain is hunted as a villain for the slaying of Esclados. This difference between a hero and a prisoner is important in shaping the widely different relationship between each knight and his lady; Erec is from the beginning master in his marriage, where Yvain is the underling. But in this paper differences are deliberately slighted in favor of similarities and parallels. To summarize to this point: the initial adventures of Erec and Yvain have in common Arthur's weakness, a solitary adventure (rather than a sharing in the general adventure of Arthur and his court), a hospitable *vavassor* with a lovely daughter, a giant/dwarf, and a fight motivated by the desire to overcome shame, this fight against a not wicked opponent who is not aware of why he is being challenged.

In both **Erec** and **Yvain** the initial adventures terminate in (1) a reunion with Arthur's court, (2) the hero's marriage, and (3) a clear winding up of the narrative to this point. Erec first returns to Caradigan and marries Enide there, while Yvain first marries Laudine in her own land and then receives the visit of Arthur and his knights. Although the order is different the same elements of wedding and reunion with Arthur are present. As for winding up the story, **Erec** began with the decision to hunt the white stag and the offense to Guinevere's damsel; the two plots were interwoven when it was decided that the bestowal of the kiss, the prerogative of the one who should kill the stag, would await Erec's return; both plots are resolved when Arthur bestows the kiss on Enide. Chrétien expressly signals this as an ending in line 1844: "Ci fine li premerains vers." **Yvain,** on the other hand, began with Calogrenant's story and Kai's taunting (the latter in 71-85 and 590-611); these matters are resolved when Yvain has slain Esclados and tumbles Kai.

The hero has now reached what Woods calls his "pinnacle of happiness," and most readers would find nothing wrong if the story should end here. Erec and Yvain have departed from Arthur's court, independently avenged a dishonor and proved their valor, made a successful marriage, and returned to the company of Arthur. There seems no need for more, no need to disturb the pleasant equilibrium that has been achieved—and yet in both romances Chrétien does exactly that.

Between the wedding and the time the hero sets out on a new series of adventures, the romances have three common elements: (1) the hero provides additional proof of his prowess by distinguishing himself in tourneying; (2) the hero is taunted for uxoriousness, and sets out to disprove this; (3) he is shown to be guilty of a fault, and sets out to work off his guilt. In **Erec** the order in which these appear is (1), followed by (2) and (3) in combination; that is, the fault of which Erec is guilty is uxoriousness. The great tournament which is held after the wedding of Erec and Enide would seem to establish Erec's valor for all time:

> Or fu Erec de tel renon
> Qu'an ne parloit se de lui non,
> Ne nus n'avoit si buene grace:
> Il sanbloit Assalon de face,
> Et de la langue Salemon,
> Et de fierté sanbloit Sanson,
> Et de doner et de despandre
> Fu parauz le roi Alixandre.
>
> [2263-70]

Yet when they return to Erec's own country he loses interest in such matters:

> Mes tant l'ama Erec d'amors
> Que d'armes mes ne li chaloit,
> Ne a tornoiemant n'aloit,
> N'avoit mes soing de tornoiier;

> A sa fame aloit donoiier.
>
> [2434-38]

This leads, justifiably, to the general report that Erec is *recreant* (2555), which so saddens Enide that Erec notices and thus learns of the low esteem into which he has fallen. Accepting the judgment as correct (2576-77), he immediately orders Enide to prepare to set out with him. He refuses all other company, saying that he intends to go alone (2692-95).

In **Yvain** the elements listed above occur differently, in the order (2), (1), (3). Following the wedding and the elaborate entertainment of Arthur and his knights, Gauvain persuades Yvain that his reputation will decline unless he comes tourneying with him:

> "Ronpez le frain et le chevoistre,
> S'irons tornoiier moi et vos,
> Que l'an ne vos apiaut jalos."
>
> [2500-2502]

Yvain is convinced by this and spends a successful year jousting in tournaments, firmly establishing his reputation (2672 ff.). Then, because he has violated his promise to return to Laudine in one year's time, he is accused of deceit by a damsel sent from her (2704-73). He knows that she is right, having already acknowledged his guilt before the damsel's arrival (2695-2703), and in his misery and self-hate he departs at once for wild terrain, completely alone (2785). In both cases the hero leaves the pleasures and company of a court for the second time; this time, however, it is not because of a desire to avenge a *honte* but because of a sense of guilt. Both men have wronged their spouses, Erec through excessive attention, Yvain through excessive neglect. They have failed, in opposite ways, to live up to the twin obligations of love and chivalry.

Also common to the two romances is the fact that when the knight sets out this time he does not look for one particular adventure but instead travels without direction, passively exposing himself to whatever adventures happen to come his way. This new beginning, prompted by a sense of guilt, initiates a series of adventures which take up the remainder of the romance and almost twice the space of what has gone before. In comparison with what follows, the earlier adventures seem trivial, of no consequence beyond the displaying of the hero's bravery and prowess that Auerbach describes as characteristic of chivalric romance [*Mimesis: The Representation of Reality in Western Literature,* trans. Willard R. Trask, 1953]. Auerbach touches only briefly, unfortunately, the moral development of a hero and the possibility that a series of adventures might display progressively higher qualities in the hero. To mention one detail that indicates such development in the romances at hand, up to the point when the hero sets out for a second time in search of adventure neither Erec nor Yvain has faced serious moral evil in an external form, though each has sensed some fault within himself. Their first adventures have been suitable contexts for a sense of shame; the succeeding adventures will be appropriate for a sense of guilt.

From this point it is not possible to trace complete parallelism, adventure for adventure, but if we treat all of the experiences of each hero between the time of his new setting forth and his final reestablishment (the return to Arthur and the coronation, for Erec; for Yvain, the return to the fountain and the reconciliation with Laudine), we can discover a number of interesting similarities. Defining an episode as any fresh encounter, involving an action, with other persons or creatures, we can speak of nine separate episodes for each hero in this interval. (pp. 128-34)

In drawing parallels we must first go back to a point in *Yvain* just prior to this series of adventures, for Erec's reunion with Arthur (adventure no. 5) has obvious parallels with Yvain's return to Arthur after his year of tourneying with Gauvain, and even with Yvain's earlier reunion with Arthur just after his marriage to Laudine. This can be simplified by noting that each hero makes two returns to Arthur, one at the time of his marriage (*Erec*, 1479-2292; *Yvain*, 2172-2638), and another after a period of adventuring or tourneying (*Erec*, 3931-4307; *Yvain*, 2680-2801). Erec's second return, now under consideration, has in common with Yvain's first reunion the contrast between Kai's rudeness and Gauvain's courtesy. When Arthur and his knights come to visit the magic fountain, Yvain tumbles the offensive Kai from his horse; this is accompanied by references to Gauvain and a lavish comparison of Gauvain with the sun (2400-2408). In *Erec* (3931 ff.) Kai tries unsuccessfully to bring the wounded and unrecognizable Erec into the company of Arthur, but when his customary coarseness leads him to use force, Erec throws him to the ground. Gauvain then tries and succeeds, with the use of tact and the trick of having Arthur move his tents into Erec's path. Also common to *Erec* (3931 ff.) and *Yvain* (2172 ff.) is the hero's concern for the horse from which he has unseated Kai. In *Erec* Kai's confession that the horse belongs not to him but to Gauvain persuades Erec to relinquish it (4055-74). Yvain takes the horse of the fallen Kai and returns it to Arthur, saying,

> "Sire! feites prandre
> Cest cheval; que je mesferoie,
> Se rien del vostre retenoie."
>
> [2272-74]

In both poems the hero shows a courtesy toward the horse and its owner which emphasizes his scorn for Kai.

Erec's second reunion with Arthur also has a clear parallel with Yvain's second reunion (2680-2801): in both cases it is Arthur who must come to the hero, instead of vice versa. In *Erec,* as we have just noted, Gauvain plays a trick on the hero, distracting him with courteous conversation while Arthur has his tents taken down and set up again directly in front of him (4112-56). Realizing that he has been outsmarted, Erec reveals himself to Gauvain and agrees to accept the hospitality and medicine of Arthur's court. Similarly, in *Yvain* (2685-93) the hero and Gauvain, after their year of successful tourneying, come to Arthur's court at Chester but set up their tents outside the town rather than lodge in the city. Arthur, in order to see them, is forced to come to their court.

Another parallel between the two romances is that both Erec and Yvain are cured by medicine which comes from Morgan, the sister of Arthur. The king sighs when he sees the wounds which Erec has received in the successive attacks on his life, and he has him treated with the *antret* (plaster) which Morgan gave him. Its power is such that it can heal any wound within a week, provided it is applied daily (4218-28). Yvain, on the other hand, is not suffering from physical wounds but from madness—a mark of the greater depth of this romance. The two damsels of the Dame de Noroison find him naked and asleep in the forest, clearly mad. The lady recalls that she has at home an ointment given to her by Morgan which is capable of curing any madness. In a curious episode which I have discussed elsewhere [in "The Ointment in Chrétien's *Yvain*," *Mediaeval Studies* (1969)], one of the damsels cures Yvain by applying the ointment to his entire body, even though in so doing she disobeys her lady's strict instructions to put it only on his temples.

The first five adventures of Erec (2795-4307) and the first five episodes in Yvain's life (2814-3484) in the second phase of the romances are not otherwise strikingly similar in story motifs. In general, however, they represent the same stage in the hero's career, which we might label Rehabilitation. By the time these series of adventures have been completed, the problem or fault which initiated them has apparently been solved. On four successive occasions Enide has disobeyed Erec, and saved his life, by warning him. After the fourth time, however, we read:

> Cil la menace,
> Mes n'a talant que mal li face;
> Qu'il aparçoit et conoist bien
> Qu'ele l'aimme sor tote rien,
> Et il li tant que plus ne puet.
>
> [3765-69]

Following this adventure (the defeat of Guivret) comes the interval at Arthur's court, and again it seems to the reader that the romance could well end. Enide's love for Erec, which he doubted from the time she confessed her uneasiness about the rumors of his slackness, has been successfully demonstrated, and on his part Erec has given sufficient refutation of the rumors. Both have been tested (cf. 4921, "Bien vos ai del tot essaiiee") and both have passed. In addition, Erec's wounds have been cured by Morgan's plaster. Again we have come to a point in the romance where we can ask, what need for more?

In *Yvain* there has been a similar rehabilitation. The hero has recovered from his madness, has performed two acts of valor and assistance (the defeat of Count Alier, the rescue of the lion), and has returned home, or at least as far as Laudine's magic fountain. He sees his former error and repents it:

> Au revenir mout fort se blasme
> De l'an, que trespassé avoit.
>
> [3528-29]

Why does he not now pour water on the slab and force Laudine's hand, as he does later on? In the answer to that question lies a key to the meaning of the structure of these romances. For the second time in both poems the reader feels he is close to an ending, and yet both start off once again, into a third series of adventures. This time the hero sets out with a trusted companion: Yvain has the lion, Erec has Enide (whom he was testing before and therefore did not fully trust). The immediate problem which troubled each hero before has now been overcome—and yet it is perhaps this very fact which is our clue to the structure of new starts which is axiomatic both for Chrétien and for his heroes. Having recognized a fault in themselves and having struggled to make up for it, Erec and Yvain must now perform disinterested service for their fellowmen, acts of charity unrelated to their immediate needs and problems.

The first adventure for both Erec and Yvain in this new series . . . is a fight with a giant or giants: Erec rescues Cadoc de Tabriol from two giants who were beating him with whips as he sat nearly naked and bound on a horse. Yvain rescues the four sons of Gauvain's sister from a giant who has them whipped by a dwarf as they ride on horses, bound and in rags. Also common to both romances is the fact that the hero first hears about the plight of the giants' victims from someone close to the victims. Erec learns from the mistress of the captured knight, Yvain from the father of the four sons. Several new elements enter the romances with this episode: (1) the hero fights a superhuman creature for the first time, and (2) he undertakes a deed of charitable valor, not simply because it is thrust upon him and he cannot avoid it, but because he is petitioned to give help. The initial adventures of both heroes were deliberate and comparatively trivial in effect. Following the crisis in their lives, they reacted more than acted: Erec's first four adventures were simply matters of self-defense, in which he had no choice but to fight; Yvain was a guest in the castle of the Dame de Noroison and was thus obliged to answer the attack of Count Alier. To be sure, his rescue of the lion was closer to a deed of voluntary charity, but was not a response to a human plea for assistance. With the slaying of the giants, Erec and Yvain freely perform needed service for others for the first time.

Following his rescue of Cadoc from the giants, Erec falls into a deathlike swoon because of loss of blood. Enide reproaches herself for what she takes to be his death and decides to slay herself with his sword. She draws the sword from its sheath and begins to contemplate it (4670-71) when Count Oringle rides up and has his men take the sword from her. This Pyramus-and-Thisbe motif is paralleled in *Yvain* when the hero and the lion return by chance to the magic fountain (3485-3525). Yvain swoons, not from wounds but—in character with this romance—because of his distress at seeing again a reminder of his guilt. He falls and grazes his neck on his sword. The lion, thinking him dead, takes the sword with his teeth, leans it across a fallen tree, secures it, and prepares to rush against it. Just at this moment, fortunately, Yvain revives and the lion halts his planned suicide.

[The heroes' seventh adventures] are both rescues of women in trouble. Count Oringle is beating and threatening Enide (4819-52), whom he has married by force, when Erec recovers from his swoon and slays him. Yvain rescues Lunete from being burned to death by defeating the seneschal who had accused her of treachery, together with his two brothers. These three knights are then burned on the pyre intended for Lunete (4570-75). In each adventure the hero dispatches a knight who has mistreated a woman who is close to him and has aided him.

Taking adventures 8 and 9 together, we see that the similarities appear in a reversed or chiastic order. Erec's fight with Guivret (8) and Yvain's fight with Gauvain (9) are both single combats between close friends who do not recognize each other. In addition, each is the most difficult battle that the hero fights. Erec is thrown from his horse by Guivret and is on the point of being killed when Enide intervenes and begs for mercy (5021-46). Yvain, after exchanging blows with Gauvain all day, is the first to admit that his opponent (still unrecognized) had dealt him harder blows than he had ever received. Fortunately, in both poems the combatants discover each other's identity before ultimate damage is done, and they enjoy a happy reunion.

Likewise, adventure 9 in *Erec* (Joie de la Cort) and 8 in *Yvain* (Chastel de la Pesme Avanture) have many things in common, beginning with the fact that both episodes have their ultimate origin in visits to the Other World. Even apart from their sources and lingering traces of fairy enchantment and disenchantment, however, the two episodes have many surface likenesses which are probably more important for Chrétien's purposes. In both cases the hero and his companions are on their way somewhere (Erec to join Arthur, Yvain to fight for the disinherited sister) when they come by chance to a town which contains a dangerous adventure. Both heroes are discouraged from undertaking the adventure. Erec is warned by Guivret (5419-46, 5461-63), by the inhabitants (5517-25), and by King Evrain (5608-41); Yvain by the rude townspeople (5115-35) and by the elder, courteous lady (5145-74). Each hero gives as the reason for staying the fact that it is late and he is in need of a night's lodging (*Erec,* 5449-53; *Yvain,* 5166-67). The custom of each place is that errant knights must be the guests of the lord—the townspeople are forbidden to receive them (*Erec,* 5479-92; *Yvain,* 5155-58). Thus both Erec and Yvain are entertained by the gracious yet imperious lord of a town containing a dangerous adventure which the hero voluntarily embraces, in spite of the fact that everyone assures him that the outcome will be fatal. Both adventures have been undertaken, with fatal results, by a series of predecessors to the hero. And both adventures have a story behind them: after he has been defeated by Erec, Mabonagrain tells him of his betrothal and the promise which committed him to defend the garden against all comers (6047-6117); Yvain, on the other hand, learns of the king of the Isle of Maidens and his agreement to deliver thirty maidens annually to the two devils (5256-5337) *before* he fights the devils. Each of these stories turns on the unhappy results of a man's promise, from which he can be released only by the hero's successful completion of the adventure.

Furthermore, in these adventures the defeat of the opponent brings with it relief to a great number of persons, not just one. Yvain liberates the 300 damsels who have been doing needlework at slave labor terms, earning four deniers (one-third of a sou) instead of the twenty sous a week that they deserve. Erec is told by Mabonagrain that his victory will not only release him but also bring great joy to the whole court:

> Mout avez an grant joie mise
> La cort mon oncle et mes amis,

Qu'or serai fors de ceanz mis;
Et por ce que joie an avront
Tuit cil qui a la cort seront,
JOIE DE LA CORT l'apeloient
Cil qui la joie an atandoient.

[6118-24]

Each adventure also has something of the supernatural about it: in *Erec* the garden in which the adventure takes place is surrounded by a magic wall of air, grows flowers and fruits all year round (though the fruits can only be eaten there), and produces all types of spices and roots useful in medicine (5739-64); the two demons whom Yvain fights have supernatural shields which cannot be cut by any sword (5622-24). Even such a detail as a row of sharp, pointed stakes is common to both adventures (*Erec,* 5774-86; *Yvain,* 5191-92). Finally we might note that one result of each adventure is that the person most responsible for the adventure is in some way dissatisfied: Mabonagrain's lady is upset when she fears that now she will see less of her lover (6192-6229); the king of the Isle of Maidens offers Yvain his daughter, and is rude in his discontent when Yvain refuses (5699-5770).

These adventures (Joie de la Cort in *Erec,* Chastel de la Pesme Avanture in *Yvain*) are reminiscent of the first adventures of each hero—the hospitable host with a lovely daughter (though the daughter is missing in Joie de la Cort), the forebodings of defeat, the disruption of a custom by means of the defeat of a knight who had maintained it—but the differences between the later adventures and the earlier are a measure of the heroes' growth. Yvain's combat with Esclados over the magic spring and Erec's combat with Yder over the sparrow-hawk were prompted, as we saw, by the desire to repair their honor. Subsequent adventures were either in self-defense or in response to a request for aid. In Joie de la Cort and Pesme Avanture, however, there is almost no motivation at all on the hero's part—he just comes upon the adventure by chance, while he has some other destination on his mind, and is not put off by discouraging remarks. Once he is in the town, Yvain is obliged to fight the two devils whether he wants to or not (5334-37). Erec has more choice in the matter, but decides to attempt the adventure when he knows nothing about it except its name and the fact that it is dangerous. Bezzola's description of the Joie de la Cort as "l'aventure cherchée" [in *Le sens de l'aventure et de l'amour,* 1947] is misleading; Erec "seeks" it only when he is already there and when he has no idea of what good or evil might be the result. The casual manner with which Erec and Yvain enter these great adventures ironically underscores the successful outcome and the great good that is achieved. With a minimum of intent they achieve a maximum of benefit, bringing relief not just to themselves or to one or two, but to a large number of people. Their good fortune suggests that through their third stage of adventures they have reached the internal maturity required to perform deeds of general welfare.

Following this series of adventures each hero makes a return, Erec to Arthur's court and his eventual coronation in Nantes, Yvain to the magic fountain where he creates another tempest and is reconciled with Laudine through the agency of Lunete. Erec, of course, has already been reconciled with Enide, but Yvain is still estranged from both his wife and his country, so that for him the twofold return is necessary. The ending of *Yvain* is the more dramatic, for the problem of coming to terms with Laudine remains unsettled until the very last lines of the poem. There is no final denouement in *Erec*—the death of his father and his coronation are predictable events which do not resolve any problems. The similarity between the two romances lies in the fact that the hero's adventures have come to an end, his worth has been amply demonstrated, and it remains simply to restore him to his deserved position. In these last scenes the hero has nothing more to do; his role is now essentially passive. It is the death of Erec's father which brings about the coronation, and it is the machinations of Lunete which bring about Yvain's restoration.

If, however, we pursue for a moment the idea that the plot of *Erec* is complete with the episode of the Joie de la Cort, while *Yvain* is not finished until the reconciliation with Laudine, we can notice a similarity between these two "final" episodes. Both have to do with the relaxing of a woman's harsh attitude toward her husband, an attitude based on the enforcement of an arbitrary decision. Mabonagrain's wife had made him promise to remain in the garden and defend it against all comers, and he was bound by that promise. Laudine had made Yvain promise to return within one year, and when he failed to return, her love promptly turned to hate (2564-67) Both of these arbitrary decisions are reversed or overcome in the final episodes, making it possible to say that both romances end with the establishment of a mature relationship.

The main points which these two romances have in common can be summarized:

1. The hero, as a consequence of separating himself from a court in which King Arthur appears weak, is entertained by a gracious *vavassor* with a lovely daughter, encounters a man of unnatural size (dwarf or giant), and—as something of a trespasser—defeats a strange knight in order to avenge a *honte.*

2. The hero then (*a*) marries a lovely lady and (*b*) is reunited with Arthur's court. The introductory narrative is wound up at this point, and a peaceful equilibrium, on which the romance could well end, has been achieved.

3. This equilibrium is shattered when the hero is accused of a fault—a fault connected with the fear or reality of uxoriousness.

4. The hero acknowledges his guilt and sets out alone, or nearly alone, on a new set of adventures.

5. These adventures have certain parallel motifs, such as the Pyramus-Thisbe motif, the faithful companion who keeps an all-night vigil, and the cure by medicine from Morgan, Arthur's sister.

6. After a number of episodes (five by this reckoning), the hero seems to have done enough to return comfortably to the previous equilibrium, and the narrative is arranged in such a way that the ending is tantalizingly near (Erec has forgiven Enide and been reunited with Arthur, Yvain is

cured of his madness and has returned to Laudine's spring).

7. Yet Chrétien sends each hero through an additional series of four adventures in which he performs deeds of charity and prowess exceeding previous achievements.

8. These last four adventures include (*a*) a rescue from giants on the petition of an intimate of the victim(s), (*b*) the deliverance of a woman close to the hero from cruel treatment, (*c*) an incognito fight with a close friend, and (*d*) an elaborate episode which the hero seems to enter casually and which leads to the release of a whole community from the oppression of a custom which has bound it for a number of years (seven in **Erec,** ten in **Yvain**).

9. The hero is returned to full status as husband and lord of his land.

These points of similarity have been coaxed out of the two romances without regard for the differences which make them each a unique work. As much or more could be written about these differences as has now been written about their similarities, but suffice it to say here that **Yvain** is the more mature work and states a more profound problem. In **Erec** the hero and heroine have disappointed each other: Enide has registered a lack of confidence in Erec's valor by listening to the talk of his slackness, and his own negligence is responsible for this talk. Reparation is then needed on both sides (thus they travel together): Erec needs proof of her love, and she needs proof of his valor. In **Yvain** the fault is on one side, and it is more serious than either Erec's or Enide's: he has broken a promise, failed in his loyalty. His affliction is accordingly more serious and he has a longer road to travel before he is restored to his wife. But both romances follow the same pattern of early success, commission of a fault, rehabilitation, and restoration at a higher level.

The structure which **Erec** and **Yvain** have in common may be contrasted with that shared by **Lancelot** and the **Conte del Graal,** in which a hero (nameless for the first 3,500 lines) is specially marked to fulfill one main adventure (freeing the prisoners from the land of Gorre, healing the Fisher King). Both Lancelot and Perceval make an unwitting mistake which hinders their progress, though it also schools them in their devotion. Their adventures are balanced by those of a secondary figure (Gauvain) who is exceptionally worthy but lacks the special commitment and election which characterizes the hero. A major difference is that Perceval develops significantly as he moves toward religious devotion, while Lancelot remains almost static in his passion for Guenevere, but both are marked by a deep commitment and are meant to fulfill one particular adventure.

The structure of **Erec** and **Yvain** is that of a progress through stages. On one level this progress has to do with the relations between the sexes and the problem of the conflicting demands of love and chivalry. Both Erec and Yvain begin at the court of a uxorious king, experience uxoriousness or the threat of it in themselves, and are finally secure in marriages in which private passion and public welfare find full and equal expression. Concurrent with this is an ethical development from action because of a

sense of honor, to humiliation and action atoning for a fault, to disinterested action on behalf of others.

This second level has echoes of higher versions of the progress of the soul. Erich Auerbach and R. W. Southern [in *The Making of the Middle Ages,* 1959] have commented on the resemblances between Chrétien's romances and the stages of Cistercian mysticism, though they tend to see these resemblances merely as expressions of parallel movements. "The religious and the romantic quests were born in the same world . . . and drew in part on the same sources of inspiration, but they were in the twelfth century kept rigidly apart" [Southern, p. 255.] H. B. Willson, on the other hand, studying Hartmann von Aue's versions of **Erec** and **Yvain,** argues for an analogical relationship between them and Christian patterns of thought. "The exile of Erec and Enite from courtly society reflects analogically the exile of humanity from the paradise of similitude with God. Courtly society is universalized, as it were, to represent the community of mankind within the wider unity of the divine *ordo.* The duty of chivalrous manhood is to realize its true self by overcoming sin through *caritas,* to redeem itself and others by selfless sacrifice" ["Sin and Redemption in Hartmann's *Erec,*" *Germanic Review* (1958)]. Willson's theory may apply equally to Chrétien, who as a twelfth-century writer would have found it difficult to keep the romantic and religious worlds rigidly apart. It is natural to expect that Chrétien's descriptions of the progress of a knight will have some resemblance to formulas of Christian progress, perhaps especially those of Saint Bernard, for whom the progress of the soul toward God was an incessant topic.

In *The Steps of Humility* Bernard describes the three steps to truth. The first is knowledge of self, or humility, "that thorough self-examination which makes a man contemptible in his own sight." The second step is knowledge of others, which leads to love and compassion. The third step is knowing God. "Since there are therefore three steps or states of truth, we ascend to the first by the toil of humility, to the second by the emotion of compassion, to the third by the ecstasy of contemplation" (chap. 6, para. 19). These stages correspond to the second, third, and fourth degrees of love as Bernard describes them in *On Loving God:* (1) love of self, (2) love of God for the sake of self, (3) love of God for God's sake, (4) love of self only for God's sake. This is one of four different divisions of love in the writings of Bernard, according to Etienne Gilson, [in *The Mystical Theology of Saint Bernard,* trans. A. H. C. Downes, 1940], who has also explicated their basic pattern: a beginning in carnal love, or love of self; then an apprenticeship in humility, by which one learns compassion; "now compassion is charity, and charity is the Holy Spirit, the Third Person of the Trinity. Thus is man led to a more and more intimate and complete union with the life of the Three Divine Persons, and, we may add, he is now ready for the supreme initiation, should it please the Father to bestow it on him." The careers of Erec and Yvain bear no analogies to the final stage or mystic vision, which is totally self-denying and seldom granted in this life, but they do resemble the three earlier stages by which man begins in self-love and rises, by means of humility, to service of others and love of God. I suggest that

Chrétien had such analogies in mind when composing these romances. (pp. 135-43)

Robert G. Cook, "The Structure of Romance in Chrétien's 'Erec' and 'Yvain'," in Modern Philology, Vol. 71, No. 2, November, 1973, pp. 128-43.

Karl D. Uitti   (essay date 1973)

[*Uitti is an American scholar and the author of* Linguistics and Literary Theory *(1969) and* Story, Myth, and Celebration in Old French Narrative Poetry, 1050-1200 *(1973). In the following excerpt from the latter work, he describes Chrétien's technical virtuosity as displayed by his use of the romance form in* Cligés, *paying particular attention to the theme of appearance versus reality.*]

[In] *Yvain,* Chrétien's novelistic perspective is enunciated by the development of certain attitudes already present in Wace as well as by what in fact turns out to be the poeticization, or internalization, of the exordium motifs one finds in straight "historical" works and also in contemporary romances. *Yvain* poeticizes the commonplaces with which . . . so many of the "wise" texts of the *matière antique* begin, e.g., the suitability, or pairing, of letters and good manners. Chrétien's own *bele conjointure* is proclaimed implicitly by virtue of being built right into the astonishing juxtapositions with which *Yvain* opens and which determine its unfolding. (Even Arthur's knights and ladies are astounded when he leaves the table!) (pp. 156-57)

[To examine these matters more closely,] I propose to focus especially upon *Cligés,* the romance dating from ca. 1176, according to A. Fourrier, and consequently the one to precede immediately *Lancelot* and *Yvain.* (Most authorities agree that *Lancelot* and *Yvain* were probably composed at about the same time, possibly even jointly, between 1176 and 1181, so that it makes sense to consider *Cligés* as the proper predecessor to *Yvain* [J. Frappier, *Chrétien de Troyes,* 1968].) Even more significant, however, is the fact that *Cligés,* as Frappier has suggested, is surely the romance in which Chrétien displays the greatest technical virtuosity. This work shows what he was capable of in that range, and it does so in a fashion that will permit us to understand better his accomplishments in the later texts. Furthermore, *Cligés* is perhaps the purest and most accomplished "romance" among Chrétien's creations, the one work that takes the romance possibilities (in this sense as opposed to novelistic ones) about as far as they will go. Conversely, *Lancelot* and, to a lesser degree, *Perceval* may, I believe, be usefully seen as attempts to deepen and render more "serious" the romance form. Chrétien attempted this deepening by making use of the novelistic means that he perfected in *Yvain,* but that, of course, were not entirely suitable to his goals in either *Lancelot* or *Perceval; Cligés,* meanwhile, remains more completely gratuitous.

A brief plot summary may be helpful. The handsome and generous young Byzantine prince, Alexandre, obtains permission from his father the emperor to visit Arthur in Britain. On a trip with Arthur's court to Brittany, Alexandre and Soredamor, the lovely maiden-in-waiting to Guenevere, see each other and fall in love; neither dares speak. Meanwhile Arthur is betrayed by Angrés, to whom he had confided the kingdom of England during his absence. Alexandre distinguishes himself in the battles of reconquest and marries Soredamor. She gives birth to Cligés. The parents take their son and remove to Greece, where Alexandre expects to claim the throne now occupied by his brother Alis. The two agree to let Alis continue his reign but only on condition he not marry, in order that, eventually, Cligés might inherit the throne. Alexandre and Soredamor die. Urged on by his barons, Alis decides to break his vow and marry Fénice, the charming daughter of the emperor of Germany. When they meet, Cligés and Fénice fall in love with each other. Fénice confesses her love to Thessala, her sorceress nurse, who prepares a drink that will make Alis mistakenly believe he has enjoyed his wife's favors on their wedding night. Cligés behaves heroically, saving Fénice from a kidnap attempt. Deeply in love, he does not quite dare declare his passion, except somewhat obliquely when he takes leave of Fénice in order to visit Arthur's court. In Britain he triumphs over most of Arthur's knights—he even equals Gauvain—but he cannot forget Fénice. He returns to Greece and proclaims his love. Fénice reciprocates but refuses to live in adultery. She will instead feign death and will be buried in a specially designed (and very luxurious) tomb, where she and Cligés can be together. After duping three *fisiciens* from Salerno, Fénice is entombed and fifteen months of joy ensue. However they are eventually found out and obliged to escape to Britain, where they raise a great army. But the news of Alis' death arrives and the two lovers are married and crowned. Subsequently, the romance concludes,

Erec defeats one of the robber-knights, as Enide looks on. (Paris, B.N., f.fr. 24403, fol. 142r.)

Greek emperors have found it expedient to keep careful watch on their spouses.

The success of *Cligés* as romance depends on the degree of superiority we are consciously willing to confer upon the fashioning as opposed to the materials; "form" and "content" are contrasted. In itself the plot is absurd. Poeticized in the romance—that is, so long as we understand explicitly that we are meant to be conscious at all times that we are coping with a romance-type plot—then and only then does it give off its flavor of ironic persiflage and delicate humor. (The procedure reminds one of *Candide.*) Chrétien exploits here the resonances of literary convention. Thus, though many have said that *Cligés* is a kind of anti-*Tristan*—indeed Fénice herself declares that she is unable to "acorder / A la vie qu'Isolz mena" (3110f.)—it is not a simple "answer," or alternative, to the Tristan legend; *Cligés* depends on *Tristan* and the way this dependence functions constitutes its response: it transforms more thoroughly into gratuitous romance forms key elements of the Tristan story and its implications, in a sense trivializing it by stressing that *Tristan* too is a romance. After all, Fénice is hardly Yseut's moral superior. Similarly, as opposed to *Érec et Énide, Cligés* does not depict an Arthurian magic or mythology. There is no mysterious and wonderful Celtic Joie de la Cort to amplify or deepen the romance's dimensions. However, just as in *Érec,* Arthur's court constitutes here the courtly place *par excellence;* King Arthur is the greatest king of all and, interestingly, Queen Guenevere plays the go-between who facilitates the marriage of Alexandre and Soredamor, a bit as she had done in bringing Érec and Énide together. The Arthurian world "imitates" itself here within the framework of Chrétien's *œuvre;* it functions as its romanesque model had functioned. Guenevere does what she had done in *Érec et Énide* and the fact that she does so is integrated into the economy of *Cligés.* Indeed this may be one of the reasons explaining Chrétien's cataloging his works at the start of *Cligés.* His very literary experience—the sum total of his work—is poeticized. At any rate, instead of occupying an ambiguous position at once in the romance and as an extension of the romance, the Arthurian world merely serves the romance in *Cligés.*

Technical virtuosity becomes a matter of poetic economy in the case of *Cligés.* In the first part of the romance Arthur's court, Alexandre's acts of prowess, and the love of Alexandre and Soredamor are purely literary motifs that are once again combined in order to make literature. The higher degree, or greater quantity, of literary consciousness displayed and utilized in *Cligés* has, in fact, important qualitative repercussions. Alexandre goes off in search of adventure. All knights in romances do just that. (So will Alonso Quijano one day.) We recall that Alexandre's military effectiveness at Arthur's court is characterized by liberal use of ruse—and, incidentally, like his namesake, our hero is known for his generosity—and this too is typical of romance. In a very Greek fashion he and his companions disguise themselves in order to get into Angrés' castle. One is reminded, quite maliciously, of Troy; also, Tristan was famous for his trickery. Alexandre falls in love and proud Soredamor reciprocates his passion. This love occurs in a décor as romanesque as possible: a boat, at sea, exactly like Tristan and Yseut. Critics have pointed out that the play on *amer* (love), *la mer* (sea), and the sickness of love (confused by Guenevere with seasickness and consequently misconstrued), a kind of *annominatio* (540ff.), throws back to the Tristan story. But our lovers remain chaste; in this they oppose, quite symmetrically, Tristan and his beloved.

Various kinds of symmetry characterize the first part of *Cligés;* these underscore the text's artifice. In her first love monologue (469ff.) Soredamor describes what she feels according to Ovidian convention: love enters through the eyes which, in this manner, "betray" the heart. The images are antithetical, centered on the concept of madness (*folie*):

> "Doloir? Par foi, donc sui je fole,
> Quant par lui voel ce qui m'afole.
> Volantez don me vaigne enuis
> Doi je bien oster, se je puis.
> Se je puis? Fole, qu'ai je dit?"
>
> (503ff.)

In his parallel monologue Alexandre takes up the same image:

> "Por fol, fet il, me puis tenir.
> Por fol? voiremant sui ge fos,
> Quant ce que je pans dire n'os."
>
> (618ff.)

Brought to the fore precisely within the rhetorical context of love casuistry and displayed almost ostentatiously, these parallelisms help proclaim the particularly romance character of *Cligés.* Chrétien uses romance convention as epitomized, say, in texts from the *matière antique* like *Énéas, Alexandre,* and *Troie;* this use implicitly proclaims the filiation of *Cligés* to that tradition. Both Alexandre and Soredamor are troubled; the chaste pride of the girl balances the hero's timidity. They are "worthy" of each other. But before their penchant for one another may be satisfied, Angrés must be defeated, and the false news of Alexandre's death must be circulated and disproved. We know that all this will lead to marriage (as, indeed, was the case of *Érec et Énide*), but—and I insist once again—we are supposed to focus on the manner in which the story unfolds. Nothing is more romance-like than the long monologues in which, with so perfect a conventionality that the effect is almost one of parody, the minds and hearts of the protagonists are explored in order to reveal a possible discrepancy. Thus Soredamor's great monologue (889-1038), coming after the narrator's depiction of her troubled *corage* (865ff.), illustrates brilliantly the romancer's technical competence. Her situation is entirely conventional: she is the young-maiden-in-love. Her rhetoric, as though to illustrate the *tançons* disturbing her, is based entirely on antithesis and oppositions. In this fashion a kind of dialectic or dispute is formed, and this allows Soredamor to sound out more deeply her soul:

> "Mes volantiers, se je savoie,
> Plus sage et plus bel le feroie.
> Par foi, donc ne le hé je mie.
> Et sui je por itant s'amie?
> Nenil, ne qu'a un autre sui.
> Et por coi pans je donc a lui,

Se plus d'un altre ne m'agree?"

(905ff.)

Similarly, the etymological figure in which Soredamor—and the romance—can fully indulge prompts the maiden, who, like many of her counterparts in OF romances of the *translatio studii* type is highly intelligent, even a bit learned, to recognize her love by equating it with the realization of her own identity:

> "Por neant n'ai ge pas cest non [Soredamor]
> Que Soredamors sui clamee.
> Amer doi, si doi estre amee,
> Si le vuel par mon non prover".

(953ff.)

She continues charmingly and very literarily in this "technical" and bookish image:

> "Et autant dit Soredamors
> Come sororee d'amors.
> Doreüre d'or n'est si fine
> Come ceste qui m'anlumine".

(971ff.)

Confronted with this kind of romance love—and let us not confuse it with *amour courtois*—scholars have been tempted to call it cold and calculated, an *amour de tête.* Certainly the expressive artifice is calculated and very knowingly put together, but the context of this intellectuality remains very much the romance, not the character. Maidens like Soredamor, Fénice, or Lavinie (*Énéas*) do not fall in love in a reasonable, intellectual way. However, they do attempt to assimilate this new passion into their understanding and, like Soredamor here, they often are depicted in their self-analysis as proceeding step by step, quite explicitly, from an initial amorous confusion to a conscious stock-taking and, finally, to an active decision. We are interested in this process and in the means by which it is revealed. Because of our technical concern some readers have been led to deny passion its rightful role even though, quite clearly, Soredamor and her lover suffer the same sweet pangs of passionate love as do Tristan and the blond Yseut. What *Cligés* is hinting at, however, is that the legend of Tristan and Yseut should also be seen as a romance, that the love of Tristan and Yseut is a story, like that of Alexandre and Soredamor, of, especially, Cligés and Fénice. This is the nature (and, we observed, the relevance) of *Cligés* as a critical commentary upon *Tristan,* a commentary quite different from that offered by *Érec et Énide.*

The fashion in which the adventures of Alexandre and his love for Soredamor are recounted strips this material of all "history" and even of "historical illusion." If everything here is more perfectly gratuitous, it follows quite logically that the second step, the "main story" of their son Cligés, must be at least as *romanesque,* if not more so. We recall Alexandre's return to Byzantium and his rather surprising agreement with the usurping Alis. (This agreement is essential, though, to avoid transforming the second part of the romance into a somber, and banal, *Vengeance Cligés.*) Note that as soon as the boy is installed at his uncle's court (like Tristan in Mark's palace), his parents conveniently die. Love, ruses, but chastity and honor, as well as a number of technical devices: orphan nephew dearly loved by a doting uncle, important play of reality

and appearances—all this is clearly established in *Cligés* before the emperor's departure for Germany.

It has been said that the "German" part of *Cligés* constitutes a development of certain political and matrimonial projects that Frederick Barbarossa attempted unsuccessfully to bring off in league with the Greek emperor towards 1170-1174. This is quite plausible. Chrétien might easily have felt free to combine here allusions to certain real happenings with the literary, very *Tristan*-like, and dramatic motif of the matrimonial embassy. By working historical events into the texture of the romance in a manner analogous to his utilization of the *Tristan* data, Chrétien contributes at once to the piquancy of his tale and to the trivialization—the game—it is called upon to bring off; the romance is all the more ironically "true-to-life." At the same time, of course, Chrétien furthers his plot: Cligés and Fénice meet; they may act out their drama within the contexts which were set up by the romance and, of course, largely determined by the story of Alexandre and Soredamor. Like Cligés' parents (and like Tristan and Yseut), Cligés and Fénice are deeply in love, but unlike Alexandre and Soredamor (however, like Tristan and Yseut), marriage is impossible because Alis (like Mark) stands in the way. This *impasse* suffices to provoke the introduction of Thessala's potion of chastity; the potion is structurally "justified." Fénice's body will belong *in reality* only to the man who possesses her heart, though, *in appearance,* she is a loyal and devoted wife. Meanwhile, Cligés dedicates his feats of prowess (in Germany as well as at Arthur's court) to his beloved. Possibly to avoid excessive seriousness at this juncture, the poet-narrator plays increasingly with his material; he intervenes with witty and explicitly literary commentary, turning his romance even from this angle into an ostensibly self-conscious object. Thus, during the tournament at Arthur's court, where Cligés so handsomely distinguishes himself, he refuses to enumerate the knights present (as Wace had done in the Arthurian *Fêtes de cour* scene from *Brut* [10,236ff.] and, indeed, as Chrétien himself, in imitation of Wace, had done in his description of the courtly *fastes* in *Érec et Énide*):

> Devers Galinguefort revint
> Li plus de la chevalerie.
> Cuidiez vos or que je vos die
> Por feire demorer mon conte:
> "Cil roi i furent, et cil conte,
> Et cil, et cil, et cil i furent?"

(4586ff.)

The play of reality and appearances may be considered simultaneously a theme and a motif in *Cligés.* Since, virtually by definition, such play constitutes a properly novelistic *theme,* it is used in *Cligés* as a motif, gratuitously, for its own sake, and, if I may be permitted the seeming paradox, in this way it turns out to be once again an authentic theme—refracted, so to speak, through the romance's various technical contexts. (It is analogous to the similarly contrived theme-motif pattern of, say, "optimism" in *Candide* or "honor" in *Orlando Furioso.*) As we observed, Alexandre loves Soredamor and is loved in return by her. We know this because the novelistic mechanism allows us to penetrate beyond mere appearance into the intimate being of the character (though only insofar as, and in the ways, this being concerns the romance: plot, thematic structure, etc.). However, love produces visible effects; according to the Ovidian convention embraced by most twelfth-century romancers, the lover pales or blushes, his breathing is troubled. Guenevere observes this *malaise* in our young heroes, but, in a delicious play on the theme of appearances vs. reality, she confuses the symptoms of love with those of seasickness! Appearances, we see, do indeed deceive! Yet, conversely, this is also a comment upon the authentic nature of passionate love. Whereas in the more properly novelistic *Érec et Énide* Chrétien attempted to establish a kind of correlation between reality and appearances—after all, Érec's idleness, resulting from his love and the voluptuous delights he enjoys with the apparently Dido-like Énide, does constitute a danger signal—in the first part of *Cligés* everything is centered on the fictional techniques to be used in getting Alexandre and Soredamor together; the problem will be compounded in the case of Cligés and Fénice.

By continuing to follow in this manner the development of the reality-appearances motif in *Cligés,* we stand a better chance of grasping this fiction's special kind of intensity. Let us look at a few key texts.

First, Fénice's complaint. Cligés has just left for Arthur's court, but in taking leave of Fénice (to whom he has not yet revealed his love, nor she to him), he declares:

"Mes droiz est qu'a vos congié praigne
Com a celi cui ge sui toz."
(4282f.)

She analyzes this statement in a very romance-like way, a bit scholastically:

A li seule opose et respont,
Et fet tele oposition.
(4364f.)

Herself in love, she is very impressed by Cligés' half avowal of devotion:

"Cligés par quele entancion
'Je sui toz vostres' me deïst,
S'Amors dire ne li feïst?
De quoi le puis je justisier?"
(4366ff.)

Motif and theme seem to combine here, for, in her monologue, Fénice attributes Cligés' words and tears to a variety of different causes. The transition is a masterpiece;

"Par foi, donc m'a cil maubaillie
Qui mon cuer a en sa baillie,
Ne m'aimme pas, ce sai je bien,
Qui me desrobe et tost le mien.
Jel sai? Por coi ploroit il dons?
Por coi? Ne fu mien an pardons,
Asez i ot reison de quoi.
N'en doi neant prandre sor moi,
Car de gent qu'an aimme et conoisse
Se part an a molt grant angoisse.
Quant il leissa sa conoissance,
Si en ot enui et pesance,
Et s'il plora, ne m'an mervoil.
Mes qui li dona cest consoil,

Qu'an Bretaigne alast demorer,
Ne me poïst mialz acorer.
Acorez est qui son cuer pert.
Mal doit avoir qui le suen pert,
Mes je ne le desservi onques
Ha, dolante, por coi m'a donques
Cligés morte sanz nul forfet?"
(4419ff.)

Fénice goes on from her memory of Cligés to rather more general considerations, and then returns to her own situation. She knows her own suffering, but what do Cligés' tears *really* mean? What is hidden behind these signs? She is caught up in her own romance.

Our second example is perhaps the capital text in the entire story: Fénice's avowal to Cligés of her love and of her maidenly reality (despite her outwardly apparent status as a married lady). Everything has built up to this confrontation. The "reality" is of course close to that of Tristan and Yseut; indeed it departs from the prototype in a direction leading to parody. Fénice's diction reinforces this impression:

"Qu'ainz vostre oncles n'ot en moi part,
Car moi ne plot, ne lui ne lut.
Onques ancor ne me conut,
Si com Adanz conut sa fame.
A tort sui apelee dame,
Mes bien sai, qui dame m'apele
Ne set que je soie pucele."
(5176ff.)

We cannot take seriously Fénice's declaration of moral purpose, except insofar as it renders possible at last the union of the storybook couple of whom we have become fond, the "natural" *dénouement* of the romance. Her conduct is legitimate only in a romance world; note the play on the pretension to exemplary value claimed by so many romances of the *translatio studii* type:

"Vostre est mes cuers, vostre est mes cors,
Ne ja nus par mon essanplaire
N'aprendra vilenie a faire."
(5190ff.)

And:

"Se je vos aim, et vos m'amez,
Ja n'en seroiz Tristanz clamez,
Ne je n'an serai ja Yseuz."
(5199ff.)

Chrétien is careful once again to reinforce the romance quality of all this by having Cligés quote learnedly from the legend of Troy when he proposes flight to Arthur's court as a solution to their dilemma (5239ff.), and by having Fénice, in reply, first quote from *Tristan* and then Saint Paul! The romance context intensifies and becomes even more pure; the play of realities and appearances turns out to be still more perfectly gratuitous. Thus, Saint Paul's doctrines concerning chastity are invoked to justify Fénice's playing dead!

The solution proposed by Fénice is unadulterated romance; the philtre, the feigned death, the refuge for the lovers. (One recalls that other *locus amœnus,* the isolated cave, where Tristan and Yseut dwelt in peace, the powerful topic of lovers against the world. The total artifice of the refuge-tomb in which Cligés and Fénice spend fifteen months of bliss—there is running hot water!—contrasts with the rustic simplicity of Tristan's cave; nevertheless Cligés seems here to see through this simplicity, down to the essential artificiality of the topos.) In any case the romance is ready to take off.

Reality and appearances, truth and lies, indeed, right and wrong—all these remain subject to the needs of the romance (and to its conditioning), especially starting with Fénice's confession of love. She pretends to be ill:

> L'empererriz, sanz mal qu'ele ait,
> Se plaint et malade se fait,
> Et l'empereres qui la croit
> De duel feire ne se recroit
> Et mires querre li envoie,
> Mes el ne vialt que nus la voie,
> Ne les leisse a li adeser.
> Ce puet l'empereor peser
> Qu'ele dit que ja n'i avra
> Mire fors un qui li savra
> Legieremant doner santé,
> Quant lui vendra a volanté.
> Cil la fera morir ou vivre,
> An celui se met a delivre
> Et de santé, et de sa vie.
> De Deu cuident que ele die,
> Mes molt a male entancion,
> Qu'ele n'antant s'a Cligés non:
> C'est ses Dex qui la puet garir.
> Et qui la puet feir morir.
>
> (5627ff.)

These very sophisticated lines are important: They confirm the light tone, the gentle irony that pervades the latter part of the romance. As though he were elaborating a symmetrical counterpart, a happy ending, to contrast with the pathetic and sad story of Tristan, Chrétien gives free rein to lightness and humor. A kind of *fabliau* quality is exploited, not only in the witty *double-entendres* we have just read but also in certain comic episodes, e.g., when Thessala obtains a urine specimen from a dying woman in order to deceive Fénice's doctors:

> Li mire vindrent an la sale,
> L'orine voient pesme et male,
> Si dit chascuns ce que lui sanble,
> Tant qu'a ce s'acordent ansanble
> Que ja mes ne respassera,
> Ne ja none ne passera,
> Et se tant vit, dont au plus tart
> An prandra Dex l'ame a sa part.
> Ce ont a consoil murmuré.
> Lors a dit et conjuré
> L'enpereres que voir an dïent.
>
> (5677ff.)

Reality and appearances, truth and fiction!

Then there is Fénice's death, with all the lamenting. The funeral scene is doubly a *scene* since, first of all, it occurs in a romance and, secondly, it is put on, or staged, even within the fiction. Chrétien plays along with his public and everyone has a good time. It is pleasant to appreciate gratuitously, not with sadness but rather with gleeful irony, funereal eloquence (5718ff.). The scene is artfully con-

structed, reminding one of the burial of Esclados-le-Roux in **Yvain.**

The episode of the three physicians from Salerno adds to the narrative accumulation of this descriptive fresco. This episode is a kind of amplification upon the event of Fénice's "death." Through their sadism the doctors—pure villains like their equally "correct" and righteous counterparts, the jealous courtiers and mean dwarfs in *Tristan*—prove to be detestable and richly deserve the punishment inflicted upon them by the outraged town ladies. (Does Chrétien subvert to his comic purposes here the "psychology" of the love tribunals of his time?) This new *fabliau* helps him round out his narrative with yet another variation on the motif of reality and appearances. Besides, we all know that Thessala will find a balm to restore Fénice to her former health and beauty.

The poet-narrator's irony becomes, to say the least, ambivalent and ambiguous when the romance seems to carry over to the real world, that is, when the reader is tempted to make the transfer in his celebration of Cligés' joy. The text guards against such a transfer by seemingly encouraging it. The narrator utilizes a typical hyperbole to evoke the lovers' pleasure and its possible moral counterpart:

> Certes, de rien ne s'avilla
> Amors, quant il les mist ansanble;
> Car a l'un et a l'autre sanble,
> Quant li uns l'autre acole et beise,
> Que de lor joie et de lor eise
> Soit toz li mondes amandez;
> Ne ja plus ne m'an demandez.
>
> (6252ff.)

But by playing with the perspective—"it seems *to them* when they kiss and embrace each other that, because of *their* joy and happiness, the entire world is better off"—Chrétien stresses that they are living a romance, perhaps, in fact, that to a degree all such lovers live a romance and that love, so conceived, is "romantic." This ought not to be taken seriously, that is, outside the romance context. Once again the nature of this text as fiction shapes what it says and, concomitantly, provides an insight into the purposes Chrétien assigns to this kind of fiction: **Cligés** is largely a romance given over to telling us what romances are and what they can do.

Chrétien's technical mastery in **Cligés** is brilliant; moreover, it is intended to be brilliant. He pulls out all the stops. A catalogue of devices used by him in this romance would adequately fill a handbook of rhetoric. Furthermore, the ostensibly bookish frame of reference—*Tristan, Énéas, Statius, Troie,* and Wace—within which plot and characterization are achieved both accentuates and utilizes the high degree of literary consciousness built into the fiction. No wonder, then, that **Cligés** deserves to be seen as the prototype of a kind of sparkling, humorously ironic, and delicately contrived fiction so much in favor toward the close of the twelfth century and at the start of the thirteenth. One thinks of *Floire et Blanchefleur, Amadas et Idoine, Blancandrin, Aucassin et Nicolete,* and others. The character of Soredamor has been viewed by at least one critic, A. Micha, as the "type de l'orgueilleuse d'amour" and described as the model for characters in some of the above-mentioned texts as well as in *Ipomédon* and *Le Bel Inconnu*. Certainly, *Cligés* shares with *Amadas et Idoine* a similarly "literary" and "ironic" tone in respect to the Tristan myths from which they derive and against which they react *as romances*. *Cligés* is never "profound"; that is its main point, of course, and, one is tempted to add, its profundity. Rather than having "méconnu la vérité humaine et tragique du *Tristan*" (Frappier), Chrétien does quite the opposite: he recognizes and isolates in *Cligés* the gratuitous romance hidden in the legend. He has hardly committed what Frappier called "un gauchissement du sujet véritable"; on the contrary, by providing it with an authentic romance form he has deepened the subject's meaning and, coincidentally, he has done much to widen the possibilities open to narrative fiction. Not only . . . do the later romances profit from the kind of technical mastery Chrétien explores and perfects in *Cligés,* but—and perhaps more significant for the subsequent development of the European narrative—*Cligés* stands at the head of a tradition that counts Ariosto, Cervantes, Voltaire, and Sterne among its more recent representatives.

The specifically literary artistry deployed in *Cligés* tends to undercut, then, the *matière* (here both that of Greece and the "vain" Breton matter); indeed the very concept of "content" is rendered problematic. However, such undercutting allows the romance to develop in conformity with its own purposes, gratuitously, as we saw, and with the literary resonances we observed. In *Cligés* Chrétien de Troyes is less the poetic philologist than his *confrères* of the *Alexandre* or *Thèbes* tradition—less even than Wace, whom, however, Chrétien resembles the closest—but he goes one step further: he clearly identifies his work in general with their spirit. This identification is what is surely meant by Chrétien's reference in his Prologue to the *translatio studii* and to the pairing of *clergie* and *chevalerie*. He is consistent in his reshaping, or celebration, of chivalric "ideals" according to the rhetoric and structures of romance fiction. Instead of serving a "history" he serves a literary tradition, a tradition that allows him to see through certain moral claims or propositions at the same time he can exploit in amusing ways a fine gamut of tales. This is, I think, the interpretation that ought to be given to Chrétien's rephrasing in the Prologue to *Cligés* of the familiar topos we had noticed in Wace (*Rou*) and elsewhere:

> Par les livres que nos avons
> Les fez des anciens savons
> Et del siegle qui fu jadis.
>
> (25ff.)

In short, it does not seem to me to be out of place or anachronistic to apply the label "anti-novel" to *Cligés,* especially since in tone, plot, and characterization it cultivates a flatness quite unlike (and even opposed to), say, *Érec et Énide* (a far more novelistic response to *Tristan*, . . .) or *Yvain* and *Perceval.* Yet, as we all know, opposites tend to attract, or influence, one another. The preoccupation with technique that so characterizes *Cligés* will hardly be shaken off in subsequent texts. If anything Chrétien states even more explicitly in his later prologues—implicitly in *Yvain,* quite explicitly in *Lancelot* and *Perceval*—the im-

portance of his craftsmanship. With *Cligés* Chrétien has proved his master's skill in the narrative; perhaps, even, he has gained a certain independence from the same bookish tradition he poeticized in *Cligés.* Full control must imply a degree of detachment. He has certainly demonstrated his independence, his irony, with respect to the values and social myths indulged in by his patrons. Finally, he has formulated an unmistakable narrative point of view, a kind of narrative "I," that, to be sure, capitalizes upon the literary self-consciousness of the genre within which he has chosen to work, but also exploits the possibilities open to such self-consciousness. With *Cligés* and its technical focus Chrétien achieves a deepening, a thickening, I should say, in his narrative art. (pp. 157-73)

> *Karl D. Uitti, "Chrétien de Troyes," in his* Story, Myth, and Celebration in Old French Narrative Poetry: 1050-1200, *Princeton University Press, 1973, pp. 128-231.*

Luttrell on Chrétien as the originator of the Arthurian romance:

The twelfth-century renaissance brought great developments in art, literature, and thought, and the example of the Latin classics and the practice of Latin composition stimulated the birth of the French romance, as a book narrative in verse for the entertainment of the well-bred. It reached its prime in the series by Chrétien de Troyes, the father of Arthurian romance, a title which is justified whether or not he was the first to bestow the conditions of written poetic composition on what had been a form of story-telling practised by professional entertainers, the tale of adventure associated with Arthur's court. For his *Erec et Enide* is the first romance we have whose hero rides on adventure in the imagined heroic age when Arthur holds sway, and to those who came after him Chrétien was the master of the form. Much in the luxuriant growth of Arthurian story can be traced directly from him, and when derivation from tales that Chrétien drew on is assumed, the likely shape of these is in fact determined by our conception of what he did with them.

> *Claude Luttrell, in his* The Creation of the First Arthurian Romance: A Quest, *Edward Arnold, 1974.*

Ruth Harwood Cline   (essay date 1975)

[*Cline is an American translator and member of the International Arthurian Society who has translated three of Chrétien's romances. In the excerpt below from the introduction to her translation of* Yvain, *she presents an overview of the "poetic language and vivid style" of* Yvain.]

Chrétien de Troyes was the creator of the Arthurian romance as a literary genre: he was the first known writer in Western Europe to put the Celtic legends of King Arthur and his knights into the long romance form in order to illustrate themes from the twelfth-century codes of love and chivalry. His five romances, *Erec and Enide, Cligès,*

Lancelot, Yvain, and *Perceval,* were written between 1160 and 1190, a period in France of great interest in British legends and folklore. Chrétien was considered an outstanding poet in an exceptionally rich period of literary creativity, and his romances were sensationally successful in the courts of Western Europe and Italy and were translated and imitated into the fifteenth century. Apart from their profound influence upon European literature, Chrétien's romances are outstanding in themselves, as poetry, as well-constructed and entertaining tales of love and adventure, as perceptive studies of human psychology and emotion, and as portraits of mankind's struggle to attain the earthly ideals of self-perfection and joy. (p. xi)

Yvain; or, the Knight with the Lion is often considered to be Chrétien de Troyes's masterpiece, and it is one of the best constructed, most captivating tales in medieval literature. The story of the lord Yvain, his beautiful wife, and his devoted lion was carried as far north as Iceland and is preserved in seven manuscripts (Paris B.N. 794, Guiot copy; Paris B.N. 1433; Paris B.N. 1450; Paris B.N. 12560; Paris B.N. 12603; Rome Vatican 1725, Chantilly 432) and two fragments (Montpellier and Annonay). This romance has maintained its high place in medieval literature, not only because of its dramatic adventures, fine analyses of sentiment, and appealing themes, but also because of its poetic language and vivid style.

In the first part of the romance, after hearing his cousin Calogrenant's account of a disastrous visit to a magic, storm-making fountain, the courageous lord Yvain establishes his reputation at King Arthur's court by riding alone to the fountain, braving the storm, slaying the defender of the fountain, and with the help of a maiden, Lunette, marrying the knight's beautiful and wealthy widow. After entertaining King Arthur and the court in his new domain, Yvain receives his wife's permission to leave her, and promising to return within one year, he departs with his friend Gawain to achieve even greater successes at a round of tournaments.

Carried away by his triumphs, Yvain forgets his promise and overstays the year. His wife rejects him utterly, and his grief drives him insane. Naked, starving, and amnesic, Yvain lives like an animal in the forest until he is befriended by a charitable hermit and cured of his madness by the lady of Noríson. A neighbor, Count Alier, has been attacking her property, and Yvain rallies her men and wins the war to repay her. After this victory Yvain rescues a lion from a serpent, assumes another identity, and as "the Knight with the Lion," devotes himself to the service of women in need. With the lion's help he rescues Gawain's niece and nephews from degradation or death by slaying a giant, Harpin of the Mountain, and then upon the same day rescues Lunette from death by fire by overcoming her three accusers. Disguised as "the Knight with the Lion," Yvain talks afterward with his wife and learns that the time for their reconciliation is not yet at hand.

Yvain's next triumph takes place at the Castle of Evil Adventure, where with the lion's help he rescues three hundred captive maidens by slaying two gigantic demons. He returns to King Arthur's court to defend the property rights of the younger daughter of the lord of the Black Thorn and fights incognito against Gawain, his closest friend and the best knight in the world, with whom he ties. After the battle, when his dual identity is revealed, Yvain, the Knight with the Lion, receives greater acclaim than ever before. He has also become worthy of his wife's forgiveness, which he returns to the fountain to seek, and the romance ends with their reconciliation.

Chrétien de Troyes derived the material for his romances from three sources: the British legends of King Arthur and other heroes of Celtic folklore, the French epics of Charlemagne and his knights, and the Greek and Roman myths and legends. *Yvain*'s origins are Celtic: *Yvain* is a form of *Owain,* who according to Chrétien's source commanded an army known as "The Ravens" in the sixth century, and with his father Urien, a historic king of the border district of Rheged, acquitted himself so valiantly against the Angles that King Arthur awarded him the kingdom of Scotland. Both Owain's and Urien's names were preserved in Welsh folklore. In the earlier legends Urien wooed and won the fairy of a fountain, who, with her friends, would take the form of an army of ravens to assist her son Owain in battle. As the legend was retold over the centuries, Owain supplanted his father as the wooer of "the Lady of the Fountain," whose traditional name *Laudine* is derived from the Latin name of Scotland. A shorter version of the tale of Yvain, Laudine, and the lion, "The Lady of the Fountain" was a well-established part of the repertoire of the Welsh bards (known today as *The Mabinogion*) and may have a common source with Chrétien de Troyes's romance.

Despite its traditional sources *Yvain* is not an imitation of a Celtic legend, but an original creation of the twelfth century. Yvain and his lady act in accordance with the edicts of courtly love, which were codified by Andreas Capellanus at a later date. The observations and the debates of the courts of love are interspersed throughout the romance, and a clerical antifeminism appears side by side with idealization of the lady. The romance mirrors twelfth-century society, from the sensual charm of an aristocratic house party to the miserable conditions of a silk workshop. As is often the case in medieval literature, some minor characters are presented in disproportionate detail, and many major characters are not described or named until long after they appear. The narrator is always present, commenting and forewarning, and never hesitating to interrupt the story with a discussion of love, which his listeners greatly enjoyed.

Above all, Chrétien meant to be entertaining, and the widespread popularity of his romances shows that he succeeded. His language is polished and elegant, his tone is witty, his descriptions of festivals and battles are colorful, and his debates are marvels of dialectic reasoning. He enlivens the romance with puns, proverbs, and parodies; he exaggerates and understates; he is by turns ironic and playful. His most fantastic scenes are described in meticulous detail, with distance, time, and cost carefully noted to give an aura of realism to the marvelous. The story's pace is swift, and many of the incidents are so amusingly told that at first the reader may not realize their deeper significance.

An important theme in **Yvain** is the portrayal of courtly love in marriage: an interesting idea since the prevailing opinion was that the legal obligations and enforced proximity of marriage accorded ill with a freely given, inspirational emotion, particularly one which made the lover submit to his lady's commands. Nonetheless the relationship between Yvain and his wife is one of courtly love, and their difficulties arise, not because of Yvain's pursuit of glory, but because of his broken promise to return within one year, his failure to prove a love he knew was being tested. Interpreting Yvain's forgetfulness as lack of love, the lady accordingly withdraws her own. As she will never knowingly admit Yvain to her presence again, his only hope lies in becoming a different person: establishing another identity and winning a finer reputation, which the lion helps him to do. At the end of the romance when the lady consents to see "the Knight with the Lion," Yvain has a chance to plead for forgiveness, which the lady grants to reconcile the knight and his lady as she had promised to do.

The lion however is far more than a helpful pet, and the role of the lion is one of the most disputed questions in the analysis of **Yvain.** Jean Frappier notes that in the Middle Ages the lion symbolized courage tempered by humility and, in the profane order, the perfect knight; in the spiritual order, Saviour Christ. Yvain's lion seems to fill all these roles in turn. Yvain never lacked courage, but he was indeed wanting in humility, and another theme of the romance is the rehabilitation of a knight who, at a pinnacle of worldly glory, commits the deadly sin of pride and loses what is most precious to him, the terrestrial joy of his lady's love. After sinking to the level of wild beasts, mind gone, body weakened from exposure, Yvain learns humility, both from the lion's example and from sharing credit for the victories with him, as the name "the Knight with the Lion" implies. It is equally true that Yvain pursues and attains the goal of becoming a perfect knight throughout the romance and that the presence of the lion is interpreted everywhere as an indication of Yvain's worth as a knight, of his noble birth and great courage.

But at a deeper level, one of the lessons which Yvain learns is that, splendid fighter though he is, he is nothing in himself. Without the help of a charitable society he would have died insane in the forest, and without the help of God, whose aid is requested before every battle except the early ones, he would never have survived his combats with gigantic or supernatural foes. Julian Harris observes that the theory of the judicial trial by combat was that God sided with the Right, and the lion, entering the fray after Yvain, despite his best efforts, realizes that he cannot win, does seem to play the role of Christ. Together they fight increasingly dangerous battles for greater rewards; their final triumph over the demons is on a supernatural plane. Before the fight with Gawain, Yvain shows that he realizes he owes his strength and his victories to God. Without help from the lion he ties with the best knight in the world, surpasses him in courtesy, and as a perfect Christian knight, returns to his lady and is forgiven. (xii-xvi)

For medieval poets the form was as important as the content of their poems, and even the less exacting verse form

of narrative poetry (rhymed octosyllabic couplets) influenced the poet's way of expressing his ideas. Chrétien de Troyes depended upon rhyme and meter to establish the swift pace of his romances. He used poetical images and metaphors, and frequently he employed the poetic device of rephrasing and repeating an important idea to fix it against the forward movement of the poem. . . . As a poet he was an innovator, responsible for making the narrative verse form more flexible by using enjambment and by breaking the couplet, for varying the traditional rhymes and assonance with identities and very rich rhymes, and for enriching and expanding the vocabulary of his time. Perhaps with a verse translation people who do not read Old French easily [would] be able to see Chrétien de Troyes in a different light and to appreciate his important role in the development of the Arthurian romance in French and English literature. (pp. xvi-xvii)

> *Ruth Harwood Cline, in an introduction to* Yvain: or, The Knight with the Lion *by Chrétien de Troyes, translated by Ruth Harwood Cline, The University of Georgia Press, 1975, pp. xi-xvii.*

Raymond H. Thompson   (essay date 1979)

[*In the following excerpt, Thompson suggests that courtly love is presented as a confining force in Chrétien's romances when the heroes devote themselves to love rather than the good of society.*]

At the conclusion of Chrétien de Troyes' **Le Chevalier de la Charrete,** we read:

> Godefroiz de Leigni, li clers,
> a parfinee *La Charrete;*
>
> . . . par le boen gré
> Crestïen, qui le comança:
> tant en a fet des lors an ça
> ou Lanceloz fu anmurez,
> tant con li contes est durez.
> Tant en a fet, n'i vialt plus metre
> ne moins, por le conte mal metre.
>
> (vv.7102-3, 7106-12)

In choosing to leave his hero thus cut off from society, Chrétien is falling back upon a motif which he employs regularly in his poetry: the isolation and confinement of the knight whose devotion to his lady outweighs his willingness to serve society as a whole.

The pattern begins in **Erec et Enide.** This poem opens with the story of how Erec chastises the arrogant Yder. Pride which scorns the rights of others is a *desmesure* which endangers society. Erec, by abasing Yder's pride, performs a service to society for which he is rewarded with the love of Enide. Unfortunately, once wed, Erec neglects the deeds which will benefit the commonweal:

> Mes tant l'ama Erec d'amors,
> que d'armes mes ne li chaloit,
> ne a tornoiemant n'aloit.
>
> (vv. 2430-32)

Instead he thinks only of his wife,

si an fist s'amie et sa drue;
en li a mise s'antendue,
en acoler et an beisier;

(vv. 2435-37)

The court thus becomes a self-chosen prison in which the hero is confined by his love for his lady. There is nothing to prevent Erec's departure other than his own attachment to Enide, for it is not her wish that he forsake deeds of arms. Yet so beguiled is he that he only realizes he stands condemned by all for dereliction of knightly duty when Enide herself discloses the general opinion. Erec is shocked into immediate action, setting forth with his lady like a true knight errant, "ne set ou, mes en avanture" (v. 2763).

Unfortunately, Erec's departure is as much prompted by anger and hurt pride as by the desire to resume his service to society, and he must suffer severely before he is purged of his own folly. Nevertheless, deeds like the rescue of a knight from two cruel giants help to restore the balance of order and justice, and so earn him the right to his redemption. Erec's return to his rightful role in society is celebrated by his encounter with Mabonagrain, who is confined from the outside world by love for a lady, just as was Erec. Whereas Erec has since served society well by his deeds of valour, Mabonagrain is compelled, by an oath to his mistress, to remain in a garden until he should be defeated in combat:

"par ce me cuida a delivre,
toz les jorz que j'eüsse a vivre,
avoec li tenir an prison."

(vv. 6045-47)

Mabonagrain does not know the nature of the lady's request when he grants her a boon, but he emphasizes that he acceded quite readily, for no true lover can deny the wishes of his mistress. Although unhappy when he learns that he has promised to remain in the garden until he should be defeated in combat, Mabonagrain confesses that he kept his displeasure secret lest she withdrew her love, a prospect he fears above all else. Thus he is obliged to remain in the garden, wherein "par nigromance" (v. 5692) every kind of songbird sings sweetly amidst a profusion of flowers, fruits, and spices. Yet for all the sensual delight it brings, this love deprives society of a valuable servant. His prowess benefits only the lady since it serves to keep him firmly by her side. Once Mabonagrain is defeated by Erec, he is free of his oath and can turn his abilities in more useful directions, as the great joy of the general populace signals.

The physical confinement in which Erec and Mabonagrain place themselves is not strict in that others may visit them although they cannot depart. Both knights are tied by their love for a lady, but they are not deaf to the call of their duty to serve society as knights errant. Once Erec remembers this duty, the very excess of his response suggests remorse at his neglect, while Mabonagrain, though unwilling to oppose his lady's wishes, remains unhappy at her choice. This "social conscience" is reflected by the degree of social contact both can maintain, social contact that is significantly absent from Jehan's tower in *Cligés.*

Here Cligés and Fenice are completely isolated from the outside world. Indeed, were the lady's presence revealed all would be lost, for she is the wife of the Emperor Alis who believes her dead. When the pair are accidentally discovered, they are forced to flee the emperor's vengeance. Although Cligés is free to leave the tower, he does so but rarely, so deeply is he enamoured of Fenice.

Once again it is society which suffers from this preoccupation with his mistress, as Cligés' career shows. While he can win honour under his lady's eyes he is prompted to many acts of rash courage in the campaign against the Saxons. However, when the pursuit of chivalry takes him from the side of his beloved, his enthusiasm wanes; filled with love-longing he leaves Arthur's court, where "S'a fet mainte chevalerie' (v. 5012).

Talanz li prant que il s'an aille,
Car trop a fet grant consirree
De veoir la plus desirree
C'onques nus puisse desirrer,

(vv. 5020-23)

However, this love affair goes beyond the mere weakening of society by the withdrawal of the knight's service, for it threatens to engulf the entire realm in civil war and its attendant destruction, already demonstrated in this romance by the rebellion of Count Angrés against Arthur.

The lovers seek to evade their social responsibilities in this remote tower with its sheer walls and single concealed entrance, but the futility of such a course is suggested by the artificiality of the environment. The windowless interior is illuminated by artificial lighting and painted vaults replace real views, while the attached garden is dominated by an exotic grafted tree. Reality intrudes into this escapist fantasy when they are discovered and forced into the outside world once again. The lovers finally take fitting places in society, ruling as emperor and empress. Yet the latter does not escape the poet's ironic comment upon her tainted reputation, for, unlike Erec and Enide, this pair have done little to earn social acceptance. Civil war is only avoided by the death of Alis, whose initial injustices in refusing to yield the throne to his older brother and then marrying despite his promise precipitate the crisis. Although thematically appropriate, this development is fortuitous.

However, Arthur, the deceived husband in *Le Chevalier de la Charrete,* cannot be so conveniently removed from the scene. This would offend not only tradition but, more importantly, justice, for unlike Alis the king is guilty of no serious offence. He passively leaves to others the task of rescuing Guenevere from Meleagant, and if not ungrateful he is certainly forgetful of the service Lancelot performs in saving the queen. Nevertheless, at worst he can be blamed for weakness; he deprives no one of their rights. Rather it is Lancelot and Guenevere who betray Arthur, the husband of one and feudal lord of both. Moreover, Lancelot compounds his offence by the trick oath he swears in defence of Guenevere's innocence. The deceit practised by Lancelot to defend the queen from the charge of adultery offends against the spirit, if not the wording, of the oath, especially since in his enthusiasm to protest his mistress' innocence he not only calls down divine vengeance upon whoever lies but also prays that God may bring the truth to light. It is significant that when the trial by combat begins, the antagonists are quickly separated before any decision can be reached.

Just as Lancelot's conduct is less justifiable from the point of view of social justice than is that of Erec, Mabonagrain, or even Cligés, so the tower in which he is imprisoned is the most isolated of all. He lacks even the solace of his lady, for he is completely alone, his abode known only to his bitterest foe. The doors are walled up so that "n'i remest huis ne antree / fors c'une petite fenestre" (vv. 6138-39). His prospects of winning social approval for his relationship with Guenevere are as hopeless as the conditions of his confinement, for he, not Arthur, is the one who has offended against his oath. If Guenevere is to become Lancelot's wife, it can only be through the destruction of Arthur and all his noblest followers. And the destruction of the court would eventually diminish the stature of the lovers, since Lancelot would no longer be its foremost champion, nor Guenevere its foremost lady. Thus there can be no real escape from the prison imposed by Lancelot's adulterous relations with the queen. The situation is hopeless. Furthermore, this suggests that Chrétien abandoned the poem when he did precisely because there could be no solution to Lancelot's dilemma, further evidence of the poet's basic disapproval of *fin' amor.*

The confining force of *fin' amor* does not operate in Chrétien's **Yvain,** where the hero's offence is to neglect his duties to his wife rather than to over-indulge his love at the expense of other responsibilities. Once Yvain is made aware of his failure, he quits Arthur's court for the woods where, after losing his senses, he wanders at large. His fate thus is the reverse of that which befalls the too-fond lovers of the earlier romances. While all are punished for their lack of social responsibility by banishment from the ordered society of the court, the punishment differs in that Yvain wanders unrestrained in the wilderness, whereas the others are confined in an artificial prison. The chaos of disorder replaces the prison of the senses. Redemption is achieved finally after service to society as represented by a series of abused damsels and ladies; thereafter, Yvain can resume his proper station at the courts both of Arthur and of his wife.

The threat of imprisonment occurs twice in Chrétien's **Perceval.** On the first occasion, Gawain is engaged in wooing the sister of the King of Escavalon when he finds himself besieged in the tower by the outraged citizenry. On the second, after triumphing over the dangers at the Castle of Marvels, he is invited to remain there as ruler and protector of the ladies who dwell therein. In neither case is Gawain in serious danger of being trapped in a prison of love. While far from averse to an affair with an unattached damsel, he never, throughout his long literary career, shows any interest in giving up the roving life of a knight errant in order to serve one lady. Gawain's relationship with the damsel of Escavalon is little more than a courteous dalliance, and he rejects out of hand the insistence that he remain at the Castle of Wonders. However, the former adventure, in which Gawain is unaware that he is wooing the sister of a vengeful enemy until he is attacked by the angry townspeople, recalls Cligés' escape from reality in the

arms of another fair lady until he too is discovered; and his situation in the Castle of Marvels recalls that of Mabonagrain in his magical garden, reluctantly confined, though free to fight against intruders. The dangers posed by the prison of the senses thus are not forgotten, and Gawain's successful avoidance of them despite difficulties should be seen as more of a tribute to this stalwart champion than is normally allowed him.

Whether the Grail Castle was intended to fit into this pattern remains conjecture. It is tempting to view it as a spiritual alternative to the sensual prison, a mystical vision of the heavenly kingdom which the true Christian will attain once released from this petty and confining life. Only in God's service does one find perfect freedom. However, given the incomplete condition of Chrétien's poem, such a development remains but an unrealized possibility.

The pattern scrutinized in this study reveals the dangers that lie in wait for Chrétien's knights when they neglect their duty to serve society. As the fate of Yvain warns, love must be paid its due, for love sanctified by marriage is a vital element in the social fabric. However, the demands of love must not be allowed to supersede broader responsibilities, and it is this awareness which prompts Enide's lament over her husband's *recreantise.* When the joys of love turn into the selfishness of sensual indulgence, then the amorous refuge is transformed into a prison. This transformation is marked on the one hand by the isolation of the lovers, which grows with their neglect of social obligations; and on the other by the initial increase in emphasis upon details which appeal to the senses: the birdsong, flower and spices of Mabonagrain's garden, and the grafted tree and painted murals of Jehan's tower replace the more general magnificence of King Lac's court. However, these details are the product of magic and artifice, sustained by isolation from a reality that inevitably intrudes. Erec must do harsh penance as a knight errant; Mabonagrain tastes bitter defeat in combat; Cligés becomes a hunted traitor who threatens his own kingdom with civil war. Yet the severest penalty is reserved for Lancelot, who finds not only that his tower is the most isolated and confining, but also that the sensual delights have vanished like dust. One small window allows the cold light of day to illuminate plain stone and meagre fare. And it is here that Chrétien chooses to leave his hero, for Godefroi reports, chillingly, that "n'i vialt plus metre / ne moins, por le conte mal metre" (vv. 7111-12). Like the knight in Keats' "La Belle Dame Sans Merci", Lancelot has awakened from the illusory dream-world of passionate love to taste the harsh reality of the prison of the senses. (pp. 249-53)

Raymond H. Thompson, "The Prison of the Senses: 'Fin' Amor' as a Confining Force in the Arthurian Romances of Chrétien de Troyes," in Forum for Modern Language Studies, *Vol. XV, No. 3, July, 1979, pp. 249-54.*

Deborah Nelson   (essay date 1981)

[*In the following excerpt, Nelson contends that Enide's dual role in* Erec and Enide—*as both* amie *("lover")* and femme *("wife") to Erec—constitutes an important theme in Chrétien's narrative: the difference between courtly love and married love.*]

Many critics define the unifying theme of **Erec et Enide** in terms of an evaluation of Erec's character and experiences and consider Enide merely as an extension of her husband's personality. The character of Enide, however, demands close scrutiny on its own merit, especially since Chrétien presents a major portion of the tale from her point of view. It is Enide to whose interior monologues the reader listens, and it is her torment and fear of abandonment with which he identifies. Even before she appears on the scene, Chrétien foreshadows her arrival from his first reference to the hunt of the White Stag. With the decision of the court to await Erec's return to award the kiss of the White Stag to the most beautiful maiden, the stage is set for his encounter with and his winning of Enide. Even though the author states that Erec is the subject of his story (v. 19), this character, in fact, maintains a consistent distance from the reader to the point that his motivations remain as mysterious to the reader as they do to Enide. When he angrily commands Enide to put on her most elegant dress and mount her finest horse (vv. 2576-79), the reader shares her bewilderment. Erec has obviously been troubled by Enide's informing him of the rumors at court about his neglect of chivalric duties, but at no time does Chrétien have Erec reveal his feelings either to Enide or to the reader. Similarly, Erec never discloses his reasons for ordering Enide to ride ahead of him and forbidding her to speak to him. Along with Enide, the reader can only speculate concerning the nature of her test.

Throughout the *roman,* Erec remains a powerful but stiff figure who challenges and defeats in combat numerous knights while always observing the conventional rules of honor. On the other hand, Enide displays a delicate sensitivity in her reactions to all situations, whether she simply blushes prettily, or cannily senses the danger inherent in a situation, as in the encounter with the first nobleman who plots Erec's death (vv. 3308-3517). Enide's reactions are strikingly human, especially in contrast with those of Erec who, as a character of extremes, merely fights fiercely or makes love joyfully.

Although Erec evolves socially from a loner, who prefers the company of the queen to that of his fellow knights engaged in hunting, to a more outgoing leader and king of his own country, the changes which occur in Enide's status are much more dramatic. She rises from the position of the rag-clad daughter of a poor *vavasor* to become the *amie* and then the *femme* of a knight of King Arthur's court and finally to attain the rank of queen. The ease of Enide's transition from *pucelle* to *amie* is exemplified in the text by her discarding the rags she wore to court and her being dressed in fine garments chosen by the queen herself (vv. 1567-1620). Surprisingly though, Enide's role as *amie* does not terminate with her marriage to Erec and her assumption of the duties and responsibilities of *femme,* and soon one focal point of the plot develops around the inherent conflict in her dual roles. Unlike the situation in Marie de France's *Eliduc* where the roles of *amie* and *femme* are neatly divided between Guilliadun and Guildeluëc, Enide must try to fulfill both roles, which are mutually exclusive in the sense that one is dominating while the other is submissive. Chrétien himself presents another variation on the theme in **Le Chevalier de la charrette** where Guenivere is, like Enide, simultaneously *amie* and *femme,* but to different men (respectively Lancelot and Arthur).

In comparison to his later treatment of Guenivere and to Marie de France's portrayal of Guilliadun, Chrétien underplays Enide's position as *amie.* Whereas Erec renders the most traditional kind of love service in winning the sparrowhawk tourney for Enide, neither he nor Enide suffer the torments of love described at length in both *Eliduc* and **Le Chevalier de la charrette.** Erec simply expresses to her father in a rational and practical manner his desire to marry Enide, and on the way to Cardigan, where Erec will present Enide to King Arthur's court, the young couple realize that they are in love (vv. 1463-96). Despite Erec's avowed love for her, Enide never emerges as the demanding and unreasonable *amie* seen in Guenivere, who sets impossible tasks for Lancelot and whose will must not only be obeyed without question but whose whims must even be anticipated. Likewise, the princess Guilliadun enjoys the attention showered on her by Eliduc and his declarations of love while she expects his acquiescence to her capricious desire that he return to steal her away from her father's kingdom. By comparison to these two contemporary *amies,* Enide's passiveness recalls that of Eliduc's wife.

Bound to Eliduc by marriage vows and the deep-seated affection that results from a positive long standing relationship, Guildeluëc provides little competition for the exciting attachment her husband forms for his *amie,* based more tenuously and superficially on physical attraction. Physical beauty also forms the basis of Erec and Enide's mutual attraction, and Chrétien recounts the unabashed eagerness with which they both await their wedding night. However, their love for each other develops beyond this preliminary stage. No such development is attempted or even considered in *Eliduc* or **Le Chevalier de la charrette.**

As Erec and Enide's relationship evolves, Enide's status also changes. With her marriage, Enide gave up forever the title of *pucelle,* which implies virginity as well as youth and a certain vulnerability, for the names of *dame* and *femme,* which denote her rank in the eyes of the world, in that she no longer depends on her father for sustenance but on her husband. However, she retains the more ambiguous title of *amie,* which describes the quality of her rapport with her spouse. This ambivalent relationship cannot endure indefinitely. It is not possible for Enide at the same time to the same man to be a dominant *amie* (like Guenivere to Lancelot and Guiliadun to Eliduc) and a subservient *femme* (like Guildeluëc to Eliduc and Guenivere to Arthur).

The catalyst which tips the uneasy balance takes the form of court gossip concerning Erec's *récréance* or reluctance to fight. Enide's regret and inner suffering which result from reporting this gossip to Erec indicate a subtle awareness of the imminent change in her status. At this point her life as *amie* terminates and her life as *femme,* subject to the whims of her husband and based on obedience and loyalty to him, commences. Without ever having exercised the full power of *amie* over her lover, she must be subservient to Erec as *femme.*

In order to assume totally the identity of wife, Enide undergoes severe testing at the hands of her husband. Unexpectedly, she emerges victorious from the ordeal by thoughtful disobedience to Erec's orders, and not by total submission. Enide's first refusal to obey Erec occurs the first night they spend on the road, when she balks at her husband's suggestion that she sleep while he guards the horses. This directive, which contrasts sharply with the harshness he has shown her all day, reflects the spirit of their recently defunct *amie-amant* relationship and reveals the ambivalence of Erec's feeling for her. Very significantly, Enide wins out as *femme* in her insistence that she stand watch and even covers Erec with her coat (vv. 3084-96). It can be no accident that Chrétien here illustrates the shifting relationship between his two protagonists, especially since in the Mabinogion's *Gereint Son of Erbin,* which is thought to share a common source with *Erec et Enide,* Gereint orders Enide to watch the horses while he sleeps.

Enide also deliberately disobeys Erec each time she warns him of the approach of attacking horsemen. The adventures on the road consistently serve to test her loyalty and obedience to her husband, but while she always remains true to him, she must disobey him in order to demonstrate her loyalty. In contrast to Erec's grumbling tolerance of her behavior, the second count attracted to Enide by her beauty demonstrates immediately after her and Erec's marriage his intention to countenance no disobedience whatsoever from his wife when he slaps her for refusing to eat her dinner at his command. Although when he asked her earlier if she were the *amie* or the *femme* of the unconscious knight, he did not react to her response "l'une et l'autre" (v. 4651), he obviously wishes to point out the total lack of ambiguity in his rapport with her.

Enide's successful evasions of the attempts of the two lustful counts to woo her away from her husband confirm even for Erec the great extent of her faithfulness to him. The doubts he harbored were based on the fact than an *amie* is not expected to remain faithful to a lover, while a *femme* must exhibit constant and conspicuous loyalty. Enide was always prepared to assume whatever role would please Erec, but he had to come to terms with himself in order to define their relationship. His aberrant behavior and unreasonable demands therefore reflect the inner turmoil which precedes his reassurance.

Immediately following their reconciliation, Erec for the first time addresses Enide as "ma dolce sœur" (v. 4882). And again when taking leave of her before entering the magic garden to battle the knight, Erec prefaces his words with "Bele douce suer, gentix dame lëax et sage" (vv. 5784-85). The term *sœur* has replaced *amie* to describe the quality of her relationship with her husband while *dame* continues to denote her status in the eyes of the world.

Despite the sincerity of Erec's declaration to Enide as they flee the castle of the Count de Limors: "Or vœl estre d'or en avant, / ausi con j'estoie devant" (vv. 4888-90), their relationship can never return entirely to its former state.

In fact, the perpetual *amie* in the garden of the *Joie de la Cour* episode illustrates the folly and potential destructiveness inherent in continuing indefinitely such a shallow relationship, while the tears shed by the *demoiselle* at the release of her lover reflect the nostalgia of Enide for her former role of *amie* which has now ended forever.

Although it has been noted that courtly writers are "unable to speak of a love that grows or develops or deepens" and can "speak only of a love that begins" [John C. Moore, "Love in Twelfth-Century: A Failure in Synthesis," *Traditio,* 24 (1968)], Chrétien deals directly in *Erec et Enide* with the growth of love which follows early infatuation and demonstrates that married love differs profoundly from the *amie-amant* relationship. He chooses to combine the Provençal literary conventions, already well-established by his time, with the tradition of wife-testing to write a story of a love based initially on physical attraction but which after marriage acquires the elements of trust and loyalty to develop into a higher and mutually gratifying sentiment. (pp. 358-63)

> *Deborah · Nelson, "Enide: 'Amie' or 'Femme?' " in* Romance Notes, *Vol. XXI, No. 3, Spring, 1981, pp. 358-63.*

L. T. Topsfield (essay date 1981)

[*Topsfield was an English scholar of medieval and modern European literature whose writings include* Troubadours and Love *(1975) and* Chrétien de Troyes: A Study of the Arthurian Romances *(1981). In the excerpt below from the latter work, he discusses both Chrétien's "inheritance" and his "legacy": first the cultural and literary traditions that influenced Chrétien, then the influence of his own romances on other works.*]

In the sense that all great works of literature and art are inevitably the product of time, place and the creative genius, Chrétien was singularly fortunate, for he was the heir to an era of spiritual and artistic reawakening and to the two centuries of cultural stirrings which had preceded it. If, as seems probable, he composed *Erec et Enide* about 1170, he came to the fore at a moment particularly suited to his talent for assimilating, adapting and building upon some of the major innovations in thought and literature of the earlier twelfth century in France. This century was clearly one of the great formative periods in the history of European civilisation, a true age of Renaissance which had turned for inspiration directly or indirectly to Greece and Rome, to Plato and Aristotle, Virgil, Seneca, Cicero and Quintilian, to Horace, Martial and Ovid, to Boethius and St Augustine, and, with quickening interest, to the resources of Hispano-Arabic thought and science. This amalgam of new learning, especially at Chartres, was no passive clerical preoccupation. Permeating lay society, it bore the mark of a vital curiosity, seeking models for its creative spirit, accepting ideas, themes, knowledge from all quarters, Celtic, Moorish, Classical and Christian. This was a curiosity which was concerned both with the reality of the idea and the natural phenomenon. It extended to the living reality of creation, to plants and animals as well as to their mythology and symbolical reality. It embraced the 'wholeness' of existence, the belief in the principle of *universitas,* the basic unity and oneness of God's creation. It inspired the faith and inventive genius which in the new cathedrals blended stone and glass with the vision of the infinite.

This vision of the infinite, of *universitas* and supreme union with God, also found expression in the work of Bernard of Clairvaux, the son of a Burgundian nobleman, who with a following of four brothers and twenty-seven friends entered the new monastery at Cîteaux and within two years had established at Clairvaux the abbey which he made into one of the great spiritual centres of Europe. Bernard, who was abbot of Clairvaux from 1115 until his death in 1153, preached and wrote 'in order to reach people's hearts', and his faith in the life of positive *caritas,* together with the warmth and brilliance of his style and imagery furnished rich inspiration to the developing literatures of Europe, and especially to the romances on the theme of the Grail.

'The lyre of poetry', says Alanus de Insulis, in his *De Planctu Naturae,* written possibly as late as 1178-80, 'sounds a false note on the superficial, literal shell of a poem, but, deeper within, it conveys to those who can hear it the secret of a higher understanding, so that, with the externals of falsehood cast away, anyone who would interpret the poem may discover the sweeter essence of truth secreted inside it'. Behind this eloquence there lies a commonplace principle of medieval, and especially twelfth-century thought. Words, however pleasing, are dross. Gold lies in the meaning which they enshrine. The art of discerning such meaning is the main purpose and joy of *lectio,* the reading and especially the understanding of what is being read. In the vernacular literature of twelfth-century France, in the metaphysical poetry of the troubadours, and in Chrétien's later romances, the fictions of poetry are harnessed to the quest for philosophical truth. And this vital literary process was recognised by the learned men of the day, as witness the *Mendacia poetarum serviunt veritati* of John of Salisbury, a leading thinker and administrator at the court of Henry II Plantagenet.

This alliance between the new learning of the schools, especially at Chartres, the brilliance of Christian, especially Cistercian thinking, and the literary genius of poets such as the troubadour Marcabru (*c.* 1130-*c.* 1150) and Chrétien de Troyes, constitutes a major advance in the evolution of European literature in the vernacular, introducing a new philosophical mode of poetry and narrative romance which reaches beyond Dante on the one hand and the whole Arthurian and courtly cycle of romances on the other, to the present day.

This new mode of vernacular poetry appears for the first time at the very outset of the twelfth century in the court of the first troubadour Guilhem VII Count of Poitou, IX Duke of Aquitaine. This court, which was associated with all the earliest troubadour poetry, had long been famous for its interest in learning and letters. Guilhem the Great, the third count of Poitou who reigned from 993 to 1030, was renowned throughout Western Europe for his wisdom. His literary tastes are evident in the allusive imagery which he uses in his letters to conceal confidential matters from the uninitiated. During his long and peaceful reign over the vast lands of Poitou and Aquitaine, he was on terms of friendship with Odilon of Cluny and with Fulbert, the founder of the cathedral school at Chartres, whom he persuaded to accept the treasurership of the cathedral at Poitiers. This link between Chartres and the court of Guilhem the Great was reinforced when Fulbert sent his pupil, Hildegarius, to establish the famous episcopal school at Poitiers. The practical influence of the 'new' learning of Chartres, and its ideas of classical humanism and natural philosophy were not confined to the schoolroom. They are apparent in the letters of idealised love which passed between Peter Damian and Agnes, daughter of Guilhem the Great, Empress of Germany from 1043, and her sister-in-law Hermensent. Reflections of these philosophical ideas are even more apparent in the poetry of the earliest troubadours.

Not the least remarkable quality of this poetry at Poitiers is that in its beginnings it was deeply concerned with the moral and philosophical questions of man's existence. Thematically, it was based on a series of antitheses, of conflicts between ways of life which are fruitful or sterile, ways of thinking and living which are whole or fragmented, of joys which are ephemeral or durable. It was concerned with the conflicting rules of reason and desire, order and impulse, the needs of the community and the individual, and also with the nature of carnal, mental and spiritual love, of illusion and reality, of nothingness, and the wisdom of folly.

These themes can be related to Christian and Stoic ideas, to the view of human love expressed in the *De natura et dignitate Amoris* of the Cistercian William of St Thierry, to Chartrian concepts of rational happiness and of man's awareness of his place in the natural order. They are used by the troubadour Marcabru in order to fashion both his ideal of *Fin'Amors,* a love which unifies physical and mental desire and spiritual aspiration, and his ideal of *cortesia,* the sum total and the outward expression of all the courtly virtues. These include *Jovens,* youthfulness of spirit, *Jois,* the quest for happiness in life, *Valors,* innate courtly virtue, and the concept of *conoissensa,* the power of discerning the good from the bad, the true from the false, the real from the illusory. It is this faculty of discrimination which shows a man the right path to follow and enables him through the rational quality of *mesura* to direct himself to a real life suited to his talents, his position in life and his *natura,* the essence of each individual human being as it exists within the natural order of created things. These moralising ideas of Marcabru, and especially his concepts of *Fin'Amors* and *mesura,* greatly influenced the evolution of troubadour lyric poetry, and, in so doing, supplied one of the foundation stones of European courtly literature.

It is even more remarkable that many ideas from contemporary philosophical thought are apparent already in the burlesque poetry of Guilhem IX. The treatment he affords them is exactly opposite to that of Marcabru. In the quicksilver flash between laughter and seriousness, wisdom and bawdy folly, Guilhem satirises the methods of scholarly debate and the moral and philosophical terms, *Malvestatz, Proeza, Leis* 'the natural law of all creatures', *Jovens, Amors* and *Jois,* which were almost certainly current in his day at the court of Poitiers, and even before that time if we are to judge from his satirical treatment of his aunts Agnes the Empress and Hermensent and Peter Damian in his licentious poem of the ginger cat, *Farai un vers pos mi sonelh* (v).

From the poetry of Guilhem IX and Marcabru we can see that there already existed at the court of Poitiers, before 1100, a lively interest in philosophical notions about man's quest for happiness (*jois*) and an awareness of an ultimate, transcendental happiness (*lo mielhs*) which may have been an adaptation to profane love of the *summum bonum* of Boethius. We can also see in both poets, though treated in opposite ways, a sense of the moral conflict in life between *Proeza,* an excellence of virtue based on order, and its opponent, the vice of recreancy and disorder which is *Malvestatz.*

It was largely from the cultural traditions which had evolved over two centuries at the court of Poitiers that the noble society of Chrétien's day drew its ideal of a rational and ordered way of life based on *mesure,* the ability to act, in given circumstances, in a way most appropriate to one's temperament, qualities or status. To this ideal of *mesure,* the rational progeny of *savoir,* a gentle dose of *folie* might be added in order to salt and define its quality. And behind this ideal of rational courtliness and the *folie* of fantasy and impulse, there existed in Chrétien's day the weighty *curialitas* of the functional court of Henry II, of the administrators and men of learning such as John of Salisbury who, in his *Policraticus,* advocated a morality of Roman *gravitas* based on a sense of responsibility towards oneself and the good of the community.

It is scarcely surprising that this rationally ordered society, with its own flights of fancy towards *folie,* should have found in Arthurian romance an idealised mirror-image of itself, an embellished reflection of the infinite possibilities of knightly adventure, love and heroism, observed against the exotic back-cloth of the Celtic tradition. Courtly reason and *savoir* could find release for its imagination in the Other World, the summons of a Celtic king to an earthly hero, of a fairy mistress to her lover. It could escape from the trials of *Fin' Amors* in the tragedy of the uncontrollable Tristan-type passion imposed by a *geis* or spell, in the theme of a mortal abducted to the Other World, of a fairy mistress rewarding the lover who defends her magic garden or fountain, of abundance turned into waste land.

For the knightly, dynastic and Arthurian side of Chrétien's literary inheritance, and for the origins of the romance genre in French, we must turn away for the moment from the court of Poitou and move northwards to England, where the Norman usurpers sat uneasily on the throne of Edward the Confessor. It is this royalty, at first uncertainly established then immensely powerful though still torn by family dissension, which under Henry II Plantagenet was to have an electrifying effect on the literature of twelfth-century France.

The Norman kings of England had clearly inherited the taste of their Viking ancestors for historico-epic narrative. They were also impatient to establish the legitimacy of their royal functions, and for this purpose they encour-

aged the historical endeavours of their scholars and writers. The first real landmark in this dynastic literature which sought to link the new Norman royalty with its illustrious predecessors, is the *Historia Regum Britanniae* of Geoffrey of Monmouth. His work, the inheritor of a tradition of historical narrative, is original in its flattering view of the Norman conquest as retribution meted out to the Anglo-Saxons for their invasion of Celtic Britain. Its sequence of dedications reflects the shaky state of the English crown. It was first dedicated soon after the death of Henry I in 1135 to his natural son Robert of Gloucester 'illustrious through his exploits and learning'. Following the swing of political change, it was then dedicated to Robert and to Waleran of Beaumont, a supporter of Stephen, and then, probably in 1136 and certainly before 1138, to King Stephen and Robert of Gloucester jointly. Geoffrey claims, though improbably in the view of many scholars, that his work is a plain translation into Latin of a 'very ancient book in the British language' *britannici sermonis librum vetustissimum,* given to him by Walter, Archdeacon of Oxford. He uses Gildas and Bede, Livy and Nennius to sketch the story of the Kings of Britain from Brutus, who landed at Totnes in Cornwall with a band of Trojans, to the death of Cadwallader in A.D. 689. Geoffrey's main importance for us is that he introduced the stories of Lear, Cymbeline, Merlin and Arthur, who, he says, was the son of Utherpendragon and gained victories over the Saxons, Norwegians, Gauls and Romans. Geoffrey's *Historia* supplied Arthurian material to Gaimar for his vernacular *Estoire des Engleis,* but its influence on later writings concerned with the Arthurian tradition, the so-called *matière de Bretagne,* was greatly augmented by the translated version of it, together with the new theme of the Round Table, in the *Roman de Brut* which Wace dedicated to Eleanor of Aquitaine in 1155.

At this point the cultural traditions of Poitou and Britain are effectively united. In 1137, Eleanor, the granddaughter of the first troubadour, Guilhem IX of Aquitaine, had succeeded in her own right to the immense territories of Poitou and Aquitaine which stretched from the Atlantic to Auvergne, from Poitou to the Pyrenees. It is not surprising that in this same year she was married to the young prince Louis who within a month of the wedding succeeded to the throne of France as King Louis VII. Eleanor bore two daughters by him, Marie de France who later became the Countess of Champagne and Chrétien's patroness, and Alice of Blois. Eleanor's energy and ebullience were, however, ill-suited to the ways of Louis VII, and, after their marriage was annulled, Eleanor, now at the age of thirty, wed in 1152 the dynamic young Henry, Count of Anjou and Duke of Normandy, who within two years was crowned Henry II Plantagenet of England. This tumultuous marriage, marked by bouts of active warfare, between husband and wife, father and sons, sons and sons, produced Henry the Young King, King Richard the Lion Heart, Geoffrey, Count of Brittany, and the gifted but ill-fated King John of England. By uniting England, Wales, and later Ireland with the western half of France, it also produced the so-called Angevin Empire and sowed the seeds of three hundred years of bloodshed between France and England.

For French literature, however, the marriage of Eleanor and Henry was of major importance. It joined the vigorous traditions of philosophical and courtly poetry in Poitou to the obsessive interest of the English royalty in the 'history' of its dynastic origins. It also provided through Henry II and Queen Eleanor an immensely important source of patronage and stimulus for narrative and poetic creation. Henry II, great-grandson of the Conqueror, was a brilliant man, a tireless soldier, administrator and law-giver, an intellectual who surrounded himself with men of great intellect. Eleanor, Queen in turn of two great countries, Duchess of Aquitaine and Countess of Poitou, an astute and daring politician, an authority on courtly behaviour, a leader, when need arose, of her troops in the field, remained true to her Viking descent from Adele, the sister of Rollo. But for our present purpose her importance lies especially in her encouragement of the love lyric of the troubadours in the Provençal tongue, or the *langue d'oc,* and of the new and evolving genre of the romance in Northern French, or the *langue d'oïl.*

The influence of Eleanor was almost certainly active in a major transformation which began to take place in troubadour poetry between 1150 and 1170. The early metaphysical poetry in the closed style, such as we find in Marcabru, was concerned with the problems of the human condition, with the quest for a supreme, unknowable happiness, with *Fin'Amors* as an abstract ideal of Love, a 'fount of goodness which illumines the world'. This allusive poetry gradually yields to the fashion for courtly compositions in the clear style, dominated by the physical presence of the idealised lady and epitomised by Eleanor's most illustrious troubadour Bernart de Ventadorn. Bernart's songs, composed between about 1145 and 1180, are intensely lyrical but have a far more restricted vocabulary than those of Marcabru. For Bernart, *Fin'Amors* is the loyal love offered in submission to the exalted, physical lady or *domna*. It rejoices in her idealised beauty and virtues. It seeks fulfilment in equal and mutually shared physical delight (xv, 29-32). Though Bernart has within him a form of *mesura* which allows him to recognise his fine folly of feeling, it is irrational feeling, the oblivion of the mind, the moment of ecstatic identification with the skylark, the nightingale or the lady, which for him is purest joy. He is the *fis amaire,* the true lover who desires, has desired and will desire one woman alone (xxx, 1-7 and 43-6), and he rejects Marcabru's concept of *mesura* as a rational force which must control these desires (xv, 33-5). The attitudes to love of Marcabru and Bernart de Ventadorn are both of fundamental importance for the development of courtly literature in Europe, and it is in their concepts of *Fin'Amors* that Chrétien de Troyes will find the inspiration for his treatment of the love affair between Guenevere and Lancelot.

Yet Chrétien's richest legacy was to be gathered from the *matière de Bretagne,* which came to him from two separate though related narrative traditions. One of these traditions took the form of Celtic lays which drew on the stories and customs of Ireland and Wales and celebrated, among other happenings, the deeds of Arthur's knights and of Tristan and Yseut. These lays had been known in France, especially in Poitou, from the later years of the

eleventh century, and had spread rapidly into Italy and Catalonia. We must first, however, consider briefly the cultivated and literary tradition of Arthurian and Classical narrative which, fostered by the Angevin courts of England-Aquitaine, provided a major basis for the genre of the romance in France.

Some fifteen years of rapid evolution in this genre still separated the influential *Roman de Brut* or *Geste des Bretons,* which Wace dedicated to Queen Eleanor in 1155, from the **Erec et Enide** of Chrétien de Troyes. But Wace's star waned, and he abandoned the *Roman de Rou,* or *Geste des Normans,* written between 1160 and 1174, when Henry II gave the same task to his more fashionable rival Benoît de Sainte-Maure.

Though Benoît, in the 43,210 octosyllabic rhyming couplets of his *Estoire des ducs de Normandie,* carried the history of the Normans down to Henry I, he is better known for his *Roman de Troie,* again in octosyllabic couplets, composed between 1154 and 1173, and dedicated to Eleanor, 'riche dame de riche rei', between 1160 and 1170. This romance drew its material from the *Historia de excidio Trojae* written about A.D. 550 by Dares Phrygius who was reputed to have fought for the Trojans, and from the *Ephemeris belli Trojani* (c. A.D. 330) of Dictys Cretensis who, it was claimed, had fought for the Greeks. The *Roman de Troie* is usually thought to be the last of three romances by different authors which are sometimes called the *triade classique.* These romances, together with the very successful *Roman d'Alexandre* and numerous lays on classical themes attest to the contemporary popularity in courtly circles of heroic subjects from Classical Antiquity.

The first in date of these three classical romances was the *Roman de Thèbes,* composed between 1150 and 1156, and based largely on the *Thebais* of Statius, though flavoured with elements from the Northern French epic or *chanson de geste.* But a yet greater influence on the development of the romance genre was exercised by the *Roman d'Eneas,* composed in ten thousand octosyllabic couplets by an unknown Norman about 1156. Apart from the opening scenes and the Dido episode, the *Roman d'Eneas* strays far from Virgil's text and intention. It neglects Virgil's theme of the high destiny which impels Eneas to found a new city and a new royalty to compensate for the waste land of Troy. Its characters are devitalised and empty of the affection and tenderness which Virgil lent them. Yet, despite the flatness of its narrative passages and the trivialisation of Eneas' motives, there were two major reasons why it should appeal to a contemporary courtly audience in France. Both these reasons stem from the expanded love affair between Lavinia and Eneas which the poet added to Virgil's story. In Lavinia, courtly society was offered an archetypal example of the damsel who recognises and controls the Ovidian fears and doubts of love and finds happiness through declaring herself to the beloved. In this respect Lavinia is the precursor of Fenice in Chrétien's **Cliges.** The second reason is the clear contrast which is established between the nature, quality and results of the loves of Dido and Lavinia for Eneas. Dido's uncontrollable passion compels her to forswear her vow of widowed chastity, to destroy herself and bring her country to ruin. The fresh, mutual love of Lavinia and Eneas accords with all the individual and social demands of courtly *mesure.* Though the terms of their falling in love may be Ovidian, the two lovers are shown to be wholly suited to each other by their youthful devotion, temperament and nobility of birth. Their marriage is also not only a love match but a dynastic triumph, promising order and happiness for the lands they will inherit and auguring well for a new dynasty which will rule the recently united lands of Eleanor and Henry II Plantagenet. This elementary *conjointure* or 'joining together' of the two love episodes in the *Eneas,* and the embryonic *sen* or underlying meaning which they imply, mark an important step forward in the evolving genre of the courtly romance. In these important respects, the *Eneas* points the way ahead to the art of Chrétien de Troyes in his first romance **Erec et Enide.**

What was a *roman* or romance? In the Carolingian Renaissance the word *romanice* had been used to express the meaning 'in the vernacular', as distinct from *latine.* In the twelfth century the form *romanz* is used regularly as an adverb, adjective or noun. The phrase *et en romans et en lati,* literally 'both in romance and in latin', which occurs in the first troubadour Guilhem IX, implies the desire for self-expression to the limit of one's capacity, for example in prayer. Used in negative constructions, it implies complete taciturnity.

Romanz, used as a noun, can refer to speech in the vernacular, to a translation into the vernacular, or a vernacular literary work. A lively twelfth-century interest in the legends of ancient Greece and Rome, of Apollonius, Alexander, Hero and Leander, Cadmus, Jason and Julius Caesar, led to the commissioning of translations into romance of the latin versions of classical texts, or even of the texts themselves. Equally strongly, as we have seen, Norman and Plantagenet dynastic interest in the ancient kings of Britain encouraged translations into romance from writings such as the *Historia* of Geoffrey of Monmouth which prompted the *Roman de Brut* of Wace.

From the 'schoolroom' task of translation into romance to the creative embellishment of the text was an easy step, and so the romance as 'translation' merged inevitably into the romance as narrative literary genre. Embellishment was inspired at first by a desire to update knowledge of the past and to write for the benefit and ornamentation of present life. Twelfth-century writers and their patrons followed the great thinkers of the day in their awareness of the giants on whose shoulders they perched. Alexander, Eneas, Arthur and, more especially, his knights are recreated in their imagination as contemporary figures of knightly and courtly excellence. It is this process of adaptation of the translated work, by additions such as the Round Table in Wace's *Brut* and the expanded Lavinia episode in *Eneas,* the introduction of marvellous objects and happenings, of the carbuncle, the precious light-giving stone, of magic animals and the wealth of the Celtic tradition, which determines the character of the romance in the second half of the twelfth century. When Chrétien writes **Erec et Enide** about 1170, the genre has moved beyond the state of being a translation or an adapted and embellished translation into a romance language. It may still draw its

material from Byzantine sources, from Classical Antiquity, the *matière de Rome,* or from the *matière de Bretagne,* but it is now ready to be fashioned, and recited or read aloud, according to the interests of its audience and its poet. As a romance of love and adventure, such as *Floire et Blancheflor,* it may serve as a pleasing courtly diversion, and this is also partly true of the weightier and more tragic Tristan stories in the versions of Beroul and Thomas. With Chrétien de Troyes, however, a dichotomy occurs in the genre of the romance. This dichotomy has many similarities to the existing division in troubadour poetry between works composed with a courtly or a metaphysical intention. With Chrétien de Troyes a new form of romance evolves and achieves, through the creative intention and the ideas which inspire it, an independent identity which is quite separate from that of its sources and from the contemporary *romans d'aventure.* This higher form of romance is characterised by its *sen* or underlying meaning and by the *conjointure,* the jointing together of incidents, and of incident and dialogue, through which the *sen* is revealed. In this respect, this form of romance differs also from the *estoire,* the 'story' or 'history' and from the *conte* which is usually a short tale about a single happening or an *aventure* and its consequences.

The different roles of the *estoire, conte* and *romanz* are acknowledged by Chrétien in the opening lines of his **Cliges:**

> Ceste estoire trovons escrite,
> Que conter vos vuel et retreire,
> An un des livres de l'aumeire
> Mon seignor saint Pere a Biauvez.
> De la fu li contes estrez,
> Don cest romanz fist Crestiiens.
> (18-23)

> This story which I wish to
> tell and relate to you do we
> find written in one of the books
> from the book-cupboard of my
> beloved lord Saint Peter at
> Beauvais. From this history
> was drawn the tale from which
> Chrétien created this romance.

Though the *conte* of **Cliges** was of Greco-Byzantine origin, Chrétien set his romance within the framework of the court of Arthur in Britain which we find in Geoffrey's *Historia* and Wace's *Brut.* An Arthurian framework also exists for the other four romances, but . . . it is less martial, less robust and becomes increasingly decadent. This change in attitude may have reflected Chrétien's growing disenchantment with the courtly and knightly values of the society around him. Another reason, however, was that he was drawing his *matière* or subject-matter from a separate and richer source. This was the oral and written tradition in which ancient Irish and Welsh tales were retold and refashioned without the constraints of the Norman and Angevin dynastic ambitions which had affected the 'literary' transmission of the Celtic Arthurian tradition by Geoffrey of Monmouth and Wace, among many other writers. It is from this less adulterated source that Chrétien inherits figures such as Erec, Mabonagrain, Meleagant and Giflet, and the weaknesses and vices of Kay and King Arthur, together with the whole mythology of the Celtic supernatural tradition.

Details of the written works in which the ancient Irish tales were transmitted and blended with Welsh traditions, are available elsewhere and have no place here. Briefly, it may be said that they extend from the Welsh poem the *Gododdin* of about A.D. 600, through the account by Nennius (*c.* A.D. 800) of Arthur's victories over the Anglo-Saxons, the *Annales Cambriae* (*c.* 955) which record, under the years 516 and 517, Arthur's victory at Badon and his death with Medrant at the battle of Camlann; through *The Spoils of Annwn* (tenth century), *The Black Book of Camarthen,* which lists Arthur's warriors, through the prose love story *Kulhwch and Olwen* (*c.* 1100) to the *Vita Gildae* of Caradoc of Llancarvan, relating the abduction of Guenevere by Melvas, and the Welsh prose tales of *Geraint, Owain* and *Peredur,* which show respectively a marked similarity to Chrétien's **Erec et Enide** and **Yvain,** and a loose relationship with **Perceval.** These three Welsh romances, together with *Kulhwch and Olwen* and other tales, are found in the *Mabinogion,* in two Welsh collections, the *White Book of Rhydderch,* written down about 1300-25, and the *Red Book of Hergest,* from about 1375 to 1425.

There is evidence that tales from this Celtic tradition were transmitted orally and were popular in France from about 1100, or even earlier. William of Malmesbury, in his *Historia Regum Anglorum* of 1125, declares that trifles of the Bretons, *nugae Bretonum,* were current in his day about Arthur, 'a man worthy not to be dreamed about in false fables but to be proclaimed in truthful works of literature'. He also tells of the discovery in south-west Wales, about 1087, of the tomb of Arthur's nephew Walwen (Gawain). In 1155, Wace also speaks of the many tales which the Bretons tell about the Round Table.

From 1100 onwards, and especially in Brittany, Poitou and its neighbours, the names of Arthurian heroes occur regularly in historical documents in France. A Gawain is attested in 1110, a Tristan in 1113, the name Arthur from as early as 814. And the references in French and German romances to Breri or Bleheris (Blihis, Bliheris, Pleherim) 'who knew the epic deeds and the stories of all the kings and counts of Brittany, and retold them to the Count of Poitiers', possibly Guilhem IX, the first troubadour, cannot be easily discounted, especially as Bleheris may be the Bledhericus whom Giraldus Cambriensis described as *famosus ille fabulator,* and may even be Bledri ap Cadivor, a Welsh nobleman allied to the Normans, who lived from about 1070 to 1140 and was given the appellation of *Latinarius* or 'interpreter'.

That courtly interest in the romance in the last third of the twelfth century embraced not only the Classical but the Celtic tradition is clear from the *Tristan* of Thomas, the *Ille et Galeron* of Gautier d'Arras, and the lays of Marie de France who states her poetic purpose: 'To prevent ourselves from falling into vice, we must study and understand and begin some difficult task. So I began to think of composing some fine story and of making a translation from latin into romance. But so many others have undertaken this sort of work that I should thereby have gained little reputation' (*Lais,* Prologue). So Marie turned her thoughts to the lays which she had heard, and in order to keep their memory fresh, retold them in a rhymed narrative, which she calls a *conte:*

> M'entremis des lais assembler,
> Par rime faire e reconter.
>
> (Prologue, 47-8)

She defines her sources:

> Les contes ke jo sai verrais,
> Dunt li Bretun unt fait les lais
> Vos conterai assez briefment.
>
> (*Guigemar,* 19-21)

I will relate to you, without too much amplification, the authentic stories of which the Bretons have composed their lays.

She describes her method:

> De un mut ancïen lai bretun
> Le cunte e tute la reisun
> Vus dirai, si cum jeo entent
> La verité, mun escïent.
>
> (*Eliduc,* 1-4)

Working from a very ancient Breton lay, I will tell you the story in my own words and its whole theme, according to the authentic truth as I, in my mind, believe it to be.

Lai may come from Old Irish *laíd* or *loíd* which in Old Irish sagas denoted the passages of speech inset into the story of adventure. If this is the case, *lai* may have been originally a lyrical passage of speech as opposed to the pure narrative, the *conte* about the *aventure.* Later it came to denote the short narrative poem itself. It seems probable that the older narratives originated in Ireland, and were inherited by the Bretons who made of them their lays which Marie was now rendering into *contes* in French, without undue amplification but with the sense of the story, the *reisun,* as she saw it, 'brought out' or, in other words, invented and then imposed in gentle fashion on the original tale.

This particular Celtic tradition, unlike the more learned literary one, not only provided stories of individual heroes, heroines and villains, to writers such as Marie de France, Beroul, Thomas and Chrétien de Troyes, but furnished them with the even more important legacy of Celtic myth. The fundamental principle of this mythology lies in the acceptance of a close and continuous relationship between this earthly human world and the Other World. No impassable barrier separates the two worlds and there is between them a frequent interchange of human and otherworldly beings. Gods, fairy maidens, can come to live in various forms in this world, especially at the seasonal festivals. Men, summoned by a fairy spirit, or by a ruler who needs assistance, may venture on a quest into the Other World.

This Other World is represented in two ways. It may be situated in the islands of happiness, youth and abundance, a place of wondrous fruits and divine drinks such as the island of Avalon. Alternatively, it may be the subterranean world of the Tuatha De Danann, a fairy people, thought to be the inhabitants of old Ireland who fled from earlier invasions. These Tuatha were believed to be guard-

Lancelot in a horsecart, followed by Gawain and squires (MS 806, fol. 158).

ians of the traditions of the ancient civilisation, and the custodians of the Talismans or Magic Objects which endowed their possessor with powers of sovereignty and abundance.

The Tuatha De Danann are linked with human beings by *geasha,* the plural of *geis* which means 'spell'. This *geis* is important in Celtic literature in which motivation to action comes from outside the characters. Negatively, the *geis* is a form of taboo such as the denial to a human being of the right to sleep two nights consecutively in the same place. Positively, the *geis* is extremely important, as the compulsion laid on a human to act, endure trials, undertake quests, and also to fall irrevocably in love. This element of supernatural power inflicted on a human being goes back to the eighth or ninth centuries of the Celtic tradition, and is symbolised in the twelfth century by the love potion intended for the ageing Mark which Brenguain inadvertently gives to Tristan and Yseut, this love triangle of uncle, wife, nephew being also a traditional Celtic pattern.

In Celtic literature themes involving journeys are a commonplace, and are of three kinds. There are abductions (Irish *aitheda*), journeys in a ship to the Magic Islands of the Other World (*imrama*), undertaken because of a *geis* imposed by a fairy mistress, and there are journeys to the Other World beneath the Hills (*echtrai*), in which the earthly hero may conquer palaces, help a king and return victorious with the Magic Objects or Talismans which are important for our understanding of the romance of *Perceval.*

Chrétien de Troyes has a Shakespearian talent for absorbing and refurbishing the ideas he inherits, and for responding to and refashioning courtly taste. He is his own man, adept at irony, wary of the static and conventional, preferring movement and progress. Having taken hold of his materials, his 'story', the themes of the Celtic supernatural, the philosophical or religious ideas of his day and current views of courtesy and knighthood, he pares and shapes them, diminishing or increasing their importance entirely in accordance with the underlying theme or *sen*

and the dramatic purpose of a particular work. And when in *Cliges* and *Erec et Enide* he adds a topical note, he appears to have adapted historical truth to suit his narrative needs. (pp. 1-16)

Chrétien gathers in an abundant legacy from his twelfth-century predecessors, and their Classical, Christian, courtly and Celtic inheritance. From the philosophers and theologians he takes their belief in the principle of *universitas,* the basic unity of God's creation, and, within this wholeness, man as an individual of inexhaustible interest in his conflicts, temptations, and passions, his *cupiditas* and search for *caritas.* Chrétien also inherits the dialectical method of the schools in which opposites are juxtaposed, compared, contrasted and analysed. For Good to be recognised, Evil must be understood. To know wisdom, folly must be detected. And in this process honour is contrasted with baseness, reality with illusion, love of God with self-love. Such use of antithesis is a device of medieval description, found in twelfth-century Arts of Rhetoric. It plays a major part in the poetry of the early troubadours, and also in Chrétien's romances in which folly precedes wisdom, pride goes before humility and shame, and misery before self-knowledge and joy. In Chrétien's 'whole' view of life, comedy keeps company with sorrow, burlesque with seriousness, and irony lightens and enhances idealism. Truth may be discerned in the vision of the world upside-down. The actual world may be illumined by the supernatural world with which it coexists. A rational man in the courtly tradition may seek security of mind and discover a higher, mystical truth which enriches or disturbs that serenity. Chrétien's acquaintance with the principles of rhetoric and dialectic, and the intellectual distance from his material which this gave him, allowed him to interweave in his romances a higher *sen* through which objects, characters and events are raised from the level of the immediate and the particular to that of the universal. This intellectual coolness which disguises personal feeling nevertheless enhances the value of Chrétien's convictions when these finally become apparent.

Chrétien's intellectual distance from the courtly and

knightly values of his day becomes increasingly evident in his later works. He could scarcely have belonged to a more talented or 'courtly' court than that of Marie de France, the Lady of Champagne for whom he composed **Lancelot.** Marie was clearly well acquainted with the etiquette of behaviour which had been established at the court of her mother Eleanor of Aquitaine, and which was 'recorded' with gentle irony, probably at Marie's request, in the *De Amore* of Andreas Capellanus. This *art de plaire* was essentially a projection into courtly social life of the abstract ideals of *Jois, Valors, Jovens, Mesura* and *Proeza* which had been extolled earlier by Marcabru. It cherished elegant conversation and manners and a positive and joyous attitude to life through which each individual contributed to the communal Joy of the Court. It was a system which revolved round the idealised presence of the lady or *domna,* and in its emphasis on the courtly and social rather than the metaphysical essence of *Fin'Amors,* on reputation rather than individual joy, it fashioned for itself a cadre of convention which hampered the higher and wider aspirations of mind and spirit. Gace Brulé, the archetypal *amant martyr* and major lyric poet at the court of Champagne, came to terms with these constraints. Chrétien, like many contemporary troubadours such as Peire d'Alvernhe, Raimbaut d'Aurenga and the later Arnaut Daniel, appeared to accept them outwardly while reacting quietly and effectively against them.

Despite the outward clarity of his narrative, Chrétien is an essentially enigmatic writer. He understates, implies, suggests. His negative opinions are indicated as subtly as his positive views, as his *antancion,* the direction or purpose given to each work, and the *conjointure* through which he reveals his ideas on love, knighthood and the quest for happiness, on man's relationship to man and to God. (pp. 18-20)

. . . . .

When we consider Chrétien's five romances in the round, we can see a sharp division in style and intention between the first two, *Erec et Enide* and *Cliges,* and the last three. This division corresponds in many ways to the distinction in contemporary troubadour poetry between the *trobar leus* or clear style, which was concerned with courtly reality, and the *clus* or allusive, metaphysical style. In *Erec et Enide* and *Cliges* Chrétien is involved with the affairs of this world, with love which leads to dynastic marriage, with the issues of personal and social order and disorder, with the conflict between wisdom and folly, between the reality and the illusion of earthly living. In the interval between *Cliges* and the first part of *Yvain,* which in its beginnings almost certainly preceded *Lancelot,* a major change occurs. The rational and benevolent optimism which had inspired *Erec et Enide,* and, also, though tinged with a sharper irony, *Cliges,* has diminished. The naive belief in the divine *ordo* of life, in which knowledge, experience and reason offer guidance to an idealised and general concept of joy, gives way to a closer and more realistic view of life as a conflict which is not to be resolved in a facile or comforting manner. Hints of such uncertainty are apparent in *Cliges.* They play a major part in *Lancelot, Yvain* and *Perceval.*

In these later romances there is a constant dramatic tension which defines the characters, illuminates the action and gives infinite range to Chrétien's meaning. This tension arises from a conflict between two contrasting views of life. On the one hand, there is the *simplece* of the personality which is a whole within itself, and which, because it is aware of itself and its identity, can respond with intuitive generosity to the demands of life and so achieve a wider wholeness with its surroundings. In such an ideal personality natural virtue and happiness abound, untouched by the tarnish of self-interest. In contrast, there is the personality which adheres to the patterns of virtue and morality formulated by courtly society and, in so doing, surrenders its pristine purity. Such a personality, lacking true *Franchise* or nobility of mind and spirit, constrained by its environment, tainted in varying degree by self-interest and the assumptions of *vaine gloire,* is fragmented.

It is in terms of this conflict that Chrétien becomes increasingly concerned with a theme which he had adumbrated in *Erec et Enide.* This is the struggle of an individual who allows conventional moral values to disguise his true self, and who, wakened from this complacency to a crisis of self-doubt and even madness, regains peace of mind in a sense of identity and oneness with life. In *Lancelot* and *Perceval* Chrétien expands this individual struggle into an allegorical conflict between the Good of this world and the Evil which he admits can never be suppressed. To allow for a wide development of this struggle between the powers of Good and Evil, Chrétien changes the thematic form of these romances from a bipartite to a tripartite construction. His language in *Yvain,* as well as in *Lancelot* and *Perceval,* sheds the unadorned simplicity of *Erec et Enide,* and in its imagery of the Cart, the Lion, the Grail and Lance, reaches out to moral and spiritual values which place Chrétien in the forefront of European literature. Chrétien's mind has abandoned the certainties of *Erec et Enide* and the happiness to be attained through temporal order. In *Perceval,* or *Percevax le viel* in ms. B, he progresses to a 'whole' view of life which can embrace secular anarchy and the persistence of Evil and yet find the *summum bonum* of spiritual order.

The allusive reaching out to seize the imagination of the audience according to its level of perception and experience can be related to the art of the metaphysical troubadours such as Marcabru, Peire d'Alvernhe and Arnaut Daniel. These poets in the *clus* and *ric* styles interwove in their works extra levels of meaning, often with Christian moralising or philosophical significance, and used words as entities in their own right, with their own particular smooth or harsh sounds and rich overtones of meaning. In the years around 1170 this creative poetry was in retreat before the spreading waves of courtly poetry in the clear style. It is not improbable that Chrétien was aware of the controversy about this issue among the troubadours of his day. It is clear, however, that his romances move from what the troubadours would have called the 'clear' style of the romance genre, typified by the *Eneas,* and by *Erec et Enide* and *Cliges,* towards a mature 'close', 'rich' style which gives us Chrétien's most memorable scenes, such as the Sword Bridge, the Grail Procession or the

Three Drops of Blood on the Snow. The symbolical description of sceptre and cloak in the Coronation scene in **Erec et Enide** has been transformed into an imaginative art in which the narrative genre of the romance becomes a form of three-dimensional poetry.

This art is apparent also in the concealed and enigmatic combinations of themes, myths and beliefs which have a separate and parallel existence within their own individual frameworks. The Grail Procession may evoke thoughts of Christian or of Celtic traditions, or of the religions of ancient Rome and Egypt. This profusion of different auras, of patterns of thought and mythology, lends richness to the texture of both **Lancelot** and **Perceval.** It also helps us to understand Chrétien's purpose in avoiding the definable in order to prompt the imagination of his audience to move outwards in an expanding universe of the spirit. In the allusive method all is implicit, nothing is earthbound or static. Yet there is intellectual control in the imaginative pattern which Chrétien presents to his audience. Each separate aura, mythology or level of meaning, whether Christian, Celtic, courtly or knightly, preserves its particular virtue which may then be added to and so may enrich the quality of the others.

In the later romances, Chrétien sees life as a cosmic unity of conflicting influences, divine and profane, spiritual and material, good and evil. Though he sees the conflict with clarity, he defines it in oblique and enigmatic fashion through deeds and words which reveal the unspoken thoughts and feelings in his characters. It is through the opposing qualities of Lancelot and Meleagant, of Perceval, Gawain and Guiromelant that he establishes a sense of his disgust at the destructiveness of evil, of his mistrust of the narrowly rationalistic and codified view of life, and his faith in the visionary experience.

As Chrétien progresses from the symbolism of the sceptre to that of the Grail, from a belief in the virtues of knowledge and sovereignty, and the temporal order they offer, to the certainties of the spiritual life, his treatment of the themes of love and knighthood deepens and matures. This evolution in Chrétien's view of life is independent of, and, as in the case of **Lancelot,** may conflict with and so enrich his narrative material. Yet the basic, unifying *sen* in his work remains unchanged. It stems from the conviction that deeds and words take their quality from the quality of the intention which motivates them. The more selfless their intention, the greater the possibility of happiness and peace of mind for the doer. The more self-interested the purpose, the more inevitable the spiral of social and personal misery.

In Chrétien's view of life the concept of *bien* and *Leauté* is of primary importance. . . . Briefly stated, *bien* in this context appears to be the goodness associated with the intuitive or 'natural' virtue of the person who is endowed with *simplece,* or the immediacy of true and virtuous human feeling, with humility, self-abnegation and *caritas.* Allied to *Leauté,* it confronts the common enemy *Mauvestié. Leauté* is the quality of fidelity to a *lei* or law. It may vary from obedience to a courtly, feudal or knightly law, to submission to the *lei* which is the basis, the very essence of natural virtue. Such *Leauté,* which has connotations of

Christian goodness, pity and *caritas,* is akin to the natural *lex* divinely bestowed on man. It transcends the conventional courtly and knightly virtues epitomised by Gawain. It alone can check the forces of evil, whether these appear as the courtly *Desleauté* of Kay, the anti-social violence of Yder, Mabonagrain or Guiromelant, or the irredeemable wickedness of Meleagant and his henchmen. This ideal of a 'natural' *bien* and *Leauté* which are innate in man and woman, and so both individual and universal, and the human aspiration towards their rediscovery, is the essential *sen* of Chrétien's romances. In this lies his right to be called a poet of *universitas.* It is this quality, apparent also in the *simplece* of his style, the tonality of his language, his evocation of atmosphere, drama and comedy, which assures the lasting influence of his work.

In what was one of the most important centuries in the history of European civilisation, Chrétien's achievement was unique. His sequence of great Arthurian romances established the romance as the major literary genre for the depiction of the weaknesses and triumphs, baseness and idealism of individual man faced with the problems of the human condition. Chrétien's work inspires and influences the great medieval German romances such as the *Erec* and *Iwein* of Hartman von Aue, the *Parzival* of Wolfram von Eschenbach. And his influence reaches out in reverse direction to the traditional Celtic stories of Erec, Yvain and Perceval contained in the *Gereint, Owein* and *Peredur* of the later Welsh *Mabinogion.* It spreads to the south, to Spain, Italy, Provence, to the troubadours, and more particularly to the thirteenth-century poet of *Flamenca* who not only follows Chrétien's linear, expository and allusive methods of indicating meaning but approves and mocks his idealism. Chrétien's real triumph, however, lies in his failure to finish the **Perceval.** The consequence of this was that the Grail theme, together with the equally 'unfinished' story of Lancelot and Guenevere, inspired within fifty years a sequence of French Arthurian romances which, through the genius of Sir Thomas Malory and other writers, immeasurably enriched English, European and world literature.

The temptation offered by the unfinished Grail story prompted numerous *Perceval Continuations* which probably used a source or sources related to those followed by Chrétien. The anonymous *First Continuation* or pseudo-Wauchier (*c.* 1200) continued the Gawain adventures; the *Second Continuation* (*c.* 1200), by an unknown writer working under Wauchier de Denain, continued the Perceval adventures; the *Third Continuation* (*c.* 1233-7) by Manessier was intended as a completion of Chrétien's work and established Perceval, the nephew of the Fisher King, as his successor in the Grail Castle; and the *Fourth Continuation* (*c.* 1233) by a Gerbert, probably Gerbert de Montreuil, author of the *Roman de la Violette,* concluded in 17,000 lines the adventure of Perceval's broken sword.

Shortly after 1200, Robert de Boron gave a fresh direction to the development of the Grail theme. He also wrote a *Merlin,* which was intended to link the stories of Joseph and Arthur and of which five hundred lines have survived, and a *Perceval* which exists in a prose version known as the *Didot-Perceval,* but the work which concerns us here is his *Roman de l'Estoire dou Graal.* This work, composed in a flat and clinical style, is a milestone in the evolution of the Grail tradition. Whereas Chrétien had suggested the Celtic and Christian associations evoked by the Grail, and had emphasised the function of the Grail and its contents, rather than the importance of the Grail as an object in its own right, Robert de Boron defined it with thirteenth-century precision as the Chalice in which the Holy Blood, gathered by Joseph of Arimathea, was transported to Britain as a symbol of the power which would convert the country to Christianity. The idea of the Grail as an aid to Christian conversion occurs also in the early thirteenth-century prose romance of *Perlesvaus.* But the culminating work of the Grail theme and of the whole Arthurian tradition is undoubtedly the *Prose Lancelot* or Vulgate Version which was probably written in Champagne between 1220 and 1230 by several hands under a central direction. It had five branches: Robert de Boron's 'history' of the origins of the Grail and its journey to Britain; the story of Merlin, also from Robert de Boron; the story of Lancelot; the *Queste del saint Graal;* and the *Mort Artu.* The *Queste,* under clear Cistercian influence, makes explicit what was implicit in Chrétien de Troyes. Arthur's knights are tested and divided into a worldly and a spiritual knighthood. The three Elect among the spiritual knights, Galahad, Perceval and Bohort, are entrusted with the mission, which they accomplish, of returning the Holy Grail to Jerusalem. In the *Mort Artu,* the worldly knighthood of Arthur, Gawain and his court is torn apart by the adulterous love of Guenevere and Lancelot, and when finally betrayed by Mordred, destroys itself on the battlefield of Salisbury Plain. Excalibur is hurled into the lake. Arthur dies.

The unique quality of Chrétien's achievement shines more brightly beside such spiritual and worldly conclusiveness. His poetic intention in the later romances becomes clearer. He is not a man who accepts absolutes such as the immaculate Galahad, nor even a Holy Grail in which the most secret mysteries of God are revealed. Chrétien allows himself only to give us intimations of our mortality and immortality, and of the almost ungraspable wholeness of a human condition which embraces cruelty and *caritas.* Such poetic intimations are the true legacy given to us by Chrétien, together with an image of the ideal which 'slips through and evades us', but which, when present, we cannot fail to recognise. (pp. 301-07)

> *L. T. Topsfield, in his* Chrétien de Troyes: A Study of the Arthurian Romances, *Cambridge University Press, 1981, 367 p.*

Peter S. Noble   (essay date 1982)

[*In the excerpt below, Noble suggests that Chrétien disapproved of the theme of* Le Chevalier de la Charrete *and that, through irony and humor, he "subtly used the 'matière et san' imposed on him to illustrate the weaknesses of courtly love."*]

Le Chevalier de la Charrete differs from all Chrétien's other romances as he deliberately disclaims responsibility for both the *matiere et san,* presumably the plot and the interpretation. This could, of course, be a graceful tribute to the Countess Marie and her patronage but when it is coupled with the fact that Chrétien did not finish the work and handed it over to Godefroiz de Leigni to finish, it must assume greater significance. Certainly Godefroiz seems to have worked with Chrétien's good will;

> car ç'a il fet par le boen gré
> Crestïen, qui le comança:
>
> (7106-07)

and may well have been guided by Chrétien in the planning of the last section. It is still strange to say the least that Chrétien should both disclaim responsibility for the inspiration for the romance and fail to finish it. If it is then looked at in relation to the other romances which he wrote, it can be seen that it is undoubtedly different. In *Erec et Enide, Cligés* and *Yvain* there can be no doubt that Chrétien sees marriage as the ideal state for lovers. In *Cligés* the Queen stresses the advantages of marriage, as the only condition in which love will endure (2266-69). In *Le Chevalier de la Charrete* there is no question of marriage and there cannot be, as the lovers are the Queen, already married to Arthur, and one of the leading knights of Arthur's court. If Chrétien had wanted to extol the virtues of unmarried love before, he had ample opportunity in the affair of Cligés and Fénice, who, however, end respectably married. It seems possible therefore that the theme was not entirely to Chrétien's liking, which would explain his care in making clear the source of the plot and the interpretation and his failure to finish it. The fact that he was working on *Yvain* at much the same time, a romance for which he seems to be entirely responsible and which was more to his taste, would also help to explain his passing the work on to Godefroiz so that he could concentrate on the plot which appealed to him more.

At first sight Chrétien treats the theme of the love of Guinevere and Lancelot with all due seriousness. The poem opens with the abduction of Guinevere and if the Foerster text is followed, Guinevere first mentions that someone other than her husband is interested in her fate at line 211.

> "Ha! Ha! se vos ce seüssiez
> ja, ce croi, ne l'otroiesiez
> que Kex me menast un seul pas."
>
> (211-13)

This does not apply to the Guiot text where the corresponding line reads:

> Ha! rois, se vos ce seüssiez . . .
>
> (209)

which cannot apply to Lancelot. The first version makes better sense as there seems to be no reason why Guinevere should whisper such a comment about her husband, but every reason why she should whisper it about Lancelot, although she is careful not to name him. Lancelot himself appears on the scene shortly afterwards when he begs a horse from Gauvain and without waiting to choose the better horse leaps onto the nearer one to save every possible second and rides off to try to rescue his lady. His own horse immediately drops dead from exhaustion, and Gauvain shortly afterwards finds the second horse dead at the scene of a great combat, suggesting that the knight had unsuccessfully attempted a rescue. Immediately after this comes the first test of Lancelot's love. He is on foot when he encounters the cart, which Chrétien is careful to explain brings great shame on any who enter into it. Nevertheless as the dwarf driving it will only consent to give any news of the Queen to anyone who will get into it. Lancelot after a brief inner struggle mounts the cart. Chrétien makes it clear that there is a struggle between common sense and love, which love very rapidly wins.

> mes Reisons, qui d'Amors se part,
> li dit que del monter se gart . . .
> N'est pas el cuer, mes an la boche,
> Reisons qui ce dire li ose:
> mes Amors est el cuer anclose
> qui li comande et semont
> que tost an la charrete mont.
>
> (365-74)

Gauvain, who is not in love, considers such an act to be 'molt grant folie' so that the contrast is clearly drawn between the lover, completely in the power of love, and the man who is still in control of his reactions.

The strength of his love is further emphasised when he sees the Queen from the window of the castle where he and Gauvain have spent the night. He follows her with his eyes until she disappears from sight, and when he can no longer see her, he contemplates dashing himself to pieces on the ground below.

> Et quant il ne la pot veoir,
> si se vost jus lessier cheoir
> et trebuchier a val son cors;
>
> (565-67)

Only the intervention of Gauvain prevents him from committing the crime of suicide and Gauvain manages to drag him back. He cuts a rather ridiculous figure at this point, emphasised by the acid comments of their hostess who thinks that he has disgraced himself to such an extent that he would be better dead than alive as no happiness can come to him in the future.

The ridiculous aspect of his behaviour is not stressed unduly, and shortly afterwards the lover is contrasted favourably with Gauvain who chooses the easier route to the Land of Gorre leaving the more difficult route to Lancelot, who accepts this uncomplainingly. As soon as he is on his own, Lancelot falls into a deep meditation, his whole mind concentrated on the thought of the Queen.

> et cil de la charrete panse
> con cil qui force ne deffanse
> n'a vers Amors qui le justise;
> et ses pansers est de tel guise
> qui lui meïsmes en oblie,
> ne set s'il est, ou' s'il n'est mie,
> ne ne li manbre de son non,
> ne set s'il est armez ou non,
> ne set ou va, ne set don vient;
> de rien nule ne li sovient
> fors d'une seule, et por celi
> a mis les autres en obli;
>
> (711-22)

This long list serves not only to bring out Lancelot's absorption in his amorous thoughts, but also by its overemphasis to make him seem a little ridiculous. Superficial-

ly he is the perfect lover absorbed in the contemplation of his lady, but given the circumstances his lack of commonsense and practicality suggest that Chrétien is viewing him with a certain irony. This is confirmed by the following scene, where Lancelot is quite unaware of the threats of the knight at the ford and remains oblivious of his existence until he is knocked off his horse into the water, cutting a decidedly laughable figure. He has to run after his shield and lance which were floating away and catch his horse before he can joust with his attacker. The moment the action begins, however, any trace of mockery disappears, and he is shown as a formidable warrior. Chrétien allows himself a brief smile at Lancelot's expense, but does not prolong it so as to make it too obvious and offend those who would interpret Lancelot's behaviour as a model for the courtly lover.

Lancelot is promptly subjected to another test by the Hospitable Damsel who demands that he should sleep with her. Very reluctantly he consents, but after the meal is confronted with the attempted rape of his hostess and has to decide whether to rescue her which might jeopardise his search of the Queen. His dilemma becomes comic as he struggles to reach his conclusion.

> honiz sui se je ci remaing.
>
> (1105)

He has no choice but to rescue his hostess, which he does only to be faced with the test of his fidelity when he has to get into bed with the maiden. Neither of them undresses completely, and it is clear from the way in which he completely ignores her, that Lancelot is not in the least aroused. Chrétien puts it more poetically, saying that he has no heart, as his own heart is elsewhere.

> Li chevaliers n'a cuer que un
> et cil n'est mie ancor a lui,
> einz est comandez a autrui
> si qu'il nel puet aillors prester.
>
> (1228-31)

No woman can distract Lancelot from his thoughts of Guinevere as his behaviour on the ride with his hostess illustrates.

> Cele l'aresne, et il n'a cure
> de quan que ele l'aparole,
> einçois refuse sa parole;
>
> (1332-34)

He is only roused from his thoughts when he realises that she is leading him away from the straight path. As he insists on returning to it, he finds the stone by the fountain where lies the beautiful comb. When the damsel finally tells him that the comb is Guinevere's, he almost faints from the sudden attack of passion, so violent that his companion dismounts to come to his aid. This forces his recovery, and so as not to embarrass him the girl pretends to have been rushing to get the comb. She is given the comb but he keeps the strands of hair, belonging to Guinevere, which he worships.

> qu'il les comance a aorer,
> et bien .c^m. foiz les toche
> et a ses ialz, et a sa boche,
> et a son front, et a sa face;

n'est joie nule qu'il n'an face;

> (1462-66)

Again this scene can be interpreted on two levels. Superficially Lancelot is behaving like a perfect courtly lover, adoring some token of his mistress in her absence, as it will serve to remind him of her. Compared with it earthly treasures are valueless. On another level, however, just as in the scene at the ford, the exaggerated reaction and behaviour make the reader wonder if Chrétien is wholly serious in this approach to Lancelot. The courtly lover is, after all, behaving almost blasphemously in worshipping other gods and despising the saints. By very slightly overdrawing the picture so that Lancelot could be accused of *demesure,* Chrétien hints that there may be some reservations in his approach to courtly love, although he is very careful not to let them emerge too obviously.

The inspiration of love is shown to be very great, for Lancelot is able to cross the Sword Bridge thanks to the power of love. He is warned about the perils which he faces, and Chrétien makes it clear what a formidable obstacle the bridge is. Lancelot is badly cut in the process, as he has to remove his armour to complete the crossing successfully. As a true lover he even finds pleasure in his pain.

> A la grant dolor c'on li fist
> s'an passe outre et a grant destrece;
> mains et genolz et piez se blece,
> mes tot le rasoage et sainne
> Amors qui le conduist et mainne,
> si li estoit a sofrir dolz.
>
> (3110-15)

The power of love has carried him across the bridge, but there is also the virtue in his own character, for King Bademagus has been watching and knows that only a man free from baseness could do it.

> que ja nus passer n'i osast,
> a cui dedanz soi reposast
> malvestiez qui fet honte as suens
> plus que proesce enor as suens.
>
> (3173-76)

To Bademagus' surprise, Lancelot despite his wounds, which the King thinks need several weeks to heal, proposes to fight Meleagant just as soon as possible, although to please the King he agrees to postpone the joust until the next day. Lancelot is showing all the impatience of the true lover. Because of this very impatience when the battle starts Meleagant gets the upper hand because Lancelot is feeling the effects of his wounds. He does not realise that the Queen and her maidens are watching him, until one of the maidens, guessing the reason why he has undertaken this battle, finds out his name from the Queen and shouts at him to take note of the presence of the Queen, hoping that this will inspire him.

The result is not quite what she intended as Lancelot will not take his eyes off the Queen and so has to fight under an even greater handicap.

> Ne, puis l'ore qu'il s'aparçut
> ne se torna ne ne se mut
> de vers li ses ialz ne sa chiere,
> einz se desfandoit par derriere;

> (3675-78)

For a few moments the audience are treated to the spectacle of Lancelot waving his sword about behind his back to keep off the attacks of such a skilful and dangerous knight as Meleagant, while keeping his eyes fixed on the Queen. The maiden has to intervene again to put an end to this way of behaving which she describes as 'folemant' and instruct Lancelot on how best to cope with Meleagant. One of the best knights in the world has to be told how to conduct his defence by a girl! Even Lancelot feels ashamed that everyone has seen that he was getting the worst of the fight, but by following the instructions he is able to combine watching Guinevere with the business of defeating Meleagant. Lancelot is inspired by love but, as the girl's comment makes clear, to excess. The sight of the Queen has given him new strength and he is able to control the battle exactly as he wants.

> et force et hardemanz li croist,
> qu'Amors li fet molt grant aïe . . .
> Amors et haïne mortex,
> si granz qu'ainz ne fu encor tex,
> le font si fier et corageus . . .
> devant la reïne sa dame
> qui li a mis el cors la flame . . .
>
> (3720-50)

As everyone can see that he is now playing with Meleagant, the King asks Guinevere to intervene, which she is willing to do. Lancelot shows yet another trait of the lover by displaying perfect and instant obedience.

> Molt est qui aimme obeïssanz,
> et molt fet tost et volentiers,
> la ou il est amis antiers,
> ce qu'a s'amie doie plaire.
>
> (3798-801)

At the risk of his own life Lancelot stops fighting, as he has heard what the Queen wishes, and would not for anything cross her.

He is all the more shaken therefore at his reception by the Queen when she refuses to speak to him. Bademagus rebukes her for her behaviour towards the man who has risked his life to save her, but Lancelot humbly accepts his dismissal, although neither he nor Kay can provide any explanation for it, and all are puzzled by the Queen's coldness towards Lancelot. Guinevere's true feelings about Lancelot are only revealed when she hears the rumours of his death. Her immediate reaction is to kill herself, as she blames herself for her harsh treatment of him during his life. She holds herself responsible for his death and regrets bitterly that they have never lain naked together. She quickly decides thereafter that it would be wrong to kill herself as in that way she would be at peace whilst it would be better for her to live on and to mourn for Lancelot, a mourning which she admits she would find sweet.

> Mialz voel vivre et sofrir les cos
> que morir et estre an repos.
>
> (4243-44)

As a result of her grief a rumour of her death reaches Lancelot, who immediately decides to die as in that way he can be united with Guinevere. His attempt is much more serious for he tries to hang himself, but fails, and the whole scene becomes slightly bathetic as those with him do not at first realise what he has tried to do and think that he has only fainted. Ironically he attributes her anger to the fact that he had mounted the cart, which he argues she ought to take as proof of his love and devotion, but the distress of both is soon turned to joy when they hear the truth. Lancelot is made to seem more sympathetic to the reader at this point. For all the farcical element in his botched suicide, his reactions are so spontaneous and whole-hearted that the depth of his love becomes apparent. In Guinevere the initially sincere feeling seems to be replaced by a rather more calculated decision as she finds reasons for staying alive, anticipating even a melancholy pleasure from her decision. She is delighted at the thought that Lancelot would have killed himself for her, although she would have been sorry if it had happened.

Their reconciliation is complete as soon as they set eyes on each other, for the Queen welcomes him in a way which makes clear that she has forgiven him. Lancelot then finds the courage to ask why she had publicly humiliated him and is told that it is because he had hesitated to get into the cart. He abases himself, admitting that she is quite justified, although before he had thought that her anger stemmed from the fact that he had actually got into the cart. He wishes to talk to her more privately and is told to come at night to the window where they can talk. For all her sensuous thoughts when she thought he was dead, Guinevere explicitly excludes anything other than talking or kissing at the window, not so much because she is unwilling as because it would be impossible with Kay lying wounded in the Queen's room. The meeting takes place but both are frustrated. Their frame of mind is made clear by 'a desmesure'.

> De ce que ansanble ne vienent
> lor poise molt *a desmesure,*
> qu'il an blasment la ferreüre.
>> (4594-96) (my italics)

Lancelot proposes to remove the bars, and the Queen assents, prudently withdrawing to her bed so that if Kay should wake, she will not be involved. Guinevere for all her love has not lost her sense of caution. Once within Lancelot worships as if at a shrine.

> si l'aore et se li ancline,
> car an nul cors saint ne croit tant.
>> (4652-53)

Chrétien makes a telling comparison between the intensity of their love, confirming what has already been obvious for some time.

> et s'ele a lui grant amor ot
> et il c. mile tanz a li
> car a toz autres cuers failli
> Amors avers qu'au suen ne fist;
>> (4662-65)

Their love has now become completely physical and sensual, and yet Lancelot still treats the affair in a near religious way.

> Au departir a sploié
> a la chanbre, et fet tot autel

con s'il fust devant un autel.
>> (4716-18)

Lancelot behaves in a way that is nearly blasphemous, but Chrétien does not criticise him overtly. There is nothing that is inconsistent in this scene with the rest of Lancelot's character as illustrated so far. He is a man of great enthusiasm, completely under the power of his lady and of his love for her. He has finally received the greatest reward in her power. It is little wonder that his reaction should be as exaggerated as his other reactions had been earlier when he found the hairs in her comb or when he heard the rumours of her death. Chrétien presents this reaction very baldly with no comment or expansion of the lines quoted. As a result they stand out amongst the other, more conventional reactions of distress at leaving the beloved, and Chrétien may be indicating his disapproval by allowing them to shock without any comment or explanation.

The result of their affair is that Meleagant suspects the Queen of adultery with Kay and fights Lancelot in a judicial combat to prove this. Naturally he is about to be defeated because he has got the wrong man, when once again the Queen shows her authority over Lancelot when she stops him fighting at Bademagus' request. This is despite Lancelot's oath.

> que se il hui venir me loist
> de Meleagant au desus,
> tant m'aïst Dex et neant plus
> et ces reliques qui sont ci,
> que ja de lui n'avrai merci.
>> (4980-84)

He is as ever completely submissive to the slightest whim of the Queen, whatever the risk may be for himself, as once again Meleagant is not willing to stop fighting and would like to take advantage of Lancelot's defencelessness. After this combat the lovers separate as Lancelot goes in search of Gauvain, who has failed to reach Gorre even by the easier route and illustrates the inadequacies of the man who is not inspired in contrast to Lancelot who is inspired by love.

Again the Queen has to suffer agony when she hears news that Lancelot is missing but this time she has to show joy for the safe arrival of Gauvain while concealing her grief over Lancelot. Only with the arrival of the forged letter announcing his safe arrival at Arthur's court is her joy restored, and she and her companions are ready to leave the land of Gorre to return to the court. There the forgery is discovered, and although the King is distressed about Lancelot, he is so delighted by the return of the Queen that his grief is turned to joy.

> quant la rien a que il plus vialt,
> del remenant petit se dialt.
>> (5357-58)

The lovers do not meet again until the tournament at Noauz which Lancelot is permitted to attend anonymously by the wife of his goaler, the seneschal. He starts very impressively but as soon as he receives a message from the Queen telling him to do 'au noauz', he becomes the worst knight on the field and is humiliated. The Queen is delighted at this exhibition of her authority and exercises it again on the next day rejoicing over Lancelot's submissive reply.

> . . . 'Des qu'ele le comande,
> li respont, la soe merci.'
>
> (5856-57)

Now that the Queen is sure,

> que ce est cil cui ele est tote
> et il toz suens sanz nule faille.
>
> (5874-75)

she is prepared to allow him to do his best which command he receives with the same courtesy. The Queen rejoices in her possession, overhearing all the marriageable girls longing for this knight in the scarlet armour and knowing that he is not interested in any of them, having just proved yet again, at the expense of his own dignity and reputation, how great his love and devotion are.

There is no further meeting between the lovers in the section written by Chrétien which ends where Lancelot is shut up in the tower. In Godefroiz' continuation Lancelot is involved with Bademagus' daughter, and his behaviour towards her differs greatly from the way he behaved to the unmarried women he met in Chrétien's part of the poem.

> La pucele beise et acole . . .
>
> (6678)

He goes on to pledge himself to her.

> Par vos sui de prison estors,
> por ce poez mon cuer, mon cors,
> et mon servise, et mon avoir,
> quant vos pleira, prandre et avoir.
>
> (6683-6)

He does not mention love, but he has gone further than ever before to any woman but the Queen. It is possible to interpret this as little more than the conventional service of a knight to a lady who has done him a service, but it seems very fulsome. The point is not developed and when Lancelot reaches the court to take up Meleagant's challenge, the attention shifts back to the Queen. She shares in the general rejoicing at Lancelot's return, but her common sense and discretion are very much in control.

> li rois, li autre, qui la sont,
> qui lor ialz espanduz i ont,
> aparceüssent tost l'afeire,
> s'ainsi, veant toz, volsist feire
> tot si con li cuers le volsist;
> et se reisons ne li tolsist
> ce fol panser et cele rage,
> si veïssent tot son corage;
> lor si fust trop granz la folie.
> Por ce reisons anferme et lie
> son fol cuer et son fol pansé;
>
> (6837-47)

Godefroiz finishes with the lovers on this note, for the rest of the poem is concerned with the defeat and death of Meleagant, but the Queen in this last appearance is fulfilling the role of the courtly lover, determined to preserve secrecy, showing 'mesure' as she controls her emotions, experiencing great *joie* at the sight of her lover (6824) and planning his reward when the time and place are appropri-

ate. There is nothing inconsistent in this presentation of her character with the character which Chrétien developed in the previous 6,000 or so lines. Guinevere is never as unrestrained or as innocent in her love as Lancelot is in his, but she, of course, is in the more dangerous position and has to be careful. She has probably learnt her lesson from the incident of the blood-stained sheets, which she and Lancelot were able to turn to their advantage unlike Tristan and Iseult from whose story the incident is clearly taken. Guinevere presumably had no wish to resemble Iseult in too many other ways.

As can be seen *Le Chevalier de la Charrete* is very different from Chrétien's other romances. It is concerned with an adulterous love affair, in which neither of the lovers considers marriage. Neither lover expresses any remorse for what they do and there is no thought given to the cuckolded husband. Guinevere seems in fact to be the model wife. At the beginning of the poem she is presented as the loyal consort of Arthur ready to humiliate herself to help him, and so it is a considerable surprise to discover that she has a lover, even if only a platonic one at this point. Once she is back at Arthur's court, it is clear from his delight that he has no suspicions about her, while her intention at the end is to ensure that he should have no cause to suspect her infidelity. She exercises throughout the poem written by Chrétien the role of the *dompna*. She is imperious, distant, demanding and socially superior. Lancelot, as her lover, shows his readiness to make any sacrifice for her. He serves her with patience, humility and obedience. He finds his inspiration in her, and life without her cannot be contemplated. When she finally grants him his reward, he treats it as a sort of religious experience and worships the very bed in which they commit adultery. The language is unfailingly courtly, and on one level Chrétien has written a romance which is a description of a highly successful and extremely passionate courtly affair. The relationship between the lovers conforms to the demands of courtly love; the behaviour of the male partner shows the power of love, and even if his behaviour is felt on occasion to be exaggerated, he is after all an idealised lover in a mythical world. He need not conform to reality in every facet.

On another level, however, it can be argued that even within the courtly code Lancelot is not a wholly satisfactory lover. He undoubtedly lacks *mesure*. His uncontrolled reactions at the sight of the Queen or at the discovery of her hair could well betray their love. His attempted suicide at the news of the death of the Queen again shows an uncontrolled reaction. He is even willing to lose his worth for the sake of the Queen, and this was a sacrifice the lover was not normally called upon to make. This also reflects badly on the Queen for the truly courtly lady did not humiliate her lover. Guinevere seems at times to exercise her power for the love of exercising it, so that in a sense she abuses it. Thus she too lacks *mesure*, although she is very much in control of herself in other respects. These points are not stressed by the author, but they are there in the poem and suggest a certain degree of dissatisfaction with the courtly code.

This impression of dissatisfaction is further strengthened

by the flashes of humour which keep appearing in Chrétien's part of the poem. It is noticeable that humour is almost entirely lacking from the last section by Godefroiz de Leigni. As already indicated Chrétien more than once seems to mock Lancelot. On several occasions he is made to seem a figure of fun, as when he twice attempts suicide and fails each time. The first occasion, when he tries to throw himself out of the window, is particularly pointed as his hostess draws to the attention of the audience how much better it would be if he actually succeeded. His daydreaming to such an extent that he is knocked off his horse into a ford and then has to run and retrieve his weapons before he can fight his aggressor is another risible episode. Again his behaviour in his fight with Meleagant is comic, as is the idea that a great knight should need instruction on how to win his fights from one of the Queen's maidens. The humorous scenes are all fairly short, and the humour is not emphasised, as they are usually followed by a more serious episode, showing Lancelot to advantage, which adds variety to the narrative. Nevertheless the humour is there, very similar to the humour in *Yvain,* where the dignity of the hero is punctured, and the ideals of the courtly court of Arthur are shown to be hollow. In *Le Chevalier de la Charrete* the grand passion of Lancelot is shown to have its comic side, and in this way the figure of the hero is cut down to size. He is not superhumanly perfect; rather he has his failings and his weak points, mostly caused by the intensity of his love, which is discreetly criticised through his humour. The love felt by Lancelot not only inspires him and causes him great happiness. It makes him look ridiculous, act like a fool and on occasion lose his reputation.

Guinevere too is not immune from criticism. It has already been suggested that she is not an ideal courtly *dompna* as she abuses her power over Lancelot. She does not show *mesure* in her treatment of him in the same way as she does when considering her own emotions. This abuse of the love which Lancelot feels for her makes her seem an unsympathetic character, and the calculating element in her personality adds to this impression. She finds very good reasons for staying alive after the death of her lover whereas he in the same situation immediately attempts suicide. She is careful to minimise the risk when Lancelot breaks into her room by withdrawing to bed during the crucial few minutes as he rips the bars out of the window. Chrétien himself makes it clear that great as her love is, it cannot match the love felt by Lancelot. Godefroiz confirms this impression of a calculating woman when at the end of the poem he has her carefully deciding to reserve her welcome until she and Lancelot are alone together. Some of this is of course common prudence, but the contrast is made with the generous, unquestioning and uncalculating love of Lancelot, and it is not to Guinevere's advantage. She is well able to manipulate husband and lover simultaneously, and as a result seems to be rather too much in control of the situation to be wholly attractive.

She is, presumably, not at all worried by the considerations that troubled Fénice [in *Cligés*]. As far as one can tell from the poem, she is a wife to Arthur as well as a mistress to Lancelot and so is guilty of exactly the crime denounced by Fénice. Two men share her body, while one

has her heart. Whether this is completely true is of course open to question, as Guinevere never indicates that she does not love Arthur, and it is certain that Arthur loves her. Guinevere is in many ways the model wife. She will go on her knees to Kay at Arthur's request to try to maintain the unity of the court. No comment is made on her feelings at the moment of her return to Arthur from the Land of Gorre. Chrétien does perhaps try to lessen the impact of the adultery by placing it in the Land of Gorre, which is even more remote than Arthur's court. Arthur is not present and although it is not quite a case of out of sight, out of mind, he is certainly not considered at all during the episode. The Queen seems to be almost a free woman, and at this point in the poem she is not physically involved with the King. The implication of Godefroiz' remarks, however, is that once both she and Lancelot are back at the court, she has every intention of continuing the affair, which will put her in the position of Iseult with her husband and her lover both possessing her. If Chrétien was sincere, as he seemed to be, in *Cligés,* where such behaviour was denounced and held up for censure, why should he now write about it, apparently complacently in *Le Chevalier de la Charrete?* Part of the answer must be because it was the 'matière et san' given to him by the Countess Marie. Another part of the answer may be that his complaisance was superficial, as he took pains to dissociate himself from the 'matière et san', and failed to complete the poem, which may well indicate reluctance or a loss of interest.

Confirmation of this suggestion, that Chrétien's enthusiasm for the poem was cool, may be found in some of the other elements in the poem. The humour which suggests that he did not take the pretensions of courtly love too seriously has already been mentioned. The possibility that the lovers are not quite such perfect examples of courtly love has also been considered. To all this should be added what can be deduced about Chrétien's attitudes from the other romances which predate or were written at the same time as *Le Chevalier de la Charrete.* From them it can be argued that Chrétien was no friend to courtly love. He abhorred the idea of adultery and preferred to stress the advantages of marriage. Chrétien was also perfectly capable of writing a romance with several layers of meaning. It can be argued that this is particularly true of *Yvain,* which is a straight adventure, a quest for identity, a highly symbolic account of the pursuit of an ideal, a mocking criticism of the claims of Arthur's court to represent *courtoisie* and a love story. The same is surely true of *Le Chevalier de la Charrete.* On one level it is an account of the courtly love affair of Lancelot and Guinevere, which is carried to such a point of idealism that it could only happen in a mythical otherworld such as the Kingdoms of Gorre and Logres. For those who look beneath the courtly surface, however, Chrétien by his use of humour and exaggeration is suggesting that a courtly affair is not the ideal which it seems. The effect of power on the character of the lady is shown to be unpleasing, while the man is reduced to a state of abject submission where his own self-respect and dignity are less important to him than his love. Chrétien is well able to use the elements of a courtly affair but he attempts to turn them against themselves by showing their harmful effects on those involved.

Thus it can be argued that far from writing a poem which extols *amour courtois,* in **Le Chevalier de la Charrete** Chrétien has subtly used the 'matiere et san' imposed on him to illustrate the weaknesses of courtly love. If this theory is accepted, then this romance is not so different from the other romances as it appears at first glance. Although it does not extol the virtues of marriage, it does bring out the drawbacks of the rival code of courtly love. The attitude of quiet criticism expressed through gentle humour and the characterisation of the main characters is very similar to the attitude expressed in **Yvain.** Chrétien's views on love are not greatly altered by the ideas in **Le Chevalier de la Charrete.** (pp. 65-79)

> *Peter S. Noble, in his* Love and Marriage in Chrétien de Troyes, *University of Wales Press, 1982, 108 p.*

Nigel Bryant   (essay date 1982)

[*In the following excerpt, Bryant examines the fundamental theme of* Perceval, *maintaining that it was Chrétien's plan "to depict a knight's development from a point of total innocence and ignorance"—a plan which is further carried out by the continuators of the story.*]

It is not hard to see why Chrétien's unfinished story of the Grail proved such a compelling one, for its fundamental theme could hardly have been bolder, clearer or more movingly simple, or more important to its medieval audience. It is about the making of a knight—in the most complete sense. It is not by chance that the story begins with a boy who has been brought up in a remote forest with no knowledge whatever of the world of knighthood, and with only the haziest understanding of matters religious—he does not even know what a church is, let alone a knight's hauberk, shield or lance. Chrétien's plan is so forthright and sweeping that he sets out to depict a knight's development from a point of total innocence and ignorance.

In the early episodes of [**Perceval**] Chrétien skilfully exploits the comic potential of this ignorance; but there is at the same time something deliberately unsettling in Chrétien's depiction of the innocent leaving his mother collapsed in a heap outside her house, almost assaulting a girl to take her ring, and killing a knight to get his arms. It becomes hard to distinguish between the innocent and the primitive.

The first steps towards improving the innocent boy's ways are taken by a knight named Gorneman de Gorhaut; but it is extremely important that, although the boy takes to knighthood like a fish to water, Gorneman's instruction is primarily *martial* and secular. So that when the new knight encounters his first great adventure, freeing Blancheflor from her enemies Engygeron and Clamadeus, he shows how immensely talented he is as a warrior; but his next great adventure, his visit to the Fisher King's castle, is a disaster; he is as yet utterly inequipped to plumb the secrets of the radiant Grail and the mysterious bleeding lance. Immediately afterwards, in a piece of brilliantly emphatic symbolism, Chrétien shows the new knight Perceval breaking the sword given to him by the Fisher King with the very first blow he strikes. The significance of the broken sword motif was not lost on the continuators, who introduced the mending of a broken sword at the Fisher King's castle as the principal test of a knight's worthiness to learn the secrets of the grail and the lance. In the First Continuation Gawain twice fails to repair it, although on the first occasion it initially *looks* to be perfectly joined, just as Gawain looks on the face of it to be a very worthy knight indeed; and at the end of the Second Continuation Perceval succeeds in repairing it—except for a notch on one edge: he is still not quite worthy to know the truth. 'From this test,' says the Fisher King, 'I know for sure that, of all men now living in all the world, there is none of greater worth than you in combat or in battle; but you have not yet done enough to have God bestow on you the praise, esteem and courtesy, the wisdom and the chivalry, to enable us to say that of all knights you were the most endowed with all high qualities.' And the true meaning of the Broken Sword is made plainest of all by Gerbert de Montreuil who, unlike Manesier in his Continuation, was not content to leave the notch in the Broken Sword's blade. In terms reminiscent of Saint Bernard of Clairvaux, the great Cistercian who was a driving force behind the Crusades, Gerbert has a hermit explain to Perceval that 'a knight's sword has two cutting edges: do you know why? It should be understood . . . that one edge is for the defence of Holy Church, while the other should embody true earthly justice. . . . But know this: Holy Church's edge is broken, while the earthly edge cuts indeed . . . and a knight who carries such a sword is deceiving God; and if he does not mend his ways, the gate of Paradise will be closed to him.' Gerbert, indeed, has Perceval break yet another sword while hammering on a gate which is locked to him, the gate of a ring of wall inside which he can hear great rejoicing; and Perceval is told afterwards by the smith Triboet that 'you broke it at the gate of Paradise.' By the end of the Second Continuation, then, Perceval has done as much as can be done in the secular, martial sense—the 'earthly edge' is mended—but he has still more to achieve before the symbolic sword is whole: before, that is to say, he is a *complete* knight.

The importance of the spiritual alongside the martial in the development of a knight, symbolised so powerfully by the Broken Sword, is a constantly recurring theme. Chrétien makes the point very clearly with the episode, strikingly thrust into the midst of Gawain's adventures, where Perceval suddenly reappears after five years of random feats of chivalry. 'Perceval . . . had lost his memory to such a degree that he no longer remembered God. April and May passed by five times—that's five whole years—without him entering a church or worshipping God or His cross. . . . That's not to say that he stopped seeking deeds of chivalry: he went in search of strange, hard and terrible adventures, and encountered so many that he tested himself well. In five years he sent sixty worthy knights as prisoners to King Arthur's court. That was how he spent five years, without a thought for God. It is all very well gallivanting around defeating knights, but there is the matter of God. Perceval is so lost, indeed, that he does not even know that it is Good Friday; and when he goes, distraught, to the house of his hermit uncle to beg forgiveness for his waywardness, the hermit makes him aware that he is stained with sin: it was the sin of deserting his mother that had led to his silence when he saw the grail; and the hermit stresses the importance of church and mass, so shamefully forgotten by Perceval for five long years—not, indeed, that Perceval has *ever* really shown any great awareness of them: his ignorance of them has so far been almost as total as his earlier ignorance of a knight's military equipment.

From the point where Perceval next reappears in the romance—in the Second Continuation—he abundantly proves his *military* capabilities; what is disastrous is that he is so repeatedly unaware of how far he has to go in his *spiritual* development. He is shocked when, on a second visit to his hermit uncle's cell, his uncle deplores his killing of another knight, and he is made to realise for the first time the importance of confession. The imbalance of Perceval's development as a knight—his brilliance as a warrior but his spiritual immaturity—is perhaps best demonstrated by the episode involving the girl who is willing to tell him the way to the Grail Castle 'if you'll keep to the way and not stray from it'. The way involves crossing a fragile bridge of ivory over the river Marmonde, and the girl gives him a ring and a white mule, saying: 'As long as you have the ring on your finger, my white mule will carry you safely . . . and you need have no fear of crossing the ivory bridge'. Sure enough, the white mule carries him safely and calmly across the wafer-thin ivory bridge, while his charger—a warrior's mount—crosses behind 'with difficulty, most fearfully'. But having got across, Perceval does not follow the path to the Grail Castle at all, but promptly allows himself to be distracted into yet more feats of military prowess—albeit proving what an outstanding knight he is—in the shape of a mighty tournament at the Proud Castle; so that when he comes to return the ring and the white mule to the girl, she is literally speechless when he tells her that he has not even tried to find his way to the Grail: 'She mounted swiftly, without taking her leave, and rode off, much to Perceval's amazement. He was not quite bewildered, for he did not know which path to take or in which direction to turn to find the court of the king called the Fisher.'

Gerbert de Montreuil, whose poem is by far the most inspired and methodical continuation of Chrétien's themes, shows by his handling of the broken sword motif that he was acutely aware of how much remained to be done before Perceval was fully worthy to know the secrets of the grail and the lance. Gerbert cleverly reintroduces Gorneman de Gorhaut, Perceval's first instructor in the art of arms, to contribute to his moral development by emphasising the importance of marriage; Gerbert at the same time thus completes Chrétien's theme of the young knight's awakening to love, by having Perceval marry Blancheflor—and the marriage is chaste indeed. And most important of all, perhaps, is Gerbert's long and central episode describing Perceval's battle with the Dragon Knight, for in it Perceval becomes unmistakably a crusader. Immediately before the battle he receives a white shield with a red cross; the Dragon Knight, moreover, who is besieging the lady of the castle of Montesclaire, is not merely wicked but an infidel, a devotee of the Devil, carrying a shield with a demonic dragon's head fixed in it, which engulfs any attacker in flame; and the lady besieged at

Montesclaire is none other than the Girl of the Circle of Gold, the significance of which would not have been lost on any of Gerbert's audience acquainted with this episode's source; for in *Perlesvaus,* from which the Dragon Knight story is taken, the Circle of Gold is identified as the Crown of Thorns [*The High Book of the Grail: Perlesvaus,* translated by N. Bryant, 1978]. Even without the additional element of an infidel threat to a most holy relic, the significance of this episode's details was unlikely to be missed; and with the aid of the power of the red cross shield—which has another holy relic, a piece of the true cross, embedded in it—Perceval not only defeats the infidel but converts him, too. In a way, nothing crystallises the overall 'meaning' of **Perceval** better than this episode, for stressing the importance of a knight's spiritual development alongside his mastery of arms leads almost inevitably to making crusading the natural outlet for knightly skills. That is surely what made the grail theme such a crucial and potent one in Arthurian romance in the late twelfth and early thirteenth centuries; for the great quest for the grail portrayed in the most exciting and appealing way possible the fusion of religious ideals and a warrior ethic, at a time when the Crusades had made such a fusion the very definition of knighthood and the very object of knightly endeavour. At a time when affairs in the Holy Land were not exactly happy for the forces of Christendom, it was an important message for the poets to convey; all the more reason, too, for Gerbert to make the taking up of the red cross shield such an inspiringly awesome challenge: ' . . . no-one could find the Grail or the lance with the head that bled ceaselessly, except the first one to be able to remove the shield from the neck of the beautiful girl. But it was at his peril that any man touched it or tried to remove it unless he was the boldest man in the world, both in word and deed, and confessed of all his sins; for otherwise he would be destroyed and killed by a thousand stones, and nothing could protect him. There was an inscription upon it to that effect for the benefit of all who saw the shield and were able to read. The girl stepped into the house at once. She had been scouring many lands, both day and night, but no-one who read the inscription would lay a hand upon the shield: they did not dare to try, for it was a fearsome test indeed.'

It must be stressed, however, that any overall 'meaning' there may be in **The Story of the Grail** is nothing like as systematic as the above may suggest. The 'meaning' of the romance is not an appeal to get on the next boat to the Holy Land, any more than it is an appeal to get married and make confession and remember the power of the sign of the cross. Quite apart from the fact that there are huge digressions from the grail theme throughout **Perceval,** with a good deal of intriguing story-telling for its own sake—notably in the First Continuation, which contains two sections that are virtually separate romances—the 'meaning' is in a sense cumulative, gradually expanding from episode to episode, all following on from Chrétien's introduction of Perceval as a totally 'unmade', innocent, ignorant boy. **Perceval** shows the gradual making of a supremely fine knight in every sense—martial, moral and spiritual. And from time to time, as in the 'crusading' episode of the battle with the Knight of the Dragon, the romance was able suddenly to jolt its medieval audience into a quite unexpected realisation of the meaning of being a knight. But it is important to stress, too, that the romance can hopefully still work on a less limited level: the depiction of an individual's development is relevant not only to the twelfth and thirteenth century aristocracy. (pp. xi-xv)

> *Nigel Bryant, in an introduction to* Perceval: The Story of the Grail *by Chrétien de Troyes, translated by Nigel Bryant, D. S. Brewer, 1982, pp. xi-xvi.*

Staines on Chrétien's contribution to Arthurian romance:

The individual knight rather than Arthur is the center of Chrétien's fiction. Traditionally, the epic and the chronicle depict a nation; their characters are the embodiment of a national destiny; their ultimate concern is the nation itself. By contrast, the romance depicts the individual. Thus, in the twelfth century, Virgil's epic of national identity becomes the *Roman d'Eneas,* with the national concerns subordinated to a tale of an individual, his heroism, his loves, his adventures. The distance between the Arthur of the chronicles and Chrétien's Arthur is the distance between Arthur in a national context and Arthur as secondary to individual knights whose heroism and loves are portrayed through their adventures.

The romances of Chrétien distance the individuals from their society, allow them their own identities, and examine their understanding of both themselves and their world. In his focus on the individual, Chrétien creates the knights who will be central figures of the Arthurian world for all future generations.

> *David Staines, in an introduction to* The Complete Romances of Chrétien de Troyes, *translated by David Staines, Indiana University Press, 1990.*

W. T. H. Jackson   (essay date 1984)

[*Jackson was an English-born scholar of Germanic and comparative literature and the author of* The Literature of the Middle Ages *(1960) and* The Anatomy of Love: The Tristan of Gottfried von Strassburg *(1971). In the following excerpt, he discusses Chrétien's* Lancelot *in terms of originality and examines the poet's possible sources, particularly focusing on the Arthurian conventions as they are developed in* Lancelot.]

Chrétien de Troyes was by far the most prolific and influential writer of French narrative poetry in the twelfth century. Of his life nothing definite is known. The appellation "de Troyes" could mean that he was born there or simply that he was connected with the town and, probably, with the court of Champagne. The identification of Chrétien with a certain canon of St. Loup, near Troyes, mentioned in records in 1173, has no supporting evidence, nor has the suggestion that, since Chrétien (Christianus) was a name frequently adopted by converts, he was of Jewish origin.

Since he states expressly that Marie, daughter of Eleanor of Aquitaine, who became countess of Champagne, proba-

bly in 1164, had given him the "matière" for *Le Chevalier de la Charrette* (*Lancelot*), it seems highly probable that he was acquainted with her and hence with her court. The dedication of *Li Contes del Graal* (*Perceval*) to Phillip, count of Flanders, proves no such acquaintanceship but it does indicate that the poem was written before 1190, when Phillip left for the Third Crusade, never to return.

It is fair to assume, from Chrétien's frequent references to Ovid and other classical literature, that he had received a good grounding in the subjects of the *trivium* (grammar, rhetoric, and dialectic), but there is no direct evidence of the equivalent of a university education or of his being a cleric. Nor is it possible to determine where Chrétien gained his knowledge of the Arthurian world. Critics have found evidence in his work of his having read the *Historia regum Britanniae* (History of the kings of Britain) by Geoffrey of Monmouth and Wace's *Brut,* which is based on it, but his treatment of the Arthurian world is so different from that of the historians that it is necessary to postulate "oral tradition" and "lost sources" to explain the different treatment. His works assume knowledge of Arthurian conventions in the audience; otherwise his irony would be lost. Nevertheless, we should never lose sight of the fact that Chrétien's Arthurian romances are the earliest examples of the genre in any language, and that their influence inside and outside France was enormous. It would appear, therefore, that for contemporaries he was the first great exponent of the Arthurian romance and an author of considerable originality. There is little real evidence which would lead a modern critic to challenge that view.

At the beginning of his *Cligés,* Chrétien states that he is the author of *Erec and Enid,* of several French versions of stories from Ovid, and of **"King Mark and Iseut the Fair."** Of these only *Erec* is extant. The other works, including that of Mark and Isolde, were probably short poems, like the *Lais* of Marie de France. We can thus be sure that the first two extant romances, *Erec* and *Cligés,* were composed in that order, and that the former was written after 1164, when Marie became countess of Champagne. The next two were *Le Chevalier de la Charrette* and *Yvain.* Many critics believe that Chrétien worked on the two simultaneously, and it is impossible to determine in what order they were made available to the public. Chrétien left the completion of *Le Chevalier de la Charrette* to Godefroi de Lagny, but he did complete *Yvain,* perhaps the best structured of all his Arthurian romances. Chrétien's last work, *Li Contes del Graal* (*Perceval*) was, as we have seen, begun before 1190 but it was never finished. Godefroi de Lagny, who completed the *Lancelot,* states categorically that he did so with the approval of Chrétien. No such statements are made by the numerous authors who continued *Perceval,* and there is a strong presumption that Chrétien died before he could finish the work.

Although he wrote a few lyric poems, and a narrative poem, *Guillaume d'Angleterre,* is ascribed to him in some manuscripts, Chrétien's fame rests on his romances. It is worth repeating that there is no extant source for any of these romances. The selection of Erec and Yvain to be outstanding heroes at the Arthurian court seems to be Chrétien's own doing, for they are not so singled out in other Arthurian works, except when these are directly dependent on Chrétien's own work. There is no evidence before his poem of any tradition of a love affair between Lancelot and Queen Guinevere and his treatment of the Grail story in **Perceval** differs totally from earlier and contemporary accounts.

Clearly his originality was recognized by contemporaries. No other French author of the period had so many of his works adapted into other languages, and it is particularly significant that two of the greatest poets who wrote in Middle High German used his work. Hartmann von Aue adapted his **Erec** and wrote a German version of **Yvain** which follows Chrétien's poem in every detail. Wolfram's *Parzival,* although a very different work from **Perceval,** nevertheless stays very close to Chrétien's poem in the material of its narrative—and that in spite of Wolfram's denial that he used the work. In sum we may say that, whatever material was available to him and whatever earlier Arthurian stories he used, Chrétien has a just claim as the originator of the Arthurian romance as a literary genre.

In considering the Arthurian background of Chrétien's romances, it is important to make a clear distinction between the historical, pseudohistorical, and mythological material which is found in them and the conception of an idealized court which provided social and moral standards for Chrétien's heroes and to a large degree controlled their conduct.

The historical material has been thoroughly investigated. The earliest mention of Arthur by name is in a Welsh poem, *Gododdin* (c. 600), where a warrior is praised for his prowess, "even though he was not Arthur." Earlier works, written in Latin, such as that of Gildas (c. 540), and a succession of later authors mention battles and achievements later connected with Arthur, but the first real account of his deeds is given by the Latin historian Nennius (c. 800). From these scattered fragments of information it seems likely that there was a Welsh chieftain towards the end of the fifth century who put up a spirited resistance to the invading Saxons and who passed into legend as the king who never died but who will come again to revivify his people. The name Artorius was given to this chief. None of the early Latin accounts mentions Queen Guinevere or any of his band of warriors, but in the Welsh prose tale *Culhwch and Olwen* we do find the names of many men who later appear as knights of the Round Table. Here Arthur is a brave and determined king, ready to challenge any odds, but there is no hint of the chivalry which was later to be attributed to his court.

Many critics are of the opinion that the *stories* about Arthur and his warriors were composed largely from Celtic (including Irish) mythological material and that they were transmitted from Wales to Brittany in oral form, since the languages were mutually comprehensible in the early Middle Ages, and were later retold in French by bilingual Breton ministrels. Such an explanation about the spread of Arthurian stories throughout France and even as far as Italy during the eleventh century is perfectly plausible.

Certainly many of the names of places and important characters in the romances can be shown to be of Celtic origin and analogues of many of the motifs and individual incidents can be found in Celtic mythology or in Irish saga. But it is dangerous to push these resemblances and analogues too far. Many are of the common stuff of myth, and parallels can be found everywhere, while some of the "identifications" of names rest on the assumption of wholesale distortion, misunderstanding, and careless transmission.

It is significant that there is nothing in extant Celtic literature which could even remotely be called a romance until works appear which are clearly based on French models. The material in the *Mabinogion,* in the *Black Book of Carmarthen,* in the *Book of Taliesin,* and the *Red Book of Hergest,* even though Arthur is mentioned and motifs are found which are like those in Arthurian romance, has none of the characteristics of the romance genre. We must therefore conclude that the early Latin accounts of Arthur and the extant Celtic material do not provide a basis for the treatment of Arthur and his court which we find in the works of Chrétien and his successors. That there was an oral tradition of stories used by minstrels to entertain their audience with Arthurian tales is virtually certain, but it is highly unlikely that these works were romances. It is impossible to say whether they introduced the notion of Arthur's chivalric court, but the possibility seems remote.

It is all the more surprising, therefore, that in 1136 a work was written which offers a totally new view of Arthur's reign. Geoffrey of Monmouth finished his *Historia regum Britanniae* (History of the Kings of Britain) in that year and by 1139 there was a copy of it in the library of a monastery at Bec in Normandy. The work covers the history of Britain from the first eponymous king, Brut, until the death of Cadwallader (689). What is remarkable about the work, however, is that no less than one sixth of it is devoted to the reign of Arthur, and it is clear that its purpose is to glorify both the king and his court and the British, that is to say Celtic, origins of Britain. Geoffrey can be shown to have used Welsh sources, but much of his work is his own invention, as contemporaries such as William of Newburgh pointed out. His *Prophecies of Merlin,* for example, material from which is largely incorporated in the *History,* seems to be largely his own invention, as is the account of the conception of Arthur which has Uther Pendragon disguise himself as the husband of Ygerne. Although sources can be found for some of the accounts of battles described in the *History,* Geoffrey seems to have made up the story of the great climactic battle between Arthur and Lucius Hiberus, emperor of Rome, and, even more important, that of the final battle in which Arthur kills Modred but is mortally wounded himself. This account of the end of Arthur's reign is of great importance. Here we are told for the first time that Modred was the son of Arthur's sister (but not, as later accounts state, that he was Arthur's son), that he took Guinevere in an adulterous "marriage" while acting as governor of Britain in Arthur's absence, that he was killed only after the loss of Gawain and most of Arthur's warriors, that Guinevere went to a convent, and that Arthur was taken to Avalon to cure his wounds. Thus the Welsh tradition of his future return was preserved. It is in Geoffrey's work that we first hear of Guinevere's adultery, transferred by Chrétien to a liaison with Lancelot, whom Geoffrey does not mention.

Geoffrey's work was written as history and as history it was understood by contemporaries and later readers. It was very probably propaganda too, an attempt to counter the extravagant stories which told of Charlemagne's conquest of Britain and which thus gave "authority" to the claims to suzerainty made by French kings. With this intention is connected the most important single feature of the work, its glorification of Arthur's court as the perfection of good manners, courage, loyalty, and civilization. It would be wrong to say that it exhibits the characteristics of what we call "courtliness." The stress is still on war, politics, and conquest, not on love and individual adventure. But the court is the center of civilization and it sets standards. The following passage makes the point clear:

> For at that time Britain was raised to such a pitch of excellence that it far surpassed other kingdoms in manners, in the richness of its material goods, and in the polished behavior of its inhabitants. All the knights who had gained fame by their prowess wore the same colored clothes and arms. The women too were polished in their behavior and also wore the same kind of clothes. They would not accept the love of any knight unless he had proved himself in combat three times. Thus they became chaste and better and the knights showed more prowess in their love for them. After they had refreshed themselves at the feast, they went to the fields outside the city to take part in different sports. The knights devised a game on horseback which gave the impression of a battle while the ladies looked on from the top of the walls. The games stirred their love to a frenzy. [*The Historia Regum Britanniae of Geoffrey of Monmouth,* ed. Action Griscom, 1929.]

Here, for the first time in connection with Arthur, we have the beginnings of the idea of pleasing a lady by prowess, of the connection between love and adventure and of nobility exalted by love. It is not likely that Geoffrey knew of the new cult of love which was being developed at this time by the lyric poets of southern France, but it is not impossible that he had heard of the cult of love which shortly after is exemplified in the *Roman d'Enéas.* However this may be, it is certain that his interest in relations between the sexes at Arthur's court is concerned with manners, not with love.

Geoffrey's work was immensely influential. About 200 manuscripts are still extant and it gained further popularity from the expanded version of Wace, written in Anglo-Norman in 1155, called *Brut.* This is the first work in which the Round Table is mentioned. There is ample evidence that Geoffrey's work was used by other historians and there can be little doubt that Chrétien knew it or a version of it. It is not too much to say that the story of Arthur as the great British king, the counterpart of Alexander and Charlemagne, begins here.

It cannot be overemphasized, however, that Geoffrey's work was intended to be history. Even though later writers of literature used the work, the romances they wrote are totally different in tone. The Arthurian court which makes its first appearance in the romances of Chrétien de Troyes is totally divorced from the realities of history. Although allegedly situated in Britain, its geographical location is uncertain. Knights leave it and go to places in continental Europe without, apparently, ever crossing the Channel. Certain features, such as the Forest of Broceliande, are always near it and seem to represent rather states of mind or locations for a particular type of action than topographical features. Much more important is the fact that inhabitants of the court are always engaged in leisure pursuits. The opening of *Yvain* (the only one of Chrétien's romances which has no prologue) makes it clear that leisure was the normal state of affairs. It is well known that an "aventure," whether in fact or in story, opens every romance except *Perceval,* and so strong did the convention become that Arthur is frequently shown as refusing to start a feast until an adventure presents itself. It can thus be said justly that Arthur's court exists to give authenticity to adventures. *Perceval* is an exception because the hero actively seeks an identity at Arthur's court, whereas other protagonists already have that identification.

The important characteristic of the Arthurian court is that it has a set of values agreed upon by all its members. None of Chrétien's romances enumerates these values. They are to be deduced from the praise or blame given to the deeds performed, whether that praise or blame comes from the narrator or from other characters. The main concerns of the members of the court are with adventure and the gaining of love, or, in other words, with martial prowess devoted entirely to the honor of the individual and to gaining the affections of a lady with no thought of social considerations other than Arthurian conventions. Marriage is important only as a relationship between two people within which the nature of their love and its relation to other virtues can be tested.

If there were no more to romance than a string of adventures illustrating these qualities, it would hardly be worth serious study. Chrétien and many of his successors used the Arthurian court invented by poets for the manipulation of these qualities and for the evaluation of their usefulness to individuals and to society. Chrétien appears to have decided to use Sir Kei, who in the histories is an honest if unenlightened person, to represent a type of sterile, even brutal, Arthurianism. To him the enforcement of the superficialities of the court is of primary importance, and he regards himself as the supreme arbiter. His effect on Arthur's own conduct is often disastrous, even though the king is well aware of his defects. By his conduct he often drags the court into ignominy and himself acts as a parody of the Arthurian hero.

At the other end of the scale is Gawain. He personifies all that is best in the system. He is gallant, polished, courteous, and kind, the person against whom all others must be measured. Yet he illustrates also the weakness of the Arthurian ethos. His actions are all directed to purely Arthurian objectives and it is only incidentally that he performs acts of humanity, for example, the freeing of the ladies from the Castle of Wonders while he is pursuing the

Lancelot crossing the Sword Bridge; Guenevere with King Baudemagus; Baudemagus meeting Lancelot (MS 806, fol. 166).

love of Orgeluse. He therefore acts as a foil to such knights as Erec and Yvain who, in different ways, emancipate themselves from the self-centered Arthurian ethos.

All Chrétien's romances are concerned with love. Indeed, it is not impossible that he had a plan to show love in a different way in each of his works, for it is quite certain that Enid's love for Erec bears no resemblance to Laudine's for Yvain or Guinevere's for Lancelot. The courtly convention of love and service to the lady affects all these affairs but they are not merely examples of "courtly love." The term is a nineteenth-century invention and we should beware trying to lump together the love situations in the Provençal *canzon,* the *alba,* and the *pastorela,* all lyric forms, and that which we find in the romance. It is true that in the *canzon* the lady is idealized and that the poet regards the poems he composes to her as love service. But there is never any communication between the poet and his lady, and the whole essence of the genre is that love must be forever in suspense. This is never the situation in the romance, where love is active and progressive, and where the lady, in spite of her great power and her ability to decide the fate of her lover, for good or evil, must obey the rules and grant her love if the knight serves her faithfully and well. Love in the romance does not exist only in the imagination of the lover-persona, as it does in the lyric. Nevertheless, Chrétien makes it very clear that in his Arthurian world, love determines the conduct of both sexes in a manner that would be impossible in the real courts of his day, and that the desire to deserve love and to win it can raise both men and women to heights not otherwise attainable and also lower them to behave despicably.

The triumph of the protagonists over the conventions of the court is what makes the great romances into true works of art. At the beginning the hero acts in accordance with the courtly ethos as he understands it and achieves success. Erec, for example, concerned only with vengeance for the insult offered to him by the black knight and his dwarf takes Enid to the tournament so that he may

have a valid "courtly" reason for challenging his opponent. She is at this point no more than an excuse for prowess. But she is also very beautiful and Erec falls in love with her body but not with her. His subsequent neglect of prowess so that he can spend all his time with her shows an Arthurian imbalance which has to be corrected, but the real problem goes deeper. When he hears Enid lamenting his lack of activity, he believes that she is concerned that he is not "honoring" her with knightly prowess. In other words, he judges the event from a purely Arthurian point of view. Nor can we be absolutely sure that such a thought is totally absent from Enid's mind at the time.

Erec determines that she shall have the prowess she desires but that, instead of having the adventures recounted to her, preferably by the knights defeated by her champion, she herself must act as bait for those who are to challenge Erec. If Erec fails her, she will fall prey to those attackers, as indeed she almost does. This perversion of the Arthurian ideal leads Enid and still more Erec to reconsider the whole nature of love and the purpose of adventure, and the final incident, the so-called *Joie de la Cort* episode, shows Erec risking death to free a fellow knight from the slavery to which he has been subjected by a lady who believes that love gives her absolute power over her lover's entire life—a logical extension of the Arthurian ethos.

In *Yvain* too, Chrétien takes care to show how it is possible for a knight to realize that adventure does not exist for the sole purpose of gaining the favor of a lady but to help other women in distress who promise no reward. Yvain returns to his lady after doing long service, not to her but to others, in the guise of the Knight of the Lion. Chrétien leaves it doubtful whether the lady to whom he returns, Laudine, understands or even wishes to understand his motivations.

The progression, then, is away from Arthurian conventions. As the knight leaves the court, returns briefly, and then separates himself completely, so the knight and the lady at first think only in Arthurian terms but end by the recognition of higher values. The same is true of Perceval, who must rise above the ethos of the court before achieving a higher destiny. All three of these romances have a clear two-part structure. In the first part the hero pursues Arthurian ideals and achieves his ends triumphantly. Then follows a catastrophic event which brings about a total change of attitude and action.

It is significant that, in Chrétien's other two romances, the pattern is different. In *Cligès* the first part is about the hero's parents, who are reduced to silence about their perfectly genuine love by the tyranny of court convention and are rescued only by Guinevere's good sense. Their career gives Chrétien the opportunity to indulge in some good natured jesting at the expense of love at Arthur's court. The second part is not so good natured. It is concerned with the attempt of their son, Cligès, to win Fenice, the wife of his father's brother. She will not hear of an adulterous liaison but is quite prepared to use drugs to sham death, to be entombed, recover, and celebrate her union with Cligès in a sepulchre. When they are discovered, they flee to the only safe place, Arthur's court, where they await the death of Fenice's husband. It will be observed that, far from rising above the Arthurian ethos, Cligès and Fenice sink below it and instead of transcending Arthur's court, they take refuge in it. It seems highly probable that, .in this work, Chrétien is determined to show how the idea of love could be perverted.

The other romance which does not show a clear two-part structure is *Le Chevalier de la Charrette* or *Lancelot,* and to this we must now turn our attention.

According to his preface to the work, Chrétien undertook the *Lancelot* at the request of Marie, countess of Champagne, daughter of Eleanor of Aquitaine by her first marriage to Louis VII of France. There is considerable evidence that Marie's court indulged in elaborate discussions of the theory of love and quite possibly in games in which questions concerning love were "tried" in "courts." This interest in love as the center of civilized and particularly of aristocratic life is perhaps what prompted Marie to suggest to Chrétien the story of Lancelot and Guinevere. Where she found the material is not known. There is no extant poem or story about their love which can be dated earlier than Chrétien's romance. In fact, there are no earlier stories in which Lancelot is the hero. The earliest German works, which are not dependent on Chrétien, ascribe numerous adventures with ladies to Lancelot but none of those ladies is Guinevere. It is just possible that Chrétien may have invented the story, but it seems much more likely that Marie gave him at least an outline of it, attracted to it, perhaps, because it represents the ultimate triumph of love over the realities of power. The fate of adulterous queens and courtier-lovers in the Middle Ages and Renaissance is well documented. Adultery was treason and was punished as such. Yet in this poem the king is little better than a cringing figure who cannot guard his own wife, and she is clearly in search of a man of finer stuff and moreover one whom she can dominate while he is capable of dominating everyone else. The Arthurian ethos is here pushed to its logical conclusion: a knight whose love service is the finest imaginable, yet who is the total slave of the lady he serves, a lady whose real desire seems to be to prove her dominance whatever the consequences. There can be little doubt that she corrupts the character of the knight rather than ennobling it and from there it is but a small step to the destruction of the whole Arthurian world which is presented in the Vulgate Version of the Arthurian romances and in Malory's *Morte d'Arthur.* To assert, as C. S. Lewis [in his *The Allegory of Love,* 1936] and others have done, that the love of Lancelot and Guinevere represents the highest manifestation of "courtly love" is true only in the sense that it pushes the conventions of that love to extreme limits, indeed to the edge of parody. Before discussing the work any further, it may well be appropriate to summarize the plot.

An unknown knight interrupts the feast Arthur is holding at his court in Camelot on Ascension Day and announces that he holds captive knights and ladies whom he will release only if Arthur entrusts Guinevere to one of his knights, who must then defeat the challenger in battle. If the challenger wins, the queen joins the other captives. Kei tricks the king into giving him the task. He departs with the reluctant queen, and when the king and Gawain ride out they find his horse and broken lance. It is clear that the queen has been abducted. Gawain follows their trail and finds a horse he had lent to Lancelot lying dead. Later he comes on Lancelot himself walking behind a cart. (Lancelot is not named until much later in the poem.) The dwarf who is driving the cart bids him get in if he wants news of the queen. After hesitating two steps, Lancelot does so. He is now riding in the shameful vehicle used to take condemned men to the gallows and he suffers appropriate abuse when passing through a town. Gawain and Lancelot reach a castle where they are well entertained, but Lancelot, though warned of danger, insists on sleeping in the best of three beds, where he is almost killed during the night by a flaming lance. No explanation of the event is given by their hostess the following morning.

As Gawain and Lancelot proceed, they learn that the queen's abductor is Meleagant, son of Baudemaguz, king of Goirre. This land can be reached only by two dangerous bridges, one under the water, one made of sword blades. Lancelot decides to take the road which leads to the sword bridge. On the way there he has to defeat a knight who is guarding a ford. At first he is so lost in thoughts of Guinevere that he is unhorsed but he recovers and wins. He next encounters a lady who will give him lodging and information only if he will lie with her. He reluctantly agrees, rescues her from an "attack" by knights who prove to be members of her own household, and then lies with her only in the most literal sense of the term. She is not offended and agrees to go with him in search of the queen. Next day, he finds a comb with Guinevere's hair and worships it as he would a holy relic. In a cemetery he raises the lid of a tomb destined for him and thereby reveals himself as the liberator of the prisoners in the land of Goirre. After other adventures, Lancelot finally arrives at the sword bridge. On the opposite bank he sees two lions but after he has crawled across and severely slashed his hands and feet, he finds they have disappeared.

Baudemaguz, a kindly man, urges Lancelot to wait until his wounds are healed before fighting, but Lancelot insists on combat the following day. Weakened as he is, he is doing badly until he sees Guinevere watching from a window. Meleagant is saved only by his father's intercession but ungraciously insists on a second combat at Arthur's court.

At their first meeting, Guinevere treats Lancelot, whom she addresses by name, with marked coolness and he leaves. On hearing false reports that she is starving herself to death, he attempts suicide, and she, hearing that he is dead, repents of her anger. Lancelot is brought to see her, and she explains that he had offended her by his hesitation in getting into the cart. That night he comes to her window, forces apart the bars, and their love is consummated. The blood from his hands stains the sheets and the wretched Kei, lying wounded in the room, is accused of adultery. Lancelot now finds himself in the dubious position of defending the innocence of Guinevere and Kei by fighting Meleagant, whom he again defeats.

Lancelot now sets out in search of Gawain but is ambushed and imprisoned. Gawain has tried to cross by the underwater bridge but he slips off and is rather ignominiously fished out of the water. He learns that the queen has been rescued by Lancelot. A tournament is arranged at Logres at which certain ladies will have an opportunity to choose husbands. Guinevere agrees to attend and is escorted there by Gawain. The wife of the jailor who has Lancelot in prison is so moved by love for him that she agrees to release him to attend the tourney. He fights unrecognized and defeats all comers until Guinevere, believing she recognizes him, sends a message to him that he should lose. He does so, incurring much abuse, until she bids him win, when he carries off all honors. He then loyally returns to his prison. From this he is finally rescued by a damsel to whom he had rendered a service while on the way to the sword bridge and who proves to be Meleagant's sister. She takes him home, nurses him back to health, and keeps him with her until it is time for the combat with Meleagant at Arthur's court. Gawain is prepared to fight in Lancelot's place, but he arrives in time for the combat, fought in an idealized landscape situation near Arthur's court. After a merciless contest, Meleagant is defeated and beheaded, much to the delight of the court.

Several general characteristics may be noted at once. There is in the *Lancelot* no structure which corresponds to that of *Erec* and *Yvain,* and, to a lesser degree, *Perceval.* The hero does not ride forth on a successful adventure, win a lady, and then have the Arthurian world collapse about him. Nor, and this is more important, does he seek a different ethos, a combination of love and prowess directed to higher ends. Lancelot's attitude remains the same throughout. He is devoted to Guinevere with religious fervor, and all his efforts are directed towards serving her. He personifies the most extreme form of the Arthurian love-ethic, even when his devotion makes him betray Arthur. As Tennyson has put it: "Faith unfaithful kept him falsely true." No one can doubt his fanatical devotion and fail to be moved by it, but it is harder to feel sympathy for Guinevere. No one can blame her for the initial abduction, but her almost ruthless exploitation of her power over Lancelot raises serious questions about the nature of the love she feels for him and about the way in which Chrétien wishes us to see Arthurian behavior in the poem. Many critics believe that Chrétien undertook the task imposed on him by Marie de Champagne with great reluctance. Certainly he did not finish the work but handed over the last thousand lines or so to Godefroi de Lagny. His lack of interest may well be part of the reason for the chaotic structure of the poem, especially of the first part. Even the most favorably disposed reader cannot fail to notice the total irrelevance of many of the episodes (for example, the fiery lance) which have no bearing on later events and which the author himself never attempts to explain. Many episodes seem to be little more than an attempt to fill out the work or mark the passage of time. Even incidents which are relevant often seem like duplicates—the amorous jaileress and the amorous sister of Meleagant, for example. The structure too is often clumsy. Why, for example, is there such a long gap between Lancelot's crossing of the sword bridge and Gawain's failure at the underwater bridge?

It is not the structure, then, which gives the poem its reputation. The interest lies in the characters and the tensions between them, their relation to the Arthurian court, and their plight as human beings. There is too the power of Chrétien's poetry to bring them to life.

Lancelot is not introduced into the story as a member of Arthur's court, nor do we find out who he is until he has performed several deeds. (He is first named in line 3660.) As happens so often in Chrétien's works, the actions which determine his fate in the romance are performed without his participation and even without his knowledge. Yet the events over which he had no control, the challenge to Arthur, the rash boon granted to Kei, the abduction of Guinevere are not the real motivating forces. It soon becomes clear that Lancelot has been in love with Guinevere for some time. His appearance *outside* Arthur's court is therefore more than accidental. For almost the whole poem Lancelot never even visits the court. Only his last combat with Meleagant takes place there, at Arthur's direction, and, it will be remembered, that combat is the direct result of the challenge to the court which opens the poem, not anything to do with Lancelot's love for Guinevere. Although he is regarded as the greatest of Arthur's knights, Lancelot is in this poem an outsider, and in the later works in which he appears he never has the same close relationship to the Arthurian world that is shown by Gawain.

Lancelot's behavior in love is also worth consideration. We do not see him fall in love, as we do Erec, Cligès, and especially Yvain. There is no opportunity for us to observe the first impact on him of Guinevere's beauty—nor for Chrétien to treat us to the Ovidian symptoms of the love-disease. He is already in love when we first encounter him but only gradually do we become aware of the fact. The most telling incident is the finding of the comb with the queen's hair entangled in it. The scene is strongly reminiscent of the episode in *Cligès* where Alexander discovers that Sordamors has sewn one of her long blond hairs into his shirt and spends the night hugging and kissing a shirt. Yet the scene in *Cligès* is so treated that the reader must find it comic, whereas Lancelot's intensity of passion is clearly to be linked with mysticism and religious devotion. To Lancelot, the hair has all the power of a saint's relic, but the reader is left with the uneasy feeling that perhaps there is a similarity between his behavior and that of Alexander.

Lancelot's devotion is absolute. He dedicates himself entirely to the service of Guinevere, even if that means death or, still worse, dishonor. His love service, in other words, is not the fulfilling of an Arthurian convention but of his own inward drive. Here, and in many other respects, he is like Tristan, and it seems that Chrétien borrowed freely from the Tristan story, which he mentions in *Cligès.*

Lancelot is like Tristan too in his sensual desires. In all the romances, the consummation of love is important, but in no other story of Chrétien's is it accompanied by such images of love and violence as in the *Lancelot.* The slashing of hands and feet, the tearing apart of window bars, the blood on the sheets are typical.

Thus there is a sharp contrast between Lancelot's love and that of the Arthurian convention. His love is individual, even fanatical. Although it may conform outwardly to some of the practices of the Arthurian court, it is really opposed to them, for it has no positive social purpose. If it continues its course (a question left open by Chrétien), its only result will be to shatter the Arthurian world, as it does in later versions.

In assessing the role of Lancelot, it is useful to compare him with Gawain. Indeed, it seems that Chrétien intended us to do so. Gawain is present when the challenge is made, but Kei deprives him of any opportunity to take it up. He does the next best thing. He goes out to track the queen and her abductor and accompanies Lancelot when he finds him. Typically, he attempts the sensible crossing of the water by the submerged bridge, and, in spite of a gallant attempt, fails. His only important action is to accompany the queen to the tournament at Logres. He follows a pattern found in many romances when he offers to take the place of his friend Lancelot in combat, but he is not called upon to do so. Throughout, Gawain behaves impeccably by Arthurian standards but he achieves nothing. His role in the romance genre as the touchstone by which other knights are judged is well known. It is most prominent in *Perceval* but it is very important in *Erec and Enid* too. In the *Lancelot,* it appears as if this role has been deliberately diluted. The friendship between Lancelot and Gawain is deep and sincere, but the feeling persists that, if Gawain was the best the court had to offer, it would not be difficult for Lancelot to surpass him.

If the stature of Gawain is much diminished in comparison with the figure we find in other romances, the figure of Arthur suffers still more. When he should be paying close attention to the challenge to his court and his person, he allows his attention to be diverted by Kei and is so desperately anxious to keep him at court that he allows himself to be tricked into naming Kei as Guinevere's escort. Nor does he himself make any serious effort to recover

her. Only at the end of the poem does he revert to his customary role as a courteous master of ceremonies for a judicial combat. This was the role he played in *Erec,* but in that poem he was not faced by the personal challenge we find in the *Lancelot.* It is a commonplace of Arthurian criticism that all the romances play down the role of Arthur so that the protagonist—Erec, Yvain, Lancelot, Perceval—may appear to greater advantage. Here we may legitimately ask whether Chrétien has not lowered the stature of the king still more because of the involvement of the hero with the king's wife and lowered the stature of the court for the purpose of ironical criticism of its conventions.

The author's treatment of Kei seems to support this point of view. As we have seen, he was a bold and noble knight in the chronicles. In *Erec* and *Cligès,* his role, though not distinguished, does not make him into the coarse, ill-tempered, and even dangerous boor that we find in *Yvain* and *Perceval,* where his actions bring misery and even death to innocent people. It would appear that, in *Lancelot,* Chrétien is introducing him as the lowest representative of Arthurian values. Here his greatest fault is arrogance, reinforced with complacency. His insistence on recognition as champion of the court leads not only to the abduction of Guinevere but also to the adultery between her and Lancelot, for it is hard to believe it would have happened if she had been escorted by a better champion—or not abducted at all. It is not, therefore, unjust that, wounded though he is, Kei should be charged with adultery, and this fact is one more piece of evidence of Chrétien's ironical intent.

The role of Guinevere is subject to various interpretations. As we have pointed out, she enters into an adulterous "marriage" with Modred in the work of Geoffrey of Monmouth, but it is hard to determine the degree of her guilt. In Chrétien's other romances she is very much the arbiter of matters concerned with love at court, but there is no hint of disloyalty to Arthur. Even at the beginning of the *Lancelot,* she begs Arthur to keep Kei but she is most unwilling to leave the court. Her subsequent actions could be regarded as motivated by disgust at Arthur's weakness, but this is not likely. Lancelot's love hardly seems to come as a surprise to her, for she would scarcely be offended at his hesitation in getting into the cart if she did not know of his love. Even after the consummation of their love, Guinevere's main purpose is to demonstrate her power over Lancelot—to show it off in the conventional Arthurian form: the knight's act of love service. Her message to him to fight badly has been explained as no more than a desire to find out that the knight really was Lancelot, but, if this were so, there would be no need for the farce to continue as it does. Guinevere's desire for power is stressed far more strongly by Chrétien than by others who treat the story, and this leads to the suspicion that Chrétien was here showing what happens to individuals and society when the Arthurian convention is pushed to its limits.

If one regards Guinevere, as one must regard Lancelot, as a victim of overwhelming passion, then her actions are easily explained. But all the evidence is against such an interpretation. She is always too calculating and can keep a suitable distance between her actions and any passion she may feel. She does not appear to be moved by any question of disloyalty to Arthur nor has she any hesitation in returning to court, where her affair must cease or produce a major disruption.

At the end of the work, Arthurian order has been restored. The queen and the knights are back at court, the violent intruder has been defeated and killed. Yet the reader knows that this "harmony" is a sham. Here, as so often, we must note the difference between *Lancelot* and *Erec* and *Yvain.* In the latter romances, the protagonists are different people with different values, even though the court is unchanged. There is no evidence that Lancelot and Guinevere are changed people, except that they have committed adultery, and what their future is, we do not know. Was this vagueness Chrétien's intention? Or did he mean that the Arthurian system solved nothing? The question is fascinating and insoluble. *Lancelot* remains the most enigmatic of Chrétien's romances. (pp. ix-xxxii)

> *W. T. H. Jackson, in an introduction to* Lancelot, the Knight of the Cart *by Chrétien de Troyes, translated by Deborah Webster Rogers, Columbia University Press, 1984, pp. ix-xxxii.*

Harry F. Williams   (essay date 1986)

[*In the following excerpt, Williams attempts to explore the meaning of Chrétien's* Perceval *by analysing its resemblances to* Lancelot *and the motifs and expressions found both in its prologue and text.*]

Behind the glittering facade of Chrétien's romances, superficially tales of love and adventure, lies at least one subsurface meaning, otherwise we must accept them as merely series of loosely connected episodes joined only for entertainment, a viewpoint long ago abandoned by connoisseurs. Conservative exegetes, seeking the author's intentions, discern in these stories literal and figurative levels. Besides, the medieval reader was accustomed to seek reality beyond the veil of literature, it would seem. A story's bipartite planes are intimated in the exordium of the *Chevalier de la Charette,* where the author attributes to Countess Marie of Champagne the *matiere et san* ("meaning and plot") and to himself only his *painne et antancion* ("trouble and time").

Never is the underlying idea openly stated; it must be inferred by retrospective conceptualization. Chrétien prefers to mystify with both language and themes. Such authorial strategy promotes more audience participation, a constant preoccupation of medieval romance writers, particularly. The real import of all his fiction still fuels lively discussion, but no romance incites more debate concerning its inner meaning than does his *Conte du Graal,* the subject of theories, in excess of two dozen, which seek to elucidate its obvious symbolism and calculated ambiguity. Such characteristics lend themselves to multivalent interpretations which will continue to proliferate, but no hypothesis advanced by others seems more cogent than my own.

Here, we seek guidance for a penetration of the meaning of the *Conte du Graal* by first viewing it telescopically, then relating it to our author's total literary production, as basis for discussion of clues provided by the story's prologue to arrive at a hypothesis whose confirmation is found in the adventures of Perceval and Gauvain.

To the uncritical eye, Chrétien's Grail story presents, after an unusual prologue, a kaleidoscopic series of experiences undergone by two successive heroes whose lives and fortunes are subtly intertwined and eventually are affected profoundly by an enigmatic adventure, as each journeys through antithetical worlds.

First we accompany the naive boy Perceval, who, impelled by the expressed desire to become a knight, leaves the Waste Forest to enter the Arthurian world (from which his family had been exiled by cataclysmic events), only to be engulfed later by the supernatural Grail community. Then we follow the accomplished knight, Gauvain, who is implicitly attracted more by amatory dalliance then by chivalric exploits, as he leaves Arthur's court to wander in a kind of Waste Forest before he arrives at the Castle of Marvels in a land "whence no knight can return," vv. 6602-6603, which analogically recalls the Grail Castle.

Despite the attention paid to chivalry and love, we feel intuitively that Chrétien no longer poses in his last romance the problems faced in his previous ones; we have here a different orientation. He wrote at least five romances (if we leave aside *Guillaume d'Angleterre* of debated authenticity, for it breathes a different spirit and poses a chronological problem). A conspicuous trait of Chrétien is a penchant for harmony and order involving both individuals and society; he is a concerned observer of the human condition in both its positive and its negative aspects.

Although a virtuoso in composition, he treated remarkably few themes in his various works. Common to both *Erec* and *Yvain,* reduced to their simplest terms, are the same principal themes and problems (viz., the relative roles of love and chivalry in a young man's life), although these tales exhibit vast surface differences. He claims in the *Cligès* to have written an earlier *Tristan* story, yet the *Cligès* itself is fundamentally a Tristan tale. So, for the second time, apparently, he treated twice, although in different ways, identical problems, a procedure consonant with medieval emphasis more on form than on subject matter. It is not unreasonable, therefore, to seek connections between the *Charette* and *Graal* stories.

Each of those poems was commissioned by a patron; both lack the customary conclusions of Chrétien; they bear descriptive and suggestive titles (a characteristic shared by his *Le Chevalier au Lion*); only these two designate King Arthur's country as Logres; in them alone is a litter used for transportation. Other parallels between them include extraordinary use of suspended or denied explanations; mysterious geoscenic backgrounds; a bipartite structure (as opposed to the triptych appearance of *Erec* and *Yvain*); the respective heroes do not begin their primary quest at Arthur's court; each of the three heroes remains unmarried. Moreover, each story follows first a straight line and unfolds at a fast pace which becomes, in the second part, more leisurely and involuted. Both Lancelot and

Gauvain are tested by a perilous bed. Both fight at a ford, experience a combat delayed, suffer a humiliating experience, and each must cross a sinister river; the author abandons them while they are imprisoned.

Lancelot and Perceval fall into a love-trance; they share action with Gauvain (as did Yvain); both resist the advances of a seductive hostess, exhibit a unique singleness of purpose, seem cast in a messianic role. The career of each (and of Gauvain) is affected by meeting a father and son (Grail King, Fisher King; Garin, Herman [at Tintagel]; Bademagu and Meleagant); each travels over a stone pass; their very names play a role in their respective stories; and Arthur's cup, stolen by the Red Knight, functions like the abduction of Guenevere. Their main theme seems identical: the protagonist leaves the everyday world to spend time, for a specific purpose, in a mysterious land which must have been, in the author's mind, a heteroclitic Otherworld. They cross and recross the boundary between life and death; they are involved in a kind of resurrection. Although often warned of the dangers, Lancelot and Gauvain, in their respective stories, consciously penetrate this other realm, Lancelot in successful search for his abducted mistress, Guenevere, whom he frees and thus illustrates courtly love; Gauvain out of curiosity liberates the enchanted castle but becomes thereby a prisoner in it. Perceval unconsciously enters the Otherworld, he is not warned, and he fails to fulfill his mission: to answer the questions about the Grail and the Lance, i.e., to discover the meaning of Life and Death. Perceval is ignorant of his destiny; are we not all? The future is unknown except for the fact that people are mortal and ultimately they experience death, yet still one goes on, from experience to experience, and fails to be unduly disturbed by the inevitable end. After Perceval's failure to penetrate the mystery of Life and Death, Gauvain is charged with seeking the key to Death (the Lance) and he too fails, but their actions illustrate the existence of faith, the fact that hope is eternal, that man will continue to dream of solving, and continue to fail to solve, the ultimate riddle of humankind. Lancelot succeeds (as did Hercules, certain Celtic heroes, and Christ); Perceval and Gauvain fail (as did classical Orpheus and Perseus). Such numerous correspondences and this fundamental contrast between the *Chevalier de la Charette* and the *Conte du Graal* must point to the message of each.

The *Chevalier de la Charette* in addition to being predominantly an exposition of courtly love, involves a victorious mission in a hostile region ("whence no stranger returns," v. 645) strongly reminiscent of the Celtic Otherworld. Might not the Perceval story be a failed Otherworld quest, with the love interest subordinate? Such a reversal of viewpoint is typical of *Erec* and *Yvain;* to cite but one example, the Knight with the Lion is responsible for the disharmony in his married life whereas Enide bears that responsibility in the earlier story. Chrétien's attitude is not always positive: Calogrenant fails and Yvain triumphs at the fountain; Cligès does not reconcile chivalry and love service; Gauvain fails and Lancelot succeeds in the *Chevalier de la Charette* poem. While writing this romance, Chrétien was obviously absorbed in Celtic mythology and so he had Lancelot complete successfully his Otherworld

mission. Later, influenced more by Christian tradition, and doubtlessly familiar with mythical Orpheus' failure to accomplish his quest in the Underworld, he has his new heroes, Perceval and Gauvain, involved less in love casuistry or high chivalric deeds and more in eschatology. As in the *Chevalier de la Charette,* the basic problem posed in the *Conte du Graal* seems to be the eternal one of Life and Death.

This problem is subtly indicated not only by Chrétien's total literary production, but also in the prologue to his Grail story by such *topoi* as number symbolism, significant evocations of individuals, and meaningful upheaval of the old social order.

In the exordium to the *Conte du Graal,* Chrétien's references to Holy Writ create immediately an atmosphere antithetical to that of the *Chevalier de la Charette,* as much as to say: Celtic mythology is here subordinate to Christian dogma. And he contrasts basic qualities of two questers—the virtues of the living Christian, Philip of Alsace, who furnished the book which inspired this romance, and the vices of the dead pagan Alexander the Great. This expressed hierarchy of two different worlds recalls to the attentive reader the unmentioned fact of Philip's interest in the material life of his country and the spiritual life of Christians everywhere (twice he went on crusade to the East and eventually died there) and Alexander's sowing, throughout the known world, of death and destruction. Thus is set up a dichotomy that will be continued throughout the romance. Do not Perceval and Gauvain resonate with Philip and Alexander? The underlying message is undoubtedly dyadic in nature.

Initial verses present curious repetitions of two concepts clamoring for attention: sowing and charitableness. One interpretation of charity might well be here: "Be charitable to this work." The concept of the first verb used (*semer*) is repeated, literally or figuratively, six times (and three more in the introductory scene). Such insistence surely recalled to medieval audiences the biblical parable of the sower, which contains the injunction: "He that hath ears, let him hear. . . . Take heed, therefore, how ye hear" [Matthew 13:3-9; Mark 4:3-14; Luke 8:5-18].

I hear in the *Conte du Graal* Chrétien's account of a quest doomed to failure, just as Alexander lacked the qualities necessary to enter Christian heaven. The hidden message, clued in part by the parable cited, is this: all generations, both sexes, any individual, the young and the mature, are all involved in a Dance of Death, all journey to a common end. Observe therefore the principal Christian virtues, of which charity is the greatest, and seek not to unriddle the eternal enigma of Life and Death. This ultimate secret is withheld from mortals. This theory is corroborated by both the Perceval and the Gauvain parts of the story.

The exuberant life of the immature country boy Perceval is abruptly changed by his first encounter with merchants of death—five knights in search of five others riding with three girls. He learns then from his mother that his father and two brothers died in the service of chivalry and that she wanted to shield him from the same fate. The story begins with reference then both to life and death and to a troubled world.

The disharmony in Perceval's life is but one item in the disoriented social order sketched in the romance. At the death of Uterpendragon (father of Arthur), people were killed, impoverished, disinherited, and exiled. At that time, we learn later, Uter's wife went to Roche de Canguin where she welcomes, with her daughter and granddaughter, her grandson Gauvain. Since Perceval was two years old at the time of his exile, and since the Grail King (Perceval's uncle) had retired to the inner room 11, 12, 15, 20 years before Perceval's visit (the time varies in the MSS), and since Perceval is now about 14 years old, inasmuch as he is ready for knighthood, then the Grail family was probably displaced at the same time as Perceval's was. The Waste Forest, the Grail Castle, and the Roche de Canguin would then be fragments of the previous Arthurian world; perhaps even the Hermit Uncle went to his hermitage then. Arthur too was certainly affected, and he may be considered in exile, if not dead, at least spiritually, since he is so strangely apathetic toward the Red Knight. But life went on in the various places of exile, as Christians are taught to expect life after death, although this fictional otherlife is corporeal rather than spiritual. Only an after-life could restore order to such social fragmentation in life.

The atmosphere of Christian life and death in the Grail Castle is suggested by the procession's form (a cross), and by its passage into the inner room to serve the holy man a single wafer, his only nourishment. This wafer recalls Christian communion, symbolic of the body of Christ. The procession passes between the bed and the fire, each of which suggests both life and death. The Grail objects are of white or red colors (symbols of life and death). The Grail Castle questions suggest symbolically life and death: whom does the Grail serve? (the Grail King, says the Hermit later) and why does the Lance bleed? (question unanswered). At table the diners eat flesh of dead animals. Contrastive are the castle life in the evening and the dead atmosphere next morning when Perceval finds himself alone.

Little effort is required to interpret the Blood-on-the-Snow scene as symbolic of life and death. Even Perceval's ecstasy is a kind of death, and death threatens the three successive knights who try to dispel his revery. The colors involved here, which recall to Perceval the complexion of Blanchefleur, remind us not only of her mortality but also of the Grail scene and of the Red Knight.

Spiritually dead, Perceval meets near the Hermitage three women and ten knights, thirteen people who came to worship on Good Friday, anniversary of the death of Christ. They remind us of the Waste Forest scene: five knights in pursuit of five others and three girls. In or near the Castle of Marvels are met particularly the three queens and five men besides mysterious Silverleg and newly-arrived Gauvain: boatman, Guiromelant, Orgueilleux du Passage à l'Étroite Voie, Greoreas, and his nephew; the reader is left to wonder whether these are the eight people sought initially by the five questing knights. This and other tantalizing questions are no more elusive than the mystery of life and death.

The Christian context of this life-death theme extends then from the prologue through the successive lessons provided by the mother, Gornemant, and the Hermit Uncle, i.e., the entire Perceval story, whereas the Gauvain section, except for the use of empty formulas, conspicuously lacks it, as did Alexander the Great, of course. The theme's context is now less religious but the theme continues to be dominant.

The prologue's contrastive views of two individuals mirror the separate careers of Perceval and Gauvain. Actions and character of each predispose the audience to accept without undue disappointment their fate. Failure of the two heroes in their primary quests was anticipated by the failure of Alexander to measure up to Philip, as well as by the catastrophe which struck Uter's realm, and by secondary quests of our protagonists: knighthood by Arthur and reunion with mother; finding the maid of Montesclaire and fighting contracted but postponed duels.

The three generations evoked in the prologue and initial scene (Alexander, Philip, and Perceval; Uter, Arthur, Perceval) are reflected by three at the Grail Castle (Grail King, Fisher King, and the latter's niece) and at the Castle of Marvels (Uter's wife [who died 60 years before], Lot's wife [dead for 20 years], and the latter's daughter). Even at the Hermitage are multiple generations apparently (Hermit, priest, and acolyte). Such insistence on generations as well as genealogies must surely be accounted for in the meaning, as much as the evocation of both life and death.

Three women influence Perceval's life strongly: his mother (close and afar), the Tent Lady (before and after the Grail scene), Blanchefleur (in fact and in retrospect). Three others serve the tale's economy: the Laughing Girl, his girl cousin, the Loathly Damsel. Male figures who further his development are Arthur, Gornemant, and the Hermit Uncle. Informative (again in different ways) are twice three individuals or groups: the questing knights, the Red Knight, Org.uilleux de la Lande, charcoal seller, Clamadeu and Enguigeron, the Grail people. This last group includes the two men rulers and one corporeally absent but psychologically present woman (niece), and the Grail procession consists of three boys, two girls. At Blanchefleur's Castle is both a convent and a monastery. Rulers meeting Gauvain at the Castle of Marvels are three women, and five men are in its orbit. Pilgrims at the Hermitage include both sexes. Gauvain encounters on his travels as many women as men. This staging of both sexes must be significant for the whole story.

The relentless march of time is shown not only by the multiple generations depicted but also by glimpses into a past and a future of Arthur, Perceval, Gauvain, the Grail Castle, and the Castle of Marvels. This aspect of time is prefigured in the prologue by comparison of Count Philip and King Alexander and verbally underscored later by the mother, the *cousine,* the Loathly Damsel, and Guiromelant. Arthur's world was of course disturbed by the upheaval in Uter's Kingdom which Perceval's mother recalls. One of the questing knights tells Perceval in the Waste Forest that Arthur knighted him five years previously. The charcoal seller tells the boy that Arthur has just defeated Rion des Iles. At story's end Arthur is being summoned to witness Gauvain's combat with Guiromelant. Past, present, and future merge meaningfully.

Perceval learns from his mother part of his ancestry. Later meetings with other relatives reflect parts of his prehistory: Fisher King, Hermit Uncle, and girl cousin. His Hermitage experience is a projection into the future [Rupert T. Pickens, *The Welsh Knight: Paradoxicality in Chrétien's Conte del Graal,* 1977]. Perceval's wandering five years in vain search of the Grail Castle suggests eternity, as does his circuitous route (the Hermitage is a pendant to the Waste Forest).

Gauvain is challenged by three enemies who defer combat: Escavalon whose father Gauvain had killed, Greoreas the rapist whom Gauvain had forced to eat with dogs for a month, with this hands tied behind his back, and Guiromelant who lost a cousin to Gauvain and a father to Gauvain's father. Is not life a deferral of death?

Gauvain's final quest and ultimate fate (like that of the historical Alexander) in the *Conte du Graal* is clearly in the land of the dead, one aspect of the Celtic Otherworld. Perceval's adventure at the Grail Castle is not so explicitly depicted, but it is mysterious, enigmatic, unreal, and is sufficiently analogous with the Castle of Marvels to be considered as located in the Otherworld. The most cogent etymology of Perceval's name, which is closely bound to his Grail adventure, is Perce-val, he who pierced the vale. He entered and left the Otherworld without restoring the harmony of his family or of the world. Why? This liberating role is reserved in Christian thought only to Christ.

Instead of one hero succeeding and the other failing, as in the *Chevalier de la Charette,* now both fail although in different degrees. Gauvain has a measure of success, for he does dispel the enchantments of the Castle of Marvels, but he is now a prisoner there, and he never finds the Bleeding Lance. His mission may be termed failure in success; Perceval's, on the other hand, may be called success in failure, for his *échec* at the Grail Castle is transcendental. His career and Gauvain's remind us to accept with biblical Job certain tests whose reason is known only to God.

Gauvain is Perceval's double. The former's career forms both contrast and complement to the latter's. Perceval goes upward, as indicated in part by the three sets of lessons he gets, from zero to infinity, and Gauvain goes downward, from infinity to zero. Perceval the boy leaves his mother in the Waste Forest to find in Gornemant a father figure whom he quickly leaves at the height of his reputation. Gauvain goes from Arthur's court, the pinnacle of chivalry, and suffers through situations, each more ridiculous than the preceding one, to find at the end his mother, whom he wants to leave but cannot. Perceval goes from a matriarchal milieu to a patriarchal one; Gauvain does the reverse. To the three male members of Perceval's family who are dead and from whom no more is heard contrast three female dead relatives of Gauvain who inhabit the Castle of Marvels. The immature Perceval and the mature Gauvain are, in a different way, as contrastive as Philip and Alexander in the prologue; it might be argued that Gauvain's career begins where Perceval's leaves

off. This viewpoint on the two heroes also suggests the author's intention.

Each of the three preliminary abodes which Perceval and Gauvain respectively pass represents a stage in his upward or downward spiral. Perceval travels quickly and alone from Arthur to Gornemant to Blanchefleur; Gauvain goes slowly and always with a companion past Tintagel, Escavalon, Galvoie. Both the Grail Castle and the Castle of Marvels give the impression of being suspended in time, with infinite past and future. Hither will come both men and women. Through the Grail Castle will doubtlessly pass individuals like Perceval who will be close to the great mystery. In the Castle of Marvels will be permanent residents like Ygerne and later her grandson Gauvain. The disharmony in this romance could be removed only by a resurrection.

So, our hypothesis, kindled by patterns of Chrétien's art and strengthened by resemblances between his *Chevalier de la Charette* and his *Conte du Graal,* is supported by subsequent reflections of motifs found in the latter's prologue. Confirmation of our theory results from post-prologue expressions and motifs, implicit or explicit, when subjected to logic or analogy.

Despite the voluminous research already devoted to the *Conte du Graal,* scholars have not noted sufficiently, in print at least, certain structural details of importance. Perceval left his mother, met the Tent Lady, fought the Red Knight near Arthur's court, received instruction from Gornemant, succored Blanchefleur, and then arrived at the Grail Castle. His adventures after that high point are analogous to the prior sequence. He left his *cousine* (whom he made unhappy as he had done his mother), met the Tent Lady again (and "repaired" the wrong he had done her), fought near Arthur's court Keu (whose arrogance reminds us of the Red Knight), acquired knowledge and aided others from a five-year experience as Knight Errant (compare the Gornemant and Blanchefleur episodes), and then came to the Hermitage (which is analogous to both the Grail Castle and the Waste Forest). Such a route suggests his career is ended; further adventures of his would be superfluous; Chrétien never intended to return to Perceval's story (the most defensible interpretation of vv. 6514-6518: "De Percheval plus longuement / Ne parole li contes chi, / Ainz avrez molt ançois oï / De monseignor Gavain parler / Que rien m'oiez de lui conter"). He had gone from real life to a symbolic death after a brief visit to the Otherworld.

His post-Grail experiences are introduced by a proverb (as the romance had begun with another): v. 3630, "Les mors as mors, les vis as vis," which Perceval utters after guessing his name and learning from his cousin about his mother's death. Significantly the cousin does not challenge the name he divines, only its qualifier "li Galois." Since she knew the significance of the Grail Castle, she must have known the import of his name and realized that he had come close to the dividing line between life and death, and now knew the meaning of mortality, which young people find difficult to comprehend.

Perceval disappears from the story after agreeing to stay

at the Hermitage through the weekend, doing penance for his confessed sins. He took communion on Easter Sunday and presumably departed the next day. The only other explicit mention of confession and communion is when Greoreas demands them (vv. 6971-6979). Our author is so fond of tripling motifs that we may expect another reference to these Christian activities. Such an occurrence is implicit in the position of the Hermitage episode. It takes place in the middle of Gauvain's four main adventures. Perceval reached his Hermit Uncle only after wandering for five years and after we learn about Gauvain's experiences at Tintagel and at Escavalon, which last only a couple of days. Such arching of the two careers must surely mean that we are to apply the Hermitage adventure to both heroes. Each has now finished his earthly destiny without knowing it.

At the end of the romance, Arthur is summoned to the tourney to be held at Roche de Canguin. This will mark the third entry on the scene of the King. There is no doubt he will come to the land of the dead, for his time will have arrived to join his relatives already there. And there is no other place except the Otherworld for Perceval to be, since his career is obviously over.

In the *Conte du Graal,* Chrétien de Troyes devotes his talents to the problem of life and death. The teachings of man, woman, or church cannot deliver us from human bondage nor enable us to penetrate the final mystery. No other theory of the meaning of our story explains so satisfactorily as this one the careers of Perceval and Gauvain. (pp. 145-57)

> *Harry F. Williams, "The Hidden Meaning of Chrétien's 'Conte du Graal',"* in Diakonia: Studies in Honor of Robert T. Meyer, *edited by Thomas Halton and Joseph P. Williman, Catholic University of America Press, 1986, pp. 145-57.*

Evelyn Mullally (essay date 1988)

[*In the excerpt below, Mullally outlines the historical and literary circumstances which must, in her opinion, be considered in order to appraise Chrétien's method of narration in his romances.*]

The rediscovery of Chrétien de Troyes in the nineteenth century has given rise, over the last hundred years or so, to a vast quantity of critical work devoted to him. He is now firmly established as the most important vernacular writer of the twelfth-century renaissance. As a Frenchman, he was at a decided advantage, for the twelfth century in France was like no period before or since. With the single exception of law, in which the Italians took the lead, this was a renaissance dominated by the French, who influenced the whole course of European culture by their revival of art, architecture, philosophy, theology, music and literature.

Chrétien, a native of Troyes in Champagne, was patronized by two powerful nobles, the Countess of Champagne and the Count of Flanders; he was thus well placed to compose the courtly literature that characterized his time.

His five romances are important in the history of European literature: *Erec et Enide* is the earliest known Arthurian romance; *Cligès* provides the earliest, most sustained and most hostile commentary on the legend of Tristan and Iseut; the *Chevalier de la Charrette* is the earliest known version of the story of Lancelot and Guinevere; the *Chevalier au Lion* is Chrétien's most original work, widely exploited by later romancers, and his *Conte del Graal* is the earliest known romance about the Grail.

As well as being the most original of twelfth-century romancers, Chrétien is also the most accessible. *Erec et Enide,* for example, is so close to modern literary preoccupations that it has been claimed as the first European novel [Pierre Gallais, "De la naissance du roman: à propos d'un article récent." *Cahiers de civilisation médiévale* 7 (1964)]. Nevertheless, the very attractiveness of Chrétien's work is its most treacherous aspect when we come to examine his romances critically. We know nothing of his life, nothing of the circumstances in which he wrote, apart from the few meagre scraps of information we can glean from the texts themselves. We cannot hope to read his romances with exactly the same literary sensibilities as his first audiences heard them eight hundred years ago, but we can take a few reasonable precautions against anachronism in our response.

First of all, it is essential to replace Chrétien in his context as a writer. Great innovator though he was, he did not create the matter of his fictions *ex nihilo.* Nor was he writing alone in a literary void. True, when we turn from the earlier narratives of the twelfth century to Chrétien's romances, his originality makes a powerful impact. Here, everyone must feel, is a truly creative artist, a master of his material who handles his subjects with complete confidence. Yet much of the material he worked on already existed in oral or written form.

Chrétien's debt to orally-transmitted literature cannot be assessed with any precision. At an unknown number of removes, he may well have drawn on the literatures of countries as far apart as Ireland and Iran. Unfortunately, the exploration of these possible links is hampered both by the obscurity of the surviving texts and by problems of transmission, and the results of over a century of investigations, though they have shed fascinating light on comparative mythology and folklore, tend to lead us away from Chrétien's texts rather than elucidating his literary techniques.

We are on surer ground with the surviving texts of Chrétien's own country and century, and with the classical and post-classical texts with which every educated person in the twelfth century was familiar. Chrétien is very much a man of his time in this respect: in his prologue to *Cligès,* he shows himself to be conscious of France's pre-eminence in chivalry and culture and proud to place himself in a tradition that he, like his contemporaries, traced back to Greece and Rome. In the same prologue he alludes to his debt to Ovid, for he mentions his translations of the *Ars Amatoria* and of some of the *Metamorphoses.*

Chrétien is also aware of the native French tradition of the *chanson de geste* which had come to maturity in the earlier part of his century. In *Erec* he alludes to a character in the William of Orange cycle. In *Cligès* and *Yvain* he alludes to the legend of Roland. His own narratives, however, are far removed from the epic tradition of the chanson de geste. The transition from the epic, which first flourished in the early part of the twelfth century, to the romance which dominated the later part, is an intriguing and complex literary phenomenon. It may be characterized as a move in predominant interest from the heroic to the romantic, that is, from celebrating the exploits of a leader and his men to narrating the adventures of an individual knight, from depicting a male-dominated environment to showing a newer one in which women have an important role, and a change from the native and historic or would-be historic to the remote and exotic. On a formal level, it is a move away from the ponderous accumulations of assonating 'laisses' to the light and fluent rhythms of the octosyllabic rhyming couplet.

Half-way between epic and romance are the narrative poems written in the middle years of the century, the so-called romances of antiquity: the *Roman de Thèbes* and the *Roman d'Eneas,* both anonymous, and the *Roman de Troie* by Benoît de Sainte-Maure. All these poems are based on epics, but on the epics of remote countries in the distant past which could be treated with romantic exoticism. All are largely concerned with the epic theme of heroic warfare, but they are also all written in the octosyllabic rhyming couplets that will become characteristic of romance; they all give at least an episodic importance to their female characters, and they all betray their debt to Ovid in their analyses of women's feelings. A couple of anonymous short tales from the *Metamorphoses* also survive: *Narcisse* and *Piramus et Tisbé* both concentrate on the analysis of tragic love. The short romance of *Floire et Blancheflor* is both more exotic and more optimistic. Chrétien had some acquaintance with all of these works and was undoubtedly keenly interested in the productions of his contemporaries and rivals, Gautier d'Arras and Thomas.

He was also aware of the new style of love-lyric being written by the troubadours of southern France. Two lyrics survive which are generally believed to be his, and in one he reproduces the sentiments of the greatest of the Occitan love poets, Bernard de Ventadour. Chrétien is a narrative rather than a lyric writer, however, and his most characteristic use of lyric themes will be to transpose them on to the plane of romance, as he does in *Lancelot.*

Chrétien assuredly had some knowledge of the great source-book of Arthurian legend, Geoffrey of Monmouth's *Historia Regum Britanniae,* though it may have been through the medium of Wace's translation, the *Roman de Brut.* It is also possible that he knew a later work by Wace, the *Roman de Rou.* The Arthur of Geoffrey and Wace is still a heroic figure: his vast conquests are reminiscent of Charlemagne's. When we meet him again in Chrétien's first romance, his character and function have both been radically transformed.

Another legend Chrétien was very familiar with and made conscious efforts to transform was the story of Tristan and Iseut. He alludes to it explicitly in *Erec* and tells us in the *Cligès* prologue that he himself had written something

(now lost) about King Mark and Iseut la Blonde. It is the most pervasive, one could say the most obsessive, of Chrétien's literary influences and, perhaps even more than Ovid, helps to shape his concept of love. Tristan is undoubtedly a heroic figure but it is in his story that love becomes the dominant theme, perhaps for the first time in twelfth-century narrative literature. It is here that the critical encounter of the heroic and romantic occurs. Indeed, as Joseph Bédier put it [in his *Le Roman de Tristan par Thomas*]: "Entre la *Chanson de Roland* et le roman d'*Erec,* si *Tristan* n'existait pas, il faudrait l'inventer."

It is in *Erec,* his earliest work, that Chrétien shows, naturally enough, the clearest traces of a good twelfth-century education: he mentions Macrobius, he shows some acquaintance with Boethius and perhaps also with Chalcidius, and displays his competence in the art of rhetoric. It has been suggested that he also came under the influence of his contemporaries who wrote in Latin: Bernard Silvester, John of Salisbury, Alain de Lille. His fellow romancer Thomas alludes to the work of Petrus Alfonsi and it is possible that Chrétien knew it too. He is certainly familiar with a number of literary attitudes expressed by Giraldus Cambrensis and Walter Map and it is even possible that he had some echo of the letters of Abelard and Heloise.

The literature that he might have been aware of is very considerable indeed. We cannot, of course, always be sure that he in fact knew all that he could have known. Marie de France, for instance, who must have been roughly contemporary with him and who shows the same acquaintance with Ovid, Boethius and Wace, shows no awareness of Chrétien, nor he of her. Nevertheless, even when no source relationship can be established, it is still instructive to compare the way Chrétien solves his narrative problems with the way his contemporaries solved theirs.

Our first task, of course, is to determine what his problems were. It is in this area, more than anywhere else, that the traps of anachronistic sensibility lie in wait for us. For a start, to be original was considered shameful rather than praiseworthy. Chrétien can boast of making his *Erec et Enide* into a masterpiece while making it plain that an Erec story is already familiar to his audience. Marie de Champagne, if no-one else, knew what was going to happen in *Lancelot,* the romance she had personally commissioned; as for *Cligès* and *Perceval,* Chrétien claims that he got the material for them out of existing books and, even though he tells us nothing further about his authorities, the last thing he wants is for us to think that he invented the plots.

It is also unlikely that one of Chrétien's concerns as a narrator was the modern preoccupation with suspense. If the plot is not new, what true suspense can there be? We find, for example, that Benoît de Sainte-Maure, as if to pre-empt all suspenseful interest in his immense *Roman de Troie,* prefaces it with nearly seven hundred lines of summary so that no part of his narrative can take us by surprise.

More radically still, we have to face the possibility that Chrétien's romances contain nothing of what we mean when we talk about psychology. There is no trace in his works of any kind of Romantic perception of the individual valued simply as an individual rather than for his intrinsic worth. Those critics who are most concerned with the psychological dimension of fiction tend to favour *Erec* and *Yvain,* the romances in which there is the highest level of what is now called "human interest."

Perhaps the most delicate problem is the one of tone. The prevailing tone of our own culture is ironic. But can we be sure that an author as remote as Chrétien is in harmony with our ideas of the absurd, or that when he chooses to distance himself from his narrative, he is doing it for the same reasons as a writer might in the twentieth century?

The rational solution would be to read Chrétien's works in the light of the expectations proper to their genre, the romance. The problem here is a historical one: Western European romance cannot be traced back any farther than Chrétien himself. The authors of the romances of antiquity laid the foundations, but the first fully-fledged romance, the first full-length narrative to cut all ties with the classical or Carolingian past, is *Erec et Enide.* To define rules for Chrétien on the basis of what he appears to have invented is simply to beg the question.

Reading Chrétien's texts, therefore, requires a negative approach in the first instance. We need to read him in a passive state of receptivity, with minds emptied as far as possible of any narrative expectation. The most important romance in this respect is *Erec,* for it is in his first romance that Chrétien lets us know, both explicitly and implicitly, what he considers to be the norms of his narrative. If, then, in this ideal state of suspended expectation, we listen to the way Chrétien goes about telling a story, it becomes apparent that the method of narration he chooses is linked with the particular bias he is giving his theme, and that the preoccupation he betrays in each narrative causes him to adapt his material in a particular way or alter his presentation of character or action.

Chrétien as a narrator is primarily concerned with bringing together the formal and thematic elements at his disposal in such a way as to enhance the overall sense of his narrative. . . . [His] methods vary considerably from one romance to the next, but within each tale the narrative technique is a unifying principle, or at least a principle of continuity. The widespread concern with deciding how many sections Chrétien's narratives should be divided up into has begun to seem excessive. For a writer so explicitly concerned with *conjointure,* it is of more interest to see how he links his episodes together.

Leaving aside Chrétien's last work, the unfinished *Conte del Graal,* which raises so many special problems that it would require a study all to itself, Chrétien's first four romances offer a substantial field of investigation into the development of his techniques as a narrator. Certain sections of the romances are of obvious importance in any analysis of technique. Chrétien's prologues, which have deservedly attracted a good deal of attention, are a continual source of enlightenment. Likewise the opening scene of each romance merits special attention, for it is here that the author establishes the norms of his narrative though they

sometimes contradict what the prologue has led us to expect. The way in which the central characters are introduced is a matter of considerable importance, for it is on them that our narrative expectations will be focussed. Then the author's interventions and comments are of undeniable importance, though they are often absent when we might welcome them and disconcerting when they are included. It goes without saying that the explicit preoccupations of the author must be given particular analysis in determining how he adapted his material for his purpose, though an author's stated intentions are far from exhausting the possible significance of his work. (pp. 1-7)

It is illuminating to compare Chrétien's narrative technique with that of writers we know preceded him. When he repeatedly adapts the same situation borrowed from one of the tales in the *Metamorphoses,* when he exploits from a new angle one of the numerous episodes of the Tristan story available to him, when he gives a new slant to well-worn anti-feminist material, then indeed we can be sure of seeing him assert his personality as a writer. Even though the relative chronology is uncertain, when we find another writer of the period solving a narrative problem one way and Chrétien solving it differently, we still learn something about his art, for it is where he is most unlike others that he is most himself. He may simply be preferring one style to another, or he may have some aesthetic or moral objection to the available material. His preference may be a purely formal one and, having set out with a specific narrative purpose in mind, he subordinates all incidental material to his overall plan. We cannot assume that what is characteristic of Chrétien in one romance will be characteristic of him throughout his career. Even a superficial reading of his romances reveals the range of their matter, so it is not unreasonable to expect change and variety in their manner. All these considerations . . . help us to do justice to Chrétien as a craftsman. (pp. 7-8)

> *Evelyn Mullally, in an introduction to "The Artist at Work: Narrative Technique in Chrétien de Troyes," in* Transactions of the American Philosophical Society, *Vol. 78, No. 4, 1988, pp. 1-8.*

William W. Kibler   (essay date 1991)

[*Kibler is an American scholar of French language and literature whose works include* An Introduction to Old French *(1984). In the excerpt below, he presents a general overview of the contemporary opinion concerning Chrétien's life, work, sources, and artistic achievement.*]

Writing in the second half of the twelfth century, Chrétien de Troyes was the inventor of Arthurian literature as we know it. Drawing from material circulated by itinerant Breton minstrels and legitimized by Geoffrey of Monmouth's pseudo-historical *Historia Regum Britanniæ* (History of the Kings of Britain, *c.* 1136-37), Chrétien fashioned a new form known today as courtly romance. To Geoffrey's bellicose tales of Arthur's conquests, Chrétien added multiple love adventures and a courtly veneer of polished manners. He was the first to speak of Queen Guinevere's affair with Lancelot of the Lake, the first to mention Camelot, and the first to write of the adventures of the Grail—with Perceval, the mysterious procession, and the Fisher King. He may even have been the first to sing of the tragic love of Tristan and Isolde. All of these themes have become staples in the romance of King Arthur, and no treatment of the legend seems complete without some allusion to them.

Yet we know virtually nothing about this incomparable genius, the author of the five earliest Arthurian romances: *Erec and Enide, Cligés, The Knight of the Cart* (*Lancelot*), *The Knight with the Lion* (*Yvain*), and *The Story of the Grail* (*Perceval*). The few references to a 'Crestien' or 'Christianus' unearthed in archival documents cannot with any certainty be related to our author, so we can know him only through his own writings. And even here we are at some remove from Chrétien himself, for the manuscripts that preserve his works all date from at least a generation after the time he composed them. (p. 1)

The [large] number of manuscripts of Chrétien's works that have come down to us from the medieval period is eloquent testimony to his popularity and importance, although from numerous fragments we can suspect that even more manuscripts were destroyed than have been saved. His romances are most often found in manuscript collections, like [the Bibliothèque Nationale] 794 and 1450, that contain pseudo-historical accounts of ancient history, to which the Arthurian material was purportedly linked, or in manuscripts containing a wide variety of other courtly romances. His unfinished *The Story of the Grail* is found most frequently with its verse continuations. . . .

From manuscript evidence we know that both *The Story of the Grail* and *The Knight of the Cart* were left unfinished by Chrétien. Many believe that he abandoned *The Knight of the Cart* because he was dissatisfied with the subject matter, which may have been imposed on him by his patroness, Marie de Champagne; and most critics accept that *The Story of the Grail* was interrupted by Chrétien's death, or by that of his patron, Philip of Alsace, Count of Flanders. The other romances—*Erec and Enide, Cligés,* and *The Knight with the Lion* were completed by Chrétien. Three additional narrative poems have been ascribed to him, with varying degrees of success. Despite the doubts of its most recent editor (A. J. Holden 1988), many believe that the hagiographical romance *William of England,* whose author names himself Crestïens in its first line, is by our poet; on the other hand, attempted attributions to Chrétien of *Le Chevalier à l'épée* (The Knight with the Sword) and *La Mule sans frein* (The Unbridled Mule), two romances found with *The Story of the Grail* in MS Berne 354, have not met with widespread acceptance. In addition to these narrative works, Chrétien has left us two lyric poems in the courtly manner, which make him the first identifiable practitioner in northern France of the courtly lyric style begun by the troubadours in the South in the early years of the twelfth century.

In the prologue to *Cligés,* his second romance, Chrétien includes a list of works he had previously composed:

Cil qui fist d'Erec et d'Enide,
Et les comandemanz d'Ovide

Et l'art d'amors en romanz mist,
Et le mors de l'espaule fist,
Del roi Marc et d'Iseut la blonde,
Et de la hupe et de l'aronde
Et del rossignol la muance,
Un novel conte recomance
D'un vaslet qui an Grece fu
Del lignage le roi Artu.

[1-10]

[He who wrote *Erec and Enide,* who translated Ovid's *Commandments* and the *Art of Love* into French, who wrote [**"The Shoulder Bite"**], and about King Mark and Isolde the Blonde, and of the metamorphosis of the hoopoe, swallow, and nightingale, begins now a new tale of a youth who, in Greece, was of King Arthur's line.]

Since this prologue mentions only *Erec* among his major romances, it is assumed that *The Knight of the Cart, The Knight with the Lion* and *The Story of the Grail* all postdate *Cligés.* From this listing it seems established that early in his career Chrétien perfected his technique by practising the then popular literary mode of translations and adaptations of tales from Latin into the vernacular. The *'comandemanz d'Ovide'* is usually identified with Ovid's *Remedia amoris* (Remedies for Love); the *'art d'amors'* is Ovid's *Ars amatoria* (Art of Love), and the *'mors de l'espaule'* is the Pelops story in Ovid's *Metamorphoses,* Book 6. These works by Chrétien have all been lost. However, the *'muance de la hupe et de l'aronde et del rossignol'* (the Philomela story in *Metamorphoses* 6) is preserved in the late thirteenth-century *Ovide moralisé,* a lengthy allegorical treatment of Ovid's *Metamorphoses,* in a version that is most probably by our author.

Chrétien also informs us in this passage that he composed a poem *'Del roi Marc et d'Iseut la blonde'.* As far as we know, this was the first treatment of that famous Breton legend in French. Chrétien does not tell us whether he had written a full account of the tragic loves of Tristan and Isolde, and scholars today generally agree that he treated only an episode of that legend since Mark's name, and not Tristan's, is linked with Isolde's. But we are none the less permitted to believe that he is in some measure responsible for the subsequent success of that story, as he was to be in large measure for that of King Arthur. Indeed, in his earliest romances Chrétien seems obsessed with the Tristan legend, which he mentions several times in *Erec and Enide* and against which his *Cligés* (often referred to as an 'anti-Tristan') is seen to react.

In the prologues to his other romances (only *The Knight with the Lion* has no prologue) Chrétien often speaks in the first person about his poetry and purposes. He gives us the fullest version of his name, Crestïens de Troies, in the prologue to *Erec,* and this designation is also used by Huon de Mery in the *Tornoiement Antecrist,* by Gerbert de Montreuil in his *Continuation* of *The Story of the Grail* and by the anonymous authors of *Hunbaut, Le Chevalier à l'épée,* and the *Didot-Perceval.* In the prologues to *Cligés* (1.45), *The Knight of the Cart* (l. 25), and *The Story of the Grail* (l. 62), and in the closing lines of *The Knight with the Lion* (l. 6821), he calls himself simply Crestïens. The fuller version of his name given in *Erec* suggests that he was born or at least spent his formative years in Troyes, which is located some one hundred miles along the Seine to the south-east of Paris and was one of the leading cities in the region of Champagne. The language in which he composed his works, which is tinted with dialectal traits from the Champagne area, lends further credence to this supposition.

At Troyes, Chrétien most assuredly was associated with the court of Marie de Champagne, one of the daughters of Eleanor of Aquitaine by her first marriage, to King Louis VII of France. Marie's marriage in 1159 to Henri the Liberal, Count of Champagne, furnishes us with one of the very few dates that can be determined with any degree of certainty in Chrétien's biography. In the opening lines of *The Knight of the Cart,* Chrétien informs us that he is undertaking the composition of his romance at the behest of 'my lady of Champagne', and critics today agree unanimously that this can only be the great literary patroness Marie. Since she only became 'my lady of Champagne' with her marriage, Chrétien could not have begun a romance for her before 1159.

Another relatively certain date in Chrétien's biography is furnished by the dedication of *The Story of the Grail* to Philip of Flanders. It appears that, sometime after the death of Henri the Liberal in 1181, Chrétien found a new patron in Philip of Alsace, a cousin to Marie de Champagne, who became Count of Flanders in 1168 and to whom Chrétien dedicated his never-to-be-completed grail romance. This work surely was begun before Philip's death in 1191 at Acre in the Holy Land, and most likely prior to his departure for the Third Crusade in September of 1190. Chrétien may have abandoned the poem after learning of Philip's death, or his own death may well have occurred around this time.

Apart from the dates 1159 and 1191, nothing else concerning Chrétien's biography can be fixed with certainty. Allusions in *Erec* to Macrobius and the Liberal Arts, to Alexander, Solomon, Helen of Troy and others, coupled with similar allusions in other romances, suggest that he received the standard preparation of a *clerc* in the flourishing church schools in Troyes, and therefore must have entered minor orders. The style of his love monologues, particularly in *Cligés,* shows familiarity with the dialectal method of the schools, in which opposites are juxtaposed and analysed, as well as with the rhetorical traditions of Classical and medieval Latin literature. It is possible, however, that he derived his style and knowledge of Classical themes uniquely from works available to him in the vernacular, without having undergone any special training in Latin, since all of the Classical stories to which he alludes had been turned into Old French by 1165. The elaborate descriptions of clothing and ceremonies in several of his romances can likewise be traced to contemporary works composed in French, particularly to Wace's *Roman de Brut* and the anonymous *Eneas* and *Floire et Blancheflor.*

Circumstantial evidence also strongly suggests that Chrétien spent some of his early career in England and may well have composed his first romance there. References to English cities and topography, especially in *Cligés* but indeed in all of his works, show that the Britain of King Arthur was the England of King Henry II Plantagenet. Moreover, there is a close link between Troyes and England in the person of Henry of Blois, abbot of Glastonbury (1126-71) and bishop of Winchester (1129-71). This prelate was the uncle of Henri the Liberal of Champagne, at whose court we have seen Chrétien to have been engaged. Henry of Blois had important contacts with Geoffrey of Monmouth and William of Malmesbury, two medieval Latin writers who, more than any others, popularized the legends of King Arthur that Chrétien was to introduce to the aristocratic public.

An even closer tie to Henry II's England has been proposed in the case of *Erec and Enide,* in which the coronation of Erec at Nantes on Christmas Day may be a reflection of contemporary politics. In 1169 Henry held a Christmas court at Nantes in order to force the engagement of his third son, Geoffrey, to Constance, the daughter of Conan IV of Brittany. This court had significant political ramifications for it assured through marital politics the submission of the major Breton barons, a submission Henry had not been able to attain by successive military campaigns in 1167, 1168 and 1169. The guest list at the coronation of Erec includes barons from all corners of Henry II's domains but, significantly, none from those of his rival Louis VII of France. Two other details from this coronation scene lend credence to such an identification: the thrones on which Arthur and Erec are seated are described as having leopards sculpted upon their arms, and the donor of these thrones is identified as Bruianz des Illes. Leopards were the heraldic animals on Henry's royal arms, and Bruianz des Illes has been positively identified as Henry's best friend, Brian of Wallingford, named in contemporary documents as Brian Fitz Count, Brian *de Insula,* or Brian de l'Isle. It thus seems plausible that *Erec* was composed at the behest of Henry II to help legitimize Geoffrey's claim to the throne of Brittany by underscoring the 'historical' link between Geoffrey and Arthur. This would place its composition shortly after 1169 while memories of the Nantes court were still fresh. Such a dating corresponds well with what we know about the composition of Chrétien's other romances, which most critics now place in the 1170s and 1180s.

Since Chrétien gave the fuller version of his name in the prologue to *Erec and Enide* we must assume he was away from the region of Troyes at the time of its composition, and it now seems reasonable to speculate that he was in England at the court of Henry II, where he would have had ample opportunity to learn of the new 'Matter of Britain' that was then attaining popularity there. *Erec,* a brilliant psychological study, appears to have been the earliest romance composed in the vernacular tongue to incorporate Arthurian themes. This poem posed a question familiar to courtly circles: how can a knight, once married, sustain the valour and glory that first won him a bride? That is, can a knight serve both his honour (*armes*) and his love (*amors*)? Erec, caught up in marital bliss, neglects the pursuit of his glory until reminded of his duties by Enide, who has overheard some knights gossiping maliciously. Accompanied by her, he sets out on a series of adventures in the course of which both he and his bride are tested. The mixture of psychological insight and extraordinary adventures was to become a trademark of Chrétien's style and of the Arthurian romances written in imitation of his work. And Chrétien would reconsider the question of *armes* and *amors* from a different perspective in *The Knight with the Lion.*

Chrétien's second major work, *Cligés,* is in part set at Arthur's court, but is principally an adventure romance based on Græco-Byzantine material, which was exceedingly popular in the second half of the twelfth century. This romance, which exalts the pure love of Fenice for Cligés, has been seen by many as a foil to the adulterous passion of Isolde for Tristan. Among the numerous textual parallels adduced to support this contention, especially in the second part of the poem, are Fenice's relationships with her husband (Alis) and sweetheart (Cligés) and her expressed views on love and marriage, the nurse Thessala's similarity to Brangien, John's hideaway and the Hall of Images, the love potion, and lover's lament. However, the poem is even more interesting to us for its use of irony, its balanced structure and its psychological penetration into the hearts of the two lovers. Here, as elsewhere, Chrétien shows the influence of Ovid, the most popular Classical writer throughout the twelfth century. And again Chrétien shows his ability to exploit popular material in a highly original manner.

It is now generally agreed that *Cligés* dates from about 1176. Although the subject matter is wholly fictional, scholars have found intriguing analogies in several of its situations to contemporary politics between 1170 and 1175. The intrigues that brought the Byzantine Emperor Manuel Comnenus to power over his elder brother, Isaac—who, like Alexander, received only the title—are remarkably akin to the situation by which Alis comes to the throne of Constantinople rather than his older brother Alexander. In the poem, the projected marriage of Alis to the daughter of the German emperor is, *mutatis mutandis,* an echo of the projected marriage between Frederick Barbarossa's son and Manuel's only daughter, Maria. As in the poem, Frederick received the Byzantine ambassadors at Cologne. And it was at Regensburg, also evoked in the poem, that Marie de Champagne's parents met the Byzantine ambassadors during the Second Crusade. Chrétien's audience would not have failed to identify the fierce Duke of Saxony to whom Fenice was originally promised with Henry the Lion, Duke of Saxony since 1142 and a cousin of Frederick Barbarossa, with whom he was generally at odds. In 1168 Henry the Lion was married to Mathilda of England, a half-sister of Marie de Champagne, but this did not keep Marie's husband, Henri the Liberal, from supporting Frederick in his struggles against his cousin. Although Chrétien freely modified these events to his own artistic ends, it seems clear that the court of Marie and Henri de Champagne would have been aware of these matters and intrigued and flattered by allusions to them.

The relationship between Chrétien's third and fourth romances, which were most likely composed in the late 1170s, is complex. There are several direct references in *The Knight with the Lion* to action that occurs in *The Knight of the Cart,* particularly to Meleagant's abduction of Guinevere and the subsequent quest by Lancelot. Yet at the same time, the characterization of Sir Kay in the early section of *The Knight of the Cart* seems explicable only in terms of his abusive behaviour in *The Knight with the Lion.* Further, the blissful conjugal scene between Arthur and Guinevere at the beginning of *The Knight with the Lion* seems incomprehensible after events in *The Knight of the Cart.* These contradictory factors have led recent scholars to propose that the two romances were being composed simultaneously, beginning with *The Knight with the Lion* then breaking off to *The Knight of the Cart,* which itself was perhaps completed in three parts. According to this theory, as it has been progressively refined and widely accepted, Chrétien wrote the first part of *The Knight of the Cart* then turned it over to Godefroy de Lagny to complete. Dissatisfied with the contrast between the two sections, Chrétien himself would then have composed the tournament section to harmonize the two parts.

The Knight of the Cart tells of the adulterous relationship of Lancelot with Arthur's queen, Guinevere. Its central theme, the acting out in romance form of a story of *fin'amors,* has generally been attributed to a suggestion by its dedicatee, Marie de Champagne, for it is in stark contrast to Chrétien's other romances, which extol the virtues of marital fidelity. For this reason, scholars today often find in *The Knight of the Cart* extensive irony and humour, which serve to undercut the courtly love material and bring its theme in line with those of Chrétien's other romances. Its composition, and *The Knight with the Lion* with it, marks an important stage in the development of Chrétien's thought, for he turns away in these works from the couple predestined to rule to the individual who must discover his own place in society.

Many critics consider *The Knight with the Lion* to be Chrétien's most perfectly conceived and constructed romance. In it he reconsiders the question of the conflict between love and valour posed in *Erec,* but from the opposite point of view: Yvain neglects his bride (*amors*) in the pursuit of glory (*armes*). Unlike Erec, who sets off for adventure accompanied by his bride, Yvain sets out alone upon his series of marvellous adventures in order to expiate his fault and rediscover himself. He eventually meets up with a lion which, among other possible symbolic roles, is certainly emblematic of his new self.

Chrétien's final work, begun sometime in the 1180s and never completed, was and still is his most puzzling: *The Story of the Grail.* Controversy continues today over whether or not Chrétien intended this romance to be read allegorically. Even those who agree that his intent was indeed allegorical argue over the proper nature and significance of the allegory. His immediate continuers, Robert de Boron and the anonymous author of the *Perlesvaus,* clearly assumed that the allegory was a Christian one. Unfortunately, death apparently overtook Chrétien before he could complete his masterwork and clarify the mysteries of the Grail Castle.

In the prologues to most of his romances, Chrétien alludes to a source from which he took his story. In *Erec,* he says that his source was a 'tale of adventure' that professional *jongleurs* were wont to mangle and corrupt, but that he would relate in 'a beautifully ordered composition'. Though no direct source for this, or any other of his romances, has been identified, there exists a general parallel to *Erec* in the story of the Welsh *Mabinogion* called *Gereint Son of Erbin*. This tale contains the episodes of the stag hunt, the joust for the sparrow-hawk, Enide's tears, the quest with Enide's repeated warnings for Gereint (Erec), the lecherous count, the 'little king' Gwiffred Petit (Guivret le Petit), and even a small-scale Joy of the Court. This relatively late Welsh prose tale, dating probably from the thirteenth century, could not have influenced Chrétien, and marked differences in details, tone and artistry suggest that it was not directly influenced by Chrétien's work either. Together, however, they attest to an earlier common source, which most critics now assume to have been Celtic in origin and oral, rather than written.

In the prologue to *Cligés,* Chrétien states that his source was a written story in a book from the library of St Peter's church in Beauvais. Again, Chrétien's precise source is unknown, though he drew heavily on Ovid, Thomas's *Tristan,* and the Old French *Roman d'Eneas* for his depictions of the nature and effects of love in this romance. The motif of feigned death occurs in other medieval works, notably in the thirteenth-century Old French romance *Marques de Rome,* in which the hero is likewise named Cligés. Much of the first part of this romance is surely of Chrétien's own invention, whereas analogies with the Tristan story seem to structure the second half.

Chrétien claims in his prologue to *The Knight of the Cart* that he was given the source material by the Countess Marie. If that is true, then she probably conveyed to him a popular Celtic abduction story, or *aithed.* In these mythological tales a mysterious stranger typically claims a married woman, makes off with her through a ruse or by force, and carries her to his otherworldly home. Her husband pursues the abductor and, after triumphing over seemingly impossible odds, penetrates the mysterious kingdom and rescues his wife. Guinevere is the subject of such an abduction story in the Latin *Vita sancti Gildæ* (Life of St Gildas) by Caradoc of Llancarvan (*c.* 1150), which contains much Celtic mythology. She is carried off by Melwas or Maheloas, lord of the *æstiva regio* (land of summer), to the *Urbs Vitrea* (City of Glass, alleged to be Glastonbury in Somerset). From there she is rescued by King Arthur with the aid of the Abbot of Glastonbury. However, this story is far removed from that by Chrétien and has no role for Lancelot. It is intriguing to speculate—but impossible to prove—that the Countess suggested the love relationship between Guinevere and Lancelot.

For *The Knight with the Lion,* which does not have a prologue, Chrétien claims in his epilogue to have given a faithful rendering of the story just as he had 'heard it told'. Like Erec, *The Knight with the Lion* has an analogue in the Welsh *Mabinogion* in a story known as *Owein,* or *The Lady of the Fountain,* which reproduces the plot of Chrétien's romance very closely up to the episode in which Lunete is saved from the stake, then diverges radically to the end. Like *Gereint Son of Erbin,* this tale dates from the thirteenth century and could not have influenced Chrétien. Nor does it appear to have been influenced by *The*

Knight with the Lion, but attests rather to an earlier common source, probably oral, that Chrétien may have known from bilingual Breton storytellers he may have encountered in England, or later in France. In addition to the general parallel furnished by *The Lady of the Fountain,* there are many individual motifs that can be traced to Celtic influence. Foremost among these are the episodes of the spring and of the town of Dire Adventure, which are closely analogous to a Celtic otherworld myth in which a hero follows a previous adventurer into a mysterious fairy kingdom defended by a hideous giant; he leaves again for his own land, breaks his faith with the fairy and loses her, then goes mad. With the legend of the spring Chrétien has skilfully blended another fairy motif that is also most likely to be of Celtic origin: the fairy enchants a mortal who must remain at her side to preserve some fearful custom until he is replaced by another who in turn continues it. This motif is found in its purest form in *Erec*'s 'Joy of the Court'.

As was the case with *Cligés,* Chrétien cites a specific written source for his *Perceval:* 'the Story of the Grail, whose book was given him by the count' (Philip of Flanders). No one knows what this book contained, nor indeed whether it ever actually existed. At any event, it was not the *Peredur* story from the *Mabinogion* which, like the analogues for *Erec* and *The Knight with the Lion* cited earlier, was too late to [have] been known by Chrétien. Numerous theories have been proposed to explain the origins of this, Chrétien's most mystifying romance, but none has met with widespread acceptance. The stories of Perceval and of the Grail seem originally to have been independent, and were perhaps amalgamated by Chrétien for the first time. Many motifs can be traced back to Celtic and Classical sources, but here and in his other romances Chrétien adapts his source materials in accord with the artistic needs of his own composition and the accepted mores of his time. He combines mysterious and magical elements from his sources with keenly observed contemporary social behaviour to create an atmosphere of mystery and wonder that is none the less securely anchored in a recognizable twelfth-century 'present'.

To fully appreciate Chrétien's achievement, it is important to place his romances in the broader context of twelfth-century literary creativity and sensitivity. Although Latin was still the predominant language for literary production well into the twelfth century, by Chrétien's day it was slowly being supplanted in France by the vernacular language known today as Old French. This 'translation' of learning from Classical lands and languages to France and the vernacular is mentioned by Chrétien in the same *Cligés* prologue from which we quoted earlier:

> Par les livres que nos avons
> Les feiz des anciiens savons
> Et del siecle qui fu jadis.
> Ce nos ont nostre livre apris,
> Que Grece ot de chevalerie
> Le premier los et de clergie.
> Puis vint chevalerie a Rome
> Et de la clergie la some,
> Qui or est an France venue.
> Deus doint qu'ele i soit retenue . . .

[27-36]

[Through the books we have, we learn of the deeds of ancient peoples and of bygone days. Our books have taught us that chivalry and learning first flourished in Greece; then to Rome came chivalry, and the sum of knowledge, which now has come to France. May God grant that they be maintained here . . .]

This movement implies a significant desire to bring literature and learning to those with little or no knowledge of Latin. That many were engaged in this undertaking is clear from the testimony of Chrétien's contemporary, Marie de France, writing in the general prologue to her *Lais* that she 'began to think of working on some good story and translating a Latin text into French, but this would scarcely have been worthwhile, for others have undertaken a similar task' (*The Lais of Marie de France*). The earliest romances, the so-called romances of Antiquity—the *Roman d'Eneas, Roman de Thèbes,* and *Roman de Troie*—were adaptations respectively of Virgil's *Aeneid,* Statius's *Thebaid,* and the late Latin Troy narrative attributed to Darys and Dictys. Ovid's tales of *Narcissus* and *Piramus and Thisbe* were also done into Old French at this same time. This early period of French literature likewise witnessed the translation of religious treatises, sermons, and books of proverbial wisdom, as well as a number of saints' lives. The evidence of a thirst for every sort of knowledge is provided by the many scientific and didactic works that appeared in French for the first time in the twelfth century: lapidaries, herbals, bestiaries, lunaries, Mirrors for Princes, and encyclopaedic works of all kinds.

Chrétien's prologues, as well as numerous allusions in his poems, offer ample proof of his familiarity with this material. In the prologue to **The Story of the Grail** he compares the generosity of his patron to that of the great Alexander. This same romance contains a reference to the loves of Aeneas and Lavinia, an affair that is given more play in the Old French *Roman d'Eneas* than in Virgil's *Aeneid.* In *Cligés* Chrétien compares King Arthur's wealth to Alexander's and Caesar's, and notes the similarities between Alis's and Alexander's situation and that of Eteocles and Polynices in the *Roman de Thèbes.* Also in *Cligés,* he compares Thessala's knowledge of magic with that of the legendary Medea and alludes to Paris's abduction of Helen of Troy, which was played out in the *Roman de Troie.* In **The Knight of the Cart,** he mentions the tragic love tale of Piramus and Thisbe. *Erec,* his first romance, is however the richest in classical allusions, for there we find references to Alexander, Caesar, Dido, Aeneas, Lavinia, Helen and Solomon, as well as to the late Latin writer Macrobius.

In moving from doing translations to composing original works on non-Classical themes, Chrétien was merely emulating a popular twelfth-century tendency. Beginning early in the century, there was a great creative movement that saw the appearance of a number of forms and works that had no Latin antecedents. The first original Old French genre to flourish was the *chanson de geste,* which featured epic themes generally centred around the court and times of Charlemagne. In MS Bibl. Nat f. fr. 24403, Chrétien's *Erec* is curiously bracketed by two *chansons de*

Hunting scene, possibly Arthur in pursuit of the white stag. (Paris, B.N. f.fr. 24403, fol. 119r.)

geste: Garin de Montglane and *Ogier le Danois.* Chrétien's comparison of Yvain's skill in battle to that of the legendary Roland (ll. 3239-41) is good proof of his knowledge of the most famous of the *chansons de geste.* And Chrétien, as we have seen, practised the other great original genre of the twelfth century, the courtly lyric. While lyric poetry certainly existed in Latin, a wholly different inspiration informs the love-lyrics of the southern French troubadours. In their poetry love becomes an art and an all-subsuming passion. The lady becomes a person to be cherished, a source of poetic and personal inspiration, rather than simply a pawn in the game of heredity.

The love tradition of the southern French troubadours moved northward in the second third of the twelfth century as a result of political developments, especially the two marriages of Eleanor of Aquitaine, first to King Louis VII of France in 1137 and then in 1152 to the future Henry II of England. With her she brought a number of courtiers and poets who introduced the southern tradition of 'courtly love' into the more sober North. Her daughters, Marie de Champagne and Alis de Blois, were both important arbiters of taste and style like their more illustrious mother, and fostered literary activities of many kinds, in both Latin and the vernacular, in their central French courts.

The very notion of 'courtly love' (or *fin'amors*) as it was practised and celebrated in medieval literature remains even today a complex and vexed question. As it is depicted in troubadour poetry, the Tristan story and Chrétien's **The Knight of the Cart,** it is an adulterous passion between persons of high social rank, in which the lovers express their profoundest emotions in a highly charged and distinctly stylized language. Both lovers agonize over their condition, indulging in penetrating self-examination and reflections on the nature of love. Although the refinement of the language gives the love an ethereal quality it is sensual and non-Platonic in nature, and for his sufferings the lover hopes for and generally receives a frankly sexual recompense. This, at any rate, is love as it appears in *The Knight of the Cart.* But was such love actually practised in the courts of twelfth-century France? Here critics are loosely divided into two opposing camps: the *realists,* who believe that such an institution did exist in the Middle Ages and is faithfully reflected in the literature of the period; and the *idealists,* who believe that it is a post-Romantic critical construct and was, in the Middle Ages, at most a game to be taken lightly and ironically.

In *The Knight of the Cart,* Lancelot seems to substitute a religion of love for the traditional Christian ethic, even going so far as to genuflect upon leaving Guinevere's bedchamber. Yet nowhere is there any direct condemnation of his behaviour, either by the characters or the narrator. Realists see in Lancelot the epitome of the courtly lover. For them, Marie de Champagne was a leading proponent of the doctrine of *fin'amors,* which was practised extensively at her court. To illustrate and further this concept, she commissioned Andreas Capellanus to draw up the rules for love in his *De arte honeste amandi* and her favourite poet, Chrétien, to compose a romance whose central theme was to be that of the perfect courtly-love relationship. But Chrétien never completed his romance, an indication perhaps that he was not in sympathy with the theme proposed to him by the Countess.

Idealists agree that the subject matter of *The Knight of the Cart* did not appeal to Chrétien, but allege different reasons. Citing the fact that adultery was harshly condemned by the medieval Church, they argue that what we today call 'courtly love' would have been recognized as idolatrous and treasonable passion. Lancelot must be seen as a fool led on by his lust, rather than his reason, into ever more ridiculous and humiliating situations. The idea of Lancelot lost in thoughts of love and being unceremoniously unhorsed or duelling behind his back to keep Guinevere in view could only be seen as ludicrous.

Most realists today will concede a degree of ironic humour in the portrayal of Lancelot, but contend that the question of morality is a moot one: the love is amoral, rather than immoral. Sensitive to the attacks of the idealists, they now downplay the importance of Andreas Capellanus, whose concept of 'pure love' has led many commentators astray, and stress the distinctions between periods and works. The love portrayed by Dante or in Chaucer's *Book of the Duchess* is of another period and qualitatively different from that of the troubadours and trouvères. Indeed, love in the poems of the northern French trouvères is itself distinct from that of the troubadours. And love as it is portrayed in the other romances by Chrétien is different from that in *The Knight of the Cart.* In all his other romances he appears as an advocate for marriage and love within marriage, constructing *Erec, Cligés* and *The Knight with the Lion* around this theme, and showing in all the disadvantages of other types of relationships.

Not only do Chrétien's prologues give us invaluable information about the poet himself, they also tell us a great deal about how he viewed his role as artist. In the prologue to *Erec,* Chrétien tells us that he *tret d'un conte d'avanture/une molt bele conjointure* ('from a tale of adventure / he draws a beautifully ordered composition'). This *conjointure* has been variously translated 'arrangement', 'linking', 'coherent organization', 'internal unity', etc., but always implies that Chrétien has moulded and organized materials that were only inchoate before he applied his artistry to them. Already in his first romance, and repeatedly in his later work, Chrétien shows himself to be conscious of his role as a literary artist, a 'maker' or 'inventor' who fashions and gives artistic expression to materials that have come to him from earlier sources.

In speaking of *un conte d'avanture* in the singular and with the article, Chrétien implies that he conceived of his source as a single work, rather than as a collection of disparate themes or motifs. He goes on to inform us that other storytellers, the professional jongleurs who earn their living by performing such narrative poems before the public, were wont to *depecier et corronpre* ('mangle and corrupt') these tales. Chrétien, on the other hand, clearly implies that he has provided a coherent structure for his tale, a structure that most critics today agree is that of a triptych. Like the traditional triptych altarpiece, Chrétien's *Erec and Enide* has a broad central panel flanked by two balanced side-panels. The first panel, which Chrétien refers to as *li premiers vers* ('the first movement', l. 1808), comprises ll. 27–1808 and weaves together the episodes of the Hunt of the White Stag and the Joust for the Sparrowhawk. The final episode, known as the Joy of the Court, forms an analogous panel of approximately the same length as the first, ll. 5321-6912. The central panel of his triptych, ll. 1809-5320, is by far the largest and most important, covering the principal action of the poem.

Erec, like the other romances that followed with the exception of *Cligés,* was arranged around the motif of the quest. In each of his romances Chrétien varied the nature and organization of the central quest. In *Erec* it is essentially linear and graduated in structure, moving from simple to increasingly complex and meaningful encounters. But already in *Erec* Chrétien was experimenting with a technique for interrupting the linearity and varying the adventures, a technique he would employ with particular success in *The Knight with the Lion* and *The Story of the Grail,* and which would be used extensively in the prose romances: interlacing. In its simplest manifestations, as it functions twice in *The Knight with the Lion,* interlacing involves the weaving together of two distinct lines of action: each time Yvain begins an adventure, it is interrupted so that he can complete a second before returning to finish the first. In the first instance, Yvain is on his way to defend Lunete, who has been condemned to die for having persuaded her mistress to marry the unfaithful Yvain. He secures lodging at a town that is besieged by the giant Harpin of the Mountain and, though it nearly causes him to be too late to save Lunete, he remains and defeats the giant. In the second instance, Yvain agrees to defend the cause of the younger daughter of the lord of Blackthorn, who is about to be disinherited by her sister. But before the combat with her champion, Gawain, can be concluded, Yvain is called to enter the town of Dire Adventure and free three hundred maidens who are forced to embroider for minimal wages in intolerable conditions. The same pattern recurs in *The Story of the Grail,* where Chrétien cuts back and forth between the adventures of Gawain and those of Perceval. The adventures in *The Knight of the Cart,* on the other hand, are organized according to the principle of *contrapasso,* by which the nature of the punishment corresponds precisely to the nature of the sin: having hesitated to step into the cart, Lancelot must henceforth show no hesitations in his service of ladies and the queen.

In the midst of the interlace in *The Knight with the Lion,* Chrétien introduces a complex pattern of intertextual references designed to link that poem to *The Knight of the Cart,* which he was composing apparently simultaneously. In the town besieged by Harpin of the Mountain, Yvain learns that the lord's wife is Sir Gawain's sister, but that Gawain is unable to succour them because he is away seeking Queen Guinevere, who has been carried off by 'a knight from a foreign land' (Meleagant) after King Arthur had foolishly entrusted her to Sir Kay. This is a direct allusion to the central action of *The Knight of the Cart,* and interweaves the plots of the two romances. Gawain cannot see to his own family's welfare in *The Knight with the Lion* because he is concurrently engaged in a quest in *The Knight of the Cart.* During the second interlace pattern of *The Knight with the Lion,* the elder sister arrives at Arthur's court just after Gawain has returned with the queen and the other captives from the land of Gorre, and it is specifically noted that Lancelot 'remained locked in the tower'. This second direct reference to the intrigue of *The Knight of the Cart* refers, perhaps deliberately, to the point at which Chrétien abandoned this romance, leaving its completion to Godefroy de Lagny. This intertextual technique did not have the success of the interlace, but attests like it to an acute artistic awareness on the part of Chrétien to the structuring of his romances. This technique of intertextual reference could also be seen as an attempt by Chrétien to lend depth or consistency to this work, setting each romance in a broader, more involved world (a technique used later in the *Lancelot-Graal,* where events not specifically recounted in that work are alluded to as background material). In Chrétien's case it might even be seen as self-promotion, encouraging the reader or listener of one romance to seek out the other.

Chrétien's artistry was not limited to overall structure, but extends as well to the details of composition. In all of his romances Chrétien shows himself to be a master of dialogue, which he uses for dramatic effect. With the exception of *Cligés,* where the lengthy monologues are frequently laboured and rhetorical, his often rapid-fire conversations give the impression of a real discussion overheard, rather than of learned discourse. The pertness and wit of Lunete, as she convinces her lady first to accept the slayer of her husband as her second mate and then to take him back after he has offended her, are often cited and justly admired. Erec and Enide's exchanges as they ride along on adventure show both the tenderness and irritation underlying their relationship. In *The Knight of the Cart,* the conversations between Meleagant and his father quite accurately set off their opposing characters through their choices of vocabulary and imagery, and the words used by

Lancelot with the queen vividly translate his abject humility and total devotion. In *The Story of the Grail,* Perceval's youthful *naïveté* comes across in his questions to the knights and his conversation with the maiden in the tent. In that same romance the catty exchanges between Tiebaut of Tintagel's two daughters could not be more true to life. Chrétien gives his dialogues a familiar ring through his choice of appropriate vocabulary and a generous sprinkling of proverbial expressions. In Erec's defiance of Maboagrain, he incorporates five proverbial expressions in only ten lines of dialogue (ll. 5873-82), using traditional wisdom to justify and support his current course of action. In the opening scene of *The Knight with the Lion,* Calogrenant shrugs off Kay's insults by citing a series of proverbs, and shortly thereafter Kay himself uses proverbial wisdom to insult Yvain. Proverbs and proverbial expressions occur in the other romances as well, where they are particularly prevalent in the monologues and dialogues.

Chrétien's use of humour and irony has been frequently noted, as has his ability to incorporate keenly observed realistic details into the most fantastic adventures. Like the dialogues, the descriptions of persons and objects are not rhetorical or lengthy, but are precise, lively and colourful. His portraits of feminine beauty, though they follow the typical patterns of description, nevertheless provide variety in their details. Chrétien even had the rare audacity to make one of his heroines (Lunete in *The Knight with the Lion*), a brunette rather than a blonde! Even more striking in their variety, however, are the portraits of ugliness: the physical ugliness of the wretched maiden with her torn dress and the grotesque damsel on her tawny mule in *The Story of the Grail,* the churlish herdsman in *The Knight with the Lion,* or the psychological ugliness of Meleagant.

Chrétien also excels in his descriptions of nature—of the plains, valleys, hills, rivers and forests of twelfth-century France and England. Natural occurrences such as the storm in Brocéliande forest early in *The Knight with the Lion,* followed by the sunshine and singing of birds, or the frightening dark night of rain the maiden later rides through in search of Yvain, are vividly evoked in octosyllabic verses of pure lyric quality. Castles, such as that of Perceval's tutor Gornemant of Gohort, perched on their rocky promontories above raging rivers, with turrets, keeps and drawbridges, are all in the latest style of cutstone construction. Gawain's Hall of Marvels in *The Story of the Grail* has ebony and ivory doors with carved panels, while the one into which Yvain pursues the fleeing Esclados the Red is outfitted with a mechanized portcullis. In *Erec* in particular Chrétien treats with consummate skill the activities, intrigues, passions, and colour of contemporary court life. This romance is filled with lavish depictions of garments, saddles and trappings, and ceremonies that give proof of his keen attention to detail and his pleasure in description. Justly famous is the elaborate description of Erec's coronation robe (ll. 6698-763), on which four fairies had skilfully embroidered portrayals of the four disciplines of the quadrivium: Geometry, Arithmetic, Music and Astronomy. His depiction of the great hall and Grail procession in *The Story of the Grail* is filled with specific details, which are richly suggestive and create an aura of mystery and wonder. In his descriptions, as in much of what he writes, Chrétien tantalizes us with details that are precise yet mysterious in their juxtapositions. He refuses to explain, and in that refusal lies much of his interest for us today. His artistry is one of creating a tone of wonder and mystification. What is Erec's motivation? Why does Enide set off on the quest in her best dress? Did Lancelot consummate his love with Guinevere? What is the significance of Yvain's lion? What is the mystery of the Grail Castle? In his prologue to *Erec and Enide,* Chrétien hints at a greater purpose behind his story than simple entertainment, but he deliberately refuses to spell out that purpose. And near the end of the romance, as Erec is about to recount his own tale for King Arthur, Chrétien significantly refuses to repeat it, telling us in words that apply equally well to all his romances:

> Mes cuidiez vos que je vos die
> quex acoisons le fist movoir?
> Naie, que bien savez le voir
> et de ice et d'autre chose,
> si con ge la vos ai esclose.
>
> [ll. 6432-36]

[But do you expect me to tell you the reason that made him set out? No indeed, for you well know the truth of this and of other things, just as I have disclosed it to you.]

All the answers we may require, Chrétien assures us, are already embedded within the *bele conjointure* he has just opened out before us with such consummate artistry. In considering these details one must resist the temptation to seek an allegorical or symbolic interpretation for each one. Borrowing constantly from a reserve of symbols, Chrétien, like his contemporary listener or reader, would have been aware of the symbolic potential of certain terms, or certain numbers, animals or gems. But these symbols are handled delicately and naturally, with no continuous system. Chrétien was not writing a sustained allegory, such as the *Romance of the Rose* or the *Divine Comedy.* Contrary to pure allegory, his symbolic mode is discontinuous and polyvalent: it does not function in a single predictable manner in each instance, and one interpretation does not necessarily preclude another. Rosemond Tuve (1966) says, writing of such works: "Though a horse may betoken undisciplined impulses in one context, a knight parted from a horse in the next episode may just be a knight parted from a horse'. The symbol may change meaning freely and associatively, or include several meanings in a single occurrence, or even disappear altogether. Where allegory was an organized science in the Middle Ages, symbolism was an art in which poetic sensitivity, imagination and invention played a significant part.

Among Chrétien's greatest achievements must be counted his mastery of the octosyllabic rhymed couplet. Although our translations are into prose, our usual medium today for a lengthy narrative, Chrétien naturally employed the medium of his own day, which had been consecrated before him by use in the rhymed chronicles and the romances of antiquity from which, as we have seen, he drew so much of his inspiration. The relatively short octosyllabic line with its frequent rhyme could become monotonous in untalented hands, but Chrétien manipulated it with great freedom and sensitivity: he varies his rhythms;

adapts his rhymes and couplets to the flow of the narrative, rather than forcing his syntax to adhere to a rigidly repeating pattern; uses repetitions and wordplay, anaphora and enjambments; combines sounds harmoniously through the interplay of complementary vowels and consonants; and he uses expressive rhetorical figures to highlight significant words. He was fond of rhyming together two words which in Old French had identical spellings but wholly different meanings, and was likewise fond of playing upon several forms of the same or homonymous words, as in the following passage from *Erec:*

> Au matinet sont esvellié
> si resont tuit aparellié
> de monter et de chevauchier.
> Erec ot molt son cheval chier,
> que d'autre chevalchier n'ot cure.
>
> [ll. 5125-29]

[They awoke at daybreak and all prepared again to mount and ride. Erec greatly prized his mount, and would not mount another.]

(pp. 2-20)

Certainly no translation can hope to capture all the subtlety and magic of Chrétien's art. But one can hope to convey some measure of his humour, his irony and the breadth of his vision. He was one of the great artists and creators of his day, and nearly every romancer after him had to come to terms with his legacy. Some translated or frankly imitated (today we might even say plagiarized) his work; others repeated or developed motifs, themes, structures and stylistic mannerisms introduced by him; still others continued his stories in ever more vast compilations. Already in the last decade of the twelfth century his *Erec and Enide* had been translated into German as *Erek* by Hartmann von Aue, who in the first years of the thirteenth century also translated *The Knight with the Lion* (*Iwein*). At about the same time Ulrich von Zatzikhoven translated *The Knight of the Cart,* also into German (*Lanzelet*). But his greatest German emulator was Wolfram von Eschenbach, who adapted Chrétien's *The Story of the Grail* as *Parzival,* one of the finest of all medieval romances, in the first decade of the thirteenth century. There were also direct adaptations of this romance into Middle Dutch and Old Welsh.

In the fifty years from 1190 to 1240 Arthurian romance was the prevailing vogue in France, and no writer could escape Chrétien's influence. Some, like Gautier d'Arras and Jean Renart, deliberately set out to rival him, fruitlessly attempting to surpass the master. Others—the majority—flattered his memory by their imitations of his work. Among the motifs first introduced by Chrétien that are found in more than one romance after him are the tournament in which the hero fights incognito (*Cligés*), the sparrow-hawk contest (*Erec*), the abduction (*The Knight of the Cart*), Sir Kay's disagreeable temperament (*Erec, The Knight of the Cart, The Story of the Grail*), and the heads of knights impaled on stakes (*Erec*).

His incompleted *The Story of the Grail* sparked by far the greatest interest. In the last decade of the twelfth century two anonymous continuators sought to complete the poem. The first took it up where Chrétien left off, continuing the adventures of Sir Gawain for as many as 19,600 lines in the lengthiest redaction, but never reaching a conclusion. The second continuator returned to the adventures of Perceval for an additional 13,000 lines. In the early thirteenth century the romance was given two independent terminations, one by Manessier in some 10,000 additional lines, and the other by Gerbert de Montreuil in 17,000 lines.

Meanwhile, also in the late twelfth century, Robert de Boron composed a derivative verse account of the history of the Grail in three related poems—*Joseph d'Arimathie, Merlin, Perceval*—of which only the first survives intact. It tells of the origin of the Grail, associating it for the first time with the cup of the Last Supper, and announces that it will be carried to the West and found there by a knight of the lineage of Joseph of Arimathea. 'Robert's *Perceval* (now totally lost) would have recounted how this knight found the Grail and thereby put an end to the 'marvels of Britain'. The second poem, now fragmentary, links the others by changing the scene to Britain, introducing Arthur and having Merlin recall the action of the first and predict that of the second. Robert's poems were soon replaced by prose versions, notably the so-called *Didot-Perceval*. In the early thirteenth century there was a second prose reworking of Chrétien's Grail story, known as the *Perlesvaus,* by an anonymous author who also knew the work of Robert de Boron and both the First and Second Continuations.

Chrétien's influence can still be felt in the vast prose compendium of the mid-thirteenth century known as the *Lancelot-Graal* or the Vulgate Cycle (1225-50), which combined his story of Lancelot's love for the queen (**The Knight of the Cart**) with the Grail quest (**The Story of the Grail**), and was the source of Malory's *Le Morte D'Arthur,* the fountainhead of Arthurian material in modern English literature. However, the success of the *Lancelot-Graal* ironically marked the decline of Chrétien's direct influence. As prose came to replace verse as the preferred medium for romance and the French language continued to evolve from Chrétien's Old French to a more modern idiom, his poems were forgotten until the rediscovery of their manuscripts in the nineteenth century.

Thanks to Malory, the Arthurian materials were never lost sight of so completely in England, and Tennyson's *Idylls of the King* reflect the vogue for Arthuriana in the Romantic period. Today in both England and America there is a renewed and lively interest in the Arthurian legends that Chrétien was the first to exploit as the subject matter for romance. All those who have celebrated and still celebrate King Arthur and his Knights of the Round Table—from the anonymous authors of the *Lancelot-Graal* through Malory and Tennyson to Steinbeck, Boorman and Bradley today—are forever in his debt. (pp. 20-2)

> *William W. Kibler, in an introduction to* Arthurian Romances *by Chrétien de Troyes, translated by William W. Kibler, Penguin Books, 1991, pp. 1-22.*

FURTHER READING

I. Bibliographies of Chrétien

Kelly, Douglas. *Chrétien de Troyes: An Analytic Bibliography.* London: Grant & Cutler, 1976, 153 p.
Comprehensive bibliography of Chrétien scholarship.

II. General Critical Studies

Artin, Tom. *The Allegory of Adventure: Reading Chrétien's "Erec" and "Yvain."* Cranbury, N. J.: Associated University Presses, 1974, 264 p.
Explores the analogic relation between Erec and Yvain's chivalric adventures and biblical events. Artin contends that Chrétien's notion of love and adventure is sacred as well as secular.

Colby, Alice M. *The Portrait in Twelfth-Century French Literature: An Example of the Stylistic Originality of Chrétien de Troyes.* Geneva: Librairie Droz, 1965, 204 p.
Overview of the structure, content, and rhetorical background of Chrétien's characterizations, highlighting his deviations from and contributions to the period.

Duggan, Joseph J. Afterword. In *"Yvain: The Knight of the Lion,"* by Chrétien de Troyes, translated by Burton Raffel, pp. 205-26. New Haven, Conn.: Yale University Press, 1986.
Considers Chrétien's principal works within their cultural context.

Guyer, Foster Erwin. *Romance in the Making: Chrétien de Troyes and the Earliest French Romances.* New York: S. F. Vanni, 1954, 285 p.
Study of Chrétien's contribution to the development of the romance genre.

——. *Chrétien de Troyes: Inventor of the Modern Novel.* New York: Bookman Associates, 1957, 247 p.
Hailing Chrétien as the "inventor of the novel," Guyer attempts to restore him to his "proper historical position" as a "great genius" in world history.

Haidu, Peter. *Aesthetic Distance in Chrétien de Troyes: Irony and Comedy in "Cliges" and "Perceval."* Geneva: Librairie Droz, 1968, 272 p.
Explores the grammatical and rhetorical theories inherited by the Middle Ages from classical antiquity which influenced Chrétien's choice of stylistic devices.

Hunt, Tony. "Tradition and Originality in the Prologues of Chrestien de Troyes." *Forum for Modern Language Studies* VIII, No. 4 (October 1972): 320-37.
Compares Chrétien's prologues with corresponding passages in various redactions of his romances in order to illustrate his poetic novelty.

Lacy, Norris J.; Kelly, Douglas; and Busby, Keith, eds. *The Legacy of Chrétien de Troyes,* Vol. I. Amsterdam: Rodopi, 1987, 342 p.
Discerns the extent to which Chrétien influenced the development of the courtly romance genre during the thirteenth century and beyond.

Laurie, Helen C. R. *Two Studies in Chrétien de Troyes.* Geneva: Librairie Droz, 1972, 225 p.
Considers the various influences on Chrétien's thought, especially Vergil's *Aeneid.*

Lewis, C. S. "The Romance of the Rose." In his *Allegory of*

Love: A Study in Medieval Tradition, pp. 112-56. Oxford: Clarendon Press, 1936.

>Acknowledges Chrétien as the first Arthurian author to impart a psychological component to medieval allegory, which, Lewis claims, has led readers to appreciate Chrétien's works as both adventure stories and serious romances.

Loomis, Roger Sherman. *Arthurian Tradition and Chrétien de Troyes.* New York: Columbia University Press, 1949, 503 p.

>Discusses Chrétien's literary artistry and examines Celtic themes expressed in his romances.

Noble, Peter S., and Paterson, Linda M., eds. *Chrétien de Troyes and the Troubadours.* Cambridge: St. Catherine's College, Cambridge, 1984, 282 p.

>Collection including several essays regarding Chrétien's romances and his presentation of the Arthurian material.

Nolan, E. Peter. "Mythopoetic Evolution: Chrétien de Troyes's *Erec et Enide, Cligés,* and *Yvain.*" *Symposium* XXV, No. 2 (Summer 1971): 139-61.

>Compares Chrétien's narrative strategies from three of his romances, noting a shift toward ironic realism in his style.

Staines, David. Introduction to *The Complete Romances of Chrétien de Troyes,* translated by David Staines, pp. ix-xxix. Bloomington: Indiana University Press, 1990.

>Provides a general overview of Chrétien's life and works and a brief history of his sources.

Woods, William S. "The Plot Structure in Four Romances of Chrétien de Troyes." *Studies in Philology* 50, No. 1 (January 1953): 1-15.

>Examines the plot in four of Chrétien's works, concluding that they have a common framework (a hero's attainment and subsequent loss of joy) which contributes to the intricacy of the romances.

Zaddy, Z. P. *Chrétien Studies: Problems of Form and Meaning in "Erec," "Yvain," "Cligés" and the "Charrete."* Glasgow: University of Glasgow Press, 1973, 196 p.

>Series of essays dealing with the form, content, and complexity of interpretation posed by four of Chrétien's most popular romances.

III. *Cligés*

Curtis, Renée L. "The Validity of Fénice's Criticism of Tristan and Iseut in Chrétien's *Cligés.*" *Bibliographical Bulletin of the International Arthurian Society* XLI (1989): 293-300.

>Questions whether or not Chrétien modeled his *Cligés* on the Tristan legend. Curtis argues that although Chrétien was familiar with *Tristan und Isolde,* he did not set out to write a story about ill-fated love.

Lonigan, Paul R. "The *Cligés* and the Tristan Legend." *Studi Francesi,* No. 53 (1974): 201-12.

>Dismisses the notion that Chrétien's *Cligés* is a rewriting of the Tristan epic. Lonigan asserts that *Cligés,* unlike *Tristan und Isolde,* is "an exquisitely contrived bit of parlor amusement" rather than a tragic tale of ill-fated love.

Robertson, D. W. "Chrétien's *Cligés* and the Ovidian Spirit." *Comparative Literature* VII, No. 1 (Winter 1955): 32-42.

>Examines Ovid's influence on Chrétien.

Shirt, David J. "*Cligés:* Realism in Romance." *Forum for Modern Language Studies* XIII, No. 4 (October 1977): 368-80.

>Elaborates on both the extra-textual and structural realism attributed to *Cligés* by previous critics.

IV. *Erec et Enide*

Nitze, William A. "Erec and the Joy of the Court." *Speculum* XXIX, No. 4 (October 1954): 691-701.

>Asserts that *Erec* is largely Chrétien's own creation, a "notable work of art with a definite idea or situation to which the main characters . . . all revert."

Sturm-Maddox, Sarah. "The *Joie de la Court:* Thematic Unity in Chrétien's *Erec et Enide.*" *Romania* 103, No. 4 (1982): 513-28.

>Asserts that the opening section (*"li premiers vers"*) and the final adventure (*"Joie de la Court"*) in Chrétien's *Erec et Enide* are analogous in their "comparing and contrasting two different ideals of love while exploring the implications of these ideals for the courtly society that serves as their context."

Vance, Eugene. "Selfhood and Substance in *Erec et Enide.*" In his *From Topic to Tale: Logic and Narrativity in the Middle Ages,* pp. 28-40. *Theory and History of Literature,* Vol. 47, edited by Wlad Godzich and Jochen Schulte-Sasse. Minneapolis: University of Minnesota Press, 1987.

>Proposes that in *Erec et Enide,* Chrétien sought to maintain the "precocious harmony" of Western culture, employing Aristotelian rationalism and neoplatonic mysticism to reconcile the transcendent and immanent aspects of human experience.

V. *Lancelot*

Condren, Edward I. "The Paradox of Chrétien's *Lancelot.*" *Modern Language Notes* 85 (1970): 434-53.

>Investigates Chrétien's ironic treatment of the love tradition. Though the poem may be constructed around a theme common to the medieval romance genre, Condren points out that the poem depicts an "inverted" social condition "where the wrong people or the wrong values control one action after another."

Cross, Tom Peete, and Nitze, William Albert. *Lancelot and Guenevere: A Study on the Origins of Courtly Love.* Chicago: University of Chicago Press, 1930, 104 p.

>Outlines the story of Lancelot and Guenevere in *Lancelot,* noting the tale's Celtic origins and thematic evolution.

de Looze, Laurence N. "Chivalry Qualified: The Character of Gauvain in Chrétien de Troyes's *Le Chevalier de la Charrette.*" *The Romanic Review* LXXIV, No. 3 (May 1983): 253-59.

>Examines Freudian and Jungian imagery and symbolism in *Lancelot.* De Looze maintains that Gauvain's failure to integrate knighthood and love is rooted in an inability to deal with the feminine world.

Morgan, Gerald. "The Conflict of Love and Chivalry in *Le Chevalier de la Charrete.*" *Romania* 102, No. 2 (1981): 172-201.

>Focuses on the treatment of love and chivalry in *Lance-*

lot, which, Morgan asserts, reveals the coherence of Chrétien's literary effort as a whole.

VI. *Perceval*

Burns, E. Jane. "Quest and Questioning in the *Conte du graal.*" *Romance Philology* XLI, No. 3 (February 1988): 251-66.

> Ponders Chrétien's intent in writing the Grail romance. Burns maintains that the tale is purposefully ambiguous and paradoxical, suggesting that for Chrétien, "there is a significant difference between meaning . . . and a definitive or monolithic truth."

Cosman, Madeleine Pelner. "The Education of Perceval: A Brave Man Slowly Wise." In her *The Education of the Hero in Arthurian Romance,* pp. 49-100. Chapel Hill: University of North Carolina Press, 1965.

> Analyzes the artistic aspects of Perceval's education. Cosman argues that the character's intellectual development is of greater significance to the poem than his chivalric adventures.

Holmes, Jr., Urban T., and Klenke, Sr. M. Amelia. *Chrétien, Troyes, and the Grail.* Chapel Hill: University of North Carolina Press, 1959, 230 p.

> Searches out the meaning of Chrétien's *Perceval,* "the cause which rendered the Quest of the Grail the most significant masterpiece of the Middle Ages."

Owen, D. D. R. "The French Master: Chrétien de Troyes" and "The First Grail Romance." In *The Evolution of the Grail Legend,* pp. 102-29, 130-64. Edinburgh: Oliver and Boyd, 1968.

> Discusses Chrétien's place in medieval French poetry and in the tradition of the Grail legend. These chapters furnish a brief biographical and critical overview as well as an examination of *Perceval* as the first account of the Grail story in romance form.

VII. *Yvain*

Brown, Arthur C. L. "Chrétien's *Yvain.*" *Modern Philology* IX, No. 1 (July 1911): 109-28.

> Analyzes Chrétien's *Yvain* as a fairy-mistress story of Celtic origin.

Brown, George Hardin. "Yvain's Sin of Neglect." *Symposium* XXVII, No. 4 (Winter 1973): 309-21.

> Presents prevalent twelfth-century concepts of behavior which help to explain Yvain's "sin," that is, his failure to return as promised to his new wife after a year fighting tournaments with Gawain.

Kratins, Ojars. *The Dream of Chivalry: A Study of Chrétien de Troyes's "Yvain" and Hartmann von Aue's "Iwein."* Washington, D. C.: University Press of America, 1982, 231 p.

> Probes the place of Chrétien's *Yvain* in the Arthurian tradition and examines it as a moral fable intended to instruct chivalric society regarding matters "which can only be understood with the heart."

Lacy, Norris J. "Organic Structure of Yvain's Expiation." *The Romanic Review* LXI (1970): 79-84.

> Structural analysis of *Yvain,* focusing particularly on the interconnectedness between the various scenes dealing with Yvain's heroic adventures.

Nitze, William A. "Yvain and the Myth of the Fountain." *Speculum* XXX, No. 2 (April 1955): 170-79.

> Deals with the variety of opinions regarding the composition of Chrétien's *Yvain.*

Uitti, Karl D. "Chrétien de Troyes's *Yvain:* Fiction and Sense." *Romance Philology* 22, No. 4 (May 1969): 471-83.

> Scrutinizes the various twelfth-century narratives available to Chrétien in his composing *Yvain,* postulating several theories for his choosing one type over another.

Gottfried von Strassburg

fl. c. 1210

German poet.

INTRODUCTION

Gottfried is widely acknowledged as a leading German poet of the Middle Ages: second, in most critics' estimation, only to Wolfram von Eschenbach. His literary reputation is based on a single work, *Tristan und Isolde* (*Tristan and Isolde*), a chivalric romance of Celtic origin connected with the cycle of Arthurian legend. Literary historians point out that while Gottfried's adaptation is a masterpiece of the German courtly epic, the genre itself had been introduced into that nation's literature a century earlier by Heinrich von Veldeke and further developed by Gottfried's contemporary, Hartmann von Aue. The general outline of *Tristan and Isolde* as well as its narrative style and essential plot elements are derived from a twelfth-century French version of the epic composed by the Anglo-Norman poet Thomas of Brittany. Scholars assert, however, that the originality of Gottfried's poem lies in its unprecedented refinement of rhyme, rhythm, and language, and in the poet's ability to render a story of overpowering erotic passion in terms of religious mysticism. The inspiration for German composer Richard Wagner's 1859 opera *Tristan und Isolde,* Gottfried's courtly epic is generally considered the highest achievement of German chivalric poetry.

All known biographical information concerning Gottfried is inferred from his work. Critics surmise that he was a learned man, versed in Latin and French, and that he must have received a sound classical and theological education typically provided by the monastic schools of the Middle Ages. Gottfried was familiar with the poetry of Ovid and Vergil, and employed many Latinate proverbs and classical references in his work; he was equally versed in religious literature, as evidenced by his use of sacred imagery drawn from the Bible and ecclesiastical authors, especially the French Christian mystic Saint Bernard of Clairvaux. Since Gottfried's *Tristan and Isolde* is a chivalric romance, historians assume that he must also have been acquainted with the customs and manners of courtly and knightly life, though most believe that Gottfried himself was not a member of the nobility since in various documents he is typically addressed using the scholarly title *Meister* rather than the aristocratic *Herr.* Some have suggested that Gottfried might have been an amanuensis in the service of a nobleman or bishop. Scholars concur that he died sometime during the composition of *Tristan and Isolde* and that the epic was completed within the same century by two German poets, Ulrich von Türheim (c. 1240) and Heinrich von Freiberg (1290). As to the date of *Tristan and Isolde,* critics infer that Gottfried's portion

Gottfried (third from right), from a medieval tapestry. (Bildarchiv)

was written about 1210, based on a celebrated passage at the beginning of the poem, the "literary excursus," in which Gottfried breaks his narrative to offer his opinion of his contemporaries.

In the Prologue to *Tristan and Isolde,* Gottfried informs the reader that he was aware of and searched through many versions of the legend, both Latin and French, to find a "true and authentic" depiction of Tristan. During the twelfth century, the tale of Tristan and Isolde was widely known and cited. Troubadour Bernart de Ventadour lamented that, in the absence of his lover, he was like a Tristan without his Isolde, and the poet Marie de France adapted a Tristan episode in her *Lais.* French poet Chrétien de Troyes claimed to have written a work dealing with the legend, but no trace of it has been preserved. There are, however, several other extant versions of the story. Around the last third of the twelfth century, the Norman-French poet Béroul composed his *Roman de Tristan,* making reference to an *estoire,* or history, of the legend which served as his source. Scholars note that a Tristan romance composed in 1180 by the German poet Eilhart von Oberge also seems to confirm the existence of such a prototype since Eilhart drew from the same source as Béroul. Another of Gottfried's forerunners, Thomas of Brittany, whom Gottfried hails as a "master-romancer," composed his Tristan story around 1170, probably at the request of someone at the court of Henry II of England. Only a few fragments and a lengthy passage of some eighteen hundred lines of his rendition survive. Unlike the courtly versions of Eilhart and Béroul, which view the adulterous love of Tristan and Isolde as dishonorable, Thomas's work depicts their love as ennobling, a perspective shared and enlarged by Gottfried. Though many German and French editions of *Tristan and Isolde* appeared over the centuries, the only exposure that the English-speaking world had to Gottfried's poem was through Wagner's opera. In 1898 Jessie L. Weston produced the first English translation of the work, which was followed by Edwin H. Zeydel's 1948 edition. Twelve years later, A. T. Hatto offered the first complete verse translation of the epic; judged by scholars a faithful rendering of the original, it remains the most highly regarded version of *Tristan and Isolde* in English.

Gottfried's epic commences with the story of Tristan's conception and birth. Tristan's father, Rivalin of Parmenie, travels to the court of King Mark of Cornwall, where he wins the love of Blancheflor, the king's sister. They elope to Parmenie; shortly thereafter, Rivalin is killed in battle, and Blancheflor dies in giving birth to Tristan. Rual, Rivalin's faithful marshal, adopts Tristan and rears him as his own son. Tristan is an extraordinarily gifted boy, accomplished in all aspects of chivalry by the time he is fourteen. Abducted by Norse merchants, he lands on the coast of Cornwall and makes his way to King Mark's castle, where he amazes the court with his musical abilities. Four years later, Rual discovers Tristan and discloses his true parentage. Adopted as an heir by his uncle, King Mark, Tristan is raised to the rank of a knight during a ritual known as the *schweitleite*. Returning to Parmenie, Tristan searches out his father's killers and conquers the country. Upon Tristan's return to Cornwall, King Mark informs him that King Gurmun of Ireland and his brother-in-law Morold have imposed a tribute on Cornwall; unfortunately, no one has the courage to face Morold in battle. Tristan accepts this challenge and is victorious, but sustains a wound which no one can heal except Morold's sister, the Irish queen. Under the name of Tantris and disguised as a minstrel, Tristan goes to Dublin. There he wins the affections of the young Irish princess Isolde; in return for lessons in music and languages, Morold's sister (Isolde's mother) heals his wound. Now cured, Tristan excuses himself with the lie that he has a wife at home and departs for Cornwall.

In an attempt to prevent Tristan from becoming Mark's successor, jealous nobles persuade the king to marry. Isolde is selected to be his bride and Tristan is sent back to Ireland as an envoy. Isolde, however, recognizes Tristan as Tantris, and when she discovers that Tristan killed her uncle Morold, her love turns to hatred. After her father consents to King Mark's marriage proposal, Isolde travels with Tristan to Cornwall. During the voyage they mistakenly drink a love potion which Isolde's mother had intended for her daughter and King Mark. Their enmity is instantly transformed into love. With the help of Isolde's maid, Brangane, Tristan and Isolde conceal their love from Mark; when the wedding night arrives, a disguised Brangane is substituted for Isolde. One adventure follows another as the lovers continue to deceive the king. Eventually they are discovered and flee the kingdom to take refuge in a cave, or *minnegrotte* ("love grotto"). A second discovery takes place, and Tristan escapes to the court of the Duke of Arundel. There he finds himself drawn to the duke's daughter, Isolde of the White Hands. At this point Gottfried's poem abruptly ends and is picked up by his successors, Ulrich and Heinrich. Though Tristan loves Isolde, he marries Isolde of the White Hands. Having been wounded by a poisoned spear, he sends a messenger across the sea to fetch the "blonde" Isolde, his true love, for only she can cure him. If she returns, the ship is to bear a white sail—if not, a black one. When the ship carrying the blonde Isolde is sighted by Tristan's wife, she deceives her husband by telling him that the sail is black. As the blonde Isolde arrives, she finds her paramour already dead and then she, too, dies of grief. King Mark, after learning of the secret love potion that made Tristan and Isolde fall in love, has their bodies brought to Cornwall for burial. On Isolde's grave he plants a vine and on Tristan's a rose, so that as they grow, they entwine.

Critics agree that the greatness of Gottfried's *Tristan and Isolde* lies in its portrayal of erotic passion. Some contend that Gottfried was not concerned with upholding social standards or celebrating marital love as do such other classic Arthurian romances as *Parceval, Erec,* and *Yvain;* rather, they claim, he employed the courtly romance genre to imbue adulterous love with pathos and to elevate it to a level which only the *edele herzen,* or "noble hearts," could comprehend. In the Prologue, Gottfried clearly states that his work is intended for a select group: those who have the education, manners, and beauty of body and spirit which allow them to grasp and partake of the tragic love of Tristan and Isolde. Gottfried's intent, according to scholars, was to affirm illicit love even though it usually disrupts social order, breaks family bonds, and causes isolation, pain, and death. This higher love is not concerned with momentary pleasure and self-gratification; it is eternal, mutual, and life-giving, or as Gottfried puts it, "bread for the living." Although the lovers perish at the story's end, Gottfried asserts in the Prologue that their love will "live on though they are dead." As C. Stephen Jaeger has written, Gottfried "transformed this class-bound, optimistic, occasionally trivial genre [of courtly romance] into the vehicle of a dark and tragic, profound and transcendent view of love."

To sanctify his vision of illicit love, Gottfried incorporated religious imagery drawn from Christian doctrine, ritual, and liturgy into his work. The use of the image of bread to describe Tristan and Isolde's nourishing love has strong eucharistic overtones, as many scholars have pointed out. Further, Gottfried parallels the death of the lovers with the death of Christ: as Jesus died for the life of the world, so the lovers' deaths provide sustenance for noble hearts. The use of religious imagery is most apparent in the cave of lovers scene. Situated in the wilderness, the traditional place of encounter with God, the cave itself is described in a naturalistic manner. But the architectural elements of the dwelling also function symbolically, with the bare walls representing love's simplicity, the green floor love's constancy, and the crystal bed love's purity. Critics such as Friedrich Ranke and Jaeger maintain that Gottfried's cave functions allegorically as a Byzantine temple or a Gothic cathedral, with vaulted arches culminating in a crowned keystone, and the crystal bed reminiscent of an altar. While in the forest, the lovers lead an austere life, deprived of food and worldly comforts. They are likened to Christian saints who sustain themselves with a more perfect spiritual diet consisting only of transcendent love which flows from their eyes. Gottfried, in fact, calls them "sufferers" or martyrs and holds them up as examples for all noble hearts. As the believer finds shelter from the temptations of the secular world in the church building, so the lovers find refuge in the cave, where they enjoy an idyllic life free from the threat of King Mark, whom Gottfried depicts as the chief representative of a social order which values the civil bond of marriage over true love.

Many scholars also cite Gottfried as the first romance writer to impart an intellectual and artistic component to love. Literature and music play a prominent role in *Tristan and Isolde,* and Gottfried goes to great lengths to portray Tristan as a consummate artist: his education includes training in speech, good manners, and foreign languages, in addition to riding, hunting, wrestling, and fighting. Tristan is also a skilled musician, a master of stringed instruments who, upon his arrival at King Mark's court, dazzles the assembly with his playing. Likewise, at the Irish court he wins favor through his recitation and music. Gottfried's concept of the role of the artist in society, as evidenced by his presentation of Tristan, has engendered much critical commentary. W. T. H. Jackson has written that "Gottfried conceived of the artist as one who could use excellent material, in this case music and lyric poetry, to dominate an audience and bend it to his will." Music dominates the preliminary stage of Tristan and Isolde's courtship, with Tristan playing the role of Isolde's tutor. Jackson has asserted that Tristan's "greatest gift is that when he finds an equally gifted woman, he can communicate his power to her and thus eliminate the necessity of any kind of performance." Art is also of paramount importance in the cave of lovers scene; while in the cave, the lovers read sad tales from Ovid and play the lute. While affirming the value of art in general, Gottfried's epic reflects the ancient and medieval belief that music is the highest of the arts since it speaks directly to the soul. As Gottfried writes, "the strains of both harp and tongue, merging their sound in each other, echoed in the cave so sweetly."

Gottfried's literary excursus offers valuable insight into his poetic values, for there he criticizes Wolfram for his obscure and sometimes vulgar phraseology, and praises Hartmann for his ability to convey a story's theme clearly, elegantly, and smoothly. Commentators concur that Gottfried deliberately imitated Hartmann's style, cleverly employing double meanings throughout his *Tristan and Isolde* which allow for more complex characterization. For example, when Isolde, in an attempt to hide her deception from Mark, hires assassins to kill Brangane, who has surrendered her virginity on Isolde's behalf, Brangane, discovering Isolde's plot, sends a greeting "in such terms as a young lady [virgin] owes to her mistress." Since she is no longer a virgin, Brangane's ambiguous formulation allows her to maintain her loyalty to Isolde while simultaneously striking at her conscience. Gottfried's poetic virtuosity is also apparent in his use of metaphors drawn from such diverse fields as the tailoring trade, landscape, mythology, and hunting, and in his handling of rhetorical devices. He was fond of combining antithetical terms to create a chiasmus (a construction that reverses its main elements), and in the Prologue, Gottfried fashioned an acrostic in which the first letter of each stanza spells out DIETRICH, the name of his patron. Finding Hartmann's use of the rhymed couplet monotonous, Gottfried broke its repetitiveness in *Tristan and Isolde* with iambic strophes, giving his poetry a rich lyrical quality. As Calvin Thomas has written, Gottfried "was an artist of rare quality. As a chooser of words and a fashioner of pleasing couplets he has no superior."

Gottfried was virtually unknown to English-speaking readers prior to Weston's translation, but his work has elicited lively critical dialogue ever since. In the early twentieth century some critics attacked the poem as blasphemous and immoral because of its lofty depiction of adulterous love, while others, notably Daniel B. Shumway, lauded the epic's grandeur and beauty which, in Shumway's opinion, "have placed the poem in the first rank of the literature of the world." Scholars universally concur that Gottfried was faithful to the traditional sources of the epic, and surpassed all other renditions in the novelty of his rhyme, language, and moral philosophy. In 1944 August Closs first probed Gottfried's psychological insights into love and introduced the concept of Gottfried's "two worlds": the "higher world" of permanence, perfection, and harmony, to which Tristan, Isolde, and all noble hearts belong; and the "lower world" of King Mark and lesser hearts which is characterized by temporality, pleasure, and disorder. Since the appearance of Closs's study, commentators have continued to explore these themes. Jackson has noted the importance of the arts, especially music, in the epic, and has challenged readers to appreciate the ways in which Gottfried's *Tristan and Isolde* differs from the works of the poet's contemporaries, emphasizing that, "Gottfried writes in the genre of the [courtly] romance, but his work is not of it." Madeline Pelner Cosman and Michael Batts have analyzed the epic as a parody of chivalry and civil marriage, while such other recent critics as Wilson and Jaeger have investigated Gottfried's use of Christian mysticism in *Tristan and Isolde* as a way to bridge the abyss between the sacred and the secular and lead the individual to higher virtues. As Jaeger has pointed out, "Gottfried distinguishes himself from all his contemporaries in courtly poetry by combining the brilliance of classical inspiration (the luster of gold) with the 'depth' of Christian spirituality (the transparency of jewels)."

Throughout the centuries, scholars have extolled *Tristan and Isolde* for its serious and moving depiction of illicit love, pointing out that no other poet before the Renaissance treated the topic of love from such a variety of perspectives and with so much psychological depth as Gottfried. As R. S. Loomis has remarked, *Tristan and Isolde* "is except for the *Canterbury Tales* and the *Divina Commedia,* the greatest poem of the Middle Ages."

PRINCIPAL ENGLISH TRANSLATIONS

The Story of Tristan and Iseult (translated by Jessie L. Weston) 1898

Tristan and Isolde (translated by Edwin H. Zeydel) 1948

Tristan (translated by A. T. Hatto) 1960

Tristan and Isolde (translated by A. T. Hatto; second edition revised and edited by Francis G. Gentry) 1988

Gottfried von Strassburg (essay date c. 1210)

[*In the following excerpt from his Prelude to* Tristan and Isolde (*written c. 1210*), *Gottfried discusses the relation of criticism to art and informs his readers that his translation of the Tristan legend is meant for "noble hearts," those who can welcome both the joy and tragedy of love.*]

If we failed in our esteem of those who confer benefits on us, the good that is done among us would be as nothing.

We do wrong to receive otherwise than well what a good man does well-meaningly and solely for our good.

I hear much disparagement of what people nevertheless ask for. This is niggling to excess, this is wanting what you do not want at all.

A man does well to praise what he cannot do without. Let it please him so long as it may.

That man is dear and precious to me who can judge of good and bad and know me and all men at our true worth.

Praise and esteem bring art on where art deserves commendation. When art is adorned with praise it blossoms in profusion.

Just as what fails to win praise and esteem falls into neglect, so that finds favour which meets with esteem and is not denied its praise.

There are so many today who are given to judging the good bad and the bad good. They act not to right but to cross purpose.

However well art and criticism seem to live together, if envy comes to lodge with them it stifles both art and criticism.

O Excellence! how narrow are thy paths, how arduous thy ways! Happy the man who can climb thy paths and tread thy ways!

If I spend my time in vain, ripe for living as I am, my part in society will continue to fall short of what my experience requires of me. Thus I have undertaken a labour to please the polite world and solace noble hearts—those hearts which I hold in affection, that world which lies open to my heart. I do not mean the world of the many who (as I hear) are unable to endure sorrow and wish only to revel in bliss. (Please God to let them live in their bliss!) What I have to say does not concern that world and such a way of life; their way and mine diverge sharply. I have another world in mind which together in one heart bears its bitter-sweet, its dear sorrow, its heart's joy, its love's pain, its dear life, its sorrowful death, its dear death, its sorrowful life. To this life let my life be given, of this world let me be part, to be damned or saved with it. I have kept with it so far and with it have spent the days that were to bring me counsel and guidance through a life which has moved me profoundly. I have offered the fruits of my labour to this world as a pastime, so that with my story its denizens can bring their keen sorrow half-way to alleviation and thus abate their anguish. For if we have something before us to occupy our thoughts it frees our unquiet soul and eases our heart of its cares. All are agreed that when a man of leisure is overwhelmed by love's torment, leisure redoubles that torment and if leisure be added to languor, languor will mount and mount. And so it is a good thing that one who harbours love's pain and sorrow in his heart should seek distraction with all his mind—then his spirit will find solace and release. Yet I would never advise a man in search of pleasure to follow any pursuit that would ill become pure love. Let a lover ply a love-tale with his heart and lips and so while away the hour.

Now we hear too much of one opinion, with which I all but agree, that the more a love-sick soul has to do with love-tales the more it will despond. I would hold with this opinion but for one objection: when we are deeply in love, however great the pain, our heart does not flinch. The more a lover's passion burns in its furnace of desire, the more ardently will he love. This sorrow is so full of joy, this ill is so inspiriting that, having once been heartened by it, no noble heart will forgo it! I know as sure as death and have learned it from this same anguish: the noble lover loves love-tales. Therefore, whoever wants a story need go no further than here. I will story him well with noble lovers who gave proof of perfect love:

> A man, a woman; a woman, a man:
> Tristan, Isolde; Isolde, Tristan.

I am well aware that there have been many who have told the tale of Tristan; yet there have not been many who have read his tale aright.

But were I now to act and pass judgment as though I were displeased by what each has said of this story, I would act otherwise than I should. This I shall not do; for they wrote well and with the noblest of intentions for my good and the good of us all. They assuredly did so well-meaningly, and whatever is done well-meaningly is indeed good and well done. But when I said that they did not tell the tale aright, this was, I aver, the case. They did not write according to the authentic version as told by [Anglo–Norman poet] Thomas of Britain, who was a master-romancer and had read the lives of all those princes in books of the Britons and made them known to us.

I began to search assiduously both in Romance and Latin books for the true and authentic version of Tristan such as Thomas narrates, and I was at pains to direct the poem along the right path which he had shown. Thus I made many researches till I had read in a book all that he says happened in this story. And now I freely offer the fruits of my reading of this love-tale to all noble hearts to distract them. They will find it very good reading. Good? Yes, profoundly good. It will make love lovable, ennoble the mind, fortify constancy, and enrich their lives. This it can well do. For wherever one hears or reads of such perfect loyalty, loyalty and other virtues commend themselves to loyal people accordingly. Affection, loyalty, constancy, honour, and many good things besides, never endear themselves anywhere so much as when someone tells a love-tale or mourns love's tender grief. Love is so blissful a thing, so blessed an endeavour, that apart from its teaching none attains worth or reputation. In view of the many noble lives that love inspires and the many virtues that come from it, oh! that every living thing does not strive for sweet love, that I see so few who, for their lover's sake, will suffer pure longing in their hearts—and all for the wretched sorrow that now and then lies hidden there!

Why should not a noble mind gladly suffer one ill for a thousand boons, one woe for many joys? He that never had sorrow of love never had joy of it either! In love, joy and sorrow ever went hand in hand! With them we must win praise and honour or come to nothing without them! If the two of whom this love-story tells had not endured sorrow for the sake of joy, love's pain for its ecstasy within one heart, their name and history would never have brought such rapture to so many noble spirits! Today we still love to hear of their tender devotion, sweet and ever fresh, their joy, their sorrow, their anguish, and their ecstasy. And although they are long dead, their sweet name lives on and their death will endure for ever to the profit of well-bred people, giving loyalty to those who seek loyalty, honour to those who seek honour. For us who are alive their death must live on and be for ever new. For wherever still today one hears the recital of their devotion, their perfect loyalty, their hearts' joy, their hearts' sorrow—

This is bread to all noble hearts. With this their death lives on. We read their life, we read their death, and to us it is sweet as bread.

Their life, their death are our bread. Thus lives their life, thus lives their death. Thus they live still and yet are dead, and their death is the bread of the living.

And whoever now desires to be told of their life, their death, their joy, their sorrow, let him lend me his heart and ears— he shall find all that he desires! (pp. 41-4)

> *Gottfried von Strassburg, in his* Tristan, *translated by A. T. Hatto, Penguin Books, 1960, 374 p.*

Jessie L. Weston   (essay date 1898)

[*An English writer and scholar, Weston was an authority on medieval legend and literature, and is best known for her work* From Ritual to Romance *(1920), which provided the basis for T. S. Eliot's poem* The Waste Land. *In the following excerpt taken from the introduction to her English translation,* The Story of Tristan and Iseult, *she acknowledges Gottfried's accomplishment and praises his version of the epic as "the work of a man of superior genius and real literary skill."*]

The poem [***Tristan and Iseult***] . . . is the work of Gottfried von Strassburg, one of the most famous of German mediæval poets, and was composed about the year 1210.

Of the poet himself we know practically nothing; he does not, like [German poet] Wolfram von Eschenbach, reveal his own name, or his position in life; and we look in vain in his work for those quaintly suggestive asides by which Wolfram takes his readers into his confidence, and reveals himself while he unfolds his story. But while the vigorous and original personality of Wolfram von Eschenbach, his depth of thought and loftiness of ideal, have stamped the *Parzival* with a character that has rendered it the masterpiece of German mediæval literature, and incomparably the finest romance of the Grail cycle, it must be conceded that Gottfried was the superior in literary skill—and knew it.

In a notable passage in the ***Tristan*** . . . the writer passes in review his literary contemporaries, living and departed, placing in the first rank [German poet] Hartmann von Aue, whom he praises highly for the ease and "crystal" purity of his style; while he sarcastically alludes to one whom he leaves unnamed, as so obscure that a commentator is needed to make his meaning clear! There has never been any doubt that the poet thus pilloried was Wolfram, and that it is to Gottfried's strictures Wolfram alludes in the *Willehalm*.

And we must admit that Gottfried justifies himself as a critic. As a master of language he is infinitely the superior of his contemporaries. Truly he had an inspiring story to tell, a story of which the poignant pathos and enduring charm have captivated the fancy and thrilled the hearts of countless generations. There is no nation that does not know the story of Tristan and Iseult; no important European literature of which it does not form a part; and to Gottfried von Strassburg belongs the honour of having most adequately told the world's greatest love-tale.

Doubtless a large measure of his success was due to the fact that he had before him a version of the story differing in some respects from that popularised by the wandering minstrels, and the work of a man of superior genius and real literary skill. The fragments of the poem of Thomas of Brittany (the Anglo-Norman writer who was Gottfried's source) which have descended to us are marked by much beauty of thought and style: in the ***Tristan*** of Gottfried we have that rare combination, the work of a true poet translated by one who was himself a greater poet. Never did a fine story fall into hands more capable of doing it justice.

Unhappily Gottfried did not live to complete his work, and of those who at a later date essayed the task [Ulrich von Türheim and Heinrich von Freiberg] not one was his equal in literary skill. We know, however, from the concluding portion of Thomas's poem that in his version the story ended in the manner of the other poems, *not* in that of the prose version represented by Malory; and we cannot but regret that we have not Gottfried's version of the great closing scene. We can only imagine what his genius would have made of that most pathetic situation in mediæval romance. (pp. vii-xi)

> *Jessie L. Weston, in an introduction to* The Story of Tristan and Iseult, *Vol. 1, by Gottfried von Strassburg, translated by Jessie L. Weston, New Amsterdam Book Company, 1898, pp. vii-xvi.*

W. Scherer   (essay date 1899)

[*Scherer was a German educator, author, and literary historian. In the excerpt that follows, he lauds Gottfried's poetic skill, judging his German treatment of the Tristan legend superior to the French version.*]

Gottfried was a man of genius and a great artist, but he was a virtuoso in style, and carried polish and elegance to extremes; he exaggerated intellectual subtlety, and delighted in antithesis and conceits of language. His sense of metrical harmony was less delicate than [German poet] Hartmann's, and his periods, admirable as they are, show less freedom and more effort at rounding and finish than the easy-flowing sentences of his predecessor. He had all Hartmann's delicacy without his simplicity. Gottfried is rhetorical, and overlays his narrative with a network of reflections. He is fond of obtruding his own personality and opinions upon his readers, and he strives after originality. He seems never to have written a love-song himself, and he mocks at the trivial laments of the Minnesingers ["troubadours"]. He declines to describe a festival or a tournament, because it has been done so often by others, but he gives in detail the best manner of dressing a hunted stag, because this was something new, and also gave him an opportunity for displaying his knowledge of the technical expressions involved, and of their etymology. He is generally careful not to weary us with the description of garments and outward appearances, but yet he occasionally goes further into these details than the author of 'Iwein' and further than the rules of epic poetry would allow.

Notwithstanding Gottfried's efforts after originality, he had no other artistic means at his disposal than those which he had inherited from Hartmann and the French poets, and he had as little power as Hartmann of inventing a story. He borrowed his *Tristan and Isolde* from a French poem, which he followed almost slavishly, even where he would have done better to differ from it. The actual poem which he made use of is lost, and we only know it from abbreviations. Since the time when [German poet] Eilhard von Oberge had written his poem of *Tristan and Isolde* after a French model, new poets in France had taken up the story afresh, and refined its incidents. Gottfried's work was far superior to Eilhard's, with which he was acquainted, both through the greater perfection of his French original and also through the greater perfection of his own style. No French treatment of the story, as far as we know,

has attained to the artistic perfection of Gottfried's *Tristan;* it was reserved for a German to give a classical form to this famous mediæval legend, which in human interest and life-like characters far surpasses the Arthur-romances. Gottfried's refined diction, his flowing language and rich imagery, were admirably adapted for the description of an overpowering passion and its destructive effect on character. The irresistible force of love is symbolised in the legend by a powerful love-potion. While German heroic poetry of the twelfth century freed itself as much as possible from fabulous elements, the Celtic stories which were introduced into German literature from France again revived a whole world of marvels. The enlightenment of the earlier period gave place to a romantic delight in the supernatural and improbable. By means of a magic potion Tristan becomes forever attached to Isolde. The love which thus arises is an overruling passion, triumphing over the greatest difficulties, and asserting itself in defence of right and law. It leads to deceit and immorality, and yet from a certain point of view it is a moral power, for though an egoistic passion it yet goes contrary to egoism. Such a passion makes a man endure all the agonies of longing and the most terrible dangers without flinching, and developes in him all the energy of devotion and self-sacrifice. It makes him bad, but never vulgar. But love is not the exclusive theme of the legend or of Gottfried's poem; it also presents us with a glorious picture of chivalry in its first bloom. The hero first appears at the court of his uncle Mark in Cornwall as a charming clever boy, who wins all hearts. He has perfect manners, and is an excellent chessplayer, huntsman, musician, and poet. In a word, he is 'höfisch' (chivalrous) through and through. After being dubbed a knight by Mark, he avenges his father's death on Morgan of Brittany. He then conquers Morold of Ireland, and thus frees Cornwall from a humiliating poll-tax. He kills a dragon in Ireland, makes peace between that country and Cornwall, and wins the Irish Princess Isolde the Fair for his uncle. But on board the vessel which is conducting the bride to her future home, Tristan and Isolde, through an unfortunate accident, drink the love-potion meant for Isolde and Mark. The mischief cannot be counteracted, and their passionate love makes them faithless to Mark, and gradually corrupts all who are connected with them. Tristan flies to the continent, enters military service, becomes acquainted with a second Isolde, Isolde the Whitehanded, and marries her; but he cannot forget the fair Queen of Cornwall, he visits her again and so makes the second Isolde miserable. Being wounded in some adventure he secretly summons his beloved to come and cure him. But his plans are frustrated by Isolde the Whitehanded, and Mark's wife dies on Tristan's dead body.

This is the complete story, but Gottfried's poem breaks off suddenly in the midst of the sophistic monologue in which Tristan resolves to marry; the completion of the work is said to have been prevented by the poet's death, about the year 1210.

The original intention of the legend seems to have been to show how noble knighthood may be ruined by passion; but Gottfried von Strassburg and his predecessors did not give this interpretation to the story. The German poet selected the theme with a distinct object. In all probability he was not a nobleman by birth, but wished to make himself appear as aristocratic as possible. He must have received a careful education, for he borrows from the classical writers, especially from Ovid, who has written so much of love, and when he takes a very high flight he introduces classical mythology. He is well acquainted with French, but he parades his knowledge of it till it becomes wearisome, and even goes so far as to speak of his fatherland only as Allemagne, 'Almanje.' He adopts as gospel the easy-going, tolerant view of life held by the nobility, defending it with the inexorable logic of a fanatical apostle, and actually declaring that without love no one can possess either virtue or honour. He recognises no bounds for the desires of men, except the public opinion of refined society, which for its part allows everything that does not create a painful sensation. There is no hint of any higher code of morals than this. Hartmann had already spoken of the gallantry of God, which makes him grant the requests of beautiful women; but Gottfried's God even helps Isolde the Fair, in deceiving her husband, and in falsifying the ordeal by Divine judgment. Gottfried is not content with describing passion faithfully, but he takes the part of the guilty lovers against the outwitted King Mark. All charms are heaped upon Tristan and Isolde, and the King is made to appear mean and contemptible in various ways.

The fact that the author is evidently writing with a purpose in view, i.e. that of defending the chivalrous philosophy of life even in its utmost extremes, introduces an element of stiffness into this otherwise sensational narrative. Moreover the author cannot free himself from that tendency to personify abstract qualities, which is one of the characteristics of the chivalrous epics, and this tendency often betrays him into artificial conceits. For instance, Tristan is armed for the fight, not like Aeneas, by Vulcan, but by Magnanimity, Goodness, Reason, and Culture. Again, in describing the woody Grotto of Love where Tristan and Isolde live for a time in banishment, Gottfried not only paints each detail, but makes each bear some reference to love; in this he resembles the mediæval commentators on the Bible, who not only took the words of the text literally, but also gave them an allegorical meaning.

In his attitude towards questions of literary art too, Gottfried appears as a conscious theorist, who wishes to enforce his opinions. In one often-mentioned passage of his poem he drops the thread of his narrative to enter on an argument with his poetical contemporaries, and set forth his own principles of art; he is describing the ceremony of dubbing Tristan a knight, when he suddenly stops to declare that he does not mean to emulate his predecessors in the description of the feast, and then goes on to speak not only of the epic poets who preceded him, but also of the lyric poets, who have nothing to do with the matter. The characteristic sketches which he draws of them are certainly most brilliant, and furnish the finest examples of the intellectual acuteness and delicate touches which could at that time be applied in literary criticism. He mentions with admiration Hartmann von Aue, Blicker von Steinach, (only known to us by a couple of songs,) Heinrich von Veldeke, Reinmar von Hagenau and Walther von der Vogelweide. On the other hand, he speaks in terms of the strongest disapproval of an unnamed writer [German poet Wolfram von Eschenbach], whom he compares to a conjuror or a juggler, a man who seeks out dark sayings, and who ought to send out an interpreter with each of his tales. Gottfried, for his part, will only adjudge poetic laurels to the writer whose diction is smooth as a level plain, which a man of simple understanding can traverse without stumbling. (pp. 157-61)

W. Scherer, "Hartmann von Aue and Gottfried von Strassburg," in his A History of German Literature, *Vol. 1, edited by F. Max Müller, translated by Mrs. F. C. Conybeare, Charles Scribner's Sons, 1899, pp. 145-61.*

An excerpt from *Tristan and Isolde*

Now that those two, both maid and man,
Isolt she, and he Tristan,
Had drunk the potion, lo, straightway,
Without an instant of delay,
The World's Unrest was with them there,
Love, ever ready to ensnare
The hearts of lovers swiftly gliding
Into their hearts and there abiding.
Ere they could rally their amazed
And overtaken hearts, Love raised
Her triumphing banner, and her sway
Laid on them both, without gainsay.
They who had hitherto been twain
Became as one, so never again
To part. Their thoughts were now no more
Contrary-minded as before.
Isolt's enmity was gone.
Love, reconciling them, had drawn
Their hearts together, cleansed, and free
From every trace of enmity,
So that each to the other was
As clear as is a looking-glass.
Between them they had but one heart.
What grieved her was an aching smart
To him, and this her grief renewed.
Being one, they were alike imbued
With pain and pleasure both, yet still
They kept concealed their mutual will.
And the cause thereof was doubt and shame.
She was ashamed, he felt the same
As she did. Then she was not sure
Of him, nor did he feel secure
Regarding her. Their hearts were set
Blindly on one desire, and yet
For both it was no easy thing
To break the silence, and to fling
The veil aside, which each one drew
Masking what each desired and knew.
                                        [11,711-44]

Gottfried von Strassburg, in Medieval German Lyrics, *translated by Margaret Fitzgerald Richey, Oliver and Boyd, 1958.*

Daniel Bussier Shumway (essay date 1904)

[*In the essay below, Shumway responds to the criticism that Gottfried's* Tristan and Isolde *is immoral. The poem, he contends, is less a discussion of marital infidelity than a meditation on the meaning of honor and virtue.*]

Few poems of German literature have given rise to so various and contradictory opinions as has Gottfried's ***Tristan und Isolde.*** Virtually all critics agree as to the beauty of the descriptions and the mastery of the niceties of style. The melodious flow of the verse, the limpid beauty of the language, and his surprising power of psychological analysis have earned for Gottfried the title of a master of his art and a high rank among German poets of any age. Few writers have excelled him in the ability to paint the conflicting emotions of the heart under the stress of an overpowering passion. Many of the older critics, however, rendered their tribute of praise almost in spite of themselves, for all this manifold beauty was in their minds only the attractive cloak for gross immorality and excited only aversion and disgust. The severe condemnation which the legend received at the hands of the poet [Robert] Southey [in his introduction to *The Byrth, Lyf and Actes of Kyng Arthur,* 1817], for example, is too well known to need more than a passing mention. His attitude is pardonable when one remembers that he was acquainted with the tale only in the crude, unpolished English version of *Sir Tristrem.* One is, however, surprised at the harsh criticism passed on Gottfried's poem by so able and, as a rule, so just a critic as Karl Lachmann, who [in his *Auswahl aus den mhd. Dichtern des 13. Jh.*] said of it: "anderes als üppigkeit oder gotteslästerung boten die hauptteile seiner weichlichen, unsittlichen erzählung nicht dar." Massmann likewise, in his edition of Gottfried, expressed himself in terms hardly less severe. Groote, who was one of the first to protest against the severe criticism of the poem, tried to condone the sin of the lovers by declaring that Isolde was married to Marke only in appearance and that Tristan was her real husband. In this he was followed by Simrock in his translation of Gottfried. That this view, however, is untenable, everyone who has read the poem attentively is well aware. Later critics, therefore, have contented themselves in the main with emphasizing the fact that Gottfried has taken a story of crime and low intrigue and transformed it into a poem of surpassing beauty. This is true enough, although much of the credit for doing this belongs in all probability to Gottfried's source, the French poet Thomas. This evidence is, however, largely æsthetic in character, and is not valid in the sphere of morality. The proofs must be sought rather in the motive which inspired the author, and in the difference of attitude on questions of morality and custom existing between mediæval and modern times. It is, therefore, the purpose of this study to consider the subject from these two points of view, to institute an inquiry into Gottfried's motive in writing the poem, to investigate his method of depicting the love scenes and his attitude toward the legend, and lastly to bring as much light to bear upon his conceptions of honor and virtue as may be gleaned from what he himself tells us in the poem.

Taking up first the question of motive, it will be generally admitted, I think, that in the realm of literature this is a prime factor in deciding questions of morality. It is not so much the incidents narrated, but the way in which they are told and the purpose animating the author, which form the final court of appeal. The historian or the literary artist may deal with the most delicate subjects, if his purpose be to instruct or admonish. To select only one of the many examples which suggest themselves to the mind: the so-called problem plays of modern literature may be disagreeable, they may depict a side of life whose existence we would gladly deny, but only a complete misconception of their purpose can lead us to call them immoral. When, however, a writer becomes purposely suggestive, when the motive is no longer to point a moral, but to appeal to depraved tastes, to excite the senses by veiled allusions or by detailed descriptions of erotic scenes, then we are forced to admit that he has been guilty of immorality which no art, however skilful, will excuse.

When we consider Gottfried's poem from this point of view, we find that it belongs to the first category. It is the narrative of an overpowering passion from which it is impossible for the victims to escape, which overthrows the barriers of honor and virtue, renders the lovers miserable despite their love, and finally leads to their tragic death. That Tristan was predestined for such a life of sinful love is clearly pointed out by Gottfried. Had the poet lived in the nineteenth century, he would have talked a great deal about environment and inherited predispositions. Having had the misfortune of being born over six hundred years before Darwin and the modern scientific school, he did what was virtually the same thing—he gave the detailed history of Tristan's parents to show that he was predestined for such a life by being a child of love. Furthermore, when the name Tristan is given to the hero, Gottfried comments upon its appropriateness, deriving it from the French *triste* ["sadness"]. "Behold," he exclaims, "what a sad life was given to him to live!" Unfortunately, the poet did not live to complete his work, but we know from the English *Sir Tristrem* and the Norse saga how Thomas finished the story, and there is not the slightest doubt but that Gottfried would have ended the poem in a way which would have made it perfectly clear that the tragic death of the lovers was the necessary consequence of their sin, and the atonement for it. In fact, he indicates this in ll. 2011-15, where he remarks:

> Sehet an den trûreclîchen tôt,
> der alle sîne herzenôt
> mit einem ende beslôz,
> daz alles tôdes übergenôz
> und aller triuwe ein galle was;

"a death which surpassed all other deaths and which contained more bitterness than any other sorrow." This passage occurs near the beginning in the description of Tristan's christening and strikes at once the keynote of the whole poem.

Gottfried's purpose is, therefore, to depict the course and the tragic consequences of a sinful love. In no case does he endeavor to present this love in an attractive or alluring light—quite the contrary. Toward the end of the poem his comments upon honor and virtue in women become more and more frequent. It is as if he felt his end approaching and did not wish to leave the world in doubt as to his attitude toward the story. Thus, after Tristan is banished from Marke's court, the poet remarks that no good woman would give up her honor to save her life. A few lines farther he adds: "There is no more beautiful thing in the world than a woman who is devoted to *mâze* [i.e., moderation]. The man who is loved by such a woman is the possessor of every earthly joy and carries a living paradise in his heart. He has no cause for anxiety and need not desire to exchange his life for that of Tristan, for a faithful wife does more for her husband than ever Isolde did for Tristan." Surely no words could express more clearly the critical, nay condemnatory, attitude of the poet toward the legend. Again, in another passage, just after the lovers have yielded to their fatal passion, he moralizes at some length upon infidelity in love. "We have a false conception of love," he tells us. "We sow weeds and expect roses and lilies to spring up, and this cannot be; we must reap what we sow. We sow love with falseness and dishonesty, and so it bears only evil and pain. Real love has been banished and we have naught but the name."

Let us now turn to the consideration of the second point, that of method, and inquire how Gottfried has treated the love scenes in the poem. This, as has already been brought out, is of the greatest importance in judging of the morality of a piece of literature, for it gives us additional and important evidence as to the motive of the author. The question in Gottfried's case is doubly important, since the character of the story is such that a poet who delights in depicting scenes of passion has ample opportunity in the course of the narrative to indulge his bent to the full. A study of Gottfried's poem from this point of view reveals at once the fact that the poet observes the utmost delicacy in dealing with erotic situations. He introduces love scenes only where he cannot avoid them without departing from the story, and when he does introduce them, it is done so simply, so charmingly, that we cannot take offense. Take, for example, the love scene between Tristan's Rivalin and Blancheflour. It was necessary for the poet to describe this scene in some detail in order to show that Tristan was a child of love. Here was a chance to indulge in description of the most erotic character. But what do we find? A scene so artless and so touching in its simplicity and delicacy that one must search far to find its equal. Overcome by her grief at Rivalin's supposedly fatal wound, Blancheflour falls in a swoon upon the edge of his couch. Her sweet presence revives in the dying hero the almost extinct spark of life. Their lips meet in kisses and then the poet adds simply:

> dâ nach so was vil harte unlanc,
> unz daz ir beider wille ergie,
> und daz vil süeze wîp enpfie
> ein kint von sînem lîbe.

—ll. 1320-23.

So, much was necessary, as stated, to show the character of Tristan's conception; the rest is left to the imagination of the reader. Here there is certainly no attempt at passionate, or even suggestive, description, and yet this is the most detailed of all the love scenes of the poem. What would not a Wieland or a Byron or a d'Annunzio have made of this episode?

Further, when after drinking the fatal potion Tristan and Isolde have confessed their mutual love and Brangaene consents to provide them with an opportunity to meet rather than see her mistress pine away, and Tristan steals softly to Isolde's darkened cabin, we should expect of a mediæval poet a most detailed description of the scene. Gottfried, however, merely relates how the physician Love took the lovesick Tristan by the hand and led him to the bedside of Isolde and gave him to her and her to him as medicine. Love bound their hearts so firmly, he tells us, that they could never be severed. Then, instead of describing the scene further, he begins a long rambling discussion of two hundred lines on the character and the effects of love, in the course of which he condemns a passion based upon treachery and deceit, and sings the praises of a love coupled with fidelity. When he finally returns to the lovers, it is only to remark that they succeeded in curing one another of their sorrow and pain.

Again, no incident in the poem has given more offense than the substitution of Brangaene for Isolde. This is not the place to justify its introduction, as we are concerned here only with Gottfried's method of treatment. Suffice it to say that he found the incident in the original, and that it seemed to offer the only way by which Brangaene might save the reputation of her mistress and make good her negligence which had brought upon the lovers their fatal passion. Now how does Gottfried treat so difficult a scene? Brangaene at first refuses thus to debase herself and consents only after repeated urging, and because she feels that she must pay the penalty of her carelessness and at any cost save the honor of Isolde, for whose happiness the queen had made her responsible. There is no detailed description of the scene. The poet hastens to assure us that Brangaene's thoughts were "lûter unde guot," and that she slipped away as soon as the object of the substitution had been accomplished.

In the other recorded instances of meetings between the lovers Gottfried contents himself, as a rule, with the mere mention of the fact, as, for example, in the series of rendez-vous in the orchard during Marke's absence. Here we read merely that they met without detection eight times in as many days. In the beautiful idyl of the *Minnegrotte* we find lengthy descriptions of nature, of the arrangement of the grotto, of the manner in which the lovers passed their days, but not even the mention of a love scene, although the opportunity to introduce such a passage could not have been more favorable. Had Gottfried been fond of indulging in erotic descriptions, he would not have allowed so favorable a chance to pass unused.

Judged, therefore, from the standpoints of motive and method, Gottfried must be exonerated from much of the blame attached to him. There are still some objections, however, which remain to be answered. Chief among these is the fact that the poet does not directly pose as a moralist and that he does not censure the lovers more severely. It has been pointed out that Marke, the deluded husband, plays the part of a stupid fool who deserves to be deceived for his credulity, and that those who act as spies upon the lovers are not represented as champions of morality, but are accused of a lack of courtly breeding (*unhövescheit*).

This is to some extent true, but it does not prove Gottfried's frivolity as conclusively as has been claimed. Those who make this criticism quite forget that a piece of literature must be judged from the viewpoint of the time and place in which it was written. Not only customs, but also the conceptions of honor and virtue, vary from age to age and may be different in different parts of the world, or in different classes of society.

The people of the Middle Ages, and especially those classes among whom chivalry took its rise had a more naïve way of looking at things than we today. Their ideals were often totally different from ours and resembled more those of the ancient world. The moral value of absolute truthfulness does not seem to have been appreciated by them any more than by the Greeks, who admired above all things craftiness and cunning. Tristan of our poem is just such a character as Ulysses or Pylades. With a quiet smile on his lips and with an ingenuity which astonishes us, he invents again and again the most plausible stories to account for the condition in which he found himself at a given moment. Thus, when he had been carried off by Norwegian traders and landed on an unknown coast, he tells the pilgrims whom he meets that he had lost his way while hunting in the neighborhood. Not only does he invent the story, but he describes the circumstances with such minutiæ that he is at once believed. That we are expected to admire him for his ready invention is evident from the words with which the episode is introduced. Again, on his second trip to Ireland Tristan goes boldly on shore, although he knows that the Irish have sworn to kill all men from Kurneval, trusting to his skill in deceiving to preserve him from harm. He makes no pretense of concealing his purpose from his fellow-travelers, but says frankly: "I must lie to them today to the extent of my ability." Such examples occur frequently, and might be largely multiplied if space would permit.

That not only Gottfried, but also his contemporaries, justified such deceit is shown by the fact that Tristan was universally considered as a model of courtly breeding. As strict a moralist as Thomasin von Zirclære holds him up as a pattern for the young to follow. Similar characters are found in the *Iwein* of [German lyric poet] Hartman von Aue, whom Gottfried took as his model. Thus the waiting maid Lunette and the young squire, who successfully deceived their mistress and induced her to marry the hero, are highly extolled. Further, the maid who cured Iwein of his madness is called wise because she tells a falsehood (*lügemaere*) to account for the disappearance of the salve used in the cure.

Another feature in which the age of chivalry differed from modern times, and which has a still closer bearing upon the question of Gottfried's morality, was the stress laid upon the strict observance of a formal courtly etiquette (*hövescheit*). Provided a man followed its dictates to the letter, other qualities were of little importance. This was, after all, only natural, for it was courtly breeding which had gradually transformed the semi-barbarous western lands into a semblance of culture and civilization. It alone distinguished often the knight from the *vilein* or boor, the noble of the twelfth and thirteenth centuries from his war-like but uncouth ancestors. The courtly poets are, therefore, continually using the phrase *durch hövescheit* in commenting upon the fine breeding of their heroes. Even more popular epics, such as the *Nibelungenlied,* make similar use of it. Now, one of the worst infringements of this formal etiquette is tale-bearing. No matter what happened, courtly etiquette demanded that a knight should be able to hold his tongue. The poems of the minnesingers are full of severe condemnation of the envious *merkaere,* who disturbed the peace of lovers. Gottfried, we find, takes the same view. He accuses the knight Marjodo and the dwarf Melot, who betray Tristan to Marke, of *unhövescheit* and scores them in no measured terms. He begins chap. 24 with a long homily on the despicableness of false friendship in general and that of Marjodo in particular, and even goes so far as to call the knight a dog and the dwarf a serpent, although he usually avoids such expressions as being uncourtly. We find [German poet] Eilhart taking exactly the same view in his version. In fact, he waxes still more indignant at the "boorishness" of the knight, whom he calls a coward (*zage*), and whom he wishes the devil would drown in the Rhine for his false friendship toward Tristan. His statements are called *nîdesch lugenmære,* although they are only too true.

With an unsurpassed beauty and melody of verse, with a marvelous knowledge of the human heart, and a searching analysis of motives and emotions, Gottfried has succeeded in giving us a poem which will stand for all time as one of the few great tragedies of love. . . .

—Daniel Bussier Shumway

Still another conception which we must thoroughly understand in order to avoid misjudging Gottfried's poem is the courtly use of the word *êre,* which seldom meant "honor" in the modern acceptation, but generally signified "reputation," the respect in which a person was held. Honor with us is mainly subjective; in the poems of chivalry it is principally objective. It was synonymous with outward appearances, and so long as these were kept, *êre* was untarnished. This is clearly brought out in Gottfried's poem. When, for example, Isolde succeeds in triumphantly standing the test of the hot iron, the poet remarks that her *êre* was restored, whereas from a modern point of view the deceit to which she had recourse dishonored her more than ever. Again, when the lovers are banished from the court, they do not grieve on account of their guilt toward Marke, but solely because the discovery of their sinful love had brought upon them the loss of their reputation at the court. And when Marke concludes to take them back into favor, they rejoice especially over their restoration to *êre.*

Most characteristic for the courtly conception of honor is

the attitude of the lovers after drinking the love potion. The thought that it would be more honorable to accept the consequences of their love does not seem to have occurred to them. In their minds it was decidedly less dishonorable to deceive Marke than to cause a public scandal. Tristan had promised to obtain the hand of Isolde for his uncle, and this promise must be kept or he would be dishonored, i.e., would lose his *êre*. The poet does not leave us in the slightest doubt as to which was the correct course for Tristan to pursue. Line 12511 he remarks:

swie sanfte uns mit der liebe sî,
so müezen wir doch ie dâ bî
gedenken der êren.

Again, a few lines farther down (12517-22) he continues:

swie wol Tristande tæte
daz leben, daz er hæte,
sin êre zôch in doch dervan.
sîn triuwe lag im allez an,
daz er ir wol gedæhte
und Marke sîn wîp bræhte.

Love and honor are in conflict, and although the former had conquered before, now honor is triumphant and love is forced to give way for the time being. A modern poet would have treated the subject in the very opposite manner. He would have shown that true honor demanded above all absolute truthfulness, and would have made Tristan confess to Marke the secret of his love, and either allowed him to suffer the consequences of betraying the king's confidence, or, if the story was to end happily, would have made Marke magnanimous enough to pardon Tristan's fault and renounce all claims to Isolde. Gottfried, however, is a child of his time, and we cannot expect him to exhibit feelings and hold ideals different from those of his contemporaries. It is, therefore, unjust to call him immoral because he places *êre*, i.e., reputation, above absolute truthfulness.

Another characteristic difference existing between modern times and the age of chivalry which must be borne in mind in judging of Gottfried's poem is to be found in the attitude toward the passion of love. Civilization was cruder, men were more naïve in those days, and their passions were not held in check by considerations of propriety and of society as in our time. Love was supreme, and few ties, however sacred, could stand before it. The many *tagelieder* of the Middle High German and the *albas* of Provençal literature are not creations of a depraved morality, but expressions of the belief that love carried with it its own justification under all circumstances. The prevailing custom of marrying young girls, often against their will, for family or state reasons to men whom they often had never seen had resulted in the gradual degradation of marriage. The question as to whether love could exist between husband and wife we find being discussed and gravely decided in the negative. The frequent lack of congeniality led husband and wife to bestow their affections elsewhere. Such secret love naturally attracted the adventurous spirit of the knights, and the prudence and cunning necessary to escape detection possessed a similar charm for the woman of leisure. The result was that violations of the marriage tie were not considered so heinous nor were they so severely punished as in a stricter age.

An interesting example of this is to be found in MS R of Raimbaut de Vaqueiras's poem *Carros,* where the marquis finds his wife asleep in the arms of the troubadour, much as Marke discovers Tristan and Isolde. Instead of avenging his honor on the spot, the marquis merely substitutes his cloak for that of Raimbaut, as Marke does with the swords in the grotto scene, and leaves the lovers undisturbed. When the troubadour awakes and sees that he has been detected, he proceeds at once to the injured husband and begs his pardon. This the latter grants, with the remark that he forgave the theft this time, but that it must not occur again. Such indifference on the part of the marquis seems incredible to us. It offers, however, a most striking parallel to our poem, and at the same time a commentary on the lack of spirit which Marke exhibits.

The susceptibility of woman to love is the favorite theme of the troubadours. [Twelfth-century French poet] Arnaut Daniel once declared that there was no woman who did not wish to yield and who would not, if rightly wooed. It was considered wrong, however, to yield lightly to the solicitations of the lover. Eilhart expresses this view clearly when he makes one of Isolde's ladies-in-waiting indignantly spurn the advances of Kehenis. Gottfried likewise is far from being an apostle of indiscriminate love. If, however, love already exists between a man and a woman, if it has proved too strong for them, if they have been forced to surrender to their passion, then it is foolish to have further scruples in the matter. This is the feeling of the age of chivalry, and Gottfried makes this clear when he remarks, that those who have gone so far that all strangeness between them has ceased to exist are thieves of their own happiness if they do not give themselves over to the enjoyment of their love. This is such a matter of course for Gottfried that he wastes no further words upon it. The intrigues and deceit necessary to procure the enjoyment of this love he considers deplorable, but nevertheless justifiable. If, then, love be thought to be an overpowering passion to which everyone must yield whom it makes its prey; if, moreover, it be so supreme that no obligation, however binding, can stand before it, then the actions of Tristan and Isolde are certainly less reprehensible from this point of view than when judged by our moral standard. From the standpoint of courtly chivalry, Gottfried's Tristan is in many respects the ideal lover, devoted to his mistress and faithful to the end. He is no gay, wanton butterfly fluttering from one flower to another, but a man whose whole life is filled with this one passion—his love for Isolde.

Whatever, therefore, may be the general opinion of the immorality of the legend in its cruder forms, it must be evident from the arguments adduced that no blame attaches to Gottfried, unless indeed we go so far as to censure him for choosing such a subject for poetic treatment. Granted, however, the right to select such a theme—and no less a man than [German poet Johann von] Goethe was a strong champion of the freedom of the poet in this respect—then we must concede that Gottfried has sought throughout to lift the tale out of the realm of the commonplace into the sphere of the ideal, that under his pen the story of a guilty passion becomes a grand picture of two souls struggling against an overpowering love, which draws them slowly but surely together and from which there is no possibility of escape—a love which renders its possessors, not happy, but miserable, and which finally ends in their tragic death. We have seen that the poet does not hold the lovers up as examples for us to imitate; on the contrary, he pauses again and again to sing the praises of virtue and moderation (*mâze*) in woman. His views on honor and love, which differ so radically from ours, find their explanation in the attitude of the age of chivalry touching these points. His motive has been shown to be pure, and the evident intention to refrain from all mention of unpleasant or gross thoughts, and the delicacy with which scenes of the most intimate character are depicted, suffice finally to clear him of the least suspicion of immorality. With an unsurpassed beauty and melody of verse, with a marvelous knowledge of the human heart, and a searching analysis of motives and emotions, Gottfried has succeeded in giving us a poem which will stand for all time as one of the few great tragedies of love, and which must disarm criticism except on the part of those who fix their eyes obstinately on one point and thus fail to see the grandeur of the struggle and the beauty of the description which have placed the poem in the front rank of the literature of the world. (pp. 423-36)

> *Daniel Bussier Shumway, "The Moral Element in Gottfried's* Tristan und Isolde," *in* Modern Philology, *Vol. 1, No. 3, January, 1904, pp. 423-36.*

Calvin Thomas   (essay date 1909)

[*Thomas was an American educator who wrote and edited several works on Germanic languages and literature. In the following excerpt, he notes Gottfried's adherence to the traditional sources of the Tristan legend*

King Mark kisses Tristan.

and concludes that "while Gottfried lacked high seriousness . . . , he was an artist of rare quality."]

[Gottfried von Strassburg] was frankly and at all times a poet of this world. If he ever passed through spiritual crises or brooded painfully over the mysteries of sin and redemption, there is no trace of it in his writings. Of the life of Gottfried von Strassburg almost nothing can be made out with certainty. He was a minnesinger of some repute, but his fame rests on his love-intoxicated romance of *Tristan,* in which he followed the French trouvère, Thomas of Brittany. When he had written nearly twenty thousand verses and carried the story to the point of Tristan's entanglement with the second Isold, his work was interrupted by death. He seems to have died about 1210.

Of the French *Tristan,* by Thomas the Trouvère, only a few fragments have been preserved; but as we have an English translation and a Norse translation, it is possible to judge with some confidence as to Gottfried's merit in the way of originality. So far as the mere narrative is concerned, he followed his original pretty faithfully. His introduction shows that he felt the pride of an honest craftsman in telling the story as he had found it in the best authority, without falsifying the tradition with inventions of his own. He wished to reproduce its incidents, and its characteristic savour, letting the whole argument develop in a natural human way out of one all-subduing passion. He had no fancy for the eccentric, and [German poet] Wolfram's "wild tales" were an offence to him. On the other hand, within the limits of a tolerably faithful rendering, there was abundant room for comment and reflection, and here it is that Gottfried shows a distinct poetic individuality. He has not Wolfram's depth, but he is a more even artist than Wolfram, in whom there are long and dreary stretches of sheer rubbish. Gottfried never falls far below the level of his own best.

The introduction to *Tristan* is mainly a warm eulogy of the love romance as pabulum for noble souls. Gottfried avers that he does not write for hard worldlings, but for those who know what love is and gladly bear its pain for the sake of its joy. Such, he thinks, will have great satisfaction in reading of the immortal pair, Tristan and Isold. In the telling of the story the non-moral character of the original is faithfully preserved. From the first moment of their surrender to the delirium of passion, Tristan and Isold have no rule of conduct other than to avoid detection. A large part of the poem is taken up with the tricks and stratagems by which the adulterous queen evades or allays the suspicions of her simple-minded husband, and the stories are told without care for their moral aspect. Gottfried is not in the least anxious lest the depravity exhibited by his hero and heroine may forfeit the reader's sympathy. They wrap themselves in lies, plot to murder the all too faithful Brangäne, and make God himself the accomplice of their iniquity. But it is all told as if such things did not signify when set over against their great love and their monumental fidelity to one another.

The tone of *Tristan* is serious, yet nothing is taken seriously but carnal love. The famous episode of the ordeal of God is significant. King Marke, harassed by suspicion, demands that Isolde prove her innocence by taking the hot iron in her hand. In her distress the guilty queen resolves to appeal to God, hoping that he will be "courteous" to a woman and help her out of her strait. After prayer a happy thought occurs to her. She writes to Tristan, asking him to present himself in disguise on the day of the trial. He does so, appearing as a shabby pilgrim. She selects the pious-looking stranger to carry her from the boat, and on the way she whispers to him that he is to stumble and fall with her in his arms. Then she goes to church and makes public oath that she has never lain in the arms of any man save the poor pilgrim in whose embrace all the world has just seen her. After this she handles the hot iron unscathed. "Thus," says Gottfried,

> Thus was the truth made manifest
> To all the world by valid test
> That Christ, in Heaven, the Worshipful,
> Is like a sleeve—adjustable—
> Adapts himself with pliant ease,
> Takes any shape that one may please;
> Is ready at the heart's desire
> To help the saint or help the liar.

This sounds rather blasphemous, but there is elsewhere no trace of free-thinking in Gottfried. Probably the shaft was aimed not at religion, but at the clerical humbug of the ordeal as a means of determining guilt and innocence.

But while Gottfried lacked high seriousness and was content to portray chivalry on its earthly side, he was an artist of rare quality. As a chooser of words and a fashioner of pleasing couplets he has no superior. Take him where one will, he is always graceful, lucid, readable. Sometimes, indeed, his fondness for the striking phrase and melodious jingle betrays him into mere poetic fooling. (pp. 78-81)

> *Calvin Thomas, "The Exotic Romances of Knighthood," in his* A History of German Literature, *1909. Reprint by Kennikat Press, 1970, pp. 65-85.*

August Closs   (essay date 1944)

[*An Austrian educator and author, Closs was a scholar of German literature. In the following excerpt from the introduction to his edition of* Tristan and Isolde, *he offers an evaluation of Gottfried's originality and poetic technique, lauding the poem as one of "the immortal treasures of the world's literature."*]

Gottfried's ***Tristan und Îsolt*** (about 1210) belongs to the immortal treasures of the world's literature. His lyrical epic still makes a direct appeal to us to-day, for it is at once personal and impersonal as every true work of art should be.

After more than seven hundred years ***Tristan und Îsolt*** provides a mine of material for the student of comparative literature—a material rich in legends, fairy tales, mythological, Celtic and Classical motifs, whilst modern poets are still irresistibly drawn to the fierce and passionate tale that underlies the mediæval romance. But indeed the very graceful form in Gottfried's case clothes a sensibility and ideas of unexpected profundity which verge on the meta-

physical and make his poem appear almost as the gospel of a religious faith, the religion of *Minne* ["love"]. (p. xvi)

Among the mediaeval Tristan romances Gottfried's poem stands out as the unrivalled masterpiece. He is no mere translator who refashions his material with supreme skill. In contrast to his source, [Anglo–Norman poet] Thomas, he modifies the form rather than the motifs. Gottfried's originality lies in his artistic style, his interpretation of emotions, in the grace and musical beauty of his work. (p. xxxii)

The main problem which concerns us is the question of Gottfried's poetic originality. . . . Instead of describing directly, he often suggests the spiritual meaning of his poem to us through the form, as for instance in his introductory lines in which Gottfried from an almost scholastic tone works up to the pregnant expression:

> *ein senedære, ein senedærîn*
> *ein man, ein wîp; ein wîp, ein man,*
> *Tristan, Îsôt; Îsôt, Tristan.*

All external things have fallen away, the reader stands ready to be initiated into the whole mystery of *Minne*, which is in fact to Gottfried almost a substitute for religion. With Gottfried the *love-potion* is no longer reason and excuse, it is a poetic symbol, and Gottfried perhaps kept the love-drink because it made an excellent climax. Love-potion or not—the climax in his ***Tristan und Îsolt*** was bound to come. A careful study of the text will confirm this. Îsolt's interest in his *lîp alsô gebære* (10031) and her curiosity about Tristan's weapons are surely far more than objective inquisitiveness as to his birth and station in life; or does it smack of modern psychology to interpret her prolonged fury against him as something more than loyalty to Môrolt, anger at the deceit, and wounded pride? Then in the love-potion scene the manner in which she pushes him away (11574ff.):

> *. . . habet iuch hin,*
> *tuot iuwer arme hin dan!*
> *ir sît ein harte müelîch man . . .*

when he tries to comfort and embrace her,—all this combines to create a crescendo that we feel the outbreak of their passion inevitable. This does not mean that [German poet] Wolfram in contrast to Gottfried lacks all form. If the classical serenity of Gottfried, who lived in the borderland between France and Germany, has much in common with Thomas in his poetic art and seems remote from Wolfram's expressive, rugged style which is so often claimed as characteristically German, we must not forget that Mozart who too in some ways recalls Gottfried perhaps more poignantly than any other artist, also represents *one* side of the German's dual nature.

Thomas and Gottfried enhance the psychological content of the saga, but Gottfried is more steeped in its spiritual aspect than Thomas. We may claim that the Prelude was contributed by Gottfried, although the nucleus of many passages is to be found in [Thomas's French translation of the courtly epic, c. 1170]. The acrostic (1-44), which acts as a sort of captatio benevolentiae, reminds one of similar passages in the works of mediaeval poets. A further original contribution are lines 45-70, which were however inspired by a few lines in Thomas 3126/30:

> A tuz amanz saluz i dit,
> As pensis e as amerus,
> As emvius, as desirus,
> As enveisiez e as purvers,
> A tuz cels ki orunt ces vers.

Gottfried speaks from his own experience (71-100) while Thomas (3136/44 and 1087) denies any personal experience; see also Gottfried 101-118, 167-186, 187-242. His request (239ff.) that his audience should lend an indulgent ear to his story, is a literary tradition of the age. The Prelude is so significant, for here, as we have noticed, he reveals the moral and literary interpretation of his life and work. Gottfried's mood is one of mingled joy and sorrow (204/5):

> swem nie von liebe leit geschach,
> dem geschach ouch liep von liebe nie.

Thus the mood of the lovers too alternates from joy to sorrow. Death alone can bring them relief (18348): *ein lîp, ein leben daz sîn wir.* In this way Gottfried reveals the profound tragedy of his Tristan; it is the alliance of life and death (62ff. + 233ff.). But our poet lifts the tragedy from the aesthetic to an almost religious plane by allowing the lovers to yearn for the consummation of their love in death (12502ff.): *dirre tôt der tuot mir wol, / solte diu wunneclîche Îsôt / iemer alsus sîn mîn tôt, / sô wolte ich gerne werben / umb' ein êweclîchez sterben*—an unmistakable anticipation of [German composer] Richard Wagner's *Liebestod,* although Gottfried's lighter even slightly frivolous tone is peculiarly his own, with its haunting Mozartian quality—hovering between joy and anguish, frivolity and the profound. (pp. xl-xli)

A detailed comparison of Thomas and Gottfried shows that the latter was also an outstanding and careful psychologist. Gottfried's conception of love is not merely sensual, but love has for him a profoundly spiritual quality, which can be intensified until it becomes mystic. The clear motivation of Gottfried's poem has long been recognized [as in French scholar F. Piquet's *L'Originalité de Gottfried von Strassburg,* 1905]. He depicts most charmingly the gradual awakening to love, Îsolt's maidenly shyness when she tries to approach her lover as if by chance (11941ff. *Tristan und Îsolt*). Gottfried endeavours to motivate events more skilfully than his source, as for example the scene with the cowardly steward, after Tristan has slain the dragon. Here Gottfried introduces the Cornish knights, whom Môrolt had taken captive at the Irish court and describes their reunion with their relatives (11177) *die von Kurnwâle ze Îrlant / ze zinse wâren gesant.* Gottfried also gives a more satisfactory explanation why there is a sword between Tristan and Îsolt: both fear that Mark will discover them (17402): *wan sî des angest hæten.* . . . Again Gottfried deepens the tone of Thomas's work in some places: King Mark and Brangæne, who is here not merely Îsolt's maid but her companion, are depicted with extraordinary sympathy. Mark is filled with (16539) *disem blinden leide.* He exiles the lovers, but for the time being conquers his jealousy and misery. The nobility of his character is revealed in the farewell scene. He can force physi-

cal separation upon the lovers, but he can never separate their hearts (16577/8): *und enkan doch an iu beiden / die liebe niht gescheiden.* He knows that it is no longer possible for the three of them to live together. Therefore he decides to stand back (16616): *disiu gemeinde ist bœse.*

On the other hand Gottfried condenses: *e.g.* the lament at the death of Blanscheflûr (1852/3), and the medical details of Tristan's healing (7939ff.). Gottfried's tone is even more courtly than that of Thomas: *e.g.* Tristan does not drink of the love-potion first but courteously hands it to Îsolt. Gottfried carefully avoids uncourtly phrases [*rede, diu niht des hoves sî* (7958)]. We must, however, not forget that it is far easier to improve upon a good source (like Thomas) than to create a work of great artistic value from an uncouth tale. (pp. xlii-xliii)

Gottfried's originality is shown most of all in his moral philosophy, the courtly *morâliteit* (8008ff.), by which the courtly *moralitas* is meant, not the New High German word *Moral.* His ideal is the classical καλοκαγαθια ["nobility"] which can only be attained in the most sacred moments in the life of men or nations. Riwalîn is ruined through his want of *mâze* (265f.): *ûf gêndiu jugent und vollez guot, / diu zwei diu füerent übermuot.* The girl Îsolt is instructed in that *morâliteit* which ennobles her (8028ff.): *wol gesite, / schôn' und reine gemuot, / ir gebærde süeze unde guot.* Music and poetry form part of her courtly instruction (3687ff., 7813ff., 7991ff., 8068ff.). Without *morâliteit* no one can have honour or possession (8022). It teaches mankind to serve and win the favour of God and the World: *got unde der werlde gevallen* (8017), but Gottfried lays more stress on the second—world; we must, however, not forget that this very world has a double nature, an inner and outer aspect, and it is the inner world which Gottfried exalts; *cf.* his Prelude.

He acknowledges that *Minne* is the force which dominates man's life. *Minne* is the source of *hovesite* ["honor"], indeed of all virtues (187ff.):

> lieb' ist ein alsô sælic dinc,
> ein alsô sæleclîch gerinc,
> daz niemen âne ir lêre
> noch tugende hât noch êre.

Without *Minne* there is no honour. She is an enchantress who ensnares her victims (11912). She is mistress of the world (11715ff., 11769ff.). She not only increases the torment of love (101f.), but also intensifies pleasure and alleviates pain. *Minne* is *virtus et passio* (204ff.). In love's grief he finds bliss (116/7). A *zornelîn* ["passion"] (13073) is also necessary: *cf.* Publilius Syrus: *"Amantium irae amoris integratio est"* ["Passionate love is integral love"]. . . . Finally *huote* ["control"] (17875ff.) is lamentable: a chaste lady needs no watcher, while others are only incited by prohibition (17953). Gottfried expresses his doctrine of love at least three times. We hear how *Minne* is kindled, how she acts and what she does in the heart of those who can love truly: *cp.* Riwalîn and *Blanscheflûr* (679ff.), *Tristan und Îsolt* 11711ff., 13021ff. and 18953ff.

Gottfried was indeed bold to adopt symbols from religious allegory for his own love-allegory of the Minnegrotte: 16683ff. and 16927ff. Although Gottfried sees in God the sum of all virtues, his ideal is fundamentally aesthetic. His God is a "courtly" God who, even at the time of the ambiguous oath, sides with Îsolt. The Minnegrotte of Thomas, as we have already mentioned, becomes in Gottfried's poem a wonderful palace. Gottfried's continuator, Ulrich, discarded it again. We cannot say that Gottfried's descriptions in this part of the epic are realistic: Tristan and Îsolt have no need of food (16819/20); the bliss of love fills their lives. (How difficult it is to justify the fact that Îsolt later returns to her husband!) Gottfried drew this allegory of *la fossiur' a la gent amant* (16704) from the symbolism of the church: the rounded vault of the grotto represents the single-heartedness of love, the breadth love's boundless power, the height noble-mindedness, the white wall purity, the floor constancy; through the three windows (kindness, humility, good breeding), the light of honour shines into the house of love. Entrance is granted only to *edeliu herzen*, who possess delicacy of feeling. No mediaeval German poet has ever gone further than Gottfried in making a religion of love. In this lofty conception of love the difference between Gottfried and [German poet Wilhelm] Eilhart and [French poet] Béroul and the Celtic legends emerges most clearly. In the stories of Deirdre-Naisi or Grainne-Diarmaid woman is nothing but a destructive force which against his will brings man to his ruin. In Eilhart and Béroul the love-potion is the excuse for the lovers' sin—which is therefore a sort of accident. [Gertrude] Schoepperle [in her *Tristan and Isolt: A Study of the Sources of the Romance,* 1913] rightly maintains: "It is no doubt due to the fact that Lancelot did not blindly drink the poison of love, but sought the cup of his own will, that he superseded Tristan in the favour of many twelfth-century readers". But in Gottfried's **Tristan und Îsolt** Tristan takes the burden of responsibility and their doom on his own shoulders (12505f.): *sô wolte ich gerne werben / umb ein êweclîchez sterben,* though there is still a slight trace of the conventional conception of the love-potion, but we must remember that symbol and reality cover each other very closely in the mediaeval mind: *cf.* Gottfried's *diz laster* (12147)! Gottfried's conception of fatality lingers on to modern times [English poet Charles] Swinburne: *Tristram of Lyonesse, the Sailing of the Swallow:*

> Their Galahault was the cup, and she that
>   mixed;
> Nor other hand there needed, nor sweet speech
> To lure their lips together; each on each
> Hung with strange eyes and hovered as a bird
> Wounded, and each mouth trembled for a word;
> Their heads neared, and their hands were drawn
>   in one,
> And they saw dark, though still the unsunken
>   sun
> Far through fine rain shot fire into the south.
> And their four lips became one burning mouth.

The love-potion is . . . a symbol in Gottfried's poem, see 9996ff. . . . Gottfried's love potion does not cause love, but symbolizes it. The cause of love is thus no longer external, but lies in the souls of the characters themselves who are bound to each other by a love which though unlawful in the eyes of the world, is in reality decreed by fate and enriches them with the perfect harmony of their hearts. Mark lacks this harmony; therefore his union with Îsolt

is in the deepest sense immoral; according to the laws of the *edeliu herzen* Mark bears more guilt than Tristan. The pathos of the old spirit of revenge in the old Irish stories is almost lost in Gottfried. Mark realizes that honour and loyalty are powerless under the spell of love (11771ff.). Therefore he allows them to go to the forest, and God himself sides with the lovers and gives His consent to their doctrine of love: 14641ff., 14657ff., 14710ff., 15548ff., especially 15651ff. (pp. xliii-xlv)

Delight in beauty and grace, in exquisite form, subtle mannerism and polished speech provide a balance to the virile ascetic defiance of the fighter. Thus Gottfried von Strassburg seeks to maintain harmony on the brink of the abyss.

—*August Closs*

Many classical references are to be found in Gottfried, *cf.* 4895-6 *des wâren Êlikônes, / des oberisten trônes,* 4729 *Pegases,* 4788 *Orphêes zunge,* 4806 *Zithêrône* 1, 4930 *Vulkân,* 4948 *frou Cassander,* 8278ff. (*cf.* Vergil, *Aeneid*), 17193 (*cf.* Ovid's *Heroides*) or 8268ff.:

> *als ich ez an den buochen las,*
> *diu von ir lobe geschriben sint,*
> *Aurôren tohter unde ir kint,*
> *Tintarides diu mære,*
> *daz an ir eine wære*
> *aller wîbe schônheit*
> *an einen bluomen geleit:*
> *von dem wâne bin ich komen,*
> *Îsôt hat mir den wân benomen . . .*

How much Gottfried was attracted by classical ideas is seen in his predilection for proverbs drawn from Latin sources. . . . Also the love-potion was not unknown to classical literature, *cf.* Ovid's *Ars Amatoria* II 106-7:

> Non data profuerint pallentia philtra puellis,
> Philtra nocent animis vimque furoris habent.

The invocation to Apollo and the Muses (4851ff.) in Gottfried's time was a bold stroke. Gottfried calls on *Apolle und die Camênen, / der ôren niun Sirênen /* to inspire him so that his song shall rise to the highest summit: *hin widere z' Êlikône / ze dem niunvalten trône,* and thus heaven almost appears a paradise for aesthetes: *und mîne bete erhœren / oben in ir himelkœren* (4903-4). Nevertheless the Church was awake to the spirit of antiquity, in so far as it could be of service to religion: Latin was the language of the Church; the seven arts formed the basis of education in the monastic schools where classical authors were read: Cicero, Ovid, Horace, Vergil, Seneca; further the stories of Alexander and Troy, also Publilius Syrus ("der berühmteste Mimendichter zu Cäsars Zeit, liebte es, seinen Stücken ethische Sentenzen einzuflechten, welche . . . den Knaben zum Auswendiglernen aufgegeben wurden") and Apollonius of Tyre. Besides this, Middle High German literature was enriched by a stream of important influences coming from the Orient through the crusaders, and from Arabian culture in Spain and indirectly through the South of France. The author of *Tristan und Îsolt* was more deeply steeped in the spirit of antiquity than any other medieval German poet. His perfect clarity of form sometimes caused him to fall into virtuosity. He also does not lack in proverbial phraseology, *cf.* 3641, 16874, 16880.

An excerpt from Gottfried's literary excursus to *Tristan and Isolde*

[During] my lifetime and earlier, poets have spoken with such eloquence of worldly pomp and magnificent trappings that had I at my command twelve times my inspiration, and were it possible for me to carry twelve tongues in my one mouth, of which each could speak as I can, I should not know how to begin to describe magnificence so well that it had not been done better before. Knightly pomp, I declare, has been so variously portrayed and has been so overdone that I can say nothing about it that would give pleasure to anyone.

Ah, how Hartmann of Aue dyes and adorns his tales through and through with words and sense, both outside and within! How eloquently he establishes his story's meaning! How clear and transparent his crystal words both are and ever must remain! Gently they approach and fawn on a man, and captivate right minds. Those who esteem fine language with due sympathy and judgement will allow the man of Aue his garland and his laurels.

But if some friend of the hare, high-skipping and far-browsing, seeks out Poetry's heath with dicing terms, and, lacking our general assent, aspires to the laurel wreath, let him leave us to adhere to our opinion that we too must have a hand in the choosing. For we who help to gather the flowers with which that twig of honor is entwined to make a floral wreath, we wish to know *why* he asks. Since if anyone lays claim to it, let him leap up and add his flowers! We shall judge from them if they grace it so well that we should take it from the poet of Aue and confer the laurel on him. But since none has yet come who has a better claim, then in God's name let us leave it as it is! We shall not allow anyone to wear it whose words are not well-laved, and his diction smooth and even; so that if someone approaches at the trot, well-poised and with an upright seat, he will not stumble there. Inventors of wild tales, hired hunters after stories, who cheat with chains and dupe dull minds, who turn rubbish into gold for children and from magic boxes pour pearls of dust!—these give us shade with a bare staff, not with the green leaves and twigs and boughs of May. Their shade never soothes a stranger's eyes. To speak the truth, no pleasurable emotion comes from it, there is nothing in it to delight the heart. Their poetry is not such that a noble heart can laugh with it. Those same story-hunters have to send commentaries with their tales: one cannot understand them as one hears and sees them. But we for our part have not the leisure to seek the gloss in the books of the black art.

Gottfried von Strassburg, in his Tristan, *translated by A. T. Hatto, Penguin, 1960.*

But it is in the construction of his lines and choice of words that he proved his greatness as an artist.

The introductory lines are divided ingeniously into verses, the so-called *ungesungene Deklamationsstrophik.* Gottfried's metre is usually alternating and full of harmony. . . . (pp. xlvii-xlviii)

His style is a direct development of that of [German poet] Hartmann von Aue, whose crystal clear presentation of the *sin* (material) he praises. The content of a work must, as Gottfried says, have internal and external beauty: in the moulding of the material and the words. In this exquisite harmony of form and content Gottfried has attained the supreme degree of perfection in Middle High German lyric poetry. The plasticity of his characters, events and nature is unique: 534ff., 551ff., 585ff., 4767ff., 17143ff.; 6626ff.: Tristan on horseback, 10889ff.: Îsolt's appearance at the Irish court; further single plastic features, so for instance when the boy Tristan sweeps back his hair and is too weak to move the deer (2846 *sîn schœne hâr daz streich er nider . . .*), and the fascinating picture of the Rhine which becomes a small stream when divided into five arms (19445-6 *sus wirt der michele Rîn / vil kûme ein kleinez rinnelîn*). Gottfried's love-epic is composed for the *edeliu herzen,* as he himself emphasizes. But his aesthetic world does not exclude heroic knighthood. We can see this for instance in the combat with Môrolt. Tristan is a warrior and a minstrel. In the most recent version of the tale [Hannah M. M. Closs, *Tristan,* 1940], this undeniable duality in the hero's nature is emphasized and developed to a psychological problem.

Delight in beauty and grace, in exquisite form, subtle mannerism and polished speech provide a balance to the virile ascetic defiance of the fighter. Thus Gottfried von Strassburg seeks to maintain harmony on the brink of the abyss. For this reason his *Tristan und Îsolt* with its exquisite sublimation of passion remains for us to-day, even after Richard Wagner's *Liebestod,* an inexhaustible source of inspiration. (pp. xlix-l)

> *August Closs, in an introduction to* Tristan und Isolt: A Poem *by Gottfried von Strassburg, edited by August Closs, Basil Blackwell, 1944, pp. xvi-l.*

Edwin H. Zeydel   (essay date 1948)

[*An American educator, translator, and author, Zeydel wrote several works on German literature and history. In the excerpt below, taken from the introduction to his English translation of Gottfried's* Tristan and Isolde, *he presents the poem as a literary production of great significance in the history of Western civilization.*]

That the romance of *Tristan and Isolde* by Gottfried von Strassburg is one of the truly great masterpieces of the Middle Ages, and indeed one of the supreme achievements of world literature, has frequently been attested by critics of many lands. The American scholar, Roger Sherman Loomis, has said [in his *The Romance of Tristram and Ysolt by Thomas of Britain,* 1931] that it "is, except for the *Canterbury Tales* and the *Divina Commedia,* the greatest poem of the Middle Ages." The British scholar, Margaret

F. Richey, writes [in her *Essays on the Medieval German Love Lyric,* 1943]: "Gottfried, not Walther, was the nightingale of perfect note. His romance of Tristan is as much song as story and has been rightly spoken of as a 'Hohelied der Minne,' a high song of love." August Closs, Austrian by birth and British by adoption, the latest editor of the work, says [in his *Tristan und Isolt, a Poem by Gottfried von Strassburg,* 1944] that it "belongs to the immortal treasures of the world's literature," that "among the medieval Tristan romances Gottfried's poem stands out as the unrivalled masterpiece," and that this work, "with its exquisite sublimation of passion, remains for us today, even after Richard Wagner's *Liebestod,* an inexhaustible source of inspiration." The French authority, F. Piquet, in a learned appreciation which already for over two generations has been considered a standard work on Gottfried and his poem [*L'Originalité de Gottfried de Strasbourg dans son Poème de Tristan et Isolde,* 1905], finds that, far from being a mere imitator or adapter, Gottfried is a great original poet. Finally, the many words of praise which the German critics have bestowed upon this unique achievement may perhaps be best epitomized by a phrase of Reinhold Bechstein, one of the eight German editors of the work. In the introduction to his edition [*Gottfried von Strassburg, Tristan,* 1930] he calls it a "golden poem."

In view of its undisputed position among literary masterpieces, it is highly surprising that Gottfried's **Tristan and Isolde** is practically unknown in the English-speaking countries—this despite the fact that Wagner's opera, based upon it and, in the final analysis, inspired by it, is one of the most beloved works of the world's operatic repertory. The only approximate access to Gottfried's poem through the medium of English is furnished by Jessie L. Weston's prose abridgment [*The Story of Tristan and Iseult*], published in 1899. While this rendering is faithful to Gottfried's meaning, it must necessarily fail to give the reader the faintest inkling of the very heart of his work—its form, its artistry, its whole spirit. At best a prose translation of so poetical a work as **Tristan and Isolde** might be compared with a pressed flower or an impaled butterfly.

There are many reasons why Gottfried's work has been prized as a great masterpiece ever since about 1215, when probably death forced him to leave it unfinished. It is based upon a fierce and passionate old tale which was already very popular in Europe when Gottfried took it up. But he refined it with all the good taste, subtlety, and grace of a consummate artist. Gottfried lived at the very height of the classical age of the German courtly romance and minnesong. This was the age in which Walther von der Vogelweide wrote his immortal lyrics and polemical songs; the age of Gottfried's great master, Hartmann von Aue, who helped to popularize the Arthurian legends in German literature and wrote that little gem on the theme of vicarious sacrifice, *Der arme Heinrich,* or *Poor Henry;* the age in which Gottfried's rival, Wolfram von Eschenbach, usually called the greatest of the court romancers, created his *Parzival,* a poem unique in many respects among lay works of the Middle Ages.

It was Gottfried who turned the crude old tale of the two hapless lovers, Tristan and Isolde, into a perfect mirror of that courtly culture introduced into France at the court of Eleanor of Poitou and soon disseminated to the courts of Central and Southern Germany, and of Austria, and prevailing throughout Western Europe from about 1150 to 1250. Already one of the best-told and richest tales in the wonderful storehouse of medieval narrative literature, it became in Gottfried's hands a unique panorama of passionate love-romance, minstrelsy, adventure, knightly battles royal, and keen moral and psychological observation. We find ourselves in a world of perfect medieval *courtoisie.* It does not surprise us that even God, who on the occasion of the ambiguous oath (Chapter XXIV) sides with Isolde, is "courtly" toward the damsel in distress. Nor is this the only sly satirical touch in Gottfried's poem.

Gottfried endowed the story with artistic power and psychological depth. He gave it a well-nigh perfect aesthetic form, suggesting rather than describing ideas, meanings, and emotions. In his hands the import of the tale assumes both personal and impersonal significance. The author informs his work with delicate sensibility and profundity of thought, and he instills a strain of rationalization, so dear to the Middle Ages. Yet it is not asceticism, abstinence, or even continence that Gottfried preaches, but rather the glorification of *Minne,* or love, as the gospel of a grandiose new faith. Dame Love, or *Minne,* is here the ruling force in human life, the source of all virtues. She allures and tempts but she also causes untold grief and distress. And the love potion is not a mere mechanical device to induce love, but, according to some, a symbol of the power of *Minne,* decreed by fate, overriding the conventions of the world, and bringing to her victims not only the perfect harmony of love but also constant tribulation and sorrow. And from *Minne* and the potion we are, at length, carried on to the allegory of the love-grotto (Chapter XXVII), drawn directly from the symbolism of the medieval Church.

Gottfried's power of depiction, too, is keen, and his language noted for its crystal-like clarity. He has succeeded in casting a magic spell of verbal music over his poem, marked not only by pure, haunting end-rhymes, now masculine now feminine, by the relief of the standard four-beat iambic line by three-beat lines, and by occasional four-line strophes, but also by ringing internal rhymes, rich alliterative and repetitive effects, bold contrasts, and subtle use of words in many shades of meaning. Form and content are perfectly matched. These, in brief, are the chief features of Gottfried's **Tristan and Isolde** which have made it a perennial favorite. (pp. 3-6)

> *Edwin H. Zeydel, in an introduction to* The "Tristan and Isolde" of Gottfried von Strassburg *translated by Edwin H. Zeydel, Princeton University Press, 1948, pp. 3-18.*

A. T. Hatto   (essay date 1959)

[*An English educator, translator, and editor, Hatto is a recognized authority in German studies who has written several works on medieval German poetry. In the following excerpt from the introduction (written in 1959) to his*

English translation of Gottfried's Tristan and Isolde, *he offers an overview of the poet's life and work, noting, in particular, Gottfried's mystical conception of love.*]

The *Tristan* of Gottfried von Strassburg (*fl.* 1210) has every right to be considered the classic form of the [courtly] romance. Few European poems of comparable length from Virgil to the present day can have so much formal artistry to show, alternating with purest narrative. Much of the verbal beauty of the original is inevitably lost in translation, but it is with some satisfaction that I offer readers of English the first unabridged rendering of Gottfried's *Tristan* and indeed of any masterpiece of this great generation of German poets, in a form which (whatever its defects) is not intrinsically absurd—plain prose.

By a curious fate the names of [Anglo–Norman poet] Thomas and Gottfried have, many years after their deaths, come to be as inseparable as the rose-bush and the vine (or, as some say, the hazel and the honeysuckle), which by virtue of the love/potion grew above the lovers' graves; not only because Gottfried chose Thomas's *Tristran* as his source, making a far more marvellous thing of it than it had ever been before, but because the surviving text of the one begins where the other's leaves off. Gottfried died when he had covered no more than five-sixths of the story; and now only the last sixth of Thomas's completed poem remains, and even then with some gaps. But by adding one part to the other, we are able to tell the tale to an end in the only way of which Gottfried would have approved—through Thomas, his chosen source, to whose narrative data he remains loyal to an astonishing degree, considering his own genius, and whom he admired as surely as he surpassed him.

Except that later writers tell us Gottfried's name, we know nothing about him but what we can learn from his poem and from two philosophical strophes of no great distinction. In the opening acrostic, Gottfried appears to dedicate his poem to one Dieterich, but this person has not been identified. Later poets and collectors of poetry give Gottfried the title not of 'hêr', which would in the first place indicate a knight, but of 'meister', that is, one who has concluded a prolonged course of study at an ecclesiastical centre of learning. We do not know it for a fact: but Gottfried is most readily imagined as a member of the urban patriciate of Strassburg, a class of men who, by the beginning of the thirteenth century, were growing in wealth and self-assurance and were soon to play a part in literature. Gottfried does not share the knights' condescension towards the merchant class, but on the contrary uses such expressions as 'courtly' or even 'noble merchant', which to a petty knight like Wolfram von Eschenbach, great poet though he was, would have been a contradiction in terms. Gottfried seems to be looking back to his own exacting education when he writes of Tristan's: 'This was his first departure from his freedom. . . . In the blossoming years, when the ecstasy of his springtime was about to unfold and he was just entering with joy into his prime, his best life was over . . . the frost of care (which ravages many young people) descended on him and withered the blossoms of his gladness!' Gottfried was assuredly highly trained in theology, law, and rhetoric, but we cannot guess how he was employed after finishing his education. One sugges-

tion which is as plausible as any is that he was in the local urban or episcopal secretariat. Whether or not he was ever engaged on confidential missions, his treatment of certain incidents in his story shows him to have been the shrewdest of diplomats, though some scholars have dubbed him 'non-political'. His understanding of French can safely be said to be perfect. It may have come from study in France.

Gottfried was a very cultured man. He was well read in Latin, French, and German literature. He is one of the greatest stylists, if not the greatest, in German literature of any period. His rare gift for language enabled him to transpose every formal artifice from the medieval Latin *ars poetica* into German and to invent others of his own. His virtuosity in such matters is astonishing. His classical allusions are more accurate than those of most who wrote in the vernacular at this time, and, what is more important, they are far more suggestive in tone. Classical poetry and mythology appealed to his fancy mightily. It is as if he had a premonition of the Renaissance. For inspiration he invokes not God, the Supreme Poet of more pious authors, but Apollo and the Nine Muses, at a time when most laymen thought of Apollo as a member of the Moslem 'Trinity'. He was utterly devoted to music, which echoes through his story. In his literary excursus he appears not only as a critic and aesthete but also as a judge of *Minnesang* ["love song"], the double art of words and melodies. He was deeply versed in hunting-lore and no doubt a keen hunter, so that his distinction between 'those who were skilled in the chase' and 'those who wished to pass the time hunting' contains a sly dig. Altogether, we may rely on it that he was adept in all those graces which make for good breeding in society. It is remarkable that, at a time when the petty nobility of the Hohenstauffen era were acquiring social refinement with an *élan* of which only upstarts are capable, this townsman of Strassburg presents us with an ideal of courtly life more brilliant and accomplished than any. Gottfried beat the knights at their own game. He will scarcely have succeeded in doing so without drawing on the culture of their tutors, the priests.

Gottfried's attitude towards that other aspect of knightly endeavour, the art of chivalry, suits what we already know of him. He affects not to wish to compete with knightly poets in descriptions of arms and battles. 'If you wish to know the details of the tournament you must ask the squires—it was they who arranged it.' But in fact, in his own manner, he can be as vivid as Wolfram and shows some slight trace of his influence. In the scene in which Tristan is knighted, Gottfried of course presents chivalry as a splendid ideal; but in action it is shorn of its glory. Instead, he gives us shrewd calculation. With knights, the stress is on tactics; and he is always careful to show how a mere man might slay a giant or a monster by a combination of luck, opportunism, and piecemeal disposal. In his story the archangels do not invisibly lay low thousands for the hero at a flourish of his sword, as in crusading narratives. As to Arthurian romance, we may assume that Gottfried had seen through its follies, for he steers clear of them all. Thomas places Tristran a generation later than King Arthur and Gottfried does nothing to change this.

Unlike his great counterpart Wolfram, Gottfried never

laughs from the heart, but he smiles now and again. He had a subtle, scathing wit, and we shall never plumb the depths of his irony. The way in which the two Isoldes dispose of the Steward's pretensions to the younger is masterly: the older woman is cool and assured and plays him like a fish on a line; the girl shelters behind her mother and is rude and waspish; the Steward blunders from trap to trap. We see Gottfried in a lighter vein, too, in the scene in which Melot the Dwarf tries unsuccessfully to ensnare Tristan with a forged message from Isolde. Here the humour is delicate and restrained—till Melot runs on to the barb. Nevertheless, there are other passages in which Gottfried goes too far with his mockery, notably at the end of the Morold episode, where the big man is returned to his king in pieces. Gottfried's taunts on the carved-up state of a warrior who has fought bravely, if arrogantly, would be unthinkable in a poet like Wolfram, who often risked his life in the field (as Gottfried probably did not), and they confirm our suspicion that Gottfried's was not a magnanimous nature. In keeping with this, there is another revealing passage in which Gottfried sophistically cuts Tristan in half to share between his two 'fathers', Mark and Rual. He argues that a man is compounded of his wealth and his person: take the former away, and you will have but half a man. There is much wisdom here; but it has a distinctly worldly flavour.

Apart from his doctrine of love, which must soon engage our attention, Gottfried tells us little of himself, and even then he keeps his mask. Although he brings God and the Church into his story more frequently perhaps than any of his contemporaries, he strikes the reader as correct in such matters but no more. He is as cool on this subject as he is ardent on that of love, and, indeed, the language in which he conveys his thoughts on love often draws on the language of religion in its intensest form. Thus it follows that his views on love and religion must be treated together.

Since Gottfried is so reticent it is not surprising that some of those most concerned to elicit his *personalia* should have put him on the rack of their scholarship and obtained the confessions they required. Some found that he was an atheistical mocker and blasphemer, others an art-loving hedonist of strangely recent type, others a Catharist heretic leading a double life, others an anti-Christian demonist, and yet others a mystical amorist. It cannot be said too emphatically that there is not a shred of evidence in favour of any of these labels, and that there is some evidence against them. But whatever we learn of him, it is never to be forgotten that we learn it by his grace, not by violation of his poem.

The way to an understanding of Gottfried's story lies through his Prologue, and, with less assurance, through the discourses which accompany his story at critical points, since these are often opportunist in character.

In the first forty lines of his Prologue, Gottfried makes a modest beginning. They deal with the relation of criticism to art, and are formed into succinct quatrains in the gnomic manner which use the subtlest play on forms and meanings, above all in the rhymes, and whose opening letters make an acrostic. One discerning critic has had the

courage to say that Gottfried, who is so very brilliant elsewhere, has attempted too much here, so that the matter has suffered from the form. Certainly these forty lines are hazardous to interpret and, divested of their verbal brilliance in translation, make a dull beginning to such a poem. (pp. 4-13)

Gottfried [in his Prologue] informs his listeners that he has decided to busy himself with something that will bring pleasure and contentment not to courtly society at large, since it was bent on having a good time, but to a select circle of 'noble hearts' who accepted and even welcomed love in the totality of its antitheses—the sweet and the bitter, joy and sorrow, life and death. To such a mode of life he is so fervently devoted that he will be damned or saved with it. To those of like mind he proposes to tell a tale that will half-assuage their pain, such being the function of a love-story: he will tell of Tristan and Isolde. After gracefully acknowledging the existence of other versions of the story and the good intentions of their authors, he names his source, the *Tristran* of Thomas, as the authentic version, and he clearly means to adhere to it. And now, in lines of classic beauty with a rhythmic flow that rises to incantation, he reveals his amatory doctrine. A tale of true love ennobles the spirit, reinforces constancy, and enhances life's good qualities; and this is because love is so blessed a thing that, unless love instruct him, no one has worth or honour. How tragic, then, that all but a few are doomed to lose love's benefits because they will not bear its sorrows! For . . .

> swem nie von liebe leit geschach,
> dem geschach ouch liep von liebe nie.

'He that never had sorrow of love never had joy of it either!' Joy and sorrow were ever inseparable in love. We must win honour and glory with the two or go to perdition without them. Had not the lovers of whom this story tells endured sorrow for the sake of love, they would never have comforted so many. Although they are now dead, their sweet name lives on, ever-renewed for the living.

> Their death, their life are our bread.
> Thus lives their life, thus lives their death.
> Thus they live still and yet are dead,
> And their death is the bread of the living.

The liturgical nature of this language is startlingly obvious. The difficulty is to say just which sacred context Gottfried had in mind, though we must remember that poetic language may embrace several contexts at once. Is the allusion direct to such canonical sayings as 'I am the living bread . . . If any man eat of this bread he shall live for ever; and the bread that I give is my flesh, which I shall give for the life of the world'? Does it come from the liturgy? Or does it come from sources derived from these?

Careful study in recent years has revealed that, while it would be foolish to discount powerful echoes from the Scriptures and the liturgy, our passage and others like it are derived from only one source with any consistency, namely, from the language of the mystics and, above all, from that of St Bernard in his *Sermons on the Song of Songs*, mystically interpreted.

Just as St Bernard in his Prologue offers 'bread', that is,

solid nourishment for the spirit, to the experienced initiates who can digest it, so Gottfried offers the 'bread' of his story to the band of noble hearts who alone are fit to receive it. Another parallel which, no doubt, gave life to our passage was this, that just as the priest preached a sermon before the Eucharist in order to awaken an intense desire for the Body of Christ in the communicants, so Gottfried in his Prologue excites the longing of his listeners for the 'bread' of the tale of Tristan, the tale of martyred love.

The architectural features of the Lovers' Cave, to which Tristan and Isolde withdraw on being banished by King Mark, show similar treatment by Gottfried. They are given allegorical interpretations recalling the traditional allegorization of the Christian Church as a building. The roundness of the Cave betokens Simplicity; its breadth the Power of Love; its height Aspiration; and so on. But, again, closer and more convincing analogies have been found to link them with a mystical interpretation of the 'Cubicle' in which the Soul suffers Union with God; and, most strikingly, with a mystical interpretation of the Tabernacle, which accounts, among other things, for the Bed.

Within the precincts of their Cave the lovers take no food: they nourish themselves merely by gazing at one another. To recur to the language of the mystics, they are consumed by one another like Christ and the Soul, and, consuming, are sustained. Like the Blessed in Paradise, they are rapt in the beatific vision and, in the words of the Book of Revelation, 'They shall hunger no more, neither thirst any more.' They may also, though less compellingly, be regarded as love's anchorites, who are nourished by invisible manna.

Gottfried's 'noble hearts' (an expression he is the first to use in German) have a close parallel in the 'noble soul' of the mystics, as has their capacity to suffer for love. 'Noble' in mystical contexts means raised to the divine plane—for how else could the Soul unite with God? The novelty of Gottfried's secular usage lies in the fact that the word for 'noble' normally took its meaning from rank in feudal society, not from qualities of the heart. Half a century before the Bolognese [poet] Guido Guinizelli conceived his humane and thus anti-feudal philosophy of the *cuore gentile,* the Strassburger Gottfried formulated his doctrine of the *edelez berze,* which similarly opened the doors to those of the highest culture, whatever their social origins. But behind both Gottfried and Guinizelli we may suspect medieval Latin authors.

A crowning analogy with the language of the mystics is found in the words in which Gottfried formulates the bond that unites the lovers, words that seek to bridge the antitheses which dominate the lives of ordinary men and women. Though these and other pairs of words ring in our ears throughout his poem, it is not they but their fusion that is of supreme importance to Gottfried. 'What I have to say does not concern that world and such a way of life; their way and mine diverge sharply. I have another world in mind which together in one heart bears its bitter-sweet, its dear sorrow, its heart's joy, its love's pain, its dear life, its sorrowful death, its dear death, its sorrowful life. To this life let my life be given, of this world let me be part, to be damned or saved with it.' When one comes to such

passages one wonders why one ever thought of translating, so poor is the return. For the rhythm of Gottfried's verse, the music of his rhymes binds opposites together triumphantly, strange though it all is in logic. I quote the passage here, so that the reader may form some idea of what is lost:

> *Der werlde und diseme lebene*
> *enkumt min rede niht ebene:*
> *ir leben und minez zweient sich.*
> *ein ander werlt die meine ich,*
> *diu samet in eime berzen treit*
> *ir süeze sur, ir liebez leit,*
> *ir liebez leben, ir leiden tot,*
> *ir lieben tot, ir leidez leben:*
> *dem lebene si min leben ergeben,*
> *der werlt wil ich gewerldet wesen,*
> *mit ir verderben oder genesen.*

Such passages convince us that Gottfried is in deadly earnest and that this is not an example of the clever dialectic of love to which one is accustomed in other medieval poems, much though a prose rendering might suggest it.

It is clear from these examples that whatever other religious matter Gottfried has drawn on, the one consistent theme is that of twelfth-century mysticism. The question now arises as to how to use this insight. In the form of the crassest alternatives: was Gottfried merely utilizing the ready-made language of the mystics, those pioneers in the discovery of the inner self, in order to say things about love that had never been said before? Or was he preaching a new religion of love while at the same time rejecting Christianity, or at least Christian teaching on love? Much depends on the answer.

Lest the reader should imagine that the conception of love which Gottfried recommends as lofty and difficult of attainment is a form of 'platonic' love, it must be said at once that it is grounded in willing and full surrender on both sides. Gottfried has some curt words for prudish lovers who deny themselves to each other. On the other hand, the love which he conceives is far from being the mere worship of the instincts as with certain modern authors. Between lovers, at least, constancy and other good qualities are demanded to their highest degree, and, if need be, the suffering entailed by true love must be borne with fortitude. Thus Gottfried's ideal of love presents a fusion of the sensual and the spiritual; how successfully I leave others to judge.

Was Gottfried utilizing religious language or preaching a new religion? To begin with, one may concede that his attitude and language imply a new *cult* of love. This in itself would amply account for his appropriation of religious and, above all, mystical language, since such language was a highly developed vehicle of ecstasy, anything short of whose intensity clearly would not have suited Gottfried. But was he preaching a religion? Surely not. His pronouncements concern relations between lovers, while those of religion concern communities. Gottfried uses scathing words on current amorous behaviour. He says that deceived husbands have only themselves to blame, for they are blinded by lust; that the closekeeping of women is abominable, since it incites them to evil courses—rather should they be trusted; that love is hounded to the far corners of the earth, or goes begging from door to door. But when we examine such statements, we find that they do not amount to a coherent and positive system, and sometimes contradict each other. They are based on ready-made home-truths, however cleverly Gottfried elaborates them. Trenchant though such observations are in themselves, they offer no prospect of reform in any social sense. If Gottfried thought that his cult of love contained the seeds of universal regeneration between the sexes he does not say so; rather does he place his hopes in a minority. One doubts whether his heroic conception of love, so securely founded on suffering, could survive in conditions where all could wed as they pleased. Lovers as Gottfried conceived them can no more do without the Jealous One's doorkeepers, spies, and 'slanderers' (who seem always to tell the truth) than revolutionaries without the police. In an ideal world free of *mésalliance* such as Gottfried implies but never describes, his lovers would go to pieces for sheer lack of opposition: they are heroes of the Resistance, of the underground army of love. It is well observed that they should leave their paradise of their own free will in the episode of the Cave of Lovers in order to resume their hunted life, which must inevitably end in separation.

In the absence of any positive statements on Gottfried's part, we must imagine him to have been resigned to the existing social order and to have accepted it as a fact of life that an absolute attachment of lovers must often or always run counter to society and find its own way of survival in desperate opposition to it. He does not say so explicitly, but there is small risk in believing him to have thought that the social order and the mighty passion of love were facts of the creation for whose conflict he was not responsible, and, moreover, that the solution offered by the clergy (of whose whole apparatus he was master) was far from satisfactory. It would be unsafe to go any further. This does not necessarily make him a heretic, though his outlook might well have gained in freedom from the mutual attrition of Christianity and Catharism in his native Strassburg in his own lifetime. Schooled in medieval and in some classical learning, Gottfried may have been a lover who could think for himself on what mattered most to him—no unusual thing in a great poet, though not very common then.

It would be hard to assert that Gottfried is anything more than correct in religious matters. He can draw a majestic picture of the power of God as it reveals itself in a tempest. He most affectionately sets heavenly crowns on the heads of that happy pair, Rual and Floraete, when they are dead. But in other contexts he cannot escape the suspicion of using the name of God lightly, or on occasion of making a mere narrative device of it, even to the point of slickness. After burying Rivalin he commends his soul to God and smartly transfers our interest to the sad death of Blanche-flor on giving birth to Tristan, only to repeat the process with her and conclude with the pointed phrase: 'And now let us tell what God did with the babe that had neither father nor mother'. He executes such manoeuvres almost too adroitly and leaves us wondering. His characters sometimes voice sentiments which we may fairly claim as his. A case in point is Tristan's fluent assumption of the

role of David to Morold's Goliath, prior to their duel. For Tristan tries to assuage the Cornishmen's fears by the argument that if a warrior who stakes his life in a good cause falls in battle, then a swift death and a people's long-drawn agony are rated differently in Heaven and on earth. In the sequel we learn that God did succour Tristan against Morold; but he came to Tristan's aid only at the last moment after a sharp reminder from Gottfried, and even then was but one ally among three.

Gottfried's alarming comment on the outcome of Isolde's trial by ordeal for adultery, in which Heaven seems to uphold her innocence, has often been adduced in discussions of his theological position. Indeed it is even now regarded, quite mistakenly, as the key passage for this purpose. When the red-hot irons leave Isolde's hands unscathed, Gottfried observes: 'Thus it was made manifest and confirmed to all the world that Christ in His great virtue is pliant as a windblown sleeve. He falls into place and clings whichever way you try Him, closely and smoothly, as He is bound to do!' Surviving rituals of such trials show that what was expected to be 'manifested' was not the nature of any member of the Trinity but the divine judgement of the case. *Tristan* was written in about 1210. Five years later the Lateran Council forbade the clergy to consecrate trials by ordeal. The Church has never liked to be less than five years behind well-informed public opinion, and it suits our situation excellently to suppose that this brilliant poet of an enlightened and somewhat rationalistic circle in the Bishop's town of Strassburg should be indulging in irony (as so often elsewhere) at the expense of those who still believed in ordeals.

There is no compelling reason to regard this passage in its context as blasphemous, or heretical or demoniac, or indeed as anything more sensational than the utterance of an intelligent and alert man who was indifferent enough in religious matters to be critical of pious excess among the ignorant. It is as if he suspected that the clergy were not on such intimate terms with their Maker as their words and behaviour implied and—despite the one occasion when the Deity thwarted the plans of young Tristan's abductors with a storm at sea—believed that God does not intervene in human affairs by fits and starts, but holds aloof till the appointed day. It has further been well observed that, in contrast to almost any comparable poem of Gottfried's day, there is no passage in *Tristan* in which its author shows a positive relationship towards any member of the Trinity but the first. Various explanations are possible, but we have no means of choosing between them.

To conclude this discussion, which, in the absence of a common opinion, it was not possible to spare the reader, it can be said that although Gottfried is propagating an esoteric cult of worldly love by means of a story as if predestined for it, and with an intensity which others devoted to the joy or the salvation of their souls, he is not preaching a new religion, nor challenging the Church head-on. Instead, he seems to emerge as a scholar, lover, sceptic, and poet with a rare power of taking words from other spheres, both emotional and rational, and suiting them to the ever-changing needs of his story, a story of passion beyond the law.

The rack and the police filing-system are not the best means of getting truth out of dead poets. There is far more to be learnt about reticent authors by trying to visualize their situation as they take their work in hand. We know that Gottfried used as his source the poem of a lesser artist, but that, for reasons of literary integrity as he understood them, he meant to keep to the story. He might smile to himself over some of the matter to be recounted, but as a question of principle he made the best case he could for it. In other words, his attitude towards his story was that of an advocate. His heart was most assuredly in all that had to do with love, and here his pleading is inspired. But where the tale goes against him, laying some strain on his advocacy, we find him cool and calculating and at times even specious. He makes damaging admissions against his clients only when he must. When Isolde asks Brangane, who is still a virgin, to do duty for her at the nuptials, Gottfried's brief comment, 'Thus Love instructs honest minds to practise perfidy, though they ought not to know what goes to make a fraud of this sort', lays the blame on Lady Love's shoulders which (we see) are broad as well as handsome. Having disposed of the matter, he never hints at guilt again, except to say that it was Mark's fault that he was deceived, because he closed his eyes—the lovers concealed nothing! Isolde's success with her doctored oath at her ordeal must also have left Gottfried exposed; but, as we have seen, he extricates himself brilliantly by means of scathing irony. This advocacy of Gottfried's makes it very difficult to penetrate to the man, and it is more profitable to study him where he reveals himself all the time—in his work, as an artist.

Gottfried's *Tristan* lies half-way between romance and novel. Its archaic narrative matter, often frankly pure fairy-tale, is set in motion by Gottfried with as much realistic psychology as it will bear. For whole stretches one feels that one is reading a novel—and then the old tale reasserts itself. At times we find him shaking his head over the story's love of the irrational, either obliquely through irony, as when dealing with monsters, or directly, as when he ridicules a widespread variant to the effect that a swallow chanced to bring a golden hair from Ireland to Cornwall, leading to the marriage of Isolde. We often have the feeling that Gottfried was more mature in outlook than he was permitted to show by the literary media of his time. Having made his choice, he adhered faithfully to the convention that a writer does not foist tales of his own imagining on a credulous public, as he accused Wolfram von Eschenbach of doing. He names his source and keeps to it, deepening here, broadening there, adding circumstantial detail and always embellishing and embroidering.

If Gottfried's *Tristan* does not arrive at being a novel, of which literary form Gottfried was no doubt capable but at which he was not aiming, it has nevertheless passed beyond romance. Nor are we losers by it. Of the two, novel and versified romance, the latter was better suited to Gottfried's unique gift of lyrical narrative. The one structural weakness which a modern critic might be tempted to ascribe to his work, were he to apply our standards to it, would be that the discrepancy between the traditional plot and Gottfried's deep understanding of human motives at times leads us to question the consistency of some characters.

A case in point is Isolde's attempt to have Brangane murdered soon after the latter has saved Isolde's reputation and perhaps her life by the sacrifice of her own virginity in Mark's bed. But for the unforeseeable compassion of Isolde's agents, the deed would have been done beyond recall. However sincerely Isolde may have repented her action, she was morally a murderess. The motive for her attempt is her fear that Brangane, once having tasted the pleasures of the bed, might conceive a liking for them and seek to oust her by exposing her. This reveals Isolde as inhumanly ruthless and utterly unworthy of a story whose confessed purpose was to show us an exemplary pair of lovers, unless we admit that love takes absolute precedence over moral considerations even to the point of murder. Gottfried does not say as much, but instead eludes the problem, which was none of his seeking. It was his source which demanded of him that he recount Isolde's attempt on Brangane's life as best he might, and this he does brilliantly within the confines of the episode. But we cannot always rhyme it with other episodes, at least with those prior to the drinking of the potion.

Yet Gottfried is not beyond all hope of rescue. For, although as a young princess Isolde had been nurtured most tenderly under the eyes of a discerning mother at a court of great refinement, Gottfried has nevertheless prepared us for her pitiless attempt on Brangane. Two hundred and fifty lines back he has made it not Tristan's or Brangane's but Isolde's idea that her cousin should replace her at the nuptials. It is but a short step from the violation of a friend's integrity to the destruction of her life. In turn, the substitution of Brangane for Isolde was dictated by fear for her life, a fear made resourceful by love; and this was all because love had forced Isolde to surrender to Tristan. For its part (as Gottfried tells the tale) love had come because Tristan and Isolde had chanced to drink a magic draught together. Thus the chain of human motivation holds as far back as this, till we are suddenly face to face with magic; which suggests that, if the consistency of Isolde's character has been impaired by anything at all, it was by the direct action of the philtre as much as by the apparently incongruous events of the tale. But, in fact, far from being no more than an uncouth survival from a cruder age (as it was historically), the Brangane episode is an integral part of the events which arise from the drinking of the potion, and is wholly congruent with that fateful act, showing as it does how swiftly love can drive Isolde to the depths. In the Brangane episode the malign aspects of love as it was released by the philtre are shown to the full in action. And how sudden was that release!

> *Nu daz diu maget unde der man,*
> *Isot unde Tristan,*
> *den tranc getrunken beide, sa*
> *was ouch der werlde unmuoze da,*
> *Minne, aller berzen lagærin.*

Now when the maid and the man, Isolde and Tristan, had drunk the draught, in an instant that arch-disturber of tranquillity was there, Love, waylayer of all hearts.

The brief but menacing syllable 'sa' ('at once') on which the two halves of the poem hinge, the carefree and the enamoured, marks the opening of a box that can be compared to Pandora's: the passion of love flies out, and with each of its heroic virtues comes a vice—arrogance, deceit, treachery, ingratitude, and finally the will to murder.

If we compare the scene in which Tristan lies helpless in his bath and Isolde ponders whether she shall avenge her uncle Morold's death on Tristan then and there, we observe that she finds it impossible to carry out the deed. Sentimental critics, wise in the wisdom of latter-day psychology, attribute Isolde's inability to kill Tristan to her being more or less unconsciously in love with him, even before drinking the love-potion, a conception which was foreign to Gottfried. Gottfried's own explanation, which one may be excused for preferring, despite its not being entirely free from prevarication, is that Isolde's womanly instincts forbade her to kill. Between this passage and her attempt on cousin Brangane's life something must have happened to Isolde. That the potion was indeed the true cause of the lovers' passion and of all that followed from it and no mere outward symbol will be shown by other means below. But we have learned enough to understand that, for some time, the potion changed Isolde's character much for the worse.

We may not leave Isolde without dwelling on one further trait. Like Eve in the popular medieval interpretation of the scene in Genesis, Isolde is the one who first overcomes the lovers' sense of shame by leaning her elbow against Tristan; it is she who entices her Adam to her orchard at great risk in the noonday heat and so brings about their discovery, separation, and fall from happiness; it is she again who, at the moment of parting, restrains Tristan from too hasty a leave-taking and solemnly pronounces the doctrine of their identity, as priestess of their amorous cult. Gottfried rates woman lower than man as a being of spirit and intelligence, but concedes her the priority in love.

Tristan's character shows no such apparent break as Isolde's. Conceived when his father seemed mortally wounded, born to sorrow by a mother who died in childbirth at the news of his father's death, Tristan was destined to be a tragic lover. In German law (but not in English law, which Thomas may have followed) Tristan was a bastard, since he was conceived out of wedlock, a state which no subsequent marriage of his parents could legitimize. On being set ashore in Cornwall the boy lied his way to safety with the utmost assurance. He soon proved himself as an infant prodigy at court in all imaginable accomplishments and ousted the Chief Huntsman and the Master Musician from their positions of preeminence without any sign of compunction. During his struggle with Morold as an initiate to knighthood, Tristan showed great political foresight, as well as courage, as in all his subsequent dealings with the anti-Tristan party at court. When he went to Duke Morgan to claim a fief which his father had held and was reminded of his illegitimacy, he forced the argument round to where Morgan cast aspersions on his mother, thus offering Tristan the one chance of 'righting' his bad case in law, which he promptly seized; for without warn-

ing he dispatched Morgan with ruthless efficiency, and later defeated his army, so that his *de facto* position was unassailable. Next, in pursuit of higher honours at the court of his maternal uncle, Tristan virtually abandoned his own loyal Parmenians—and commended them piously to God. Gottfried himself is so sensitive to the impression this might make that he washes his hands of Tristan's action by means of a literary device. His audience is represented as insisting that Tristan should pursue his ambitions, regardless of his obligations to Parmenie, and the poet acquiesces.

Thus after Tristan has drunk the love-potion it does not strike us as unthinkable that he should succumb to its effects after a sharp struggle with Loyalty and Honour. And we must in any case regard this pair as a rhetorical convenience, because, when Gottfried has to unite Tristan and Isolde for the first time, Loyalty and Honour lose to Love; whereas, when Gottfried has to land the lovers in Cornwall at a time when they were free to go to Tristan's country, Loyalty and Honour (for what they are worth) are momentarily in the ascendant—probably the poorest piece of work in the story. Now come a series of intrigues which make it clear that no one less adroit and unconcerned for moral issues than Tristan has been since childhood (despite his upbringing by honest Rual) could ever have stayed near his mistress so long. And when at last he is caught in flagrant delict and goes into exile, he singes his wings in a new flame under the fatal fascination—so we are told—of the lady's name, Isolde of the White Hands. Gottfried's description of the passing disintegration of Tristan's love for Isolde the Fair to the point where he can marry, but not love, the other Isolde, is masterly; but we are aware that Tristan's loyalty even within the sacred bond of love has received a permanent scar.

The characters of Tristan and Isolde thus oscillate between the ideal, if judged by amatory standards, and the criminal, if judged by others. Gottfried barely hints whether he regards this as inevitable; but in his Prologue to *Parzival*, Wolfram von Eschenbach shows that he has noticed the discrepancy. In Wolfram's eyes there is but one standard of loyalty, which reveals Gottfried's lovers to be false.

The account of the loves of Tristan's parents, Rivalin and Blancheflor, makes one of the finest short stories in German of any period. Clearly Tristan has inherited some of his parents' qualities. They fall madly in love with each other without the aid of a love-potion and give themselves up to their passion with the same disregard for the consequences as Tristan and Isolde, and with an even more reckless disregard for their lives. But the father is far less circumspect than his son. He is mettlesome, ambitious, and revengeful, to his own undoing. He has been excellently described as 'constitutionally incapable of doing anything but loving and fighting. He is improvident in the extreme.' Blancheflor's reason is flooded to drowning by warm emotions. Having abandoned her whole future to the dashing Rivalin's whim, she reminds him apologetically of the plight in which she would find herself, were he to go away and leave her, and finds a swift and at last adequate response in her lover's impetuous heart.

The shadows in Gottfried's ideal pair are deepened by contrast with the happily married couple Rual and Floraete, who move with ease in courtly society and yet remain uncorrupted and touchingly devoted to Tristan, their fosterling and overlord, who belongs to quite another world. Brangane and Curvenal, too, are patterns of loyal love towards their respective principals, the former especially in that, having failed to guard the potion well, she pays the price in full on demand, and even pardons her would-be murderess. (Thomas, however, in a later scene which Gottfried did not reach, shows Brangane turning against her mistress when the load becomes too heavy for her.) In the minor character Marjodo there is a well-conceived change of behaviour. A friend of Tristan's and a secret admirer of Isolde, he becomes their implacable enemy on discovering that the Queen is not so unattainable as he had thought, so that, withered by jealousy, he descends from being Tristan's bosom-friend to the level of Melot, the insidious dwarf, to make a pair who henceforth hunt together as the Serpent and the Cur.

The most problematic figure is that of Mark. He sets the tone of a court famed for its gaiety and high breeding, qualities which are not always borne out in later episodes, in which his barons intrigue against Tristan. We find Mark magnanimous and then ever more devoted to the child of his sister's elopement, both before and after discovering his identity, often against his own political interest, about which he does not seem to care. His love of pleasure shows its first signs of weakness, as Gottfried tells the tale, when he fails to detect the deception at his nuptials—'one woman was like another to him'. At first he will not credit the rumours linking the names of the two he loves best in the world. But when suspicion grows and it is time for him to act, he is blinded by lust for his beautiful Queen and will not see the truth. At length, in language of great nobility and tinged with a tragic quality that we meet with only here, yet somewhat undermined by its belatedness, Mark stands aside from their company of three and banishes the lovers, not finding it in himself to harm them. Soon, at the flimsiest sign of Isolde's innocence, Mark falls victim once again to his desire for the wife who does not love him. He wavers for a long time in suspicion and doubt, unable to make up his mind, till at last crass certainty tears illusion from his eyes. The last we hear of him in Gottfried's unfinished poem is that instead of killing the lovers in the act as the law (both written and unwritten) would have allowed or even required, he returns to the Palace to fetch witnesses; but finding Tristan gone and with him all proof of the deed, he is lectured by his councillors, after an ineffective show of annoyance, into taking Isolde back as a woman who has been much wronged.

Thomas had raised the figure of Mark from that of a royal cuckold given to black fits of rage to one who was for ever in doubt because he could find no proof by which to convict his dear ones. Gottfried no doubt perceived that such a figure harboured tragic possibilities. This may well be one of the reasons why he fixes the guilt on Mark so squarely—only the lovers must have his listeners' sympathy, he has none to spare for a rival. Altogether, the men and women of the Middle Ages had little sentiment to spare for husbands. For these and other reasons Mark can

at best be a pathetic, but not a tragic, figure. It is our gentler, or should one say less robust, modern outlook alone which suspects that he might be otherwise.

Some further light is thrown on the situation by an inquiry into the nature of the love-potion. Was it a cause of love, or a mere symbol of the passage from unconscious to conscious love? Tristan and Isolde are certainly occupied with each other in some way prior to drinking the potion, and it would be very modern and therefore very profound of Gottfried to have them unconsciously in love. But unfortunately, if one combs this part of the story, one finds no explicit statement to this effect, so that any who assume it are without question placing psychological constructions on the narrative of a poet who was well able to do this for himself. They do so at their own risk. It was seen above that Gottfried's motive for Isolde's failure to kill Tristan in his bath was her womanly nature. The woman who kills is a she-devil, like Kriemhild in the *Nibelungenlied*. After Isolde's admiration of Tristan's handsome looks and physique as he sits naked in his tub before she has discovered his identity, this somewhat ambiguous motive of her womanhood is disappointing, but it must be borne. Other comparable scenes occur, in which a reader of *Peg's Paper* might detect unconscious love, as, for example, on board ship shortly before the mishap with the philtre, when Isolde rejects Tristan's respectful and strictly permissible familiarities (compare how Hermione gives her hand to Polixenes in [William Shakespeare's] *The Winter's Tale* in all innocence and propriety according to the fashion of the times). In such scenes Gottfried plays with his listeners. He executes a double finesse. For he knows as well as they that the two must fall in love. He has told us twice over that they are fated to do so, when on two occasions Isolde was the first to discover her future lover. He, too, knows of unconscious love, and half tempts us to jump to conclusions. But, in fact, with the conventions at his disposal, he adheres closely to the tradition of his story, namely that it was a philtre which made his lovers fall in love.

At first sight it would seem that no philtre is needed to involve two high-spirited young people in a fatal passion, since Tristan's parents Rivalin and Blancheflor fall in love in much the same way without one. But their tragedy is brought about by Rivalin's arrogance, which is external to their love; and although they ran away from one court, they might easily have lived at another had Rivalin not fallen in battle. The loves of Rivalin and Blancheflor nevertheless do offer a clue to the problem. Rivalin's falling in love is compared to the ensnarement of a free bird on the limed twig, an image which [English poet Geoffrey] Chaucer uses later in his *Troilus:*

> For love bigan his fetheres so to lyme . . .
> [I, 353]

Like Claudius's 'limèd soul' in [Shakespeare's] *Hamlet,* Rivalin struggles to be free, but is more engaged. And when Gottfried comes to tell of the fruitless efforts of Tristan and Isolde, especially of the latter, to free themselves from the insidious clinging of love, he renews this image. There were no hints of unconscious love in Rivalin before Blancheflor sighed at him; so that this parallel alone is

enough to suggest that there was no unconscious love between Tristan and Isolde. But Gottfried was more explicit.
Before Tristan has finally won Isolde for his uncle at the
court of Dublin, she is compared to the free falcon on its
bough that turns its gaze where it pleases, an image rich
in associations with medieval German love-poetry. In this
same scene Isolde is also referred to as Love's bird of the
chase. Later, this image too is revived; but now Isolde has
drunk the draught, she has been caught in the lime (as falcons were sometimes caught in practice), and has succumbed; so that her predatory eyes, now in company with
her heart, go out to one man alone, her fated lover Tristan.
Thus it would seem that any change in Isolde's character
must be attributed to the potion.

The inference is clear. At the Irish court, Isolde, the falcon
on her bough, was fancy-free. But now, thanks to the fateful error with the potion, she is Love's captive. There is
proof that Gottfried uses symbols in this way. For in Marjodo's dream a mighty boar ranges from the forest,
plunges up to Mark's bedchamber and fouls the royal
linen with his foam at the very moment when Tristan is
lying in the Queen's arms. Looking back over the story we
recall that the device on Tristan's shield at his knighting
ceremony is precisely that of the Boar, just as the boar of
Troilus' dream tallies with the heraldic Boar of his rival
Diomede in Chaucer. These magnificent images of the
Boar and the Falcon are used sparingly but consistently
by Gottfried in his *Tristan.*

It would be fair to say that although Gottfried employs the
love-philtre symbolically (how could it fail to symbolize
fatal passion?), this does not preclude it from being the
cause of Tristan and Isolde's love. In Thomas's version
Mark also drinks of the potion. But Gottfried will have
none of that. He causes Brangane to throw the cursed fatal
flask into the sea so that Mark should be unable to drink
of it. For what part could sensual Mark have in the unique
and heroic passion of which Tristan and Isolde are the
martyrs? And be it noted: when the ships put to land, the
sea is such that they can make good headway, but, as the
love-drink falls into its lap, we are told that it is wild and
raging! Evidently the sea has claimed something very potent and out of the ordinary. This innovation of Gottfried's, slight in itself yet highly significant in effect, must
serve for many other instances of his discreet yet far-
reaching changes.

One final word remains to be said on Gottfried's attitude
towards love. Although, while the tale is on, Chaucer sym-
pathizes warmly with his pair of lovers in *Troilus,* he takes
it all back at the end and again in his last will and testament. It is possible, though very unlikely, that Gottfried
might have done so, had he finished his story. He seems
to have committed himself too deeply. But because of the
mask that he wears we shall never know for sure. One feels
in the end that he was an idealist and also a pessimist in
love. He tells us that he has known the passion since his
twelfth year, has found his way to the Cave (though he
never went to Cornwall), and blundered up to the Bed,
without ever resting on it. Even his lovers, who do repose
there, do not stay there long, but resume their place of
'honour' in society, after which Tristan's love is to suffer

cruel attrition. Gottfried has prepared us for this. For
when Love brings the pair together for the first time, he
discreetly engages our attention in a discourse on love as
love had come to be—cheapened, prostituted, and hounded to the corners of the earth. Gottfried despairs from the
outset of the ability of the common herd to attain it. But
even the hopes which he places in his chosen band of noble
hearts appear slender.

Comparison with his source shows that Gottfried was
tactful in his handling of the lovers' amours beyond what
we might expect in a man of his generation. To the modern
mind the relationship of the three, and then four, main
characters is unpalatable. As soon as a situation of this
sort threatens to arise in the *Forsyte Saga* on Soames's reassertion of his rights, [English author John] Galsworthy
stages Bosinney's exit—scarcely credibly for us—by having him run over by a hansom-cab. From a natural delicacy of feeling and in the interests of the beauty of the tale
as he wished to tell it, Gottfried passes over disturbing elements as lightly as he can; whereas Thomas, always the
analytical psychologist, tends to wallow in outraged feelings.

To place Gottfried's *Tristan* in its true perspective it must
be stressed that it is but one of four great narrative poems
in medieval German, the others being the *Parzival* and the
Willebalm of Wolfram von Eschenbach, and the epic *Nibelungenlied,* all written within twenty years of one another at the beginning of the thirteenth century. Together
with the songs of leading Minnesinger like Heinrich von
Morungen, Walther von der Vogelweide, and Neidhart
von Reuental, these longer poems make an age of great literature as yet unsuspected by readers of English at large.
German genius has sometimes been over-cried in its native
land, so that where there is a hindrance to its appreciation
as here—only a discipline as exacting as that of classical
studies will unlock the door to it—others have taken the
line of least resistance and ignored the just claims to their
attention of this fascinating poetry. Even that great master
of medieval literatures, [literary critic] W. P. Ker, shows
few signs of having savoured the poetry of the Hohenstauffen age of Germany. Here, then, is a lost world of the
imagination awaiting discovery by the curious, and here,
as a beginning, is Gottfried's *Tristan,* which, unless I have
sadly betrayed it, should bring a shock of delight to those
who were expecting an Arthurian romance, a Tennysoni-
an idyll, or a Wagnerian melodrama; or who imagined
that in the year A.D. 1210 Germany was still altogether in
the Dark Ages. (pp. 13-31)

> *A. T. Hatto, in an introduction to* Tristan *by
> Gottfried von Strassburg, translated by A. T.
> Hatto, Penguin Books, 1960, pp. 7-35.*

W. T. H. Jackson   (essay date 1962)

[*An English educator and author, Jackson was a renowned paleographist and specialist in medieval studies.
He wrote several works dealing with the literature of the
Middle Ages, notably* The Anatomy of Love: The Tristan of Gottfried von Strassburg *(1971). In the following
essay, he examines the importance of the arts in Gott-*

Tristan, the learned knight.

fried's courtly epic and asserts that Tristan is depicted
as exemplifying every Christian in his struggle to achieve
union with the divine through music.]

Although the thinkers of the Middle Ages did not develop
any theories about the function of the artist which can be
compared with those of Plato or the Romantics, they had
definite views on art and its relation to society. Art in its
broadest sense had for them an ethical and social function
which inevitably became part of the grand design of the
universe. None of the great writers of romance is without
consciousness of this function. In the creation of the Arthurian romance in particular they were fully aware of
their responsibilities, but they interpreted them in differing ways. It seems to me that Gottfried von Strassburg realizes most fully the intellectual aspects of his responsibility and takes most note of the esthetic theories which justified the arts, and in particular music, as beneficial for
Christian men and women and as leading towards that
harmony of the spirit with the eternal which was regarded
as the highest good.

It should hardly surprise us that Gottfried should show
this awareness. Of all the German courtly poets, he gives
immeasurably the greatest evidence of formal learning—

his knowledge of the classics, his skill in the formal style
which we rather unwisely persist in calling rhetoric, his
acquaintance with French literature, and his grasp of mystical theology and its terminology—all these stamp him as
formally trained, as a *magister* or *dominus*. Whatever the
compiler of the manuscripts of lyric poetry may have
meant when he called Gottfried "meister," we shall be
safer to interpret the word as "magister" than as merely
a bourgeois of Strassburg. An earlier generation of critics
saw in Gottfried's nonaristocratic status the reason for his
failure to describe the ceremony of Tristan's knighting and
for his disagreements with Wolfram von Eschenbach.
Such views are unsound, as I hope to show. More recently
Wolfgang Mohr [in his *"Tristan und Isold als Künstlerroman,"* *Euphorion* LIII (1969)] has sought to interpret
Tristan und Isold as a *Künstlerroman* but only in the limited sense that its hero behaved as a *Spielmann* and that his
attitudes and activities were those of that class. There is
some truth in this, but I shall attempt to go further and
to indicate that the quarrel with [German poet] Wolfram
was a fundamental disagreement on the nature and purpose of the courtly epic. The omission of the *swertleite*
["knighting ritual"] and the insertion of the passage of literary criticism in its stead thus become a rejection of the
type of knight whom Wolfram and, even more, other writers made their hero and the substitution of one whose approach to life and above all to love was based on criteria
quite different from theirs. Gottfried's contempt for his
fellow-writer is well known. He describes him as "vindære
wilder mære, der mære wildenære," a description whose
form is as significant as its content, for in describing Wolfram as an inventor of wild tales and a poacher of stories
Gottfried graphically portrays the confusion in the cross-
fusion of his words. What Wolfram lacks is a sense of
form, of disciplined structure, in a word, artistry. Wolfram's reply is revealing: "Schildes ambet ist min art," I am
a man of my weapons, not of the pen, a man of action, not
an intellectual. His much quoted denial of his ability to
read falls into the same category of anti-intellectual statements. Nor should we overlook the passage in which he
makes mocking reference to the man caught naked in his
bath:

> disiu aventiure
> vert ane der buoche stiure
> e man si hete vür ein buoch,
> ich wære e nacket ane touch,
> so ich in dem bade sæze
> ob ich des questen niht vergæze.

The allusion to Tristan's unfortunate situation when
trapped by Isold is surely very obvious. Wolfram and Gottfried knew that they could not agree on the *raison d'être*
of the courtly epic. They were using the form for completely different purposes.

Even more significant than these chance remarks is the
passage of literary criticism in which the references to
Wolfram are found. The *swertleite* was the introduction of
a young man not only to knighthood but to a whole new
way of life. The ceremonial marked for him the path he
was to tread and the ideals towards which he was to strive.
It is interesting to note that the author of the *Nibelungenlied* felt it incumbent upon him to have a *swertleite* for his

hero, however awkwardly such an event sat with his source material and his story. Since he was intent on imparting a courtly veneer to his work, he had to introduce Siegfried to knightly society and, as we might expect, the emphasis is on the ceremonial rather than on the physical and moral preparation necessary. Parzival does not have an official *swertleite,* but there is a detailed account of the various stages of his training by Gurnemanz and of his knighting.

Tristan receives his sword at a ceremony at his uncle's court, an event which might be expected to call forth Gottfried's finest powers of description—if he were writing a courtly romance in the normal sense. But he refuses to describe it. His ironic apology that he cannot compete with those who have done so before is no more convincing than the view of those who assert that he, a bourgeois, would not know the details of the ceremony. Gottfried was not usually lacking in information, particularly information which could be found in books—and even in his own source, Thomas of Britain. We must regard his refusal as deliberate and equally deliberate his insertion of a long passage of what can only be called literary criticism. There is little logic in the substitution unless we observe that Gottfried wished to discuss not knightliness but the literature of knighthood, not the knight's physical prowess, his ability to win victories or his success as a "courtly lover," but rather the knight as a man, as a sensitive being, a thinker and artist.

Gottfried has already given us several clues that he is not writing a courtly epic in the normal sense of the term. In the prologue he points out that he has nothing against previous writers of the Tristan story, indeed that he appreciates their efforts and knows that they wrote "niwan us edelem muote," with the best of intentions. But he adds that few have told the story aright and that he will himself write for the "edelen herzen," that is, for hearts above the normal courtly audience which wants only pleasure. These remarks are usually taken to mean that his treatment of the love theme would be different, and that he was writing for a select audience which would be able to appreciate his novel approach to the subject. This interpretation is no doubt correct, but it does not exclude another aspect of Gottfried's work, namely, that he wished to stress the artistic and intellectual approaches to love. His transition in the literary criticism passage is smooth enough; he states that knightly glory has been so frequently described that it has been worn out by speech and that he could give no pleasure to anyone by further attempts. [German poet] Hartmann von Aue, he says, knew how to color and ornament the subject both outwardly and inwardly (note that he has moved from the *swertleite* to knighthood in general), and he thus pays his respects to the master who understood the outward and inward meaning of courtly romance—in the accepted sense of the term. In his genre and style, Hartmann is unapproachable. For Wolfram he has nothing but scorn, but it is worth noting that it is mainly to his style that Gottfried is alluding, to his side leaps and high jumps on the field of words. Gottfried is soon done with the narrative poets. Although he mentions Heinrich von Veldecke as well as Hartmann, it is as a lyric poet that he praises him. Far more attention is paid to the lyric

poets—one hundred thirty lines against seventy—and in describing them the stress is upon the musical aspects of their work. For, says Gottfried, speaking of Walther von der Vogelweide, the music is in the mode which comes from Cithaeron, where the goddess of love holds sway both within and without, for she [Music] is the mistress of the chamber of that court; she shall be the leader of the "nightingales," of whom Walther is now the greatest. The meaning of the passage is clear—music is the way to love, and it descends from Aphrodite and the stream of Helicon to be the inspiration of the *Minnesänger* ["troubadour"], even if the mythology becomes a little confused in the process. After a brief glance at Tristan, who is still unready for his initiation, Gottfried returns to his theme, the need of inspiration and skill in words for the poet and in particular the need for inspiration from classical sources, from Apollo and the Muses. Finally we are told what Tristan is to be equipped with—not arms but "muot unde guot, bescheidenheit und höfschen sin." The exact nature of these virtues is not easy to determine, but it is certain that they are moral and intellectual qualities, not physical ones.

This playing down of the physical aspects of Tristan's character is found throughout the poem. Naturally, Tristan is an excellent knight in the normal sense of the term. His prowess in arms is far above that of any contemporary. He defeats Morolt and Morgan, dragons and giants, but in none of these actions does Gottfried stress his hero's bravery and some of his actions are definitely not in the best knightly tradition. As Petrus W. Tax has shown, much of the description of Tristan's combats seem to imply mockery of knightly standards.

A few examples must suffice to show the aspects of his hero which did interest Gottfried. Let us first note that his father Riwalin is almost always described in sensual and external terms:

> "seht" sprachen si "der jungelinc
> der ist ein sæliger man:
> wie sælichliche stet im an
> allez daz, daz er begat!
> wie gar sin lip ze wunsche stat!
> wie gant im so geliche in ein
> diu siniu keiserlichen bein!
> wie rehte sin schilt zaller zit
> an siner stat gelimet lit!
> wie zimet der schaft in siner hant!
> wie wol stat allez sin gewant!
> wie stat sin houbet und sin har!
> wie süeze ist aller sin gebar!
> wie sælichliche stat sin lip!
> o wol si sæligez wip,
> der vröude an ime beliben sol!"
>
> (704-719)

Gottfried places these words in the mouths of those who see Riwalin. This is the impression that he makes on a courtly audience when they first see him. Almost every line is an emotional exclamation at a different feature of his appearance and physical prowess and it is worth noting how often the word "sælic" and its compounds are associated with him. He is the happy, worldly knight rejected by Gottfried in his prologue, at least so far as the courtly audience which sees him is concerned. The passage just quoted should be compared with the careful description of the first impression which Tristan makes on the same court some years later (see below).

The dominant features of Tristan are made apparent as soon as Gottfried begins to describe his education. He is handed over to a wise man and begins the study of books. (There is an obvious parallel here with the story of Vergil and Lucinius as there is later with Apollonius of Tyre.) This study of books, we are explicitly told, was the beginning of his sorrow:

> der buoche lere und ir getwanc
> was siner sorgen anevanc;
> und iedoch do er ir began
> do leite er sinen sin dar an
> und sinen vliz so sere
> daz er der buoche mere
> gelernete in so kurzer zit
> dan ie kein kint e oder sit.
>
> (2085-92)

He also learned music and other arts, but his accomplishments in such skills as riding and fencing, are merely listed. No comment is made on their importance for his later life.

Tristan's first contact with Mark's court comes about through his meeting with the huntsman and his knowledge of hunting ceremonial a fairly common device in medieval works, but the impression he makes on the court is entirely due to his skill as an artist and musician:

> a Tristan, wære ich alse duo!
> Tristan, du maht gerne leben:
> Tristan, dir ist der wunsch gegeben
> aller der vuoge, die kein man
> ze dirre werlde gehaben kan."
> Ouch macheten si hier under
> mit rede michel wunder:
> "hora!" sprach diser, "hora! sprach der
> "elliu diu werlt diu hœre her:
> ein vierzehnjærec kint
> kan al die liste, die nu sint!"
>
> (3710-20)

There is the same quality of exclamatory surprise here, but the qualities admired and the attitude are different. The courtiers wish that they could be like Tristan but they know they cannot. It is not his beauty or physical strength that they admire, but his skill and knowledge, his *liste,* a term of many meanings. He is the *niuwe spilman,* the fresh face and the new type at court. The admiration he excites is increased by surprise that a person of his age should be capable of such feats, both in playing and singing and in knowledge of foreign languages. He is the infant prodigy, the young genius who knows more than grown men, and the effect of his skill and knowledge is to turn all men to his favor. Even here, however, the classical connection is not forgotten. It is the story of Pyramus and Thisbe that he sings, the *locus classicus* for unhappy love. Tristan is well aware of the burden imposed on him by his learning. The simple physical joys of the uncomplicated knight will never be his:

> wan ritterschaft, also man seit,

> diu muoz ie von der kintheit
> nemen ir anegenge
> oder si wirt selten strenge.
> daz ich min unversuohte jugent
> uf werdekeit unde uf tugent
> so rehte selten güebet han,
> daz ist vil sere missetan
> und han ez an mich selben haz.
> nu weiz ich doch nu lange daz:
> senfte und ritterlicher pris
> diu missehellent alle wis
> und mugen vil übele samet wesen.

Tristan goes on to say that if he had known before how things would stand with him, he would have organized his life differently. (He is still only fourteen!) There are other passages where it is made clear that the kind of training which Tristan had received was incompatible with the duties of a knight as they are normally understood. Tristan was bound to suffer for not being as other men are. The arts, and in particular the music which he loves and which is part of his being, do indeed give him a fuller life but one where, as Gottfried has already observed, sorrow and joy combine and sorrow predominates.

We must discuss in some detail the arrival of Tristan in Ireland, for it is central to the study of Tristan as artist. The hero has left Cornwall in a ship, and when he is near the coast, he has himself put into a small boat with only his harp—no weapons, no rich possessions. He is now dependent entirely on his music, and when a boat approaches, it is his music which draws a group of interested hearers, and, ultimately, Isold's own tutor, even though, as Gottfried emphasizes, the music he is playing, while technically superb, is that of a lifeless man. We are told that the tutor who hears him had already imparted to Isold over a period of years his own skill in music and the book-learning which he possessed. In other words, she had already received the normal education for a girl of her station from the court chaplain. The tutor soon recognizes in Tristan a skill far above his own and out of pity and admiration recommends him to his mistress, Isold's mother. She promises to cure Tristan but strikes a bargain—that he shall undertake to teach her daughter. Clearly he could teach her daughter only something exceptional, above the common run of playing skill and reading which she already possessed. The lines which describe this scene are so full of double meaning that they defy translation. Tristan, whose playing in the boat had been so lifeless, now plays

> niht alse ein lebeloser man,
> er vieng ez lebelichen an
> und alse der wol gemuote tuot.
>
> (7825-27)

He played no longer as a lifeless man—a man without liveliness. He was to be cured of his bodily wound and attain life once again, but that life was to be different, as the queen says with double implication:

> dar umbe wil ich dir din leben
> und dinen lip ze miete geben
> wol gesunt und wol getan:
> diu magich geben unde lan,
> diu beidiu sint in miner hant.
>
> (7855-59)

She can indeed give and refuse, but which action will produce which result is deliberately left unclear. Tristan for his part expresses his joy that he could be cured through music, but the phrase "mit spil genesen kan" could equally well mean "flourish through music," or "through my playing," or "through play." No educated listener could fail to be reminded of the story of Abélard and Héloïse, for there too a brilliant young man was called upon to instruct a sensitive girl, with dire results for both. Gottfried has altered his source material considerably in this scene, for in Thomas of Britain's version, if Brother Robert represents him accurately, the younger Isold asks to hear Tristan play and then herself asks for him as an instructor. The kind of instruction she receives is described only in general terms. Nor can we ignore the strong troubadour and *Minnesänger* tradition of the wound of love which was curable only by the person who had inflicted it. Gottfried seems to have written the whole of this scene with the double background of instruction and the wound-cure motif in mind. Tristan's bodily cure is succeeded by an incident in which other wounds, less easily curable, are inflicted.

We have already noted that Tristan's instruction of Isold goes beyond what she had already learned from the chaplain. In the account of the instruction which follows two elements predominate, music and *moraliteit*. We are given a description of Isold's acquisition of outstanding technical skill in playing and singing in various languages. But it is on the effects of music which Gottfried dwells, and to these we must now turn our attention. To understand them we must look at the statements on the esthetics of music which, we may safely assume, were known to Gottfried. As so often is the case in medieval studies, we must begin with [medieval philosopher] Boethius, for he incorporated the theories of Plato and the Neoplatonists into his treatise on music as well as the views of the Greek theorists. His *De institutione musica* was the basis of all medieval studies of the subject and was certainly read by any student who had progressed as far as Gottfried. For Boethius music was the queen of the arts and hearing the highest of the senses. Music embodied that harmony which found its loftiest expression in the music of the spheres, inaudible to mortals but expressing external cosmic harmony. Beauty as perceived by the senses was regarded by medieval writers as transitory and external. As the documents quoted by De Bruyne show, the deeper, truer beauty lies in the universal design, in harmony and proportion. (Perhaps this is why number relationships are important apart from the symbolic associations of the numbers themselves.) Music, more than any other of the arts, reflects this harmony and proportion. Boethius remarks [*in his Anicii Manlii Torquali Severini Boetii, de institutions musica libri quinque*]: "Nulla enim magis ad animum disciplinis via quam auribus patet." The ears are the best way for the disciplines to reach the mind. The very word *consonantia* can refer to music, to harmony of character, and to eternal harmony. Cassiodorus is even more definite about the priority of music than his great contemporary: "Haec cum de secreto naturae, tamquam sensuum regina, tropis suis ornata processerit, reliquae cogitationes exsiliunt omniaque facit eici ut ipsam solummodo dilectet audiri."

We can trace the effects of these pronouncements very clearly in Gottfried's work—the effect on Mark and his court, on the strangers in Ireland, on the Queen and Isold. It is through music, not through knightly prowess that Tristan makes his way. But this alone would do little more than confirm Mohr's statement that Tristan is essentially a *Spielmann* and place him in the same category as a score of other medieval heroes. Tristan teaches Isold a great deal more than mere musical skill. Gottfried constantly emphasizes that he improves her, and he reinforces this statement with details of her progress by naming the forms—*pastourelle, rotruange, chanson, reflet.* He stresses the "foreignness" of this accomplishment:

> leiche und so vremediu notelin,
> diu niemer vremeder kunden sin,
> in franzoiser wise
> von Sanze und San Dinise.

His reference to Saint Denis is interesting when we remember that the school there was in the forefront of the great innovations in musical theory of the later twelfth century.

Isold, in other words, is being elevated by Tristan to his own high level of musical accomplishment, not only in practice but in theory, which latter, according to contemporary writers, was by far the more important branch. I am reluctant to run the risk of being accused of reading into Gottfried's text meanings which could not possibly be there, but I cannot refrain from noting that the musical theories of the twelfth century recognized a distinction between two kinds of performed music, *musica practica pura,* which was designed to appeal to the senses and move through them, and *musica practica mixto* or *musica theoretica practica* designed to appeal to the higher faculties. The division corresponds to the well-known separation of perception by sight into the *sensus et imaginatio,* perceived by the *oculus carnis,* and *ratio et intelligentia,* perceived by the *oculus rationis et oculus contemplationis.* Isold's instruction is obviously concerned with *musica practica pura,* as we can see from Gottfried's careful description of its effects, a description which naturally has strong resemblances to the scene in which Tristan's impact on Mark's court was described.

> Wem mag ich si gelichen
> die schœnen, sælderichen
> wan den Syrenen eine,
> die mit dem agesteine
> die kiele ziehent ze sich?
> als zoch Isot, so dunket mich,
> vil herzen unde gedanken in,
> die doch vil sicher wanden sin
> von senedem ungemache.
> ouch sint die zwo sache,
> kiel ane anker unde muot,
> zebenmazene guot:
> si sint so selten beide
> an stæter wegeweide,
> so dicke in ungewisser habe,
> wankende beidiu an und abe,
> ündende hin unde her,

sus swebet diu wiselose ger,
der ungewisse minnen muot,
reht als daz schif ane anker tuot
in ebengelicher wise.

(8085-8105)

Isold is able so to move the senses of her audience through her playing that all their emotions are concentrated on love. A careful examination of the simile shows, however, that there is a destructive element in the music she sings. The Sirens led ships to crash upon the rocks and destroy themselves. So Isold's music arouses the senses, awakens love which had never been suspected, and causes the hearers to lose control both of emotion and thought.

The passage which follows details the effects even more precisely and we should note that there is more than emotion involved:

diu gevüege Isot, diu wise,
diu junge süeze künigin
also zoch si gedanken in
uz maneges herzen arken,
als der agestein die barken
mit der Syrenen sange tuot.
si sanc in maneges herzen muot
offenlichen unde tougen
durch oren und durch ougen.
ir sanc, dens offenliche tete
beide anderswa und an der stete,
daz was ir süeze singen,
ir senftez seiten clingen,
daz lute und offenliche
durch der oren künicriche
hin nider in diu herzen clanc.
so was der tougenliche sanc
ir wunderlichiu schœne,
diu mit ir muotgedœne
verholne unde tougen
durch diu venster der ougen
in vil manic edele herze sleich
und daz zouber darin streich,
daz die gedanke zehant
vienc unde vahende bant
mit sene und mit seneder not.
Sus hæte sich diu schœne Isot
von Tristandes lere
gebezzeret sere.

(8106-34)

Isold is described as "the wise" and the effects of her singing are combined with the effects of her personal beauty. As so often in Gottfried's work, there is a double effect both in the emotion described and in the language used. The obvious impact is through the sounds of the music, the secret effect through Isold's presence; the first impact is on the senses, the second on the thoughts. Immediately after this passage we are told that Isold composed songs— as indeed we might expect from the earlier description of her instruction. She knows how to write material which will produce the effects she desires. In other words, she is showing herself the complete musician, the theorist as well as the practical performer. But when describing her impact on the members of the court, not on Tristan, Gottfried confines himself to sensual description.

That music brings *consonantia* to Tristan and Isold can hardly be denied. But there is more. Let us return once more to Boethius, this time for his definition of a musician. A musician, he says, is a person who understands modes and rhythms, types of songs, combinations, and everything which will be discussed later in his treatise. He should also know the works of the poets according to the theory and method proposed and suited to music. Thus he does not regard mere performers or even poets as complete musicians. Only those who have also mastered the theory are really worthy of the title. It will be noted that either Tristan or Isold could meet these qualifications, according to the way Gottfried describes them. In the teaching of Isold, Tristan has taken the first step towards their ultimate harmony. He raises her to the same musical level which he has himself already attained; he gives her the power over men which his own music gave to him. But this is not all. Gottfried stresses that he also teaches her something called *moraliteit,* "diu kunst diu leret schœne site." There have been numerous attempts to explain the meaning of this term, none of them very successful. Gottfried seems to have introduced the word to German and would hardly have done so if he had intended by it nothing more than "polite education" or even training for the courtly virtues. By the introduction of a word new to his audience he clearly meant to call their attention to the fact that Isold was acquiring a quality different from those normally taught to young ladies of the court circle. His careful description confirms this:

da solten alle vrouwen mite
in ir jugent unmüezic wesen.
moraliteit daz süeze lesen
deist sælic unde reine.
ir lere hat gemeine
mit der werlde und mit gote.
si leret uns in ir gebote
got unde der werlde gevallen:
sist edelen herzen allen
zeiner ammen gegeben,
daz si ir lipnar unde ir leben
suochen in ir lere;
wan sin hant guot noch ere,
ezn lere si moraliteit.

(8006-19)

It should be noted that *moraliteit* is the nurse of the *edele herzen,* the people for whom Gottfried wrote his poem and who are described in his prologue as not satisfied with a love which involves only pleasure. It is *their* nourishment and *their* life. It can hardly, therefore, be mere superficial behavior but something deeper and more permanent. It is strange that no one, to my knowledge, has called attention in this connection to another passage of Boethius: "Musica vero non modo speculationi verum etiam moralitati coniuncta est. Nihil enim tam proprium humanitati quam remitti dulcibus modis astringique contrariis."

The word *speculatio* is used throughout this treatise in the sense of "theory," that is, the study of music as an art. This, of course, is what Gottfried has been describing. But also, Boethius says, music is important for its relation to the character of man. *Moralitas* is a word hard to define exactly—it is not "morality" but the total "mores" of man, his character viewed as an abstraction. Music can affect this character, it can be soothed or aggravated, ennobled or debased. It is surely no accident that we see the double effect of music upon spirits dedicated both to the joy and the sorrow of love. Gottfried has already made clear the effects of the playing both of Tristan and Isold on a courtly audience. *Moraliteit,* however, is something higher. It links the higher spirits and pleases both the human and the divine. So, too, does Boethius describe music as linking the human and the divine, producing that *consonantia* which is a harmony both of sounds and souls. Is it too farfetched to suppose that the use of the word *moraliteit* is at least inspired by Boethius' use of *moralitas*? The fact that his description of the training in music is followed immediately by the mention of this quality would seem to indicate that this is so. Harmony of character and of soul come through music.

Isold is a different person after Tristan's teaching. It is worth noting that he never performs knightly service for her, as Lancelot does for Guinevere. The episode with the dragon is almost a travesty of such affairs in courtly romance, for Tristan kills the dragon without intending it as a service. If the action had any importance, it was to win Isold for Mark! He never has to fight the seneschal, for the wretch is beaten by the production of the dragon's tongue. We have already noted the failure of the lovers and of Brangaene to put their love affair on the same level as that of a courtly intrigue. It is to the scene in the *Minnegrotte* that we must turn to see the realization of the preparation made by Tristan's instruction.

This is not the place to add anything to the enormous amount already written about the literary use of the Minnegrotte, but one or two points must be recalled. The grotto is described as quite separate from the normal world and in particular from the world of the court. This is, of course, a permanent tradition in the source material, but in most other versions the separation is one which the lovers hate and which they bring to an end as soon as they are able. Even in the work of Thomas of Britain the grotto, although pleasant enough, is not the shrine which Gottfried makes of it. All the literary devices which designate the earthly paradise appear in Gottfried's version—the *paysage idéal,* the separation by wasteland and forest, the mountains, the long journey to reach it. In this place love could attain levels which were not possible on earth. Such a view is not, of course, confined to Gottfried. We find similar use of the *hortus conclusus* motif in the Phyllis and Flora poem and in the *Roman de la Rose.* It is also to be observed that the lovers are alone—they are not in Thomas' poem. That Gottfried allegorizes his edifice, if such it can be called, by the techniques described by Hrabanus Maurus, Honorius of Autun, and later by Durandus is well recognized. But it is less often noted that the grotto itself is explicitly stated to be pagan and dedicated to the goddess of love. Classical allusions again appear, the stories which the lovers tell are those of famous couples of antiquity. Tristan and Isold have withdrawn into an idealized world many of whose elements derive from the classics and whose relation to their love is depicted by the use of allegorizing techniques similar to those employed by the Christian fathers in relating the church edifice to the soul. The virtues proclaimed, however, are those which suit Gottfried's conception of perfect love. The whole passage is an attempt to describe in allegorical terms the

shrine of love in the heart. What other meaning can we attach to the statement "Diz weiz ich wol, wan ich was da." Gottfried has himself been to the cave, he has done everything which the lovers do except lie in the crystalline bed, for there only the elect could come. But all the other experiences he has had: he has indeed frequented the grotto, that is, been in love so often that the marble at the side of the bed would show traces if it were not for its power to renew itself.

> und aber den esterich da bi,
> swie herte marmelin er si,
> den han ich so mit triten zebert:
> hæt in diu grüene niht ernert,
> an der sin meistiu tugent lit,
> von der er wahset alle zit,
> man spurte wol dar inne
> diu waren spor der minne.
>
> (17117-24)

The virtues of true love have also affected his heart—even though he has never been to Cornwall.

> diu sunnebernde vensterlin,
> diu habent mir in daz herze min
> ir gleste dicke gesant:
> ich han diu fossiure erkant.
> sit minen eilif jaren ie
> und enkam ze Curnewale nie.
>
> (17133-38)

Clearly it is not a place which Gottfried is describing, but a state of ideal love, and he is using the grotto allegory as a background for figures which would evoke in his readers a realization of the ideal state he is describing. [Lyric Christian poet] Prudentius had done something very similar, for the battle he described was in the soul, even though one would not know it from his descriptions. Gottfried's lovers are still mortal but they are shown as raised above mortal experience. They need no mortal food, as Gottfried emphasizes. But once again it is in the arts and in particular in music that their inner harmony expresses itself. As often in lyric poetry, the *paysage idéal* reflects the perfection of their state, but there is much more emphasis than usual on bird song.

> diz gesinde diende zaller zit
> ir oren unde ir sinne.
>
> (16894 f.)

We need not see here any more than the author's general stressing of the delight and satisfaction of all the senses in the state of love. Much more important is that when the lovers retire to their *kluse,* their inner shrine, they join in harmony:

> und liezen danne clingen
> ir harphen unde ir singen
> senelichen unde suoze.
> si wehselten unmuoze
> mit handen und mit zungen:
> si harpheten, si sungen
> leiche unde noten der minne.
> si wandelten dar inne
> ir wunnenspil, swie si gezam:
>
> (17205-13)

The harmony between them is complete:

ouch lutete ietweder clanc
der harphen unde der zungen,
sos in einander clungen,
so suoze dar inne
als ez der süezen Minne
wol zeiner kluse wart benant:
la fossiure a la gent amant

(17218-24)

Their music was more clear and more pure than any which had ever been heard in this shrine dedicated to the goddess of love. There is little doubt in my mind that Gottfried is here using musical imagery as he used the allegory of the church and of the *paysage idéal*. He is showing his two lovers achieving a higher harmony, the *consonantia* of which we have spoken. It is not the *consonantia* of the human soul with the universe. The lovers do not hear the music of the spheres, but here, as so often, Gottfried is applying the imagery common to the whole Christian tradition of his day to illustrate the higher love of which Tristan and Isold are the representatives. At the beginning of his study of the poem, Petrus Tax asks the very pertinent question: "ob diese *minne* eine nach der Intention des Dichters im ganzen Werk einheitliche, wandlungsunfähige Gestalt aufweist, oder aber ob Gottfried nicht vielmehr zeigen will, wie Tristan und Isolde erst allmählich, und nach vielen Rückfällen in eine ihnen eigentlich ungemäße Form der Liebe, den schmalen und gefahrvollen Weg ihrer *minne* his zum hohen Gipfel erklimmen". The thesis outlined in this paper contributes something to the solution of the problem. Both Tristan and Isold required to be trained before they were capable of the highest form of love. Tristan was trained in books and music until he was intellectually and spiritually capable. This training he subsequently imparted to Isold. I am not, of course, arguing that theirs was an intellectual love. The exact nature of the love, however interesting as a problem in itself, is not, in fact, strictly relevant. It is the means of arriving at perfect harmony which we are discussing. This harmony was achieved through and within the arts and particularly through music. Such a viewpoint does not exclude the consideration that the lovers themselves at first believed their situation to be courtly, nor that Gottfried wished to show the depth of their attraction by using the terminology of mysticism. The disrespect for the trappings of courtly romance, however, and the ironical treatment of those who follow its methods are best explained by Gottfried's determination to make his hero an artist. He is much more than a *Spielmann*, much more than a *homo ludens*, even though he incorporates many of their characteristics. The love of Tristan and Isold rests on a harmony attained through the arts, just as Gottfried, in describing the growth and flowering of their love, uses the style of the schools which forces the hearer to interpret what he hears. The quarrel with Wolfram was thus fundamental. It concerned not only the style but the attitude which style represents. Wolfram's obscurity is often humorous, often one suspects, deliberate, sometimes caused by ignorance. Gottfried uses a style of which double and triple meanings are an essential constituent. It is the style of a formally educated man, and this man was Gottfried's hero. (pp. 364-72)

W. T. H. Jackson, "Tristan the Artist in Gott-

fried's Poem," in PMLA, *Vol. LXXVII, No. 4, September, 1962, pp. 364-72.*

Richey on Gottfried's lyricism:

[Gottfried] is not known to us as a Minnesinger, but his romance of *Tristan,* upon which his fame rests, is as much song as story, and has rightly been called a 'Hohelied der Minne' [high song of love]. The music of the verse is enchanting, and the highlights of the story are to be looked for in the lyrical passages, with their ineffable blend of intellectual subtlety and emotional depth.

Margaret Fitzgerald Richey, in her Medieval German Lyrics, *Oliver and Boyd, 1958.*

M. O'C. Walshe (essay date 1962)

[*Walshe is an English educator specializing in Germanic studies. In the following excerpt, he offers a general evaluation of Gottfried's courtly epic, noting its poetic style, characterizations, and importance in the history of medieval German literature.*]

[A] great figure in the history of the court epic is Gottfried von Strassburg, whose *Tristan* forms the greatest imaginable contrast to [Wolfram von Eschenbach's] *Parzival,* considered from the point of view of style, of content, or of ethos. These two works represent in fact the opposite poles of the courtly world: whatever claims to be courtly lives and has its being somewhere between these two extremes. [German poet] Hartmann was the teacher of both poets, and it is interesting to see how the different tendencies discernible in his work are developed by Wolfram and Gottfried respectively. Hartmann was acutely conscious of the conflicting claims of the divine and the human, the next world and this, and his final 'solution' of the problem really consisted of little more than a tacit acceptance of both spheres separately. This finds its outward expression in the sharp division of his literary output into two parts: there is no serious attempt at a synthesis. But the two younger poets attempted a closer integration. Wolfram saw human life *sub specie æternitatis,* so that for his vision ideal chivalry was but the earthly reflexion of the divine. Hartmann's conditional acceptance, in *Iwein,* of the values of this world in their own sphere points towards Gottfried's elevation of the purely human into the quasi-transcendental sphere. Where Wolfram brings heaven down to earth, Gottfried invests things earthly with heavenly attributes. If Wolfram's way points forward to the mystics of the 14th century, Gottfried's points rather to the secular humanism of the Renaissance. *Tristan* is the apotheosis of earthly love.

The 12th century saw the appearance of two famous tales of love. One . . . was Chrétien's *Lancelot,* whose theme, at second hand, is perhaps the most familiar of all Arthurian themes to the English reader. The other was the story of *Tristan and Isolde.* At first glance these two tales appear very similar and seem to breathe the same spirit. Closer inspection reveals a contrast. In both works the king's nephew has a love-affair with the queen, Lancelot with Guinevere, Arthur's wife, and Tristan with Isolde, the wife of King Mark. In both works this immoral relation is (*pace* Tennyson) accepted: both arose in a *milieu* sufficiently broadminded to overlook the moral teachings of the Church for the sake of a good story. Here there is no difference of attitude. The difference lies in the relation of the lovers to each other. Lancelot is the typical lover according to the strict code of courtly love—he is subordinated to the lady, who is his mistress in more senses than one, and he is bound to obey her lightest wish without hesitation. This is the 'service' he has to perform before he can expect a reward. In *Tristan* there is no mention of 'service' and no suggestion of subordination of either sex to the other. Tristan is on a level with Isolde, both burn with the same passion; they are not the serving knight and the overweening *frouwe*, but *ein man ein wîp, ein wîp ein man*. In Walther's terminology it is a case of *ebene minne* ["noble love"]. The story is a universal tale of overmastering passion, not an artificial figment of 12th-century French feminist imagination. This was the theme which attained its classically perfect form at the hands of Gottfried von Strassburg. It is immoral, if we will, but it is universally human in its appeal.

Like Hartmann, Gottfried is known to us only from his own work and the references of later poets. Documentary evidence of his life is completely lacking. He does not even tell us his own name in *Tristan,* but since the poem is incomplete, it is possible that he would have named himself at the end. He was not a knight, for the title always given him is not *hêr* but *meister*. At one time it was believed that he could be identified with a municipal notary of Strassburg, but this has turned out to be a mistake. Nevertheless, we must assume that he belonged to some such circle, and he may well have been in the employ of the bishop or the municipality. He was certainly not a cleric, but like [German poet] Heinrich von dem Türlin a representative of the rising citizen class, though a far more cultured one. The Rhenish episcopal cities such as Cologne, Strassburg and Basle, were among the first in which the citizens became socially and politically important. In the course of time they developed their own independent culture, but to begin with they adopted the cultural forms of the still-dominant knightly caste. Certain elements of this culture were not so intimately bound up with the profession of arms that they could not be adapted to the conditions of the well-to-do *bourgeoisie*. At the same time we can see in Gottfried's case that it is rather the courtly than the strictly chivalrous element which attracts him. He had absorbed all that was finest in the secular culture of his time: he understood French as well as German (no mistakes in translation have been found in *Tristan,* although Strassburg was at that time a purely German city), and he was also thoroughly at home in the Latin literature then available. He had a wide knowledge of theology (despite his remarkably secular outlook) and had obviously had a thorough musical training. We may therefore assume that, like Hartmann, he had attended a monastery school. Who the patron was for whom he composed his *Tristan* is unknown: in an acrostic he mentions the name Dietrich, but this personage has not been identified.

Gottfried was . . . not the first to retell the *Tristan* story in German: Eilhart von Oberg had already produced a version in the 12th century. Gottfried's immediate source was the poem of the Norman Thomas de Bretagne, written in England between about 1155 and 1170, of which we possess nine different fragments from five separate manuscripts, making a total of 3144 lines. But a direct comparison of the two works is unfortunately impossible except for a small portion, as the Thomas fragments all belong to the latter part of the story, beginning shortly before the point at which Gottfried breaks off. In fact only 54 lines of the French poem can be directly compared, and these correspond to 114 lines in Gottfried. There is no doubt that the original story is of Celtic origin, though various features of the existing versions must be put to the account of later French writers. The name of the hero Tristan is certainly Celtic, and he is identified with a Pictish prince Drostan. The name of the heroine, Isolde, has been declared to be Germanic, but is in fact probably also Celtic.

The existing Tristan romances fall into two groups, which are called the minstrel version and the courtly version. The (older) minstrel version is represented in French especially by Bérol and in German by Eilhart von Oberg. The more polished courtly group embraces Thomas's work and those versions dependent on it. These are Gottfried's poem and the Norwegian prose translation *Tristrams Saga ok Ísondar,* made by the monk Robert for King Haakon V in 1226. This is artlessly written and gives only the externals of the action, omitting all the reflexions and monologues which mirror the emotions of the lovers. But it is valuable because with its aid we can check how closely Gottfried follows his source. (pp. 180-83)

We might say that what [Anglo-Norman poet] Thomas did for his source, Gottfried did in turn for Thomas. Thomas refined the crude minstrel-tale and deepened its psychology: Gottfried further refined and improved on Thomas. The *Urtristan* was, we may assume, a kind of fate tragedy. The tension lay in the conflict between Tristan's loyalty to Mark, his lord, and the fearful, dæmonic power of the love which bound him to Isolde, and from this tension the tragedy resulted. Love was here regarded as a fatal and inescapable doom. But such a conception ran counter to the views of 12th-century courtly society, for whom love was primarily neither guilt nor dæmonic force, but a positive value. Thus Thomas had to alter the motivation. Even then it did not quite fit in with fashionable theories, but Thomas did what he could: he turned the tragedy of fate into a psychological novel, putting the main stress on the analysis of the lovers' feelings. For this purpose he introduced monologues into the story which, it is true, may seem to us rather dry and pedantic. Other changes too were necessary. Crude and archaic features had to be removed or toned down, events had to be more plausibly motivated, and above all the whole had to be clothed in a dignified and fitting style, which was not without lyrical qualities. Thomas aimed to write a story for lovers, to create a work of art whose form should adequately express the feelings of the lovers. He was certainly a fine poet, if not of the very first rank. His chief fault is perhaps a certain over-intellectualism. He seems to dissect rather than feel the emotions of his characters.

Gottfried's *Tristan* was a life's work. We can be sure that he wrote no other major work, for it is highly improbable that a second great work by the famous author of *Tristan* would have disappeared so completely as not even to be mentioned by contemporaries. He must have spent many years on this one poem, polishing and repolishing it, and finally died without finishing it, having composed not quite 20,000 lines. Though he relied on Thomas, he knew other versions of the story and was critical of them. He did not completely reshape his source as Wolfram had done in his two great epics; he changed but little of the action, but deepened and refined on the psychology and laid even greater stress on the didactic element. Nevertheless the ethical problem posed by *Tristan* is a difficult one, and the varying views expressed by scholars about this are not always free from unconscious humour. One scholar has held that his 'moral laxity' is typically French, while another has seen something characteristically German in the lovers' unwavering constancy in danger and distress. It could however be urged that Gottfried was chiefly concerned to tell a story, not to point a moral.

If there is some doubt as to how to interpret *Tristan* it is not because Gottfried does not tell us what he thinks. In his prologue he makes it quite clear that he is writing for a very definite public. His *Tristan* is no more intended for the masses than is *Parzival*. Little as they otherwise have in common, both poets could have headed their works with Horace *Odi profanum vulgus et arceo*. Gottfried writes for the world of 'noble hearts'—*diu edelen herzen*. It is noteworthy that the word *edel* appears first in *Tristan* in the transferred sense, denoting aristocracy of outlook, not necessarily of birth, and it is no coincidence that Gottfried himself was not of noble origin. The *edelen herzen* are those who are prepared to take life as it is, who do not seek to live in a mere world of pleasure all the time, but who know joy and sorrow, who wish not merely to taste the joys of a fleeting amour, but who do not shrink from the pain which is inseparable from true love. He counts himself among this select company:

> Der werlt wil ich gewerldet wesen,
> mit ir verderben oder genesen.

> of that world I would be a 'worldling',
> with it I'd fain perish or be saved.

Love is for Gottfried—at least within the framework and for the purposes of his *Tristan* (perhaps a not unimportant reservation)—the central concept in his total view of life; it has an autonomous value such as is normally accorded only to religion, or at least to the same extent that the concept of chivalry has that value in *Iwein*. We must, however, take care not to over-simplify Gottfried's view of life as it is here expressed. In fact it is quite complex. In any case it is clearly a chief purpose of his to present this ideal of love in its highest perfection, and at the same time with all its problematic implications.

But the elevation of love to a kind of religion has further consequences: like every religion this love has its own morality, according to which judgements must be passed if it is to be taken at all seriously. And according to this morality it is not Tristan and Isolde who are guilty, but Marke, the deceived husband. For he knows that the wife

with whom he lives is inwardly a stranger to him and belongs, despite the Church and the law, to another. In this point Andreas Capellanus, the theoretician of courtly love, would have been on the side of the lovers, for his first rule runs: *causa coniugii ab amore non est excusatio recta*, 'the fact of marriage is no proper excuse for not loving', i.e. should not stand in the way of lovers. And although he also says 'there is nothing to prohibit one woman from being loved by two men', he also declares at another place that 'a true lover does not desire to enjoy the embraces of any other except his beloved'.

Gottfried's attitude was inevitably conditioned by the development of the story in the tradition as it reached him. Nothing, perhaps, underwent a profounder change than the love-potion. In the earliest fable the potion was presumably nothing but an instrument of fate, by means of which the lovers were destroyed. In the succeeding minstrel stage, on the other hand, it was probably little more than an external means of inaugurating an exciting action. In some versions the potion loses its potency after three or four years—an unæsthetic touch which Gottfried could not possibly have used. In point of fact in Gottfried's, as indeed even in Thomas's version, the love-potion has little more than symbolic significance. Conceivably it might almost have been dropped. But this would have meant too violent a break with tradition and, besides, the potion served one useful function as an excuse for the behaviour of the lovers, who were in its power and therefore could not help themselves.

The scene in which Tristan and Isolde partake of the unhappy potion is quite short but marvellously effective. During the crossing from Ireland to Cornwall the ship stops in port. Most of those on board go ashore, but Tristan visits Isolde, who still harbours bitter resentment against him for having killed her uncle, in her cabin. While there he asks for wine. A serving-wench brings the presumed wine:

> nein, ezn was niht mit wîne,
> doch ez im glîche wære,
> ez was diu wernde swære,
> diu endelôse herzenôt
> von der si beide lâgen tôt.

> but no, it was not wine,
> though like wine it seemed.
> It was enduring pain,
> everlasting heart's distress
> from which (at last) they both lay dead.

They both drink; then Brangæne comes in and is seized with horror when she sees the flask:

> mit tôtem herzen gie si dar.
> si nam daz leide veige vaz,
> si truog ez dannen und warf daz
> in den tobenden wilden sê:
> 'owê mir armen!' sprach si 'owê
> daz ich zer werlde ie wart geborn!'

> with a dead heart she went thither.
> she took the evil deadly flask,
> she bore it thence and cast it forth
> into the wild and raging sea:
> 'alack and woe is me!' she said, 'alas

that ever in this world I was born!'

A remarkable feature here is that the sea has suddenly become wild and raging in the harbour. Nature herself obviously takes an interest in the fate of the lovers. There follows a long description of the effects of the potion, and this is not, as in Veldeke's poem, couched in purely physiological terms, but shows real psychological insight. Love creeps into the hearts of both and conquers them before they are even aware of the fact; Isolde strives vainly in love's toils like a bird on a limed twig. Both are the prey of conflicting emotions: in Tristan love must contend with honour, in Isolde with modesty, but the issue is not in doubt, and both at last succumb and shamefaced confess their feelings. In this account Gottfried displays his virtuosity.

The high-point of the poem is reached with the description of the Grotto of Love. In the oldest versions the lovers had to flee to the woods and there endure a life of privation as the price of being together. Thomas had converted this life in the woods into an idyll by introducing the Grotto. Gottfried exploited its possibilities to the full. This grotto lies hidden in the woods, far from human habitation, and owes its origin to the days when the earth was inhabited by giants. Gottfried gives it a splendid natural setting and describes its architecture in detail. It is dedicated, like a pagan temple, to the Goddess of Love. It is adorned throughout with precious stones and has a marble floor. Tiny windows above let in the light, and the entry is guarded by a bronze door. The lovers subsist here without food, sustained by love alone—just as the inhabitants of Munsalvæsche are sustained by the power of the Graal. In reply to possible objections, Gottfried says that he too has once lived on love. After explaining the symbolism he concludes: 'I too know the grotto, though in all my life I have never been in Cornwall.'

The parallel between Wolfram's Munsalvæsche and Gottfried's Grotto is unmistakable, and may even be intentional. For Wolfram the Graal Castle is certainly symbolic—but the details of the symbolism are not insisted on. The total impression is left to have its effect. Gottfried is not content to leave matters thus. Every detail is allegorically ('mystically' in the earlier medieval sense) expounded. Thus we are told that the grotto is round, without corners, because true love knows no concealment, it is lofty because it gives *hôher muot,* and so on. In like manner, in Old High German times, passages from the Bible had been interpreted, and the most erotic passages from the *Song of Songs* explained in acceptable terms. But in Gottfried's hands this theological technique was turned back on itself to create a 'theology of love'. The method was to prove popular, as we see from the *Roman de la Rose.*

The lengths to which Gottfried was prepared to go in apparently subordinating religion to the service of love can be seen in the famous passage describing Isolde's ordeal. She has to prove her innocence by carrying a red-hot ploughshare in her hand. First of all she prays to Christ for aid, and then she thinks of a plan to deceive the court. Tristan appears, disguised as a pilgrim, at the place where the ordeal is to take place. Marke and Isolde arrive in a small boat, and the presumed pilgrim offers to carry Isolde

ashore. In doing so he stumbles and falls with her still in his arms. Thus Isolde is able to swear that she has lain in the arms of no man but Marke and, of course, the poor pilgrim whom all have seen carrying her ashore! Thereupon she takes the glowing ploughshare in her hand, and it does not burn her:

> dâ wart wol goffenbæret
> und al der werlt bewæret,
> daz der vil tugenthafte Krist
> wintschaffen als ein ermel ist,
>
> there it was made manifest
> and proven to all the world
> that Christ the virtuous
> is pliant as a windblown sleeve.

a remark which astonishes us in a medieval poet. This has been interpreted as a deliberately anti-religious utterance, but it is far more likely that it reflects rather Gottfried's rejection of the barbarous and antiquated custom of the ordeal, which in any case was soon to be condemned (1215) by the Lateran Council.

One is perhaps slightly surprised to discover that *Tristan* is also, among so many other things, a didactic work. In the description of the young Tristan's education we learn a great deal about medieval pedagogical methods and, paradoxical as it sounds, we find in *Tristan* more information about the courtly code of morality than in any other medieval epic. On the occasion of Tristan's investiture Marke gives his nephew good advice, while the continuation of the passage also contains the first piece of literary criticism in the German language. Then, too, Tristan, disguised as the minstrel Tantris, is engaged by the Irish queen to instruct her daughter, and it is here that we find the famous formulation of the whole courtly moral code: *Got und der werlt gevallen.* Pleasing the world, i.e. *le monde,* the courtly world, is the same as possessing *êre,* enjoying the respect of one's fellow men. The tragedy of love in *Tristan* lies not least in the fact that it is ultimately incompatible with 'honour' in this sense. Therefore those who are existentially committed to the world of the 'noble hearts', for whom the morality of *Tristan* is valid, must finally perish with this world. In this context the demands of religion are overtly considered as little as they are in *Iwein,* but by implication they are called into question. Thus Gottfried's real attitude is not so easy to define, and some scholars have been led into strange speculations. Recent attempts to connect his outlook with that of certain contemporary heretical movements are not very convincing. What is more certain is that he was familiar with 12th-century mystical trends, whose language he echoes. But it is unsafe to regard *Tristan* as altogether a confessional work, except in so far as Gottfried made it a vehicle for his æsthetic ideals. Nor can we avoid the suspicion that some things in *Tristan* are intended as a polemical counterblast to *Parzival,* the *mystique* of which Gottfried found distasteful. There are many indications that the rival poets sharpened their wits on each other, and Wolfram, too, gave as good as he got. It is likely, for instance, that Wolfram's portrayal of Sigune as a martyr of love is in opposition to Gottfried's Isolde, whose martyrdom he regarded as spurious.

Gottfried's characterisation reveals both his strength and his weakness. Just as the morality of *Tristan* is relative to the basic conception, so too its psychological truth tends to fluctuate according to the distance of each episode from the central theme. Brilliant though Gottfried's psychological penetration is, it is like a searchlight which he switches on when he is interested. It does not play so continuously as Wolfram's on great and small alike. It illuminates, but, except in the moments of greatest intensity, it scarcely warms. Thus the characters of the poem tend to remain somewhat frozen in splendid but rather conventional attitudes except at the peaks of the inner action. Gottfried idealises them just as Hartmann tends to do, but the idealisation is æsthetic rather than ethical.

In his youth Tristan appears far too much of a model boy to be entirely acceptable, and he later develops a little too much into the perfect knight and accomplished man-of-the-world who masters all arts to perfection, to be entirely credible. He is the glass of fashion, the mould of form; he is inventive and resourceful (*listec*) and skilled of body, able like Odysseus to find a way out of any situation. But he seems curiously devoid of inner life when we compare him with Parzival. Nor is it possible to discover in his actions any higher ethical motivation, though he shows loyalty to Marke and suffers from the conflict which the drinking of the potion imposes on him. From then on, of course, his only loyalty is to Isolde, and at the end he wavers even in this. There is a certain contrast with Isolde here, who becomes more attractive to us precisely towards the end, owing to her more unconditional loyalty to Tristan. In fact she makes a more distinctly human impression just because she is less idealised. Her radiant beauty—nowhere described in detail—is without blemish like that of other medieval heroines, but her character is not free from human faults or even from distinctly evil traits. She is easily moved to anger, as we learn quite early from the scene in which she wishes to kill Tantris/Tristan because he slew her uncle, and her desire to do away with the faithful Brangæne from a quite unfounded fear of betrayal does not endear her to us. Beneath the courtly surface she has a slightly dæmonic aspect, doubtless a heritage from earlier versions of the story.

King Marke is perhaps a more sympathetic character on the whole, whether Gottfried intended this or not. He is noble and generous, a wise ruler, and he loves both his nephew and his wife above all else, and for long refuses to listen to the rumours which are being spread about them. As a deceived husband he plays an unheroic role, no doubt, but here too his indecision springs from his love for both Tristan and Isolde. He does not want to know the truth, and when finally no further doubt is possible, Gottfried remarks that he was happier when he could still doubt. In Thomas's version, Marke too had partaken of the potion and was therefore condemned to blind love. Gottfried eliminated this feature, thereby enabling himself to show Marke as a relatively free agent; yet Marke's love for Isolde, blindly sensual though it be, is so deep that he can forgive her everything. This may be weakness, but it is a feature not lacking in human warmth. A favourite character of Gottfried's is Brangæne, the sharer of the lovers' secret and unwitting cause of the tragedy. Despite

Isolde's attempt to reward her loyalty with treachery, she still remains ever ready to help the lovers out of every predicament. Tristan's companion Kurvenal is her male counterpart, but has much less to do in the story. Such lesser characters too, as the faithful Rual, who brought up Tristan as a child and cared for his heritage, are little individualised: though carefully and sympathetically drawn, they remain conventional, not endowed with the individual life we find in similar characters in *Parzival*.

For formal beauty of style Gottfried's *Tristan* is unsurpassed among German epic poems of the Middle Ages—at least if we discount Wolfram's haunting *Titurel* fragments. On this account he has jocularly been called the greatest French poet of the Middle Ages. His verse is extremely melodious, and in fact the claim has been made that a kind of musical compositional principle can be found in it. Occasionally the ornamentation may appear a little too heavy and he seems to become excessively mannered, but in general he exercises a wise restraint and avoids this danger. We have here a hint of the later Italian *dolce stil nuovo*. But this style attests not only his good taste, but also his learning. The elaborate use of the figures of rhetoric betrays his scholastic training. There are plays on words, acrostics which run through the whole poem at certain points, and the decorative quatrains which effectively introduce the whole and round off important sections. The music of his verse, indeed, seems often to flow on effortlessly with a Mozartian grace. (pp. 184-92)

> M. O'C. Walshe, "The Classical Court Epic," in his Medieval German Literature: A Survey, Cambridge, Mass.: Harvard University Press, 1962, pp. 134-92.

H. B. Willson   (essay date 1964)

[*In the essay below, Willson discusses Gottfried's prologue to* Tristan and Isolde, *identifying elements of Christian mysticism in the poet's attempt to reconcile the divine and mortal aspects of love.*]

In the prologue to his *Tristan* Gottfried von Strassburg distinguishes between two worlds. One of them seeks only joy and is unwilling and unable to endure sorrow:

> als die, von der ich hoere sagen,
> diu keine swaere enmüge getragen
> und niwan in vröudon welle sweben:
> die laze ouch got mit vröuder leben!

Not for this world has he composed his story but for another,

> diu samet in eime herzen treit
> ir süeze sur, ir liebez leit,
> ir herzeliep, ir senede not,
> ir liebez leben, ir leiden tot,
> ir lieben tot, ir leidez leben. . . .

This world is that of the *senedaere*, who have *edele herzen* ["noble hearts"] or *edeler muot*.

Although there has been a great deal of speculation as to what the poet means by this opposition of the two worlds and as to its significance in relation to the story he tells of the love of Tristan and Isolde, we do not yet have a full understanding of the inspiration and intention behind it. The concept of the *edelez herze* remains controversial. In what does the nobility consist? In how far is one justified in considering it to be an analogy of the mystical 'edele Seele'?

As yet, the indebtedness of Gottfried's **Tristan** to Bernardine mysticism is by no means universally accepted, although much evidence has been adduced in favour of the theory. In view of this uncertainty, it would seem useful to point out a close parallel with Gottfried's 'seekers after joy' to be found in [medieval spiritual writer] St Bernard, and to try to ascertain whether or not the poet is inspired by it.

In his *De Gradibus Humilitatis et Superbiae* (cap. XII) St Bernard says: 'Proprium est superborum, laeta semper appetere, et tristia devitare, juxta illud: Cor stultorum ubi laetitia (*Eccle.* VII, 5)'. Pride leads men always to seek joy and to flee sorrow. He goes on to explain what he means: when a man has descended the first two grades of pride the joy for which he continually sighs is interrupted by the unhappiness he feels when he sees good in others, for he finds the humiliation it reflects on him intolerable. He therefore goes to the opposite extreme and tries to draw particular attention to his own merits, while at the same time detracting from the merits of others. In so doing he seeks to perpetuate his own joy and remove the cause of his sorrow. As a result vain joy, the third degree of pride, begins to possess him whom joy and sorrow previously shared each in its turn. Such people cannot bear to hear others extolled and so they sing their own praises at the expense of others. Only in this way can they deceive themselves into thinking and believing that they are superior to their fellows.

The fact that both Gottfried and St Bernard refer to persons who seek only joy prompts the question: does this imply an *analogia entis* or does it merely reflect a 'structural' similarity with mystical thought, intentionally employed in order to demonstrate an *analogia antithetica,* of the kind suggested by Gottfried Weber [in his *Gottfrieds von Strassburg Tristan und die Krise des hochmitte lalterlichen Weltbildes um 1200,* 1953]? Or is the parallel only coincidental? The answer can only be reached through an examination of the prologue and its relationship to the poem, together with a comparative scrutiny of St Bernard's text.

The **Tristan** prologue begins as follows:

> Gedaehte man ir ze guote niht,
> von den der werlde guot geschiht,
> so waerez allez alse niht,
> swaz guotes in der werlde geschiht.
> Der guote man swaz der in guot
> und niwan der werlt ze guote tuot,
> swer daz iht anders wan in guot
> vernemen wil, der missetuot.
>
> (1 ff.)

Praise must be given where it is due. One should not detract from the worth of those who have benefited the world in which they live. They should be remembered with honour. Anyone who fails to give such credit com-

mits an offence against his fellows. The same idea is repeated a few lines further on:

> Tiur unde wert ist mir der man,
> der guot und übel betrahten kan,
> der mich und iegelichen man
> nach sinem werde erkennen kan.
>
> (17 ff.)

But there are many people who pervert values, turning good into evil and evil into good:

> Ir ist so vil, die des nu pflegent,
> daz si daz guote zübele wegent,
> daz übel wider ze guote wegent:
> die pflegent niht, si widerpflegent.
> Cunst unde nahe sehender sin
> swie wol diu schinen under in,
> geherberget nit zuo zin,
> er leschet kunst unde sin.
>
> (29 ff.)

However good a person's critical faculty may be, however acute his judgement, they will be perverted if he allows envy and jealousy to influence him. If people are jealous of others and their achievements they will undoubtedly fail to give credit where it is due.

A great deal of common ground between Gottfried and St Bernard may thus be observed. In the passages quoted both stress the importance of recognizing the merits of others and the iniquity of allowing envy and jealousy to detract from them. In particular, Gottfried shares the idea of perversion with St Bernard: good is turned into evil and evil into good, which is in tune with St Bernard's remark that proud people try to conceal their own defects while detracting from the merits of others. Gottfried does not, it is true, mention pride, which, according to St Bernard, is the root cause of such behaviour, but he uses the word *nit* and immediately continues:

> Hei tugent, wie smal sint dine stege,
> wie kumberlich sint dine wege!
> die dine stege, die dine wege,
> wol ime, der si wege unde stege!
>
> (37 ff.)

To the specific vice of envy is opposed the general term 'virtue'. The implication is that those who detract from the worth of others, the envious ones who allow their judgement of others to be perverted, fail to show the virtues which make for concord and harmony between human beings, of which *caritas* ["charity"] is the supreme example. Envy, like pride, is a mortal sin, and St Bernard's text makes it clear that he regards pride as a source of envy. It would therefore seem very likely that Gottfried, although he does not actually mention it, has *superbia* ["pride"] in mind, the sin which is characteristic of the human condition since the Fall and leads to all other sins. *Superbia* and *caritas* are opposites. For him, as for St Bernard, those who seek only joy are those who do their utmost to avoid the sorrow of seeing others praised. Their whole joy lies in their own imagined worth and excellence. They make no attempt to overcome the original sin of pride.

St Bernard goes on to give some typical features of the behaviour of people who are possessed by what he calls vain joy. One never sees them weeping or hears them groaning. If one observes them closely one would think either that they are entirely forgetful of their own faults, or that they have none. Levity appears in their gestures, gaiety on their faces and vanity in their step. They only seek to enjoy themselves and are always ready to laugh. For, since they try to forget everything which tends to make them look contemptible and therefore saddens them, at the same time keeping in mind those things which they think contribute to their own excellence, they cannot suppress their gaiety nor hide their vain joy. One often sees them indulging in immoderate laughter.

This emphasis on immoderation is significant: such people laugh too much and weep too little. It is clear that he does not mean that joy is bad in itself, but that there should be an equal measure of joy and sorrow. True joy cannot exist on its own without its opposite, sorrow. The parallel with Gottfried remains close. For those who seek only joy he has no use whatever. His words are addressed to those who carry in one heart

> ir süeze sur, ir liebez leit,
> ir herzeliep, ir senede not,
> ir liebez leben, ir leiden tot,
> ir lieben tot, ir leidez leben:
> dem lebene si min leben ergeben,
> der werlt wil ich gewerldet wesen,
> mit ir verderben oder genesen.
>
> (60 ff.)

He wishes to be associated with those who have an equal measure of joy and sorrow, in whom these are inextricably mingled. He is prepared to share their joy and sorrow alike, their life and their death. They are the virtuous ones, and in such virtue, the virtue of *caritas,* does their nobility of heart consist. His story is to be a comfort to them (*edelen herzen zeiner hage:* 47). He has exerted himself for the sake of this world of noble hearts, serving them out of love towards them (*der werlt ze liebe:* 46).

As its title shows, St Bernard's tract opposes the virtue of *humilitas* ["humility"] to the sinful vice of *superbia.* In the first chapter he gives a definition of humility: *Humilitas est virtus, qua homo verissima sui agnitione sibi ipsi vilescit.* It is a virtue by which man, having a true knowledge of himself, becomes contemptible in his own eyes. And he goes on to say that the fruit of humility is knowledge of the truth, which is denied to the proud. The truth is sought in ourselves, in our neighbour, and in its own nature. In ourselves when we judge ourselves and know our own misery and sinfulness, in our neighbour when we have compassion with him in *his* misery, and in its own nature when we consider it with a pure heart. Those who have compassion with their neighbour in his misery rejoice with those who rejoice and weep with those who weep. Their hearts being purified by this fraternal charity, they derive the greatest joy from contemplating truth in its own nature, for the love of which they willingly bear the sufferings of their fellows. But before one's heart can be touched with compassion for the misery of others one must first know one's own misery and know from one's own feelings how one's neighbour feels, so that one may learn from one's own experience how best to help him, following the exam-

ple of Christ, who wished to suffer so that He might have compassion. Humility, therefore, leads directly on to *compassio* ["compassion"] and *caritas.* One cannot be proud in the knowledge of one's own wretchedness, neither can one only seek joy. One rejoices with others when they are joyful and weeps with them when they are sorrowful. In one's own *passio* ["suffering"] one has *compassio* with their *passio.*

This gives us further insight into the meaning of Gottfried's prologue. He addresses himself to those of noble, or pure, hearts, for only they can see the truth. They have humility and therefore compassion. He is entitled to be considered one of them and to receive their love and compassion, because he has shown his love and compassion towards them in his efforts to compose a story which will lighten their burden of sorrow, their human misery (71 ff.). Like all men, they, and he, are in a condition of misery in this world and long to hear something which relieves their sorrow. He has provided it in his story. The 'activity' of listening to it (*unmüezekeit*) will help them:

> wan swer des iht vor ougen gat,
> da mite der muot zunmuoze gat,
> daz entsorget sorgehaften muot,
> daz ist ze herzesorgen guot.
>
> (77 ff.)

Paradoxically it is a story of suffering which will bring them relief from their own suffering:

> ein senelichez maere
> daz tribe ein senedaere
> mit herzen und mit munde
> und senfte so die stunde.
>
> (97 ff.)

The poet concedes that there might be people who think that the more sorrowful tales a *senedaere* hears the greater will be his own sorrow (101 f.). This is both logical and in a sense true, but one thing makes it difficult to believe that this is all there is to be said:

> swer innecliche liebe hat,
> doch ez im we von herzen tuo,
> daz herze stet doch ie dar zuo.
> der innecliche minnen muot,
> so der in siner senegluot
> ie mere und mere brinnet,
> so ie er serer minnet.
>
> (111 ff.)

By this he means that the suffering of a *senedaere,* or noble heart, is the product of his own intense, ardent love, a *passion* which leads him to seek after perfect joy in the midst of his earthly misery. The more ardently one loves the more sorrow it gives to the heart, and yet the more ready the heart is to love. Why should this be so? He gives the answer:

> diz leit ist liebes alse vol,
> daz übel daz tuot so herzewol,
> daz es kein edele herze enbirt,
> sit ez hievon geherzet wirt.
>
> (116 ff.)

Reference back to St Bernard clarifies and confirms this: the reason why the sorrow of this ardent love is so full of joy, and why the evil of this sorrow does the heart so much good, is that the passionate love of a *senedaere* is for his neighbour and for the truth. With his neighbour he shares sorrow and joy, which fraternal charity ennobles and purifies his heart so that he contemplates the truth in its own nature. It is for the love of this truth and the joy that it brings that he bears the sorrows of his neighbour. Every noble heart must seek this purification, which Gottfried expresses by *geherzet*. This is why

> der edele senedaere
> der minnet sendiu maere.

> (121-2)

The *passio-compassio* concept emerges clearly here: the *senedaere* feels *compassio* for the *passio* of those who suffer in the story in their quest for perfect love and joy, who are themselves *senedaere*. He shares their suffering and so finds joy, as they, the characters, find joy in their suffering. In the story he is about to tell his hero and heroine, Tristan and Isolde, are the *senedaere* with whom his audience of *senedaere* must suffer, for whose *passio* they must have *compassio* (123 ff.). In telling a story concerning the sorrows of these two, who love ardently and strive to achieve perfect love, he is giving his audience the opportunity to find joy in the suffering they share with them and in the vision of the union of perfect love which they enjoy.

After introducing his hero and heroine by name (130) Gottfried tells his audience that, although there are many who have told of Tristan and Isolde, not many have told the tale correctly. However, he will not be uncharitable towards these, for they were of *edeler muot* (141) and had the best intentions. Far from detracting from their merit he will show his own humility and his love for them by acknowledging that they exerted themselves for the good of the world. Yet only [poet] Thomas von Britanie told the correct version and he, Gottfried, intends to follow this, also with the best intentions towards those of noble hearts (167 ff.). He then proceeds to explain how this *senemaere* will benefit them, his world of noble hearts, and in so doing enlarges on what he has already said concerning love and its effect on such noble hearts.

Of his story he says:

> ez liebet liebe und edelt muot,
> ez staetet triuwe und tugendet leben,
> ez kan wol lebene tugende geben.

> (174 ff.)

In other words, it will ennoble the heart through love, which will be made more like itself and enduring, and so help towards a virtuous life, for it is a story of *reine triuwe* (178). When a *getriuwer man,* that is, one who has a noble heart and feels love for others, hears such a story he loves *triuwe* and other virtues all the more, and these virtues are never more loved than when heart's love is told of and when compassion is shown for heart's sorrow (180 ff.). Only love can give virtue and honour and yet so few strive after heart's love and are prepared to bear it towards another person, all because of the miserable sorrow it sometimes brings. This sorrow is indeed miserable in comparison with the infinite joy love gives:

> War umbe enlite ein edeler muot

niht gerne ein übel durch tusent guot,
durch manege vröude ein ungemach?

> (201 ff.)

In love sorrow and joy are inseparable. One cannot attain honour and praise among one's fellows without love, which must contain both joy and sorrow (204 ff.).

In this highly rhetorical exposition of the virtue and virtues of love the word *liebe,* both in its basic form and in derivatives, is of frequent occurrence, while *triuwe* also appears several times. *minnen* occurs once (207) and other prominent words are *staete, ere* and *tugent. leit* is opposed to *liebe.* This concentration on the concepts of love and virtue provides ample confirmation of the above interpretation of the earlier part of the prologue. *liebe, triuwe, minne, tugent, ere,* all these are closely associated; indeed, they merge into each other at the highest level of meaning. This universal breadth of the concept of love can only be that of *caritas,* the supreme virtue from which all others flow. In *caritas* love, joy, and sorrow meet; heart's love is joy because heart's love is sorrow. It is the joy found in the sharing of the sorrow of one's neighbour. It cannot be disputed that *liebe* and *minne,* for example, do not mean simply love between the sexes. If this were so the above passage, and indeed the entire poem, would be lacking in continuity with the first part of the prologue, where the emphasis, as we have seen, is on love and compassion for one's neighbour. Only if *liebe, minne,* and *triuwe* are given the widest possible meaning throughout the prologue, namely *caritas,* can it be seen and understood as a coherent and integrated whole. Its unity is the unity of *caritas.* And it is for this very reason that Gottfried's conception of *caritas,* of love in the fullest and truest sense, must be said to comprehend and embrace sexual love, if that love is essentially *getriuwe,* that is, 'caritative'. A *friunt* (197) is a fellow human being with whom one has a caritative relationship, with whom one is prepared to share sorrow and joy, whether or not this relationship springs from heterosexual attraction. In the case of Gottfried's hero and heroine it is in fact the *passio* of sexual love with which the audience must have *compassio.* If they had not suffered for the sake of love, sorrowed for the sake of joy, reconciling both opposites in one heart, many noble hearts would have been deprived of their joy in the *senemaere* of their love (211 ff.).

The close affinity of all this with St Bernard's ideas, and through him with Christian mystical thought, seems beyond doubt. Gottfried's prologue is dominated by the *caritas* concept, of which *humilitas* and *compassio* are an integral part. Mystical paradox and reconciliation of opposites are much in evidence. Poet, audience (or that part of it which is prepared to listen with the right attitude of mind and heart), and characters are united in a bond of mutual love. All belong to the community of noble hearts because of their readiness to suffer and share suffering in seeking after love and joy. In an analogical sense, the poet is inviting his audience to partake with him of a 'communion'. Just as the sufferings of Christ are shared in the Eucharist, just as the faithful feel *compassio* for Him whose *passio* gave life and joy to mankind, and find joy in this sharing of His suffering, the suffering of love, so also the poet's virtuous audience are invited to share the *passio* of Tristan and Isolde. For their sufferings, their life and death, are the bread of life of all noble hearts:

> Ir leben, ir tot sint unser brot.
> sus lebet ir leben, sus lebet ir tot.
> sus lebent si noch und sint doch tot
> und ist ir tot der lebenden brot.
>
> (237 ff.)

They lived and died so that those who came after might live by the example of their undying love. Like the sweet name of the Redeemer

> ir süezer name der lebet iedoch
> und sol ir tot der werlde noch
> ze guoter lange und iemer leben
> den triuwe gernden triuwe geben
> den ere gernden ere.
>
> (223 ff.)

In the fullest sense, then, the *Tristan*-prologue is sacramentally conceived. The world of noble hearts to whom the poet appeals for compassionate attention is a world in which love, the New Law of *caritas,* holds sway. He contrasts it deliberately with the 'world' in a more generally accepted sense, a world dominated by the original sin of pride which separated and still separates it from its divine creator, who is Love. A *senedaere* is one who has overcome the sin of pride and is able, in his humility, to share the emotions of others, particularly that of sorrow. He is united in a bond of *triuwe* and *liebe* with his fellows. The fortunes and misfortunes of others are more important to him than his own. He is concerned not with division, conflict, and separation, but with union and communion with others like himself, and with God. Like [German poet] Wolfram in his *Parzival*-prologue, Gottfried is insisting on the importance of fraternal charity in his audience. The prologue tells us, above all, how the poet feels towards his own characters and how he expects his audience to react to them and their vicissitudes of sorrow and joy.

This clear indication of the poet's own attitude, which he also expects his hearers to adopt, is, of course, of crucial importance for the interpretation of *Tristan.* It is basically and essentially a Christian attitude and as such precludes any possibility of an interpretation which does not start from a Christian premiss. If the full implications of the supreme Christian virtue of charity are acknowledged the way lies open to a deeper understanding of the relationship between the prologue and the story it introduces.

In the story itself, in fact, further striking evidence of the poet's basic attitude of *caritas,* which he shares with St Bernard, may be observed. In his *Sermones de Cantica Canticorum* (cap XXIV) St Bernard refers as follows to what he calls the 'detestable vice of detraction':

> Everywhere, even in the choir of maidens, such are found who watch closely the actions of the Bride, not to imitate them, but to detract from their merit. . . . You see them walking apart, drawing together and making little knots, where they indulge themselves without restraint in insolent words and scurrilous whispers. . . . They associate themselves together in order to speak ill of their neighbour and are united to cause disunion. They form among themselves

friendships full of unfriendliness, combine under a common impulse of malignity, and make odious cabals.

He sums up: 'For everyone who slanders his neighbour gives proof, in the first place, that he is wholly devoid of charity.'

Gottfried condemns, in remarkably similar terms, this same lack of charity towards the lovers shown by Melot and Marjodo:

> Ich spriche daz wol überlut,
> daz keiner slahte nezzelkrut
> nie wart so bitter noch so sur
> alse der sure nachgebur,
> noch kein angest also groz
> alse der valsche husgenoz.
> ich meine daz zer valscheit:
> der vriunde vriundes bilde treit
> und in dem herzen vint ist,
> daz ist ein vreislich mitewist.
>
> (15,047 ff.)

Such people, says Gottfried, have honeyed tongues, but hearts filled with poisonous envy. Tristan also speaks of these two, against whom he finds it necessary to warn Isolde, as *eiterslangen in tuben bilde* (15,088). It is clear that Gottfried conceives Melot and Marjodo as being concerned only to detract from the merit of the lovers, they feign friendship but are full of unfriendliness. They are 'bitter neighbours', devoid of charity. Marjodo is also called *der nidege* (13,637) and in 15,100 Melot is designated as a *slange* and Marjodo as a *hunt*. These two form an odious cabal and are united to cause disunion, associating themselves together to speak ill of their neighbours. Marke, too, who has the same initial as Melot and Marjodo, is said to be part of this conspiracy:

> sus triben si dri diz maere.
> Melot und Marke und Marjodo,
> bizs under in gevielen do
> mit gemeinem rate dar an:
> würde min her Tristan
> von dem hove gescheiden,
> man möhte an in beiden
> die warheit offenbaere sehen.
>
> (14,274 ff.)

This unholy 'trinity' acts in concert to bring about the discomfiture of the lovers. They are three-in-one, but their unity is bent on producing discord.

There can be little doubt that Gottfried is here dependent on St Bernard, as he is in the prologue. Melot and Marjodo are closely watching the actions of the lovers, just as the detractors closely watch the actions of the mystical Bride, with a view to detracting from their merit. They are filled with poisonous envy while speaking with honeyed tongues. Elsewhere St Bernard speaks of the *virus detractionis,* the *lethale poculum detractionis,* while detractors are said to have vipers' tongues and to be hateful to God. Gottfried is even found to be echoing St Bernard's *videte detractores, videte canes* when he refers to Marjodo as a dog.

An earlier passage in the poem also reveals Gottfried's attitude to hatred and envy (8395 ff.). There he says that a worthy man (*der biderbe*) is always exposed to these, since worthiness and envy are as close as mother and child. The one unfailingly engenders the other. His meaning is plain: the world in which we live is a sinful world and pride, envy and hatred are part of man's heritage as a result of original sin. All the more reason, he implies, why we should try to overcome these vices so deeply rooted in us. They lead to detraction, the slandering of one's neighbour. Those who strive to be virtuous should be praised for their goodness.

The poet's exhortation to his audience to show *caritas,* his obvious disapproval of hatred and envy in relations between human beings, clearly indicates that in his opinion Tristan and Isolde should not be disparaged, but are thoroughly deserving of compassion. But why should their behaviour entitle them to the sympathy of the audience? Do they not frequently resort to lying, deceit and trickery, conducting themselves in a manner which scarcely betokens charity towards their fellows? Is their relationship not selfish and exclusive, promoting discord rather than concord? Why should such an adulterous relationship be viewed sympathetically, as opposed to arousing the moral indignation of the audience? Is there nothing to be said for the efforts of Marke, Melot, and Marjodo to expose and break up such an alliance?

These are the very pertinent questions which raise doubts in the minds of those who find it difficult to accept the thesis of the analogy of the carnal love of Tristan and Isolde with mystical love, as portrayed, for example, in St Bernard or the Victorines. The essential 'immorality' of their love seems to conflict with Christian ethical teaching, whether Catholic or Protestant, medieval or modern, particularly since marriage is a sacrament blessed by the Church. Are Tristan and Isolde not sinners, and worthy of censure and punishment?

For Gottfried, as for any reader of his **Tristan,** the mainspring of the poem is the direct opposition between the legal marriage contract of Marke and Isolde and the 'illicit' love of Tristan and Isolde, induced by the magic power of the potion. Queen Isolde, who compounded it, intended that it should be drunk by Marke and Isolde on their wedding night, so that they might become one in undying love. The mistake and its consequences provide a vital clue to the interpretation of the poem. Gottfried is obviously convinced that a mere contract between two persons does not amount to love, and therefore does not make a true marriage. Something more is needed, namely love, and the potion would have given it, but instead Marke and Isolde drink ordinary wine together (12,647 ff.), which had no such effect. By this pointed contrast between the potion and ordinary wine the poet makes it quite clear that the marriage of Marke and Isolde is totally devoid of love. The undying love which should have been infused into their relationship by the potion becomes instead characteristic of that between Tristan and Isolde, who have not entered into a legal marriage contract. It is patent that Gottfried is here heavily dependent on mystical thought: according to St Bernard mystical love is not a contract but an affection. The poet transfers this essential motif from the sphere of spiritual to that of carnal love. Isolde's marriage

to Marke is a formal arrangement without substance or content. Gottfried places the strongest possible stress on this contrast between contract and affection in order to leave no doubt in the minds of his listeners as to the true nature of the love between hero and heroine. It is an analogue of mystical love, which neither can nor will accept any containment or limitation, any formal restriction. It is without measure. The very essence of mystical love is that it is violent and passionate. It is characteristic of those who are inflamed by it that that they will do everything in their power to overcome all obstacles and impediments to its complete fulfilment. Since the lovers are completely dominated by this violent love, and since there could be no greater impediment to their union than Isolde's contract to Marke, Tristan and Isolde are doomed to suffer. Such is the *passio* of love, from which they cannot escape. Their *senen* is produced by an overwhelming desire which cannot be satisfied, a desire for perfect love, for total and permanent union with each other. But only on the voyage home to Cornwall and in the *Minnegrotte* can they be united for a brief spell without outside interference. After these short-lived periods of ecstasy they must return to the world of the court, where they are surrounded by watchful eyes and wagging tongues. They suffer anguish and torture in their attempts to reconcile their honour and their passion. Ultimately they must separate.

In Gottfried's view Isolde's marriage tie with Marke is the symbol of the world which prevents the lovers from realizing their ideal of perfection in love, and is thus directly analogous to the 'world' in mystical thought, a world which constantly reasserts its claim on the soul seeking the heavenly bliss of the *unio mystica.* For this reason the love of Tristan and Isolde, like the love of the mystical Bride and Bridegroom, is not and cannot be perfect love. Both loves are governed and conditioned by the 'vicissitudes' of earthly life, limited and confined by the world. Joy is not possible without attendant sorrow in this vale of tears, bedevilled by sin. Human beings are themselves sinful and they cannot therefore at any time in mortal life realize the transcendental ideal of love to the full. A noble heart, however, a *senedaere,* approaches nearer to this ideal than one who belongs to the world which only seeks joy. The latter has no ideal of love. The love of *ir aller werlt* is a travesty of true love, for which Minne herself cannot be blamed (12,248 ff.). Such love is *geluste under gelange* (17,800). Love herself is not of this world, but of transcendental origin, and only we *valschen minnaere, der Minnen trügenaere* (12,311-12) are to blame if she is often degraded and humiliated to the lower order of the sinful world in which we live. Marke, says the poet, is blinded to true love by *geluste* and *gelange,* but this is not the fault of Tristan and Isolde. The responsibility for the *erlosez leben* which Marke and Isolde live together is placed upon the shoulders of the former (17,753 ff.). Isolde never wished to marry him (12,402). Women cannot be blamed for the blindness induced in men by *geluste* and *gelange* (17,783 ff.).

In contrast, the love of Tristan and Isolde is characterized by *staeter friundes muot* (12,269) and *inneclichiu triuwe* (220). This enduring and, by definition, transcendental quality distinguishes it from the love of such as Marke.

But, unhappily, the world and all that pertains to it is not eternal but transient, and accordingly the fulfilment of their love is impossible in the environment of Marke's court and in the context of Marke's marriage to Isolde. That the lovers should be forced to lie and deceive in order to demonstrate their essential oneness is a direct consequence of the *huote* imposed on Isolde. *huote* is *diu ware suht der minne, der Minnen viendinne* (12,196 ff.). They cannot but behave in such a way if they are to prove their *triuwe* and *staete* to each other, to display the enduring character of their love. Their own endurance, their suffering, is in the very nature of that affection. They are the victims of an error for which they themselves are not responsible. The tragedy of their situation is that, as a result of drinking the potion, they are drawn irresistibly together, but cannot be permanently joined because of the hostility of their environment. The methods they use in their attempts to achieve union are forced upon them by the world, by the *huote* which cramps the freedom of love. Their *list* is necessary if they are, even for a short time, to transcend the limitations and confinement of the world, but neither they nor their love can be held primarily responsible for those limitations. Love cannot be free in this world.

All this may be said in defence of the lovers, and Gottfried says it, both explicitly and by implication, but, paradoxically, there is another side, of equal importance. The poet is perfectly well aware that their love itself, for all its transcendental characteristics, partakes also of these very limitations and imperfections of the world. It is carnal love, of the flesh, and the flesh is mortal and sinful. Tristan and Isolde are human beings and therefore sinful by nature. The carnality of their love is in direct conflict with their longing for complete and lasting union. They cannot completely transcend the world and yet remain in it. The flesh must die. The paradox of their love is that it is both transcendental *and* immanent, eternal and 'temporal', of divine origin (like all love) and yet human. It cannot be divorced from the world which the lovers are continually striving to overcome in their *triuwe* and *staete* to each other. Their inability to avoid behaviour lacking in charity towards their fellows is inseparable from the fact that their love is of this world and that they are in it; it is inherent in the eating of the apple in Paradise and for this they, like all human beings, must bear responsibility and suffer the punishment of death. *Amor carnalis,* whatever form it may take, cannot be dissociated from sin and death. Yet they are surely redeemed by their strivings to achieve the ideal of the true love which transcends mortality. By these very strivings they qualify as *senedaere,* as noble hearts.

Gottfried's two worlds in his prologue are therefore clearly demarcated one against the other. The first is the world of those who seek only joy, a world in which love is often perverted and distorted, shackled by conventions devoid of genuine substance and truth. It is a 'dualistic' world in direct opposition to Heaven, a world of sin, pride and envy. In such a world hostile to enduring love and, indeed, to anything enduring, Tristan and Isolde are destined to suffer and die, like all human beings, since their love is basically carnal. The imperfections and limitations of the world of sin are the cause of their deaths, just as they caused the death of the Redeemer himself. Gottfried's world of noble hearts, on the other hand, is a 'gradualistic' world of humility, compassion and *caritas.* Only in this latter world can true love find a place, and that only to a limited degree, in accordance with the conditions prevailing in earthly life, but the difference is that it is a world given the promise of redemption and eternal life in the humility, compassion and *caritas* of Christ, who died and rose again. In such a world the death of Tristan and Isolde for love gives life to others who come after and are inspired by their *triuwe* and *staete* unto death. The difference between the two worlds may also be expressed in Wolfram's terms: the world of sin is all black, but the world of noble hearts is *parrieret,* both black and white, reconciling the 'vicissitudes' or *schanzen* of *liep* and *leit, leben* and *tot,* spiritual and carnal, mortal and immortal, sin and redemption, God and man, as does Christ himself in his love. The one world is completely cut off from God by sin, but the other has a direct link with Heaven through *caritas.*

The paradox of the reconciliation of divine and mortal, of transcendent and immanent, which is fundamental to Christian belief and inherent in the mystical love relationship, is therefore also an essential feature of the relationship between Tristan and Isolde. This is what makes the analogy supremely valid. It involves no perversion of the Christian viewpoint. Though not perfect, since it is of the flesh, their love participates in the perfection of divine *caritas.* It is not *either* virtuous *or* sinful, but *both* virtuous *and* sinful. The acknowledgement of the *parrieren,* the vicissitudes, of the love of hero and heroine brings to light the full meaning of the poem. Tristan and Isolde suffer a *passio* analogous to the original *Passio,* which was made necessary by sin and yet brought redemption to sinners. Christ himself and his Passion are *parierret,* a paradox which is one of the deepest mysteries of the Christian faith. In the world of the flesh the measureless *triuwe* of Christ led to the 'disorder' of the Crucifixion; analogically, the 'inordinate' *triuwe* of the lovers to each other, which is in direct conflict with their carnal love, produces disorder in the lower order of human life and so leads to their suffering and deaths. On the human plane carnal 'love without measure' inevitably produces *inordinatio.* Only in a higher order, where carnality would be transcended, would the *unmaze* of their love, paradoxically, be 'ordinate', could they become eternally one with each other in God. It is this very *parrieren* which dictates the combined divinity and humanity of Gottfried's message in his prologue: if God showed his compassion for a sinful world which rebelled against him, so much the more should man show his compassion for his fellows in their suffering and sin, which is inseparable from the human condition. Basically carnal, and therefore 'black', though the love of hero and heroine may be, they should nevertheless be the recipients of *compassio* and *caritas* and, indeed, be praised and honoured for the transcendent goodness and 'whiteness' of their *triuwe* and *staete.* As St Bernard puts it, sinful man should not be indignant at the sins of sinful man, but should show the affection of compassion, though he is more prone to do the first than the second. Only compassion can forge the link between the lower and the higher order.

Thus it may be seen that Gottfried's intentions can only be fully revealed if both prologue and poem are viewed in terms of an *analogia entis*. Neither makes any sense at all without this assumption. In the prologue the poet tries to convey to his audience his conception of the unity of himself, his listeners and his characters in the *corpus mysticum* of noble hearts, a unity flowing from *caritas,* the *caritas* shown by the God who came to save sinners. He is concerned to put them in a suitable frame of mind. Now that he has exerted himself to present his characters in a way acceptable to lovers of *senemaere,* they must cooperate with him and show their compassionate interest. They must prepare themselves to partake of the 'communion' which the reading of the story represents, the bread of life he is offering them in his tale of love. They must be reverent; only those who can show this reverence and appreciate the tale in its full sacramental significance are fit to participate and to enjoy the fruits of participation. (pp. 595-607)

> *H. B. Willson, "Gottfried's 'Tristan': The Coherence of Prologue and Narrative," in* The Modern Language Review, *Vol. LIX, No. 4, October, 1964, pp. 595-607.*

W. T. H. Jackson   (essay date 1970)

[*In the essay below, Jackson offers an appraisal of Gottfried's literary excursus in* Tristan and Isolde. *He contends that Gottfried, unlike his contemporaries, employed the courtly romance genre in order to expose its inadequacies and limitations as a vehicle for depicting transcendent love.*]

Literary criticism of any sort is unusual in medieval writing. When works are cited or discussed, it is usually to help a student to formalize his own endeavors, and the authors used for the purpose are those beyond criticism, that

Tristan teaches Isolde to play the harp.

is, the classical writers who have long been canonized. Any mention of contemporary authors is rare and when it occurs at all it is usually inspired by either affection or rancor and does not constitute literary criticism in any real sense of the term. Style or even poetic method is never discussed. There were, of course, numerous "Arts of Poetry" in Latin and in some of the vernaculars but these are works written with the express purpose of providing rules of poetic composition. They are prescriptive, not critical.

In view of this absence of even the most rudimentary literary criticism in the work of contemporaries, it is surprising to find embedded in a courtly romance an apparent digression which seems at first sight to be a review of the present state of the poetic art, complete with all the touchiness and prejudice which one associates with artists talking about their rivals' work. The passage has actually been called "Gottfried's literary criticism" and it is, of course, best known for its caustic references to a writer who is almost certainly Wolfram von Eschenbach. But does the passage in fact constitute literary criticism? Gottfried was not the kind of artist who dropped his theme to make asides, particularly asides of 456 lines. Nor, when the passage is inspected closely, is there much literary criticism in it. Very few authors are mentioned, and, as I hope to show, they are mentioned in a specific order with a very definite purpose in mind. The whole passage is an organic part of the romance, a carefully integrated discussion of the means of telling Tristan's story within the story itself.

There is no need to spend very long in discussing the reasons for the substitution of a literary excursus for a description of a formal ceremony of knighting. Gottfried says that the subject has been treated ad nauseam (although there are no such descriptions in the works of Hartmann and Wolfram), but that is not his real reason for avoiding the subject. Tristan is, for Gottfried, a literary figure or . . . an artist. It would have been perfectly suitable to show his father Riwalin going through the ceremonies of investiture but to do so for Tristan would have been an offense against his nature. Here is the very point on which Gottfried and Wolfram disagreed most violently, for Parzival is the literary representation of a true knight, while Tristan is a literary figure, an artist who assumes the form of a knight because the chivalric romance was the principal literary genre of the day. If Tristan is to be made a knight, he must be made a literary knight, and it will be necessary to endow him not with the sword and spurs of the fighting man but with the qualities needed in a romance and furthermore in a romance of a very special kind. Here we must observe very closely. We are told that thirty other young men are to be knighted with Tristan, and their clothes—that is, their vestments, their new acquisitions or, allegorically, the qualities they take on when they become knights—are these:

> daz eine, daz was hohe muot;
> daz ander, daz was vollez guot;
> daz dritte was bescheidenheit,
> diu dise zwei zesamene sneit;
> daz vierde daz was höfscher sin,
> der naete disen allen drin.
>
> (ll. 4567-72)

[The first was noble spirit, the second material

goods, the third, discretion, which tailors these two into one. The fourth was courtly sense, which sewed for them all.]

Now all these are so-called courtly virtues, the qualities we associate with Hartmann's heroes. They have no special relevance to Tristan in his principal role in the poem. Gottfried makes this point perfectly clear by his (unnecessary) introduction of the other thirty young candidates for knighthood. The qualities listed are those which Tristan shares with all knights in all romances. Gottfried does not condemn them. In the spirit of his own prologue, he accepts them as desirable and praiseworthy—but they are simply not sufficient for Tristan. In his description of the way in which these qualities are applied, Gottfried indicates his feeling that they are superficial:

> der hohe muot der gerte,
> daz volle guot gewerte,
> bescheidenheit schuof unde sneit,
> der sin der naete ir aller cleit
> und andere ir feiture,
> baniere and covertiure
> und anderen der ritter rat,
> der den ritter bestat.
> swaz so den ros und ouch den man
> ze rittere geprüeven kan,
> der geziuc was aller sere rich
> und also rich, daz iegelich
> einem künege wol gezaeme,
> daz er swert darinne naeme.
>
> (ll. 4575-88)

[Noble spirit desired, material goods fulfilled the desire, discretion created and tailored, sense sewed all their garments and other accessories, their pennants and their cases and all the other chivalric trappings that go with a knight. Their accountrements were all very rich in respect to horse and man, so rich that each would have been fit for a king's knighting.]

The stress on externals is obvious—*cleit, covertiure, rich*—and the point is made that these were trappings for "ritter." This is what a normal literary investiture would be like but it is not for Tristan. The candidates are all ready with "bescheidenlicher richeit," but how is Gottfried to accommodate the description to what he wants in *his* story? Twice he stresses the necessity of suiting his words to this type of narration (ll. 4596, 4599) and points out that many authors have described "werltliche zierheit, von richem geraete" and also "ritterlichiu zierheit." This is precisely what Gottfried does not intend to do. But it is what Hartmann von Aue can do perfectly.

Now let us try to find out what it is that Hartmann is so good at. It is not that he tells the story of Tristan, for there is no evidence that he ever did, nor is there any reason for regarding him as an expert in describing knightly ceremonial, for we have no such descriptions in his works. He tells a relatively uncomplicated story, the knightly comedy of which Gottfried speaks in his preface. His words are clear—the well-known "cristalline wortelin"—and his "sense" is irreproachable:

> swer guote rede ze guote
> und ouch ze rechte kan verstan

> der muoz dams Ouwere lan
> sin schapel und sin lorzwi.
>
> (ll. 4134-37)

[Anyone who can understand fine writing with the right attitude and with judgment must grant the man of Aue his wreath and laurels.]

The correspondence with the words of the first two sections of Gottfried's preface is unmistakable:

> Der guote man swaz der in guot
> und niwan der werlt ze guote tuot,
> swer daz iht anders wan in guot
> vernemen wil, der missetuot.
>
> (ll. 5-8)

[If a good man does anything with good intentions and desiring only to benefit the world, then anyone who takes this in any spirit but that of fairness is doing wrong.]

Hartmann is one of those good men who write good stories with happy endings, whose sense is clear, whose language is pleasant and polished—and whose work is shallow. This description of Hartmann von Aue is not perhaps as flattering as many of his admirers believe. He is placed first in the list of writers, nearest to the thirty candidates for knighthood, because his work corresponds most closely to their characteristics. He also bears another of the stigmata by which Gottfried indicates half-approval—all the epithets referring to his style are visual—*durchverwet, durchzieret, figieret, luter, reine, cristalline* (dyes, ornaments, fashions, clear, pure, crystalline) and constantly the references to flowers. We are reminded of the description of Riwalin and the impression he made on the court, and especially on the ladies of the court, when he arrived in Cornwall. That impression was purely visual, as Gottfried's images show:

> "seht," sprachen si, "der jungelinc
> der ist ein saeliger man:
> wie saelicliche stet im an
> allez daz, daz er begat!
> wie gar sin lip ze wunsche stat!
> wie gant im so geliche in ein
> diu siniu keiserlichen bein!
> wie rehte sin schilt zaller zit
> an siner stat gelimet lit!
> wie zimet der schaft in siner hant!
> wie wol stat allez sin gewant!
> wie stat sin houbet und sin har!
> wie süeze ist aller sin gebar!
> wie saelecliche stat sin lip!
> o wol si saeligez wip,
> der vröude an im beliben sol."
>
> (ll. 794-809)

["Look," they said, "that young fellow is *divine*! How *divinely* all his actions become him! What a perfect body he has! His legs are positively imperial and how smoothly they move together! His shield stays glued to his side all the time, his spear looks so beautiful in his hand—his clothes suit him so well and look at his head and hair! How sweet his whole bearing! His person is really divine—and fortunate the woman who can have her joy of him!"]

For courtly ladies enjoyment of details through the eye leads inevitably to speculation about Riwalin's potentiality as a lover. There is strong evidence throughout the poem that Gottfried associates visual imagery with the court of which Mark is the ruler and hence with literary courtliness.

Gottfried does, however, stress that within his sphere Hartmann is supreme. Furthermore, he is classical in his clarity and simplicity, in contrast to Wolfram, who is muddy and complex. It should be emphasized that Gottfried regards Wolfram as competing with Hartmann, not with himself. Hartmann knows how to write a perfect, classical, courtly romance. Wolfram does not. Furthermore, in his use of unclassical diction and imagery Wolfram attracts the untaught and inexperienced and makes them reject the pure classical tradition. Obscurity, in this type of writing, is the cardinal offense. It is obvious that Gottfried is not prepared to admit that Wolfram is attempting anything but a straightforward courtly romance, even though he was too intelligent not to have realized that *Parzival* was a different kind of work. In particular, he will not admit that interpretation is needed to understand the poem. The work is obscure and in need of explanation not because it is subtle but because its author has no sense of style, unlike Gottfried's own work, which needs interpretation because it has several levels of meaning. Gottfried thus takes up a somewhat intransigent position—that the chivalric romance reaches perfection in a clearly presented story in classical diction and that the values presented in such a story are to be taken at their face value. The opinion is of interest to all who study medieval romance and one wonders whether Chrétien de Troyes was of the same opinion and if this is the reason for his frequent use of irony in handling the genre.

The passage on Bligger von Steinach is remarkable in several ways. It describes him as a narrative poet, a "dyer," a user of color imagery. Once again we are concerned with the poetry of description and visual imagery. Yet there are differences. The ideal of clarity and translucence gives way to that of rich stuff of embroidery. The fringes are Greek—perhaps Byzantine—and the words are not pure and clear in themselves but are made pure by fairies who dip them in their well. This must mean that some process of transmutation is needed before the "sin" is apparent. The stress is still on "wort und sin," as it was in the description of Hartmann, but in the exact middle of the description of Bligger, at a point which marks exactly one third of the length of the excursus, a new element is introduced which I would like to think is significant, namely sound imagery. Typically, Gottfried uses stylistic devices to call attention to the new element:

> sin zunge, diu die harpfen treit,
> diu hat zwo volle saelekeit:
> daz sint diu wort, daz ist der sin:
> diu zwei, diu harpfen under in
> ir maere in vremedem prise.
>
> (ll. 4705-09)

[His tongue has a harp in it and possesses two perfect delights—his words and what inspires them. These two between them play out their tale upon the harp with rare quality.]

The midpoint of the description of Bligger and the one-third point of the excursus falls at *saelekeit.* Pivoted about it are repetitions of "harpfen" and "zwei," in slight variation. The two elements are still "wort" and "sin" but the additional element of harmony has been added. The fact that the harp appeared on the family escutcheon of Bligger von Steinach merely enhances the allusion. The rest of the discussion is perhaps best described as a eulogy of Bligger's poetic technique, a subject which is never raised in connection with Hartmann von Aue. The final image is that of flight, not the flight of a singing bird, the nightingale, but of an eagle. The progression toward soaring and music is clear. Hartmann, although limpid, is earthbound. Bligger is borne by his own words in eagle's flight. Heinrich von Veldeke is carried aloft by Pegasus, the true classic inspiration, from whose hoofmarks there sprang the stream of Helicon.

With Heinrich von Veldeke we move into a new phase. Bligger von Steinach is known to us only through a few doubtfully ascribed lyrics; we know nothing of the narrative poem mentioned by Gottfried. Yet it is clear that, like Wolfram and Hartmann, he was both lyric and narrative poet. Heinrich, as we know from his extant work, was active in both fields, and Gottfried chooses to stress the fact, although he had ignored the lyric efforts of Hartmann and Wolfram. In the description of Heinrich the words "wort" and "sin" have become adjectival—"rederich" and "sinnic"—not by any means the same thing, and for the first time there is definite mention of the *Minnesang.*

> der sprach uz vollen sinnen;
> wie wol sanc er von minnen!
> wie schone er sinen sin besneit!
> ich waene, er sine wisheit
> uz Pegases ursprunge nam,
> von dem diu wisheit elliu kam.
>
> (ll. 4727-32)

[He spoke from complete inspiration. How well he sang of love! How well he brought measure to his inspiration! I believe he drew his poetic skill from Pegasus' spring from which all such skill comes.]

Wisheit here is surely not wisdom but poetical skill. Once again there is strong stress on the classical origin of all true poetry, but this time the element of singing, of music is introduced. Gottfried clearly regards Heinrich as an innovator, as the man who had introduced into German literature the true forms of poetry. Is he alluding to narrative or lyric? The last line of the description gives the clue:

> . . . daz die den wunsch da brechent
> von bluomen und von risen
> an worten unde an wisen.
>
> (ll. 4748-50)

[. . . and they break off whatever flowers and blossoms they want, in words and music.]

The combination "wort und wise" is used so frequently in lyric poetry that it is almost impossible to escape the conclusion that *Minnesang* is what is meant here. As if to confirm this, Gottfried moves, without further comment, to the discussion of "nightingales."

Thus Gottfried has taken us from a eulogy of Hartmann von Aue, whom he regards as a narrative poet of pure courtly romance, through a vicious aside on the subject of Wolfram, whom he chooses to regard as a Hartmann *manqué*, to Bligger von Steinach, mainly narrative but with lyric possibilities, to the man who indeed wrote narrative poetry but whose fame rested on having introduced into German literature the lyric tradition of Provence and the *langue d'oïl* which itself derives from classical sources. The movement from word to music, from the visual to the aural, is very clear. The description of the poets is in accordance with Gottfried's normal pattern of coupling the visual with courtly narrative and music with the higher faculties which transcend the courtly.

Gottfried begins the talk of nightingales and promptly rejects many of them, for I read the couplet

> der nahtegalen der ist vil,
> von den ich nu niht sprechen wil.
>
> (ll. 4751-52)

[There are many nightingales of whom I do not wish to speak now.]

as excluding the majority, not as a mere statement that there are many nightingales and that he will not talk about them. What he is saying is that most lyric poets are not suitable for inclusion in his literary discussion and in fact he selects only two, Reinmar von Hagenau and Walther von der Vogelweide. The selection from the point of view of a modern critic would be rather odd. Heinrich von Morungen would seem a better choice than Reinmar and Walther is hardly a conventional *Minnesänger*. But we must remember that Gottfried is not discussing the words of the lyrics, which constitute the only part of them still extant, but rather the combination of words and melody, *wort and wise,* which to him and his contemporaries together formed the true *Minnesang*. If either of the parts could be regarded as more important than the other, it was probably the melody. His reason for the exclusion of many lyric poets is very similar to his reason for making courtly narrative inferior to his own:

> durch daz sprich ich niht anders da,
> wan daz ich iemer sprechen sol:
> si kunnen alle ir ambet wol
> und singent wol ze prise
> ir süeze sumerwise
> ir stimme ist luter unde guot
> si gebent der werlde hohen muot
> und tuont reht in dem herzen wol.
>
> (ll. 4754-61)

[Therefore I shall say of them only what I always have to say: they all know their trade and sing their sweet songs of summer in praiseworthy fashion. Their voices are clear and good, they give the world inspiration and spread warmth in our hearts.]

Note the repetition of the words "ambet," "luter," "guot," etc., which we found in the description of Hartmann von Aue and in particular the expression "ir süeze sumerwise." This and the statement "si gebent der werlde hohen muot" indicate the connection between these lyric poets and the group mentioned in the preface:

> ine meine ir aller werlde niht
> als die, von der ich hoere sagen,
> diu keine swaere enmüge getragen
> und niwan in vröuden welle sweben.
>
> (ll. 50-53)

[I don't mean the world of all those people of whom I hear it said that they cannot stand any hardship and wish only to float along in bliss.]

They are the poets of the joyous, unthinking love, the Maytime love of Riwalin and Blanscheflur in its first stages. Yet there is a difference. The emphasis is on music, not words, and this heightens the artistic effect, as the repeated *guot/muot, vogelsanc/gedank* motif shows.

These nightingales are differentiated from the named *Minnesänger* by a rather unusual device, the introduction of an assumed listener who interrupts Gottfried with the line:

> nu sprechet umb die nahtegalen.
>
> (l. 4774)

[Now tell us about the nightingales.]

The word *die* should here be regarded as a demonstrative rather than a mere definite article. The author intends to talk about *the* nightingales, the ones that matter, not merely about all nightingales, for Gottfried has been doing that ever since he first mentioned the subject. *The* nightingales are the poets who sing of a love which is not pure joy:

> die sint ir dinges wol bereit
> und kunnen alle ir senede leit
> so wol besingen und besagen.
>
> (ll. 4775-77)

[They are all well trained and can express their yearning pain in words as well as music.]

The important word is *senede,* which has not appeared in the previous references to lyric poetry or indeed in any of the discussion of narrative poetry. Its appearance marks the first time that the theme of mixed joy and sorrow, Gottfried's professed main theme, has been associated with poetry. In both the description of Reinmar von Hagenau and that of Walther von der Vogelweide the stress is entirely on music and the imagery is aural. Words are mentioned very rarely. Gottfried uses a line reminiscent of Walther von der Vogelweide in describing the activities of these poets, "so wol besingen und besagen," compared with Walther's "ze Osteriche lernte ich singen unde sagen" but after that he mentions only melodies:

> (ich meine aber von ir doenen
> den süezen, den schoenen),
>
> . . . . .
>
> ich waene, Orphees zunge,
> diu alle doene kunde,
> diu doenete uz ir munde.
>
> (ll. 4785-86; 4790-92)

[(I mean their sweet, their lovely sounds) . . . I really think that Orpheus' tongue, which was master of all music, sounds forth from her mouth.]

It is clearly music which conveys the joy and sorrow of love. Two other features are worthy of note, the stress on love and the repetition of the idea of mixed joy and sorrow. Gottfried leaves no doubt in the mind of his audience that the lyric poetry he is referring to is love poetry only and furthermore love poetry which is in the direct classical tradition. In his praise of Walther von der Vogelweide, he explicitly excludes all lyric which is not in this tradition:

> (ich meine aber in dem done
> da her von Zytherone,
> da diu gotinne Minne
> gebiutet uf und inne)!
>
> (ll. 4807-10)

> [(I mean in that mode from Mount Cithaeron where the goddess of love holds power both within and without)!]

Presumably he is excluding both Walther's *Mädchenlieder* and his political songs. Only love poetry is worthy of true melody:

> diu wiset si ze wunsche wol,
> diu weiz wol, wa si suochen sol
> der minnen melodie.
> si unde ir cumpanie
> die müezen so gesingen,
> daz si ze vröuden bringen
> ir truren unde ir senedez clagen:
> und daz geschehe bi minen tagen!
>
> (ll. 4813-20)

> [She gives them exactly the right directions, she knows where to look for the melody of love. May she and her company sing in such fashion that they turn their sadness and yearning complaints into joy—and may it happen in my time!]

Thus the hope of the perfect combination of music and words to express love lies with the company of lyric poets but it is not apparently realized as yet. The goddess love is to guide them, the same goddess who appears as the guardian of the *Minnegrotte* later in the poem.

There are several important implications in Gottfried's judgments on lyric poetry. Reinmar and Walther are the highest practitioners of the art; they lead a company which is devoted to love poetry; they are musicians rather than writers of verse; they approach the true classical concept of love more closely than any other poets. Yet it is also made clear that neither of them is capable of the expression of the highest type of love, Tristan love. It is hoped that Walther will be able to inspire his company to attain the goal of successful combination of melody with the joy and sorrow of love but there is no certainty that he will be able to do so.

What has Gottfried said about the poetry of his day? The narrative poets have shown great skill in the presentation of love at court. The lyric poets are charming in the same way and two of them show promise that one day lyrics will be written which will attain the ideal of combining fine music with the understanding of the true nature of love. Yet it is clear that the picture is imperfect. None of the poets reaches the highest goal. Music stands higher than words, but no contemporary form is truly capable of the expression of love as Gottfried understands it. Literature, in other words, has failed. And this is the reason for the relatively sudden transition to the person of Tristan and

not only to his person but to a clear statement that all of this literary preparation is insufficient to make a literary knight of him:

> Nu han ich rede genuoge
> von guoter liute vuoge
> gevüegen liuten vür geleit.
> ie noch ist Tristan umbereit
> ze siner swertleite.
>
> (ll. 4821-25)

> [Now I have presented my kind audience with enough talk about the skill of these good people. But Tristan is still not ready for his knighting.]

In other words, even though I have produced all the accepted literary devices and types of today, this is still insufficient to make a knight of Tristan in the sense that I would like it. As so often in the poem, the depiction of the character or place—for example, the *Minnegrotte*—is far less important in the literal than in the allegorical sense. We may note in passing that the *vuoge/gevüege* compounds are often uncomplimentary words for Gottfried, as may be seen in the bitterest passage in the whole work, the trial by hot iron:

> da wart wol goffenbaeret
> und all der werlt bewaeret,
> day der vil tugenthafte Crist
> wintschaffen alse ein ermel ist:
> er vüeget unde suochet an,
> da manz an in gesuochen kan,
> alse gevuoge und alse wol,
> als er von allem rehte sol.
>
> . . . . .
>
> daz wart wol offenbare schin
> an der gevüegen künigin.
>
> (ll. 15733-40, 15745-46)

> [Thus it was revealed and testimony given before the whole world that Christ, that most virtuous man, will flap in every breeze, just like a sleeve. He will fit in and cling on in any way you wish Him to, as close and tight as you please. . . . This was made perfectly clear by the example of the subtle queen.]

The kindest translation would be "pliant." There is at least a suspicion here that Gottfried means that he has provided enough conventionalities for courtly people.

If, then, the accepted literary means are insufficient, what is Gottfried to do? At first sight he seems to doubt his own ability to do more:

> ine weiz, wie in bereit:
> der sin wil niender dar zuo;
> son weiz diu zunge, waz si tuo
> al eine und ane des sinnes rat
> von dem sir ambet allez hat.
>
> (ll. 4826-30)

> [I don't know how to prepare him. My inspiration fails, and thus my tongue doesn't know what to do, all alone and with no advice from the inspiration that gives it its task.]

At first the passage seems to be a conventional humility formula, but why, at this stage, would he introduce such a passage, particularly when we consider that at the point where such a formula might be in place, that is in the preface, he was neither humble nor formulaic. Closer examination reveals that his words are not conventional. He once again uses the word/sense combination and gives the reason why the combination does not function properly here.

> dem man, der niht wol reden kan,
> kumt dem ein rederischer man,
> im erlischet in dem munde
> daz selbe, daz er kunde.
>
> (ll. 4835-38)

[When a man who cannot speak well encounters a fluent speaker, even what he could say dies on his lips.]

Who is this "redericher man"? Not one of Gottfried's contemporaries but almost certainly Tristan himself. Gottfried is deprived of the power of speech when faced with the necessity of presenting such a fluent and talented individual as his main character and in the end he can think of nothing better than to write smoothly as the best of his contemporaries do. I have little doubt that these latter remarks are intended ironically. After all, Gottfried has made it clear on several occasions that he regards his work as unique. It is in the matter of making Tristan into a literary knight that his invention fails, not in the telling of Tristan's love story.

He now turns directly to Apollo and the classical Muses for inspiration. Again he ironically underestimates his abilities. Many men have been granted the full measure of the Muses' inspiration—we may well ask who they are, for Gottfried does not tell us—but Gottfried asks for only a tiny drop to restore him to the path of rectitude.

> und mag ouch ich den da bejagen,
> so bewalte ich mine stat da wol,
> da man si mit rede behalten sol.
> der selbe trahen der eine
> der ist ouch nie so cleine,
> ern müeze mir verrihten,
> verrihtende beslihten
> beidiu zungen unde sin,
> an den ich sus entrihtet bin.
>
> (ll. 4880-88)

[And if I can obtain that drop, I shall be in control of the situation so far as that can be done in words. That same single drop, small though it may be, will put straight again both my tongue and my inspiration, in respect of which I have strayed, ordering them and smoothing them as it does so.]

Poor Gottfried! He has lost his verbal skill and to show us how completely it has vanished he produces some neat plays on *verrihten* and *entrihten* but does not tell us what is the right and the wrong way.

I am not, of course, implying that Gottfried is being ironical at the expense of the Muses or the stream of Helicon. Throughout his work he makes it quite clear that he regards all true poetry as originating in the classical tradition. What is conspicuously absent here is the constant reference to music which we find, for example, in the references to classical poetry made in the *Minnegrotte* scene.

It is words that he mentions in the literary excursus, words which are like gold, words which are like gems—all of them visual, not aural, images. The words they inspire are those of courtly poetry.

It is worth noting that the poets of the high Middle Ages, both French and German, regarded their poetry as directly descended from classical and even preclassical times. It is significant that the earliest courtly romances in the French vernaculars are the *Roman de Thèbes* and the *Roman d'Énéas,* followed by the *Roman de Troie.* These are all earlier than any extant Arthurian romance. An even clearer statement of the position is made in the German poem *Moriz von Crâun,* where it is explicitly stated that the courtly virtues came from Troy through ancient Greece to Rome, where they were temporarily submerged by the wicked Nero to emerge again under Charlemagne. Gottfried may well be referring to this tradition in his references to classical inspiration.

The conjecture is perhaps strengthened by his next observation. He has now received everything he asked for, a small drop of inspiration from the Muses and the power to use words, and he tells us what the result will be:

> Nu diz lat allez sin getan,
> daz ich des allez si gewert,
> des ich von worten han gegert,
> und habe des alles vollen hort,
> senft allen oren miniu wort,
> ber iegelichem herzen schate
> mit dem ingrüenen lindenblate,
> ge miner rede als ebene mite,
> daz ich ir an iegelichem trite
> rume unde reine ir straze
> noch an ir straze enlaze
> dekeiner slahte stoubelin,
> ezn müeze dan gescheiden sin,
> und daz si niuwan ufe cle
> und uf liehten bluomen ge . . .
>
> (ll. 4908-22)

[Now let us suppose that all this has been done, that I have been granted all that I have asked for in respect to words and that I have a full supply; that my words please every ear, give shade to every heart with the deep green linden leaf; if it goes along at the same pace as my speech and clears and smooths its path and leaves not a speck of dust in its way that has not been removed and that it never moves except on clover and bright flowers . . .]

This passage should be compared carefully with the earlier one which deals with Hartmann and Wolfram. It will be noted that the same visual imagery is present. Wolfram can provide—or tries to provide—shade with the bare stick instead of with the "meienblat." In other words, he is incapable of using the style which will delight the audience for courtly narrative. (Gottfried constantly connects the linden tree or the flowering May with courtly poetry.) Even the dust of which Wolfram makes his "mergriezen" is carefully swept out of the way by Gottfried. The inspiration of the Muses and the stream of Helicon will, in other words, enable him to write courtly comedy, the happy ending, the type of poetry at which Hartmann excels—but there is still no evidence that it will allow him to treat adequately the story of Tristan and Isolde. He has already used such techniques to the full in telling the story of Riwalin and Blanscheflur, whose love was precisely of that character. It would seem that Gottfried is stating that he will need the help of the Muses in writing in the style of Hartmann.

Yet this way is already well trodden—and so is the next possible way, even though it is of a totally different kind. The preparation of a warrior's arms by a god, Hephaistos or Vulcan, is a *topos* in classical epic, and the most famous example of it is the description of the shield of Achilles. I know of no way in which medieval writers could have had direct knowledge of this passage, since it does not appear in the *Ilias Latina,* but there are plenty of similar descriptions in Latin poems [e.g. Homer's *Iliad* and Vergil's *Aeneid*], of which by far the most accessible to medieval writers was the description of the arms of Aeneas. The arming of the hero marks an important stage in his career. The gift of arms of divine origin sets him apart from other warriors, however brave, and he is shown as a person far superior to all contemporaries. According to this system, we would have to assume that Tristan now stood before his greatest test, the conflict with Duke Morgan, and that his characteristics were indicated by the wild boar on his shield, the mark of courage, and the fiery dart of love on his helmet. These would be the normal characteristics of the knight-in-love, and every author would use these or similar symbols for his hero. Gottfried does not in fact say that he is doing or will do this but merely that he would do so if he were to adopt the classical convention. The reference to the production of clothes by Cassandra has puzzled generations of commentators, for no classical author ascribes to her any special skill in weaving. Her gift was that of prophecy with no one believing what she said. If Gottfried is not simply making an error here—and that is quite likely—he must be referring to the interpretation of the hero's future through special wisdom, that is, allegorical interpretation. In fact the matter is of little ultimate importance, for the author makes it clear that this system too is inadequate:

> was haete daz iht ander craft
> dan alse ich die geselleschaft
> Tristandes e bereite
> ze siner swertleite?
>
> (ll. 4961-64)

[What other effect could this have (than the one I produced) earlier when I was equipping Tristan's company for knighthood?]

All of the devices would be excellent to describe Tristan's company but not Tristan himself. The best the poet can do is to fall back on his earlier description and endow his hero with the four qualities of the literary knight which he has already mentioned—*muot, guot, bescheidenheit, höfscher sin.* So Tristan, so far as his literary knighthood is concerned, is back with his companions and we may well ask why Gottfried has gone to all this trouble to reject every literary possibility of describing adequately how his hero became a knight. The key, surely, lies in the following passage:

> sus si Tristan geleitet

> ze hove und ouch ze ringe,
> mit allem sinem dinge
> sinen gesellen ebenglich,
> ebenziere und ebenrich:
> ich meine aber an der waete,
> die mannes hant da naete,
> niht an der angebornen wat,
> diu von des herzen kamere gat,
> die si da heizent edelen muot,
> diu den man wolgemuoten tuot
> und werdet lip unde leben:
> diu wat wart den gesellen geben
> dem herren ungeliche.
> ja weizgot der muotriche,
> der eregire Tristan
> truoc sunderlichiu cleider an
> von gebare und von gelaze
> gezieret uz der maze.
> er haetes alle an schoenen siten
> unde an tugenden übersniten.
> und iedoch an der waete,
> die mannes hant da naete,
> dan was niht underscheidung an;
> des truoc der werde houbetman
> in allen geliche.
>
> (ll. 4986-5111)

[So let Tristan be led to court and to the joust exactly like all his companions in all his accoutrements, with the same trim and the same richness. I am talking, of course, about the clothes sewn by human hands, not about those he was born with, the ones that come from the wardrobe of the heart, the ones called "nobility," which make a man of spirit and dignify person and life. *These* clothes were not the same for the lord and his companions. God knows, Tristan, spirited and ambitious as he was, wore quite unusual clothes and in bearing and ease of manner he was quite unusually distinguished. He was far superior in fine manners and qualities. But in the clothes that were sewn by human hands there was no distinction. The superior wore the same clothes as everyone else.]

Tristan is exactly like his companions in matters pertaining to the court and to fighting. Exactly like them indeed—there are three compounds with *eben-*—except that Gottfried is using one of his favorite stylistic devices, repeating words within a line and over successive lines to show harmony in one way and conflict in the other. Tristan is like his companions only in externals, the qualities which can be imparted by human agency and those which can be and have been adequately dealt with by the accepted literary types. Only in things which are not visible, the indescribable qualities, was he different. Gottfried uses the words "sunderlichiu cleider" in the sense that they are special and apart, peculiar to Tristan. Yet obviously they cannot be seen, since Gottfried stresses the fact that in outward appearance Tristan was indistinguishable from his fellows.

The imagery is extremely complex. We should not forget that the *descriptio ad vestitum* was a rhetorical commonplace—Chaucer's squire is an excellent example of its use—and the figure depends on the assumption that a man's character may be observed from his clothes. Yet

Tristan's clothes reveal only a part, and that the least important part, of his character. Even the other candidates have allegorical as well as material clothes, the four qualities in which they are dressed. Thus their appearance is allegorized in terms of their milieu. As a Christian puts on the whole armor of God, so they put on the whole armor of literary courtliness. They are, we may say, in the courtly mainstream. This, I believe, is what Gottfried means by "wort und sin," and it is clear that he regards it as conventional enough. Tristan looks like his companions and so far as his visible trappings are concerned, he can be allegorized in the same way. He is, after all, the hero of a romance whose external form follows that of Hartmann and others. He fights in tournaments and wins a lady.

It is the invisible clothes which distinguish him from all other heroes. Since "invisible clothes" is a contradiction in terms, we must understand a third level of meaning, qualities which indicate character and which are purely his own. The rhetorical commonplace itself has been allegorized and now we have a *descriptio ad veslitum sine vestitu.* If this were the only example of such a proceeding in the poem, I might be accused of farfetched interpretation, but surely Gottfried's famous mention of his own visit to the *Minnegrotte,* even though he had never been to Cornwall, falls into the same category. He is not allegorizing the *Minnegrotte* at that point—all the allegorizing has already been done—but allegorizing his own allegory in terms of the Christian allegory of the church. To understand the true significance of the *Minnegrotte,* the reader must be aware of the Christian allegories and make a comparison between the Christian understanding of the church and Gottfried's reference to it, in other words, allegorize an allegory. Only thus can the *Minnegrotte* experience have the same meaning for the *edele herzen* ["noble hearts"] as the church building has for a Christian.

Gottfried is always most careful to show the different levels at which Tristan appeals to different audiences. I need only mention the contrast between his impact on the Irish court when he is introduced in his own person in order to reveal the falsity of the seneschal's claims (11. 11102 ff.), which is conveyed entirely by visual imagery, and the impression made on Mark's court, which is intellectual, and on Isolde, which is musical. It is worth noting that very similar techniques are used to show Isolde's varying impact. The audience at the knighting ceremonies could not see what Tristan's real qualities were. They were perceptible only to those who could see beneath the externals. They could not be imparted by any human agency or ceremony.

Thus the literary excursus proves to be literary criticism, and the humility formula far from humble. Gottfried has selected two topoi of literary narrative, the knighting found in some courtly romances and the arming which is found in classical epic. Each of them, properly used, should throw some light on the character of the hero. Yet a study of the leading narrative poets reveals that they are capable of description only when they rely on visual imagery. Brilliant though their surfaces may be they can reveal only those qualities which make for chivalric prowess. They cannot depict a Tristan in his full stature. The lyric poets have different powers and a day may come—but has not come yet—when the combination of words and music will be able to render the complexion of a Tristan in its full terms. Nor is the classical arming adequate. Even with all of the powers of the Muses to aid it, it still can do no more than represent a hero who will succeed in gaining victory at a decisive point in his career.

Thus, so far as literary forms are concerned, there is nothing that can be done. The best of contemporary writing will show Tristan to be just like his companions and the audience will think he is just a polished knight. (Most critics and readers before Ranke and Schwietering fulfilled this prophecy of Gottfried's very neatly.)

Yet Gottfried is, after all, writing a poem about Tristan and Isolde, and there is no reason to think that he believed himself incapable of the task. Like Horace, he dares to enter new regions to do things previously unattempted. He will use new and intenser forms of imagery, particularly musical imagery, to show the different qualities (the *lugenden* of l. 5006) which Tristan possesses. These will not be those of a knight, so there is no point in stressing investiture, but of an artist—hence the literary excursus. It is the artistic method we are discussing here. Then why bring up the question of knighting at all? Because Gottfried was well aware that he was writing a knightly romance. He could use no other genre, for without the ironic contrasts between Tristan and the normal knight many of his effects would be lost. He deliberately underrated or refused to recognize the originality of the work of Wolfram von Eschenbach. His own purpose was to show the inadequacy of the genre, to indicate that he could find none better, and then to take the reader into his confidence and ask him to look carefully at what he found in the **Tristan** and thus appreciate in what ways the poem differed from the work of

---

Cosman on Gottfried's view of the courtly romance genre:

What does Gottfried mock and how does he do it? As these are exemplified in the romance literature of his day, Gottfried laughs at traditional chivalry and traditional *Minne* [love]. His parody consists in isolating one action or part of an action, together with its expected decorations, from its traditional Arthurian milieu and inserting into it a character or action from another. By deliberate inversion, or inflation, or introduction of realistic detail into a stock romance context, Gottfried achieves his parodistic smile. His is a playful blasphemy against serious romance canons and a usage of its patterns for purposes other than those for which they were developed. In mockery, as in his elaboration of the concept of the learned knight, Gottfried denies the very characteristics of the genre and achieves greatness in that denial. . . . [Courtly] romance may be the vehicle but not the consummate expression of an exposition of mystical love. Gottfried's deviations from the characteristic romance patterns signal the excellence of his achievement.

Madeleine Pelner Cosman, in her The Education of the Hero in Arthurian Romance, *University of North Carolina Press, 1965.*

contemporaries. The poem is, after all, written for *edele herzen* who live in courts but are not of them. Tristan and Isolde too live in courts but are not of them. As he had indicated in his prologue, Gottfried writes in the genre of the romance but his work is not of it. The literary excursus is an organic part of the poem, for it shares with the preface the task of indicating to the audience how the whole work must be read. (pp. 992-1001)

W. T. H. Jackson, "The Literary Views of Gottfried von Strassburg," in PMLA, *Vol. 85, No. 5, October, 1970, pp. 992-1001.*

Michael S. Batts (essay date 1971)

[*Batts is an English educator specializing in Germanic studies. In the following excerpt, he asserts that Gottfried composed his courtly epic for an educated and experienced audience who could appreciate his satire of knighthood and the civil bond of marriage.*]

[The] problems of finding a basis for the interpretation of a medieval work are numerous, and . . . not the least [is] the distinction between the desire of an author to be understood and the contemporary understanding of his work. . . . [We] must also consider the "message"—to use an unpopular term—which Gottfried wished to convey to his audience, and this naturally includes a consideration of the public to which this message was directed. In order to begin more logically with the latter point, we must turn to the prologue, in which Gottfried first establishes a relationship with his audience. This passage is sufficiently important to be quoted *in extenso:*

> If I spend my time in vain, ripe for living as I am, my part in society will continue to fall short of what my experience requires of me. Thus I have undertaken a labor to please the polite world and solace noble hearts—those hearts which I hold in affection, that world which lies open to my heart. I do not mean the world of the many who . . . are unable to endure sorrow and wish only to revel in bliss. . . . What I have to say does not concern that world and such a way of life; their way and mine diverge sharply. I have another world in mind which together in one heart bears its bitter-sweet, its dear sorrow, its heart's joy, its love's pain, its dear life, its sorrowful death, its dear death, its sorrowful life (41-63).

In the first place, it is not necessary to assume, as has sometimes been done, that Gottfried does not want, or does not expect, his work to be read by any but those to whom he specifically addresses himself. He merely states that the labor he had undertaken is for the sake of those among whom he numbers himself. He is writing for those who, like Tristan and Isolde, understand that in life and love, joy and sorrow are inextricably commingled, that life and love cannot be understood or appreciated unless these two are fully accepted. Only those who have grasped this will understand the full meaning of his work and find solace in it. Since they experience joy and suffering, they will find comfort in his work, and especially lovers; for those who suffer the pleasures and pangs of love will be both comforted and inspired by reading of others' joys and torments. Gottfried's work would, then, naturally, be "caviare to the general," but he must have expected it to be read also by those who did not fully understand it. Indeed, there is a certain irony in the fact that those who read the work without great depth of understanding will not have perceived that they were being satirized.

It would certainly also be wrong to see in the world to which Gottfried particularly addresses himself and of which he counts himself a member, an organized and esoteric group, a religious society or sect, or even a select few recognizable within society. In the first place, the possible audience was restricted to what would now be called the "upper classes," including the aristocracy both ecclesiastical and lay. The so-called masses did not exist as an audience for courtly works and certainly not for a man like Gottfried. Gottfried speaks to the "man of leisure," the educated and experienced man of the world. . . . For the moment it is important to consider first the majority which Gottfried satirizes and rejects and which must nevertheless have also formed a part—and presumably a major part—of his actual audience. This majority consists of—to use modern terminology—the pleasure-seeking crowd, the average, unthinking man.

The only large "class" which existed and which counted was, of course, the knightly class, and it is of the typical members of this class that Gottfried is thinking. They spent their time in hunting and hawking, in feuding and tourneying, in arranging pageants and banquets, in administering the affairs of state or their own estates as best they could and often without enthusiasm. This would be a common view of the function of knighthood, despite the imposing list of duties which they swore to undertake on receiving the accolade. In this work, Gottfried portrays knights as either courageous failures or poltroons. The only exception is Tristan, and he, as we shall see, breaks every rule in the book. Rivalin is a perfect example of chivalry, but one who "over-indulged himself in pleasures dear to his heart and did entirely as he pleased" (262-64), who "lived for the sake of living" (304). The results of his rash behavior are—after the initial success against Morgan—catastrophic. He rushes to the aid of Mark and is severely wounded. Later he is killed by the man whom he had previously attacked on pretext and defeated. Gottfried disposes of him somewhat cynically, indicating by the manner in which his demise is portrayed that this was no very great loss: "It has come to pass, it has to be: the good Rivalin is dead. No more is required of them [his followers] than to pay the dues of a dead man, for there is nothing else to be done" (1703-9).

Rivalin's counterpart is Mark who represents the inactive type, in contrast to the overly active Rivalin. Mark is an example of the *roi-fainéant* ["idle King"] but without the redeeming strength of character that enabled King Arthur to make his court a veritable center of chivalry. His early submission to Ireland is excused as the result of his minority; but by or even before the time Rivalin arrives there, he is clearly of age and has undertaken nothing. When Rivalin arrives, he is arranging a splendid pageant. it is not said to what extent Mark participates in the campaign in which Rivalin is wounded. Later, when Tristan comes to the court, Mark is so impressed by his qualities that he entreats him to stay, not as a knight, but rather as a courtier—"you can do everything I want"—and becomes to a large degree dependent for his pleasures on Tristan.

The arrival of Morold throws the whole court into a panic and no one—least of all apparently Mark—is willing to risk his life. They all prefer, as Tristan points out, a dishonored life (having bartered their children to save it) to the risk of death, but at least an honorable death. These same knights are later portrayed as being terrified by Tristan's proposal to take them with him to Ireland and yet cunning enough to advise the King in order to obtain their own ends—to displace Tristan—and later to maintain their popularity by recommending him to recall Isolde from the grotto. Yet by these and others, such as the dwarf Melot, the King is persuaded first one way and then another. If Rivalin was headstrong, selfwilled, and rash, he at least made decisions and attempted to carry them out boldly. Mark seems devoid of any strength of character. His true nature is gradually exposed as he becomes more and more involved in the relationship with Tristan and Isolde.

The most striking evidence of Gottfried's attitude toward knighthood, its pomp and circumstance and the disparity between theory and practice, is contained in the description of the knighting of Tristan. Gottfried begins this passage in a stereotyped manner with a complaint of his inability to do justice to the description of such a ceremony, and instead of making the attempt, he does not describe the ceremony, but instead provides his audience with a short history of the literature of the past two generations. This and the following bombastic outline of how he would describe Tristan's preparations if he could—liberally larded, as it is, with references to classical mythology—must have been largely unintelligible to all but the most educated minority. But the more galling aspect is surely the sovereign artistry which he displays and which so obviously would have enabled him to describe the ceremony he so pointedly claims to be unable to describe.

The greater irony lies, however, in the definition of the aims of knighthood which Gottfried, nevertheless, introduces at the close of this passage. Mark, the weak and pleasure-loving Mark, advises Tristan: "Be modest and straightforward. Be truthful and well-bred. Always be kind to the poor; to the rich always be proud. Cultivate your appearance. Honor and love all women. Be generous and loyal and never tire of it . . ." (5027-36). The irony of this counsel lies not so much in the fact that the audience knows full well what kind of relationship will develop between Mark and Tristan, but in the fact that Tristan proceeds to discard every one of these honorable precepts in the action to follow. His modesty is rarely in evidence except as a form of mock modesty, as he willingly allows his talents to be drawn out and displayed. He is rarely straightforward, preferring, at all times, to tell untruths in order to gain advantage. The precept of honoring and loving all women he has no chance to put into practice, since he is never in a situation to help anyone but Isolde in defeating the steward. Certainly his behavior toward his uncle's wife and his later treatment of Isolde Whitehand accord ill with his oath. Tristan maintains or discards his loyalty at will.

As an example of the subtlety with which Tristan, with little or no consideration for veracity, turns every situation to his advantage, let us consider the passage in which—after all the untruths he has been telling come to light through the discovery of the damaged sword—he explains to Queen Isolde and her daughter his mission to Ireland:

> After my first voyage here, when I was cured, I sang your praises continually to my Lord Mark, till my prompting turned his thoughts so strongly toward you that he summoned the resolution for the deed, but only just, and I will tell you why. He feared your enmity, and in any case wished to stay single for my sake, so that I could succeed him when he died. But I urged him against it until he began to give way to me .
> (10, 551-66)

This is a very subtle but nonetheless distinct distortion of the truth. Tristan had begged Mark to marry only because he feared for his own life, and Mark gave way only because Tristan threatened otherwise to leave him. The King, then, chose Isolde partly because she had been praised by Tristan but primarily because he thought this would make a marriage impossible—hardly a flattering thought for Isolde! As Tristan puts it, it not only sounds better to the Isoldes, he also displays himself in an advantageous light. On other occasions—to mention a few only in passing—Tristan cuts down Morgan without warning (having concealed his weapon under his cloak) and takes advantage of Morold's temporary weakness to cripple him and then pours scorn on his helpless adversary. He also takes advantage of a friendly and not seriously intended offer on the part of his friend Gilan, in order to extort from him his favorite dog in precisely the same manner in which Gandin had tricked Mark out of Isolde. On that occasion Tristan had had hard words for his uncle.

Tristan is, in other words, always successful, not merely as an artist, but equally in his prowess as a knight. His success sets him apart from the average knight and indicates the difference in quality between the world to which he belongs and the average world, *"ir aller werlt."* The average man, either ineffectually engaged in mundane matters or engrossed in the pursuit of amusement and the pleasures of the body, is surpassed in every way by this *elite,* even in those areas which have no great meaning for them. To a certain extent, this superiority may be said to be an innate gift, something not to be acquired by everyone; but in large measure it is also the result of early, intense, and continued cultivation of mind and spirit. Such training does not make one less able to function on the lower level. On the contrary, it endows one with superior abilities in wordly matters but deprives one of interest in them. It is at this point that we must return to the question of education.

Gottfried lays great emphasis on Tristan's education (2056ff.), which comprised instruction in the arts, specifically languages, literature, and music. Perhaps it is significant that Gottfried says "that in addition to these"

(2103)—thereby placing the others in perspective?—he learned the chivalric accomplishments of riding, fencing, hunting, and so forth. Although the beginning of his studies is called "the beginning of his cares" (2086), yet there is no suggestion of deprivation. On the contrary, it is clearly understood that, once in the ban of these studies, Tristan developed an inborn propensity to the very highest level. In turn, Tristan instructs Isolde in the arts which he has acquired, although, of course, in this case the instruction is restricted specifically to the finer arts of language, literature, and music. She too had had an excellent education even before his arrival, but it was still inadequate. Under Tristan's tutelage she develops her innate talents with great rapidity to a level of accomplishment that astonishes the world.

In particular Gottfried speaks of *"moraliteit,"* a term that has stirred up considerable discussion. This study is defined by Gottfried as "a good and wholesome thing. Its teaching is in harmony with God and the world. In its precepts it bids us to please both, and it is given to all noble hearts as a nurse, for them to seek in her doctrine their life and their sustenance" (8009-017). This rather vague definition of the French term *moralité*—defined in the Old French dictionary as *bon sens*—seems to mean the art of maintaining always and in every situation an amiable disposition, a pleasing and winning way, of adopting an attitude that will maintain one's honor and win one esteem, no matter how difficult or desperate the situation. The "morality" of this may be questionable, but it seems to suggest that faculty by means of which the *elite* of which Gottfried speaks remains perfectly in control of any situation and pleasing to God and man—in which there is presumably no religious implication. This is the quality which enables Tristan and Isolde to carry through and carry off their various deceits without prejudice either to their reputation at court or their conviction of being in the right.

That Mark does not belong to this world is only too evident. He represents an inferior world, and his nature unfolds itself in the course of the conflict for the possession of Isolde, who stands between Tristan and Mark, bound to the one by genuine love and to the other by the moral, social, and legal code. At first, Mark is too gross to notice the difference between Brangane and Isolde. Later he is too engrossed in physical possession to perceive that Isolde loves his nephew. Persuaded now by his enemies, now by the lovers, he vacillates between suspicion of their guilt and implicit belief in their innocence. When he finally begins to suspect on his own account, he can only turn from private to public advisers, demonstrating his complete inability to appreciate the nature of love. But up to this point, and then through the ordeal episode, Gottfried does not outrightly condemn his behavior, but rather exposes it as pitiful. Mark's guilt does not really begin to grow until after the lovers have returned from the grotto.

Mark's determination to regain Isolde is motivated entirely by physical desire and not by any genuine belief in her innocence. Although this is not expressly stated, it is implied by the attitude of his councilors who fall in with his obvious desire to have Isolde back without being convinced by the reason which is given. The hypocrisy which

Gottfried condemns in Mark lies in his setting spies to hinder a love which he publicly claims does not exist. He pretends blindness which—says Gottfried—comes from purely sensual lust and passion. The meaning of the scenes following the return from the grotto is very fully explained by Gottfried in his lengthy sermon based on the text: "A virtuous woman needs no guardian." His argument is basically that the distrust which leads to the surveillance of an honest woman breeds distrust in her, to the extent of driving her to provide a reason for the lack of trust. In other words: prohibition breeds the crime.

Mark, of course, cannot help himself and forces the catastrophe. The tragic quality of the ensuing episode, therefore, lies in the destruction of what is great and good by inferior motives. Mark, it is true, suffers as well; and in a limited way Gottfried shows some sympathy for him. He has always tried to find the truth and has been unconvinced until, knowing the truth in his heart, he shuns it and tries to destroy it. At this point, he unintentionally finds the truth unequivocally demonstrated before his eyes, with the result that his life too is destroyed: "He no longer fancied, he knew. . . . All his past efforts to rid himself of doubt had now ended in living death" (18,222-30). For Tristan and Isolde there is tragedy, for they are thrown off balance by the circumstances which surround them and are trapped into falling below the true level of their existence. As a result they are punished by separation, but, while they must endure love's suffering in isolation, with only a remote hope of eventual reunion, at least they have this love to sustain them; Mark has nothing.

The end would thus seem tragic in the sense that Tristan and Isolde have irrevocably lost the chance of real happiness, and nothing related after this point can alter that. The question, therefore, arises as to whether or not Gottfried viewed this kind of love as inevitably leading to conflict and tragedy, and whether he is presenting this story as a precept or as a warning. To answer these questions we must recall the words of the prologue and remember how Tristan and Isolde spent their days in the grotto. Gottfried had earlier said:

> I have offered the fruits of my labor to this world
> as a pastime, so that with my story its denizens
> can bring their keen sorrow half-way to allevia-
> tion and thus abate their anguish. . . . It is a
> good thing that one who harbors love's pain and
> sorrow in his heart should seek distraction with
> all his mind—then his spirit will find solace and
> release. . . . This sorrow is so full of joy, this ill
> so inspiring that, having once been heartened by
> it, no noble heart will forego it. I know as sure
> as death and have learned it from this same an-
> guish: the noble lover loves love-tales (45-122).

Although he does not specifically say so, it must be assumed that the love tales to which Gottfried refers are tales of "tragic" love, just as his own story. Certainly when they are in the grotto, Tristan and Isolde tell each other tales of the tragic love affairs of the past even though there is at that moment no suggestion of imminent tragedy. And yet they must know that there can be no lasting fulfillment for them, for they cannot completely escape from the world with which they are in conflict, as were the lovers of whom they tell. Such love as they speak of and such loves as theirs cannot, however, be destroyed, no matter how much it may be obstructed and saddened by the world. It outlasts death by being passed on to future generations. If their love does not find permanent fulfillment in life, at least they achieve momentary exaltation and maintain it undiminished into death. In their death their love, then, finds another kind of fulfillment, for it now lives on in others and provides the sustenance which enables future lovers to bear similar adversities. In this way, their love, though apparently tragic in its immediate result, triumphs over the inferiority of the world which uncomprehendingly rejects it, and it is no tragedy for those with understanding. Their life is tragic only insofar as it partakes of the tragic imperfection of the whole human race, which can never attain a perfect state or find complete fulfillment in human existence, but must always stumble and fall anew.

The conflict between the lovers and the world which Mark represents is certainly inevitable. Gottfried advocates that those who have the necessary insight into this situation should cultivate their esthetic sensibilities through literature and music and should withdraw as much as possible from mundane responsibilities. He advocates this for both man and woman so that the woman becomes an equal partner in the experience, with the right to make her own choice. But since it is Mark who represents the world as it is, the lovers' conflict with him means a clash with the existing social order. In the simplest possible terms: Gottfried is on the side of illicit love against the legal husband. How is this to be understood?

In looking at this question it is important to avoid thinking in terms of twentieth-century morality and advisable also to pass over the question of the attitude toward marriage in Gottfried's time. Rather we should look first toward the literature of Gottfried's day, and the ideals expressed there, and compare these with Gottfried's work and the views which he proffers. Of the two great forms of literature at the beginning of the thirteenth century, minnesong had as its basis the love of a man for a woman who was either his superior in life and, for that reason, unapproachable, married to another or, for some other reason, unattainable. In the most extreme case, a man could be in love with a woman he had never seen. It is true that in earlier works erotic love breaks through and reappears subsequently with [German lyric poet] Walther von der Vogelweide. In addition there was one form—the dawn song—in which the situation was always the same (the parting of lovers at dawn) and always presupposed physical union. The basic element remained, however, the cultivation of a purely spiritual love.

In the courtly epic, the other great literary form of the period, there is emphasis on action rather than contemplation, and the knight, by his prowess, wins and marries the lady. The idea of love is here completely different, for the lady is won without wooing and the result is marriage, whereas in minnesong she is always wooed but never won and the result is normally rejection, certainly never more than a form of distant encouragement. The story of Tristan might, therefore, be considered as a classic minnesong situation: the knight in love with the wife of another, her station also being above his. But Gottfried cuts right through the conventional posturing and emphasizes that their love became complete only after their physical union, while the husband, who is normally ignored in minnesong, is portrayed in detail as ignoble and essentially guilty. The relationship which is compounded by the epic situation of Tristan having in fact risked his life to "win" the lady, leads not to marriage or to courtly spiritual love but to "courtly adultery."

While it is true that morality, in the sense of conventional chivalric posturing, means little to Gottfried, it is not necessary to see in the outcome of his story either a condemnation of marriage and approval of adultery or a condemnation of adultery as leading inevitably to tragedy. Nowhere in Gottfried's work is there a suggestion that love cannot lead to marriage or that it must result in tragedy, if one of the partners is already married. Tristan and Isolde are exemplary and represent the utmost limits of human endeavor both in their love and in the obstacles which it must face. Never has the world known such lovers, but never have lovers been beset by so many difficulties or persecuted by such base enemies. Although Gottfried portrays character with due respect for verisimilitude, he is nevertheless concerned to portray Mark and his supporters as representative of the worst elements of the lower world—gross sensuality, envy, and pure evil—the most complete denial of the values for which he stands. By so doing, he establishes the primacy of the love bond over the (civil) marriage bond; but this is done without intent to undermine authority, either juridical or ecclesiastical.

Tristan and Isolde are, therefore, exemplary in spirit only. A knowledge of the manner in which they nurture and maintain their love, in spite of the evil forces marshaled against them, will sustain others in their lesser suffering, in the burden of life and the torments of love; just as the mystic and the monk are uplifted and strengthened by reading the lives of saints and martyrs who have gone before them. For Gottfried, the essential thing is that the noble in spirit should preserve love from debasement by a sensual and materialistic society and should foster and spread the appreciation of the true nature of love, its supreme and eternal virtue. Should the other world refuse to recognize the existence of Gottfried's world and, in its jealousy, set about deliberately to destroy it, then the world of the spirit, the true spirit of love, should supersede the degradation of marriage which, in Gottfried's eyes, is the equivalent of purchasing a wife, of "love . . . for sale in the open market" (12,296), whereas in truth:

> Love is so blissful a thing
> so blessed an endeavor,
> that apart from its teaching
> none attains worth or reputation. (187-90)

(pp. 76-86)

Michael S. Batts, in his Gottfried von Strassburg, *Twayne Publishers, Inc., 1971, 182 p.*

King Mark finds the lovers in the forest.

C. Stephen Jaeger (essay date 1973)

[*An American educator and authority on German literature, Jaeger has written extensively on the legend of Tristan and Isolde, including a study entitled* Medieval Humanism in Gottfried von Strassburg's Tristan und Isolde *(1977). In the following excerpt, he elucidates the tradition behind the crown of virtues in the Cave of Lovers allegory, arguing that the image of the crown represents Gottfried's belief that secular literature, as well as the Bible and the writings of the church fathers, could lead the reader to "love of higher virtues."*]

The keystone at the top of Gottfried's cave of lovers is capped with a marvelous piece of workmanship: a crown encrusted with jewels. Gottfried calls this finely wrought crown "the mold of virtues", *der tugende goz*. The crown is not a part of the cave allegory; its function is quite different from the other architectural elements of the cave. The walls, the floor, the crystal bed all function allegorically: they "are", or they signify something—the roundness of the walls is love's simplicity, the breadth is the strength of love, the crystal represents the clarity and brilliance of love. The crown, however, does not stand for any quality of love, but rather it mediates between those in the cave and certain beings, *die ob uns in den wolken swebent / und uns ir schin her nider gebent*. Its jewels gather up the virtues and glory of these beings in the clouds and pass them down to the lowly spirit fluttering about on the floor below. *Hoher muot* ["higher spirit"] does not require such mediation, since of its own strength it can soar up into the clouds, (*diu hoehe, deist der hohe muot, / der sich uf in die wolken tuot*, yet even *hoher muot* is drawn upwards to the crown, and in striving for this goal it can overcome every obstacle. The power of the crown is most apparent in its effect on *niderer muot* ["lowly spirit"]. Gottfried includes himself and his readers in this group, and, as if we stood in the cave with the author as our guide, he speaks of the influence of the crown on us who are not exalted lovers:

> . . . *wir, die nidere sin gemuot,*
> *der muot sich allez nider tuot*
> *und an dem estriche swebet,*
> *der weder swebet noch enclebet* . . .

We of *niderer muot* gaze upwards at the masterpiece; its radiance startles us from our lethargy, so that our spirit grows wings, and flies upward to bring forth praise of virtue. The "lowly spirit" takes from the sight of the crown the strength necessary to transcend its sluggish, earthbound state, a strength which flows from certain beings in the clouds: their celestial radiance passes through the jewels of the crown and penetrates to the spirit below, summoning it upward to love of virtue.

This paraphrase of **Tristan,** 16939-62, serves to clarify a difficult passage in the poem, a passage which had been the victim of considerable misunderstanding, until E. W. Theissen and W. N. Vlaming proposed an accurate translation [in 1930], showing that the twice repeated *ir* of lines 16955-56 must be understood as demonstratives, referring forward to the relative clause of the next two lines. The proper translation of 16955-58 is, (we look up at the piece of work) "which depends on the virtues and descends from the glory of those who soar above us in the clouds

and send down their radiance to us." This translation makes us aware of the presence of transcendent beings above the cave, a presence earlier concealed from view by misunderstanding of the text. . . . An understanding of the tradition behind Gottfried's image of the crown of virtues will substantiate Theissen and Vlaming's estimation of the passage. The present essay proposes to study the image of the crown, its history and its place within Gottfried's work as a whole.

The crown with its anagogic beckoning to the dull spirit, the image of the soul sprouting wings, celestial beings who pass their virtue and glory in the form of light down to the world of mortals—these elements of Gottfried's image are closely connected with theories of mystic contemplation in 12th century theology. But they have a long history, which we intend to sketch in broad outline.

The roots of Gottfried's image reach back as far as the 3rd century neoPlatonists and their most important representative, Plotinus. It will suffice for our purposes if we begin with a figure into whom the channels of neo-Platonist thought funneled, St. Denis, the pseudo-Areopagite. St. Denis [in his *De Caelesti Ierarchia*] bequeathed to the Middle Ages a conception of the heavens in which the celestial heights consist of nine tiers of angels beyond which, ultimately, God resides. From God emanates the divine light, which pours down over the successive steps of the hierarchy in what [French philosopher] Etienne Gilson calls [in his *History of Christian Philosophy in the Middle Ages*, 1955] an "illuminative cascade", infusing with light all levels of creation, from the seraphim who reside next to God and burn with the brilliance of His light, down to the lowliest creatures on earth, plants and insects. The divine light weakened progressively in its descent, and the position of each living creature in the heavenly and earthly hierarchies is determined by the degree to which he partakes of the divine illumination. For one strain of mysticism in the Middle Ages, the contemplative in seeking the path to God, envisioned his task as a process of rising by stages along this difusion of light. Denis describes various modes of ascent: the way of analogy, the way of negation, and mystic ecstasy. The first two belong together, since they both involve the use of mediation to gain insight into the invisible mysteries of God. When we attempt to understand God either by the created things of nature, or by the words of holy scripture, then we are raised by mediation to the contemplation of the Divine. St. Denis says that the divine light can only penetrate to us, as mortals, when clothed in material symbols:

> *Etenim neque possibile est, aliter lucere nobis divinum radium, nisi varietate sacrorum velaminum anagogice circumvelatum . . .*

When we follow the words of scripture, we are led upwards to enlightenment and the praise of the Divine:

> *Haec arcana temperanti silentio honorantes, ad lucentes nobis in sacris eloquiis splendores intendamus, et ab ipsis in lucem ducamur ad thearchicos hymnos . . .*

The function of scripture described in this passage is very close to that of Gottfried's crown. The crown draws us upwards to the light of the "beings in the clouds", and in our ascent we give praise to virtue; Scripture, says St. Denis, draws us to the beams of heavenly light which shine forth from the Bible, to give praise to the heavens (*ad thearchicos hymnos*). The use of such mediation is the lowest of the three ways of approaching God, says St. Denis, since inherent in it is the danger of seduction by earthly images:

> *In quidem enim pretiosioribus sacris formationibus consequens est et seduci auriformes quasdam aestimantes esse caelestes essentias, et quosdam viros fulgureos, decora indutos vestimenta, candide et ignee innocueque resplendentes . . .*

Simple souls, *qui nihil visibilibus bonis altius intelligunt*, are seduced by the beautiful images in scripture to this crude equation of the images with the heavenly spirits which they most inadequately represent. In order to avoid this danger, the writers of scripture resorted to images so dissimilar to the things they were intended to describe that not even the simplest of human beings could believe that they truly described heaven: multi-colored horses, bow-bearing arch-generals, many headed monsters, and the other grotesqueries of the Book of Revelations. The contemplation of such images allows us to observe what God is not, and thus approach some understanding of heaven by negation. Though negation is preferable to analogy, ultimately both of these methods are inadequate; in this life nothing can be absolutely affirmed or denied concerning God. The higher means of attaining knowledge of God is through mystical ecstasy, which requires that the seeker abandon all earthly images and all reliance on human reason. St. Denis counsels his fellow priest, Timothy, to whom the tract on *Mystical Theology* is directed,

> *. . . circa mysticas speculationes corroborato itinere et sensus desere, et intellectuales operationes, et sensibilia et invisibilia, et omne non ens, et ens; et ad unitatem, ut possibile, inscius restituere ipsius, qui est super omnem essentiam et scientiam.*

But the unmediated approach to God is reserved for the initiate; this path is closed to men who cling to earthly images and human understanding.

These modes of contemplation—the mediation of images and unmediated, ecstatic flight—provide the basic framework within which the mystic strove to understand the properties of God. Analogy and negation are the paths of those who are lower in spirit, those who require the use of human reason; ecstasy is the means of the practiced mystic, the initiate, to attain *unio mystica*. No one would, of course, maintain that the world of mortal beings and mutability was absolutely unreliable as a way to God; St. Paul himself had said [in Romans 1:20],

> *Invisibilia enim ipsius, a creatura mundi, per ea quae facta sunt, intellecta, conspiciuntur: sempiterna quoque ejus virtus, et divinitas . . .*

But for most medieval thinkers, the knowledge of God through His creatures remains on the level St. Denis had assigned it, an inferior means, to be used by men who partake to a lesser degree of the divine illumination. (pp. 95-9)

The Dionysian scheme of the cosmos generated a set of imagery to describe the contemplation of the Celestial: the mind ascends through the realms of the intelligences and the intelligible virtues, through the nine spheres of angels, along a trail of light emanating from God. Each soul ascends as it is best able, according to the degree of divine illumination it has received (or, through exercise, acquired). The world of men, like the world of angels, is divided into hierarchies. Those who are least illuminated require the use of earthly mediators—phenomena of nature, earthly beauty, or the *convenientes figurationes* of scripture—in order to break from the earthly realm into the heavenly. Men of the world, insofar as they seek illumination, require the mediation of those things which they can understand in order to gain insight into those things which they cannot. Anagogic imagery normally describes the process of mediation from the ascetic point of view. From the point of view of the initiate, and so men who must avail themselves of the lower path are described with various negative epithets: *the carnal populace, mens hebes* [stupid minds]. Initiates ascend without mediation, directly along the trail of divine light.

We are accustomed, particularly since Curtius' work [*European Literature and the Latin Middle Ages*, translated by W. R. Task, 1963], not to ask about the ultimate origin of poetic commonplaces. We regard the "topoi" of classical antiquity as elemental forms of expression, whereas they are themselves the expressions of archetypal forms of thought. In the case of Gottfried's crown of virtues, we have isolated an instance where a commonplace is traceable to its root in Christian thought. Gottfried's image of the crown is the first instance of anagogic imagery in secular literature of which I am aware. But such imagery is not uncommon in the poetry of the later Middle Ages and of the Baroque. We now turn to a few examples from these periods.

An image in [German poet] Albrecht von Scharfenberg's description of the Grail temple [in his *Der jüngere Titurel*] deserves a brief mention. He imputes an anagogic function to the statue of the four evangelists:

> *swelch oug iz da was sehende, daz wart zu got in groze vroud geleitet, also daz si da gedahten hin zuo dem himel trone und elliu dinc versmahten, di den menschen roubent solcher crone*

The stance of the ascetic reveals itself here. The mediation of the statues is a means which the beholder is meant to rise above and abandon; once he has, with its help, seen the throne of God, thenceforth he disdains all earthly objects. . . .

A work that applies anagogic imagery consistently is [Italian poet] Dante's *Paradiso*. Dante has built the entire metaphysics of mystic contemplation into the structure of the last book of the *Divina Commedia*. The poet's ascent through the various spheres of heaven proceeds along the beam of the divine light. In the opening canto, when Dante and Beatrice ascend from earth into the first sphere of heaven, Beatrice gazes directly into the sun, but Dante cannot endure its brilliance, and he gazes instead into the eyes of Beatrice:

> *Beatrice tutta nell 'etterne rote*

fissa con li occhi stava; ed io in lei
le luci fissi, di là su remote.

In this way they rise from earth to the first sphere of heaven. Dante and his guide partake of different degrees of illumination: Beatrice, the initiate, can rise to heaven unmediated; Dante, the mortal, requires mediation to rise from his earthbound state into the lower celestial realms. In this case the mediation comes through the eyes of a woman. It is clear that the eyes of Beatrice are the means which draw Dante upward through the spheres of heaven. Later he tells Cacciaguida that *li occhi della mia donna mi levaro,* namely from the mount of the earthly paradise into heaven and then from one heavenly light to the next. This is possible, not only because of the immanent power of the lady's beauty, but also because divine Joy shines through her (*il piacere etterno, che diretto / raggiava in Beatrice, dal bel viso*). Dante's idea of representing the eyes of Beatrice as the mediators which raise Dante through the heavens represents a fusion of two traditions: the ethical value of a lady's love and the anagogic function of earthly beauty. The former developed among the poets of courtly love; the latter was espoused by speculative mystics. This fusion of traditions shows us the ultimate meaning of anagogic imagery as Dante and Gottfried apply it: it represents the integration of the worldly and the divine, the profane and the sacred. The eyes of Beatrice and the crown of virtues symbolize the authors' conviction that earthly love and beauty can serve as the means to elevate the mind to celestial heights.

The framework of mystic contemplation lends itself to this fusion with the courtly motif of the moral value that flows through the eyes of the lady: the relation of the "lowly spirit" to earthly mediators offers a neat parallel to the subordinate position of the lover to the beloved. [Italian poet] Petrarch adapted anagogic imagery joined with the courtly love tradition, and made it into one of the commonplaces of his sonnets and canzoni, particularly in the poems in praise of his lady's eyes. Through Petrarch, the motif of the anagogic power of the lady's eyes passed into the sonnets of the Renaissance and Baroque. (pp. 105-07)

Clearly we must regard the crown of virtues as an element quite distinguishable from the rest of the cave allegory in **Tristan.** F. Ranke, in his essay relating Gottfried's techniques to the allegorical interpretation of the church building [*Die Allegoric der Minnegrotte in Gottfrieds Tristan,* 1925] did not, of course, regard separately the component parts of the cave; he understood them as all having derived from the same sources. Some recent studies have shown that it is important to regard each element of the cave of lovers and its environs separately. The present study hopes to strengthen this dawning awareness. The following comments will demonstrate that it is decisive for the interpretation of the cave of lovers episode to realize that Gottfried consciously joins elements from different traditions in this section of the poem.

In the last decade the interest in the cave allegory as a parody of Christian forms his diminished; scholarship has cautiously moved away from Ranke's approach to focus on the secular and literary sources of the cave and its environs. Rainer Gruenter [in his "Das wunnecliche tal," *Eu-*

phorion 55 (1961): 341-404] has studied the close connection between the landscape of the grotto and that of the "locus amoenus" of classical and Middle Latin poetry. And Herbert Kolb, in his essay, *'der minnen hus'* [*Euphorion* 56 (1962): 229-47], has attacked Ranke's time-honored theory that the cave allegory is indebted directly to the forms and techniques of cathedral allegory. Kolb has shown that Gottfried assembled the cave out of structural elements which also occur in 'temples of Love' in Old French love allegories. The walls, the floor, the impossibly complicated door have counterparts in French works; the crystal bed, in which Gottfried Weber [in his *Gottfrieds von Straussburgs Tristan und die Krise des hochmittelalterlichen Weltbildes un 1200,* 1953] saw a profound perversion of the Eucharist, provided repose for a number of French lovers around the time that it was finding its way into the Minnegrotte. The origin of the cave is disquietingly pagan: Gottfried has heathen giants build it as a secret place to carry on their love affairs. In a good many particulars, then, the scene and architecture of the cave of lovers is pagan, classical, secular.

The thoroughly Christian image of the keystone is not brought into this setting randomly, attracted along with other elements all borrowed at the same time from the conventions of church allegory. The crown of the keystone alone remains as an element which is unquestionably of Christian origin. Kolb makes no mention of the keystone in his essay, and with good cause: he is trying to establish the sources of the cave allegory as purely literary, and the presence of the crown of virtues contradicts his basic premise. Kolb wants to see the cave as a unified structure with no disparate—that is, Christian—elements. The crown of virtues is, to speak from Kolb's point of view, a disparate element, but far from producing a dissonance in the style of the scene, the presence of this particular Christian element amidst the secular surroundings is very meaningful: Gottfried integrates two previously opposed traditions in the architecture of his cave of lovers. The crown with its anagogic beckoning caps the secular architecture of all the cave beneath. The crown establishes a continuity between the pagan setting, the secular architecture and the celestial beings soaring above us in the clouds. Earthly and Heavenly meet at this point. There can be no more striking and transparent symbol of the joining of the secular sphere and the Christian cosmos that the image of *hoher muot* sprouting wings and flying upwards to give praise to celestial virtue; the quintessential spirit of the knight and lover raises itself by the machinery of mystic contemplation into the heavens. Gottfried has applied the crown meaningfully within the tradition of contemplation from which it sprang: it is a mediator by which we rise through earthly things to heavenly.

Seen in this light, the composite architecture of the cave represents a statement of the poet's intentions not only in the Minnegrotte episode, but in the work as a whole. This indication of Gottfried's intentions is certainly a subtle one, but not one veiled in a dark poetic conceit. The crown and its effect must have been immediately recognizable to the educated among Gottfried's readers, since it relies on the most common scheme, St. Denis', of the architecture of heaven and the means of contemplating its realms. If the image does indeed contain a statement of Gottfried's intentions, then what are they? Here we stand for a moment before a danger: we face the question "analogia antithetica" or "analogia entis"? I am inclined to believe, with Herbert Kolb ["Zur Allegorie der Minnegrotte in Gottfrieds *Tristan*," *Euphorion* 56 (1962): 229-47] that the question is superfluous and misleading. Gottfried's work does not place us before such extremes. His intentions in *Tristan und Isolde* are to integrate *hoher muot* into the Christian cosmos; to graft secular poetry onto the tree of Christian tradition (to use an image of which Gottfried himself is fond). This is not to say that the work is a poem of fervent Christian piety. Gottfried's sympathies are undoubtedly with the world of *hohe minne, edele herzen* ["higher love," "noble hearts"], minstrelsy, learning and the hunt. His intention is to bring the world of the romance into the service of Christianity, to make of his characters mediators which serve to lead the mind of the reader to the experience of sublime love and loyalty, and thus strengthen these virtues in him. This is precisely the benefit which Gottfried promises the reader in his prologue:

> ez ist in sere guot gelesen,
> guot? ja, innecliche guot:
> ez liebet liebe und edelt muot,
> ez staetet triuwe und tugendet leben,
> ez kan wol lebene tugende geben;

We know that the mere sight of Isolde is morally improving:

> 'der Isot under ougen siht,
> dem liutertz herze unde muot,
> reht als diu gluot dem golde tuot:
> ez liebet leben unde lip.'

and it is a short step from this "topos" to the idea that the love of a woman serves a Christian purpose, an idea we see ripened to maturity in the works of Dante. The Christian purpose is admittedly shallow in Gottfried's work; the joining of the two realms is indeed a graft. The secular work suddenly claims for itself the position of a Christian endeavour; the cave of lovers opens the work, through the crown, onto the Christian cosmos. But Gottfried's *Tristan* is not an "integument" which clothes Christian mysteries. Its Christianizing amounts to little more than a blessing spoken over the characters of the romance. We might paraphrase the symbolic statement of the crown as follows: "Tales of love have their place in the Christian cosmos: they are mediators which lead us into the lower realms of heaven. Here is where the story of Tristan and Isolde functions as a 'good work', for it can raise us to these heights" [12200-208]. This is precisely the message of the tradition which stands behind the crown: mediation does not lead us to the vision of God; its goals are modest. It leads us only to the realm of the virtues.

When we ask whether the work represents an antithetical or a proper analogy to orthodox Christianity, then we impose a false criterion on it; we demand that it yield up some secret which it does not contain; we ask the poet whether he is a fervent believer or a fervent iconoclast, when he is neither. We fail to take into account the hierarchic pattern of thought in a gradualistic system, whereby all levels of existence represent varying stages of the Good,

whereby men of low spirituality avail themselves of the means appropriate to them to raise themselves— slightly—along the ladder of illumination. We have been led to apply this question partly because Gottfried does in fact combine Christian forms with an adulterous love situation, and this is a bold idea. But we have shown above one instance in which Dante likewise fuses a Christian tradition with a convention of courtly love. Certainly the role which he assigns to Beatrice also is a bold idea. But it is preposterous to suppose that Dante intended the figure of Beatrice as an antithesis to the Virgin as mediatrix. There is a difference of degree between Dante's and Gottfried's fusing of Christian and secular motifs, not a difference of kind. Both poets expand Christian mythology by grafting secular elements into it. In the case of Gottfried the graft is superficial: the connection with the Christian sphere shines through the work at a few points, but Christian motifs, concepts, intentions are not built into the structure of the work, as they are in Dante's *Paradiso*. But in both cases the process of joining previously hostile traditions is essentially the same. The boldness in Gottfried's image of the crown is this: it represents a claim that secular literature is capable of providing "convenientes figurationes" to lead the mind of the reader to love of higher virtues; secular literature claims for itself a role previously restricted to Holy Scripture, the writings of the church fathers and of the most illumined theologians.

The line of *Tristan* research of which Ranke, Schwietering and Weber [*Gottfrieds von Strassburg "Tristan" und die Krise des hochmittelalterlichen Weltbildes um 1200*, 1953] are the most prominent representatives cannot be brushed aside as easily as the last section of this study perhaps seemed to indicate. Does the crown of virtues really mediate between secular and Christian values? Are "those who soar above us in the clouds" the angels and beings which populate the Christian heavens, or are they the celestial creatures of a schismatic cosmos based on Minne as the highest good? Weber's arguments of a crisis in medieval culture around 1200 could be applied with equal validity to interpret this Christian element of the poem as yet another parody of religious forms. I see the crown of virtues as the symbol of the poet's striving to integrate classical and secular forms with Christian ones. This interpretation would be a tenuous one, if it were not for another passage in *Tristan* which confirms it, Gottfried's literary excurse.

One of Gottfried's main concerns in the literary excurse is sources of inspiration, both his own and those of his contemporary poets. In the imagery with which Gottfried describes the style of his fellow poets, he imputes to each of them (with two exceptions, which I will account for presently) a pagan or classical source of inspiration. The genius of Blicker von Steinach seems to have been spun by fairies, purified and brightened in their well. Veldeke's source is a classical one:

> ich waene, er sine wisheit
> uz Pegases urspringe nam . . .

Reinmar's inspiration is likewise classical—he sings with the tongue of Orpheus:

> Ich waene, Orphees zunge,
> diu alle doene kunde,

diu doenete uz ir munde.

Walther has his love songs straight from Venus, the goddess of love. Then we come to Gottfried himself. He turns first to Helicon, the home of Apollo and the nine muses, and begs them for a single drop from their well of inspiration. This one drop, he says, will pass his words through the crucible of the muses and rarify them marvelously like Arabian gold. But then there is a remarkable change in the direction of his plea: he transfers it from the home of the muses to "the true Helicon, the highest throne". Again, it is Herbert Kolb who has shown that *der ware Elicon* can only mean the Christian heaven, the celestial heights, which, as a source of inspiration is the figural fulfillment of the pagan Helicon. The preceding study of the crown of virtues suggests a possible answer to Kolb's question,

> Welchen Sinn und Zweck sollte es haben, daβ Gottfried zweimal hintereinander, zuerst in antikischer, sodann in Christlicher Weise von den Überirdischen die Gabe der Dichtkunst erfleht?

Gottfried turns from the secular traditions of his contemporaries to draw his inspiration ultimately from the Christian heaven. But it is not the case that he rejects the ministrings of Apollo and the muses; his words are first burnished (this is his prayer) in the crucible of the muses, refined like gold, then they receive the translucent quality which divine inspiration can provide (*durchliuhtec als ein erweltiu gimme.*) Classical inspiration is equated with the qualities of gold, Christian with the qualities of jewels. It is quite appropriate: the classical tradition gives him a brilliance and radiance of style, but the mind stops at the surface, cannot penetrate gold. Christian inspiration gives depth, transparency to his style; it allows the mind to penetrate beyond the brilliant surface of the work.

The gold and jewels in the imagery of the literary excurse form a convenient bridge back to the gold and jewels of the crown of virtues. Both the crown and Gottfried's style attempt to lead the soul through material and worldly things to spiritual things. The cave of lovers is surrounded with the scenery of the classical "locus amoenus", the cave is constructed out of allegorical elements common to Old French love allegories, and the edifice is crowned with a masterpiece of Christian workmanship which leads to the celestial heights. Thus the classical and pagan is crowned with the Christian. Similarly, Gottfried's fellow poets in the literary excurse are inspired by the secular and classical tradition in poetry, whereas Gottfried himself seeks his inspiration in a harmonious blending of classical and Christian sources. Gottfried sees himself, in contrast to many of his contemporaries, as a poet who strives to integrate the two. It is significant that the only two poets mentioned in the excurse to whom Gottfried does not impute a secular source of inspiration are the two who have struggled in their works with the problem of integrating the worldly and the Divine: Hartmann and Wolfram. And Gottfried carefully qualifies his statement about Walther to show that the classical source applies only to his love songs (*ich meine aber in dem done / da her von Zytherone . . .*). (In the case of Wolfram, however, Gottfried was clearly not motivated purely by philosophical considerations in remaining silent about his source of in-

spiration.) The caution in formulation, Gottfried's selectivity, indicate that the classical references are meaningfully applied: those who sing "as if" inspired by classical sources are in fact basically secular poets.

In the two passages which are generally recognized as Gottfried's most genial and original creations, we find this impulse to integrate the classical with the Christian tradition, the secular with the religious sphere. Undeniably these two passages contain a kind of statement of purpose; they indicate in what directions the poet's intentions lie. But it is impossible to conclude from them that the poet has imparted anything more that a gloss of Christian purpose to the work. Both are deft and daring poetic ideas, but their efficacy remains for the most part in the poetic sphere. They represent artful and (in the case of the crown) learned claims of Christian purpose, flourishes of Christian sentiment. Gottfried certainly did not fashion the ethos of his work in accordance with Christian orthodoxy. But the crown of virtues indicates to us that he was not averse to doing so, that he sought to guide the work, as he had received it from Thomas of Brittany, in that direction. (pp. 110-16)

> *C. Stephen Jaeger, "The Crown of Virtues in the Cave of Lovers Allegory of Gottfried's 'Tristan'," in* Euphorion, *Vol. 67, 1973, pp. 95-116.*

Jackson on Gottfried's Tristan as artist:

It appears . . . that Gottfried conceived of the artist as one who could use excellent material, in this case music and lyric poetry, to dominate an audience and bend it to his will. His concept is, in fact, very close to our own idea of the great classic actor who can impose his interpretation of a play upon his audience or even of a political orator who imposes his ideas not by rational argument but by eloquent presentation and emotional force. It should be remembered that Tristan is spoken of as an original composer only once, although he may have composed some of the songs he performed. When he is in a state of total mental confusion over his attitude to the two Isoldes; he composes a song which he intends to celebrate Isolde the Fair but which is taken by all the members of Kaedin's court to be in praise of Isolde White Hands. His composition, therefore, brings confusion and irrationality of a very different kind from that brought about by his performances and it is a state in which he is by no means the dominant figure. . . .

Gottfried does not think of his artist-hero as a composer or creator but as an interpreter and a person who understands music. Any composing he does is incidental to his interpretation. The artist is far above the common minstrel and equally far above the lords and barons who make up courtly society. He can use his power of interpretation and his ability to communicate music to impose his will on such people. Yet his greatest gift is that when he finds an equally gifted woman, he can communicate his power to her and thus eliminate the necessity of any kind of performance. In their own world performance ceases and is replaced by true harmony.

> *W. T. H. Jackson, in his* "Artist and Performance in Gottfried's *Tristan," Tristania,* 1975.

C. Stephen Jaeger   (essay date 1988)

[*In the essay that follows, Jaeger presents an overview of the cultural and literary context of Gottfried's* Tristan and Isolde, *noting especially the poet's masterful combining of classical elements with Christian spirituality.*]

Tristan is a work that mocks our popular conceptions of the Middle Ages: an "age of faith," an age of chivalry, a gloomy, dark, and reactionary society welded into a unity by fear or love of authority, by intellectual and spiritual homogeneity. The uniqueness of *Tristan* is evident if we try to fit it into these categories.

It was an age of faith: it may have been that for monks, but here are some of the passages from *Tristan* that tell us something about the poet's attitude to religion: when Isolde carries the glowing iron to test her loyalty to her husband and is not burned, God attests to her innocence, even though she is guilty as sin and has sworn a false oath to maintain the illusion of innocence. God apparently accepts the illusion; in any case, forced by the ordeal to render judgment, He comes down on her side. Gottfried comments, "Thus it was made manifest and confirmed to all that Christ in His great virtue is pliant as a windblown sleeve. He falls into place and clings, whichever way you try Him. . . . He is at the beck of every heart for honest deeds or fraud." The lovers' cave where Tristan and Isolde live during their banishment is a kind of spiritualized temple of love, whose architecture Gottfried explains allegorically: its roundness stands for Love's simplicity; its height for aspiration; the greenness of the marble floor for constancy, and so forth. It is a well known form of allegorizing in the high Middle Ages, but not in tales glorifying adulterous love. Gottfried borrowed it from the forms of cathedral allegory. At the end of his prologue he tells us that the story of Tristan and Isolde "is bread to all noble hearts. With this their death lives on. We read their life, we read their death, and to us it is sweet as bread. . . . Thus they live still and yet are dead, and their death is the bread of the living." It is a turn of thought borrowed from the sacrament of the Eucharist; the story of Tristan and Isolde takes on the quality of the body of Christ: through the death of those it represents it gives life to the living.

So, Gottfried's use of Christianity, its God, and its most sacred forms, is puzzling at best, outrageous at worst. He seems to be sanctifying an adulterous love affair by applying the forms of orthodox religion to it. But the work did not cause a scandal and Gottfried did not end at the stake, and so it is best to say that we do not understand his attitude to Christianity.

It was an age of chivalry: Gottfried's contemporaries were writing narratives, courtly romances, about knights who ride around seeking adventure, proving themselves, shaping their identities, and winning honor for their ladies by fighting with other knights, giants, wizards, dwarves, and dragons. In *Tristan,* chivalric prowess is not very important. Tristan does not learn to fight until the ripe old age of eighteen, and then he fights some very unchivalric bat-

tles: fully armed, he attacks his father's liege lord and kills him, though the latter has neither weapons nor armor. He conquers the Irish champion Morolt, hacks up his body, and places the pieces in a sack to be sent back to Ireland, even though Morolt had offered Tristan quarter, friendship, and a cure for his poisoned wound earlier in the battle when he was at his mercy. In the early parts of the romance, Tristan makes his way and establishes himself at court by his skills as courtier and artist: hunting skills, mastery of music and foreign languages, diplomacy, and statesmanship. The showplace of the story and the testing ground of the hero is the king's court, not the field and the forest typical of Arthurian romance. Apart from intellectual attainments, the other skill most important to Tristan is cunning and trickery, a quality which the Middle High German vocabulary does not distinguish too sharply from wisdom and knowledge.

All this is highly unchivalric, and again one wonders why the work did not cause scandal to those who held to a knightly code of behavior. Arthurian romance is unfailingly optimistic, at least every romance that Gottfried might have known.

Society was unified by an authority seen as God-given, hence above question: Gottfried depicts the court of Cornwall as teeming with intriguers, a staging place for plots and counterplots. He represents the king of Cornwall and uniter of England as a shallow, sensual, materialistic, and sentimental cuckold. The unquestioned value in this work is the love of hero and heroine for each other. Never mind that that love is politically subversive, never mind that disloyalty of vassal to king is seen as a kind of special distinction of the vassal. What is important here are the feelings of two "superior" individuals, two "noble hearts," for each other, not the stability of the social order.

If there are medieval categories into which the romance fits conveniently, they are yet to be found and formulated. Add this to the fact that Gottfried wrote in a style so elegant that it was not to be matched in Germany until the late eighteenth century, that his education is clearly far superior to any contemporary, and one is tempted to ask whether the whole thing is not the product of some nineteenth-century forger. It is in any case one of those unique works of genius that presents itself to the modern reader as if the period it is set in were just historical costume. It is not narrowly bound by the forms of thought, characterization, and representation that hedged in other contemporary works.

When Gottfried von Strassburg began this work which sanctifies a forbidden and destructive love, he had a number of earlier versions to draw on that condemned it. He inherited the basic outline of the story from rather primitive versions from the second half of the twelfth century by the German Eilhart von Oberge and the Norman-French poet Béroul, and these probably go back to early Celtic tales of a sorceress-queen who enslaved an unwilling lover by means of a magic potion. In the twelfth-century "pre-courtly" versions, the love potion is still seen as a demonic force, the love itself as a fateful catastrophe that engulfs and holds the lovers against their own will. They recognize its immorality, condemn it, but are powerless against the force of its magic. In a particularly ungallant gesture, Eilhart has the love potion wear off after four years. The version of the tale that Gottfried himself recognized as the "true" one came from an Anglo-French poet, Thomas of Brittany, who probably wrote for the court of Henry II of England and Eleanor of Aquitaine. This poet conceived of the adulterous love as lofty and ennobling. Gottfried adopted Thomas's conception, and outdid his "master," spiritualizing the love, depicting the court and its representatives as envious intriguers and the king himself as shallow, weak, lustful, and materialistic. The courtly poets produced versions that are against the social order and for the lovers.

An introduction to the story of Tristan and Isolde does better to start in social than in literary history. Any work of literature that outlives its contemporaries begins in life and human experience, and should be seen as a distillate of that experience, not as an artifact of literary history. Literature was lived before it was written down. Earlier writers were at pains to mask this fact. It is a kind of indiscretion after all. Medieval poets were especially good at concealing the experiences on which their poems were based, and preventing the reader from asking where these stories had their beginnings in life. To a medieval romancier transported magically into the eighteenth century, it would have seemed like a betrayal of trade secrets when Goethe proclaimed that his poetic works were fragments of a great confession. The pre-Romantic author did not want the real source of his stories discovered: he wanted them to appear before the reader with the objectivity of myth or the authority of sacred history, or both. If they were true, they were not personal; if somebody wrote them himself, then they were a kind of lying. Therefore works of literature were costume productions staged and set as though without an author, and a long tradition of scholarship that reduced literary study to history of motifs and forms cooperated in ignoring or blurring the reality to which medieval literature refers.

For courtly poets of the high Middle Ages and beyond, Arthurian legend was the grand costume room and prop chest. Here they found their elaborate disguises which they shaped to fit their scenario and cast of characters: the courteous and amorous knight errant, the menagerie of dwarves, giants, dragons and enchanters, all those damsels, cruel or in distress, vengeful or submissive; the enchanted forests and castles, the storms of Broceliande and the mists of Avalon.

To help us ignore him, the courtly poet said nothing about himself. Gottfried von Strassburg is a name to us. It occurs nowhere in the text of his poem *Tristan und Isolde,* unless we want to take the cryptic G, with which the first word of the poem begins, as the initial of his name. We only know his full name because later poets mentioned it in praising his work. No historical document mentions a poet Gottfried von Strassburg. What we know about him as a person is nothing, and it does not matter. What counts is his understanding of human affairs, love, sensibility, court behavior, his conception of education, of the relations of lover and beloved, of courtier and ruler, of husband and wife. His poem tells us his experience of these

things in such intimate detail that it requires the discreet masking of chivalric legend.

To approach Gottfried von Strassburg and his work, we do well to begin with the social context of the work, the prince's court, and with the economy of ideas and values that functioned there, its typical experiences and its cast of characters. This is where Gottfried's story of Tristan and Isolde lived before it was written down. It defines itself by the contrast to courtly convention.

If the private experience behind Gottfried's tale is lost to recovery, the representative experience is not. Court society of the twelfth and early thirteenth century was swept by a wave of fashion in manners and ethics, and its most dramatic symptom is the emergence of a code of behavior called "courtliness." Such a code had existed at courts ecclesiastical and secular at least since the mid-eleventh century. But in the middle of the twelfth, something quite radical happened: a code of court behavior—fine speech, delicacy of feelings, with and urbanity—was preached to the lay nobility, to dukes, counts, and even normal soldiers, at least the ones who rode on horseback and defined themselves as professional militia. And the men who fashioned and propounded the code of courtly behavior, ordinarily classically educated court clerics, created a medium that became probably the most powerful instrument of education ever forged: the courtly romance. This literary form creates the figure of the chivalric-courtly knight serving his lady and mankind. It put forward an ideal that until that time had next to no counterpart in reality, and the ideal became a wildly popular fashion, both in literature and in life.

> [Gottfried] introduced forms of expression and ideals from the humanistic schools of France into German courtly romance, and transformed this class-bound, optimistic, occasionally trivial genre into the vehicle of a dark and tragic, profound and transcendent view of love.
>
> —*C. Stephen Jaeger*

With this ideal of the civilized knight came a new form of love. A cult of love fashionable at the courts of southern France gave impetus to the courtly education of knights. In any case, a cult of refined love made common cause with the trend toward the education and refinement of knights, and the result is what has come to be called "courtly love." At its shallowest it was a court game. At its best it was one of the most brilliant programs of education any age ever conceived. Men "fell in love" with ladies who refused them their love until they had proved themselves worthy of it. That might mean that they must learn to speak well, wash, clean their fingernails and mind their manners, defer to ladies, wear lace shirts and tight-fitting pants. It might also mean that they must fight battles in the name of their lady and win victories, conquer villains, wizards, and giants. That at least is the form "love service" could take when transformed into fiction. "Courtly Love" was a fiction even when it was practiced in reality. Court society lives from such fictions, and in a sense every appearance at court, every encounter, every conversation, was a staged and choreographed event. If it took its style from some literary tradition, so much the better. This playful aestheticizing of everyday life at court becomes much more dramatically visible in the later Middle Ages and Renaissance, when lords and ladies replayed scenes from Arthurian romance as the content of their festivals and pageants and occasionally even in the course of everyday life. At the "accession day tilts" in honor of the coronation of Elizabeth I of England, her courtiers presented themselves as combatants in staged jousts within the fiction that each was a disguised knight engaged in some amorous adventure in the service of his lady-love, the queen. Even serious or trivial acts of administration had to be stylized according to chivalric models. Sir Walter Raleigh, confined in the Tower of London for marrying without the Queen's consent, writes Elizabeth a letter requesting his release and casting himself in the role of Orlando Furioso driven mad from excessive love, and that means, for the queen. But he was not suggesting a liaison; rather he was just speaking the idiom within which gentlemen presented their petitions and requests to the queen: courtly-chivalric love.

In its twelfth-century beginnings, "courtly love" probably tread a precarious line between a court game and a socially acceptable mask for lust, and occasionally even for genuine feelings. The courtly romance lives from the idiom of courtly love: adventure in the service of one's lady love, love as an educating force, love as the force which drives men on to great deeds.

But it is easy to see how the emotion of love could be trivialized and exploited by its integration into a court game or a program of civilizing. Some of the best romances arose in opposition to the debasing of love. In Wolfram von Eschenbach's *Parzival,* probably the greatest of medieval romances, and one against which Gottfried polemicized in his "literary excursus" in **Tristan,** the landscape is littered with the bodies of knights and ladies who suffer because of the practices of love service. Parzival's cousin Sigune spends her life lamenting over the dead body of her friend, Schionatulander, whom she had refused to love until he performed various adventures to prove his love for her. The Grail King Anfortas suffers from an incurable wound received because he served a lady for her love against the laws of the Grail society, though very much in conformity to the rules of courtly love.

That is the background against which we should see Gottfried's conception of love. He says, in an important passage just after the love potion,

> They are right who say, 'Love is hounded to the ends of the earth.' All that we have is the bare word, only the name remains to us: and this we have so hackneyed, so abused, and so debased, that the poor, tired thing is ashamed of her own name and is disgusted at the word. . . . Shorn of all honor and dignity she sneaks begging from house to house. . . . Love, mistress of all hearts, the noble, the incomparable, is for sale in the open market.

So it would seem if we read the court poetry celebrating courtly love. What bolsters true love and loyalty are the tales of great lovers from the past, those who have lived and died for love. In the idyll of the cave of lovers, Tristan and Isolde themselves read the love tragedies of Ovid: Pyramus and Thisbe, Biblis, Dido and Aeneas. In his prologue, Gottfried offers his story to that elite group he calls "noble hearts." They are different from that ignoble crowd, "who are unable to endure sorrow and wish only to revel in bliss . . . I have another world in mind which together in one heart bears its bittersweet, its dear sorrow, its heart's joy, its love's pain, its dear life, its sorrowful death, its dear death, its sorrowful life." He has projected these qualities onto King Mark, who is that pleasure seeker brought low by his shallow, debasing view of love, and has made of Tristan and Isolde the noble lovers so loyal that they die for love.

Another odd and perplexing feature of Gottfried's ideal of love is his use of sickness, wounds, and physical suffering as a metaphor for longing and fulfillment. Occasionally the experience of love and physical illness merge in the events of the story. Tristan is conceived when his mother comes to her lover, Rivalin, at night in the guise of a physician supposedly to cure a mortal wound. She is admitted, and ministers to the dying man by making love to him. He is miraculously cured, and the deathbed becomes the (pre-)nuptial bed on which the hero is conceived. When Tristan and Isolde make love for the first time, Gottfried says, "Love the physician led Tristan, her sick one, by the hand: and there, too, she found her other patient, Isolde. She quickly took both sufferers and gave him to her, her to him, to be each other's remedy." It makes good sense within this metaphor that the love potion is seen as a kind of poison which joins them together and spells their eventual death. Love is both poison and cure, both suffering and happiness. But once we know the meaning with which Gottfried has invested the motif of poison and incurable wounds, what are we to say of Tristan, near to death from the poisoned wound he received in the battle with Morolt, arriving in Ireland to receive his cure at the hands of Queen Isolde, the mother of his future lover? He floats up to the city walls playing his musical instrument; the sweet sound of the music mingles with the stench of his ripe wounds, and both waft over the walls of the city and announce his arrival. Is Gottfried here playing with the metaphor, love is a kind of sickness? He is at the very least playing on the rich overtones with which the motifs, love, sickness, wounds, poison, music, are imbued. Against that background, the poisoned wound cured by a woman named Isolde must be seen as a kind of replaying of the curing of his father and his own conception, and at the same time a foreshadowing of the love potion, the love-sickness-to-death it causes, and his "cure" from Princess Isolde. This is just one of the many forms in which Gottfried's idea that love is both joy and suffering expresses itself.

Tristan is a romance of the court, a courtier's tragedy. The prince's court is the social or institutional context of this work, and if we read Gottfried's poem against what we can learn of actual court life of the period, it helps us approach an understanding of some of the problems in the work: the character of Tristan, for instance, this trickster-artist-intellectual-lover.

His debut at Mark's court in Cornwall is a showpiece of courtier virtues. Abandoned on the Cornish coast by the Norwegian sailors who had kidnapped him, he meets the king's hunting party as they are flaying their quarry, a hart. Tristan, a fourteen-year-old boy at the time, steps up boldly and chides them for cutting up the animal in an uncourtly way. They ask him to show them the custom of his own land, and he agrees. He takes off his coat, rolls up his sleeves, and lays back his hair, while all the Cornishmen, in the spell of this showman, watch in awed admiration. Then he proceeds to "excoriate" the hart, shows them other rare hunting customs and introduces them to the French vocabulary of the hunt. Finally, he arranges the members of the hunt party in a formation that reproduces the physical form of the hart, and with himself and the master huntsman at its head, crowned with wreaths, the parade sets off solemnly and amid trumpet peals, for the king's court. It is a scene that must be read against the background of court pageantry and the royal entry, a form of courtly presentation that derives from the forms of the ancient Roman triumphal procession.

On the way to court, the huntsmen ask him who he is. He answers that he is the son of a merchant, though he himself and the reader are well aware that he is the son of the lord of Parmenie. At court, Tristan listens one day to the playing of a musician, the best in Cornwall. He comments on the performance in a way that indicates he knows a thing or two about music. The musician asks him whether he himself can play, and Tristan replies that he once could, but now has grown so rusty that he dare not. (Remember, he is fourteen years old at the time.) The musician urges him until he finally, reluctantly, takes up the instrument—and plays so well that they are all amazed. The king asks him whether he plays other instruments. He answers that he cannot. The king presses him. Tristan relents. He admits, unwillingly, that he knows every sort of stringed instrument. The one he knows best, the *sambjut,* has never even been heard of in Cornwall. The court again breaks into fervent praise of this child prodigy. The king asks whether he knows other languages than the ones he has heard him sing (French, Latin, and English). Tristan answers that he knows a few others "tolerably well." Then he is addressed in every language known at the court—Norwegian, Irish, German, Scottish, and Danish—and handles himself in each like a native. Again he inspires awed admiration, as if he were a virtuoso on a stage.

And that is just what the courtier is at the moment of his debut. Baldesar Castiglione was to describe this complex of strategies and virtues in his *Book of the Courtier* (1528). He called his calculated underplaying of talents *sprezzatura,* a kind of behavior aimed at winning the favor of the prince and warding off the envy of the court. It is a disdainful attitude toward one's own talents, "which conceals all artistry and makes whatever one says or does seem uncontrived and effortless . . . we can truthfully say

that true art is what does not seem to be art, and the most important thing is to conceal it."

By his many talents, his charm, his affability, he wins the love of King Mark and rises swiftly to become the king's favorite, eventually the heir of the kingdom. Gottfried was so interested in the figure of the young Tristan, his youth, education, his rise to prominence in Cornwall, his diplomacy, his skill in facing intrigues, that fully half of the (unfinished) poem is devoted to the events prior to the drinking of the love potion. The work is in large part devoted to representing the success of a talented courtier. The second part, the love story, shows his struggle to maintain this position while deceiving the king, and his eventual fall. In this sense it is appropriate to call the story, which is hard to categorize in known narrative genres, a courtier's tragedy.

An introduction to Gottfried's *Tristan* is not complete without some discussion of the poet's place in the contemporary literary scene. If we know that place particularly well, it is because Gottfried himself indicated it in the passage called his "literary excursus." He introduces it just before the ceremony of Tristan's knighting as an answer to the question, how were the clothes made for Tristan and his thirty companions? It is an elegantly oblique answer. I, Gottfried says, cannot speak well of knightly splendor, since so many earlier writers have outdone me on that score. And he proceeds to mention and praise these other poets: he gives Hartmann von Aue the laurel wreath, and his phrasing projects an image of himself as a kind of *arbiter elegantiarum,* a judge of poetry—and a haughty one, well aware of his own superior position—empowered to pass judgment on his contemporaries, crown this one, damn that one. He proceeds to damn an unnamed poet who has pressed his claim to the laurel wreath too boldly: his style is uneven, obscure, and deceptive, like the performances of carnival tricksters who produce pearls from dust and deceive the minds of children. This poet is undoubtedly Wolfram von Eschenbach, the one of Gottfried's contemporaries whose work in the judgment of posterity measures up to or surpasses Gottfried's. He goes on to praise Heinrich von Veldeke, Reinmar von Hagenau, Walther von der Vogelweide, and others. The passage represents the first piece of literary criticism in the German language, and from it we can learn a great deal about the aesthetics of Gottfried's poetry. For instance, he praises Hartmann for his "crystalline words," and his ability to adorn his tale "both inside and out" with words and meanings. It is not hard to imagine what it means to adorn the outside of the tale: presumably elegance of diction, richness of visual and auditory detail, the external adornments of the story. But what is the "inside" of the tale? Clearly, Gottfried sees a level of meaning beyond plot and story in Hartmann, and what he admired in this poet he developed in his own writing. The "inner meaning," the ideal of "crystalline" diction and transparent narration is evident in Gottfried's own work especially where he uses the device of allegory. Gottfried is the first vernacular poet to make any consistent use of allegory. He explains the architecture of the cave of lovers as an allegory of the virtues of love; he describes Tristan's fight with Morolt as a battle of two armies: Morolt with the strength of four men opposes Tristan and his three allies: Fighting Spirit, Justice, and God. Abstractions become participants, and Tristan receives his poisoned wound when he fights by himself aided only by his Fighting Spirit. He wins the victory only when God and Justice join him. The meaning to which these "crystalline" words point is that a knight fighting solely for the sake of fighting, without a higher purpose, is bound to lose; but fighting for a cause, for God and Justice, he is bound to win.

In the invocation that ends the literary excursus, Gottfried reveals something like a poetic program underlying his work. In praising his contemporaries, he assigns to each of them a pagan or classical source of inspiration: Hartmann wears the laurel wreath, the emblem of Apollo; Veldeke takes his inspiration from the well of Pegasus; the fabric of Blicker von Steinach's tales is spun by the fairies and purified in their well; Reinmar sings with the tongue of Orpheus; Walther has his love songs from the Goddess Venus. Gottfried himself is speechless in the face of all the eloquent men he has conjured up, and in his embarrassment he turns for help to Helicon, the home of the muses and Apollo: may they send him a single drop of inspiration to burnish his words to the luster of Arabian gold. But then in a second call for inspiration he turns to "True Helicon," "the highest throne," and requests from those beings "up there in their heavenly choirs" an inspiration that will make his speech "transparent as an exquisite gem." This second invocation has caused some problems of interpretation, which are solved when we see the tradition of the double invocation. It is a form common to the humanist poets of the twelfth century as well as to those of the fifteenth and sixteenth. The poet calls first on the classical inspirers, Apollo and the Muses, then turns for his ultimate inspiration to the higher inspirer, a Christian source, "true Apollo," God, Christ, the Holy Spirit, or some representative of the Christian realm. We find variants of this double invocation in Dante, Petrarch, Pico della Mirandola, Erasmus, and in the visual arts in Raphael's great fresco of "Parnassus" in the Vatican chamber, Stanza della Segnatura. The form has a clear and fixed meaning for the humanist: it represents the harmonic cooperation of the classical and the Christian traditions in poetry, and that, it is quite clear, is the sense in which Gottfried meant it. He distinguishes himself from all his contemporaries in courtly poetry by combining the brilliance of classical inspiration (the luster of gold) with the "depth" of Christian spirituality (the transparency of jewels). The use to which he put the latter is beside the point.

This is the best insight the work gives us into Gottfried's conception of his own role as poet, and it states fairly well the role modern scholars assign to him: he was a humanistically educated cleric with a vast knowledge of classical antiquity and of contemporary court life. He introduced forms of expression and ideals from the humanistic schools of France into German courtly romance, and transformed this class-bound, optimistic, occasionally trivial genre into the vehicle of a dark and tragic, profound and transcendent view of love. (pp. vii-xviii)

> *C. Stephen Jaeger, in a foreword to* Tristan and Isolde *by Gottfried von Strassburg, edited by Francis G. Gentry, revised edition, Continuum, 1988, pp. vii-xviii.*

FURTHER READING

Anson, John S. "The Hunt of Love: Gottfried von Strassburg's *Tristan* as Tragedy." *Speculum* XLV, No. 4 (October 1970): 594-607.
  Explores the metaphorical use of the hunt as a symbol of Tristan's search for perfect love.

Bekker, Hugo. *Gottfried von Strassburg's "Tristan": Journey through the Realm of Eros.* Columbia, S.C.: Camden House, 1987, 303 p.
  Considers *Tristan and Isolde* as a "story of a developmental journey." Bekker concludes, based on an examination of symbolism, language, and poetic devices, that human sexuality is a principal theme of the epic.

Cosman, Madeleine Pelner. "The Education of Tristan: Music and Manners Make the Man." In her *The Education of the Hero in Arthurian Romance,* pp. 3-48. Chapel Hill: University of North Carolina Press, 1965.
  Analyzes the artistic aspects of Tristan's education. Cosman argues that the character's intellectual development is of greater significance to the poem than his chivalric adventures.

Dayan, Joan C. "The Figure of Isolde in Gottfried's *Tristan:* Toward a Paradigm of *Minne.*" *Tristania* VI, No. 2 (Spring 1981): 23-36.
  Examines the character of Isolde as a symbol of divine love. The romance of Tristan and Isolde, Dayan asserts, traces the progression of love from the corporeal to the spiritual.

Gray, Wallace. "Tristan." In his *Homer to Joyce,* pp. 105-25. New York: Macmillan Publishing Co., 1985.
  Views Gottfried's *Tristan and Isolde* as a masterful combination of epic, romance, and novel. Gray holds that the work heralds the birth of Renaissance Humanism in its belief in individual worth and possibility of change, and also serves as a paradigm for the Western romance novel in its use of the adulterous love triangle.

Jackson, W. T. H. *The Anatomy of Love: The "Tristan" of Gottfried von Strassburg.* New York: Columbia University Press, 1971, 280 p.
  Discusses the incompatibility between Gottfried's mystical conception of love as found in *Tristan and Isolde* and the society in which he lived.

———. "Artist and Romance in Gottfried's *Tristan.*" *Tristania* I, No. 1 (November 1975): 3-13.
  Explores the importance of music in *Tristan and Isolde.* Jackson argues that Gottfried's Tristan uses his musical skill to win the love of Mark and Isolde, and that music gives expression to the mystical harmony of the lovers, Tristan and Isolde.

Jaeger, C. Stephen. *Medieval Humanism in Gottfried von*

Strassburg's "Tristan und Isolde." Heidelberg, Germany: Carl Winter, 1977, 194 p.

Approaches Gottfried's epic from the point of view of the history of literary forms. Jaeger offers historical background on the legend with an explanation of some of the forms and ideas found in Gottfried's work.

Kunzer, Ruth Goldschmidt. *The "Tristan" of Gottfried von Strassburg: An Ironic Perspective.* Berkeley: University of California Press, 1973, 221 p.

Investigates irony in *Tristan and Isolde* through an analysis of narrative structure, characterization, and language. Kunzer contends that irony is the basis of the poem rather than Christian mysticism or anti-Christian demonism.

Loomis, R. S. Introduction to *The Romance of Tristram and Ysolt, by Thomas of Britain.* New York: E. P. Dutton and Co., 1923.

Contains references to Gottfried's contribution to the Tristram and Ysolt legend.

Picozzi, Rosemary. *A History of Tristan Scholarship.* Berne, Switzerland and Frankfurt, Germany: Herbert Lang and Co., 1971, 168 p.

A survey of the ideas and accomplishments of Gottfried critics who, since the late eighteenth century, have dealt with the legend of Tristan and Isolde and, particularly, with Gottfried's rendering.

Ponsoye, Pierre. "Aspects of Tristan Esoterism." *Yearbook of Comparative Criticism* IV (1971): 162-80.

Analyzes the various versions of the Tristan legend. Ponsoye concludes that though the versions differ in form and language, all share a common rhythm, structure, and theme.

Schoepperle, Gertrude. *"Tristan and Isolt": A Study of the Sources of the Romance,* second edition. 2 vols. New York: Burt Franklin, 1960.

A comprehensive study of the origins of the Tristan legend.

Snow, Ann. *"Wilt, Wilde, Wildenaere:* A Study in the Interpretation of Gottfried's *Tristan." Euphorion* 68 (January 1969): 365-77.

A linguistic analysis of the multiple meanings of the word *wilde* [wild] and the significance of the hunting metaphor in Gottfried's *Tristan and Isolde.*

Stevens, Adrian and Wisbey, Roy, eds. *Gottfried von Strassburg and the Medieval Tristan Legend: Papers from an Anglo-North American Symposium.* Arthurian Studies XXIII; Publications of the Institute of Germanic Studies, vol. 44. Suffolk, England: D. S. Brewer and The Institute of Germanic Studies, 1990, 284 p.

A collection of essays by such critics as August Closs, Michael Batts, and H. B. Willson, dealing with the complexities of interpreting Gottfried's epic.

Willson, H. B. "The Old and the New Law in Gottfried's *Tristan." Modern Language Review* LX, No. 2 (1965): 212-24.

Compares Gottfried's epic with the biblical narrative of the adulterous woman (John 8). Wilson maintains that Gottfried viewed the romance of Tristan and Isolde in spiritual terms, as a fulfillment of Christ's command to "love thy neighbor."

Layamon

fl. c. 1200

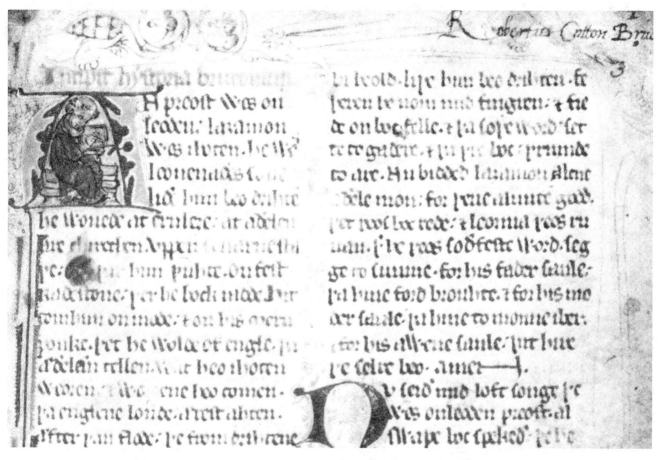

First page of Layamon's Brut *from the British Library Cotton Caligula A.ix manuscript.*

(Also transliterated as Lawemon or Lawman) English poet.

INTRODUCTION

Known for his *Brut,* a verse chronicle of Britain's legendary history, Layamon is considered the first important writer in Middle English. Although his work is not the earliest rendering of the heroic tales of Britain—it is a loose paraphrase of the twelfth-century French *Roman de Brut* (c. 1155) by Robert Wace, itself a translation of Geoffrey of Monmouth's *Historia Regum Britanniae* (c. 1136)—Layamon's *Brut* is significant as the first English poem written in the native language after the Norman Conquest (1066). The chronicle also contains the earliest known appearance in English of the legend of King Arthur, much expanded and embellished with fairy and supernatural lore. Not easily categorized into one of the typi-cal medieval genres, the *Brut* has most often been dubbed Britain's heroic, national epic.

All that is known about Layamon's life was provided by the author himself in the opening lines of his *Brut.* He introduces himself as Layamon, a priest and the son of Leovenath, or Leuca, an Anglo-Saxon name from which the poet's nationality has been deduced. Layamon mentions a church at "Ernley," on the banks of the Severn river near Radestone, as his residence. The village of Lower Areley, also called Areley Kings or Areley Regis, near Worcester and the Welsh border, matches this description and is believed to be the "Ernley" of Layamon's *Brut.* Based on a reference in his text to Wace's *Roman de Brut,* scholars have suggested that Layamon must have been writing at the turn of the thirteenth century. Layamon states that Wace presented his work to Eleanor of Aquitaine, who "was" the queen of King Henry II; commentators have thus inferred that Layamon must have composed his poem after the death of Henry II in 1189 and before (or possibly soon after) Eleanor's death in 1204.

Although the original manuscript of the *Brut* no longer exists, there are two manuscript copies of the work, both in the British Library and both apparently dating from the late thirteenth century or shortly thereafter. The B. L. Cotton Caligula A. ix manuscript (referred to as the A-text) is believed to be the closer to Layamon's lost original as well as the earlier and more complete of the two texts, despite some significant gaps. Its language is archaic and it is written almost completely in English; critics have maintained that Layamon clearly tried to avoid borrowing French words from his source since there are fewer than ninety words of French origin in the A- and B-texts combined, which total more than 56,800 words. The transcriber of the second manuscript, the B. L. Cotton Otho C. xiii (referred to as the B-text), modernized the text by replacing much of its antiquated language, substituting words then in current use, and adding phrases derived from French. The Otho manuscript also includes the passages missing from the Caligula text. The *Brut* was not translated into modern English until 1847, when Frederic Madden published *Layamon's "Brut"; or, Chronicle of Britain.* Despite certain problems that resulted from his attempt to integrate the two versions of the text, this edition remained the most widely cited and the only complete translation of the *Brut* until recently. A few scholars have offered selections from the *Brut* in the twentieth century, but none attempted to translate the work as a whole again until Donald G. Bzdyl produced his *Layamon's "Brut": A History of the Britons* in 1989.

Layamon took for his subject the reigns of the Briton kings and their heroic struggles against the Anglo-Saxons. The *Brut* chronicles Britain's history on an epic scale, from the landing on Albion of Brutus, the mythical great-grandson of Aeneas and the first king of the Britons, to the routing of Cadwalader by the Saxons in 689. Layamon writes that he patterned his work on three sources: Wace's *Roman de Brut,* also known as the *Geste des Bretons;* an English book by St. Bede; and another, supposedly written by Austin and St. Albin. Scholars are reasonably certain that St. Bede's book is the *Ecclesiastical History* (c. 732), but there has been much debate over the identity of the third book; however, the evidence suggests that Layamon depended only on the first source, Wace, as his model for the *Brut.* A court poet who translated Geoffrey of Monmouth's Latin work into French, Wace expanded the narrative to include the newly popular elements of romance and chivalry. Layamon reversed the process of modernization in adapting Wace's text for an English audience, presenting early English history as an heroic, but austere and brutal age. Critics have noted that despite the pervasive violence and bloodthirstiness evident in Layamon's *Brut,* there is nevertheless a hint of sensitivity in it missing from Wace's work: Wace's heroes are more chivalric, but they are colder and less sympathetic to the poor and the old than Layamon's otherwise fiercer characters.

Layamon's most significant alteration of his source was to greatly expand the role of Arthur. One third of the *Brut* focuses on Arthur and many of Layamon's additions to the *Roman de Brut* were made in this section of the work. Arthur, Layamon's main character, was apparently his ideal hero. He was a benevolent monarch, a Christian de-

voted to the Virgin Mary, and an accomplished and charismatic leader; but more importantly to Layamon, he was a war hero, and in the *Brut* he resembles nothing more strongly than a primitive Germanic chieftain. Layamon's saga of Arthur's reign relates many new episodes now famous in the Arthurian legend, including the making of the Round Table and its properties, the bestowal of gifts by the fairies at Arthur's birth, and the fuller, more imaginative account of Merlin's conception. Critics have noted that Layamon's originality was often the result of his interweaving of supernatural elements taken from French and Welsh folklore with realistic military details in the *Brut,* and his use of both pre-Christian and Christian elements in the characterization of Arthur.

Critics have primarily noted the poem's somber tone and militaristic images, and Layamon's use of a more archaic poetic style than that of his predecessor, Wace. Despite his reliance on alliteration and the half-line structure, Layamon's verse exhibits some poetic conventions unknown to the Anglo-Saxon tradition—for example, rhyme and assonance—while his alliteration often falters and he never uses the typical Old Norse device of the kenning (a metaphorical compound word or phrase also used in Anglo-Saxon poetry). Scholars therefore believe that Layamon's poetry resembles a popular verse form, possibly related to oral tradition, rather than classical Old English poetry. Nevertheless, his style has often been likened to that of Old English battle poetry, especially because of his incorporating of heroic images and well-known epic similes reminiscent of *Beowulf* (c. 8th century). As a result of its many formal ambiguities and the vast nature of its subject matter, critics have been unable to agree on the genre of the *Brut,* variously referring to it as a chronicle, a national epic, or, simply, a poem. However they ultimately classify the *Brut,* commentators have praised Layamon's vivid, imaginative scenes and the dramatic tension present in his work, as well as his sense of concrete detail, genuine portrayal of emotion, evocation of mood, and innovative use of direct speech.

Much of the scholarship on Layamon has centered around his departures from Wace's text. Critics contend that it is nearly impossible to discuss the *Brut* without examining its sources, and there has been a lively debate about the extent and nature of Layamon's borrowings from and revisions of earlier works. Many scholars have favorably assessed Layamon's modifications and additions, emphasizing his talent for depicting action scenes with simplicity and emotional intensity. Literary historians have also focused on the nationalistic aspect of the *Brut.* Although the verse form Layamon used in the *Brut* was influenced by foreign elements, Layamon, an Anglo-Saxon, seems to have written deliberately for an Anglo-Saxon public, in its own language. The *Brut* is also Anglo-Saxon in temper and style, using common native expressions rather than the language of the Anglo-Norman court and embodying such Anglo-Saxon values as bravery and loyalty. Still Layamon portrays the Britons (the enemies of his own people), as the heroes of his narrative, and describes with relish the numerous defeats of the Saxons. Scholars have struggled to reconcile this apparent contradiction in Layamon's allegiance. Most have maintained that Layamon intended the *Brut* to be a national history, demonstrating to the Anglo-Saxons of a post-Norman Conquest society that unification of competing races was possible and, indeed, part of a necessary process for the attainment of nation-hood. Other critics, however, have characterized the *Brut* as a testament to Layamon's accordance with the belief that the round of wars in Britain represented divine punishment for the sins of each race, with the eventual downfall of the Britons furnishing a moral analogy to the relatively recent conquest of the Anglo-Saxons by the Normans. In recent studies of the *Brut,* commentators have continued to examine the issue of emerging national consciousness in England, emphasizing Layamon's portrayal of Arthur and his role in sixth century Britain as key elements in this process.

Today Layamon's *Brut* is most valued for its significant additions to the Arthurian tradition and for its historical importance to English literature as a whole. The epic scope and poetic quality of Layamon's work inspired Henry Cecil Wyld to judge the *Brut* "incomparably the greatest achievement in English poetry between the Anglo-Saxon period and Chaucer."

PRINCIPAL ENGLISH EDITIONS

Layamon's "Brut,"; or, Chronicle of Britain; A Poetical Semi-Saxon Paraphrase of The "Brut" of Wace [translated by Frederic Madden]   1847

"Layamon's *Brut*" [in *Arthurian Chronicles,* translated by Eugene Mason, edited by Ernest Rhys]   1912

Layamon's Arthur: The Arthurian Section of Layamon's "Brut" [partial translation by W. R. S. Barron and S. C. Weinberg]   1989

Layamon's "Brut": A History of the Britons [translated by Donald G. Bzdyl]   1989

Layamon   (poem date c. 1200)

[*In the following excerpt from the opening lines of the* Brut *composed around the year 1200, Layamon tells of his inspiration to undertake the composition of the work.*]

> There was a priest in the land who was called Layamon;
> he was the son of Leovenath—God be merciful to him!
> He lived at Areley by a noble church
> on the bank of the Severn—he thought it pleasant there—
> close to Redstone; there he read books.
>   It came into his mind, an excellent intention of his,
> that he would relate the noble origins of the English,
> what they were called and whence they came
> who first possessed the land of England
> after the flood sent by God,
> which here on earth destroyed all living things it came upon,

> save Noah and Shem, Japhet and Ham,
> and their four wives who were with them in the ark.
>   Layamon travelled far and wide throughout this land,
> and collected the excellent books which he took as a model.
> He chose the English book which St Bede composed.
> He chose another in Latin composed by St Albin
> and the good Austin who introduced baptism here.
> He chose a third book and placed it with the others,
> a book which a French cleric
> called Wace, who could write well, had composed
> and presented to the noble Eleanor
> who was the great King Henry's queen.
>   Layamon laid these books down and turned the pages;
> he looked on them with pleasure—God be gracious to him!
> He took quill pens in his hand and wrote on parchment
> and set down together the most truthful words,
> and compressed the three books into one.
>   Now Layamon begs every good man,
> for the sake of almighty God,
> that he should read this book and study these writings,
> that he should repeat in full these truthful words
> for the soul of his father who begot him,
> and for the soul of his mother who gave birth to him,
> and for his own soul that it may be the better for it. Amen.

(p. ix)

Layamon, in an excerpt from Layamon's "Arthur": The Arthurian Section of Layamon's "Brut" *(Lines 9229—14297), by Layamon, edited and translated by W. R. J. Barron and S. C. Weinberg, Longman, 1989, p. ix.*

Thomas Tyrwhitt   (essay date 1775)

[*In the excerpt below, Tyrwhitt briefly comments on Layamon's place in English literary history and his attempt at writing rhyming poetry.*]

. . . I have not been able to discover any attempts at rhyming poetry, which can with probability be referred to an earlier period than the reign of Henry the Second. In that reign Layamon, a priest of Ernleye, near Severn, as he calls himself, translated (chiefly) from the French of Wace a fabulous history of the Britons, entitled **Le Brut,** which Wace himself, about the year 1155, had translated from the Latin of Geoffrey of Monmouth. Though the greatest part of this work of Layamon resembles the old Saxon poetry, without rhyme or metre, . . . he often intermixes a number of short verses of unequal lengths, but rhyming together pretty exactly, and in some places he has imitated not unsuccessfully the regular octosyllable measure of his French original. (pp. lxvii-lxix)

Thomas Tyrwhitt, "An Essay on the Language

and Versification of Chaucer," in The Canterbury Tales of Chaucer, Vol. I *by Geoffrey Chaucer, edited by Thomas Tyrwhitt, 1775. Reprint by James Nichol, 1860, pp. xxxv-xcvi.*

Henry Morley   (essay date 1888)

[*Morley was an English journalist influential in the development of English literature as a subject for academic study. He began writing a twenty-volume history,* English Writers, *but finished only half by the time of his death. His criticism was largely historical and biographical in nature. In the following excerpt, Morley offers a general overview of Layamon's* Brut, *placing the work in the context of the known facts of the poet's life.*]

While in Transition English (known commonly as Early English) change was being . . . made at different rates of progress, there had long ceased to exist a cultivated literary class among the English that might have studiously maintained the old purity of inflexion. As at this day the German peasantry confuse the genders, and clip the inflexions of their language, so doubtless First-English was confused and clipped by the main body of the people, even in the best days of its literature. But when Norman influence ruled over literature, and the best native writers used either Latin or Norman-French, complexities of gender and inflexion must needs go the way of nature rather faster than they usually do, but as they all sooner or later must go in the language of a vigorous and active people.

Nevertheless, if its voice was out of fashion for a few years, there had been no pause in the working of the Anglo-Saxon mind; and among all the signs of intellectual advancement that mark the busy period of Henry II.'s reign, not the least is the recognition of an English song in its own native tongue. The early gleemen had been represented, no doubt, by an unbroken line of story-tellers and amusers who were welcome at the firesides of the people, chanted songs of adventure and miracles of saints by the wayside and at village ales, and wherever there was holiday resort of men. But the literature of the people was, for more than a hundred years after the Conquest, left to perish on their lips. They who were rich enough to pay for written transcripts cared only for works addressed in Latin to the educated world, or to the court in French. Till the end of the twelfth century there was no demand among the rich, in castle or cloister, for written copies of the legends, tales, and songs that passed from lip to lip among the people. But when the fusion becomes more complete, when French and Latin literature of the twelfth century has become more and more national, the stream of native literature that had for a time been flowing underground rises again to the surface and flows on and broadens, and becomes the main stream into which all others flow. It was Layamon, priest of a rural district, in whose work we have at the beginning of the thirteenth century the first MS. record, after the Conquest, of a poem in the language of the people; and of this work also the inspiration is to be traced back to that mock history of Geoffrey of Monmouth which rose suddenly as a bright spring of romance in the midst of a wilderness of record, and wherever it went quickened the blossoming of fancy from the ready soil.

Layamon, the son of Leovenath—called in the later text of his poem Laweman the son of Leuca—was a priest who read the services of the Church at Ernley, on the banks of the Severn, near Redstone. The place is now called Areley, or Areley Kings, and is about three and a half miles from Bewdley, in Worcestershire. The later of the two texts of his poem, doubtless in error, makes him say that "he dwelt at Ernley, with the good knight, upon Severn." Of his life no more is known. Of his book, he says that he compiled it from three sources—namely, a book in English, by Saint Bede; another in Latin, by Saint Albin and Austin; and a book in French, by a clerk named Wace, who presented it to Eleanor, Henry II.'s Queen. To obtain these three books he says that he travelled "wide over land." If the English book be the translation of Bede's *History* ascribed to Alfred, he has taken from it only the story of Pope Gregory and the Anglo-Saxon captives at Rome; and he differs from it in many places even when he is not copying from Wace. Of what is meant by the Latin book of Albinus and Austin there can be only remote conjecture. Sir Frederic Madden, the first editor of Layamon, whose Introduction to his ***Brut*** I am now following, thinks that Layamon may have supposed, by confusion, the Albinus of Canterbury, who gave Bede information, to be the author of the original Latin of Bede's *History,* and that he further confused St. Augustin with the authorship. But that is hardly possible. The "errors of equal magnitude" to which Sir Frederic refers are errors in early history, that a man might well make without being therefore judged unable to read the most obvious fact in the books he has been taking particular pains to obtain. The reference, I think, must be to some other work of which there is no MS. extant. But the third authority, Wace's *Brut,* was the work chiefly used by Layamon, and of this the English poem is, in fact, an amplified translation. It is doubled in length. Wace's *Brut* contains 15,300, Layamon's 32,250 lines. The addition consists partly of speeches put with dramatic effect into the mouths of persons of the story, partly of a very considerable extension of the Arthurian romance, names of persons and places being supplied, and the interpolations of new matter being sometimes to the extent of a hundred lines and more. Among the many legendary additions, for example, is that of King Arthur's being taken after death to Avalon. In his dying speech to Constantine he says, according to Layamon—

> "I will fare to Avalun, to the fairest of all maidens, to Argante the Queen, an elf most fair, and she shall make my wounds all sound; make me all whole with healing draughts. And afterwards I will come again to my kingdom and dwell with the Britons with mickle joy." Even with the words there approached from the sea a little short boat floating with the waves; and two women therein wondrously formed; and they took Arthur anon, and bare him quickly, and laid him softly down, and forth they gan depart. Then was it accomplished that Merlin Whilom said, that mickle care should come of Arthur's departure. The Britons believe yet that he is alive, and dwelleth in Avalun with the fairest of all elves, and the Britons ever yet expect when Arthur shall return.

(pp. 205-08)

Layamon has completely kept, after the introductory line or two, himself and his own time out of the story that is really a poem in his hands. It is not easy, therefore, to assign to his work an exact date. In telling of Leir and of Caer-Leir, or Leicester, that he is said to have founded, Layamon says that "of yore it was a most noble burgh, and afterwards there fell towards it very much sorrow, so that it was all destroyed through slaughters of the people." This may be supposed to refer to its destruction by the forces of Henry II. in 1173. Again, in telling of King Ebraue, after whom the burgh he founded was called Eborac, he says, "afterwards came foreign men and named it Eoverwic, and the northern men, not long since, through an ill practice, called it Yeork." In another passage, within not many lines of the end, he thus ascribes to King Ina the establishment of Peter's pence: "Inne was the first man that began Peter's penny. When Inne, the king, was dead, and his laws done away, then ceased the tribute here five-and-sixty years, until that Athelstan arrived into this land, and had dwelt here full fifteen years. The king kissed his feet and greeted him fair, and eft the same tribute granted that Inne, the king, did ere; and so it hath stood ever since in this land—the Lord knoweth how long the law shall last!" In 1205 King John and his nobles resisted the Pope's mandate for its collection. In the beginning of his work, too, Sir Frederic Madden, who calls attention to these points, adds that Layamon says Wace presented his book to Eleanor, who *was* Henry's queen, inferring from this that either Henry, or both he and Eleanor, must then have been dead. But, it is argued, Henry died in 1189 and Eleanor in 1204. The date of the composition of Layamon's ***Brut*** is, therefore, on this as well as the other grounds, placed, by common consent, a few years after the year 1200. I do not doubt the accuracy of the conclusion thus arrived at; but no argument is to be founded on the expression "Eleanor, who was Henry's queen," unless it be admitted that Layamon wrote this poem after his own death, for his very first lines tell that "There was a priest in the land who was named Layamon."

Layamon, priest and teacher—like Wace he was *clerc lisant*—in a rural district, was among those who spoke the language of the country with the least mixture of Norman-French. In the earlier of the two MSS. of Layamon, written in the thirteenth century, Sir Frederic Madden found that the English of the poet contained fewer than fifty words derived from the Normans, and some even of those which he found may have come direct from Latin. . . .

. . . [Several] of these words had been used more than half a century before in the Saxon Chronicle. The second MS. of Layamon, written about a generation later, drops about twenty of the French words in the early text, and introduces rather more than forty others, of which a few had long been in familiar use. (pp. 209-11)

In the two texts, containing together more than 56,800 lines, there are thus but ninety words of French origin to be found.

Battles are described in the old way. In Layamon's ***Brut,*** as in Cædmon or *Beowulf,* there are few similes, and those which occur are simply derived from natural objects, as the lion, the boar, the crane, hail, &c. There is the same

use of a descriptive synonym for man or warrior. There is the old depth and earnestness that rather gains than loses dignity by the simplicity of its expression, often in colloquial form. There is the old alliterative manner, too, with greater freedom in the use, sometimes the two letters of alliteration are in the second half line instead of the first, sometimes there are two in each half line, sometimes only two in the whole line. There are traces of assonance, with here and there a little slide into full rhyme, that had by imitation both of Latin and of French verse already found its way into songs of the people, the accent being placed with equal justice on the alliterative and upon the rhyming syllable. The rhyming couplets are described by Mr. Guest [in his *History of English Rhythms*] as founded on the models of accentuated Anglo-Saxon rhythms of four, five, six, or seven accents, those of six and five accents being used most frequently, but with changes made at will by the poet from the shortest to the longest. (pp. 211-12)

By what motive was the country priest impelled to produce these six-and-fifty thousand lines of English verse? He had not, like Wace, the commission of a queen. No liberal Count of Flanders cared for him. No king or courtier, having Wace's *Brut* within his reach in what was then accounted the vernacular of literature, would ask a country priest to turn it into English verse. The introduction to the second manuscript of Layamon's poem says that he dwelt at Ernley, now Areley Kings, with "the good knight." If that phrase be interpolated, not by error but by accurate tradition of a lord of the manor who was remembered after death not by his name, but by his character, as the "Good Knight," we know so much the more of Layamon's home in his parish. But no good knight bade him produce an English *Brut.* If his labour had been inspired by any patron, he must have named the patron in the poem. And Layamon has not done that, but, on the contrary, he has explicitly asserted that the task was one of his own choosing. The thought occurred to him and took strong possession of him—"it came to him in mind and in his chief thought—that he would tell the noble deeds of the English."

He was a priest remote from courtly towns, and living near to what were then the Welsh Marches. His parish of Areley Kings, west of the Severn, between Bewdley and Stourport, is now a hamlet with rather fewer than six hundred inhabitants. As it is a rectory worth at the present time about four hundred guineas a year, we may reasonably assume it to have been of old a country living that gave simple competence to any quiet student priest. Such a priest undoubtedly was Layamon. That is shown by the complete forgetfulness of self which, after the usual opening lines, causes his personality to vanish from so long a poem, and by the kindly temper of those first lines. It may be remembered, for example, how they end with addition to the usual request of payment from the reader or the hearer by a prayer for the writer's soul, of a tender thought also "for his father's soul that brought him forth, and for his mother's soul that bore him to be a man."

Layamon was a modest, pious English priest, who loved his country, and enjoyed traditions of its ancient time.

Having the true fine natural spirit of a poet and a scholar, he was among the many in almost every part of Europe who had their imagination kindled by Geoffrey of Monmouth's patriotic fictions. He had discoursed much and pleasantly with his neighbours, for his mind was stored with the oral tradition only to be gathered in familiar social talk; and when he translated Wace's *Brut* he added not only fresh legends of his own gathering, but new touches to the old. This he did partly by use of the stories he himself had heard, partly by setting Wace's pictures in the light of his own fancy. His account, for example, of the wrestling on the Cornish Down between Corineus and the giant Geomagog, shows how Layamon could on occasion translate Wace's verse into more life-like poetry.

Again, Layamon's ***Brut*** shows that his piety was that of a refined man, unobtrusive. He misses glaring opportunities for preaching, where he has too right an instinct of art to stale the freshness of a legend; as in his delivery of the odd record of Ebrauc's surpassing excellence as the first man who enriched England by plundering his neighbours. He drops reflections here and there; if the poem be read it gives the impression that its writer was a pious priest; and yet in all its six-and-fifty thousand lines there are nowhere to be found ten, if anywhere five, consecutive lines of interpolated preaching.

From his work, then, we have a right to infer that this earliest poet in our modern tongue was a devout, gentle, and affectionate parish priest, who loved his home and his country, and was friend as well as spiritual counsellor to the small flock of rustic parishioners, whose boys he taught and whose good will satisfied all but his intellectual wants.

Then "it came to him in mind and in his chief thought that he would tell the noble deeds of the English;" so he made a pilgrimage out of his parish for the books in foreign tongues whose native story it had "come into his mind" to write in native verse. And when he had them, is there a student who does not feel the simple and charming touch of nature in his record, "Layamon laid before him these books, and turned over the leaves, lovingly he beheld them, may the Lord be merciful to him"?

Can we doubt in what spirit the good country priest and poet bent day by day over his long labour, and can we doubt who were his public? In all those thousands of lines chiefly written with a French original beside him are to be found only three or four dozen words of French origin. And yet in translation from the French others were tempted irresistibly to the adoption of French words and phrases, and Layamon, too, was a French scholar. But father Leovenath, and the old mother who bore Layamon to be a man, perhaps were not French scholars, and they, if they lived with him, as it is likely that they did, were the critical chiefs of his public. The rest of the world about his parsonage knew nothing but English. And although Layamon cannot have been without his human desire to be remembered generously by his countrymen, as he who first put the traditions of their ancient glory into English song—and his work was, perhaps, planned to yield fresh matter for chant at rustic festivals by the minstrels and story-tellers who still brought literature to the common

ear—the best success he saw was among his simple Areley people. (pp. 227-30)

Henry Morley, "Layamon," in his An Attempt Towards a History of English Literature: From the Conquest to Chaucer, Vol. III, *Cassell & Company Limited, 1888, pp. 202-31.*

An excerpt from Layamon's *Brut*

þa yet cleopede Arður,   aðelest kingen:
Yurstendæi wes Baldulf   cnihten alre baldest;
nu he stant on hulle   and Auene bihaldeð,
hu ligeð i þan stræme   stelene fisces;
mid sweorde bigeorede   heore sund is awemmed;
heore scalen wleoteð   swulc gold-faye sceldes;
þer fleoteð heore spiten   swulc hit spæren weoren.
þis beoð seolcuðe þing   isiyen to þissen londe,
swulche deor an hulle,   swulche fisces in wællel' (10638-45)

(Then Arthur, noblest of kings, continued: 'Yesterday Baldof was the boldest of warriors; now he stands on the hill and looks upon the Avon, sees how steel fish lie in the river trammelled with swords, their swimming impaired; their scales gleam as if they were gilded shields; their fins drift in the water like spears floating there. This is a marvellous thing come to pass in this land, such beasts on the hill, such fish in the water!')

Layamon, in his Brut, *edited and translated by W. R. J. Barron and S. C. Weinberg, Longman Group, 1989.*

Henry S. Pancoast   (essay date 1907)

[*In the excerpt below, Pancoast presents the* Brut *as one of the best examples of "the singular fusion of languages and literatures."*]

[At] the opening of the thirteenth century there are signs that the English language is beginning to win back its literary importance. A great change in the political importance of England, at the beginning of that century, marks the beginning of a new epoch. For one hundred and forty years England had been ruled by foreign kings. Now, in 1204, King John lost nearly all his lands on the Continent, a territory comprising three-fifths of modern France. England could no longer be regarded as the dependency of a foreign power; it was the chief, almost the only dependency of the crown, free once more to follow the bent of its own genius. When John lost Normandy, the antagonism between the English and the Normans had already disappeared. For generations they had lived together in the same island; they had intermarried; they had fought side by side against a foreign enemy; many Normans had learned to speak English, and many English could both speak and write in French. Now, cut off from the rest of the world, they were to draw even closer together, and force the *Great Charter* of liberty from their king.

Some time during these early years of the thirteenth century, English poetry, which had showed but little sign of life
since the *Song on the Battle of Maldon* (991), suddenly
revived in the ***Brut*** of Layamon (cir. 1205). The end of a
foreign rule in England and the rebirth of a true English
poetry are thus almost exactly contemporaneous. All that
we know of Layamon, he tells us himself in the opening
lines of his poem. He was a parish priest in North Worcestershire, and dwelt at Earnley (now Ernley Regis) on the
banks of the river Severn. There "came to him in mind and
in his chief thought that he would of England tell the
noble deeds." So he got books, among others the *Brut* "of
the French Clerk that was named Wace," and retold in
English the legendary history of Britain. Layamon tells us
very little about himself, yet his few words make him very
real and human to us. No one who loves books will doubt
that this country priest was a true book-lover. He tells us
that he had "to take a wide journey over the land" to obtain "the noble books" which he "took for a pattern." We
may imagine him returning in triumph with his treasures
to his quiet home by the Severn, and settling to work with
a tranquil mind. "Layamon laid down these books and
turned the leaves, he beheld them lovingly. May the Lord
be merciful to him! Pen he took with his fingers and wrote
a book skin, and the true words set together, and the three
books compressed into one." Layamon speaks of using
three books, but he relied chiefly on one. His ***Brut,*** a metrical chronicle of the legendary history of Britain, is based
mainly on Wace's book, as Wace's *Brut* was based on the
history of Geoffrey of Monmouth. There is a vein of true
poetry in it, unwieldly as it seems, and it is notable as
marking the entrance of many famous stories into English
literature. Let us look for a moment at the significance of
this extraordinary poem. From one aspect it is almost like
a voice from the England of Cædmon or of Cynewulf. Its
vocabulary is almost wholly English, as hardly fifty words
of French origin are to be found in its thirty thousand
lines. At times we recognise the true fighting spirit of the
old English battle-song. Yet, from another aspect, the
poem bears witness to the influence of those foreign elements which had already entered deeply into English life
and literature. Layamon lived near the Welsh border, and
there, where the land of the Englishman almost touched
the land of the Celt, he pondered over a Norman's version
of a Celtic legend. Layamon's chief material is thus not
English, but Norman or Celtic; and his theme is not the
glory of English, but of British heroes. It would be hard
to find a better example of the singular fusion of languages
and literatures. A Norman *trouvère* and an English poet
vie with each other in singing the praises of British Kings.
The stories, which Wace the Norman had taken from
Geoffrey the Welshman, are now retold by Layamon the
Englishman. Three men, of three races, recite the ***Brut;***
each uses a different language,—the Welshman, Latin; the
Norman, French; until finally the work is taken up by the
Englishman, and this foreign material is made contributo-
ry to English literature. (pp. 84-7)

*Henry S. Pancoast, "From the Norman Con-
quest to Chaucer," in his* An Introduction to
English Literature, *third edition, Henry Holt
and Company, 1907, pp. 72-103.*

Lucy Allen Paton   (essay date 1912)

[*In the following excerpt, Paton locates Layamon's* Brut
in the context of the early Arthurian chronicles.]

To Wace we owe [a] debt, for the *Roman de Brut* served
as the direct source for one of the greatest members of the
Arthurian literature of any period. This is the ***Brut,*** written in the first half of the thirteenth century, after the year
1204, by Layamon, an English priest of the country parish
of Lower Arnley in Worcestershire.

> There was a priest in the land, who was named
> Layamon; he was son of Leovenath—may the
> Lord be gracious to him!—he dwelt at Ernley,
> at a noble church upon Severn's bank,—good it
> there seemed to him—near Radestone, where he
> books read. It came to him in mind, and in his
> chief thought, that he would tell the noble deeds
> of the English; what they were named, and
> whence they came, who first possessed the En-
> glish land, after the flood that came from the
> Lord. . . . Layamon began to journey wide
> over this land, and procured the noble books
> which he took for pattern. He took the English
> book that Saint Bede made; another he took in
> Latin, that Saint Albin made, and the fair Aus-
> tin, who brought baptism in hither; the third
> book he took, and laid there in the midst, that
> a French clerk made, who was named Wace,
> who well could write; and he gave it to the noble
> Eleanor, who was the high King Henry's queen.
> Layamon laid before him these books, and
> turned over the leaves; lovingly he beheld
> them—may the Lord be merciful to him!—pen
> he took with fingers, and wrote on book-skin,
> and the true words set together, and the three
> books compressed into one. Now prayeth Laya-
> mon, for love of the Almighty God, each good
> man that shall read this book and learn this
> counsel, that he say together these soothfast
> words, for his father's soul, who brought him
> forth, and for his mother's soul, who bore him
> to be man, and for his own soul, that it be the
> better. Amen!

With these words Layamon introduces us to his book and
to himself; in fact they contain the sum total of our information about his life. But they put us at once into sympathy with the earnest, sincere student, who wrote, not like
Geoffrey and Wace, for the favour of a high-born patron,
but for the love of England and of good men and his few
hardly-won and treasured books. Of these books Wace's
Brut received the lion's share of his attention, and he made
little or no use of the others that lay before him. He followed Wace's poem in outline, but he succeeded in extending its 15,300 verses to 32,241, by giving a free rein to his
fancy, which he often allowed to set the pace for his pen.
For Layamon in his retired parish, performing the monotonous and far from engrossing duties of a reading clerk,
lived in reality a stirring life of the imagination. Back in
the Saxon past of England his thoughts moved, and his
mind dwelt on her national epic heroes. Not only in his
language, which belongs to the period of transition from
Anglo-Saxon to Middle English, but in his verse and
phraseology, he shows the influence of earlier Anglo-
Saxon literature. The sound of the *Ode on Athelstane's*

Victory and of *Beowulf* is in our ears as we read his intense, stirring lines. Wars and battles, the stern career of a Saxon leader, the life of the woods and fields attracted him far more than the refinements of a Norman court, and by emphasising the elements that were most congenial to himself he developed an entirely different picture from that presented by either Geoffrey [of Monmouth, author of *Historia Regum Britanniae,*] or Wace. Writing with intense interest, he lives and moves and has his being among the events that he is narrating, and is far too deeply absorbed in his story to limit himself to the page that he has before him. Given a dramatic situation, the actors become living personalities to him, and he hears impassioned words falling from their lips in terse phrases such as he never found in the lines of Wace. Uther Pendragon, in a deadly battle against the Irish invaders under Gillomar and Pascent, slays Gillomar, then overtakes Pascent:—

> And said these words Uther the Good: 'Pascent, thou shalt abide; here cometh Uther riding!' He smote him upon the head, so that he fell down, and the sword put in his mouth—such meat to him was strange—so that the point of the sword went in the earth. Then said Uther, 'Pascent, lie now there; now thou hast Britain all won to thy hand! So is now hap to thee; therein thou art dead; dwell ye shall here, thou, and Gillomar thy companion, and possess well Britain! For now I deliver it to you in hand, so that ye may presently dwell with us here; ye need not ever dread who you shall feed.'

Arthur leads his men close to the hosts of Colgrim, the leader of the Saxon invaders:—

> Thus said Arthur, noblest of kings: 'See ye, my Britons, here beside us, our full foes,—Christ destroy them!—Colgrim the strong, out of Saxonland? His kin in this land killed our ancestors; but now is the day come, that the Lord hath appointed that he shall lose the life, and lose his friends, or else we shall be dead; we may not see him alive! . . . ' Up caught Arthur his shield, before his breast, and he gan to rush as the howling wolf, when he cometh from the wood, behung with snow, and thinketh to bite such beasts as he liketh. Arthur then called to his dear knights: 'Advance we quickly, brave thanes! all together towards them; we all shall do well, and they forth fly, as the high wood, when the furious wind heaveth it with strength.' Flew over the [fields] thirty thousand shields, and smote on Colgrim's knights, so that the earth shook again. Brake the broad spears, shivered shields; the Saxish men fell to the ground. . . . Some they gan wander as the wild crane doth in the moorfen, when his flight is impaired, and swift hawks pursue after him, and hounds with mischief meet him in the reeds; then is neither good to him nor the land nor the flood; the hawks him smite, the hounds him bite, then is the royal fowl at his death-time.

Layamon lets his imagination display itself not merely in the dramatic speeches that he puts into the mouths of his actors; he occasionally composes a long incident, as in the story of the coronation of Constans, of the announcement to Arthur of Mordred's treachery, and in the very striking account of Arthur's election to the throne of Britain and his reception of the messengers who come for him. "Arthur sate full still; one while he was wan, and in hue exceeding pale; one while he was red, and was moved in heart. When it all brake forth, it was good that he spake; thus said he then, forthright, Arthur, the noble knight: 'Lord Christ, God's Son, be to us now in aid, that I may in life hold God's laws.' " But in general Layamon's expansions of Wace are merely slight additions or modifications, sufficient in number, however, to go far in doubling the size of the volume. His great change is that which I have already mentioned, the spirit in which the story is conceived, and this is best illustrated, perhaps, in the person of Arthur himself. For Arthur is no knight-errant, but a grim, stern, ferocious Saxon warrior, loved by his subjects, yet dreaded by them as well as by his foes. "Was never ere such king, so doughty through all things." He stands in the cold glare of monarchy and conquest, and save in the story of his birth and of his final battle he is seldom, if ever, seen through the softer light of romance. But Layamon is the only source for the story of which we hear nothing in the later romances, and which is generally attributed to a Teutonic origin, that elves came to Arthur's cradle and gave him good gifts—to be the best of knights, a rich king, long lived, abounding in "virtues most good." Layamon, too, gives a truly Celtic version of Arthur's disappearance from earth. Two fairy maidens bear the wounded king in a boat from the battle-field over the sea to Argante, the queen of Avalon, who will make him whole again. "And the Britons ever yet expect when Arthur shall return." This story, and also Layamon's very important account of the establishment of the Round Table, which is vastly more complete than Wace's, bear unmistakable marks of a Celtic origin. Layamon, in fact, living as he did near the Welsh border, naturally shows familiarity with current Welsh tradition. His work has a high value in the vexed question of the origin and growth of Arthurian romance; for it proves the existence of genuine Welsh tradition about Arthur, and makes untenable the position of those critics who maintain that the Arthurian legend had an independent development only on the continent.

Layamon's contributions to our knowledge of the Arthurian material are, however, comparatively small, since he augmented his original in the main by passages inspired by his own imagination. His additions may be called poetic rather than legendary. Partly because of its Saxon character his **Brut** never attained wide popularity, and it had little effect upon the cycle; but it remains one of the most truly great literary achievements in the field of both Arthurian chronicle and romance.

Our three most important Arthurian chroniclers, Geoffrey, Wace, and Layamon, were all men of marked individuality and ability; each lives for us with as distinct a personality as if we had far more than our very imperfect knowledge of the details of his life. Geoffrey, a clever combiner, a highly-gifted narrator and scholar, born at a happy hour, gave the Arthurian legend a definite literary form, brought permanently together independent elements of tradition, and contributed enormously to the popularity of the cycle. Wace, the professional author, the scrupulous antiquarian and naïve poet, carefully refined the material of Geoffrey, and dressed it in the French costume of courtly life. Layamon, the intense and imaginative English priest, transformed it by the Saxon spirit, and divesting it of its courtly elegance, filled it with greater simplicity and force. (pp. xii-xvi)

Lucy Allen Paton, in an introduction to Arthurian Chronicles *by Wace and Layamon, edited by Ernest Rhys, translated by Eugene Mason, Everyman's Library, 1912, pp. vii-xx.*

Andrew Lang (essay date 1912)

[*Lang was one of England's most powerful men of letters during the closing decades of the nineteenth century, and is remembered today as the editor of the "color fairy books," a twelve-volume series of fairy tales introduced with* The Blue Fairy Book *(1889) and ending with* The Lilac Fairy Book *(1910). The stories in these volumes were drawn from various world cultures, the outgrowth of Lang's extensive research into early languages and literature in an attempt to find cultural affinities in the folktales, myths, and legends of otherwise disparate societies. A romantic vision of the past imbued Lang's writings, coloring his work as a translator, poet, and revisionist historian. In the following excerpt, Lang praises Layamon's poetic abilities, citing echoes of ancient Greek literature in the* Brut, *and especially focusing on its romantic aspects.*]

Thanks to Geoffrey [of Monmouth], at last, some time about 1200-1220, came an English poet, Layamon, a true poet (now and then), whose work reminds us occasionally at once of the Greeks whom he had never read, of masters whom he did not know; and of the things most romantic in the verses of the last great poet of England. Layamon, the author of **The Brut,** had no ambition; he had no hope of gain; the king and the courtiers would never hear of him.

Layamon was an English priest in a quiet country parish, not far from the Welsh Border, at Ernley, near Radestone, on the Severn, as he tells us. Yet the new French culture had reached him and inspired him; he gave it to Englishmen in their own English language and he is therefore readable: is more than a mere name. It "came into his mind" to tell the history of England, in verse, and he says that he travelled far to get the books of Bede (in Anglo-Saxon), "the fair Austin and St. Albin," in Latin, and the book made in French by a French clerk, Master Wace, "who well could write". "Lovingly he beheld these books," but, in fact, he only used one of them, namely Wace's *French* version (1155) of Geoffrey of Monmouth's romance. Wace had altered Geoffrey as he pleased, and Layamon took the same liberty with Wace; his book is twice as long as that of the French clerk; he also inserted many things not to be found in the text of Wace as now printed, but derived partly from still unprinted manuscripts of Wace, partly from other sources; perhaps from Welsh legends known to this priest who dwelt beside the Severn. Wace added to Geoffrey's account of Arthur, the story wherever he found it, of "The Table Round," so shaped that the knights could not quarrel about the high-

est place. Layamon adds that the Fairy ladies came to Arthur's birth—as in a very old belief, found in ancient Greece and ancient Egypt—and that they later carried him away to Avalon, there to be healed of his wounds.

He calls the fairy Queen "Argante," possibly a French corruption of a Breton name. His account of the birth of the enchanter Merlin, "No man's son," is romance itself. Merlin's mother, who had become a nun, knew not who was her child's father, only that in her dreams there came to her "the fairest thing that ever was born, as it were a tall knight, all dight in gold. This thing glided before me and glistened with gold. Oft me it kissed, and oft embraced."

What can be more romantic than this tale of the golden shadow of love that glides through the darkling bower—told by a nun with bowed head, shamefast! We are reminded of the lines in which Io, in Æschylus, tells of the shadowy approaches of Zeus, the king of gods; and the voice that spoke to her in dreams.

The Greeks had another such tale of the gold that fell in the tower of Danaë before the birth of Perseus. The origin of Layamon's story may be in some ancient Celtic myth of the loves of gods and mortal women, and of Merlin, son of a god.

From his shadowy nameless father, Merlin received his gift of prophecy, and, from the first, foretold the Passing of Arthur.

In Layamon's poem we find what does not occur in the older Anglo-Saxon poems, such as *Beowulf,* the use of similes in the manner of Homer, whose warriors charge like lions, hungry, and beaten on by wind and snow. Thus, too, in Layamon's verse,

> Up caught Arthur his shield, before his breast,
> and he 'gan to rush as doth the howling wolf
> when he cometh from the wood, flecked with
> snow, and thinketh to seize what beasts he will.

Arthur defeats the Saxons, and drives them from the ford of the river, through the deep marshland,

> And as the wild crane in the fen, when the falcons follow him through air, and he wearies in his flight, but the hounds meet him in the reeds;
> as *he* can find no safety whether in field or flood, even so the Saxons were smitten in ford and field, and went blindly wandering.

These similes give clear, vivid pictures of life in fen and forest, and enliven the poem in the true epic way, and Layamon gives, perhaps, the first English picture of an English fox-hunt. In his poem, Guinevere does not love Launcelot, but the traitor Modred, and when Modred is defeated by her husband, Arthur, she flies to Caerleon, where "she hooded her and made her a nun," and her end is unknown.

In the last great battle in the west, both hosts fall—it is a field of the dead and dying. Arthur bears fifteen wounds. He is alone with Constantine, to whom he entrusts his kingdom.

> "But I will pass to Avalun, to the fairest of all

maidens, to Argante the Queen, an elf most beautiful, and she shall make my wounds all whole with draughts of healing. And afterwards I will come again to my kingdom."

Then came floating from the sea a little boat, and two women therein, shaped wonderfully; and they took Arthur anon, and bore him to that boat, and laid him softly down, and went their way. Bretons believe that he liveth yet, and wonneth in Avalun, with the fairest Queen of Faery.

Do we not already seem to hear the voice of Tennyson's weeping queens, as the king floats into the night?

Romance has come to England, and from the mingling of races and tongues—Celtic, French, English—an English poet has been born: a man who sees with the eyes of imagination, and who can make us share his visions of the golden shadow that was father of Merlin; of the wolf with the snow caked on his matted hide as he rushes from the wood; of the hawking party in the fens; of the battle by the tidal waters of the west.

Layamon is full of promise of good things to come, as in his description of Goneril and her husband, when she begins to grudge to her father, King Lear, the expensive service of his forty knights; while her husband feebly opposes her unnatural avarice. (The story of Lear is also in Geoffrey of Monmouth, and is based on a common folk-tale.)

Again, when Layamon's Arthur laughs over the slain Colgrem, ". . . Lie there, now, Colgrem; high hadst thou climbed this hill, as if thou wouldst win heaven, now shalt thou fare to hell, and there find thy kinsfolk, . . . " we are carried back to the boasts over the dead that Greeks and Trojans utter in the *Iliad*. But these great touches are rare in the 30,000 lines of Layamon, the mass of his poem "is blank enough".

Layamon thought himself a chronicler in rhyme, a historian; in his book he has many tales, not that of Arthur alone; he has dull passages in plenty, none the less the good priest has many qualities of the great poet. (pp.48-51)

Andrew Lang, "Layamon's 'Brut'," in his History of English Literature from "Beowulf" to Swinburne, *1912. Reprint by Longmans, Green and Co., 1928, pp. 48-59.*

John S. P. Tatlock (essay date 1923)

[*Tatlock was an American educator known as a Chaucer scholar. In the excerpt below, he examines Layamon's extensive use of epic formulas in the* Brut.]

In Layamon's poem commonly called **Brut** there is an extraordinary profusion of epic formulas, full of flavor and charm, contributing as much as anything to the marked individuality of the poem. The same or similar phrases are used again and again, as a rule in the same or similar circumstances, or to describe the same person or action. . . . A phrase is considered a formula when it occurs three times or more in this poem; two occurrences may be accidental, but three are becoming habitual. Other occurrences could doubtless be found, and also other formulas, but we [find it best to] exclude mere stock-rimes, and in

general phrases so inevitable that they would not have been felt as formulas by Layamon or his auditors, however often repeated. (pp. 494-95)

Some formulas are highly poetic and probably original; others . . . may have been traditional in poetry; a few are colorless, commonplaces of daily speech. It is difficult to draw the line between what would stand out to Layamon and his auditors as a distinct formula, and what was a common obvious expression of no individuality, even though often repeated. Certain ones are especially used with the name of a particular person, invariably for the sake of alliteration or rime. But Layamon had few principles about his formulas. He avoids nothing, and uses them just as it happens. Nothing could be more elastic or protean than his practice.

Some formulas are nearly petrified, others vary much, some so much that they verge into mere stock rimes, with no consciousness of being formulas at all. The variations are usually for the plain purpose of adaptation to new conditions in the sense or the verse. Variation for the rime is commoner than for the alliteration. At times discrimination and even subtlety is shown in alteration or inversion; force or irony is gained through memory of the usual form. Often the variation seems merely wanton, shows little sense of rhythm or of the value of words; perhaps Layamon's verbal memory lacked exactness. In matters of style he had frequent happy thoughts, but was slapdash, neither sophisticated, recollected, nor wary; occasionally he seems as if feeling his way up to a standard form, and accordingly formulas are least abundant in the early part of the poem (they are most abundant in the middle); but there is little indication that in devising his formulas he groped about for perfection, and then held it.

In the use of the formula Layamon found two chief conveniences,—for the verse and for the narrative. Though his poem contains many lines with neither rime nor alliteration, he preferred to have one or the other, and sometimes both. The half-line formulas often contain alliteration and usually afford alliteration or a rime (strict or easy-going) for the other half-line, and all of the full-line formulas contain either alliteration, oftener rime, or sometimes both. Another service to the verse is expletive. Unlike Anglo-Saxon poets, Layamon dislikes to begin a new sentence in the middle of a line, and a well-sounding tag makes this unnecessary. This is why the short formulas are commonest in the second half-line, and often have more sound than sense. Again, there was an obvious convenience in having an agreeable form of words all ready when for the second or twentieth time he told of the death of a king or the summoning of an army. It was obvious to use it when one knew no reason why one should not. In the absence of a more sophisticated desire for novelty, the liturgical instinct had its way. And though he was far from critical and self-conscious, he presumably felt the formula style harmonious with his broad and elemental manner. His formulas are magnifying and imposing, no mere convenience, but often a means of embellishment. Doubtless his auditors too found a pleasure in the mere repetition, as children feel in *The Three Bears* and *The House that Jack Built*, or even as we feel in recognizing a recurring *motif* in music. Nevertheless, he sometimes seems to weary of a particular formula, and certainly sometimes passes over opportunities to use it, or varies it wantonly. In spite of the convenience and pleasure he found in the practice, he is not wholly mechanical.

The literary effect for the modern reader will depend on himself. Modern poets, highly conscious, avoid favorite phrases, and show their individuality in subtler ways. Readers very modern in taste may find Layamon's usage rude or even helpless (though they might beware of flouting Homer at the same time). Others will find great charm in it. Sometimes this is a quaintness in the idea or words, perhaps supplied by some later association, for usually quaintness is in the eye of him who looks. Other formulas have intrinsic interest and beauty, which justify their repetition, like *Drihten, Maryen, Ofte-wo, Slayen-dayen.* Some are singularly vivid, like the formulas *Brac, Hayel, Libben.* Layamon has originality and distinction of style. The modern feels less pleasure than the medieval in mere recognition of the familiar, but will appreciate the epic breadth which the formulas promote, and may even relish them as a mark of a strong literary individuality. They promote unity, in so linear and prolonged a narrative, by recalling earlier situations or roughly enforcing characterization. They suit the alliterative verse, *staccato,* with its strongly-marked units and rare *enjambement,* neither restless nor nimble. No doubt they are used too much, but as one reads they seem by no means so common as when they are collected, nor do they give an effect of helplessness. (pp. 511-14)

John S. P. Tatlock, "Epic Formulas, Especially in Layamon," in PMLA, *Vol. XXXVIII, No. 3, September, 1923, pp. 494-529.*

Jones on the vernacular nature of the *Brut:*

While not indifferent to romance, as several significant additions to the Arthurian part of his story will show, Layamon wrote his ***Brut*** as a frankly patriotic English epic. Wace's work is almost as artificial and exotic a product as the poetical romances; it was designed as a contribution to the polite literature of the Norman aristocracy. Layamon, dwelling in seclusion on the banks of the Severn, where "it was good to be," was fired by an ambition "to tell the noble deeds of England," and to tell them in the English tongue. His poem is the first articulate utterance of the native English genius reasserting itself in its own language after the long silence which succeeded the Conquest. Although he borrows most of his matter from Wace, Layamon, in manner and spirit, is much nearer akin to the robust singers of the Old English period than to the courtly French poet. The simple force and vividness of the primitve English epic reappear in descriptions of battle scenes and of heroic deeds. Even the poet's diction is scrupulously pure English. And Arthur, who, in the hands of the professional romancers, had already become all but an alien to his fatherland, is restored to his rightful place as the champion of Britain. . . .

W. Lewis Jones in The Cambridge History of English Literature, *edited by A. W. Ward and A. R. Waller, G. P. Putnam's Sons, 1907.*

Emile Legouis   (essay date 1929)

[*A French scholar and philologist, Legouis is the author of* Chaucer *(1913),* Edmund Spenser *(1923),* Wordsworth in a New Light *(1923), and the acclaimed* Histoire de la littérature anglaise *(1924;* A History of English Literature, *1926), written with Louis Cazamian. In the following excerpt from the latter work, Legouis finds fault with Layamon's pronounced but "mistaken" patriotism, yet praises his version of the* Brut, *deeming him a transitional figure in English literature.*]

In the last quarter of the twelfth or in the first years of the thirteenth century Layamon, a priest of Ernley, on the Severn and near the Welsh border, put Wace's *Brut* into English verse for the benefit of his fellow-countrymen. Wace, with the curious mind and the detachment of an Anglo-Norman trouvère, had followed Geoffrey of Monmouth's fabulous history of the Britons, and had therefore glorified that people at the expense of their Saxon adversaries. And Layamon, or Laweman, a pure German by race and tongue, faithfully repeated this story, as though he were ignorant of his own origin. His sympathies are all with the Britons; the Saxons are for him barbarians whose victories grieve him sorely and whose defeats delight him. It is not astonishing that he has scandalised modern English historians, almost to the point of being dubbed traitor. Freeman, the historian of the Norman Conquest, cannot enough despise the Anglo-Saxon who betrays his race, whose national heroes are not Alfred and Hengist, but Brutus, the descendant of Æneas, and the famous King Arthur. None the less, Layamon's patriotism is as ardent as it is mistaken. His error draws attention to the fact that the two races who had been enemies were already inextricably fused. They constituted a new unity which was already the English nation, and had England for its place and symbol. It is because he sees the Britons as legitimate owners of England that Layamon makes common cause with them against the Saxons, whom he regards as invaders, and there is not a doubt that when he speaks of the Saxons he is secretly thinking of the Normans, the oppressors of his fellow-countrymen.

Layamon is, on the whole, a faithful translator. He contributes nothing new except certain passages of Arthurian legend. These principally reflect the developments of this legend in the half-century which separated him from Wace, yet he deserves honour for first revealing some of the most poetic touches in the story. Living, as he did, on the Welsh March, he may have had direct access to traditions of which his forerunners were unaware. Most of his additions are, however, accepted nowadays as either based on a text of Wace other than that printed, or borrowed from the lost *Chronique rimée* of Geoffrey Gaimar.

Nevertheless, Layamon is no mere translator. He cannot be classed among the trouvères, with their curiosity and the simple amusement they found in their own fine tales. He is a scop, and has kept something of the epic mood and the wild, impassioned note of Anglo-Saxon poetry, together with part of its vocabulary, a rhythm which still hesi-

tates between rhyme and alliteration, and certain traces of
the ancient mythology and the sombre, ancestral enthusiasm for war. He is, moreover, the first writer to weave
about King Arthur a fairy lore of which there is hardly a
word in Geoffrey of Monmouth or in Wace. He is more
at his ease than they in the realm of the marvellous. When
he tells the story of the passing of the king we seem to be
listening to Malory:

> When these words were spoken,
> There came thither wending,
> A little boat moving,
> On the waters it floated,
> And two women in it,
> Wondrously formed;
> And lo! they took Arthur,
> And swiftly they bare him,
> And softly him down laid,
> And forth 'gan their sailing.
> Then was it accomplished
> What Merlin said whilom,
> That great woe would follow
> On Arthur's forthfaring.
> Still think the Britons
> That Arthur yet liveth
> And dwelleth in Avalon
> With the fairest of all elves;
> Still wait the Britons
> For Arthur's returning.

Very far from attaining to Wace's easy fluency, correctness and courtliness, Layamon, awkward and blunt, yet
has a plebeian way which is not unpleasing. He recurs to
the massive ironies of the Anglo-Saxon epic. Thus he tells
how the British King Uther, with Arthur's help, defeated
his brother Pascent, who together with Gillomar, the savage Irish invader, attempted to dethrone him. At the moment when Uther has wounded Gillomar to death and Arthur has slain Pascent the poet's voice has the very tones
of the *Ode of Brunanburh*:

> On the head he smote him
> So that he down fell,
> In his mouth his sword thrust—
> Uncouth his dinner—
> So went the sword's point
> In the earth beneath him.
> And then spake Uther,
> "Pascent, now lie there,
> Now hast thou Britain,
> To thy hand hast won it.
> So is now hap to thee;
> Therein death hath come to thee;
> Dwell shalt thou therein
> With thy fellow Gillomar,
> And well enjoy Britain.
> To you I deliver it;
> Ye twain may presently
> Dwell in the land with us;
> Nor dread ye ever
> Who food will give ye."

Such passages, occurring in a chivalrous romance, show
the transitional character of Layamon's curious version of
the Arthurian story. He was at once the last of the scops
and the first of the English trouvères. (pp. 86-9)

*Emile Legouis, "From the Norman Conquest
to Chaucer (1066-1350)," in* A History of English Literature *by Emile Legouis and Louis
Cazamian, translated by Helen Douglas Ir-
vine, W. D. MacInnes, and Louis Cazamian,
revised edition, The Macmillan Company,
1929, pp. 56-99.*

Henry Cecil Wyld   (essay date 1930)

[*Wyld was an English educator and philologist, and the
author of works on such subjects as comparative philology, dialects, and historical grammar. In the excerpt
below, he discusses the general characteristics of Layamon's style, contending that despite the lack of attention
given it, the* Brut *"is incomparably the greatest achievement in English poetry between the Anglo-Saxon period
and Chaucer."*]

The great work known as Layamon's **Brut** is not nearly
so well known as it deserves to be among students of English poetry. The reasons for this are partly its great
length—it runs to 32,241 half-lines—partly the fact that
it is only available, in its entirety, in a single edition, the
splendid one of Sir Frederick Madden, now more than
eighty years old, and not always easy to come by, and lastly the apparent uncouthness and strangeness of the language.

And yet, and this should be said at once, the **Brut** is incomparably the greatest achievement in English poetry
between the Anglo-Saxon period and Chaucer. For variety
of interest, vigour, and spirit, Robert of Brunne, though
greatly inferior to Layamon in poetical quality, can alone
be compared to him. The only other work in verse of approximately the same date as the **Brut,** and nearly equal
to it in bulk, the *Ormulum,* is so notoriously devoid of
those graces of diction and imagery which distinguish the
Brut, that it is negligible as poetry, and whatever interest
it may possess for the student of literature is confined to
such as attaches to an unsuccessful metrical experiment.
To borrow a phrase of Johnson's, "it cannot be read without reluctance." The metrical version of *Genesis and Exodus* which belongs to a later part of the thirteenth century,
though redeemed from the dullness of a mere paraphrase
by the occasional flashes of vividness and of genuine
human feeling, can with difficulty be brought within the
sphere of poetry.

The outstanding quality of Layamon's work, and this is
found on every page, almost in every line, is the essential
poetical character of the diction. We feel in reading the
work, as we feel in reading Anglo-Saxon poetry, that it is
the deliberate intention of the writer to be poetical, and to
produce something which shall appeal to the imagination
and the emotions. It is this consciousness that he is writing
poetry, and not merely telling a story or enforcing a moral,
that leads Layamon to employ a diction which for the men
of his time was deeply tinged with heroic and romantic associations, "words," as Dr. Johnson says, "refinded from
the grossness of domestic use." Layamon's language is not
merely the ancient speech of Englishmen, almost free, at
least in the older text, from foreign elements, it is the language of their old poetry, as Madden well says [in his preface to the **Brut; or, Chronicle of Britain**], "at every mo-

ment reminding us of the splendid phraseology of Anglo-Saxon verse." Layamon is thus in the true line of succession to the old poets of his land.

His vocabulary and his spirit are theirs. His poetry has its roots, not merely in the old literary tradition, but also, like this, in the essential genius of the race.

The intensity of feeling, the wealth of imagery, the tender humanity, the love of nature, the chivalrous and romantic spirit, which distinguish the poetry of Layamon would give him a high place among the English poets of any age. His copious, varied, and picturesque vocabulary, so rich in association, and often so suggestive of mysterious beauty, gives his work a lasting value possessed by no other Middle-English poetry before Chaucer, disfigured as so much of of this is by an unredeemed flatness, insipidity and matter-of-factness in thought and expression. (pp. 1-2)

Layamon's **Brut** is sometimes referred to as a translation of the Norman poem [the chronicle of Wace, also titled the *Brut*]. This is true to the extent that, in the main, the episodes in the latter follow those in Wace's work, the names of persons, places, and weapons are usually faithfully preserved, though not infrequently the form of these is considerably modified; the general subject and order of the narrative are reproduced, and sometimes several lines on end are faithfully rendered. But the English poem is very far from being a line for line translation. The number of lines in Wace is 15,300, less than half that of Layamon.

How is it that the "translation" is double the length of the original? The extra space is accounted for in two ways: first, by the numerous episodes and scenes which Layamon introduces without any corresponding passages in Wace; secondly, by the innumerable touches, sometimes occupying only a few lines, with which he heightens the effect of Wace's rather bald narrative, touches that express human feeling, and reveal the sentiments and passions of the actors, which add picturesque descriptive details of an action—a fight, a carouse, the arming of a hero for battle, a sea voyage—or which show the poet's feeling for external nature.

Of the actual additions of episodes not dealt with by Wace at all, and consisting of anything from ten or twenty lines to ten or twenty pages of the printed text, Madden's list occupies about two pages of his Introduction. One of the finest of these original episodes is the splendid description of the hunting down of Childric, in which the fugitive king is compared to a fox pursued by hounds. This leads quite naturally to a highly spirited and inspiring account of a fox-hunt, so typically English in subject and feeling.

We shall have occasion to quote some passages from this exciting chase later on. . . . Another passage which illustrates at once how Layamon expands and embellishes the text of Wace, and the way in which he introduces new matter is the noble account of Arthur's death and passage to the Valley of Avalon. (pp. 5-6)

The essential kernel of the story in Wace is contained in the lines:

> En Avalon se fist porter

> Por ses plaies mediciner.

Few will dispute the poetical value of Layamon's expansions and additions—the speech of Arthur to his kinsman, part of which reminds us somewhat of Beowulf 's last address to Wiglaf (*Beow.* 2813-16); the picturesque touch whereby Arthur himself announces the manner of his passing and his expected return; the fair queen of the elves, and her healing drenches; the little ship driven by the waves in which the king is laid gently down by the two women in wondrous attire. Finally, instead of the matter-of-fact humming and hawing of "Maistre Gasse," Layamon contrives to create just such an atmosphere of wonder and mystery concerning the ultimate fate of Arthur as we find in the concluding lines of the account of the passing of Scyld:

> Men ne cunnon
> secgan to soðe, sele rædende,
> hæleð under heofenum, hwa þæm hlæste onfeng
>   (*Beow.* 50-2).

We may compare the French and English poems almost where we will, and we shall find, here a word or two inserted, there a few lines added in the latter, which enliven the narrative and make it more picturesque and interesting. In the first few lines of the poem the words *alðeodisc wif,* "a foreign woman," occur in reference to Helen (I. 4. 20), which are not suggested by anything in Wace; a few lines further on, describing the voyage of Æneas to Italy, the English poet tells how. . . . "The ships travelled far and wide across the wintry sea; amid clouds and storms, they endured tribulations." There is nothing of this in Wace.

The story of King Lear and his daughters occupies in Wace about 413 lines on pp. 81-98 in Vol. I [Le Roux de Lincy edition, 1838]; in Layamon we have 810 half-lines on pp. 124-158 in Vol. I [Madden's edition, 1847]. In spite of some noble scenes in the earlier part of the story, the French poem records the coming of the old King to take refuge with Cordelia in cold, dry and very brief terms. In the English version the episode, though treated with dignity and restraint, is full of human interest and natural emotion. Whereas Wace (Vol. I, pp. 95-96) merely relates that on his arrival in France Lear sent a messenger to his daughter to announce his coming, and that the queen, very properly, supplied him with a castle to live in, clothes to wear, and other comforts, Layamon tells us the words used by the envoy to the queen in some detail, adding the characteristic touch, that when she heard of her father's troubles, and that he had come to seek her, "long she sat silent, she flushed where she sat upon the bench, as it had been from wine"—

> þe quene Cordoille: seæt longe swþe stille,
> heo iward reod on hire benche: swilche hit were
>   of wine scenche
>   (I. 150. 6-9).

and how . . . "her thoughts burst forth altogether; it was good that she spoke." Then she thanks Apollin that she hears such good tidings, that her father is alive and is come to her. Only then she sets about planning his comfort and arranges for splendid gifts to be sent him—"her dear father; the things he likes best, food and drink, and fair garments, hounds and hawks and valuable horses, forty household retainers noble and powerful, and nobly clad; make him a good bed, and bathe him often and let him blood, little and often," and so on (I, 151). In due time Lear arrives in excellent fettle, is nobly received by his son-in-law, kisses his daughter, and they all sit down to a feast amid general rejoicings, to the sound of trumpets and pipes, in the hall behung with purple and gold, while minstrels sing to the notes of fiddles and harps (I. 153-54). All this detail is pure Layamon.

As a last example of the English poet's heightening of the colours of his original, we may take the quarrel, and reconciliation, through the intercession of their mother, of the brothers Brennus and Belyn.

Belyn the elder became king of Britain on the death of their father, King Dunwal, but had granted Brennus a part of his kingdom beyond the Humber to hold in vassallage. After a time Brennus, misled by evil councillors, rebelled against his brother, and attempted to seize the whole kingdom for himself, but was defeated and driven overseas to Burgundy, where he was well received, and later on married the duke's daughter. On the death of his wife's father, Brennus succeeds him and makes an excellent king. But he remembers how his brother had deprived him of his former kingdom, and determines to attack Belyn in his own country. Having summoned his army, Brennus embarks, and subsequently lands in Britain. Belyn is informed of his brother's arrival, raises his forces, and marches against him. Everything is staged for the great battle, and now our episode opens (see Lay. 1. 213, and Wace, I. p. 132). The old queen, mother of the rival kings, was still alive. She inquires where Brennus is to be found, and arrives just as he is putting on his armour. She runs to him and throwing her arms around him kisses him again and again. A moving speech follows, which up to a point is pretty closely rendered by Layamon from Wace. The queen reminds Brennus that he and his brother are both her sons and have both been suckled at the same breast, that he is in the wrong in having broken his oath of fealty to Belyn, and implores him not to harry the land with foreign troops, but

> Ah leoue sune Brennes: bei þi starke þone
> leie adun þin hære-scrud: & þin rede sceld,
> and þi sper longe: & þi swerd stronge,
> and ilef þire moder: and leoue þine broðer
>   (I. 216, 7-14).

It is in the expansion of the next few lines that Layamon shows his independence and originality. Wace reads (2863, p. 136, Vol. I.):

> Quant Brennes sa mère entendi
> Pitié en ot, si la crei.
> S'espee et puis son hiaume osta
> Et de l'auberc se despoilla
> Devant sa gent el camp sali,
> Et Bélins refist altresi.
> Et la mère les assembla,
> Entrebaisier les commanda,
> Onques ni ot conte conté
> Dès qu'ele lor a commandé,
> Si s'alerent entrebrachier
> Et dolcement entrebaisier
> Ensi fu li guerre accordée

> Et l'ire des frères finee.

Layamon starts off with a touch of nature not found in Wace:

> Vrnen hire teares: ouer hire leores;
> Brennes þat isæh: and seoryede on his heorte,
> Let gliden his gare: þat hit grund sohte;
> he scæt his riche sceld: feor ut in þene feld,
> awei he warp his gode breond: & of mid þere
>   burne.
> Brennes and his moder: mildeliche ferden
> in ænne bradne feld: and Belin him toyennes.
> þa weop þe breoðer: and swa dede þe oðer.
> þa spec þe moder: milde mid muþe—
> yit buð mine leoue sunen: liðeð to-somne,
> and iwurðeð sæhte: and euer on blisse.
> cusseð and cluppeð: cuðie meies.
> cnihtes yit beoð boðe kene: while ich wes quene
> nis noht un-huhtlic: incker moder inc hateð.
> þer heo hom custen: þe weren kinges bearn
> bifeoren þa twam ferden: freondscipe makeden.
> bemen þer bleowen: blisse wes on folke
>   (I. 216. 15-217.24).

It will be felt, I think, that the English version transcends the French in picturesqueness and human interest. It is the sight of his mother's tears, not only her words, which moves Brennus. Then the action of letting his spear slip from his grasp, followed by the impulsive hurling of his shield far out into the field, is a true and natural touch.

Note also the effectiveness of the inverted word-order, and the almost colloquial idiom—"away he flung his good sword, and off with his corslet." Then there is a fitting formality in the adjournment of Brennus and his mother to a spacious field where the brothers meet, and a naturalness in their tears. The old queen's homely remarks as she thrusts her sons into each other's arms, "There! you are my own good boys again! your mother would not ask you to do what was unbecoming," put the final touch to the reconciliation as the brothers embrace before the armies; and then, in characteristic English fashion, horns are sounded, and a banquet is enjoyed to the sound of pipes and the song of minstrels—"Thus was Brennus reconciled with his brother":

> þer weore segge (O. gleomenne) songe: þer were
>   pipen imangge
> þa wes swa muchel murehðe: þat ne mihte heo
>   beon na mare.
> þus iwarð Brennes: sæht wið his broðer
>   (I. 218. 1-6).

There is no word of feast or song in Wace, who hustles the brothers off to London immediately they have made it up without giving them time for supper.

These few examples perhaps illustrate sufficiently the free way in which Layamon deals with the text of Wace in those passages where he is actually following the French writer and not importing totally new episodes.

I pass now to examine more at large the qualities of Layamon as a poet. It will be convenient to consider these under certain general heads, such as references to the phenomena of external Nature; reflexions on life, and on human nature; chivalrous ideas and ideals; descriptions of human actions, especially of battles, voyages, hunting, rejoicings in the halls of princes; ceremonial and pageantry.

In many cases the illustrations will be drawn from portions of the work added by Layamon, in others from the English poet's amplifications of a few lines or phrases in Wace. Where the suggestion for the passage quoted is to be found in Wace, this will be indicated; where no reference is made to the French poet, it may be assumed that the ideas expressed in the quotations are wholly due to Layamon.

The love of external Nature is highly developed in Layamon, as in the older English poets, and there is no mistaking his keen enjoyment of it. He constantly brings in references to the sea, waves, storms, mountains, rocks, woods, animals, with a specific intimacy usually altogether absent from the corresponding passage in the French text, if indeed there be any hint there at all of such matter. How delightful and full of gaiety are the lines on the coming of summer to town!—

> þa weoren bliðe spelles: In Arðures hallen.
> þer wes hareping and song: þa weoren blissen
>   imong,
> þa æstre wes agonge: & Aureril eode of tune,
> and þæt gras was riue: & þat water wes liðe,
> And men gan spillien: þat Mai wes at tune
>   (II. 593. 23-594-9).

This is all based on two matter-of-fact lines in Wace:

> En avril quant estre entra,
> En Angleterre trespassa
>   (II. 93. 2-3).

Simile is more freely used on the whole than in Anglo-Saxon poetry, and is invariably drawn from the objects or processes of Nature. There is a fine comparison of a surging host of fugitives to "a lofty wood when the wild wind shakes it violently":

> swa þe hæye wude
> þenne wind wode: weieð hine mid mæine
>   (II. 421. 17-19).

Arthur rushing impetuously upon his enemies is compared to "the fleet wolf when he sallies from the wood, bedecked with snow, purposing to devour such beasts as he fancies":

> sea þe runie wulf
> þenne he cumeð of holte: bihonged mid snawe
> and þencheð to biten: swulc deor swa him likeð
>   (II. 421. 5-9).

The speed with which a man leaps upon his horse is twice compared to that of a spark flashing from the fire:

> Cador sprong to horse: swa spærc of fure
>   (II. 478. 10-11).

He (Arthur) "sprong forð an stede: swa sparc deð of fure" (II. 565. 8-9). He pursues Childeric "neh alswa swiðe: swa þe fuyel flieð" (II. 473. 2-3).

Hengest leaps to the fight "as though it were a lion" (II. 267. 1-2).

Arthur among his foemen is "like the wild boar when he finds many swine among the mast":

> swa bið ðe wilde bar
> þenne he i þan mæste: monie (swin) imeteð
>   (II. 469. 5-7).

Edwin becomes terribly enraged "as is a boar (at bay) in the wood when the hounds surround him" (III. 217. 4-8). Arrows fly "as thick as falls the snow" (III. 94. 14-15); or again, "as thick was their flight as though it were hail" (II. 100. 13-14). The hosts of Octa pour in at his summons "like hail that falls" (II. 183. 10-11).

The most elaborate simile in the whole poem is that in which Arthur, having brought Childeric to that point of desperation when he sends envoys to sue for peace, and to promise that he will trouble Arthur and his country no more, but will sail away, compares him to a hunted fox. "Then Arthur laughed loudly. Thanks be to the Lord who rules our destinies, that Childeric has had enough of my country. He hath divided up my land among his knights, forsooth, and thought to drive me out of my country, to make me contemptible and to have my kingdom, to have destroyed my kindred, and to condemn my people":

> Ah of him bið iwurðen swa bið of þam voxe,
> þenne he bið baldest ufen an þan walde,
> & haueð his fulle ploye & fuyeles inoye.
> for wildscipe climbið and cluden isecheð,
> i þan wilderne holyes him wurcheð.
> fare wha swa auere fare: naueð he næuere nænne
>   kare.
> he weneð to beon of duyeðe: baldest alre deoren.
> Þenne siyeð him to: segges vnder beoryen
> mid hornen mid hunden: mid hayere stefenen.
> hunten þar talieð: hundes þer galieð,
> Þene vox driveð: yeond dales and yeond dunes.
> he ulihþ to þan holme: and his hol isecheð.
> i þan uirste ænde: i þan holte wendeð.
> þenne is þe balde uox: blissen al bidæled,
> and mon him to-delueð: on ælchere heluen;
> þenne beoð þer forcuðest: deoren alre pruttest.
> Swa wes Childeriche: þan strongen and þan
>   riche
> he þohten al mi kinelond setten an his ayere
>   hond.
> ah nu ich habbe hine idriuen to þan bare dæðe.
> whæðer swa ich wulle don: oðer slæn oðer ahon.
>   (II. 450 16-452. 23.)

There is no mistaking the gusto of all this. Layamon had evidently assisted at many a hunt, had heard the view-halloo, and the music of hounds in full cry, and had seen the fox dug out. For the moment he is much more interested in the fox than in the fate of Childeric.

The entire episode from which this passage comes is one of the most spirited and interesting in the whole of Middle English poetry, with its extraordinary variety of incident, action, scene, mood, and sentiment. Among so much that is attractive I must only mention one more passage in the present connection, the remarkable lines in which Arthur depicts Baldulf, one of Childeric's companions, standing on a hill and gazing down into the waters of the Avon. "He sees how his dead knights are lying like great steel fish below the waters of the stream, no longer able to swim indeed, their scales are gleaming as it were gold-plated shields, and their fins afloat, as it were spears. Wondrous things indeed are seen in the land—such a deer upon the hill, such fish in the water!"

> Yurstendæi wes Baldulf: cnihten alre baldest.
> nu he stant on hulle: and Auene he bi-haldeð,
> hu liyeð i þan stræme: stelene fisces.
> mid sweorde bi-georede: heore sund is awem-
>   med.
> heore scalen wleoteð: swulc gold-fage sceldes.
> þer fleoteð heore spiten: swulc hit spæren
>   weoren,
> þis bið seolcuðe þing: isiyen to þissen londe
> swulche deor an hulle: swulche fishes in walle
>   (II. 471. 15—472. 6).

There is a fine passage in which Brutus is represented as contemplating with delight the beauties and attractions of Britain. The lines are a rendering of a passage in Wace (Vol. I. p. 60) which is little more than a cold impersonal enumeration of mountains, woods, streams, and so on, without any underlying feeling. Layamon's version seems to be inspired by the warm personal attachment of an Englishman to the varied beauties and graces of the natural features of his native land, upon each of which he dwells with loving satisfaction. It is impossible not to feel that the poet is voicing his own emotions when he says:

> Thus Brutus pondered, and beheld the people;
> he beheld the mountains fair and lofty; he beheld
> the meadows that were so broad; he beheld the
> waters and the wild deer; he beheld the fish, he
> beheld the birds; he beheld the pasture lands and
> lovely woods—he saw the woods how they
> flourished, he saw the corn how well it grew; he
> looked upon all the country, and it was dear to
> him in his heart
>   (II. 85. 6-21).

We have only to compare the English with the French original of this passage, to perceive at once the difference between the true poet and the conscientious writer of Chronicles.

Layamon often enlivens his narrative, and makes it more real, by adding at least some particulars of the landscape amid which an action takes place. The detailed account of Loch Lomond, its sixty islands with their rocks and eagles, of the deep valleys which surround it, and the streams which flow into it (see II. 489.11—491. 9), is translated pretty faithfully from Wace (II. p. 60), and is found also in Geoffrey of Monmouth (Bk. x. ch. 6). The English poet, however, has added some characteristic lines (II. 489. 11-20):

> þat is a seolcuð mere: iset a middelærde
> mid fenne & mid ræode: mid wætere swiðe
>   bræde,
> mid fiscen and mid feoyelen: and mid uniuele
>   þingen.
> þat water is unimete brade: nikeres baðieð inne;
> þer is æluen ploye: in atteliche pole.

It is impossible not to think, on reading this, of the horrible pool in Beowulf, where Grendel and his mother had their habitation. Not only does the general erriness of the

place recall the Anglo-Saxon description, but some of the words and phrases used occur in this. (pp. 7-14)

We seem to get down to the heart of wild life amid wild surroundings as the poet tells how, when Constantine landed at Totnes,

> the Britons heard of it where they couched in pits, or lurked amid stocks and stones, hiding like badgers in woods and waste places, among heath and fern, so that one could hardly find a Briton, except it were fast enclosed in a castle or stronghold. But when they heard that Constantine was in their country, then there came forth from the mountains many thousand men; they leaped from the woods like deer, and marched on London. Many hundred thousand pressed forward, by road, or through forests. And brave women donned men's clothes and rallied to the army
>   (II. 110. 18-111. 17).

We may conclude our account of Layamon's treatment of scenery with his description of Caerleon and its surroundings before its destruction:

> In those days men deemed there was no city so fair, or so widely famed, as Caerleon by Usk, unless it were the famous city of Rome. Indeed there were many who said that Caerleon was a more splendid city than Rome, and that Usk was the fairest of all rivers:

> Medewes þer weoren brade: bihalues þere bury-
>   he
> þer wes fisc þer wes fuyel: & fæiernesse inoye.
> þer wes wude and wilde deor: wunder ane monie
> þer wes al þa murhðe: þe æi mon mihte of
>   þenche
>   (II. 596. 12—597.7).

Layamon shows the same interest in wild animals, and beasts of the chase, as is found in Anglo-Saxon literature—see examples in several passages already quoted—and the characteristic Nordic love of "hundes and haukes: and derewurðe horses" (I. 151. 17-18). A very English touch reveals the knights' care for their chargers before a battle—"heo wipeden hors leoue: mid linnene claðe; here steden heo scoiden" (II. 512. 20-22). A most engaging passage tells how a body of knights before an attack, rested for the night in "a wood, an exceeding fair spot, in a deep valley, secluded on all sides. And when the dawn came and the deer began to stir, they rode forth singing, so blithe were they" (III. 72. 9-18). We have here no mere literary flourish, but a genuine delight in the life of the woods.

There is a beautiful little picture of a hunted "crane," or more probably a heron, to which the Saxon host, routed and scattered by Arthur, is compared:

> Some wandered hither and thither as doth the wild heron over the moor-fen when he can no longer fly strongly, and the fleet hawks are after him, while the fierce hounds are waiting for him in the reeds. He can find refuge neither on land or water, for the hawks will strike, and the hounds will seize him. Then the royal bird is doomed whichever way he takes
>   (II. 422. 21—423. 9).

When the Trojans land in France the first clash of arms comes because their chief Corineus insists, in spite of the prohibition of the King of Poitou, on hunting in the royal forest. The scene, which is very briefly described in Wace (I. 40-41), is much amplified by Layamon, chiefly in order to give more details of the hunt and its disastrous close. . . . (pp. 14-16)

Leaving the treatment of landscape and animated nature, we may now pass to the sea and journeys upon it. Apart from casual references to this or that person going to, or coming from, the sea, it is solely in connection with voyages that Layamon mentions the ocean. As a dweller in an inland county he may well have had no first-hand knowledge of the sea, though he apparently knew something of the art of sailing.

Perhaps the most elaborate description of a sea voyage is that of Ursula, daughter of Athionard, "lord of this land," whose father

> þohte heo to sende: ouer sæ stræmes
> in to Bruttaine londe: to Conaan þan stronge
> (II. 73. 11-14).

The plan, however, miscarried owing to a dreadful storm which arose after the ships got out of the Thames. An account of the journey is given in Wace, I.p 285, but, as usual, the most picturesque and moving lines in our version are additions by Layamon. . . . (p. 16)

The comparison of the tumultuous waves to burning towns is remakable and orginal. The poet probably has in his mind the flying clouds of spray which he sees as resembling great volumes of drifting smoke. The same simile is found in I. 195. 12-13. It is a characteristic human touch, of which there are so many in Layamon, to refer to the strange cry of terror and appeal which no man born could hear, no matter how hard-hearted, or how stout a warrior he might be, without compassion for such immense calamity.

Of quite a different kind was the voyage of the treacherous Childeric whom Arthur, having defeated him, allows to depart on the understanding that he will return to his own country and give no more trouble. . . . (p. 17)

As might be expected from so spirited and romantic a poet, Layamon handles the whole subject of war, and every aspect of martial action, with peculiar vigour and picturesqueness. From the arming and equipping of his hero to the final victorious rush which scatters the enemy, no detail is missing that can lend colour or majesty to the principal characters, and bring into relief their valour, their bodily strength, and their greatness of soul. The speeches of the leaders are inspiring, and we watch with growing excitement each cut and thrust and parry in the fight itself. The scene is splendidly staged, often amid romantic surroundings, and the action is carried through in true heroic manner. Layamon visualizes a scene and a situation, and often records the impressions of the actors in the drama with a glowing imagination and a sense of the picturesque that are quite beyond Wace. A good example

of this is the sudden discovery by the Roman army of King Arthur's host ready to give battle:

> The Roman people saw all the valleys, all the uplands, all the hills, dotted with helmets; they saw the lofty banners fluttering in the wind—sixty thousand warriors bore them—they saw the shields flash and the corslets gleam, the gold-embroidered cloaks, the stern men and the prancing horses. The very earth shook. The Emperor marked the king where he was encamped by the wood-shaw.

> iseyen alle þa dales: alle þa dunes,
> alle þa hulles: mid helmes biþahte,
> hey here-mærken: hæleðes heom heolden,
> sixti þusend: þrauwen mid winde;
> sceldes blikien: burnen scinen
> palles gold-faye: gumen wiðe sturne;
> steden lepen: sturede þa eorðe.
> þe keiser isah þæne king fare: þer he was bi wude
>   scaye.
>
> (III. 90. 6-21.)

As in ancient heroic poetry, the arms of the hero, and the ceremony of putting them on before some momentous fight, are described with some minuteness. There are two elaborate descriptions of the arming of Arthur, the first occasion being before the fight against the Saxons at Bath, the second before Arthur's single combat with King Frolle of France. In the first of these Layamon follows Wace pretty closely, but adds certain important details. Perhaps the most significant is the statement that his corslet had been made by a cunning "elvish" smith:

> he dude on his burne: ibroiden of stele,
> þe makede on aluisc smið: mid aðelen his crafte;
> he wes ihaten Wijgar: þe witeye wurhte
> (II. 463. 13-18).

With this compare Beowulf's allusion to his corslet:

> Onsend Hygelace yif mec hild nime
> beadu-scruda betst, þæt mine breost wereð
> hægla selest; þæt is Hrædlan laf,
> Welandes geweorc
>
> (*Beow.* 452-55).

Also the reference to Beowulf's "white helmet, adorned with gems, and girt with a coronet":

> swa hine fyrn-dagum
> worhte wæpna smið
>
> (*Beow.* 1451-2).
> (pp. 18-19)

The arming of Arthur for his fight with Frolle is given with minute and splendid detail, and the account seems to be entirely Layamon's own. Wace's story of the combat is in vol. II. pp. 85-89, and differs so much in treatment from that of Layamon that it is very difficult to compare them. Here is his description of the process of arming:

> Arthur the strong took his weapons in hand, he threw upon his back a very costly robe, a linen shirt, and a purple tunic; a precious corslet woven of steel. He set upon his head a good helmet; at his side he hung his sword Caliburne; he covered his legs with hose of steel, and put upon his feet his right good spurs. The king in his ar-

mour (weden) leapt upon his steed, and they reached him a good shield entirely made of ivory. Into his hand they gave a strong shaft at the end of which was a serviceable spearhead. This was made at Carmarthen by a smith called Griffen—Uther had owned it who was king here formerly. When he was armed the brave king rode forth, and those present could see the mighty king and how gallantly he rode. Since the world was established, nowhere was it told that ever so fair a man went out upon a horse as was King Arthur the son of Uther. Behind the king there rode forty hundred valiant warriors in the first troop, noble captains in steel armour, gallant Britons busy with their weapons (II. 575. 19—577. 20).

There are numerous examples of leaders rallying and urging on their followers in battle—both brief cries of encouragement under stress of battle, and of more formal utterances. . . . (pp. 19-20)

A few examples of Arthur's personal prowess in battle must suffice:

> And Arður him seolf arnde biforen al his ferde,
> Arður þe ræie: Ron nom an his honde;
> he stræhte scaft stærcne: stiðimoden king
> his hors he lette irnen: þa ðe eorðe dunede
> sceld he braid on breosten: þe king wes abolyen.
> He smat Borel þene eorl: þurh ut þa breosten
> þat þæ heorte to-chan
>   (II. 467. 15—468.4).

To such purpose does Arthur lay about him that he drives the enemy "to the flood," where twenty-five hundred are slain, and "Avon's stream is all bridged with steel" (II. 469. 14-17)—that is, with the bodies of men in armour.

> Arðou igrap his sweord riht: & he smat ænne
>   Sexisc cniht
> þat þe sweord þat wes swa god: æt þan to þen
>   at-stod,
> & he smat enne oþer: þa wes þas cnihtes broðer,
> þat his helm and his hæfd: halden to grunde;
> þenne þridde dunt he sone yaf: and enne cniht
>   atwa clæf
>   (II. 474. 4-13).

No wonder that, as the poet adds, "then were the Britons exceedingly encouraged, and laid on to the Saxons":

> His brode swærd he up ahof: and hærdliche
>   adun sloh,
> and smat Colgrimes ðat hælm: þat he amidde
>   to-clæf,
> and þere brune hod: þat hit at þe breoste at-stod
>   (II. 475. 17-22).

> And he sweinde touward Baldulfe: mid his
>   swiðren honde
> & swipte þat hæued of: forð mid þan helme
>   (II. 475. 23—476.3).

To turn from the exploits of individuals to the turmoil of general battle, there is no lack of dash and vigour in the onslaughts described in the poem. High courage and endurance in the fight are displayed by high and low alike:

> þa wes æuer ælc cheorl: al swa bald alse an eorl,

> & alle þa gadelinges: alse heo weoren sunen
>   kinges
>   (II. 90. 3-6).
>   (p. 21)

In the various battles described by Layamon we find the same sort of detail as in the Anglo-Saxon poets: the mad rush of the opposing forces, the clash of sword with sword, the ringing of sword and spear against shield and helmet, the splintering of lances, the thunder of horses' hoofs, which shakes the earth and makes the welkin ring, the blare of trumpets, the hail of arrows, the fall of doomed men, the cries of agony and of triumph. The grey wolf howling over the stricken field, and the eagles and ravens eager for their prey, which play so large a part in the battle scenes of the older poets, are absent from Layamon. On the other hand, we have here streets and streams running with blood, which, I think, do not figure in Anglo-Saxon battle poetry. (p. 22)

After one battle we are told how "gilded shields lay scattered about the fields." (III. 62. 19-20). In another, after the usual hewing of lofty helmets, clashing of shields and splitting of burnies—"warriors fell, saddles were emptied. There was a cry among the host, the earth resounded, the brooks ran red with blood; men fell, their faces grown pale in death. Thus they fought (literally 'dealt') the whole day long, right up to the evening" (III. 220. 19-221. 8.) So it goes on, in fight after fight, generally with some new touch in each. But the above are representative of the type. (pp. 22-3)

[The manners and customs of the halls of . . . princes as exhibited by Layamon] bear a striking resemblance to those depicted in Beowulf. There can, I think, be little doubt that the ancient habits survived in the castles of the great, and that Layamon, although he may trick out his descriptions with literary graces derived from our oldest poetry, has yet given a first-hand picture of manners as he actually saw them in the early times of English chivalry. (p. 23)

Wace's references to the founding of the Round Table, which he specifically calls both *Roonde Table* and *Table Roonde,* and to the members of the Order, are much briefer than those of Layamon. Madden regards the passage in II. 531-542, which deals with the events immediately leading up to the foundation of the Order, with the making of the actual Table itself, and incorporates the remarks . . . concerning the legends that had grown up concerning the Table, and about Arthur and his knights, as perhaps one of the most remarkable and curious instances which occur of the additional matter engrafted by Layamon on the text of Wace.. . . . It is worth nothing that Layamon never uses the French name by which the Table was afterwards known, and which he might well have taken from Wace, but contents himself with the homely English *bord.* . . .

The more we read the **Brut,** the more are we impressed by the versatility of the author. Layamon is gifted with an inexhaustible flow of poetical language; he has a powerful and beautiful imagination, a tender and graceful fancy, a never-failing vigour and gusto, a wide sympathy with, and enjoyment of, every phase of life and action. He never fails to interest the reader, whether his theme be drawn from his rich stores of legendary lore, from his own observation of nature, or whether it be a battle or a banquet.

Layamon is essentially an English poet. He is strongly moved by the old romantic stories of his native land. He loves her mountains and moors, her woods, her streams; he is in intimate touch with the wild life that stirs within them. He enters as keenly as any of his countrymen into the excitement of the chase; he loves horses, hawks, and hounds. He knows how to invest his descriptions of battles and pageants, of ceremonies and feasts and minstrelsy, with the glow and splendour of chivalry, and the glamour of romance. The colours seem as fresh to-day as when the pictures were painted. When the poet chooses to exhibit the feelings and emotions of his characters in relation to the situation in which they find themselves, he does it simply, naturally, and with a noble dignity and restraint, witness the scene where Cordelia hears of her father's sorrows, and his arrival in France, or the reconciliation of Brennus and Belyn, or the passage where Arthur learns that he is the son of Uther Pendragon:

> For dead is Uther Pendragon, and thou art Arthur his son. Dead also is that other, Aurelien, his brother. Thus they told him the news, and Arthur sat silent. For a while he grew pale, and weak in all his body; for a while he was flushed, and sorrowed much in his heart. At last his thoughts broke from him—it was well that he spoke.
>
> (II. 411. 1-11)

We have in the **Brut** an intensely vivid world of external nature, of human action, and of human joys and griefs; we find an untiring interest in the earthly life and affairs of men. Of strong religious and devotional feeling, or of solicitude concerning the future state of man, and his relation to eternity, I find small trace in this poem. Such a spirit, or attitude of mind, is not perceptible even as a background of the poet's thought. But if there is no expression of specific religious belief, and no avowedly moral intention, the whole atmosphere of the poem is lofty, chivalrous, and noble. Nor do we ever doubt that the writer is a man of a high and generous nature, with a true reverence for whatsoever things are lovely and of good report, and rich in every human quality which goes to make a man and a poet. (pp. 28-30)

> *Henry Cecil Wyld, "Layamon as an English Poet," in* The Review of English Studies, *Vol. VI, No. 21, January, 1930, pp. 1-30.*

Jorge Luis Borges   (essay date 1952)

[*An Argentine short story writer, poet, and essayist, Borges was one of the leading figures in contemporary literature. In his literary criticism, Borges is noted for his insight into the manner in which an author both represents and creates a reality with words, and the way in which those words are variously interpreted by readers. With his fiction and poetry, Borges's critical writing shares the perspective that literary creation of imaginary worlds and philosophical speculation about the world itself are parallel or identical activities. In the following excerpt*

from an essay written in 1952, Borges maintains that Layamon is a poignant figure "who was the last Saxon poet and never knew it."]

[Emile] Legouis has seen the paradox of Layamon but not, I believe, his pathos. The introduction to the **Brut,** written in the third person at the beginning of the thirteenth century, contains the facts of his life. Layamon wrote:

> There was in the land a priest named Layamon; he was the son of Leovenath (may God have mercy on his soul!), and he lived in Ernley in a noble church on the banks of the Severn, a good place to be. He hit upon the idea of relating the exploits of the Englishmen, what they were named and where they came from and which ones arrived on English soil after the flood. Layamon traveled throughout the land and acquired the noble books that were his models. He took the English book made by St. Bede; he took another in Latin made by St. Albin and St. Augustine, who brought us the faith; he took a third and placed it in the middle, the work of a French cleric named Wace, who knew how to write well, and gave it to the noble Leonor, queen of the great Henry. Layamon opened those three books and turned the pages; he looked at them lovingly—may God have mercy on him!—and picked up the pen and wrote on parchment and summoned the right words and made the three books into one. Now Layamon, for the love of God Omnipotent, begs those who read this book and learn the truths it teaches to pray for the soul of his father, who begot him, and for the soul of his mother, who bore him, and for his own soul, to make it better. Amen.

Thirty thousand irregular verses proceed to recount the battles of the Britons and especially of Arthur against the Picts, the Norse, and the Saxons.

The first impression, and perhaps the last, given by Layamon's introduction is of infinite, almost incredible, simplicity. The childish habit of saying *Layamon* and not *I* enhances that impression, but behind the candid words the emotion is complex. Layamon is touched not only by the subject matter of the songs, but also by the somewhat magical circumstance of seeing himself singing them; this reciprocity corresponds to the "Illo Virgilium me tempore" of the *Georgics* or to the beautiful "Ego ille qui quondam" that someone prefaced to the *Aeneid*.

A legend picked up by Dionysius of Halicarnassus and adopted famously by Virgil states that Rome was founded by men of the race of Aeneas, the Trojan who battles Achilles on the pages of the *Iliad*. Similarly a *Historia Regum Britanniæ* dating from the beginning of the twelfth century attributes the founding of London ("citie that some tyme cleped was New Troy") to a great-grandson of Aeneas called Brutus, whose name would be perpetuated in Britannia. Brutus is the first king in the secular chronicle of Layamon; he is followed by others, who have known a very diverse fortune in literature: Hudibras, Lear, Gorboduc, Ferrex and Porrex, Lud, Cymbeline, Vortigern, Uther Pendragon (Uther Dragon's Head), and Arthur of the Round Table, "the king who was and will be," as his mysterious epitaph says. Arthur is mortally wounded in his last battle; but Merlin, who in the *Brut* is not the son of the Devil but the son of a silent phantom of gold loved by his mother in dreams, prophesies that he will return (like Barbarossa) when his people need him. The restless hordes, the "pagan dogs" of Hengest (the Saxons who were scattered over the face of England from the fifth century onward) wage war against him in vain.

It has been said that Layamon was the first of the English poets; it is more correct and more poignant to think of him as the last of the Saxon poets. The latter, converted to the faith of Jesus, applied the harsh accent and the military images of the Germanie epics to that new mythology (in one of the poems of Cynewulf, the Twelve Apostles resist the onrush of swords and are skilled in the manipulation of shields; in the Exodus, the Israelites who cross the Red Sea are Vikings); Layamon subjected the courtly and magical fictions of the *Matière de Bretagne* to that same rigor. Because of the subject, he is one of the many poets of the Breton Cycle, a distant colleague of that anonymous writer who revealed to Francesca da Rimini and to Paolo the love they felt for each other without knowing it. In spirit he is a lineal descendant of those Saxon rhapsodists who reserved their felicitous words for the description of battles and who did not produce a single amatory stanza in four centuries. Layamon has forgotten the metaphors of his ancestors; in the *Brut,* the sea is not the whale's path, nor are the arrows vipers of war, but the vision of the world is the same. Like Stevenson, like Flaubert, like so many men of letters, the sedentary cleric takes pleasure in verbal violence; where Wace wrote, "On that day the Britons killed Passent and the Irish King," Layamon amplifies:

> And Uther the Good said these words: "Passent, here you will remain, for here comes Uther on his horse!" He hit him on his head and knocked him down and put his sword in his mouth (giving him a food that was new to him) and the point of the sword disappeared into the ground. Then Uther said: "Now it is well with you, Irishman; all England is yours. I deliver it into your hands so that you may stay here and live with us. Look, here it is; now you will have it forever."

In every line of Anglo-Saxon verse there are certain words, two in the first half and one in the second, that begin with the same consonant or with a vowel. Layamon tries to observe that old metrical law, but the coupled octosyllables of the *Geste des Bretons* by Wace—one of the three "noble books"—continually distract him with the new temptation to rhyme, and so after *brother* we have *other* and *night* after *light*. The Norman Conquest took place around the middle of the eleventh century. The *Brut* dates from the beginning of the thirteenth, but the vocabulary of the poem is almost purely Germanic; there are not fifty words of French origin in thirty thousand verses. Here is a passage that is scarcely a prefiguring of the English language and has notable affinities with the German:

> And seothe ich eumen wulle
> to mine kineriche
> and wunien mid Brutten
> mid muchelere wunne.

Those were Arthur's last words. Their meaning is: "And then I shall go to my kingdom and I shall dwell among Britons with great delight."

> The subjects of the earlier epics were the exploits of a hero or the loyalty that warriors owe to their captain; the real subject of the *Brut* is England.
>
> —*Jorge Luis Borges*

Layamon sang with fervor about the ancient battles of the Britons against the Saxon invaders, as if he were not a Saxon and as if Britons and Saxons had not been, since Hastings, conquered by the Normans. The fact is singular and permits several conjectures. Layamon, son of Leovenath (Leofnoth), lived not far from Wales, the bulwark of the Celts and the source (according to Gaston Paris) of the complex myth of Arthur; his mother could very well have been a Briton. This is a likely conjecture, but it cannot be verified, and it is perhaps not very significant; one could also suppose that the poet was the son and grandson of Saxons, but that intimately the *jus soli* was stronger than the *jus sanguinis.* . . . Another possibility is that Layamon, perhaps unwittingly, gave the Britons of the *Brut* the value of Saxons, and the Saxons the value of Normans. The enigmas, the *Bestiary,* and the curious runes of Cynewulf prove that such cryptographic or allegorical exercises were not alien to that ancient literature; but something tells me that this speculation is fantastic. If Layamon had thought that the conquerors of yesterday were the conquered of today, and the conquerors of today could be the conquered of tomorrow, I believe he would have utilized the simile of the Wheel of Fortune, which appears in the *De Consolatione;* or he would have had recourse to the prophetic books of the Bible, not to the intricate romance of Arthur.

The subjects of the earlier epics were the exploits of a hero or the loyalty that warriors owe to their captain; the real subject of the *Brut* is England. Layamon could not foresee that two centuries after his death his alliteration would be ridiculous ("I can not geste—rum, ram, ruf—by lettre," says a character in Chaucer) and his language, a rustic jargon. He could not suspect that his insults to the Saxons of Hengest were the last words in the Saxon language, destined to die and to be born again in the English language. According to the Germanist [W. P.] Ker, he scarcely knew the literature whose tradition he inherited; he knew nothing of the wanderings of Widsith among Persians and Hebrews nor of the combat of Beowulf in the bottom of the red marsh. He knew nothing of the great verses from which his own were to spring; perhaps he would not have understood them. His curious isolation, his solitude, make him, now, pathetic. *"No one knows who he is,"* said León Bloy. Of that intimate ignorance no symbol is better than this forgotten man, who abhorred his Saxon heritage with

Saxon vigor, and who was the last Saxon poet and never knew it. (pp. 158-62)

Jorge Luis Borges, "The Innocence of Laya- mon," in his Other Inquisitions: 1937-1952, *translated by Ruth L. C. Simms, University of Texas Press, 1964, pp. 158-62.*

Dorothy Everett   (essay date 1955)

[*Everett was an English educator and medieval scholar. In the following excerpt, she discusses the qualities of early alliterative verse present in Layamon's* Brut, *particularly noting its similarities to Old English heroic poetry.*]

A great deal of Middle English poetry, and some of the best of it, witnesses to the vitality of a poetic tradition which begins, for us, in the eighth century, but which, to judge from *Beowulf,* was even then well established. This tradition is rooted in the kind of blank verse usually known today as 'alliterative verse', the verse which the fourteenth-century poet of *Sir Gawain and the Green Knight* described as 'linked with true letters, as has long been the custom in the land'. To Middle English poets, however, the tradition meant more than the verse form. Even in Old English poetry it is clear that there existed a stock of alliterating words and phrases on which poets were accustomed to draw. There were, too, certain fixed habits of composition, intimately connected with the nature of the alliterative line; notably a cumulative method of description, the piling up of phrases, usually a half-line in length and often similar in construction, each of which makes its contribution to the total impression. When, therefore, the rhythm of alliterative verse beat in a poet's mind, it brought with it a manner to some extent predetermined and a store of words and phrases, some of them age-old and many not known outside alliterative verse.

There are other things too, less easy to define, which the tradition meant to the Middle English poet. The verse, largely perhaps through its special diction, seems to have carried with it memories of the subjects and scenes that had most interested its earlier users—some memory, however blurred, of the ancient heroic system centring in the Lord and his hall which is pictured in *Beowulf,* and a clearer memory of certain kinds of descriptions—of battles, of scenes of revelry in the hall, of voyages and storms at sea, of terrors natural and supernatural. Hence Middle English poets often write as if they had an inherited knowledge of how such things could be effectively presented.

The marks of this tradition appear in alliterative poetry of the whole of the Middle English period, though naturally one poet differs greatly from another in what he takes and what he leaves. (pp. 23-4)

The nature of Layamon's *Brut* (dating in all probability from the last years of the twelfth century) suggests that its author knew earlier verse which, in subject, had things in common with Old English heroic poems; and more certain evidence of the existence of such verse is provided by a few rough alliterative lines belonging to a version of the story of Wade which are included in a thirteenth-century Latin sermon. Some of the verse known to these twelfth- and thirteenth-century writers may have been composed near to their own time, but much of it could have been, and some of it must have been, Old English verse orally transmitted, sometimes over a long period of time, and more or less modernized in language and metre in the course of transmission—a process which would explain some of the characteristics of the verse and diction of Middle English alliterative poetry. (pp. 25-6)

A basic condition of all Old English verse is that the metrical stresses fall on the first or stem syllable of a word, and it is because this continues to be so in Middle English that the same alliterative phrases could survive as rhythmic units for centuries, in spite of the many metrical and linguistic changes that took place. (p. 27)

Early Middle English verse has one peculiarity of its own, which seems to have accompanied, and was perhaps caused by, the use of rhyme or assonance to link the half-lines. In many of the rhyming lines there is a more or less regular alternation of stressed and unstressed syllables, so that they sound like rough couplets, as in the following line from Layamon's *Brut:*

> Leófe fæder dúre swa bíde ich gódes áre,

or in

> Hire fáder héo wolde súge seóþ, wére him léf
>   wére him láþ.

Such lines can have alliteration or not, and the half-lines can have two, three, or four stresses, three being the most usual number. Their appearance in alliterative verse has been taken to mean that poets of this period found it hard to keep the rhythms of alliterative verse unaffected by that of Middle English couplet metres derived from French; but, since a similar tendency appears in the late Old English lines on Alfred and Godwin, it is likely that it was a natural development in 'popular' verse. In any case, the fact that fourteenth-century alliterative verse is free from it may suggest that, in the early period too, there was some verse that was more correct.

Obviously Middle English alliterative metre was essentially a poorer vehicle of expression than Old English 'classical' metre. Middle English poets found it harder to avoid monotony and to achieve subtle effects. In addition, in the early period, they were hampered by the uncertainty of rhythms resulting from the tendency just described.

Layamon's *Brut,* the most important alliterative poem of the early period, does not escape these dangers. Its rhythms are, for the most part, rough and insecure; and when they appear more settled, as occasionally in passages that are strongly reminiscent of Old English poetry, they are monotonous. The following passage has the merit of vigour, but if it is set beside comparable lines in Old English (for instance *The Fight at Finnsburuh,* 28-30), it is clear what the later form of verse has lost in variety and flexibility:

> Heven here-marken, halden to-gadere,
> Luken sweord longe, leiden o þe helmen,
> Fur ut sprengen. Speren brastlien,

Sceldes gonnen scanen, scaftes to-breken.

Yet, in spite of the deficiencies of his metre, Layamon can describe the passing of Arthur so that his readers are compelled to feel its mystery:

> Aefne þan worden, þer com of see wenden,
> Þat wes an sceort bat liðen, sceoven mid vðen;
> And twa wimmen þerinne, wunderliche idihte.
> And heo neomen Arður anan, and aneouste hine
>   uereden,
> And softe hine adun leiden, and forð gunnen heo
>   liðen.
> Þa wes hit iwurðen þat Merlin seide whilen,
> Þat weore unimete care of Arthures forð-fare.
> Bruttes ileueð yete þat he bon on live,
> And wunnien in Aualun mid fairest alre aluen.
> And lokieð euere Bruttes yete whan Arthur
>   cumen liðe.

Or, in a different vein, he can present Arthur as the ferocious warrior rushing upon his foes:

> Up bræid Arður his sceld foren to his breosten,
> And he gon to rusien swa þe rimie wulf
> Þenne he cumeð of holte, bihonged mid snawe,
> And þencheð to-biten swulc deor swa him likeð.
> Arður þa cleopede to leofe his cnihten,
> 'Forð we bilive, þeines ohte!
> Alle somed heom to! Alle we sculleð wel don!'
> And heo forð hælden, swa þe hæye wude
> Þenne wind wode weieð hine mid mæine.

Such passages will indicate that Layamon's poem has an interest of its own in addition to its historic interest as the first English work to tell the story of Arthur.

Layamon's subject, as he announces it at the beginning of his poem, is the history of the people 'who first possessed the land of the English'. It is, in fact, the history of the Britons as told by Geoffrey of Monmouth some time between 1130 and 1138 in his *Historia Regum Britanniae.* For the most part, however, Layamon was not directly indebted to Geoffrey, but to the Norman poet Wace who, some twenty years later, retold Geoffrey's history in verse in his *Roman de Brut,* completed in 1155. Layamon mentions Wace as one of his sources, adding a detail unknown elsewhere, that Wace gave his book 'to the noble Eleanor who was queen of Henry the mighty king (Henry II)'; but he also speaks of two other sources, 'the English book which Bede made' and another in Latin made by 'St. Albin and the fair Austin who brought baptism hither'. He is undoubtedly referring to the Old English and the Latin versions of Bede's *Ecclesiastical History;* but he does not appear to have made much use of these books, and the manner in which he refers to them suggests that he wished to lend the authority of great names to his own work rather than that he was familiar with the books he supposed they had written. The latest opinion is that, apart from some echoes of Geoffrey's Book vii (which contains the Prophecies of Merlin) almost everything in Layamon's story comes from Wace (as we know him), supplemented constantly by his own imagination. The views of earlier scholars, that he drew upon Welsh tradition, or that he knew an expanded, and now lost, version of Wace's *Brut,* have little to support them.

The history of the Britons, as related by Layamon, Wace, and Geoffrey, opens with a reference to the flight of Aeneas from Troy and a brief record of his descendants in Italy. So the high lineage of the British kings is established; for Brutus, the great-grandson of Aeneas, will be the founder of their dynasty and the Britons can claim a common Trojan ancestry with the Romans. Later in the history, the kinship of the two races is recognized by Julius Caesar, who says—in Layamon's words—'alle we comen of ane kunne'. We are told much of Brutus, of his exile after he had accidentally killed his father, and how, after many adventures, he came at last, by the advice of the goddess Diana, to the fair land of Albion which, when he had taken possession of it, he called Britain after his own name.

In the long story of Brutus's successors, some reigns are passed over rapidly, but matters of real significance in the history of the British race are treated at length. The more fully developed narratives are concerned with the conflict between Belinus (Belin) and his brother Brennius (Brenne), their reconciliation and their conquest of France and Rome; Caesar's invasion of Britain, the resistance of Cassibellanus and various later conflicts of the Romans and the Britons; the first coming of the Saxons under Hengest and Horsa; the life of Arthur. Even in Geoffrey, however, the tale of Lear and his three daughters seems to have been elaborated for its own sake, and a few more—the story of St. Ursula and her virgins, for instance—are developed by Wace or by Layamon simply because they are good stories or, in the case of St. Ursula, already famous.

Arthur is of first importance in all three versions. The story of his life is told in great detail—particularly his wars and conquests and his last fight against Modred. In addition, his reign is introduced by a very full account of his ill-fated family; of the treacherous killing of the monk-king Constans (Constance), the vengeance taken by his brothers Aurelius and Uther, the reign of Aurelius and his death by poison, the succession of Uther, his love for Ygerna (Ygerne), wife of Gorlois, Duke of Cornwall, the begetting of Arthur, and finally Uther's death, again treacherously contrived. Throughout this section one is aware of the mysterious figure of Merlin, mostly retired and unseen, but emerging at critical moments to give help by advice, by practising strange arts and by his knowledge of the future. More than once he prophesies the coming of Arthur. If, as has been recently argued, Geoffrey is careful not to describe Merlin as a magician, there seems little doubt that Wace and Layamon believed him to be one.

The history of the Britons does not end with Arthur, but continues, on a less exciting level, till the time of Cadwallader, when the Britons had become worn out with incessant war and with famine. Cadwallader, warned by God that the Britons shall no longer reign in Britain, went to Rome and died there (689). The Saxon Athelstan then ruled all England, and the Britons—in Layamon's words—came to Wales and lived 'dispersed among the rocks and cliffs, the churches and monasteries, the woods and mountains', henceforth to be called, not Britons, but Welsh.

This is a long story as Geoffrey tells it; it becomes longer in Wace, and much longer still in Layamon. Each successive writer, besides expanding the statements in his original, also adds completely new matter—Layamon much more often than Wace. Some of the most interesting additions are concerned with Arthur. Wace is the first writer ever to speak of the Round Table; Layamon alone tells how the fairies took Arthur at his birth and bestowed many gifts upon him and how in the end they carried him to Avalon to their queen Argante. But interesting as these additions are, they are less important when the two later versions are judged as poetry, than the transformation which the history undergoes with each retelling. Wace evidently wished to make the 'history' intelligible and attractive to sophisticated and more or less cultured readers by interpreting it in terms which they could appreciate. So, for instance, he begins his account of the qualities of Arthur with the statement,

> Chevaliers fu mult vertuus,
> Mult fu preisanz, mult glorius,

> ['He was a very valiant knight, full of honour
> and renown,']

and he proceeds to endow him with the virtues of a chivalric knight who surpassed all other princes in 'curteisie', 'noblesse', 'vertu', and 'largesce'. Wace makes the most of the first meeting between Uther and Ygerne, describing Uther sitting at the feast with his thoughts constantly upon her, looking sideways at her, smiling, making 'signs of love', while Ygerne behaves in a manner neither encouraging nor disdainful—a scene likely to interest those who, a very little later, were to be delighted by the love-romances of Chrétien de Troyes. Wace took pains, too, to write in a style calculated to please his readers, a style . . . marked by a discriminating use of simple rhetorical devices, notably some forms of verbal repetition. His verse is smooth and careful and he uses the literary French of his day, which would have been familiar to the Norman court in England and in Paris.

Layamon was in many ways the antithesis of Wace. What he tells of himself at the beginning of his poem implies a man living a simple life, remote from the world which Wace knew. There was, he says, a priest called Layamon who lived

> at Ernleye, æt æðelen are chirechen,
> Vppen Seuarne staþe—sel þar him þuhte—
> Onfest Radestone, þer he bock radde.

> ['At a noble church at Areley, near Redstone,
> upon the banks of the Severn where he read the
> Bible—pleasant it seemed to him there.']

The suggestion of provincialism, rusticity almost, derived from Layamon's own statement seems to be confirmed by several facts. He writes in a dialect which is likely to have been that of the county he lived in, in a verse form peculiar to the conquered English. His diction includes words and phrases traditional in such verse and it is almost free from French words, a fact the more remarkable when it is remembered that he must have pored long over Wace's French. He shows no knowledge of French literature other than Wace's poem, though by his time some famous French Arthurian romances had been written. Yet he cannot have been completely provincial and inexperienced. He himself tells us that he had travelled widely through England to obtain books to help him with his poem; he succeeded in getting Wace's book, and, by some means or other, he learnt that Wace had given a copy of it to Queen Eleanor. If he had not read widely in French, he had at least, to judge by his understanding of Wace, a good knowledge of the language. There are even signs that he had some knowledge of the technique of poetic composition as understood by educated writers, or at least that he was capable of learning something about it from his study of Wace.

It is possible, therefore, that his verse form and diction are the result, not of inability to write otherwise, but of a conscious preference for what was traditional among the English. A clear statement of this cannot be found in his poem, but this is not surprising for the nature of his history did not allow him to express partiality for his own people. It does give him an opportunity to praise his country, and this he does in lines, which while agreeing with Wace's in their main substance, are fuller and more appreciative. Two of his additions to Wace are possibly significant. Immediately after he has recorded (following Wace) that Gurmund gave land to the English and for over a hundred years Christianity was not known there, he interpolates the story of Gregory and the English slaves ('Truly you are English, most like to angels; of all people who live on earth, your race is the fairest'); and on one occasion he goes out of his way to disparage the Normans who 'destroyed this people'. If it seems incongruous that he should have chosen to retell the history of the Britons, including their long struggle against the invading Saxons or English—Layamon sometimes uses the terms interchangeably—the lines which follow his remarks about the Normans provide a hint of the attraction it held for him. He is speaking of London and of the various names it has had under its various conquerors, and he remarks:

> Swa is al þis lond iuaren for uncuðe leoden
> Þeo þis londe habbeð biwunnen, and eft beoð
>   idriuen hennene;
> And eft hit biyetten oðeræ, þe uncuðe weoren.

> ['So has all this land fared because of foreigners
> who have conquered this land, and then are driven hence; and then others won it who were foreigners.']

This seems to show that the Saxon conquest of Britain interested him as a parallel to the Norman conquest of which he and his countrymen were still conscious. However, the most compelling reason for his interest in British history was in all probability that it made abundantly clear that his country, whatever its misfortunes, had had a long and often glorious past.

Certain it is that, whether by deliberate choice or not, Layamon converted the French *Brut* into a poem that is astonishingly English—English, that is, in the sense that its conceptions and its manner constantly reflect the earlier poetry of England. The passage corresponding to Wace's description of Arthur is significant. Of the qualities which Wace attributes to him, Layamon mentions only his bravery and his liberality. He evidently felt that the best indication of Arthur's greatness was the wealth and standing of his household, for he tells us that each of his cup-bearers, and his chamberlains ('bur-þæinen') and his porters had gold for their backs and their beds; he then adds 'He had never a cook who was not a very good warrior, nor ever a knight's servant who was not a bold thane'. These lines, for which there is no hint in Wace, convert Arthur into the kind of lord (*hlaford*) described in *Beowulf*, whose household consists of thanes of noble birth, his equals in rank.

What Layamon tells us of the doings of kings and their warriors also reminds us of the earlier poetry. Warriors vow to do great deeds in battle and are bound by their vaunts. Frollo has to face Arthur in single combat because 'he had made his vaunt [his *beot*, the same word as in Old English] before his whole host'. A brief reference in Wace to a banquet is developed into the lines:

> He wende into halle and his haleðes mid him
> alle.
> Bemen heo bleowen, gomen men gunnen cleo-
> pien.
> Bord heo hetten breden, cnihtes setten þerto;
> Heo æten, heo drunken; dræm wes i buryhen.

> ['He went into the hall and all his warriors with him. Trumpets were blown, merriment proclaimed. They ordered tables to be set up. Knights sat at them; they ate and drank. There was revelry in the castle.']

Layamon's description of the arming of Arthur is of special interest because, while his list of arms agrees fairly closely with Wace's and he even includes some of the same details about them, yet his conception of them is markedly different:

> Þa dude he on his burne ibroide of stele,
> Þe makede on aluisc smið mid aðelen his crafte;
> He wes ihaten Wygar, þe Witeye wurhte . . .
> Calibeorne his sweord he sweinde bi his side,
> Hit wes iworht in Aualun mið wiyelefulle craf-
> ten.
> Halm he set on hafde, hæh of stele;
> Þeron wes moni yimston, al mid golde bigon;
> He wes Vðeres, þas æðelen kinges,
> He wes ihaten Goswhit, ælchen oðere vnilic.

> ['Then he put on his mail-coat of linked steel, which a fairy smith had made with excellent skill; it was called Wygar, and Witeye made it. He hung by his side his sword Excalibur; it was made in Avalon by magical arts. A high helmet of steel he placed on his head, on which was many a precious stone, all encompassed with gold. It had been Uther's, the noble king's. It was called Goosewhite, and was unlike any other.']

This calls to mind, not Wace's matter-of-fact descriptions, nor any of those in French and English romances, but rather the arming of Beowulf ('the war-corslet linked by hand, . . . the gleaming helmet encircled by lordly chains, as a weapon-smith had made it in olden times'). It calls to mind, too, other allusions to weapons in Old English poetry; in particular, the fairy smith Witeye recalls We-

land, the cunning smith of heroic legend, and justly so, if Witeye is the Old English Widia, son of Weland.

Some echoes of Old English poetry appear in unlikely places, as when Loch Lomond is set in the fen-land (like Grendel's mere) and has nickers bathing in it! In descriptions of sea-journeys and battles, as might be expected, these echoes are constant and all-pervasive. But it is Layamon's battle-descriptions that show most clearly the hold the older poetry had over him. He does not attempt to individualize a battle by describing the disposition and movement of armies. Instead, he gives himself over to the memories of battles he knows in poetry, and, by means of the old methods and phrases, he creates an impression of battle—its noise, confusion, and excitement—as in the lines from Arthur's last fight. He has, it is true, a nearer precedent for his cumulative method of description in Wace, for he too piles up numbers of parallel phrases, but the almost completely different details which the two poets select for mention (for instance, in their accounts of the battle of Julius Caesar against Cassibelaunus) make it clear that it is not Wace that Layamon is thinking of. Layamon's descriptions are not to be despised. They are more stirring than many carefully worked out accounts, and though the objection that all his battles are alike is unanswerable, it is rather the number of them that gives rise to it than his method.

These memories of 'far-off things, And battles long ago' are inextricably bound up with the verse and the old words and phrases through which he learnt of them. But it should not be thought that the words meant to him just what they did in Old English heroic poetry. In *Beowulf* such words as *hæleþ* ['warrior'] and *duyuþ* have reference to a particular kind of society; but *duyuþ*, which in certain passages in *Beowulf* meant 'a body of tried retainers', 'comitatus', is mostly used by Layamon in the vaguer sense of 'body of men, host of warriors'. And so it is with many other of the old words; something of their meaning has gone and they have become less pregnant, more generalized. It cannot be assumed, either, that Layamon made the same connexions as we do, if we know heroic poetry. When, for instance, he applies the term 'Godes wiðersaka' ['Adversary of God'] to the giant Geomagog, he need not intend to connect him with Grendel, descendant of the evil brood of Cain, of whom the same term is used. For, however much he may remind us of Old English heroic poetry, it is most unlikely that he knew what we know. Nowhere are the similarities between Old English poetry and his poem like those between a model and something directly imitated from it. The relationship is always much less clear-cut. Even when he is most reminiscent, Layamon gives an impression of only half-recalling what he reminds us of—an impression similar to that made by the dimmed meaning of the old words he uses, and explicable in both cases if the old conceptions and words reached him not as the result of reading, but of continued oral transmission. Since, as has been shown, Layamon's verse-form is related not to 'classical' Old English verse, but to the 'popular' type, it is reasonable to suppose that it was from 'popular' verse, orally handed down, that he got his reminiscences of early heroic poetry. Presumably Layamon acquired his loose, repetitive, easy-flowing style from the same source;

but all that can be said is that it seems to have some relation to that of the 'popular' verses in the *Anglo-Saxon Chronicle* and to that of Middle English writings in the verse-form related to the 'popular' type, especially the *Departing Soul's Address* and the *Proverbs of Alfred*. On the one hand devices characteristic of 'classical' Old English verse (litotes and 'kennings', for instance) are lacking or rare in all these writings, and their style is altogether less close-packed, owing in part to a more sparing use of compound words. On the other hand, the Middle English writings have in common certain forms of repetition, in particular the repetition of formulas, and some of the same expressions appear in two or more of them. The early, non-alliterative romance *King Horn* also has these characteristics. Some of the resemblances have been thought to point to direct borrowing, by the **Brut** from the *Proverbs,* for instance, and by *King Horn* from the **Brut;** but this would not be inconsistent with the view that these early Middle English writings had behind them a common style deriving from oral poetry.

This assumption would explain what may be called Layamon's basic style; but some of his best effects depend either on similes which have no parallel in any surviving Old or early Middle English verse, or on what appear to be original uses of the repeated formula.

Layamon's repeated formulas (often referred to as 'epic formulas') are the most conspicuous feature of the style of his poem. Layamon must have known this device in the verse with which he was familiar, for he often used it as others did, but he also developed it for his own purposes. Of the many simple formulas which recur, some frequently, throughout the whole poem, a number can be paralleled in late Old English or early Middle English. Such are the many 'fill-ups', used to complete a line ('widen and siden', 'nu and æver mare'), statements making a transition in the narrative ('þe king hine biþohte wat he don mahte'); descriptive phrases like 'æðelest alre kingen', 'Bruttene deorling'. Also to be included here are phrases which seem to be attached to certain circumstances or events, like 'feollen þæ fæie' ['The doomed men fell'], so common in battle-descriptions, or 'wind stod at wille' ['The wind blew as they desired'] often included in an account of a voyage; and also formulas which have the effect of summarizing an action, like 'balu wes on folke' ['Woe came upon the people'] frequently used as a comment on defeat in battle. Parallels to some of these can be found in *King Horn* where the couplet (or slight variations of it) 'þe se began to flowe ['The tide began to flow in.'] And Horn Child to rowe' occurs several times in describing a voyage; and in the Worcester *Departing Soul's Address* where there is a refrain-like repetition of the summarizing line, 'Al is reowliche þin siþ efter þin wrecche lif ['All pitiful is thy departure after thy wretched life']. Here, however, it has a more important function than Layamon's summarizing formulas, since it emphasizes a main idea of the poem.

So far Layamon's repetition of formulas seems to be merely a conventional trick, and it is often a tiresome one to modern readers. But when some one formula is confined to a particular story or episode, for which it has been spe-

cially selected, it can be effective: and it is in these instances that Layamon seems to be most original.

The stories of Vortiger and of Leir and his daughters provide examples of the effective use of formulas. In the long account of Vortiger's treachery and ultimate downfall, recurring descriptive phrases act like a ground-bass, drumming home the craftiness and guile of the man. At the first mention of his name, before we know anything about him, Layamon remarks 'yæp mon and swiðe war' ['A crafty man and most wary'], and he repeats this, with variations, several times while he tells how Vortiger succeeded in getting the monk Constans made king. Once Constans has been crowned, Vortiger plots against him and contrives that he shall be slain by a company of Pictish knights, whom he then openly accuses of murder so that the Britons are roused and kill them. Throughout these doings the recurrent phrase is 'þe swike wes ful derne' ['Who was a most secret traitor']. But already, before this, Layamon has slipped in the phrase 'of ufele he wes wel iwar' ['He was well practised in evil'] which, with variations, is to be used of Vortiger almost to the end of his story. Its use even when Vortiger is himself being deceived by Hengest may seem careless and meaningless, but it could be intended as an ironical reminder, as if Layamon repeatedly said 'remember, thus is the Vortiger who betrayed Constans'. At any rate, Layamon was well aware what he was doing at the end of this episode, for, just as Hengest's treachery is about to be fully revealed, he suddenly changes the formula, while keeping an echo of its earlier form and exclaims, 'Her he wes to unwar!' ['Here he was too unwary'].

In the story of Leir and his daughters, formulas serve a slightly different purpose—that of linking various parts of the narrative. It is one which lends itself naturally to this kind of treatment and there are several verbal echoes between the different parts of it, both of phrases and of keywords. In the first part Layamon drives home the falseness of Gornoille and Regan, and Leir's folly in trusting them, by reiterating the word *Lesinge,* 'lie'. Leir 'believed his daughter's [Gornoille's] lie'; 'all her [Regan's] lie her father believed': 'Cordoille heard the lies which her sisters spoke to the king' and she swore that she would speak 'soþ' to her father. This last statement is caught up again towards the end of the tale when Leir laments, 'Soþ seide Cordoille, for cuð hit is me nouþe' ['Cordoille spoke truth; now I know it'], and again, 'truth the young woman spoke', 'but my daughter spoke the truth . . . and both her two sisters told me lies'. There is a hint for these later repetitions in Wace, though Wace does not, like Layamon, use repetition to link the earlier and later scenes. The formula which provides the most effective link in Layamon's story has no parallel in Wace. It is first used when the husbands of Gornoille and Regan decide that they will take over the rule of the country and that Leir, while he lives, shall be supported by them

> Dæies and nihtes, mid feowerti hired cnihtes;
> And heo him wolden finden haukes and hundes
> Þat he mihte riden yeond alle þanne þeoden

> ['By day and by night, with forty men of his household, and they would provide for him

hawks and hounds so that he could ride all over
the country.']

Just after this we are told that he went to Scotland and was
received by Gornoille and her husband 'mid feowerti hired
cnihtes, mid horsen and mid hundes'. Gornoille's complaint to her husband soon follows:

> He halt here fauwerti cnihtes, daies and nihtes;
> He haveþ her þas þeines and alle heore swaines,
> Hundes and havekes.
>
> ['He maintains here forty knights, day and night;
> he has these thegns here, and all their serving-
> men, hounds and hawks.']

Much later in the story comes the last echo. Cordoille,
having been told of Leir's plight by his servant, bids him
go back to her father and provide for him richly. He is to
buy for him fine clothes and 'hundes and havekes and
durewurðe ['valuable'] horses' and is to maintain in his
house 'feowerti hired cnihtes'.

In the stories of Vortiger and of Leir Layamon uses his repeated phrases organically, in the one instance to ensure
some continuity of impression throughout a very long narrative, in the other to bring out similarities and contrasts
between various parts of the story and so to make the reader conscious of its essential movements. This would seem
to indicate some sort of artistic awareness; and there are
similar indications in Layamon's use of his most striking
similes. While brief simple similes occur throughout the
poem, the longer and more impressive ones are all concentrated in one part of it—the account of Arthur's wars
against Colgrim, Baldulf, and Childrich. The earlier part
of this account contains the long exultant speech in which
Arthur compares Childrich to the fox who climbs seeking
the rocks in the wild places, making holes for himself,
carefree, because he believes himself the boldest of all animals. 'But then men below the hills come towards him
with horns and hounds, with loud cries. . . . They drive
the fox over hill and dale. He flees to the cliff and seeks
his hole. . . . Men on every side dig towards him. There
the proudest of all animals is then most wretched. So was
it with Childrich, the strong and mighty.' In the later stage
of the war, when Childrich and his men are forced to flee
across the river Avon with Arthur in pursuit, we are told
that so many Saxons lie dead in the river that 'al wes
Auene stram mid stele ibrugged' ['The whole river Avon
was bridged with steel']. Childrich, Colgrim, and Baldulf
climb to the hill above Bath and Arthur again exults: 'Yesterday was Colgrim the bravest of all men; now is he like
the goat' who 'high on the hill fights with his horns when
the fierce wolf approaches him.' He then taunts Baldulf
and Childrich in similar fashion, each speech echoing the
beginning of the first: 'Yesterday was Baldulf . . . ', 'Yesterday was Childrich . . . ', and each elaborated by a
comparison. The one addressed to Baldulf is the most remarkable:

> Yursterdæi wes Baldulf cnihten alre baldest;
> Nu he stant on hulle, and Auene bihaldeð,
> Hu ligeð i þan stræme stelene fisces
> Mid sweorde bigeorede. Heore sund is awem-
>   med,
> Heore scalen wleoteð swulc gold-faye sceldes;

Þer fleoteð heore spiten, swulc hit spæren
   weoren.

['Yesterday was Baldulf the boldest of all
knights. Now he stands on the hill and looks
upon Avon—how steel fishes lie in the river, girt
with swords. Their swimming is impaired. Their
scales gleam like gold-decked shields. There
float their fins as if they were spears.']

The effectiveness of this image depends on the reversal of
the normal order of its terms which has the effect of slow-
ing down the comprehension of it. We see with Baldulf the
river filled with gleaming fish, and only gradually comes
the recognition that these fish are dead warriors.

Layamon's account of the wars against Childrich and his
allies, in which these speeches occur, is one of the most
original passages in his poem. It has a wealth of incident
and detail much of which is not even hinted at in Wace's
much shorter and more sober version. In Layamon's
imagination the whole action evidently became momentous and exciting, and the concentration in this story of
elaborate similes, together with the use of such formal devices as the parallelism of Arthur's taunting speeches, are
signs that he felt a heightened style to be appropriate to
it.

To judge from this account, and from his best uses of the
repeated formula, Layamon had some notion of suiting his
style to his matter and of using stylistic devices for his own
ends: that is to say, he possessed some degree of artistic
consciousness, and, perhaps, even some knowledge of the
art of poetry as it was understood in his own time and set
out in manuals of instruction. This second suggestion runs
counter to the usual view of Layamon, and it cannot be
held to be proven by these examples alone. It is possible
that more light might be thrown on his knowledge by a
thorough study of his various kinds of repetition, both of
formulas and of important words; but it would be necessary to take into account not only what he may have found
in native poetry, but also how far he was influenced by
Wace, with whom repetition of some kinds is a favourite
device, and from whose practice he certainly learnt more
than has been recognized.

Yet, whatever Layamon may have known of the art of poetry, and whatever skill he may display in some parts of
his work, artistry is not pre-eminent among his qualities.
He is too lacking in restraint and discretion. The very devices which he can use well, he will at times use carelessly,
even to the point of spoiling his own good effects, as when
he says of Hengest, 'Hengest was of ufele war', which,
though true, is disturbing when the reader has come to feel
that this kind of phrase belongs particularly to Vortiger.

His great gift is for imagining scenes of action. Arthur's
wars against Childrich provide plenty of examples of his
power of imagining warlike scenes, but he can also create
others quite different from these, and by different means.
At the climax of Arthur's story, when he has defeated the
Emperor of Rome, Layamon prepares for the coming
change in Arthur's fortunes by narrating some events
which are not in Wace. He describes the arrival of a knight
from Brittany with news of Modred. Arthur talks to him
for a long time but the young knight will not tell the truth

about Modred. Next morning Arthur relates a dream which he takes to be a warning of evil, and he ends the recital with the lament 'I know surely that all my joy has gone, and for as long as I live I must endure sorrow. Alas, that I have not here Wenhaver, my queen.' At last the knight tells Arthur of Modred's treachery and then Layamon brings the scene before us, conveying in a few simple statements, more or less parallel in form, the effect of the news on Arthur's court:

> Þa sæt hit al stille in Arðures halle.
> Þa wes þer særinæsse mid sele þan kinge.
> Þa weoren Bruttisce men swiðe vnbalde vor þæn.
> Þa umbe stunde stefne þer sturede;
> Wide me mihte iheren Brutten iberen;
> And gunnen to tellen a feole cunne spellen
> Hu heo wolden fordeme Modred and þa quene.

['Then all was still in Arthur's hall. Then there was sorrow for the good king. Then were the Britons exceedingly downcast thereby. Then after a while voices stirred there; on all sides could be heard the cries of the Britons and in many different speeches they told how they would destroy Modred and the queen.']

Layamon's sensitiveness to the emotional quality of a scene appears particularly in moments of tension or suspense. There is an example in his version of the legend of St. Ursula. At first he follows Wace, describing the departure from the Thames of Ursula and the great company of virgins, and the terrible storm that came upon their ships and wrecked many of them; but at this point he introduces a scene that is not in Wace, though he mentions the persons concerned in it—Wanis and Melga. Layamon tells us that these men, who were outlaws, had come out from Norway and, knowing the signs of the weather, had laid up in an island:

> And swa heo leien i þan æit-londe, and iseyen þat weder stronge.
> Iseyen scipen an and an, while ma, while nan,
> Þeonne feowere, þenne fiue; sellic heom þuhten a þissen liue
> Whæt weoren þa yemere scipen þa yeond þa sæ weolken.

['And so they lay up in that island and watched the fierce storm. They saw ships one by one, at times more, at times none, then four, then five; it seemed to them a marvel what the wretched ships might be that tossed on the sea.']

There is a feeling of suspense here, even if one does not know that Ursula is to fall into the hands of these ruthless men. What is more notable, however, is that by a simple scene, apparently of his own invention, Layamon brings home the utter helplessness and abandonment of the women, which is to him the essence of their pitiful story. It is this instinct for the essential quality or significance of a story, or of an episode or description, and the power to make the reader feel it, that gives Layamon a claim to be regarded as a poet, in spite of the obvious defects of his work. These are not limited to its rough metre and a style that is often slack and careless. The work suffers, too, from the disadvantages of the chronicle form which Layamon

received from his predecessors. These might have been less apparent if Layamon had been able to make Arthur, the most important figure in his history, more human and credible. But he cannot present a complete personality, nor even a complete epic hero. He can, on separate occasions, show Arthur being fearless, impetuous, self-willed, often savagely ferocious, once or twice merciful to women in distress; but these traits appear singly, each in connexion with some one action, and they remain the materials for a character, rather than part of one.

This incapacity of Layamon's is to some extent obscured by his ability to make the reader feel the emotions of his people, as he does with Cordoille, in the story of Leir. He does this largely, though not entirely, by describing their physical manifestations. Cordoille sits very still after she has made her reply to her father, and when he has given his judgement she goes to her room and is 'shamefast' ('mortified'); she is silent and turns red when, at the end of the story, Leir's man comes to ask for her help. But her emotions arise naturally from her situation; they are not peculiar to her as an individual. Layamon's awareness of them is part of his power of rising to a situation, particularly to a moment of tension.

Since his history contains many kinds of stories and situations, this power of his means that his poem does not lack variety of interest. As occasion offers he can present the mystery of the supernatural; in the story of Arthur's birth, for example, and of his passing and in some passages about Merlin. In his accounts of war he shows heroic and violent action and bloodthirsty sentiments; his theme is suffering and pity in such stories as those of St. Ursula and of Leir. Like most of the Old English poets, however, he is not interested in romantic love; here he even tones down what little Wace has to offer.

Layamon's **Brut,** the most considerable and by far the best of the early Middle English alliterative poems, was written in the west of England, in Worcestershire, and this is pre-

---

Wilson on Layamon's *Brut*:

There can be little doubt that the **Brut** is one of the most significant of Middle English poems. In spirit, in vocabulary and in metre it is a continuation of the Old English alliterative tradition. The more specifically English characteristics have been emphasized, . . . but Layamon has also been influenced, though to a lesser extent, by the contemporary French romance. The fact that he writes a history in verse instead of prose is due to the influence of his French source, and many of his characters, despite their links with the old Germanic heroes, are beginning to show the influence of the French romances of chivalry. At first sight the length of the poem is discouraging and naturally enough the excellence of the best parts is not uniform. Nevertheless the variety of interest, the vigour and the poetic imagination which we find in the great scenes make it one of the best of the Middle English poems.

R. M. Wilson in his *Early Middle English Literature, Methuen & Co. Ltd., 1939.*

cisely where the native alliterative verse might be expected to flourish most vigorously and to survive longest. (pp. 27-45)

Dorothy Everett, "Layamon and the Earliest Middle English Alliterative Verse," in her Essays on Middle English Literature, *edited by Patricia Kean, Oxford at the Clarendon Press, 1955, pp. 27-45.*

Walter F. Schirmer   (essay date 1957)

[*In the essay below, Schirmer compares Layamon's* Brut *with the histories of Geoffrey and Wace and contends that because Layamon "tried to build up an heroic epic reminding us of Anglo-Saxon poetry and intended to constitute a national epic," his work is different from those of his predecessors.*]

Layamon's **Brut,** according to J. E. Wells 'the most prominent of the English Chronicles', is a free and amplified 'translation' of Wace's *Romanz de Brut* or *Geste des Bretons* which, in its turn, is a 'French verse-'translation' of Geoffrey of Monmouth's *Historia Regum Britanniae.* Thus the same material is treated in three works belonging to different literary categories, each of which has to be considered in comparison with the other two in order to point out its peculiar quality.

Geoffrey's *Historia* is a Latin prose chronicle, written about 1136 and dealing with the supposed history of Britain from the fall of Troy to the death of Cadwallader in 689. It caused a great stir as it contained a detailed account of an almost unknown period. Though Geoffrey was severely criticized by later historians because he 'contra fidem historicae veritatis deliravit,' as William of Newburgh put it, most chroniclers accepted his narration more or less as a recital of facts, and the legend of the English national hero Arthur took firm root in the minds of the people. Geoffrey could not foresee the historical influence of his book and the immense Arthurian literature following in its wake, but—as I have tried to prove elsewhere (in a paper read at the International Conference of University Professors of English, Cambridge, August 1956)—he knew exactly what he was setting out to do. In a critical political situation, viz. the threat of civil war after the death of Henry I, he wanted to strengthen the *Reichsidee* of the Norman empire by an appeal for unity; the heroic history of the ideal Kingdom of Arthur and its downfall was meant to be a lesson and a warning. Accordingly the *Historia regum Britanniae* is a political tract intended for that time, in the guise of an historical work, just as Livy's *Libri ab urbe condita* are historical work with a political message.

The success of Geoffrey's book, although it was due to its contents, was helped by the literary skill of the writer. The *Historia* has an almost epic structure; more than half of it is devoted to the Arthurian story and Geoffrey is gradually building up to this climax from the very beginning, see the oracle given to Brutus:

Hic de prole tua reges nascentur: et ipsis
Totius terrae subditus orbis erit. (I, 11)

This prophecy is fulfilled by the conquests of Arthur and the apex of his career in the Whitsuntide or coronation festival at Caerleon. Then, dramatically, the Roman challenge interrupts everything, and, after hope has been renewed by Arthur's victorious campaign in Gaul, comes the catastrophe: Modred's treason and Arthur's death. Then the story dies away in resignation with the report of the unfortunate followers of the hero-king. This structure is very different from the continuous annalistic account of the contemporary Anglo-Latin chroniclers. Of course, Geoffrey has to adapt himself to that method, too, as he proposes to write a 'historia', but even there, as E. Faral points out (in *La Légende Arthurienne,* Paris, 1929) and that is why he calls Geoffrey's work an 'épopée nationale', there is a well-balanced succession of lists of Kings and detailed accounts of persons or events. Thus the story of Brutus and Locrinus is followed by a long list of kings, then comes the story of Leir and his daughters, whereupon there follows again a list of kings, then the story of Belinus and Brennius is given in detail and so on throughout the book. Halfway, as J. S. P. Tatlock remarks (in *The Legendary History of Britain,* Berkeley, 1950), in the prophecies of Merlin, the narration pauses, allowing a retrospective and prospective view similar to the *Aeneid* where there is also in the middle a prophetic vision of things to come. Thus, even from a literary point of view, Geoffrey's *Historia* is an epoch-making work.

When Henry II (or his Queen Alienor) ordered Wace to write a French verse-translation of Geoffrey's *Historia* he was probably thinking of the political significance of the book which in a vernacular version might prove still more effective. The Frenchman Wace, however, a professional writer with an uncommon 'talent de peintre et de conteur' (as his editor Ivor Arnold says), will have been equally struck by the literary merits of the famous book. In any case, his 'translation' called *Roman de Brut* which, in 1155, he presented to Queen Alienor (according to Layamon 42) is unlike its source and must be considered as a work of his own. Of course, the historical material was already given and he could not change the recital of facts given in the *Historia,* but the emphasis he laid on the story and the flowing short couplets, the tinkle of rhyme and the rhetorical devices transform the learned historical work into an entertaining novel.

Wace, like every medieval writer, knows that a story is made more attractive if its truth is asserted, but as he is a matter-of-fact Frenchman this 'realism' has a peculiar tinge:

Ne vuil sun livre translater
Quant jo nel sai interpreter. (7539 ff.)

Consequently he omits the mysterious prophecies of Merlin but adds factual information of his own, mostly topographical details, but also Arthur's institution of the Round Table (9747 ff.) which appealed to him not as a legendary motif but as a chivalrous one. Whatever else he reports from Celtic or Breton tradition, e.g. Arthur's return (13275 ff.), he introduces or winds up with the remark 'si la geste ne ment' or 'ne sai si. . . .'. A temperament like Wace's feels quite at home when he has to deal with reality which is shown most advantageously in the brilliant descriptions of everyday life which he grafts on to the material derived from Geoffrey. Arthur's return from Paris (10171 ff.) and his embarkation at Southampton for the Roman campaign (11190 ff.) are vividly described and make the reader as it were an eye-witness. Such scenes of medieval life which we find ever and anon in his narrative enliven the *Brut* and they reach perfection in the picturesque description of the festival at Caerleon (10337 ff.). With his command of an admirable vocabulary Wace is also able to describe, in a graphic style, battles (e.g. 12539 ff.; 13080 ff.), a siege (9970 ff.) or a storm at sea (6040 ff.).

Bearing in mind that medieval narrative art is mainly concerned with such descriptions, as is borne out by Geoffroi de Vinsauf 's *Poetria nova* (in E. Faral's *Les Arts poétiques du Moyen Age,* Paris, 1924), it is easily understood that Wace's *Brut* set a pattern and had a lasting influence. It is neither a political work nor an historical one but a 'romanz', which means a more or less historical narration in the vernacular. It is actually the first of the long line of romances which were to follow, especially in French, and which constitute a vital part of medieval literature.

In order to understand this importance of Wace's *Roman de Brut* one point has still to be stressed which I have carefully omitted so far, as we shall have to deal with it in detail later on, namely the courtly atmosphere. The heroic material derived from Geoffrey becomes in Wace's hand interwoven with many strands of chivalrous material. That is what Wace was interested in, whereas as a Frenchman he stood rather aloof from the Britons and Saxons and their warlike exploits. For this reason the *Roman de Brut* produces a literary forking point. On the one hand it gave rise to the romance proper, mainly represented by the French 'roman courtois', which comprises the many stories of the knights of the Round Table, Gawain, Lancelot, Tristan and so on; on the other hand it transmitted the heroic material of Geoffrey's *Historia* which was taken up by Layamon and, one and a half centuries later, by the English author of the alliterative *Morte Arthure.*

Layamon's **Brut,** which was probably finished by 1205 or about 1200, is chiefly drawn from Wace though perhaps not from the version that has come down to us but from another, probably later recension, which included some additional material mainly from Breton sources. Be that as it may, the general impression is that of a totally different work. This is already shown by its outward appearance. Wace has 14866 lines, Layamon's A-text has 32241 short lines (as printed by Sir Frederic Madden) or rather 16121 long lines, for it is written in Old English alliterative verse, though in a curiously Protean form (as J. E. Wells terms it), as syllable-counting and rhyme are equally taken into account. It is, however, far removed from the smooth lines of Wace, much more vigorous and in keeping with his intention 'þat he wolde of Engle: þa æðelæn tellen' (13 ff.); he says 'Engle' not Britons and once (14242) 'Bruttes' is used as a synonym for 'the English'. Thus, in the very beginning we get a notion of the author's patriotic spirit, a term which could not be applied to Geoffrey's dynastic interests and much less to Wace's cosmopolitan ideals of chivalry. Layamon is proud to belong to the people which had been so heroic and glorious in the past. He tells that

past emotionally, ecstatically like a bard. With him, Arthur is the great conqueror of foreign realms, the greatest of all, 'Nes næuer ar swulc king' (22979), overcoming giants and flinging defiance at the potentates of the earth, even at the mightiest of them all, the Emperor of Rome. Prophesying his birth, Merlin speaks of Arthur as an almost superhuman being 'so long as is eternity, he shall never die; the while that this world standeth, his glory shall last (MS. B: men will of him tell) and he shall in Rome rule the thanes' (18848 ff. in Madden's translation). Whenever Arthur is spoken of, the author is apt to use the bardic tone which is customary in heroic poetry. (pp. 15-18)

These preliminary remarks concerning the general impression, which may have reminded us of the Anglo-Saxon scop, will put us in the proper mood for an unprejudiced study of the epic which, to judge from the bibliographical lists, has more often been dealt with from a linguistic or prosodic point of view than from a literary one. My proposition is to follow in the steps of the late J. S. P. Tatlock (in the work quoted above) and F. L. Gillespy (in the *California Publications in Modern Philology,* III, 4) in order to show that Layamon, though he derived from Wace and handled the same material as Geoffrey, is different from either as he tried to build up an heroic epic reminding us of Anglo-Saxon poetry and intended to constitute a national epic. This can be proved by a closer comparison of the three works, the main characteristics of which we have outlined.

The most striking difference, that of bulk, proves less instructive than might be expected as Layamon's additions are to be found in all parts of his work and must have been inserted for varying reasons. The sparrow-incident in the story of the burning of Cirencester (29223-92) is an element of story-telling. The long enumeration of the pagan gods Hengest believes in (13897 ff.) is probably meant to stress the Christian standpoint ('oure bilefues me beoþ loþe' 13942-48). The legends about the institution and construction of the Round Table (22895-955), merely alluded to by Wace, are told *in extenso* on account of their miraculous elements. This and the wish to promote the hero to the highest rank is also the reason for the substantial additions to many passages dealing with Arthur, e.g. Merlin's prophecy of Arthur's birth (18762 ff.), Arthur's fight with Childric, which takes up nearly 200 lines (22261-456) against 4 in Wace (9358 ff.)—as do also Arthur's victories over the four Northern Kings (22525-674), which again Wace dispatches in a few lines (9703 ff.). Most impressive is Layamon's insertion of how Arthur learns of Modred's treason (27992 ff.). For Wace's report (13437 ff.) he substitutes an intense scene of tension: a messenger arrives, he is well received by Arthur who expects good news. Then Arthur tells his dream, the meaning of which is cautiously hinted at by the messenger, whereupon Arthur bursts out that he never suspected 'þat æuere Moddred mi mai wolde biswiken. . . . no Wenhauer mi quene'. Then at last the messenger breaks the bad news.

This shows the meaning of most, and the poetically most important, of Layamon's additions. He is not content to give a continuous account of the incidents as Wace does, he wants to create scenes of dramatic tension, and the means by which this is effected are direct speech or dramatic dialogue. Hundreds of lines are taken up by direct speeches and dialogues which have no parallel in Wace. But they have a parallel in *Beowulf*. The messenger is a well known figure in *Beowulf* and the reports of the coast guard (237 ff.), of Wulfgar (333 ff.), of Beowulf himself (1652 ff.) and of Wiglaf (3077 ff.) are similar to the scene mentioned above or to the report of Gawain or Walwain before the Romans (26260 ff.). To intensify action speeches are often broken up into dialogues. The first meeting of Igerne and Uther in Gorlois' guise (19043 ff.) becomes a short but vivid scene by means of dialogue, the poisoning of Uther is another and outstanding example of such dramatization (19626-815 against Wace 8938 ff.). Fighting-scenes are always interrupted and intensified by direct speeches, dialogues and exclamations: Octa (19472-507), Caesar (7383 ff.), Queen Genuis (9808-65) and, most effective, the various speeches uttered by representatives of both parties in the great struggle between Arthur and Rome.

We need not give more examples to show that these speeches and dialogues are more than merely a stylistic device; they are an adequate expression of Layamon's conception of what the Arthurian story meant to him and what he wanted to communicate to his readers. It is almost the opposite of Wace's entertaining art. His stress on feeling, energy, heroic achievements puts him closer to Geoffrey than to Wace, and turning to the chivalrous elements he seems to reverse the process the story underwent in Wace's hands.

Wace, who wanted to please his patron, Queen Alienor, tried to give a courtly colouring to the heroic material of the *Historia*. Though he could not justify the only love-story it contained, Guinevere's adultery, which Geoffrey called 'nefanda' and which he dismissed with the words 'de hoc quidem. . . . Gaufridus tacebit' (XI, 1), the adulterous queen could be withdrawn from too severe reproaches by showing her repentant:

> Mielz volsist morte estre que vive.
> Mult fud triste, mult fud pensive. (13213 ff.)

In the same way Igerne is idealized: 'Curteise esteit e bele e sage' and Uther desired her because 'en ot oï parler / E mult l'aveit oï loer' (8575). Courtly love and chivalry are the main themes in the greatly expanded description of Arthur's festival at Caerleon (10491 ff.), and in order to make Arthur appear as the perfect knight his cruelty is toned down and he is called 'li bons reis' (11897).

This courtly atmosphere disappears in Layamon's rendering: Arthur is no longer the centre of a chivalrous court but, as already in Geoffrey's *Historia,* the mighty conqueror of the world (22979). Layamon is not afraid to tell of his cruel doings, his threat to destroy the Irish 'with fire and with steel' (22269), his killing the whole population of Winchester (28440 ff.), the cruel punishing of his own subjects (22827 ff.), his terrifying rage which keeps his followers in awe so that they do not dare to tell him bad news (24891). The different impression we get from Wace's and Layamon's **Brut** is made clear by a close comparison of the text. Wace's description of the festival at Caerleon is not only shortened from 91 to 31 lines (W. 10525-616; L. 24695-727) but chivalrous terms like 'curteisie' and 'mesure' (e.g. W. 10334) are either left out or are replaced by words with a wider significance: 'bohorder' (W. 10525) becomes 'aernen' (24695), 'escremir' (W. 10527) becomes 'lepen' (24697), and in many places 'curteis' is translated by 'wel idon' or 'of tuhtle swiðe gode' (22239). In some passages we do not have a translation but a free rendering (e.g. W. 10337 ff.; L. 24421 ff.) which substitutes his favourite words: 'selcuth', 'sellic', 'wunder', which have anything but a chivalrous aura.

It is obvious that, about the year 1200, the English language ran short of words equivalent to the French chivalrous terms with their delicate shades of meaning. But it is equally obvious that Layamon's intention lay in a different direction. He wanted to glorify the bygone age of heroism and to lament its decline. There his vocabulary is far richer than Wace's. For 'sea' which Wace can but render by 'mer' and 'marine' we find in Layamon 'saltne stræm', 'sæ flode', 'sæstreme', 'sæbrimme', 'wilde þissere watere.' For 'death' we find the recurrent terms 'bale-siþ', 'dæþ-siþ', 'wæi-siþ', 'fæie-siþ', 'forþ fere', which either recall Old English expressions (e.g. 'bealu-siþ' in *Exodus*) or bear resemblance to them (e.g. 'forþ siþ' in *Guthlac*, 'fæge-hus' in *Elene*). The often repeated word 'fæie'—doomed to die—conveys to our imagination the tragic atmosphere of the Anglo-Saxon epic (e.g. in *Beowulf*: 'fæge and geflymed', 'fæge gefealleþ'). Equally rich is Layamon's vocabulary for 'warrior': 'here gume', 'here kempe', 'wæl kempe', 'here dring', 'beorn', 'hæleþ', 'scalc', which also remind us of the many similar synonyms in Old English poetry. We hear of 'Brutus and his duyede', as in *Beowulf* of 'Hroþgars duguþ'; the evil adversary Geomagog is called 'godes wiþersaka' (1808) and 'scaþe', as Grendel 'godes andsaca' and 'hearm-scaþa'. Similar to the practice in *Beowulf* the king is called 'leod king', 'gumene lauerd' or 'kine lauerd', the queen 'leodene læfdi', and the hall, which in *Beowulf* is called 'winsele', reverts as 'wunsele'. It would be tiresome to give more examples of the many similarities between Layamon's language and Old English poetic diction, which extend even to the religious sphere: for Arthur's prayer after he heard of Modred's treason recalls *Caedmon's Hymn:* 'Ældrihten godd: domes waldend / All middel-ærdes mund' (28205). This characteristic of Layamon's style has already been pointed out by J. S. P. Tatlock in a list of 128 epic formulae which occur 1500 times (*P.M.L.A.* 38 [1923] p. 494 ff.).

Heroic deeds, steadfastness, grim death in battle move Layamon's mind, as may be shown by a last quotation. In Uther Pendragon's battle with the Irish under Gillomar and Pascent, Uther kills Gillomar and says to Pascent:

> "Pascent, thou shalt abide; here cometh Uther riding." He smote him upon the head, so that he fell down, and he thrust the sword into his mouth—such meat to him was strange—so that the point of the sword went into the earth. Then said Uther "Pascent, lie now there; now thou hast Britain all won to thy hand. So is now hap to thee; therein thou art dead; dwell ye shall

here, thou and Gillomar thy companion, and possess well Britain . . . " (18097 ff.).

There is nothing of all this in Wace who merely says that the Irish were beaten and Gillomar killed (8360 ff.).

Layamon's imagination is kindled whenever he has to tell of battles, and if we compare his way of describing them with that of Wace another difference strikes us. When Wace is brilliant, giving the impression of an onlooker with picturesque details, Layamon's emotional rendering tends to split up the general description into scenes of single combat, which again reminds us of the Anglo-Saxon poets. Take, for instance, the battle between the usurper Hengest and the lawful heir Aurelius (W. 7679-838; L. 16294-537), where Wace is less interested in the single combat of the two antagonists than in their argumentative speeches; or take the great decisive battle between Arthur and the Saxons (W. 9272-362; L. 21057-479), which gives Wace an opportunity to show his rhetorical skill in description by giving a graphic picture of Arthur's armour, whereas the actual fighting, which does not much interest him, is almost forgotten. In both cases Layamon makes us share the emotions of the adversary as well; his imagination is wholly taken up by the dramatic turns in the fighting, with words that convey a tenseness of atmosphere. The same result is reached, as we have already seen, by the insertion of dramatic dialogues and exclamations of the fighters or by an intensifying retardation. A striking example for this is the description of the Romans lying in ambush while the Britons with their prisoners come unsuspectingly singing while they ride (26946). Here for more than 100 lines (26847-963) the reader is kept in suspense before the fighting begins and all the while the uncertainty of the outcome creates a dramatic tension.

The difference between the two works is a difference of style, not one of greater or less literary ability. Wace's *Brut* has already all the salient traits of the romance whereas Layamon's work over and over again shows the characteristics of the heroic epic. In his poem there breathes a stern, warlike world without the gentler touches of Norman chivalry which find room even in Geoffrey's *Historia* and which colour the whole of Wace's romance. That is why we are so often reminded of the Old English epic poems. Even glimpses of natural scenery are interspersed, similar to the Anglo-Saxon poetry and very different at the same time, for they rarely convey a gloomy or menacing aspect of nature but add a light, clear, homely tinge to the heroic picture. Where Wace simply mentioned the fact 'Le jour emprés' (493), we read in Layamon 'A marewen þa hit dai wes: and þa niht to-dælde' (833) or 'an ane time: þat þe dai wes liht: and þe sunne wes swiþe briht' (7237). . . . Wace's factual lines 'En Avril, quant esté entra' (10173) Layamon expands to the following picture of spring: 'When Easter was gone, and April went from town, and the grass was rife, and the water was calm and men gan to say that May was in town' (24195 ff). When Brutus, for the first time, beholds his new English home Wace for once gives a detailed picture (1209-14) but it remains an anaphoric enumeration repeating ten times the word 'vit' (—he saw), a rhetorical 'feu d' artifice' which Layamon by expanding turns into an emotional picture of home (2004-16).

More characteristic even than the use of these glimpses of natural scenery is the different handling of the epic simile. Wace makes rare use of them, he prefers a simple comparison and generally takes it from the stock of European rhetorical tradition. This is the case in the numerous comparisons of heroes in battle to a lion tearing a flock of sheep. None of these comparisons is taken over by Layamon. We come closer to what a Frenchman or Englishman of the 12th Century may have actually seen when the giant Dinabuc is compared with a hunted wild boar who turns on the huntsman (W. 11519). Here again Layamon drops the comparison though he is rather fond of hunting similes. In this way Arthur is likened to a wolf when he pursues Colgrim (20123), Corineus fights 'swa þe rimic wulf' (1546), Bedevere grows wrathful like a wild boar (25832) and the same is said of Brutus (1697), King Eadwine (30319) and Childric (21261). The frequency of such comparisons recalling an actual hunting scene is remarkable and often they become real similes by some words sketching the situation, for instance: 'Childric is wrath as the wild boar when he in the beech-wood meeteth many swine' (21261).

Four of these similes recalling scenes of hunting or beast-life he may have witnessed himself are as long and detailed as Homeric similes. They are the simile of the wild crane when speaking of the Saxons put to flight (20163 ff.), the passage of Childric compared with the hunted fox (20839 ff.) extending to 40 lines, the simile of the goat attacked by the wolf (21300 ff.) and, in the same speech by Arthur, the derisive comparison of Childric with the huntsman fleeing before the deer (21335). I should like to quote at least one of these similes to show their peculiar quality. 'The beaten Saxons they gan wander as the wild crane doth in the moorfen when his flight is impaired, and swift hawks pursue after him, and hounds with mischief meet him in the reeds; then is neither good to him, nor the land nor the flood; the hawks him smite, the hounds him bite, then is the royal fowl at his death time' (Sir Frederic Madden's translation).

Of course, these similes are aids to an imaginative visualization but the main purpose is to intensify the mood. This may be proved by a last group of comparisons mainly working on our imagination and therefore gaining extraordinarily in power of intensification. Leir enraged at Cordelia is likened to a black cloth (3070), the storm-driven waves of the sea are compared with flames of burning houses (4578), of Cador or of Arthur jumping on their horses is said 'swa sparc deþ of fure' (21482, 23508). Similarly the rushing motion and not the picture of a rout is conveyed by the words, 'they forth fly as the high wood when the furious wind heaveth it with strength' (20134 ff.). Finally, the picture and an imaginative transcendence of it is given in the haunting passage: 'Yesterday was Balduf of all knights boldest, now he standeth on the hill and beholdeth the Avon how the steel fishes lie in the stream! Armed with swords, their life is destroyed. Their scales float like gold-dyed shields; there float their fins as if it were spears' (20132 ff.). Passages like these show what rare kind of poet Layamon was, how far his *Brut* is removed from the well-ordered, well-told, rational source he translated or rather transformed.

This brings us to a last distinctive characteristic: the element of wonder and supernatural agents. It is already conspicuous in Geoffrey's *Historia* owing to its political purpose. The Diana-oracle gives a divine authorization to the new settlers in Britain and contains a prophecy of the coming Norman empire which is strengthened by the prophetic utterances of the all-important figure of Merlin. His prophecies are not confined to Arthur and his time, they are meant for the present time and for the future. The sceptical Wace does not quite know what to do with these supernatural elements; he calls Diana a devil (637) and omits the greater part of Merlin's prophecies which fill the whole book VII of Geoffrey's *Historia*. If he makes more of Avallon and Arthur's return it is because he, as a story-teller, does not want to miss an attractive motif of a fairy-tale. Geoffrey, of course, had to be reticent as the return of a Celtic king did not fit in with his rôle as an archetype of the Norman dynasty.

Layamon is equally far removed from Geoffrey's *Reich-sidee* and political intention as from Wace's matter-of-factness. His imagination is captured by the wondrous world of the past. His whole account of Arthur is steeped in the miraculous. When Arthur is born he is given presents by elves who promise him that he shall become the best of knights and the richest of kings (19284 ff.). Elves have dug the mysterious lake in Scotland, the description of which makes us remember the very phrasing of the description of Grendel's moor-lake in *Beowulf* (L. 21998 ff.; *Beow.* 1372 ff.). Arthur's sword Caliburn is forged by the elf-smith Wygar (21137) and his spear is made by Griffin at Kairmerþin, Merlin's town (23783). Merlin in Layamon's poem is not merely a sorcerer as in Wace, he becomes an instrument of fate. His wisdom is put on a parallel with God's infinite knowledge (23837) and many times his prophecies are alluded to, so that all happenings seem to be directed by supernatural forces. The moving of the gigantic rocks of Stonehenge which Geoffrey explained by the superior technical skill ('ingenium artis') of Merlin, becomes a solemn scene of magic art witnessed in awe and at a distance by all the bystanders: 'Uther drew him back and assembled his knights, so that none there remained near the stones, as far as a man might cast a stone' (17424) and Merlin draws the magic circle by going round three times. We constantly feel the presence of a supernatural world.

Wace's remark, that the wondrous things told of Arthur are 'ne tut mençunge ne tut veir' (9793) is given an opposite meaning in Layamon's adaptation: 'It is not all sooth nor all falsehood that minstrels sing; but this is the sooth respecting Arthur the king' (22976). Arthur's first dream (G. X, 2; W. 11245 ff.; L. 25579 ff.) which in Wace's rendering loses all impressiveness—he replaces Geoffrey's 'cuius murmure tota litora intremebant' by 'mult lai, mult fort, mult gros, mult grant; Mult esteit d'orrible façun' (11248 ff.)—in Layamon's version is told by the king himself and his agitation is felt in the cluster of adjectives 'wunderlic', 'sturnlic', 'laþlic', 'feondlic' etc. and in the beat of the somewhat irregular alliterative lines.

Arthur's death forms the apex of Layamon's poetic art of conjuring up a miraculous scene. Geoffrey tried to catch the style of a chronicle. 'Arturus rex fataliter vulneratus est qui illinc ad sananda vulnera in Avallonis advectus cognato suo Constantino, filio Cadoris ducis Cornubiae, diadema Britanniae concessit, anno ab incarnatione dominica quingentesimo quadragesimo secundo' (XI, 2). Wace is the perfect story-teller. He says: 'If the chronicle speaks truth Arthur himself was mortally wounded. He caused him to be borne to Avalon for the healing of his wounds. He is still there awaited by the Britons for as they say and deem he will return and live again. Master Wace who wrote this book cannot say more about his death than was spoken by the prophet Merlin. Merlin said of Arthur, if I read aright, that his end should be hidden in doubtfulness' (13275 ff.). Layamon is the magician; in his report of Arthur's death rings the epic note of fate: Arthur was wounded wondrously much. Then came to him a lad, who was of his kindred; he was Cador's son, the Earl of Cornwall; Constantine the lad hight, he was dear to the king. Arthur looked on him, where he lay on the ground, and said to him with sorrowful heart: "Constantine, thou art welcome; thou wert Cador's son. I give thee here my kingdom and defend thou my Britons ever in thy life, and maintain them all the laws that have stood in my days, and all the good laws that in Uther's days stood. And I will fare to Avalun, to the fairest of all maidens, to Argante the queen, an elf most fair, and she shall make my wounds all sound; make me all whole with healing draughts. And afterwards I will come again to my kingdom, and dwell with the Britons with mickle joy". Even with the words there approached from the sea that was a short boat, floating with the waves; and two women therein, wondrously formed; and they took Arthur anon, and bare him quickly, and laid him softly down, and forth they gan depart. Then it was accomplished that Merlin whilom said, that mickle sorrow should be after Arthur's departure. The Britons believe yet that he is alive, and dwelleth in Avalun with the fairest of all elves; and the Britons ever yet expect when Arthur shall return. Was never the man born, of ever any lady chosen, that knoweth of the sooth, to say more of Arthur. But whilom was a sage hight Merlin; he said with words—his sayings were sooth—that an Arthur should yet come to help the English. (28589 ff. Sir Frederic Madden's translation)

It is a pity that the story does not break off here but goes on to tell the sad fate of Arthur's successors. Layamon—that is the only reproach he cannot be spared—like so many medieval writers, knew nothing of literary form, arrangement of parts, artistic structure. Geoffrey's carefully built-up structure, which we tried to indicate, could be neglected by Wace as his delightful chatty way of story-telling leads us on from scene to scene like a big road running over hill and valley and past many towns and crowded scenes. Layamon's scenes, which are more numerous and more sharply defined, stand out like unconnected blocks, the more so as his style is less flowing, more vigorous and dramatically effective, sometimes even jerky. The parts his narrative may be divided into: lines 1-18532 dealing with the early history from the fall of Troy to the begetting of Arthur; 18533-28651 dealing with the story of Arthur; 28652-32241 dealing with the history from Arthur's death to the expulsion of the Britons by Æthelstan, are too lengthy and do not hold the reader's attention. But these weaknesses are outweighed by poetic merits. For Layamon was a poet. His **Brut** stands out as the nearest approach to epic achievement between *Beowulf* and Chaucer. (pp. 18-27)

Walter F. Schirmer, "The Presidential Address 1957," in M. H. R. A.: Annual Bulletin of the Modern Humanities Research Association, *No. 29, November, 1957, pp. 15-27.*

Roger Sherman Loomis (essay date 1959)

[*Loomis was an American educator and scholar of Arthurian legend and medieval literature whose principal publications include* Celtic Myth and Arthurian Romance *(1927),* Arthurian Tradition and Chrétien de Troyes *(1949), and* Arthurian Literature in the Middle Ages *(1959), which he edited. In the following excerpt, he examines Layamon's additions to Wace's* Brut, *focusing on such elements of his verse as handling of stylistic conventions, alliteration, rhyme, and simile.*]

[The] opening passage of the famous Middle English poem, generally known as the **Brut,** tells us that its author was a parish priest at Arley Regis, Worcestershire, in the Severn valley. His use of 'was' in reference to Eleanor as queen of Henry II implies that Henry at least must have been dead, perhaps Eleanor also. If the latter alternative be accepted, the poem must have been written after 1204, but Tatlock [in his *Legendary History of Britain*] assembled evidence which pointed rather to the reign of Henry's son, Richard I, 1189-99. Tatlock also pointed out that, though the name of Layamon's father was Saxon, that of Layamon himself, meaning 'law man', was of Scandinavian origin and at this time was recorded only in the old Danelaw. Probably, then, there was a Scandinavian strain in the poet's family. But it is not necessary to accept Tatlock's theory, based on this fact and the poet's display of knowledge about Irish matters, that Layamon was born in Ireland of a Saxon father and a Scandinavian woman, and spent part of his youth there before he came to England and settled at Arley. Surely an English priest with any curiosity would know of SS. Columkille (Columba), Brendan, and Bride, and would not have had to be born in Ireland to know that the natives when summoned to battle removed their breeches, for, after the Norman conquest of Ireland began in 1169, Irish fighting habits, especially one so bizarre, would have been common topics for conversation in England.

On one point Layamon's introduction is misleading; he made almost no use of Bede's *Ecclesiastical History of the English People,* either in King Alfred's translation or in the original Latin (which scholars agree is meant by the book of SS. Albin and Augustine). He probably had every intention of doing so when he started, but since Wace's book went back to the beginnings of Britain, he had to rely at first on that, and finding it easier to stick to it than to conflate it with Bede, he forgot about his promise to the reader. Ironically enough, the poet who set out to celebrate the noble deeds of the English followed through to the end a book in which that race is held up to execration, for Layamon's poem is substantially a free paraphrase of

Wace. Ironically, too, it uses the language, the poetic form, and the style of the people it disparages.

It is generally recognized that Layamon employed the verse form and the conventions, not of the great Anglo-Saxon masterpieces but of the popular poetry of the eleventh and twelfth centuries, the medium of the humbler minstrels who succeeded the courtly *scops* and learned clerics. The basic verse form is still the alliterative line with four accents and a slight pause in the middle, but the alliteration is quite irregular, in many lines absent, and the lines are longer. Moreover, the hemistichs are often linked by assonance or rime, a feature which had already appeared in the Anglo-Saxon *Judith*. In all these respects Layamon's **Brut** shows a close likeness to the *Proverbs of Alfred,* written somewhat earlier.

The influence of Wace may be seen in the increasing use of rime as the poem proceeds, and in the effective employment of simile, a device very rare in Anglo-Saxon poetry. Wace has a few short comparisons, for example: 'As the proud lion, which has long been starved, kills rams, kills ewes, kills lambs, great and small, just so did the Britons'; 'They [a Roman troop] were without a commander, like a ship without a steersman, which the wind drives wherever it wishes when there is no one who keeps it on its course.' Layamon seems to have taken the hint from these passages (though, oddly enough, he does not paraphrase them), and from Merlin's prophecy that Uther's son will be 'like a boar fierce in battle', and he introduced many similes as consciously as did Homer. 'As a whirlwind does in the field when it raises the dust high from the earth, so Ridwathlan rushed on his foes.' Again, we read that Arthur 'rushed like the fierce wolf, when he comes from the wood behung with snow, and thinks to bite such beasts as he pleases'. When the Saxons were routed, 'some wandered as the wild crane does in the moor-fen when his flight is impaired and swift hawks pursue him and hounds meet him cruelly in the reeds. Then neither land nor water is good to him; hawks smite him, hounds bite him; then the royal fowl is doomed on his way.' Again, when at Bath Arthur gazed on the mail-clad corpses of the Saxons lying in the river, Layamon put in his mouth this mocking shout: 'Yesterday was Baldulf boldest of all knights; now he stands on the hill and beholds the Avon, how steel fishes lie in the stream. . . . Their scales float like gold-painted shields; their fins float as if they were spears!' This same battle of Bath inspired three other similes: the wild boar meeting the swine in the beech wood, hunters running the fox to earth and digging him out, and the goat defending himself with his horns against the wolf. Nothing seems to have stirred Layamon's imagination to these vivid flights except the triumphs of his ancestral foes.

Similes account only in very small part, however, for the fact that the English poet expanded Wace's 14,800 verses to 32,200 hemistichs. Though he omitted many trifling details and condensed the narrative of Arthur's embarkation for Normandy—one of Wace's purple passages—to six lines, yet he more than made up for these cuts by his looser style and his inventions. Epic formulas, of which Tatlock [in his "Epic Formulas, Especially in Layamon," *PMLA* XXXVIII, No. 3 (September 1923)] counted more than

125, serve as padding. On a voyage 'wind stod an willen' (the wind stood in the desired quarter); during a battle 'monie þer weoren faeie' (many there were doomed). Again and again Arthur is styled 'noblest of kings'. Some of these stereotyped phrases once had vigour but lose it through constant reiteration.

Far more important both in bulk and in significance are the many elaborations due simply to Layamon's feeling for the concrete and the dramatic, which has already been noted in his similes. Wace says merely that after Arthur had defeated Lucius he caused the body of the emperor to be taken and watched with great honour and sent it to Rome on a bier. Layamon specifies that Arthur had a tent pitched in a broad field, had the body of Luces borne there and covered with gold-coloured palls and watched for three days while he had a long chest made, covered with gold. When the body had been placed in it, he sent it under the escort of three kings on a lofty bier to Rome.

Most vital and original are the additions which describe behaviour, express feelings in speech, and even supply dramatic incidents. For instance, Wace tells the story of the poisoning of Uther by Saxon spies in general terms and uses no direct discourse. Layamon is very specific, introduces six speeches, and sets the action at Winchester. He invents the scene where the spies, dressed as almsmen, wait in the street for the king's dole. They hail a knight of the royal household, complain that they have been starving since the Saxons took their lands, and are now singing prayers for King Uther. The knight reports their complaint to Uther, and at his bidding they are admitted to his household. It is a fresh and realistic handling of an ironic situation.

Arthur's portentous dream which forecasts the treachery of Modred has been often noted as one of Layamon's best additions to Wace, and though the idea was perhaps traditional, since we have variant versions of such a dream in texts which are not based on Layamon, the handling seems very characteristic of his manner. Arthur dreamed that he was sitting astride the roof of a hall with Walwain before him. Modred came with a battle-axe and hewed the posts which upheld the building, and Wenhaver pulled down the roof so that Arthur fell and broke his right arm. Gripping his sword in his left hand, Arthur smote off Modred's head so that it rolled on the floor, and he hacked the queen to pieces.

This last detail illustrates one of Layamon's strangest and strongest idiosyncrasies, for this man of God was a barbarian at heart. He seems to belong in a milieu where the softening influences of woman-worship and courtesy were unknown. Whereas Wace attributes to Gawain the sentiment that 'for friendship (*amistié*) and for their mistresses knights perform deeds of chivalry', the Saxon poet deletes the mistresses. He seems to approve of Arthur's wholesale punishment of the kindred of those who quarrelled at his Yuletide feast: the males were to lose their heads, the females their noses. The code which protects ambassadors from outrage had little sanctity for Layamon, for whereas Wace said merely that the Britons in anger would have insulted and rebuked the Roman embassy if Arthur had not interrupted, Layamon has the Britons leap on the Ro-

mans, clutch them by the hair, and throw them to the ground before Arthur stops them. Over and over again the priest of Arley repeats gleefully the curses which consigned the enemies of the Britons to hell. Even his humour has a grim flavour, for when Uther killed Pascent by driving a sword into his mouth, the poet remarks, 'such food was strange to him'.

Though many critics have ignored this ferocious streak, Tatlock candidly called it Layamon's 'most intense and personal trait' [*Legendary History*]. He suggested that it was due to the poet's hypothetical Irish blood and contrasted it with what he termed 'the thoroughly Christian or at least restrained' character of Anglo-Saxon poetry. But even Tatlock had to admit that the *scop* in his battle-pieces exulted in slaughter; and the clerics who composed *Exodus* and *Judith* displayed a similar taste for blood. Racial distinctions are notoriously hazardous, and Layamon's brutality, ruthlessness, and hatred of the heathen, which Tatlock would derive from the Irish, may be matched abundantly in the *chansons de geste*.

Let us return to the subject of Layamon's additions and consider three which have provoked both curiosity and controversy. The first tells how, when Arthur was born, 'alven' (fays) took him and bestowed on him three gifts—strength, dominion, and long life. Some readers have been struck by the Germanic word *alven* and have been reminded of the coming of the Norns at the birth of Helgi. But though the word is Germanic, the concept is widespread. The same story of the fays and their gifts is told of Arthur by the second continuator of *Perceval,* and of Floriant and Ogier the Dane by other French poets, who most significantly speak of Morgain la Fée as chief of the ladies and tell how, when the hero comes to die, she transports him to her island home. Since three French poets knew this tradition and could not have got it from Layamon, evidently it was a French legend. If one wishes to trace it back to a Celtic source, one may find it surviving in Breton folk-lore. Sébillot was told in 1880 that the fairies called Margots bestowed gifts on the new-born infants of noble houses and predicted what they would become [*Traditions et Superstitions de la Haute Bretagne, 1882*].

The second passage is the exquisite account of Arthur's departure. Wounded in his last battle with a broad spear, he spoke to Constantine, his kinsman:

> 'I will fare to Avalun, to the fairest of all maidens, to Argante the queen, a fay most fair. She shall make my wounds all sound, make me all whole with healing potions. Then I will come again to my kingdom and dwell with the Britons with great joy.' Even with the words, there came from the sea a short boat gliding, driven by the waves, and two women therein wondrously clad. They took Arthur at once and bore him in haste and laid him down softly and moved away. . . . Bretons believe yet that he is alive and dwells in Avalun with the fairest of all fays.

The closest parallel is again furnished by a French text, the *Didot Perceval,* which relates that Arthur, wounded by a lance, announced to Constantine that he would not die, but would be conveyed to Avalon to have his wounds tended by Morgain, his sister. The author adds a reference to the Wild Hunt and the Breton hope of Arthur's return. This story of Arthur's passing is, of course, closely related to that of the fays at his birth, and Giraldus makes it certain that it came from the Bretons since he credits it not to his countrymen, the *Wallenses,* but to the 'fabulosi Britones et eorum cantores'.

The third passage concerns the fight over precedence at Arthur's Yuletide feast and the making of the Round Table by a Cornish carpenter. Layamon paraphrased Wace's reference to the Bretons and added the description of the fracas. He added also that the Table could seat 1,600 men and yet could be carried about wherever Arthur rode. Layamon, too, must have read of the Round Table in French, or listened to a tale told by a Breton *conteur.*

The evidence regarding these three passages is consistent and plain: their sources were not in the poet's own brain but in Breton stories, related in French, either orally or in manuscript. This is corroborated by the fact that the name which Layamon gives to one of Modred's sons, Melyon, matches the name Melehan which is given him in the Vulgate *Mort Artu,* and which is likewise applied to the hero of a Breton lai. There is nothing to support the conjecture that Layamon picked up his Celtic matter from the Welsh, nor has research revealed any manuscript of Wace's *Brut* which included these additions, as Immelmann and Bruce postulated [in Layamon, *Versuch über Seine Quellen,* 1906, and *MLN* XXVI (1911), respectively]. It would appear that the tales were so familiar, so fascinating, and so widely believed that Layamon could hardly help including them.

Yet in spite of this demonstrated Breton influence and of a more questionable Irish or Scandinavian inheritance, Layamon is essentially, as Wyld maintained [in his "Layamon as an English Poet," *The Review of English Studies* VI, No. 21 (January 1930)], an English poet. To be sure, the claim that his sea-pieces carry on the tradition of the Anglo-Saxon *Seafarer,* or that Arthur's waking the giant of Mont St. Michel before attacking him shows a peculiarly English ideal of sportsmanship, cannot be accepted, for only S. Ursula's voyage is described in more than landlubber commonplaces, and Huon of Bordeaux was as chivalrous as Arthur. Nevertheless, anyone who has read much in the earliest English poetry will feel at home with Layamon, in spite of the looser lines, the presence of rime and assonance, and the rarity of kennings. The vocabulary is overwhelmingly Saxon; only 150 Romance words occur. There is a wealth of synonyms for 'warrior', 'sea', 'go', &c. The nickers that haunt Grendel's mere in *Beowulf* bathe in Layamon's Loch Lomond. There are *scops* in both poems, and there is *dream* (joy) in hall. Both poets, though Christian, accept the idea of an inexorable doom involved in the Saxon word *faege,* Middle English *feye,* Scottish *fey.* Though Layamon's use of the kenning is confined almost entirely to phrases descriptive of the Deity, he achieves at one point such an agglomeration of these as to rival Caedmon's *Hymn.* Here is Caedmon:

> Þa middangeard moncynnes weard,
> Ece dryhten, æfter teode
> Firum foldan, frea ælmihtig.

While Caedmon managed to get three kennings into three lines, Layamon got five!

> Laverd drihten crist, domes waldende,
> Midelarde mund, monnen froure,
> Þurh þine aðmode wil, walden ænglen . . .

Perhaps the most startling survivals of the old native tradition are certain details of Arthur's arming for the battle of Bath. Wace, following Geoffrey, had mentioned the sword Caliburne, the shield Pridwen, the spear Ron, and a hauberk without name. Layamon says this byrnie was made by an elvish smith, calls it Wygar, and adds 'þe witeye wurhte', which may mean either 'which a wizard wrought', or, 'which Witege wrought'. Now Widia, as Kittredge observed [in *Modern Philology;* i (1903)], was in Germanic legend the son of the famous artificer Weland. Arthur's helm, too, Layamon calls Goswhit, i.e. 'Goosewhite'. It cannot be wholly a coincidence that *Beowulf* 's byrnie was wrought by Weland and that we read of his 'hwita helm'.

Thus we find Layamon employing the traditions of his ancestors to glorify their most redoubtable foe. He even exults in the fulfilment of the forecasts which he had met presumably in some form of Geoffrey of Monmouth's *Prophetiae Merlini* and had applied to Arthur: 'In ore populorum celebrabitur, et actus eius cibus erit narrantibus.' 'Pectus eius cibus erit egentibus, et lingua eius sedabit sicientes.' Twice Layamon paraphrases them. 'Of him shall gleemen sing gloriously; of his breast shall eat noble *scops;* of his blood shall men drink.' 'Gleemen will make a table of that king's breast, and very many *scops* will sit at it and eat their fill ere they depart thence, and draw out wine-draughts from that king's tongue, and drink and revel day and night.' Surely it was a happy prophecy, for Arthur has been the hero not only of Welsh bards and Breton *conteurs* but of some of the great poets of England, of whom Layamon himself was the first. (pp. 104-11)

> *Roger Sherman Loomis, "Layamon's 'Brut',"* in Arthurian Literature in the Middle Ages: A Collaborative History, *edited by Roger Sherman Loomis, Oxford at the Clarendon Press, 1959, pp. 104-11.*

C. S. Lewis (essay date 1963?)

[*Lewis is regarded as a formidable logician and Christian polemicist, a perceptive literary critic, and—perhaps most highly—as a writer of fantasy literature. Also a noted academic and scholar, Lewis held posts at Oxford and Cambridge, where he was an acknowledged authority on medieval and Renaissance literature. A traditionalist in his approach to life and art, he opposed the modern critical movement toward biographical and psychological interpretation, preferring to practice and propound a theory of criticism that stresses the author's intent rather than the reader's presuppositions and prejudices. In the following excerpt from a posthumously published collection of essays, Lewis discusses the most important differences between the* Brut *of Wace and that of Layamon.*]

It is easy to explain why Layamon's **Brut** has few readers.

The only text [Ed. F. Madden, 3 vols. 1847] is almost un-obtainable; the poem is long; much of its matter is dull. But there are very good reasons for overcoming these obstacles. One is that Layamon is much easier than most Middle English poetry: far easier than Dunbar or *Pearl* or *Gawain,* yet not flattering the beginner, as Chaucer does, with a deceptive appearance of easiness. But secondly—and this is the reason most to my mind—the **Brut** is well worth our attention in its own right. The dull passages are a legacy from its known sources; its vividness, fire, and grandeur, are new. And sometimes—rarely, I admit—it reveals, in a flash, imaginative power beyond the reach of any Middle English poet whatever.

As everyone knows, the ultimate source of Layamon's subject-matter is Geoffrey of Monmouth's *Historia Regum Britanniae* (1147). It was a foundation quite unworthy of the structure raised upon it. Geoffrey is of course important for the historians of the Arthurian Legend; but since the interest of those historians has seldom lain chiefly in literature, they have not always remembered to tell us that he is an author of mediocre talent and no taste. In the Arthurian parts of his work the lion's share falls to the insufferable rigmarole of Merlin's prophecies and to the foreign conquests of Arthur. The latter are, of course, at once the least historical and the least mythical thing about Arthur. If there was a real Arthur he did not conquer Rome. If the story has roots in Celtic Paganism, this campaign is not one of them. It is fiction. And what fiction! We can suspend our disbelief in an occasional giant or enchantress. They have friends in our subconscious and in our earliest memories; imagination can easily suppose that the real world has room for them. But vast military operations scrawled over the whole map of Europe and excluded by all the history we know are a different matter. We cannot suspend our disbelief. We don't even want to. The annals of senseless and monotonously successful aggression are dreary enough reading even when true; when blatantly, stupidly false, they are unendurable. Whether Geoffrey intended all this stuff as political propaganda for our continental empire or merely as a sop to national vanity, we neither know nor care. It is either way deplorable, and it is what Geoffrey chiefly wants to tell us about Arthur. He has of course included better things, but his own contribution is a mere disfigurement. The decided contempt which it gives me for Geoffrey has the paradoxical effect of making me readier to believe that the *Historia* is filled with valuable deposits of tradition, both legendary and historical. Wherever I meet anything that I think good as story or probable as history (and I meet both fairly often) I feel sure that Geoffrey did not make it up.

After Geoffrey came Wace, the Norman, who was born in Jersey and made Canon of Bayeux by Henry II. He died, perhaps, about 1175. He is remembered by everyone for his account of Taillefer riding before William the Bastard's army at Senlac and singing the Song of Roland; this comes in his *Roman de Rou.* In 1155 he retold Geoffrey's matter in octosyllabics as the *Geste des Bretons,* which we, following the manuscripts, know as the *Roman de Brut.* He certainly did not regard himself as a writer of what we should call romance. His attitude to his material is rather that of a historian to an unreliable, yet by no means worth-

less, document. He thinks it is partly true, partly false. He is anxious to avoid errors. He has even been at the pains of investigating a fountain in Broceliande where the fays were said to appear, and his comment (in the *Roman de Rou*) on the negative result of the experiment is well known: 'Wonders I sought but I found none; a fool I returned, a fool I went.' But in another way he is not in the least like a historian. He feels perfectly free to touch up his original, describing, as if he had been an eyewitness, scenes he never saw and supplying vivid details from his own imagination.

After Wace, Layamon, whose **Brut** was probably written before 1207. He tells us he was priest at Ernleye (now King's Arnley) on the Severn. It *com him on mode,* came into his head, to relate the noble deeds and origin of the *Engle.* He travelled far and wide and secured these books as his sources: the 'English book' made by Bede (i.e. the Anglo-Saxon version of the *Ecclesiastical History*), a book by 'Seint Albin and the feire Austin', and a book by a 'French Clerk' called Wace. The second item in this catalogue is puzzling. It is generally taken to be Bede's Latin original of the very same book which, in Anglo-Saxon, makes Layamon's first item. I find it difficult to be content with this theory, but the question is not very important since Layamon actually makes extremely little use of Bede in any shape or form. Wace is the only one of his three authors who really counts. Perhaps when the poet mentioned all three books in his poems—for those days, and for a man in his humble station, they were a costly library, which he *leofliche bi-heold* [lovingly beheld]—he expected to use them much more than he actually did.

But we cannot next proceed, as we used to do with Chaucer and *Il Filostrato,* to get a text of Wace, collate it with the English **Brut,** and thus try to isolate Layamon's original work. It is generally accepted that Layamon worked from a redaction of Wace, contaminated by other versions of the story. And it seems clear to me, as to others, that he was in touch with real Welsh or (less often) English traditions. Thus he knows, and could not learn from Wace, the name of Arthur's helmet *Goswhit* (21147) and his shield *Pridwen* (21152), and of the smith Griffin who made his spear (23783). In a passage peculiar to himself (13562-90) he gives to the Pict who murdered King Constance the name Gille Callæt, which is unknown to both Wace and Geoffrey. It is too good a name for a Pict to have been invented by a writer so unphilological as Layamon, who elsewhere cheerfully gives the names Ethelbald and Ælfwald to two 'Britons' who revolted against 'Gracien'. The passage in which he does so (12253 *seq.*) is also significant. No one else relates this revolt; but Layamon's very clear localization of it in East Anglia—no county patriotism would tempt him thither—suggests that a historical tradition of some far later rebellion may underlie it. There are, too, places where Layamon unexpectedly agrees with Geoffrey against Wace. At 1275 his *pritti dawes* confirms Geoffrey's figure, and our text of Wace reads *trois jors.* This might be a mere accident. More importantly, at 14050 Layamon and Geoffrey both tell us that Lindesey was the fief given by Vortigern to Hengest, and Wace—in our *textus receptus*—does not. Since Layamon is generally thought to have made no use of Geoffrey, and certainly does not mention him, this passage suggests a source, probably British, common to both. It is certainly difficult not to suppose Welsh poetry behind the following prophecy about Arthur:

> Of him scullen gleomen godliche singen.
> Of his breosten scullen æten aðela scopes.
> Scullen of his blode beornes beon drunke.
>
> (18856-61)

> [Of him shall minstrels sing finely. Of his breast noble poets shall eat; on his blood, heroes be drunk.]

Geoffrey, doubtless from the same source, had said 'His deeds will be meat to their tellers', but Layamon gives more.

We thus know neither what (exactly) Layamon's MS of Wace contained nor from what other sources, oral or written, he supplemented it. I believe, myself, that many, or even most, of those passages peculiar to the English *Brut* which I shall mention are in fact Layamon's own. But I must not assume this. In order to avoid committing myself I shall therefore speak no more of Layamon but simply of the *Brut,* of the text itself. Who, or how many people, or in what proportions each, made it what it is, is a question I cannot answer. This inability of course frustrates our curiosity as scholars, and it puts out of use our characteristically modern critical habits. There is no question here of finding the single author, totally responsible for his work of art, and expressing his unique personality through it. But this frustration is instructive, and it is fortunate that the text which meets us at the very threshold of Middle English poetry should so clearly render the modern approach impossible. If criticism cannot do without the clear separation of one work from another and the clear unity of the individual author with the individual text, then criticism of medieval literature is impossible.

The metre of the *Brut* has often been described and I shall not deal with it at length. Sometimes for a line or so it conforms to the classical Anglo-Saxon pattern:

> æðela inwurðen,
> wihte wal-kempen, on heora wiðer-winnan.
>
> (776-8)

> [To be valiant—tough death-warriors—against their enemies.]

At the opposite extreme we get

> He makede swule grið, he makede swulc frið
> monien layen gode, þe lond swuððen stode.
>
> (4254-7)

> [He made such peace, he made such order, many good laws, that thereafter the land was steady.]

Internal rhyme had appeared in *Maldon* and was (like consonance) regular in certain Old Norse metres: the real novelty is the absence of alliteration. To an ear trained on *Beowulf,* a text which oscillates thus may at first be as repulsive as 'monkish hexameters' were to the Humanists. But one grows reconciled to it in the end; and not, I think, only because one's standards have been lowered by habituation. The types of classical Old English half-line are, after

all, blocks of pure speech rhythm. So are the half-lines of the *Brut's* new rhymed (or consonanced, or assonanced) lines. Hence they lie down together not uncomfortably. There is no real parallel to the jarring effect we should get if alcaics were suddenly introduced among elegiacs or octosyllabics amid blank verse. There is, too, a tendency for one norm or the other to predominate over fairly long stretches. Battle-pieces, appropriately, often keep close to the old metre. The new, often used for pathetic, derisive or gnomic comment, has its own rustic pungency. Notice its effect in the following where it comes after two lines of fairly pure alliterative verse:

> 'And yif þu him abidest he þe wule binden,
> quellen þine leoden and þi lond ayen'.
> Ofte wes Arþure wa; neuere wurse þene þa.
>
> (20379-84)

> ['And if you await him he will make you prisoner, kill your people, and hold your land.' Often had Arthur been in woe; never worse than at that moment.]

If the *Brut* is only partially Anglo-Saxon in metre, it is almost wholly so in style. Expressions that recall the old poets meet us at every turn: *Godes wiðer-saka* (1808; of Gogmagog), *mid orde and mid egge* (5202), *sæ-wierie* (6205), *weorld-scome* (8323), *gumene ælder* (12178)

> [God's enemy. With point and edge. Sea-weary. World-shame. Lord of men.].

If they are not always exact reproductions, this makes them more interesting. It shows that the poet is not merely imitating, as Claudian, say, imitated the Augustans, but working in a live tradition. Hence his resemblance to his predecessors is not limited to vocabulary. Arthur's prayer, with its accumulation of more or less synonymous phrases (almost *kenningar*), comes in the very accents of Hrothgar:

> Lauerd drihten crist, domes waldende,
> midelarde mund, monnen froure,
> þurh þine aðmode wil, walden ænglen.
> Let þu mi sweuen to selþen iturnen.
>
> (25567-74)

> [Lord, master, Christ, prince of glory, protection of middle earth, comfort of men, by thy gracious will, prince of angels. Make thou my dream turn to good.]

The *Brut* is Anglo-Saxon in style for the best reason: because it is Anglo-Saxon in temper. Its outlook, its most recurrent emotions, its sense of values, all belong to the old order.

This brings us to an instructive paradox. In the opening lines the *Brut* promises to tell the history of the *Engle* (13): actually it tells that of the Britons when they had been conquered, killed, and dispossessed. Even if the word *Engle* is merely a careless slip, it is no bad symbol of what is to follow. This poem, while Anglo-Saxon in style and temper, is wholly British in its conscious sympathies. For those Germanic invaders who were Layamon's real ancestors and whose language he wrote, the *Brut* has hardly a good word to say. They are treacherous, heathen hounds. Best deal with them as Aldolf did with Hengest when he swiped off his head, gave him good burial after his own heathen fashion (for he was after all a brave fighter) and then

> bad for þere sæule þat hire neuere sæl neore.
> (16723-4)

[Prayed for his soul that bliss should never come to it.]

We may suspect that the ***Brut*'s** view of the English invaders against whom Arthur fought has been much coloured by memories of a far more recent invasion. At l. 7116, significantly, it speaks of the Normans coming to England *mid heore nið crafte* [*With their evil strength (or* cunning)]. But no such explanation for its British partialities is really needed. Centuries later when we no longer had cause to hate the Normans we still somehow accepted the Britons (as represented by Geoffrey) for our ancestors and delighted in this supposed link with Arthur, Cassibelaune, Brennes, and the Trojans. The consciousness of race, or (if you prefer) the illusion of race, seems hardly to have existed. Nor is race much use to us as critics. If there was a historical Arthur he was probably a Roman. His legend is Celtic in origin. The particular handling of it which we are now considering is the adaptation, thoroughly Anglo-Saxon in spirit, of a Norman poem. Its later dissemination is the work of French poets and romancers. Its modern developments are almost exclusively English and American. We should use a very misleading metaphor if we said the legend had a Celtic 'kernel'; 'for, when he hath the kernel eate, who does not throw away the shell?' If we threw away what is not Celtic we should have left something other than the Arthurian legend which has really mattered.

From what has already been said it will be obvious that the ***Brut*** is a very different poem from Wace's *Geste* as we have it, and must have been very different from any redaction of Wace which we can imagine. The mere language determines this. *Feollen þa fæie* [the fated ones fell (14038)] has a ring which nothing could have in French octosyllabics. The habitual images and attitudes of the English poem add another difference. An angel, or that early aviator King Bladud, has, not wings, but a *feðerhome* [Feather-jacket of swanskin] (2874, 25871). Heroes may speak of their exploits in the devout manner of Beowulf himself: *godd hit me iuðe þat ich hine igripen habben* [God granted me that I have caught him] (16549). Characters give one another a great deal of advice, sometimes, as may be thought, portentously, but sometimes, as in the old poetry, with magnificent weight—

> Nu þu ært al ane of aðele þine cunne.
> Ah ne hope þu to ræde of heom þat liggeð dede.
> Ah þenc of þe seoluen. Seolðen þe beoð yiueþe;
> for selde he aswint þe to him seolue þencheð.
> (17934-41)

[Now thou alone art left of thy noble kindred. But hope not to get counsel from those that lie dead, but take heed to thyself. Good will befall thee. For seldom he fails who takes heed to himself.]

But the differences go far beyond this kind of thing. The ***Brut*** is much more archaic and unsophisticated than the *Geste*. One can easily believe that Wace was familiar with real, contemporary courts and camps. But the ***Brut*** sees all its battles in terms of the heroic past. Strategical features are blurred or omitted. Instead, we get the warhedge standing like a grey wood, faces turning pale, many a grey-haired warrior hewn with sword, broad-bladed spears broken and cloven shields—

> Heowen hardliche hælmes gullen,
> falewede feldes of fæie blode.
> And þa heðene saulen helle isohten.
> (18316-21)

[They hewed hardily, helms resounded, fields were discoloured with fated blood, as the souls of heathens set out for hell.]

It paints its courts in equally old-fashioned colours. In the *Geste* as we have it the Roman ambassadors are true diplomats, elderly men, well-dressed, carrying olive branches, walking slowly and behaving with much dignity. In the ***Brut*** they are

> þeines ohte mid palle bi-þehte.
> Hæye here-kempen, hehye men on wepne.
> (24741-4)

[Valiant thanes, clad in pall, high battle-warriors, high men with weapons.]

The Norman gaiety and lightness do not get into the ***Brut*** at all. There is a striking example a few lines later when Arthur consults with his lords about his answer to the Romans. It is a delightful scene in Wace. The King holds his council in a stone keep called the Giant's Tower. As they go up its spiral stair, Cador, who was a man of jokes, calls out merrily to Arthur who happens to be in front of him. This threat from Rome, he says, is welcome. We have had far too much peace lately. It softens a man. It encourages the young bachelors to spend too much time dressing, with an eye to the ladies. Gawain, overhearing this, says Cador need not bother his head about the young men. Peace after war is very pleasant. So is love. Bright eyes teach chivalry. Thus they jested. Now turn to the ***Brut***, 24883-972. First, by a tiny touch, it alters the whole lighting. It cannot mention the tower without adding

> An ald stanene weorc; stiðe men hit wurhten.
> (24885-6)

[An old stone work; tough men made it.]

With this characteristically Beowulfian glance at the remoter past everything becomes at once darker, graver, more wintry. There is no prattle on the stairs. When everyone is seated in his place, Cador rises and expresses his view about the corrupting influence of peace in a set speech, seriously. Then Walwain *wraððede hine swide* [Was very angry (24951)]. His praise of peace has nothing to do with ladies' eyes—

> God is grið and god is frið þe freoliche þer
> haldeð wið,
> and godd sulf hit makede þurh his godd-
> cunde—
> (24957-60)

[Good is peace and good is quiet for him who

uses them nobly; and God Himself made it through His Deity]

and there is nothing sportive about his disagreement with Cador. It is a real strife, a *flit* (24966), and Arthur, as if he knew that swords might be out in a minute, has to cry out

Sitte adun swiðe, mine cnihte alle.
And ælc bi his lifen luste mine worden.

(24969-72)

[Sit down, I tell you, my knights all. Let each, on his life, hear what I shall say.]

Equally instructive are the different eulogies which the *Geste* and the **Brut** give of Arthur. In Wace he is one of Love's lovers. He founded those courtesies which courts have followed since. He lived in great state and splendour. In the **Brut**, *he wes þan yungen for fader, þan alden for frouer* [To the young he was a father, to the old a comforter] (19936-7). Thus everywhere the **Brut** is heavier, more serious, more plangent than its Norman counterpart. Provided that we carefully define for ourselves the sense in which we are using the word, we may say that it is more barbaric and less civilized.

We must not misunderstand this. It has to be admitted that the **Brut** at one point (22841 *seq.*) introduces an atrocity of which Wace and Geoffrey are innocent. But it was something done in hot blood. In general the **Brut** is a kinder work than the *Geste*. It is both fiercer and more tender. The Norman courtesy can be callous, the Norman lightness can be cynical; the **Brut** is, at bottom, more sensitive. Its favourite heroes, if rough-hewn, remember the sufferings of common men. Its Brennes, as soon as he has conquered Rome, starts repairing the war damage, prevents a massacre, forbids plunder, and summons back the refugees (*flæmen*) with the assurance that they shall have peace and live under the laws of their own country (5938-69). Its Vortimer, at his accession, undertakes to emancipate all slaves (14852). Its Arthur resolves that if he conquers France,

Auere ælche ærmen mon þe æð scal iwurðen,
and wurchen ic wulle muchel godes wille.

(23741-4)

[Always every poor man shall find his lot the easier, and I mean to do great God's will.]

It may, no doubt, be suspected that the sympathies of the **Brut** here reflect the humble condition of its author. But they are not confined to the poor. It dwells lovingly on Arthur's discharge of his veteran knights when he bade them go with joy and repent their sins, never carrying weapons more, but living the rest of their days religiously. It extends even to Pagans—provided, of course, they are not Saxons—as in its lament for Julius Caesar

Wale þat eæuere ei sucche mon in to eælde
sculde gan.

(7223-4)

[Well-away that every any such man had to go in to Hell!]

And to the Caesar whom it thus laments it independently

attributes courtesy and chivalry in his treatment of the captured Cassibelaune (8942 *seq.*). It alone shows us Ygærne, in private, sorrowing for the lives which Uther's love for her will cost (18616 *seq.*). Its conceptions are sometimes finer than those of Wace. Androgeus, though a traitor fighting against Cassibelaune, warns his men to take the king alive and give him no wound, 'for he is my lord and kinsman' (8605).

Another distinction of the **Brut** is its love for the supernatural. It knows that a fairy smith, *on aluisc smið*, made Arthur's byrnie (21131). Wace, following Geoffrey, had peopled Loch Lomond with prophetic eagles; the **Brut** adds

uniuele þinge.
Þat water is unimete brade; nikeres þer badieð
inne,
þer is æluene ploye in atteliche pole.

(21744-8)

[Unchancy things. The water is immensely wide; nikeres (aquatic monsters) bathe therein, there is play of elves in the dreadful pool.]

Of another strange water it adds *alfene hine dulfen*, elves dug it (21998). It interpolates the statement that as soon as Arthur came on earth elves took and enchanted the child and gave him their gifts (19253 *seq.*). It could have learned from the *Geste* that Arthur after his last battle was carried to Avalon for the healing of his wounds and that the Britons still look for his return thence. The **Brut** likes the passage so well that it reproduces it twice (23067 *seq.*, 28610-41), making us much surer than Wace had done that Avalon is a fairy country, since Arthur is taken thither by Argante 'the queen', 'the fairest of all elves'. Let us notice, however, that the **Brut**'s marvels are not all Celtic. The fairy smith was called Wygar. The *nikeres* and their pool might have come straight out of *Beowulf*. And the word I have translated 'elves' has to do duty both for the *fées* of continental tradition and for our own more formidable *ylfe*.

So far I have been speaking of differences between the **Brut** and the *Geste* which are not necessarily differences of poetic merit. Except in the scene between Cador and Gawain, where the *Geste* is in my opinion superior, a man might reasonably prefer either. Certainly if a Gigadibs could have existed among the Normans and had deigned (and been able) to read the **Brut** he would truly have said that it 'lacked contemporaneity'. I now turn to those of its peculiarities which seem to me to be also superiorities.

First of all, it might have been written by someone who had read Aristotle and learned that a narrative poet ought to speak as much as possible through the mouths of his characters and as little as possible through his own. Again and again where our text of Wace merely says that people issued such and such orders, or had such and such disputes, or gave one another such and such news, the **Brut** sets them talking. I should say there was twenty or even thirty times as much dialogue in it as in the *Geste;* besides prayers, soliloquies, and the like. It is often extremely vigorous. Arthur's speech (20825-98) after the submission of Childric is a good example.

But of course the author (or authors) of the **Brut** did not need to have read Aristotle. This reiterated use of the dramatic method is part and parcel of the general intensity with which it grasps all that it treats. It is far more committed, more engaged, closer to its matter, than the *Geste*. It shows us happening what the *Geste* often merely records. It knows how everyone looked and behaved: how Corineus, after his great speech on the ingratitude of Locrin, brought down his axe and shattered the stone the King stood on (2311); how Godlac, on hearing of his mistress's marriage, swooned in his chair and the courtiers threw cold well-water on his face (4516 *seq.*); how Pantolaus and his crew must have appeared after their long voyage, with their tattered clothes and their indifference to decency (6271 *seq.*). No one who has ever watched for the return of the fishing fleet after bad weather will miss the graphic reality of the following, where the two vikings watch the storm-tossed fleet of Ursula coming in:

> And swa heo leien i þan æit-londe and iseyen þat
>   weder stronge;
> iseyen scipen an and an, while ma, while nan,
> þeonne feowere þenne fiue. . . .
>
>   (12033-7)

[And thus they lay in the island and saw the wild weather; saw ships—one—and one—sometimes more—sometimes none—then four—then five.]

The *Brut's* certainty as to what you would have seen if you had been present creates character. We are perhaps told of too many people

> Þeo hit up bræc hit wes god þat he spec—
>   (5431-2 *et passim*)

[When it came out, what he said was good]

though it certainly brings vividly before us a certain type of slow starter. Far more interesting is the process whereby Merlin—little more than a name in the *Geste*—becomes impressive in the *Brut*. In both texts he tells Uther how to get the monoliths for Stonehenge. This is a mere necessity of the plot. The *Brut* adds

> Þus seiden Mærlin and seoððen he sæt stille
> alse þeh he wolde of worlden iwiten.
>   (17232-5)

[Thus said Merlin and then sat still as though he were going out of the world.]

He is liable to such stillnesses. On another occasion, having been asked a question, he

> sæt him stille longe ane stunde,
> swulc he mid sweuene swunke ful swiðe.
> *Heo seiden þe hit iseyen mid heore ayen æyen*
> þat ofte he hine wende swulc hit a wurem
>   weore. . . .
>   (17906-13)

[Sat still for a long time as though he were labouring hard with a dream. Eye-witnesses said that he often turned the way a snake would.]

Whether this is how wizards (what we'd call mediums) really behave, I don't know, but I think the passage would carry immediate conviction even without the line I have italicized. It is, however, the real masterpiece. Here is an-

other. After Uther's death Wace merely tells us that the bishops and barons sent a message to Arthur calling upon him to be King. *Tantamne rem tam negligenter?* The *Brut* tells us how three bishops and seven knights sought the youth out (he was only fifteen) in Britanny, and gives their speech. Then

> Arður sæt ful stille.
> Ænne stunde he wes blac and on heuwe swiðe
>   wak;
> ane while he wes reod and reousede on heorte.
> Þa hit alles up brac hit wes god þat he spac.
> Þus him sæide þer riht Arður þe aðele cniht,
> 'Lauerd crist, godes sune, beon us nu a fultume,
> þat ich mote on life goddes layen halden.'
>   (19887-99)

[Arthur sat very quiet. Now he was pale and very drained of colour; now he grew red and was moved at heart. When it all came out, what he said was good. Thus in that place spoke Arthur the good knight: 'Lord Christ, Son of God, help us that while I live I may keep God's laws.']

It will be noticed that in all these quotations there is hardly anything that could be called poetical adornment. I doubt whether the poet was thinking about poetry; it sounds more as if his only object were to make sure that we should see exactly what he had imagined. We may even doubt how far he knew that he was working from imagination. But the *Brut* can be good in a different vein. I spoke a while back of its close adherence to the Anglo-Saxon type of poetry. But in one important way it departs from that type. The simile was almost (not quite) unknown to the Anglo-Saxon poets. It is frequent in the *Brut*. Some of its similes are short and easily found. Troops muster thick as the falling hail, *alse hayel þe ualleð* (14517 *et passim*): Ridwathlan rushes on his enemies as a *þode* or whirlwind, carrying a dust-cloud, falls in a field (27645); at an angry meeting many a stout Briton had *beres leches*, boar's looks (22281-2); or (less obviously) an army advances 'as if all the earth would catch fire' (20643-4). But besides these we find similes of the Homeric or 'long-tailed' type; fittingly, since the *Brut* is, in its manner and temper though not in its art, the most Homeric poem in English. One would much like to know where its long-tailed similes come from. If they had any literary model it has been fully assimilated; they do not read at all like the stanza-long, laboured similes in which Spenser thought he was being Virgilian. They smell of real country and first-hand observation. As here:

> Up bræid Arður his sceld foren to his breosten
> and he gon to rusien swa þe runie wulf
> þenne he cumeð of holte bi-honged mid snawe
> and þencheð to biten swulc deor swa him likeð.
>   (20120-7)

[Arthur hitched up his shield before his breast and began to rush like the howling(?) wolf when it comes, all hung with snow, out of the wood, and means to get its teeth into any beast that pleases it.]

A moment later—for, as in Homer, and more than in Virgil, the similes tend to bunch—he tells his men that their enemies will fly

swa þe hæye wude
þenne wind wode weieð hine mid mæine—
(20135-7)

[As the tall wood when the mad wind tosses it
with its strength.]

and after that comes the longer and more complex simile
of the crane flying broken-winged from the hawks to be
met among the reeds by hounds, so that neither land nor
water will now save it, for the hour of the noble bird
(*kinewurðe foyel*) is come (20163-75). That of the goat
pursued by the wolf (21301-15) is too long to be quoted.
It is remarkable for being, at the end, mortised back into
the main narrative (I think Homer never does this) by Arthur's triumphant cry that he himself is the wolf and Colgrim the goat (21315).

It will be noticed that all these come from the Arthurian
section of the *Brut,* and it is there, I believe, that its addition to, and transformations of, any possible source we
know, are most continuous. Our text of Wace reads, in
comparison, like an epitome; it gives a skeleton: nearly all
the flesh is supplied by the *Brut.* This is of course most obvious in the very long and frequent passages which have
no analogue at all in the French; but it is no less instruc-
tively seen where the two texts are close. In the following,
where Merlin's mother tells how he was begotten, I have
italicized what is peculiar to the *Brut.*

Þa ich wes an uore *fiftene yere,*
Þa wunede ich on bure, *on wunsele mine,*
maidene mid me, wundre ane uæire.
Þenne ich wæs on bedde iswaued *mid soft mine*
slepen,
þenne com [me] biuoren *þa fæirest þing þat wes*
iboren,
swulc hit weore a muchel cniht al of golde idiht.
Þis ich isæh *on sweuene alche niht on slepe;*
þis þing *glad me biuoren* and *glitene on golde.*
Ofte hit me custe, ofte hit me clupte. . . .
(15700-17)

[When I was, long since, *fifteen years old, then*
I lived in my bower, in my chamber of delight, my
maidens with me, wonderfully fair. When I was
in bed, plunged in my soft sleep, then there came
before me *the loveliest thing ever born—like a tall*
knight all decked with gold. This I saw *in dream*
each night in my sleep. This thing *moved before*
me and *glimmered in gold.* Often it kissed me,
often embraced me.]

It will be apparent how much the *Brut* has shaded and
softened and beautified the story, making it both more
credible and more tolerable. The young princess is put in
her right setting, with her *wunsele* and her maids: the
image of sheltered royal girlhood—sheltered, at least,
from all merely human lovers—is built up. Her own experience is all dim, half a dream, something between sleep
and waking. And the daemon is the loveliest thing ever
born.

But I have kept to the end two touches that seem to me
proofs of yet higher power. One turns on two words. We
are twice told, of a storm at sea, that the waves were like
'burning towns' (or villages): *alse tunes per burnen* (4578),
tunes swulche per burnen (11978). It may be the phrase of

a longshoreman rather than a sailor; waves out at sea are
less likely to give this particular appearance. But I do not
think I shall ever again see a breaker coming in against the
wind without remembering the burning towns. The image,
so far as I know, never occurs before or after the *Brut.* It
embodies a quality of eye and imagination which I believe
we never meet in Langland, Chaucer or Gower. My other
example is more complex. Arthur, exulting over the Saxon
rout, looks down on the Avon and sees

Hu ligeð i þan stræme stelene fisces
mid sweorde bi-georede; heore sund is awemmed,
heore scalen wleoteð swulc gold-faye sceldes,
þer fleoteð heore spiten swulc hit spæren
weoren.

(21323-30)

[How steel fishes lie in the stream, girt with
sword; their swimming is spoiled, their scales
float like gold-bright shields, their fins drift there
as if it were spears.]

Coleridge and Wordsworth would have made this the text
for a full dissertation on the esemplastic faculty. First, the
imagination turns the mail-clad, hence silvery-gleaming,
dead into fishes. Then, assuming the fishes as a basis, by
way of a simile within a simile, it half turns them back into
knights, comparing the wooden shields and spear-shafts
(which would of course leave the bodies on the river bed
and float on the surface) to scales and fins. And it does this
not as the romantic imagination might, for its own sake,
but under the influence of a strong, bitter, and probable
passion. (pp. 18-33)

C. S. Lewis, "The Genesis of a Medieval
Book," in his Studies in Medieval and Renais-
sance Literature, *edited by Walter Hooper,*
Cambridge University Press, 1966, pp. 18-40.

Tatlock on the epic nature of the *Brut*:

Lawman's poem is one of the landmarks in English literary
history, in spite of its borrowed matter. It has been given no
adequate defined position, and so few people have dwelt on
its high merit and freshness that one fancies few have read
it with absorption and a leisured mind. Here Arthur makes
his first appearance in English, Arthur with his court who
through medieval romance, Spenser, nineteenth century poetry, to E. A. Robinson, has become the nearest figure we
have to a racial hero, for by his connection with the land,
and his embodiment of our religion and our ideals, and by
our own mixed blood, he has become accepted as English,
or at least we accept him as British just as we accept the
word British for our own descent. By reason of Arthur's position as its climax as well as of the long line of other traditional heroes, events and associations, and of its breadth of
treatment, simplicity, intensity, enthusiasm, accord with
the supernatural, vitality of imagination, elevation and
sometimes nobility and religious feeling, the poem is the
nearest thing we have to a traditional racial epic.

J. S. P. Tatlock in his The Legendary
History of Britain, *University of*
California Press, 1950.

Michael Swanton   (essay date 1987)

[In the following excerpt, Swanton characterizes Laya-mon's Brut *as "the most sweeping and detailed history of the island that had ever been attempted in the English language," and focuses particularly on Layamon's por-trayal of Arthur.]*

[Whether] or not interpreted as the scourge of God, the merest acquaintance with the history of the nation would recognize [the Norman invasion of England] as merely part of a lengthy cyclic pattern. Native authors with na-tional concerns who now found themselves unable to exe-crate the foreign invader, or to speak of contemporary events, in an acceptably public form, might turn with greater safety and circumspection to the glories of the na-tion's remoter past.

The first and perhaps most impressive vernacular *essai* of this kind was Layamon's ***Brut***—a large-scale, ambitious survey of national history—significantly in the language of a subject race. Layamon's theme is stated clearly in the opening lines:

> Hit com him on mode, ond on his mern þonke,
> þet he wold on Engle þa æðelæn tellen,
> wat heo ihoten weoren ond wonene heo comen
> þa Englene londe ærest ahten.
>
> (ll.6-9)

[It came into his mind, and into his fine imagina-tion, that he would tell of the noble origins of the English—what they were called and whence they came who first possessed England.]

Choosing a larger and more heterogeneous canvas than the single incidents dealt with in *Judith* or [*The Battle of*] *Maldon* and a more complex theme than that which en-gaged the author of *Guthlac A,* he set out to construct a genuinely national epic: the most sweeping and detailed history of the island that had ever been attempted in the English language, plotting the rise and fall of the British people from their arrival under their eponymous founder Brutus to their final dispersal in the face of the Saxon colo-nization. The shape of his work was determined largely by the Anglo-Norman *Romanz de Brut* which the Jerseyman Robert Wace dedicated to Eleanor of Aquitaine and which was in turn adapted from the immensely successful *Historia Regum Britanniae* by Geoffrey of Monmouth. Layamon's ***Brut*** represents a substantial literary achieve-ment, although somewhat difficult of access, partly be-cause of its size (at some sixteen thousand lines five times the length of *Beowulf,* embracing an enormous sweep of history, and involving an exceptionally comprehensive cast-list), and partly because the verse chronicle is an un-familiar and uncertain literary category, although it has much in common with modern historical romance in which the dividing line between historical fact and histori-cal fiction is unreal and unimportant.

Layamon's epic falls into three, unequal parts. The first nine thousand lines or so begin with the legendary founda-tion of the nation by the descendants of Aeneas who fled from the fall of Troy eventually to discover a giant-infested Albion, and continues through the various vicissi-tudes of Roman times until the disastrous rule of the treacherous Vortigern and the arrival of the Saxons under Hengest. The central part may properly be regarded as an Arthuriad, beginning with the 'prophecies of Merlin' (omitted by Wace but available in Geoffrey) and the be-getting of Arthur by Uther Pendragon on Ygerne through the machinations of Merlin; going on to chronicle the events of Arthur's reign which represent the height of British achievements—first the successful rout of the Sax-ons, and then further conquests which lead to suzerainty over the whole of Europe—and culminating in the submis-sion of Rome itself, at which point the treachery of Ar-thur's nephew Mordred leads to the slaughter of the knights of the Round Table and the death of Arthur him-self (ll.9229-14297). There follows a substantial coda of some two thousand lines dealing with the sad fate of Ar-thur's successors, until the final dispersal of the native British tribes with the death of Cadwallon in 689—and consolidation of English power under Æthelstan (ll.14298-16095).

Far less episodic than at first it might seem, the shape of history Layamon perceives is a recurrent pattern of land and people subject to continual conquest, through which the unique personality of Britain survives time and time again. His is a national and not a racial history; *jus sol ni sanguinus,* the story is not of the Britons but of the land of Britain. Just as the typical 'Englishman' is content to include among his forebears Boudicea, William the Con-queror, William of Orange, or a host of Hanoverian sover-eigns, very soon the colonial Normans would speak of themselves as 'English', even before they spoke the lan-guage. The terms 'England' and 'the English' are semanti-cally tolerant, frequently considered synonymous with 'Britain' and 'the British', often to the distress of racially conscious Celts. For Layamon the terms 'English' and 'British' are interchangeable. Although the historical cir-cumstances cannot avoid the fact that they seem to be major opponents, they are opponents only as part of a pro-visional pattern of transient fortune. The inescapable facts of Germano-Celtic hostilities in the land, and of their eventual outcome, have large implications which are not lost on Layamon as the representative of a recently con-quered race, which had now to come to terms with a new set of alien masters, absorbing and eventually submerging them in their own 'nationality'. Although Layamon's story is of the past, he will naturally dress it in terms which are meaningful to his age. The landscape, both physical and emotional is a twelfth-century feudal one, of castles, siege-works and jealously guarded deer-preserves (ll.713f); sub-Roman Winchester is offered its 'freedom' as if it were an early medieval borough (l.14171).

The traditional theme of earthly mutability persists strongly, although the image of the ruin is no longer viable since by the twelfth century so many ancient towns were either lost from view altogether, or totally rebuilt, with their past affirmed only by historians. Unlike the Wander-er's affective nostalgia therefore, Layamon's sentiment is an antiquarian one, symptomized by his constant concern to explain the origins of topographical names together with the events associated with them. Onomastic precision, albeit often technically inaccurate, lends a convincing air of concrete corroboration quite different from either the imagined world of *Beowulf* or the topographical exactitude of *Maldon*. More than a mere gazetteer, it serves to develop a complete personality of Britain. His summary of the history of London in this respect characterizes his theme (ll.3528f). The name of the town constantly changes as a result of successive waves of new conquerors; it is called first 'New Troy', then Kaer-Lud—which its greatest developer named after himself so that he might be remembered, but such is the transience of human wishes that:

> Seoððen her com uncuð folc faren in þessere
> þeode
> ond nemneden þa burh Lundin an heore leode-
> wisen.
> Seoððen comen Sæxisce men ond Lundene heo
> cleopeden,
> þe nome ileste longe inne þisse londe.
>
> (ll.3543-46)

[Afterwards there came foreign people into this realm and named the town Lundin in their native language. Afterwards Saxon men came and called it Lundene, a name which lasted for a long time in this land.]

The recurrent phrase *Seoððen her com* marks the rhythm of successive change until Layamon's own times when, revealing partisan sentiment:

> Seoððen comen Normans mid heore nið-craften
> and nemneden heo Lundres; þeos leodes heo
> amærden.
>
> (ll.3547-48)

[Afterwards came the Normans with their evil power and named it Lundres; they harmed this nation.]

But this is merely an expected part of the regular development of the pattern:

> Swa is al þis lond ivaren, for uncuðe leoden
> þeo þis londe hæbbeð bi-wunnen and eft beoð
> idriven hennene.
> And eft hit bi-yetten oðeræ þe uncuðe weoren,
> ond falden þene ælden nomen æfter heore wille
> of gode þe buryen and wenden heore nomen
> swa þat his her burh nan in þissere Bruttene
> þat habbe hire nome æld þe me arst hire on-
> stalde.
>
> (ll.3549-55)

[So has all this land fared as a result of foreign nations who have conquered this land but were later driven away. And later others who were foreigners gained it, and suppressed the old names of fine towns as they wanted, and changed their names, so that there is here in Britain no town that has its old name that men gave it first of all.]

The realm of Albion has been held in turn by successive waves of invaders: giants, Britons, Saxons in turn, and now in the writer's own time by Normans. But the implication is clear, that all conquerors are themselves eventu-

ally conquered—or absorbed—and it is implicitly understood that the Norman yoke is unlikely to prove permanent. As Merlin says, speaking prophetically of the dragons whose conflict shakes the foundations of Vortigern's fortress—with first the white and then the red dragon wounded in turn and retiring into their holes beneath the foundations so that 'no man saw them afterwards'—what should this betoken, but 'kings that are to come, and their fight and their adventure—and their fated folk' (ll.7999-8000). There is no doubt as to the eventual outcome. Whatever the result of a momentary contest, it is clear that there are always kings to come, and equally that their people are doomed to fall. Both theme and sentiment are traditional—the lesson of *Deor, Wanderer* and *The Ruin* writ large. Whatever the personal achievement of these kings—in an awesome roll-call of a hundred or so rulers, great and small, virtuous or immoral—their end must be the same. All achievements of even the best or most authoritarian of rulers are impermanent. The whole cycle had begun with a reversal of fortune, with refugees fleeing from a once-great and impregnable city now in ruins. Thereafter the larger shape of the rise and fall of nations merely reflects the fate of individuals as king after king is raised to power only to be brought low by treachery, folly, or merely old age. Individuals like King Lear tossed by fortune from power to poverty and back to riches again, experience constant reversal. It offers plentiful scope for irony. The Saxon leader, Childeric, so recently master of the land, now disastrously defeated by Arthur, remarks:

> 'Oft hit ilimpeð a veole cunne þeoden
> þer gode cnihtes cumeð to sturne fihte
> þat heo aerest biyiteð after heo hit leoseð—
> ond al swa us to-yere is ilumpen here
> ond æft us bet ilimppeð yif we moten livien.'
>
> (ll.10364-68)

['It will often happen among many races of people where fine knights come to a fierce fight, that they who first win afterwards lose—and that is just what has happened to us here now, and again better may befall us, if we live.']

Brought finally to bay at Mount Badon, the Saxons are mocked by Arthur as 'yesterday's men' in a cumulative incantation of reversion:

> 'Yesterday Colgrim was the bravest of all men.
> Now . . . '
>
> (ll.10628-29)
> 'Yesterday Badulf was the boldest of all knights.
> Now . . . '
>
> (ll.10638-39)
> 'Yesterday the Emperor (Childeric) was the
> bravest
> of all kings. Now . . . '
>
> (ll.10646-47)

The anarchic circumstances against which the violent and power-hungry nobles jostled one another in pursuit of their ambitions must have seemed no more capricious than the recent history of Layamon's own times from Conquest to Anarchy. The Christian warrior like Arthur may occasionally acknowledge that the outcome of a battle lies in the hands of the Lord of Hosts. But it seems an unconvincing piety—the pattern of history motivated more by the caprice of inscrutable fate than a benevolent providence. Nevertheless, Layamon the country priest will end his epic on a pietistic note: 'whatever may be hereafter, happen what may, may it be God's will. Amen'. (ll.16094-96).

Whereas the stories of many kings are passed over summarily—Hudibras, Lear, Gorboduc, Lud, 'Old King' Cole, Cymbeline—the circumstances leading up to the accession of Arthur are treated in full. In this the figure of Vortigern, his career very much enlarged from Wace, plays the role of chief villain: wicked steward and tyrannical ruler by turns, perverting the good order of the realm by the introduction of alien mercenaries—first Picts and then Saxons—pursuing merely personal rather than national advancement and displaying a treacherous disregard for the welfare of his own people. The disapprobation expressed by the narrative voice is emphatic. Whereas Geoffrey or Wace do not allow their personal preferences markedly to obtrude on the narrative, we are left in no doubt of where Layamon's sympathies lie, conveying an absolute sense of right and wrong. Of Vortigern's rise to power he remarks by way of anticipation: 'the beginning was unpleasant—and so was the end' (l.6621). Vortigern plots the downfall of the pious King Constance with a degree of Machiavellian openness.

> Þa isæh Vortiger—*of muclen ufele he wes wær*—
> þat Constanz þe king ne cuðe of londe na-þing
> for he nefde ileorned naver nane lare
> buten in his munstre þat munec scolde drigen;
> Vortiger þat isæh—þe Wurse him wes ful neh—
> ofte he hine bi-ðohte wæht he don mahte,
> hu he mihte mid læsinge i-quemen þan kinge.
> Nu þu miht iheren hu þes swiken him gon varen.
> Weoren of Brutlonde þa bezste alle dæde.
>
> (ll.6626-34)

[Then Vortigern—he was familiar with great wickedness—saw that Constance the king knew nothing about the world because he had never learned about anything except what a monk performs in his monastery; Vortigern saw that—the Devil was very close to him—and he often wondered, incited by power, how he could flatter the king with lies. Now you can hear what this deceit did for him. The best men of Britain were then all dead.]

The italicized phrase, or variants of it, is associated with the name of Vortigern so regularly that as an expected collocation it can be employed to special rhetorical effect. When the name Vortigern first appears, it is accompanied by the narrative aside, *yæp mon ond swiðe war* [a crafty man and very wary] (l.6487), repeated with variations thereafter (ll.6536, 6569, 6588, 6593) until it forms an expected formulaic collocation, merely confirmed by a significant variant to stress Vortigern's decidedly Machiavellian character—*of ufele he wes wel iwar* [he was well aware of (familiar with) evil] (ll.6615, 6626, 6669, 6691, 6899, 6929, etc.)—until finally deceived by the Saxon mercenary leader Hengest, the betrayer betrayed, the poet remarks laconically with an ironic recall of the same formula: *her he wes to un-war,* [here he wasn't wary enough!] (l.7601).

Having perverted the Pictish mercenaries to his own peculiar service:

> 'Ye scullen habbe seolver ond gold, þe bezste hors of þis lond,
> claðes ond fæire wif; eore wille ich wulle drigen;
> ye sculleð beon me leofve, for þa Bruttes me beoð laðe;
> lude ond stille ich wulle don eore wille
> yifye wulleð in londe halden me for laverd.'
>
> (ll.6683-87)

['You shall have silver and gold, the best horses in the land, clothes and beautiful women; I will perform your will; you shall be dear to me, for the Britons are hateful to me; loud and soft I will do your will if you will maintain me as lord in the land.']

Vortigern contrives that they shall slay the monk-king, Constance, on the paltry excuse that he has provided insufficient beer-money. Then when the Picts come to present Vortigern with the head of Constance, he falls to the ground in a pretence of despair, thus inciting the British to assault the Pictish community in a wholesale pogrom, taking no captives but slaying even their chamber-servants, cooks, and boys (ll.6842-45). Vortigern reigns supreme for a time but the Picts of the North remain vengeful, becoming increasingly dangerous:

> He wes wod he wes wild, he wes ræh he wes bald;
> of alle þinge he hæfde his iwille—but þa Peohtes neoren nævere stille
>
> (ll.6857-58)

[He was mad, he was wild, he was cruel, he was bold; he had his way in every respect—except the Picts were never peaceful.]

added to which there is talk of an attack by the monk-king's surviving brothers, Aurelius Ambrosius and Uther Pendragon. And thus it is that, ever an opportunist, hearing of the arrival of Saxon ships in the Thames, Vortigern invites Hengest's men to intervene. Although heathen, the Saxons are explicitly acknowledged to be 'the finest men that ever came here' (ll.6885-86). They are clearly superior physically, better equipped, better clothed, than Vortigern's retinue, and by implication morally superior: 'Vortigern's court was held in contempt; the Britons were sorry for such a sight' (ll.6980-81). Although heathen, Hengest represents a moral agent, working as it were under the old rather than the new law: 'the most courteous of all knights who lived under heathen law in those days' (ll.7209-10). The formulaic collocation associated with the name of Hengest is one of clear approval: 'finest of all knights' (ll.6933, 6955, 6967, etc.). Despite their heathen nature, which Vortigern himself declares is an abhorrence, he urgently needs their protection against both his former friends the Picts, and increasingly his own alienated people, who now favour the accession of Constance's kin. Hengest contrives that his beautiful daughter Rowenna should come forcibly to the notice of the king—who finally apostatizes in marrying her according to heathen custom; and 'when he had disgraced himself on her, gave her London and Kent' (l.7184).

As the Britons begin to desert Vortigern, Layamon creates an almost sympathetic picture of the king's embarrassment, awkwardly caught between two worlds and the conflicting demands of personal and national pride. After all, he *has* invited the Saxons, he *has* contracted a marriage alliance; now 'How, for shame, could I shun them so soon, and drive my dear companions from the land?' (ll.7289-90). Layamon's use of direct speech is particularly effective, informing his received materials with a dramatic, almost Shakespearian access to historical events. What it loses in genuine historical perspective, it gains enormously in concrete and dramatic immediacy, allowing us to glimpse the faces of important men—the history-makers—at critical moments in their lives, focusing on scenes of stress or exhilaration so as to identify the all too human element in decisions effecting the fate of nations. Yet despite this human insight, the characters Layamon portrays—even those who figure prominently like Vortigern or Arthur—do not develop fully realized personalities but remain two-dimensional Platonically conceived Romanesque personae engaged in a series of situations which display only unmixed motives or emotions, where the connecting strand is narrative rather than psychological.

Very soon Vortigern's land is so full of heathen foreigners (ll.7255-57) that the British cause can be identified with Christendom in the starkly racial terms of crusading times. Layamon refers to the Saxon idols—indiscriminately—and of course anachronistically—simply as 'Mahomet', (ll.7279, 14583), much as a century later the author of *Arthur and Merlin* would term the Briton's pagan enemies not Saxons but 'Saracens'. This simplistic black-and-white framework conveys an absolute sense of right and wrong, which permits the ferocious intolerance characteristic of the era in which Layamon lived, compared with which the actions of Judith or Byrhtnoth, Assyrian or Viking, pale into decent defensiveness.

The *Brut* reflects the stark realities of wholesale warfare at a time when in the torture-chambers of twelfth-century baronial castles the devils of Guthlac had become in reality indistinguishable from men, and it was openly said that Christ and his saints slept. Having sacked and burned the city of Cirencester, the Saxon leader executes savage reprisals:

> Gurmund falde þa munstres and an-heng alle þa
>   munkes;
> of cnihten he carf þe lippes, of madenen þa tittes;
> preostes he blend; al þis folc he scende;
> ælcne bilefved mon he lette bi-limien;
> and þus he gon to taken on, and fordude al þisne
>   Cristindom.
>
> (ll.14651-55)

[Gurmund pulled down the monasteries and hanged all the monks; from knights he cut off the lips, and from girls the breasts; priests he blinded; he injured the whole people; each man left behind he deprived of his limbs; and he carried on in this fashion and destroyed all this Christendom.]

But such ferocity is by no means confined to the heathen protagonist. Layamon's Christians are never in doubt as to their Christian duty: it is to slay 'heathen hounds'. Wishing to serve Christ the better, the governor, Lucius, at whose request missionaries had first come to Britain, simply has slain all those who refuse baptism, converting by force as if they were twelfth-century captive Saracens or Jews (l.5073). Self-righteous intolerance would readily extend to gratuitous cruelty. Adolf of Gloucester urges Aurelius to let his lads use the captive Hengest as target practice in their games of archery (ll.8261-62); but Bishop Aeldadus demands to have him cut to pieces in the market-place, throwing the pieces about the streets, citing an obscure Old Testament precedent in justification (ll.8289f). If Hengest's remains are eventually buried according to pagan custom, it is not so much to honour a worthy if mistaken opponent, but to ensure—as they explicitly pray—that his soul should go to hell (ll.8344-46). In general the religious sentiment now expressed seems to be fundamentally one of dutiful service in return for divine patronage. The *miles Christi* is no longer the loving and faithful member of Christ's comitatus, but a feudal retainer. Aurelius vows to worship God *provided* he enables him to defeat Hengest—striking a pragmatist's bargain (ll.8121-29).

If in some respects Layamon falls into simple epic amplification, so that armies of many thousands are said to take the field, to be slaughtered in as great numbers, he realistically depicts scenes of horror unknown—or at least unadmitted—in earlier battle-poetry. In one battle six thousand are said to be trodden to death by horses alone—unseated knights wandering dazed through fields that are so full of blood no one can see where to strike, until it is decided to move to a fresh site (ll.13703-21).

Since the victor of a conflict can now deem his foe unquestionably vicious, impulsive, savage mockery which serves to degrade and dehumanize a defeated enemy is apparently acceptable. When Uther Pendragon, having knocked down Vortigern's son, drives a sword through his mouth and into the ground, the narrator remarks coolly 'such food was unfamiliar to him' (l.9028). Arthur will address dead or dying foes with 'gameful words' (l.10693). In such a world the traditional beasts of battle anticipating carnage are forgotten; instead, it is the men who are pictured as bestial—a natural development of action and image. The early Britons hide like badgers, leap like deer out of the woods (ll.6395-402), whither at the end they return to live like wild animals in the wastelands where, hostile and suspicious, Guthlac finds them. Warriors are urged to have the heart of a boar, the cunning of a raven (l.15169). Arthur rushes on the Saxon:

> swa þe runie wulf
> þenne he cumeð of holte, bihonged mid snawe;
> ond þencheð to biten swulc deor swa him likeð.
> (ll.10041-43)

[like the fleet wolf when he comes out of the forest, hung about with snow, intent on devouring whatever animals he wishes.]

This extended network of images recurs throughout, but most effectively in a closely packed sequence serving to heighten the excitement of Arthur's final rout of the Saxons with startling force. After seven thousand are slain in the waters of the River Dunglas, the remnant wander through the fen like noble but faltering heron caught between hawks in the air and hounds in the reeds (ll.10061-67). Childeric is hunted down like a fox through the wood of Calidon in a graphic simile sustained through some sixteen lines (ll.10398-413). During the culminating battle thousands of Saxons have been cut down crossing the Avon. Looking down on the river from Mount Badon the Saxon leader Badulf sees:

> hu ligeð i þan stræme stelene fisces
> mid sweorde bi-georede; heore sund is awem-
>   med;
> heore scalen wleoteð swulc gold-faye sceldes,
> þer fleoteð heore spiten swulc hit spæren
>   weoren.
>
> (ll.10640-43)

[how in the stream there lie steel fish, girt with swords; their ability to swim is impaired; their scales are gleaming just like gold-plated shields, their fins are floating as if they were spears.]

We might have expected another simile; instead, the logic of the equation is presented in a shocking and effective order. What Badulf sees from his vantage-point are merely so many fish that happen to look like dead warriors. We, of course, know all too well the dreadful reality. Well might the poet add:

> þis bið seolcuðe þing isiyen to þissen londe:
> swulche deor an hulle, swulche fisces in wælle!
>
> (ll.10644-45)

[This is a remarkable thing come to pass in this land: such a beast on the hill, such fish in the water!]

In the end remarks Layamon, the Saxon hunter flees from the beast he was accustomed to hunt (ll.10647-50).

A gamut of human motives are realistically acknowledged. Deceit and cowardice, merely hinted at in *Judith* or *Maldon,* are now fully expounded. A Christian king and *swiðe goud cniht* who has sent thousands of heathen hounds to hell (ll.14572-74), does not hesitate to abandon his defeated retine to death at the hands of the enemy, creeping away on all fours as though wounded (ll.14629-30). Another can apparently admit to having stolen away from his army by night to sleep with his wife (and incidentally because his enemy has such a large force), urging her to bed quickly with the lame excuse that it will improve national morale (ll.9495-501). The softer side of reality is also admitted. The possibility of manly tears is acknowledged, Aurelius's knights weeping at his death, akin to the dignified distress of knightly mourners figured on thirteenth-century English sculptured tombs (l.8884). In a well-observed human picture, two reconciled brothers impulsively throw away their weapons and fall to tears like the children they are, as their mother urges them to kiss and make up: 'You are my dear sons . . . both of you brave knights' (ll.2532-43). The emotional effect of such stories on the contemporary audience is known.

In an unstable world where violence and treachery are commonplace, the virtue of strong, even ruthless, kingship is clear. Layamon's summary of Arthur's rule: 'pleasant enough where he had his will, but exceedingly stern with those who went against it' (ll.11235-36), is strongly reminiscent of the Chronicler's view of William the Conqueror. To be an effective king, it seems that one must be not merely loved but feared (ll.13526-27). Arthur's knights are of course brave and good; they are also threatened and coerced; those summoned to join his army render their service not out of love or loyalty but on pain of death or loss of limbs, or of being burned alive (ll.11131, 14231-32). Layamon's leaders—Arthur not excepted—are even less considerate of their men than Byrhtnoth, consigning thousands to death. Like William, or any contemporary feudal ruler, Arthur is quite prepared to harry his own land to bring a disobedient people violently to heel—reducing Winchester to blood-stained rubble for having given a fugitive enemy temporary shelter (ll.14195-99). Arthur's ferocity is not confined to potential enemies; his retribution against those who break his peace is terrible—whoever they may be. His horrendous response when a drunken Christmas party degenerates from throwing bread rolls to end in knife-play, is to have the knight responsible for starting it promptly dragged to a swamp and drowned, his kinsmen beheaded, and their womenfolk mutilated—their noses cut off so as to destroy their beauty. (And these are the circumstances which lead to the institution of the Round Table!) After this prompt and terrifying execution the merriment resumed at Arthur's behest sounds a somewhat hollow note (ll.11367-420).

Arthur's ferocious reputation ultimately proves a weakness. As excess of proper awe causes men to fear him, the king is distanced, even alienated from those who should serve him, in a manner reminiscent of the eastern despot Holofernes. When Arthur is disturbed by a portentous dream, there is no knight who dares ask him how he feels, or dares offer an unacceptable interpretation 'for fear of losing the limbs he loves' (ll.12792-93). Such isolation renders Arthur not only morally but politically vulnerable. Deprived of necessary counsel at critical moments, he is thus at least partially responsible for his own downfall. Finally, on the eve of his most dreadful reverse, a messenger critically withholds unwelcome news, delaying revelation of his nephew Mordred's treason—his liaison with Guinevere and usurpation of the kingdom—even declaring that there is nothing to worry about in the king's dreams, the significance of which is patently transparent to all except Arthur, who is reluctant to believe its obvious import (ll.13971ff).

Neither Arthur nor any of his knights (although undeniably presented as strong and virtuous) display any of the chivalric qualities they assumed for Wace—who presumably wished to satisfy the courtly expectations of his patron, Eleanor. The Roman ambassadors who demand historically justifiable tribute from Britain are not treated honourably like the Viking herald at Maldon, but thrown to the ground by Arthur's knights, who tear them by the hair and threaten worse (ll.12393-98). Layamon has neither the vocabulary nor the mind to treat such sentiments as *curtesie.* The idiom of chivalry was as yet semantically and socially inaccessible to an English audience. The romantic fiction of knight-errantry by which the young squires at the Angevin court thought to measure their lives was differently perceived through English eyes; from the point of view of a subject people, the all-too-familiar mounted soldiery were unlikely to have appeared in all respects the *chevalers* of courtly French romance.

Nevertheless there are already clearly present in Layamon's portrayal elements of the Arthur of romance: the British hero, appropriated by English and Norman in turn, who would capture the public imagination of all Europe. More than merely the greatest of British kings, Arthur is different in kind from the long roll-call of rulers depicted in the *Brut.* His conception is supernaturally contrived by Merlin, the first and arguably the greatest wizard to figure in English literature. Engendered on a nun by an incubus (ll.7835f, 8538), Merlin is a somewhat dangerous agent through whom the supernatural approaches the knightly world. When he moves the enormous rocks of Stonehenge, it is significant that the court stands well back outside the magic circle Merlin draws (8697f). But the supernatural potential remains largely undeveloped. At Arthur's birth elves are present, although they bestow virtues: wealth, long life, and generosity, rather than the enchanted rings and magical paraphernalia of fairy romance (ll.9608-15). Arthur's weapons and armour are of course remarkable, but not more so than Beowulf 's. If Beowulf 's byrnie was said to have been Weland's work, Arthur's is attributed to the 'elvish smith' Widia (identifiable as Weland's son by Beadohild . . . ; ll.10543-45). Remote and dangerous lakes are infested with the same sort of watermonsters we hear of in *Beowulf,* but they are not directly encountered by human agents. The only dragons seen are in dreams; and the giant of Mont-St-Michel, if gross in size and manners, is very corporeal, and even more credible than Grendel.

After Arthur's final disastrous battle against Mordred—the Round Table dispersed, his kingdom destroyed—the mortally wounded king is borne away to the mysterious Isle of Avalon by elvish maidens. The atmosphere of mystery surrounding his ultimate destination is not dissimilar to that surrounding the departure of Scyld Scefing. But Arthur believes that the elves can heal him of his wounds, and that he will return to rule the Britons in peace and prosperity (ll.14277-82). We know of course that this is unreasonable. However great Arthur may be, within or without the fictive structure he is subject to the same inexorable law of mutability as that long roll-call of kings who have been, are, or are to come, and whose achievement, however great, has come to naught. No mere Arthuriad, Layamon's history of the Britons significantly does not end with the passing of Arthur but goes on to tell the sad fate of his successors. Arthur's greatness might delay, but cannot avert, the iterated pattern of 'And then . . . '. It is undeniable that belief in Arthur's survival and ultimate return was an article of faith among the Celts (ll.14290-92) and the cause of nationalist brawls in Cornwall and Brittany. A persistent cause of political disquiet, it is not insignificant that Angevin pressure was brought on the monks of Glastonbury to search for Arthur's grave—the discovery of which was reported in 1190. But although Arthur was now officially 'dead', the Celtic predilection for such 'Trojan fantasies' would persist well into the thirteenth century. Whereas Wace declared himself personally

doubtful as to the story of Arthur's survival, Layamon is non-committal, acknowledging the tension present between the credible, albeit enlarged, world of history, and the world of romance. At Arthur's birth Merlin had prophesied that he should never die, but poets and minstrels would feed from his body and men be drunk with his blood in a game that should last them until the world's end (ll.9406f, 11494f). It is clearly Arthur's reputation rather than his person which is in consideration, since it is only in imagination that the inexorable process of mutability may be defied. But the literary amalgam of reality and fiction could not prove stable, and the Arthur of romance precipitates out from the chronicle. (pp. 174-87)

> *Michael Swanton, "An Assured Heroism," in his* English Literature before Chaucer, *Longman, 1987, pp. 142-92.*

Jeff Rider   (essay date 1989)

[*In the following excerpt, Rider assesses Layamon's depiction of Merlin, comparing it with Wace's treatment of that character, and discusses Layamon's reworking of Wace's poem as an expression of protest against Norman hegemony.*]

Wace's *Roman de Brut* and Layamon's adaptation of it have been closely compared a number of times, and "canonical" characterizations of the two texts and the two poets were established as early as 1906. Wace was quintessentially Norman, a professional writer who enjoyed royal patronage. Layamon was "a thorough mediæval Saxon," a rustic priest who wrote to please himself, perhaps out of a sense of patriotism.

Layamon's thorough, even militant, "Englishness" has long been observed in his textual practice—his language, poetic form, and figures—and in his imaginative reworking of certain characters and episodes. Dorothy Everett [in *Essays on Middle English Literature,* 1955] and E. G. Stanley [in "Layamon's Antiquarian Sentiments," *Medium Aevum* 38 (1969)] have also explained how a militant Anglo-Saxon could have moral and political reasons for choosing to translate a Norman, anti-Anglo-Saxon poem. What has not been done, and what I would like to do here, is to show that the moral and political motives which led Layamon to choose to rewrite Wace's poem in an archaic English idiom also oriented him toward the poetic material in a way fundamentally different from Wace. Layamon's new orientation toward this material is reflected in a distinct preference for fictional discourse over historical discourse and is most evident in his reimagining of Wace's Merlin and of the relationship between Merlin and the kings he serves. A study of Layamon's transformation of Merlin can thus show us how more effective romancing—a shift away from historical discourse toward fictional discourse—may have moral and political import.

A study of Layamon's transformation of Wace's Merlin can inform us in other ways. It can show the complexity of Layamon's response to the *Roman* and the thoroughness with which he reinvested it with new values and meanings. It can tell us more about Layamon's attitude toward his historical circumstances and help us give life to those circumstances. It can, finally, help us to a better understanding of the poem's social function, the role it could play for Layamon and for English men and women like him, and to a fuller explanation of the reasons why the English priest undertook to rewrite the French cleric's poem.

The fundamental lineaments of the Merlin of Wace's *Roman* and Layamon's **Brut** go back to Geoffrey of Monmouth's *Historia regum Britanniæ*. In this work Merlin functions as prophet, sage, and wizard to three kings; his most important actions are his prophecy of Arthur's birth and career and his use of magic to bring about Arthur's conception. Merlin's dual role of prophet and wizard puts him in a peculiar position which Robert Hanning has summed up like this: "His use of his special power to perform magic deeds . . . puts him temporarily in control of national progress, as with Arthur's conception. At such moments, Merlin exemplifies human greatness creating history and its own destiny. Since, however, he has predicted Arthur's coming in his vatic seizure, he acts here too as an agent of inexorable history, bringing to fruition that which he knows must happen. It might be said that Merlin is Geoffrey's symbol for the artist-historian; whose insight into predetermined history gives him some control over the historical process." [*The Vision of History in Early Britain*, 1966]. Layamon clearly appreciated Merlin's unique position. In a scene not found in Geoffrey's *Historia* or Wace's *Roman,* Layamon has Merlin share his foreknowledge with a messenger Uther has sent to him to ask if he will come to the king: "Uther [says Merlin] desires the beautiful Ygærne, Gorlois' wife; he desires her greatly. But he will never obtain her, never at any time, except through my stratagem, for there is no more faithful woman in this world. Nevertheless, he shall possess the beautiful Ygærne and he shall engender in her one who will rule widely." Merlin is the linchpin of history. He reveals history, he shapes it, and yet he is its creature, merely tracing its preexisting shape.

Merlin's ambiguous relation to history is mirrored in his ambiguous heritage. He is the offspring of a Welsh princess, who will later become a nun, and an incubus demon, one of those spirits who, as Geoffrey relates, live "between the moon and the earth" and "have partly the nature of men and partly that of angels, and when they wish assume mortal shapes and have intercourse with women." Layamon expands on this somewhat, adding that these demons "make fun of the folk. Many a man they often trouble in dreams and many a beautiful woman soon gives birth through their power and many a good man's child they beguile through magic." These demons—who are not to be confused with devils, for, Layamon insists, "they do not much harm" (Ne doð heo noht muchel scaðe)—are good examples of what C. S. Lewis, [in *The Discarded Image*, 1964], termed the *longævi:* "They are marginal, fugitive creatures. They are perhaps the only creatures to whom the Model does not assign, as it were, an official status. Herein lies their imaginative value. They soften the classic severity of the huge design. They intrude a welcome hint of wildness and uncertainty into a universe that is in danger of being a little too self-explanatory, too luminous." (The Model is Lewis's conception of "the medieval synthesis itself, the whole organisation of their theology, sci-

ence, and history into a single, complex, harmonious mental Model of the Universe.") It is surprising, paradoxical almost, to find the offspring of an incubus demon at the center of history.

It is, moreover, important to recognize the tension inherent in this state of affairs. Merlin is by nature a marginal, unofficial, fugitive, ambiguous figure. The space devoted to him in the narrative is small. Yet his existence and powers are absolutely fundamental for the course of history, which, in a quasi-historical work of this kind, is identical with the narrative. The kings whose succession is the subject of the history are his masters, yet they depend on his vision and help. Merlin is implicitly in competition with the kings and is to some degree a threat to them. History, their story, could easily become Merlin's story: the narrative could easily be displaced from the historical center toward the fictional margin. Bound by history yet shaping it, Merlin represents the free play of language and historical imagination within historical writing, a force potentially independent of the line of kings. In the portion of Geoffrey's *History* which immediately precedes Arthur's advent, history and the narrative thus have, potentially, two poles: Merlin, who reveals and shapes events, and the succession of kings who act them out.

Layamon and Wace differ strikingly in their reactions to this tension. Wace, by and large, makes Merlin subject to the kings and downplays his importance. Layamon, on the other hand, increases Merlin's status and importance at the same time that he makes him more elusive and independent: the tension between the two poles is thus enhanced and the focus of power in this relationship shifts decidedly toward Merlin. Aspects of this difference are evident in the very first scene in which we encounter the prophet. When Merlin's mother is called upon to explain his birth, Wace has her say: "When I was somewhat grown, something, I do not know if it was some ghostly illusion, often came and kissed me closely. Like a man I heard it speak, and it felt like a man to me, and several times it spoke with me, but it didn't show itself at all. It came near to me this way often and often came to kiss me, and it lay down with me and so I conceived; I have never known another man. I bore this boy." Layamon has Merlin's mother say that when she was fifteen and still at home,

> when I was in bed asleep, sleeping softly, then the most beautiful thing that was ever born used to come before me; it looked like a tall knight, dressed all in gold. I saw this each night in a dream while I was sleeping. This thing glided before me and glistened with gold; it often kissed me and often embraced me; it approached me often and came very close to me. When this was at an end and I looked at myself, I thought these things strange: I found my food distasteful, my limbs awkward. I thought it strange and wondered what might be the cause. Then at last I understood that I was with child. When my time came I had this boy.

Layamon increases the incubus's furtiveness by making it a creature of sleep and dream, but he has also imagined the scene more completely and concretely. He takes care to locate these events in time and space (the mother was fifteen, at home, in her room—Wace has none of these details), and he makes the incubus more brilliant and striking. Layamon's episode is at once more mysterious and better drawn; it moves away from historical discourse toward fictional discourse.

The various other aspects of Layamon's transformation of Wace's Merlin can be summarized under three general categories which will be discussed in turn below. These categories are: (1) locating Merlin; (2) his status and role; and (3) the representation of his prophetic powers.

Finding Merlin and obtaining his aid are relatively easy in the *Roman*. When Wace's Aurelie wanted to see Merlin, "the king had him sent for at Labanes, a spring, which was in Wales, very far away—I don't know where it is, because I have never been there. He came to the king who had commanded him to come." Similarly, when Wace's Uther is besieging Gorlois and wants Merlin's help, the wizard is directly at hand in Uther's camp and the king "sent for Merlin and had him come" (Fist mander e venir Merlin [line 8682]). Wace's kings know where Merlin is; they send for him, and he comes obediently at their command.

Layamon's kings have a much rougher time of it. First, they must go to great efforts and expense to find Merlin. Layamon's Aurelie

> sent his messengers through his whole kingdom, and ordered every man to ask about Merlin; and if he should find him, to bring him to the king; he would give him land, both silver and gold, and carry out in the world whatever he wanted. The messengers began to ride wide and far. Some went straight north, and some went out south, some went straight east, and some went straight west; some went on until they came to Alaban, which is a spring in Wales. [Merlin] loved the spring and often bathed in it. The knights found him there where he was sitting by the shore.

In Layamon's version of the second episode, Merlin is not in Uther's camp but must be located "with cunning" (mid liste) through a hermit who is bribed to bring Merlin to the king. In another episode, one not found in the *Roman*, Uther is simply unable to locate the wiseman: "The king had men ride wide and far. He offered gold and treasure to each traveling man, to whoever might find Merlin throughout the land. He attached great importance to this, but he heard nothing of him."

Layamon's kings do not know where Merlin is, and they have trouble finding him. Since he tells both Aurelie's messenger and the hermit that he knew in advance of their coming and since he cannot be located on one occasion, it would seem that Merlin is found only when he wants to be. Once he is found, moreover, it is not at all certain he will agree to do what the king wants. He is, the kings clearly feel, someone they must flatter and seduce. Thus when Aurelie's messengers discovered Merlin by the spring, they "greeted him courteously" (faeire . . . hine igraetten)], called him "wisest of men" (monnene wisest), and delivered this message: "Through us a good king

greets you. He is named Aurelie, the noblest of all kings. He earnestly asks you to please come to him, and he will give you land, both silver and gold." These messengers were also "afraid that he would flee" (afæred, þat he fleon wolde). When Merlin agrees to see Uther out of love for the hermit, the latter weeps and kisses him; and his tears and gratitude suggest that he, too, was afraid Merlin might not go to the king. The point of all this, I take it, is that Merlin is completely independent of Layamon's kings, who cannot, like Wace's kings, simply order him to come.

Once Merlin has—obediently—responded to their summons, Wace's kings do treat him quite well. Aurelie "received him with great honor, made much joy at his coming, greatly treasured him" (l'ad mult enuré; / A grant enur le recuilli, / Mult le joï, mult le cheri [lines 8018-20]) and "requested" and "prayed" the prophet to tell him something of the future, rather than commanding him to do so. Wace's Uther likewise "prayed" Merlin to help him, "implored his mercy," and offered to recompense him for his aid.

Layamon's wizard, however, has a still higher status. Aurelie addresses him "with fair words" (mid fæire . . . worden); Uther speaks to him "with very gentle words" (mid swiðe softe worden) and calls him "dear friend" (leoue freond). When Aurelie heard of Merlin's imminent arrival, writes Layamon, "never before in his life had the king ever been so happy at the arrival of any man who came to him. The king got on his steed and went riding out, and all his knights with him, to welcome Merlin. The king met him and greeted him courteously, he embraced him, he kissed him, and he made him his friend. There was great joy and laughter among the people on account of Merlin's arrival, who was the son of no man." The joy which is described here is public rather than individual or private, and Merlin is clearly perceived to be more here than the curious prophet from whom Wace's Aurelie wants to hear wonders. The king's and people's joy at Merlin's coming is the joy which greets the arrival of a powerful ally, a rescuer, a savior; and such joy is based, in part anyway, on a fear that he might not come.

Merlin has a political importance in this last scene which is also seen at other points in the ***Brut*** and is utterly lacking from the *Roman*. While Uther is commanding an army sent to repel an invasion, a strange comet appears. When the king saw the comet, "his heart was filled with sorrow and he was strangely frightened, as were all the great many men who were in the army. Uther called Merlin, and asked him to come to him, and thus said to him with very gentle words: 'Merlin, Merlin, dear friend, prove yourself and tell us about the token that we have seen; for I do not know what in the world shall come of it. Unless you can advise us we must ride back.' Merlin is again presented here in a public context and as a last resort, a savior; if he cannot give counsel, no one can, and the army must turn back. Wace, in contrast, mentions only that Uther "marveled greatly" (forment s'en merveilla [line 8305]) at the comet, was alarmed by it, and begged Merlin to say what it signified. There is no mention of the army or of turning around; Merlin is Uther's private wiseman, without a public function.

After he has interpreted the appearance of the comet, Merlin disappears without a word from the *Roman.* Layamon turns this silence into an overt absence: "While he [Uther] was king, and chose his ministers, Merlin went away; he never knew where, never in the world, nor what became of him. The king and all his people were grieved, and all his courtiers mourned because of this." The universal sorrow at Merlin's disappearance is a further witness to his public, savior-like role. His disappearance, moreover, is remarked and mourned at a time when Uther is establishing his rule and choosing his ministers, implying that Merlin would have been one of them. Merlin's political importance is also clear from the effect of his absence: when news of his disappearance reaches the Saxon leaders, it encourages them to invade Britain yet one more time (this is their motivation only in the *Brut*). When Merlin reappears, thanks to the hermit's efforts, Uther goes out to him before he reaches the camp and says, "Merlin, you are welcome! Here I set in your hand all the counsel of my land, and you must advise me in my great need. . . . And unless I have your advice you will soon see me dead." Uther offers to make Merlin prime minister, as it were, and appeals to him once more as a savior and last resort. Throughout his appearances in the *Brut,* then, Merlin is seen as possessing a power and a status which make him in some sense the kings' equal or even their superior. The kings are forever seeking to ally Merlin to them but can do so only on his terms. His power is, finally, supreme.

Merlin's greater independence and special status in Layamon's text are also mirrored in his increased otherworldliness. He seems only partly to inhabit this world and is therefore all the less subject to its authorities and laws. Wace has very little to say about this aspect of Merlin. Only once do we get a rather perfunctory description of anything like a trance. Asked to explain the meaning of the comet, "Merlin was greatly troubled, sad at heart, and spoke no word. When his spirit came back to him, he greatly lamented and greatly sighted: 'Ah, God,' he said, 'what great sadness.' " Layamon describes the scene this way: Merlin sat still for a long time as though he were struggling greatly with a dream. Those who saw it with their own eyes said that he often twisted as if he were a worm. At last he began to awaken, then he began to tremble, and Merlin the wise man spoke these words: 'Wellaway, wellaway! Great is the sorrow in this world, that has come to this land. Where are you, Uther? Sit down here before me, and I will tell you of sorrows enough.' After he had explained the comet's meaning, writes Layamon, "Merlin began to doze, as if he wanted to sleep" (Merlin gon to slume, swulc he wolde slæpen). Wace has no such detail: we simply hear no more of Merlin after he is done explaining.

Layamon adds two other such moments to his poem. When Aurelie's messengers found Merlin by the spring, he made no answer to their courteous greeting and was silent so long that they were afraid he would run away. When he finally spoke, Layamon says that "it all broke forth" (hit alles up brac) and Merlin prophesied to the

messengers. Likewise, after Merlin had finished prophesying to Aurelie, he "sat still, as though he would take leave of the world. The king had him brought into a beautiful room" (sæt stille. / al-se þeh he wolde, of worlden iwiten. / Þe king hine lette bringen, into ane fære bure).

These scenes of prophecy, which Layamon has imagined much more clearly and fully than Wace, help make the Merlin of the *Brut* far more mysterious and unworldly than his counterpart in the *Roman.* Merlin's question, "Where are you, Uther?" which, as Frances Gillespy pointed out [in "Layamon's *Brut:* A Comparative Study in Narrative Art," *University of California Publications in Modern Philogy,* 1916], indicates that "he apparently gropes for the king who is near him," and Aurelie's having Merlin led to a room (because he is incapable of guiding himself ?) are particularly nice touches. Wace has nothing more to say about Merlin once he has finished prophesying, but Layamon always takes care to complete the scene and frame the prophecy with descriptions of the prophet. This desire for imaginative completeness is further evidence of Layamon's movement toward fictional discourse.

Merlin's abstraction or unworldliness is also evinced by his lack of concern with material things. To Aurelie's messengers, Merlin replies: "I don't care about his land, his silver, nor his gold, nor his clothes, nor his horses; I have enough myself " (Ne recche ich noht his londes, his seoluer no his goldes. / no his claðes no his hors, miseolf ich habbe inowe [BL 8510-11; M 17051-54]). To Uther he says: "I will not possess any land, neither silver nor gold; for I am in counsel the richest of all men, and if I wished for possessions, then I should become the worse in power." These are again Layamon's additions—additions which show his greater engagement with his material, his fictionalization of it, and his insistence on Merlin's distance from the world.

Layamon's Merlin is distinctly better imagined, more prominent, and better integrated into the work than Wace's figure. His prophetic gift and trance are more fully circumstantiated, his comings and goings are better noted, and his political role in the British *regnum* is markedly greater. Layamon's Merlin differs from Wace's most, though, in his elusiveness. He is hard to find; he is beyond coercion, beyond royal command, not to be bought. His spirit seems to hold commerce with another realm. We know more about Layamon's prophet than we do about Wace's, but the more we know, the less he seems knowable. He is fugitive, always on the verge of drifting away—physically or in spirit. When he is present, therefore, he is the center of attention; no longer secondary or subservient, he is welcomed as a savior and receives offers of gifts and service from others. He is a power in this world and a link to another, living ambiguously between the two.

In Merlin's increased independence from royal power; in this increased tension between the historical, political center and the visionary, fictional margin; in Layamon's movement away from historical discourse toward fictional discourse, we see not only more effective romancing but also a reflection of the difference between Wace's and Layamon's circumstances. On the one hand we have the Norman court poet at the heart of a Norman empire; on the other there is the Saxon parish priest at the empire's edge. Just as Layamon's linguistic archaizing was not an innocent yearning for the good old days but a political gesture whose modern equivalent would be something like an exhibition of traditional Palestinian crafts on the occupied West Bank, so in Merlin's elusiveness and independence we find the representation of feelings of resistance, of defiance of what was Norman, royal, central, predetermined.

Layamon's transformation of Merlin demonstrates and epitomizes the English poet's movement away from historical discourse toward fiction, a movement which represents Layamon's feelings of defiance and resistance toward the central, Norman authority in exactly the same way that Merlin shows increased independence from royal power, but on a larger level. In Layamon's time historical discourse was traditionally viewed as "a narrative of things which were done," and as an account of "true things which were done." It was contrasted with fiction, with "fable," which "contains things neither true nor verisimilar" [Cicero, *Rhetorica ad Herennium*] and which was considered an account of "things not done, but made up," of "things which were neither done nor can be done, for they are against nature" [Isidore of Seville, *Etymologiarum sive originum libri xx*]. History, that is, was the discourse of the real, the natural, the probable, while fiction was the discourse of the imaginary, the un- or supernatural, the unlikely. To write history—to write about the real, the natural, the probable—was in some sense for Layamon to write about the Normans: the "things that had been done," after all, had led to the Norman conquest. The greater independence and importance Layamon accords to the prophet-wizard Merlin are a sure sign of the poet's shift toward fiction, toward the imaginary, the unlikely, the supernatural.

The tension between Merlin and the kings—between the fictional margin and the historical center—and the shift toward fiction are conspicuous in the episode of Arthur's conception. Gorlois has shut himself in one of his Cornish castles and locked Ygærne in Tintagel. After a week of assaults, Uther has still failed to take Gorlois's castle and, he swears, "I desire the beautiful Ygærne so much that I cannot go on living" (swa swiðe me longeð, þat ne mai i noht libben. / after þere faire Ygærne). Yet there is little he can do, for Tintagel is "closed tightly all around with sea cliffs, so that it cannot be taken by any man" (mid sæ-cliuen, faste biclused. / þat ne bið he biwunne, þurh nanes cunes monnen), and Ygærne herself "is good, a most faithful woman" (is wel idon, a swiðe treowe wimmon).

Stymied and dying of desire, Uther turns to Merlin. After reminding the king that "there is no knight, however noble, of any land, who can unfasten the gates of Tintagel with force" (Nis nan cniht swa wel iboren, of nane londe icoren. / þe mi[d] strengðe of Tintaieol, þe yeten mihten un-tunen), Merlin unfolds his stratagem: through his "leech-craft" and "magic" (leche-craft, wiyel), Merlin will make Uther's appearance, speech, and the rest exactly like Gorlois's. The transformed Uther is freely admitted to Tintagel and to the unsuspecting Ygærne's bed. That night Arthur is conceived. The next day Gorlois is defeat-

ed and killed; Tintagel surrenders shortly afterward, and Uther and Ygærne marry.

A little reflection shows us that the circumstances of this episode were created precisely to permit a final demonstration of Merlin's powers and give him a role in Arthur's conception. The difficulty of Merlin's task in this episode is stressed, and the efficacy of his "magic" and "power" is contrasted with the futility of royal and knightly "strength." This mention of "power" (craft) takes us back to the incubi, their moral ambiguity, and their powers of deceit and illusion ("many a beautiful woman soon gives birth through their power" [craft]). Such power, deceit, illusion, and moral ambiguity—precisely the qualities of which secular fiction was accused—thus lie at the heart of history and are the sine qua non of its progress. Finally, then, the succession of kings and the progress of history depend utterly on Merlin's supernatural, fictional powers: the "things which were done" depended utterly on "things which were neither done nor can be done, for they are against nature."

Merlin's principal narrative role in the **Brut** is to announce and assure the advent of Arthur; and Merlin, the work's second pole, disappears from the poem after Arthur is conceived. Arthur himself seems to inherit Merlin's prophetic role, foreseeing his own fate in two dreams, the second of which is found only in the **Brut.** The two poles of the work, represented by Merlin and the succession of kings he serves, are united in Arthur, who is, in a sense, the son of both Uther and Merlin, of both history and fiction.

With the advent of Arthur and the disappearance of Merlin, Layamon's relation to what is royal, central, and predetermined shifts radically. The center is no longer occupied by the conquering Normans; in Arthur, the son of both Uther and Merlin, Layamon finds an image of the doomed English under their last kings. Thus it is that Layamon can write, at Arthur's mysterious disappearance, that "formerly there was a wise man named Merlin. He said with words—his sayings were true—that an Arthur should yet come to help the *English,*" seeing in him the promise of an English savior. Layamon, that is, found in Wace's poem a rehearsal and denunciation of his ancestors' sins *and,* in his ancestors' British opponents, an image of his own people's past greatness and the promise of its restoration. An Arthur would yet come who, like the Arthur of the **Brut,** would encompass and unite fiction and history, Merlin and the kings, the two poles of society, the displaced Saxon margin and the empowered Norman center. Layamon's transformation of Merlin increases the tension between the work's two poles; his Arthur provides an imaginative representation of the resolution of this tension.

In Layamon's reworking of Wace's poem, in this move toward fiction and away from history, an imaginative space opens up, a space where Layamon could represent and try to resolve some English tensions. The **Brut** was first intended as a celebration of England's past and the English past. It permitted Layamon to recall the English conquest of Britain, to find in the Britons an image of the valiant but doomed English, to see the Norman conquest as a divine punishment of the English for their past misdeeds, and to attribute the Norman victory to God's aid rather than to the unaided strength of the Normans. In the relationship between Merlin and the kings, Layamon could express some of the feelings of defiance and resistance to Norman hegemony that he and other English men and women must have experienced, and he could shift the balance of power in that relationship—in fiction at least—away from the royal, Norman center. In the *Brut,* in imagination at least, Layamon could resolve some of these feelings, foreseeing the day when he and others like him would no longer feel alienated from the central authority.

In reworking Wace's poem, Layamon represented some of the tensions inherent in his historical circumstances together with their resolution. It was precisely because the French poem offered him the opportunity to represent and imaginatively resolve these tensions that he chose to rewrite it, and in the process of representing and imaginatively resolving these real, historical tensions—tensions which could not be so represented and resolved in action—he necessarily produced a more effective fiction. What could not be worked out in action he worked out in literature: a representation of the world, transformed by the power of fiction, where a king depends on Merlin to engender his story. (pp. 1-12)

Jeff Rider, "The Fictional Margin: The Merlin of the 'Brut'," in Modern Philology, *Vol. 87, No. 1, August, 1989, pp. 1-12.*

W. R. J. Barron and S. C. Weinberg (essay date 1989)

[*In the excerpt below, Barron and Weinberg provide an overview of the cultural context of the* Brut, *Layamon's relationship to his literary sources, the characterization of Arthur in the poem, and the* Brut's *status as a national epic.*]

Whether the *Brut* was written ten years before the turn of the century or twenty years after will have made little difference to the cultural context at the level of English life familiar to a country priest. In his western backwater social circumstances changed slowly, and everywhere in England the political conditions established by the Norman Conquest had long been accepted and absorbed. Those who understood such matters recognised that the Conqueror had had some claim to the throne; simpler men regarded his victory at Hastings as God's judgement in his favour, and he legitimised it by exacting the formality of election by the Witan, the old royal council. The bitterness of the Anglo-Saxon aristocracy, robbed of its patrimony, did not outlive the generation decimated at Hastings, proscribed for their resistance to the Conqueror there or in the regional rebellions of the early years, deprived of their lands and so of their rank, power and prosperity. All passed to the Conqueror's kinsmen and followers, Normans, Bretons, Flemings, who had supported him in his military adventure. Their numbers were small; by the end of William's reign (1087) some fifteen hundred held estates in England, representing between one and two per

cent of the population. But they were widely dispersed and, under the king, their power was absolute.

The power of the Church passed, with its lands and treasures, out of English hands. Odo of Bayeux, the Conqueror's brother, distributed benefices to Norman churchmen and by the end of the reign, when only two Englishmen held estates directly from the king, only one native bishop, Wulfstan of Worcester, still retained his see. Lesser men had less to lose; what shocked them was not the replacement of one ruling class by another, but the thoroughness with which the new masters exploited their conquest, the ruthless efficiency with which the Domesday survey (1086) listed every acre, every ox in the kingdom, the rapacity which carried off crucifixes, shrines, altar plate and embroideries to adorn continental churches or Norman dinner-tables.

As memories of the Conquest faded in the course of the twelfth century, it was not the illegal actions of foreigners of which all classes complained, but the punctiliousness with which their new masters enforced English law for their own advantage. Absolute monarchical rule was imitated at local level in the new stone castles whose holders administered justice to the tenants they armed and mounted as their followers in war. The social relationship was familiar to Englishmen accustomed to group themselves in peace and war about a chieftain who was often their kinsman as well as lawgiver. But the new feudal system formalised what had been a voluntary association of social equals; lesser thanes who might once have headed a warband of their own were forced into dependence by the high costs of mounted warfare, and many yeomen farmers, deprived of their lands, sank into serfdom.

Socially dominant and widely dispersed, the seigneurs exerted an influence out of all proportion to their numbers, their Norman entourage living closely and working daily with their English sub-tenants, village reeves, childrens' nurses and other domestic servants. The age was one of comparative peace, after centuries of Islamic and Viking threat to Europe, when an unprecedented rise in population facilitated forest clearances, marsh drainage, the use of heavier ploughs and the foundation of thousands of new villages. The consequent increase in trade and the flourishing of the towns allowed some Englishmen to rise in the world and achieve a degree of social independence: skilled craftsmen, merchants, goldsmiths who were bankers to the barons, the minters of coin who continued to come from traditional English families. As their wealth increased, their daughters married into Norman families; English women of good family had made such marriages since the Conquest. Slowly the two peoples began to mingle, to share common values, to forget their different racial origins.

The social situation was mirrored in the linguistic, evolving slowly from age to age, area to area, with a complexity too great to be recorded in detail. The conquerors had no nationalistic bias against English; though William abandoned his personal effort to learn the language, he continued its administrative use in the first generation. But with the displacement of the old ruling class, the spoken language diversified into the dialects of a land-bound peasantry which the new rulers had no incentive to learn. Their Norman French assumed any administrative function for which Latin was inappropriate: pleading in the lawcourts, the keeping of estate records and household accounts, the education of nuns. It was also the language of polite society which any Englishman hoping to rise in the world— surviving thanes anxious for assimilation with their peers, native clergy seeking preferment, the higher servants on baronial estates—had to master as perfectly as possible. For some two centuries it retained its dominance as an island-wide vernacular, spoken by all who aspired to power in any sphere, increasingly cut off from its continental roots, slowly evolving into Anglo-Norman.

But the great mass of Englishmen knew no more of it than the occasional word of command thrown at them or a snatch of song picked up from the castle servants. Gradually their weight of numbers told and their masters became increasingly, if at first casually, bilingual. The children of mixed marriages carried into adult life a smattering of the mother-tongue learnt in the nursery. Conscientious Norman clerics, if they hoped to be effective at parish level, needed English as administrators even if they left preaching to the ill-educated native clergy. Great churchmen, civil servants as much as priests, and the great nobles, crown officers as much as landed magnates, with whom they did formal business in Latin, might use French and English at other levels of their complex lives.

The early thirteenth century, when Layamon seems most likely to have been parish priest of Areley Kings, was a turning point in the shifting balance between the three languages. In 1204 Normandy was lost to the English crown in a dispute with the king of France as nominal overlord, forcing those with feudal holdings in both countries to decide where their allegiance lay and abandon their estates in one or the other to younger brothers. England had meanwhile acquired, through marriage or conquest, vast territories in south-west France which kept her in constant conflict with the emergent nation-state whose dialect, Francien, was increasingly the medium of French cultural dominance in western Europe. Anglo-Norman, in its insular isolation, seemed increasingly a provincial dialect to be replaced in the education of the nobility, whose children now had to be taught the class idiom, by continental French. Though its social prestige had begun to wane, Anglo-Norman relinquished its administrative function reluctantly, sphere by sphere, over the centuries as English again became the language of government, lawcourts, schools and eventually, in the age of Chaucer, of courtly literature. Its eventual triumph was still far off in the age of Layamon; to his contemporaries its literary renaissance would have seemed highly improbable.

With the hindsight of our modern perspective, the future of English literature seems no more in doubt than that of the language. Since the mass of the people continued to speak English, their need for entertainment and instruction would ensure its ultimate return to literary use. But whatever form it took in the post-Conquest centuries, the literature of an under-class was unlikely to find more than accidental and fugitive record in written form. Some scriptoria at least went on copying those forms of pre-Conquest

literature whose social function remained valid: the *Anglo-Saxon Chronicle,* a historical record given national status by Alfred the Great (871-99), was continued at local level, surviving until 1154 at Peterborough Abbey; the homilies which Ælfric, Abbot of Eynsham (*c.* 955-*c.* 1020), wrote for the spiritual instruction of laymen and uneducated clerics, lived on in the south-west well into the twelfth century. From the west too came the *Katherine*-group of religious texts (lives of Katherine and other female saints, a treatise on virginity, devotional pieces to the Virgin and Christ— in highly wrought prose full of the rhythmical and alliterative effects of Old English verse), and the *Ancrene Wisse,* a practical and devotional guide for anchoresses revised for use by a wider community of female recluses. The practical function of such texts in the education of female religious was to keep their influence alive for centuries to come; the Old English prose tradition had survived the Conquest. Poetry, when it was again recorded in any quantity, wore the metrical dress of the French tradition—chiefly the octosyllabic couplet—ornamented with features of Anglo-Saxon verse, but showing a native wit, some learning and an English idiom, enriched with borrowed terms, wholly at home in the new forms. It was polite, the product of minor monastic houses or the grammar schools attached to them, but not courtly.

The court of the Normans and Angevins spoke the language and shared the tastes of the French-dominated courts of western Europe. The oldest surviving copy of the national epic, *La Chanson de Roland,* said to have been sung on the battlefield at Hastings, was made in England. For a century and more there was little to distinguish continental and insular literature; the same patrons employed writers on both sides of the Channel and the literary traffic in a revolutionary age was not all one-way. The court of Henry I (1100-35) produced, under the patronage of his queens, a novel amalgam of saint's life, adventure story and spiritual vision in the *Voyage of St Brendan,* the oldest *Bestiaire* in the French language, and a verse history of the reign. Henry II's queen, Eleanor of Aquitaine, dedicatee of Wace's *Brut,* was also patroness of Benoit de Sainte-Maure's *Roman de Troie;* her husband was most probably the king to whom Marie de France dedicated her *Lais,* some, if not all, written in England. Of the earliest versions of the Tristan story, precursors of the full-blown *roman courtois,* one was certainly, the other most probably composed there. To the end of the Middle Ages French was to remain an acceptable literary language at the English court.

Both vernacular traditions drew freely upon Latin, the medium of the common intellectual culture of western Christendom. England had had its place in that tradition as beneficiary and contributor ever since the establishment of the Christian missions in Kent in the last years of the sixth century and in Northumbria early in the seventh. In the monastic schools of Canterbury and at Wearmouth, Jarrow and York, Latin and Greek were taught as well as anywhere in the western world. From them missionaries and scholars went out to spread the faith in Germany and teach in the palace-schools of Charlemagne's empire. The northern tradition faded after the Danish invasions and the destruction at York of the largest library in Europe;

the southern contributed to Alfred's revival of English culture in resistance to Danish barbarism.

The Conquest was to involve England in the intellectual revival of the twelfth century, by which time men of native stock had returned to leadership of the Church and English clerics moved freely between cathedral schools and nascent continental universities. Their learning, intended for the service of religion, also served the needs of the state, and their Latinity, shaped in the schoolroom by models drawn from classical antiquity, inevitably absorbed and reflected some of the associated values. A typical example, John of Salisbury (c. 1115-80), educated under Abelard at Paris and later Bishop of Chartres, believed the ethical teaching of Horace and Cicero compatible with the Christian faith and regarded Virgil as expressing, in allegorical form, the truth of all philosophy. Others might warn about the insidious influence of pagan authors, but their style was redolent of the very works they warned against. And style as well as learning could bring advancement at court; men like Walter Map (c. 1140-1210) and Giraldus Cambrensis (1147-1223) served Henry II as civil servants but also as entertainers writing history, pseudo-history, anecdote and folklore with wit and elegance. Others wrote poetry with the epic pretensions of their classical models, such as Joseph of Exeter's *De Bello Troiano* in which ancient history is strongly coloured with medieval romance. It was this sphere of clerical learning in the service of courtly entertainment, remote from the world of a provincial parish priest, which, somewhat improbably, saw the genesis of Layamon's *Brut.* (pp. xii-xvi)

. . . . .

What has been said of Wace's *Brut,* might, with variation of terms, be said of Layamon's poem: the narrative sequence, the thematic sweep, the sense of historical conviction derive from Geoffrey; but Layamon has coloured the whole with the spirit, the atmosphere, some of the expressive means of Old English epic. No one seriously doubts that Wace's version was the intermediary: but Layamon's text, at 16,095 long lines, each roughly equivalent to an octosyllabic couplet, is more than twice as long. The disparity is such, passage after passage having no counterpart in Wace, that it has been suggested Layamon's source must have been some version of the *Historia* other than Wace's *Roman:* an extended text of Wace incorporating material which might account for the additions in Layamon, or the lost version of Gaimar, or some other lost redaction of Geoffrey. The supposition is a somewhat backhanded compliment to Layamon, valuing the additional material as too significant to have originated with a provincial English poet. But if Gaimar's version contained such interesting additions and showed anything of Layamon's dramatic sense—and his *Estorie des Engleis* makes the latter unlikely—it is difficult to see why it should have been displaced by Wace's less detailed text. The manuscripts of Wace so far analysed show comparatively trifling variations, verbal rather than narrative or thematic; and, whatever other lost redactions may have contained, it is difficult to believe that the archaic, traditional character of Layamon's *Brut,* to which much of the additional matter notably contributes, can have been inherited from

a French source. In the future, fuller knowledge of the vernacular versions of the *Historia* may clarify the source of individual episodes; it is unlikely to account for the extent and nature of the additions in Layamon.

Layamon source studies have, to some extent, been distorted by concentration upon a number of passages which seem to offer support for various theories of the cultural influences upon the poet and, in particular, about the origin and transmission of the Arthurian legend. A characteristic instance is the presence at Arthur's birth of *aluen* who bestow on him gifts of valour, dominion and long life (9609-15). Supernatural intervention in the life of mortals suggests Celtic influence, traced by some scholars to Breton sources preserved only in late folklore form, by others to Irish legends of fairy gifts bestowed upon heroes, supporting a theory, not generally accepted, that Layamon was of Scandinavian-Irish origin and shows personal knowledge of Irish matters. But in Norse legends also, the Norns preside over birth and foretell the destiny of princes and, though there is nothing conclusive in the Germanic origin of the term *aluen* (often used to translate names of classical nature-spirits—dryads, naiads, nymphs), Layamon may equally well have drawn upon Germanic tradition. The concept of gift-giving fays is probably too widespread to be traced to a particular tradition without more precise detail than Layamon gives.

Other apparent additions also suggest that Layamon was embroidering upon established tradition rather than conflating differing versions or freely inventing. But for the few lines in Wace on the making of the Round Table (9747-60), he would no doubt have been credited with drawing directly on the Celtic traditions concerning it to which Wace alludes. Yet Wace's text supplies the essential framework for Layamon's much longer passage (11345-464); the implication that Arthur had the table made in response to the rivalry for pre-eminence among his followers apparently suggested to Layamon the contention for places in a hierarchical seating order, the blows which might follow, the throwing of loaves and wine-bowls, and the extreme punishments merited by the ringleaders. His excited imagination reflects not so much the regressive barbarism of which he has been accused as contemporary reality. The punishments are those for treason, an act of violence in the sovereign's presence threatening the stability of the state—a danger still reflected in the regulations of the Palace of Westminster, red tape in the cloakrooms for the hanging of swords, the two sword-lengths separating Government and Opposition benches in the chamber—and are extended to kinsmen and womenfolk on the accepted basis that treason is an inheritable taint in the blood. The initiative taken by one of Arthur's hostages to suppress the riot with the only weapons available, the carving knives laid before the king, is reminiscent of those occasions in Anglo-Saxon literature when hostages make common cause with their captors under assault. That the suggestion for the building of the table comes from a Cornish carpenter may imply a localised version of a common Celtic legend, but the precision of detail which gives sixteen hundred as the number of those who could be seated round it is as characteristic of Layamon's love of the concrete as the making of a sequence of scenes full of dialogue from Wace's outline narrative is typical of his dramatic instinct.

Other passages which have attracted interest because they provide additional details of key episodes of the Arthurian legend have a similar air of extrapolation within a widely diffused tradition. To Wace's bare mention of Arthur's departure to Avalon (13277-8), Layamon adds that there his wounds will be healed by the fay Argante (14277-80), identified with his sister Morgan in French romance where the same details are given. Their occurrence there might suggest that she was associated with Avalon in Breton legend, but does not rule out the possibility that the association was also part of the Celtic tradition more immediately available to Layamon. Another instance of imaginative extrapolation which owes little or nothing to Celtic tradition is Arthur's dream of the treachery of Modred and Guenevere (13981-14021), inserted by Layamon after news of it has been brought but not yet revealed to the king. The passage reduplicates the earlier dream in which Arthur, during the crossing to France, sees a dragon defeat a bear in combat, a dream which his attendants fear to interpret as ill-omened. The tension created by the uncertain significance of the dream is repeated here by the reluctance of the messenger to admit that it relates to the news he has so far concealed, though the imagery makes its meaning clear: Arthur dreams that he bestrides a great wooden hall with Gawain seated before him as champion, royal sword in hand; Modred hews through the supporting pillars while Guenevere pulls down the roof, and, as the hall collapses, king and nephew fall, Arthur breaking his right arm and Gawain both of his; but, taking his sword in his left hand, Arthur cuts down the traitors. Structurally and thematically the episode echoes Geoffrey; its imagery, reminiscent of the Anglo-Saxon hall as the seat of royal power and the associated concept of the *comitatus* as royal bodyguard and defender of the nation, seems unlikely to have come from Gaimar's Anglo-Norman version or from an extended text of Wace. The later part of the vision is blurred by reuse of the animal imagery of the earlier dream, obscure in significance; but the combination of the general tradition of prophetic dreams, Geoffrey's imagery and thematic application, and the inventive employment of English images is characteristic of Layamon.

His presentation of Arthur's armour (10542-62) represents a similar amalgam: to the general concept of the hero's arms as emblems of his valour exploited by Geoffrey in a passage (§147) where names drawn from Celtic tradition are given to Arthur's shield, sword and spear, a passage barely changed in Wace, Layamon adds further details of Celtic origin (that the sword Caliburn was made by magic skill in Avalon) and of Germanic colouring (that Uther's helmet was called Goswhit and his corslet Wygar made by Witege (Widia), son of the magical weapon-smith Weland). And when he returns to Arthur's equipment on a later occasion (11856-70), without warrant from Wace, he attributes the spear Ron, inherited from Uther, to the Carmarthen smith Griffin. Appreciating the significance of the hero's arms being made by specially skilled, even supernatural smiths, inherited from various ancestors, given individual names, Layamon clearly felt free to embellish

the arming convention from the variety of racial traditions available to him in the melting-pot of post-Conquest England.

It is natural that, living where he did, he should be assumed to have drawn on Welsh sources for additional details of the Celtic Arthur. There are some details which suggest such an origin: the comment that Caerleon was accursed (12114); the statement that the battle between Arthur and Lucius was the third greatest ever fought (13717), as if referring to one of the triads in which Welsh tradition listed significant events or persons in threes as an *aide-mémoire* in recalling their stories; the Saxons' curious threat to make a bridge of Arthur's backbone, to lay his bones in the doorway of the hall where all men must pass (10473-9), reminiscent of the story in the *Mabinogi* of Bran the Blessed who used his body as a bridge on which his army might cross to Ireland. None offers conclusive proof, only the possibility that elements of Celtic tradition, widely dispersed in western Europe, were most readily available to Layamon in Wales, of whose geography he shows some knowledge.

Equally the few trifling details in which his version seems closer to that of Geoffrey than of Wace prove no direct knowledge of the *Historia,* the disparity often disappearing when the Wace variants are consulted. But there are undeniable echoes of Merlin's Prophecies which Wace omitted: to Merlin's bare announcement in the *Roman de Brut* that Uther shall have his way with Ygerne, wife of Earl Gorlois, Layamon adds his pronouncement that the child to be born of their union should have immortal fame, should rule in Rome, and should never die:

> 'Of him scullen gleomen　godliche singen;
> of his breosten scullen æten　aðele scopes;
> scullen of his blode　beornes beon drunke.
> Of his eyene scullen fleon　furene gleden;
> ælc finger an his hond　scarp stelene brond.
> Scullen stan walles　biuoren him tofallen;
> beornes scullen rusien,　reosen heore mærken.'
>
> (9410-16)

('Of him shall minstrels splendidly sing; of his breast noble bards shall eat; heroes shall be drunk upon his blood. From his eyes shall fly sparks of fire; each finger on his hand shall be a sharp steel blade. Stone walls shall fall down before him; men shall tremble, their banners fall.')

In the *Historia* (§112.2), it is said of the Boar of Cornwall, champion of the oppressed British against the invading Saxons—manifestly Arthur: '*In ore populorum celebrabitur et actus eius cibus erit narrantibus*' ('It shall be extolled in the mouths of its peoples, and its deeds will be as meat and drink to those who tell tales'); and at §115.26 it is said of the Boar of Commerce, feasibly associated with Arthur: '*Pectus eius cibus erit egentibus et lingua eius sedabit sitientes*' ('Its breast will be as food to the hungry and its tongue will assuage the thirst of those who are dry'). These two sentences seem to have been conflated in Layamon's passage, but the extrapolation from the concept of a hero's reputation serving as meat and drink to the bards who sing of him to the Eucharistic imagery of a Saviour on whose body and blood his people are spiritually nourished is typical of the verbal exaltation which overcomes Layamon in moments of heightened thematic interest. The image of Arthur's fingers as blades of steel seems a similar imaginative invention, but the picture of him as a ruler of Rome before whom stone walls shall fall may echo another sentence in the Prophecies (§112.2): *'Tremebit Romulea domus seuitiam ipsius et exitus eius dubius erit'* ('The House of Romulus shall dread the Boar's savagery and the end of that House will be shrouded in mystery').

The combination of invention and extrapolation is characteristic; so also is the repetition of this passage at a later moment of exaltation, the founding of the Round Table (11489-517), with variation of terms which queries further the form in which Layamon can have known the Prophecies. It is combined there with Merlin's prognosis that the British would refuse to credit Arthur's death when he should later depart to Avalon, while his prophecy that the walls of Rome should fall down before the king is echoed at the moment when he is about to launch his final attack upon the empire (13964-70).

These echoes of the Prophecies, though sufficiently close to Geoffrey's text to imply a literary rather than an oral origin, are yet so vague as to suggest something recollected from memory rather than immediately based upon a text consulted. The same might equally be true of the only incident in Layamon's **Brut** which appears to derive from Bede, Pope Gregory's famous encounter with Anglo-Saxon slaves in the Roman forum which inspired the Augustinian mission for the conversion of their island. An episode so vital to the Christian history of the country might, however, have been widely enough diffused in popular tradition to account for its appearance in the **Brut** (14695-728). But there is some indication in the forms of Anglo-Saxon names given by Layamon, much more consistent and authentic than the variable, often almost unrecognisable, forms given in the Wace manuscripts, that Layamon had direct access to a text of the *Historia Ecclesiastica,* the original Latin or the Anglo-Saxon translation, either of which could have supplied more correct models. Two other apparent borrowings from Anglo-Saxon sources suggest where he might have had access to either text or both. There is a possibility that Layamon may have drawn upon the homilies of Ælfric, Abbot of Eynsham, in condemning idolatry when Brutus visits the Temple of Diana after the fall of Troy (569-637), and in his account of Vortigern's resort to sacrificing a child without a father to ensure the completion of his tower of refuge in the Welsh mountains (7721-880) where there may be echoes of matter associated with Ælfric's condemnation of the killing of illegitimate children. The echoes in both cases are scattered and inexact, like vague memories of earlier reading. Layamon may have read the homilies at Worcester where a large library of Old English manuscripts, including many Ælfric texts, was still preserved in the thirteenth century.

The source evidence, imprecise though it still is, suggests that Layamon felt free to embellish his version of a masterwork, Geoffrey's *Historia,* with whatever his imagination found relevant among the materials, literary, oral and personal, stored in his mind. His treatment of Wace is characteristically medieval, unrestrained by any inhibiting respect for the integrity of the work or the authorial property of those who had preceded him, assuming the right, the duty to bring to it anything which would make it more meaningful, more persuasive for the particular audience for which he intended it. The liberty which Wace himself had assumed Layamon carried much further, yet without significant narrative additions, alterations or rearrangements in sequence. The great difference between their versions is not in matter but in the manner of narration, most characteristically in reduplication of incidents, imaginative extrapolation of given material, dramatisation of narrative in action, dialogue, formal speeches, extended similes, repeated formulae of imagery and expression. Repeatedly and constantly, the English **Brut** loses touch with the French text, sometimes for hundreds of lines, yet without introducing anything markedly alien or inappropriate to the context of the original. The effect is of effortless extrapolation from the known to the unknown, from familiar outline to intimate and novel detail.

> **The narrative expansion and imaginative intensity with which Arthur is treated in the *Brut* indicates his importance in Layamon's interpretation. . . .**
>
> **—Barron and Weinberg**

The opening episode of the Arthurian section, the fathering of the hero, contains a characteristic example of narrative reduplication. In Wace, when Uther, frustrated in his passion for Ygerne, is advised to send for Merlin, the seer appears within a few lines (8676-82), having been with the royal army. The English adds a sequence of highly dramatised scenes, some seventy lines in all (9361-430): Uther confides in his thane Ulfin who tells him that there is a hermit with the army who knows Merlin, ' "where he lies each night under the heavens; and Merlin often spoke with him and told him wondrous things" ', and if they could win him over the king might gain his desires. At Uther's request, the hermit 'journeyed into the land to the west, to a vast forest, a wilderness where he had lived full many a year, and in which he had often encountered Merlin'. There he finds Merlin eagerly expecting him since, as he reveals in a long speech, he knows everything that has passed since the hermit left for the royal camp, including why he is so urgently needed: ' "Uther is filled with longing for the lovely Ygerne, greatly besotted with the wife of Gorlois. But it will never happen, as long as time shall last, that he shall win her save by my magic skill; for there is no truer woman in this mortal world." '

Though not found in Wace, this is not truly invention on Layamon's part; in outline it reduplicates an earlier episode when Merlin is missing in a moment of need. Aurelius, Uther's brother and predecessor, seeks advice on a suitable monument to commemorate the British chieftains treacherously massacred by Hengest near Salisbury, and sends messengers far and wide who ultimately find Merlin by a fountain deep in Wales (8473-526). To this episode in Wace (8003-16), Layamon adds the king's promise of land and treasure, Merlin's rejection of all gifts, his fore-knowledge of the mission to find him and of the coming death of Aurelius. These features recur in the reduplicated episode, as if Layamon were echoing his own version rather than Wace's, culminating in Merlin's foretelling of the winning of Ygerne and the future greatness of her son Arthur. The reduplication serves to reintroduce Merlin after an absence prolonged by the increased scale of the English version and renew his association with the mysterious west, to demonstrate his powers as a seer, and create narrative tension by allowing him to prophesy the seemingly impossible, Uther's winning of the virtuous Ygerne. The characteristic reuse of materials adds little that is new, narrative or thematic; but the patterned repetition places the vital prophecy, original with Layamon, at the climax of a long, highly dramatised sequence of preparatory material.

The episode which follows, leading to Uther's death and the succession of Arthur, shows the same sense of climax achieved by vivifying Wace's outline narrative with dramatic action cumulative in its emotional effect upon the reader. Wace describes how the Saxons, unable to overcome Uther in war, send spies disguised in ragged dress who, failing to get within striking distance of the king, poison the well from which he drinks and so kill him (8951-9000). Layamon, taking his imaginative clue from the ragged dress, sends the assassins to court disguised as beggars who, at the royal alms-giving, claim charity as men of worth brought to ruin by Saxon exactions: ' "Neither fish nor flesh ever comes into our bowl, nor any kind of drink save a draught of water, nothing but water alone—that is why we are so lean." ' In a sequence of dramatised scenes, full of dialogue, they are fed, clothed and lodged by Uther, overhear his doctor order a chamberlain to protect the well from falling rain, poison it and, when its water is brought to Uther in golden bowls, he drinks and dies (9797-882). The dramatisation underscores the irony, Layamon's invention, that Uther died by the hands of those who had enjoyed his charity, treachery characteristic of the Saxons in his presentation. Its principal effect is to highlight the climax which immediately follows Uther's burial at Stonehenge: in Wace, Arthur is crowned within four lines (9009-12), while Layamon makes an emotive scene of the boy's reaction to the news of his father's death:

Þus heo gunnen tellen and Arður sæt ful stille;
ænne stunde he wes blac and on heuwe swiðe wak,
ane while he wes reod and reousede on heorte.
Þa hit alles up brac hit wes god þat he spac;
þus him sæide þerriht Arður, þe aðele cniht:
'Lauerd Crist, Godes sune, beon us nu a fultume,
þat ich mote on life Goddes layen halden.'
(9923-9)

(Thus they spoke and Arthur sat quite still; one moment he was pale and quite lacking in colour, next instant he was red, with heartfelt grief. When it all burst out, what he said was fitting; Arthur, the noble knight, at once spoke thus:

'Lord Christ, son of God, be a help to us now, that I may uphold God's laws throughout my life.')

Such additions contribute to theme by emphasis, others by accumulation at much greater length. Arthur's early campaigns of foreign conquest occupy some seventy lines in Wace (9659-730) where, following his defeat of Gillomar, King of Ireland, the rulers of the Orkneys, Jutland, and Winetland come to him in his next conquest, Iceland, offering submission. Over some two hundred and thirty lines (11103-336), Layamon elaborates the pattern of the Irish campaign: brief conflict followed by a long speech of submission by the king, offering tribute, hostages, his sons to serve the conqueror, confirmed upon the relics of Irish saints; and Arthur's benign response accepting the hostages as guarantors of fidelity, remitting half the tribute and promising his protection. The same pattern is then repeated for each of the rulers in turn, omitting the initial fighting and diminishing slightly in length, varying the terms of submission but cumulatively reinforcing the picture of Arthur as ruthless in conquest and gracious in victory, characteristic of Layamon's presentation of the king. To the modern mind the repetitions may be tedious; to the medieval they may well have seemed ceremonious and fitting celebrations of the first foreign triumphs of a national hero.

In terms of Layamon's use of sources they confirm the general impression of a combination of narrative dependence and creative independence in the elaboration and dramatisation of Wace's outline by reduplication, extrapolation and the importation of congruent detail from other traditions. No doubt the more closely the imported detail conformed to the experience, personal and cultural, of the audience, the more effectively it served Layamon's purpose; but it is scarcely surprising that, in a multi-cultural society, so little of it can be traced to a specific source. This combination of narrative dependence and piecemeal originality has suggested a particular method of composition:

> . . . we infer that he took in good-sized masses of Wace's poem and let them settle down in his imagination and stimulate its own creation; hence his great expansion, especially after the early part . . .; hence also his frequent small changes of order, his occasional contradictions of Wace, and forgetful dropping of very good passages, his constant insertion of precise numbers, fresh proper names, and other concrete detail often highly lifelike, perceptive, emotional—dialogue, speeches and the like, often epic in breadth, good cheer, ideality, adapted to the recitative manner. [J.S.P. Tatlock, *The Legendary History of Britain*, 1950]

Such a method of composition might well explain the varying estimates of Layamon's dependency upon Wace, extensive in terms of matter, much less so in literary expression. (pp. xxviii-xxxvi)

. . . . .

The narrative expansion and imaginative intensity with which Arthur is treated in the ***Brut*** indicates his importance in Layamon's interpretation; but his place in the dynastic pattern and his personal characterisation were pre-determined by Geoffrey of Monmouth. In the line of British heroes founded by Brutus he comes after the high point of Brenne and Belin's conquest of Rome when, with Maximian's withdrawal of the best of the nation for his continental campaigns and the consequent Saxon invasion, the ultimate fate of Britain is already fixed. His personal role as the supreme national champion is heightened by the underlying threats, never wholly forgotten, of foreign invasion and domestic treason. For such a role Geoffrey had time-honoured models in Alexander and Caesar, world-conquerors struck down at the height of their power, and in Charlemagne, though as founder of that empire with which the Angevins were to contend the possession of France rather than the legendary Charlemagne of the *chansons de geste,* old and wise, figure-head rather than active warrior. The legend of Alexander's mysterious, divine parentage perhaps suggested the illicit siring of Arthur by the aid of magic; his youthful accession, his personal prowess and the scale of his conquests may also owe something to the classical model. Charlemagne provided precedent for a secular leader in a patriotic cause against pagan forces uniting his followers by generosity and good government. But these external literary influences need have done no more than strengthen the concept of Arthur inherited from Welsh tradition: valiant war-leader, good Christian devoted to the Virgin Mary, inspiring his followers by his personal prowess, his valour expressed in his arms with their ancient names and reputations. Unrestrained by historical record, Geoffrey has created the figure of an ideal king in whom, nonetheless, many aspects of contemporary monarchy are reflected.

The idealised portrait was clearly acceptable to Layamon, though he chose to emphasise certain features and to reflect different aspects of reality. Many of his additions and elaborations heighten the idealisation of Arthur. The echoes he introduces from Geoffrey's Prophecies of Merlin establish his undying fame even before he has been born:

> 'Longe beoð æuere,   dæd ne bið he næuere;
> þe wile þe þis world stænt,   ilæsten scal is
>   worðmunt;
> and scal inne Rome   walden þa þæines.'
>
>   (9406-8)

('As long as time lasts, he shall never die; while this world last his fame shall endure; and he shall rule the princes in Rome.')

Another of his creative initiatives, invoking the tradition of gift-giving deities at the birth of a prince, defines the sources of Arthur's greatness as warrior, king and long-living, generous patron:

> heo yeuen him mihte   to beon bezst aire cnih-
>   ten;
> heo yeuen him anoðer þing,   þat he scolde beon
>   riche king;
> heo yiuen him þat þridde,   þat he scolde longe
>   libben;
> heo yifen him, þat kinebern,   custen swiðe gode
> þat he wes mete-custi   of alle quike monnen;
>
>   (9610-14)

(. . . they gave him strength to be the best of

all knights; they gave him another gift, that he should be a mighty king; they gave him a third, that he should live long; they gave him, that royal child, such good qualities that he was the most liberal of all living men;)

The armour which is the emblem of his knighthood is given more explicit magical associations than in Wace or Geoffrey:

> þa dude he on his burne   ibroide of stele
> þe makede on aluisc smið   mid aðelen his
>   crafte;
> he wes ihaten Wygar   þe Witeye wurhte.
> His sconken he helede   mid hosen of stele.
> Calibeorne his sweord   he sweinde bi his side;
> hit wes iworht in Aualun   mid wiyelefulle craf-
>   ten.
>
>   (10543-8)

(. . . then he put on his corslet of woven steel which an elvish smith had made by his noble skill; he who made Wygar was called Witeye. He protected his legs with hose of steel. At his side hung his sword Caliburn; it was made in Avalon by magic arts.)

And the numinous element is increased by the invention of Arthur's second dream (13981-14021); though modelled at least in part upon the first, uninterpreted omen (12764-93), the king reveals his own understanding of it by his concern for the absent Guenevere who, in a dream, he had cut to pieces for her complicity in Modred's treason. Finally, at his departure to Avalon, he admits foreknowledge that the *aluen* who blessed him at birth promise healing for his fifteen terrible wounds and eventual return to his kingdom (14277-82). But though greatly increased by Layamon, the element of the occult is not thematically engaged; Arthur is not supernaturally guided in his mission as national messiah, as his predecessors were by Merlin whom Arthur never meets. It merely adds a gloss of fairy prince to his more realistic roles as war-leader, world conqueror, lawgiver and Christian king.

In the medieval manner, Arthur is characterised in relation to those roles rather than in terms of individuality; others are characterised only in relation to him as beautiful, passive consort, loyal or traitorous nephews, obedient followers, rebellious underlings, imperious or humbled opponents. Nor is there any development in his presentation; at his accession aged fifteen, he is already wholly himself—'and the years had all been well employed, for he was fully mature' (9931). Immediately afterwards, at his coronation, his regal personality is sketched in terms which are to remain constant throughout his reign:

> Þa þe Arður wes king   —hærne nu seollic
>   þing—
> he wes mete-custi   ælche quike monne,
> cniht mid þan bezste,   wunder ane kene;
> he wes þan yungen for fader,   þan alden for
>   frouer,
> and wið þan vnwise   wunder ane sturnne;
> woh him wes wunder lað   and þat rihte a leof.
> Ælc of his birlen   and of his bur-þæinen
> and his ber-cnihtes   gold beren an honden,
> to ruggen and to bedde   iscrud mid gode webbe.

Nefde he neuere nænne coc   þat he nes keppe swiðe god,
neuær nanes cnihtes swein   þat he næs bald þein.
Þe king heold al his hired   mid hæyere blise;
and mid swulche þinges he ouercom alle kinges,
mid ræhyere strengðe   and mid richedome;
swulche weoren his custes   þat al uolc hit wuste.
Nu wes Arður god king;   his hired hine lufede
æc hit wes cuð wide   of his kinedome.

(9945-61)

(When Arthur was king—now listen to a marvellous matter—he was generous to every man alive, among the best of warriors, wonderfully bold; he was a father to the young, a comfort to the old, and with the rash extremely stern; wrong was most hateful to him and the right was always dear. Each of his cup-bearers and his chamberlains and his footmen bore gold in hand, wore fine cloth on back and bed. He never had any cook who was not a good warrior, never any knight's squire who was not a bold thane. The king kept all his followers in great contentment; and by such means he defeated all kings, by fierce strength and by generosity; such were his virtues that all nations knew of it. Now Arthur was a good king; his followers loved him and it was known far beyond his kingdom.)

The ambivalence, benevolence and sterness, ferocity and generosity, is Layamon's addition to the blander portrait in Wace and Geoffrey, and he occasionally restates it aphoristically as the key to Arthur's personality:

Arður wes wunsum   þer he hafde his iwillen,
and he wes wod sturne   wið his wiðer-iwinnen.

(11235-6)

(Arthur was gracious whenever he achieved his purpose, and he was terribly stern with those who opposed him.)

As such, it manifests itself in each aspect of his multiple role.

His function as lawgiver, foretold by Merlin before his birth, sworn to by the young king at the moment of his accession, is periodically renewed at national hustings, exercised in foreign territories whose conquest is confirmed by the establishment of British law, and finally forms the basis of his charge to his successor, Constantin:

'Ich þe bitache here   mine kineriche;
and wite mine Bruttes   a to þines lifes,
and hald heom alle þa layen   þa habbeoð istonden a mine dayen,
and alle þa layen gode   þa bi Vðeres dayen stode.'

(14273-6)

('I here entrust my realm to you; and you defend my Britons as long as you live, and maintain for them all the laws that have been in force in my day, and all the good laws which existed in Uther's time.')

But though the king is presented as the fountain of justice,

justice is as often equated with punishment as with mercy. The punishments decreed by Arthur for those who started the riot which led to the making of the Round Table seem very rough justice indeed:

'Nimeð me þene ilke mon   þa þis feht ærst bigon,
and doð wiððe an his sweore   and drayeð hine to ane more,
and doð hine in an ley uen   þer he scal liggen;
and nimeð al his nexte cun   þa ye mayen iuinden
and swengeð of þa hafden   mid breoden eouwer sweorden.
Þa wifmen þa ye mayen ifinden   of his nexten cunden,
kerueð of hire neose   and heore wlite ga to lose;
and swa ich wulle al fordon   þat cun þat he of com.'

(11393-400)

('Seize that man who first began this fight, put a cord about his neck and drag him to a marsh, and thrust him into the bog where he shall lie; and seize all his close kin whom you can find and strike off their heads with your broad swords. The women of his immediate family whom you can find, cut off their noses and let their looks be ruined; and so I will utterly destroy the race from which he came.')

But violence within the court, threatening the king's peace and the stability of the nation, is treason—for which Arthur imposes the traditional penalty: ' "mid horsen todrayen þat is elches swiken layen" ' (11406). The infectious nature of treason, which justifies the killing of the traitor's kin, is demonstrated in the closing days of Arthur's reign when Modred, having seduced the citizens of Winchester from their loyalty to the king, betrays them in turn, slipping away with his forces and leaving the city to Arthur's punishment:

And Arður Winchestre   þa burh bilai wel faste
and al þat moncun ofsloh   —þer wes soryen inoh!
Þa yeonge and þa alde,   alle he aqualde.
Þa þat folc wes al ded,   þa burh al forswelde,
þa lette he mid alle   tobreken þa walles alle.
Þa wes hit itimed þere   þat Merlin seide while:
'Ærm wurðest þu, Winchæstre;   þæ eorðe þe scal forswalye!'
Swa Merlin sæide   —þe witeye wes mære.

(14195-202)

(And Arthur besieged the town of Winchester very closely and slew all the inhabitants—great was the sorrow there! He killed them all, both young and old. When the people were all dead, the city completely destroyed by fire, then he caused all the walls to be destroyed utterly. Then was it come to pass there as Merlin once prophesied: 'Wretched shall you be, Winchester; the earth shall swallow you up!' Thus spoke Merlin, who was a true prophet.)

Such passages have been cited as evidence of Layamon's sadistic temperament and the unsophisticated nature of his English audience. But an audience, many of whose members may have been born in an age of civil war, remembering the anarchy under Stephen when in the strongholds of baronial freebooters such tortures were inflicted that, according to the *Anglo-Saxon Chronicle,* 'men said openly that Christ and all his saints were asleep', might well have found Layamon's picture of a strong and ruthless ruler both realistic and attractive. Though the antique native roots of his idiom may have darkened that picture with epic colouring suggesting a return to more primitive values, the spectacle of Arthur wooing and coercing his followers to rally to the defense of the nation ('And whoever stayed away should suffer mutilation; and whoever came willingly, he should become rich'), restraining them when they assault the Roman ambassadors in his court (a detail not in Wace), and calming violent disputes between his closest kinsmen in council no doubt seemed admirable exercise of authority in the interests of the nation. Layamon wrote in an age when fear and favour were equally instruments of government and admits their parity in Arthur's methods of control:

> Alle Brut-leoden   luueden Arðuren.
> Alle heom stod him æie to   þat wuneden a þan
> ærde;
>
> (13526-7)

(All the people of Britain loved Arthur. All who dwelt in the land stood in awe of him;)

If he acknowledges the darker side of feudal polity to a greater degree than Wace, it is perhaps because the vividness with which his imagination pictures the reign of Arthur instinctively clothes it in the circumstances of his own age. Ultimately he undermines the heroic image he has been at such pains to create by distancing the king from those who should advise and support him. When the king has his first portentous dream, no one dares to offer an interpretation which might disturb his feudal lord 'lest he should lose limbs which he valued' (12792-3); and the messenger who brings news of Modred's treachery critically delays its delivery and even denies the significance of Arthur's second prophetic dream:

> þa andswarede þe cniht: Lauerd, þu hauest un-
> riht;
> ne sculde me nauere sweuen   mid soryen arecc-
> hen.
> þu ært þe riccheste mon   þa rixleoð on londen
> and þe alre wiseste   þe wuneð under weolcne.
> Yif hit weore ilumpe,   swa nulle hit ure Drihte,
> þat Modred, þire suster sune,   hafde þine quene
> inume
> and al þi kineliche lond   isæt an his ayere hond,
> þe þu him bitahtest   þa þu to Rome þohtest,
> and he hafde al þus ido   mid his swikedome,
> þe yet þu mihtest þe awreken   wurðliche mid
> wepnen,
> and æft þi lond halden   and walden þine leo-
> den,
> and þine feond fallen   þe þe ufel unnen,
> and slæn heom alle clane   þet þer no bilauen
> nane.'
>
> (14022-34)

(Then the knight answered: 'Lord, you are mistaken; one should never interpret dreams ominously. You who rule in this land are the most powerful and the wisest of all who dwell upon earth. If it should have happened, as our Lord forbid, that Modred your sister's son had seized your queen and taken into his own possession your entire kingdom, which you entrusted to him when you planned to go to Rome, and he had done all this by his treachery, still you might fittingly avenge yourself by force of arms, and possess your land again and rule your people, and destroy your enemies who wish you ill, kill them one and all that none of them survive.')

Such adulation rings hollow on the eve of Arthur's last campaign—against fellow Britons.

The dangers of internal dissension are never entirely forgotten: a sudden passion for a loyal subject's wife may precipitate civil war, rivalry for pre-eminence at court lead to riot, quarrels erupt between trusted lieutenants in council. Arthur imposes his authority by using the political means of a feudal age: personal example, public ceremonial, royal largess, state religion. His military prowess is demonstrated both as tactician marshalling forces from all over his empire against the might of Rome, and as national champion fighting the Roman tribune in single combat. Both roles originate with Geoffrey, but Layamon has developed them with vigour and imaginative realism. The single combat, four times longer than in Wace, results from a challenge issued by the enemy leader in the confidence that Arthur will refuse, 'for if Frolle, King of France, had known that Arthur would grant him what he had requested, he would not have done so for a ship full of gold'. Their meeting on an island in the Seine is treated with all the formality of a trial by combat, and victory over an opponent of equal valour is won by Arthur's personal prowess:

> þær Bruttes wolden   ouer water buyen
> yif Arður up ne sturte   stercliche sone
> and igræp his sceld godne,   ileired mid golde,
> and toyaines Frolle   mid feondliche lechen;
> breid biforen breosten   godne sceld brade.
> And Frolle him to fusden   mid his feond-ræse
> and his sweord up ahof   and adunriht sloh,
> and smat an Arðures sceld   þat he wond a þene
> feld.
> Þe helm an his hæuede   and his hereburne
> gon to falsie   foren an his hafde,
> and he wunde afeng   feouwer unchene long—
> heo ne þuhte him noht sær   for heo næs na
> mare—
> þat blod orn adun   ouer al his breoste.
> Arður wes abolye   swiðe an his heorte
> and his sweord Caliburne   swipte mid maine,
> and smat Frolle uppen þæne hælm   þat he atwa
> helden
> þurhut þere burne hod   þat hit at his breoste
> atstod.
> Þa feol Frolle,   folde to grunde;
> uppen þan gras-bedde   his gost he bilæfde.
>
> (11951-69)

(The Britons would have crossed the river then had Arthur not instantly leapt up, grasped his fine shield with its golden rim and, raising his good broad shield before his chest, advanced upon Frolle with hostile intent. And Frolle rushed at him in fierce assault and, raising his sword and striking downwards, smote upon Arthur's shield so that it fell to the ground. The helmet on his head and the chain-mail on his forehead beneath gave way, and he received a wound four inches long—since it was no greater it did not seem painful to him—so that the blood ran down all over his chest. Arthur was greatly enraged at heart, and swinging his sword Caliburn with force, struck Frolle upon the helmet so that it split apart right through the coif of mail and the sword lodged in his chest. Then Frolle fell, stricken to the earth; upon the grassy ground he yielded up his life.)

As in the other battle passages, Layamon relishes the violence, the bodies cut in half, the sword lodging in the teeth of a cloven skull, the showers of arrows 'thick as falling snow', the streams of blood flowing along the forest paths, the wounded soldiers wandering over the wooded countryside. The contrast with Wace's comparatively bland and generalised battle pieces owes more, perhaps, to Layamon's preference for concrete detail and the vividness of his vocabulary than to the sadistic interests with which he is sometimes credited.

On another occasion when the king defends his people against an evil force, he evokes the beastliness of the Giant of Mont St Michel vividly (12960-13040), but not more grotesquely or at greater length than Wace (11450-598) whose comparison with Arthur's combat with the giant Riun, collector of royal beards, Layamon reduces to a bare allusion. But there is a significant contrast: in Wace's account, Arthur hopes to take the giant unawares; Layamon says 'Arthur would never attack him while asleep lest he should later suffer reproach'. Layamon has been said to lack appreciation of chivalry, yet he elaborates descriptively the few lines in the *Roman de Brut* telling how the body of the emperor Lucius was returned to Rome, recognising the honour due to a worthy opponent who 'had been a very brave man while he lived' and underscoring the irony of Arthur's message that the golden coffin was the only tribute he would send the Romans.

Layamon's appreciation of the place of ceremonial in medieval governance seems no less acute than Wace's: Arthur's arming is as splendid, his councils as formal if often more impassioned, his crown-wearing at Caerleon no less detailed, ceremonious or courtly, even if his followers show more interest in field sports and ball games than in the gambling and board games of Wace. The English poet is no less aware of the refinements of court life than the French, except in the matter of courtly wooing where he does no more than lip-service to Wace's rare passages of *amour courtois*. Where he omits such references, as when Gawain praises peace as conducive to amorous dalliance, it is in favour of a different idealism based on social good rather than personal happiness:

'for god is grið and god is frið þe freoliche þer
    haldeð wið—
and Godd sulf hit makede þurh his Godd-
    cunde—
for grið makeð godne mon gode workes wurc-
    hen
for alle monnen bið þa bet þat lond bið þa
    murgre.'
                                        (12455-8)

('. . . for peace and quiet are good if one maintains them willingly—and God himself in his divinity created them—for peace allows a good man to do good deeds whereby all men are the better and the land the happier.'!)

Ceremonial occasions display the unity and magnificence of the Round Table and the royal munificence which underpin both. Arthur rewards loyal service with kingdoms and castles, dismisses aged knights with rich gifts, restores forfeited lands to pardoned rebels (though not to traitors or perjurers), and feasts his followers to the sound of trumpets. Much of the detail is merely echoed or elaborated from Wace, but Layamon's understanding of the role of generosity in Arthur's regality is apparent from his initial characterisation: 'The king kept all his followers in great contentment; and by such means he defeated all kings, by fierce strength and by generosity'.

Religious observance plays an important part in Arthur's public life: clerics bless his enterprises, keep vigil before he fights Frolle, celebrate his victories; he, in turn, nominates archbishops, rebuilds ruined churches, takes oaths upon the relics of saints. Repeatedly, earnestly and with every appearance of sincerity he invokes divine aid: at the moment of his accession when he prays for help in upholding God's laws all his life, addressing, before every battle, the Virgin whose image he bears on his shield and, on waking in terror from an ominous dream, calling on Christ by formulaic titles as old as the oldest English verse:

'Lauerd Drihten, Crist, domes waldende,
midelarde mund, monnen froure,
þurh þine aðmode wil, walden ænglen,
let þu mi sweuen to selþen iturnen!'
                                        (12760-3)

('Christ, our Lord and Master, Lord of destinies, Guardian of the world, Comforter of men, Ruler of angels, let my dream, through your gracious will, lead to a good end!')

But here too prayer is a public act in the hearing of his men, just as elsewhere God is invoked in a political act as Arthur is about to execute youthful German hostages in a moment of anger against their leaders:

'Ah, swa me hælpen Drihten þæ scop þæs
    dæies lihten,
þerfore he scal ibiden bitterest alre baluwen,
harde gomenes   —his bone ich wulle iwurðen!
Colgrim and Baldulf beiene ich wulle aquellen,
and al heore duyeðe dæð scal iðolien.
Yif hit wule ivnnen Waldende hæfnen,
ich   wulle   wurðliche   wreken   alle   his
    wiðer-deden.
Yif me mot ilasten þat lif a mire breosten,
and hit wulle me iunne þat iscop mone and
    sunne,
ne scal nauere Childric æft me bicharren!'
                                        (10515-24)

('But, so help me God who created the light of day, he shall suffer for it the most bitter affliction, harsh treatment—I will be his slayer! I will kill both Colgrim and Baldolf, and all their followers shall suffer death. If the Ruler of Heaven grants it, I will fittingly avenge all his wicked deeds. If life endures within me, and He who created sun and moon grants it, never again shall Childric deceive me!')

Since Arthur, the public figure, has no inner life, there is no indication of his personal faith, even in moments of greatest anguish: when he learns of the treachery of Modred and Guenevere—it is Gawain who invokes God's law in vowing their destruction; when he laments Gawain's own death; or in the slaughter at Camelford. Christian and magical elements having coexisted in his public life as easily as the roles of feudal sovereign and fairy prince in his persona, it comes as no surprise that he invokes the fairy Argante for his bodily healing and that it is Merlin who, like some Old Testament prophet, predicts his messianic return:

> Nis nauer þe mon iboren   of nauer nane burde
>   icoren
> þe cunne of þan soðe   of Arðure sugen mare.
> Bute while wes an witeye   Mærlin ihate;
> he bodede mid worde   —his quiðes weoren
>   soðe—
> þat an Arður sculde yete   cum Anglen to fulste.
>   (14293-7)

(No man ever born of noble lady can tell more of the truth about Arthur. But there was once a seer called Merlin who prophesied—his sayings were true—that an Arthur should come again to aid the people of England.)

It seems ironic that Arthur's messianic return, the hope of the British, should here be promised to the English whose ancestors were their bitterest foes. The unexpected twist raises the issue of Layamon's central theme and the literary category to which the *Brut* belongs. The difficulty of definition arises partly from the unfamiliarity of modern critics with the concept of a verse chronicle neither factually historical nor yet an obvious literary construct with traditional criteria of form and content. The problem originates with Geoffrey whose *Historia,* definable today as a pastiche chronicle, fascinated its original audience precisely because it illuminated the dark past of their society with a certainty warranted by all the apparatus of academic historiography. Where modern readers of such a pastiche would expect to be given some perspective to encourage appreciation of the ironic disparity between the fictive material and its factual presentation, the completeness of the illusion seems to have been a large part of its appeal for medieval readers, even for those contemporary chroniclers who yielded reluctantly to its fascination. Certainly neither Wace nor Layamon betrays any hint of ironic detachment towards the *Historia;* their concern is to make its matter yet more relevant and convincing to their particular audiences. Categorisation is complicated, in Layamon's case, by his use of elements of poetic idiom associated in Old English tradition with works of epic character. But the surviving fragments of that tradition include nothing of the scale and historical scope of the *Brut,* whose idiom suggests compilation and extrapolation from a variety of models rather than inheritance of an established epic medium. If Layamon's poem is to be judged as a national epic, it must be on other grounds than continuity of national tradition, either of idiom or theme. The very fact that the elements in his idiom which lend it epic colouring stemmed from that society cast as the racial foe in the *Brut* suggests the improbability of thematic inheritance, just as the variety of its components reflects the period of cultural fusion in which the work was written.

The *Brut* also lacks the formal criteria of the wider epic tradition from which it was cut off by Geoffrey's imitation of Latin chronicle only faintly coloured with Virgilian overtones; without the learning and the literary self-consciousness of a Joseph of Exeter, Layamon probably lacked access to and possibly interest in the classical models. So his work shows nothing of the structural complexity, the variety of perspective, the thematic concentration of Virgilian or Homeric epic. Equally it lacks the episodic organisation of *Beowulf* and the *Chanson de Roland.* In contrast, the narrative is swift, spare, uncomplicated in motivation, the narrator occasionally weakening concentration by his interventions. But the formal characteristics of epic vary greatly from age to age, culture to culture. Essential characteristics common to acknowledged examples of the genre include great length, seriousness of treatment, concentration upon themes and values vital to a particular society, especially to its military survival, demonstrated in the careers of charismatic heroes of exceptional gifts and prowess. There can be no question that the *Brut* is of epic scale and scope, covering in over sixteen thousand lines some two thousand years of history. Nor can there be any doubt of its seriousness of purpose or thematic power; despite its narrative linearity and a certain thinness of texture, the underlying theme persists of a noble society, born out of disaster, striving at times for mere survival, at others for total dominance, only to fall again into disaster. The stature of its heroes, Brutus, Brenne, Belin, Aurelius, Uther, Arthur, and the extent to which each embodies the national cause, is manifest. That it celebrates multiple aspects of charismatic leadership and personal prowess in a variety of heroes, rather than a Beowulf, a Roland or a Cid, associates it with the *Iliad.* That it ends in heroic failure, leaving a shadow hanging over the future of the national cause need not invalidate it as epic; so do *Beowulf,* and the *Roland.* Nor need the fact that it transmutes repeated failure into national glory and perverts historical fact in the process, since the *Roland* also shows the power of the patriotic imagination to transform disaster into triumph just as the *Iliad* demonstrates how the accretion of legend can transform a grain of fact into an epic myth. Nor should it be devalued as epic by its origin in the *Historia* whose myth-making is a conscious process, since the *Aeneid* also is a literary artefact with specific models in mind and conscious designs upon the patriotism of its audience. That the *Brut* has not been seriously considered as an epic may suggest that its literary quality cannot bear comparison with these classic examples of the genre. But that in turn may reflect the extent to which its appreciation has been limited by the nature of the texts available, and its impact upon national tradition through English chronicles and the alliterative poetry of the later Middle Ages been underestimated because of lack of research.

But there is, perhaps, a more fundamental reason why its epic character has remained undefined. Each of the admitted masterpieces of the genre has come to be identified with a specific culture, composed at the moment when that culture achieved national identity, establishing or inventing its glorious origins, celebrating past triumphs, used as a rallying cry in crisis, a paen in victory (like the *Roland* at Hastings), transmuted by time into a cultural symbol. For Layamon's **Brut** no such national status seems possible, dealing as it does with a defeated and slighted culture in the language of its conquerors. Unless, that is, its fundamental theme is not culture but country, not race but land. It may not be merely a verbal slip which promises Arthur's return to aid the English, since Layamon initially declares his intention to 'relate the noble origins of the English, what they were called and whence they came who first possessed the land of England' (7-9), announcing his subject as the land and his starting point as the coming of its first inhabitants. The history of the island is then outlined as that of its successive conquerors who, each in turn, changed its name and gave it their own:

þis lond was ihaten Albion   þa Brutus cum heron;
þa nolde Brutus namare   þat hit swa ihaten weore,
ah scupte him nome   æfter himseluan.
He wes ihaten Brutus; þis londe he clepede Brutaine,
and þa Troinisce men,   þa temden hine to hærre,
æfter Brutone   Brutuns heom cleopede;
and yed þe nome læsteð   and a summe stude cleouieð faste . . .
Heora ayene speke Troinisce   and seoððen heo hit cleopeden Brutunisc;
ah Englisce men hit habbeð awend   seoððen Gurmund com in þis lond.
Gurmund draf out þe Brutuns   and his folc wes ihaten Sexuns,
of ane ende of Alemaine   Angles wes ihaten;
of Angles comen Englisce men   and Englelond heo hit clepeden.
þa Englisce ouercomen þe Brutuns   and brouhten heom þer neoðere
þat neofer seoððen heo ne arisen   ne her ræden funden.

(975-81, 987-93)

(This land was called Albion when Brutus arrived here; Brutus did not wish that it should any longer be so called, but he made a name for it in keeping with his own. He was called Brutus; this land he called Britain, and the Trojans who had made him their leader called themselves Britons after Brutus; and the name yet endures and remains still in some places . . . They afterwards called their own Trojan language British; but the English have changed it since Gormund came into this country. Gormund drove out the Britons and his people were called Saxons, from a region of Germany called Anglia; from Anglia came the English and they called the land England. The English overcame the Britons and brought them into subjection so that they never rose again nor prospered here.)

The country's multi-cultural past is exemplified in the changing names of its capital, called 'Troye þe Newe' by Brutus, later Trinovant, then Kaerlud in honour of King Lud, changed to Lundene by the English and by the French to Lundres:

þus is þas burh iuaren   seoððen heo ærest wes areræd,
þus is þis eitlond   igon from honde to hond
þet alle þa burhyes   þe Brutus iwrohte
and heora noma gode   þa on Brutus dæi stode
beoð swiðe afelled   þurh warf of þon folke.

(1032-6)

(Thus has this city fared since it was first built; thus has this island passed from hand to hand so that all the cities which Brutus created have been brought low and their proper names which they bore in the days of Brutus obliterated through change of peoples.)

The detailed location of the narrative in the British Isles originates with Geoffrey who uses scores of place-names to relate the wide-ranging action to regions, rivers, towns and ports familiar to his comparatively mobile, ruling-class audience, and to add to the illusion of historical perspective by borrowing, occasionally perhaps inventing, traditions associating place-names with persons or events in his story or by evoking their association with Roman history. The technique obviously appealed to Layamon's antiquarian temperament and he extended it, adding further place-names and giving additional details about others. He betrays understandable ignorance of continental locations but special, no doubt personal, knowledge of south and west England and south Wales. The effect, as the wide-ranging action shifts from Loch Lomond to Stonehenge, from the Humber to the Severn, Dumbarton to Teignwic, York to Exeter, is of a legend rooted in known places, a familiar landscape. For Layamon's provincial audience many of the British names may have seemed as exotic as Mont St Michel, Bayeux, Poitiers, Autun and the Great St Bernard, some of which places lay in territories ruled or claimed by their Angevin masters. Citizens of a would-be imperial power, their patriotism may have been roused by evocative names and distant conquests just as later English audiences were by Kipling's tales from the Raj, with scarcely more knowledge of geographical setting and historical reality. Just as the Normans, to judge from the success of Wace's *Brut,* took pleasure in a legend which made them heirs to imperial claims rivalling those their French contemporaries had inherited from Charlemagne, so the English could take pride in the same shadowy claims to the Roman inheritance.

In an age when most men were land-bound and feudal states were often transient groupings of military or marital acquisitions, patriotism was rooted in place of origin and feudal allegiance rather than in nationality, race or language. As territories changed hands, men's enduring allegiance was to the land which gave them their feudal status and their living, and to any ruler whose firm possession of it promised stability and protection. The ruler, however unwelcome initially, inherited with the land the feudal hierarchy of land-holders, the mutual rights and privileges which bound each to each, the immemorial usages which constituted its identity, the myths and legends which provided its historical roots. The Normans, who called themselves English even before they spoke the language and resented royal recruitment of their continental cousins for the suppression of unrest at home, rapidly identified themselves with the traditions of the land they had conquered. For the defeated English there was every temptation to sublimate their humiliation by associating their circumstances with those of the British whom they had similarly overwhelmed and displaced. To what extent that was a conscious process with Layamon, for whom the terms 'British' and 'English' seem interchangeable, cannot be determined. His constant demonstration and vilification of the viciousness of the Saxons and comparatively rare and benign references to the Angles suggests that he intended a distinction between the former as the Germanic invaders and the latter as the ancestors of the English—though he acknowledges their Germanic origin also. But his occasional references to Arthur as 'King of England' and the apparent modelling of his cognomen 'Bruttene deorling' on the medieval title for Alfred the Great, 'England's darling' may show a conscious intention to encourage his English-speaking compatriots to identify themselves with the British both as victors and victims. His lively and inventive version of Geoffrey's unified history of the island made it a more vivid and effective focus for patriotism in which all races could associate themselves with the victorious British and identify the foreign invader, whatever his nationality, as the perennial enemy. The tragedy in which it ends is the tragedy of a particular race, but as a national epic its underlying message is that all conquerors are themselves eventually conquered. So, just as the occasional disaffection of Arthur's followers and the treachery of Modred imply moral reasons for the Norman Conquest, the defeat of the Saxons may prefigure the eventual overthrow of the most recent invaders. Though Layamon could not have foreseen it, their overthrow was already implict in the sources, language and poetic medium of his **Brut,** exemplifying that cultural fusion which was to be the future of Britain. If Layamon's work is a national epic, its subject is Britain—with all the ambivalence the name has acquired across the centuries.

Arthur has become the symbol of that ambivalent national identity, embodying the land, its racial fusions, its traditions of law and justice, its Christian faith and its resistance to foreign invasion. Geoffrey's *Historia* which gave academic respectability and wide-spread currency to that symbol has nothing to say of the hope of the British that Arthur will return to lead them. But by stating within the same sentence that the king was mortally wounded at Camlann and that he was carried off to Avalon so that his wounds might be tended, Geoffrey acknowledges, with politic ambiguity, the myth of Arthur's return already current when he wrote (§178). Wace, in his account (13275-98), openly admits its currency, but hints at personal doubts by citing Merlin as prophesying merely that Arthur's end would remain uncertain. In Layamon's version (14288-97), the hope of the British is reasserted, supported by a positive prophecy of Merlin for whose truthfulness the poet vouches. Writing for an English audience, he had less to fear from official disapproval than those whose patrons belonged to the ruling class. The power of the messianic myth to cause unrest in a multiracial society had already been demonstrated before Geoffrey wrote: the chronicler Herman of Laon tells how, when canons of that

city visited Bodmin in 1113, doubts cast by one of their servants on a Cornishman's assertion that Arthur still lived led to a near riot. Shortly afterwards, a commentator on the Prophecies of Merlin remarked that in Brittany anyone who doubted Arthur's survival would be lucky to escape stoning. The historian, William of Malmesbury, noted how the absence of a known grave for Arthur encouraged what he regarded as trifling fables about his survival. Meanwhile the restless Welsh, in frequent rebellion against Angevin authority, looked to Arthur as their expected leader in the reconquest of the island said, by Geoffrey, to have been prophesied by Merlin (§115.20).

The political solution was to find the grave; in 1191, the monks of Glastonbury, prompted by Henry II, discovered in the abbey cemetery, an oak coffin said to contain giant bones worthy of an epic hero and a lead cross inscribed: *Hic iacet sepultus inclitus Rex Arturius in insula Avalonia* (Here lies buried the renowned king Arthur in the isle of Avalon). But the power of a myth which embodies the dreams of a society was demonstrated across the centuries to come as the funerary inscription changed form to reflect what each age wished to believe. In the most influential of Arthurian texts, *Le Morte Darthur* (c. 1470), which was to carry the legend triumphantly into the modern world, Sir Thomas Malory wrote:

> Yet som men say in many partys of Inglonde that kynge Arthure ys nat dede, but had by the wyll of oure Lorde Jesu into another place; and men say that he shall com agayne, and he shall wynne the Holy Crosse. Yet I woll nat say that hit shall be so, but rather I wolde sey: here in thys worlde he chaunged hys lyff. And many men say that there ys wrytten uppon the tumbe thys: *Hic iacet Arthurus, Rex quondam Rexque futurus* (Here lies Arthur, once king, who shall be king hereafter).

The dream lived on and was to go round the world. Already in the twelfth century the commentator [formerly thought to be Alain de Lille] on the Prophecies of Merlin saw the process well advanced:

> What place is there within the bounds of the empire of Christendom to which the winged praise of Arthur the Briton has not extended? Who is there, I ask, who does not speak of Arthur the Briton, since he is scarcely less known to the peoples of Asia than to the Cornish and Welsh, as our pilgrims returning from the east inform us? The peoples of the east speak of him as do the peoples of the west, though separated by the breadth of the whole earth. Egypt speaks of him, and the Bosphorus is not silent. Rome, queen of cities, sings his deeds, and his wars are not unknown to her former rival Carthage. Antioch, Armenia and Palestine celebrate his feats. [*Prophetica Anglicana*]

In that process Layamon, parish priest of Areley Kings, played an honourable if, as yet, not fully appreciated part. (pp. xliii-lvi)

W. R. J. Barron and S. C. Weinberg, in an introduction to Layamon's "Arthur": The Arthurian Section of Layamon's "Brut" (Lines

9229-14297), *edited and translated by W. R. J. Barron and S. C. Weinberg,* Longman, 1989, pp. viii-lviii.

FURTHER READING

Blake, N. F. "Rhythmical Alliteration." *Modern Philology* 67, No. 2 (November 1969): 118-24.
    Represents Layamon's *Brut* as an example of both the close connection between poetry and prose during the early Middle English period and of a poetic form called "rhythmical alliteration."

Bøgholm, N. *The Layamon Texts: A Linguistical Investigation.* Travaux du cercle linquistique de Copenhague, vol. III. Copenhagen: Einar Munksgaard, 1944, 85 p.
    A detailed linguistic study offering commentary on Layamon's vocabulary and orthography, among other topics.

Bzdyl, Donald G. Introduction to *Layamon's "Brut": A History of the Britons,* translated by Donald G. Bzdyl, pp. 1-32. Medieval & Renaissance Texts & Studies, vol. 65. Binghamton, N.Y.: Center for Medieval and Early Renaissance Studies, 1989.
    Defines the factors responsible for the neglect of Layamon's *Brut* and discusses the difficulty of assigning it to a particular genre. Bzdyl also includes general commentary on Layamon's life and the *Brut.*

Davis, H. S. "Layamon's Similes." *The Review of English Studies* XI, No. 42 (May 1960): 129-42.
    Explores Layamon's use of similes, especially long similes, and its bearing on Geoffrey of Monmouth's credibility.

Donoghue, Daniel. "Layamon's Ambivalence." *Speculum: A Journal of Medieval Studies* 65, No. 3 (July 1990): 537-63.
    Attributes the disparity between the style and content of Layamon's *Brut* to cultural ambivalence, maintaining that Layamon "remains caught between the old and the new, the Anglo-Saxon and the Anglo-Norman, in an age of competing allegiances, and from his middle position he balances the oppositions within the scheme of a historiographical tradition more complex than most of his modern admirers have allowed."

Fletcher, Robert Huntington. "Did Layamon Make Any Use of Geoffrey's *Historia?*" *PMLA* XVIII (1903): 91-4.
    Disagrees with the theory that Layamon was not influenced in any way by Geoffrey of Monmouth's chronicle, pointing to certain episodes in Layamon's *Brut* that correspond to Geoffrey, but not to Wace.

Guest, Edwin. "Chapter III." In his *A History of English Rhythms,* Vol. II, pp. 94-131. London: William Pickering, 1838.
    Examines the dialect used by Layamon in the *Brut.*

Heather, P. J. "Layamon's *Brut.*" *Folklore* XLVIII, No. 4 (December 1937): 339-65.
    Discusses the legends and folklore present in the *Brut.*

Jones, Gwyn. Introduction to *Wace and Layamon: Arthurian Chronicles,* translated by Eugene Mason, pp. v-xii. London: J. M. Dent & Sons, 1962.
    Traces the literary history of Arthurian legend in the twelfth century, beginning with Geoffrey of Monmouth and ending with Layamon.

Keith, W. J. "Layamon's *Brut:* The Literary Differences between the Two Texts." *Medium Ævum* XXIX, No. 3 (1960): 161-72.
    Examines differences in literary quality between the two manuscripts of Layamon's *Brut.*

Kirby, I. J. "Angles and Saxons in Layamon's *Brut.*" *Studia Neophilologica* XXXVI, No. 1 (1964): 51-62.
    Contends that Layamon's *Brut* is cohesive as a work of art, despite the accusations of inconsistency and traitorship sometimes leveled against Layamon for portraying his people, the Anglo-Saxons, as the villains in his poem.

Le Saux, Françoise H. M. *Layamon's "Brut": The Poem and Its Sources.* Cambridge, England: D. S. Brewer, 1989, 244 p.
    An in-depth study of the relationship between Layamon's *Brut* and its sources.

Loomis, Roger Sherman. "Notes on Layamon." *The Review of English Studies* X, No. 37 (January 1934): 78-84.
    Disputes the Celtic origin of many of Layamon's additions to his translation of Wace's *Brut.*

Noble, James. "The Larger Rhetorical Patterns in Layamon's *Brut.*" *English Studies in Canada* XI, No. 3 (September 1985): 263-72.
    Contends that Layamon continued the Old English poetic tradition in his rhetorical practices.

Shichtman, Martin B. "Gawain in Wace and Layamon: A Case of Metahistorical Evolution." In *Medieval Texts & Contemporary Readers,* edited by Laurie A. Finke and Martin B. Shichtman, pp. 103-19. Ithaca, N.Y.: Cornell University Press, 1987.
    Explores the characterizations of Gawain in Wace's *Roman de Brut* and Layamon's *Brut,* maintaining that the development of this plot element "indicates the directions that these works take as metahistories."

Stanley, E. G. "Layamon's Antiquarian Sentiments." *Medium Ævum* XXXVIII, No. 1 (1969): 23-37.
    Analyzes differences in dialect and language between the two manuscripts of Layamon's *Brut.*

Swart, J. "Layamon's *Brut.*" In *Studies in Language and Literature in Honour of Margaret Schlauch,* edited by Mieczyslaw Brahmer, Stanislaw Helsztynski, and Julian Krzyzanowski, pp. 431-35. Warsaw: PWN-Polish Scientific Publishers, 1966.
    Offers general commentary on the genre and classification of Layamon's *Brut.*

Turville-Petre, Thorlac. "The Origins of the Alliterative Revival." In his *The Alliterative Revival,* pp. 1-25. Cambridge, England: D. S. Brewer, 1977.
    Appraises the alliterative techniques used by Layamon in the *Brut.*

Visser, Gerard Johannes. *Layamon: An Attempt at Vindication.* Assen, The Netherlands: Van Gorcum & Co. N. V., 1935, 100 p.

Identifies Layamon's Latin, Welsh, and Norman sources.

Willard, Rudolph. "Layamon in the Seventeenth and Eighteenth Centuries." *Studies in English* XXVII, No. 1 (June 1948): 239-78.
Presents a survey of early Layamon scholarship.

The Alliterative *Morte Arthure*

Circa Fourteenth Century

English poem.

INTRODUCTION

The alliterative *Morte Arthure* is regarded as a masterpiece of medieval English poetry. Drawing on a stock of formulas and conventions common to works of the fourteenth-century Alliterative Revival that gave rise to such classics as *Sir Gawain and the Green Knight* and *Pearl, Morte Arthure* employs these elements in a tale of war and heroism especially well-suited to the weighty rhythm and onomatopoeic effects of alliterative verse—a poetic form characterized by the repetition of like sounds. Although most other Arthurian narratives feature the characters of the Round Table in stories of courtly love and chivalry, *Morte Arthure* traces in particular the rise and fall of Britain's Arthur, a warrior king whose exploits constitute the primary focus of the work.

After briefly summarizing Arthur's imperial conquests, the poem relates his confrontation with the fictional Roman emperor Lucius Iberius. Through a group of envoys Lucius demands that Arthur pay tribute for warring on Roman lands. After consulting with the knights of his Round Table, Arthur makes preparations for battle with Rome. As he sails for the continent, he falls asleep in his cabin and has a dream that philosophers later interpret to portend Britain's victory. Arthur's subsequent march through France features his heroic battle with a cannibalistic giant, whom he destroys singlehandedly, and reaches a high point with the king's victory over Lucius and his forces, who had advanced from Italy for a counterattack. Following his victory over the Roman emperor, Arthur engages in a series of campaigns, declaring his intention to rule the entire earth; a second dream, however, foretells a change in the king's fortunes. Shortly thereafter, Arthur learns that Mordred, whom he had appointed regent, has usurped his throne in England and has fathered a child to Queen Guinevere. Arthur hastens back to Britain, where he wages war with Mordred and his forces. Although the rebel faction is defeated, Arthur and Mordred exchange mortal swordstrokes; realizing that he will not recover, Arthur appoints a successor and seeks absolution before his death.

The author of the alliterative *Morte Arthure* is unknown. Like other Arthurian narratives, it is based on the chronicles of Geoffrey of Monmouth, Robert Wace, Layamon, and others. Although the first direct mention of Arthur occurs in the ninth-century *Historia Britonum,* Geoffrey's *Historia Regum Britanniae,* an immensely popular chronicle written about 1137, is credited as the primary source of the Arthurian legend. Geoffrey established Arthur as a great medieval monarch—a conqueror reminiscent of

Arthur is mortally wounded. From an illustration in Wace's Roman de Brut *(1155).*

Alexander the Great and a model of chivalry and Christian piety; Wace added an account of Arthur's knights of the Round Table, and Layamon contributed dream and fairy motifs. The twelfth-century French poet Chrétien de Troyes influenced many later adaptations of the Arthur story when he amplified the role of the knights; in his version, their deeds of valor were inspired by courtly love rather than a quest for fame, and the lover-hero replaced the warrior-hero in virtually all subsequent Arthurian tales. The alliterative *Morte Arthure,* however, rejected the romance tradition initiated by Chrétien, reintroducing an ethos based on the military heroism featured in the chronicles.

Morte Arthure was most likely written during the last half of the fourteenth century. Scholars generally cite the latest possible date for the work as 1440—the year inscribed on the oldest extant manuscript. They further note that the poem could not have been completed before 1310, the date of one of its sources, the French romance *Voeux de Paon.* Allusions within *Morte Arthure* to events marking the reign of England's Edward III (1327-77), as well as its use of literary conventions typical of the period of Richard II's rule (1377-99), suggest a date within the last four decades of the fourteenth century for the composition of the poem. The text preserved by the Yorkshire scribe Robert of Thornton in the manuscript dated 1440 was published for the first time more than four centuries later in J. O. Halliwell's 1847 edition, *The Alliterative Romance of the Death of King Arthur.* Subsequent versions of the poem by Edmund Brock (1871) and Mary Macleod Banks (1900) were faithful to Thornton's manuscript and made *Morte Arthure* more readily available. Erik Björkman's German edition, published in 1915, was the first to feature extensive commentary, notes, textual analyses, and other marginalia, and also incorporated numerous disputed emendations into the poem's Middle English text. Another significant edition of the work is that of John Finlayson, whose *Morte Arthure* (1967) presents an abridged version of the poem and includes his highly-regarded commentary. Valerie Krishna's 1976 critical edition of the poem is presently considered the standard text.

The alliterative *Morte Arthure* is the only significant Arthurian narrative that is not modeled on the French courtly romance tradition. Dorothy Everett noted that, while the poem does include monsters, prophetic dreams, and other elements that "belong wholly to the world of romance," they are "treated in a matter-of-fact way, as necessary 'properties' " of a story that had been redefined in romance versions. Finlayson has suggested that the *Morte Arthure* more closely resembles the *chanson de geste* or "story of great deeds"—an early French genre exemplified by the epic *Song of Roland*—than any Arthurian romance. Like the *chanson de geste, Morte Arthure* is an heroic poem focusing on deeds of valor associated with war and political allegiance; the knights in this poem are driven by loyalty to their overlord and a desire for fame rather than by love for a woman. Moreover, *Morte Arthure*'s realistic descriptions of time and place and seemingly objective presentation of events are consistent with the tone and epic style of the *chanson de geste,* as well as of the poem's chronicle sources.

A wealth of commentary on elements of tragedy and moral persuasion in *Morte Arthure* was prompted by William Matthews's seminal study *The Tragedy of Arthur,* in which the critic defined the poem as "a classic of the medieval tragedy of fortune." Several commentators, including Finlayson, have agreed that the poem is structured in the symmetrical, rise-and-fall manner of medieval tragedy, noting many parallel passages throughout the work. The most notable of these are Arthur's two prophetic dreams, foretelling his rise to and fall from world dominance. The second dream, a microcosm of the themes and structures in the poem, features Arthur's symbolic ascent to the highest seat on the wheel of fortune. Although the worthiest of nine conquerors who had either experienced or aspired to this position, Arthur is thrown down when the duchess of the wheel withdraws her favor. Noting that numerous passages in the work associate God with fortune, destiny, and chance, Matthews focused on a portion of Arthur's dream in which the ancient conqueror Alexander remorsefully acknowledges the sins that prompted his own fall, concluding: "For [Alexander], and by implication for all the others, the duchess-of-the-wheel is an agency of God's justice, and what has brought [Alexander] low, seemingly into eternal damnation, is not chance but his own sins of vainglory and cruelty." Many critics have agreed that *Morte Arthure* has a distinctly moral tone but have varied considerably in their characterizations of the didactic intent for the poem. John Gardner was among those who have viewed hubris as the cause of Arthur's fall, asserting: "[Arthur's] tragedy is that he forgets that a king

acts as God's servant, not as master in his own right." Russell Peck has suggested that Arthur was ultimately victimized by his own selfish, willful behavior; others have contended that Arthur's fall is retribution for his unchivalrous conduct in waging unjust wars. Such conclusions have led many scholars to examine the work as a political allegory, prompting speculation that the poet may have intended the work as a protest against British imperialism during the reign of Edward III.

The premise that the moral message in *Morte Arthure* is expressed through the sins and punishment of Arthur has been challenged by some commentators, who argue that the king's greatness in the poem is undiminished by his downfall. Central to their argument are stylistic analyses of the poem that highlight the poet's depiction of Arthur as alternately benevolent and vengeful, chivalric and avaricious. For example, Larry D. Benson has noted that "in his dying speech [Arthur] is the noble king still, arranging for the future government of his kingdom and giving orders that Mordred's children be slain and left unburied." Benson regards the poem as a philosophic commentary on the human condition—the inevitability of changes of fortune and of death. According to this view, the same zeal that prompted Arthur's deeds of heroism also sparked the rashness that positions him for his fatal encounter with Mordred—the moral of the poem being the need to recognize, as Benson has written, "the frailty of this world and to turn instead to a faith in heaven."

While critics continue to debate elements of the theme, structure, and genre in *Morte Arthure,* they are virtually unanimous in their estimation of the poem's literary merit. Acknowledging the stylistic flaws summarized by Everett as "excess," among them "long, overloaded descriptions" that "slow down the narrative considerably," Gardner has written: "The virtues of the *Morte Arthure* are those of the medieval warhorse: it is slow and somewhat clumsy, sometimes inelegant, but large and powerful; and like the warhorse it holds with absolute firmness to its course."

PRINCIPAL ENGLISH EDITIONS

The Alliterative Romance of the Death of King Arthur (edited by J.O. Halliwell) 1847

Morte Arthure; or, The Death of Arthur (edited by Edmund Brock) 1871

Morte Arthure: An Alliterative Poem of the 14th Century, from the Lincoln MS. (edited by Mary Macleod Banks) 1900

Morte Arthure (abridged; edited by John Finlayson) 1967

The Alliterative Morte Arthure, The Owl and the Nightingale, and Five Other Middle English Poems in Modernized Version (edited by John Gardner) 1971

The Alliterative Morte Arthure: A Critical Edition (edited by Valerie Krishna) 1976

Morte Arthure: A Critical Edition (edited by Mary Hamel) 1984

King Arthur's Death: The Middle English Stanzaic Morte Arthur and Alliterative Morte Arthure (edited by Larry D. Benson) 1986

Mary Macleod Banks (1900)

[*In the following excerpt from the introduction to her edition of* Morte Arthure, *Banks describes the work as one of the foremost contributions to the alliterative revival in fourteenth-century English poetry.*]

The **Morte Arthure** is an outcome of the alliterative revival of the fourteenth century, and has many features in common with other poems of its time. It bears certain very definite resemblances to products of the courtly school, such as its machinery of dreams and allegory, its glory of jewels, glowing colour and princely splendour, its long lists of things delightful to mediæval ears, of courtiers, kings and banquetings, and its conventions, tributes to smiling meadows, streams, and birds of song. But its resemblances to the poems of the revival are closer, more firmly wrought into the texture of the work; they embrace many of its special excellences.

Like the other alliterative poems it is written in the metre of Old English poetry, and contributes to one of the artistic phenomena of history. Like them, too, it marks a movement which has a value beyond that of its artistic form. For the revival of the old heroic line was a thing which stirred the hearts of poets at an hour of national quickening, and beat true to a pulse strengthened by consciousness of power in the people at large. It is as significant of the time as Wicliffe's sermons or any of the social and political changes reflected in legislation of those years. It was not a mere literary affectation. What remains of it is written chiefly in dialects of the North and West, where tradition might well be vigorous, but where scholarly trifling would be least in vogue. It was rejected by the courtly poets, and by the master Chaucer, whose artistic making bears the stamp of foreign ideals, and it was cherished by Langland, who wrote for the people, studying their methods, and by the authors of the popular drama, where literary eccentricities would have been out of place if not impossible. Recognition for the verse-forms of our forefathers may spring to-day from the wider humanism which is our dower, but we may doubt whether the Humanism of Europe in the time of the second and third Edwards would have listened to alliterative poetry, even if the influence of that urbane spirit could have penetrated to the borders of Logres. The thunder-tones of the old gods had been too lately silenced, the philosophic debate of the schools was not disposed to pause for a retrospect across the years of strife. Not to schools or courts need we look for the explanation of the revival of native art, but rather to an impulse engendered of the national mood, which led poets to the adoption of a form of verse known to the people and alive in familiar versions of the songs of more adventurous days.

The metre of these poems is modelled, not on the original type, but on the alliterative line as it revealed itself to ears fast losing the sense of inflectional syllables, and transformed by the shortening, lengthening and slurring of sounds which altered their values for stress; it has every sign of study of contemporary forms, and the many variations from the earlier pattern which four hundred intervening years of linguistic change had brought. Here and there we are surprised and startled by alliterative phrases which are like echoes from the older poets of a kind not found in the rhyming romances, but there is little evidence that the style of Old English poetry had been studied in connection with them. We find few traces of the spirit of the older epic in the style of these later poems, and the binding together by alliteration of English words with those from Romance sources would strengthen the belief that the measure was preserved where the language in which it was first known had become unintelligible, and where the masterpieces of pre-conquest poetry were unknown.

In the **Morte Arthure** the measure is in many respects more artistically successful than in some other poems of the same class; it finds a kindred theme in war and the achievements of a national hero, and regains something of its old swing and resonance; it moves more freely here than when weighted with moral illustration as in *Piers Plowman,* or tipped with the fairy quills of romance as in *Sir Gawayne and the Grene Knight;* it vibrates with the tramp of fighting legions.

The poets of the revival were not content with the well-worn vocabulary of their rhyming contemporaries, they have an unmistakable freshness of style and a boldness in culling words from the many sources at their command which conscientious compilers of glossaries often wish had been a little less enterprising. The **Morte Arthure** has these merits of freshness and variety; its vocabulary is one of the most interesting, one of the fullest of all. It is often uncompromisingly technical, for the poet delights in realities and solid facts, and it abounds in idiom and forcible, homely phrase. Its author takes pleasure in the wilder aspects of life; he has none of those descriptions of tempest, raging seas, and winter snow which have made *Sir Gawayne, Cleanness and Patience,* and the *Destruction of Troy* famous, but he too relishes the keen air of the crags, and knows the power of the "wagande wynde owte of the weste." He puts all his strength into his pictures of stirring multitudes, of revellings and monsters, of the strife on the stream and the crashing of battle-coggs.

He is minute in matters of detail, only Langland or Deguileville could have rivalled him in his sketch of the giant of Mont St. Michael, or of Cradok's pilgrim-dress, contrasted as it is with the brilliant state of the man whose undoing he is about to proclaim. The cheap simile and metaphor of the rhyming romances is cast aside, the poet enumerates his points of interest swiftly and vividly, using his "lists" with rare success. (pp. 123-25)

There is an observance of common things, sympathy with men in their daily occupation, and a grasp of fact, for which we should look in vain to any other poet of the time but Chaucer himself; this is amply illustrated by the lines describing the bustle of the start out to sea from Sandwich . . . , or the boys chasing the boar at the gates of Como . . . , or the king in his barge . . . , or the mariners chatting of their "termys" before the battle at sea.

The story is almost untouched by romance; it is that of the chroniclers with a few additions from other sources. Well in keeping with the subject is the lordly opening where Arthur appears flushed with the pride of conquest like Veronese's Alexander amidst the profusion of his banquets. The "gabs" of the lords in the Giant's Tower have an actuality which is of the style of the chronicles, not of romance; they might have been recorded by Froissart.

The *Morte Arthure* has little of the spirit of romance, we find that only in an allusion here and there, and in the Gawayne episode. The men known to modern readers from Malory and Tennyson, there moving under a mystic heaven or caught in the toils of impossible undertakings, are here burly warriors who love conquest, banquets, and the service of their lord. The ideals of *Amadis of Gaul* would have been incomprehensible to them. They know nothing of Broceliande or the Grail, and are not troubled by the prophecies of Merlin and the knightly quest. Here is war without the wantonness, the dragon's wing without the faery charm. There are added touches of horror, like those of the *Mysteries of Udolpho,* but there is none of the mystery and the elfin gleam which have fallen upon later travellers in Arthur's realms. It is a far cry from Malory to Spenser, but the gap between the *Morte Arthure* and Malory's book, which embodies most of its story, would be more difficult to bridge over. Arthur in Avalon has a surgeon from Salerno to search his wounds, and is buried to the mourning of pontifical dirges amidst "blacks" and conventional trappings of woe. We hear no hint of his coming again, or of that barge which seems to float for ever along the horizon of romance. Launcelot is one of the "lesse men," and, like his fellow-lords, has thoughts only of war with Lucius. The form of narrative is positive, it leaves little to suggestion. The characters are highly individualised and carefully drawn, the poet finds his chief interest in them; but when was the typical romancer ever led away from the one essential, incident, to a consideration of his characters? The manner is nowhere that of romance, the development is on entirely different lines; one might liken the originality of treatment to that of Chrestien de Troyes, but Chrestien's again is a different spirit, more courtly and chivalrous in tone.

Gawayne's position is, according to the English tradition, second in importance to Arthur alone, only Cador comes near him in weight, and Cador has been carefully studied, his character is clearly worked out. It is well to have a *Morte Arthure* where Gawayne has his due, he soon became a shadow, and as "Gawayne the Hende" was looked upon as a convenient figure for pageants. The northern poets bring him into special prominence; he is one of the few heroes of romance who receive sympathetic notice in the *Canterbury Tales.* (pp. 125-27)

[The] author is worthy of his place as a contemporary of Chaucer, and is none the less deserving of praise because he elected to clothe his creation in a garb less courtly than that which was to pass on to future poets as the royal robe of English song. And his measure was not without subtle influence on later styles, we hear its beat in the lines of Coleridge and Scott, and note its free movement in Elizabethan verse as in the lyrics of Burns; many wood-notes in English poetry bear witness to the native power of the old metre of the *Morte Arthure.* (p. 127)

Mary Macleod Banks, in an introduction to

Morte Arthure: An Alliterative Poem of the 14th Century, *edited by Mary Macleod Banks, Longmans, Green and Co., 1900, pp. 123-30.*

Dorothy Everett   (essay date 1953?)

[*Everett was an English educator and critic who specialized in medieval studies. In the following excerpt from an essay published posthumously, she provides an overview of the theme, style, and content of the alliterative* Morte Arthure.]

The *Morte Arthure* is, in subject and treatment, a thoroughly masculine work. Its heroic theme resembles those beloved by the Old English poets. Arthur is the mighty conqueror, haughty to his enemies, generous to his knights, and undaunted in defeat; his sole occupation, and that of his men is fighting; courage and loyalty are the virtues they prize. The temper which they (and the poet) admire is well illustrated in the speech of Sir Idrus when, in the last battle, Arthur bids him rescue his father, who is hard pressed:

> He es my fadire in faithe, forsake sall I neuer,
> He has me fosterde and fedde and my faire
>   bretheren . . .
> He commande me kyndly with knyghtly wordes,
> That I schulde lelely one þe lenge and one noo
>   lede elles;
> I sall hys commandement holde, yif Crist wil me
>   thole.
> He es eldare than I, and ende sall we bothen,
> He sall ferkke before, and I sall come aftyre.
> Yiffe him be destaynede to dy todaye one þis
>   erthe,
> Criste comly with crown take kepe to hys saule.

In all that concerns the relations between Arthur and his knights resemblances to Old English heroic poetry are striking. The knights, some of them Arthur's kinsmen and all of them ready to boast of their high lineage, are councillors as well as warriors, like the picked band of tried men, the *duguþ,* who in *Beowulf* support Hroþgar. Like them, they make their vaunts about the great deeds they will do in battle, and receive from their lord rewards for their valour. The speech of Sir Cader, encouraging his men to brave a great army of the Romans, reads like a fourteenth-century version of one from *The Battle of Maldon.* 'Think', he cries, 'on the valiant prince who has ever enriched us with lands and honour . . . given us treasure and gold and many rewards, greyhounds and fine horses. . . . ' How much of this is due to the Middle English poet we do not know, but if, as the latest opinion holds, he got his story from a French romance, or combined material from several romances, it seems likely that he developed it on lines that were traditional in English heroic poetry, as Layamon had done before him.

But the monsters encountered in *Morte Arthure* are not those of *Beowulf,* even though the same or similar phrases are sometimes used of them. In place of the indefinite but immensely suggestive description of Grendel, that misshapen haunter of the waste lands, that 'helle gast' of the brood of Cain, who is evil and terrifying even today, the *Morte Arthure* has the giant of Mont St. Michel, presented with a wealth of definite details which, horrible as they are, yet fail to terrify. The giant's kirtle, 'spun in Spain' and 'garnished in Greece' and bordered with beards of slain kings, is a fancy befitting the story of Jack the Giant-killer rather than a thing to be believed in. More impressive is the description of the giant as Arthur first sees him:

> He lay lenand on lange, lugande vnfaire,
> Þe thee of a manns lymme lyfte vp by þe haunche;
> His bakke and his bewschers and his brode lendez
> He bekez by þe bale-fyr and breklesse hym semede;
> Þare ware rostez full ruyde and rewfull bredez,
> Beerynes and bestaile brochede togeders,
> Cowle full cramede of crysmede childyre;
> Sum as brede brochede, and bierdez þam tournede.

Other marvels in the story—the prophetic dreams, the balm that heals Sir Priamus and Sir Gawayne—belong wholly to the world of romance, and are treated in a matter-of-fact way, as necessary 'properties' of the story. Nor are these the only features traceable to the romances. The poem opens according to pattern, with a prayer and a call for attention; there are the expected descriptions of feasts, of clothing, of the arming of knights. The stigmatization of Arthur's enemies, even in Britain, as Saracens reflects the familiar romance conflicts between Christian and Saracen, and, though in the earlier part of the story Arthur fights merely for personal glory, he enters upon his last campaign displaying a banner on which is 'a chalke-whitte mayden And a childe in hir arme þat chefe es of hevyne,' and his end is marked by Christian devotion. Of the gentler virtues comprised under the term 'courtesy', he and his knights show little trace, however, in spite of the opening description of them as 'Kynde men and courtays and couthe of courte thewes.' More characteristic of them are the grim jests they make in battle, as when Arthur cuts through the knees of the giant Golapas, crying, 'Come down and speak to your companions. You are too high by half, I promise you truly. You shall be more convenient in height, with my Lord's help.' This recalls similar jests in the Icelandic sagas, and demonstrates how superficial the relation between this poem and the romances of chivalry really is.

For this is a tragic tale, 'þat trewe es and nobyll.' Fittingly, it is given a firm foundation in time and place. So, Arthur justifies his rage at the summons to appear before the Roman Emperor Lucius by an 'historical' account of his ancestors' lordship over Rome; and the stages of his own journey thither are so clearly indicated that it would be possible to trace them on a map. Descriptions are solid, for the most part realizable in terms of the known. In recounting the siege of Metz, the poet specifies the siege instruments that were brought up and suggests the resulting destruction by details that come home to present-day readers perhaps even more than they did to the fourteenth century:

> Stone-stepells full styffe in þe strete ligges,

> Chawmbyrs with chymnés and many cheefe innes
> Paysede and pelid down playsterede walles.

Constantly a scene is brought to life by some realistic detail, as when the sheriffs 'sharply shift' the commons to make room for the great lords who are to embark for the expedition against Lucius, or, as when Arthur, having climbed to the top of Mont St. Michel, lifted his visor and 'caughte of þe colde wynde to comforthe hym seluen' (a touch that did not escape Malory). There are details like this in the accounts of battles, but they are mingled with others, more conventional and less real, for the tradition of such descriptions in alliterative poetry is too strong to be ignored. Here is a characteristic passage:

> Than the Romaynes and the rennkkez of þe rounde table . . .
> Foynes ful felly with flyschande speris,
> Freten of orfrayes feste appon scheldez.
> So fele fay es in fyghte appon þe felde leuyde,
> That iche a furthe in the firthe of rede blode rynnys.
> By that swyftely one swarthe þe swett es byleuede,
> Swerdez swangen in two, sweltand knyghtez
> Lyes wyde-opyn welterande on walopande stedez.

In all descriptions there is much use of the cumulative method, detail being piled on detail, often in phrases of similar construction, as in Old English poetry. But the poet of **Morte Arthure** is less restrained than the best of the Old English poets, and his long, overloaded descriptions slow down the narrative considerably. It is noticeable how often Malory improves upon him by selecting only the most significant of the details he offers. A sense of overelaboration is increased by some of the poet's tricks of style and metre. Often he uses the same alliterating sound for several lines on end, for as many as ten on one occasion; or he will begin consecutive lines with the same phrase or rhythm. Phrases and even whole lines from one passage are repeated in another, not usually for the purpose of linking sections of the narrative, as in some alliterative poems, but merely to produce a sort of echo. In one instance only is this repetition justified by its effect. When Arthur tells his council of Modred's treachery, which he has just learnt from Sir Cradok, his repetition of several of Sir Cradok's phrases helps to convey his stunned horror at the news. In general the effect of these various kinds of repetition is like that of a battering-ram. The mind wearies of what it feels to be a continual striving to impress. Excess is, indeed, the great defect of the poem, and not only in matters of style. There are too many giants, almost all 'engendrede of fendez' ('begotten of devils'); there are too many speeches at the opening council, and here, and elsewhere, they are too long; there is far too much fighting.

But a distinction must be made between the earlier and later parts of the poem, for in the later, though from line to line the method of narration is not essentially different, the tale is made far more engrossing. It may be that the poet turned to a fresh source for the last part of his tale . . . ; or it may be that the incidents are in themselves so stirring that they called forth in the poet powers which do not appear in the earlier part. Whatever the reason, the story moves more purposefully from the point where Arthur, nearing the end of his victorious progress through Europe, stands at the top of the St. Gotthard pass looking down upon Lombardy, and cries, 'In yon pleasant land I think to be lord.' Descending into Italy, he receives at Viterbo the Pope's message that he will crown him sovereign in Rome. That very night he has a dream in which he sees eight kings clinging to Fortune's wheel and striving in vain to reach a silver chair. Fortune sets Arthur in the chair, but at midday she turns against him. A philosopher tells him that the kings are eight of the Nine Worthies, all renowned conquerors in their day. Arthur himself will be the ninth; he is now 'at the highest', and will achieve no more. Arthur rises and goes out alone 'with anger in his heart', and almost at once he sees a man, dressed as a pilgrim and hastening on the road to Rome, who proclaims himself Sir Cradok, a knight of Arthur's chamber, come from Britain to tell him that Modred has had himself crowned king and has taken Guinevere for his wife. Arthur quickly calls a council and, then, leaving a few knights to guard his conquests, he hurries back through Italy, Germany, and Flanders to take ship for Britain.

In this climax of the story the events are so ordered as to bring out the drama inherent in them, and they are related without digression, indeed, with a certain urgency, which is not lost even in the long account of the dream. After this, even though the excitement of the unexpected is lacking, the poet remains to the end in control of his story. He achieves a fine contrast between the maddened fighting and violent end of Gawain and the slow grief-stricken tributes of his slayer, Modred, and of Arthur. In Arthur's lament, the most widely quoted passage in the poem, the repetitive, cumulative style is at its most effective:

> Þan the corownde kyng cryes full lowde:
> 'Dere kosyn o kynde, in kare am I leuede,
> For nowe my wirchipe es wente and my were en-
>   dide.
> Here es þe hope of my hele, my happynge of
>   armes,
> My herte and my hardynes hale one hym
>   lengede,
> My concell, my comforthe, þat kepide myn
>   herte!
> Of all knyghtes þe kynge þat vndir Criste lifede,
> Þou was worthy to be kynge, þofe I þe corown
>   bare,
> My wele and my wirchipe of all þis werlde riche
> Was wonnen thourghe sir Wawayne and
>   thourghe his witt one!'

Vowing to avenge Gawain, Arthur pursues Modred to Cornwall, and, after fierce fighting, slays him, but receives his own deathwound. The rest of the poem is on a quieter note. Arthur laments his fallen knights, and asks to be carried to Glastonbury to the Isle of Avalon, where, after calling for a confessor, he dies, saying 'In manus'. The poet concludes: 'So ends King Arthur, as writers tell, who was of the kin of Hector, the son of the king of Troy.' Characteristically, this 'true' tale knows nothing of a mystic boat with wailing women, nor of the prophecy that Arthur shall return to the Britons.

The poem, as a whole, is animated by an energetic and powerful imagination, not always sufficiently kept in check. Though the poet lacks subtlety, he has a sure sense of the dramatic, and never fails to recognize the significant moments in his story. He has, particularly at such times, a clear mental picture of action (though he is not capable of subtle or consistent characterization), and he understands the emotions that prompt it or arise from it. He knows, too, the value of contrast in bringing out the emotional quality of a scene or an action. Even in the earlier, less stirring parts of the poem perception is quickened by such contrasts as the Roman messengers bowing in knightly fashion before delivering the Emperor's summons and then, suddenly terrified at Arthur's anger, 'crouching like dogs' before him, or Arthur, when he is discovered wounded after his terrific fight with the monstrous giant of Mont St. Michael, telling his knights that his sword and shield lie on the top of the crag together with the giant's club, and asking simply that they should go and fetch them. (pp. 61-7)

> *Dorothy Everett, "The Alliterative Revival," in her* Essays on Middle English Literature, *edited by Patricia Kean, Oxford at the Clarendon Press, 1955, pp. 46-96.*

William Matthews   (essay date 1960)

[*Matthews was an Anglo-American educator, editor, biographer, and critic specializing in medieval studies. In the following excerpt from the epilogue to his analysis of Arthur as a tragic hero in the alliterative* Morte Arthure, *Matthews examines allusions in the poem to historical figures and events, speculating that the work may have been intended as an imaginative protest against British imperialism.*]

That **Morte Arthure** is one of the great achievements of alliterative poetry and deserves to be reckoned with *Pearl, Piers Plowman,* and *Sir Gawain and the Green Knight* has seldom been questioned. . . . [It] should also be set side by side with *Troilus and Criseyde* as a classic of the medieval tragedy of fortune. Artistically, it lacks the perfection of *Sir Gawain* or of Chaucer's masterpiece. Its chronicle-like versions of battles and campaigns and its tendency toward episodic digression might be excused by the nature of its sources or justified by medieval fashions in narrative and rhetoric, but they still tend to divert attention from the main narrative and from the principal theme. The realism of the poem does not always sit easily with its supernatural elements; the vocabulary is occasionally local and uncouth; and the triphammer rhythms are sometimes so continuingly energetic as to get wearisome. But these are minor blemishes on a poem that is admirable for its solid construction and rugged strength, its richness in language, subtle imagery, the vivid descriptions, dialogue that is finely varied, a pervasive irony that engages both the reader's mind and his feelings, the sensitive gradation of its tragic mood, and, above all, the brilliant originality of its characterization and of an interpretation that revitalizes one of the great themes of romance. The poem is the product not only of masterly craftsmanship but also of a powerful imagination, powerfully moved, and its effectiveness in its own times is evident from the later works that respond to its originality and its passion.

In recounting Arthur's career as a conqueror, Geoffrey of Monmouth and his chronicler-offspring had not shunned the brutalities of war. To a modern conscience, the operations against the Scots and Picts, for example, would surely fall into the pitiless category of genocide. But Arthur's liquidations of enemies and barbarians raise no doubts in most chroniclers' minds: they are as righteous, praised just as highly, as his Christian commiseration in permitting a miserable remnant to survive in their native squalor. For almost all English historians, Arthur was the paragon of English kings. The few medieval chroniclers who do tarnish with criticism the necessities of his heroic campaigns are moved less by moral scruples than by unbritish partisanship or scholarly scepticism.

Morte Arthure, therefore, drawing for the first time a critical portrait of the national hero on the basis of deep concern with the moral problem of war, is distinctly a minority report.

So marked an originality must express the poet's own feelings. That he was not alone in his sentiments about imperial war has . . . been observed. Uncustomary applications of the moral imagination are so often triggered by troubled occasions in a writer's own world and time, however, that it is tempting to seek for something within the unknown poet's experience that may have given rise to his troubled interpretation of the death of Arthur and the passing of his golden world. Reading social significance into the anonymous poetry of far-off ages is a procedure that rarely convinces anyone but the reader himself. But with *Morte Arthure* it seems almost inescapable to venture toward the *bête glattissant* of contemporary allusion in quest of some fuller lease on the poem's truth. If for the remainder of this [essay], therefore, the earnest and patient reader finds himself committed to a journey through the scholarly wasteland, and if at its end he should feel that he has been vouchsafed nought but fewmets of the dragon (or even the traces of some other beast whatever), may he while shaking his head cross himself kindly, remembering that wodewoses and shapechangers inhabit not only the land of Logres: they are even more endemic in the bifocal world of academic Pellinores.

As for the source of the poem, it seems most likely to have been French and to have been composed during the first half of the fourteenth century. When compared with the story narrated by Geoffrey, Wace, and Layamon two centuries before, *Morte Arthure* shows many additions and changes, and although, contrary to common critical assumption, it was not totally impossible for a medieval English poet to be as original as a French one, there are several indications that for some of these alterations the poet must have been indebted to an untraced French work written not long before.

The most obvious is the poem's peculiar concern with France and the abnormal sympathy it displays for England's old enemy. A dozen times and more, France and Frenchmen are referred to in compliment: "douce Fraunce," "flour of rewmes," "the freke men of Fraunce,"

and the like. In the foray at Metz Arthur commits his forces to a young French leader and even speaks of his men as Frenchmen. And in the interpretation of the king's dream, it is his crimes against France that are singled out for condemnation, and the expiation is to be made there:

> Fownde abbayes in Fraunce, þe froytez are
> theyn awen.
> Fore Froill, and for Ferawnt, and for thir ferse
> knyghttis,
> That thowe fremdly in Fraunce has faye beleuede.

On the literary side, despite its basis in the chronicle tradition, the poem displays intimate knowledge of Arthurian themes that had developed in the French prose romances. Some of the important minor characters, Ywain, Erec, Idrus, Cleges, Lancelot, and others, belong solely to the romance tradition. The naming of Arthur's sword of peace as Clarent may derive from his battle cry "Clarent!" in the *Estoire de Merlin*. The symbolism of Gawain's death is seemingly related to the religious interpretation of the Grail that had been begun by Robert de Boron and continued in the romances of the Vulgate Cycle. The relationship of the poem to the corresponding section of the *Mort Artu* is particularly close. Mordred's tarnished birth and Florent's being the son of Gawain probably derive from that romance, and so too does the death duel between Mordred and Arthur. Guenevere's grief at Arthur's departure, her fear that she would never see him again, Lancelot's vengeance on Mordred's children, Gawain's burial and Arthur's lament are all described in that French romance in terms that recall the alliterative poem. Among larger resemblances, it is interesting that in the prose *Lancelot* the fantasy of world conquest crops up: Galehot, disturbed by dreams of serpents, confesses to Lancelot the mad ambition to conquer all the world that had led him to build his great prison, L'Orgueilleuse Emprise—"Et iou auoie empris tant a conquerre que iou y metroie C et L roys dessous ma seignorie. Et quant iou lez auroie tous conquis, si les ameneroie tous o moi en chest chastel. Et lors mi feroie couronner." This folly was inspired by the vainglory of Fame—"pour chou que tous li siecles parlast de moi apres ma mort." Galehot fully expects the complete reversal that ensues: "Nus beubans nest si haut montes quil ne soit aussi tost bien bas descendus." Provocative as it is, this analogue is somewhat remote, but there is more likelihood that one inspiration for the courageous but madly vengeful Gawain of the poem is the Gawain of *Mort Artu,* whose passion to avenge upon Lancelot the death of Gaheriet brings death to himself and ruin to the Round Table: "Biaus niés," says Arthur, "grant damage ma fait vostre grand folie."

An alliance of the romance and chronicle traditions such as these details suggest seems more likely to have been effected in France than in England, and the same impression is given by the Alexander motifs that are introduced into the narrative and the borrowings from *Les Voeux du Paon* and *Li Fuerres de Gadres:* they would not have been impossible for a fourteenth-century English poet, but they would have been easier for a French writer of the period that produced *Perceforest* and its mingling of Arthurian and Alexandrian heroes.

Reinforcing this impression from the literary subject is the strong evidence of the language. Some names appear in French form: *Boice, Kayon, Cadors,* and so on, the poet uses a scattering of French grammatical constructions, and the poem is remarkable for an exceedingly large French vocabulary. A checking of scattered passages shows frequencies ranging from 15 per cent to 22 per cent, almost twice as high as the percentages in similar samples taken from other English poems of the time. On a nonfrequency basis, the glossary to Björkman's edition [1915] reveals a heavy preponderance of French words, and even if one excludes the many words for feasting, warfare, armor, costume, law, and shipping, which might conceivably have been known to the poet through social life and fashion, the French vocabulary is abnormally rich. Many French words in the poem were rare or unknown in the literary language of the time. Over a score of them are cited in the *O.E.D.* solely from *Morte Arthure* or are not recorded at all, e.g., *As armes!* and *Fy a debles!* and *avires* "turns towards," *dictour* "spokesman," *encroysse* "to go on crusade," *erchevesques* "archbishops," *fawnelle* "chestnut horse," *laundone* "field," *pastorelles* "herdsmen," *roo* "wheel," *sertes* "obligations." A dozen more occur first in the poem, often long before the next use, e.g., *credance* "ambassador's document," *genatours* "light horsemen," *hotche* "to strike," *pome* "globe," and *toge* "cloak." And, adding to the peculiarly Gallic coloration of the language are numerous words that, although they were also used by other fourteenth-century writers, were scarcely familiar in the literary vocabulary of the time, e.g., *ayele* "grandfather," *arborye* "wood," *enhoril* (enourle) "to surround," *nurry* "nursling," *masondewe* "hospital," *roy* "king," *somercastell* "howdah," or *stotaye* "to become foolish." Rich as is the poet's diction in other areas, too, it is unlikely that he could have relied solely upon his own linguistic resources for this French vocabulary: far more probable is it that much is the result of his use of a French source.

Such a source might go far to explain the poet's criticism of the greatest of British kings. If it is also assumed that the French source was critical of Arthur and contained some of the major additions to the traditional story, then it is possible to make some deductions about its date of composition and the emotional climate in which it was written.

It must have been written at least as late as the thirteenth century, for *Morte Arthure* employs several knights who had been brought into the Arthurian world by Chrétien de Troyes and his romance followers and also reflects the religious interpretation of the Vulgate Cycle. A date as late as the early part of the fourteenth century is indicated by the use of elements from *Les Voeux du Paon,* which was written by Jacques de Longuyon about 1312. And, since the accepted dating of *Morte Arthure* is some time in the second half of the fourteenth-century, it must follow that the terminal dates for the composition of the postulated French source are 1312 and, say, 1375; and a reasonable narrowing would give 1330-1360.

In those years began the Hundred Years' War and with it the bitterness against the English invasions, French civil wars, and indeed war in general. . . . And how such an

emotion could be transferred to Arthur may be seen in Laurent de Premierfait's version of the fall of Arthur in *Les Cas des nobles hommes et femmes,* written about 1400. Contrary to the wholly eulogistic account of the king that appears in Lydgate's adaptation, Boccaccio had not been entirely uncritical in his original version of the tragedy. After the victory over Lucius, Arthur had become inflated with the pride of conquest, and it was while he was in this state of weakness that Fortune prepared his fall: "Et quum illi cessisset victoria in omissum desyderium recidens occupaturus ampliora processit. Set elato iam parabatur occisus. Dum igitur armis interiora Galliae infestaret: Modredus eius ex concubina filius . . . " and so on. This criticism of Arthur's pride and his conquests in France is emphasized markedly in the French adaptation:

> Or aduint que artur obtint en armes victoire contre le consul rommain et les siens. Si rechei artur en desir de faire guerre et conqueste de pays la quelle chose il auoit delaisse. Et proceda a occuper pour soy et conquerir plus grans terres et plus amples seignories. Mais au roy artur esleue et orgueilleux fortune ia auoit apreste le trebuchet. Car tandiz que le roy artur guerroioit et malmenoit par ses batailles les principales prouinces de gaules qui estoient subiectes aux romains, mordret vn sien fils . . . " and so on.

The theory that the poem had a French source which was inspired by the happenings of the early years of the Hundred Years' War might serve of itself to explain not only some of the literary and linguistic features of *Morte Arthure* but also the unusualness of its view of Arthur's career as a conqueror. It would certainly be the better part of valor to stop with that generalization. But there are details in the poem, not explainable by the influence of Alexander stories, that seem to point directly to historical events more recent than the time of Arthur and perhaps to a topical allusion in the poem as a whole.

Morte Arthure follows medieval literary habit in translating the manners of its characters to its own time: armor, costume, tactics, meals, shipping, conversational idiom, are all those of the fourteenth century. More significant than this customary modernization, however, is the addition to the traditional story of several names that seem to belong to a period near to the time of the poem's composing, for they may have been meant to suggest to the audience a parallel in contemporary affairs.

The pagans of Prussia and the liegemen of Lithuania who appear so often in the poem, mostly in connection with Gawain's foray at Metz, surely owe their surprising appearance in the Arthurian world to the crusades of the Teutonic Knights in 1350-1380—holy wars in which it was the fashion for the young aristocrats of England and Europe to win their chivalric spurs. The giants of Genoa who lend their might to Lucius only to be cut down to Arthurian size seem kin to the famous Genoese crossbowmen whose terror was diminished by the longbows of England at Crécy and Poitiers. The Danes who aid Mordred do not appear in the chronicles, but they bring to mind the plans of Waldemar III to reconquer the land once held by his ancestors Canute and William and the great Danish raid on the English coast that is reported by John of Reading for June, 1363.

The countess of Crasyn bears an unusual name that is possibly relevant to Quercy and the southern French campaigns of Edward, the Black Prince. The Montagues who fight side by side with Gawain against Mordred are no Arthurians; but a famous family of that name fought prominently in Edward III's Scottish wars, and one of its members took the lead in capturing Roger Mortimer in the company of his mistress, Edward II's queen. Wallingford Castle, where, according to the poem but not according to any other Arthurian chronicle or romance, Arthur kept the sword of peace that Guenevere betrayed into Mordred's hands, is a castle associated particularly with Edward II and Edward III. It was given to Edward II's favorite, Piers Gaveston, and was thereafter attached to the duchy of Cornwall; on Gaveston's death Queen Isabella received the castle and at Christmas 1326 held high festival there with her paramour Mortimer; and the Black Prince lived there for a time after his marriage to Joan of Kent. These facts suggest a deliberate parallelism between the treason of Guenevere and Mordred and the treason of Isabella and Mortimer that was settled by the energy of the new king Edward III. Somewhat more loosely, the naming of Arthur's second sword as Clarent matches the Arthurian name Clarence that was assumed by Edward's son Lionel; and the appearance of Hainault, Brabant, Flanders, and Holland among Arthur's imperial possessions brings to mind the extension of English power that resulted from Edward III's marriage to Philippa of Hainault and his partnership with Jan van Artevelde.

In addition to the associations between these added names and events of the earlier fourteenth century, some incidents familiar in the Arthurian story are treated in a fashion that may have been meant to evoke the memory of some of the most celebrated occurrences of that time.

Arthur's wars parallel generally and often in detail Edward III's campaigns in the earlier stages of the Hundred Years' War. Both wars began with disputes over homage and casuistical British claims to lordship abroad, Arthur claiming through Constantine and others of his remote ancestors, Edward through Isabella his mother. Arthur's freeing of the duchess of Brittany from the imperialistically inclined giant of St. Michel has some counterpart in Edward's support in 1342 of the embattled Joan of Montfort who fought so pluckily to uphold the tenure of her imprisoned husband against the monkish but brutal Charles of Blois, his rival in claiming the duchy of Brittany.

Despite its series of heroic duels and its ultimate debt to Geoffrey or Wace, the description of Arthur's battle at Sessoynes is manifestly based upon a fourteenth-century art of warfare. In many details it closely matches the battle of Crécy. In other versions Arthur's battle with Lucius occurs near Autun in Burgundy, but the alliterative poet associates it with northern France. Just as Arthur marches from Barfleet by the "blythe stremes" toward Chastell Blanke on his way to his meeting with Lucius, just so Edward's army passed through Barfleet, reached the Seine at Castle Rocheblanche, and crossed the Somme at Blanche-Tague on its way to Crécy. The locale of both battles was similar: between river and wooded hillside near a city in a northern French valley. Arthur's disposition of his forces on the hillside was much like Edward's: three battles on foot, the best knights in the van, with archers on either side of them, and cavalry in reserve. Genoese formed an important part of the opposed army in both engagements, and the fact that Edward entrusted his right wing to the Prince of Wales, with Welsh spearmen in support, is paralleled by the role of the Welsh king, Sir Valyaunt (a character who is missing from other versions of the battle of Sessoynes), as chieftain of the check in the fight against Lucius. Arthur's tactics, a repulse by the longbowmen followed by a charge of cavalry, were also Edward's. And the details with which the poet embroiders the traditional account of the disposition of Lucius' body may be matched by the ceremonial honors that were paid to John of Bohemia, whose corpse was dressed in fine linen, encoffined, set on a horse litter, and, under a cover of cloth of gold, carried to burial. But, even though such resemblances are striking enough, what is most persuasive that the poet was envisaging an Anglo-French conflict is that in one line he refers to the enemy as being French— "and faughte with the frekkeste þat to Fraunce langez."

If this battle was intended to mirror Crécy, then the siege of Metz that follows immediately may possibly reflect the siege of Calais, 1346-1347. Apart from general similarities that might be expected in any description of medieval sieges, there is one detail in the poem which generally recalls what is perhaps the most famous incident in the siege of Calais. When the burghers of the city approached the great chair where Edward was sitting under a scarlet canopy of state, Queen Philippa and her ladies were also present, according to Froissart, and, when all other pleas for mercy had failed, the queen fell to her knees and persuaded the king to forego his vengeance upon Calais and its citizens. In comparable fashion, after Metz has been taken, the poet describes an incident quite unlike anything else in his work: the countess of Crasyn and her ladies kneel to Arthur, who is mounted "on a couerede horse comlyli arayede," and successfully beseech him for forgiveness for the city and its people.

The sea battle in which Arthur wins his first victory over Mordred also recalls one of the two great sea fights of Edward's reign. In the engagement fought in August, 1350, and generally known as Espagnols-sur-mer, Edward won a famous victory over a fleet of Spanish privateers. The details of that battle and of the king's part in it, as described by contemporary chroniclers, resemble the description of the fight off Southampton that appears in the poem, and the similarities are made the more impressive by the facts that in one line the poem refers to Mordred's forces as "Spanyolis" and that Arthur's banner is there described as combining his traditional Virgin and Child with a device that matches the second division, "gules charged with five crowns, *or*," of the standard of Edward III. Arthur's banners, states the poet, were:

> betyn of gowles,
> With corowns of clere golde clenliche arraiede,
> Bot þare was chosen in þe chefe a chalke-whitte
>   mayden
> And a childe in hir arme, þat chefe es of hevyne.

The Arthur of the alliterative poem, it has been argued, was drawn with an eye to Alexander the Great. It is no contradiction of that opinion to suggest that the poet's gaze may also have been on a conqueror nearer to his own time. Most of the parallels outlined above, and particularly such details as the Spaniards of the sea battle, the French at Sessoynes, the Montagues who fought against Mordred, the association of Guenevere and Mordred with Wallingford, the armorial bearings of Arthur, point toward the fourteenth-century king whose character and proceedings match most nearly the hero of *Morte Arthure* and who is portrayed allegorically in another fourteenth-century alliterative poem, *Wynnere and Wastour.*

> **"The Arthur of the alliterative poem, it has been argued, was drawn with an eye to Alexander the Great. It is no contradiction of that opinion to suggest that the poet's gaze may also have been on a conqueror nearer to his own time."**
>
> **—William Matthews**

That monarch is Edward III, the admired, patriotic, and ambitious warrior who by arms, diplomacy, and match-making sought to recover the possessions lost by his weakling father and to extend his dominion over most of western Europe. Edward's conquests and hopes agree fairly closely with the catalogue of possessions with which the poem begins and the wars and ambitions it goes on to describe, and his character and tastes were in many ways those which distinguish the hero of the poem. The great ruler whom the messengers describe in their report to Lucius, handsome, beaver-bearded, magnificent in costume, wealth, and entertainment, but given to terrifying outbursts of anger, might have been drawn from Edward—handsome and well built, wearing a flowing beard of berry-brown hue, delighting in splendid raiment and the ceremony of feasts and office, and prone to short-lived fits of rage. The passion for hawking and hunting that leads Arthur to foreswear this greatest of pleasures until he has revenged Gawain was also Edward's passion: even on campaign he took with him small armies of falconers and huntsmen, "dont il alloit chacun jour ou en chasse ou en riviere, ainsi qu'il lui plaisoit" wrote Froissart. Arthur was disposed to prodigal generosity, to alternations of compassion and cruelty, and these also were traits of Edward, whose extravagances were notorious and whose sieges and conquests were no less cruel than Arthur's. Twice at least, with the unfortunate London carpenters whose scaffolds fell during a state procession and with the burghers of Calais who held out against his siege, it was only the pleas of Philippa that dissuaded him from savage vengeance against simple folk who had frustrated his will; and the character of his French campaigns may be judged from the words of Petrarch, written soon after a journey to Paris in 1361—"Everywhere was a melancholy emptiness and devastation; everywhere fields uncultivated and barren; everywhere homes ruined and deserted, except where they were surrounded by the walls of cities or castles; in every place the melancholy tracks of the English and the new and horrible scars left by their swords." The courage and rashness of the British king in the siege of Metz and in his last fight with Mordred were also characteristic of the Plantagenet king, manifested in the sea battle of Espagnols-sur-mer or his offer to settle the war with Philip in single combat. Edward's energy as a young man, his decisiveness in battle, his skill as a tactician and incompetence as a stategist, are all marks of the Arthur of the poem, and so too is his religiosity. Despite his troubles with the pope, Edward, like Arthur, was orthodox and devout, unwearied in pilgrimage, lavish in religious foundations. Arthur's imperial ambition, which left his land defenseless, was the seed of both a national and a personal disaster. And as Edward's similar *fata morgana* year after year bled his countrymen white, criticism of his senseless and profitless campaigns increased. "In spite of the superficial encomiums of the chroniclers," declared [James Mackinnon, in his *History of Edward III,* 1900], "it is certain that Edward came to be widely unpopular." His military successes, like Arthur's, brought him within reach of the emperor's crown: upon the death of his old ally Ludwig of Bavaria in 1347, the German electors offered their support to his imperial candidacy. Nevertheless, as Tout sums up his career [in his *History of England from the Accession of Henry III to the Death of Edward III,* 1905], "His ambition transcended his resources, and before he died even his subjects were aware of his failure."

Unusual as many of these traits are of Arthur, it is likely that most of them might be matched in other fourteenth-century rulers besides Edward: warlike ambition, anger, cruelty, courage, religiosity, and a passion for the chase were scarcely idiosyncrasies of any one medieval monarch. But for the English king the similarities have special point, for to compare him with Arthur was almost a commonplace in his own day. "Never had there been such a king since the days of Arthur, King of Britain," wrote Froissart, who also recalled an occasion at Berkhampstead when an ancient knight expounded to the Queen's ladies—correctly as it turned out—the prophecies of Merlin: "According to him, neither the Prince of Wales nor the Duke of Clarence, though sons to King Edward, will wear the crown of England, but it will fall to the House of Lancaster."

Comparison of Edward with Arthur appears in the chronicles of the Canon of Bridlington, Robert of Avesbury, Thomas Walsingham, Adam of Usk, and others. And indeed the association was fostered by the king himself. In battle he was inclined to conduct himself as if he were Lancelot, he gave one of his sons a name from Arthurian romance, and he carried to its climax the Arthurian cult which his thirteenth-century forbears had fostered with an eye to its value in their claims to the crown of all Britain. In 1279, on the occasion of the knighting of his three sons by Edward I, Roger Mortimer had held a great Round Table at Kenilworth. Five years later, Edward—from whose manuscripts Rustician of Pisa made his abridgement of the Arthurian romances—had celebrated his conquest of Wales and liquidation of its princes by holding a Round Table in Carnarvonshire at which the chivalry of Europe competed and the king was presented with the newly discovered crown of Arthur. In 1328, Roger Mortimer, first earl of March and at that time the *de facto* ruler of England, imitated his grandfather with a Round Table at Bedford. These Arthurian evocations, splendid as they were, were outshone in magnificence by the Round Table that Edward III produced in 1344. On New Year's Day, he sent heralds with invitations into the courts of France, Burgundy, Hainault, Scotland, Flanders, Brabant, and Germany. Beginning on St. George's Day, the celebration consisted of four days of extravagant entertainment and tournament, culminated by a great feast at which Edward and Philippa wore crowns in the pattern of the Pentecostal feast described in Geoffrey of Monmouth. On the fifth day, after Mass, the king swore solemnly to restore Arthur's Round Table and to hold a celebration at Windsor every year at Pentecost, and in February he commanded the construction of a circular building, two hundred feet across, in which the banquet for these annual celebrations should be held. The building was never completed, but so famous and so politically potent was the Arthurian gesture that it immediately inspired Philip of France to set up a rival Round Table in his own land—his practical objective being thereby to woo away Germanic arms from Edward's support.

If, from these familiar facts, it seems plausible that a French writer of the time might have been inspired to draw a portrait of Arthur in the likeness of Edward III, there are also good reasons to believe that he might simultaneously have drawn them both in the image of Alexander. The alliterative *Morte Arthure,* it has been argued, is heavily indebted to the most popular of fourteenth-century extensions of the Alexander story, *Les Voeux du Paon,* and it is therefore highly suggestive for the present argument that the best known of the French derivatives from De Longuyon's romance deals unequivocally with Edward III and his campaigns in France. This work is *Les Voeux du Héron,* a poem written some time after 1340, possibly by a Picard or Flemish writer. It describes how, one day in September, 1338, Robert of Artois, an exile at the court of Edward III, contrived by an ingenious plot to provoke a fearful war in which knights were killed, women widowed, and churches destroyed. Robert roasts a heron that he had caught, brings it to the king's table, and by declaring that it was fitting to present so cowardly a bird to a king who had let himself be deprived of his French inheritance, goads Edward and his knights into making vows on the heron. Edward swears to defy the French king, to invade France and set the whole country to the flame, to conquer like Alexander. In turn, similar vows, one or two lighthearted but most of them belligerent and savage, are proclaimed by the earl of Salisbury, Walter de Manny, the earl of Derby, the earl of Suffolk, Jean de Fauquemont, John of Beaumont, and Queen Philippa. Their speeches are adapted from the vows on the peacock by Alexander's douzepers in De Longuyon's poem, but, as Professor Whiting has proved [in his "The Vows of Heron," *Speculum* XX (1945)], they are also cleverly adapted to the actual behavior during the years 1333-1340 of the persons making the vows. Commonly the poem has

been interpreted by historians as a pro-English piece reflecting the warlike aspirations of brave men. In fact, it is anti-English and anti-war. "To call it a 'pacifist' poem would be perhaps to go too far," writes Professor Whiting, "but the frequent references to the misfortunes and hardships of war are striking . . . *Les Voeux du Héron* is neither 'pretty and playful,' 'French romance of the next generation,' nor 'une agréable fiction,' but a grimly satirical document, which, when the Hundred Years' War was just beginning, foreshadowed what it was in the main to be, a struggle productive only of destruction, frustration, and suffering." Its resemblances to *Morte Arthure,* we may add, are patent. Not only does it draw from the same Alexander romance and sometimes employ similar phraseology in the vows, but its attitude toward war and, if our identification is correct, toward Edward III is also very much the same.

It is fair to conjecture from this analogy that the French source that has been postulated for *Morte Arthure* was, like *Les Voeux du Héron,* inspired both by the story of Alexander and his douzepers as it was related by De Longuyon and by the bitterness and anti-war feeling aroused by Edward's invasion and the cruelties of the early campaigns of the Hundred Years' War. But, although such a view of Arthur and Edward would have been natural enough in a French poet of the period 1340-1350, it is somewhat surprising to find it reproduced in an English poem of the second half of the fourteenth century. For almost all English writers, Arthur was the nonpareil of English kings, immune from criticism of any kind. And, as for Edward III, it was a rare Englishman indeed who found anything to condemn in his manner of waging warfare, especially when it led to such triumphs as Crécy and Poitiers. Criticism of both kings would have been easier for a Scottish poet, and there is something in *Morte Arthure*'s view to support the old claim that the poem was written in southern Scotland. But *Morte Arthure* displays no noticeable northern patriotism (it once even speaks disparagingly of "scathell Scotlande"); although it is understanding of Mordred, it is still hostile to that Scottish hero; it makes nothing of the Scottish origin of Mordred and Gawain his brother; and its criticism of Arthur is less hostile than that of Fordun and most other Scottish chroniclers, tempered by admiration and by an English-style patriotism that inclines the poet to reiteration of "our king" and "our men." And, although the general run of its language is not against Scottish composition, the poem contains a few forms which have been held by recent students to prove that its dialect has been altered and that it was originally composed in the northwest of England, perhaps in Lancashire or near Carlisle.

Short of more certain knowledge, therefore, as to when, where, and by whom the poem was composed, there seems no way of arriving at a special social explanation for its originality. The simplest and probably the most satisfactory way of meeting the dilemma is to recognize that the poet was a man of courageous independence and to guess that he may have composed his work soon after 1375, when the piled-up misfortunes of John of Gaunt had added Pelion to the Ossa of Edward's failures in France and when the ordinary Englishman was weary of the tragic futility of his rulers' imperial conquerings. This was the period, just before Edward's death, when, as Tout has stated, ". . . even his subjects were aware of his failure." In such a social temper, a French work that criticized the Arthurian imperialism might have proved attractive to an English poet of sturdy mind as a springboard from which to launch his own protest against the folly and unchristian cruelty of unjustified wars of the kind conducted by Alexander, Edward, and Arthur of Britain. (pp. 178-92)

> *William Matthews, in his* The Tragedy of Arthur: A Study of the Alliterative "Morte Arthure," *University of California Press, 1960, 230 p.*

Larry D. Benson   (essay date 1966)

[*Benson is an American educator and critic specializing in medieval studies. In the following essay, he argues that the alliterative* Morte Arthure *is a medieval tragedy featuring conventions peculiar to its period, and as such cannot be categorized within traditional genres. All text citations are to Brock's 1871 edition of* Morte Arthure.]

The alliterative **Morte Arthure** is not a complicated poem; a bold simplicity of structure and action is its chief virtue, and it speaks wisely and directly about the meaning of heroism and defeat. Yet the **Morte Arthure** has proved very difficult for modern readers to understand and appreciate, and its critics disagree not simply on what the poem is about but on what it is—romance, epic, or tragedy. Their difficulty, and ours, is that the **Morte Arthure** is emphatically a poem of its own time and place, simple in design but complex in the moral attitude that derives from the late Gothic ability to maintain contradicting attitudes and to derive aesthetic pleasure from the tension of unresolved conflicts. But we know so little about such art and as critics we are so professionally committed to finding unity even in diversity that we seek other contexts and traditions in which to judge the poem, without realizing that by the very act of classification we impose on the work a set of expectations that it was never meant to fulfill. We try to think of it as a "romance," and then, finding that expectation frustrated, we suppose that the poem must be some sort of anachronism—the last Old English epic or the first Elizabethan tragedy.

Perhaps our trouble is that so many of us come to the **Morte Arthure** with our ideas about Arthur and his court already formed on romances such as *Sir Gawain and the Green Knight* or the works of Malory and with our conception of the noble life in the Middle Ages built on that complex of ideas about love and battle that we call "chivalry." To read the alliterative **Morte Arthure** is to see Arthur in another light altogether, a harsher, stronger light, undimmed by the chivalric mist in which the romancers enclosed him. This is an Arthur who is pre-eminently heroic, a king whose most noble title is "conqueror," who knows little of tournaments but a great deal about war and nothing of courtly love but everything of friendship and loyalty.

Consequently, the world of the **Morte Arthure** is more austere than the word "Arthurian" usually implies, and the poem seems in many ways closer to Old English heroic verse than to romantic tales of Arthur by writers such as the author of the stanzaic *Mort Arthure*. The version of Arthur's death in that romance has become the "accepted" version, the one Malory consciously preferred to that in our alliterative poem, perhaps because Arthur himself in the stanzaic *Mort Arthure* appears in his "accepted," romantic version. In the alliterative **Morte Arthure,** however, as in the older heroic poetry, the principal concerns are feasting and fighting, the tone is serious, relieved by occasional touches of grimly ironic humor (as when Arthur tells the giant Golopas, whom he has cut off at the knees, that he is now handsomer by half), and the outcome is a defeat. Before each battle Arthur's knights boast of the deeds they will do in vows that seem to echo the *beots* of Old English warriors, and their relation to their leader is similar to that of the Anglo-Saxon *comitatus*. As Dorothy Everett has remarked [in her *Essays on Middle English Literature*, 1955], the speech of Sir Cador, encouraging his men to attack the Romans, "reads like a fourteenth-century version of one from *The Battle of Maldon*".

> Thynk one the valyaunt prynce that vesettez vs
> ever,
> With landez and lordsheppez, whare vs beste
> lykes;
> That has vz ducherés delte, and dubbyde vs
> knyghttez,
> Gifene vs gersoms and golde, and gardwynes
> many,
> Grewhoundez and grett horse, and alkyne gamnes,
> That gaynez tille any gome, that vndyre God
> leuez.
>
>   (1726-31)

Furthermore, Arthur's motives are those of an Anglo-Saxon hero—conquest, revenge, generosity to his friends, and implacable hatred to his foes. For him revenge is more important than that practice which must have done much to alleviate the horror of medieval war, the chivalric institution of ransom:

> Thane the kyde conquerour cryes fulle lowde,
> "Cosyne of Cornewaile, take kepe to thi selfene,
> That no captyne be kepyde for none siluer,
> Or sir Kayous dede be cruelly vengede!"
>
>   (2261-4)

"Cruelly" is the key word here, for Arthur is undeniably cruel. When he sends the dead emperor back to Rome, he is not only paying homage to a worthy opponent; he is creating the occasion for a grim jest, sending the body instead of the taxes demanded:

> "Here are the kystis," quod the kynge, "kaire
> ouer the mownttez;
> Mette fulle monee that ye haue mekylle yernede,
> The taxe and the trebutte of tene schore wynteres,
> That was tenefully tynte in tyme of oure elders.
> Saye to the senatoure, the ceté that yemes,
> That I sende hyme the somme, assaye how hyme
> likes!
>
>   (2342-7)

Localities in the *Morte Arthure*

Map of places referred to in the Morte Arthure. *From Valerie Krishna's 1976 edition of the poem.*

Only to Guenevere does he grant forgiveness, and even that is tinged with irony—"Yife Waynor hafe wele wroghte, wele hir betydde!" (v. 4325). To all others he is unyielding, and his revenge on Mordred goes beyond both of their graves, for in his last speech, as he feels his own death coming on, he gives orders regarding Mordred's children:

> And sythene merke manly to Mordrede chil-
>   drene,
> That they bee sleyghely slayne, and slongene in
>   watyrs;
> Latt no wykkyde wede waxe, ne wyrthe one this
>   erthe.
>
>   (4320-22)

This warrior king, with his passion for revenge, is closer to the Arthur of Layamon's *Brut,* himself an Old English hero, than to the Arthur who appears in Malory or in the stanzaic *Mort Arthure.* Yet the hero of our poem is not as anachronistic as the fact seems to imply, for the alliterative *Morte Arthure* does not look back from romance to a more heroic age; it looks away from romance to medieval life itself. By the fourteenth century romance and chivalry were primarily literary concerns, frameworks for ceremony rather than guides for conduct, and even Malory's life was closer to that which pulses in the lines of the *Morte Arthure* than to that reflected in his own work. Probably Froissart himself, the "chronicler of European chivalry," would have recognized the contemporary spirit of Arthur, for in his own chronicles the brutal lines of medieval militarism are only occasionally softened by acts of chivalry and the fighting men are more often simple warriors than polished *chevaliers.*

In Froissart's account of the battle of Poitiers, for example, we see the Black Prince, who came closest to embodying the chivalric code, in a situation relished by both the author of the *Morte Arthure* and the Anglo-Saxons—a hero and his followers beset by a much larger group of foes. The Prince rises to the occasion with a speech that would be as suitable in an Old English epic or in the *Morte Arthure* as it is in Froissart's *Chronicles:*

> Now, sirs, though we be but a small company as
> in regard to the puissance of our enemies, let us
> not be abashed therefor; for the victory lieth not
> in the multitude of people but whereas God will
> send it. If it fortune that the journey be ours, we
> shall be the most honoured people of all the
> world; and if we die in our right quarrel, I have
> the king my father and brethren, and also ye
> have good friends and kinsmen; these shall re-
> venge us.

When the battle is joined, Sir James Audley, fulfilling a vow like those in our poem, takes the vanguard and displays a ferocity that the Prince later rewards with great gifts; "for that day he never took prisoner, but always fought and went on his enemies." That day, too, Lord John Clermont, "was beaten down and could not be ransomed, but was slain without mercy." The Black Prince is as fierce and unmerciful as any of his followers, and when he comes upon Duras, his enemy Cardinal Perigord's retainer, his grim sense of humor matches Arthur's: "Sirs, take the body of this knight on a targe and bear him to Poitiers, and present him from me to the cardinal of Perigord, and say how I salute him by that token."

Such acts are undeniably cruel, but they earned the Black Prince the admiration of all Europe. Likewise, Froissart and his readers probably did not think it evil that Edward II marched through France with such violence that the country was "brent, exiled, robbed, wasted, and pilled," for they knew that in a ruler, though the romances sometimes disguise the fact, cruelty is almost a virtue, and the just king is necessarily cruel. [The critic adds in a footnote, "We must remember that when the word 'cruel' appears in the *Morte Arthure* it usually has the meaning 'stern, unyielding.' "] In *Piers Plowman* Langland upbraids Edward II not for destroying parts of the French countryside but for sparing any of it at all, and he uses the example of Saul, who earned the enmity of God for failing to massacre all the Amalekites, "Man, woman, and wif, child, widow, and bestes." When Arthur orders Mordred's children to be slain, he is not merely indulging in an archaic passion for complete revenge; he is doing his duty as a good medieval king by seeing that "No wykyde wede waxe, ne wyrthe one this erthe."

Though Arthur is too clearly a fourteenth-century king to fit into the fictional past of romance or the heroic past of epic, he is undeniably a "tragic" figure, and the best recent criticism of the poem has focused our attention on that aspect of the poem. But if it is true that our poem is, as William Matthews calls it, *The Tragedy of Arthur,* it is nevertheless tragedy as the late medieval period understood that term when [in Alfred Harbage's words] "a proliferating body of mortuary verse" told sad tales of the death of kings, good and bad alike, to show the fickleness of this world:

> Tragedie is to seyn a certeyn storie,
> As olde bookes maken us memorie,
> Of hym that stood in greet prosperitee,
> And is yfallen out of heigh degree
> Into myserie, and endeth wrecchedly.
>
>   (*Monks Pro,* 1973-77)

The difficulty is that when we think of tragedy we think in Aristotelian terms, and if we classify a work like the *Morte Arthure* as tragedy and think furthermore that it is a very good work, almost unconsciously we begin trying to justify our judgment by discovering Aristotelian elements in it. The plot, we think, must be well-made by classic standards, and so we look for a "suitable antagonist" or for some logical way of accounting for all the parts of the plot, including the siege of Metz and Gawain's encounter with Priamus, and we either fail to find them and thereby discover that the *Morte Arthure* is poorly constructed or, perhaps more disturbing, we do find them and discover that our fourteenth-century poet is an artist of Jamesian subtlety. We scrutinize the hero for a "tragic flaw" and discover it in the *hamartia* of Arthur's incestuous engendering of Mordred, thereby revealing the poet's carelessness, since he fails to mention this essential fact. Or closer to the truth, we look for evidence of justice in the hero's fall, and we find it in Arthur's "excess."

But medieval tragedy needs none of these elements. Behind Chaucer's famous definition stands the medieval conviction that all human possessions—power, love, life—are transitory, that their loss is inevitable and painful, and therefore that those who have the greatest share of human goods—those who stand in "heigh degree"—will most painfully lose them. As we can see from Chaucer's *Monk's Tale* or from its source in Boccaccio, the villain is the human condition itself, with death and the unforeseen chances of life (which medieval writers called "Fortune") the agents of a hero's downfall. The hero, like all men, will inevitably fall to death or wretchedness even though he be flawless, for the lesson of medieval tragedy is simply that man is not the master of his own destiny. Indeed, the tragic hero is apt to be better than other men, the greatest of lovers or the noblest of kings, the exemplar of a way of life, for the more one deserves continued success in love or war, the more stunning the fall, and the more forceful the lesson of Boethius' *Consolation of Philosophy,* of the *ubi sunt* lyrics, or of medieval sermons—that the only remedy for this universal situation is to recognize the frailty of this world and to turn instead to a faith in heaven.

Consequently, if a medieval tragic hero has a fault, it is not so much in himself as in the code to which he has given allegiance, and the only significant moral choice is the original decision to strive for worldly success. To give one's allegiance to an earthly code—to love, to kingship— is to suffer from moral blindness, but it is also necessary to achieve the excellence that we mortal men admire and that the world, wretched though it may be, requires. This is the complexity of the ***Morte Arthure,*** a moral complexity that will seem to us only a confusion if we seek the neatness of later works. Arthur does suffer from a form of *démesure,* and an interpretation of the poem that fails to recognize this must ignore that important speech in which the "philosopher" interprets Arthur's dream and tells him flatly:

> I rede thow rekkyne and reherse vn-resonable
> dedis,
> Ore the repenttes fulle rathe alle thi rewthe
> werkes!
> Mane, amende thy mode, or thow myshappene,
> And mekely aske mercy for mede of thy saule.
> (3452-55)

But, on the other hand, to consider only this aspect of the action, the rise and fall of the hero as "man," is to overlook the other, equally important side of the action, the accomplishments of the hero as king. In the same speech that the philosopher admonishes Arthur for his "vn-resonable dedis" he praises him for those very deeds:

> This salle in romance be redde with ryalle
> knyghttes,
> Rekkenede and renownde with ryotous kynges,
> And demyd one domesday, for dedis of armes,
> ffor the doughtyeste that euer was duelland in
> erthe.
>
> (3440-43)

The mention of Doomsday seems to imply that even God admires these earthly deeds.

The tension in a work like the ***Morte Arthure*** is thus not between good and evil, between the "excess" of earthly kingship and the virtue of renunciation; the tension is be-tween two goods, between the Christian detachment that is necessary for ultimate happiness even on this earth and the complete engagement with an earthly ideal that is necessary for heroism. That is why we finally admire the medieval tragic hero for the very qualities that lead to his fall. One could wish that Macbeth had been less ambitious or Hamlet more resolute, but who could wish that Troilus were a less perfect lover, Arthur a less noble king?

> "Arthur's fall is the result not of any flaw
> in himself but of a flawed ideal, the
> worldly ideal of heroic kingship that, like
> all worldly ideals, leads even its finest
> adherents to the inevitable turn of
> Fortune's wheel and a tragic fall."
>
> —*Larry D. Benson*

There is no doubt that Arthur's warlike deeds do lead him into moral blindness, for our poet uses the fall of this ideal conqueror as a means of probing for the weakness in the ideal of conquest itself. The structure of the narrative reflects the parallel between the rise of Arthur's material fortunes, as he earns the fame that will last until Doomsday, and the decline in his spiritual state, as he performs his "unreasonable" but admirable deeds. At the beginning of the poem we see Arthur as the perfect ruler, carefully providing for the well-being of his people as he sets out to avenge their past wrongs and prevent any future injuries from the Romans. There is irony in his appointment of Mordred as regent, despite Mordred's own protestations, for it shows us that even the greatest king cannot read the future and realize that he is thus causing more misery for his people at home than he can ward off by his expedition abroad. But Arthur's intentions are above reproach, as they are in his first adventure on the continent, the fight with the giant of Mont St. Michel. There Arthur is at his best, in single combat overcoming the monster that has ravaged his lands and then distributing the giant's treasure among his people, taking care that none has cause to complain of his share. His campaign against Lucius and his monstrous pagan allies is almost a parallel restatement of this initial adventure, though greater in magnitude.

Even in the first skirmish of that campaign, however, we have an adumbration of the poem's end, for Gawain's headstrong slaying of Gayus at the Emperor Lucius' table foreshadows the headstrong landing that leads to his death, and when Gawain dies, as Arthur recognizes, the King must die too. After the second skirmish, the Romans' ambush of Idrus, we are shown the first hint of internal discord in the Round Table when Arthur unjustly rebukes his knight, a rebuke that Idrus answers by pointing out Arthur's own error in judgment—an indication that even our ideal king is not infallible and perhaps an allusion to the fatal error in trusting Mordred. Finally, in the third and last battle of the campaign Kay and Bedevere, Arthur's companions on his journey to Mont St.

Michel, are left dead on the field, and we have the first of the burials that are to become a recurrent motif in the last part of the poem. Arthur is the good king, conquering as his state in life demands, but his conquests, good in themselves and a necessary goal for him and his knights, lead inevitably to the end of all conquest; their cost is the senseless violence of Gawain's slaughter of Gayus (a betrayal of the emperor's hospitality), the thoughtless rebuke of such faithful servants as Idrus, and the death of Arthur's most loved knights.

Once Lucius is defeated the havoc of Arthur's war becomes even more apparent, as Arthur, with endless and complete conquest his only goal, turns next not on a foreign foe but on one of his own disloyal vassals and begins the siege of Metz. Though the one battle at Metz is fought against the remainder of Lucius' pagan army, it is Gawain who battles those pagans and converts Sir Priamus; Arthur directs the siege, fighting against Christians, and the poet's description of that siege brings home to us the horrors of fourteenth-century warfare:

> Thane boldly thay buske, and bendes engynes,
> Payses in pylotes and proues theire castes;
> Mynsteris and masondewes they malle to the
>   erthe,
> Chirches and chapelles chalke-whitte
>   blawnchede.
> Stone [s]tepelles fulle styffe in the strete ligges,
> Chawmbyrs with chymnés, and many cheefe
>   inns,
> Paysede and pelid downe playsterede walles;
> The pyne of the pople was peté for to here!
>   (3036-43)

The invasion of Italy, separated from this passage by only a few dozen lines, is characterized by Florent's sudden assault on Como, when the idyllic scene of shepherds driving their flocks to pasture and boys shouting at a boar is shattered by Florent's striking and stabbing men: "ffowre stretis, or thay stynte, they stroyene fore euere" (3127). Arthur himself "turmentez the pople," creates woeful widows, "And alle he wastys with werre, thare he awaye rydez" (3153-56).

Yet the poet's attitude is more ambivalent than the simple condemnation of Arthur that critics have taken these passages to be. It is clear that the poet, like other fourteenth-century writers, wants us to see the wastefulness and potential sinfulness of war, but it is also clear that he wants us to admire Arthur even in the midst of this war. Whatever the effects of Arthur's campaign, his cause is just; Mordred, the lord of Metz, and even the Romans (275-79) are usurping his just rights, and most of his enemies are pagans, making his wars a kind of crusade and justifying Gawain's faith that if he and his men die in such a struggle "We salle be hewede vn-to heuene, or we be halfe colde" (4091).

Even when he is forced to fight Christians he remains a model of earthly kingship. His siege engines mercilessly bombard Metz, but he, like Edward I at the siege of Calais, heeds the pleas of a woman and spares the populace. He wants only to punish the traitor, and he gives orders to his troops that must have made them the ideal medieval army

of occupation (3078-83). His armies brutally ravage the Italian countryside, but he is eager to make peace, and when the new ambassadors from Rome arrive, he treats them with noble feasting that recalls the opening banquet of the poem, when the first embassy came to demand tribute for Lucius.

But he also remains the conqueror, and when the Roman crown is offered to him, he exultingly contemplates yet new conquests and proclaims,

> We salle be ouerlynge of alle that one the erthe
>   lengez!
>   (3211)

Here Arthur is at his most "unreasonable," blindly ignoring the limitations of his condition, and here, if we are considering the poem from the Aristotelian viewpoint, is the *hybris* that leads to the tragic fall. But in this same speech Arthur is also the most admirable of conquerors, for the goal that he envisions is the most virtuous a medieval king could propose—the reconquest of Jerusalem and the avenging of Christ's death:

> We wille by the Crosse dayes encroche their
>   londez!
>   . . . . .
> Syne graythe ouer the grette see with gud mene
>   of armes,
> To reuenge that renke that one the rode dyede!
>   (3212-17)

We know that Arthur's end is near, that he is now at the zenith of Fortune's wheel and will inevitably fall, not because of some fate seeking retribution for his sins, and not because God's justice demands that he be punished for the excesses of his campaign, for his cruelty is necessary even in a just war and he remains noble in his kingship. He will fall because the zeal essential to the attainment of his present success has led him to forget his own mortal limitations; the moral of tragedy, as Chaucer's monk tells us, is "Lat no man truste on blynd prosperitee." He has acquired a touch of *surquidrie,* the supreme overconfidence that begins to reveal itself when he rides so near the walls of Metz that his own men object and then brushes off their concern with the assurance that "Salle neuer harlotte haue happe, thorowe helpe of my Lorde, / To kylle a corownde kynge with krysome enoynttede" (2446-47). He learns later that his confidence is misplaced when he is "Rebukkede with a rebawde" (4283), Mordred. By that time he has also learned that he is not his own master, that he can act only "Tille Drightene and derfe dede hafe done qwate theme likes" (4008), He has lost Guenevere, been betrayed by Mordred, the man he most trusted, and suffered the death of Gawain, the man he most loved.

In romances such as the stanzaic *Mort Arthure* or Malory's account of Arthur's death, the final scene is softened by the prospect of Arthur's return and the whole fall of the Round Table is enveloped with an air of repentance and forgiveness that makes the end more pathetic than tragic. At the end of our poem Arthur is dead and will not return; the Isle of Avalon is the monastery at Glastonbury, where he is received not by fairies but by surgeons who attempt and fail to heal his wounds. And there is no repentance. Arthur has done what he must, and he has remained true to his ideals; his sorrow is not for his sin but for the good warriors that he has led to death, and, far from repenting that he lusted to be "ouerlynge of alle," he thanks God for granting him "the ouer-hande of alle other kynges" (4300). In his dying speech he is the noble king still, arranging for the future government of his kingdom and giving orders that Mordred's children be slain and left unburied. The author leaves us to recognize that Arthur's fall is the result not of any flaw in himself but of a flawed ideal, the worldly ideal of heroic kingship that, like all worldly ideals, leads even its finest adherents to the inevitable turn of Fortune's wheel and a tragic fall. At the end of the manuscript in which our poem is preserved some later scribe has added the words that appeared on Arthur's tomb at Glastonbury—*rex quondam rex que futurus.* But these words are from that other, now more familiar tradition. The hero of the alliterative *Morte Arthure* is no king of faery; he is an Arthur seen within the context of the fourteenth century and judged from that late medieval point of view. He can never return again.

Nor can the kind of poem that the *Morte Arthure* is easily return to us again, for we have lost the ability to maintain contradictory viewpoints, sincerely admiring and just as sincerely rejecting worldly ideals. That is why so much criticism of this poem is at once valuable and incomplete; we insist on choosing between ideals and neatly subordinating one to another. That Gothic ability to maintain the tension of conflicting viewpoints accounts for the aesthetic strength of even so simply constructed a work as the *Morte Arthure* and allows the poet to create a hero who with his dying breath orders a terrible revenge on Mordred's children and who yet can say "I fore-gyffe alle greffe" and dies with *In manus* on his lips. (pp. 75-85)

> *Larry D. Benson, "The Alliterative 'Morte Arthure' and Medieval Tragedy," in* Tennessee Studies in Literature, *Vol. XI, 1966, pp. 45-87.*

John Finlayson   (essay date 1967)

[*Finlayson is an educator and critic who has written extensively on the alliterative* Morte Arthure. *In the following excerpt from the introduction to his edition of* Morte Arthure, *Finlayson discusses the poem's theme, characterization, tone, and style.*]

Morte Arthure is an isolated work. There is nothing quite like it in the literature of the Alliterative Revival, despite superficial resemblances to the *Destruction of Troy* and *Alexander* poems. It is frequently judged as if it were a *romance,* but it is, in fact, a rare example of a mode of poetry which had been replaced by the *romance.* The nearest comparable work is the Old French *chanson de geste,* the *Chanson de Roland.* The sentiments of our poem are almost purely heroic: the emphasis on the loyalty of his men to Arthur, and of Arthur to them; the attitudes to war and battle, which are almost identical with those in *Beowulf* and the battle of Maldon; the close relationship of Arthur to Gawain, which parallels Charlemagne's relationship to Roland; the almost total absence of 'love-interest', despite the dominance of courtly love in contemporary literature; the stereotyped laments by Arthur on the death of Ga-

wain, which closely resemble that of Charlemagne for Roland—these are all clear indications that we are in the heroic, not the romantic world. The English poem bears a great similarity in subject-matter, attitude and structure to the *chansons de geste* of the Charlemagne cycle. This cycle is concerned with nationalism, the glories of war, with warrior-heroes and a warrior king, and in addition to all this has a strong religious tone. In all of these areas the alliterative poem parallels the *Chanson de Roland.* That the prime subject of *Morte Arthure* is war and the glories of war will be obvious enough from the narrative progression, from the zest of the battle descriptions (as well as from their multiplicity) and the enthusiasm of the knights when war is first mooted. In keeping with the serious purpose of the *chanson de geste,* our author is at pains to point out the justice of Arthur's wars and to create the impression of Arthur as a pious king, a champion of Christianity. In most of the medieval works on chivalry, five main causes of war are defined: three of these, namely, for justice, against oppression and against usurpation, are lawful; the other two, for revenge or aggression, are wilful. While in the chronicle sources there is some doubt as to the absolute justice of Arthur's cause and a strong hint of the desire for conquest being the dominant motive, the author of the alliterative poem stresses the insult to Arthur's honour which arises from the Emperor's letter and emphasizes Arthur's historical right to tribute from Rome, because of his ancestor Constantine—

> 'He conquerid be crosse be craftez of armes,
> That Criste was on crucifiede, that kynge es of
>   heven.'
>
>   (285-6)

Thus, by implication, Arthur's claim has some sort of religious justification or sanction which is not mentioned in the chronicles. Arthur's war against the Romans fulfils one of the categories of lawful war. His destruction of the giant is motivated by his desire to free his vassals from oppression, the second category of lawful war (cf. 842-51). The war against Modred clearly falls into the third category of lawful war, that against usurpation. After defeating the Romans, Arthur embarks on a series of conquests which have no direct connection with his professed reason for going to war; that is, he now indulges in wars of aggression which, according to the handbooks of chivalry, are not lawful but wilful. That the character of Arthur's wars has changed is confirmed by the philosopher's interpretation of the king's second dream:

> 'Freke', sais the philosophre, 'thy fortune es
>   passede . . .
> Thow has schedde myche blode and schalkes
>   distroyede,
> Sakeles in cirquytre in sere kynges landis . . .
> I rede thow rekkyn and reherse unresonable
>   dedis,
> Or the repenttes full rathe all thi rewthe
>   werkes.'
>
>   (3394-3453)

When tragedy does come, it is brought about partly because Arthur has departed from the path of justice.

Not only are the themes and preoccupations of *Morte Arthure* very similar to those of the *Chanson de Roland,* but the structure also parallels that of the Old French poem. To date, the alliterative poem has been considered to be rather a loose, rambling work, similar in its lack of form to the other 'chronicle-romances' and pseudo-histories, but a closer examination reveals that, like the *Roland* (which is considered to have a unity of subject and an internal cohesion that distinguishes it from other *chansons*), it falls into four distinct sections, each of which, since the poem was intended for oral narration, provides a natural break from which the poet could continue his recital at a later time. The four sections of the *Chanson de Roland* demonstrated by Jean Rychner are:

    i The Prelude to the Roncevaux
    ii The Roncevaux
    iii The Baligant episode
    iv. The Judgment of Ganelon

The four sections into which *Morte Arthure* appears to divide are:

    i The Prelude to the War with the Romans (1-553).
    ii War with the Romans (554-2393). This section includes the combat with the giant which, although almost a section in itself, is closely related to the higher unity of the poem, the concept of the Christian warrior king, and is locally of importance in presenting Arthur as a Christian champion.
    iii Arthur's further conquests and the Gawain-Priamus episode (2394-3217).
    iv War with Modred
                                    (3218-4346).

The Prelude to the Roncevaux has much in common in motifs with *The Prelude to the Wars with the Romans*. Section ii of *Morte Arthure* has a fairly close resemblance to Section ii of the *Roland,* as have certain parts of Section iv. Other parts of Section iv in the alliterative poem bear a resemblance to Sections ii and iii of the *Chanson de Roland.* In both poems there is a section which *seems* to interfere with the formal unity of the work, but just as the Baligant episode in the *chanson de geste* is necessary to establish Charlemagne and the victory of Christianity, so section iii of *Morte Arthure* is necessary for the development of Gawain and to provide a reason for Arthur's final tragedy.

Theme

Morte Arthure, then, is deliberately heroic in its themes, sentiments and structure, and cannot be judged according to the criteria used for evaluating and enjoying such poems as *Sir Gawain and the Green Knight* and *Ywain and Gawain.* Though the extent to which a work of art conforms to a particular *genre* is a legitimate critical interest and, to an audience aware of and responsive to form, may provide part of the entertainment and meaning, a poem must provide or create its own particular, unique interest which may be related to but cannot be totally dependent on the associations of a tradition. The attraction of *Morte Arthure* lies partly in the richness of the vocabulary and the technical virtuosity of the descriptions of battles, giants, dreams, sea-battles or certain moments of heightened dramatic tension, such as Arthur's anger at Lucius's message or the heroic sentiments of young Sir Idrus who refuses to leave Arthur's side even to save his own father. *Morte Arthure* is not just another patchy medieval narrative. On the contrary, it is a unified structure in which these descriptive passages are directed towards the exposition of the main theme. The overall theme of the poem is the Rise and Fall of a Christian warrior-king: in outline it is, in fact, a medieval tragedy such as Chaucer's Monk defines, 'a certeyn storie'

> Of hym that stood in greet prosperitee
> And is y-fallen out of heigh degree.

The Monk's stories are all of great kings, such as Alexander, brought low by the capricious workings of 'false Fortune'. In *Morte Arthure,* however, the idea of medieval tragedy is modified to come much closer to a modern concept of tragedy. There is a reason for the tragedy and the instruments of the fall are present when the 'greet prosperitee' is dominant. In the Monk's tragedies, the greatness of the figures who are brought low is assumed from their historical fame, but in *Morte Arthure* the greatness is created in the poem, so that Arthur's fall may be not just another example of the inevitable Fall through pride of a superhuman conqueror, but the true tragedy of a conqueror who has unfolded before our eyes both as conqueror and as man, whose glory and weaknesses have been present to us in the poem.

The Character of Arthur

While the overall design of the poem, then, is that of the medieval tragedy, within this structure the interest lies in the gradual exposition of the nature of the hero. In heroic poetry, the heroes are men of superior ability, presented and accepted as being greater than other men. Much of the interest lies in what happens to them, but an equal interest lies in their characters, for a hero is not simply a man raised above others; he is also the representative of a people or a way of life, and his glory and Fall portray the potential glory and the perpetual Fall of mankind. Arthur is 'heroic', but he does not conform to any one 'type' or 'kind' of hero. All heroes are not of a single kind:

> Just as there is more than one kind of human excellence, so there is more than one kind of hero. The different kinds reflect not only different stages of social development but the different metaphysical and theoretical outlooks which the conception of a hero presupposes [C. M. Bowra, in *Heroic Poetry,* 1952].

To say that Arthur is a heroic figure is not to say very much, and may even be misleading, since certain characteristics of the hero, such as the desire to display prowess, regardless of cause, and reckless, often foolish bravery, are played down in Arthur and attributed instead to certain of his knights—as in the case of Cador (ll. 1920 ff.)—with a strong hint of criticism of these particular characteristics. For Arthur is not only 'heroic', he is also a king and, to a limited extent, a chivalrous knight; not only these, but also the champion of Christendom against the forces of evil and the pagan world. He may be said to comprehend many of the differing characteristics of Beowulf, Roland and Charlemagne.

Immediately after the introductory twenty-five lines, we are confronted with Arthur the conqueror, Layamon's 'rihchest alre kinge under gode seolve'. The list of his conquests is long and impressive, and immediately brings the hero before us almost at the height of his powers. There is no hint in this poem of the 'romantic', faery elements we find in Layamon's *Brut*. This makes the Arthur of the alliterative *Morte Arthure* similar to Wace's hero in that both are seen basically as human beings, kings and leaders, possessed of great, but essentially human powers. The first section of the poem (ll. 1-553) serves roughly the same function as the opening scenes of a play: it establishes the position of the hero through its picture of Arthur's court and the extravagant feast which occupies the centre of the proceedings; the abrupt entry of the 'senators' with their arrogant embassy has almost as disruptive an effect as the entry of the Green Knight into Arthur's court in *Sir Gawain* and, as in the latter poem, dramatically reveals the nature of the forthcoming action. Arthur's controlled anger, courteous treatment of the ambassadors and subsequent consultation of his knights quickly establish the moderation, courtesy and readiness to take counsel which are the marks of the medieval 'wyse prince'. The method of exposition is already established as dramatic, not analytic. This method prevails throughout most of the poem; only rarely are we told what a character feels without reference to appearance or action. The succeeding scenes in which Arthur assembles his hosts, takes his leave of a weeping Guinevere, appoints Modred regent, and embarks for France are quite complex: the assembly of armies and embarkation create an atmosphere of bustle and martial colour which, besides evoking similar pictures from contemporary descriptions of the Hundred Years' War, establish quite firmly that we are in the real world, not the unreal world of *romance;* Arthur's leave-taking of Guinevere introduces a 'romantic' note which renders even more ironic his appointment as Regent of Modred, who had asked to be excused. Thus, mainly through action and speech, the Prelude vividly presents the mood, situation and chief protagonist.

The author next proceeds to establish Arthur's personal stature—as opposed to what we assume from his court, conquests and position—so that his Fall, when inevitably it occurs, may be not only the tragedy of a medieval king, but also of a person who has been present to us within this poem. The episode which brings Arthur most strikingly before us in his 'heroic' stance is his combat with the giant of St Michael's Mount (840 ff.). This fight has been regarded by most critics as just another of the many 'giant-killing' episodes in medieval literature, intended to show Arthur as knight-errant; but its position in the poem, the manner in which it has been developed from its source, and the nature of the description indicate that, far from being merely one unimportant incident in a formless chronicle poem, it is a central part of a fairly well-constructed narrative. In this episode Arthur is shown as a combination of Christian ruler and ideal *chanson de geste* hero, with the inevitable influence of courtly ideas—especially in his sympathy for the captive 'duches' (868-79). His generosity in disposing of the giant's treasure (1214-17) and his absolute bravery are qualities which, though often assumed to be *romance* characteristics, the

romance and the *chanson de geste* have in common. The monster (called 'Dinabuc' in Wace) is more than simply a gigantic human like Porrus in the *Wars of Alexander* or an uncouth creature like the Monster herdsman in *Ywain and Gawain;* there is a strong suggestion in the *Morte Arthure* giant of a Grendel-like combination of arch-fiend and human reprobate, for what is stressed most in the monster is not simply the sensational aspect of his appearance, such as his size (though this is not ignored), but rather his anti-Christian conduct, the eating of baptized children (844-5), and the general disorder he creates among Arthur's people. One of the greatest differences between Old and Middle English narrative poetry is the difference in the technique of description. Where warriors and monsters in O.E. literature tend to be described in traditional evocative terms which operate through association, such as kennings, the Middle English poet, even when using traditional epithets, is more concrete, detailed and direct in his descriptions, whether of people or things. In *Beowulf* the poet is concerned not so much with particulars as with the idea of a monster and, therefore, relies on 'vague horror and undefined dread'. The terror produced by Grendel and his mother derives as much from their bleak, monster-haunted surroundings as it does from the vagueness of their portrayal. The Middle English poet, on the other hand—especially in the fourteenth century, as we can see by comparing twelfth and fourteenth century manuscript illuminations—is writing in an age in which the visual arts are concerned not only with the conceptual, but also with the individual and actual. The poet of *Morte Arthure* is concerned not only to convey those emotions and ideas associated with monsters in general, but also to represent the details of one particular member of the species. Moreover, it is a commonplace of Middle English literature that those things or people whom the author wishes to be considered evil, dangerous or despicable are nearly always described in all the details of their ugliness. Chaucer's less savoury characters are an obvious example. Given this difference in approach between the OE and the ME poet, it can be seen that the elaborate description of the giant is intended to bring home to the audience the magnitude of Arthur's task, and correspondingly to enhance his final achievement by making the encounter more than simply an 'aventure', elevating it to a universal struggle against evil, for Dinabuc, being 'engerderde of fendez', is as much of a 'helle gast' as Grendel. It is significant in this description not only that he is extremely ugly, but also that his ugliness is described in terms of wild animals, i.e. those creatures removed from Man's dominion after the Fall. Moreover, those animals have moral associations of which the audience would be aware, and these associations implicitly accrue to the giant. The particular attributes of the giant place him in the category of those animals and monsters inimical to Man, unlike the Herdsman in *Ywain and Gawain:* he is a cannibal, ugly, kidnapper of women, an *incubus* and a bringer of death, since he ravished and murdered the duchess (978-9). The giant in this poem is, therefore, a very potent symbol of Evil, the unnatural and death, and this combat, besides being dramatically interesting, establishes Arthur as at once the champion of Christianity against Evil, epic hero and redeemer of his people, defender of ladies in distress

(1200-7), and generous monarch. Thus, in **Morte Arthure** his actions are released from the bounds of pseudo-history, and spread beyond the limits of the individual to have social, moral and universal implications. Moreover, Arthur's victory is owed not purely to his own prowess, but to Providence. At the moment when Arthur is in distress, the attention switches to the 'balefull bierdez' who serve the giant. They pray for his deliverance and, a few lines later, Arthur succeeds in killing the monster with his dagger (1148), a weapon defined in chivalric handbooks as signifying 'trust in God'. It is at this point that Arthur is called 'Governour undyr Gode . . . to whom grace is graunted' (1200-7), which suggests a strong parallel between Arthur and David. Like David, he is later to suffer a fall from grace.

The first 800 lines of the poem present the picture of Arthur the conqueror, the ruler of a glittering court, who is about to embark on a just war. The giant-episode then fills out the picture of Arthur as an individual in such a way that, despite his infrequent appearances until the last battle, his presence is felt throughout the poem; it also makes it quite clear that at this point Arthur is not only a great conqueror, but is also, more significantly, the champion of Christianity and redeemer of his people. The piety ascribed to Gawain and Arthur at the end of the poem (and their lives) is thus part of the deliberate pattern and not merely, as it tends to be in *romance,* a convention.

The development of Arthur's character and, therefore, of one of the chief interests of the poem is not confined to exposition through speech and action; dramatic contrast forms one of the principal devices of the poem, on both the local and the overall level. Arthur's character is enhanced by contrast with that of two of his knights, Cador and Gawain: both these knights are presented as recklessly brave. Cador is the first to display this characteristic and is reprimanded by the king for it (1922-7); later, Gawain indulges in similar behaviour and is praised by Arthur (3029-31). This varying attitude does not represent a difference in Arthur's regard for the two knights, but is instead related to a change in situation and values. Arthur's reprimand comes when the character of his wars is still lawful, his praise when his wars are wilful. By itself, this is an insignificant detail, but it forms part of that larger contrast of attitudes which plays a role in the 'meaning' of the poem. It is through Gawain's character that the change in values and contrasts of character are best seen. The Gawain of this poem bears little relationship to any of the *romance* Gawains. The encounter with Priamus serves to establish Gawain's 'prouesse', but it is important to notice that the whole atmosphere of this episode contrasts markedly with the dominant tone of the earlier sections of the poem and with the war against Modred. The Gawain-Priamus episode is a typical *roman d'aventure* encounter: the hero rides out 'wondyrs to seke' in a conventional spring landscape, encounters a strange knight with whom he breaks a lance. The whole incident follows the 'unreal world' rituals of *romance*. At this point, Gawain is no longer the national warrior, maintaining his king's cause and justice, as he was during the Roman wars, but is now the individual *'chevalier errant'* whose actions have no socio-political motivation but are simply an end in

themselves, related only to the individual's need to 'prove' himself. In this world, the combatants are not enemies but simply opponents or rivals in an elaborate, if dangerous, game. In some respects, this encounter serves to contrast the purposeless ritual of the typical *romance* combat with the serious, political and religious context of the whole poem. This change of atmosphere from *chanson de geste* to *romance* comes, significantly, at the point where Arthur's wars have ceased to be lawful and have become wars of conquest. Later, Gawain engages in the feat of reckless bravery mentioned earlier, and his death is occasioned by this same heedlessness. In other words, as the character of Gawain becomes more important in the poem, so too does the motif of reckless bravery develop. While the major theme of Arthur's greatness, the justness of his wars and his championship of the right is developed, a minor theme is announced, a theme which is at first hardly apparent, but gradually grows in significance as the narrative progresses. Cador's welcoming of the war with Lucius (252-8) and his own reckless exploits give a hint of later developments, but this element of *desmesure* is not given prominence until the moment when the sin which is to cause Arthur's fall is introduced. Instrument and cause of this tragedy unite here to foreshadow the final tragedy.

Arthur's second dream, that of the Wheel of Fortune, makes explicit what has so far been implicit in some of the elements discussed above. Structurally, this dream balances the first dream, which preceded the fight with the giant. Poetically, it associates **Morte Arthure** with the impressive dream visions of the fourteenth century, and the images of violence (Fortune's sudden anger and overthrow of kings, the wolves lapping the blood of the knights of the Round Table) disturbingly evoke the theme of the arbitrary actions of Fate which cut across the pattern of normal order, as in the *Knight's Tale*. It is to the spilling of innocent blood, as well as the earlier slaying of Frollo—that is, blood spilt in wilful wars—that the 'philosophre' attributes Arthur's forthcoming fall:

> 'Thow has schedde myche blode   and schalkes distroyede,
> Sakeles in cirquytrie   in sere kynges landis.'
>
> (3398-9)

Among the innocent blood to be spilt is also that of Gawain which, as Arthur laments, 'es sakles of sin', for Gawain 'es sakles supprysede for syn of myn one' (l. 3986). Through his 'sin' Arthur has killed not only 'Froill', 'Ferawnt' and others, but has also destroyed his own honour by indirectly causing the death of Gawain who represented his glory:

> 'For nowe my wirchipe es wente,   and my were endide . . .
> My wele and my wirchipe   of all this werlde riche
> Was wonnen thourghe sir Wawayne   and thourghe his witt one.'
>
> (3957-64)

This consciousness that his glory, represented by the knights of his Round Table, is destroyed runs through all his last speeches (cf. 4088ff.; 4155-60) and is finally made explicit in his prayer after the burial of his knights, where the constantly reiterated theme is:

> 'in care am I levyde;
> All my lordchipe lawe in lande es layde
> undyre. . . . '
>
> (4275-90)

Maddened by his grief at the death of Gawain, Arthur rejects the advice of those who counsel him to await reinforcements, and recklessly attacks the larger army of Modred. It is this reckless disregard of odds, for which he had reprimanded Cador, that brings about Arthur's own destruction, as it had destroyed Gawain. Thus Arthur's end comes not as an inexplicable twist of Fortune, but as the inevitable retribution for his sins, of which Modred is the direct, and Arthur's reckless engagement of a superior force the indirect, instrument. Nevertheless, the tone at the end of the poem is not that of a moral *exemplum*, as it is at the end of the *Wars of Alexander*. What predominates is the author's imaginative sympathy with the last heroic stand of Gawain and Arthur, the poetic validity of Gawain's last address and Arthur's elegiac lament over Gawain, the firmness of the faith with which they face death, and the sorrow over the destruction of a civilization. It is an ending which is consistent with the predominantly heroic tone of the poem and belongs to the type of the *Chanson de Roland*, a tragic, heroic close.

Concrete Visualization

Like most heroic poems, **Morte Arthure** leaves the reader with a dominant impression of violent action—splintering lances, flashing swords, warriors rushing together or falling 'fey in the feld'. The essence of the *chanson de geste* is dramatic action, and in our poem this action is rendered vivid both by the heavy onomatopoeia of the alliteration and the intensely visual nature of the descriptions. Even in the galloping rush of the battle descriptions, our eyes are constantly drawn to swords 'like flames flashing on helmets', the sparks which fly when a shield is struck, the red runnels of blood which run in the field. Most of these details are expressed in formulas and are commonplaces of heroic literature, yet they succeed in presenting the action as something concrete and immediate. The technique of description in the battle scenes is mainly impressionistic—small details such as the above are caught for a moment, but do not impede the swift rush and clash of battle. The author rarely troubles himself with details of strategy, nor does he interrupt the action to provide us with a detailed description of a hero, as *romances* frequently do. Instead, by mentioning again and again the slashing of swords, the breaking of breast-plates, the girding of grim men, he conveys the idea of 'battle', the sound and fury of combat as it strikes the individual engaged in fighting, rather than detached appreciation of manoeuvres conveyed to the spectator or analysed by the military historian.

In addition to the constant sense of movement and the quick impressionistic presentation of details, the **Morte Arthure** presents its readers with a wealth of static descriptions which rival those of *Sir Gawain*. In these, the technique is very different from that of the battle descriptions. Instead of the quick heroic epithet, the significant detail, we are given a minutely itemized account of the object depicted. Something of the ceremony and display of medieval life is conveyed by the way in which the author names and describes things. For example, the list of dishes served at Arthur's feast impresses by its plentitude and the exotic nature of some of the food. By the time one has passed from the 'pacokes and plovers in platers of golde' (182) to the 'condethes full curious all of clene silvyre' (201) one is dazzled by the splendour and wealth of Arthur's court, as are the Roman ambassadors. The richness of the detail dramatically conveys Arthur's power at a very early stage in the poem. This description, like most others in **Morte Arthure**, is affective in function; it both provides a local centre of interest for the audience of an intensely visual nature and, at the same time, contributes to the total structure of the poem by adding to our already growing sense of the wealth, power and civilization which Arthur represents.

The elaborate nature of the description of the feast, the minute itemizing of each feature, are characteristic of medieval rhetorical art. The same techniques, the same interest in precise detail, richness of colour and material, is to be observed in the portrayal of Arthur's arming before his fight with the giant (ll. 900-19) and of his dress before he receives news of Modred's usurpation (ll. 3456-75). Each of these descriptions occurs just before a significant event in Arthur's career; they are not purely ornamental, but have a function which can best be understood with a little knowledge of the nature of medieval rhetorical art. Briefly, in the works of the theoreticians of medieval rhetoric, description (*descriptio*) of persons is divided into two parts—outward appearance and inner qualities. The two are not, of course, divorced, since the outward appearance of a character is taken to be intimately linked to his inner qualities, that is, a handsome warrior will almost inevitably be a good person. Outward appearance is in turn divided into detailed description of features, body and dress. **Morte Arthure** pays hardly any attention to details of physical appearance—this belongs more to dream vision and romance—but concentrates on dress, mainly armour. The elaborate richness of armour and dress, besides giving the poem concreteness and feeding the audiences' love of colour and wealth, is also a method of expressing visually the rank and importance of the character. In addition, the formality of the elements of the description—based as they are on stereotyped models—produces a sense of order and power, of that order which is in one case threatened and in the other about to be overthrown.

Probably the most formalized of descriptions in medieval literature—apart from those of feminine beauty, of which there is no example in our poem—are landscapes, in particular, spring landscapes which are normally to be found as the prelude to a love story, an adventure or a dream vision. Medieval poets very rarely attempt to describe an *actual* landscape. In most cases they elaborate, according to certain rhetorical rules of style, on a number of formal elements. These elements in themselves—flowers blooming, trees in bud, birds singing, waters murmuring and winds blowing warmly—convey the essentials of spring. By simply mentioning these features, the medieval poet—because of the long traditions of such descriptions—could rely on conveying the idea of spring. However, most frequently poets amplify the details—the dexterity with which they could amplify being a mark of their skill. On the whole, therefore, medieval descriptions of landscape are to be distinguished from one another not by their larger elements, but by the details of their elaboration. There are four landscape descriptions in *Morte Arthure.* The first three (ll. 920-32; 2501-12; 2670-7) are of the Ideal Spring Landscape type which formed the principal motif of natural description from classical times to the sixteenth century, but in the first there is a great deal of factual enumeration of birds and animals which gives the scene a quality of actuality. In the second, the detailing of the places through which the knights pass is rendered by a mingling of impressionism and concreteness, imparting to the landscape a 'realism' which is heightened by the sensuous description of the 'mede':

> And in the mornynge miste   one a mede falles
> Mawen and unmade   maynoyrede bott lyttyll
> In swathes down,   full of swete floures.
>
> (2506-8)

In this type of description the formal structure expresses the essential motif *Spring* and its almost inevitable association in medieval narrative poetry with adventure or love, or both, but at the same time the particular rendering conveys a reaction to the scene which is almost subjective, the mood of knights riding blithely towards adventure. Each of these scenes is a prelude to a particular episode of the poem, the most elaborate (920-32) preceding the most significant single episode in *Morte Arthure,* Arthur's fight with the giant.

Being a *chanson de geste, Morte Arthure* is essentially a poem of motion, broken, occasionally and briefly, by moments of stasis, such as the descriptions already mentioned. There is, however, one large section of the poem—the dream of the Wheel of Fortune which precedes the news of Modred's treachery (3230-3455)—in which heroic action is suspended and description of action gives way to detailed portrayal of place and people. This section is the turning-point of the poem and Arthur's fortunes, and the only protracted episode of non-heroic, non-chivalric event. Arthur's dream begins in a manner typical of dream visions—the dreamer finds himself alone in a strange place:

> 'Me thoughte I was in a wode   willed myn one.'
>
> (3230)

This conventional opening evokes the serious atmosphere associated with alliterative dream-poems such as *Piers Plowman* and *Death and Life.* However, having evoked these traditional associations, the *Morte Arthure* poet rapidly particularizes the dream by introducing a nightmare element which is not to be found in any of the well-known dream visions. The wild beasts, ominously lapping the blood of the Round Table knights, from whom Arthur flees, foreshadow the end of the dream, when he is dashed from his throne, and the end of the poem. The landscape in which Arthur finds himself is not simply of an idealized spring type. Here we have 'vynes of silver' and 'grapis of golde', as well as 'all froytez . . . that floreschede in erthe'. This rich combination of idealized reality and natural sce-

nery conceived of in terms of precious metals places it in the tradition of Earthly Paradise descriptions. Though the separate parts of this dream-setting can quite easily be assigned to a tradition, their combination here is quite remarkable, providing a very effective contrast of the terror and disorder suggested by the 'wilderness' section with the lush fruitfulness and order of the dream meadow or Earthly Paradise. The nearest parallel in alliterative literature is Gawain's journey in *Sir Gawain* through Wirral and arrival at Bercilak's castle. In both alliterative poems, encounters with savage animals in a wild landscape are followed by arrival at a place of some splendour and beauty which, deceptively, appears to be a haven from the forces of evil and disorder. This atmosphere of splendour and beauty is reinforced by the description of the Wheel of Fortune and the portrayal of the Goddess Fortuna which resembles that of Langland's Lady Mede in its emphasis on the richness of her dress. This whole episode—the Other World landscape, the portrayal of Fortune, the vignettes of the Worthies on the Wheel—is full of concrete visualization of place and people, of colour and wealth, which gives reality to this 'unreal' world of dream. It is, in fact, this ability to present actions and scenes concretely to the eye which is one of the marks of the *Morte Arthure* poet.

Verse

Most medieval poetry was written to be read aloud to an audience, and this condition, together with the nature of the audience, naturally affects verse technique. Close-textured verse and subtle echoes of previous lines do not lend themselves well to oral presentation; instead, a poem read aloud must make its effects in a broad, readily discernible way. The maintenance of a regular rhythm rather than delicate variations on a central rhythmical pattern will obviously tend to be favoured in verse delivered orally. *Morte Arthure* is one of the more impressive of a number of poems composed in the North and Midlands during what has been called the Alliterative Revival. The heavy, regular, onomatopoeic effect of the alliterative line is eminently suited to public declamation, and its ability to render scenes of violence and action vividly makes it even more suitable for heroic poetry. At the same time, of course, the evidence of *Sir Gawain, Pearl, Piers Plowman* and the dream descriptions and elegiac passages of *Morte Arthure* establishes that alliteration does not necessarily limit the poet either to simple subjects or crude poetic effects.

Over the years, editors and critics have noted that many similarities of phrases are to be found among the alliterative poems. At first, these correspondences often led to theories of common authorship, but later it was realized that the alliterative poets had a common stock of phrases. More recently, it has been realized that the similarities in diction and phrase to be observed in alliterative poems are the result of their being composed for oral delivery, through the use of poetic formulas. In the last thirty-five years it has been demonstrated that, among communities largely unaffected by mass-communications and containing a high proportion of illiterate or semi-literate people, much poetry, especially of the heroic type, is both rendered and composed orally; that is, the poet will have in his head a basic plot which he will deliver to his audience directly—the moment of delivery will be the moment of composition. For such a method of composition to function well, there must be a store of poetic material on which the poet can draw at will. Clearly, the nature of alliterative poetry and of the audience to which it was delivered meets most of the conditions just described. The exception to this statement is that, since most alliterative works have known sources to which they can often be closely related, line by line, the moment of delivery is *not* in their case the moment of composition. From the evidence of manuscript transmission, it is clear that the alliterative poets were literate and wrote down their compositions—though not necessarily in exactly the form in which we now possess them. While composing, however, they would appear to have drawn on a common stock of alliterative formulas to express the events drawn from their source material, and in some cases to have created new formulas on the model of those with which they were familiar. Despite this difference, however, the main principles formulated by those classical scholars who first defined oral-formulaic composition are still largely relevant to an understanding of alliterative *romances* and *chansons de geste*. The seminal work on this method of composition is that of Milman Parry on Homeric literature ["Studies in the Epic Technique of Oral Verse-Making," *Harvard Studies in Classical Philology* XLIII (1932)]. Parry divides the store of poetic material into two categories: 'themes' and 'formulas'. The 'themes' are a group of ideas or motifs which occur regularly not simply in any given poem, but also in most poems of any one *genre*. For example, in heroic poetry single combat, arming of knights, laments for dead heroes, exhortations to armies, arrival of ambassadors, pursuit of a fleeing enemy, and so on, are all frequently recurring episodes, and some of them occur also in *romances*. 'Formulas' are the stock phrases used to express these stereotyped motifs. Briefly, Parry's theory of oral-formulaic composition is that the oral poet (or a literate poet using the same technique) makes his verse by choosing from a vast number of fixed phrases which he has heard in the poems of other poets.

> Each one of these phrases does this: it expresses a given idea in words which fit into a given length of the verse. Each one of these fixed phrases, or formulas, is an extraordinary creation in itself. . . . The formulas . . . are not each of them without likeness to any other; in that case the technique would be far too unwieldy. They fall into smaller groups of phrases which have between them a likeness of ideas and words, and these in turn fall into groups which have a larger pattern in common, until the whole diction is schematized in such a way that the poet, habituated to the scheme, hits without effort, as he composes, upon the type of formula and the particular which, at any point in his poem, he needs to carry on his verse and his sentence.

The continual use of formulas is, as C. S. Lewis pointed out [in his 1942 "Preface" to *Paradise Lost*], not necessarily a second best on which the poets fall back when inspiration fails them. The use of formulas is due as much to the needs of the audience as to the requirements of the reciter. The formulaic nature of the themes and language would enable the audience to concentrate on the narrative development, on the larger 'meaning' which the poet is trying to convey, while at the same time making any individual variation stand out more significantly. To say that a theme or phrase belongs to the oral-formulaic tradition does not, of course, mean that we are obliged to suspend normal literary judgments on the poetic worth of poems composed in this tradition. It does, however, mean that we have to alter our criteria of evaluation. In the past, many alliterative works have been dismissed for their lack of originality in diction and imagery, for their repetitiousness. It is still possible to make such statements, as long as we realize that the type of originality in diction and imagery we can legitimately expect of a poet working deliberately in a formulaic tradition for oral delivery is very different from that which we can find in a poet whose compositions are meant chiefly to be read privately by someone who can pause any length of time over one line or phrase and has the whole poem spatially before him at all times. We must first of all, therefore, accept that the poet is working in a particular convention, and then try to decide how he is using that convention: whether he is simply repeating in a bald and possibly inappropriate way a well-worn formula, or moulding a formula creatively (by elaboration of elements or combination with other formulas) to his particular needs. The main difficulty in making these distinctions at the moment lies in our inadequate knowledge of the conventions. Oakden's collection of formulas deals only with half-lines, whereas it is clear that many formulas cover a line or even a group of lines. Until formulas have been tabulated for a fair number of the more important alliterative works, our judgments about the 'originality' of any alliterative poet's use of language must necessarily be rather tentative, though this in no way alters our assessment of how immediately effective any given line or group of lines is. At least forty alliterative formulas occur regularly in the pseudo-chronicle romances, and by comparing the **Morte Arthure** poet's use of a formula with its employment in another or others, it is possible to distinguish quite clearly between them on artistic grounds.

In poetry of a heroic nature the most important and most frequently used formulas are based on verbs of action. One of the most frequently employed verbs to express the idea of *striking* is *gird*. *Gird* occurs with extreme frequency in another alliterative work, *The Destruction of Troy* [cited edition is that of G. A. Panton and D. Donaldson, 1869], where it is often coupled with *grip*, as in

> Gryppet a grym toole, gyrde of his hede.
> (938)

This formula is repeated in 1340, 1377, 940, 6586, 6768, 7471, 7787 and, no doubt, in many other lines. To the two constant elements *gird* and *grip*, it can be observed that a third variable element is generally added. In the example quoted, the third element is *grym*, though this is sometimes replaced by *grounde*. Never, in *The Destruction of Troy*, is there any further elaboration of the formula. In **Morte Arthure** the formulas are basically the same, but the handling of them is rather different:

MA ll.
1369-70   He gryppes hym a grete spere and graythely
           hym hittez;
           Thurghe the guttez into the gore he gyrdes
           hym ewyn.
2526-7   A grete spere fro his grome he grypes in
           hondes
           Gyrdes ewen overe the streme on a stede
           ryche.
2948-9   Thane sir Gawayne was grefede and grypys
           his spere
           And gyrdez in agayne with galyarde knygt-
           tez.
3757-61   Bot sir Gawayne for grefe myghte noghte
           agaynestande
           Umbegrippys a spere and to a gome rynnys,
           That bare of gowles full gaye with gowtes of
           sylvere;
           He gyrdes hym in at the gorge with his grym
           launce;
           That the grownden glayfe graythes in son-
           dyre.

Where in *The Destruction of Troy* the formula is concentrated in one line, the **Morte Arthure** poet takes the basic pattern and expands it, not simply by adding meaningless half-lines or filler-phrases, but by using associated ideas and thus extending the significance of the formula. In all the examples shown, the constants are *gird* and *grip,* as in the *Troy,* but these are spread over two lines in the first three, and over three in the fourth. To these two constants has been added a third *a . . . spere,* which is the object of the verb *grip,* and in the first two quotations at least it forms an alliterative element, 'a grete spere'. By the addition of 'spere' the **Morte Arthure** poet has narrowed down the formula from one evocative of general battle to one expressing the motif of single combat with lance. In the fourth example, the poet has developed what could be called an elaborated formula where the 'g' alliteration is sustained for five lines, yet does not obscure the main idea expressed by the formula, namely that Gawain 'umbegrippys a spere' and 'gyrdes' his enemy. This elaborated formula owes most of its elements to the formulaic tradition: the elements *ground, grym, grete spere* are all variables on the basic collocation of *gird* with *grip* in *The Destruction of Troy.* Thus, of the five lines of the elaborated formula, four are part of the family of formulas associated in alliterative poetry with *gird* in collocation with *grip.* The third line of the formula, 'That bare of gowles full gaye with gowtes of sylvere', seems to be an additional piece of elaboration entirely due to the individuality of the author, though demonstrating at the same time the strong influence of the rhetorical convention of amplification of descriptive detail.

Thus, although the **Morte Arthure** poet and the author of *The Destruction of Troy* are using the formulaic technique of composition, there are quite obvious differences of style and quality. The *Troy* poet uses only single-line formulas and does not follow one formula with others which are associated with it verbally. His poem, therefore, frequently seems very haphazard, each line being a unit in itself and related to the others only in a general way. The lack of alliterative patterns and of formulaic development make it unlikely that the poem was ever intended primarily for recitation. In **Morte Arthur,** as in the *Iliad, Beowulf* and the *Chanson de Roland*—all poems of a kind which can be recognized by its use of repetitions and formulas— formulas are not usually employed singly; they are either expanded in an original manner by the poet, or are grouped with associated formulas using the same alliteration or the same verb, as in the elaborated formula I examined above, which is also a complete motif, namely that of single combat with a lance.

As one might expect in a heroic poem, formulas expressing combat and motion are very frequent. The most common are to be found associated with the following verbs:

> bowe, boune, braid, busk, cayre, fell, lenge,
> schokke, schunt, schot, skape, slit, sley, spede,
> strike, stroy, swelt, swap, swing, venge, wound.

Some of these formulas appear in **Morte Arthure** with considerable frequency, others only two or three times, but an interesting feature is that they tend to occur in groups or clusters. In many cases, the formulas are constructed on the same alliteration, so that in this poem we characteristically find extended passages of up to eight lines (and sometimes even more, e.g. 2889-97, 3300-9) alliterating on one letter. This not only has the effect of unifying and highlighting a particular motif, but is also clearly an exhibition of the sheer virtuosity of the artist. Most of these clusters of formulas constructed on the same alliteration are combinations of traditional formulas, modified and elaborated by our poet. The oral-formulaic poet is not confined to modifying or repeating traditional phrases; he may also frequently create new formulas. Though our knowledge of oral-formulaic tradition in Middle English is so limited that any statements must be tentative, it does appear that the **Morte Arthure** poet is creative not only in combining and elaborating, but also in inventing new formulas to meet the particular requirements of his poem. One of the most elaborate of these is a formula expressing the motif of knights of the Round Table riding into battle. It appears in its most elementary form in ll. 4117-18:

> Redily thas rydde men of the rownde table
> With ryall raunke stele rittys theire mayles.

It is not, of course, surprising to find *riding* and *round table* frequently associated in an Arthurian poem. However, in our poem the association of the two frequently generates an extended sequence of 'r' alliterations, and the alliterative elements are so stereotyped as to suggest they are formulas. In the most extended examples (e.g. 1472-5, 2790-5, 2878-81, 2983-8) it can be observed that besides *ride* and *round table* there are several other elements which express the heroic motif of battle between mounted knights, and in so doing have created an extended formula which has no parallel in the other chronicle poems, or indeed in Arthurian poems like *Sir Gawain.* Not only is the formula created elaborate; it is also sufficiently flexible to allow the author to impart to an essential, heroic motif a high degree of particularity. It will be observed that the position and number of formulaic elements in any one example is varied, and also that other elements, such as 're-tenuz' (2921), 'raskaile' (2881) and 'roselde' (2880, 2793), are introduced which are not formulaic and thus add particular significance to a general motif.

Clearly, the **Morte Arthure** poet's mastery of the alliterative medium consists of more than the mere ability to recite a greater range of 'r' alliterations than the authors of other alliterative poems. His genius consists of being able to achieve three effects simultaneously: (1) the onomatopoeic effect, which is especially important in poetry intended for oral narration, (2) the evocation of particular types of heroic action, which would be familiar to and expected by his audience, and (3) the particularization of the general motif. Although formulaic composition limits the poet, it does not preclude individual creation. The limitation imposed is one of theme and the restrictions are those of a discipline rather than of a tyranny. For example, battle scenes in heroic literature are very stereotyped. In alliterative, oral-formulaic poetry they will appear even more so. Distinction in literary value will then have to be made on the local arrangement of events, the particular use of individual formulas and the cumulative effect. In the particular analysis of battle scenes it will be observed that what is being described is not one unique incident or individual action, but rather a series of conventional, expected, archetypal actions in which the aim is to give the impression of action, rather than to crystallize one particular moment of action or time. What the poet is doing is putting loosely together a number of ready-made shapes to form a design or pattern of a particular sort, in this case, of *battle.* Creating his own original shapes would not be, as it would in the modern artist, his central preoccupation. Moreover, this is typical of the alliterative chronicle poems. Now and again, certain details of strategy are given and the antagonists differ, so that the narrative thread may be maintained, but apart from these things one battle is much like another and was evidently expected to be so, even in more sophisticated or courtly works such as *The Knight's Tale,* where the battle between Palamon and Arcite could quite easily come from an alliterative, formulaic poem.

The poetry of **Morte Arthure** will be found to lie in broad effects: the ability to create action and violence by massive, blocked lines; the heavy richness caused not by one particularly apposite phrase but an accumulation of detail; the emphasis of a motif by the employment of a number of phrases which all express the central idea, though in different words. As C. S. Lewis remarked about primary epic, oral poetry 'is not built up of isolated effects; the poetry is in the paragraph; or in the whole episode'. The main strength of formulaic poetry, apart from its suitability to oral narration and its ability to express the expected in a formal manner, resides in the greater richness of meaning which tradition lends to individual words and phrases. Associations with other poems using the same formula will affect their meaning in the work under discussion and the work will thus acquire the kind of many-toned significance which is inherent in poetry based on traditional formulaic techniques. (pp. 11-30)

John Finlayson, in an introduction to Morte Arthure, *edited by John Finlayson, London: Edward Arnold, 1967, pp. 1-34.*

Arthur encounters the giant of St. Michael's Mount. From an illustration in Wace's Roman de Brut.

John Gardner   (essay date 1971)

[An American author best known for his philosophical novels, Gardner was also a noted medievalist. In the following excerpt from his edition of the Morte Arthure, *he assesses the poet's artistry, highlighting prominent themes in the work.]*

The greatness of the **Morte Arthure** is of a different kind from that of *Pearl* and *Sir Gawain and the Green Knight.* The *Gawain*-poet constructs elegant lines, brilliantly manipulating alliterative patterns, rhythms, and consonant and vowel relationships for maximum interpenetration of sound and sense, and he elaborates imagistic and symbolic patterns as well as any poet in the English tradition. He creates vital and unique characters, develops irony, pathos, and, above all, humor with a master's finesse and never slips for an instant into lapses of taste. By comparison, the man who wrote the **Morte Arthure** may seem crude. Rhythm in the **Morte Arthure** is often merely serviceable. Like the *Gawain*-poet, the **Morte Arthure**-poet uses what may be described as a sprung five-stress line with four-beat variants, and he is fond (though less fond than the *Gawain*-poet) of crossed alliteration, superabundant alliteration, and the like; but in **Morte Arthure** the line sometimes lapses from superb music to what must be called slogging through the job. The poet has certain phrases, such as "as hym lykez," which he uses repeatedly (as might an oral poet) to fill out a line, and even if one grants that these phrases are appropriate to the theme of the poem—for they are—they are obtrusive. The poet's imagery is often powerful and vivid—the dragon and bear in Arthur's first nightmare, for instance—but at times it is mechanical. As for symbolism, it is of a different kind entirely from that of the *Gawain*-poet. Instead of subtle juxtapositions of imagery, which serve to introduce ironic

MORTE ARTHURE   **CLASSICAL AND MEDIEVAL LITERATURE CRITICISM, Vol. 10**

comment or develop allegorical implications, the *Morte Arthure*-poet generally uses bold, stark symbols not easily missed or misunderstood, and bold shifts of genre which throw basic attitudes into ironic juxtaposition—"heroic" against "romantic," "worldly" against "religious." The characterization is carefully worked out but, despite the poet's labor, not impressive compared to characterization in *Sir Gawain*. The humor in the *Morte Arthure* is gallows humor, a far cry from the dazzling, civilized humor of the *Gawain*-poet; and his moments of pathos (for instance when Arthur leaves Guinevere or when Arthur learns of the death of a duchess) are seldom completely successful.

These differences are to a large extent the results of a more basic difference in the way the two poets apprehend reality; in other words, they emerge because of the kinds of subject matter each poet chooses. The virtues of the *Morte Arthure* are those of the medieval warhorse: it is slow and somewhat clumsy, sometimes inelegant, but large and powerful; and like the warhorse it holds with absolute firmness to its course. What the poet directly or indirectly borrows from Geoffrey of Monmouth and Wace, his principal forerunners in the chronicle tradition, he tightens, alters, or expands to suit his own purpose, and his artistic purpose is impressive. If the *Morte Arthure* suffers by comparison to *Sir Gawain and the Green Knight,* the reverse is also true: *Sir Gawain* is a more perfect poem, but one of a lesser kind.

Sir Gawain is a sophisticated Christian comedy—a "romance"—which has little place for the heroic. It is no doubt true that if Gawain had not passed his test at the castle of temptation he would have lost his head; but Gawain does pass his test, in effect (as we were sure he would), and does not lose his head. Indeed, the very idea of the heroic is turned into comedy in *Sir Gawain*. Everywhere in heroic literature we read of centuries-old monsters brought low at last by some outstanding warrior—a Beowulf or Siegfried. How absurd, one might argue, that a monster which has tormented the world for a thousand years should be slain in the end by a paltry mortal! For the *Gawain*-poet, heroic deeds are often "too tedious to tell," or if they must be told are often recounted tongue in cheek. (Gawain does of course behave heroically at times, and the poet does not always mock him.) The goods affirmed in *Sir Gawain and the Green Knight* are for the most part civilized and Christian values: splendid counterpanes, jewels, dinners; courtly manners and entertainments; charity, loyalty, humility. These are affirmations appropriate to what Edmund Burke would call "the beautiful." They are not affirmations appropriate to "the sublime"—that is, art which seriously concerns itself with the awesome, the terrible, or, in a word, the antihuman. If we accept the general point of view advanced by Professors Höltgen and Matthews, the *Morte Arthure* is a tragedy and affirms the universal human defiance of those outer and inner forces which would destroy all that is best in the human. The poem has what *Sir Gawain* was never meant to have: power. The *Morte Arthure*-poet makes occasional mistakes, but his large, grim vision and the passion of his affirmation limit the importance of the mistakes.

Moreover, the mistakes are generally defensible because

> "The virtues of the *Morte Arthure* are those of the medieval warhorse: it is slow and somewhat clumsy, sometimes inelegant, but large and powerful; and like the warhorse it holds with absolute firmness to its course."
>
> —**John Gardner**

of the difficulty of the thing attempted and the limitation of the poet's models. With a little effort almost any man can achieve sublime vision—the powerfully charged intellectual and emotional sense of the godlike value of the human and the dreadful power of the antihuman, whether we conceive the antihuman as the realm of the old Germanic monsters, or abstract evil, or the indifference of the universe. For a sophisticated man, the difficulty lies in finding a sufficient dramatic vehicle for sublime emotion. Artists have proved repeatedly that it is virtually impossible to make monsters real if one does not believe in them. Compare the fabulous elements in the "Owain," in the *Mabinogion,* to the artifices in Chrétien's *Yvain.* Or compare the monsters in *Beowulf* to the giants of the *Morte Arthure.* We do not see Grendel but only the reactions of the men who see him, for the *Beowulf*-poet (or perhaps the tradition from which he draws) knows for certain that monsters exist but has no clear idea what they look like. The monsters in the *Morte Arthure* are made up—or, to speak precisely, are carefully culled from earlier romances for a new, allegorical use. Not really believing in them, the poet makes them stand primarily as symbols of all that is hostile to man—bestiality, cannibalism, rape, tyranny, ugliness, brute force, stupidity, allegiance to the devil. The most terrible monsters, he suggests, are those inside men, here specifically the monstrousness of spirit in such men as the wicked Lucius of Rome. Such deformity will in time infect even the archetype of royal virtue, King Arthur, whose later degenerate nature the St. Michael's giant foreshadows.

Presenting the St. Michael's giant, the poet works in language which associates the giant with tyranny, identified later with the tyranny of Lucius and that of Arthur at the peak of his power. Consider the language here for instance:

> Then King Arthur answered the ancient woman:
> "I have come from the conqueror, the courteous and noble,
> As one of the noblest men among Arthur's knights,
> A messenger sent to amend these wrongs for the people,
> To speak with this mighty master who guards the mountain,
> And treat of terms with this tyrant, by the treasure of lands,
> To buy a truce for a time, until better may come."
>
> (ll. 985-91)

Speaking of the giant as a "mighty master" (in the original, *maister mane*) and ironically describing himself as a messenger from Arthur's court who comes seeking truce, Arthur sets up an analogy between his dealings with the giant and normal diplomatic dealings. The old woman with whom he speaks answers that the giant "cares for neither rents nor for burnished gold" (l. 994; in the original: *ffor bothe landez and lythes ffulle lyttile by he settes;/Of rentez ne of rede golde rekkez he neuer . . .*). Arthur himself, in his dealings with the Romans and again with Mordred, will care for neither rents nor "rede golde"—but for nobler reasons. Ingenious juxtapositions and grim humor are hallmarks of this poet's technique, and all the subtlety of his thought derives from his fascination with the underlying similarities in things superficially disparate or the essential moral differences within things which outwardly resemble one another. The trouble with the St. Michael's Mountain scene, in short, is that the scene works intellectually as a comment upon other scenes in the poem, but lacks the powerful illusion of reality found elsewhere in the poem. There is, however, good reason for the *Morte Arthure*'s partial failure at this point—its setting in the chronicle tradition and its consequent false realism in the treatment of occasional borrowings from works of fantasy. No other scene in the poem, I think, is flawed in this way, including the romantic Priamus-Gawain scene, and there are many truly magnificent scenes—Arthur's two dreams and the whole of the opening and closing sections of the poem.

The theme of the *Morte Arthure* is pride, a theme intimately related, here as everywhere in medieval literature, to the idea of Fortune—and the poet's chief technique, as I have said, is careful juxtaposition of character against character, scene against scene. The most elaborate critical discussion of the poem is that of Professor William Matthews [in his *The Tragedy of Arthur: A Study of the Alliterative Morte Arthure*, 1960]. It would be a misuse of space here to summarize the whole of Matthews's argument. I will simply outline it and mention certain problems raised by his reading. By internal analysis, Matthews shows that Arthur is a tragic hero whose flaw from the outset is hubris; he argues that the St. Michael's Mount giant is in a sense a figure of what Arthur will become at the height of his pride; and he claims that in the end Arthur tends to think of himself as almost another Christ. He shows in detail that certain elements of Arthur's characterization identify him with Edward III, so that the poem may be read as a criticism of that king. Then, on the theory that no English poet would dare to criticize his king in this way, Matthews suggests unconvincingly that the poem was originally a French work. Two important reviews labored to demolish Matthews's reading—the reviews by J. L. N. O'Loughlin and John Finlayson [in *Medium Ævum*, 32 (1963) and *Review of English Studies*, n.s. 14 (1963), respectively]. Both pointed out that if one looks at the *Morte Arthure*-poet's sources in chronicle tradition one finds that this poet consistently heightened Arthur's wisdom and virtue, giving him every possible flattering epithet—"free," "noble," "worthy," and so forth—and by subtler means as well. At least through roughly the first

half of the poem it is impossible to take these epithets as ironic. One of the reviewers pointed out that the whole argument that Arthur comes to think of himself as another Christ (an overstatement of Matthews's position) rests on Arthur's single phrase, natural in its setting, expressing a wish that he could "die for you all [his knights]." On this last point Matthews may nevertheless be right, of course; some literary evidence is visceral. Having thrown out Matthews's reading, both reviewers return to the traditional view that Arthur falls because of his sin of incest in engendering Mordred, and for no other cause whatever. (There is no suggestion of Arthur's incestuous begetting of Mordred in Geoffrey's *Historia,* Wace's *Brut,* or Lazamon's *Brut,* nor is it clearly hinted in the *Morte Arthure.*)

But Matthews was essentially correct, and Professor Höltgen, in his article, "König Arthur und Fortuna" [*Anglia* 75 (1957)], supports Matthews's reading. Both Matthews and Höltgen seek to understand the poem by reading carefully what it says, not by imposing on it a meaning assumed from Arthurian tradition. For Höltgen, Arthur falls through trust in Fortune; and what this means, in terms of the medieval tradition of Fortune, is that Arthur falls through mistaken faith in the stability of the things of this world (a form of pride). Riding higher and higher on Fortune's wheel, Arthur forgets that he must go down again. His tragedy is not so much that he proudly climbs to the heights of Fortune (it is partly that, but the climb is largely an effect on Arthur's very nature as worthiest of the Nine Worthies). Mainly his tragedy is that he forgets that a king acts as God's servant, not as master in his own right. As a result, he lapses in lawful chivalry (as Finlayson has shown), and so, when the downswing of Fortune's wheel comes, he goes down raging, ruining even his own homeland and vassals.

The idea of Fortune is at the heart of the poem, and not only in the sense that Arthur's dream of Fortune's wheel marks the tragic turning point. The idea of inevitable change is the central dramatic principle of the work. The poem begins when Lucius of Rome is at the height of his power and when Arthur has just finished winning back the vast system of holdings and tributes which rightfully belong to his house. Their clash, the fall of Lucius, and the eventual fall of Arthur in his turn come inexorably. Again and again, the end of the poem (the fall of Arthur) ironically echoes the beginning (Arthur's bringing down of first a giant, then Lucius), showing the change in Arthur's situation. Some of these echoes take the form of identical actions by Arthur which have opposite meanings. For instance, in the opening scene King Arthur's ferocious look terrifies the envoys of Emperor Lucius, who have insulted Arthur into wholly righteous indignation; near the end of the poem, when Arthur's fortune has changed and his legitimate pride has become corrupt, leading him into wars of aggression (Finlayson's point), the same look silences Arthur's own Round Table. Other echoes identify the now-corrupted Arthur with Lucius and his like. Early in the poem Arthur is advised to put down his arms and wear only his kirtle as he approaches an unmerciful giant (the dream-symbol of the giant in Arthur's first nightmare is at the same time a symbol of Lucius, according to Arthur's interpreters); later Arthur himself is approached in exactly this way by his victims. Similarly, the giant savagely demands Arthur's beard, and Arthur later shaves the beards of his Roman prisoners to shame them. The wanton destruction wrought by the overweening Lucius has its direct parallel in Arthur's destructions near the end of his career:

> Now Arthur turns, when the time is right, to Tuscany,
> And he swiftly storms those towns with their lofty towers;
> He casts down mighty walls, wounds gentle knights,
> Topples towers, and torments the people,
> Makes many a splendid widow sing out woe
> And often sink down weary, weep, wring her hands.
> He wastes all with war, whatever his force rides past,
> And all their wealth and their dwellings he turns to destruction.
> Thus they spring on and spread, and spare but little,
> Spend without sparing what took long years to save.
>
> (ll. 3148-58)

Pivotal details midway through the poem prepare for the king's drastic change. Lucius is unexpectedly ennobled when he behaves toward Arthur's messengers with the same lordly restraint Arthur showed in his dealings earlier with the messengers of Lucius. Lucius, we discover here, is perhaps not as vicious as he seemed. And at about the same time that we are forced to modify our attitude toward Lucius, we must begin to modify our attitude toward Arthur. The Romans crying out against Arthur speak with apparent sincerity; indeed they sometimes echo the very words of Arthur's men in their complaints against Lucius:

> I scorn King Arthur and all his noble barons
> Who thus unjustly occupy these realms,
> Betraying the emperor, his earthly lord,
> All the array of the royalty of the Round Table
> Is cried against with rage in many a realm;
> He holds his revels now with Roman rents,
> But soon he'll explain himself, if all goes right with us.
>
> (ll. 1661-67)

All these sentiments have been expressed against Lucius by Arthur's men, and in almost the same language, in the council in the Giants' Tower at the start of the poem.

The same technique of comparison informs the poet's development of the relationship between Arthur's single combat with the St. Michael's giant and his war with Lucius. Various details, some straight, some ironic, identify Arthur's battle with the giant as a holy cause. The king tells Bedevere and Kay that he is seeking a saint's shrine; later the knights mock the dead "saint" and jokingly compare returning home with his remains to returning with holy relics (ll. 1163-68). The poet dilates on the idea of crossing oneself for safety (ll. 961-68, 1041); and the giant is identified with demonic or infidel forces: he is repeatedly called a "fiend," he "martyrs" children, etc. The fight is associated not only with righteous religious battle, a cru-

sade, but also with war for political order. The giant is a "tyrant," a "powerful master," a bad vassal (cf. l. 1172, *"Be sekere of this sergeaunt, he has me sore greuede!"*—*sergeaunt* here having the meaning "vassal" or "petty lord") with whom Arthur says he will "treat for a truce." Lucius too is a tyrant, a rebel to Arthur's legitimate claim as overlord—if the claim is in fact legitimate—and he has the support of infidels and giants "engendered by friends." (After Caesar's conquest, the legitimacy of Arthur's claim is open to question. The poet's audience probably knew this and could probably consider the claim in the light of its intimate knowledge of more recent claims and counterclaims to continental territories such as Normandy and Guyenne, and even to England.) Lucius and the giant are guilty of the same crimes: Arthur fights both "by-cause of his people," i.e., to protect his people, and also because both seek tribute, Lucius a tribute of rents, the giant a more barbaric and shameful tribute, Arthur's beard. And in both cases it is Arthur's sense of his own proper dignity—as well as his responsibility—which motivates him to fight. There are still other parallels between the two battles. For instance, after destroying the giant, Arthur distributes his treasure just as, after conquering cities, he will distribute treasures and rents. But there is also a significant, though subtle, contrast: Arthur takes no credit for his victory over the giant. It was not a man's deed, he says, but God's or the Virgin's (ll. 1208-10), and in the place of the battle he erects a holy shrine. No parallel details appear when he has won his continental war; on the contrary, he resolves to go "avenge" the man who died on the cross (l. 3215), almost as though he were an equal. The lack of a parallel is no oversight. In a scene emphatically contrasting Arthur's behavior and Sir Gawain's, Gawain does give the honor of victory to God, though Priamus, his victim, would give it to Gawain (cf. ll. 2630-43, esp. l. 2643). And on the other hand, when the two beaten Romans kneeling in their kirtles ask Arthur's mercy "for the love of him who has lent you lordship on earth," Arthur says he will give mercy by his *"own* grace" (ll. 2312-18)— and grim mercy at that. As he moves through the last stages of his invasion Arthur of course himself "torments the people." (l. 3151). Exactly like the giant and like Lucius, he makes women despair and weep and wring their hands, ravages the land, takes treasures, "spoils without mercy." Both Arthur's philosophers and Arthur himself will repeatedly speak later of Arthur's "cruel deeds." Professor O'Loughlin's argument, then, that Arthur did nothing wrong except in engendering Mordred is as untenable as Matthews's argument that Arthur was wrong from the start. Yet it is true, as we shall see, that Arthur's incest is significant.

Large structural contrasts of the sort I have been mentioning, all emphasizing change, are supported throughout by details which illustrate in imagistic form the conflicts and oppositions which account for the doubleness of Fortune. On his way to fight the giant of St. Michael's, who has murdered a beloved lady, Arthur and his men pass a beautiful meadow. The poet's description of the place ironically recalls descriptions in the poetry of courtly love:

> They rode along the river that ran so swift,
> Where trees arched out above with regal boughs;

The roe and the reindeer ran there recklessly,
Revelling there in the thickets and wild rose
    trees;
The groves were all in bloom with brilliant flow-
    ers,
With falcons and cock pheasants of flaming
    hues;
And all the birds there flashed as they flew on
    their wings,
And there the cuckoos sang out clear in the
    groves,
And with every kind of joy they cheered them-
    selves;
The notes of the nightingales rang out sweetly
    there
As they struggled against the thrushes, three
    hundred at once,
And what with the murmur of the water and
    singing of birds
One might have been cured who had never been
    well in his life.

                           (ll. 919-31)

In courtly-love poetry, the image of an earthly paradise where birds sing, flowers bloom, and a beautiful river flows, customarily emphasizes the unchanging nature of the place or at least the apparently unchanging nature. (For a typical example, see Chaucer's *Parliament of Birds*, ll. 183-210.) Similar descriptions abound in medieval literature—elsewhere in Chaucer, in the works of the *Gawain*-poet, in Dante and in the works of lesser continental poets. . . . A standard ironic treatment of the image is that in which the garden seems immutable but in fact is not. So in Chaucer's *Legend of Good Women* (prologue), the earth has *forgotten* its "pore estat," has put winter out of mind and now sings with false confidence. It is this strain in the tradition which the **Morte Arthure**-poet employs for his own purpose. His lines on the idyllic scene (just quoted) are built of oppositions: the contrasting images of the swift river and the motionless, regal boughs; the images of hunting bird and game bird; the combative cuckoos, nightingales, and thrushes—traditional debaters. Through this scene where contrasting natures harmlessly war, a scene conventionally associated with love and revelation, Arthur and his men ride to battle far more deadly than that in which the songbirds are engaged.

The same conventional image of the seeming earthly Paradise appears later (ll. 2670-75), immediately—and ironically—followed by a discovery that Sir Gawain is mortally wounded, and afterward followed by a contrasting image of the true Paradise the waters of which can raise the dead. The warning seems clear: beware the beauties and glories of mere earth.

An even more impressive yet simpler imagistic contrast comes when the splendidly garbed King Arthur meets humbly dressed Sir Craddock on the highway to Rome. As Matthews points out, Arthur's dress is an imagistic indication of his overweening pride at this point; or, to put the matter another way, the contrast of Arthur's dress and that of Sir Craddock, newly arrived from England, shows dramatically that Arthur's fortune is not what he thinks it: back home his power is crumbling. In wishing to push on beyond the original holdings of his house, and in taking all the credit himself, Arthur has begun to think with overweening pride. He imagines his power can increase indefinitely.

From the standard medieval point of view, pride is a deadly sin, the chief of the seven. But it would be a mistake to impose the standard opinion, in its usual very simple form, on the **Morte Arthure.** The poem is orthodox, but its vision is not a simple one. Here pride takes three forms. First there is that legitimate sense of dignity and importance a great conqueror experiences after bringing a vast empire to the rule of Christian law. He takes just and reasonable pride not only in his own accomplishments but also in the achievement of his men, and his insistence upon his dignity is not a matter of selfishness but the mark of his power and an effect of his deep love for his people. The opening catalog of Arthur's conquests—a longer catalog than one finds in any of the earlier Arthurian works—is introduced specifically to establish Arthur's legitimate greatness; and the whole scene in which Arthur consults his knights indicates his love for them and theirs for him, as well as the legitimacy of his anger at Lucius's unjustified demand for tribute. The splendid feast Arthur gives for the envoys has in it all the waste and show lamented in *The Parliament of the Three Ages* and in *Winner and Waster*, and perhaps it points forward to that selfish pleasure which will mark Arthur's later corruption, but it is entirely legitimate by virtue of its purpose: by means of this display of wealth and power Arthur hopes to dissuade Lucius from attacking him. Arthur's harsh and vindictive treatment of the messengers from Rome may foreshadow a later cruel streak, but it is not cruelty here; it is justified by purpose. Lucius is to understand that Arthur can make a dangerous enemy. But as the poem progresses—as I have said—the inner or moral meaning of events begins to be obscure. For instance, midway through the poem Arthur delivers a speech on the inappropriateness of a king's ransoming prisoners. His position is unselfish insofar as gathering ransom is mere acquisitiveness—the very fault to which Arthur will come when he adopts his plan of world conquest (or so his philosophers tell him)—but the speech also may reflect the king's exaggerated sense of his personal dignity. Since captives are unworthy of audience with kings, he says, they ought to be exiled or thrown into dungeons to await the king's decision. Soon after this we encounter Arthur's opinion, delivered with great scorn to a soldier at his side, that no mere archer could possibly be so blessed by Fortune as to strike a king or his horse. The notion is not especially uncommon in medieval thought, but Arthur's attitude, his rash faith in his own luck, his faith that it will support him even in technically illegal wars, nevertheless parallels the pride of young Priamus and stands in striking contrast to Gawain's attitude. Having overthrown the "proud" (as the poet insists) young Priamus, Gawain seeks to preserve Priamus's dignity by declaring that he, Gawain, is no one important, merely a tailor to the king, so that Priamus has lost no honor to another knight. Priamus is incredulous at the thought that he might be beaten by a commoner and at last forces Gawain to admit his true identity. But even when Gawain has done so, Gawain insists that the honor is God's, and that the victory is only luck (l. 2642), implying that Priamus might as easily have been lucky.

As Matthews rightly argues, by this time there is a touch of selfish pride even in King Arthur's magnanimity. At the siege of Metz the king graciously grants his peace not only to the ladies who come to beg mercy but to every man, woman, and child in the city; but the poet emphasizes details which throw ironic light on the kindness of the king. Arthur delivers his mercy from high on a splendidly covered horse, and he is dressed in his most glorious apparel. The siege itself, moreover, is presented in curious terms:

> Then boldly they attack and they bend back
>   their engines
> Loaded heavy with stones, and they prove their
>   casts;
> Convents and hospitals they smash to the earth,
> And the fairest of churches and lovely chalk-
>   white chapels;
> Huge stone steeples come smashing down into
>   the streets
> And chambers with wide chimneys, and many
>   chief halls;
> And they smashed and pelted down those plas-
>   ter walls,
> And the grief of the people was a pitiful thing to
>   hear!
>
>   (ll. 3034-41)

These are the only details selected. The siege is just and necessary, but the poet's whole focus is on the accidental destruction of the innocent—converts, hospitals, churches, homes.

The legitimate pride with which Arthur began resulted in defensive, hence justifiable, war against Lucius, a usurper and a tormenter of Arthur's people. But Arthur's decaying pride leads him, as I have said, to plan a war of conquest: he intends to capture all the world, revel on its tributes, and at last avenge the Knight who was murdered on the cross. Mordred's treason cancels that plan—Arthur's wheel has begun to descend—and King Arthur is driven to the final pitch of sinful pride, and emotion at once noble and terrible, which is to say, tragic. Though still described with flattering epithets, he becomes now, as did Achilles once, raw outrage, neither selfish nor selfless in the usual sense of selflessness. He does not fight his final battle for the sake of his people—indeed, the Round Table is against the rash action which is certain to destroy the kingdom. Arthur fights out of personal wrath, to avenge the death of a man he loved and destroy a world intolerable to those who affirm—sinfully, from a Christian point of view—the supreme value of the human. His vengeance vow is profoundly personal, particularly if one compares the formal vows of Cador and the rest at the start of the poem, or the vows of Gawain. Here pride has gone mad, but the madness is unquestionably noble. Vanished utterly is the objective and reasonable concern with justice for his people, the concern displayed in his first formal council in the Giants' Tower; and gone, too, is the concern with wise strategy which once made Arthur lash out at the rash young Sir Cador. What is left is rage: at the pagan and demonic forces which circle his kingdom on every side, at Mordred and all who have betrayed from within, and at himself, finally for his own "cruel deeds," which he takes to be the cause of his downfall. And so he kills Mordred, dies himself, and leaves the kingdom in ruin.

The earlier scenes in the **Morte Arthure,** full of boasts and vows of revenge, battles, deaths, and moments of tenderness, may operate at first mainly as adventure. But these scenes gain new interest when one rereads them after finishing the poem, for nothing here is mere filler. The boasts and vows in the earlier scenes establish the basis for boasts and vows with very different moral implications. The battle scenes set up the favorable view of war which the poem is to reverse and establish the importance of thematically significant characters, especially the model knight, Sir Gawain; and the early battle scenes at the same time elaborate the complex revenge motif. Guinevere's farewell to Arthur intensifies the effect of her later betrayal; but, more important, it lays the groundwork for contrasting farewells—Kay's leave-taking at the time of his death, Gawain's splendid last speech to his men, Mordred's farewell over the dead Gawain, Arthur's angry farewell to Mordred, and the nation's farewell to Arthur at the end of the poem.

Moreover, when one looks more closely at the earlier scenes, one discovers that they are the work of a poet with a keen sense of dramatic method. Consider the glorification of Arthur in the opening movement. The poet's brief "argument" of the poem (ll. 12-25) insists on the virtue and dignity of his characters. They were "loyal in their religion" (*lele in theire lawe,* a phrase which can have wider meaning than my translation preserves); they were circumspect in their works, kind, courteous, aware of the customs of court, and earned many honors. Here as everywhere in the poem, the poet's emphasis is on the greatness of Arthur which makes his fall so terrible. He of course says nothing yet of the reasons for Arthur's fall—they are allowed to emerge dramatically as the poem progresses. But the fact that he does not include them in his argument should not be construed as evidence that he is indifferent to them. The poet's argument ignores the whole final third of the poem—the fall from greatness. In lines 26-51 the legendary sway of Arthur at the height of his power is considerably increased from earlier tradition, and it is moved back in time: the poet gives it to Uther Pendragon, Arthur's father. Arthur is thus transformed from an empire builder, a man who might be suspected of overweening pride, to a defender and protector of his own. Here and elsewhere, the borrowings from Charlemagne and Alexander romances are one of many indications of the English poet's concern with elevating Arthur above all other worthies. Now the poet shifts from a list of conquests already made to conquests being made. And finally, with the pause provided by Arthur's Christmastime revels at Carlisle, the poet shifts from summary to fully elaborated dramatic presentation. His last strictly general remark in this section has the right weight as a terminus and is interesting in other ways as well: "Never in any man's time was more festivity / Made in the western marches in midwinter." The lines (76-77) invite comparison with the lines in the later *Sir Gawain and the Green Knight* in which Gawain remarks that he has never seen such a kill of deer "this seven years in the winter season." In *Sir Gawain* the emphasis is on the unnatural, perhaps magical winter abundance. In the **Morte Arthure** the emphasis is rather on the extraordinary, even heroic, but not unnatural, glory of Arthur's feast.

Arthur's revels are interrupted by a senator from Rome, and here the poet finds new ways of glorifying Arthur. The senator addresses Arthur boldly, as he would address a petty vassal in Lucius's name, and Arthur responds with a look of wrath which makes the mighty Romans cower before him. The Romans beg to be forgiven, claiming they merely do their duty to Lucius, whom they fear. Arthur not unnaturally calls them cowards and says: "There is a certain man in this hall [who] if he were sorely vexed, you would not look [at] once for all Lombardy." Thus with a grimly ironic circumlocution and then a direct slap, Arthur answers the senator's excuse. By "a certain man" he of course means himself: the allusion to Lombardy is a bald reference to what Arthur takes for the real reason for the senator's coming—his hope of winning some feudal estate from his emperor. The sneering charge is one Arthur makes repeatedly—for example again at l. 460. The cowardly messenger's next words instantly admit that Arthur is indeed a greater king than Lucius—"You're the lordliest man I have ever looked upon!"—an exclamation easily construed as another lapse in faith to Lucius, motivated by fear of the even greater King Arthur. But the messenger's fear is not introduced merely for comic effect. His fear contrasts with Arthur's respect for the great Lucius, whom he does not fear but whose messengers he honors for the sake of Lucius's noble blood. There is no suggestion, in this early scene, of overweening pride in Arthur: the poet rules that out by every possible means, including Arthur's consultation with his men (a traditional detail). Arthur's wrath is greater here than in the source, but this does not point to a tragic flaw. The poet's heightening of the King's anger increases the importance of Arthur's setting personal vengeance aside (ll. 150-51).

After seven days of feasting and entertaining the Roman senator, showing him an apparent friendliness which encourages him to bring up his business once again with "austeryne wordez"—somber, grave, or grievous words— Arthur suddenly and terribly changes his manner, showing his true colors. Acting with full consent of his parliament, he speaks to the senator with bald scorn. He mocks Rome's power, then directly mocks the senator and his company, comically rushing him out of the country, feigning revulsion at the "obscene" habits of foreigners. The senator again shows his timidity (ll. 467-74). Then the poet rings a change: the senator boldly stands up to King Lucius (ll. 514-52), asserting Arthur's greatness, even his virtue. The senator is not a complete coward after all; what he has heretofore shown is natural fear of a man of extraordinary power.

The poet's characterization of the senator is only one of many devices introduced for Arthur's glorification. In lines 212-15 the poet speaks of Arthur's goblets, made of gold and studded with gems, which are proof against any poison. The idea here—a medieval commonplace—is that by their nature precious jewels will either cancel the effect of poison or else explode at its touch. (The same idea appears in the alliterative *Purity*.) Notice the lines which immediately follow:

> And the conqueror stood, himself, in gleaming array,

> All clad in clean gold colors, together with his knights,
> And wearing his diadem there on that splendid dais,
> And was judged the mightiest monarch alive on earth.
>
> (ll. 216-19)

The implied analogy between the goblets and the king is difficult to miss: both are clad in gold; whereas the cups have gems, Arthur has his diadem; the cups even share Arthur's most obvious quality in the opening movement of the poem, righteous wrath: "For the bright gold, in its wrath, would burst into pieces." Arthur in his wrath, on the other hand, "casts colors" (*keste colours*) and burns like a glowing coal, as would a gem (ll. 117-18).

But glorification of Arthur is not the poet's only concern in the opening movement. If Arthur is the greatest of the Nine Worthies, a man in whom there can be no poison (as the juxtaposition of the goblets and the king appears to suggest), he will finally prove no more invulnerable to Fortune's power than other men. His eventual fall is foreshadowed and in part explained in the opening movement, and again the poet's main technique is subtle juxtaposition. Consider carefully lines 553-691. At first glance we see only contrast. The poet focuses on Lucius's assembling of his forces (ll. 553-623), then on Arthur's assembling of his. Lucius's tyrannical power is emphasized; Arthur, in contrast, speaks with Parliament's sanction at the feast of St. Hilary, one of the four terms when common-law cases were traditionally heard. But the passage on Lucius's preparations ends with emphasis on monstrous progeny— giants "engendered by fiends," witches and warlocks, often viewed in the Middle Ages (as is Malory's Merlin) as the offspring of devils; the Arthurian section ends with focus on Mordred. The poet does not insist on the dangerous potential of Mordred; he does not need to—the story is familiar to his audience. But much is said of his watching over Guinevere (he will later become her lover), and the phrase "childe of my chambyre," which has a number of meanings, is in one sense grimly fitting. For all his great virtue, Arthur is tainted by an old mistake. Gross and obvious bastardy is associated with Lucius's forces, but Arthur's house is also subtly infected.

Arthur's dream of the dragon and bear prepares in another way for his fall. Medieval tradition on the dragon is of a double nature: the dragon is sometimes identified in scriptural exegesis with creative power or monarchy (much as in Chinese tradition), sometimes with destruction and/or evil. See Ezek. 29:3, 32:2, where the dragon is an emblem of Egypt; Jer. 51:34, where it is the emblem of Nebuchadnezzar. In Isaiah it is repeatedly used as an emblem of destruction, as it is in Rev. 12:3 ff and elsewhere. It is sometimes identified with the Eden serpent (see Exod. 7:9-12) or directly with the devil. So in Chaucer, the *Canon's Yeoman's Tale*. The bear in exegetical tradition is an emblem of ferocity second only to the lion, but unlike the lion it is not used in scripture as an emblem of proper or righteous ferocity. It attacks sheep, sheep being in turn an emblem of mankind, God's flock; and the fact that it should at last be subdued was one of the wonders of the Messiah's kingdom. Because of the bear's upright stance, etc., the bear is viewed in folk tradition as a deformed sort of man.

The imagistic identification of the dragon with Arthur, the bear with the St. Michael's giant and also with Lucius's host (ll. 823-25) is carefully worked out. The dragon is beautiful and stately as well as terrible in its strength (ll. 760-72, 786-98); the bear is gross and misshapen, easily identified with the unnaturalness of Lucius's army (ll. 611 ff.) and with the ugliness of the St. Michael's giant, who is also stocky, bowlegged, and foamy-mouthed (ll. 1073-1102). The traditional ambiguity in the image of the dragon—an ambiguity perhaps inherent in the image—is obviously fitting for a king who is the very model of royal virtue but will one day become tyrannical. The ambiguity comes clear, of course, only when we have the hindsight afforded by the last third of the poem. But there are hints, at least, earlier. When the Viscount of Valence charges the Welsh King (ll. 2049 ff.), he carries a dragon "As a sign that our sovereign lord [Arthur] should be destroyed . . . For there can be nothing but death where the dragon is raised." The explication of the heraldic symbol is at least curious set beside the philosopher's explication of the dream symbol.

As a footnote to the above discussion of the poet's sense of the dramatic it might be added that even when the poet is not at his best his scenes have many attractive features. The poet can handle battle scenes better than can many a writer, certainly better than Malory, and he knows how to handle many kinds of fighting—on the battlefield, in the siege of a city, or on warships. The deploying of forces, the skirmishes, mass battles, and single encounters all come through distinctly and forcefully, controlled by a skillful alternation of panoramic and close-up camera shots. To present-day taste the poet's fervent patriotism and partisanship—shown in his frequent use of phrases like "our knights," "our valiant barons," or "our king"—may be distracting; but the poet is surely right. He is not merely cutting down psychic distance but is also insisting that the battle is between the powers of light and the powers of darkness. Lucius's army is an army of pagans, devils, and monsters. His hosts ride not on horses, normally, but on camels and elephants. (The point is Matthews's.) The phrase "our king" and the flattering epithets continue to ring out emphatically even after the fighter of devils has become, himself, a kind of devil, and the tragic irony is impressive.

The poem of course gains additional interest from the fact that its central character is partly drawn from life. As I have said . . . the character of King Arthur is in part based on the character of King Edward III. The list of Arthur's conquests at the start of the poem does not follow the list found in the chronicles but is influenced by the list of Edward's claims or conquests; many of the names in the poem are not Arthurian but belong to Edward's time—the Montagues, for instance—and many of the enemy armies are not traditional enemies of Arthur but enemies of Edward—the Prussians, Lithuanians, and Genoans. Arthur's battle at Sessoynes closely matches Edward's battle of Crécy, and Arthur's siege of Metz parallels Edward's siege of Calais. One parallel pointed out by Matthews is

particularly striking. Just as at Metz Arthur grants mercy to the countess and her ladies, so at Calais King Edward, sitting under a scarlet canopy of state, granted mercy to Queen Philippa and her ladies. There are also interesting lesser details, for instance the description of Arthur's beard in *Morte Arthure,* which recalls the description of Edward's beard in *Winner and Waster.* We need not pause over all the parallels. It is enough to say that if the reader takes upon himself as well as he can the psychological set of the poet's original audience, the *Morte Arthure* becomes an even richer experience. The battle scenes lose the repetitiveness they sometimes have as art-in-isolation; the exclamations of "our king" gather still greater force; and the dissolution resulting from Arthur's pride—and prophesied as the outcome of Edward's pride—takes on greater immediacy. This is not to say that the power of the poem lies chiefly in what may have been its immediate political purpose. It is to say that the reader who enters into the situation behind the poem—here as in the case of, say, Yeats's "Easter, 1916"—will appreciate more than the reader who does not. (pp. 239-56)

John Gardner, "The Alliterative Morte Arthure," in The Alliterative Morte Arthure, The Owl and the Nightingale and Five Other Middle English Poems, *edited by John Gardner, Southern Illinois University Press, 1971, pp. 239-56.*

Russell A. Peck   (lecture date 1975)

[*Peck is an American educator and critic. In the following essay, originally delivered as a lecture in 1975, he discusses the alliterative* Morte Arthure *as a tragedy that warns of the dangers of selfishly willful behavior. Text citations are to Krishna's 1976 edition.*]

"Be war of wylffulnesse . lest wondris arise."
—*Mum and the Sothsegger*

Lucius's messengers arrive at Arthur's banquet. From an illustration in Wace's Roman de Brut.

The latter part of the fourteenth century was marked by disenchantment with virtually every institution invented by man. Like so much of the literature of this chaotic period, the alliterative *Morte Arthure* is imbued with a deep concern about what constitutes virtuous behavior. God "schelde vs fro schamesdede and synfull werkes" (l. 3), says its opening prayer, "and gyffe vs grace to gye and governe vs here" (4). The poet would study government, but rather than attack institutions, he directs his attention to personal behavior, the government of ourselves. In this regard he is typical of his age, where moral positions tend to be introspective and self-critical. Like Gower, Chaucer, Langland, and the political moralists at the end of the century, he espouses the idea that the chaos man sees about him is caused by man himself. As Gower puts it in the *Confessio Amantis*:

> man is overal
> His oghne cause of wel and wo.
> That we fortune clepe so
> Out of the man himself it groweth.

Like other writers of his day, the poet of the *Morte Arthure* singles out the will as the faculty which most determines an individual's life. His poem is a masterful study of willfulness and the wonders it can conjure.

For fourteenth-century literary men, Boethius is the principal spokesman on matters of the will. A brief review of his ideas proves helpful in establishing some of the premises within our poem. The *Consolation of Philosophy* is a treatise on personal government in which a person is likened to a king who has sovereign rights over the kingdom of his soul. If he rules that kingdom well, he enjoys happiness and steadfastness. Good rule is partly a matter of self-knowledge (the remembering of who you are) and partly a keeping of balanced perspective on one's own good and the greater good, supremely embodied in God Himself. Paradoxically, then, man's power over his kingdom is not exclusively his own, but is contingent upon God's power. The sovereignty is his own only through his own right choices which enable him to participate in the *summum bonum*. Good rule requires an awareness of discrete boundaries between what is one's own and not one's own.

Intimately tied up with these Boethian ideas of good rule are two subtopics, fate and tragedy, which likewise figure largely in literature dealing with the will. Gower, for example, follows Boethius when he asserts in the *Vox Clamantis*:

> Each man shapes for himself his own destiny, incurs his own lot according to his desire, and creates his own fate. And thus a free mind voluntarily claims what it does for its various deserts in the name of fate. In truth, fate ought always to be handmaiden to the mind, from which the name itself which will be its own is chosen.

If fate is what one chooses, then tragedy is that condition when the will, through wrong choices, isolates the soul from its proper good, so that it feels wretched and lost. The will may rationalize its misery, placing the blame elsewhere (on Fortune, perhaps), but that very rationalization is symptomatic of its own indiscretion which is the efficient cause of its misery.

A dramatic moment near the beginning of the *Consolation* poses this configuration of ideas with admirable brevity. Lady Philosophy has just heard Boethius' lament about his imprisonment and the unjust charges brought against him. Fortune, it seems, has been his malicious enemy. Lady Philosophy replies:

> Whan I saugh the . . . sorwful and wepynge, I wiste anoon that thow were a wrecche and exiled; but I wyste nevere how fer thyn exil was yif thy tale ne hadde schewid it me. But certes, al be thow fer fro thy cuntre, thou n'art nat put out of it, but thow hast fayled of thi weye and gon amys. And yif thou hast levere for to wene that thow be put out of thy cuntre, thanne hastow put out thyselve rather than any other wyght hath. For no wyght but thyselve myghte nevere han doon that to the.

Several points here have bearing upon the alliterative *Morte Arthure:* (1) The soul, in governing itself, must know and maintain its true residence. (2) Fortune has no power over man's true country. The only way a man may be exiled is by his own willful departing. (3) Such a departure, not Fortune, is the cause of wretchedness. (When Fortune subsequently offers her famous *de casibus* definition of tragedy, she is describing an effect, not a cause.) (4) Exile is largely a matter of disorientation, a forgetting of what is properly one's own, or a misidentification of rightful possessions. Seeking to possess something which is not rightly its own, the will dispossesses itself. (5) When the will makes its misidentifications, it substitutes its own fantasies for true realities. These are the "wondris" which the Sothsegger speaks of when he warns young rulers to beware of "wylffulnesse." By approaching the *Morte Arthure* as a study of willful behavior we come close to its heart and its author's intention. Such an approach, moreover, exemplifies one of the later fourteenth-century's major topics, the dangers of willfulness.

The poet takes his story from the chronicles of Wace and Layamon, rather than the later, more popular romances. Perhaps his reason is that he wants the story to seem more like history. He develops his plot as a sequence of events, each of which requires decisions of Arthur or his knights and imposes consequences on that which follows. It is noteworthy that the poem's opening announcement of its subject (12-25) speaks of the glorious deeds of Arthur, his war with Lucius, and the conquest of Rome, but makes no mention of the poem's disastrous outcome. Perhaps the point of that omission is to avoid making the plot seem fated from the beginning. The fate of each character and the outcome of the poem will be determined by the characters themselves, who as the plot progresses, will get "what them likes." I mention the familiar tag because it occurs in various forms over a hundred times in the poem and is one of the poet's principal devices for focusing attention on willfulness. (The second most common tag, the reflexive pronoun in its intensive form—himselven, themselven, myselven, etc.—has something of the same effect and is often used in conjunction with the "as him likes" tag.)

Because the plot is designed to unfold as Arthur shapes his fate, I shall conduct my analysis according to the sequence of events as the poet introduces them. But first I would call attention to one other plotting device which the poet uses to create irony and a heightened sense of impending tragedy. The plot of the poem falls into two main parts of about the same length: (1) the events leading up to the Battle of Sessoine and the defeat of Lucius; and (2) the events which follow that victory. The main difference between the parts lies in Arthur's motive for fighting. In the first half he is primarily concerned with defending his lands, title, and people from a usurper. After the victory his motive becomes personal revenge. Revenge, as John Finlayson has noted, is not (according to chivalric manuals) a lawful reason for war. More important for our purposes, in Boethian psychology, revenge, like any form of tyranny or aggression, stems from a willful misunderstanding of what is rightfully one's own. Consequently, the actions of the second half of the poem tend to reflect deluded judgment and to parody the more rationally oriented events of the first part. William Matthews and others have noted the rising and falling action of the poem as Fortune turns away from Arthur. But the plotting is more intricate than that. The poet has arranged situations within the two parts geometrically in a hysteron proteron fashion, where the first event ties up with the last (which is a reverse of the first), the second with the next to the last, the third with third to last, and so on:

1. Arthur at his Christmas banquet, surrounded by joyous knights.	13. Dying Arthur, surrounded by his dead knights.
2. The council of Arthur and his knights.	12. Arthur's refusal to call a council at the request of Sir Wichere.
3. Dream of the dragon, which bodes well, and the crossing of the channel to France.	11. Dream of Fortune, which bodes ill, and the crossing of the Channel to England.
4. Arthur's holy battle with the Giant of Gene, who despoils the land, devours Christians, and rapes women. Arthur founds a church on the crag.	10. Arthur despoils Italy, torments the people, makes widows aplenty, and destroys churches.
5. Gawain's purposeful embassy to Lucius.	9. Gawain passes time somewhat idly in the Priamus interlude.
6. Presumptuous Sir Cador risks lives to win glory. Gets scolded by king.	8. Presumptuous Arthur works "naked" beside the walls of Metz. Gets scolded by Sir Ferrer.

7. The Battle of Sessoine. Arthur's victory, and the beginning of his defeat.

These structural antitheses are not absolutely symmetrical, but they are sufficiently parallel to call attention to themselves and create ironies which resound throughout the second part, as Arthur's behavior becomes progressively more arbitrary. The hysteron proteron structure, where acts parody former acts, focuses attention on the crucial central scene, where Arthur's motives become clouded and, instead of returning home with victory, he turns to seek revenge for the death of Sir Kay.

The *Morte Arthure* begins, as we have noted, with an elab-

orate prayer which defines the poet's intent to help men learn to govern themselves. In emphasizing the need for right governance "in this wrechyd world" (5), the prayer directs our attention to the poem's central motif, and by presenting God as a king beyond history who maintains his feudal court in "the kyngdom of Hevyne" (6), it establishes a model of kingship which is beyond fortune. The poet stresses God's glory and graciousness. The reflexive pronoun tag occurs three times in the prayer, not to indicate God's willfulness but his gracious self-possession and shared self as he shields men "thurgh grace of Hymseluen" (1) and calls men "Ewyre . . . to byde in blysse wyth Hym seluen" (8). The idea seems to be that God knows his own place and through his generosity enables men to know and govern theirs. In Boethian terms, self-possession is the antithesis of exile, where a man's will drives him away from what is truly his own.

The opening scene is designed to show Arthur as a powerful and wise king. There can be no question of his kingliness, if kingliness is measured by success. In one swift catalogue of conquests he recovers all the lost lands of his ancestors (26-47). Having secured lands "ynowe" (45), he rests for a season "to solace hym seluen . . . as hym beste lykes" (54-55). But he is more than a conqueror. He founds the city of Caerleon. In the chronicle sources Caerleon is a well-established city to which Arthur retires to enjoy its splendor. Perhaps the *Morte Arthure* uses the founding of the city as a sign of Arthur's generative behavior. In his treatise *On Kingship* St. Thomas Aquinas designates city-building as the principal duty of a creative king. Arthur would seem to be such a ruler. At his Christmas feast he shares his magnificence in high style with his great company of dukes, earls, doucepeers, archbishops, "and oþer ynowe" (67) at Carlisle. In addition to restressing his having plenty "ynowe" (45, 67), the poet, by use of other recurring tags, emphasizes Arthur's having accomplished his will—he rules "as hym lykys" (32), sojourns "as hym best lykes" (55), assembles his courtiers "to see whenn hym lykyde" (63) while they bow and "buske when hym lykys" (69). He won his lands "at hys will" (33), "by drede of hym seluyn" (46), "fre til him seluyn" (34), so that now he may surround himself with the courtiers he "commaundez hym seluyn" (71). As if to allay any doubts we might have of the completeness of Arthur's satisfaction, the poet says there "whas neuer syche noblay in no manys tym / Mad in myd-wynter in þa weste marchys" (76-77). The greater the magnificence here, of course, the more stark the contrast at the end of the poem, where, hysteron proteron, Arthur stands desolate among his dead knights, with nothing "as hym beste lykes." Our study will be to discover how he got from one state to the other.

Certainly, if a king is to rule, he must have his own will. The success of his rule will depend largely, however, upon his personal ability to govern that will. One recalls the Sothsegger's advice to young rulers to "be war of wylffulnesse . lest wondris arise." It is precisely when one has his will that he is most likely to be challenged. The splendor of the scene at Carlisle is comparable to the Christmas feast in *Sir Gawain and the Green Knight*, where amidst all its plenty that court is confronted with wonders. In the chronicle sources of the *Morte Arthure*, the embassy from

Lucius comes at Whitsunday. Perhaps our poet chose the midwinter season to suggest a time of pending, a time when the court's blessings stand out against an otherwise barren scene. The challenge from without comes as a jolt to Arthur and his court. As the first course of their banquet is being served, the Romans appear "sodanly" (80) and boldly assert their demands. Arthur meets the challenge as a good king should, with balance and courtesy. He entertains the Roman senator well, allows him seven days to see England's glories, and sees to it that his desires are satisfied. He gives him an allowance to "spende what þe lykys" (162) and wines "ynow" to try "whoso lykes" (205). Assured that the senator has all he wants "for solauce of hym seluen" (239) in "thees barayne landez" (224), Arthur calls his own counselors to him, thus showing further his wisdom as ruler. Christine de Pisan [in *Les Faites d'Armes*] observes that a prince may take up arms to obtain justice for himself once he has consulted impartial counselors. Though Arthur's counselors are far from impartial, he himself shows good judgment as he weighs their advice carefully, warning them against haste and headlong action. When the impetuous Sir Cador "lughe on hym luffly with lykande lates" (248) at the prospect of getting back to war instead of lying around like "losels," Arthur warns him:

> . . . thy concell es noble;
> Bot þou arte a meruailous man with thi mery
>   wordez;
> For thow countez no caas, ne castes no forthire,
> Bot hurles furthe appon heuede, as thi herte
>   thynkes.
>
> (259-62)

Arthur shows balanced judgment. Instead of leaping after the words of the "meruailous man," he would "trette of a trew towchande þise nedes" (263). He measures his rights against those of Lucius, observing that if ancient titles are the issue he has as much claim to the title of Rome as Lucius. Rather than succumb to Lucius' demands, Arthur will meet him in the field to defend his own. After the council, Arthur pays tribute to his knights for their support and acts decisively with the embassy. In fact, his kingly presence is so overwhelming that, even after they have returned to Rome to report to Lucius, the Romans are terrified and spontaneously praise him.

This initial image of Arthur as king is altogether positive. He is awesome in power, magnanimity, counsel, and firm decision. The next situation in which his judgment is tested is more subtle. Since he must travel abroad he must choose a lieutenant to look after the realm in his absence. This is an important moment, especially in a literature dealing with Boethian ideas of self-possession (home) and willful wandering (exile). The mere fact that a king travels abroad does not mean, of course, that he is a willful wanderer. . . . There are many examples of kings in medieval literature who govern so well that their authority is in no way diminished by their physical absence. Nevertheless, there is always the possibility that in setting off to seek wonders abroad one will discover the greatest wonder of all, the loss of his homeland.

The **Morte Arthure** explores Arthur's choice of Mordred as lieutenant in much greater detail than the chronicle sources. The poet carefully obscures any hints that Mordred might be a poor choice. In Layamon, with the first mention of Mordred, the poet curses him as "forcuþest monnen," noting that "treouþe nafde he nane . to nauer nane monne." Our poet's Mordred is a good man, mild of speech and conscientious. He is loyal to Arthur and worried about his ability to bear the burden of so large a responsibility, wondering if Arthur might not be wiser to choose some more warlike man. If there is an identifiable fault in the choice it lies in Arthur's insistence that Mordred take the job, want it or not. Aquinas, in keeping with Boethius' notion of right rule and proper domain, warns that the tyrant who seeks his own private good at the expense of his citizens is the worst of all rulers. Similarly, Dante argues that a good king is one who guarantees the free choices of his people, mankind being at its best when it is most free. Arthur is careless of Mordred's prerogatives, announcing publicly his choice of "me sybb, my syster son, Sir Mordrede hym seluen, / Sall be my leuetenaunte" (645-46), even before speaking to Mordred. Arthur presumes upon his kinship. The sources avoid mentioning Mordred's kinship to Arthur at this point. They would obscure the blood tie, if possible, for it seems embarrassing. Our poet stresses it, for it seems honorable. Mordred addresses Arthur as "my sybbe lorde" (681), and Arthur replies:

> Thowe arte my neuewe full nere, my nurrée of
>   olde,
> That I haue chastyede and chosen, a childe of
>   my chambyre;
>
> (689-90)

and "for the sybredyn of me" (691) insists that Mordred undertake the task. Mordred's desire to be excused of the charge should not be taken as hypocrisy. Arthur's insistence demands scrutiny, however, for his threats leave Mordred no choice:

> . . . foresake noghte þis offyce;
> That thow ne wyrk my will, thow watte whatte
>   it menes.
>
> (691-92)

It is the first time Arthur has acted arbitrarily in the poem or been willfully highhanded. But although Arthur's aggressiveness might be disturbing in an assessment of his personal wisdom, it seems in keeping with his regal power, and the poet does not question it here. There will be other acts more willful before we learn the shortcomings of this present judgment. Though Arthur's insistence is arbitrary, from the evidence the poet offers we must conclude at this point that Arthur's choice of his kinsman was sound.

On behalf of Arthur's judgment, we might note the explicitness with which he instructs his lieutenant in his powers and obligations (none of these details occurs in the chronicles): Mordred is to have complete authority throughout Arthur's lands. He must also look after Gaynor to see that she lacks nothing "þat hire lykes" (653). He must attend the king's personal estates, keep his castles well equipped, and make appointments ("ordayne thy seluen") of chancellors, chamberlains, auditors, judges, and other officers according to his own judgment—"chaunge as þe lykes"

(660). He should act justly under God, he should look after the treasury, and in the event of Arthur's death, he should be king. Or, if Arthur should return safely, then Arthur will make Mordred his heir,

> When I to contré come, if Cryste will it thole;
> And thow haue grace gudly to gouerne thy seluen,
> I sall corowne þe, knyghte, kyng with my handez.
>
> (676-78)

These are powerful promises by Arthur. He is to be commended for his guidelines, though his constraint of Mordred's will to the office, then the giving him such unrestrained liberties within that office, are perhaps questionable.

A portion of the departure scene is devoted to Arthur's farewell to Gaynor. It also is original with our author and contributes to our perception of Arthur's governance. Gaynor is presented as a loving person, but one who is fearful and generally weak. Arthur reassures her by reminding her that she has in the past "mekyll praysede" (711) Mordred and that he "sall be thy dictour . . . to doo whatte the lykes" (711-12). The dramatic irony of the passage is poignant, not only for Arthur, but Mordred and Gaynor as well. At this crucial moment the poet gives the first hint that all may not be well. As Arthur leaves, Gaynor swoons, and we are told: "cho sees hym no more" (720). The half-line's closed syntax creates a disconcerting sense of finality and leaves us wondering what wonders might arise to prevent Arthur's happy return.

The next hint which calls into question Arthur's decision occurs as he sleeps in his boat and dreams of the dragon and the bear. The philosophers who accompany Arthur assure him that the dragon signifies himself and that he will destroy the bear, that is, some tyrant or giant, who torments his people. They ignore, however, that part of the dream which says that the dragon "come dryfande ouer þe depe to drenschen hys pople" (761). The dream seems to suggest the possibility that Arthur might destroy his own. We tend to forget the phrase, however, for even though Arthur seems momentarily in the hands of fortune as his boat floats on the water, he soon lands safely and the meaning of the dream as the philosophers glossed it unfolds. "A grett geaunte of Geen, engenderde of fendez" (843) torments Arthur's people, and he rescues them.

The poet takes pains to present Arthur as a model Christian king in the encounter with the giant. He heightens the religious implications of the conquest, by making the giant specialize in devouring "fawntekyns" and Christian maidens. In the chronicles the giant is simply a rapist who is swiftly dispensed with by a combined effort of Sir Bedevere, Sir Kay, and Arthur. The issues in the *Morte Arthure* are entirely different. As Arthur undertakes the task "by my selfe one" (937) and "for rewthe of þe pople" (888), his quest has overtones of a religious mission. He arms himself ceremonially and sets Sir Bedevere and Sir Kay to pray. The giant, with his kirtle "bordyrde with the berdez of burlyche kyngez" (1002), is the epitome of willful usurpation. The "wafull wedowe" (950), who tells Arthur of the giant's crimes, typifies those bereft by the usurper. The giant wants Arthur's beard, and, to pass the time until he gets it, sups on "seuen knaue childre, / Choppid in a chargour . . . with pekill and powdyre of precious spycez, / And pyment full plenteuous of Portyngale wynes" (1025-28), then rapes to death the serving girls. He does not even have enough manners to sit up when he eats, but luxuriously lolls "lenand on lang" (1045), warming his bare backside at the fire as he crunches on a man's thigh.

The ensuing battle is a *tour de force* of alliterative excitement and comic grotesquerie. The giant lands the first blow, striking Arthur on the crest. The king is undaunted, however, for his strength lies not in earthly symbols but in "þe crafte of Cryste" (1107). He uses his wits, gets under the monster's guard, and stabs him through the brain. Unfortunately, the brain seems to be no vital organ in this fiend, for the blow scarcely fazes him. Arthur's next blow is more lethal as he hits "Iust to þe genitales and jaggede þam in sondre" (1123). That makes the sex-fiend roar and thrash fiercely. So Arthur stays in close and

> Swappez in with the swerde þat it þe swang brystedd;
> Bothe þe guttez and the gor guschez owte at ones,
> Þat all englaymes þe gresse one grounde þer he standez.
>
> (1129-31)

This provokes the giant to throw away his club, embrace Arthur in his deadly grip, and wrestle him all the way down the hill onto the flood marshes. Arthur finally slays him with his dagger, which, as Finlayson observes [in the York Medieval Texts edition of *Morte Arthure*, 1967], probably signifies "trust in God," while the not yet raped (and thus still living) maidens pray that Christ keep Arthur from sorrow. Though Sir Kay and Sir Bedevere fear the king is lost, when they finally pry him from the monster's death grip he has only three broken ribs.

None of these details is found in the chronicles. The point of their invention (besides their comic violence, so artfully maintained throughout the passage) is perhaps twofold. First, they dramatize the ideal Christian prince in his struggle to defend his people against the willful aggression of evil tyrants. Arthur has fought alone, but not on his own:

> "it was [he says] neuer manns dede, bot myghte of Hym selfen,
> Or myracle of Hys Modyr, þat mylde es till all."
>
> (1210-11)

He shares the glory of the event with the people as he "Cristenly carpez" with them, distributes the giant's treasure to the "comouns of the countré" (1215), keeping only the kirtle for himself, and commands a church to be built on the crag to commemorate the martyred duchess. There is a second effect produced by the passage, however, which cannot be recognized until the later part of the poem when Arthur himself becomes a tyrant and "turmentez þe pople" (3153), "wroghte wedewes full wlonke wrotherayle synges" (3154), "stroyene for euere" their cities (3127), and "spoylles dispetouslye" 3159) the countryside. There Arthur's activities remind us of the giant of Gene, and we wonder if Arthur has not, after all, added his beard to the usurper's aegis. Perhaps the one relic he claimed after the battle reflects even so soon in the poem an incipient over-reaching. Likewise, the giant's first blow to his crest, though incidental in the battle, perhaps anticipated the blow Arthur's truly kingly nature suffers when he gives way to willfulness. The image of Arthur locked in the monster's death grip perhaps prefigures what is in store for Arthur should he stop fighting to defend the innocent in the name of God in order to seek revenge by his "awen strenghe" (2472). Then he becomes victim of his own tyrannical acts and ends up comparing himself to the "wafull wedowe" (4285) rather than the saintlike victor.

But those events are far away from the scene where Arthur, with good Christian intent, slays the Giant of Gene. That he himself might become tyrannical has been scarcely suggested. Certainly he is guilty of no actions which would qualify as "shamesdedes." During the early conduct of the war Arthur continues to behave like a responsible leader. The question of right judgment and just cause as opposed to willful action the poet centers around the headstrong Sir Cador. Charged with the responsibility of conveying prisoners to Arthur in Paris, Sir Cador sidesteps his mission in order to win glory against unfavorable odds. His recklessness costs him several of his best knights. When he reports to Arthur, the king is grieved:

> Sir Cador, thi corage confundez vs all!
> Kowardely thow castez owtte all my beste
> knyghttez.
>
> (1922-23)

Sir Cador defends himself boldly against the scolding— "Karpe whatte yow lykys" (1929)—and reprimands Arthur for criticizing him after he has faced danger doing his "delygens todaye" (1934) on the king's behalf.

Arthur does not emerge from the dispute very well. His authority seems shaken, and he himself confused about what constitutes virtuous behavior. One of Arthur's most attractive qualities is his great love and loyalty to his men. But it is also his point of weakness. When Cador questions that love, Arthur reverses his position and gives him complete endorsement. He goes even further. In a flood of affection he names Cador and his children to be his heir. In his loving outburst Arthur seems to forget his larger office. In promising the kingdom to Cador, he thoughtlessly breaks his pledge to his forgotten kinsman Mordred. Arthur has no reason to believe that Mordred is not performing his "delygens" at home. If he did suspect infidelity he would be obliged to return home to set the matter straight. In his eagerness to appease Sir Cador, he breaks faith with his lieutenant. War deeds matter more than peaceful commitments. The battlefield usurps the rights of home.

Though Arthur's judgment as king has been seriously compromised at this juncture, his greatness as conqueror grows more luminous. The poet delights in showing what a clever military leader the king is. Arthur tricks Lucius into attacking him from a disadvantageous position. When his own men need support he backs them vigorously, nobly confronting the giant Golopas, whom he cuts down to size by lopping off his legs. Arthur's personal entrance into the fray sets the Romans to flight. But it is here that the turning point of the poem occurs. Here, at the poem's exact center, Sir Kay receives his deathblow: "At þe turnyng that tym the traytoure hym hitte" (2173). Kay is the first of the men really close to the king to be slain. The poet takes what had been a passing reference in the chronicles and turns it into his crux. The "turnyng that tym" makes all the difference to Arthur. Mortally wounded, Sir Kay "weyndes to þe wyese kyng and wynly hym gretes" (2185). He asks for fitting burial and requests that he be remembered to the queen, the "burliche birdes" of court, and his "worthily weife, þat wrethide me neuer" (2191). His recollection of the English court adds a domestic poignancy, reminding us of the homeland which they are theoretically defending. Arthur, in his great love of his men, is enraged over Kay's death, and thinks more of revenging the dead man than heeding his dying words. He swiftly defeats Lucius (though not without losing Sir Bedevere, his cup-bearer), and gives vent to his wrath by refusing ransom to his enemies, whom he mercilessly slaughters so that "Sir Kayous dede be cruelly vengede" (2264). He ships the corpses of Lucius and his senators to Rome in lieu of the tribute they had demanded—"assaye how hym likes!" (2347)—along with an announcement that the war the Romans wanted will now come to Rome—"be ware yif yow lykes" (2370). In his anger, Arthur would ram their willfulness down their throats.

It is noteworthy that the poet interrupts his narrative at this point to announce the date of the victory:

> In the kalendez of Maye this caas es befallen;
> The roy ryalle renownde, with his Rownde
> Table,
> One the coste of Costantyne, by þe clere
> strandez,
> Has þe Romaynes ryche rebuykede for euer.
>
> (2371-74)

Arthur has his victory. The rhetorical finality of the passage demarcates a major section of the plot. From this juncture Arthur fights in what he chooses to think of as his own cause. That cause is not a return home, but a seeking of revenge.

The second half of the poem differs from the first in subtle shifts in tone and kind of events. Where in the first we had a series of episodes in which Arthur exercised judgment, we now have a sequence of progressively vain actions marked by lack of judgment. After his victory over Lucius, instead of returning with his kingdom intact, Arthur calls a war council. This council contrasts sharply with the council at Carlisle when he began his foreign campaign. Here, instead of listening to his counselors and weighing what they say against his own understanding of causes, he "karpes in the concell" and "comandez them" what to think (2392ff.). He says he has heard of a knight "that I haue cowayte to knawe" (2397), whose lovely lands he would like for himself: "I will that ducherye devyse and dele as me lykes" (2400). His motive seems more like that of the tyrant Lucius than a just ruler.

In the first half of the poem, when knights became reckless, Arthur cautioned them. Now the situation is reversed: Arthur becomes the reckless one, to the consternation of his knights. In the siege of Metz, Sir Ferrer cautions Arthur against the "foly" (2432) of fighting without armor so near the walls. Arthur's nakedness before the wall might be interpreted in several ways: first, as a sign of his recklessness; second, as a sign of his neglecting to put on God's armor as he had done when he fought the Giant of Gene; and third, as an indication of his lack of regard for his own men, whom he now slightingly calls "gadlynges" (2443). Outraged at Sir Ferrer's suggestion, Arthur mocks him as a "fawntkyn" who will be "flayede for a flye þat on thy flesche lyghttes" (2441). There was a time when Arthur defended "fawntekyns." Now that term becomes one of derision. Scorning Sir Ferrer as a coward, he boasts his own fearlessness—"I am nothyng agaste" (2442). Ironically, it is just now that Arthur begins to have something to fear. His greatest recklessness lies not in his prancing before the wall "sengely in thy surcotte" (2434), but in his attitude toward himself. His crown, instead of signifying his reverence, constancy, good name, and common domain, becomes an excuse, a privilege which he thinks sets him apart from the common lot. "Sall neuer harlotte haue happe . . . to kyll a co-rownde kyng with krysom enoynttede!" (2446-47), he boasts. That is one bit of political philosophy which fourteenth-century Englishmen knew to be patently false. Fortune is no respecter of vaunted anointments.

As the Battle of Metz gets underway, Arthur, for the first time in the poem, fails to accomplish his will. In contrast to the fight with the Giant of Gene, where Arthur fought with the strength of God, he tries to win this one on his own. Though his army breaks down the gate and almost secures a garrison "be theire awen strenghe" (2472), they are forced to retreat. Instead of victory they settle for a siege. The battle at Metz is not mentioned in the chronicles, which direct Arthur south through Burgundy. By having Arthur turn east to conquer lands along the way, the poet emphasizes Arthur's growing ambition. The episode becomes a symbol of vanity, as Arthur lays siege to the cities of the world while neglecting his own land.

As commentary on the emptiness of Arthur's aggression, the poet inserts into the middle of the episode the interlude of Gawain and Priamus. Finlayson has noted that the interlude has the markings of a *chanson d'aventure,* as Gawain, to pass the time during the siege, sets out "wondyrs to seke" (2514). The *chanson d'aventure* formula was popular among fourteenth-century English writers who, in their concern over disintegration of social and political values, found the blame in the willful behavior of men seeking their fortune. Like other poems of this kind, the Priamus interlude calls attention to the will wandering in Fortune's domain, and suggests the need for behavior accountable to truths beyond Fortune. Both Priamus and Gawain are fortune hunters. After wounding each other, they discover that they must rely on each other's help if either is to recover. The cure is dramatically ironic as we think ahead to Arthur's wound by his kinsman, a wound for which he finds no cure.

Following this vignette of mutual dependence, the poet shifts back to the capture of Metz, emphasizing the satisfaction Arthur gets in his victory:

> Thus in Lorayne he lenges, as lorde in his awen,
> Settez lawes in the land, as hym leefe thoghte.

And one þe Lammese Day to Lucerne he wendez,
Lengez thare at laysere with lykyng inowe.
(3092-95)

Arthur's actions have become a kind of idleness, a self-indulgent lingering. He thinks he is increasing his possessions, but in truth he is calling things by their wrong names. As he sets laws according to his pleasure, what he is really changing is his own definition of king. In becoming a tyrant, he dispossesses himself. With his true country abandoned, he is less "lorde in his awen" than he imagines. Nor can he expect much love from the woeful widows.

With each new conquest Arthur *thinks* he is greater, though his actions prove increasingly vain. The poet dramatizes his swelling vanity by inventing a scene on top of Mount Goddard, from which Arthur contemplates Lombardy stretched at his feet:

> When he was passede the heghte, than the Kyng houys
> With his hole bataylle, behaldande abowte,
> Lukand one Lumbarddye, and one lowde melys,
> "In yone lykand londe, lorde be I thynke."
> (3106-9)

Would that thinking could make it so. Recall Petrarch's famous letter describing his ascent of Mont Ventoux, where the vastness of the scene reminded him that the world is vanity and that his proper study should be the maintaining of his soul. Our poet's point is similar: the prospect is an epitome of surquidry, as Arthur, lacking Petrarch's insight, imagines himself lord of that vast domain.

The Italian battles that ensue are even more reckless than the siege of Metz. When Arthur first set out for Rome after his victory of Sessoine, he vowed not to attack church properties. Now he plunders at will, church and countryside alike. The poet emphasizes Arthur's dissipation as he revels "with riche wyne" and

> . . . riotes hym selfen,
> This roy with his ryall men of þe Rownde Table,
> With mirthis and melodye and manykyn gamnes—
> Was neuer meriere men made on this erthe!
> (3172-75)

Arthur's joy is indeed presumptuous, for by this time he has cause to be the saddest man on earth. As he presses on, the "konyngeste cardynall" of Rome approaches him, hoping to stop the onslaught by promising Arthur the crown and all rites on Sunday eight days hence. That prospect boosts Arthur's joy to a new pinnacle as he gloats: "Now may we reuell and riste, fore Rome es oure awen" (3207). In his imagination he sets the coronation on Christmas day. His choice of date juxtaposes his wish with the Christmas festivity at the outset of the poem where Arthur, in his splendor at home, had assembled his counselors to consider their defense against Lucius. Somehow that court, which had seemed so magnificent, has become pale and forgotten. Rome gets its tribute from England after all, as Arthur imagines how he will dwell there and

> Ryngne in my ryalltés, and holde my Rownde
> Table,
> Withe the rentes of Rome, as me beste lykes.
>
> (3214-15)

The vanity of his aspiration might be compared to that of Charlemagne in the *Chanson de Roland,* with his hopes of being crowned in Saragossa. Like that other worthy, Arthur is seeking the wrong city. The poet clinches Arthur's megalomania with the fantasy that after his coronation he will then retake Jerusalem, "to reuenge the Renke that on the Rode dyede" (3217). Arthur would not only rule the world; he would undertake God's task as well.

The placing of Arthur's second dream immediately after his plan to avenge God undercuts the heroics of Arthur's wondrous fantasy. The review of the nine worthies is not a catalogue of heroic achievements. Rather, it is an emblem of Fortune's fools. Fortune lures Arthur to his place atop the wheel by appealing to his desires, then whirls the wheel and destroys him. Such is the tragedy of Fortune, as a man of high estate falls to wretchedness. But that fall, as Fortune describes it, is only a surface aspect of the real tragedy. The real loss began when Arthur stopped defending his homeland and willfully sought possessions that were not his own. His exile appears metaphorically in the dream as a wilderness entangled by vines and filled with wolves, swine, and other beasts which devour his knights. That wood is a place of his own making: "Me thoughte I was in a wode willed myn one" (3230). The philosophers who gloss the dream leave no doubt about its meaning:

> Thow has schedde myche blode and schalkes
> distroyede,
> Sakeles, in cirquytrie, in sere kynges landis.
> Schryfte the of thy schame and schape for thyn
> ende;
> Thow has a schewynge, Sir Kynge—*take kepe
> yif the lyke;*
> For thow sall fersely fall . . . *þe froytez are theyn
> awen.*
>
> (3398-3403; italics mine)

Rather than "vertous lywynge" (see lines 3-5), Arthur's conquest turns out to be "schamesdede." His fate is the fruit of his own willful behavior, but the tragedy lies in his misunderstanding of his proper domain. His geographical displacement is simply a manifestation of his psychological disorder.

Immediately following the dream, Arthur learns of the rebellion in England. In the chronicles the informer is not named. Our poet identifies him as Sir Craddok, "kepare of Karlyon" (3512), and makes a pilgrim of him. Caerleon, which Arthur established "be assentte of his lordys" (60) at the beginning of the poem, is an emblem of peace, the gift of a generous king to his people. Its abandonment by its keeper reflects the situation of all England, which has been abandoned by Arthur. That the keeper is an outcast is commentary on the lack of good government at home. That he is a pilgrim to Rome suggests that there might be other reasons for seeking that city besides conquest. Although Craddok was knight of Arthur's own chamber and says, "Me awghte to knowe þe Kynge: he es my kydde lorde" (3509), he fails to recognize Arthur behind all his "riche wedys" (3493). His failure to know his

lord is more a commentary on Arthur than it is on Craddok. The Arthur he knew has become unrecognizable.

The conclusion to the *Morte Arthure* differs from the chronicles in several ways, but especially in the poet's treatment of Mordred and Gawain. The highly original presentation of these two vassals provides, as did the Craddok episode, a commentary on Arthur unique to this poem. The poet's sympathetic treatment of Mordred defies one of the strongest traditions in the whole of the Arthurian canon. We have seen how Mordred was presented at the outset as a dutiful though somewhat put upon kinsman. We also noted that Arthur breaks his pledge to Mordred by naming Cador his heir. None of this excuses Mordred, of course, when he betrays Arthur's trust, marries Gaynor, "corownde hym seluen" (3525), and "haldys his awen" (3541). Nevertheless, he is no simple villain. Only once does the poet call him "traytoure be tresone" (3782); the more common label is "Sir Mordrede the Malebranche" (4062, 4174), a title that reflects as much on Arthur, his progenitor, as it does upon Mordred. Mordred's loving care for Gaynor seems to be based on mutual affection. Not only do they marry, but they also have children, a detail found in neither of the chronicles. And, as Matthews notes, there is no precedent for his letter of concern to Gaynor, after Arthur attacks. His most sympathetic treatment occurs, however, at that very moment when we might expect the poet to reprehend him, at the slaying of Sir Gawain. Mordred kills Gawain in self-defense and is immediately filled with remorse. When King Frederick asks the identity of the fierce opponent, Mordred laments:

> "He was makles one molde, mane, be my
> trowthe;
> This was Sir Gawayne the gude, þe gladdeste of
> othire,
> And the graciouseste gome that vndire God lyf-
> fede,
> Mane hardyeste of hande, happyeste in armes,
> And þe hendeste in hawle vndire heuen riche,
> Þe lordelieste of ledyng qwhylls he lyffe myghte,
> Fore he was lyone allossede in londes inewe;
> Had thow knawen hym, Sir Kyng, in kythe
> thare he lengede,
> His konynge, his knyghthode, his kyndly
> werkes,
> His doyng, his doughtynesse, his dedis of armes,
> Thow wolde hafe dole for his dede þe dayes of
> thy lyfe."
>
> (3875-85)

Perhaps one way the poet thinks to praise Gawain is by putting his eulogy in the mouth of his enemy, but the speech goes far beyond praise. Its deep-felt statement of personal loss is an insight into brotherhood as profound as any Arthur himself arrives at. As Mordred turns weeping from the fray, he curses not Arthur, but rather the time "þat euer his werdes ware wroghte siche wandrethe to wyrke" (3889). Sighing for his "sybb blode," he leaves the battle, pierced to his heart with remorseful remembrance of the joyous Round Table. He avoids Arthur as best he can, but finally is trapped, wounded by Sir Marrock, and then slain by Arthur, who cuts off his hand, an inch from the elbow, and, after Mordred faints, impales him through the vent in his armor. The literary effect of such grisly details is markedly different from those gory alliterative quatrains when Arthur slew the Giant of Gene or the Giant Golopas. There is small joy in Arthur's victory over Mordred, his son.

Perhaps the poet's positive treatment of Mordred stems from his desire to associate him with his kinsman Sir Gawain, who is in some ways, like Mordred and Sir Craddok, an unwitting victim of Arthur's willfulness. All three of these vassals end up stranded in England by an absent Arthur, though Gawain, like Mordred, is as well a victim of his own choices. The chronicles give little attention to Gawain's death. We are merely told that he is slain while establishing the beachhead. Our poet greatly enlarges the scene, making it the crux in Arthur's defeat. After winning a stunning sea victory, Gawain succeeds in landing a small troop. Though he fights against overwhelming odds, he secures a "grene hill" (3768) which, we are told, he might have maintained had he sat tight—"he had wirchipe, iwys, wonnen for euer" (3769). But Gawain sees Mordred among the enemy, and his desire for revenge overcomes him. With a "grete wyll" (3774) he charges. As his men become entangled and slain, Gawain becomes increasingly desperate. The poet emphasizes his madness: seeing his men destroyed, "what for wondire and woo, all his witte faylede" (3793); "alls vnwyse, wodewyse, he wente at þe gayneste" (3817); "his reson was passede. / He fell in a fransye for fersenesse of herte" (3825-26); "hedlyngs he rynys" (3829). The poet compares him to a lion:

> Alls he þat wold wilfully wasten hym selfen;
> And for wondsom and will all his wit failede,
> That wode alls a wylde beste he wente at þe
>   gayneste.
>
> (3835-37)

He then draws a moral exemplum: "Iche a wy may be warre be wreke of anoþer" (3839). The epitome functions in two ways. First, Gawain is literally self-destroyed as he throws himself upon the fallen Mordred. His folly anticipates Arthur's own wild encounter with Mordred where the king, blind to the warning which the poet saw dramatically implicit in Gawain's death (3839), rushes to his own mortal wound. Second, if we think of reason as man's kingly part, Gawain dies in a state without a king. The poet embellishes the idea by leaving the king literally at sea. In the chronicles Arthur is fighting on shore at the time of Gawain's death. Our poet deliberately separates them, as if to create an emblem of headlessness.

It is the pattern of Boethian philosophical tragedy that the hero-victim becomes progressively isolated. Not only does his willfulness make him victim of Fortune, but it also removes him from the security of his rightful place. We have seen Gawain and Mordred die in isolation. The most desolate scene of all, however, is Arthur's death. The poem's conclusion is a study in barrenness. The poet has deliberately removed from the story all references to Merlin and his faery world, which were so prominent in the chronicles. There is no prophetic hope of a world beyond or a world to come which will make all things right. There is only Arthur, a "wafull wedowe" amidst a field of corpses. Much of the sadness at the end lies in the fact that Arthur,

for all his destructiveness and ambition, is a great warrior with a profound love of his men. The two moments which shape his fate most decisively are the deaths of his loved ones, Sir Kay and Sir Gawain. The poet fixes our attention on this sympathetic quality in Arthur during the last battle, when Arthur, seeing Ewain in trouble, tells Idrus (Ewain's son) to go help his father. Idrus refuses, saying that his father had instructed him not to depart from Arthur's side under any circumstance. Overwhelmed with compassion Arthur cries out:

> "Qwythen hade Dryghttyn destaynede at his
>   dere will,
> Þat he hade demyd me todaye to dy for yow all."
>
> (4157-58)

He would rather die for his men than have for a lifetime all the lands Alexander conquered (4159-60). The problem is that Arthur's deeply felt love, though noble, is only part of what is required of a good king. It may be a heroic gesture to destroy oneself for the sake of a loved one, but it is not the mark of a good leader. Without kingly governance of the will, all the deep compassion comes to grief.

Sorrow is a forgetting, says Lady Philosophy. In his grief over Gawain's death Arthur equates Gawain with his own sufficaunce (see 3956-60, where Arthur equates Gawain with "my wirchipe," "hope of my hele," "my herte and my hardynes," and "my concell, my comforthe, þat kepide myn herte"). Filled with self-hatred, he feels dispossessed: "I am vttirly vndon in myn awen landes" (3966). But a good king must be in full possession of himself. The incipience of Arthur's dispossession goes back clearly to his departure from England, where his naming of his lieutenant and heir was as much an act of will as tact. His personal security later becomes threatened when, in his exchange with Sir Cador, he forgets his own good counsel and, in response to Cador's declaration that he was fighting for Arthur, somewhat sentimentally makes him his heir. Repeatedly thereafter, Arthur ignores good counsel in the illusion of brotherhood, all the while losing his good men. Like Gawain, who had a choice of whether to stay on his hill or willfully attack his "sybb blode," Arthur is given one last opportunity to choose his fate, as Sir Wichere advises him to call a council. But Arthur is determined in his revenge. It is ironic that in destroying Mordred, Arthur finds no peace, only corpses. "A traytoure has tynte all my trewe lordys" (4281), he laments. But the question of who has done the betraying is not easily answered.

The dying Arthur goes to Glastonbury, where a surgeon of Salerne "enserches his wondes" (4311), but no cure can be found. Lady Philosophy observes, "Yif thou abidest after help of thi leche, the byhoveth discovre thy wownde." The bottom of Arthur's wound eludes "discovery." Unlike the Priamus scene, where the enemies discovered that they were really brothers, Arthur leaves no enemies alive. After disposing of Mordred, he calls his confessor, forgives Gaynor, and dies—but not until he sends out men to destroy Mordred's children. The slaughter of the children is perhaps his most empty act of all, for they are the closest blood kin he has. Having slain his only son, he now slays his grandchildren. R. M. Lumiansky has suggested [*Medieval and Renaissance Studies,* ed. John M. Headly, 1967] that Arthur regains the magnanimity, courage, and magnificence of "Christ's knight" at the end of the poem. I find it difficult to see much fortitude in his behavior. Though he searches his wound, despite his prayer of victory and his *In manus,* he fails to see very deeply into it. His fate is about as wretched as it can be. Instead of invoking the "once and future king" epitaph, the poet directs our attention the other way, tracing Arthur's lineage back to Troy and "Ectores blude." The allusion hearkens back to the dream of Fortune's wheel with its unflattering description of Hector. Such a conclusion goes deliberately against the courtly propaganda of the time which would see the royalty of England as being descended from Arthur and claiming a glory that goes all the way back to Troy. Instead, the tone, like that of other late fourteenth-century English poems, looks upon the myth of Trojan descent as a dubious honor, the tale of a city destroyed by its own folly. One part of the conclusion's starkness lies in the fact that we as audience have, like Gawain and even Mordred, found a nobility and grandeur in Arthur, his loyalties, and his aspirations. That has all been destroyed at the end of the poem, where we find a bereft community of dignitaries and ladies "buskede in blake" (4339) putting Arthur in the ground and weeping at the tomb: "whas neuer so sorowfull a syghte seen in theire tym" (4341). Another part of the starkness lies in the Boethian reasoning whereby we see that Arthur, whom we have loved and by whom we have been thrilled, shaped his own fate. The wonder we are left with at the end is not that of a world glossed by Merlin, or embellished by some redemptive virtue. The wonder is the bleak scene itself. (pp. 153-78)

> *Russell A. Peck, "Willfulness and Wonders: Boethian Tragedy in the Alliterative 'Morte Arthure',"* in The Alliterative Tradition in the Fourteenth Century, *edited by Bernard S. Levy and Paul E. Szarmach, The Kent State University Press, 1981, pp. 153-82.*

James L. Boren   (essay date 1977)

[*In the following essay, Boren analyzes the "narrative design" of the alliterative* Morte Arthure, *comparing it with that of other narrative poems written during the reign of England's Richard II (1377-99). According to Boren, recognition of* Morte Arthure *as an example of this Ricardian genre contributes to a better understanding of the work's themes. All text citations are to Brock's 1871 edition.*]

It should be of more than casual concern that critics have differed so widely in their identification of the generic tradition in which the author of the Middle English alliterative **Morte Arthure** chose to write, for the issue involves more than literary classification: generic identification conditions (and may even determine) our perception and understanding of the details of a literary text. Most recently cases have been made for the poem as a "tragedy of fortune," a *chanson de geste,* and as an *exemplum* illustrating the virtue of fortitude, but generic identification has not led to a convincing exposition of narrative structure. For example, in identifying **Morte Arthure** as a *chanson de*

Arthur battles Roman emperor Lucius. From an illustration in Wace's Roman de Brut.

geste, John Finlayson [in his "Introduction" to *Morte Arthure,* 1967] has attempted to account for all the incidents of the poem within a four-part narrative scheme. This divisioning functions to support his argument that the poem structurally parallels the *Chanson de Roland,* but he indicates an awareness of the problem of incorporating Arthur's fight with the giant of St. Michael's Mount, "almost a section in itself," into the section devoted to the war with Lucius, and his outline in general is dependent upon thematic interpretation of the poem. Earlier critics generally pursued a thematic analysis of the poem, finding its unity solely in the dominant character of Arthur, but even the poem's most recent editor has written that "The alliterative **Morte Arthure** is not a complicated poem; a bold simplicity of structure and action is its chief virtue . . . " [Larry D. Benson, *Tennessee Studies in Literature* 11 (1966)]. I should like to argue, however, that the **Morte Arthure** poet wrote such a distinctive sense of narrative structural design, a design which exhibits features common to the central narrative tradition of late fourteenth-century England.

In *Ricardian Poetry,* J. A. Burrow attempts to define the narrative features in the works of Chaucer, Gower, Langland and the *Gawain*-poet which, taken together, might constitute a period style. He observes that "The basic unit of Ricardian narrative is the single episode. . . . The episode may be narrated at length or briefly; but whatever its scale, it will be set within some strongly-marked 'enclosing' form. A poem may consist of one such episode or several," and he concludes: "The structures, like the narrative techniques and the significations, are clearly and deliberately articulated." Earlier in his study, he contends that "Ricardian poets show a strongly literary sense of form and structure in their handling of text divisions."

Burrow excludes *Morte Arthure* from his discussion of
Ricardian poetry, commenting that "writers, such as the
author of the alliterative *Morte Arthure,* may find their
place in a view of the period more comprehensive than
mine," but the poem, as I shall try to show, does exhibit
features which Burrow has termed Ricardian: significant
narrative devices demarcating distinct narrative segments
function to condition the meaning of each episode, raising
the episodes to the status of *exempla.*

Morte Arthure can be seen to be comprised of the following segments: .

> Introduction, lines 1-77.
> I. The preparations for war, lines 78-839.
> II. The fight with the giant of St. Michael's
>   Mount, lines 840-1221.
> III. The war with Lucius, lines 1222-2385.
> IV. The wars of conquest, lines 2386-3175.
> V. The dream of Fortune, lines 3176-455.
> VI. The war with Modred, lines 3456-4341.
> Epilogue, lines 4342-46.

This outline of the poem acknowledges the poet's clear use
of narrative demarcations: five of the sections begin with
the arrival of figures bearing messages which affect the
course of subsequent events, and, in the other section, the
poet replaces the messenger(s) with a council of Arthur's
knights. The respective defining features of the six sections
are thus:

> I. The ambassadors from Rome.
> II. The Templar.
> III. The messengers from the Marshall of
>   France.
> IV. Arthur's council before the siege of Metz.
> V. The cardinal from Rome.
> VI. Sir Cradok.

These text divisions not only reinforce the generally recognized thematic emphasis which the poet has given to Arthur's fight with the giant (section II), but, more significantly, add emphasis to those sections (IV and V) which
are the poet's own contribution to the traditional story of
Arthur's fall. In this narrative scheme, an added dimension of meaning results from the clear juxtaposition and
thematic balance of episodes, and the variation in delineating devices emphasizes the pivotal nature of Arthur's
council at the beginning of section IV.

In section I, Arthur first appears to us in the role of conqueror, appointing kings for his realm, dubbing knights,
setting the people at peace, and founding the city of Caerleon. It is there, during the great Christmas festivities, that
the ambassadors of Lucius Iberius, Emperor of Rome,
suddenly appear before Arthur and demand tribute-
homage to Rome for the lands Arthur holds. The poet
carefully develops the confrontation between Arthur and
the ambassadors, and, as John Finlayson has aptly observed, "Arthur's controlled anger, courteous treatment
of the ambassadors and subsequent consultation of his
knights quickly establish the moderation, courtesy and
readiness to take counsel which are the marks of the medieval 'wyse prince.' The method of exposition is already established as dramatic, not analytic." It is the appearance
and challenge of the Roman ambassadors which dramati-

cally initiate the action of the first section of the poem and
establish the character of the British king.

The second section of the poem begins with the arrival of
the Templar, whose appearance at this juncture is more
than just a "religious touch." John Finlayson has discussed the battle with the giant as being especially important in the thematic development of the poem, and John
Gardner [in his "Comments on the Poems," appended to
his 1971 translation of *Morte Arthure*] has observed many
of the more significant thematic and verbal parallels between this section and later actions in the narrative. Despite the fact that the poet has devoted only 382 lines to
this episode, it is clearly a locus of a number of motifs and
a touchstone for their interpretation. That the poet intended Arthur's behavior in this episode to be a model of right
conduct which foreshadows his subsequent victory over
Lucius is generally accepted; that elements in the episode
ironically hint at Arthur's later decline from virtue is less
often realized. Recognition of the Templar as the differentiating figure which begins this section makes one aware
of the thematic ambiguity of the subsequent narrative.

The story of the rise and spectacular fall of the Templars
has continued to be a controversial subject, and questions
still remain concerning the motives which prompted Philip IV of France to initiate in 1307 the inquisition which
led to the destruction of this celebrated order of knights.
But, in fourteenth-century England, the story of the fall
of the Templars came to be treated generally as an *exemplum* on the perversion of noble ideals through covetousness—an idea to which Langland had cause to refer in lamenting the social conditions of his own time:

> And now is werre and wo   and ho so "whi" as-
>   keth,
> For couetyse after a croys   the croune stant in
>   golde.
> Bothe riche and religiouse   that rode thei hon-
>   ouren
> That in grotes is y-graue   and in golde nobles.
> For couetyse of that croys   clerkes of holy-
>   churche
> Schullen ouer turne as Templars duden   the
>   tyme aprocheth faste.
> Mynne ye nat, lettered men,   hou tho men hon-
>   ourede
> More tresour than treuthe?   ich dar nat telle
>   the sothe
> How tho corsede Crystine   catel and richesse
>   worshepeden;
> Reyson and riytful dome   the religious dam-
>   nede.

In the late fourteenth century, with the memory of the
Templars' fall still vivid, a reference to that disgraced
order could not be without significance. As a representative of an order of real knights which achieved at its height
a level of honor and power not unworthy of the legendary
knights of the Round Table, the Templar functions to
foreshadow Arthur's later decline from the ideals of conduct exemplified in this episode. It is the Templar's appearance which renders especially ominous Arthur's
choice of spoils from amidst the treasure hoard of the slain
giant. Arthur's trophies—the giant's club and his kirtle
made from the beards of slaughtered kings—are the sym-

bols of unjust power and the shameful tribute demanded by tyrants. But, while the appearance of this messenger clearly adumbrates Arthur's later decline, in this specific episode the remembered history of the Templars would seem to effectively contrast with and thereby accentuate the exemplary nature of the king's actions. If the Templar represents the triumph of covetousness over nobility of purpose, Arthur's reply to the Templar's account of the giant's abduction of the Duchess of Brittany suggests quite the opposite:

> "I had leuer thane alle Fraunce, this fyftene wynter,
> I hade bene be-fore thate freke, a furlange of waye,
> Whene he that ladye had laghte and ledde to the montez:
> I had lefte my lyfe are cho hade harme lympyde!"
>
> (ll. 872-75)

In section II, the selection of the Templar as an introductory figure evidences the poet's sophisticated awareness of articulating techniques.

In the third section of the poem, the poet introduces the messengers from the Marshall of France to mark the beginning of warfare with Lucius. It is their speech (ll. 1235-62) which first suggests a parallel between the crimes of the giant and Lucius' invasion of France, and the thematic parallel of sections II and III is further emphasized by the messengers' appeal to Arthur as a defender of the oppressed. At the end of the second section, Arthur had ordered the distribution of the giant's treasure "To comouns of the contré, clergye and other" (l. 1215), and, at the beginning of the third section, the messengers tell Arthur that the forces of Lucius "Confoundez thy comouns, clergy and other" (l. 1245). The messengers clearly serve as a differentiating structural device, but they also intensify both the real and symbolic opposition of Arthur and Lucius at this point in the narrative.

Having established a pattern of narrative differentiation in the first three occurrences of messengers, the poet significantly deviates from that pattern in the beginning of the fourth section of the poem. As John Finlayson has argued, it is in this section that Arthur embarks upon a campaign of personal conquest only tenuously related to the issues which brought about the war with Lucius, and this campaign seems unsupported by the legal and moral justifications of the earlier warfare. The variation in the introductory device serves to emphasize this change, for, at the beginning of the fourth section, the poet has substituted Arthur's council before the siege of Metz (ll. 2386-415) for the arrival of messengers. In direct contrast to the earlier council in which Arthur solicited advice concerning the Roman ultimatum (section I, lines 249-406), here Arthur is the only one to speak, announcing his plans to attack the rebel Duke of Lorraine and to invade Italy. The emphasis in this scene is upon the exercise of Arthur's will in triumph: the poet's employment of this council seems to suggest that power has rendered the king unwilling to listen to any voice but that of his own desires. In the first three sections the messengers function to prompt a confrontation between Arthur and worldly adversity; subsequent to the fourth section the messengers function implicitly to confront Arthur with the spiritual consequences of his own deeds.

At the end of the fourth section Arthur rests his army outside Viterbo and awaits the reaction of the senators of Rome. But, when the Roman response does come to Arthur at the beginning of the fifth section, it is borne not by a senator but by a cardinal in the role of papal emissary. Before the siege of Metz, Arthur had affirmed that " 'yif we spare the spirituelle, we spede bot the bettire' " (l. 2414), but, in the subsequent assault, Arthur's siege machines batter the city:

> Mynsteris and masondewes they malle to the erthe,
> Chirches and chapelles chalke-whitte blawnchede.
> Stone stepelles full styffe in the strete ligges.
>
> (ll. 3038-40)

And now (ll. 3179-80) the cardinal's words suggest that Arthur is warring against the community of Christendom—not just the Romans but the Church of Rome and the Pope himself. With the acceptance of eight score children as hostages, Arthur becomes like the giant of St. Michael's Mount (the victimizer of children), and, when he orders the slaying of the child hostages if Rome fails to pay tribute, he manifests a covetousness as perverted as that of the fallen Templars. Arthur is on the verge of that fall foreseen in his dream of Fortune (ll. 3227-393) which dominates the fifth section of the poem.

When Arthur recounts that dream to the philosophers in his entourage, he is told that his good fortune has passed (l. 3394), and his actions are condemned:

> "Thow has schedde myche blode, and schalkes distroyede,
> Sakeles, in cirquytrie, in sere kynges landes;
> Schryfe the of thy schame, and schape for thyn ende!"
>
> (ll. 3398-400)

Arthur is urged to repent and " 'ffownde abbayes in ffraunce' " (l. 3403), that is, implicitly, to return to an earlier pattern of exemplary conduct evidenced in the fight with the giant of St. Michael's Mount. After that encounter Arthur had built a church and established a convent as a memorial to the victory granted through the will of God and, indirectly, to the just and pious actions which made the king worthy of that bestowal of grace (see ll. 1218-21). But, having been condemned by his philosophers, Arthur is nevertheless unrepentant as he dresses himself in elaborate scarlet garments and stalks out alone upon the field.

At the beginning of section VI, Arthur's brilliant clothing, indicative of his unrepentant state, significantly contrasts with the somber appearance of Sir Cradok, a humble pilgrim, and Arthur's failure to recognize this long-time friend and counselor as he travels to Rome is perhaps symbolic of his inability to recognize the need for repentance. But, at first, Cradok also fails to recognize the king, even though, in response to Arthur's questions, he says: " 'Me awghte to knowe the kynge, he es my kydde lorde' " (l.

3509). While it is reasonable that Arthur might not recognize the knight Cradok in the unusual guise of a pilgrim, it is just as reasonable to expect that Cradok would recognize Arthur, who is dressed extraordinarily but still as a king might be dressed. That Cradok does not recognize Arthur suggests some fundamental alteration in the appearance of the king. In this case (as with the extreme case of the giant) the physical seems to mirror the spiritual, and Cradok's failure to recognize Arthur may be indicative of his (Arthur's) spiritual degeneration. The moral contrast between the two figures is as complete as their contrasting physical appearances would suggest: while Cradok is on the road to Rome to seek the pardon of the Pope, Arthur is on that same road in the role of aggressor and as a threat to those same spiritual powers. Just how far Arthur's fortunes have declined is made clear in Cradok's speech (ll. 3523-55), for the king is without a kingdom: Modred has seized the throne and taken Arthur's queen. The encounter with Cradok serves not only to initiate the concluding section of the poem (the war against Modred) but to suggest a spiritual failure which lies at the heart of Arthur's conquests after the defeat of Lucius.

Despite some uncertainty about the range of materials which influenced the *Morte Arthure* poet, it would appear that his story is substantially that derived from the twelfth-century pseudo-historical tradition of Geoffrey of Monmouth, Wace and Layamon. But consideration of those narratives suggests that the structure I have described is the poet's own contribution to the traditional story and a key to the meaning with which he has invested the account of Arthur's fall. The first of the differentiating figures, the emissaries from Lucius (section I), is clearly enough derived from the chronicles: Geoffrey mentions twelve anonymous envoys, Wace twelve anonymous elders, and Layamon twelve anonymous knights. But only Layamon uses messengers at subsequent narrative turning points: in *Brut* an anonymous knight meets Arthur in France and brings word of the giant's ravages, and, following the victory over Lucius, another anonymous knight is introduced to tell of Modred's treason. While John Finlayson may be correct in his conclusion that Wace's *Le Roman de Brut* was the primary source for *Morte Arthure,* Layamon's *Brut* may have contributed more than hitherto has been suspected to the structural design of the fourteenth-century poem. But the *Morte Arthure* poet seems to have exploited what was only potential in Layamon's work. He first substituted a Templar for Layamon's anonymous knight (section II), and then extended the pattern of demarcation, adding the messengers from the Marshall of France to mark the beginning of warfare with Lucius (section III). In the following two sections (IV and V)—which are the poet's own contribution to the traditional story—he continued the pattern of demarcating features, and, in the final section (VI), substituted for Layamon's second anonymous messenger the dramatic encounter with Sir Cradok.

In this reading of the poem, the *Morte Arthure* poet's sense of structure is revealed in his expansion, intensification, and modification of narrative features inherited from the chronicle tradition, and his sole departure from his carefully developed narrative scheme (the substitution of

Arthur's council at the beginning of the fourth section) assumes even greater significance by calling special attention to that section which is currently a focus of controversy in *Morte Arthure* criticism. As John Finlayson has observed, his interpretation of the poem differs markedly from that of William Matthews on the issue of whether Arthur's wars are progressively unlawful from the beginning of the poem or whether they become unlawful only after the victory over Lucius. Citing medieval theories of warfare, Finlayson has argued that Arthur's attack on Metz is the turning point in the poem, and the structural design of the poem supports Finlayson's interpretation: in section IV Arthur's wars become unlawful, and the variation in the delineating device signals that change. Thus both intrinsic and extrinsic criteria establish the pivotal nature of this fourth section of the poem.

This structural analysis of the narrative design raises another significant question: whether we should accept any generic identifications arising from thematic interpretations which ignore or depreciate the structural design of the poem. The *Morte Arthure* poet wrote with a distinctive sense of structure unique in comparison to the twelfth-century chronicle treatments of the story but quite consistent with characteristics of late fourteenth-century Ricardian poetry. The undeniable exuberance and expansiveness of the narrative should not blind us to the carefully structured episodic design which encapsulated the poet's vision of Arthur's fall. (pp. 310-17)

> *James L. Boren, "Narrative Design in the Alliterative 'Morte Arthure',"* in Philological Quarterly, *Vol. 56, No. 3, Summer, 1977, pp. 310-19.*

Karl Heinz Göller   (essay date 1981)

[*In the following essay, Göller examines depictions of war, allusions to contemporary issues, and the use of literary conventions in* Morte Athure, *contending that the work is essentially an "anti-romance." All text citations, unless otherwise indicated, are to Krishna's 1976 edition.*]

The *AMA* [*Alliterative Morte Arthure*] has been classified by literary critics as a romance, an epic, and a *chanson de geste,* as well as a tragedy, an *exemplum* of the virtue of fortitude, and a *Fürstenspiegel.* There are sound arguments for each of these categories, and this alone is proof of the fact that it is impossible to ascribe the poem to a single literary genre. Like many other masterpieces of world literature, the *AMA* defies neat pigeon holing. (p. 15)

A historian [John Barnie in his *War in Medieval English Society,* 1974] recently called the poem 'quite unique in fourteenth-century English romance'. If it could at all be called a romance, it is one with a very peculiar twist to it. The *AMA* has outgrown its genre historically. While still clinging to its traditional framework, stock characters and themes, it has become its own opposite. This is particularly evident in the light of its contemporary near relation, the so-called stanzaic *Morte Arthur,* with its love story and pure romance character. When compared with works of this kind, the *AMA* can and should be called an anti-romance. This term, of course, is not meant to designate a new literary genre, an undertaking which would be more than difficult. Even the problem of defining romance, with its immense spectrum of applications, has never been satisfactorily solved. Suffice it to say that 'romance' is generally regarded as [according to the *Shorter Oxford Dictionary*] 'a fictitious narrative . . . of which the scene and incidents are very remote from those of ordinary life.'

In the case of the *AMA* the figures and events are taken from a literary tradition which was at the time and even is today connected with what could be called prototypical romance. But this is only a very thin veneer, a kind of historical drapery, which—for large portions of the poem—is insufficient to disguise the contemporaneity of the main characters and their actions. Since Neilson ['*Huchown of the Awle Ryale' the Alliterative Poet*, 1902] there has been general agreement that in the *AMA* familiar literary figures are used to represent contemporary rulers and the problems of the time; the degree and scope of this reciprocal relationship, however, have remained controversial.

At the same time, familiar literary genres of romance are criticised or even satirised, having become nothing more than empty clichés, widely divorced from any historical or contemporary reality. The poet seems particularly interested in unmasking the trivialised and romanticised form of literary portrayal of war and heroism, by confronting it with the moral and physical results of real war. Thus the *AMA* is in two respects an anti-romance: it ushers in personalities and problems of contemporary life in the costume of distant centuries; but even more important, it destroys commonplaces of chivalry and knightly warfare through inversion, irony and black humour.

The figures and events are traditionally familiar but they have undergone a sea-change. Arthur is still the admired head of state, but is shown to be morally corrupted by his growing power, Lancelot is no longer the most prominent and best knight of the Round Table; instead he is placed on a par with Valyant, Ewayn and Loth, and there is no love intrigue with Guinevere. Gawain is the leading figure among the knights, but he is far from being a perfect model of knighthood. He is arrogant and frivolous, acts rashly and impetuously, usurps command and oversteps his power. His metaphors are hardly courteous, for he promises to subdue the enemy to a state of meekness likened to the 'bouxom' willingness of a bride in bed (2858).

In the *AMA,* the opening boudoir scene of the stanzaic *Morte Arthur* (Arthur and Guinevere lie in bed, chatting about bygone adventures) has been replaced by the battlefield. A tragic parting before the king leaves for war marks Arthur's relationship with his wife. Guinevere in her turn wickedly conspires with Mordred and even bears him two children although she is usually represented as barren. Mordred is no simple traitor. He regards himself as a rightful pretender to the crown; in the final battle he changes his arms accordingly and wears the three leopards of England.

In the *AMA* the reality of war in all its gruesomeness and the contemporaneity of the fourteenth century clash heavily with the world of romance. Nearly all the stereotype

scenes of courtly literature are recognisable, but they are embedded in new contexts and ridiculed either by comic-ironic parody or by confrontation with the historical reality of the fourteenth century. Indeed the burden of a topical allusion weighs so heavily that Arthur appears almost as a contemporary fourteenth century king.

Even those episodes which up to the present have been seen as pure romance, e.g. the Priamus episode (2501-2715), achieve, by virtue of the poet's subtle use of irony and inversion of traditional motifs, the very opposite effect. Romance is negated and even reduced to absurdity. Of overall importance is the poet's attitude towards war. Two souls dwell in his breast, for he is simultaneously a patriot and an opponent of war—at times holding positions that would nowadays be called pacifist. This dichotomy is responsible for the ambivalence of the poem in matters Arthurian. The king is at one and the same time the greatest ruler that has ever lived on earth and yet a doomed soul.

The overall message of the poem can only be seen against the background of Arthurian tradition as a whole. From the very beginning the figure of King Arthur had strong political implications. This was already true of Geoffrey of Monmouth's *Historia Regum Britanniae,* which saw King Arthur as an incarnation of the idea of the Empire. Most English kings after the conquest have regarded themselves as lawful heirs and successors of King Arthur. An entire series of kings had no objections against being styled as *Arturus redivivus.* Henry III led his troops under the Arthurian banner of the dragon. Edward I was an 'Arthurian enthusiast' and held jousts and tournaments which he called 'Table Rounds'. The same is true of Edward III, the founder of the Order of the Garter:

> [he] toke pleasure to newe reedefy the Castell of Wyndsore, the whiche was begonne by kyng Arthure; and ther firste beganne the Table Rounde, wherby sprange the fame of so many noble knightes throughout all the worlde.

John Lydgate called Henry V 'of knyhthode Lodesterre, . . . Able to stond among the worthy nyne', which recalls King Arthur as the most famous of the Worthies. Particularly the Tudor and Stuart kings were connected with King Arthur. Henry VII called his first-born son Arthur. In the seventeenth century the designation 'Arthurian' was practically synonymous with 'royalist'. Thus Arthurian literature always had a political cast, whatever the period. It follows that during the fourteenth century and after, the audience of the *AMA* would have expected topical allusions to the reigning English monarch.

Thus it also seems quite likely that Arthurian poets, and among them almost certainly the author of the *AMA,* used their work as a vehicle for political instruction, as a 'mirror for magistrates' or *Fürstenspiegel.* This should not tempt us to read the *AMA* as a *roman à clef,* or to draw a one-to-one relationship between specific historical personalities and major figures in the poem.

The poem is a literary work which illustrates parallels and analogies to historical persons and events by means of an imaginative story (parable). The events of the Hundred

Years War obviously form the background of the poem, but fourteenth century disillusionment with royal war and its consequences has been transferred to a faraway and fictitious world usually having romantic associations, and therefore well suited to make the miseries of the age stand out in relief.

Even as early as the beginning of the fourteenth century, chroniclers regarded the idea of a society based on chivalry as no more than a fiction. The ideals of the poets and the moralists became more and more remote from reality, and, conversely, the code of chivalry was increasingly reduced to a mere alibi—to a literary bauble and a social game. Thus in 1344 King Edward III vowed to found an Order of knights based on the code of honour of King Arthur and his Round Table, although, only two years earlier, French propaganda had accused him of raping the Countess of Salisbury in a most uncourteous fashion.

In various passages historical persons and events are reflected in a recognisable way. Thus the author mentions that Arthur holds a large council before his decision to wage war, just as English kings were accustomed to do. The response of Arthur's councillors in this matter is described in a way similar to political discussions in England preceding the Hundred Years War, where the idea of war was greeted enthusiastically.

The mention of the Commons (274) is of particular note in this connection. Arthur refuses to recognise Lucius' demand for tribute because the alleged rights of this Roman Emperor cannot be based on treaties with English kings; on the contrary, they have been granted the Romans by the 'comons': They 'couerd it of comons, as cronicles telles.' (274) The word *comons,* in this context, refers to the representatives of the shires and the boroughs. Thus English parliamentary history is reflected here. During the fourteenth century the commons gained more and more power over king and nobles in the approval of tax levies—not, of course, without resistance on the part of the king. This is also evident in King Arthur's incriminating remark on the commons, which must be seen as a reflex of the tensions between the king and nobility on the one hand and the commons on the other.

Further details support the conclusion that the poet used concrete events of the fourteenth century to give the work a contemporary veneer. Thus he states that Arthur's ceremonial sword Clarent was kept in Wallingford Castle, a place which is not mentioned anywhere else in Arthurian literature. There may be no traditional connection of Arthur (or Guinevere) with Wallingford, but there certainly is one with the royal family, since it belonged to the Black Prince from 1337 onwards. Various ladies of the royal house were quartered in Wallingford Castle during the fourteenth century, as for instance Edward III's mother Isabella; the wife of the Black Prince, Joan of Kent; and Richard II's second wife, Isabella of France. It is therefore not surprising that Guinevere, King Arthur's wife, is connected with Wallingford in the poem. Arthur's wardrobe was located there, and it was in this castle that Guinevere took unlawful possession of Arthur's sword Clarent and passed it to Mordred.

A similar connection to historical events can be seen in the cryptic formulation of the poet that the Duchess of Brittany who had been abducted by the giant of Mont St Michel is a relative of Arthur's wife ('thy wyfes cosyn', 864). Geoffrey and Wace refer to the giant's having ravished Helen, the niece of Arthur's kinsman, Howel. Layamon describes the abducted lady as the daughter of Howel, a nobleman of Brittany. It is highly probable that the poet of the *AMA* is alluding to the Duchess of Brittany and that the contemporary audience would have interpreted his words as an allusion. She is referred to as the king's 'wyfes cosyn' and the poet emphasises this relationship by the special tag, 'knowe it if þe lykez.' (864). Neilson tried to establish a relationship between Philippa of Hainault, Edward III's wife, and Jean de Montfort, one of the claimants to the Duchy of Brittany, but he had to admit that 'Pedigrees are troublesome things, and I do not profess them.' Neilson overlooked the fact that there were two claimants to the Duchy in the fourteenth century. The problem of succession in Brittany was a matter of bitter dispute which marked the beginning of the wars between France and England. In the eyes of the French, Jeanne de Penthièvre was the true Duchess of Brittany and she was actually related to Philippa by her marriage to Charles de Blois. Edward III supported Jean de Montfort, while Philip, king of France, went to the aid of Jeanne de Penthièvre. The poet's explicit reference to the Duchess of Brittany as a relative of Arthur's wife is probably an indication that he intended to allude to Edward III's involvement in Brittany.

The detailed description of warfare in the *AMA* is a significant feature with a close connection to the historical background of the period. Contemporary methods of waging war are recognisable in a great number of passages. Thus, for instance, Arthur's tactics in the battle of Sessoyne have been viewed as parallels to the commands and the strategy of Edward III at the battle of Crécy, for instance the development of bowmen, which in the period was both revolutionary and decisive for the outcome of a battle. Some passages have given rise to speculation that Arthur had his knights dismount, as Edward had done at the battle of Crécy. Similarities have also been seen in the battle-array of Arthur's troops. The great sea battle at the end of the poem has been compared to the sea battle of Winchelsea, at which Edward conquered a Spanish fleet. The author of the *AMA* says quite unexpectedly that Spaniards ('Spanyolis', 3700) went overboard, when he should have spoken of the Danes who were Mordred's mariners (3610, 3694). These, in turn, have been associated with the Danish plunderers who ravaged the English coast during the Hundred Years War.

The poet of the *AMA* gives evidence of his knowledge of the martial laws of his time. The conditions under which the Roman ambassadors are guaranteed their safety and granted free passage are much the same as those given to historical embassies during the fourteenth century. When Arthur promises the Duchess of Lorraine a dowry for herself and her children from the revenues of the estates of her husband, who himself will have to remain a prisoner until the end of his life, he is implementing a common practice of the time (3088-9). This is very similar to the situation which arose after Edward III had given his daughter away in marriage to Enguerrand de Coucy in return for his promise of absolute loyalty. As a dowry the couple were given a number of estates in England. When Coucy went over to the French king in 1379, Isabella was given his English estates to provide for her and her children.

The personal names of the figures also remind the reader of historical personages. Among the companions of Gawain are men called Montagu ('Mownttagus', 3773). This family played a dominant rôle during the reigns of all three Edwards. William Montagu, second earl of Salisbury, fought at the battles of Crécy and Poitiers and was one of the original Knights of the Garter. In conclusion it can be said that there is a close relationship between historical persons and events and their reflection in the poem.

In addition to these direct allusions to figures and events, which were more or less undisguised and thus easily recognisable to a contemporary audience, there are indirect allusions and references which are communicated by means of irony and other literary devices, some of them very sophisticated and subtle. Since appreciation of such passages is only possible in the light of the historical background of the time, modern readers are no longer in a position to recognise the significance of all the veiled or ironic allusions made by the poet.

An obvious example of this kind of irony occurs when Arthur receives the senators from Rome and a banquet is prepared for them which Arthur claims is but 'feble' fare (226). From the exceedingly detailed description of the actual meal served, it is obvious that Arthur's understatement is intentional. The senator says that Arthur is the 'lordlyeste lede þat euer I one lukyde' (138). Through the long list of dishes served at the feast the poet highlights Arthur's weakness for luxury and pomp, a fact of particular significance in the light of contemporary prohibitions. Edward III had passed a law limiting the number of courses with the object of reducing expenditure on rich food: 'no man, of what estate or condition soever he be, shall cause himself to be served in his house or elsewhere, at dinner, meal, or supper, or at any other time, with more than two courses, and each mess of two sorts of victuals at the utmost, be it of flesh or fish, with the common sorts of pottage, without sauce or other sort of victuals . . . '. In the light of this Statute, the king's banquet was highly immoderate and even illegal, an allusion which a contemporary audience would most certainly have understood. Almost the same meal is put on the Waster's table in *Wynnere and Wastoure,* so that there can be little doubt that the king, be it Arthur or Edward, was considered a glutton and a waster *par excellence.*

The poet's descriptions of the king's rich dress are in all likelihood a form of covert irony intended to reveal his disapproval of the sumptious fashions of the time. Although King Edward himself had passed one law in 1336 and a second one in 1363 relating to 'the outrageous and excessive apparel of divers people against their estate and degree to the great destruction and impoverishment of all the land', he failed to moderate his own dress. The Monk of Malmesbury criticised this extravagant fashion in his *Chronicle,* denouncing it as more fit for women than men.

After Arthur's dream of the Wheel of Fortune, there is a detailed description of his marvellous clothes. The poet admires them only on a superficial level. After Arthur's fall from the Wheel, when he has been told to repent, they appear in a negative light in comparison with those of the pilgrim, Cradoke, who scathingly comments to Arthur, whom he does not recognise: whoever you think you are, for all your rich clothes and finery, you cannot stop me from going on my pilgrimage to Rome, despite the war that is going on (cf. 3492-6).

A strange comparison between war and pilgrimage runs in the form of an undercurrent through the whole work. At the beginning of the poem, Arthur's knights all swear by the vernicle, the kerchief of St Veronica, that they will wage war in Italy and kill Lucius. Obviously there is a connection between Italy and St Veronica's veil because it was displayed in St Peter's at Rome. At the same time the vernicle was the symbol of those who made the pilgrimage to Rome. The overt irony of the vernicle motif lies in the fact that Arthur's knights all swear a sacred oath, as if they were going on a pilgrimage, but their true intent is slaughter.

In the light of Cradoke's later mention of a pilgrimage to Rome despite war, and in view of the irony of the sham-pilgrimage in the episode of Mont St Michel, topical allusions seem highly probable, e.g. to the exposition of Veronica's veil in 1350, or to the fact that King Edward III forbade his subjects to go to Rome for the Jubilee because of the war.

> **"In the alliterative *Morte Arthure* the reality of war in all its gruesomeness and the contemporaneity of the fourteenth century clash heavily with the world of romance."**
>
> —*Karl Heinz Göller*

In spite of what has been said by Benson [in his *Malory's 'Morte Darthur',* 1976] concerning the relationship of romance and reality in the fifteenth century, it is safe to say that the idea of warfare based on chivalric laws was recognised as outdated by the fourteenth century. War had developed its own laws which were no longer compatible with the lofty sentiments of idealistic dreamer-poets.

The author of the *AMA* is certainly not one of them as becomes evident in his conscious departure from the traditional motifs, stylistic devices and stereotypes of classical and post-classical Arthurian romance, whenever these stand in the way of his intention to expose and even *explode* the myths of romance. He makes use of older literary traditions, e.g. the chanson de geste, in which he apparently sensed the presence of a kindred spirit. An outward sign of this is his use of the alliterative long line, which differs from that found in other *Arthurian* works of the alliterative revival.

Even the criteria of language, e.g. vocabulary, metre, and stylistic devices, seem intended to convey a certain message. This is true even if the alliterative mode was not chosen to express resentment against the court of London and its French bias, as has been suggested. The alliterative long line is an unsuitable vehicle for the gentler tone of the typical romance. For the same reasons the author has abandoned the *aventure* structure which is an essential feature of other Arthurian prose and verse romances. Only two episodes of this kind remain, and they must be completely redefined, namely Arthur's battle with the Giant of Mont St Michel (840-1221) and the Priamus episode (2501-2715).

The battle of Arthur with the giant of Mont St Michel has been called [by J. P. Oakden in his *Alliterative Poetry in Middle English,* 1930-5] a 'purely romantic element in the story'. It is certainly the poet's major expansion of the episode as recounted by Geoffrey, Wace and Layamon and is an entertaining mock *aventure* which serves something of the purpose of the inversion or even parody of a knightly combat. There is the traditional setting, a *locus amoenus,* Arthur's arming, and the romance situation of a damsel in distress to be rescued. But neither the damsel, nor the giant are true to orthodox romance. The giant is a preposterously grotesque monster whose body is a weird conglomeration of parts drawn from twelve different animals, ranging from a boar to a badger. Obscenity was taboo in medieval courtly literature, yet the poet describes the giant's unshapely loins and does not omit the fact that he was not wearing breeches, reminding us of the devils in medieval mystery plays. In the fight Arthur severs this 'myx's' (cf. 989) genitals with his sword. After a rough-and-tumble wrestling match which is very far removed from chivalric battle, he eventually succeeds in subduing his opponent. Arthur does not even strike the final and fatal blow himself. Instead he asks Bedever to stab the giant to the heart.

The damsel is no less a personage than the Duchess of Brittany herself whom the giant abducted while she was out riding near Rennes (853). The duchess in the poem is not rescued in true Arthurian spirit, and the poet spares us no details when he explains that the giant 'slewe hir vnslely and slitt hir to þe nauyll'. (979). The battle with the giant of Mont St Michel is certainly a very twisted 'romantic element in the story'. Arthur's humour and irony, the emphasis on bawdy and grotesqueness, all this turns the episode into a burlesque *aventure.*

As far as the Priamus episode is concerned, the poet has set it between two grim battles, and the result is what may be called "structural irony.' His purpose is obvious. He wants to highlight the frivolity and triviality of knightly combat in order to use it as a foil for the brutality of war. In the episode, even the wound that Gawain inflicts upon Priamus is highly fantastic and bears no comparison with those of the battlefield. Gawain splits the knight's shield in two and wounds him so seriously that his liver is exposed to the sunlight (2560-1). Gawain, on the other hand,

has no drop of blood left in his veins (2697). When Gawain and Priamus clash swords, flames flash from their weapons and their helmets. Priamus' and Gawain's wounds are treated with the magic water of Paradise which Priamus carries with him in a golden phial and the knight is as fit as a fish ('fische-halle', 2709) after four hours.

By bringing romantic fiction into a strongly realistic context, the author is confronting the audience with the idea that chivalric jousting was nothing more than a ridiculous game. Finlayson seems to have had something similar in mind when he spoke [Modern Philology 61 (1963)] of an implied 'detrimental judgement on this particular form of chivalric action.' By inserting this romantic *aventure,* the poet relativises the whole concept of romance, setting it in a world of reality. Romance as a literary genre is ironised by its use as a foil juxtaposed to hard facts.

But not only structural irony is instrumental in debunking the clichés of romance; the poet's descriptional mannerisms also serve purposes which differ greatly from those of the usual portrayal of knightly combat. The way which the poet chose to describe the actual fighting on the battlefield evokes disgust in the reader today. The hideous details have little to do with knightly *courtoisie.* War historians have pointed out that battle strategy had basically changed in the fourteenth century, and that chivalric single combat had been replaced by mass battle in which the old norms of conduct barely played a part. Revolting and disgusting injuries to the human body are described in detail. When Sir Floridas kills Feraunt's kinsman, a mixture of entrails and excrement falls at the horse's feet (2780-3). The liver and lungs of a foe remain on the lance when it is pulled out of his body (2168). The ground is red and slippery with the blood of the dead. The dying lie torn open, while others writhe in agony on their horses (2143-7).

It is notable that the author seems to have been mildly obsessed with wounds 'below the belt'. As has already been noted, Arthur enrages the Giant of Mont St Michel by slicing his genitals off. When he kills the Viscount of Valence, the place of injury is described by using the pubic region as a point of orientation, even though it seems superfluous to do so: The spear penetrates the short ribs one span above the genitals (2060-1). In view of this little idiosyncrasy of the poet's, mention of a knight named 'Ienitall' (2112) need not necessarily be regarded as a slip of the pen in want of emendation. Many editors have proposed corrections, and Krishna changes 'Ienitall' to 'Ionathal'. Most likely 'Ienitall' was a highly telling name, or a Freudian slip on the part of either the author, or the scribe.

The terrible descriptions of death are not to be found in the sources or forerunners of the *AMA,* although Old Norse Tales, French *chansons de geste* and English chronicles (e.g. Layamon's *Brut*) are not exactly squeamish when describing combat and bloodshed. The purpose of such descriptions in the *AMA* seems evident. Obviously they enhance the heroism of Arthur's men. The greater the opponent, the worse a death he deserves. Revenge mobilises the knights' last atom of strength. In literature as on the battlefield, the death of a foe was a source of pleasure for a fourteenth-century knight. In his *Chronicle*, Geoffrey le Baker of Swinbroke describes how the Black Prince, then a sixteen-year old boy, won his first honours at Crécy, serving as an example of chivalry to his comrades by brutally killing the enemy.

The audience is, however, confronted not only with the heroism of Arthur's men, but also with their tragic death. Lines 2146-52 are a lament for all those killed in war: Fair faces are disfigured, and bloodstained dying men lie sprawling on the ground; others, mortally wounded, are carried off by their galloping mounts. Gawain, 'the gude man of armes' (3858), is killed by Mordred, who stabs a knife into his brain (3856-7). Sir Lionel's skull is split open, the wound is as large as the breadth of a hand (2229). Sir Kay is killed from behind by a cowardly knight who pierces his flanks with a spear, breaking open his bowels and spilling his entrails (2171-6).

One further feature which, among others, is responsible for the anti-romantic character of the **AMA** is the poet's peculiar brand of humour which at times approaches a form similar to what we now call black humour. This term is applied to a technique in which 'grotesque or horrifying elements are sharply juxtaposed with humorous or farcical ones' [according to K. Beckson and A. Ganz's *Literary Terms: A Dictionary,* 1975], a literary feature that is by no means a modern phenomenon. As B. J. Friedman put it: 'I have a hunch Black Humor has probably always been around, always will.' According to Mathew Winston, who draws a line between the absurd and grotesque shades of the technique, the grotesque form of black humour is 'obsessed with the human body, with the ways in which it can be distorted, separated into its component parts, mutilated, and abused.'

It is this very obsession with the human body and the ways it can be mutilated and distorted which forms one of the characteristics of the poet's narrative. A farcical element is introduced when the mutilation is ludicrously improbable. When Arthur kills the Egyptian prince who has slain Sir Kay, he first cuts both him and his horse clean in two, in a vertical direction, disembowelling the horse (2197-2203). Then Arthur in his rage meets another foe whom he strikes in two, this time horizontally. There is a comically grotesque picture of the man's torso toppling to the ground, while his horse gallops away with the lower half of his body. This is followed by the ironical, even farcical comment of the narrator: 'Of þat hurte, alls I hope, heles he neuer' (2204-9).

Several of the so-called tags contain snide comments by the narrator, which relativise the gruesome descriptions. It is certainly ridiculous to say that a knight 'rode no more' after a spear has pierced his heart and he has fallen dead to the ground (2792-5). Another knight is described as speechless (2063) after a spear has pierced him, and splent and spleen stick to the spear (2061). Lucius is injured by a lance piercing his paunch. His stomach is decorated with the pennant of the lance, while the tip of the weapon juts out half a foot beyond his back (2073-80), and yet he is not dead. One hundred and fifty lines later Lucius reappears, obviously still alive, with the lance presumably still through him (2220).

When Arthur kills the giant Golapas, he first cuts him clean in two at the knees, and there is a grotesque picture of his upper half toppling down and a pair of legs standing on their own (2133-9). This is the same kind of description as that used by Heller in *Catch-22* when Kid Sampson is sliced in two by the propeller of a plane: ' . . . and then there were just Kid Sampson's two pale, skinny legs, still joined by strings somehow at the bloody truncated hips, standing stock-still on the raft for what seemed a full minute or two before they toppled over backward into the water finally with a faint, echoing splash and turned completely upside down so that only the grotesque toes and the plaster-white soles of Kid Sampson's feet remained in view.'

Arthur calls out to Golapas in a grimly ironic tone that he'll make him even more handsome, and with that he cuts the giant's head off his torso—a macabre jest. The poet's comment is an ironic use of a proverb 'Thus he settez on seuen with his sekyre knyghttez' (2131); to 'set on seven' is an allusion to the creation of the world in seven days, and the phrase was transferred to men doing wonders and miracles. To compare slaughter with God's creation stops just short of blasphemy.

Arthur himself has a weird, macabre sense of humour. After his victory against Lucius, he has the bodies of the emperor and of sixty senators and other knights embalmed and wrapped in silk and then in lead to preserve them. The coffins are strapped on camels and other mounts; the emperor's coffin is put on an elephant, a macabre bow to his higher rank. The king then calls an assembly saying to the captives 'Here are the chests with the taxes you wanted. This is the only tribute Rome will get from me' (2341-7). Arthur's word seems a grim joke, but one in keeping with the times. Froissart describes a similar form of cynicism in his *Chronicle:* 'Than the prince sayd to two of his squyers and to thre archers, Sirs, take the body of this knyght on a targe and bere him to Poycters, and present him fro me to the cardynall of Pyergourt, and say howe I salute hym by that token.' In the poem, Cradoke, the pilgrim, says he is going to Rome to get his pardon from the Pope, war or no war, and that he will probably come across Arthur who is waging war there, that 'noble' Lord with his 'awfull' knights (cf. 3493-3502). On the surface he utters admiring words for his king, but there is a second layer of meaning in which he criticises him for waging war, and thus stopping pilgrims from going to Rome. A contemporary audience would have appreciated the allusion to war versus pilgrimage. Finlayson talked [in his 'Introduction' to a 1967 London edition of **Morte Arthure**] of Arthur's 'just' war turning into an 'unjust' one. There can be no doubt that the poet is saying that *every* war is unjust. It is not only the knights on the battlefield who lose their lives, but innocent people who suffer as a result. For the civilian population, plundering and pillaging are martyrdom. For the heroic aggressor, war is glory. In his *Tree of Battles* (1387), Honoré Bonet utters his discomfort and displeasure at the suffering of the people:

> My heart is full of grief to see and hear of the great martyrdom that they inflict without pity or mercy on the poor labourers and others who are incapable of ill in word or thought; who toil for

men of all estates; from whom Pope, kings, and
all the lords in the world receive, under God,
what they eat and drink and what they wear.
And no man is concerned for them . . .

There was at least one who cared: the author of the *AMA,*
who says that it is the 'comouns of þe countré, clergye and
oþer, Þat are noghte coupable þerin, ne knawes noght in
armez' who suffer (1316-17).

At the very beginning of the poem, the problem of how
to justify war from a moral point of view is discussed. But
although Arthur points out that legal justification for war
is necessary, the Council disregards Arthur's reasoning
and revenge is their only interest. Arthur is swayed by his
knights and makes no further mention of the legal problem, thinking back on his own fame, honour and riches
which he attributes to his men's heroism. So war begins
and the black side of battle is skilfully portrayed by the
poet with subtle change of perspective. In the first half of
the poem, the author presents himself during long passages as one of Arthur's men. He also gives us a bird's eye
view of the battlefield as seen by the victor. The apparent
patriot talks of 'oure cheualrouse men' (1880, 2989), 'our
lele knyghttez' (2998), 'oure valyant biernez' (1958) and
uses other admiring epithets.

Morte Arthure.

An alliterative Poem of the 14th Century

from

The Lincoln MS.

Written by

Robert of Thornton.

Edited, with Introduction, Notes, and Glossary, by

Mary Macleod Banks

Longmans, Green, and Co.,
39 Paternoster Row, London
New York and Bombay
1900

Title page of Mary Macleod Banks's edition of Morte Arthure.

From Arthur's siege of Metz onwards, the author changes
his position and is less willing to identify himself with Arthur's men. In his final lament for Arthur it is characteristic of his attitude towards 'his' sovereign that he no longer
speaks of 'our king' but of 'this comlyche Kynge' (3218)
and says bluntly 'Thus endis Kyng Arthure' (4342), with
no romantic idea of his return from Avalon.

In describing Arthur's war in Tuscany the poet uses such
words as 'wastys' (3156), 'vnsparely' (3160) and 'dispetouslye' (3159) which are an obvious indication of his criticism of the wastefulness of war. It is Arthur who causes
misery: 'wandrethe he wroghte' (3157) and he 'turmentez
þe pople' (3153). Lines 3032-43 are similar to a description
of a *chevauchée* in Edward's reign where villages were pil-
laged and burnt and everything devastated. The poet exclaims: 'The pyne of þe pople was peté for to here' (3043).
After this brutal assault, the common people are seen
streaming out of the town into the woods, helpless refugees clutching their goods and chattels (3068-71). In
Metz, ministers, hospitals, churches and chapels are
struck down and razed to the ground, and of course, houses and inns as well (3038-42). When the city of Como is
besieged, the poet mentions poor people and herdsmen
who are leading the swine to pasture (3120-1). Arthur's
men slay everyone in their path (3126). Eventually, all
upper Italy is laid waste. Here, as in many other countries,
Arthur 'has schedde myche blode and schalkes distroyede,
Sakeles, in cirquytrie' (3398-9).

The *AMA* poet was not alone in his condemnation of war.
Gower, Wycliff, Brinton, Langland, Chaucer and Hoc-
cleve are some of the names associated with the attack on
war in the second half of the fourteenth century. Gower
bitterly criticised the aristocrats for their greed and covetousness: 'It is nothing to you if the downtrodden people
bewail their sufferings, provided that the general misfortune brings in money to you.'

The discussion was by no means restricted to court circles
in London. The *AMA,* among other works, is proof of the
fact that wider circles in England had become involved in
the concern about the evils of war. Philosophers and theologians had fully recgonised the devastating consequences
of war. They were aware of the misery it inflicted on the
common people. And yet they were still convinced that
war was unavoidable because of man's inherent imperfection. For this reason it was not war itself that was called
into question, but the justness or unjustness of individual
conflicts. In numerous publications legal scholars attempted to codify the laws of war, and in so doing
achieved such widespread recognition in Europe that their
work can be regarded as the beginning of international
martial law.

Wycliffites, however, adopted a progressively more radical
position in regard to the question of war. Several of Wycliff's pupils and followers voiced the opinion that war
was sinful, whatever the reason behind it. Thus they concluded that war was unjustifiable—both from the secular
and from the spiritual point of view. This revolutionary
doctrine was made public in the famous Twelve Conclusions, which were nailed on the doors of Westminster Hall

and St Paul's while Parliament was in session (1395). The most important points were as follows:

> þe tende conclusiun is, þat manslaute be batayle or pretense lawe of rythwysnesse for temporal cause or spirituel with outen special reuelaciun is expres contrarious to þe newe testament, þe qwiche is a lawe of grace and ful of mercy. [. . .] But þe lawe of mercy, þat is þe newe testament, forbad al mannisslaute: *in euangelio dictum est antiquis, Non occides* [in the gospel it was said to them of old time, Thou shalt not kill; cf. Matt. 5, 12]. And [. . .] knythtis, þat rennen to hethnesse to geten hem a name in sleinge of men, geten miche maugre [displeasure] of þe king of pes; for þe mekenesse and suffraunce oure beleue was multiplied, and fythteres and mansleeris Ihesu Cryst hatith and manasit. *Qui gladio percutit, gladio peribit* [all they that take the sword shall perish with the sword; cf. Matt. 26, 52].

Such partial statements, which from the point of view of the twentieth century would be styled pacifist, were regarded as a shocking provocation. Together with other Lollard tenets, they were condemned as heretic by the Pope and the English bishops.

It is probable that the author of the *AMA* was familiar with such ideas, although he was not a Lollard himself. From the very beginning of his poem he is critical of war and all things pertaining to it. In this respect he is unorthodox for his time. The poet exemplifies this message through the figures of Arthur and Gawain. Both live by the sword and die by the sword, and thus fulfil the Biblical passage quoted in the Xth *Conclusion:* 'They that take the sword shall perish with the sword.' At the same time, the fate of King Arthur is a warning example for the medieval concept of *contrapasso:* 'per que quis peccat, per idem punitur et ipse.' ('Wherewith one sins, therewith shall he be punished.')

The *AMA* must be viewed as a kind of *Fürstenspiegel*, one not necessarily directed towards a historically identifiable ruler. It is a typological admonishment to every monarch involved in war. Arthur, in his pride and arrogance, has raised the banner of the dragon, meaning war, and has shed the blood of the innocent. The philosopher tells him: 'Thow has schedde myche blode and schalkes distroyede, Sakeles, in cirquytrie.' (3398-9).

It is one of the unsolved problems of this puzzling work, that the criticism levelled against unjust wars does not diminish the poet's enthusiasm for the description of war. The subject fascinated him, not only because he was more than familiar with the rich tradition of English heroic poetry. And yet all these heroic and war-like deeds are, in his opinion, proof of human iniquity and vainglory. Just as St Augustine admired the achievements of the great pagan philosophers, so, too, the poet of the *AMA* admired the war-like deeds of Arthur and his knights. Nevertheless he also views them as being 'awke' (13), and therefore *praeter viam* and sinful.

In conclusion we can say that the poet has used the conventions of romance, and the traditional personages and themes to present the problems of his own age. The *AMA*

is a kind of death knell, a lament on the ideal of knightly ethos which is unmasked as a fiction incompatible with the reality of war and with Christian ethics. But King Arthur will not rise again in this world, for war has felled him like any other mortal. The subject of the entire poem is the Death of Arthur, and as such it is also entitled *Morte Arthure* in two places: at the beginning and end of the manuscript. Much like Henry II, the poet evidently wanted to see Arthur safely in his grave, and therewith refute the myth of Arthur's second coming.

But even Chrétien de Troyes had voiced the premonition that Arthur's fame would last forever: 'I agree with the opinion of the Bretons that his name will live on for evermore.'

In a very similar way the poet has the philosopher say to King Arthur:

> 'This sall in romance be redde with ryall knyghttes,
> Rekkenede and renownde with ryotous kynges,
> And demyd on Domesdaye, for dedis of armes,
> For þe doughtyeste þat euer was duéllande in erthe;
> So many clerkis and kynges sall karpe of youre dedis,
> And kepe youre conquestez in cronycle for euer.'
>
> (3440-5)

This statement stands unreconciled beside the *vanitasvanitatum* topos of the poem. Therefore it is by no means incomprehensible, or even illogical, that the scribe affixed the following inscription to the manuscript:

> Hic jacet Arthurus, rex qondam rexque futurus.
>
> (pp. 15-29)

> *Karl Heinz Göller, "Reality Versus Romance: A Reassessment of the 'Alliterative Morte Arthure'," in* The Alliterative Morte Arthure: A Reassessment of the Poem, *edited by Karl Heinz Göller, D. S. Brewer, 1981, pp. 15-29.*

Michael W. Twomey   (essay date 1986)

[*In the following essay, Twomey contrasts the ideals represented by Arthur's Round Table with fourteenth-century civic and ecclesiastical convictions in an examination of Arthur's heroic intentions and the "unjust wars" he waged. Text citations are to Hamel's 1984 edition.*]

Although there is some disagreement whether Arthur's career in the Alliterative *Morte Arthure* [*MA*] is truly tragic, it is generally agreed that his " 'rewthe werkes' " (3453), the unjust wars for which the philosopher chides Arthur when he interprets the dream of Fortune's wheel, begin with the siege of Metz and continue at least until Arthur's conquest of Rome. And although critics hold that during this period Arthur's wars of conquest are unjust, the questions of why they are unjust and of what relation they have to Arthur's final battle, against the treacherous Mordred, so far have been only partially answered. John Finlayson [in *Chaucer und seine Zeit: Symposion für Wal-*

ter F. Schirmer, 1968] and Russell A. Peck [in *The Alliter-ative Tradition in the Fourteenth Century,* edited by Levy and Szarmach, 1981], the first to examine closely Arthur's motives for waging war, have adduced evidence from four-teenth and fifteenth century treatises on chivalry which suggests that Arthur's wars become unjust when they be-come willful. Peck points out that Arthur's conquests begin out of revenge for Kay's death. However, a reading of the poem in the light of legal principles and of laws gov-erning just war, that is to say, from the point of view of civil and ecclesiastical authority, reveals not only the poet's intimate knowledge of the laws of war (these legal details are emphasized in *MA* but not in its sources), but his rich and ironic examination of the ethical problems in-herent in heroic kingship. The literary, chivalric ideal of the Round Table is measured against late fourteenth cen-tury legal and theological ideals of monarchic govern-ment. Because the character of Arthur is presented in a psychologically complex fashion, the transition from just to unjust war which accompanies Arthur's decline is not sudden but gradual. The siege of Metz, regarded as the first of Arthur's unjust wars, is an execution of justice against a contumacious vassal, although Arthur's conduct during it is reckless; on the other hand, because of its un-just motives, even Arthur's battle with Mordred lacks full legal sanction. Given the poet's extensive use of both con-temporary and literary allusion, his knowledge and use of the law should not be surprising. Although he is a deeply engaged man of his times who is morally opposed to un-checked monarchic power, the poet neither descends into polemic nor denies sympathy to his hero.

The action of *MA* is set in motion by Lucius's demand for tribute (86-115, esp. 102-03, 112-15), against which the poet carefully justifies Arthur's title as sovereign and un-derscores the legality of Arthur's war against Rome. Lu-cius claims tribute on the grounds of Britain's subjection to Rome in Julius Caesar's time; moreover, he accuses Ar-thur of treasonous violence against the Roman people. Ar-thur's counterclaim is that his ancestors Belyn and Brenne (MS. T's "and Bawdewyne the thyrde" is disrupted) ruled the Empire for 160 years (!) in succession, and were suc-ceeded by Constantine the Great (271-87). Though con-fusing, Arthur's claim is based upon the line of kings stretching from Hector through Aeneas to Brutus and Uther Pendragon—the Trojan genealogy by which the poet himself, in the poem's closing, reckons Arthur's place in history. This claim is reinforced by the Christianity of Arthur's empire, *imperium* being translated to the Chris-tians at Constantine's conversion. Although Lucius's claim is of greater antiquity because it goes back to Julius Caesar, and although Arthur's father Uther Pendragon did not rule in Rome, Arthur considers himself legal sov-ereign partly on the basis on the concept of *translatio im-perii,* the medieval historical idea that legitimate rulership of the known world had been passed from the Hebrews to the Greeks (or the Trojans) to the Romans and thence to the Christian West. In England the idea was particularly tenacious, since Englishmen saw themselves as descen-dants of Aeneas through the eponymous founder of Brit-ain, Brutus. Thus, when Lucius presses his claim, because Arthur believes that he holds title to his ancestors' lands he has already subdued most of Western Europe (26-51).

Seen in this light, his campaigns south into Italy are not so much conquest as reconquest of rebellious territories.

The poet's frequent use of the epithet "emperor" for Lu-cius allows for the hovering suggestion—perhaps in reflec-tion of the actual complications arising in titular dis-putes—that Lucius's claim has some validity. But the legal evidence beyond Arthur's claims about his right to rule es-tablishes him as a divinely-appointed king. Arthur has been crowned and anointed with chrism (142), two an-cient and important signs of legal kingship. In the four-teenth century, although sacramental consecration had been replaced by less indelible anointment, the ceremony of crown and chrism nevertheless had great constitutional value, since it made the difference between a usurper and a king. Legally, Edward III became king the moment Ed-ward II was deposed, but Henry IV succeeded Richard II as king only when crowned and anointed. The legitimacy of Arthur's status as king is also supported by his position as an heir. In late medieval thinking, the motto "nemo po-test facere se ipsum regem" ["no one can make himself king"] described the theory that kings could only be born, not made. The English legal treatise called Glanville quali-fied this theory with another: that "solus Deus heredem facere potest" ["only God can make an heir"], which meant that the true validation of a king was in the birth of an heir. With God's approval so guaranteed, the coro-nation only confirmed what was already fact and law. Sim-ilarly, canon law maintained that a king assumed his au-thority upon accession, by virtue of his status as an heir, rather than at coronation. In England, precedent for this doctrine was established by Edward I, who ruled with full authority and dated his regnal years from the moment of his accession at the death of Henry III in 1272; he was not crowned until 1274. Arthur's right to rule is therefore di-vinely guaranteed in two ways: first, by Arthur's status as Uther Pendragon's heir; second, by Arthur's coronation and anointment with chrism. Arthur also rules in accor-dance with conciliar advice and consent, which is one of three modes of popular participation in monarchic gov-ernment. Before declaring war on Lucius, he takes council from "lordes of his lygeaunce . . . justicez and juggez and gentill knyghtes" (244, 246), Arthur's closest circle of re-tainers. When one by one they call for war to redress inju-ries done by Roman aggressors, Arthur defers action until he has obtained popular consent from the three estates (337-46, 415-18). As we shall see, the importance of this legal evidence of the king's right to rule is not simply that is justifies Arthur's war against Lucius, but that despite it, Arthur falls, equivocating his right to do battle with Mor-dred; in a sense, at the end of the poem, Arthur takes Lu-cius's place and Mordred Arthur's.

At the beginning of *MA* then, because of his valid claim to the throne and his just exercise of authority, Arthur is in a favorable position for waging just war. By looking closely at when and why Arthur's wars become unjust, it is possible to see that although Arthur has a right to wage war against the Duke of Lorraine, who is a contumacious vassal, and in Lombardy, where his knights were am-bushed, the chief reason that Arthur turns south after de-feating Lucius is *cupiditas* "desire". The battle with the Duke and the siege of Metz are thus ambiguously just and tainted. They are just because the same justifications as for the war against Lucius obtain for them. They are tainted because they are tinged with desire for the beautiful lands of Lorraine and Lombardy. The best way to begin demonstrating this is briefly to examine how the poet applies late medieval laws governing just war to Arthur's campaigns.

Isidore of Seville's definition of the just war (*Etymologiae* 18.1), which was incorporated into Gratian's *Decretum* (pars 2, causa 23, q. 2, c. 1) and canon law generally, was that "Iustum bellum est quod ex praedicto geritur de rebus repetitis aut propulsandorum hostium causa" ["just war is that which is waged on valid authority, either to regain things lost or to drive out invaders"]. Unjust war, on the other hand, "est quod de furore, non de legitima ratione initur. De quo in *Republica* Cicero dicit (3.35): 'Illa iniusta bella sunt quae sunt sine causa suscepta' " ["is what is begun out of passion, not out of lawful reason; about which Cicero says in his *Republic:* 'unjust wars are those which are undertaken without good reason' "]. What constituted a good reason for just war was worked out more specifically later on; of late medieval authorities Raymond of Pennaforte's *Summa de poenitentia* is typical. Here are found five conditions for the just war: 1) war's only object must be self-defense or the protection of property; 2) war may be waged only when no other way of achieving the object can be found; 3) war may be waged only out of a desire for justice, not out of hatred or greed; 4) only laymen may fight in a war—clergymen are forbidden to bear arms; 5) war may be waged only by one who has the authority to do so, such as a sovereign prince or the Roman Church.

Of course, all princes argue that their wars are just. Lucius's argument against Arthur is essentially a claim that Arthur is a rebel guilty of *lèse majesté* and criminal violence against Roman lands and people. Since in Lucius's eyes Arthur is guilty of contumacy, a capital crime, Lucius wishes to wage a legal war in execution of justice, his claim supported by his belief that he is the legitimate Roman Emperor. But if, as seems to be the case, Arthur is legally the sovereign prince of Britain, his war against Lucius is further justified by its meeting all five conditions for just war: 1) it is just with regard to its object because it seeks redress for injury to Arthur's knights and possessions (these wrongs are listed in detail by Arthur's knights before Arthur goes to consult with his parliament, and include rapes, robberies, and ambushes [247-394]); 2) it is just with regard to its cause since it is in self-defense and there is no recourse but to fight; 3) it is just with regard to its intention since in order to re-establish law in the empire Arthur must put down rebellion; 4) it is just with regard to the persons engaged in it because it is fought only by seculars; 5) it is waged on valid authority because Arthur is a sovereign prince.

The justness of Arthur's war against Lucius is demonstrated symbolically in Arthur's single combat with the giant of Mont St. Michel, who foreshadows Lucius and his host. The giant, a tyrant (842, 878, 991), is one of a race of Genoan giants, whom recently Lucius has deployed in the mountains of France (556-61) and whom Arthur's knights encounter later in open battle with Lucius (2889 ff.; cp.

375, 559). Thus, although the giant has prevailed at Mont St. Michel for seven years (846), he is clearly Lucius's man. The giant's status as a tyrant—a legal term for an unjust prince who may legally be opposed—and his crime of cannibalism figuratively suggest Lucius and his predatory offenses against Arthur's lands and people. Appropriately, the giant was " 'engenderde of fendez' " (843), and so has a lineage that stretches back to archetypal Biblical crimes of murder and rebellion. As a giant, he is a descendant of Cain and a member of the race for whose sins God brought down the deluge in Genesis 6. The battle with the giant of Mont St. Michel takes on further significance from its setting: traditionally, St. Michael is the captain of the heavenly host and, in Apoc. 12:7-9, the arch-defender against heavenly treason. Defeating the giant is not a chivalric *aventure* but an important step in just war against Lucius.

Divine approval is an important factor in just war, for open war is judicial combat on a large scale. And since one kind of just war is against pagans who threaten Christian society, the *MA* poet further justifies Arthur's war against Lucius by characterizing Lucius's army as largely made up of heathens, Saracens, and giants (599, 612, 624, 1260, etc.) and by emphasizing, through oaths and prayers, the Christianity of Arthur and his followers (296-99, 308-11, etc.). This reflects a tendency from the thirteenth century on to view just wars legally and morally as crusades. However, the holy-war element in Arthur's campaigns also helps to justify the battle with the Duke of Lorraine, in which Arthur's adversaries are again fiends, apostates, and Saracens. Feraunt is the devil's son (2761), and hence the half-brother of the Genoan giants; Raynalde of Rhodes is "rebell to Criste—/ Peruertede with paynyms þat Cristen persewes" (2785-86); the Duke of Lorraine himself, who rides on a camel (2941), is accompanied by a troop of "paynymes of Pruyslande" (2835); and there are Saracens everywhere, as Priamus warns Gawain (2815-16, cp. 2906, 2974, 2992). As if he were a crusader, Gawain urges his men on with the cry, " 'The fekyll faye sall faile, and falssede be distroyede!' " (2860), and he can be assured of victory even though he is outnumbered thirty to one, ignores Florent's advice to flee the battle, and refuses Priamus's offer of assistance.

The holy-war element in Arthur's campaign against the Duke is complemented by several more down-to-earth legal considerations. Because he is a Roman sympathizer, the Duke is a contumacious vassal, as Arthur alleges shortly before the siege of Metz: " 'The renke rebell has bene vnto my Rownde Table, / Redy aye with Romaynes at ryotte my landes' " (2402-03). The poet calls the Duke's men "renayede wreches" (2913). Arthur's war against the Duke is thus a war to enforce justice on a contumacious vassal, a form of just war. Even though actual warfare was often (perhaps even usually) in violation of the laws of war, Arthur once again demonstrates an exemplary legality at the siege of Metz. Often, the siege began with a demand for surrender. If this was refused, the encamped army might begin the assault on the town. In *MA* there is no time for preliminaries, since the inhabitants of Metz fire vollies of arrows at Arthur's troops as soon as they approach the city (2424-27). The open battle in the suburbs of Metz then legally gives way to assault on the town (2464-81). However, Arthur waits before beginning the assault, sending Florent and Gawain out for provisions, and it is only when they return instead with prisoners from the battle with the Duke that Arthur launches his attack on the town (3032). Although it might seem that instead Arthur ought to give the inhabitants of Metz another opportunity to surrender, he is not legally obligated to do so, since the town has already shown itself guilty of *lèse majesté,* a capital offense, and Arthur's war against Lorraine is not a titular dispute, as was his war against Lucius, but an execution of justice. Once the assault begins no quarter need be given, and since it is up to the commander whether or not to accept terms of surrender, it is merciful of Arthur to accept surrender from the Countess of Crasyn (3044-61), the legality of the surrender being guaranteed by Arthur's receipt of the keys to the city, by which he obtains *seizin* 'legal posession' of it (3064-65). It was widely held that in siege warfare goods might be seized and captives enslaved; but by forbidding his soldiers to harm the inhabitants (3057-59), Arthur is enforcing the law which forbids spoil after surrender. In fact, Arthur goes beyond the law, generously offering reparations which, not incidentally, will also ensure the goodwill of his re-conquered subjects (3072-77). The only persons punished are the Duke and his loyal followers, whom Arthur sends to prison in Dover (3066-67).

Thus far I have tried to show that Arthur's claim to his throne and his conduct of the wars against Lucius and the Duke of Lorraine have sound legal footing. The problem now is to determine when and why Arthur begins to defy the law, since this will demonstrate how legal theory and literary characterization combine in the portrayal of Arthur's tragic decline. Only after the siege of Metz does the transition to unjust war appear sudden and dramatic, for in the attack on Lombardy, which follows the siege of Metz by only a few lines, all the legal justifications for battle, which the poet has thus far been careful to provide, are silently omitted. As far as we know, Como has done Arthur no offense; there is no Lucius-faction hiding there; and since Arthur has already defeated Lucius the city is already his. When Arthur attacks Como, he does so as if it were a rebellious town, but without any of the preliminaries required by the laws of siege warfare. The only fighting in the suburbs this time is that "Boyes . . . bourden full heghe / At a bare synglere that to þe bente rynnys" (3106-07). (These lines echo ironically Arthur's boast before charging the Genoan giants: " 'I wende no Bretouns walde bee basschede for so lyttill — / And fore bare-legyde boyes þat on the bente houys!' " [2121-22].) Como seems to be *hors de guerre,* yet Arthur launches an "enbuschement" (3099) without even hoisting banners and issuing war cries, the usual signs of war that until now Arthur's troops have consistently displayed. The only concession to law is that Arthur holds off the attack until the herdsmen and farmers have left the city for their daily work. According to [Honoré Bonet's *Tree of Battles,* ca. 1375], these trades are protected by the Church's safe-conduct, because "all manner of folk live off their labor . . . [and because such men] have no concern with war or with harming anyone." Arthur turns his troops loose to plunder and destroy once they are inside the city

gates: they "stekes and stabbis thorowe that them ayaynestondes — / Fowre stretis, or þay stynte, they stroyen fore euere" (3110-11). It is no wonder that "all þe contré and he full sone ware accordide" (3133); and when the Lord of Milan hears of Arthur's attack and victory at Como he prudently hastens to pay homage to Arthur, arriving at Como laden down with tribute. In order to guarantee his reader's disapproval of the Tuscan campaign, the poet conflates the sequence of events and presents it from the point of view of Arthur's innocent victims (3150-63).

When the Roman cardinals petition for peace (3176 ff.) we recall that before attacking Metz, when he pledged to establish an eternal law in Lombardy, Arthur promised his protection to all the papal lands (2406-15). However, this pledge is conditional and pragmatic, for it comes out of Arthur's desire for success rather than out of any implicit regard for the Church: " 'Yif we spare the spirituell, we spede bot the bettire; / Whills we haue for to speke, spille sall it neuer' " (2414-15). It is therefore not surprising that when Arthur has conquered all of Europe he ignores his pledge, accepting as hostages eightscore children against the Pope's promise to crown and anoint him emperor (3176-90). In an expansive moment, flushed with success, Arthur commands the hostages to be treated royally (3208-09), but when he must hastily leave Rome for Britain, he orders Howell and Hardolf to hang the hostages if Rome defaults on its rents or does not give him *seizin* on the appointed day (3587-90). Arthur would punish the Church for Roman civil recalcitrance; indeed, he would willingly break his pledge of non-aggression to the Church, flying in the face of provisions in canon and civil law which forbid hostilities against the Church. Even Arthur's intentions to crusade in the Holy Land, interrupted by Mordred's rebellion, are potentially illegal. According to the *Tree of Battles,* "the Church has the right to wage war . . . on Saracens and Jews when they constitute a threat to Christian society," not because they disbelieve or do not know the Gospels, "and if we cannot make war on them so that they may receive Holy Baptism, why should we do it on account of their possessions? Truly, reason does not command this." Further, in order to crusade, one must first secure the Church's permission, which at this point Arthur does not bother to obtain.

Although Arthur's defect manifests itself as willful conquest, its cause may be located in Arthur's passions, which Arthur so indulges that he gives way completely to unreason and thus, in the legal terms laid out earlier, disqualifies himself from waging just war. A hint of Arthur's tendency to indulge his passions is revealed in his appetite for feasting and dress, which a recent review of research calls a "weakness of luxury and pomp." Arthur's banquet for the Roman senators closely resembles Waster's in *Wynnere and Wastoure* and far exceeds the limits imposed by a statute of Edward III. Likewise, Arthur's rich attire resembles that of fourteenth century fops, about which Edward III also passed sumptuary laws. In Christian psychology, the result of this inner disorder is sin, which is why the philosopher interpreting Arthur's second dream urges Arthur not only to abandon unjust war (3397-99) but also to examine his conscience, confess his sins, and do penance (3400, 3452-55). Had Arthur's wars been just, not only would he have committed no sin, but such sins as already stained his soul would have been forgiven. In the works of Augustine and, later, in canon law and in treatises of chivalry—indeed, everywhere the subject was argued— the passion out of which unjust war arose was desire (*cupiditas*), either for conquest or for vengeance; hence, to suggest the increasingly sinful motive of Arthur's campaigns, the poet characterizes Arthur's desire for conquest through the image of concupiscence of the eyes, the beginning of the soul's fall into sin. Though Arthur may have legal reasons for war, he is also strongly seduced by the beauty of Lorraine and Lombardy: Lorraine is " 'louely' " (2399), while Lombardy is " 'lykande to schawe' " (2406), as Arthur announces before attacking Metz. Then, when he emerges from the Alps to see Lombardy stretching out beneath his eyes, Arthur says aloud: " 'In yone lykande londe lorde be I thynke' " (3093).

Arthur's passion does not suddenly arise during the campaign in Lorraine, though, for it has been present throughout in another form: the loyalty ethos of the Round Table. In his war council, Arthur shows this loyalty by adopting his knights' causes as his own, although he prudently refrains from their enthusiasm for war. For instance, when Cador exults over the opportunity to renew the Round Table's tarnished chivalry in war, Arthur gently rebukes him for thinking with his heart (259-62). Nevertheless, the king indulges his knights' boasting, for he recognizes that, rash as it may be, it is a necessary spur to the heroism on which his reputation and power depend:

> 'Alweldande Gode   wyrchipe yow all
> And latte me neuere wanntte yow   whylls I in
>   werlde regne;
> My menske and my manhede   ye mayntene in
>   erthe,
> Myn honour all vtterly   in oæer kyngys landes,
> My wele and my wyrchipe   of all þis werlde
>   ryche.'
>
> [397-401]

It is commonly held that Arthur's *desmesure* arises during the siege of Metz—at which Arthur indulges his belief in his invincibility, saying, " 'Sall neuer harlotte haue happe, thorowe helpe of my Lorde, / To kyll a corownde kynge with krysom enoynttede' " (2446-47)—and culminates in his claim that " 'we sall be ouerlynge of all þat on the erthe lengez!' " (3211). What has been overlooked is that these words hark back to Arthur's war council, as if in proclaiming them Arthur were recalling Aungers' loyal praise: " 'Thow aughte to be ouerlynge ouer all oþer kynges, / Fore wyseste and worthyeste and wyghteste of hanndes—The knyghtlyeste of counsaile þat euer coron bare!' " (289-91). The Italian campaign discussed above as an unjust war is, in another light, the fulfillment of a loyalty oath that Arthur made before crossing the English channel. Then, hearing the Welsh king recount a Roman ambush on him at Pontremoli in Lombardy while he was on pilgrimage (324-29), and egged on by Ewan, Arthur had vowed to " 'myne doun þe wallez' " there (351-52).

The dividing line between just wars fought in redress of injuries and unjust wars fought out of desire to avenge loyal retainers is a thin one, indeed. It is in response to this bond of loyalty with his knights that Arthur rides off into battle seeking revenge when one of Lucius's men kills Kay in battle (2171 ff.). In so doing, he falls into a melancholy frenzy from which he does not recover: "Thane remmes þe riche kynge fore rewthe at his herte, / Rydes into [þe] rowte his dede to reuenge" (2197-98). In the moment of loyalty he casts aside legal reasons for battle and yields to personal motives, becoming as guilty of thinking with the heart as Cador had been earlier. Arthur's self-indulgent response to Kay's death contrasts with the pity he feels for the victims of the tyrannical giant of Mont St. Michel: "Thane romyez the ryche kynge for rewthe of þe pople" (888). Equally important, it foreshadows the despair Arthur feels when Idrus's loyal offer to fight to the death alongside him prompts him to realize that the loyalty ethos of the Round Table requires the deaths of all his knights:

> Þan remys the riche kynge   with rewthe at his
>   herte,
> Hewys hys handys one heghte   and to þe heuen
>   lokes:
> 'Qwy then [ne] hade Dryghttyn destaynede   at
>   His dere will
> þat he hade demyd me to-daye   to dy for yow
>   all?
> That had I leuer than be lorde   all my lyfe tym
> Off all þat Alexandere aughte   qwhills he in
>   er the lengede!'
>
> [4155-60]

In the "rewthe at his herte" Arthur feels over Kay's death begin the " 'rewthe werkes' " (3453; note the poet's use of "rewthe werkes" in 3894 for Mordred's rebellion) of which the philosopher later exhorts Arthur to repent; but it is only now that Arthur, as if in single combat, defeats Lucius (2246-55). Describing him in action, the poet calls Arthur "manly in his maly[n]coly" (2204), thereby recognizing the paradoxical relationship between the excess in Arthur's passions and his achievement of *menske* and *manhede* as a king. If in his war council and on the battlefield (e.g., with Cador in 1922-27) Arthur restrains and rebukes his knights' rashness, Arthur himself is its source; indeed, in several places after Arthur adopts the revenge motive his knights have to restrain *him*. Disorder in the body politic begins in the body natural of the king. If Arthur's *de iure* fall begins when he turns from just to unjust war, the reasons for this turn lie much further back, in the character of the king and in the ethos by which he defines himself as King Arthur of the Round Table. It is an inevitable fall which simply has found its occasion.

> **"If Arthur's *de iure* fall begins when he turns from just to unjust war, the reasons for this turn lie much further back, in the character of the king and in the ethos by which he defines himself as King Arthur of the Round Table."**
>
> —*Michael W. Twomey*

The melancholy frenzy engendered by his loyalty to Kay enables Arthur to defeat his enemy even as it disqualifies him from waging just war. Arthur's descent into passion further marks his descent into illegitimacy because of the fundamental relationship between law and reason in medieval legal philosophy. All positive law—the laws of war, for example—comes from natural law and ultimately from divine law. Natural law is perceived through the faculty of reason, which is the image of God impressed in man. Hence, in the Middle Ages law is not primarily statutes, as it is today, but the immutable moral principles that derive from natural and divine law. It is reason that places man above beasts in the natural order; the fall from reason—both in theological and in legal contexts—is the descent into the bestial, the unnatural. As John of Legnano says in the *Tractatus de bello* [ca. 1360], unjust war is against nature because those who wage it are controlled by *sensus* rather than *intellectus*. The philosopher refers to this doctrine when he calls Arthur's unjust wars " 'vnresonable dedis' " (3452). It is therefore highly suggestive that in Arthur's last battle, where he encounters the rebellious Mordred, Arthur and Gawain are characterized as beasts. The poet notes that Arthur's hair is beaver-colored (3630); and when Arthur, still on board ship, hears of Gawain's death he hastens to shore, deep in anguish, "als a lyon" (3922). In his turn, Gawain, whose passionate outbursts initiate the hostilities in Arthur's war against Lucius (1302 ff.), is also characterized as a lion when in a state of high passion. When all his wit fails (3793), he charges Mordred's troops: "alls vnwyse wodewyse he wente at þe gayneste" (3817). The poet observes as Gawain fights that "Thare myghte no renke hym areste: his reson was passede. / He fell in a fransye for fersenesse of herte. . . . / Letande alls a lyon, he lawnches them thorowe" (3825-26, 3831). The moment of greatest pathos in *MA* is also the moment of the poet's severest indictment of Arthur's heroic kingship. As Arthur embraces the corpse of Gawain so closely and so long that he bloodies his beard, the poet remarks that Arthur appears "alls he had bestes birtenede and broghte owt of life" (3972). This striking image fulfills the prophecy of Arthur's first vision, which he dreamt before fighting the giant of Mont St. Michel. The dragon in that dream is Arthur himself, "dryfande ouer þe depe to drenschen hys pople" (761): this line, the poet's general interpretation of the dream, points beyond the philosopher's reading, which is restricted to the battles with the giant and with Lucius. In the end, heroic kingship equivocates *manhede* and *menske*. When Arthur weeps over Gawain's body that " 'he es sakles, supprysede for syn of myn one' " (3986), it is clear that the passion binding his men together in loyalty is also the passion that undoes Arthur's kingship and the entire Arthurian world.

Since by the time he hears of Mordred's rebellion Arthur has become an unjust king, it is important to note that according to fourteenth century legal theory the unjust king deposes himself *ipso facto*. No legal process is required for the deposition to be legally valid. The people's right to replace such a king, based on the principle of *vox populi, vox Dei* and called the right of resistance, was urged against both Edward II and Richard II. Arthur's tragic fall is thus complicated by the irony that Mordred, the heir apparent,

seizes Arthur's wife and stages an illegal rebellion as Arthur deposes himself by falling into unjust war. This irony is heightened when we consider that if divine approval for a king is shown by the birth of an heir, Mordred's getting a son by Guinevere (3552), which is in none of the poem's sources, could suggest divine right to rule in Arthur's place. Arthur's childlessness in turn correlates with the idea that although Arthur is a just king at the poem's beginning, at its end he lacks divine approval.

When he lands in Britain to quell Mordred's rebellion, Arthur, like Lucius at the beginning of the poem, claims lands that are not his. Both Arthur and Mordred are waging unjust war here—quite simply, because war is judicial combat writ large, if one of them were in the right, he would have survived the battle—but the poet is especially careful to underscore, through a reprise of themes from earlier in the poem, the poignancy of Arthur's end now that Arthur's right to rule in Britain has lapsed. Although Mordred's army contains Saracens (e.g., 3530, 3786 ff., 3942), the battle is no longer a holy war, regardless of Gawain's Roland-like invocations (3795-3812). Although his labels "traytour" (e.g., 3886) and "renayede renke" (3892) place Mordred in the same category of contumacious vassal as Lucius and the Duke of Lorraine (cp. 2173, where a "traitor" kills Kay, and 2913), the poet shows marked sympathy for Mordred, for example by having him deliver a heartfelt eulogy over Gawain's body, after which, in pointed contrast to Arthur, "he remyd and repent hym of all his rewthe werkes" (3894). Moreover, unbeknownst to Mordred, Arthur betrays Mordred before Mordred betrays him. In 676-78 Arthur promises to crown Mordred upon his return if Mordred keeps England wisely in his absence. However, he equivocates the promise on the battlefield when, becoming the victim of his own loyalties, he appoints Cador heir apparent (1944).

Because Arthur makes personal loyalty the ethical basis of action, it is impossible for him to rule justly and to adhere to the laws of war, since both require disinterested action on behalf of the common good. The code of personal loyalty is a kind of *cupiditas*, misplaced desire, opposed to the politicized *caritas* sanctioned by the Church as *amor patriae*. This code is the reason that once Arthur is aroused he fights only out of revenge. When he has conquered Rome, he declares that he will go on a crusade in order to " 'reuenge the Renke that on the Rode dyede' " (3217). When he learns of Mordred's treachery, his first words are not that he will return to Britain to execute justice on his rebellious vassal, but " 'I sall it revenge! / Hym sall repente full rathe all his rewthe werkes!' " (3559-60). With the latter line he applies to Mordred the very words by which the philosopher admonished him, projecting onto his nephew his own guilt in order to avoid the implications of his prophetic dream about the Nine Worthies and Fortune's wheel. Seeing the corpse of Gawain only rekindles Arthur's desire for revenge. "Than gliftis þe gud kynge and glopyns in herte" (3949) only slightly varies the line that introduced Arthur's revenge for Kay, "Thane remmes þe riche kynge fore rewthe at his herte" (2197); together, the lines point the two scenes where the deaths of Arthur's beloved knights provoke expressions of loyalty via revenge. And just as revenge for Kay's death made Arthur "manly in his melancholy," once Arthur swears never to resume life at the Round Table until Gawain's death " 'be dewly reuengede' " (4006), the conclusion will leave him, by his own sad admission, without any of the knights who "mayntenyde my manhede" and "made me manly one molde" (4278, 4279).

The poet's moving evocation of the profound irony of heroic kingship reminds us that, despite its close connection with late fourteenth century concerns, *MA* is set in the quasi-historical past of Celtic Britain, when the ethos of the *comitatus* was something more than literary fiction. In the chronicles of Geoffrey of Monmouth and Wace, the story of the fall of Arthur's empire is the climax of the larger story of the fall of the British kings. The Saxon conquest is due not only to the flaws of individual kings but to an historical law which our poet applies through Arthur's second prophetic dream, where he sees six of the Nine Worthies and then himself tumble from the Wheel of Fortune even as two successors, Charlemagne and Godfrey of Bouillon, clamber on. The point of this dream is not that Fortune suddenly interrupts Arthur's career, but that it always has been operating in it. Indeed, Fortune's operation throughout history is one of the lessons of the historical pattern of *translatio imperii* and of the scheme of the nine Worthies. *MA* sets the ethos of Arthur's Round Table against the laws of war and history in order to suggest both the historical inevitability of Arthur's fall and Arthur's own responsibility for it. (pp. 133-46)

> *Michael W. Twomey, "Heroic Kingship and Unjust War in the Alliterative 'Morte Arthure',' " in* ACTA, *Vol. XI, 1986, pp. 133-51.*

Christopher Dean (essay date 1986)

[*In the following essay, Dean examines ways in which the character Gawain in* Morte Arthure *demonstrates the compassion, loyalty, and Christian devotion characteristic of the medieval chivalric knight. Text citations are to Krishna's 1976 edition.*]

Few critics who have written on the alliterative *Morte Arthure* have addressed themselves centrally to the study of Gawain's role and character even though he is the most important figure after Arthur. Those who have differ considerably in their assessment of Gawain. On the one hand, he has been seen favorably as an ideal warrior of almost saint-like purity and as a Christ figure; on the other, he has been regarded unfavorably as a rash, passionate soldier, the epitome of reckless folly serving as a warning to all headstrong men who turn their backs on reason. A less extreme view, however, may come nearer to the truth. The significance of Gawain's character rests, not in what he is, but in how he relates to the king. Gawain's role is to complement that of Arthur by displaying those qualities which are praiseworthy in a knight but which would perhaps be unsuitable in a monarch. Taken together, the characters of the king and his nephew exemplify the late medieval ideals of noble behavior.

The author of the *Morte Arthure* makes few comments on the action of his poem or on the characters in it; consequently the reader receives little direct guidance as to how

he should judge Gawain. The few epithets the poet uses to describe him, however, are universally complimentary. He is "Sir Gaywayne þe worthye" (233, 1302), "Syr Gaweayne the gracyous" (1468), "þe knyghte noble" (4015), but most commonly he is "Sir Gawayne the gude" (2218, 3706, 3724, 3943), or "gud Gawayne, gracious and noble" (2851), or "the gude man of armes" (3858). Even if one partially dismisses these words as traditional and required by the alliteration, their cumulative effect is to praise Gawain. At one point in the poem, however, the author does make a deliberate personal comment. As Gawain dies at Mordred's hand, the poet says:

> And thus Sir Gawayne es gon, the gude man of
> armes,
> Withowttyn reschewe of renke and rewghe es þe
> more;
> Thus Sir Gawayne es gon, that gyede many
> othire.
>
> [3858-60]

The note of pity, sorrow, and regret for the passing of a noble hero is strongly evident here and indicates how the poet sees Gawain.

The structure of the poem indicates best how the reader should look at Sir Gawain. Gawain is kept as distant from the king as possible. In all the actions in which Arthur plays a significant and individual part, Gawain either does not appear—the council that decides to declare war on the Romans, Arthur's battle with the giant, the attack on Metz and the subsequent campaign in Italy, the dream of Fortune's wheel and its interpretation, the final battle against Mordred—or, where his presence must be noted as a part of Arthur's army, his role is kept as small as possible. In the main battle against Lucius, he appears for only eight lines, does nothing, and is insulted by Lucius, who rushes past him to fight elsewhere (2218-25). In the sea battle against Mordred, he appears for only two lines (3706-07). On the other hand, Gawain has three episodes in which he is the dominant figure, and in these the king has no part: the embassy that goes to the camp of Lucius, the episode with Priamus and the landing on the coast which leads to the hand-to-hand struggle with Mordred and the death of Gawain.

This separation of Arthur and Gawain, and the consequent requirement that the reader look at them alternately throughout the poem, make it inevitable that he should set the two side-by-side and compare them. At times, there is a deliberate formal contrast. Gawain meets Lucius briefly in battle but is ignored by him; Arthur meets Lucius, fights him and kills him. Gawain encounters Mordred in combat but is overcome by him; Arthur later meets Mordred and succeeds in killing him. These two comparisons are intended to establish the relative hierarchical values of Arthur the king and Gawain the subject knight.

Two other comparisons, however, indicate their equality in spite of their difference in status. The first is the matter of leadership and command. Arthur, by virtue of his position, has the right to lead, but his leadership always has political dimensions to it. He acts as a statesman when he undertakes his war with Rome only after listening to the advice of his counselors; he inspires by personal example when he encounters single-handedly the giant of Michael's Mount, the giant Golapas, and Lucius; he demonstrates his contempt for his enemies and his own invincibility when he rides unprotected near to the walls of Metz. Gawain's leadership is of a different kind. It is leadership that he takes upon himself because he is the most fitting and because his fitness is recognized by those who are with him. In the embassy to Lucius, Sir Boice is the nominal leader, but it is Gawain who hurls words of defiance at the emperor and who deliberately pushes the Romans into fighting. In the ensuing battle, Gawain again leads. He kills Sir Gayous (1352-55); he turns when the Romans follow the Britons and is the first to kill his opponent (1368-73); he rallies the Britons when they flee (1443-48); he rescues Sir Boice, who had been taken prisoner (1468-83). No blame is attached to Gawain for anything that happens in this encounter. Indeed, the king is so overjoyed at what occurred that he awards the knight who brings the news the splendid prize of "Tolouse þe riche" merely for acting as the messenger (1567). On a second occasion it is Florente who is put in charge of a foraging party, but when the group is threatened by an enemy army, Florente readily hands over his authority to Gawain: "Þe are owre wardayne, iwysse, wyrke as yowe lykes" (2740). He advises running away because the Britons are outnumbered, but the reader discovers his real fear: if he makes a mistake he will be blamed (2737). He may, indeed, have been rather relieved when Gawain took the responsibility onto his own shoulders. In any case, no one objects to Gawain's assuming command and ordering them into battle. The real test, of course, is the outcome: the Britons win an enormous victory, and a herald hurries to Arthur to tell him jubilantly that Gawain "has wonn todaye wirchip for euere" (3022). The king, as before, is overjoyed at what Gawain has done, and Gawain's decision is absolutely vindicated.

The second parallel between King Arthur and Sir Gawain is that both fight and win single-handedly battles against larger-than-life foes in contexts apart from the main story of Arthur's dynastic wars. Early in the poem, Arthur turns aside from his campaign against Lucius to fight the giant of Michael's Mount; later Gawain "weendes owtt" from the battlefield "wondyrs to seke" (2513-14). His opponent, Sir Priamus, kin to Alexander, Iudas and Iosue (2602-05), proves to be almost as marvellous, for he carries at his belt a vial "full of þe flour of þe fouur well, / Þat flowes owte of Paradice" (2705-06). Arthur fights for the kingly virtues of justice and the succoring of his people in their need; Gawain fights from motives of pure chivalry, the sheer delight of proving himself on equal terms a better man than his opponent. It is the same spirit that will not let Gawain in Malory's *Le Morte d'Arthur* allow Sir Marhaus to go unchallenged, even though Sir Uwayne warns him that he is acting foolishly: "Hit were shame to us," he said, "and he were nat assayed, were he never so good a knyght." Both Arthur and Gawain are acting worthily according to their different lights, and both are upholding principles valued highly by medieval society. In this respect Arthur and Gawain are complementary figures. Each manifests a different aspect of the medieval conception of the noble life and each represents ideals that were dear to the Middle Ages.

Arthur is a heroic and admirable king, who never forfeits the poet's esteem. Modern readers can readily applaud many of his actions; his refusal to submit to the demands of Lucius, his defense of his oppressed subjects, his mercy toward the ladies of Metz, his grief for Gawain's death, his wish to have sacrificed his own life if the lives of his men might have been spared thereby, and his impulsive desire to pursue Mordred without waiting for reinforcements. The modern reader can even appreciate his sardonic humor as he cuts Golapas down by the knees. If other actions are less readily acceptable—such as his laying waste to the cities in Italy and his killing of Mordred's children—they must be regarded in the light of fourteenth-century values and practices. As far as the particular circumstances of this poem will allow, Gawain behaves as a chivalric knight should. There is no place for love or the service of women; but other qualities, such as courage and daring in battle, the desire to excel over all other knights, total loyalty to his lord, and, by no means least, devotion to God, are all there. Gawain's actions can almost always be accounted for by appealing to the principles of chivalry.

Gawain's first speech to Lucius, condemned by some critics as arrogant, proud, or ill-tempered, sets out much that is basic to his character (1303-25). It can be divided into ten sections:

1. invoking God's name (1303-04)
2. cursing the Sultan (1305-06)
3. calling him a "fals heretyke" (1307)
4. challenging the legality of Lucius's rule over his lands (1308-10)
5. cursing him again, invoking the same curse that fell on Cain (1311-12)
6. insulting him, calling him "cukewalde" and "vnlordlyeste lede þat I on lukede euer!" (1312-13)
7. wondering why Lucius acts so evilly (1314-17)
8. telling him to leave the land (1318-19)
9. telling him that otherwise he must fight (1320-21)
10. saying that he has fulfilled his mission as ordered and demanding an answer (1322-25).

Naturally, much of this speech is occasioned by the king whose message it is. Indeed, some of the words are virtual quotations. Gawain's command to "kaire of his landes" (item 8) echoes the king's "Cayre owte of my kyngryke" (1272); his second command to "encontre hym ones" (item 9) repeats Arthur's "countere me ones" (1274); and his insulting comment that Lucius is "þe vnlordlyeste lede" (item 6) may well be inspired by Arthur's statement that Lucius "vnlordly he wyrkez" (1267). Elsewhere, Gawain follows the substance of Arthur's thought if not his actual words, as in items 4 and 7, which are Gawain's way of expressing Arthur's "letherly agaynes law to lede my pople" (1268). Charges of Gawain's intemperance derive from his use of insulting epithets such as "cukewalde" (item 6) and "alfyn" (1343), but even here he has Arthur as a model, for the king earlier had called Lucius "þat cursede wreche" (1273) and enjoined his ambassador to use "crewell wordez" (1271). Clearly, Arthur did not want a tactful message delivered.

Surprisingly, what Gawain seems to have added on his

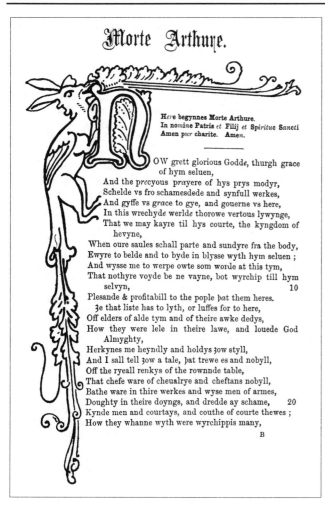

The first page of Mary Macleod Banks's edition of the poem.

own initiative is not arrogance and rudeness but all the religious overtones: the charge that Lucius is a heretic, the invocation of God's help for the British side, and the curses in God's name against Lucius for his aggression. This first episode reveals Gawain to be a loyal servant of the king who does his duty both in letter and spirit. Second, he is a forceful man who imposes himself on both friend and foe alike by the strength of his personality. Third, he is a Christian who believes that he is fighting for and with the help of God.

The Priamus interlude has been rightly identified as pure romance, the only such episode in a poem of essentially a very different nature. By changing so distinctively to another mode at this point, the poet is asking the reader to see Gawain differently from all the other men in Arthur's army. In this episode he must not be thought of as a soldier on a military campaign, but as a chivalric knight seeking adventures. The reader can, of course, insist on taking this episode realistically (though what does he then make of the water flowing out of Paradise?) and criticize Gawain as a soldier deserting his duty for his own selfish ends, but the poet gives him no reason to do so. This is a happy and successful adventure, and everything that Gawain does reflects to his credit. He defeats his foe in fair battle; he treats

him generously afterwards and does not despise him because he overcame him (as Sir Kay might have); he converts him to the Christian faith; and ultimately he brings him as an ally to Arthur's side. Here Gawain is the ideal chivalric and Christian knight.

Gawain's last episode, when he pushes ashore against immense odds and establishes a beachhead at the cost of his own life, is the one which has been seized upon most avidly by critics hostile to him. Fichte's article [in *The Alliterative Morte Arthure: A Reassessment of the Poem,* 1981] for example, is based heavily upon Gawain's actions in this scene. He begins by criticizing him for failing to concentrate his efforts on holding "þe grene hill" (3768), calling this a strategically important position. Instead, Gawain attacks the main army and is killed. Though the holding of the green hill in itself may be a small matter, the implications that stem from it are not. Since the terrain of the battlefield is not made completely clear, Fichte's assessment of the tactics may be wrong through his misunderstanding of what happened. Gawain sailed up "a gole," or small inlet, and when his ship ran aground he jumped into waist-deep water and waded ashore (3725). He stood on "þe sonde" (3728), then rushed into "the banke" (3731), which was probably the cliff at the top of the gulley into which he had sailed. The vanguard of Mordred's men was drawn up on another "banke" (3733) and to get at them Gawain's forces had to charge "ouer þe sonde" (3745). After Gawain defeated the vanguard, which fled back to the main host, he attacked the "medilwarde" (3766). Only then does the poet comment: "For hade Sir Gawayne hade grace to halde þe grene hill, / He had wirchipe, iwys, wonnen for euer" (3768-69). Does this mean, as Fichte suggests, that if only Gawain had kept as a secure base an already-won hill he would have won glory forever? Unless the "banke" of line 3733 is synonymous with the hill, no hill has so far been mentioned. Certainly, there has been no account of Gawain's men fighting their way to the crest of a hill. Further, one might ask what is so magnificent about maintaining an initial foothold that such an action would ensure permanent glory? Glory never comes from prudence. An alternative suggestion is that the "avawwarde" were positioned on the cliff top as a first line of defense but that the main body of the army was drawn up some distance back in a strategic position—most likely based on a defensible hill—and that it is the winning of this from the full army and holding it thereafter that would indeed have merited "wirchipe" forever.

It must be admitted at once that Gawain's actions were not reasonable or prudent. To take a single ship with no more than 140 men in it against an army of 60,000 has to be folly by any common-sense standards, and to try to hold a hill against such odds is just as foolish as attacking the main army head-on. Setting reason aside, however, what did Gawain's "rash" foray achieve? In numerical terms "ten thosandez" (3929) of the enemy were killed at a cost of "seuen score knyghtes" (3930), a ratio that must appeal to any general, medieval or modern. Second, King Frederick admits that Gawain's venture "has grettly greffede vs, so me Gode helpe, / Gyrde down oure gude men and greuede vs sore" (3870-71). Whereupon, fearing a subsequent attack from Arthur, Mordred retreated and so allowed the king to land unopposed, suffering no casualties at all. Such a thrust today would not bring down censure on Gawain's head; it would more likely merit the awarding of the Victoria Cross. Unfortunately, Victoria Crosses are all too often awarded posthumously.

The final scene shows in more concentrated form the same virtues that Gawain had displayed in the opening encounter in Lucius's camp. First, his loyalty and devotion to Arthur cause him to lead his men ashore under extremely dangerous circumstances and to attack Mordred fiercely, whatever the risk to his own life. The venom of his hatred is particularly evident in the ferocity of his curses: " 'Fals fosterde foode, the Fende haue thy bonys! / Fy one the, felone, and thy false werkys!' " (3776-77). His courage and bravery, of course, are as evident as ever; and if he fights in the end in a mad frenzy, it is because he realizes that death is about to overtake him without his achieving his purpose of killing Mordred. Likening his fighting to that of a wild beast (3837) is one of the more traditional epithets in a medieval poet's repertoire and indicates only the ferocity of the man's actions. It says nothing at all about his mental state.

A somewhat newer note for Gawain is his compassion and regret for the loss of his men, which links him in another way to Arthur, who throughout the poem has grieved whenever his men have been injured or killed. The ground was prepared for this element of compassion in Gawain when he earlier lamented the death of Chastelayne at the hands of Swyan of Swecy (2962-68). In this last episode, therefore, Gawain regrets the coming death of his men:

> Thane Sir Gawayne grette with his gray eghen,
> For grefe of his gud men that he gyde schulde;
> He wyste that þay wondyde ware and wery forfoughtten.
>
> [3790-92]

But his response is different from his earlier grief for Chastelayne. He cannot hope to avenge them as he did Chastelayne, but he consoles them instead with the prospect of ascending to heaven as a reward for fighting Christ's foes:

> Bes dowghtty todaye, yone dukes schall be youres;
> For dere Dryghttyn this daye, dredys no wapyn.
> We sall ende this daye alls excellent knyghttes,
> Ayere to endelesse joye with angells vnwemyde.
> Þofe we hafe vnwittyly wastede oure selfen,
> We sall wirke all wele in þe wirchipe of Cryste.
> We sall for yone Sarazenes, I sekire yow my trowhe,
> Souppe with oure Saueoure solemply in Heuen,
> In presence of þat precious Prynce of all oþer,
> With prophetes and patriarkes and apostlys full nobill,
> Before His freliche face that fourmede vs all.
>
> [3798-3808]

These are the last words from Gawain and they express most fully and deeply his religious faith. Clearly, he believes that his actions will take him straight to heaven. He ends then as he began, a Christian soldier fighting loyally for his lord against manifestly evil and pagan opponents. Upheld by his faith and trusting in God, Gawain dies at Mordred's hands.

Too much should not be made of Gawain's blaming himself for acting "vnwittyly," for this readiness to blame oneself when things go wrong and to credit others when they go right is a worthy quality in a leader. This quality is not found in Gawain alone. Only a few lines later, Arthur, with a similar disregard for the literal truth, will attribute all his success to Gawain alone: " 'My wele and my wirchipe of all þis werlde riche / Was wonnen thourghe Sir Gawayne and thourghe his witt one' " (3963-64). Such statements are expected. They are hardly objective assessments of a man's worth. More importantly, it must be remembered that this judgment of the folly of the action is Gawain's alone. It is not shared by the poet or by any other character in the poem, friend or foe.

Two eulogies spoken over Gawain's body as it lies on the shore must also be considered. The second eulogy, spoken by Arthur, might be considered first, because there is less likelihood of finding a dispassionate judgment of Gawain here than in Mordred's eulogy. Arthur laments the loss of one of his best soldiers and grieves for the death of a dear kinsman. It is to be expected, therefore, that Arthur would show more emotion and less objectivity, even if it were not already clear that he feels passionately about all his knights and cares for the injuries and deaths of them all. His unrestrained language is not out of character when he says that Gawain has died a sinless man and that with his demise all hope for success is gone. His men, however, more pragmatic and less emotionally involved than the king, rebuke him for weeping like a woman and bluntly tell him to behave "als a kyng scholde" (3979).

Because he is less blinded with emotion toward Gawain, Mordred's judgment of him is more useful as an evaluation. As Gawain's enemy and slayer, one would not expect praise from him. Yet Mordred does ascribe a very full and generous list of noble qualities to Gawain:

> "He was makles one molde, mane, be my trowhe;
> This was Sir Gawayne the gude, þe gladdeste of othire,
> And the graciouseste gome that vndire God lyffede,
> Mane hardyeste of hande, happyeste in armes,
> And þe hendeste in hawle vndire heuen riche,
> Þe lordelieste of ledyng qwhylls he lyffe myghte,
> Fore he was lyone allossede in londes inewe;
> Had thow knawen hym, Sir Kyng, in kythe thare he lengede,
> His konynge, his knyghthode, his kyndly werkes,
> His doyng, his doughtynesse, his dedis of armes,
> Thow wolde hafe dole for his dede þe dayes of thy lyfe."
>
> [3875-85]

Some of these qualities—that he was "þe hendeste in hawle" or that he did "kyndly werkes"—have not been revealed in the poem and so have to be taken on trust. However, that matters less than the overall style of the passage, a conventional eulogy for a chivalric knight that touches on all the qualities that an ideal knight ought to be remembered for. Whether he actually had them is in a sense irrelevant. The kind of eulogy that Mordred delivers recognizes the nature of Gawain and of his chivalry. That is what is important. The best parallel to it in style and manner is not, as Haas suggests [in *The Alliterative Morte Arthure: A Reassessment of the Poem,* 1981], in Anglo-Saxon poetry, but in Ector's eulogy for Lancelot where we have a similar catalog of virtues set out in similar superlative terms:

> "A, Launcelot!" he sayd, "thou were hede of al Crysten knyghtes! And now I dare say," sayd syr Ector, "thou sir Launcelot, there thou lyest, that thou were never matched of erthely knyghtes hande. And thou were the curtest knyght that ever bare shelde! And thou were the truest frende to thy lovar that euer bestrade hors, and thou were the trewest lover, of a synful man, that ever loved woman, and thou were the kyndest man that ever strake wyth swerde. And thou were the godelyest persone that ever cam emonge prees of knyghtes, and thou was the mekest man and the jentyllest that ever ete in halle emonge ladyes, and thou were the sternest knyght to thy mortal foo that ever put spere in the reeste." [*Le Morte d'Arthur* 3: 1259]

Mordred's summary of Gawain's nature and role may well stand for the author's views as revealed in the action of the poem. Gawain, as he so often is elsewhere in Middle English literature, is the supreme example of the chivalric knight, though here naturally the warlike qualities of reckless boldness in battle, complete loyalty to his king, and compassion for his fellow knights who meet death in battle are stressed rather than his more usual peacetime qualities of courtesy and love service. Even more importantly, his Christian devotion and trust, the very foundation of a chivalrous knight's way of life, is demonstrated again and again. Both in parallel and contrast, therefore, he stands with the king. Arthur shows those qualities that are the distinctive marks of a good ruler; Gawain represents the chivalric knight. Together, in a world otherwise filled with tragedy and treachery, they show that the ideals of medieval nobility exist and can be followed, whatever the consequences of doing so may be. (pp. 115-25)

> *Christopher Dean, "Sir Gawain in the Alliterative: 'Morte Arthure',"* in Papers on Language & Literature, *Vol. 22, No. 2, Spring, 1986, pp. 115-25.*

FURTHER READING

Clark, George. "Gawain's Fall: The Alliterative *Morte Arthure* and Hastings." *Tennessee Studies in Literature* XI (1966): 89-95.
  Contends that historical accounts of the Battle of Hastings in 1066 provided a model for the *Morte Arthure* poet's depiction of events leading to Gawain's death.

Eadie, J. "The Alliterative *Morte Arthure:* Structure & Meaning." *English Studies* 63, No. 1 (February 1982): 1-12.
  Disagrees with prevailing critical assessments of the alliterative *Morte Arthure,* arguing that Arthur's death is not a punishment for cruel or selfish behavior but simply an inevitable change of fortune.

Finlayson, John. "Rhetorical 'Descriptio' of Place in the Alliterative *Morte Arthure.*" *Modern Philology* LXI, No. 1 (August 1963): 1-11.
  Discusses the poet's use of *descriptio loci,* or descriptions of place, in the alliterative *Morte Arthure,* concluding that the poet was "skilled in the exposition of the courtly arts of *descriptio* [and was] consciously moulding a tradition to his own individual ends."

——. "Formulaic Technique in *Morte Arthure.*" *Anglia: Zietschrift für Englische Philologie* 81 (1963): 372-93.
  Compares the formulaic structure of individual lines of the alliterative *Morte Arthure* with similarly structured lines in two other Medieval poems: *The Destruction of Troy* and *The Wars of Alexander.*

——. "*Morte Arthure:* The Date and a Source for the Contemporary References." *Speculum* XLII, No. 4 (October 1967): 624-38.
  Disputes the prevailing critical assumption that the alliterative *Morte Arthure* was written circa 1365 and was based on events in the life of Edward III, suggesting that the poem was probably written between 1375 and 1440 and contains only indirect references to Edward.

——. "The Concept of the Hero in *Morte Arthure.*" In *Chaucer und Seine Zeit: Symposion für Walter F. Schirmer,* edited by Arno Esch, pp. 249-74. Tübingen, Germany: Max Niemeyer Verlag, 1968.
  Discusses the character of Arthur, asserting that "Arthur neither completely nor merely conforms to an epic or romance pattern of the perfect hero. . . ."

Hamel, Mary. "The 'Christening' of Sir Priamus in the Alliterative *Morte Arthure.*" *Viator* 13 (1982): 295-307.
  Examines the encounter between Gawain and Priamus in *Morte Arthure* and in Thomas Malory's "Tale of King Arthur and the Emperor Lucius."

Keiser, George R. "Edward III and the Alliterative *Morte Arthure.*" *Speculum* XLVIII, No. 1 (January 1973): 37-51.
  Argues that the alliterative *Morte Arthure* was not intended primarily as a commentary on the reign of Edward III.

——. "Narrative Structure in the Alliterative *Morte Arthure,* 26-720." *The Chaucer Review* 9, No. 2 (Fall 1974): 130-44.
  Compares the opening scenes of the alliterative *Morte Arthure* with those of Wace's *Brut,* a possible source of the poem, in order to demonstrate how the poet transformed "the austere Arthur of Wace's poem into a character his contemporaries might better understand."

——. "The Theme of Justice in the Alliterative *Morte Arthure.*" *Annuale Mediaevale* 16 (1975): 94-109.
  Argues that the medieval ideal of a just king as agent of a just God "was a decisive influence in the artist's shaping of his narrative in the Alliterative *Morte Arthure.*" According to Keiser, the poem demonstrates that "the most important conquest a man can make, in warring against injustice, is the conquest of his own will."

Krishna, Valerie. Introduction to *The Alliterative Morte Arthure: A Critical Edition,* pp. 1-38. New York: Burt Franklin & Co., 1976.

Includes an overview of stylistic, linguistic, and historical issues concerning the alliterative *Morte Arthure.*

Obst, Wolfgang. "The Gawain-Priamus Episode in the Alliterative *Morte Arthure.*" *Studia Neophilologica* LVII, No. 1 (1985): 9-18.

Examines Gawain's encounter with Priamus in the alliterative *Morte Arthure,* finding in it symbolic justification for Arthur's conquests and support for the contention that Arthur's character and morals are consistently praiseworthy throughout the poem.

O'Loughlin, J. L. N. "The English Alliterative Romances." In *Arthurian Literature in the Middle Ages: A Collaborative History,* edited by Roger Sherman Loomis, pp. 520-27. London: Oxford at the Clarendon Press, 1959.

Includes discussion of the uncertain origin of the alliterative *Morte Arthure,* "one of the masterpieces of the alliterative revival."

Parks, Ward. "The Flyting Contract and Adversarial Patterning in the Alliterative *Morte Arthure.*" In *Traditions and Innovations: Essays on British Literature of the Middle Ages and the Renaissance,* edited by David G. Allen and Robert A. White, pp. 59-74. Newark: University of Delaware Press, 1990.

Discusses the interchange of insults and bragging, known as "flyting," inherent to the medieval contest as represented in the alliterative *Morte Arthure.* Parks maintains that "even as the heroes vie with one another for personal glory, they are tacitly or explicitly negotiating the terms of the trial of arms that will determine which of them has won."

Patterson, Lee W. "The Historiography of Romance and the Alliterative *Morte Arthure.*" *The Journal of Medieval and Renaissance Studies* 13, No. 1 (Spring 1983): 1-32.

Examines *Morte Arthure* in relation to its sources. Patterson maintains that "the history of the genre and the history of the times are mutually inscribed" in the poem, "providing occasions of form and theme that allow for a meditation on the meaning of history per se—for, that is, a historiography."

Shoaf, R. A. "The Alliterative *Morte Arthure:* The Story of

Britain's David." *Journal of English and Germanic Philology* LXXXI, No. 2 (April 1982): 204-26.

Asserts that the poem's depiction of Arthur as a great but fallible king is informed by the example of the biblical King David.

Spearing, A. C. "Alliterative Poetry." In his *Readings in Medieval Poetry,* pp. 134-72. Cambridge: Cambridge University Press, 1987.

Characterizes the alliterative *Morte Arthure* as effectively developing "the heroic possibilities of alliterative verse," in a discussion of the features of the genre.

Vale, Juliet. "Law and Diplomacy in the Alliterative *Morte Arthure.*" *Nottingham Medieval Studies* XXIII (1979): 31-46.

Discusses passages of the alliterative *Morte Arthure,* contending that its author possessed a high degree of "technical (and sometimes highly specialised) knowledge of law and diplomacy. . . . "

Vaughan, M. F. "Consecutive Alliteration, Strophic Patterns, and the Composition of the Alliterative *Morte Arthure.*" *Modern Philology* 77, No. 1 (August 1979): 1-9.

Analyzes the structure of the alliterative *Morte Arthure,* claiming that the original poem "would appear to have been structured in four-line 'sentences' regularly reinforced by consecutive alliteration and combined into verse paragraphs of irregular length."

Wilson, Robert H. "Some Minor Characters in the *Morte Arthure.*" *Modern Language Notes* LXXI, No. 7 (November 1956): 475-80.

Discusses problems in identifying several minor characters in the alliterative *Morte Arthure* resulting from variations in the spelling of their names.

Ziolkowski, Jan. "A Narrative Structure in the Alliterative *Morte Arthure* 1-1221 and 3150-4346." *The Chaucer Review* 22, No. 3 (1988): 234-45.

Documents a parallel narrative structure in the first and last quarters of the alliterative *Morte Arthure.*

CLASSICAL AND MEDIEVAL LITERATURE CRITICISM

INDEXES

Literary Criticism Series
Cumulative Author Index

Literary Criticism Series
Cumulative Topic Index

CMLC Cumulative Nationality Index

CMLC Cumulative Title Index

CMLC Cumulative Critic Index

This Index Includes References to Entries in These Gale Series

Authors in the News (AITN) reprints articles from American periodicals covering authors and members of the communications media. Two volumes.

Bestsellers (BEST) furnishes information about best-selling books and their authors for the years 1989-1990.

Black Literature Criticism (BLC) provides excerpts from criticism of the most significant works of black authors of all nationalities over the past 200 years. Complete in three volumes.

Children's Literature Review (CLR) includes excerpts from reviews, criticism, and commentary on works of authors and illustrators who create books for children.

Classical and Medieval Literature Criticism (CMLC) offers criticism on the works of world authors from classical antiquity through the fourteenth century.

Contemporary Authors encompasses eight related series: *Contemporary Authors (CA)* provides biographical and bibliographical information on more than 99,000 writers of fiction, nonfiction, poetry, journalism, drama, and film. *Contemporary Authors New Revision Series (CANR)* provides updated information on active authors previously covered in *CA*. *Contemporary Authors Permanent Series (CAP)* consists of updated listings for deceased and inactive authors removed from revised volumes of *CA*. *Contemporary Authors Autobiography Series (CAAS)* presents commissioned autobiographies by leading contemporary writers. *Contemporary Authors Bibliography Series (CABS)* contains primary and secondary bibliographies as well as bibliographical essays on major modern authors. *Black Writers (BW)* compiles selected *CA* sketches on more than 400 prominent writers. *Hispanic Writers (HW)* compiles selected *CA* sketches on twentieth-century Hispanic writers. *Major 20th-Century Writers (MTCW)* presents in four volumes selected *CA* sketches on over 1,000 of the most influential writers of this century.

Contemporary Literary Criticism (CLC) presents excerpts of criticism on the works of creative writers who are now living or who have died since 1960.

Dictionary of Literary Biography comprises five related series: *Dictionary of Literary Biography (DLB)* furnishes illustrated overviews of authors' lives and works. *Dictionary of Literary Biography Documentary Series (DLBD)* illuminates the careers of major figures through a selection of literary documents, including letters, interviews, and photographs. *Dictionary of Lit-*

erary Biography Yearbook (DLBY) summarizes the past year's literary activity and includes updated and new entries on individual authors. *Concise Dictionary of American Literary Biography (CDALB)* and *Concise Dictionary of British Literary Biography (CDBLB)* collect revised and updated sketches that were originally presented in *Dictionary of Literary Biography*.

Drama Criticism (DC) provides excerpts of criticism on the works of playwrights of all nationalities and periods of literary history.

Literature Criticism from 1400 to 1800 (LC) compiles significant passages from criticism on authors of the fifteenth through the eighteenth centuries.

Nineteenth-Century Literature Criticism (NCLC) reprints significant passages from criticism on authors who died between 1800 and 1899.

Poetry Criticism (PC) presents excerpts of criticism on the works of poets from all eras, movements, and nationalities.

Short Story Criticism (SSC) offers critical excerpts on short fiction by writers of all eras and nationalities.

Something about the Author encompasses four related series: *Something about the Author (SATA)* contains biographical sketches on authors amd illustrators of juvenile and young adult literature. *Something about the Author Autobiography Series (SAAS)* presents commissioned autobiographies by prominent authors and illustrators of books for children and young adults. *Authors & Artists for Young Adults (AAYA)* provides students with profiles of their favorite creative artists. *Major Authors and Illustrators for Children and Young Adults (MAICYA)* contains in six volumes both newly written and completely updated *SATA* sketches on nearly 800 authors and illustrators for young people.

Twentieth-Century Literary Criticism (TCLC) contains critical excerpts on authors who died between 1900 and 1960.

World Literature Criticism (WLC) contains excerpts from criticism on the works of over 200 major writers from the Renaissance to the present. Complete in six volumes.

Yesterday's Authors of Books for Children (YABC) contains heavily illustrated entries on children's writers who died before 1961. Complete in two volumes.

Literary Criticism Series
Cumulative Author Index

Aleixandre, Vicente 1898-1984 ... **CLC 9, 36**
See also CA 85-88; 114; CANR 26;
DLB 108; HW; MTCW

Alepoudelis, Odysseus
See Elytis, Odysseus

Aleshkovsky, Joseph 1929-
See Aleshkovsky, Yuz
See also CA 121; 128

Aleshkovsky, Yuz .... **CLC 44**
See also Aleshkovsky, Joseph

Alexander, Lloyd (Chudley) 1924- .. **CLC 35**
See also AAYA 1; CA 1-4R; CANR 1, 24,
38; CLR 1, 5; DLB 52; MAICYA;
MTCW; SATA 3, 49

Alfau, Felipe 1902-................ **CLC 66**
See also CA 137

Alger, Horatio Jr. 1832-1899 ..... **NCLC 8**
See also DLB 42; SATA 16

Algren, Nelson 1909-1981 .... **CLC 4, 10, 33**
See also CA 13-16R; 103; CANR 20;
CDALB 1941-1968; DLB 9; DLBY 81,
82; MTCW

Ali, Ahmed 1910- .... **CLC 69**
See also CA 25-28R; CANR 15, 34

Alighieri, Dante 1265-1321 .... **CMLC 3**

Allan, John B.
See Westlake, Donald E(dwin)

Allen, Edward 1948-............. **CLC 59**

Allen, Roland
See Ayckbourn, Alan

Allen, Woody 1935- .... **CLC 16, 52**
See also CA 33-36R; CANR 27, 38;
DLB 44; MTCW

Allende, Isabel 1942- .... **CLC 39, 57**
See also CA 125; 130; HW; MTCW

Alleyn, Ellen
See Rossetti, Christina (Georgina)

Allingham, Margery (Louise)
1904-1966 .... **CLC 19**
See also CA 5-8R; 25-28R; CANR 4;
DLB 77; MTCW

Allingham, William 1824-1889 ... **NCLC 25**
See also DLB 35

Allston, Washington 1779-1843.... **NCLC 2**
See also DLB 1

Almedingen, E. M. .... **CLC 12**
See also Almedingen, Martha Edith von
See also SATA 3

Almedingen, Martha Edith von 1898-1971
See Almedingen, E. M.
See also CA 1-4R; CANR 1

Alonso, Damaso 1898-1990 .... **CLC 14**
See also CA 110; 131; 130; DLB 108; HW

Alta 1942-....................... **CLC 19**
See also CA 57-60

Alter, Robert B(ernard) 1935-...... **CLC 34**
See also CA 49-52; CANR 1

Alther, Lisa 1944-............. **CLC 7, 41**
See also CA 65-68; CANR 12, 30; MTCW

Altman, Robert 1925-............ **CLC 16**
See also CA 73-76

Alvarez, A(lfred) 1929-......... **CLC 5, 13**
See also CA 1-4R; CANR 3, 33; DLB 14,
40

Alvarez, Alejandro Rodriguez 1903-1965
See Casona, Alejandro
See also CA 131; 93-96; HW

Amado, Jorge 1912-........... **CLC 13, 40**
See also CA 77-80; CANR 35; DLB 113;
MTCW

Ambler, Eric 1909-........... **CLC 4, 6, 9**
See also CA 9-12R; CANR 7, 38; DLB 77;
MTCW

Amichai, Yehuda 1924- ...... **CLC 9, 22, 57**
See also CA 85-88; MTCW

Amiel, Henri Frederic 1821-1881 .. **NCLC 4**

Amis, Kingsley (William)
1922- ...... **CLC 1, 2, 3, 5, 8, 13, 40, 44**
See also AITN 2; CA 9-12R; CANR 8, 28;
CDBLB 1945-1960; DLB 15, 27, 100;
MTCW

Amis, Martin (Louis)
1949- ....CLC 4, 9, 38, 62
See also BEST 90:3; CA 65-68; CANR 8,
27; DLB 14

Ammons, A(rchie) R(andolph)
1926- .... **CLC 2, 3, 5, 8, 9, 25, 57**
See also AITN 1; CA 9-12R; CANR 6, 36;
DLB 5; MTCW

Amo, Tauraatua i
See Adams, Henry (Brooks)

Anand, Mulk Raj 1905-........... **CLC 23**
See also CA 65-68; CANR 32; MTCW

Anatol
See Schnitzler, Arthur

Anaya, Rudolfo A(lfonso) 1937- .... **CLC 23**
See also CA 45-48; CAAS 4; CANR 1, 32;
DLB 82; HW; MTCW

Andersen, Hans Christian
1805-1875 .... **NCLC 7; SSC 6**
See also CLR 6; MAICYA; WLC; YABC 1

Anderson, C. Farley
See Mencken, H(enry) L(ouis); Nathan,
George Jean

Anderson, Jessica (Margaret) Queale
.... **CLC 37**
See also CA 9-12R; CANR 4

Anderson, Jon (Victor) 1940- .... **CLC 9**
See also CA 25-28R; CANR 20

Anderson, Lindsay (Gordon)
1923-................... **CLC 20**
See also CA 125; 128

Anderson, Maxwell 1888-1959 ..... **TCLC 2**
See also CA 105; DLB 7

Anderson, Poul (William) 1926- .... **CLC 15**
See also AAYA 5; CA 1-4R; CAAS 2;
CANR 2, 15, 34; DLB 8; MTCW;
SATA 39

Anderson, Robert (Woodruff)
1917-..................... **CLC 23**
See also AITN 1; CA 21-24R; CANR 32;
DLB 7

Anderson, Sherwood
1876-1941 ...... **TCLC 1, 10, 24; SSC 1**
See also CA 104; 121; CDALB 1917-1929;
DLB 4, 9, 86; DLBD 1; MTCW; WLC

Andouard
See Giraudoux, (Hippolyte) Jean

Andrade, Carlos Drummond de ...... **CLC 18**
See also Drummond de Andrade, Carlos

Andrade, Mario de 1893-1945..... **TCLC 43**

Andrewes, Lancelot 1555-1626 .... **LC 5**

Andrews, Cicily Fairfield
See West, Rebecca

Andrews, Elton V.
See Pohl, Frederik

Andreyev, Leonid (Nikolaevich)
1871-1919 .... **TCLC 3**
See also CA 104

Andric, Ivo 1892-1975 .... **CLC 8**
See also CA 81-84; 57-60; MTCW

Angelique, Pierre
See Bataille, Georges

Angell, Roger 1920- .... **CLC 26**
See also CA 57-60; CANR 13

Angelou, Maya 1928-....... **CLC 12, 35, 64**
See also AAYA 7; BLC 1; BW; CA 65-68;
CANR 19; DLB 38; MTCW; SATA 49

Annensky, Innokenty Fyodorovich
1856-1909 .... **TCLC 14**
See also CA 110

Anon, Charles Robert
See Pessoa, Fernando (Antonio Nogueira)

Anouilh, Jean (Marie Lucien Pierre)
1910-1987 ...... **CLC 1, 3, 8, 13, 40, 50**
See also CA 17-20R; 123; CANR 32;
MTCW

Anthony, Florence
See Ai

Anthony, John
See Ciardi, John (Anthony)

Anthony, Peter
See Shaffer, Anthony (Joshua); Shaffer,
Peter (Levin)

Anthony, Piers 1934-............. **CLC 35**
See also CA 21-24R; CANR 28; DLB 8;
MTCW

Antoine, Marc
See Proust,
(Valentin-Louis-George-Eugene-)Marcel

Antoninus, Brother
See Everson, William (Oliver)

Antonioni, Michelangelo 1912- ..... **CLC 20**
See also CA 73-76

Antschel, Paul 1920-1970....... **CLC 10, 19**
See also Celan, Paul
See also CA 85-88; CANR 33; MTCW

Anwar, Chairil 1922-1949 .... **TCLC 22**
See also CA 121

Apollinaire, Guillaume .... **TCLC 3, 8**
See also Kostrowitzki, Wilhelm Apollinaris
de

Appelfeld, Aharon 1932- .... **CLC 23, 47**
See also CA 112; 133

Apple, Max (Isaac) 1941-........ **CLC 9, 33**
See also CA 81-84; CANR 19

Appleman, Philip (Dean) 1926-..... **CLC 51**
See also CA 13-16R; CANR 6, 29

Appleton, Lawrence
See Lovecraft, H(oward) P(hillips)

Apuleius, (Lucius Madaurensis)
    125(?)-175(?) . . . . **CMLC 1**

Aquin, Hubert 1929-1977 . . . . **CLC 15**
    See also CA 105; DLB 53

Aragon, Louis 1897-1982 . . . . **CLC 3, 22**
    See also CA 69-72; 108; CANR 28;
    DLB 72; MTCW

Arany, Janos 1817-1882 . . . . **NCLC 34**

Arbuthnot, John 1667-1735 . . . . **LC 1**
    See also DLB 101

Archer, Herbert Winslow
    See Mencken, H(enry) L(ouis)

Archer, Jeffrey (Howard) 1940- . . . . **CLC 28**
    See also BEST 89:3; CA 77-80; CANR 22

Archer, Jules 1915- . . . . **CLC 12**
    See also CA 9-12R; CANR 6; SAAS 5;
    SATA 4

Archer, Lee
    See Ellison, Harlan

Arden, John 1930- . . . . **CLC 6, 13, 15**
    See also CA 13-16R; CAAS 4; CANR 31;
    DLB 13; MTCW

Arenas, Reinaldo 1943-1990 . . . . **CLC 41**
    See also CA 124; 128; 133; HW

Arendt, Hannah 1906-1975 . . . . **CLC 66**
    See also CA 17-20R; 61-64; CANR 26;
    MTCW

Aretino, Pietro 1492-1556 . . . . **LC 12**

Arguedas, Jose Maria
    1911-1969 . . . . **CLC 10, 18**
    See also CA 89-92; DLB 113; HW

Argueta, Manlio 1936- . . . . **CLC 31**
    See also CA 131; HW

Ariosto, Ludovico 1474-1533 . . . . **LC 6**

Aristides
    See Epstein, Joseph

Aristophanes
    450B.C.-385B.C. . . . . **CMLC 4; DC 2**

Arlt, Roberto (Godofredo Christophersen)
    1900-1942 . . . . **TCLC 29**
    See also CA 123; 131; HW

Armah, Ayi Kwei 1939- . . . . **CLC 5, 33**
    See also BLC 1; BW; CA 61-64; CANR 21;
    DLB 117; MTCW

Armatrading, Joan 1950- . . . . **CLC 17**
    See also CA 114

Arnette, Robert
    See Silverberg, Robert

Arnim, Achim von (Ludwig Joachim von
    Arnim) 1781-1831 . . . . **NCLC 5**
    See also DLB 90

Arnim, Bettina von 1785-1859 . . . . **NCLC 38**
    See also DLB 90

Arnold, Matthew
    1822-1888 . . . . **NCLC 6, 29; PC 5**
    See also CDBLB 1832-1890; DLB 32, 57;
    WLC

Arnold, Thomas 1795-1842 . . . . . . **NCLC 18**
    See also DLB 55

Arnow, Harriette (Louisa) Simpson
    1908-1986 . . . . **CLC 2, 7, 18**
    See also CA 9-12R; 118; CANR 14; DLB 6;
    MTCW; SATA 42, 47

Arp, Hans
    See Arp, Jean

Arp, Jean 1887-1966 . . . . **CLC 5**
    See also CA 81-84; 25-28R

Arrabal . . . . **CLC 2, 9, 18**
    See also Arrabal, Fernando

Arrabal, Fernando 1932- . . . . **CLC 58**
    See also Arrabal
    See also CA 9-12R; CANR 15

Arrick, Fran . . . . **CLC 30**

Artaud, Antonin 1896-1948 . . . . . **TCLC 3, 36**
    See also CA 104

Arthur, Ruth M(abel) 1905-1979 . . . . **CLC 12**
    See also CA 9-12R; 85-88; CANR 4;
    SATA 7, 26

Artsybashev, Mikhail (Petrovich)
    1878-1927 . . . . **TCLC 31**

Arundel, Honor (Morfydd)
    1919-1973 . . . . **CLC 17**
    See also CA 21-22; 41-44R; CAP 2;
    SATA 4, 24

Asch, Sholem 1880-1957 . . . . **TCLC 3**
    See also CA 105

Ash, Shalom
    See Asch, Sholem

Ashbery, John (Lawrence)
    1927- . . . **CLC 2, 3, 4, 6, 9, 13, 15, 25, 41**
    See also CA 5-8R; CANR 9, 37; DLB 5;
    DLBY 81; MTCW

Ashdown, Clifford
    See Freeman, R(ichard) Austin

Ashe, Gordon
    See Creasey, John

Ashton-Warner, Sylvia (Constance)
    1908-1984 . . . . **CLC 19**
    See also CA 69-72; 112; CANR 29; MTCW

Asimov, Isaac
    1920-1992 . . . . **CLC 1, 3, 9, 19, 26**
    See also BEST 90:2; CA 1-4R; 137;
    CANR 2, 19, 36; CLR 12; DLB 8;
    MAICYA; MTCW; SATA 1, 26

Astley, Thea (Beatrice May)
    1925- . . . . **CLC 41**
    See also CA 65-68; CANR 11

Aston, James
    See White, T(erence) H(anbury)

Asturias, Miguel Angel
    1899-1974 . . . . **CLC 3, 8, 13**
    See also CA 25-28; 49-52; CANR 32;
    CAP 2; DLB 113; HW; MTCW

Atares, Carlos Saura
    See Saura (Atares), Carlos

Atheling, William
    See Pound, Ezra (Weston Loomis)

Atheling, William Jr.
    See Blish, James (Benjamin)

Atherton, Gertrude (Franklin Horn)
    1857-1948 . . . . **TCLC 2**
    See also CA 104; DLB 9, 78

Atherton, Lucius
    See Masters, Edgar Lee

Atkins, Jack
    See Harris, Mark

Atticus
    See Fleming, Ian (Lancaster)

Atwood, Margaret (Eleanor)
    1939- . . . . **CLC 2, 3, 4, 8, 13, 15, 25, 44;**
                                                    SSC 2
    See also BEST 89:2; CA 49-52; CANR 3,
    24, 33; DLB 53; MTCW; SATA 50; WLC

Aubigny, Pierre d'
    See Mencken, H(enry) L(ouis)

Aubin, Penelope 1685-1731(?) . . . . **LC 9**
    See also DLB 39

Auchincloss, Louis (Stanton)
    1917- . . . . **CLC 4, 6, 9, 18, 45**
    See also CA 1-4R; CANR 6, 29; DLB 2;
    DLBY 80; MTCW

Auden, W(ystan) H(ugh)
    1907-1973 . . . . . **CLC 1, 2, 3, 4, 6, 9, 11,**
                                                14, 43; PC 1
    See also CA 9-12R; 45-48; CANR 5;
    CDBLB 1914-1945; DLB 10, 20; MTCW;
    WLC

Audiberti, Jacques 1900-1965 . . . . . . **CLC 38**
    See also CA 25-28R

Auel, Jean M(arie) 1936- . . . . **CLC 31**
    See also AAYA 7; BEST 90:4; CA 103;
    CANR 21

Auerbach, Erich 1892-1957 . . . . **TCLC 43**
    See also CA 118

Augier, Emile 1820-1889 . . . . **NCLC 31**

August, John
    See De Voto, Bernard (Augustine)

Augustine, St. 354-430 . . . . **CMLC 6**

Aurelius
    See Bourne, Randolph S(illiman)

Austen, Jane
    1775-1817 . . . . **NCLC 1, 13, 19, 33**
    See also CDBLB 1789-1832; DLB 116;
    WLC

Auster, Paul 1947- . . . . **CLC 47**
    See also CA 69-72; CANR 23

Austin, Mary (Hunter)
    1868-1934 . . . . **TCLC 25**
    See also CA 109; DLB 9, 78

Autran Dourado, Waldomiro
    See Dourado, (Waldomiro Freitas) Autran

Averroes 1126-1198 . . . . **CMLC 7**
    See also DLB 115

Avison, Margaret 1918- . . . . **CLC 2, 4**
    See also CA 17-20R; DLB 53; MTCW

Ayckbourn, Alan
    1939- . . . . **CLC 5, 8, 18, 33, 74**
    See also CA 21-24R; CANR 31; DLB 13;
    MTCW

Aydy, Catherine
    See Tennant, Emma (Christina)

Ayme, Marcel (Andre) 1902-1967 . . . **CLC 11**
    See also CA 89-92; CLR 25; DLB 72

Ayrton, Michael 1921-1975 . . . . **CLC 7**
    See also CA 5-8R; 61-64; CANR 9, 21

Azorin . . . . **CLC 11**
    See also Martinez Ruiz, Jose

Azuela, Mariano 1873-1952 . . . . **TCLC 3**
    See also CA 104; 131; HW; MTCW

Baastad, Babbis Friis
See Friis-Baastad, Babbis Ellinor

Bab
See Gilbert, W(illiam) S(chwenck)

Babbis, Eleanor
See Friis-Baastad, Babbis Ellinor

Babel, Isaac (Emanuilovich)........ **TCLC 13**
See also Babel, Isaak (Emmanuilovich)

Babel, Isaak (Emmanuilovich)
1894-1941(?) .... **TCLC 2**
See also Babel, Isaac (Emanuilovich)
See also CA 104

Babits, Mihaly 1883-1941 .... **TCLC 14**
See also CA 114

Babur 1483-1530.................. **LC 18**

Bacchelli, Riccardo 1891-1985 ..... **CLC 19**
See also CA 29-32R; 117

Bach, Richard (David) 1936- .... **CLC 14**
See also AITN 1; BEST 89:2; CA 9-12R;
CANR 18; MTCW; SATA 13

Bachman, Richard
See King, Stephen (Edwin)

Bachmann, Ingeborg 1926-1973..... **CLC 69**
See also CA 93-96; 45-48; DLB 85

Bacon, Francis 1561-1626 .... **LC 18**
See also CDBLB Before 1660

Bacovia, George................ **TCLC 24**
See also Vasiliu, Gheorghe

Badanes, Jerome 1937-........... **CLC 59**

Bagehot, Walter 1826-1877 ...... **NCLC 10**
See also DLB 55

Bagnold, Enid 1889-1981......... **CLC 25**
See also CA 5-8R; 103; CANR 5; DLB 13;
MAICYA; SATA 1, 25

Bagrjana, Elisaveta
See Belcheva, Elisaveta

Bagryana, Elisaveta
See Belcheva, Elisaveta

Bailey, Paul 1937- .... **CLC 45**
See also CA 21-24R; CANR 16; DLB 14

Baillie, Joanna 1762-1851 .... **NCLC 2**
See also DLB 93

Bainbridge, Beryl (Margaret)
1933- .... **CLC 4, 5, 8, 10, 14, 18, 22, 62**
See also CA 21-24R; CANR 24; DLB 14;
MTCW

Baker, Elliott 1922- .... **CLC 8**
See also CA 45-48; CANR 2

Baker, Nicholson 1957- .... **CLC 61**
See also CA 135

Baker, Ray Stannard 1870-1946 ... **TCLC 47**
See also CA 118

Baker, Russell (Wayne) 1925-...... **CLC 31**
See also BEST 89:4; CA 57-60; CANR 11;
MTCW

Bakshi, Ralph 1938(?)-........... **CLC 26**
See also CA 112; 138

Bakunin, Mikhail (Alexandrovich)
1814-1876 .... **NCLC 25**

Baldwin, James (Arthur)
1924-1987 ..... **CLC 1, 2, 3, 4, 5, 8, 13,
15, 17, 42, 50, 67; DC 1; SSC 10**
See also AAYA 4; BLC 1; BW; CA 1-4R;
124; CABS 1; CANR 3, 24;
CDALB 1941-1968; DLB 2, 7, 33;
DLBY 87; MTCW; SATA 9, 54; WLC

Ballard, J(ames) G(raham)
1930- .... **CLC 3, 6, 14, 36; SSC 1**
See also AAYA 3; CA 5-8R; CANR 15, 39;
DLB 14; MTCW

Balmont, Konstantin (Dmitriyevich)
1867-1943 .... **TCLC 11**
See also CA 109

Balzac, Honore de
1799-1850 .... **NCLC 5, 35; SSC 5**
See also DLB 119; WLC

Bambara, Toni Cade 1939- .... **CLC 19**
See also AAYA 5; BLC 1; BW; CA 29-32R;
CANR 24; DLB 38; MTCW

Bamdad, A.
See Shamlu, Ahmad

Banat, D. R.
See Bradbury, Ray (Douglas)

Bancroft, Laura
See Baum, L(yman) Frank

Banim, John 1798-1842 .... **NCLC 13**
See also DLB 116

Banim, Michael 1796-1874 ...... **NCLC 13**

Banks, Iain
See Banks, Iain M(enzies)

Banks, Iain M(enzies) 1954- .... **CLC 34**
See also CA 123; 128

Banks, Lynne Reid .... **CLC 23**
See also Reid Banks, Lynne
See also AAYA 6

Banks, Russell 1940- .... **CLC 37, 72**
See also CA 65-68; CAAS 15; CANR 19

Banville, John 1945-.............. **CLC 46**
See also CA 117; 128; DLB 14

Banville, Theodore (Faullain) de
1832-1891 .... **NCLC 9**

Baraka, Amiri
1934- ... **CLC 1, 2, 3, 5, 10, 14, 33; PC 4**
See also Jones, LeRoi
See also BLC 1; BW; CA 21-24R; CABS 3;
CANR 27, 38; CDALB 1941-1968;
DLB 5, 7, 16, 38; DLBD 8; MTCW

Barbellion, W. N. P............... **TCLC 24**
See also Cummings, Bruce F(rederick)

Barbera, Jack 1945-.............. **CLC 44**
See also CA 110

Barbey d'Aurevilly, Jules Amedee
1808-1889 .... **NCLC 1**
See also DLB 119

Barbusse, Henri 1873-1935 .... **TCLC 5**
See also CA 105; DLB 65

Barclay, Bill
See Moorcock, Michael (John)

Barclay, William Ewert
See Moorcock, Michael (John)

Barea, Arturo 1897-1957 .... **TCLC 14**
See also CA 111

Barfoot, Joan 1946- .... **CLC 18**
See also CA 105

Baring, Maurice 1874-1945 .... **TCLC 8**
See also CA 105; DLB 34

Barker, Clive 1952- .... **CLC 52**
See also BEST 90:3; CA 121; 129; MTCW

Barker, George Granville
1913-1991 .... **CLC 8, 48**
See also CA 9-12R; 135; CANR 7, 38;
DLB 20; MTCW

Barker, Harley Granville
See Granville-Barker, Harley
See also DLB 10

Barker, Howard 1946-........... **CLC 37**
See also CA 102; DLB 13

Barker, Pat 1943-.............. **CLC 32**
See also CA 117; 122

Barlow, Joel 1754-1812 .... **NCLC 23**
See also DLB 37

Barnard, Mary (Ethel) 1909-...... **CLC 48**
See also CA 21-22; CAP 2

Barnes, Djuna
1892-1982 ... **CLC 3, 4, 8, 11, 29; SSC 3**
See also CA 9-12R; 107; CANR 16; DLB 4,
9, 45; MTCW

Barnes, Julian 1946-.............. **CLC 42**
See also CA 102; CANR 19

Barnes, Peter 1931-............. **CLC 5, 56**
See also CA 65-68; CAAS 12; CANR 33,
34; DLB 13; MTCW

Baroja (y Nessi), Pio 1872-1956 .... **TCLC 8**
See also CA 104

Baron, David
See Pinter, Harold

Baron Corvo
See Rolfe, Frederick (William Serafino
Austin Lewis Mary)

Barondess, Sue K(aufman)
1926-1977 .... **CLC 8**
See also Kaufman, Sue
See also CA 1-4R; 69-72; CANR 1

Baron de Teive
See Pessoa, Fernando (Antonio Nogueira)

Barres, Maurice 1862-1923 .... **TCLC 47**

Barreto, Afonso Henrique de Lima
See Lima Barreto, Afonso Henrique de

Barrett, (Roger) Syd 1946- .... **CLC 35**
See also Pink Floyd

Barrett, William (Christopher)
1913- .... **CLC 27**
See also CA 13-16R; CANR 11

Barrie, J(ames) M(atthew)
1860-1937 .... **TCLC 2**
See also CA 104; 136; CDBLB 1890-1914;
CLR 16; DLB 10; MAICYA; YABC 1

Barrington, Michael
See Moorcock, Michael (John)

Barrol, Grady
See Bograd, Larry

Barry, Mike
See Malzberg, Barry N(athaniel)

Barry, Philip 1896-1949.......... **TCLC 11**
See also CA 109; DLB 7

Bart, Andre Schwarz
   See Schwarz-Bart, Andre

Barth, John (Simmons)
   1930-...... **CLC 1, 2, 3, 5, 7, 9, 10, 14,
                  27, 51; SSC 10**
   See also AITN 1, 2; CA 1-4R; CABS 1;
   CANR 5, 23; DLB 2; MTCW

Barthelme, Donald
   1931-1989 ..... **CLC 1, 2, 3, 5, 6, 8, 13,
                  23, 46, 59; SSC 2**
   See also CA 21-24R; 129; CANR 20;
   DLB 2; DLBY 80, 89; MTCW; SATA 7,
   62

Barthelme, Frederick 1943-........ **CLC 36**
   See also CA 114; 122; DLBY 85

Barthes, Roland (Gerard)
   1915-1980 .... **CLC 24**
   See also CA 130; 97-100; MTCW

Barzun, Jacques (Martin) 1907- .... **CLC 51**
   See also CA 61-64; CANR 22

Bashevis, Isaac
   See Singer, Isaac Bashevis

Bashkirtseff, Marie 1859-1884 ... **NCLC 27**

Basho
   See Matsuo Basho

Bass, Kingsley B. Jr.
   See Bullins, Ed

Bassani, Giorgio 1916-............ **CLC 9**
   See also CA 65-68; CANR 33; MTCW

Bastos, Augusto (Antonio) Roa
   See Roa Bastos, Augusto (Antonio)

Bataille, Georges 1897-1962 .... **CLC 29**
   See also CA 101; 89-92

Bates, H(erbert) E(rnest)
   1905-1974 .... **CLC 46; SSC 10**
   See also CA 93-96; 45-48; CANR 34;
   MTCW

Bauchart
   See Camus, Albert

Baudelaire, Charles
   1821-1867 .... **NCLC 6, 29; PC 1**
   See also WLC

Baudrillard, Jean 1929-........... **CLC 60**

Baum, L(yman) Frank 1856-1919 ... **TCLC 7**
   See also CA 108; 133; CLR 15; DLB 22;
   MAICYA; MTCW; SATA 18

Baum, Louis F.
   See Baum, L(yman) Frank

Baumbach, Jonathan 1933- ...... **CLC 6, 23**
   See also CA 13-16R; CAAS 5; CANR 12;
   DLBY 80; MTCW

Bausch, Richard (Carl) 1945- ..... **CLC 51**
   See also CA 101; CAAS 14

Baxter, Charles 1947-............. **CLC 45**
   See also CA 57-60

Baxter, James K(eir) 1926-1972 .... **CLC 14**
   See also CA 77-80

Baxter, John
   See Hunt, E(verette) Howard Jr.

Bayer, Sylvia
   See Glassco, John

Beagle, Peter S(oyer) 1939-........ **CLC 7**
   See also CA 9-12R; CANR 4; DLBY 80;
   SATA 60

Bean, Normal
   See Burroughs, Edgar Rice

Beard, Charles A(ustin)
   1874-1948 .... **TCLC 15**
   See also CA 115; DLB 17; SATA 18

Beardsley, Aubrey 1872-1898 ..... **NCLC 6**

Beattie, Ann
   1947- .... **CLC 8, 13, 18, 40, 63; SSC 11**
   See also BEST 90:2; CA 81-84; DLBY 82;
   MTCW

Beattie, James 1735-1803 .... **NCLC 25**
   See also DLB 109

Beauchamp, Kathleen Mansfield 1888-1923
   See Mansfield, Katherine
   See also CA 104; 134

**Beauvoir, Simone (Lucie Ernestine Marie
   Bertrand) de**
   1908-1986 ... **CLC 1, 2, 4, 8, 14, 31, 44,
                  50, 71**
   See also CA 9-12R; 118; CANR 28;
   DLB 72; DLBY 86; MTCW; WLC

Becker, Jurek 1937-............ **CLC 7, 19**
   See also CA 85-88; DLB 75

Becker, Walter 1950-............. **CLC 26**

Beckett, Samuel (Barclay)
   1906-1989 ..... **CLC 1, 2, 3, 4, 6, 9, 10,
                  11, 14, 18, 29, 57, 59**
   See also CA 5-8R; 130; CANR 33;
   CDBLB 1945-1960; DLB 13, 15;
   DLBY 90; MTCW; WLC

Beckford, William 1760-1844 .... **NCLC 16**
   See also DLB 39

Beckman, Gunnel 1910-.......... **CLC 26**
   See also CA 33-36R; CANR 15; CLR 25;
   MAICYA; SAAS 9; SATA 6

Becque, Henri 1837-1899........ **NCLC 3**

Beddoes, Thomas Lovell
   1803-1849 .... **NCLC 3**
   See also DLB 96

Bedford, Donald F.
   See Fearing, Kenneth (Flexner)

Beecher, Catharine Esther
   1800-1878 .... **NCLC 30**
   See also DLB 1

Beecher, John 1904-1980.......... **CLC 6**
   See also AITN 1; CA 5-8R; 105; CANR 8

Beer, Johann 1655-1700............ **LC 5**

Beer, Patricia 1924-.............. **CLC 58**
   See also CA 61-64; CANR 13; DLB 40

Beerbohm, Henry Maximilian
   1872-1956 .... **TCLC 1, 24**
   See also CA 104; DLB 34, 100

Begiebing, Robert J(ohn) 1946-..... **CLC 70**
   See also CA 122

Behan, Brendan
   1923-1964 ....**CLC 1, 8, 11, 15**
   See also CA 73-76; CANR 33;
   CDBLB 1945-1960; DLB 13; MTCW

Behn, Aphra 1640(?)-1689 .... **LC 1**
   See also DLB 39, 80; WLC

Behrman, S(amuel) N(athaniel)
   1893-1973 .... **CLC 40**
   See also CA 13-16; 45-48; CAP 1; DLB 7,
   44

Belasco, David 1853-1931 .... **TCLC 3**
   See also CA 104; DLB 7

Belcheva, Elisaveta 1893- .... **CLC 10**

Beldone, Phil "Cheech"
   See Ellison, Harlan

Beleno
   See Azuela, Mariano

Belinski, Vissarion Grigoryevich
   1811-1848 .... **NCLC 5**

Belitt, Ben 1911-................ **CLC 22**
   See also CA 13-16R; CAAS 4; CANR 7;
   DLB 5

Bell, James Madison 1826-1902 ... **TCLC 43**
   See also BLC 1; BW; CA 122; 124; DLB 50

Bell, Madison (Smartt) 1957-...... **CLC 41**
   See also CA 111; CANR 28

Bell, Marvin (Hartley) 1937-..... **CLC 8, 31**
   See also CA 21-24R; CAAS 14; DLB 5;
   MTCW

Bell, W. L. D.
   See Mencken, H(enry) L(ouis)

Bellamy, Atwood C.
   See Mencken, H(enry) L(ouis)

Bellamy, Edward 1850-1898 ...... **NCLC 4**
   See also DLB 12

Bellin, Edward J.
   See Kuttner, Henry

Belloc, (Joseph) Hilaire (Pierre)
   1870-1953 .... **TCLC 7, 18**
   See also CA 106; DLB 19, 100; YABC 1

Belloc, Joseph Peter Rene Hilaire
   See Belloc, (Joseph) Hilaire (Pierre)

Belloc, Joseph Pierre Hilaire
   See Belloc, (Joseph) Hilaire (Pierre)

Belloc, M. A.
   See Lowndes, Marie Adelaide (Belloc)

Bellow, Saul
   1915- ..... **CLC 1, 2, 3, 6, 8, 10, 13, 15,
                  25, 33, 34, 63**
   See also AITN 2; BEST 89:3; CA 5-8R;
   CABS 1; CANR 29; CDALB 1941-1968;
   DLB 2, 28; DLBD 3; DLBY 82; MTCW;
   WLC

Belser, Reimond Karel Maria de
   1929-...................... **CLC 14**

Bely, Andrey .... **TCLC 7**
   See also Bugayev, Boris Nikolayevich

Benary, Margot
   See Benary-Isbert, Margot

Benary-Isbert, Margot 1889-1979... **CLC 12**
   See also CA 5-8R; 89-92; CANR 4;
   CLR 12; MAICYA; SATA 2, 21

Benavente (y Martinez), Jacinto
   1866-1954 .... **TCLC 3**
   See also CA 106; 131; HW; MTCW

Benchley, Peter (Bradford)
   1940-...................... **CLC 4, 8**
   See also AITN 2; CA 17-20R; CANR 12,
   35; MTCW; SATA 3

Benchley, Robert (Charles)
   1889-1945 .... **TCLC 1**
   See also CA 105; DLB 11

Benedikt, Michael 1935- .... **CLC 4, 14**
   See also CA 13-16R; CANR 7; DLB 5

Benet, Juan 1927-. . . . . CLC 28

Benet, Stephen Vincent
1898-1943 . . . . TCLC 7; SSC 10
See also CA 104; DLB 4, 48, 102; YABC 1

Benet, William Rose 1886-1950 . . . TCLC 28
See also CA 118; DLB 45

Benford, Gregory (Albert) 1941-. . . . CLC 52
See also CA 69-72; CANR 12, 24;
DLBY 82

Benjamin, Lois
See Gould, Lois

Benjamin, Walter 1892-1940. . . . . TCLC 39

Benn, Gottfried 1886-1956. . . . . TCLC 3
See also CA 106; DLB 56

Bennett, Alan 1934-. . . . . CLC 45
See also CA 103; CANR 35; MTCW

Bennett, (Enoch) Arnold
1867-1931 . . . . TCLC 5, 20
See also CA 106; CDBLB 1890-1914;
DLB 10, 34, 98

Bennett, Elizabeth
See Mitchell, Margaret (Munnerlyn)

Bennett, George Harold 1930-
See Bennett, Hal
See also BW; CA 97-100

Bennett, Hal . . . . CLC 5
See also Bennett, George Harold
See also DLB 33

Bennett, Jay 1912-. . . . . CLC 35
See also CA 69-72; CANR 11; SAAS 4;
SATA 27, 41

Bennett, Louise (Simone) 1919-. . . . . CLC 28
See also BLC 1; DLB 117

Benson, E(dward) F(rederic)
1867-1940 . . . . TCLC 27
See also CA 114

Benson, Jackson J. 1930-. . . . . CLC 34
See also CA 25-28R; DLB 111

Benson, Sally 1900-1972 . . . . CLC 17
See also CA 19-20; 37-40R; CAP 1;
SATA 1, 27, 35

Benson, Stella 1892-1933. . . . . TCLC 17
See also CA 117; DLB 36

Bentham, Jeremy 1748-1832 . . . . . NCLC 38
See also DLB 107

Bentley, E(dmund) C(lerihew)
1875-1956 . . . . TCLC 12
See also CA 108; DLB 70

Bentley, Eric (Russell) 1916-. . . . . . . CLC 24
See also CA 5-8R; CANR 6

Beranger, Pierre Jean de
1780-1857 . . . . NCLC 34

Berger, Colonel
See Malraux, (Georges-)Andre

Berger, John (Peter) 1926- . . . . . . CLC 2, 19
See also CA 81-84; DLB 14

Berger, Melvin H. 1927-. . . . . CLC 12
See also CA 5-8R; CANR 4; SAAS 2;
SATA 5

Berger, Thomas (Louis)
1924-. . . . . CLC 3, 5, 8, 11, 18, 38
See also CA 1-4R; CANR 5, 28; DLB 2;
DLBY 80; MTCW

Bergman, (Ernst) Ingmar
1918- . . . . CLC 16, 72
See also CA 81-84; CANR 33

Bergson, Henri 1859-1941 . . . . TCLC 32

Bergstein, Eleanor 1938-. . . . . CLC 4
See also CA 53-56; CANR 5

Berkoff, Steven 1937-. . . . . CLC 56
See also CA 104

Bermant, Chaim (Icyk) 1929- . . . . . . CLC 40
See also CA 57-60; CANR 6, 31

Bernanos, (Paul Louis) Georges
1888-1948 . . . . TCLC 3
See also CA 104; 130; DLB 72

Bernard, April 1956- . . . . CLC 59
See also CA 131

Bernhard, Thomas
1931-1989 . . . . CLC 3, 32, 61
See also CA 85-88; 127; CANR 32;
DLB 85; MTCW

Berrigan, Daniel 1921-. . . . . CLC 4
See also CA 33-36R; CAAS 1; CANR 11;
DLB 5

Berrigan, Edmund Joseph Michael Jr.
1934-1983
See Berrigan, Ted
See also CA 61-64; 110; CANR 14

Berrigan, Ted. . . . . CLC 37
See also Berrigan, Edmund Joseph Michael
Jr.
See also DLB 5

Berry, Charles Edward Anderson 1931-
See Berry, Chuck
See also CA 115

Berry, Chuck. . . . . CLC 17
See also Berry, Charles Edward Anderson

Berry, Jonas
See Ashbery, John (Lawrence)

Berry, Wendell (Erdman)
1934- . . . . CLC 4, 6, 8, 27, 46
See also AITN 1; CA 73-76; DLB 5, 6

Berryman, John
1914-1972 . . . . . CLC 1, 2, 3, 4, 6, 8, 10,
13, 25, 62
See also CA 13-16; 33-36R; CABS 2;
CANR 35; CAP 1; CDALB 1941-1968;
DLB 48; MTCW

Bertolucci, Bernardo 1940- . . . . CLC 16
See also CA 106

Bertrand, Aloysius 1807-1841 . . . . NCLC 31

Bertran de Born c. 1140-1215 . . . . . CMLC 5

Besant, Annie (Wood) 1847-1933 . . . TCLC 9
See also CA 105

Bessie, Alvah 1904-1985. . . . . CLC 23
See also CA 5-8R; 116; CANR 2; DLB 26

Bethlen, T. D.
See Silverberg, Robert

Beti, Mongo. . . . . CLC 27
See also Biyidi, Alexandre
See also BLC 1

Betjeman, John
1906-1984 . . . . CLC 2, 6, 10, 34, 43
See also CA 9-12R; 112; CANR 33;
CDBLB 1945-1960; DLB 20; DLBY 84;
MTCW

Betti, Ugo 1892-1953 . . . . TCLC 5
See also CA 104

Betts, Doris (Waugh) 1932-. . . . CLC 3, 6, 28
See also CA 13-16R; CANR 9; DLBY 82

Bevan, Alistair
See Roberts, Keith (John Kingston)

Beynon, John
See Harris, John (Wyndham Parkes Lucas)
Beynon

Bialik, Chaim Nachman
1873-1934 . . . . TCLC 25

Bickerstaff, Isaac
See Swift, Jonathan

Bidart, Frank 19(?)-. . . . . CLC 33

Bienek, Horst 1930-. . . . . CLC 7, 11
See also CA 73-76; DLB 75

Bierce, Ambrose (Gwinett)
1842-1914(?) . . . . . TCLC 1, 7, 44; SSC 9
See also CA 104; CDALB 1865-1917;
DLB 11, 12, 23, 71, 74; WLC

Billings, Josh
See Shaw, Henry Wheeler

Billington, Rachel 1942-. . . . . CLC 43
See also AITN 2; CA 33-36R

Binyon, T(imothy) J(ohn) 1936- . . . . CLC 34
See also CA 111; CANR 28

Bioy Casares, Adolfo 1914-. . . . CLC 4, 8, 13
See also CA 29-32R; CANR 19; DLB 113;
HW; MTCW

Bird, C.
See Ellison, Harlan

Bird, Cordwainer
See Ellison, Harlan

Bird, Robert Montgomery
1806-1854 . . . . NCLC 1

Birney, (Alfred) Earle
1904-. . . . . CLC 1, 4, 6, 11
See also CA 1-4R; CANR 5, 20; DLB 88;
MTCW

Bishop, Elizabeth
1911-1979 . . . . . CLC 1, 4, 9, 13, 15, 32;
PC 3
See also CA 5-8R; 89-92; CABS 2;
CANR 26; CDALB 1968-1988; DLB 5;
MTCW; SATA 24

Bishop, John 1935-. . . . . CLC 10
See also CA 105

bissett, bill 1939- . . . . CLC 18
See also CA 69-72; CANR 15; DLB 53;
MTCW

Bitov, Andrei (Georgievich) 1937-. . . CLC 57

Biyidi, Alexandre 1932-
See Beti, Mongo
See also BW; CA 114; 124; MTCW

Bjarme, Brynjolf
See Ibsen, Henrik (Johan)

Bjoernson, Bjoernstjerne (Martinius)
1832-1910. . . . . TCLC 7, 37
See also CA 104

Black, Robert
See Holdstock, Robert P.

Blackburn, Paul 1926-1971 . . . . . . CLC 9, 43
See also CA 81-84; 33-36R; CANR 34;
DLB 16; DLBY 81

Black Elk 1863-1950 . . . . **TCLC 33**

Black Hobart
  See Sanders, (James) Ed(ward)

Blacklin, Malcolm
  See Chambers, Aidan

Blackmore, R(ichard) D(oddridge)
  1825-1900 . . . . **TCLC 27**
  See also CA 120; DLB 18

Blackmur, R(ichard) P(almer)
  1904-1965 . . . . **CLC 2, 24**
  See also CA 11-12; 25-28R; CAP 1; DLB 63

Black Tarantula, The
  See Acker, Kathy

Blackwood, Algernon (Henry)
  1869-1951 . . . . **TCLC 5**
  See also CA 105

Blackwood, Caroline 1931- . . . . **CLC 6, 9**
  See also CA 85-88; CANR 32; DLB 14;
  MTCW

Blade, Alexander
  See Hamilton, Edmond; Silverberg, Robert

Blair, Eric (Arthur) 1903-1950
  See Orwell, George
  See also CA 104; 132; MTCW; SATA 29

Blais, Marie-Claire
  1939- . . . . **CLC 2, 4, 6, 13, 22**
  See also CA 21-24R; CAAS 4; CANR 38;
  DLB 53; MTCW

Blaise, Clark 1940- . . . . **CLC 29**
  See also AITN 2; CA 53-56; CAAS 3;
  CANR 5; DLB 53

Blake, Nicholas
  See Day Lewis, C(ecil)
  See also DLB 77

Blake, William 1757-1827 . . . . **NCLC 13**
  See also CDBLB 1789-1832; DLB 93;
  MAICYA; SATA 30; WLC

Blasco Ibanez, Vicente
  1867-1928 . . . . **TCLC 12**
  See also CA 110; 131; HW; MTCW

Blatty, William Peter 1928- . . . . **CLC 2**
  See also CA 5-8R; CANR 9

Bleeck, Oliver
  See Thomas, Ross (Elmore)

Blessing, Lee 1949- . . . . **CLC 54**

Blish, James (Benjamin)
  1921-1975 . . . . **CLC 14**
  See also CA 1-4R; 57-60; CANR 3; DLB 8;
  MTCW; SATA 66

Bliss, Reginald
  See Wells, H(erbert) G(eorge)

Blixen, Karen (Christentze Dinesen)
  1885-1962
  See Dinesen, Isak
  See also CA 25-28; CANR 22; CAP 2;
  MTCW; SATA 44

Bloch, Robert (Albert) 1917- . . . . **CLC 33**
  See also CA 5-8R; CANR 5; DLB 44;
  SATA 12

Blok, Alexander (Alexandrovich)
  1880-1921 . . . . **TCLC 5**
  See also CA 104

Blom, Jan
  See Breytenbach, Breyten

Bloom, Harold 1930- . . . . **CLC 24**
  See also CA 13-16R; CANR 39; DLB 67

Bloomfield, Aurelius
  See Bourne, Randolph S(illiman)

Blount, Roy (Alton) Jr. 1941- . . . . . . **CLC 38**
  See also CA 53-56; CANR 10, 28; MTCW

Bloy, Leon 1846-1917 . . . . **TCLC 22**
  See also CA 121

Blume, Judy (Sussman) 1938- . . . **CLC 12, 30**
  See also AAYA 3; CA 29-32R; CANR 13,
  37; CLR 2, 15; DLB 52; MAICYA;
  MTCW; SATA 2, 31

Blunden, Edmund (Charles)
  1896-1974 . . . . **CLC 2, 56**
  See also CA 17-18; 45-48; CAP 2; DLB 20,
  100; MTCW

Bly, Robert (Elwood)
  1926- . . . . **CLC 1, 2, 5, 10, 15, 38**
  See also CA 5-8R; DLB 5; MTCW

Bobette
  See Simenon, Georges (Jacques Christian)

Boccaccio, Giovanni 1313-1375
  See also SSC 10

Bochco, Steven 1943- . . . . **CLC 35**
  See also CA 124; 138

Bodenheim, Maxwell 1892-1954 . . . **TCLC 44**
  See also CA 110; DLB 9, 45

Bodker, Cecil 1927- . . . . **CLC 21**
  See also CA 73-76; CANR 13; CLR 23;
  MAICYA; SATA 14

Boell, Heinrich (Theodor)
  1917-1985 . . . **CLC 2, 3, 6, 9, 11, 15, 27,
  39**
  See also Boll, Heinrich (Theodor)
  See also CA 21-24R; 116; CANR 24;
  DLB 69; DLBY 85; MTCW

Bogan, Louise 1897-1970 . . . . . **CLC 4, 39, 46**
  See also CA 73-76; 25-28R; CANR 33;
  DLB 45; MTCW

Bogarde, Dirk . . . . **CLC 19**
  See also Van Den Bogarde, Derek Jules
  Gaspard Ulric Niven
  See also DLB 14

Bogosian, Eric 1953- . . . . **CLC 45**
  See also CA 138

Bograd, Larry 1953- . . . . **CLC 35**
  See also CA 93-96; SATA 33

Boiardo, Matteo Maria 1441-1494 . . . . **LC 6**

Boileau-Despreaux, Nicolas
  1636-1711 . . . . **LC 3**

Boland, Eavan 1944- . . . . **CLC 40, 67**
  See also DLB 40

Boll, Heinrich (Theodor)
  1917-1985 . . . **CLC 2, 3, 6, 9, 11, 15, 27,
  39, 72**
  See also Boell, Heinrich (Theodor)
  See also DLB 69; DLBY 85; WLC

Bolt, Robert (Oxton) 1924- . . . . **CLC 14**
  See also CA 17-20R; CANR 35; DLB 13;
  MTCW

Bomkauf
  See Kaufman, Bob (Garnell)

Bonaventura . . . . **NCLC 35**
  See also DLB 90

Bond, Edward 1934- . . . . **CLC 4, 6, 13, 23**
  See also CA 25-28R; CANR 38; DLB 13;
  MTCW

Bonham, Frank 1914-1989 . . . . **CLC 12**
  See also AAYA 1; CA 9-12R; CANR 4, 36;
  MAICYA; SAAS 3; SATA 1, 49, 62

Bonnefoy, Yves 1923- . . . . **CLC 9, 15, 58**
  See also CA 85-88; CANR 33; MTCW

Bontemps, Arna(ud Wendell)
  1902-1973 . . . . **CLC 1, 18**
  See also BLC 1; BW; CA 1-4R; 41-44R;
  CANR 4, 35; CLR 6; DLB 48, 51;
  MAICYA; MTCW; SATA 2, 24, 44

Booth, Martin 1944- . . . . **CLC 13**
  See also CA 93-96; CAAS 2

Booth, Philip 1925- . . . . **CLC 23**
  See also CA 5-8R; CANR 5; DLBY 82

Booth, Wayne C(layson) 1921- . . . . . **CLC 24**
  See also CA 1-4R; CAAS 5; CANR 3;
  DLB 67

Borchert, Wolfgang 1921-1947 . . . . . **TCLC 5**
  See also CA 104; DLB 69

Borges, Jorge Luis
  1899-1986 . . . **CLC 1, 2, 3, 4, 6, 8, 9, 10,
  13, 19, 44, 48; SSC 4**
  See also CA 21-24R; CANR 19, 33;
  DLB 113; DLBY 86; HW; MTCW; WLC

Borowski, Tadeusz 1922-1951 . . . . . . **TCLC 9**
  See also CA 106

Borrow, George (Henry)
  1803-1881 . . . . **NCLC 9**
  See also DLB 21, 55

Bosschere, Jean de 1878(?)-1953 . . . **TCLC 19**
  See also CA 115

Boswell, James 1740-1795 . . . . **LC 4**
  See also CDBLB 1660-1789; DLB 104;
  WLC

Bottoms, David 1949- . . . . **CLC 53**
  See also CA 105; CANR 22; DLB 120;
  DLBY 83

Boucolon, Maryse 1937-
  See Conde, Maryse
  See also CA 110; CANR 30

Bourget, Paul (Charles Joseph)
  1852-1935 . . . . **TCLC 12**
  See also CA 107

Bourjaily, Vance (Nye) 1922- . . . . **CLC 8, 62**
  See also CA 1-4R; CAAS 1; CANR 2;
  DLB 2

Bourne, Randolph S(illiman)
  1886-1918 . . . . **TCLC 16**
  See also CA 117; DLB 63

Bova, Ben(jamin William) 1932- . . . . **CLC 45**
  See also CA 5-8R; CANR 11; CLR 3;
  DLBY 81; MAICYA; MTCW; SATA 6,
  68

Bowen, Elizabeth (Dorothea Cole)
  1899-1973 . . . . . **CLC 1, 3, 6, 11, 15, 22;
  SSC 3**
  See also CA 17-18; 41-44R; CANR 35;
  CAP 2; CDBLB 1945-1960; DLB 15;
  MTCW

Bowering, George 1935- . . . . **CLC 15, 47**
  See also CA 21-24R; CAAS 16; CANR 10;
  DLB 53

Bowering, Marilyn R(uthe) 1949- ... **CLC 32**
See also CA 101

Bowers, Edgar 1924- .... **CLC 9**
See also CA 5-8R; CANR 24; DLB 5

Bowie, David .... **CLC 17**
See also Jones, David Robert

Bowles, Jane (Sydney)
1917-1973 .... **CLC 3, 68**
See also CA 19-20; 41-44R; CAP 2

Bowles, Paul (Frederick)
1910- .... **CLC 1, 2, 19, 53; SSC 3**
See also CA 1-4R; CAAS 1; CANR 1, 19;
DLB 5, 6; MTCW

Box, Edgar
See Vidal, Gore

Boyd, Nancy
See Millay, Edna St. Vincent

Boyd, William 1952- .... **CLC 28, 53, 70**
See also CA 114; 120

Boyle, Kay 1902- .. **CLC 1, 5, 19, 58; SSC 5**
See also CA 13-16R; CAAS 1; CANR 29;
DLB 4, 9, 48, 86; MTCW

Boyle, Mark
See Kienzle, William X(avier)

Boyle, Patrick 1905-1982 .... **CLC 19**
See also CA 127

Boyle, T. Coraghessan 1948- ... **CLC 36, 55**
See also BEST 90:4; CA 120; DLBY 86

Brackenridge, Hugh Henry
1748-1816 .... **NCLC 7**
See also DLB 11, 37

Bradbury, Edward P.
See Moorcock, Michael (John)

Bradbury, Malcolm (Stanley)
1932- .... **CLC 32, 61**
See also CA 1-4R; CANR 1, 33; DLB 14;
MTCW

Bradbury, Ray (Douglas)
1920- .... **CLC 1, 3, 10, 15, 42**
See also AITN 1, 2; CA 1-4R; CANR 2, 30;
CDALB 1968-1988; DLB 2, 8; MTCW;
SATA 11, 64; WLC

Bradford, Gamaliel 1863-1932 ..... **TCLC 36**
See also DLB 17

Bradley, David (Henry Jr.) 1950- ... **CLC 23**
See also BLC 1; BW; CA 104; CANR 26;
DLB 33

Bradley, John Ed 1959- .... **CLC 55**

Bradley, Marion Zimmer 1930- ..... **CLC 30**
See also AAYA 9; CA 57-60; CAAS 10;
CANR 7, 31; DLB 8; MTCW

Bradstreet, Anne 1612(?)-1672 .... **LC 4**
See also CDALB 1640-1865; DLB 24

Bragg, Melvyn 1939- .... **CLC 10**
See also BEST 89:3; CA 57-60; CANR 10;
DLB 14

Braine, John (Gerard)
1922-1986 .... **CLC 1, 3, 41**
See also CA 1-4R; 120; CANR 1, 33;
CDBLB 1945-1960; DLB 15; DLBY 86;
MTCW

Brammer, William 1930(?)-1978 .... **CLC 31**
See also CA 77-80

Brancati, Vitaliano 1907-1954 ..... **TCLC 12**
See also CA 109

Brancato, Robin F(idler) 1936- ..... **CLC 35**
See also AAYA 9; CA 69-72; CANR 11;
SAAS 9; SATA 23

Brand, Millen 1906-1980 .... **CLC 7**
See also CA 21-24R; 97-100

Branden, Barbara .... **CLC 44**

Brandes, Georg (Morris Cohen)
1842-1927 .... **TCLC 10**
See also CA 105

Brandys, Kazimierz 1916- .... **CLC 62**

Branley, Franklyn M(ansfield)
1915- .... **CLC 21**
See also CA 33-36R; CANR 14, 39;
CLR 13; MAICYA; SATA 4, 68

Brathwaite, Edward (Kamau)
1930- .... **CLC 11**
See also BW; CA 25-28R; CANR 11, 26

Brautigan, Richard (Gary)
1935-1984 .... **CLC 1, 3, 5, 9, 12, 34, 42**
See also CA 53-56; 113; CANR 34; DLB 2,
5; DLBY 80, 84; MTCW; SATA 56

Braverman, Kate 1950- .... **CLC 67**
See also CA 89-92

Brecht, Bertolt
1898-1956 .... **TCLC 1, 6, 13, 35**
See also CA 104; 133; DLB 56; MTCW;
WLC

Brecht, Eugen Berthold Friedrich
See Brecht, Bertolt

Bremer, Fredrika 1801-1865 ..... **NCLC 11**

Brennan, Christopher John
1870-1932 .... **TCLC 17**
See also CA 117

Brennan, Maeve 1917- .... **CLC 5**
See also CA 81-84

Brentano, Clemens (Maria)
1778-1842 .... **NCLC 1**

Brent of Bin Bin
See Franklin, (Stella Maraia Sarah) Miles

Brenton, Howard 1942- .... **CLC 31**
See also CA 69-72; CANR 33; DLB 13;
MTCW

Breslin, James 1930-
See Breslin, Jimmy
See also CA 73-76; CANR 31; MTCW

Breslin, Jimmy .... **CLC 4, 43**
See also Breslin, James
See also AITN 1

Bresson, Robert 1907- .... **CLC 16**
See also CA 110

Breton, Andre 1896-1966 ... **CLC 2, 9, 15, 54**
See also CA 19-20; 25-28R; CAP 2;
DLB 65; MTCW

Breytenbach, Breyten 1939(?)- .. **CLC 23, 37**
See also CA 113; 129

Bridgers, Sue Ellen 1942- .... **CLC 26**
See also AAYA 8; CA 65-68; CANR 11,
36; CLR 18; DLB 52; MAICYA;
SAAS 1; SATA 22

Bridges, Robert (Seymour)
1844-1930 .... **TCLC 1**
See also CA 104; CDBLB 1890-1914;
DLB 19, 98

Bridie, James .... **TCLC 3**
See also Mavor, Osborne Henry
See also DLB 10

Brin, David 1950- .... **CLC 34**
See also CA 102; CANR 24; SATA 65

Brink, Andre (Philippus)
1935- .... **CLC 18, 36**
See also CA 104; CANR 39; MTCW

Brinsmead, H(esba) F(ay) 1922- .... **CLC 21**
See also CA 21-24R; CANR 10; MAICYA;
SAAS 5; SATA 18

Brittain, Vera (Mary)
1893(?)-1970 .... **CLC 23**
See also CA 13-16; 25-28R; CAP 1; MTCW

Broch, Hermann 1886-1951 .... **TCLC 20**
See also CA 117; DLB 85

Brock, Rose
See Hansen, Joseph

Brodkey, Harold 1930- .... **CLC 56**
See also CA 111

Brodsky, Iosif Alexandrovich 1940-
See Brodsky, Joseph
See also AITN 1; CA 41-44R; CANR 37;
MTCW

Brodsky, Joseph .... **CLC 4, 6, 13, 36, 50**
See also Brodsky, Iosif Alexandrovich

Brodsky, Michael Mark 1948- ..... **CLC 19**
See also CA 102; CANR 18

Bromell, Henry 1947- .... **CLC 5**
See also CA 53-56; CANR 9

Bromfield, Louis (Brucker)
1896-1956 .... **TCLC 11**
See also CA 107; DLB 4, 9, 86

Broner, E(sther) M(asserman)
1930- .... **CLC 19**
See also CA 17-20R; CANR 8, 25; DLB 28

Bronk, William 1918- .... **CLC 10**
See also CA 89-92; CANR 23

Bronstein, Lev Davidovich
See Trotsky, Leon

Bronte, Anne 1820-1849 .... **NCLC 4**
See also DLB 21

Bronte, Charlotte
1816-1855 .... **NCLC 3, 8, 33**
See also CDBLB 1832-1890; DLB 21; WLC

Bronte, (Jane) Emily
1818-1848 .... **NCLC 16, 35**
See also CDBLB 1832-1890; DLB 21, 32;
WLC

Brooke, Frances 1724-1789 .... **LC 6**
See also DLB 39, 99

Brooke, Henry 1703(?)-1783 .... **LC 1**
See also DLB 39

Brooke, Rupert (Chawner)
1887-1915 .... **TCLC 2, 7**
See also CA 104; 132; CDBLB 1914-1945;
DLB 19; MTCW; WLC

Brooke-Haven, P.
See Wodehouse, P(elham) G(renville)

Brooke-Rose, Christine 1926- ...... **CLC 40**
See also CA 13-16R; DLB 14

Brookner, Anita 1928- ...... **CLC 32, 34, 51**
See also CA 114; 120; CANR 37; DLBY 87;
MTCW

Brooks, Cleanth 1906- .... **CLC 24**
See also CA 17-20R; CANR 33, 35;
DLB 63; MTCW

Brooks, George
See Baum, L(yman) Frank

Brooks, Gwendolyn
1917- .... **CLC 1, 2, 4, 5, 15, 49**
See also AITN 1; BLC 1; BW; CA 1-4R;
CANR 1, 27; CDALB 1941-1968;
CLR 27; DLB 5, 76; MTCW; SATA 6;
WLC

Brooks, Mel...................... **CLC 12**
See also Kaminsky, Melvin
See also DLB 26

Brooks, Peter 1938- .... **CLC 34**
See also CA 45-48; CANR 1

Brooks, Van Wyck 1886-1963...... **CLC 29**
See also CA 1-4R; CANR 6; DLB 45, 63,
103

Brophy, Brigid (Antonia)
1929- .... **CLC 6, 11, 29**
See also CA 5-8R; CAAS 4; CANR 25;
DLB 14; MTCW

Brosman, Catharine Savage 1934-.... **CLC 9**
See also CA 61-64; CANR 21

Brother Antoninus
See Everson, William (Oliver)

Broughton, T(homas) Alan 1936- ... **CLC 19**
See also CA 45-48; CANR 2, 23

Broumas, Olga 1949- .... **CLC 10**
See also CA 85-88; CANR 20

Brown, Charles Brockden
1771-1810 .... **NCLC 22**
See also CDALB 1640-1865; DLB 37, 59,
73

Brown, Christy 1932-1981 .... **CLC 63**
See also CA 105; 104; DLB 14

Brown, Claude 1937- .... **CLC 30**
See also AAYA 7; BLC 1; BW; CA 73-76

Brown, Dee (Alexander) 1908- .. **CLC 18, 47**
See also CA 13-16R; CAAS 6; CANR 11;
DLBY 80; MTCW; SATA 5

Brown, George
See Wertmueller, Lina

Brown, George Douglas
1869-1902 .... **TCLC 28**

Brown, George Mackay 1921-.... **CLC 5, 48**
See also CA 21-24R; CAAS 6; CANR 12,
37; DLB 14, 27; MTCW; SATA 35

Brown, Moses
See Barrett, William (Christopher)

Brown, Rita Mae 1944-........ **CLC 18, 43**
See also CA 45-48; CANR 2, 11, 35;
MTCW

Brown, Roderick (Langmere) Haig-
See Haig-Brown, Roderick (Langmere)

Brown, Rosellen 1939-............ **CLC 32**
See also CA 77-80; CAAS 10; CANR 14

Brown, Sterling Allen
1901-1989 .... **CLC 1, 23, 59**
See also BLC 1; BW; CA 85-88; 127;
CANR 26; DLB 48, 51, 63; MTCW

Brown, Will
See Ainsworth, William Harrison

Brown, William Wells
1813-1884 .... **NCLC 2; DC 1**
See also BLC 1; DLB 3, 50

Browne, (Clyde) Jackson 1948(?)-... **CLC 21**
See also CA 120

Browning, Elizabeth Barrett
1806-1861 .... **NCLC 1, 16**
See also CDBLB 1832-1890; DLB 32; WLC

Browning, Robert
1812-1889 .... **NCLC 19; PC 2**
See also CDBLB 1832-1890; DLB 32;
YABC 1

Browning, Tod 1882-1962 .... **CLC 16**
See also CA 117

Bruccoli, Matthew J(oseph) 1931- .. **CLC 34**
See also CA 9-12R; CANR 7; DLB 103

Bruce, Lenny..................... **CLC 21**
See also Schneider, Leonard Alfred

Bruin, John
See Brutus, Dennis

Brulls, Christian
See Simenon, Georges (Jacques Christian)

Brunner, John (Kilian Houston)
1934- .... **CLC 8, 10**
See also CA 1-4R; CAAS 8; CANR 2, 37;
MTCW

Brutus, Dennis 1924- .... **CLC 43**
See also BLC 1; BW; CA 49-52; CAAS 14;
CANR 2, 27; DLB 117

Bryan, C(ourtlandt) D(ixon) B(arnes)
1936- .... **CLC 29**
See also CA 73-76; CANR 13

Bryan, Michael
See Moore, Brian

Bryant, William Cullen
1794-1878 .... **NCLC 6**
See also CDALB 1640-1865; DLB 3, 43, 59

Bryusov, Valery Yakovlevich
1873-1924 .... **TCLC 10**
See also CA 107

Buchan, John 1875-1940 .... **TCLC 41**
See also CA 108; DLB 34, 70; YABC 2

Buchanan, George 1506-1582 .... **LC 4**

Buchheim, Lothar-Guenther 1918- ... **CLC 6**
See also CA 85-88

Buchner, (Karl) Georg
1813-1837 .... **NCLC 26**

Buchwald, Art(hur) 1925-........... **CLC 33**
See also AITN 1; CA 5-8R; CANR 21;
MTCW; SATA 10

Buck, Pearl S(ydenstricker)
1892-1973 .... **CLC 7, 11, 18**
See also AITN 1; CA 1-4R; 41-44R;
CANR 1, 34; DLB 9, 102; MTCW;
SATA 1, 25

Buckler, Ernest 1908-1984........ **CLC 13**
See also CA 11-12; 114; CAP 1; DLB 68;
SATA 47

Buckley, Vincent (Thomas)
1925-1988 .... **CLC 57**
See also CA 101

Buckley, William F(rank) Jr.
1925- .... **CLC 7, 18, 37**
See also AITN 1; CA 1-4R; CANR 1, 24;
DLBY 80; MTCW

Buechner, (Carl) Frederick
1926- .... **CLC 2, 4, 6, 9**
See also CA 13-16R; CANR 11, 39;
DLBY 80; MTCW

Buell, John (Edward) 1927-........ **CLC 10**
See also CA 1-4R; DLB 53

Buero Vallejo, Antonio 1916- ... **CLC 15, 46**
See also CA 106; CANR 24; HW; MTCW

Bufalino, Gesualdo 1920-.......... **CLC 74**

Bugayev, Boris Nikolayevich 1880-1934
See Bely, Andrey
See also CA 104

Bukowski, Charles 1920-.... **CLC 2, 5, 9, 41**
See also CA 17-20R; DLB 5; MTCW

Bulgakov, Mikhail (Afanas'evich)
1891-1940 .... **TCLC 2, 16**
See also CA 105

Bullins, Ed 1935- .... **CLC 1, 5, 7**
See also BLC 1; BW; CA 49-52; CAAS 16;
CANR 24; DLB 7, 38; MTCW

Bulwer-Lytton, Edward (George Earle Lytton)
1803-1873 .... **NCLC 1**
See also DLB 21

Bunin, Ivan Alexeyevich
1870-1953 .... **TCLC 6; SSC 5**
See also CA 104

Bunting, Basil 1900-1985.... **CLC 10, 39, 47**
See also CA 53-56; 115; CANR 7; DLB 20

Bunuel, Luis 1900-1983 .... **CLC 16**
See also CA 101; 110; CANR 32; HW

Bunyan, John 1628-1688 .... **LC 4**
See also CDBLB 1660-1789; DLB 39; WLC

Burford, Eleanor
See Hibbert, Eleanor Burford

Burgess, Anthony
.. **CLC 1, 2, 4, 5, 8, 10, 13, 15, 22, 40, 62**
See also Wilson, John (Anthony) Burgess
See also AITN 1; CDBLB 1960 to Present;
DLB 14

Burke, Edmund 1729(?)-1797........ **LC 7**
See also DLB 104; WLC

Burke, Kenneth (Duva) 1897-.... **CLC 2, 24**
See also CA 5-8R; CANR 39; DLB 45, 63;
MTCW

Burke, Leda
See Garnett, David

Burke, Ralph
See Silverberg, Robert

Burney, Fanny 1752-1840 .... **NCLC 12**
See also DLB 39

Burns, Robert 1759-1796........... **LC 3**
See also CDBLB 1789-1832; DLB 109;
WLC

Burns, Tex
See L'Amour, Louis (Dearborn)

Burnshaw, Stanley 1906-..... **CLC 3, 13, 44**
See also CA 9-12R; DLB 48

Burr, Anne 1937- . . . . **CLC 6**
See also CA 25-28R

Burroughs, Edgar Rice
1875-1950 . . . . **TCLC 2, 32**
See also CA 104; 132; DLB 8; MTCW;
SATA 41

Burroughs, William S(eward)
1914- . . . . **CLC 1, 2, 5, 15, 22, 42**
See also AITN 2; CA 9-12R; CANR 20;
DLB 2, 8, 16; DLBY 81; MTCW; WLC

Busch, Frederick 1941- . . . **CLC 7, 10, 18, 47**
See also CA 33-36R; CAAS 1; DLB 6

Bush, Ronald 1946- . . . . **CLC 34**
See also CA 136

Bustos, F(rancisco)
See Borges, Jorge Luis

Bustos Domecq, H(onorio)
See Bioy Casares, Adolfo; Borges, Jorge
Luis

Bustos Domecq, H(onrio)
See Borges, Jorge Luis

Butler, Octavia E(stelle) 1947- . . . . . **CLC 38**
See also BW; CA 73-76; CANR 12, 24, 38;
DLB 33; MTCW

Butler, Samuel 1612-1680 . . . . **LC 16**
See also DLB 101

Butler, Samuel 1835-1902 . . . . . . **TCLC 1, 33**
See also CA 104; CDBLB 1890-1914;
DLB 18, 57; WLC

Butor, Michel (Marie Francois)
1926- . . . . **CLC 1, 3, 8, 11, 15**
See also CA 9-12R; CANR 33; DLB 83;
MTCW

Buzo, Alexander (John) 1944- . . . . . . **CLC 61**
See also CA 97-100; CANR 17, 39

Buzzati, Dino 1906-1972 . . . . **CLC 36**
See also CA 33-36R

Byars, Betsy (Cromer) 1928- . . . . **CLC 35**
See also CA 33-36R; CANR 18, 36; CLR 1,
16; DLB 52; MAICYA; MTCW; SAAS 1;
SATA 4, 46

Byatt, A(ntonia) S(usan Drabble)
1936- . . . . **CLC 19, 65**
See also CA 13-16R; CANR 13, 33;
DLB 14; MTCW

Byrne, David 1952- . . . . **CLC 26**
See also CA 127

Byrne, John Keyes 1926- . . . . **CLC 19**
See Leonard, Hugh
See also CA 102

Byron, George Gordon (Noel)
1788-1824 . . . . **NCLC 2, 12**
See also CDBLB 1789-1832; DLB 96, 110;
WLC

C.3.3.
See Wilde, Oscar (Fingal O'Flahertie Wills)

Caballero, Fernan 1796-1877 . . . . . **NCLC 10**

Cabell, James Branch 1879-1958 . . . **TCLC 6**
See also CA 105; DLB 9, 78

Cable, George Washington
1844-1925 . . . . **TCLC 4; SSC 4**
See also CA 104; DLB 12, 74

Cabrera Infante, G(uillermo)
1929- . . . . **CLC 5, 25, 45**
See also CA 85-88; CANR 29; DLB 113;
HW; MTCW

Cade, Toni
See Bambara, Toni Cade

Cadmus
See Buchan, John

Caedmon fl. 658-680 . . . . **CMLC 7**

Caeiro, Alberto
See Pessoa, Fernando (Antonio Nogueira)

Cage, John (Milton Jr.) 1912- . . . . . . **CLC 41**
See also CA 13-16R; CANR 9

Cain, G.
See Cabrera Infante, G(uillermo)

Cain, Guillermo
See Cabrera Infante, G(uillermo)

Cain, James M(allahan)
1892-1977 . . . . **CLC 3, 11, 28**
See also AITN 1; CA 17-20R; 73-76;
CANR 8, 34; MTCW

Caine, Mark
See Raphael, Frederic (Michael)

Caldwell, Erskine (Preston)
1903-1987 . . . . **CLC 1, 8, 14, 50, 60**
See also AITN 1; CA 1-4R; 121; CAAS 1;
CANR 2, 33; DLB 9, 86; MTCW

Caldwell, (Janet Miriam) Taylor (Holland)
1900-1985 . . . . **CLC 2, 28, 39**
See also CA 5-8R; 116; CANR 5

Calhoun, John Caldwell
1782-1850 . . . . **NCLC 15**
See also DLB 3

Calisher, Hortense 1911- . . . . **CLC 2, 4, 8, 38**
See also CA 1-4R; CANR 1, 22; DLB 2;
MTCW

Callaghan, Morley Edward
1903-1990 . . . . **CLC 3, 14, 41, 65**
See also CA 9-12R; 132; CANR 33;
DLB 68; MTCW

Calvino, Italo
1923-1985 . . . . **CLC 5, 8, 11, 22, 33, 39;
SSC 3**
See also CA 85-88; 116; CANR 23; MTCW

Cameron, Carey 1952- . . . . **CLC 59**
See also CA 135

Cameron, Peter 1959- . . . . **CLC 44**
See also CA 125

Campana, Dino 1885-1932 . . . . **TCLC 20**
See also CA 117; DLB 114

Campbell, John W(ood Jr.)
1910-1971 . . . . **CLC 32**
See also CA 21-22; 29-32R; CANR 34;
CAP 2; DLB 8; MTCW

Campbell, Joseph 1904-1987 . . . . **CLC 69**
See also AAYA 3; BEST 89:2; CA 1-4R;
124; CANR 3, 28; MTCW

Campbell, (John) Ramsey 1946- . . . . **CLC 42**
See also CA 57-60; CANR 7

Campbell, (Ignatius) Roy (Dunnachie)
1901-1957 . . . . **TCLC 5**
See also CA 104; DLB 20

Campbell, Thomas 1777-1844 . . . . **NCLC 19**
See also DLB 93

Campbell, Wilfred . . . . **TCLC 9**
See also Campbell, William

Campbell, William 1858(?)-1918
See Campbell, Wilfred
See also CA 106; DLB 92

Campos, Alvaro de
See Pessoa, Fernando (Antonio Nogueira)

Camus, Albert
1913-1960 . . . **CLC 1, 2, 4, 9, 11, 14, 32,
63, 69; DC 2; SSC 9**
See also CA 89-92; DLB 72; MTCW; WLC

Canby, Vincent 1924- . . . . **CLC 13**
See also CA 81-84

Cancale
See Desnos, Robert

Canetti, Elias 1905- . . . . **CLC 3, 14, 25**
See also CA 21-24R; CANR 23; DLB 85;
MTCW

Canin, Ethan 1960- . . . . **CLC 55**
See also CA 131; 135

Cannon, Curt
See Hunter, Evan

Cape, Judith
See Page, P(atricia) K(athleen)

Capek, Karel
1890-1938 . . . . **TCLC 6, 37; DC 1**
See also CA 104; WLC

Capote, Truman
1924-1984 . . . . . **CLC 1, 3, 8, 13, 19, 34,
38, 58; SSC 2**
See also CA 5-8R; 113; CANR 18;
CDALB 1941-1968; DLB 2; DLBY 80,
84; MTCW; WLC

Capra, Frank 1897-1991 . . . . **CLC 16**
See also CA 61-64; 135

Caputo, Philip 1941- . . . . **CLC 32**
See also CA 73-76

Card, Orson Scott 1951- . . . . **CLC 44, 47, 50**
See also CA 102; CANR 27; MTCW

Cardenal (Martinez), Ernesto
1925- . . . . **CLC 31**
See also CA 49-52; CANR 2, 32; HW;
MTCW

Carducci, Giosue 1835-1907 . . . . . . **TCLC 32**

Carew, Thomas 1595(?)-1640 . . . . **LC 13**

Carey, Ernestine Gilbreth 1908- . . . . **CLC 17**
See also CA 5-8R; SATA 2

Carey, Peter 1943- . . . . **CLC 40, 55**
See also CA 123; 127; MTCW

Carleton, William 1794-1869 . . . . . . **NCLC 3**

Carlisle, Henry (Coffin) 1926- . . . . . . **CLC 33**
See also CA 13-16R; CANR 15

Carlsen, Chris
See Holdstock, Robert P.

Carlson, Ron(ald F.) 1947- . . . . **CLC 54**
See also CA 105; CANR 27

Carlyle, Thomas 1795-1881 . . . . . . **NCLC 22**
See also CDBLB 1789-1832; DLB 55

Carman, (William) Bliss
1861-1929 . . . . **TCLC 7**
See also CA 104; DLB 92

Carpenter, Don(ald Richard)
1931- . . . . **CLC 41**
See also CA 45-48; CANR 1

Carpentier (y Valmont), Alejo
  1904-1980 .... **CLC 8, 11, 38**
  See also CA 65-68; 97-100; CANR 11;
  DLB 113; HW

Carr, Emily 1871-1945........... **TCLC 32**
  See also DLB 68

Carr, John Dickson 1906-1977 ...... **CLC 3**
  See also CA 49-52; 69-72; CANR 3, 33;
  MTCW

Carr, Philippa
  See Hibbert, Eleanor Burford

Carr, Virginia Spencer 1929-....... **CLC 34**
  See also CA 61-64; DLB 111

Carrier, Roch 1937- .... **CLC 13**
  See also CA 130; DLB 53

Carroll, James P. 1943(?)-......... **CLC 38**
  See also CA 81-84

Carroll, Jim 1951- .... **CLC 35**
  See also CA 45-48

Carroll, Lewis .... **NCLC 2**
  See also Dodgson, Charles Lutwidge
  See also CDBLB 1832-1890; CLR 2, 18;
  DLB 18; WLC

Carroll, Paul Vincent 1900-1968.... **CLC 10**
  See also CA 9-12R; 25-28R; DLB 10

Carruth, Hayden 1921- .... **CLC 4, 7, 10, 18**
  See also CA 9-12R; CANR 4, 38; DLB 5;
  MTCW; SATA 47

Carson, Rachel Louise 1907-1964... **CLC 71**
  See also CA 77-80; CANR 35; MTCW;
  SATA 23

Carter, Angela (Olive)
  1940-1991 .... **CLC 5, 41**
  See also CA 53-56; 136; CANR 12, 36;
  DLB 14; MTCW; SATA 66; SATO 70

Carter, Nick
  See Smith, Martin Cruz

Carver, Raymond
  1938-1988 ... **CLC 22, 36, 53, 55; SSC 8**
  See also CA 33-36R; 126; CANR 17, 34;
  DLBY 84, 88; MTCW

Cary, (Arthur) Joyce (Lunel)
  1888-1957 .... **TCLC 1, 29**
  See also CA 104; CDBLB 1914-1945;
  DLB 15, 100

Casanova de Seingalt, Giovanni Jacopo
  1725-1798 .... **LC 13**

Casares, Adolfo Bioy
  See Bioy Casares, Adolfo

Casely-Hayford, J(oseph) E(phraim)
  1866-1930 .... **TCLC 24**
  See also BLC 1; CA 123

Casey, John (Dudley) 1939-....... **CLC 59**
  See also BEST 90:2; CA 69-72; CANR 23

Casey, Michael 1947-.............. **CLC 2**
  See also CA 65-68; DLB 5

Casey, Patrick
  See Thurman, Wallace (Henry)

Casey, Warren (Peter) 1935-1988 ... **CLC 12**
  See also CA 101; 127

Casona, Alejandro................ **CLC 49**
  See also Alvarez, Alejandro Rodriguez

Cassavetes, John 1929-1989........ **CLC 20**
  See also CA 85-88; 127

Cassill, R(onald) V(erlin) 1919-... **CLC 4, 23**
  See also CA 9-12R; CAAS 1; CANR 7;
  DLB 6

Cassity, (Allen) Turner 1929- .... **CLC 6, 42**
  See also CA 17-20R; CAAS 8; CANR 11;
  DLB 105

Castaneda, Carlos 1931(?)-......... **CLC 12**
  See also CA 25-28R; CANR 32; HW;
  MTCW

Castedo, Elena 1937- .... **CLC 65**
  See also CA 132

Castedo-Ellerman, Elena
  See Castedo, Elena

Castellanos, Rosario 1925-1974..... **CLC 66**
  See also CA 131; 53-56; DLB 113; HW

Castelvetro, Lodovico 1505-1571..... **LC 12**

Castiglione, Baldassare 1478-1529 ... **LC 12**

Castle, Robert
  See Hamilton, Edmond

Castro, Guillen de 1569-1631....... **LC 19**

Castro, Rosalia de 1837-1885 ..... **NCLC 3**

Cather, Willa
  See Cather, Willa Sibert

Cather, Willa Sibert
  1873-1947 ...... **TCLC 1, 11, 31; SSC 2**
  See also CA 104; 128; CDALB 1865-1917;
  DLB 9, 54, 78; DLBD 1; MTCW;
  SATA 30; WLC

Catton, (Charles) Bruce
  1899-1978 .... **CLC 35**
  See also AITN 1; CA 5-8R; 81-84;
  CANR 7; DLB 17; SATA 2, 24

Cauldwell, Frank
  See King, Francis (Henry)

Caunitz, William J. 1933- .... **CLC 34**
  See also BEST 89:3; CA 125; 130

Causley, Charles (Stanley) 1917-..... **CLC 7**
  See also CA 9-12R; CANR 5, 35; DLB 27;
  MTCW; SATA 3, 66

Caute, David 1936-............... **CLC 29**
  See also CA 1-4R; CAAS 4; CANR 1, 33;
  DLB 14

Cavafy, C(onstantine) P(eter)...... **TCLC 2, 7**
  See also Kavafis, Konstantinos Petrou

Cavallo, Evelyn
  See Spark, Muriel (Sarah)

Cavanna, Betty .... **CLC 12**
  See also Harrison, Elizabeth Cavanna
  See also MAICYA; SAAS 4; SATA 1, 30

Caxton, William 1421(?)-1491(?)..... **LC 17**

Cayrol, Jean 1911-............... **CLC 11**
  See also CA 89-92; DLB 83

Cela, Camilo Jose 1916-...... **CLC 4, 13, 59**
  See also BEST 90:2; CA 21-24R; CAAS 10;
  CANR 21, 32; DLBY 89; HW; MTCW

Celan, Paul .... **CLC 53**
  See also Antschel, Paul
  See also DLB 69

Celine, Louis-Ferdinand
  .... **CLC 1, 3, 4, 7, 9, 15, 47**
  See also Destouches, Louis-Ferdinand
  See also DLB 72

Cellini, Benvenuto 1500-1571 .... **LC 7**

Cendrars, Blaise
  See Sauser-Hall, Frederic

Cernuda (y Bidon), Luis
  1902-1963 .... **CLC 54**
  See also CA 131; 89-92; HW

Cervantes (Saavedra), Miguel de
  1547-1616 .... **LC 6**
  See also WLC

Cesaire, Aime (Fernand) 1913-.. **CLC 19, 32**
  See also BLC 1; BW; CA 65-68; CANR 24;
  MTCW

Chabon, Michael 1965(?)- .... **CLC 55**

Chabrol, Claude 1930-............ **CLC 16**
  See also CA 110

Challans, Mary 1905-1983
  See Renault, Mary
  See also CA 81-84; 111; SATA 23, 36

Chambers, Aidan 1934- .... **CLC 35**
  See also CA 25-28R; CANR 12, 31;
  MAICYA; SAAS 12; SATA 1, 69

Chambers, James 1948-
  See Cliff, Jimmy
  See also CA 124

Chambers, Jessie
  See Lawrence, D(avid) H(erbert Richards)

Chambers, Robert W. 1865-1933... **TCLC 41**

Chandler, Raymond (Thornton)
  1888-1959 .... **TCLC 1, 7**
  See also CA 104; 129; CDALB 1929-1941;
  DLBD 6; MTCW

Chang, Jung 1952-............... **CLC 71**

Channing, William Ellery
  1780-1842 .... **NCLC 17**
  See also DLB 1, 59

Chaplin, Charles Spencer
  1889-1977 .... **CLC 16**
  See also Chaplin, Charlie
  See also CA 81-84; 73-76

Chaplin, Charlie
  See Chaplin, Charles Spencer
  See also DLB 44

Chapman, Graham 1941-1989 ...... **CLC 21**
  See also Monty Python
  See also CA 116; 129; CANR 35

Chapman, John Jay 1862-1933 ..... **TCLC 7**
  See also CA 104

Chapman, Walker
  See Silverberg, Robert

Chappell, Fred (Davis) 1936-....... **CLC 40**
  See also CA 5-8R; CAAS 4; CANR 8, 33;
  DLB 6, 105

Char, Rene(-Emile)
  1907-1988 .... **CLC 9, 11, 14, 55**
  See also CA 13-16R; 124; CANR 32;
  MTCW

Charby, Jay
  See Ellison, Harlan

Chardin, Pierre Teilhard de
  See Teilhard de Chardin, (Marie Joseph)
  Pierre

Charles I 1600-1649 .... **LC 13**

Charyn, Jerome 1937- .... **CLC 5, 8, 18**
  See also CA 5-8R; CAAS 1; CANR 7;
  DLBY 83; MTCW

Chase, Mary (Coyle) 1907-1981 ...... **DC 1**
See also CA 77-80; 105; SATA 17, 29

Chase, Mary Ellen 1887-1973 .... **CLC 2**
See also CA 13-16; 41-44R; CAP 1;
SATA 10

Chase, Nicholas
See Hyde, Anthony

Chateaubriand, Francois Rene de
1768-1848 .... **NCLC 3**
See also DLB 119

Chatterje, Sarat Chandra 1876-1936(?)
See Chatterji, Saratchandra
See also CA 109

Chatterji, Bankim Chandra
1838-1894 .... **NCLC 19**

Chatterji, Saratchandra .... **TCLC 13**
See also Chatterje, Sarat Chandra

Chatterton, Thomas 1752-1770 .... **LC 3**
See also DLB 109

Chatwin, (Charles) Bruce
1940-1989 .... **CLC 28, 57, 59**
See also AAYA 4; BEST 90:1; CA 85-88;
127

Chaucer, Daniel
See Ford, Ford Madox

Chaucer, Geoffrey 1340(?)-1400 ..... **LC 17**
See also CDBLB Before 1660

Chaviaras, Strates 1935-
See Haviaras, Stratis
See also CA 105

Chayefsky, Paddy .... **CLC 23**
See also Chayefsky, Sidney
See also DLB 7, 44; DLBY 81

Chayefsky, Sidney 1923-1981
See Chayefsky, Paddy
See also CA 9-12R; 104; CANR 18

Chedid, Andree 1920- .... **CLC 47**

Cheever, John
1912-1982 ..... **CLC 3, 7, 8, 11, 15, 25,
64; SSC 1**
See also CA 5-8R; 106; CABS 1; CANR 5,
27; CDALB 1941-1968; DLB 2, 102;
DLBY 80, 82; MTCW; WLC

Cheever, Susan 1943- .... **CLC 18, 48**
See also CA 103; CANR 27; DLBY 82

Chekhonte, Antosha
See Chekhov, Anton (Pavlovich)

Chekhov, Anton (Pavlovich)
1860-1904 ...... **TCLC 3, 10, 31; SSC 2**
See also CA 104; 124; WLC

Chernyshevsky, Nikolay Gavrilovich
1828-1889 .... **NCLC 1**

Cherry, Carolyn Janice 1942-
See Cherryh, C. J.
See also CA 65-68; CANR 10

Cherryh, C. J. .... **CLC 35**
See also Cherry, Carolyn Janice
See also DLBY 80

Chesnutt, Charles W(addell)
1858-1932 .... **TCLC 5, 39; SSC 7**
See also BLC 1; BW; CA 106; 125; DLB 12,
50, 78; MTCW

Chester, Alfred 1929(?)-1971 .... **CLC 49**
See also CA 33-36R

Chesterton, G(ilbert) K(eith)
1874-1936 .... **TCLC 1, 6; SSC 1**
See also CA 104; 132; CDBLB 1914-1945;
DLB 10, 19, 34, 70, 98; MTCW;
SATA 27

Chiang Pin-chin 1904-1986
See Ding Ling
See also CA 118

Ch'ien Chung-shu 1910- .... **CLC 22**
See also CA 130; MTCW

Child, L. Maria
See Child, Lydia Maria

Child, Lydia Maria 1802-1880 .... **NCLC 6**
See also DLB 1, 74; SATA 67

Child, Mrs.
See Child, Lydia Maria

Child, Philip 1898-1978 .... **CLC 19, 68**
See also CA 13-14; CAP 1; SATA 47

Childress, Alice 1920- .... **CLC 12, 15**
See also AAYA 8; BLC 1; BW; CA 45-48;
CANR 3, 27; CLR 14; DLB 7, 38;
MAICYA; MTCW; SATA 7, 48

Chislett, (Margaret) Anne 1943- .... **CLC 34**

Chitty, Thomas Willes 1926- .... **CLC 11**
See also Hinde, Thomas
See also CA 5-8R

Chomette, Rene Lucien 1898-1981 .. **CLC 20**
See also Clair, Rene
See also CA 103

Chopin, Kate .... **TCLC 5, 14; SSC 8**
See also Chopin, Katherine
See also CDALB 1865-1917; DLB 12, 78

Chopin, Katherine 1851-1904
See Chopin, Kate
See also CA 104; 122

Chretien de Troyes
c. 12th cent. .... **CMLC 10**

Christie
See Ichikawa, Kon

Christie, Agatha (Mary Clarissa)
1890-1976 ...... **CLC 1, 6, 8, 12, 39, 48**
See also AAYA 9; AITN 1, 2; CA 17-20R;
61-64; CANR 10, 37; CDBLB 1914-1945;
DLB 13, 77; MTCW; SATA 36

Christie, (Ann) Philippa
See Pearce, Philippa
See also CA 5-8R; CANR 4

Christine de Pizan 1365(?)-1431(?) .... **LC 9**

Chubb, Elmer
See Masters, Edgar Lee

Chulkov, Mikhail Dmitrievich
1743-1792 .... **LC 2**

Churchill, Caryl 1938- .... **CLC 31, 55**
See also CA 102; CANR 22; DLB 13;
MTCW

Churchill, Charles 1731-1764 .... **LC 3**
See also DLB 109

Chute, Carolyn 1947- .... **CLC 39**
See also CA 123

Ciardi, John (Anthony)
1916-1986 .... **CLC 10, 40, 44**
See also CA 5-8R; 118; CAAS 2; CANR 5,
33; CLR 19; DLB 5; DLBY 86;
MAICYA; MTCW; SATA 1, 46, 65

Cicero, Marcus Tullius
106B.C.-43B.C. .... **CMLC 3**

Cimino, Michael 1943- .... **CLC 16**
See also CA 105

Cioran, E(mil) M. 1911- .... **CLC 64**
See also CA 25-28R

Cisneros, Sandra 1954- .... **CLC 69**
See also AAYA 9; CA 131; HW

Clair, Rene .... **CLC 20**
See also Chomette, Rene Lucien

Clampitt, Amy 1920- .... **CLC 32**
See also CA 110; CANR 29; DLB 105

Clancy, Thomas L. Jr. 1947-
See Clancy, Tom
See also CA 125; 131; MTCW

Clancy, Tom..................... **CLC 45**
See also Clancy, Thomas L. Jr.
See also AAYA 9; BEST 89:1, 90:1

Clare, John 1793-1864 .... **NCLC 9**
See also DLB 55, 96

Clarin
See Alas (y Urena), Leopoldo (Enrique
Garcia)

Clark, (Robert) Brian 1932- .... **CLC 29**
See also CA 41-44R

Clark, Eleanor 1913- .... **CLC 5, 19**
See also CA 9-12R; DLB 6

Clark, J. P.
See Clark, John Pepper
See also DLB 117

Clark, John Pepper 1935- .... **CLC 38**
See also Clark, J. P.
See also BLC 1; BW; CA 65-68; CANR 16

Clark, M. R.
See Clark, Mavis Thorpe

Clark, Mavis Thorpe 1909- .... **CLC 12**
See also CA 57-60; CANR 8, 37; MAICYA;
SAAS 5; SATA 8

Clark, Walter Van Tilburg
1909-1971 .... **CLC 28**
See also CA 9-12R; 33-36R; DLB 9;
SATA 8

Clarke, Arthur C(harles)
1917- ...... **CLC 1, 4, 13, 18, 35; SSC 3**
See also AAYA 4; CA 1-4R; CANR 2, 28;
MAICYA; MTCW; SATA 13, 70

Clarke, Austin C(hesterfield)
1934- .... **CLC 8, 53**
See also BLC 1; BW; CA 25-28R;
CAAS 16; CANR 14, 32; DLB 53

Clarke, Austin 1896-1974........ **CLC 6, 9**
See also CA 29-32; 49-52; CAP 2; DLB 10,
20

Clarke, Gillian 1937- .... **CLC 61**
See also CA 106; DLB 40

Clarke, Marcus (Andrew Hislop)
1846-1881 .... **NCLC 19**

Clarke, Shirley 1925- .... **CLC 16**

.... **CLC 30**
See also Headon, (Nicky) Topper; Jones,
Mick; Simonon, Paul; Strummer, Joe

Claudel, Paul (Louis Charles Marie)
1868-1955 .... **TCLC 2, 10**
See also CA 104

Clavell, James (duMaresq)
    1925-................... **CLC 6, 25**
    See also CA 25-28R; CANR 26; MTCW

Cleaver, (Leroy) Eldridge 1935-.... **CLC 30**
    See also BLC 1; BW; CA 21-24R;
    CANR 16

Cleese, John (Marwood) 1939-..... **CLC 21**
    See also Monty Python
    See also CA 112; 116; CANR 35; MTCW

Cleishbotham, Jebediah
    See Scott, Walter

Cleland, John 1710-1789 .... **LC 2**
    See also DLB 39

Clemens, Samuel Langhorne 1835-1910
    See Twain, Mark
    See also CA 104; 135; CDALB 1865-1917;
    DLB 11, 12, 23, 64, 74; MAICYA;
    YABC 2

Clerihew, E.
    See Bentley, E(dmund) C(lerihew)

Clerk, N. W.
    See Lewis, C(live) S(taples)

Cliff, Jimmy..................... **CLC 21**
    See also Chambers, James

Clifton, (Thelma) Lucille
    1936-................... **CLC 19, 66**
    See also BLC 1; BW; CA 49-52; CANR 2,
    24; CLR 5; DLB 5, 41; MAICYA;
    MTCW; SATA 20, 69

Clinton, Dirk
    See Silverberg, Robert

Clough, Arthur Hugh 1819-1861.. **NCLC 27**
    See also DLB 32

Clutha, Janet Paterson Frame 1924-
    See Frame, Janet
    See also CA 1-4R; CANR 2, 36; MTCW

Clyne, Terence
    See Blatty, William Peter

Cobalt, Martin
    See Mayne, William (James Carter)

Coburn, D(onald) L(ee) 1938-...... **CLC 10**
    See also CA 89-92

Cocteau, Jean (Maurice Eugene Clement)
    1889-1963 .... **CLC 1, 8, 15, 16, 43**
    See also CA 25-28; CAP 2; DLB 65;
    MTCW; WLC

Codrescu, Andrei 1946-........... **CLC 46**
    See also CA 33-36R; CANR 13, 34

Coe, Max
    See Bourne, Randolph S(illiman)

Coe, Tucker
    See Westlake, Donald E(dwin)

Coetzee, J(ohn) M(ichael)
    1940-................ **CLC 23, 33, 66**
    See also CA 77-80; MTCW

Cohen, Arthur A(llen)
    1928-1986 .... **CLC 7, 31**
    See also CA 1-4R; 120; CANR 1, 17;
    DLB 28

Cohen, Leonard (Norman)
    1934-................... **CLC 3, 38**
    See also CA 21-24R; CANR 14; DLB 53;
    MTCW

Cohen, Matt 1942-............... **CLC 19**
    See also CA 61-64; DLB 53

Cohen-Solal, Annie 19(?)- .... **CLC 50**

Colegate, Isabel 1931- .... **CLC 36**
    See also CA 17-20R; CANR 8, 22; DLB 14;
    MTCW

Coleman, Emmett
    See Reed, Ishmael

Coleridge, Samuel Taylor
    1772-1834 .... **NCLC 9**
    See also CDBLB 1789-1832; DLB 93, 107;
    WLC

Coleridge, Sara 1802-1852....... **NCLC 31**

Coles, Don 1928- .... **CLC 46**
    See also CA 115; CANR 38

Colette, (Sidonie-Gabrielle)
    1873-1954 ...... **TCLC 1, 5, 16; SSC 10**
    See also CA 104; 131; DLB 65; MTCW

Collett, (Jacobine) Camilla (Wergeland)
    1813-1895 .... **NCLC 22**

Collier, Christopher 1930-........ **CLC 30**
    See also CA 33-36R; CANR 13, 33;
    MAICYA; SATA 16, 70

Collier, James L(incoln) 1928-..... **CLC 30**
    See also CA 9-12R; CANR 4, 33;
    MAICYA; SATA 8, 70

Collier, Jeremy 1650-1726.......... **LC 6**

Collins, Hunt
    See Hunter, Evan

Collins, Linda 1931-.............. **CLC 44**
    See also CA 125

Collins, (William) Wilkie
    1824-1889 .... **NCLC 1, 18**
    See also CDBLB 1832-1890; DLB 18, 70

Collins, William 1721-1759 .... **LC 4**
    See also DLB 109

Colman, George
    See Glassco, John

Colt, Winchester Remington
    See Hubbard, L(afayette) Ron(ald)

Colter, Cyrus 1910- .... **CLC 58**
    See also BW; CA 65-68; CANR 10; DLB 33

Colton, James
    See Hansen, Joseph

Colum, Padraic 1881-1972........ **CLC 28**
    See also CA 73-76; 33-36R; CANR 35;
    MAICYA; MTCW; SATA 15

Colvin, James
    See Moorcock, Michael (John)

Colwin, Laurie 1944- .... **CLC 5, 13, 23**
    See also CA 89-92; CANR 20; DLBY 80;
    MTCW

Comfort, Alex(ander) 1920-........ **CLC 7**
    See also CA 1-4R; CANR 1

Comfort, Montgomery
    See Campbell, (John) Ramsey

Compton-Burnett, I(vy)
    1884(?)-1969 ...... **CLC 1, 3, 10, 15, 34**
    See also CA 1-4R; 25-28R; CANR 4;
    DLB 36; MTCW

Comstock, Anthony 1844-1915 .... **TCLC 13**
    See also CA 110

Conan Doyle, Arthur
    See Doyle, Arthur Conan

Conde, Maryse .... **CLC 52**
    See also Boucolon, Maryse

Condon, Richard (Thomas)
    1915-............ **CLC 4, 6, 8, 10, 45**
    See also BEST 90:3; CA 1-4R; CAAS 1;
    CANR 2, 23; MTCW

Congreve, William
    1670-1729 .... **LC 5, 21; DC 2**
    See also CDBLB 1660-1789; DLB 39, 84;
    WLC

Connell, Evan S(helby) Jr.
    1924-............... **CLC 4, 6, 45**
    See also AAYA 7; CA 1-4R; CAAS 2;
    CANR 2, 39; DLB 2; DLBY 81; MTCW

Connelly, Marc(us Cook)
    1890-1980 .... **CLC 7**
    See also CA 85-88; 102; CANR 30; DLB 7;
    DLBY 80; SATA 25

Connor, Ralph .... **TCLC 31**
    See also Gordon, Charles William
    See also DLB 92

Conrad, Joseph
    1857-1924 ...... **TCLC 1, 6, 13, 25, 43;
    SSC 9**
    See also CA 104; 131; CDBLB 1890-1914;
    DLB 10, 34, 98; MTCW; SATA 27; WLC

Conrad, Robert Arnold
    See Hart, Moss

Conroy, Pat 1945-............. **CLC 30, 74**
    See also AAYA 8; AITN 1; CA 85-88;
    CANR 24; DLB 6; MTCW

Constant (de Rebecque), (Henri) Benjamin
    1767-1830 .... **NCLC 6**
    See also DLB 119

Conybeare, Charles Augustus
    See Eliot, T(homas) S(tearns)

Cook, Michael 1933- .... **CLC 58**
    See also CA 93-96; DLB 53

Cook, Robin 1940-............... **CLC 14**
    See also BEST 90:2; CA 108; 111

Cook, Roy
    See Silverberg, Robert

Cooke, Elizabeth 1948-........... **CLC 55**
    See also CA 129

Cooke, John Esten 1830-1886..... **NCLC 5**
    See also DLB 3

Cooke, John Estes
    See Baum, L(yman) Frank

Cooke, M. E.
    See Creasey, John

Cooke, Margaret
    See Creasey, John

Cooney, Ray .... **CLC 62**

Cooper, Henry St. John
    See Creasey, John

Cooper, J. California. .... **CLC 56**
    See also BW; CA 125

Cooper, James Fenimore
    1789-1851 .... **NCLC 1, 27**
    See also CDALB 1640-1865; DLB 3;
    SATA 19

Coover, Robert (Lowell)
    1932-............ **CLC 3, 7, 15, 32, 46**
    See also CA 45-48; CANR 3, 37; DLB 2;
    DLBY 81; MTCW

Copeland, Stewart (Armstrong)
1952- .... CLC 26
See also The Police

Coppard, A(lfred) E(dgar)
1878-1957 .... TCLC 5
See also CA 114; YABC 1

Coppee, Francois 1842-1908 ...... TCLC 25

Coppola, Francis Ford 1939-....... CLC 16
See also CA 77-80; DLB 44

Corcoran, Barbara 1911- .... CLC 17
See also CA 21-24R; CAAS 2; CANR 11,
28; DLB 52; SATA 3

Cordelier, Maurice
See Giraudoux, (Hippolyte) Jean

Corman, Cid..................... CLC 9
See also Corman, Sidney
See also CAAS 2; DLB 5

Corman, Sidney 1924-
See Corman, Cid
See also CA 85-88

Cormier, Robert (Edmund)
1925- .... CLC 12, 30
See also AAYA 3; CA 1-4R; CANR 5, 23;
CDALB 1968-1988; CLR 12; DLB 52;
MAICYA; MTCW; SATA 10, 45

Corn, Alfred 1943- .... CLC 33
See also CA 104; DLB 120; DLBY 80

Cornwell, David (John Moore)
1931- .... CLC 9, 15
See also le Carre, John
See also CA 5-8R; CANR 13, 33; MTCW

Corrigan, Kevin.................. CLC 55

Corso, (Nunzio) Gregory 1930-... CLC 1, 11
See also CA 5-8R; DLB 5,16; MTCW

Cortazar, Julio
1914-1984 ..... CLC 2, 3, 5, 10, 13, 15,
33, 34; SSC 7
See also CA 21-24R; CANR 12, 32;
DLB 113; HW; MTCW

Corwin, Cecil
See Kornbluth, C(yril) M.

Cosic, Dobrica 1921- .... CLC 14
See also CA 122; 138

Costain, Thomas B(ertram)
1885-1965 .... CLC 30
See also CA 5-8R; 25-28R; DLB 9

Costantini, Humberto
1924(?)-1987 .... CLC 49
See also CA 131; 122; HW

Costello, Elvis 1955-.............. CLC 21

Cotter, Joseph S. Sr.
See Cotter, Joseph Seamon Sr.

Cotter, Joseph Seamon Sr.
1861-1949 .... TCLC 28
See also BLC 1; BW; CA 124; DLB 50

Coulton, James
See Hansen, Joseph

Couperus, Louis (Marie Anne)
1863-1923 .... TCLC 15
See also CA 115

Court, Wesli
See Turco, Lewis (Putnam)

Courtenay, Bryce 1933-........... CLC 59
See also CA 138

Courtney, Robert
See Ellison, Harlan

Cousteau, Jacques-Yves 1910-..... CLC 30
See also CA 65-68; CANR 15; MTCW;
SATA 38

Coward, Noel (Peirce)
1899-1973 .... CLC 1, 9, 29, 51
See also AITN 1; CA 17-18; 41-44R;
CANR 35; CAP 2; CDBLB 1914-1945;
DLB 10; MTCW

Cowley, Malcolm 1898-1989 ...... CLC 39
See also CA 5-8R; 128; CANR 3; DLB 4,
48; DLBY 81, 89; MTCW

Cowper, William 1731-1800....... NCLC 8
See also DLB 104, 109

Cox, William Trevor 1928- ... CLC 9, 14, 71
See also Trevor, William
See also CA 9-12R; CANR 4, 37; DLB 14;
MTCW

Cozzens, James Gould
1903-1978 .... CLC 1, 4, 11
See also CA 9-12R; 81-84; CANR 19;
CDALB 1941-1968; DLB 9; DLBD 2;
DLBY 84; MTCW

Crabbe, George 1754-1832...... NCLC 26
See also DLB 93

Craig, A. A.
See Anderson, Poul (William)

Craik, Dinah Maria (Mulock)
1826-1887 .... NCLC 38
See also DLB 35; MAICYA; SATA 34

Cram, Ralph Adams 1863-1942.... TCLC 45

Crane, (Harold) Hart
1899-1932 .... TCLC 2, 5; PC 3
See also CA 104; 127; CDALB 1917-1929;
DLB 4, 48; MTCW; WLC

Crane, R(onald) S(almon)
1886-1967 .... CLC 27
See also CA 85-88; DLB 63

Crane, Stephen (Townley)
1871-1900 ..... TCLC 11, 17, 32; SSC 7
See also CA 109; CDALB 1865-1917;
DLB 12, 54, 78; WLC; YABC 2

Crase, Douglas 1944- .... CLC 58
See also CA 106

Craven, Margaret 1901-1980....... CLC 17
See also CA 103

Crawford, F(rancis) Marion
1854-1909 .... TCLC 10
See also CA 107; DLB 71

Crawford, Isabella Valancy
1850-1887 .... NCLC 12
See also DLB 92

Crayon, Geoffrey
See Irving, Washington

Creasey, John 1908-1973.......... CLC 11
See also CA 5-8R; 41-44R; CANR 8;
DLB 77; MTCW

Crebillon, Claude Prosper Jolyot de (fils)
1707-1777 .... LC 1

Credo
See Creasey, John

Creeley, Robert (White)
1926- .... CLC 1, 2, 4, 8, 11, 15, 36
See also CA 1-4R; CAAS 10; CANR 23;
DLB 5, 16; MTCW

Crews, Harry (Eugene)
1935- .... CLC 6, 23, 49
See also AITN 1; CA 25-28R; CANR 20;
DLB 6; MTCW

Crichton, (John) Michael
1942- .... CLC 2, 6, 54
See also AITN 2; CA 25-28R; CANR 13;
DLBY 81; MTCW; SATA 9

Crispin, Edmund .... CLC 22
See also Montgomery, (Robert) Bruce
See also DLB 87

Cristofer, Michael 1945(?)- .... CLC 28
See also CA 110; DLB 7

Croce, Benedetto 1866-1952 ...... TCLC 37
See also CA 120

Crockett, David 1786-1836 ...... NCLC 8
See also DLB 3, 11

Crockett, Davy
See Crockett, David

Croker, John Wilson 1780-1857 .. NCLC 10
See also DLB 110

Cronin, A(rchibald) J(oseph)
1896-1981 .... CLC 32
See also CA 1-4R; 102; CANR 5; SATA 25,
47

Cross, Amanda
See Heilbrun, Carolyn G(old)

Crothers, Rachel 1878(?)-1958..... TCLC 19
See also CA 113; DLB 7

Croves, Hal
See Traven, B.

Crowfield, Christopher
See Stowe, Harriet (Elizabeth) Beecher

Crowley, Aleister.................. TCLC 7
See also Crowley, Edward Alexander

Crowley, Edward Alexander 1875-1947
See Crowley, Aleister
See also CA 104

Crowley, John 1942-.............. CLC 57
See also CA 61-64; DLBY 82; SATA 65

Crud
See Crumb, R(obert)

Crumarums
See Crumb, R(obert)

Crumb, R(obert) 1943-............ CLC 17
See also CA 106

Crumbum
See Crumb, R(obert)

Crumski
See Crumb, R(obert)

Crum the Bum
See Crumb, R(obert)

Crunk
See Crumb, R(obert)

Crustt
See Crumb, R(obert)

Cryer, Gretchen (Kiger) 1935-...... CLC 21
See also CA 114; 123

Csath, Geza 1887-1919........... TCLC 13
See also CA 111

Cudlip, David 1933- . . . . CLC 34

Cullen, Countee 1903-1946 . . . . . TCLC 4, 37
    See also BLC 1; BW; CA 108; 124;
       CDALB 1917-1929; DLB 4, 48, 51;
       MTCW; SATA 18

Cum, R.
    See Crumb, R(obert)

Cummings, Bruce F(rederick) 1889-1919
    See Barbellion, W. N. P.
    See also CA 123

Cummings, E(dward) E(stlin)
    1894-1962 . . . . . CLC 1, 3, 8, 12, 15, 68;
                         PC 5
    See also CA 73-76; CANR 31;
       CDALB 1929-1941; DLB 4, 48; MTCW;
       WLC 2

Cunha, Euclides (Rodrigues Pimenta) da
    1866-1909 . . . . TCLC 24
    See also CA 123

Cunningham, E. V.
    See Fast, Howard (Melvin)

Cunningham, J(ames) V(incent)
    1911-1985 . . . . CLC 3, 31
    See also CA 1-4R; 115; CANR 1; DLB 5

Cunningham, Julia (Woolfolk)
    1916- . . . . CLC 12
    See also CA 9-12R; CANR 4, 19, 36;
       MAICYA; SAAS 2; SATA 1, 26

Cunningham, Michael 1952- . . . . CLC 34
    See also CA 136

Cunninghame Graham, R(obert) B(ontine)
    1852-1936 . . . . TCLC 19
    See also Graham, R(obert) B(ontine)
       Cunninghame
    See also CA 119; DLB 98

Currie, Ellen 19(?)- . . . . CLC 44

Curtin, Philip
    See Lowndes, Marie Adelaide (Belloc)

Curtis, Price
    See Ellison, Harlan

Czaczkes, Shmuel Yosef
    See Agnon, S(hmuel) Y(osef Halevi)

D. P.
    See Wells, H(erbert) G(eorge)

Dabrowska, Maria (Szumska)
    1889-1965 . . . . CLC 15
    See also CA 106

Dabydeen, David 1955- . . . . CLC 34
    See also BW; CA 125

Dacey, Philip 1939- . . . . CLC 51
    See also CA 37-40R; CANR 14, 32;
       DLB 105

Dagerman, Stig (Halvard)
    1923-1954 . . . . TCLC 17
    See also CA 117

Dahl, Roald 1916-1990 . . . . CLC 1, 6, 18
    See also CA 1-4R; 133; CANR 6, 32, 37;
       CLR 1, 7; MAICYA; MTCW; SATA 1,
       26; SATO 65

Dahlberg, Edward 1900-1977 . . . CLC 1, 7, 14
    See also CA 9-12R; 69-72; CANR 31;
       DLB 48; MTCW

Dale, Colin . . . . TCLC 18
    See also Lawrence, T(homas) E(dward)

Dale, George E.
    See Asimov, Isaac

Daly, Elizabeth 1878-1967 . . . . CLC 52
    See also CA 23-24; 25-28R; CAP 2

Daly, Maureen 1921- . . . . CLC 17
    See also AAYA 5; CANR 37; MAICYA;
       SAAS 1; SATA 2

Daniels, Brett
    See Adler, Renata

Dannay, Frederic 1905-1982 . . . . CLC 11
    See also Queen, Ellery
    See also CA 1-4R; 107; CANR 1, 39;
       MTCW

D'Annunzio, Gabriele
    1863-1938 . . . . TCLC 6, 40
    See also CA 104

d'Antibes, Germain
    See Simenon, Georges (Jacques Christian)

Danvers, Dennis 1947- . . . . CLC 70

Danziger, Paula 1944- . . . . CLC 21
    See also AAYA 4; CA 112; 115; CANR 37;
       CLR 20; MAICYA; SATA 30, 36, 63

Dario, Ruben . . . . TCLC 4
    See also Sarmiento, Felix Ruben Garcia

Darley, George 1795-1846 . . . . NCLC 2
    See also DLB 96

Daryush, Elizabeth 1887-1977 . . . . CLC 6, 19
    See also CA 49-52; CANR 3; DLB 20

Daudet, (Louis Marie) Alphonse
    1840-1897 . . . . NCLC 1

Daumal, Rene 1908-1944 . . . . TCLC 14
    See also CA 114

Davenport, Guy (Mattison Jr.)
    1927- . . . . CLC 6, 14, 38
    See also CA 33-36R; CANR 23

Davidson, Avram 1923-
    See Queen, Ellery
    See also CA 101; CANR 26; DLB 8

Davidson, Donald (Grady)
    1893-1968 . . . . CLC 2, 13, 19
    See also CA 5-8R; 25-28R; CANR 4;
       DLB 45

Davidson, Hugh
    See Hamilton, Edmond

Davidson, John 1857-1909 . . . . TCLC 24
    See also CA 118; DLB 19

Davidson, Sara 1943- . . . . CLC 9
    See also CA 81-84

Davie, Donald (Alfred)
    1922- . . . . CLC 5, 8, 10, 31
    See also CA 1-4R; CAAS 3; CANR 1;
       DLB 27; MTCW

Davies, Ray(mond Douglas) 1944- . . CLC 21
    See also CA 116

Davies, Rhys 1903-1978 . . . . CLC 23
    See also CA 9-12R; 81-84; CANR 4

Davies, (William) Robertson
    1913- . . . . CLC 2, 7, 13, 25, 42
    See also BEST 89:2; CA 33-36R; CANR 17;
       DLB 68; MTCW; WLC

Davies, W(illiam) H(enry)
    1871-1940 . . . . TCLC 5
    See also CA 104; DLB 19

Davies, Walter C.
    See Kornbluth, C(yril) M.

Davis, B. Lynch
    See Bioy Casares, Adolfo; Borges, Jorge
       Luis

Davis, Gordon
    See Hunt, E(verette) Howard Jr.

Davis, Harold Lenoir 1896-1960 . . . . CLC 49
    See also CA 89-92; DLB 9

Davis, Rebecca (Blaine) Harding
    1831-1910 . . . . TCLC 6
    See also CA 104; DLB 74

Davis, Richard Harding
    1864-1916 . . . . TCLC 24
    See also CA 114; DLB 12, 23, 78, 79

Davison, Frank Dalby 1893-1970 . . . CLC 15
    See also CA 116

Davison, Lawrence H.
    See Lawrence, D(avid) H(erbert Richards)

Davison, Peter 1928- . . . . CLC 28
    See also CA 9-12R; CAAS 4; CANR 3;
       DLB 5

Davys, Mary 1674-1732 . . . . LC 1
    See also DLB 39

Dawson, Fielding 1930- . . . . CLC 6
    See also CA 85-88

Day, Clarence (Shepard Jr.)
    1874-1935 . . . . TCLC 25
    See also CA 108; DLB 11

Day, Thomas 1748-1789 . . . . LC 1
    See also DLB 39; YABC 1

Day Lewis, C(ecil)
    1904-1972 . . . . CLC 1, 6, 10
    See also Blake, Nicholas
    See also CA 13-16; 33-36R; CANR 34;
       CAP 1; DLB 15, 20; MTCW

Dazai, Osamu . . . . TCLC 11
    See also Tsushima, Shuji

de Andrade, Carlos Drummond
    See Drummond de Andrade, Carlos

Deane, Norman
    See Creasey, John

de Beauvoir, Simone (Lucie Ernestine Marie
    Bertrand)
    See Beauvoir, Simone (Lucie Ernestine
       Marie Bertrand) de

de Brissac, Malcolm
    See Dickinson, Peter (Malcolm)

de Chardin, Pierre Teilhard
    See Teilhard de Chardin, (Marie Joseph)
       Pierre

Dee, John 1527-1608 . . . . LC 20

Deer, Sandra 1940- . . . . CLC 45

De Ferrari, Gabriella . . . . CLC 65

Defoe, Daniel 1660(?)-1731 . . . . LC 1
    See also CDBLB 1660-1789; DLB 39, 95,
       101; MAICYA; SATA 22; WLC

de Gourmont, Remy
    See Gourmont, Remy de

de Hartog, Jan 1914- . . . . CLC 19
    See also CA 1-4R; CANR 1

de Hostos, E. M.
    See Hostos (y Bonilla), Eugenio Maria de

de Hostos, Eugenio M.
  See Hostos (y Bonilla), Eugenio Maria de

Deighton, Len . . . . **CLC 4, 7, 22, 46**
  See also Deighton, Leonard Cyril
  See also AAYA 6; BEST 89:2;
    CDBLB 1960 to Present; DLB 87

Deighton, Leonard Cyril   1929-
  See Deighton, Len
  See also CA 9-12R; CANR 19, 33; MTCW

de la Mare, Walter (John)
    1873-1956 . . . . **TCLC 4**
  See also CA 110; 137; CDBLB 1914-1945;
    CLR 23; DLB 19; MAICYA; SATA 16;
    WLC

Delaney, Franey
  See O'Hara, John (Henry)

Delaney, Shelagh   1939- . . . . **CLC 29**
  See also CA 17-20R; CANR 30;
    CDBLB 1960 to Present; DLB 13;
    MTCW

Delany, Mary (Granville Pendarves)
    1700-1788 . . . . **LC 12**

Delany, Samuel R(ay Jr.)
    1942- . . . . **CLC 8, 14, 38**
  See also BLC 1; BW; CA 81-84; CANR 27;
    DLB 8, 33; MTCW

Delaporte, Theophile
  See Green, Julian (Hartridge)

De La Ramee, (Marie) Louise   1839-1908
  See Ouida
  See also SATA 20

de la Roche, Mazo   1879-1961 . . . . . . **CLC 14**
  See also CA 85-88; CANR 30; DLB 68;
    SATA 64

Delbanco, Nicholas (Franklin)
    1942- . . . . **CLC 6, 13**
  See also CA 17-20R; CAAS 2; CANR 29;
    DLB 6

del Castillo, Michel   1933- . . . . **CLC 38**
  See also CA 109

Deledda, Grazia (Cosima)
    1875(?)-1936 . . . . **TCLC 23**
  See also CA 123

Delibes, Miguel . . . . **CLC 8, 18**
  See also Delibes Setien, Miguel

Delibes Setien, Miguel   1920-
  See Delibes, Miguel
  See also CA 45-48; CANR 1, 32; HW;
    MTCW

DeLillo, Don
    1936- . . . . **CLC 8, 10, 13, 27, 39, 54**
  See also BEST 89:1; CA 81-84; CANR 21;
    DLB 6; MTCW

de Lisser, H. G.
  See De Lisser, Herbert George
  See also DLB 117

De Lisser, Herbert George
    1878-1944 . . . . **TCLC 12**
  See also de Lisser, H. G.
  See also CA 109

Deloria, Vine (Victor) Jr.   1933- . . . . **CLC 21**
  See also CA 53-56; CANR 5, 20; MTCW;
    SATA 21

Del Vecchio, John M(ichael)
    1947- . . . . **CLC 29**
  See also CA 110; DLBD 9

de Man, Paul (Adolph Michel)
    1919-1983 . . . . **CLC 55**
  See also CA 128; 111; DLB 67; MTCW

De Marinis, Rick   1934- . . . . **CLC 54**
  See also CA 57-60; CANR 9, 25

Demby, William   1922- . . . . **CLC 53**
  See also BLC 1; BW; CA 81-84; DLB 33

Demijohn, Thom
  See Disch, Thomas M(ichael)

de Montherlant, Henry (Milon)
  See Montherlant, Henry (Milon) de

de Natale, Francine
  See Malzberg, Barry N(athaniel)

Denby, Edwin (Orr)   1903-1983 . . . . . **CLC 48**
  See also CA 138; 110

Denis, Julio
  See Cortazar, Julio

Denmark, Harrison
  See Zelazny, Roger (Joseph)

Dennis, John   1658-1734 . . . . **LC 11**
  See also DLB 101

Dennis, Nigel (Forbes)   1912-1989 . . . . **CLC 8**
  See also CA 25-28R; 129; DLB 13, 15;
    MTCW

De Palma, Brian (Russell)   1940- . . . . **CLC 20**
  See also CA 109

De Quincey, Thomas   1785-1859 . . . **NCLC 4**
  See also CDBLB 1789-1832; DLB 110

Deren, Eleanora   1908(?)-1961
  See Deren, Maya
  See also CA 111

Deren, Maya . . . . **CLC 16**
  See also Deren, Eleanora

Derleth, August (William)
    1909-1971 . . . . **CLC 31**
  See also CA 1-4R; 29-32R; CANR 4;
    DLB 9; SATA 5

de Routisie, Albert
  See Aragon, Louis

Derrida, Jacques   1930- . . . . **CLC 24**
  See also CA 124; 127

Derry Down Derry
  See Lear, Edward

Dersonnes, Jacques
  See Simenon, Georges (Jacques Christian)

Desai, Anita   1937- . . . . **CLC 19, 37**
  See also CA 81-84; CANR 33; MTCW;
    SATA 63

de Saint-Luc, Jean
  See Glassco, John

de Saint Roman, Arnaud
  See Aragon, Louis

Descartes, Rene   1596-1650 . . . . **LC 20**

De Sica, Vittorio   1901(?)-1974 . . . . . **CLC 20**
  See also CA 117

Desnos, Robert   1900-1945 . . . . **TCLC 22**
  See also CA 121

Destouches, Louis-Ferdinand
    1894-1961 . . . . **CLC 9, 15**
  See also Celine, Louis-Ferdinand
  See also CA 85-88; CANR 28; MTCW

Deutsch, Babette   1895-1982 . . . . **CLC 18**
  See also CA 1-4R; 108; CANR 4; DLB 45;
    SATA 1, 33

Devenant, William   1606-1649 . . . . **LC 13**

Devkota, Laxmiprasad
    1909-1959 . . . . **TCLC 23**
  See also CA 123

De Voto, Bernard (Augustine)
    1897-1955 . . . . **TCLC 29**
  See also CA 113; DLB 9

De Vries, Peter
    1910- . . . . **CLC 1, 2, 3, 7, 10, 28, 46**
  See also CA 17-20R; DLB 6; DLBY 82;
    MTCW

Dexter, Pete   1943- . . . . **CLC 34, 55**
  See also BEST 89:2; CA 127; 131; MTCW

Diamano, Silmang
  See Senghor, Leopold Sedar

Diamond, Neil   1941- . . . . **CLC 30**
  See also CA 108

di Bassetto, Corno
  See Shaw, George Bernard

Dick, Philip K(indred)
    1928-1982 . . . . **CLC 10, 30, 72**
  See also CA 49-52; 106; CANR 2, 16;
    DLB 8; MTCW

Dickens, Charles (John Huffam)
    1812-1870 . . . . **NCLC 3, 8, 18, 26**
  See also CDBLB 1832-1890; DLB 21, 55,
    70; MAICYA; SATA 15

Dickey, James (Lafayette)
    1923- . . . . **CLC 1, 2, 4, 7, 10, 15, 47**
  See also AITN 1, 2; CA 9-12R; CABS 2;
    CANR 10; CDALB 1968-1988; DLB 5;
    DLBD 7; DLBY 82; MTCW

Dickey, William   1928- . . . . **CLC 3, 28**
  See also CA 9-12R; CANR 24; DLB 5

Dickinson, Charles   1951- . . . . **CLC 49**
  See also CA 128

Dickinson, Emily (Elizabeth)
    1830-1886 . . . . **NCLC 21; PC 1**
  See also CDALB 1865-1917; DLB 1;
    SATA 29; WLC

Dickinson, Peter (Malcolm)
    1927- . . . . **CLC 12, 35**
  See also AAYA 9; CA 41-44R; CANR 31;
    DLB 87; MAICYA; SATA 5, 62

Dickson, Carr
  See Carr, John Dickson

Dickson, Carter
  See Carr, John Dickson

Didion, Joan   1934- . . . . . **CLC 1, 3, 8, 14, 32**
  See also AITN 1; CA 5-8R; CANR 14;
    CDALB 1968-1988; DLB 2; DLBY 81,
    86; MTCW

Dietrich, Robert
  See Hunt, E(verette) Howard Jr.

Dillard, Annie   1945- . . . . **CLC 9, 60**
  See also AAYA 6; CA 49-52; CANR 3;
    DLBY 80; MTCW; SATA 10

Dillard, R(ichard) H(enry) W(ilde)
    1937- . . . . **CLC 5**
  See also CA 21-24R; CAAS 7; CANR 10;
    DLB 5

Dillon, Eilis 1920-............... **CLC 17**
See also CA 9-12R; CAAS 3; CANR 4, 38;
CLR 26; MAICYA; SATA 2

Dimont, Penelope
See Mortimer, Penelope (Ruth)

Dinesen, Isak........... **CLC 10, 29; SSC 7**
See also Blixen, Karen (Christentze
Dinesen)

Ding Ling...................... **CLC 68**
See also Chiang Pin-chin

Disch, Thomas M(ichael) 1940-... **CLC 7, 36**
See also CA 21-24R; CAAS 4; CANR 17,
36; CLR 18; DLB 8; MAICYA; MTCW;
SATA 54

Disch, Tom
See Disch, Thomas M(ichael)

d'Isly, Georges
See Simenon, Georges (Jacques Christian)

Disraeli, Benjamin 1804-1881 ..... **NCLC 2**
See also DLB 21, 55

Ditcum, Steve
See Crumb, R(obert)

Dixon, Paige
See Corcoran, Barbara

Dixon, Stephen 1936-............. **CLC 52**
See also CA 89-92; CANR 17

Doblin, Alfred.................. **TCLC 13**
See also Doeblin, Alfred

Dobrolyubov, Nikolai Alexandrovich
1836-1861 .... **NCLC 5**

Dobyns, Stephen 1941-............ **CLC 37**
See also CA 45-48; CANR 2, 18

Doctorow, E(dgar) L(aurence)
1931-..... **CLC 6, 11, 15, 18, 37, 44, 65**
See also AITN 2; BEST 89:3; CA 45-48;
CANR 2, 33; CDALB 1968-1988; DLB 2,
28; DLBY 80; MTCW

Dodgson, Charles Lutwidge 1832-1898
See Carroll, Lewis
See also CLR 2; MAICYA; YABC 2

Doeblin, Alfred 1878-1957....... **TCLC 13**
See also Doblin, Alfred
See also CA 110; DLB 66

Doerr, Harriet 1910- .... **CLC 34**
See also CA 117; 122

Domecq, H(onorio) Bustos
See Bioy Casares, Adolfo; Borges, Jorge
Luis

Domini, Rey
See Lorde, Audre (Geraldine)

Dominique
See Proust,
(Valentin-Louis-George-Eugene-)Marcel

Don, A
See Stephen, Leslie

Donaldson, Stephen R. 1947-....... **CLC 46**
See also CA 89-92; CANR 13

Donleavy, J(ames) P(atrick)
1926-............. **CLC 1, 4, 6, 10, 45**
See also AITN 2; CA 9-12R; CANR 24;
DLB 6; MTCW

Donne, John 1572-1631 ...... **LC 10; PC 1**
See also CDBLB Before 1660; DLB 121;
WLC

Donnell, David 1939(?)-........... **CLC 34**

Donoso (Yanez), Jose
1924-............... **CLC 4, 8, 11, 32**
See also CA 81-84; CANR 32; DLB 113;
HW; MTCW

Donovan, John 1928-1992 .... **CLC 35**
See also CA 97-100; 137; CLR 3;
MAICYA; SATA 29

Don Roberto
See Cunninghame Graham, R(obert)
B(ontine)

Doolittle, Hilda
1886-1961 ... **CLC 3, 8, 14, 31, 34; PC 5**
See also H. D.
See also CA 97-100; CANR 35; DLB 4, 45;
MTCW; WLC

Dorfman, Ariel 1942-............ **CLC 48**
See also CA 124; 130; HW

Dorn, Edward (Merton) 1929-... **CLC 10, 18**
See also CA 93-96; DLB 5

Dorsan, Luc
See Simenon, Georges (Jacques Christian)

Dorsange, Jean
See Simenon, Georges (Jacques Christian)

Dos Passos, John (Roderigo)
1896-1970 ... **CLC 1, 4, 8, 11, 15, 25, 34**
See also CA 1-4R; 29-32R; CANR 3;
CDALB 1929-1941; DLB 4, 9; DLBD 1;
MTCW; WLC

Dossage, Jean
See Simenon, Georges (Jacques Christian)

Dostoevsky, Fedor Mikhailovich
1821-1881 .... **NCLC 2, 7, 21, 33; SSC 2**
See also WLC

Doughty, Charles M(ontagu)
1843-1926 .... **TCLC 27**
See also CA 115; DLB 19, 57

Douglas, Gavin 1475(?)-1522........ **LC 20**

Douglas, Keith 1920-1944 .... **TCLC 40**
See also DLB 27

Douglas, Leonard
See Bradbury, Ray (Douglas)

Douglas, Michael
See Crichton, (John) Michael

Douglass, Frederick 1817(?)-1895.. **NCLC 7**
See also BLC 1; CDALB 1640-1865;
DLB 1, 43, 50, 79; SATA 29; WLC

Dourado, (Waldomiro Freitas) Autran
1926-.................... **CLC 23, 60**
See also CA 25-28R; CANR 34

Dourado, Waldomiro Autran
See Dourado, (Waldomiro Freitas) Autran

Dove, Rita (Frances) 1952-........ **CLC 50**
See also BW; CA 109; CANR 27; DLB 120

Dowell, Coleman 1925-1985........ **CLC 60**
See also CA 25-28R; 117; CANR 10

Dowson, Ernest Christopher
1867-1900 .... **TCLC 4**
See also CA 105; DLB 19

Doyle, A. Conan
See Doyle, Arthur Conan

Doyle, Arthur Conan 1859-1930 .... **TCLC 7**
See also CA 104; 122; CDBLB 1890-1914;
DLB 18, 70; MTCW; SATA 24; WLC

Doyle, Conan
See Doyle, Arthur Conan

Doyle, John
See Graves, Robert (von Ranke)

Doyle, Sir A. Conan
See Doyle, Arthur Conan

Doyle, Sir Arthur Conan
See Doyle, Arthur Conan

Dr. A
See Asimov, Isaac; Silverstein, Alvin

Drabble, Margaret
1939- .... **CLC 2, 3, 5, 8, 10, 22, 53**
See also CA 13-16R; CANR 18, 35;
CDBLB 1960 to Present; DLB 14;
MTCW; SATA 48

Drapier, M. B.
See Swift, Jonathan

Drayham, James
See Mencken, H(enry) L(ouis)

Drayton, Michael 1563-1631........ **LC 8**

Dreadstone, Carl
See Campbell, (John) Ramsey

Dreiser, Theodore (Herman Albert)
1871-1945 .... **TCLC 10, 18, 35**
See also CA 106; 132; CDALB 1865-1917;
DLB 9, 12, 102; DLBD 1; MTCW; WLC

Drexler, Rosalyn 1926- .... **CLC 2, 6**
See also CA 81-84

Dreyer, Carl Theodor 1889-1968.... **CLC 16**
See also CA 116

Drieu la Rochelle, Pierre(-Eugene)
1893-1945 .... **TCLC 21**
See also CA 117; DLB 72

Drop Shot
See Cable, George Washington

Droste-Hulshoff, Annette Freiin von
1797-1848 .... **NCLC 3**

Drummond, Walter
See Silverberg, Robert

Drummond, William Henry
1854-1907 .... **TCLC 25**
See also DLB 92

Drummond de Andrade, Carlos
1902-1987 .... **CLC 18**
See also Andrade, Carlos Drummond de
See also CA 132; 123

Drury, Allen (Stuart) 1918-........ **CLC 37**
See also CA 57-60; CANR 18

Dryden, John 1631-1700 .... **LC 3, 21**
See also CDBLB 1660-1789; DLB 80, 101;
WLC

Dryden, John 1631-1700 .... **LC 3**

Duberman, Martin 1930-.......... **CLC 8**
See also CA 1-4R; CANR 2

Dubie, Norman (Evans) 1945-...... **CLC 36**
See also CA 69-72; CANR 12; DLB 120

Du Bois, W(illiam) E(dward) B(urghardt)
1868-1963 .... **CLC 1, 2, 13, 64**
See also BLC 1; BW; CA 85-88; CANR 34;
CDALB 1865-1917; DLB 47, 50, 91;
MTCW; SATA 42; WLC

Dubus, Andre 1936- .... **CLC 13, 36**
See also CA 21-24R; CANR 17

Eiseley, Loren Corey 1907-1977 . . . . . **CLC 7**
See also AAYA 5; CA 1-4R; 73-76;
CANR 6

Eisenstadt, Jill 1963- . . . . **CLC 50**

Eisner, Simon
See Kornbluth, C(yril) M.

Ekeloef, (Bengt) Gunnar
1907-1968 . . . . **CLC 27**
See also Ekelof, (Bengt) Gunnar
See also CA 123; 25-28R

Ekelof, (Bengt) Gunnar . . . . **CLC 27**
See also Ekeloef, (Bengt) Gunnar

Ekwensi, C. O. D.
See Ekwensi, Cyprian (Odiatu Duaka)

Ekwensi, Cyprian (Odiatu Duaka)
1921- . . . . **CLC 4**
See also BLC 1; BW; CA 29-32R;
CANR 18; DLB 117; MTCW; SATA 66

Elaine . . . . **TCLC 18**
See also Leverson, Ada

El Crummo
See Crumb, R(obert)

Elia
See Lamb, Charles

Eliade, Mircea 1907-1986 . . . . **CLC 19**
See also CA 65-68; 119; CANR 30; MTCW

Eliot, A. D.
See Jewett, (Theodora) Sarah Orne

Eliot, Alice
See Jewett, (Theodora) Sarah Orne

Eliot, Dan
See Silverberg, Robert

Eliot, George 1819-1880. . . . **NCLC 4, 13, 23**
See also CDBLB 1832-1890; DLB 21, 35,
55; WLC

Eliot, John 1604-1690 . . . . **LC 5**
See also DLB 24

Eliot, T(homas) S(tearns)
1888-1965 . . . . **CLC 1, 2, 3, 6, 9, 10, 13,
15, 24, 34, 41, 55, 57; PC 5**
See also CA 5-8R; 25-28R;
CDALB 1929-1941; DLB 7, 10, 45, 63;
MTCW; WLC 2

Elizabeth 1866-1941 . . . . **TCLC 41**

Elkin, Stanley L(awrence)
1930- . . . . **CLC 4, 6, 9, 14, 27, 51**
See also CA 9-12R; CANR 8; DLB 2, 28;
DLBY 80; MTCW

Elledge, Scott . . . . **CLC 34**

Elliott, Don
See Silverberg, Robert

Elliott, George P(aul) 1918-1980 . . . . . **CLC 2**
See also CA 1-4R; 97-100; CANR 2

Elliott, Janice 1931- . . . . **CLC 47**
See also CA 13-16R; CANR 8, 29; DLB 14

Elliott, Sumner Locke 1917-1991 . . . **CLC 38**
See also CA 5-8R; 134; CANR 2, 21

Elliott, William
See Bradbury, Ray (Douglas)

Ellis, A. E. . . . . **CLC 7**

Ellis, Alice Thomas . . . . **CLC 40**
See also Haycraft, Anna

Ellis, Bret Easton 1964- . . . . **CLC 39, 71**
See also AAYA 2; CA 118; 123

Ellis, (Henry) Havelock
1859-1939 . . . . **TCLC 14**
See also CA 109

Ellis, Landon
See Ellison, Harlan

Ellis, Trey 1962- . . . . **CLC 55**

Ellison, Harlan 1934- . . . . **CLC 1, 13, 42**
See also CA 5-8R; CANR 5; DLB 8;
MTCW

Ellison, Ralph (Waldo)
1914- . . . . **CLC 1, 3, 11, 54**
See also BLC 1; BW; CA 9-12R; CANR 24;
CDALB 1941-1968; DLB 2, 76; MTCW;
WLC

Ellmann, Lucy (Elizabeth) 1956- . . . . **CLC 61**
See also CA 128

Ellmann, Richard (David)
1918-1987 . . . . **CLC 50**
See also BEST 89:2; CA 1-4R; 122;
CANR 2, 28; DLB 103; DLBY 87;
MTCW

Elman, Richard 1934- . . . . **CLC 19**
See also CA 17-20R; CAAS 3

Elron
See Hubbard, L(afayette) Ron(ald)

Eluard, Paul . . . . **TCLC 7, 41**
See also Grindel, Eugene

Elyot, Sir Thomas 1490(?)-1546 . . . . . **LC 11**

Elytis, Odysseus 1911- . . . . **CLC 15, 49**
See also CA 102; MTCW

Emecheta, (Florence Onye) Buchi
1944- . . . . **CLC 14, 48**
See also BLC 2; BW; CA 81-84; CANR 27;
DLB 117; MTCW; SATA 66

Emerson, Ralph Waldo
1803-1882 . . . . **NCLC 1, 38**
See also CDALB 1640-1865; DLB 1, 59, 73;
WLC

Eminescu, Mihail 1850-1889 . . . . . **NCLC 33**

Empson, William
1906-1984 . . . . **CLC 3, 8, 19, 33, 34**
See also CA 17-20R; 112; CANR 31;
DLB 20; MTCW

Enchi Fumiko (Ueda) 1905-1986 . . . . **CLC 31**
See also CA 129; 121

Ende, Michael (Andreas Helmuth)
1929- . . . . **CLC 31**
See also CA 118; 124; CANR 36; CLR 14;
DLB 75; MAICYA; SATA 42, 61

Endo, Shusaku 1923- . . . . . **CLC 7, 14, 19, 54**
See also CA 29-32R; CANR 21; MTCW

Engel, Marian 1933-1985 . . . . **CLC 36**
See also CA 25-28R; CANR 12; DLB 53

Engelhardt, Frederick
See Hubbard, L(afayette) Ron(ald)

Enright, D(ennis) J(oseph)
1920- . . . . **CLC 4, 8, 31**
See also CA 1-4R; CANR 1; DLB 27;
SATA 25

Enzensberger, Hans Magnus
1929- . . . . **CLC 43**
See also CA 116; 119

Ephron, Nora 1941- . . . . **CLC 17, 31**
See also AITN 2; CA 65-68; CANR 12, 39

Epsilon
See Betjeman, John

Epstein, Daniel Mark 1948- . . . . **CLC 7**
See also CA 49-52; CANR 2

Epstein, Jacob 1956- . . . . **CLC 19**
See also CA 114

Epstein, Joseph 1937- . . . . **CLC 39**
See also CA 112; 119

Epstein, Leslie 1938- . . . . **CLC 27**
See also CA 73-76; CAAS 12; CANR 23

Equiano, Olaudah 1745(?)-1797 . . . . . . **LC 16**
See also BLC 2; DLB 37, 50

Erasmus, Desiderius 1469(?)-1536 . . . . **LC 16**

Erdman, Paul E(mil) 1932- . . . . **CLC 25**
See also AITN 1; CA 61-64; CANR 13

Erdrich, Louise 1954- . . . . **CLC 39, 54**
See also BEST 89:1; CA 114; MTCW

Erenburg, Ilya (Grigoryevich)
See Ehrenburg, Ilya (Grigoryevich)

Erickson, Stephen Michael 1950-
See Erickson, Steve
See also CA 129

Erickson, Steve . . . . **CLC 64**
See also Erickson, Stephen Michael

Ericson, Walter
See Fast, Howard (Melvin)

Eriksson, Buntel
See Bergman, (Ernst) Ingmar

Eschenbach, Wolfram von
See Wolfram von Eschenbach

Eseki, Bruno
See Mphahlele, Ezekiel

Esenin, Sergei (Alexandrovich)
1895-1925 . . . . **TCLC 4**
See also CA 104

Eshleman, Clayton 1935- . . . . **CLC 7**
See also CA 33-36R; CAAS 6; DLB 5

Espriella, Don Manuel Alvarez
See Southey, Robert

Espriu, Salvador 1913-1985 . . . . **CLC 9**
See also CA 115

Esse, James
See Stephens, James

Esterbrook, Tom
See Hubbard, L(afayette) Ron(ald)

Estleman, Loren D. 1952- . . . . **CLC 48**
See also CA 85-88; CANR 27; MTCW

Evans, Mary Ann
See Eliot, George

Evarts, Esther
See Benson, Sally

Everett, Percival
See Everett, Percival L.

Everett, Percival L. 1956- . . . . **CLC 57**
See also CA 129

Everson, R(onald) G(ilmour)
1903- . . . . **CLC 27**
See also CA 17-20R; DLB 88

Everson, William (Oliver)
1912- . . . . **CLC 1, 5, 14**
See also CA 9-12R; CANR 20; DLB 5, 16;
MTCW

Evtushenko, Evgenii Aleksandrovich
See Yevtushenko, Yevgeny (Alexandrovich)

Ewart, Gavin (Buchanan)
1916- . . . . **CLC 13, 46**
See also CA 89-92; CANR 17; DLB 40;
MTCW

Ewers, Hanns Heinz 1871-1943 . . . **TCLC 12**
See also CA 109

Ewing, Frederick R.
See Sturgeon, Theodore (Hamilton)

Exley, Frederick (Earl) 1929- . . . . **CLC 6, 11**
See also AITN 2; CA 81-84; 138; DLBY 81

Eynhardt, Guillermo
See Quiroga, Horacio (Sylvestre)

Ezekiel, Nissim 1924- . . . . **CLC 61**
See also CA 61-64

Ezekiel, Tish O'Dowd 1943- . . . . **CLC 34**
See also CA 129

Fagen, Donald 1948- . . . . **CLC 26**

Fainzilberg, Ilya Arnoldovich 1897-1937
See Ilf, Ilya
See also CA 120

Fair, Ronald L. 1932- . . . . **CLC 18**
See also BW; CA 69-72; CANR 25; DLB 33

Fairbairns, Zoe (Ann) 1948- . . . . **CLC 32**
See also CA 103; CANR 21

Falco, Gian
See Papini, Giovanni

Falconer, James
See Kirkup, James

Falconer, Kenneth
See Kornbluth, C(yril) M.

Falkland, Samuel
See Heijermans, Herman

Fallaci, Oriana 1930- . . . . **CLC 11**
See also CA 77-80; CANR 15; MTCW

Faludy, George 1913- . . . . **CLC 42**
See also CA 21-24R

Faludy, Gyoergy
See Faludy, George

Fanon, Frantz 1925-1961 . . . . **CLC 74**
See also BLC 2; BW; CA 116; 89-92

Fanshawe, Ann . . . . **LC 11**

Fante, John (Thomas) 1911-1983 . . . **CLC 60**
See also CA 69-72; 109; CANR 23;
DLBY 83

Farah, Nuruddin 1945- . . . . **CLC 53**
See also BLC 2; CA 106

Fargue, Leon-Paul 1876(?)-1947 . . . **TCLC 11**
See also CA 109

Farigoule, Louis
See Romains, Jules

Farina, Richard 1936(?)-1966 . . . . **CLC 9**
See also CA 81-84; 25-28R

Farley, Walter (Lorimer)
1915-1989 . . . . **CLC 17**
See also CA 17-20R; CANR 8, 29; DLB 22;
MAICYA; SATA 2, 43

Farmer, Philip Jose 1918- . . . . . . **CLC 1, 19**
See also CA 1-4R; CANR 4, 35; DLB 8;
MTCW

Farquhar, George 1677-1707 . . . . **LC 21**
See also DLB 84

Farrell, J(ames) G(ordon)
1935-1979 . . . . **CLC 6**
See also CA 73-76; 89-92; CANR 36;
DLB 14; MTCW

Farrell, James T(homas)
1904-1979 . . . . **CLC 1, 4, 8, 11, 66**
See also CA 5-8R; 89-92; CANR 9; DLB 4,
9, 86; DLBD 2; MTCW

Farren, Richard J.
See Betjeman, John

Farren, Richard M.
See Betjeman, John

Fassbinder, Rainer Werner
1946-1982 . . . . **CLC 20**
See also CA 93-96; 106; CANR 31

Fast, Howard (Melvin) 1914- . . . . . . **CLC 23**
See also CA 1-4R; CANR 1, 33; DLB 9;
SATA 7

Faulcon, Robert
See Holdstock, Robert P.

Faulkner, William (Cuthbert)
1897-1962 . . . . **CLC 1, 3, 6, 8, 9, 11, 14,
18, 28, 52, 68; SSC 1**
See also AAYA 7; CA 81-84; CANR 33;
CDALB 1929-1941; DLB 9, 11, 44, 102;
DLBD 2; DLBY 86; MTCW; WLC

Fauset, Jessie Redmon
1884(?)-1961 . . . . **CLC 19, 54**
See also BLC 2; BW; CA 109; DLB 51

Faust, Irvin 1924- . . . . **CLC 8**
See also CA 33-36R; CANR 28; DLB 2, 28;
DLBY 80

Fawkes, Guy
See Benchley, Robert (Charles)

Fearing, Kenneth (Flexner)
1902-1961 . . . . **CLC 51**
See also CA 93-96; DLB 9

Fecamps, Elise
See Creasey, John

Federman, Raymond 1928- . . . . . . **CLC 6, 47**
See also CA 17-20R; CAAS 8; CANR 10;
DLBY 80

Federspiel, J(uerg) F. 1931- . . . . **CLC 42**

Feiffer, Jules (Ralph) 1929- . . . . **CLC 2, 8, 64**
See also AAYA 3; CA 17-20R; CANR 30;
DLB 7, 44; MTCW; SATA 8, 61

Feige, Hermann Albert Otto Maximilian
See Traven, B.

Fei-Kan, Li
See Li Fei-kan

Feinberg, David B. 1956- . . . . **CLC 59**
See also CA 135

Feinstein, Elaine 1930- . . . . **CLC 36**
See also CA 69-72; CAAS 1; CANR 31;
DLB 14, 40; MTCW

Feldman, Irving (Mordecai) 1928- . . . . **CLC 7**
See also CA 1-4R; CANR 1

Fellini, Federico 1920- . . . . **CLC 16**
See also CA 65-68; CANR 33

Felsen, Henry Gregor 1916- . . . . **CLC 17**
See also CA 1-4R; CANR 1; SAAS 2;
SATA 1

Fenton, James Martin 1949- . . . . **CLC 32**
See also CA 102; DLB 40

Ferber, Edna 1887-1968 . . . . **CLC 18**
See also AITN 1; CA 5-8R; 25-28R; DLB 9,
28, 86; MTCW; SATA 7

Ferguson, Helen
See Kavan, Anna

Ferguson, Samuel 1810-1886 . . . . . **NCLC 33**
See also DLB 32

Ferling, Lawrence
See Ferlinghetti, Lawrence (Monsanto)

Ferlinghetti, Lawrence (Monsanto)
1919(?)- . . . . **CLC 2, 6, 10, 27; PC 1**
See also CA 5-8R; CANR 3;
CDALB 1941-1968; DLB 5, 16; MTCW

Fernandez, Vicente Garcia Huidobro
See Huidobro Fernandez, Vicente Garcia

Ferrer, Gabriel (Francisco Victor) Miro
See Miro (Ferrer), Gabriel (Francisco
Victor)

Ferrier, Susan (Edmonstone)
1782-1854 . . . . **NCLC 8**
See also DLB 116

Ferrigno, Robert . . . . **CLC 65**

Feuchtwanger, Lion 1884-1958 . . . . . **TCLC 3**
See also CA 104; DLB 66

Feydeau, Georges (Leon Jules Marie)
1862-1921 . . . . **TCLC 22**
See also CA 113

Ficino, Marsilio 1433-1499 . . . . **LC 12**

Fiedler, Leslie A(aron)
1917- . . . . **CLC 4, 13, 24**
See also CA 9-12R; CANR 7; DLB 28, 67;
MTCW

Field, Andrew 1938- . . . . **CLC 44**
See also CA 97-100; CANR 25

Field, Eugene 1850-1895 . . . . **NCLC 3**
See also DLB 23, 42; MAICYA; SATA 16

Field, Gans T.
See Wellman, Manly Wade

Field, Michael . . . . **TCLC 43**

Field, Peter
See Hobson, Laura Z(ametkin)

Fielding, Henry 1707-1754 . . . . **LC 1**
See also CDBLB 1660-1789; DLB 39, 84,
101; WLC

Fielding, Sarah 1710-1768 . . . . **LC 1**
See also DLB 39

Fierstein, Harvey (Forbes) 1954- . . . **CLC 33**
See also CA 123; 129

Figes, Eva 1932- . . . . **CLC 31**
See also CA 53-56; CANR 4; DLB 14

Finch, Robert (Duer Claydon)
1900- . . . . **CLC 18**
See also CA 57-60; CANR 9, 24; DLB 88

Findley, Timothy 1930- . . . . **CLC 27**
See also CA 25-28R; CANR 12; DLB 53

Fink, William
See Mencken, H(enry) L(ouis)

Firbank, Louis 1942-
See Reed, Lou
See also CA 117

Firbank, (Arthur Annesley) Ronald
1886-1926 . . . . **TCLC 1**
See also CA 104; DLB 36

Fisher, Roy 1930- . . . . **CLC 25**
See also CA 81-84; CAAS 10; CANR 16;
DLB 40

Fisher, Rudolph 1897-1934 . . . . **TCLC 11**
See also BLC 2; BW; CA 107; 124; DLB 51,
102

Fisher, Vardis (Alvero) 1895-1968. . . . **CLC 7**
See also CA 5-8R; 25-28R; DLB 9

Fiske, Tarleton
See Bloch, Robert (Albert)

Fitch, Clarke
See Sinclair, Upton (Beall)

Fitch, John IV
See Cormier, Robert (Edmund)

Fitgerald, Penelope 1916- . . . . **CLC 61**

Fitzgerald, Captain Hugh
See Baum, L(yman) Frank

FitzGerald, Edward 1809-1883 . . . . **NCLC 9**
See also DLB 32

Fitzgerald, F(rancis) Scott (Key)
1896-1940 . . . . **TCLC 1, 6, 14, 28; SSC 6**
See also AITN 1; CA 110; 123;
CDALB 1917-1929; DLB 4, 9, 86;
DLBD 1; DLBY 81; MTCW; WLC

Fitzgerald, Penelope 1916- . . . . . . **CLC 19, 51**
See also CA 85-88; CAAS 10; DLB 14

FitzGerald, Robert D(avid)
1902-1987 . . . . **CLC 19**
See also CA 17-20R

Fitzgerald, Robert (Stuart)
1910-1985 . . . . **CLC 39**
See also CA 1-4R; 114; CANR 1; DLBY 80

Flanagan, Thomas (James Bonner)
1923- . . . . **CLC 25, 52**
See also CA 108; DLBY 80; MTCW

Flaubert, Gustave
1821-1880 . . . . . **NCLC 2, 10, 19; SSC 11**
See also DLB 119; WLC

Flecker, (Herman) James Elroy
1884-1915 . . . . **TCLC 43**
See also CA 109; DLB 10, 19

Fleming, Ian (Lancaster)
1908-1964 . . . . **CLC 3, 30**
See also CA 5-8R; CDBLB 1945-1960;
DLB 87; MTCW; SATA 9

Fleming, Thomas (James) 1927- . . . . **CLC 37**
See also CA 5-8R; CANR 10; SATA 8

Fletcher, John Gould 1886-1950 . . . **TCLC 35**
See also CA 107; DLB 4, 45

Fleur, Paul
See Pohl, Frederik

Flying Officer X
See Bates, H(erbert) E(rnest)

Fo, Dario 1926- . . . . **CLC 32**
See also CA 116; 128; MTCW

Fogarty, Jonathan Titulescu Esq.
See Farrell, James T(homas)

Folke, Will
See Bloch, Robert (Albert)

Follett, Ken(neth Martin) 1949- . . . . **CLC 18**
See also AAYA 6; BEST 89:4; CA 81-84;
CANR 13, 33; DLB 87; DLBY 81;
MTCW

Fontane, Theodor 1819-1898 . . . . . **NCLC 26**

Foote, Horton 1916- . . . . **CLC 51**
See also CA 73-76; CANR 34; DLB 26

Forbes, Esther 1891-1967. . . . . **CLC 12**
See also CA 13-14; 25-28R; CAP 1;
CLR 27; DLB 22; MAICYA; SATA 2

Forche, Carolyn (Louise) 1950- . . . . . **CLC 25**
See also CA 109; 117; DLB 5

Ford, Elbur
See Hibbert, Eleanor Burford

Ford, Ford Madox
1873-1939 . . . . **TCLC 1, 15, 39**
See also CA 104; 132; CDBLB 1914-1945;
DLB 34, 98; MTCW

Ford, John 1895-1973. . . . . **CLC 16**
See also CA 45-48

Ford, Richard 1944- . . . . **CLC 46**
See also CA 69-72; CANR 11

Ford, Webster
See Masters, Edgar Lee

Foreman, Richard 1937- . . . . **CLC 50**
See also CA 65-68; CANR 32

Forester, C(ecil) S(cott)
1899-1966 . . . . **CLC 35**
See also CA 73-76; 25-28R; SATA 13

Forez
See Mauriac, Francois (Charles)

Forman, James Douglas 1932- . . . . . . **CLC 21**
See also CA 9-12R; CANR 4, 19;
MAICYA; SATA 8, 70

Fornes, Maria Irene 1930- . . . . . . **CLC 39, 61**
See also CA 25-28R; CANR 28; DLB 7;
HW; MTCW

Forrest, Leon 1937- . . . . **CLC 4**
See also BW; CA 89-92; CAAS 7;
CANR 25; DLB 33

Forster, E(dward) M(organ)
1879-1970 . . . . **CLC 1, 2, 3, 4, 9, 10, 13,
15, 22, 45**
See also AAYA 2; CA 13-14; 25-28R;
CAP 1; CDBLB 1914-1945; DLB 34, 98;
MTCW; SATA 57; WLC

Forster, John 1812-1876 . . . . **NCLC 11**

Forsyth, Frederick 1938- . . . . . . **CLC 2, 5, 36**
See also BEST 89:4; CA 85-88; CANR 38;
DLB 87; MTCW

Forten, Charlotte L. . . . . **TCLC 16**
See also Grimke, Charlotte L(ottie) Forten
See also BLC 2; DLB 50

Foscolo, Ugo 1778-1827. . . . . **NCLC 8**

Fosse, Bob . . . . **CLC 20**
See also Fosse, Robert Louis

Fosse, Robert Louis 1927-1987
See Fosse, Bob
See also CA 110; 123

Foster, Stephen Collins
1826-1864 . . . . **NCLC 26**

Foucault, Michel
1926-1984 . . . . **CLC 31, 34, 69**
See also CA 105; 113; CANR 34; MTCW

Fouque, Friedrich Heinrich Karl) de la Motte
1777-1843 . . . . **NCLC 2**
See also DLB 90

Fournier, Henri Alban 1886-1914
See Alain-Fournier
See also CA 104

Fournier, Pierre 1916- . . . . **CLC 11**
See also Gascar, Pierre
See also CA 89-92; CANR 16

Fowles, John
1926- . . . . **CLC 1, 2, 3, 4, 6, 9, 10, 15, 33**
See also CA 5-8R; CANR 25; CDBLB 1960
to Present; DLB 14; MTCW; SATA 22

Fox, Paula 1923- . . . . **CLC 2, '**
See also AAYA 3; CA 73-76; CANR 20,
36; CLR 1; DLB 52; MAICYA; MTCW;
SATA 17, 60

Fox, William Price (Jr.) 1926- . . . . . **CLC 22**
See also CA 17-20R; CANR 11; DLB 2;
DLBY 81

Foxe, John 1516(?)-1587 . . . . **LC 14**

Frame, Janet . . . . **CLC 2, 3, 6, 22, 66**
See also Clutha, Janet Paterson Frame

France, Anatole . . . . **TCLC 9**
See also Thibault, Jacques Anatole Francois

Francis, Claude 19(?)- . . . . **CLC 50**

Francis, Dick 1920- . . . . **CLC 2, 22, 42**
See also AAYA 5; BEST 89:3; CA 5-8R;
CANR 9; CDBLB 1960 to Present;
DLB 87; MTCW

Francis, Robert (Churchill)
1901-1987 . . . . **CLC 15**
See also CA 1-4R; 123; CANR 1

Frank, Anne(lies Marie)
1929-1945 . . . . **TCLC 17**
See also CA 113; 133; MTCW; SATA 42;
WLC

Frank, Elizabeth 1945- . . . . **CLC 39**
See also CA 121; 126

Franklin, Benjamin
See Hasek, Jaroslav (Matej Frantisek)

Franklin, (Stella Maraia Sarah) Miles
1879-1954 . . . . **TCLC 7**
See also CA 104

Fraser, Antonia (Pakenham)
1932- . . . . **CLC 32**
See also CA 85-88; MTCW; SATA 32

Fraser, George MacDonald 1925- . . . . **CLC 7**
See also CA 45-48; CANR 2

Fraser, Sylvia 1935- . . . . **CLC 64**
See also CA 45-48; CANR 1, 16

Frayn, Michael 1933- . . . . . . **CLC 3, 7, 31, 47**
See also CA 5-8R; CANR 30; DLB 13, 14;
MTCW

Fraze, Candida (Merrill) 1945- . . . . . **CLC 50**
See also CA 126

Frazer, J(ames) G(eorge)
1854-1941 . . . . **TCLC 32**
See also CA 118

Frazer, Robert Caine
See Creasey, John

Gloag, Julian 1930- .... **CLC 40**
See also AITN 1; CA 65-68; CANR 10

Gluck, Louise 1943-......... **CLC 7, 22, 44**
See also Glueck, Louise
See also CA 33-36R; DLB 5

Glueck, Louise................. **CLC 7, 22**
See also Gluck, Louise
See also DLB 5

Gobineau, Joseph Arthur (Comte) de
1816-1882 .... **NCLC 17**

Godard, Jean-Luc 1930-.......... **CLC 20**
See also CA 93-96

Godden, (Margaret) Rumer 1907-... **CLC 53**
See also AAYA 6; CA 5-8R; CANR 4, 27,
36; CLR 20; MAICYA; SAAS 12;
SATA 3, 36

Godoy Alcayaga, Lucila 1889-1957
See Mistral, Gabriela
See also CA 104; 131; HW; MTCW

Godwin, Gail (Kathleen)
1937- .... **CLC 5, 8, 22, 31, 69**
See also CA 29-32R; CANR 15; DLB 6;
MTCW

Godwin, William 1756-1836..... **NCLC 14**
See also CDBLB 1789-1832; DLB 39, 104

Goethe, Johann Wolfgang von
1749-1832 .... **NCLC 4, 22, 34; PC 5**
See also DLB 94; WLC 3

Gogarty, Oliver St. John
1878-1957 .... **TCLC 15**
See also CA 109; DLB 15, 19

Gogol, Nikolai (Vasilyevich)
1809-1852 ..... **NCLC 5, 15, 31; DC 1;
SSC 4**
See also WLC

Gold, Herbert 1924-....... **CLC 4, 7, 14, 42**
See also CA 9-12R; CANR 17; DLB 2;
DLBY 81

Goldbarth, Albert 1948-......... **CLC 5, 38**
See also CA 53-56; CANR 6; DLB 120

Goldberg, Anatol 1910-1982 .... **CLC 34**
See also CA 131; 117

Goldemberg, Isaac 1945- .... **CLC 52**
See also CA 69-72; CAAS 12; CANR 11,
32; HW

Golden Silver
See Storm, Hyemeyohsts

Golding, William (Gerald)
1911- ..... **CLC 1, 2, 3, 8, 10, 17, 27, 58**
See also AAYA 5; CA 5-8R; CANR 13, 33;
CDBLB 1945-1960; DLB 15, 100;
MTCW; WLC

Goldman, Emma 1869-1940 ...... **TCLC 13**
See also CA 110

Goldman, William (W.) 1931-.... **CLC 1, 48**
See also CA 9-12R; CANR 29; DLB 44

Goldmann, Lucien 1913-1970 ...... **CLC 24**
See also CA 25-28; CAP 2

Goldoni, Carlo 1707-1793 .... **LC 4**

Goldsberry, Steven 1949-......... **CLC 34**
See also CA 131

Goldsmith, Oliver 1728(?)-1774....... **LC 2**

Goldsmith, Peter
See Priestley, J(ohn) B(oynton)

Gombrowicz, Witold
1904-1969 .... **CLC 4, 7, 11, 49**
See also CA 19-20; 25-28R; CAP 2

Gomez de la Serna, Ramon
1888-1963 .... **CLC 9**
See also CA 116; HW

Goncharov, Ivan Alexandrovich
1812-1891 .... **NCLC 1**

Goncourt, Edmond (Louis Antoine Huot) de
1822-1896 .... **NCLC 7**

Goncourt, Jules (Alfred Huot) de
1830-1870 .... **NCLC 7**

Gontier, Fernande 19(?)- .... **CLC 50**

Goodman, Paul 1911-1972.... **CLC 1, 2, 4, 7**
See also CA 19-20; 37-40R; CANR 34;
CAP 2; MTCW

Gordimer, Nadine
1923- .... **CLC 3, 5, 7, 10, 18, 33, 51, 70**
See also CA 5-8R; CANR 3, 28; MTCW

Gordon, Adam Lindsay
1833-1870 .... **NCLC 21**

Gordon, Caroline
1895-1981 .... **CLC 6, 13, 29**
See also CA 11-12; 103; CANR 36; CAP 1;
DLB 4, 9, 102; DLBY 81; MTCW

Gordon, Charles William 1860-1937
See Connor, Ralph
See also CA 109

Gordon, Mary (Catherine)
1949- .... **CLC 13, 22**
See also CA 102; DLB 6; DLBY 81;
MTCW

Gordon, Sol 1923-................ **CLC 26**
See also CA 53-56; CANR 4; SATA 11

Gordone, Charles 1925- .... **CLC 1, 4**
See also BW; CA 93-96; DLB 7; MTCW

Gorenko, Anna Andreevna
See Akhmatova, Anna

Gorky, Maxim................... **TCLC 8**
See also Peshkov, Alexei Maximovich
See also WLC

Goryan, Sirak
See Saroyan, William

Gosse, Edmund (William)
1849-1928 .... **TCLC 28**
See also CA 117; DLB 57

Gotlieb, Phyllis Fay (Bloom)
1926- .... **CLC 18**
See also CA 13-16R; CANR 7; DLB 88

Gottesman, S. D.
See Kornbluth, C(yril) M.; Pohl, Frederik

Gottfried von Strassburg
fl. c. 1210 .... **CMLC 10**

Gottschalk, Laura Riding
See Jackson, Laura (Riding)

Gould, Lois .... **CLC 4, 10**
See also CA 77-80; CANR 29; MTCW

Gourmont, Remy de 1858-1915.... **TCLC 17**
See also CA 109

Govier, Katherine 1948-.......... **CLC 51**
See also CA 101; CANR 18

Goyen, (Charles) William
1915-1983 .... **CLC 5, 8, 14, 40**
See also AITN 2; CA 5-8R; 110; CANR 6;
DLB 2; DLBY 83

Goytisolo, Juan 1931- .... **CLC 5, 10, 23**
See also CA 85-88; CANR 32; HW; MTCW

Gozzi, (Conte) Carlo 1720-1806 .. **NCLC 23**

Grabbe, Christian Dietrich
1801-1836 .... **NCLC 2**

Grace, Patricia 1937-............. **CLC 56**

Gracian y Morales, Baltasar
1601-1658 .... **LC 15**

Gracq, Julien.................. **CLC 11, 48**
See also Poirier, Louis
See also DLB 83

Grade, Chaim 1910-1982 .... **CLC 10**
See also CA 93-96; 107

Graduate of Oxford, A
See Ruskin, John

Graham, John
See Phillips, David Graham

Graham, Jorie 1951-............. **CLC 48**
See also CA 111; DLB 120

Graham, R(obert) B(ontine) Cunninghame
See Cunninghame Graham, R(obert)
B(ontine)
See also DLB 98

Graham, Robert
See Haldeman, Joe (William)

Graham, Tom
See Lewis, (Harry) Sinclair

Graham, W(illiam) S(ydney)
1918-1986 .... **CLC 29**
See also CA 73-76; 118; DLB 20

Graham, Winston (Mawdsley)
1910- .... **CLC 23**
See also CA 49-52; CANR 2, 22; DLB 77

Granville-Barker, Harley
1877-1946 .... **TCLC 2**
See also Barker, Harley Granville
See also CA 104

Grass, Guenter (Wilhelm)
1927- .. **CLC 1, 2, 4, 6, 11, 15, 22, 32, 49**
See also CA 13-16R; CANR 20; DLB 75;
MTCW; WLC

Gratton, Thomas
See Hulme, T(homas) E(rnest)

Grau, Shirley Ann 1929- .... **CLC 4, 9**
See also CA 89-92; CANR 22; DLB 2;
MTCW

Gravel, Fern
See Hall, James Norman

Graver, Elizabeth 1964-........... **CLC 70**
See also CA 135

Graves, Richard Perceval 1945- .... **CLC 44**
See also CA 65-68; CANR 9, 26

Graves, Robert (von Ranke)
1895-1985 ... **CLC 1, 2, 6, 11, 39, 44, 45**
See also CA 5-8R; 117; CANR 5, 36;
CDBLB 1914-1945; DLB 20, 100;
DLBY 85; MTCW; SATA 45

Gray, Alasdair (James) 1934- ...... **CLC 41**
See also CA 126; MTCW

Author Index

Hoffman, Stanley 1944-........... **CLC 5**
See also CA 77-80

Hoffman, William M(oses) 1939-... **CLC 40**
See also CA 57-60; CANR 11

Hoffmann, E(rnst) T(heodor) A(madeus)
1776-1822 .... **NCLC 2**
See also DLB 90; SATA 27

Hofmann, Gert 1931-............. **CLC 54**
See also CA 128

Hofmannsthal, Hugo von
1874-1929 .... **TCLC 11**
See also CA 106; DLB 81, 118

Hogarth, Charles
See Creasey, John

Hogg, James 1770-1835......... **NCLC 4**
See also DLB 93, 116

Holbach, Paul Henri Thiry Baron
1723-1789 .... **LC 14**

Holberg, Ludvig 1684-1754 .... **LC 6**

Holden, Ursula 1921-............. **CLC 18**
See also CA 101; CAAS 8; CANR 22

Holderlin, (Johann Christian) Friedrich
1770-1843 .... **NCLC 16; PC 4**

Holdstock, Robert
See Holdstock, Robert P.

Holdstock, Robert P. 1948-....... **CLC 39**
See also CA 131

Holland, Isabelle 1920- .... **CLC 21**
See also CA 21-24R; CANR 10, 25;
MAICYA; SATA 8, 70

Holland, Marcus
See Caldwell, (Janet Miriam) Taylor
(Holland)

Hollander, John 1929-...... **CLC 2, 5, 8, 14**
See also CA 1-4R; CANR 1; DLB 5;
SATA 13

Hollander, Paul
See Silverberg, Robert

Holleran, Andrew 1943(?)-........ **CLC 38**

Hollinghurst, Alan 1954- .... **CLC 55**
See also CA 114

Hollis, Jim
See Summers, Hollis (Spurgeon Jr.)

Holmes, John
See Souster, (Holmes) Raymond

Holmes, John Clellon 1926-1988.... **CLC 56**
See also CA 9-12R; 125; CANR 4; DLB 16

Holmes, Oliver Wendell
1809-1894 .... **NCLC 14**
See also CDALB 1640-1865; DLB 1;
SATA 34

Holmes, Raymond
See Souster, (Holmes) Raymond

Holt, Victoria
See Hibbert, Eleanor Burford

Holub, Miroslav 1923-............. **CLC 4**
See also CA 21-24R; CANR 10

Homer c. 8th cent. B.C. .... **CMLC 1**

Honig, Edwin 1919-.............. **CLC 33**
See also CA 5-8R; CAAS 8; CANR 4;
DLB 5

Hood, Hugh (John Blagdon)
1928- .... **CLC 15, 28**
See also CA 49-52; CANR 1, 33; DLB 53

Hood, Thomas 1799-1845....... **NCLC 16**
See also DLB 96

Hooker, (Peter) Jeremy 1941-...... **CLC 43**
See also CA 77-80; CANR 22; DLB 40

Hope, A(lec) D(erwent) 1907-.... **CLC 3, 51**
See also CA 21-24R; CANR 33; MTCW

Hope, Brian
See Creasey, John

Hope, Christopher (David Tully)
1944- .... **CLC 52**
See also CA 106; SATA 62

Hopkins, Gerard Manley
1844-1889 .... **NCLC 17**
See also CDBLB 1890-1914; DLB 35, 57;
WLC

Hopkins, John (Richard) 1931-...... **CLC 4**
See also CA 85-88

Hopkins, Pauline Elizabeth
1859-1930 .... **TCLC 28**
See also BLC 2; DLB 50

Horatio
See Proust,
(Valentin-Louis-George-Eugene-)Marcel

Horgan, Paul 1903- .... **CLC 9, 53**
See also CA 13-16R; CANR 9, 35;
DLB 102; DLBY 85; MTCW; SATA 13

Horn, Peter
See Kuttner, Henry

Horovitz, Israel 1939- .... **CLC 56**
See also CA 33-36R; DLB 7

Horvath, Odon von
See Horvath, Oedoen von
See also DLB 85

Horvath, Oedoen von 1901-1938... **TCLC 45**
See also Horvath, Odon von
See also CA 118

Horwitz, Julius 1920-1986........ **CLC 14**
See also CA 9-12R; 119; CANR 12

Hospital, Janette Turner 1942-..... **CLC 42**
See also CA 108

Hostos, E. M. de
See Hostos (y Bonilla), Eugenio Maria de

Hostos, Eugenio M. de
See Hostos (y Bonilla), Eugenio Maria de

Hostos, Eugenio Maria
See Hostos (y Bonilla), Eugenio Maria de

Hostos (y Bonilla), Eugenio Maria de
1839-1903 .... **TCLC 24**
See also CA 123; 131; HW

Houdini
See Lovecraft, H(oward) P(hillips)

Hougan, Carolyn 19(?)- .... **CLC 34**

Household, Geoffrey (Edward West)
1900-1988 .... **CLC 11**
See also CA 77-80; 126; DLB 87; SATA 14,
59

Housman, A(lfred) E(dward)
1859-1936 .... **TCLC 1, 10; PC 2**
See also CA 104; 125; DLB 19; MTCW

Housman, Laurence 1865-1959 ..... **TCLC 7**
See also CA 106; DLB 10; SATA 25

Howard, Elizabeth Jane 1923- ... **CLC 7, 29**
See also CA 5-8R; CANR 8

Howard, Maureen 1930- ..... **CLC 5, 14, 46**
See also CA 53-56; CANR 31; DLBY 83;
MTCW

Howard, Richard 1929- ...... **CLC 7, 10, 47**
See also AITN 1; CA 85-88; CANR 25;
DLB 5

Howard, Robert Ervin 1906-1936... **TCLC 8**
See also CA 105

Howard, Warren F.
See Pohl, Frederik

Howe, Fanny 1940- .... **CLC 47**
See also CA 117; SATA 52

Howe, Julia Ward 1819-1910 ..... **TCLC 21**
See also CA 117; DLB 1

Howe, Susan 1937-.............. **CLC 72**
See also DLB 120

Howe, Tina 1937-.............. **CLC 48**
See also CA 109

Howell, James 1594(?)-1666 .... **LC 13**

Howells, W. D.
See Howells, William Dean

Howells, William D.
See Howells, William Dean

Howells, William Dean
1837-1920 .... **TCLC 41, 7, 17**
See also CA 104; 134; CDALB 1865-1917;
DLB 12, 64, 74, 79

Howes, Barbara 1914-............ **CLC 15**
See also CA 9-12R; CAAS 3; SATA 5

Hrabal, Bohumil 1914-........ **CLC 13, 67**
See also CA 106; CAAS 12

Hsun, Lu .... **TCLC 3**
See also Shu-Jen, Chou

Hubbard, L(afayette) Ron(ald)
1911-1986 .... **CLC 43**
See also CA 77-80; 118; CANR 22

Huch, Ricarda (Octavia)
1864-1947 .... **TCLC 13**
See also CA 111; DLB 66

Huddle, David 1942- .... **CLC 49**
See also CA 57-60

Hudson, Jeffery
See Crichton, (John) Michael

Hudson, W(illiam) H(enry)
1841-1922 .... **TCLC 29**
See also CA 115; DLB 98; SATA 35

Hueffer, Ford Madox
See Ford, Ford Madox

Hughart, Barry .... **CLC 39**
See also CA 137

Hughes, Colin
See Creasey, John

Hughes, David (John) 1930- .... **CLC 48**
See also CA 116; 129; DLB 14

Hughes, (James) Langston
1902-1967 .... **CLC 1, 5, 10, 15, 35, 44;**
PC 1; SSC 6
See also BLC 2; BW; CA 1-4R; 25-28R;
CANR 1, 34; CDALB 1929-1941;
CLR 17; DLB 4, 7, 48, 51, 86; MAICYA;
MTCW; SATA 4, 33; WLC

Jacobson, Dan 1929- . . . . **CLC 4, 14**
  See also CA 1-4R; CANR 2, 25; DLB 14;
  MTCW

Jacqueline
  See Carpentier (y Valmont), Alejo

Jagger, Mick 1944-. . . . . **CLC 17**

Jakes, John (William) 1932- . . . . **CLC 29**
  See also BEST 89:4; CA 57-60; CANR 10;
  DLBY 83; MTCW; SATA 62

James, Andrew
  See Kirkup, James

James, C(yril) L(ionel) R(obert)
  1901-1989 . . . . **CLC 33**
  See also BW; CA 117; 125; 128; MTCW

James, Daniel (Lewis) 1911-1988
  See Santiago, Danny
  See also CA 125

James, Dynely
  See Mayne, William (James Carter)

James, Henry
  1843-1916 . . . . . **TCLC 2, 11, 24, 40, 47;**
                           SSC 8
  See also CA 104; 132; CDALB 1865-1917;
  DLB 12, 71, 74; MTCW; WLC

James, Montague (Rhodes)
  1862-1936 . . . . **TCLC 6**
  See also CA 104

James, P. D. . . . . **CLC 18, 46**
  See also White, Phyllis Dorothy James
  See also BEST 90:2; CDBLB 1960 to
  Present; DLB 87

James, Philip
  See Moorcock, Michael (John)

James, William 1842-1910 . . . . . **TCLC 15, 32**
  See also CA 109

James I 1394-1437 . . . . **LC 20**

Jami, Nur al-Din 'Abd al-Rahman
  1414-1492 . . . . **LC 9**

Jandl, Ernst 1925- . . . . **CLC 34**

Janowitz, Tama 1957- . . . . **CLC 43**
  See also CA 106

Jarrell, Randall
  1914-1965 . . . . **CLC 1, 2, 6, 9, 13, 49**
  See also CA 5-8R; 25-28R; CABS 2;
  CANR 6, 34; CDALB 1941-1968; CLR 6;
  DLB 48, 52; MAICYA; MTCW; SATA 7

Jarry, Alfred 1873-1907 . . . . **TCLC 2, 14**
  See also CA 104

Jarvis, E. K.
  See Bloch, Robert (Albert); Ellison, Harlan;
  Silverberg, Robert

Jeake, Samuel Jr.
  See Aiken, Conrad (Potter)

Jean Paul 1763-1825 . . . . **NCLC 7**

Jeffers, (John) Robinson
  1887-1962 . . . . **CLC 2, 3, 11, 15, 54**
  See also CA 85-88; CANR 35;
  CDALB 1917-1929; DLB 45; MTCW;
  WLC

Jefferson, Janet
  See Mencken, H(enry) L(ouis)

Jefferson, Thomas 1743-1826 . . . . **NCLC 11**
  See also CDALB 1640-1865; DLB 31

Jeffrey, Francis 1773-1850 . . . . . . **NCLC 33**
  See also DLB 107

Jelakowitch, Ivan
  See Heijermans, Herman

Jellicoe, (Patricia) Ann 1927- . . . . . **CLC 27**
  See also CA 85-88; DLB 13

Jen, Gish . . . . **CLC 70**
  See also Jen, Lillian

Jen, Lillian 1956(?)-
  See Jen, Gish
  See also CA 135

Jenkins, (John) Robin 1912- . . . . **CLC 52**
  See also CA 1-4R; CANR 1; DLB 14

Jennings, Elizabeth (Joan)
  1926- . . . . **CLC 5, 14**
  See also CA 61-64; CAAS 5; CANR 8, 39;
  DLB 27; MTCW; SATA 66

Jennings, Waylon 1937- . . . . **CLC 21**

Jensen, Johannes V. 1873-1950 . . . . **TCLC 41**

Jensen, Laura (Linnea) 1948- . . . . . . **CLC 37**
  See also CA 103

Jerome, Jerome K(lapka)
  1859-1927 . . . . **TCLC 23**
  See also CA 119; DLB 10, 34

Jerrold, Douglas William
  1803-1857 . . . . **NCLC 2**

Jewett, (Theodora) Sarah Orne
  1849-1909 . . . . **TCLC 1, 22; SSC 6**
  See also CA 108; 127; DLB 12, 74;
  SATA 15

Jewsbury, Geraldine (Endsor)
  1812-1880 . . . . **NCLC 22**
  See also DLB 21

Jhabvala, Ruth Prawer
  1927- . . . . **CLC 4, 8, 29**
  See also CA 1-4R; CANR 2, 29; MTCW

Jiles, Paulette 1943- . . . . **CLC 13, 58**
  See also CA 101

Jimenez (Mantecon), Juan Ramon
  1881-1958 . . . . **TCLC 4**
  See also CA 104; 131; HW; MTCW

Jimenez, Ramon
  See Jimenez (Mantecon), Juan Ramon

Jimenez Mantecon, Juan
  See Jimenez (Mantecon), Juan Ramon

Joel, Billy . . . . **CLC 26**
  See also Joel, William Martin

Joel, William Martin 1949-
  See Joel, Billy
  See also CA 108

John of the Cross, St. 1542-1591 . . . . **LC 18**

Johnson, B(ryan) S(tanley William)
  1933-1973 . . . . **CLC 6, 9**
  See also CA 9-12R; 53-56; CANR 9;
  DLB 14, 40

Johnson, Charles (Richard)
  1948- . . . . **CLC 7, 51, 65**
  See also BLC 2; BW; CA 116; DLB 33

Johnson, Denis 1949- . . . . **CLC 52**
  See also CA 117; 121; DLB 120

Johnson, Diane (Lain)
  1934- . . . . **CLC 5, 13, 48**
  See also CA 41-44R; CANR 17; DLBY 80;
  MTCW

Johnson, Eyvind (Olof Verner)
  1900-1976 . . . . **CLC 14**
  See also CA 73-76; 69-72; CANR 34

Johnson, J. R.
  See James, C(yril) L(ionel) R(obert)

Johnson, James Weldon
  1871-1938 . . . . **TCLC 3, 19**
  See also BLC 2; BW; CA 104; 125;
  CDALB 1917-1929; DLB 51; MTCW;
  SATA 31

Johnson, Joyce 1935- . . . . **CLC 58**
  See also CA 125; 129

Johnson, Lionel (Pigot)
  1867-1902 . . . . **TCLC 19**
  See also CA 117; DLB 19

Johnson, Mel
  See Malzberg, Barry N(athaniel)

Johnson, Pamela Hansford
  1912-1981 . . . . **CLC 1, 7, 27**
  See also CA 1-4R; 104; CANR 2, 28;
  DLB 15; MTCW

Johnson, Samuel 1709-1784 . . . . **LC 15**
  See also CDBLB 1660-1789; DLB 39, 95,
  104; WLC

Johnson, Uwe
  1934-1984 . . . . **CLC 5, 10, 15, 40**
  See also CA 1-4R; 112; CANR 1, 39;
  DLB 75; MTCW

Johnston, George (Benson) 1913- . . . **CLC 51**
  See also CA 1-4R; CANR 5, 20; DLB 88

Johnston, Jennifer 1930- . . . . **CLC 7**
  See also CA 85-88; DLB 14

Jolley, (Monica) Elizabeth 1923- . . . **CLC 46**
  See also CA 127; CAAS 13

Jones, Arthur Llewellyn 1863-1947
  See Machen, Arthur
  See also CA 104

Jones, D(ouglas) G(ordon) 1929- . . . . **CLC 10**
  See also CA 29-32R; CANR 13; DLB 53

Jones, David (Michael)
  1895-1974 . . . . **CLC 2, 4, 7, 13, 42**
  See also CA 9-12R; 53-56; CANR 28;
  CDBLB 1945-1960; DLB 20, 100; MTCW

Jones, David Robert 1947-
  See Bowie, David
  See also CA 103

Jones, Diana Wynne 1934- . . . . **CLC 26**
  See also CA 49-52; CANR 4, 26; CLR 23;
  MAICYA; SAAS 7; SATA 9, 70

Jones, Gayl 1949- . . . . **CLC 6, 9**
  See also BLC 2; BW; CA 77-80; CANR 27;
  DLB 33; MTCW

Jones, James 1921-1977 . . . . **CLC 1, 3, 10, 39**
  See also AITN 1, 2; CA 1-4R; 69-72;
  CANR 6; DLB 2; MTCW

Jones, John J.
  See Lovecraft, H(oward) P(hillips)

Jones, LeRoi . . . . **CLC 1, 2, 3, 5, 10, 14**
  See also Baraka, Amiri

Jones, Louis B. . . . . **CLC 65**

Jones, Madison (Percy Jr.) 1925- . . . . **CLC 4**
  See also CA 13-16R; CAAS 11; CANR 7

Jones, Mervyn 1922- . . . . **CLC 10, 52**
  See also CA 45-48; CAAS 5; CANR 1;
  MTCW

Jones, Mick 1956(?)- . . . . **CLC 30**
See also The Clash

Jones, Nettie (Pearl) 1941- . . . . **CLC 34**
See also CA 137

Jones, Preston 1936-1979 . . . . **CLC 10**
See also CA 73-76; 89-92; DLB 7

Jones, Robert F(rancis) 1934- . . . . **CLC 7**
See also CA 49-52; CANR 2

Jones, Rod 1953- . . . . **CLC 50**
See also CA 128

Jones, Terence Graham Parry
1942- . . . . **CLC 21**
See also Jones, Terry; Monty Python
See also CA 112; 116; CANR 35; SATA 51

Jones, Terry
See Jones, Terence Graham Parry
See also SATA 67

Jong, Erica 1942- . . . . **CLC 4, 6, 8, 18**
See also AITN 1; BEST 90:2; CA 73-76;
CANR 26; DLB 2, 5, 28; MTCW

Jonson, Ben(jamin) 1572(?)-1637 . . . . . . **LC 6**
See also CDBLB Before 1660; DLB 62, 121;
WLC

Jordan, June 1936- . . . . **CLC 5, 11, 23**
See also AAYA 2; BW; CA 33-36R;
CANR 25; CLR 10; DLB 38; MAICYA;
MTCW; SATA 4

Jordan, Pat(rick M.) 1941- . . . . **CLC 37**
See also CA 33-36R

Jorgensen, Ivar
See Ellison, Harlan

Jorgenson, Ivar
See Silverberg, Robert

Josipovici, Gabriel 1940- . . . . **CLC 6, 43**
See also CA 37-40R; CAAS 8; DLB 14

Joubert, Joseph 1754-1824 . . . . **NCLC 9**

Jouve, Pierre Jean 1887-1976 . . . . . . **CLC 47**
See also CA 65-68

Joyce, James (Augustine Aloysius)
1882-1941 . . . . **TCLC 3, 8, 16, 35; SSC 3**
See also CA 104; 126; CDBLB 1914-1945;
DLB 10, 19, 36; MTCW; WLC

Jozsef, Attila 1905-1937 . . . . **TCLC 22**
See also CA 116

Juana Ines de la Cruz 1651(?)-1695 . . . **LC 5**

Judd, Cyril
See Kornbluth, C(yril) M.; Pohl, Frederik

Julian of Norwich 1342(?)-1416(?) . . . . **LC 6**

Just, Ward (Swift) 1935- . . . . **CLC 4, 27**
See also CA 25-28R; CANR 32

Justice, Donald (Rodney) 1925- . . **CLC 6, 19**
See also CA 5-8R; CANR 26; DLBY 83

Juvenal c. 55-c. 127 . . . . **CMLC 8**

Juvenis
See Bourne, Randolph S(illiman)

Kacew, Romain 1914-1980
See Gary, Romain
See also CA 108; 102

Kadare, Ismail 1936- . . . . **CLC 52**

Kadohata, Cynthia . . . . **CLC 59**

Kafka, Franz
1883-1924 . . . . . . **TCLC 2, 6, 13, 29, 47;**
SSC 5
See also CA 105; 126; DLB 81; MTCW;
WLC

Kahn, Roger 1927- . . . . **CLC 30**
See also CA 25-28R; SATA 37

Kain, Saul
See Sassoon, Siegfried (Lorraine)

Kaiser, Georg 1878-1945 . . . . **TCLC 9**
See also CA 106

Kaletski, Alexander 1946- . . . . **CLC 39**
See also CA 118

Kalidasa fl. c. 400 . . . . **CMLC 9**

Kallman, Chester (Simon)
1921-1975 . . . . **CLC 2**
See also CA 45-48; 53-56; CANR 3

Kaminsky, Melvin 1926-
See Brooks, Mel
See also CA 65-68; CANR 16

Kaminsky, Stuart M(elvin) 1934- . . . **CLC 59**
See also CA 73-76; CANR 29

Kane, Paul
See Simon, Paul

Kane, Wilson
See Bloch, Robert (Albert)

Kanin, Garson 1912- . . . . **CLC 22**
See also AITN 1; CA 5-8R; CANR 7;
DLB 7

Kaniuk, Yoram 1930- . . . . **CLC 19**
See also CA 134

Kant, Immanuel 1724-1804 . . . . . . **NCLC 27**
See also DLB 94

Kantor, MacKinlay 1904-1977 . . . . . . **CLC 7**
See also CA 61-64; 73-76; DLB 9, 102

Kaplan, David Michael 1946- . . . . . . **CLC 50**

Kaplan, James 1951- . . . . **CLC 59**
See also CA 135

Karageorge, Michael
See Anderson, Poul (William)

Karamzin, Nikolai Mikhailovich
1766-1826 . . . . **NCLC 3**

Karapanou, Margarita 1946- . . . . **CLC 13**
See also CA 101

Karinthy, Frigyes 1887-1938 . . . . . . **TCLC 47**

Karl, Frederick R(obert) 1927- . . . . . **CLC 34**
See also CA 5-8R; CANR 3

Kastel, Warren
See Silverberg, Robert

Kataev, Evgeny Petrovich 1903-1942
See Petrov, Evgeny
See also CA 120

Kataphusin
See Ruskin, John

Katz, Steve 1935- . . . . **CLC 47**
See also CA 25-28R; CAAS 14; CANR 12;
DLBY 83

Kauffman, Janet 1945- . . . . **CLC 42**
See also CA 117; DLBY 86

Kaufman, Bob (Garnell)
1925-1986 . . . . **CLC 49**
See also BW; CA 41-44R; 118; CANR 22;
DLB 16, 41

Kaufman, George S. 1889-1961 . . . . . **CLC 38**
See also CA 108; 93-96; DLB 7

Kaufman, Sue . . . . **CLC 3, 8**
See also Barondess, Sue K(aufman)

Kavafis, Konstantinos Petrou 1863-1933
See Cavafy, C(onstantine) P(eter)
See also CA 104

Kavan, Anna 1901-1968 . . . . **CLC 5, 13**
See also CA 5-8R; CANR 6; MTCW

Kavanagh, Dan
See Barnes, Julian

Kavanagh, Patrick (Joseph)
1904-1967 . . . . **CLC 22**
See also CA 123; 25-28R; DLB 15, 20;
MTCW

Kawabata, Yasunari
1899-1972 . . . . **CLC 2, 5, 9, 18**
See also CA 93-96; 33-36R

Kaye, M(ary) M(argaret) 1909- . . . . . **CLC 28**
See also CA 89-92; CANR 24; MTCW;
SATA 62

Kaye, Mollie
See Kaye, M(ary) M(argaret)

Kaye-Smith, Sheila 1887-1956 . . . . . **TCLC 20**
See also CA 118; DLB 36

Kaymor, Patrice Maguilene
See Senghor, Leopold Sedar

Kazan, Elia 1909- . . . . **CLC 6, 16, 63**
See also CA 21-24R; CANR 32

Kazantzakis, Nikos
1883(?)-1957 . . . . **TCLC 2, 5, 33**
See also CA 105; 132; MTCW

Kazin, Alfred 1915- . . . . **CLC 34, 38**
See also CA 1-4R; CAAS 7; CANR 1;
DLB 67

Keane, Mary Nesta (Skrine) 1904-
See Keane, Molly
See also CA 108; 114

Keane, Molly . . . . **CLC 31**
See also Keane, Mary Nesta (Skrine)

Keates, Jonathan 19(?)- . . . . **CLC 34**

Keaton, Buster 1895-1966 . . . . **CLC 20**

Keats, John 1795-1821 . . . . . . **NCLC 8; PC 1**
See also CDBLB 1789-1832; DLB 96, 110;
WLC

Keene, Donald 1922- . . . . **CLC 34**
See also CA 1-4R; CANR 5

Keillor, Garrison . . . . **CLC 40**
See also Keillor, Gary (Edward)
See also AAYA 2; BEST 89:3; DLBY 87;
SATA 58

Keillor, Gary (Edward) 1942-
See Keillor, Garrison
See also CA 111; 117; CANR 36; MTCW

Keith, Michael
See Hubbard, L(afayette) Ron(ald)

Kell, Joseph
See Wilson, John (Anthony) Burgess

Keller, Gottfried 1819-1890 . . . . **NCLC 2**

Kellerman, Jonathan 1949- . . . . **CLC 44**
See also BEST 90:1; CA 106; CANR 29

Kelley, William Melvin 1937- . . . . . . **CLC 22**
See also BW; CA 77-80; CANR 27; DLB 33

Knowles, John 1926- ...... **CLC 1, 4, 10, 26**
See also CA 17-20R; CDALB 1968-1988;
DLB 6; MTCW; SATA 8

Knox, Calvin M.
See Silverberg, Robert

Knye, Cassandra
See Disch, Thomas M(ichael)

Koch, C(hristopher) J(ohn) 1932- ... **CLC 42**
See also CA 127

Koch, Christopher
See Koch, C(hristopher) J(ohn)

Koch, Kenneth 1925- .... **CLC 5, 8, 44**
See also CA 1-4R; CANR 6, 36; DLB 5;
SATA 65

Kochanowski, Jan 1530-1584....... **LC 10**

Kock, Charles Paul de
1794-1871 .... **NCLC 16**

Koda Shigeyuki 1867-1947
See Rohan, Koda
See also CA 121

Koestler, Arthur
1905-1983 .... **CLC 1, 3, 6, 8, 15, 33**
See also CA 1-4R; 109; CANR 1, 33;
CDBLB 1945-1960; DLBY 83; MTCW

Kohout, Pavel 1928-............. **CLC 13**
See also CA 45-48; CANR 3

Koizumi, Yakumo
See Hearn, (Patricio) Lafcadio (Tessima
Carlos)

Kolmar, Gertrud 1894-1943...... **TCLC 40**

Konrad, George
See Konrad, Gyoergy

Konrad, Gyoergy 1933- .... **CLC 4, 10**
See also CA 85-88

Konwicki, Tadeusz 1926-..... **CLC 8, 28, 54**
See also CA 101; CAAS 9; CANR 39;
MTCW

Kopit, Arthur (Lee) 1937- .... **CLC 1, 18, 33**
See also AITN 1; CA 81-84; CABS 3;
DLB 7; MTCW

Kops, Bernard 1926-.............. **CLC 4**
See also CA 5-8R; DLB 13

Kornbluth, C(yril) M. 1923-1958.... **TCLC 8**
See also CA 105; DLB 8

Korolenko, V. G.
See Korolenko, Vladimir Galaktionovich

Korolenko, Vladimir
See Korolenko, Vladimir Galaktionovich

Korolenko, Vladimir G.
See Korolenko, Vladimir Galaktionovich

Korolenko, Vladimir Galaktionovich
1853-1921 .... **TCLC 22**
See also CA 121

Kosinski, Jerzy (Nikodem)
1933-1991 ... **CLC 1, 2, 3, 6, 10, 15, 53,**
70
See also CA 17-20R; 134; CANR 9; DLB 2;
DLBY 82; MTCW

Kostelanetz, Richard (Cory) 1940- .. **CLC 28**
See also CA 13-16R; CAAS 8; CANR 38

Kostrowitzki, Wilhelm Apollinaris de
1880-1918
See Apollinaire, Guillaume
See also CA 104

Kotlowitz, Robert 1924-........... **CLC 4**
See also CA 33-36R; CANR 36

Kotzebue, August (Friedrich Ferdinand) von
1761-1819 .... **NCLC 25**
See also DLB 94

Kotzwinkle, William 1938- ... **CLC 5, 14, 35**
See also CA 45-48; CANR 3; CLR 6;
MAICYA; SATA 24, 70

Kozol, Jonathan 1936-............ **CLC 17**
See also CA 61-64; CANR 16

Kozoll, Michael 1940(?)- .... **CLC 35**

Kramer, Kathryn 19(?)- .... **CLC 34**

Kramer, Larry 1935- .... **CLC 42**
See also CA 124; 126

Krasicki, Ignacy 1735-1801 .... **NCLC 8**

Krasinski, Zygmunt 1812-1859 .... **NCLC 4**

Kraus, Karl 1874-1936........... **TCLC 5**
See also CA 104; DLB 118

Kreve (Mickevicius), Vincas
1882-1954 .... **TCLC 27**

Kristofferson, Kris 1936-......... **CLC 26**
See also CA 104

Krizanc, John 1956-.............. **CLC 57**

Krleza, Miroslav 1893-1981 ...... **CLC 8**
See also CA 97-100; 105

Kroetsch, Robert 1927- ...... **CLC 5, 23, 57**
See also CA 17-20R; CANR 8, 38; DLB 53;
MTCW

Kroetz, Franz
See Kroetz, Franz Xaver

Kroetz, Franz Xaver 1946- .... **CLC 41**
See also CA 130

Kropotkin, Peter (Aleksieevich)
1842-1921 .... **TCLC 36**
See also CA 119

Krotkov, Yuri 1917-.............. **CLC 19**
See also CA 102

Krumb
See Crumb, R(obert)

Krumgold, Joseph (Quincy)
1908-1980 .... **CLC 12**
See also CA 9-12R; 101; CANR 7;
MAICYA; SATA 1, 23, 48

Krumwitz
See Crumb, R(obert)

Krutch, Joseph Wood 1893-1970.... **CLC 24**
See also CA 1-4R; 25-28R; CANR 4;
DLB 63

Krutzch, Gus
See Eliot, T(homas) S(tearns)

Krylov, Ivan Andreevich
1768(?)-1844 .... **NCLC 1**

Kubin, Alfred 1877-1959 .... **TCLC 23**
See also CA 112; DLB 81

Kubrick, Stanley 1928-............ **CLC 16**
See also CA 81-84; CANR 33; DLB 26

Kumin, Maxine (Winokur)
1925- .... **CLC 5, 13, 28**
See also AITN 2; CA 1-4R; CAAS 8;
CANR 1, 21; DLB 5; MTCW; SATA 12

Kundera, Milan
1929- .... **CLC 4, 9, 19, 32, 68**
See also AAYA 2; CA 85-88; CANR 19;
MTCW

Kunitz, Stanley (Jasspon)
1905- .... **CLC 6, 11, 14**
See also CA 41-44R; CANR 26; DLB 48;
MTCW

Kunze, Reiner 1933-............. **CLC 10**
See also CA 93-96; DLB 75

Kuprin, Aleksandr Ivanovich
1870-1938 .... **TCLC 5**
See also CA 104

Kureishi, Hanif 1954-............. **CLC 64**

Kurosawa, Akira 1910-............ **CLC 16**
See also CA 101

Kuttner, Henry 1915-1958....... **TCLC 10**
See also CA 107; DLB 8

Kuzma, Greg 1944-............... **CLC 7**
See also CA 33-36R

Kuzmin, Mikhail 1872(?)-1936 .... **TCLC 40**

Kyprianos, Iossif
See Samarakis, Antonis

La Bruyere, Jean de 1645-1696...... **LC 17**

Laclos, Pierre Ambroise Francois Choderlos
de 1741-1803 .... **NCLC 4**

La Colere, Francois
See Aragon, Louis

Lacolere, Francois
See Aragon, Louis

La Deshabilleuse
See Simenon, Georges (Jacques Christian)

Lady Gregory
See Gregory, Isabella Augusta (Persse)

Lady of Quality, A
See Bagnold, Enid

La Fayette, Marie (Madelaine Pioche de la
Vergne Comtes 1634-1693....... **LC 2**

Lafayette, Rene
See Hubbard, L(afayette) Ron(ald)

Laforgue, Jules 1860-1887........ **NCLC 5**

Lagerkvist, Paer (Fabian)
1891-1974 ...... **CLC 7, 10, 13, 54**
See also CA 85-88; 49-52; MTCW

Lagerkvist, Par
See Lagerkvist, Paer (Fabian)

Lagerloef, Selma (Ottiliana Lovisa)
1858-1940 .... **TCLC 4, 36**
See also Lagerlof, Selma (Ottiliana Lovisa)
See also CA 108; CLR 7; SATA 15

Lagerlof, Selma (Ottiliana Lovisa)
See Lagerloef, Selma (Ottiliana Lovisa)
See also CLR 7; SATA 15

La Guma, (Justin) Alex(ander)
1925-1985 .... **CLC 19**
See also BW; CA 49-52; 118; CANR 25;
DLB 117; MTCW

Laidlaw, A. K.
See Grieve, C(hristopher) M(urray)

Lainez, Manuel Mujica
See Mujica Lainez, Manuel
See also HW

Lamartine, Alphonse (Marie Louis Prat) de
    1790-1869 .... **NCLC 11**

Lamb, Charles 1775-1834........ **NCLC 10**
    See also CDBLB 1789-1832; DLB 93, 107;
    SATA 17; WLC

Lamb, Lady Caroline 1785-1828.. **NCLC 38**
    See also DLB 116

Lamming, George (William)
    1927- .... **CLC 2, 4, 66**
    See also BLC 2; BW; CA 85-88; CANR 26;
    MTCW

L'Amour, Louis (Dearborn)
    1908-1988 .... **CLC 25, 55**
    See also AITN 2; BEST 89:2; CA 1-4R;
    125; CANR 3, 25; DLBY 80; MTCW

Lampedusa, Giuseppe (Tomasi) di ... **TCLC 13**
    See also Tomasi di Lampedusa, Giuseppe

Lampman, Archibald 1861-1899 .. **NCLC 25**
    See also DLB 92

Lancaster, Bruce 1896-1963....... **CLC 36**
    See also CA 9-10; CAP 1; SATA 9

Landau, Mark Alexandrovich
    See Aldanov, Mark (Alexandrovich)

Landau-Aldanov, Mark Alexandrovich
    See Aldanov, Mark (Alexandrovich)

Landis, John 1950-.............. **CLC 26**
    See also CA 112; 122

Landolfi, Tommaso 1908-1979... **CLC 11, 49**
    See also CA 127; 117

Landon, Letitia Elizabeth
    1802-1838 .... **NCLC 15**
    See also DLB 96

Landor, Walter Savage
    1775-1864 .... **NCLC 14**
    See also DLB 93, 107

Landwirth, Heinz 1927-
    See Lind, Jakov
    See also CA 9-12R; CANR 7

Lane, Patrick 1939- .... **CLC 25**
    See also CA 97-100; DLB 53

Lang, Andrew 1844-1912........ **TCLC 16**
    See also CA 114; 137; DLB 98; MAICYA;
    SATA 16

Lang, Fritz 1890-1976 .... **CLC 20**
    See also CA 77-80; 69-72; CANR 30

Lange, John
    See Crichton, (John) Michael

Langer, Elinor 1939- .... **CLC 34**
    See also CA 121

Langland, William 1330(?)-1400(?) ... **LC 19**

Langstaff, Launcelot
    See Irving, Washington

Lanier, Sidney 1842-1881 .... **NCLC 6**
    See also DLB 64; MAICYA; SATA 18

Lanyer, Aemilia 1569-1645 .... **LC 10**

Lao Tzu .... **CMLC 7**

Lapine, James (Elliot) 1949-....... **CLC 39**
    See also CA 123; 130

Larbaud, Valery (Nicolas)
    1881-1957 .... **TCLC 9**
    See also CA 106

Lardner, Ring
    See Lardner, Ring(gold) W(ilmer)

Lardner, Ring W. Jr.
    See Lardner, Ring(gold) W(ilmer)

Lardner, Ring(gold) W(ilmer)
    1885-1933 .... **TCLC 2, 14**
    See also CA 104; 131; CDALB 1917-1929;
    DLB 11, 25, 86; MTCW

Laredo, Betty
    See Codrescu, Andrei

Larkin, Maia
    See Wojciechowska, Maia (Teresa)

Larkin, Philip (Arthur)
    1922-1985 ... **CLC 3, 5, 8, 9, 13, 18, 33,**
                                          39, 64
    See also CA 5-8R; 117; CANR 24;
    CDBLB 1960 to Present; DLB 27;
    MTCW

Larra (y Sanchez de Castro), Mariano Jose de
    1809-1837 .... **NCLC 17**

Larsen, Eric 1941- .... **CLC 55**
    See also CA 132

Larsen, Nella 1891-1964 .... **CLC 37**
    See also BLC 2; BW; CA 125; DLB 51

Larson, Charles R(aymond) 1938-... **CLC 31**
    See also CA 53-56; CANR 4

Latham, Jean Lee 1902-.......... **CLC 12**
    See also AITN 1; CA 5-8R; CANR 7;
    MAICYA; SATA 2, 68

Latham, Mavis
    See Clark, Mavis Thorpe

Lathen, Emma .... **CLC 2**
    See also Hennissart, Martha; Latsis, Mary
    J(ane)

Lathrop, Francis
    See Leiber, Fritz (Reuter Jr.)

Latsis, Mary J(ane)
    See Lathen, Emma
    See also CA 85-88

Lattimore, Richmond (Alexander)
    1906-1984 .... **CLC 3**
    See also CA 1-4R; 112; CANR 1

Laughlin, James 1914-........... **CLC 49**
    See also CA 21-24R; CANR 9; DLB 48

Laurence, (Jean) Margaret (Wemyss)
    1926-1987 .. **CLC 3, 6, 13, 50, 62; SSC 7**
    See also CA 5-8R; 121; CANR 33; DLB 53;
    MTCW; SATA 50

Laurent, Antoine 1952- .... **CLC 50**

Lauscher, Hermann
    See Hesse, Hermann

Lautreamont, Comte de
    1846-1870 .... **NCLC 12**

Laverty, Donald
    See Blish, James (Benjamin)

Lavin, Mary 1912-...... **CLC 4, 18; SSC 4**
    See also CA 9-12R; CANR 33; DLB 15;
    MTCW

Lavond, Paul Dennis
    See Kornbluth, C(yril) M.; Pohl, Frederik

Lawler, Raymond Evenor 1922- .... **CLC 58**
    See also CA 103

Lawrence, D(avid) H(erbert Richards)
    1885-1930 .... **TCLC 2, 9, 16, 33; SSC 4**
    See also CA 104; 121; CDBLB 1914-1945;
    DLB 10, 19, 36, 98; MTCW; WLC

Lawrence, T(homas) E(dward)
    1888-1935 .... **TCLC 18**
    See also Dale, Colin
    See also CA 115

Lawrence Of Arabia
    See Lawrence, T(homas) E(dward)

Lawson, Henry (Archibald Hertzberg)
    1867-1922 .... **TCLC 27**
    See also CA 120

Laxness, Halldor .... **CLC 25**
    See also Gudjonsson, Halldor Kiljan

Layamon fl. c. 1200 .... **CMLC 10**

Laye, Camara 1928-1980........ **CLC 4, 38**
    See also BLC 2; BW; CA 85-88; 97-100;
    CANR 25; MTCW

Layton, Irving (Peter) 1912-..... **CLC 2, 15**
    See also CA 1-4R; CANR 2, 33; DLB 88;
    MTCW

Lazarus, Emma 1849-1887........ **NCLC 8**

Lazarus, Felix
    See Cable, George Washington

Lea, Joan
    See Neufeld, John (Arthur)

Leacock, Stephen (Butler)
    1869-1944 .... **TCLC 2**
    See also CA 104; DLB 92

Lear, Edward 1812-1888 .... **NCLC 3**
    See also CLR 1; DLB 32; MAICYA;
    SATA 18

Lear, Norman (Milton) 1922- ...... **CLC 12**
    See also CA 73-76

Leavis, F(rank) R(aymond)
    1895-1978 .... **CLC 24**
    See also CA 21-24R; 77-80; MTCW

Leavitt, David 1961-............. **CLC 34**
    See also CA 116; 122

Lebowitz, Fran(ces Ann)
    1951(?)- .... **CLC 11, 36**
    See also CA 81-84; CANR 14; MTCW

le Carre, John .... **CLC 3, 5, 9, 15, 28**
    See also Cornwell, David (John Moore)
    See also BEST 89:4; CDBLB 1960 to
    Present; DLB 87

Le Clezio, J(ean) M(arie) G(ustave)
    1940- .... **CLC 31**
    See also CA 116; 128; DLB 83

Leconte de Lisle, Charles-Marie-Rene
    1818-1894 .... **NCLC 29**

Le Coq, Monsieur
    See Simenon, Georges (Jacques Christian)

Leduc, Violette 1907-1972........ **CLC 22**
    See also CA 13-14; 33-36R; CAP 1

Ledwidge, Francis 1887(?)-1917 ... **TCLC 23**
    See also CA 123; DLB 20

Lee, Andrea 1953- .... **CLC 36**
    See also BLC 2; BW; CA 125

Lee, Andrew
    See Auchincloss, Louis (Stanton)

Lee, Don L. .... **CLC 2**
    See also Madhubuti, Haki R.

Lee, George W(ashington)
    1894-1976 .... **CLC 52**
    See also BLC 2; BW; CA 125; DLB 51

Mahfouz, Naguib (Abdel Aziz Al-Sabilgi)
1911(?)-
See Mahfuz, Najib
See also BEST 89:2; CA 128; MTCW

Mahfuz, Najib . . . . **CLC 52, 55**
See also Mahfouz, Naguib (Abdel Aziz Al-Sabilgi)
See also DLBY 88

Mahon, Derek 1941- . . . . **CLC 27**
See also CA 113; 128; DLB 40

Mailer, Norman
1923- . . . . . . **CLC 1, 2, 3, 4, 5, 8, 11, 14, 28, 39, 74**
See also AITN 2; CA 9-12R; CABS 1; CANR 28; CDALB 1968-1988; DLB 2, 16, 28; DLBD 3; DLBY 80, 83; MTCW

Maillet, Antonine 1929- . . . . **CLC 54**
See also CA 115; 120; DLB 60

Mais, Roger 1905-1955 . . . . **TCLC 8**
See also BW; CA 105; 124; MTCW

Maitland, Sara (Louise) 1950- . . . . . . **CLC 49**
See also CA 69-72; CANR 13

Major, Clarence 1936- . . . . **CLC 3, 19, 48**
See also BLC 2; BW; CA 21-24R; CAAS 6; CANR 13, 25; DLB 33

Major, Kevin (Gerald) 1949- . . . . **CLC 26**
See also CA 97-100; CANR 21, 38; CLR 11; DLB 60; MAICYA; SATA 32

Maki, James
See Ozu, Yasujiro

Malabaila, Damiano
See Levi, Primo

Malamud, Bernard
1914-1986 . . . . . **CLC 1, 2, 3, 5, 8, 9, 11, 18, 27, 44**
See also CA 5-8R; 118; CABS 1; CANR 28; CDALB 1941-1968; DLB 2, 28; DLBY 80, 86; MTCW; WLC

Malcolm, Dan
See Silverberg, Robert

Malherbe, Francois de 1555-1628 . . . . . **LC 5**

Mallarme, Stephane
1842-1898 . . . . **NCLC 4; PC 4**

Mallet-Joris, Francoise 1930- . . . . . . **CLC 11**
See also CA 65-68; CANR 17; DLB 83

Malley, Ern
See McAuley, James Phillip

Mallowan, Agatha Christie
See Christie, Agatha (Mary Clarissa)

Maloff, Saul 1922- . . . . **CLC 5**
See also CA 33-36R

Malone, Louis
See MacNeice, (Frederick) Louis

Malone, Michael (Christopher)
1942- . . . . **CLC 43**
See also CA 77-80; CANR 14, 32

Malory, (Sir) Thomas
1410(?)-1471(?) . . . . **LC 11**
See also CDBLB Before 1660; SATA 33, 59

Malouf, (George Joseph) David
1934- . . . . **CLC 28**
See also CA 124

Malraux, (Georges-)Andre
1901-1976 . . . . . **CLC 1, 4, 9, 13, 15, 57**
See also CA 21-22; 69-72; CANR 34; CAP 2; DLB 72; MTCW

Malzberg, Barry N(athaniel) 1939- . . . **CLC 7**
See also CA 61-64; CAAS 4; CANR 16; DLB 8

Mamet, David (Alan)
1947- . . . . **CLC 9, 15, 34, 46**
See also AAYA 3; CA 81-84; CABS 3; CANR 15; DLB 7; MTCW

Mamoulian, Rouben (Zachary)
1897-1987 . . . . **CLC 16**
See also CA 25-28R; 124

Mandelstam, Osip (Emilievich)
1891(?)-1938(?) . . . . **TCLC 2, 6**
See also CA 104

Mander, (Mary) Jane 1877-1949 . . . **TCLC 31**

Mandiargues, Andre Pieyre de . . . . . . **CLC 41**
See also Pieyre de Mandiargues, Andre
See also DLB 83

Mandrake, Ethel Belle
See Thurman, Wallace (Henry)

Mangan, James Clarence
1803-1849 . . . . **NCLC 27**

Maniere, J.-E.
See Giraudoux, (Hippolyte) Jean

Manley, (Mary) Delariviere
1672(?)-1724 . . . . **LC 1**
See also DLB 39, 80

Mann, Abel
See Creasey, John

Mann, (Luiz) Heinrich 1871-1950 . . . **TCLC 9**
See also CA 106; DLB 66

Mann, (Paul) Thomas
1875-1955 . . . **TCLC 2, 8, 14, 21, 35, 44; SSC 5**
See also CA 104; 128; DLB 66; MTCW; WLC

Manning, Frederic 1887(?)-1935 . . . **TCLC 25**
See also CA 124

Manning, Olivia 1915-1980 . . . . . . **CLC 5, 19**
See also CA 5-8R; 101; CANR 29; MTCW

Mano, D. Keith 1942- . . . . **CLC 2, 10**
See also CA 25-28R; CAAS 6; CANR 26; DLB 6

Mansfield, Katherine . . . **TCLC 2, 8, 39; SSC 9**
See also Beauchamp, Kathleen Mansfield
See also WLC

Manso, Peter 1940- . . . . **CLC 39**
See also CA 29-32R

Mantecon, Juan Jimenez
See Jimenez (Mantecon), Juan Ramon

Manton, Peter
See Creasey, John

Man Without a Spleen, A
See Chekhov, Anton (Pavlovich)

Manzoni, Alessandro 1785-1873 . . **NCLC 29**

Mapu, Abraham (ben Jekutiel)
1808-1867 . . . . **NCLC 18**

Mara, Sally
See Queneau, Raymond

Marat, Jean Paul 1743-1793 . . . . **LC 10**

Marcel, Gabriel Honore
1889-1973 . . . . **CLC 15**
See also CA 102; 45-48; MTCW

Marchbanks, Samuel
See Davies, (William) Robertson

Marchi, Giacomo
See Bassani, Giorgio

Marie de France c. 12th cent. . . . . **CMLC 8**

Marie de l'Incarnation 1599-1672 . . . . **LC 10**

Mariner, Scott
See Pohl, Frederik

Marinetti, Filippo Tommaso
1876-1944 . . . . **TCLC 10**
See also CA 107; DLB 114

Marivaux, Pierre Carlet de Chamblain de
1688-1763 . . . . **LC 4**

Markandaya, Kamala . . . . **CLC 8, 38**
See also Taylor, Kamala (Purnaiya)

Markfield, Wallace 1926- . . . . **CLC 8**
See also CA 69-72; CAAS 3; DLB 2, 28

Markham, Edwin 1852-1940 . . . . . **TCLC 47**
See also DLB 54

Markham, Robert
See Amis, Kingsley (William)

Marks, J
See Highwater, Jamake (Mamake)

Marks-Highwater, J
See Highwater, Jamake (Mamake)

Markson, David M(errill) 1927- . . . . **CLC 67**
See also CA 49-52; CANR 1

Marley, Bob . . . . **CLC 17**
See also Marley, Robert Nesta

Marley, Robert Nesta 1945-1981
See Marley, Bob
See also CA 107; 103

Marlowe, Christopher 1564-1593 . . . . . **DC 1**
See also CDBLB Before 1660; DLB 62; WLC

Marmontel, Jean-Francois
1723-1799 . . . . **LC 2**

Marquand, John P(hillips)
1893-1960 . . . . **CLC 2, 10**
See also CA 85-88; DLB 9, 102

Marquez, Gabriel (Jose) Garcia . . . . . . **CLC 68**
See also Garcia Marquez, Gabriel (Jose)

Marquis, Don(ald Robert Perry)
1878-1937 . . . . **TCLC 7**
See also CA 104; DLB 11, 25

Marric, J. J.
See Creasey, John

Marrow, Bernard
See Moore, Brian

Marryat, Frederick 1792-1848 . . . . **NCLC 3**
See also DLB 21

Marsden, James
See Creasey, John

Marsh, (Edith) Ngaio
1899-1982 . . . . **CLC 7, 53**
See also CA 9-12R; CANR 6; DLB 77; MTCW

Marshall, Garry 1934- . . . . **CLC 17**
See also AAYA 3; CA 111; SATA 60

Marshall, Paule 1929- .. **CLC 27, 72; SSC 3**
    See also BLC 3; BW; CA 77-80; CANR 25;
    DLB 33; MTCW

Marsten, Richard
    See Hunter, Evan

Martha, Henry
    See Harris, Mark

Martin, Ken
    See Hubbard, L(afayette) Ron(ald)

Martin, Richard
    See Creasey, John

Martin, Steve 1945- .... **CLC 30**
    See also CA 97-100; CANR 30; MTCW

Martin, Webber
    See Silverberg, Robert

Martin du Gard, Roger
    1881-1958 .... **TCLC 24**
    See also CA 118; DLB 65

Martineau, Harriet 1802-1876.... **NCLC 26**
    See also DLB 21, 55; YABC 2

Martines, Julia
    See O'Faolain, Julia

Martinez, Jacinto Benavente y
    See Benavente (y Martinez), Jacinto

Martinez Ruiz, Jose 1873-1967
    See Azorin; Ruiz, Jose Martinez
    See also CA 93-96; HW

Martinez Sierra, Gregorio
    1881-1947 .... **TCLC 6**
    See also CA 115

Martinez Sierra, Maria (de la O'LeJarraga)
    1874-1974 .... **TCLC 6**
    See also CA 115

Martinsen, Martin
    See Follett, Ken(neth Martin)

Martinson, Harry (Edmund)
    1904-1978 .... **CLC 14**
    See also CA 77-80; CANR 34

Marut, Ret
    See Traven, B.

Marut, Robert
    See Traven, B.

Marvell, Andrew 1621-1678......... **LC 4**
    See also CDBLB 1660-1789; WLC

Marx, Karl (Heinrich)
    1818-1883 .... **NCLC 17**

Masaoka Shiki.................. **TCLC 18**
    See also Masaoka Tsunenori

Masaoka Tsunenori 1867-1902
    See Masaoka Shiki
    See also CA 117

Masefield, John (Edward)
    1878-1967 .... **CLC 11, 47**
    See also CA 19-20; 25-28R; CANR 33;
    CAP 2; CDBLB 1890-1914; DLB 10;
    MTCW; SATA 19

Maso, Carole 19(?)- .... **CLC 44**

Mason, Bobbie Ann
    1940- .... **CLC 28, 43; SSC 4**
    See also AAYA 5; CA 53-56; CANR 11,
    31; DLBY 87; MTCW

Mason, Ernst
    See Pohl, Frederik

Mason, Lee W.
    See Malzberg, Barry N(athaniel)

Mason, Nick 1945-............. **CLC 35**
    See also Pink Floyd

Mason, Tally
    See Derleth, August (William)

Mass, William
    See Gibson, William

Masters, Edgar Lee
    1868-1950 .... **TCLC 2, 25; PC 1**
    See also CA 104; 133; CDALB 1865-1917;
    DLB 54; MTCW

Masters, Hilary 1928- .... **CLC 48**
    See also CA 25-28R; CANR 13

Mastrosimone, William 19(?)-...... **CLC 36**

Mathe, Albert
    See Camus, Albert

Matheson, Richard Burton 1926- ... **CLC 37**
    See also CA 97-100; DLB 8, 44

Mathews, Harry 1930-........ **CLC 6, 52**
    See also CA 21-24R; CAAS 6; CANR 18

Mathias, Roland (Glyn) 1915-..... **CLC 45**
    See also CA 97-100; CANR 19; DLB 27

Matsuo Basho 1644-1694........... **PC 3**

Mattheson, Rodney
    See Creasey, John

Matthews, Greg 1949- .... **CLC 45**
    See also CA 135

Matthews, William 1942-......... **CLC 40**
    See also CA 29-32R; CANR 12; DLB 5

Matthias, John (Edward) 1941-...... **CLC 9**
    See also CA 33-36R

Matthiessen, Peter
    1927- .... **CLC 5, 7, 11, 32, 64**
    See also AAYA 6; BEST 90:4; CA 9-12R;
    CANR 21; DLB 6; MTCW; SATA 27

Maturin, Charles Robert
    1780(?)-1824 .... **NCLC 6**

Matute (Ausejo), Ana Maria
    1925- .... **CLC 11**
    See also CA 89-92; MTCW

Maugham, W. S.
    See Maugham, W(illiam) Somerset

Maugham, W(illiam) Somerset
    1874-1965 .... **CLC 1, 11, 15, 67; SSC 8**
    See also CA 5-8R; 25-28R;
    CDBLB 1914-1945; DLB 10, 36, 77, 100;
    MTCW; SATA 54; WLC

Maugham, William Somerset
    See Maugham, W(illiam) Somerset

Maupassant, (Henri Rene Albert) Guy de
    1850-1893 .... **NCLC 1; SSC 1**
    See also WLC

Maurhut, Richard
    See Traven, B.

Mauriac, Claude 1914-............. **CLC 9**
    See also CA 89-92; DLB 83

Mauriac, Francois (Charles)
    1885-1970 .... **CLC 4, 9, 56**
    See also CA 25-28; CAP 2; DLB 65;
    MTCW

Mavor, Osborne Henry 1888-1951
    See Bridie, James
    See also CA 104

Maxwell, William (Keepers Jr.)
    1908- .... **CLC 19**
    See also CA 93-96; DLBY 80

May, Elaine 1932- .... **CLC 16**
    See also CA 124; DLB 44

Mayakovski, Vladimir (Vladimirovich)
    1893-1930 .... **TCLC 4, 18**
    See also CA 104

Mayhew, Henry 1812-1887 ...... **NCLC 31**
    See also DLB 18, 55

Maynard, Joyce 1953-............ **CLC 23**
    See also CA 111; 129

Mayne, William (James Carter)
    1928- .... **CLC 12**
    See also CA 9-12R; CANR 37; CLR 25;
    MAICYA; SAAS 11; SATA 6, 68

Mayo, Jim
    See L'Amour, Louis (Dearborn)

Maysles, Albert 1926- .... **CLC 16**
    See also CA 29-32R

Maysles, David 1932-............. **CLC 16**

Mazer, Norma Fox 1931- .... **CLC 26**
    See also AAYA 5; CA 69-72; CANR 12,
    32; CLR 23; MAICYA; SAAS 1;
    SATA 24, 67

Mazzini, Guiseppe 1805-1872 .... **NCLC 34**

Mazzini, Guiseppe 1805-1872 .... **NCLC 34**

McAuley, James Phillip
    1917-1976 .... **CLC 45**
    See also CA 97-100

McBain, Ed
    See Hunter, Evan

McBrien, William Augustine
    1930- .... **CLC 44**
    See also CA 107

McCaffrey, Anne (Inez) 1926-...... **CLC 17**
    See also AAYA 6; AITN 2; BEST 89:2;
    CA 25-28R; CANR 15, 35; DLB 8;
    MAICYA; MTCW; SAAS 11; SATA 8,
    70

McCann, Arthur
    See Campbell, John W(ood Jr.)

McCann, Edson
    See Pohl, Frederik

McCarthy, Cormac 1933-........ **CLC 4, 57**
    See also CA 13-16R; CANR 10; DLB 6

McCarthy, Mary (Therese)
    1912-1989 ... **CLC 1, 3, 5, 14, 24, 39, 59**
    See also CA 5-8R; 129; CANR 16; DLB 2;
    DLBY 81; MTCW

McCartney, (James) Paul
    1942- .... **CLC 12, 35**

McCauley, Stephen 19(?)-......... **CLC 50**

McClure, Michael (Thomas)
    1932- .... **CLC 6, 10**
    See also CA 21-24R; CANR 17; DLB 16

McCorkle, Jill (Collins) 1958-...... **CLC 51**
    See also CA 121; DLBY 87

McCourt, James 1941-............. **CLC 5**
    See also CA 57-60

McCoy, Horace (Stanley)
    1897-1955 .... **TCLC 28**
    See also CA 108; DLB 9**

Moore, George Augustus
1852-1933 .... TCLC 7
See also CA 104; DLB 10, 18, 57

Moore, Lorrie .... CLC 39, 45, 68
See also Moore, Marie Lorena

Moore, Marianne (Craig)
1887-1972 ... CLC 1, 2, 4, 8, 10, 13, 19,
47; PC 4
See also CA 1-4R; 33-36R; CANR 3;
CDALB 1929-1941; DLB 45; DLBD 7;
MTCW; SATA 20

Moore, Marie Lorena 1957-
See Moore, Lorrie
See also CA 116; CANR 39

Moore, Thomas 1779-1852....... NCLC 6
See also DLB 96

Morand, Paul 1888-1976 .... CLC 41
See also CA 69-72; DLB 65

Morante, Elsa 1918-1985....... CLC 8, 47
See also CA 85-88; 117; CANR 35; MTCW

Moravia, Alberto...... CLC 2, 7, 11, 27, 46
See also Pincherle, Alberto

More, Hannah 1745-1833 .... NCLC 27
See also DLB 107, 109, 116

More, Henry 1614-1687............. LC 9

More, Sir Thomas 1478-1535 ...... LC 10

Moreas, Jean................... TCLC 18
See also Papadiamantopoulos, Johannes

Morgan, Berry 1919-............. CLC 6
See also CA 49-52; DLB 6

Morgan, Claire
See Highsmith, (Mary) Patricia

Morgan, Edwin (George) 1920-..... CLC 31
See also CA 5-8R; CANR 3; DLB 27

Morgan, (George) Frederick
1922-....................... CLC 23
See also CA 17-20R; CANR 21

Morgan, Harriet
See Mencken, H(enry) L(ouis)

Morgan, Jane
See Cooper, James Fenimore

Morgan, Janet 1945-............. CLC 39
See also CA 65-68

Morgan, Lady 1776(?)-1859...... NCLC 29
See also DLB 116

Morgan, Robin 1941-............. CLC 2
See also CA 69-72; CANR 29; MTCW

Morgan, Scott
See Kuttner, Henry

Morgan, Seth 1949(?)-1990 .... CLC 65
See also CA 132

Morgenstern, Christian
1871-1914 .... TCLC 8
See also CA 105

Morgenstern, S.
See Goldman, William (W.)

Moricz, Zsigmond 1879-1942 ..... TCLC 33

Morike, Eduard (Friedrich)
1804-1875 .... NCLC 10

Mori Ogai .... TCLC 14
See also Mori Rintaro

Mori Rintaro 1862-1922
See Mori Ogai
See also CA 110

Moritz, Karl Philipp 1756-1793 ...... LC 2
See also DLB 94

Morren, Theophil
See Hofmannsthal, Hugo von

Morris, Julian
See West, Morris L(anglo)

Morris, Steveland Judkins 1950(?)-
See Wonder, Stevie
See also CA 111

Morris, William 1834-1896 ...... NCLC 4
See also CDBLB 1832-1890; DLB 18, 35, 57

Morris, Wright 1910-... CLC 1, 3, 7, 18, 37
See also CA 9-12R; CANR 21; DLB 2;
DLBY 81; MTCW

Morrison, Chloe Anthony Wofford
See Morrison, Toni

Morrison, James Douglas 1943-1971
See Morrison, Jim
See also CA 73-76

Morrison, Jim .... CLC 17
See also Morrison, James Douglas

Morrison, Toni 1931-..... CLC 4, 10, 22, 55
See also AAYA 1; BLC 3; BW; CA 29-32R;
CANR 27; CDALB 1968-1988; DLB 6,
33; DLBY 81; MTCW; SATA 57

Morrison, Van 1945- .... CLC 21
See also CA 116

Mortimer, John (Clifford)
1923-.................... CLC 28, 43
See also CA 13-16R; CANR 21;
CDBLB 1960 to Present; DLB 13;
MTCW

Mortimer, Penelope (Ruth) 1918-.... CLC 5
See also CA 57-60

Morton, Anthony
See Creasey, John

Mosher, Howard Frank .... CLC 62

Mosley, Nicholas 1923-........ CLC 43, 70
See also CA 69-72; DLB 14

Moss, Howard
1922-1987 .... CLC 7, 14, 45, 50
See also CA 1-4R; 123; CANR 1; DLB 5

Motion, Andrew 1952-............ CLC 47
See also DLB 40

Motley, Willard (Francis)
1912-1965 .... CLC 18
See also BW; CA 117; 106; DLB 76

Mott, Michael (Charles Alston)
1930-.................... CLC 15, 34
See also CA 5-8R; CAAS 7; CANR 7, 29

Mowat, Farley (McGill) 1921- ..... CLC 26
See also AAYA 1; CA 1-4R; CANR 4, 24;
CLR 20; DLB 68; MAICYA; MTCW;
SATA 3, 55

Moyers, Bill 1934-.............. CLC 74
See also AITN 2; CA 61-64; CANR 31

Mphahlele, Es'kia
See Mphahlele, Ezekiel

Mphahlele, Ezekiel 1919-......... CLC 25
See also BLC 3; BW; CA 81-84; CANR 26

Mqhayi, S(amuel) E(dward) K(rune Loliwe)
1875-1945 .... TCLC 25
See also BLC 3

Mr. Martin
See Burroughs, William S(eward)

Mrozek, Slawomir 1930-........ CLC 3, 13
See also CA 13-16R; CAAS 10; CANR 29;
MTCW

Mrs. Belloc-Lowndes
See Lowndes, Marie Adelaide (Belloc)

Mtwa, Percy (?)-................ CLC 47

Mueller, Lisel 1924-.......... CLC 13, 51
See also CA 93-96; DLB 105

Muir, Edwin 1887-1959.......... TCLC 2
See also CA 104; DLB 20, 100

Muir, John 1838-1914 .... TCLC 28

Mujica Lainez, Manuel
1910-1984 .... CLC 31
See also Lainez, Manuel Mujica
See also CA 81-84; 112; CANR 32; HW

Mukherjee, Bharati 1940-........ CLC 53
See also BEST 89:2; CA 107; DLB 60;
MTCW

Muldoon, Paul 1951- .... CLC 32, 72
See also CA 113; 129; DLB 40

Mulisch, Harry 1927-............ CLC 42
See also CA 9-12R; CANR 6, 26

Mull, Martin 1943-.............. CLC 17
See also CA 105

Mulock, Dinah Maria
See Craik, Dinah Maria (Mulock)

Munford, Robert 1737(?)-1783 .... LC 5
See also DLB 31

Mungo, Raymond 1946-.......... CLC 72
See also CA 49-52; CANR 2

Munro, Alice
1931- .... CLC 6, 10, 19, 50; SSC 3
See also AITN 2; CA 33-36R; CANR 33;
DLB 53; MTCW; SATA 29

Munro, H(ector) H(ugh) 1870-1916
See Saki
See also CA 104; 130; CDBLB 1890-1914;
DLB 34; MTCW; WLC

Murasaki, Lady................. CMLC 1

Murdoch, (Jean) Iris
1919- ...... CLC 1, 2, 3, 4, 6, 8, 11, 15,
22, 31, 51
See also CA 13-16R; CANR 8;
CDBLB 1960 to Present; DLB 14;
MTCW

Murphy, Richard 1927-.......... CLC 41
See also CA 29-32R; DLB 40

Murphy, Sylvia 1937-............ CLC 34
See also CA 121

Murphy, Thomas (Bernard) 1935-... CLC 51
See also CA 101

Murray, Les(lie) A(llan) 1938- ..... CLC 40
See also CA 21-24R; CANR 11, 27

Murry, J. Middleton
See Murry, John Middleton

Murry, John Middleton
1889-1957 .... TCLC 16
See also CA 118

Musgrave, Susan 1951- .... **CLC 13, 54**
See also CA 69-72

Musil, Robert (Edler von)
1880-1942 .... **TCLC 12**
See also CA 109; DLB 81

Musset, (Louis Charles) Alfred de
1810-1857 .... **NCLC 7**

My Brother's Brother
See Chekhov, Anton (Pavlovich)

Myers, Walter Dean 1937- .... **CLC 35**
See also AAYA 4; BLC 3; BW; CA 33-36R;
CANR 20; CLR 4, 16; DLB 33;
MAICYA; SAAS 2; SATA 27, 41, 70, 71

Myers, Walter M.
See Myers, Walter Dean

Myles, Symon
See Follett, Ken(neth Martin)

Nabokov, Vladimir (Vladimirovich)
1899-1977 .... **CLC 1, 2, 3, 6, 8, 11, 15,**
23, 44, 46, 64; SSC 11
See also CA 5-8R; 69-72; CANR 20;
CDALB 1941-1968; DLB 2; DLBD 3;
DLBY 80, 91; MTCW; WLC

Nagy, Laszlo 1925-1978 .... **CLC 7**
See also CA 129; 112

Naipaul, Shiva(dhar Srinivasa)
1945-1985 .... **CLC 32, 39**
See also CA 110; 112; 116; CANR 33;
DLBY 85; MTCW

Naipaul, V(idiadhar) S(urajprasad)
1932- ...... **CLC 4, 7, 9, 13, 18, 37**
See also CA 1-4R; CANR 1, 33;
CDBLB 1960 to Present; DLBY 85;
MTCW

Nakos, Lilika 1899(?)- .... **CLC 29**

Narayan, R(asipuram) K(rishnaswami)
1906- .... **CLC 7, 28, 47**
See also CA 81-84; CANR 33; MTCW;
SATA 62

Nash, (Fredric) Ogden 1902-1971 .. **CLC 23**
See also CA 13-14; 29-32R; CANR 34;
CAP 1; DLB 11; MAICYA; MTCW;
SATA 2, 46

Nathan, Daniel
See Dannay, Frederic

Nathan, George Jean 1882-1958 ... **TCLC 18**
See also Hatteras, Owen
See also CA 114

Natsume, Kinnosuke 1867-1916
See Natsume, Soseki
See also CA 104

Natsume, Soseki .... **TCLC 2, 10**
See also Natsume, Kinnosuke

Natti, (Mary) Lee 1919-
See Kingman, Lee
See also CA 5-8R; CANR 2

Naylor, Gloria 1950- .... **CLC 28, 52**
See also AAYA 6; BLC 3; BW; CA 107;
CANR 27; MTCW

Neihardt, John Gneisenau
1881-1973 .... **CLC 32**
See also CA 13-14; CAP 1; DLB 9, 54

Nekrasov, Nikolai Alekseevich
1821-1878 .... **NCLC 11**

Nelligan, Emile 1879-1941 .... **TCLC 14**
See also CA 114; DLB 92

Nelson, Willie 1933- .... **CLC 17**
See also CA 107

Nemerov, Howard (Stanley)
1920-1991 .... **CLC 2, 6, 9, 36**
See also CA 1-4R; 134; CABS 2; CANR 1,
27; DLB 6; DLBY 83; MTCW

Neruda, Pablo
1904-1973 .... **CLC 1, 2, 5, 7, 9, 28, 62;**
PC 4
See also CA 19-20; 45-48; CAP 2; HW;
MTCW; WLC

Nerval, Gerard de 1808-1855 ...... **NCLC 1**

Nervo, (Jose) Amado (Ruiz de)
1870-1919 .... **TCLC 11**
See also CA 109; 131; HW

Nessi, Pio Baroja y
See Baroja (y Nessi), Pio

Neufeld, John (Arthur) 1938- ...... **CLC 17**
See also CA 25-28R; CANR 11, 37;
MAICYA; SAAS 3; SATA 6

Neville, Emily Cheney 1919- .... **CLC 12**
See also CA 5-8R; CANR 3, 37; MAICYA;
SAAS 2; SATA 1

Newbound, Bernard Slade 1930-
See Slade, Bernard
See also CA 81-84

Newby, P(ercy) H(oward)
1918- .... **CLC 2, 13**
See also CA 5-8R; CANR 32; DLB 15;
MTCW

Newlove, Donald 1928- .... **CLC 6**
See also CA 29-32R; CANR 25

Newlove, John (Herbert) 1938- ..... **CLC 14**
See also CA 21-24R; CANR 9, 25

Newman, Charles 1938- .... **CLC 2, 8**
See also CA 21-24R

Newman, Edwin (Harold) 1919- .... **CLC 14**
See also AITN 1; CA 69-72; CANR 5

Newman, John Henry
1801-1890 .... **NCLC 38**
See also DLB 18, 32, 55

Newton, Suzanne 1936- .... **CLC 35**
See also CA 41-44R; CANR 14; SATA 5

Nexo, Martin Andersen
1869-1954 .... **TCLC 43**

Nezval, Vitezslav 1900-1958 ...... **TCLC 44**
See also CA 123

Ngema, Mbongeni 1955- .... **CLC 57**

Ngugi, James T(hiong'o) .... **CLC 3, 7, 13**
See also Ngugi wa Thiong'o

Ngugi wa Thiong'o 1938- .... **CLC 36**
See also Ngugi, James T(hiong'o)
See also BLC 3; BW; CA 81-84; CANR 27;
MTCW

Nichol, B(arrie) P(hillip)
1944-1988 .... **CLC 18**
See also CA 53-56; DLB 53; SATA 66

Nichols, John (Treadwell) 1940- .... **CLC 38**
See also CA 9-12R; CAAS 2; CANR 6;
DLBY 82

Nichols, Peter (Richard)
1927- .... **CLC 5, 36, 65**
See also CA 104; CANR 33; DLB 13;
MTCW

Nicolas, F. R. E.
See Freeling, Nicolas

Niedecker, Lorine 1903-1970.... **CLC 10, 42**
See also CA 25-28; CAP 2; DLB 48

Nietzsche, Friedrich (Wilhelm)
1844-1900 .... **TCLC 10, 18**
See also CA 107; 121

Nievo, Ippolito 1831-1861 .... **NCLC 22**

Nightingale, Anne Redmon 1943-
See Redmon, Anne
See also CA 103

Nik.T.O.
See Annensky, Innokenty Fyodorovich

Nin, Anais
1903-1977 ..... **CLC 1, 4, 8, 11, 14, 60;**
SSC 10
See also AITN 2; CA 13-16R; 69-72;
CANR 22; DLB 2, 4; MTCW

Nissenson, Hugh 1933-............ **CLC 4, 9**
See also CA 17-20R; CANR 27; DLB 28

Niven, Larry .... **CLC 8**
See also Niven, Laurence Van Cott
See also DLB 8

Niven, Laurence Van Cott 1938-
See Niven, Larry
See also CA 21-24R; CAAS 12; CANR 14;
MTCW

Nixon, Agnes Eckhardt 1927-...... **CLC 21**
See also CA 110

Nizan, Paul 1905-1940.......... **TCLC 40**
See also DLB 72

Nkosi, Lewis 1936-............... **CLC 45**
See also BLC 3; BW; CA 65-68; CANR 27

Nodier, (Jean) Charles (Emmanuel)
1780-1844 .... **NCLC 19**
See also DLB 119

Nolan, Christopher 1965-......... **CLC 58**
See also CA 111

Norden, Charles
See Durrell, Lawrence (George)

Nordhoff, Charles (Bernard)
1887-1947 .... **TCLC 23**
See also CA 108; DLB 9; SATA 23

Norman, Marsha 1947- .... **CLC 28**
See also CA 105; CABS 3; DLBY 84

Norris, Benjamin Franklin Jr.
1870-1902 .... **TCLC 24**
See also Norris, Frank
See also CA 110

Norris, Frank
See Norris, Benjamin Franklin Jr.
See also CDALB 1865-1917; DLB 12, 71

Norris, Leslie 1921- .... **CLC 14**
See also CA 11-12; CANR 14; CAP 1;
DLB 27

North, Andrew
See Norton, Andre

North, Captain George
See Stevenson, Robert Louis (Balfour)

North, Milou
See Erdrich, Louise

Northrup, B. A.
See Hubbard, L(afayette) Ron(ald)

North Staffs
See Hulme, T(homas) E(rnest)

Norton, Alice Mary
See Norton, Andre
See also MAICYA; SATA 1, 43

Norton, Andre 1912- .... **CLC 12**
See also Norton, Alice Mary
See also CA 1-4R; CANR 2, 31; DLB 8, 52;
MTCW

Norway, Nevil Shute 1899-1960
See Shute, Nevil
See also CA 102; 93-96

Norwid, Cyprian Kamil
1821-1883 .... **NCLC 17**

Nosille, Nabrah
See Ellison, Harlan

Nossack, Hans Erich 1901-1978 ..... **CLC 6**
See also CA 93-96; 85-88; DLB 69

Nosu, Chuji
See Ozu, Yasujiro

Nova, Craig 1945- .... **CLC 7, 31**
See also CA 45-48; CANR 2

Novak, Joseph
See Kosinski, Jerzy (Nikodem)

Novalis 1772-1801 .... **NCLC 13**
See also DLB 90

Nowlan, Alden (Albert) 1933-1983 .. **CLC 15**
See also CA 9-12R; CANR 5; DLB 53

Noyes, Alfred 1880-1958 .... **TCLC 7**
See also CA 104; DLB 20

Nunn, Kem 19(?)- .... **CLC 34**

Nye, Robert 1939- .... **CLC 13, 42**
See also CA 33-36R; CANR 29; DLB 14;
MTCW; SATA 6

Nyro, Laura 1947- .... **CLC 17**

Oates, Joyce Carol
1938- ..... **CLC 1, 2, 3, 6, 9, 11, 15, 19, 33, 52; SSC 6**
See also AITN 1; BEST 89:2; CA 5-8R;
CANR 25; CDALB 1968-1988; DLB 2, 5;
DLBY 81; MTCW; WLC

O'Brien, E. G.
See Clarke, Arthur C(harles)

O'Brien, Edna
1936- ... **CLC 3, 5, 8, 13, 36, 65; SSC 10**
See also CA 1-4R; CANR 6; CDBLB 1960
to Present; DLB 14; MTCW

O'Brien, Fitz-James 1828-1862 ... **NCLC 21**
See also DLB 74

O'Brien, Flann .... **CLC 1, 4, 5, 7, 10, 47**
See also O Nuallain, Brian

O'Brien, Richard 1942- .... **CLC 17**
See also CA 124

O'Brien, Tim 1946- .... **CLC 7, 19, 40**
See also CA 85-88; DLBD 9; DLBY 80

Obstfelder, Sigbjoern 1866-1900 ... **TCLC 23**
See also CA 123

O'Casey, Sean
1880-1964 .... **CLC 1, 5, 9, 11, 15**
See also CA 89-92; CDBLB 1914-1945;
DLB 10; MTCW

O'Cathasaigh, Sean
See O'Casey, Sean

Ochs, Phil 1940-1976 .... **CLC 17**
See also CA 65-68

O'Connor, Edwin (Greene)
1918-1968 .... **CLC 14**
See also CA 93-96; 25-28R

O'Connor, (Mary) Flannery
1925-1964 ... **CLC 1, 2, 3, 6, 10, 13, 15, 21, 66; SSC 1**
See also AAYA 7; CA 1-4R; CANR 3;
CDALB 1941-1968; DLB 2; DLBY 80;
MTCW; WLC

O'Connor, Frank .... **CLC 23; SSC 5**
See also O'Donovan, Michael John

O'Dell, Scott 1898-1989 .... **CLC 30**
See also AAYA 3; CA 61-64; 129;
CANR 12, 30; CLR 1, 16; DLB 52;
MAICYA; SATA 12, 60

Odets, Clifford 1906-1963 .... **CLC 2, 28**
See also CA 85-88; DLB 7, 26; MTCW

O'Donnell, K. M.
See Malzberg, Barry N(athaniel)

O'Donnell, Lawrence
See Kuttner, Henry

O'Donovan, Michael John
1903-1966 .... **CLC 14**
See also O'Connor, Frank
See also CA 93-96

Oe, Kenzaburo 1935- .... **CLC 10, 36**
See also CA 97-100; CANR 36; MTCW

O'Faolain, Julia 1932- .... **CLC 6, 19, 47**
See also CA 81-84; CAAS 2; CANR 12;
DLB 14; MTCW

O'Faolain, Sean
1900-1991 .... **CLC 1, 7, 14, 32, 70**
See also CA 61-64; 134; CANR 12;
DLB 15; MTCW

O'Flaherty, Liam
1896-1984 .... **CLC 5, 34; SSC 6**
See also CA 101; 113; CANR 35; DLB 36;
DLBY 84; MTCW

Ogilvy, Gavin
See Barrie, J(ames) M(atthew)

O'Grady, Standish James
1846-1928 .... **TCLC 5**
See also CA 104

O'Grady, Timothy 1951- .... **CLC 59**
See also CA 138

O'Hara, Frank 1926-1966 ..... **CLC 2, 5, 13**
See also CA 9-12R; 25-28R; CANR 33;
DLB 5, 16; MTCW

O'Hara, John (Henry)
1905-1970 ...... **CLC 1, 2, 3, 6, 11, 42**
See also CA 5-8R; 25-28R; CANR 31;
CDALB 1929-1941; DLB 9, 86; DLBD 2;
MTCW

O Hehir, Diana 1922- .... **CLC 41**
See also CA 93-96

Okigbo, Christopher (Ifenayichukwu)
1932-1967 .... **CLC 25**
See also BLC 3; BW; CA 77-80; MTCW

Olds, Sharon 1942- .... **CLC 32, 39**
See also CA 101; CANR 18; DLB 120

Oldstyle, Jonathan
See Irving, Washington

Olesha, Yuri (Karlovich)
1899-1960 .... **CLC 8**
See also CA 85-88

Oliphant, Margaret (Oliphant Wilson)
1828-1897 .... **NCLC 11**
See also DLB 18

Oliver, Mary 1935- .... **CLC 19, 34**
See also CA 21-24R; CANR 9; DLB 5

Olivier, Laurence (Kerr)
1907-1989 .... **CLC 20**
See also CA 111; 129

Olsen, Tillie 1913- ..... **CLC 4, 13; SSC 11**
See also CA 1-4R; CANR 1; DLB 28;
DLBY 80; MTCW

Olson, Charles (John)
1910-1970 ..... **CLC 1, 2, 5, 6, 9, 11, 29**
See also CA 13-16; 25-28R; CABS 2;
CANR 35; CAP 1; DLB 5, 16; MTCW

Olson, Toby 1937- .... **CLC 28**
See also CA 65-68; CANR 9, 31

Olyesha, Yuri
See Olesha, Yuri (Karlovich)

Ondaatje, Michael 1943- .... **CLC 14, 29, 51**
See also CA 77-80; DLB 60

Oneal, Elizabeth 1934-
See Oneal, Zibby
See also CA 106; CANR 28; MAICYA;
SATA 30

Oneal, Zibby .... **CLC 30**
See also Oneal, Elizabeth
See also AAYA 5; CLR 13

O'Neill, Eugene (Gladstone)
1888-1953 .... **TCLC 1, 6, 27**
See also AITN 1; CA 110; 132;
CDALB 1929-1941; DLB 7; MTCW;
WLC

Onetti, Juan Carlos 1909- .... **CLC 7, 10**
See also CA 85-88; CANR 32; DLB 113;
HW; MTCW

O Nuallain, Brian 1911-1966
See O'Brien, Flann
See also CA 21-22; 25-28R; CAP 2

Oppen, George 1908-1984 .... **CLC 7, 13, 34**
See also CA 13-16R; 113; CANR 8; DLB 5

Oppenheim, E(dward) Phillips
1866-1946 .... **TCLC 45**
See also CA 111; DLB 70

Orlovitz, Gil 1918-1973 .... **CLC 22**
See also CA 77-80; 45-48; DLB 2, 5

Ortega y Gasset, Jose 1883-1955 ... **TCLC 9**
See also CA 106; 130; HW; MTCW

Ortiz, Simon J(oseph) 1941- .... **CLC 45**
See also CA 134; DLB 120

Orton, Joe .... **CLC 4, 13, 43**
See also Orton, John Kingsley
See also CDBLB 1960 to Present; DLB 13

Paz, Gil
See Lugones, Leopoldo

Paz, Octavio
1914- ...... **CLC 3, 4, 6, 10, 19, 51, 65;**
PC 1
See also CA 73-76; CANR 32; DLBY 90;
HW; MTCW; WLC

Peacock, Molly 1947- .... **CLC 60**
See also CA 103; DLB 120

Peacock, Thomas Love
1785-1866 .... **NCLC 22**
See also DLB 96, 116

Peake, Mervyn 1911-1968 .... **CLC 7, 54**
See also CA 5-8R; 25-28R; CANR 3;
DLB 15; MTCW; SATA 23

Pearce, Philippa .... **CLC 21**
See also Christie, (Ann) Philippa
See also CLR 9; MAICYA; SATA 1, 67

Pearl, Eric
See Elman, Richard

Pearson, T(homas) R(eid) 1956- .... **CLC 39**
See also CA 120; 130

Peck, John 1941- .... **CLC 3**
See also CA 49-52; CANR 3

Peck, Richard (Wayne) 1934- ...... **CLC 21**
See also AAYA 1; CA 85-88; CANR 19,
38; MAICYA; SAAS 2; SATA 18, 55

Peck, Robert Newton 1928- .... **CLC 17**
See also AAYA 3; CA 81-84; CANR 31;
MAICYA; SAAS 1; SATA 21, 62

Peckinpah, (David) Sam(uel)
1925-1984 .... **CLC 20**
See also CA 109; 114

Pedersen, Knut 1859-1952
See Hamsun, Knut
See also CA 104; 119; MTCW

Peeslake, Gaffer
See Durrell, Lawrence (George)

Peguy, Charles Pierre
1873-1914 .... **TCLC 10**
See also CA 107

Pena, Ramon del Valle y
See Valle-Inclan, Ramon (Maria) del

Pendennis, Arthur Esquir
See Thackeray, William Makepeace

Pepys, Samuel 1633-1703 .... **LC 11**
See also CDBLB 1660-1789; DLB 101;
WLC

Percy, Walker
1916-1990 ... **CLC 2, 3, 6, 8, 14, 18, 47,**
65
See also CA 1-4R; 131; CANR 1, 23;
DLB 2; DLBY 80, 90; MTCW

Perec, Georges 1936-1982 .... **CLC 56**
See also DLB 83

Pereda (y Sanchez de Porrua), Jose Maria de
1833-1906 .... **TCLC 16**
See also CA 117

Pereda y Porrua, Jose Maria de
See Pereda (y Sanchez de Porrua), Jose
Maria de

Peregoy, George Weems
See Mencken, H(enry) L(ouis)

Perelman, S(idney) J(oseph)
1904-1979 ... **CLC 3, 5, 9, 15, 23, 44, 49**
See also AITN 1, 2; CA 73-76; 89-92;
CANR 18; DLB 11, 44; MTCW

Peret, Benjamin 1899-1959 .... **TCLC 20**
See also CA 117

Peretz, Isaac Loeb 1851(?)-1915... **TCLC 16**
See also CA 109

Peretz, Yitzkhok Leibush
See Peretz, Isaac Loeb

Perez Galdos, Benito 1843-1920... **TCLC 27**
See also CA 125; HW

Perrault, Charles 1628-1703 .... **LC 2**
See also MAICYA; SATA 25

Perry, Brighton
See Sherwood, Robert E(mmet)

Perse, St.-John .... **CLC 4, 11, 46**
See also Leger, (Marie-Rene) Alexis
Saint-Leger

Perse, Saint-John
See Leger, (Marie-Rene) Alexis Saint-Leger

Peseenz, Tulio F.
See Lopez y Fuentes, Gregorio

Pesetsky, Bette 1932- .... **CLC 28**
See also CA 133

Peshkov, Alexei Maximovich 1868-1936
See Gorky, Maxim
See also CA 105

Pessoa, Fernando (Antonio Nogueira)
1888-1935 .... **TCLC 27**
See also CA 125

Peterkin, Julia Mood 1880-1961.... **CLC 31**
See also CA 102; DLB 9

Peters, Joan K. 1945- .... **CLC 39**

Peters, Robert L(ouis) 1924- .... **CLC 7**
See also CA 13-16R; CAAS 8; DLB 105

Petofi, Sandor 1823-1849........ **NCLC 21**

Petrakis, Harry Mark 1923- .... **CLC 3**
See also CA 9-12R; CANR 4, 30

Petrov, Evgeny .... **TCLC 21**
See also Kataev, Evgeny Petrovich

Petry, Ann (Lane) 1908- ...... **CLC 1, 7, 18**
See also BW; CA 5-8R; CAAS 6; CANR 4;
CLR 12; DLB 76; MAICYA; MTCW;
SATA 5

Petursson, Halligrimur 1614-1674 .... **LC 8**

Philipson, Morris H. 1926- .... **CLC 53**
See also CA 1-4R; CANR 4

Phillips, David Graham
1867-1911 .... **TCLC 44**
See also CA 108; DLB 9, 12

Phillips, Jack
See Sandburg, Carl (August)

Phillips, Jayne Anne 1952- ..... **CLC 15, 33**
See also CA 101; CANR 24; DLBY 80;
MTCW

Phillips, Richard
See Dick, Philip K(indred)

Phillips, Robert (Schaeffer) 1938-... **CLC 28**
See also CA 17-20R; CAAS 13; CANR 8;
DLB 105

Phillips, Ward
See Lovecraft, H(oward) P(hillips)

Piccolo, Lucio 1901-1969 .... **CLC 13**
See also CA 97-100; DLB 114

Pickthall, Marjorie L(owry) C(hristie)
1883-1922 .... **TCLC 21**
See also CA 107; DLB 92

Pico della Mirandola, Giovanni
1463-1494 .... **LC 15**

Piercy, Marge
1936- .... **CLC 3, 6, 14, 18, 27, 62**
See also CA 21-24R; CAAS 1; CANR 13;
DLB 120; MTCW

Piers, Robert
See Anthony, Piers

Pieyre de Mandiargues, Andre 1909-1991
See Mandiargues, Andre Pieyre de
See also CA 103; 136; CANR 22

Pilnyak, Boris .... **TCLC 23**
See also Vogau, Boris Andreyevich

Pincherle, Alberto 1907-1990 ... **CLC 11, 18**
See also Moravia, Alberto
See also CA 25-28R; 132; CANR 33;
MTCW

Pineda, Cecile 1942- .... **CLC 39**
See also CA 118

Pinero, Arthur Wing 1855-1934 ... **TCLC 32**
See also CA 110; DLB 10

Pinero, Miguel (Antonio Gomez)
1946-1988 .... **CLC 4, 55**
See also CA 61-64; 125; CANR 29; HW

Pinget, Robert 1919- .... **CLC 7, 13, 37**
See also CA 85-88; DLB 83

Floyd .... **CLC 35**
See also Barrett, (Roger) Syd; Gilmour,
David; Mason, Nick; Waters, Roger;
Wright, Rick

Pinkney, Edward 1802-1828 ..... **NCLC 31**

Pinkwater, Daniel Manus 1941- .... **CLC 35**
See also Pinkwater, Manus
See also AAYA 1; CA 29-32R; CANR 12,
38; CLR 4; MAICYA; SAAS 3; SATA 46

Pinkwater, Manus
See Pinkwater, Daniel Manus
See also SATA 8

Pinsky, Robert 1940- .... **CLC 9, 19, 38**
See also CA 29-32R; CAAS 4; DLBY 82

Pinta, Harold
See Pinter, Harold

Pinter, Harold
1930- ..... **CLC 1, 3, 6, 9, 11, 15, 27, 58**
See also CA 5-8R; CANR 33; CDBLB 1960
to Present; DLB 13; MTCW; WLC

Pirandello, Luigi 1867-1936..... **TCLC 4, 29**
See also CA 104; WLC

Pirsig, Robert M(aynard) 1928- ... **CLC 4, 6**
See also CA 53-56; MTCW; SATA 39

Pisarev, Dmitry Ivanovich
1840-1868 .... **NCLC 25**

Pix, Mary (Griffith) 1666-1709 .... **LC 8**
See also DLB 80

Plaidy, Jean
See Hibbert, Eleanor Burford

Plant, Robert 1948- .... **CLC 12**

Plante, David (Robert)
1940- .... **CLC 7, 23, 38**
See also CA 37-40R; CANR 12, 36;
DLBY 83; MTCW

Plath, Sylvia
1932-1963 .... **CLC 1, 2, 3, 5, 9, 11, 14, 17, 50, 51, 62; PC 1**
See also CA 19-20; CANR 34; CAP 2;
CDALB 1941-1968; DLB 5, 6; MTCW;
WLC

Plato 428(?)B.C.-348(?)B.C. ...... **CMLC 8**

Platonov, Andrei .... **TCLC 14**
See also Klimentov, Andrei Platonovich

Platt, Kin 1911- .... **CLC 26**
See also CA 17-20R; CANR 11; SATA 21

Plick et Plock
See Simenon, Georges (Jacques Christian)

Plimpton, George (Ames) 1927-..... **CLC 36**
See also AITN 1; CA 21-24R; CANR 32;
MTCW; SATA 10

Plomer, William Charles Franklin
1903-1973 .... **CLC 4, 8**
See also CA 21-22; CANR 34; CAP 2;
DLB 20; MTCW; SATA 24

Plowman, Piers
See Kavanagh, Patrick (Joseph)

Plum, J.
See Wodehouse, P(elham) G(renville)

Plumly, Stanley (Ross) 1939- ...... **CLC 33**
See also CA 108; 110; DLB 5

Poe, Edgar Allan
1809-1849 ... **NCLC 1, 16; PC 1; SSC 1**
See also CDALB 1640-1865; DLB 3, 59, 73, 74; SATA 23; WLC

Poet of Titchfield Street, The
See Pound, Ezra (Weston Loomis)

Pohl, Frederik 1919- .... **CLC 18**
See also CA 61-64; CAAS 1; CANR 11, 37;
DLB 8; MTCW; SATA 24

Poirier, Louis 1910-
See Gracq, Julien
See also CA 122; 126

Poitier, Sidney 1927-............. **CLC 26**
See also BW; CA 117

Polanski, Roman 1933- .... **CLC 16**
See also CA 77-80

Poliakoff, Stephen 1952- .... **CLC 38**
See also CA 106; DLB 13

.... **CLC 26**
See also Copeland, Stewart (Armstrong);
Summers, Andrew James; Sumner,
Gordon Matthew

Pollitt, Katha 1949- .... **CLC 28**
See also CA 120; 122; MTCW

Pollock, Sharon 1936- .... **CLC 50**
See also DLB 60

Pomerance, Bernard 1940-......... **CLC 13**
See also CA 101

Ponge, Francis (Jean Gaston Alfred)
1899-1988 .... **CLC 6, 18**
See also CA 85-88; 126

Pontoppidan, Henrik 1857-1943 ... **TCLC 29**

Poole, Josephine .... **CLC 17**
See also Helyar, Jane Penelope Josephine
See also SAAS 2; SATA 5

Popa, Vasko 1922-.............. **CLC 19**
See also CA 112

Pope, Alexander 1688-1744 .... **LC 3**
See also CDBLB 1660-1789; DLB 95, 101;
WLC

Porter, Connie 1960- .... **CLC 70**

Porter, Gene(va Grace) Stratton
1863(?)-1924 .... **TCLC 21**
See also CA 112

Porter, Katherine Anne
1890-1980 ..... **CLC 1, 3, 7, 10, 13, 15, 27; SSC 4**
See also AITN 2; CA 1-4R; 101; CANR 1;
DLB 4, 9, 102; DLBY 80; MTCW;
SATA 23, 39

Porter, Peter (Neville Frederick)
1929-.................... **CLC 5, 13, 33**
See also CA 85-88; DLB 40

Porter, William Sydney 1862-1910
See Henry, O.
See also CA 104; 131; CDALB 1865-1917;
DLB 12, 78, 79; MTCW; YABC 2

Portillo (y Pacheco), Jose Lopez
See Lopez Portillo (y Pacheco), Jose

Post, Melville Davisson
1869-1930 .... **TCLC 39**
See also CA 110

Potok, Chaim 1929-....... **CLC 2, 7, 14, 26**
See also AITN 1, 2; CA 17-20R; CANR 19,
35; DLB 28; MTCW; SATA 33

Potter, Beatrice
See Webb, (Martha) Beatrice (Potter)
See also MAICYA

Potter, Dennis (Christopher George)
1935-.................... **CLC 58**
See also CA 107; CANR 33; MTCW

Pound, Ezra (Weston Loomis)
1885-1972 ..... **CLC 1, 2, 3, 4, 5, 7, 10, 13, 18, 34, 48, 50; PC 4**
See also CA 5-8R; 37-40R;
CDALB 1917-1929; DLB 4, 45, 63;
MTCW; WLC

Povod, Reinaldo 1959-............ **CLC 44**
See also CA 136

Powell, Anthony (Dymoke)
1905-.......... **CLC 1, 3, 7, 9, 10, 31**
See also CA 1-4R; CANR 1, 32;
CDBLB 1945-1960; DLB 15; MTCW

Powell, Dawn 1897-1965 .... **CLC 66**
See also CA 5-8R

Powell, Padgett 1952-............. **CLC 34**
See also CA 126

Powers, J(ames) F(arl)
1917- .... **CLC 1, 4, 8, 57; SSC 4**
See also CA 1-4R; CANR 2; MTCW

Powers, John J(ames) 1945-
See Powers, John R.
See also CA 69-72

Powers, John R. .... **CLC 66**
See also Powers, John J(ames)

Pownall, David 1938-............. **CLC 10**
See also CA 89-92; DLB 14

Powys, John Cowper
1872-1963 .... **CLC 7, 9, 15, 46**
See also CA 85-88; DLB 15; MTCW

Powys, T(heodore) F(rancis)
1875-1953 .... **TCLC 9**
See also CA 106; DLB 36

Prager, Emily 1952-............. **CLC 56**

Pratt, Edwin John 1883-1964 ..... **CLC 19**
See also CA 93-96; DLB 92

Premchand.................... **TCLC 21**
See also Srivastava, Dhanpat Rai

Preussler, Otfried 1923-.......... **CLC 17**
See also CA 77-80; SATA 24

Prevert, Jacques (Henri Marie)
1900-1977 .... **CLC 15**
See also CA 77-80; 69-72; CANR 29;
MTCW; SATA 30

Prevost, Abbe (Antoine Francois)
1697-1763 .... **LC 1**

Price, (Edward) Reynolds
1933- .... **CLC 3, 6, 13, 43, 50, 63**
See also CA 1-4R; CANR 1, 37; DLB 2

Price, Richard 1949- .... **CLC 6, 12**
See also CA 49-52; CANR 3; DLBY 81

Prichard, Katharine Susannah
1883-1969 .... **CLC 46**
See also CA 11-12; CANR 33; CAP 1;
MTCW; SATA 66

Priestley, J(ohn) B(oynton)
1894-1984 .... **CLC 2, 5, 9, 34**
See also CA 9-12R; 113; CANR 33;
CDBLB 1914-1945; DLB 10, 34, 77, 100;
DLBY 84; MTCW

Prince, F(rank) T(empleton) 1912-.. **CLC 22**
See also CA 101; DLB 20

Prince 1958(?)-.................. **CLC 35**

Prince Kropotkin
See Kropotkin, Peter (Alekseievich)

Prior, Matthew 1664-1721.......... **LC 4**
See also DLB 95

Pritchard, William H(arrison)
1932-...................... **CLC 34**
See also CA 65-68; CANR 23; DLB 111

Pritchett, V(ictor) S(awdon)
1900-........... **CLC 5, 13, 15, 41**
See also CA 61-64; CANR 31; DLB 15;
MTCW

Private 19022
See Manning, Frederic

Probst, Mark 1925-.............. **CLC 59**
See also CA 130

Prokosch, Frederic 1908-1989.... **CLC 4, 48**
See also CA 73-76; 128; DLB 48

Prophet, The
See Dreiser, Theodore (Herman Albert)

Prose, Francine 1947-............. **CLC 45**
See also CA 109; 112

Proudhon
See Cunha, Euclides (Rodrigues Pimenta) da

Proust,
(Valentin-Louis-George-Eugene-)Marcel
1871-1922 .... **TCLC 7, 13, 33**
See also CA 104; 120; DLB 65; MTCW;
WLC

Prowler, Harley
See Masters, Edgar Lee

Pryor, Richard (Franklin Lenox Thomas)
1940- . . . . **CLC 26**
See also CA 122

Przybyszewski, Stanislaw
1868-1927 . . . . **TCLC 36**
See also DLB 66

Pteleon
See Grieve, C(hristopher) M(urray)

Puckett, Lute
See Masters, Edgar Lee

Puig, Manuel
1932-1990 . . . . **CLC 3, 5, 10, 28, 65**
See also CA 45-48; CANR 2, 32; DLB 113;
HW; MTCW

Purdy, A(lfred) W(ellington)
1918- . . . . **CLC 3, 6, 14, 50**
See also Purdy, Al
See also CA 81-84

Purdy, Al
See Purdy, A(lfred) W(ellington)
See also DLB 88

Purdy, James (Amos)
1923- . . . . **CLC 2, 4, 10, 28, 52**
See also CA 33-36R; CAAS 1; CANR 19;
DLB 2; MTCW

Pure, Simon
See Swinnerton, Frank Arthur

Pushkin, Alexander (Sergeyevich)
1799-1837 . . . . **NCLC 3, 27**
See also SATA 61; WLC

P'u Sung-ling 1640-1715 . . . . **LC 3**

Putnam, Arthur Lee
See Alger, Horatio Jr.

Puzo, Mario 1920- . . . . **CLC 1, 2, 6, 36**
See also CA 65-68; CANR 4; DLB 6;
MTCW

Pym, Barbara (Mary Crampton)
1913-1980 . . . . **CLC 13, 19, 37**
See also CA 13-14; 97-100; CANR 13, 34;
CAP 1; DLB 14; DLBY 87; MTCW

Pynchon, Thomas (Ruggles Jr.)
1937- . . **CLC 2, 3, 6, 9, 11, 18, 33, 62, 72**
See also BEST 90:2; CA 17-20R; CANR 22;
DLB 2; MTCW; WLC

Qian Zhongshu
See Ch'ien Chung-shu

Qroll
See Dagerman, Stig (Halvard)

Quarrington, Paul (Lewis) 1953- . . . . **CLC 65**
See also CA 129

Quasimodo, Salvatore 1901-1968 . . . **CLC 10**
See also CA 13-16; 25-28R; CAP 1;
DLB 114; MTCW

Queen, Ellery. . . . . **CLC 3, 11**
See also Dannay, Frederic; Davidson,
Avram; Lee, Manfred B(ennington);
Sturgeon, Theodore (Hamilton); Vance,
John Holbrook

Queen, Ellery Jr.
See Dannay, Frederic; Lee, Manfred
B(ennington)

Queneau, Raymond
1903-1976 . . . . **CLC 2, 5, 10, 42**
See also CA 77-80; 69-72; CANR 32;
DLB 72; MTCW

Quin, Ann (Marie) 1936-1973 . . . . . . **CLC 6**
See also CA 9-12R; 45-48; DLB 14

Quinn, Martin
See Smith, Martin Cruz

Quinn, Simon
See Smith, Martin Cruz

Quiroga, Horacio (Sylvestre)
1878-1937 . . . . **TCLC 20**
See also CA 117; 131; HW; MTCW

Quoirez, Francoise 1935- . . . . **CLC 9**
See also Sagan, Francoise
See also CA 49-52; CANR 6, 39; MTCW

Raabe, Wilhelm 1831-1910 . . . . **TCLC 45**

Rabe, David (William) 1940- . . . **CLC 4, 8, 33**
See also CA 85-88; CABS 3; DLB 7

Rabelais, Francois 1483-1553 . . . . **LC 5**
See also WLC

Rabinovitch, Sholem 1859-1916
See Aleichem, Sholom
See also CA 104

Radcliffe, Ann (Ward) 1764-1823 . . **NCLC 6**
See also DLB 39

Radiguet, Raymond 1903-1923 . . . . **TCLC 29**
See also DLB 65

Radnoti, Miklos 1909-1944 . . . . **TCLC 16**
See also CA 118

Rado, James 1939- . . . . **CLC 17**
See also CA 105

Radvanyi, Netty 1900-1983
See Seghers, Anna
See also CA 85-88; 110

Raeburn, John (Hay) 1941- . . . . **CLC 34**
See also CA 57-60

Ragni, Gerome 1942-1991 . . . . **CLC 17**
See also CA 105; 134

Rahv, Philip. . . . . **CLC 24**
See also Greenberg, Ivan

Raine, Craig 1944- . . . . **CLC 32**
See also CA 108; CANR 29; DLB 40

Raine, Kathleen (Jessie) 1908- . . . **CLC 7, 45**
See also CA 85-88; DLB 20; MTCW

Rainis, Janis 1865-1929 . . . . **TCLC 29**

Rakosi, Carl. . . . . **CLC 47**
See also Rawley, Callman
See also CAAS 5

Raleigh, Richard
See Lovecraft, H(oward) P(hillips)

Rallentando, H. P.
See Sayers, Dorothy L(eigh)

Ramal, Walter
See de la Mare, Walter (John)

Ramon, Juan
See Jimenez (Mantecon), Juan Ramon

Ramos, Graciliano 1892-1953 . . . . . **TCLC 32**

Rampersad, Arnold 1941- . . . . **CLC 44**
See also CA 127; 133; DLB 111

Rampling, Anne
See Rice, Anne

Ramuz, Charles-Ferdinand
1878-1947 . . . . **TCLC 33**

Rand, Ayn 1905-1982 . . . . **CLC 3, 30, 44**
See also CA 13-16R; 105; CANR 27;
MTCW; WLC

Randall, Dudley (Felker) 1914- . . . . . . **CLC 1**
See also BLC 3; BW; CA 25-28R;
CANR 23; DLB 41

Randall, Robert
See Silverberg, Robert

Ranger, Ken
See Creasey, John

Ransom, John Crowe
1888-1974 . . . . **CLC 2, 4, 5, 11, 24**
See also CA 5-8R; 49-52; CANR 6, 34;
DLB 45, 63; MTCW

Rao, Raja 1909- . . . . **CLC 25, 56**
See also CA 73-76; MTCW

Raphael, Frederic (Michael)
1931- . . . . **CLC 2, 14**
See also CA 1-4R; CANR 1; DLB 14

Ratcliffe, James P.
See Mencken, H(enry) L(ouis)

Rathbone, Julian 1935- . . . . **CLC 41**
See also CA 101; CANR 34

Rattigan, Terence (Mervyn)
1911-1977 . . . . **CLC 7**
See also CA 85-88; 73-76;
CDBLB 1945-1960; DLB 13; MTCW

Ratushinskaya, Irina 1954- . . . . **CLC 54**
See also CA 129

Raven, Simon (Arthur Noel)
1927- . . . . **CLC 14**
See also CA 81-84

Rawley, Callman 1903-
See Rakosi, Carl
See also CA 21-24R; CANR 12, 32

Rawlings, Marjorie Kinnan
1896-1953 . . . . **TCLC 4**
See also CA 104; 137; DLB 9, 22, 102;
MAICYA; YABC 1

Ray, Satyajit 1921- . . . . **CLC 16**
See also CA 114; 137

Read, Herbert Edward 1893-1968 . . . . **CLC 4**
See also CA 85-88; 25-28R; DLB 20

Read, Piers Paul 1941- . . . . . . **CLC 4, 10, 25**
See also CA 21-24R; CANR 38; DLB 14;
SATA 21

Reade, Charles 1814-1884 . . . . **NCLC 2**
See also DLB 21

Reade, Hamish
See Gray, Simon (James Holliday)

Reading, Peter 1946- . . . . **CLC 47**
See also CA 103; DLB 40

Reaney, James 1926- . . . . **CLC 13**
See also CA 41-44R; CAAS 15; DLB 68;
SATA 43

Rebreanu, Liviu 1885-1944 . . . . **TCLC 28**

Rechy, John (Francisco)
1934- . . . . **CLC 1, 7, 14, 18**
See also CA 5-8R; CAAS 4; CANR 6, 32;
DLBY 82; HW

Redcam, Tom 1870-1933 . . . . **TCLC 25**

Reddin, Keith. . . . . **CLC 67**

Robbe-Grillet, Alain
1922- ...... **CLC 1, 2, 4, 6, 8, 10, 14, 43**
See also CA 9-12R; CANR 33; DLB 83;
MTCW

Robbins, Harold 1916-............. **CLC 5**
See also CA 73-76; CANR 26; MTCW

Robbins, Thomas Eugene 1936-
See Robbins, Tom
See also CA 81-84; CANR 29; MTCW

Robbins, Tom............... **CLC 9, 32, 64**
See also Robbins, Thomas Eugene
See also BEST 90:3; DLBY 80

Robbins, Trina 1938- .... **CLC 21**
See also CA 128

Roberts, Charles G(eorge) D(ouglas)
1860-1943 .... **TCLC 8**
See also CA 105; DLB 92; SATA 29

Roberts, Kate 1891-1985 .... **CLC 15**
See also CA 107; 116

Roberts, Keith (John Kingston)
1935- .... **CLC 14**
See also CA 25-28R

Roberts, Kenneth (Lewis)
1885-1957 .... **TCLC 23**
See also CA 109; DLB 9

Roberts, Michele (B.) 1949-....... **CLC 48**
See also CA 115

Robertson, Ellis
See Ellison, Harlan; Silverberg, Robert

Robertson, Thomas William
1829-1871 .... **NCLC 35**

Robinson, Edwin Arlington
1869-1935 .... **TCLC 5; PC 1**
See also CA 104; 133; CDALB 1865-1917;
DLB 54; MTCW

Robinson, Henry Crabb
1775-1867 .... **NCLC 15**
See also DLB 107

Robinson, Jill 1936-.............. **CLC 10**
See also CA 102

Robinson, Kim Stanley 1952- ...... **CLC 34**
See also CA 126

Robinson, Lloyd
See Silverberg, Robert

Robinson, Marilynne 1944-........ **CLC 25**
See also CA 116

Robinson, Smokey................ **CLC 21**
See also Robinson, William Jr.

Robinson, William Jr. 1940-
See Robinson, Smokey
See also CA 116

Robison, Mary 1949-............. **CLC 42**
See also CA 113; 116

Roddenberry, Eugene Wesley 1921-1991
See Roddenberry, Gene
See also CA 110; 135; CANR 37; SATA 45

Roddenberry, Gene............... **CLC 17**
See also Roddenberry, Eugene Wesley
See also AAYA 5; SATO 69

Rodgers, Mary 1931-............. **CLC 12**
See also CA 49-52; CANR 8; CLR 20;
MAICYA; SATA 8

Rodgers, W(illiam) R(obert)
1909-1969 .... **CLC 7**
See also CA 85-88; DLB 20

Rodman, Eric
See Silverberg, Robert

Rodman, Howard 1920(?)-1985..... **CLC 65**
See also CA 118

Rodman, Maia
See Wojciechowska, Maia (Teresa)

Rodriguez, Claudio 1934-......... **CLC 10**

Roelvaag, O(le) E(dvart)
1876-1931 .... **TCLC 17**
See also CA 117; DLB 9

Roethke, Theodore (Huebner)
1908-1963 ..... **CLC 1, 3, 8, 11, 19, 46**
See also CA 81-84; CABS 2;
CDALB 1941-1968; DLB 5; MTCW

Rogers, Thomas Hunton 1927- ..... **CLC 57**
See also CA 89-92

Rogers, Will(iam Penn Adair)
1879-1935 .... **TCLC 8**
See also CA 105; DLB 11

Rogin, Gilbert 1929-.............. **CLC 18**
See also CA 65-68; CANR 15

Rohan, Koda .... **TCLC 22**
See also Koda Shigeyuki

Rohmer, Eric.................... **CLC 16**
See also Scherer, Jean-Marie Maurice

Rohmer, Sax .... **TCLC 28**
See also Ward, Arthur Henry Sarsfield
See also DLB 70

Roiphe, Anne Richardson 1935- ... **CLC 3, 9**
See also CA 89-92; DLBY 80

**Rolfe, Frederick (William Serafino Austin
Lewis Mary)** 1860-1913...... **TCLC 12**
See also CA 107; DLB 34

Rolland, Romain 1866-1944....... **TCLC 23**
See also CA 118; DLB 65

Rolvaag, O(le) E(dvart)
See Roelvaag, O(le) E(dvart)

Romain Arnaud, Saint
See Aragon, Louis

Romains, Jules 1885-1972.......... **CLC 7**
See also CA 85-88; CANR 34; DLB 65;
MTCW

Romero, Jose Ruben 1890-1952 ... **TCLC 14**
See also CA 114; 131; HW

Ronsard, Pierre de 1524-1585....... **LC 6**

Rooke, Leon 1934-............. **CLC 25, 34**
See also CA 25-28R; CANR 23

Roper, William 1498-1578......... **LC 10**

Roquelaure, A. N.
See Rice, Anne

Rosa, Joao Guimaraes 1908-1967... **CLC 23**
See also CA 89-92; DLB 113

Rosen, Richard (Dean) 1949-....... **CLC 39**
See also CA 77-80

Rosenberg, Isaac 1890-1918...... **TCLC 12**
See also CA 107; DLB 20

Rosenblatt, Joe .... **CLC 15**
See also Rosenblatt, Joseph

Rosenblatt, Joseph 1933-
See Rosenblatt, Joe
See also CA 89-92

Rosenfeld, Samuel 1896-1963
See Tzara, Tristan
See also CA 89-92

Rosenthal, M(acha) L(ouis) 1917-... **CLC 28**
See also CA 1-4R; CAAS 6; CANR 4;
DLB 5; SATA 59

Ross, Barnaby
See Dannay, Frederic

Ross, Bernard L.
See Follett, Ken(neth Martin)

Ross, J. H.
See Lawrence, T(homas) E(dward)

Ross, (James) Sinclair 1908-....... **CLC 13**
See also CA 73-76; DLB 88

Rossetti, Christina (Georgina)
1830-1894 .... **NCLC 2**
See also DLB 35; MAICYA; SATA 20;
WLC

Rossetti, Dante Gabriel
1828-1882 .... **NCLC 4**
See also CDBLB 1832-1890; DLB 35; WLC

Rossner, Judith (Perelman)
1935- .... **CLC 6, 9, 29**
See also AITN 2; BEST 90:3; CA 17-20R;
CANR 18; DLB 6; MTCW

Rostand, Edmond (Eugene Alexis)
1868-1918 .... **TCLC 6, 37**
See also CA 104; 126; MTCW

Roth, Henry 1906-............ **CLC 2, 6, 11**
See also CA 11-12; CANR 38; CAP 1;
DLB 28; MTCW

Roth, Joseph 1894-1939......... **TCLC 33**
See also DLB 85

Roth, Philip (Milton)
1933- ...... **CLC 1, 2, 3, 4, 6, 9, 15, 22,
31, 47, 66**
See also BEST 90:3; CA 1-4R; CANR 1, 22,
36; CDALB 1968-1988; DLB 2, 28;
DLBY 82; MTCW; WLC

Rothenberg, Jerome 1931-....... **CLC 6, 57**
See also CA 45-48; CANR 1; DLB 5

Roumain, Jacques (Jean Baptiste)
1907-1944 .... **TCLC 19**
See also BLC 3; BW; CA 117; 125

Rourke, Constance (Mayfield)
1885-1941 .... **TCLC 12**
See also CA 107; YABC 1

Rousseau, Jean-Baptiste 1671-1741 ... **LC 9**

Rousseau, Jean-Jacques 1712-1778... **LC 14**
See also WLC

Roussel, Raymond 1877-1933 ..... **TCLC 20**
See also CA 117

Rovit, Earl (Herbert) 1927-......... **CLC 7**
See also CA 5-8R; CANR 12

Rowe, Nicholas 1674-1718.......... **LC 8**
See also DLB 84

Rowley, Ames Dorrance
See Lovecraft, H(oward) P(hillips)

Rowson, Susanna Haswell
1762(?)-1824 .... **NCLC 5**
See also DLB 37

Sansom, William 1912-1976. . . . . . **CLC 2, 6**
See also CA 5-8R; 65-68; MTCW

Santayana, George 1863-1952 . . . . . **TCLC 40**
See also CA 115; DLB 54, 71

Santiago, Danny . . . . **CLC 33**
See also James, Daniel (Lewis)

Santmyer, Helen Hooven
1895-1986 . . . . **CLC 33**
See also CA 1-4R; 118; CANR 15, 33;
DLBY 84; MTCW

Santos, Bienvenido N(uqui) 1911- . . . **CLC 22**
See also CA 101; CANR 19

Sapper . . . . **TCLC 44**
See also McNeile, Herman Cyril

Sappho fl. 6th cent. B.C. . . . . **CMLC 3; PC 5**

Sarduy, Severo 1937- . . . . **CLC 6**
See also CA 89-92; DLB 113; HW

Sargeson, Frank 1903-1982 . . . . **CLC 31**
See also CA 25-28R; 106; CANR 38

Sarmiento, Felix Ruben Garcia 1867-1916
See Dario, Ruben
See also CA 104

Saroyan, William
1908-1981 . . . . . **CLC 1, 8, 10, 29, 34, 56**
See also CA 5-8R; 103; CANR 30; DLB 7,
9, 86; DLBY 81; MTCW; SATA 23, 24;
WLC

Sarraute, Nathalie
1900- . . . . **CLC 1, 2, 4, 8, 10, 31**
See also CA 9-12R; CANR 23; DLB 83;
MTCW

Sarton, (Eleanor) May
1912- . . . . **CLC 4, 14, 49**
See also CA 1-4R; CANR 1, 34; DLB 48;
DLBY 81; MTCW; SATA 36

Sartre, Jean-Paul
1905-1980 . . . **CLC 1, 4, 7, 9, 13, 18, 24,**
44, 50, 52
See also CA 9-12R; 97-100; CANR 21;
DLB 72; MTCW; WLC

Sassoon, Siegfried (Lorraine)
1886-1967 . . . . **CLC 36**
See also CA 104; 25-28R; CANR 36;
DLB 20; MTCW

Satterfield, Charles
See Pohl, Frederik

Saul, John (W. III) 1942- . . . . **CLC 46**
See also BEST 90:4; CA 81-84; CANR 16

Saunders, Caleb
See Heinlein, Robert A(nson)

Saura (Atares), Carlos 1932- . . . . **CLC 20**
See also CA 114; 131; HW

Sauser-Hall, Frederic 1887-1961 . . . . **CLC 18**
See also CA 102; 93-96; CANR 36; MTCW

Savage, Catharine
See Brosman, Catharine Savage

Savage, Thomas 1915- . . . . **CLC 40**
See also CA 126; 132; CAAS 15

Savan, Glenn . . . . **CLC 50**

Saven, Glenn 19(?)- . . . . **CLC 50**

Sayers, Dorothy L(eigh)
1893-1957 . . . . **TCLC 2, 15**
See also CA 104; 119; CDBLB 1914-1945;
DLB 10, 36, 77, 100; MTCW

Sayers, Valerie 1952- . . . . **CLC 50**
See also CA 134

Sayles, John Thomas 1950- . . . **CLC 7, 10, 14**
See also CA 57-60; DLB 44

Scammell, Michael . . . . **CLC 34**

Scannell, Vernon 1922- . . . . **CLC 49**
See also CA 5-8R; CANR 8, 24; DLB 27;
SATA 59

Scarlett, Susan
See Streatfeild, (Mary) Noel

Schaeffer, Susan Fromberg
1941- . . . . **CLC 6, 11, 22**
See also CA 49-52; CANR 18; DLB 28;
MTCW; SATA 22

Schary, Jill
See Robinson, Jill

Schell, Jonathan 1943- . . . . **CLC 35**
See also CA 73-76; CANR 12

Schelling, Friedrich Wilhelm Joseph von
1775-1854 . . . . **NCLC 30**
See also DLB 90

Scherer, Jean-Marie Maurice 1920-
See Rohmer, Eric
See also CA 110

Schevill, James (Erwin) 1920- . . . . . . **CLC 7**
See also CA 5-8R; CAAS 12

Schisgal, Murray (Joseph) 1926- . . . . . **CLC 6**
See also CA 21-24R

Schlee, Ann 1934- . . . . **CLC 35**
See also CA 101; CANR 29; SATA 36, 44

Schlegel, August Wilhelm von
1767-1845 . . . . **NCLC 15**
See also DLB 94

Schlegel, Johann Elias (von)
1719(?)-1749 . . . . **LC 5**

Schmidt, Arno (Otto) 1914-1979 . . . . **CLC 56**
See also CA 128; 109; DLB 69

Schmitz, Aron Hector 1861-1928
See Svevo, Italo
See also CA 104; 122; MTCW

Schnackenberg, Gjertrud 1953- . . . . . **CLC 40**
See also CA 116; DLB 120

Schneider, Leonard Alfred 1925-1966
See Bruce, Lenny
See also CA 89-92

Schnitzler, Arthur 1862-1931 . . . . . . **TCLC 4**
See also CA 104; DLB 81, 118

Schor, Sandra (M.) 1932(?)-1990 . . . **CLC 65**
See also CA 132

Schorer, Mark 1908-1977 . . . . **CLC 9**
See also CA 5-8R; 73-76; CANR 7;
DLB 103

Schrader, Paul Joseph 1946- . . . . **CLC 26**
See also CA 37-40R; DLB 44

Schreiner, Olive (Emilie Albertina)
1855-1920 . . . . **TCLC 9**
See also CA 105; DLB 18

Schulberg, Budd (Wilson)
1914- . . . . **CLC 7, 48**
See also CA 25-28R; CANR 19; DLB 6, 26,
28; DLBY 81

Schulz, Bruno 1892-1942 . . . . **TCLC 5**
See also CA 115; 123

Schulz, Charles M(onroe) 1922- . . . . **CLC 12**
See also CA 9-12R; CANR 6; SATA 10

Schuyler, James Marcus
1923-1991 . . . . **CLC 5, 23**
See also CA 101; 134; DLB 5

Schwartz, Delmore (David)
1913-1966 . . . . **CLC 2, 4, 10, 45**
See also CA 17-18; 25-28R; CANR 35;
CAP 2; DLB 28, 48; MTCW

Schwartz, Ernst
See Ozu, Yasujiro

Schwartz, John Burnham 1965- . . . . **CLC 59**
See also CA 132

Schwartz, Lynne Sharon 1939- . . . . . **CLC 31**
See also CA 103

Schwartz, Muriel A.
See Eliot, T(homas) S(tearns)

Schwarz-Bart, Andre 1928- . . . . **CLC 2, 4**
See also CA 89-92

Schwarz-Bart, Simone 1938- . . . . **CLC 7**
See also CA 97-100

Schwob, (Mayer Andre) Marcel
1867-1905 . . . . **TCLC 20**
See also CA 117

Sciascia, Leonardo
1921-1989 . . . . **CLC 8, 9, 41**
See also CA 85-88; 130; CANR 35; MTCW

Scoppettone, Sandra 1936- . . . . **CLC 26**
See also CA 5-8R; SATA 9

Scorsese, Martin 1942- . . . . **CLC 20**
See also CA 110; 114

Scotland, Jay
See Jakes, John (William)

Scott, Duncan Campbell
1862-1947 . . . . **TCLC 6**
See also CA 104; DLB 92

Scott, Evelyn 1893-1963 . . . . **CLC 43**
See also CA 104; 112; DLB 9, 48

Scott, F(rancis) R(eginald)
1899-1985 . . . . **CLC 22**
See also CA 101; 114; DLB 88

Scott, Frank
See Scott, F(rancis) R(eginald)

Scott, Joanna 1960- . . . . **CLC 50**
See also CA 126

Scott, Paul (Mark) 1920-1978 . . . . **CLC 9, 60**
See also CA 81-84; 77-80; CANR 33;
DLB 14; MTCW

Scott, Walter 1771-1832 . . . . **NCLC 15**
See also CDBLB 1789-1832; DLB 93, 107,
116; WLC; YABC 2

Scribe, (Augustin) Eugene
1791-1861 . . . . **NCLC 16**

Scrum, R.
See Crumb, R(obert)

Scudery, Madeleine de 1607-1701 . . . . . **LC 2**

Scum
See Crumb, R(obert)

Scumbag, Little Bobby
See Crumb, R(obert)

Seabrook, John
See Hubbard, L(afayette) Ron(ald)

Sealy, I. Allan 1951- . . . . **CLC 55**

Shiel, M(atthew) P(hipps)
    1865-1947 .... **TCLC 8**
    See also CA 106

Shiga, Naoya 1883-1971.......... **CLC 33**
    See also CA 101; 33-36R

Shimazaki Haruki 1872-1943
    See Shimazaki Toson
    See also CA 105; 134

Shimazaki Toson................. **TCLC 5**
    See also Shimazaki Haruki

Sholokhov, Mikhail (Aleksandrovich)
    1905-1984 .... **CLC 7, 15**
    See also CA 101; 112; MTCW; SATA 36

Shone, Patric
    See Hanley, James

Shreve, Susan Richards 1939-...... **CLC 23**
    See also CA 49-52; CAAS 5; CANR 5, 38;
    MAICYA; SATA 41, 46

Shue, Larry 1946-1985............ **CLC 52**
    See also CA 117

Shu-Jen, Chou 1881-1936
    See Hsun, Lu
    See also CA 104

Shulman, Alix Kates 1932- ...... **CLC 2, 10**
    See also CA 29-32R; SATA 7

Shuster, Joe 1914- .... **CLC 21**

Shute, Nevil..................... **CLC 30**
    See also Norway, Nevil Shute

Shuttle, Penelope (Diane) 1947- ..... **CLC 7**
    See also CA 93-96; CANR 39; DLB 14, 40

Sidney, Mary 1561-1621 .... **LC 19**

Sidney, Sir Philip 1554-1586....... **LC 19**
    See also CDBLB Before 1660

Siegel, Jerome 1914- .... **CLC 21**
    See also CA 116

Siegel, Jerry
    See Siegel, Jerome

Sienkiewicz, Henryk (Adam Alexander Pius)
    1846-1916 .... **TCLC 3**
    See also CA 104; 134

Sierra, Gregorio Martinez
    See Martinez Sierra, Gregorio

Sierra, Maria (de la O'LeJarraga) Martinez
    See Martinez Sierra, Maria (de la
    O'LeJarraga)

Sigal, Clancy 1926-............... **CLC 7**
    See also CA 1-4R

Sigourney, Lydia Howard (Huntley)
    1791-1865 .... **NCLC 21**
    See also DLB 1, 42, 73

Siguenza y Gongora, Carlos de
    1645-1700 .... **LC 8**

Sigurjonsson, Johann 1880-1919... **TCLC 27**

Sikelianos, Angelos 1884-1951 .... **TCLC 39**

Silkin, Jon 1930- .... **CLC 2, 6, 43**
    See also CA 5-8R; CAAS 5; DLB 27

Silko, Leslie Marmon 1948- .... **CLC 23, 74**
    See also CA 115; 122

Sillanpaa, Frans Eemil 1888-1964... **CLC 19**
    See also CA 129; 93-96; MTCW

Sillitoe, Alan
    1928- .... **CLC 1, 3, 6, 10, 19, 57**
    See also AITN 1; CA 9-12R; CAAS 2;
    CANR 8, 26; CDBLB 1960 to Present;
    DLB 14; MTCW; SATA 61

Silone, Ignazio 1900-1978 .... **CLC 4**
    See also CA 25-28; 81-84; CANR 34;
    CAP 2; MTCW

Silver, Joan Micklin 1935- .... **CLC 20**
    See also CA 114; 121

Silverberg, Robert 1935- .... **CLC 7**
    See also CA 1-4R; CAAS 3; CANR 1, 20,
    36; DLB 8; MAICYA; MTCW; SATA 13

Silverstein, Alvin 1933- .... **CLC 17**
    See also CA 49-52; CANR 2; CLR 25;
    MAICYA; SATA 8, 69

Silverstein, Virginia B(arbara Opshelor)
    1937- .... **CLC 17**
    See also CA 49-52; CANR 2; CLR 25;
    MAICYA; SATA 8, 69

Sim, Georges
    See Simenon, Georges (Jacques Christian)

Simak, Clifford D(onald)
    1904-1988 .... **CLC 1, 55**
    See also CA 1-4R; 125; CANR 1, 35;
    DLB 8; MTCW; SATA 56

Simenon, Georges (Jacques Christian)
    1903-1989 ...... **CLC 1, 2, 3, 8, 18, 47**
    See also CA 85-88; 129; CANR 35;
    DLB 72; DLBY 89; MTCW

Simic, Charles 1938-... **CLC 6, 9, 22, 49, 68**
    See also CA 29-32R; CAAS 4; CANR 12,
    33; DLB 105

Simmons, Charles (Paul) 1924- ..... **CLC 57**
    See also CA 89-92

Simmons, Dan..................... **CLC 44**
    See also CA 138

Simmons, James (Stewart Alexander)
    1933- .... **CLC 43**
    See also CA 105; DLB 40

Simms, William Gilmore
    1806-1870 .... **NCLC 3**
    See also DLB 3, 30, 59, 73

Simon, Carly 1945-............... **CLC 26**
    See also CA 105

Simon, Claude 1913-....... **CLC 4, 9, 15, 39**
    See also CA 89-92; CANR 33; DLB 83;
    MTCW

Simon, (Marvin) Neil
    1927- .... **CLC 6, 11, 31, 39, 70**
    See also AITN 1; CA 21-24R; CANR 26;
    DLB 7; MTCW

Simon, Paul 1942(?)- .... **CLC 17**
    See also CA 116

Simonon, Paul 1956(?)- .... **CLC 30**
    See also The Clash

Simpson, Harriette
    See Arnow, Harriette (Louisa) Simpson

Simpson, Louis (Aston Marantz)
    1923- .... **CLC 4, 7, 9, 32**
    See also CA 1-4R; CAAS 4; CANR 1;
    DLB 5; MTCW

Simpson, Mona (Elizabeth) 1957-... **CLC 44**
    See also CA 122; 135

Simpson, N(orman) F(rederick)
    1919- .... **CLC 29**
    See also CA 13-16R; DLB 13

Sinclair, Andrew (Annandale)
    1935- .... **CLC 2, 14**
    See also CA 9-12R; CAAS 5; CANR 14, 38;
    DLB 14; MTCW

Sinclair, Emil
    See Hesse, Hermann

Sinclair, Mary Amelia St. Clair 1865(?)-1946
    See Sinclair, May
    See also CA 104

Sinclair, May................. **TCLC 3, 11**
    See also Sinclair, Mary Amelia St. Clair
    See also DLB 36

Sinclair, Upton (Beall)
    1878-1968 .... **CLC 1, 11, 15, 63**
    See also CA 5-8R; 25-28R; CANR 7;
    CDALB 1929-1941; DLB 9; MTCW;
    SATA 9; WLC

Singer, Isaac
    See Singer, Isaac Bashevis

Singer, Isaac Bashevis
    1904-1991 ... **CLC 1, 3, 6, 9, 11, 15, 23,
    38, 69; SSC 3**
    See also AITN 1, 2; CA 1-4R; 134;
    CANR 1, 39; CDALB 1941-1968; CLR 1;
    DLB 6, 28, 52; DLBY 91; MAICYA;
    MTCW; SATA 3, 27; SATO 68; WLC

Singer, Israel Joshua 1893-1944 ... **TCLC 33**

Singh, Khushwant 1915-........... **CLC 11**
    See also CA 9-12R; CAAS 9; CANR 6

Sinjohn, John
    See Galsworthy, John

Sinyavsky, Andrei (Donatevich)
    1925- .... **CLC 8**
    See also CA 85-88

Sirin, V.
    See Nabokov, Vladimir (Vladimirovich)

Sissman, L(ouis) E(dward)
    1928-1976 .... **CLC 9, 18**
    See also CA 21-24R; 65-68; CANR 13;
    DLB 5

Sisson, C(harles) H(ubert) 1914-..... **CLC 8**
    See also CA 1-4R; CAAS 3; CANR 3;
    DLB 27

Sitwell, Dame Edith
    1887-1964 .... **CLC 2, 9, 67; PC 3**
    See also CA 9-12R; CANR 35;
    CDBLB 1945-1960; DLB 20; MTCW

Sjoewall, Maj 1935-............... **CLC 7**
    See also CA 65-68

Sjowall, Maj
    See Sjoewall, Maj

Skelton, Robin 1925- .... **CLC 13**
    See also AITN 2; CA 5-8R; CAAS 5;
    CANR 28; DLB 27, 53

Skolimowski, Jerzy 1938- .... **CLC 20**
    See also CA 128

Skram, Amalie (Bertha)
    1847-1905 .... **TCLC 25**

Skvorecky, Josef (Vaclav)
    1924- .... **CLC 15, 39, 69**
    See also CA 61-64; CAAS 1; CANR 10, 34;
    MTCW

Spengler, Oswald (Arnold Gottfried)
1880-1936 .... **TCLC 25**
See also CA 118

Spenser, Edmund 1552(?)-1599 ...... **LC 5**
See also CDBLB Before 1660; WLC

Spicer, Jack 1925-1965 ...... **CLC 8, 18, 72**
See also CA 85-88; DLB 5, 16

Spielberg, Peter 1929- .... **CLC 6**
See also CA 5-8R; CANR 4; DLBY 81

Spielberg, Steven 1947- .... **CLC 20**
See also AAYA 8; CA 77-80; CANR 32;
SATA 32

Spillane, Frank Morrison 1918-
See Spillane, Mickey
See also CA 25-28R; CANR 28; MTCW;
SATA 66

Spillane, Mickey .... **CLC 3, 13**
See also Spillane, Frank Morrison

Spinoza, Benedictus de 1632-1677 .... **LC 9**

Spinrad, Norman (Richard) 1940-... **CLC 46**
See also CA 37-40R; CANR 20; DLB 8

Spitteler, Carl (Friedrich Georg)
1845-1924 .... **TCLC 12**
See also CA 109

Spivack, Kathleen (Romola Drucker)
1938- .... **CLC 6**
See also CA 49-52

Spoto, Donald 1941- .... **CLC 39**
See also CA 65-68; CANR 11

Springsteen, Bruce (F.) 1949- ...... **CLC 17**
See also CA 111

Spurling, Hilary 1940- .... **CLC 34**
See also CA 104; CANR 25

Squires, Radcliffe 1917- .... **CLC 51**
See also CA 1-4R; CANR 6, 21

Srivastava, Dhanpat Rai 1880(?)-1936
See Premchand
See also CA 118

Stacy, Donald
See Pohl, Frederik

Stael, Germaine de
See Stael-Holstein, Anne Louise Germaine
Necker Baronn
See also DLB 119

Stael-Holstein, Anne Louise Germaine Necker
Baronn 1766-1817 .... **NCLC 3**
See also Stael, Germaine de

Stafford, Jean 1915-1979 ... **CLC 4, 7, 19, 68**
See also CA 1-4R; 85-88; CANR 3; DLB 2;
MTCW; SATA 22

Stafford, William (Edgar)
1914- .... **CLC 4, 7, 29**
See also CA 5-8R; CAAS 3; CANR 5, 22;
DLB 5

Staines, Trevor
See Brunner, John (Kilian Houston)

Stairs, Gordon
See Austin, Mary (Hunter)

Stannard, Martin .... **CLC 44**

Stanton, Maura 1946- .... **CLC 9**
See also CA 89-92; CANR 15; DLB 120

Stanton, Schuyler
See Baum, L(yman) Frank

Stapledon, (William) Olaf
1886-1950 .... **TCLC 22**
See also CA 111; DLB 15

Starbuck, George (Edwin) 1931-... **CLC 53**
See also CA 21-24R; CANR 23

Stark, Richard
See Westlake, Donald E(dwin)

Staunton, Schuyler
See Baum, L(yman) Frank

Stead, Christina (Ellen)
1902-1983 .... **CLC 2, 5, 8, 32**
See also CA 13-16R; 109; CANR 33;
MTCW

Steele, Richard 1672-1729 .... **LC 18**
See also CDBLB 1660-1789; DLB 84, 101

Steele, Timothy (Reid) 1948- ...... **CLC 45**
See also CA 93-96; CANR 16; DLB 120

Steffens, (Joseph) Lincoln
1866-1936 .... **TCLC 20**
See also CA 117

Stegner, Wallace (Earle) 1909- ... **CLC 9, 49**
See also AITN 1; BEST 90:3; CA 1-4R;
CAAS 9; CANR 1, 21; DLB 9; MTCW

Stein, Gertrude 1874-1946 ... **TCLC 1, 6, 28**
See also CA 104; 132; CDALB 1917-1929;
DLB 4, 54, 86; MTCW; WLC

Steinbeck, John (Ernst)
1902-1968 ..... **CLC 1, 5, 9, 13, 21, 34,**
45; SSC 11
See also CA 1-4R; 25-28R; CANR 1, 35;
CDALB 1929-1941; DLB 7, 9; DLBD 2;
MTCW; SATA 9; WLC

Steinem, Gloria 1934- .... **CLC 63**
See also CA 53-56; CANR 28; MTCW

Steiner, George 1929- .... **CLC 24**
See also CA 73-76; CANR 31; DLB 67;
MTCW; SATA 62

Steiner, Rudolf 1861-1925 .... **TCLC 13**
See also CA 107

Stendhal 1783-1842 .... **NCLC 23**
See also DLB 119; WLC

Stephen, Leslie 1832-1904 .... **TCLC 23**
See also CA 123; DLB 57

Stephen, Sir Leslie
See Stephen, Leslie

Stephen, Virginia
See Woolf, (Adeline) Virginia

Stephens, James 1882(?)-1950 ...... **TCLC 4**
See also CA 104; DLB 19

Stephens, Reed
See Donaldson, Stephen R.

Steptoe, Lydia
See Barnes, Djuna

Sterchi, Beat 1949- .... **CLC 65**

Sterling, Brett
See Bradbury, Ray (Douglas); Hamilton,
Edmond

Sterling, Bruce 1954- .... **CLC 72**
See also CA 119

Sterling, George 1869-1926 .... **TCLC 20**
See also CA 117; DLB 54

Stern, Gerald 1925- .... **CLC 40**
See also CA 81-84; CANR 28; DLB 105

Stern, Richard (Gustave) 1928-... **CLC 4, 39**
See also CA 1-4R; CANR 1, 25; DLBY 87

Sternberg, Josef von 1894-1969..... **CLC 20**
See also CA 81-84

Sterne, Laurence 1713-1768......... **LC 2**
See also CDBLB 1660-1789; DLB 39; WLC

Sternheim, (William Adolf) Carl
1878-1942 .... **TCLC 8**
See also CA 105; DLB 56, 118

Stevens, Mark 1951- .... **CLC 34**
See also CA 122

Stevens, Wallace
1879-1955 .... **TCLC 3, 12, 45**
See also CA 104; 124; CDALB 1929-1941;
DLB 54; MTCW; WLC

Stevenson, Anne (Katharine)
1933- .... **CLC 7, 33**
See also CA 17-20R; CAAS 9; CANR 9, 33;
DLB 40; MTCW

Stevenson, Robert Louis (Balfour)
1850-1894 .... **NCLC 5, 14; SSC 11**
See also CDBLB 1890-1914; CLR 10, 11;
DLB 18, 57; MAICYA; WLC; YABC 2

Stewart, J(ohn) I(nnes) M(ackintosh)
1906- .... **CLC 7, 14, 32**
See also CA 85-88; CAAS 3; MTCW

Stewart, Mary (Florence Elinor)
1916- .... **CLC 7, 35**
See also CA 1-4R; CANR 1; SATA 12

Stewart, Mary Rainbow
See Stewart, Mary (Florence Elinor)

Still, James 1906- .... **CLC 49**
See also CA 65-68; CANR 10, 26; DLB 9;
SATA 29

Sting
See Sumner, Gordon Matthew

Stirling, Arthur
See Sinclair, Upton (Beall)

Stitt, Milan 1941- .... **CLC 29**
See also CA 69-72

Stockton, Francis Richard 1834-1902
See Stockton, Frank R.
See also CA 108; 137; MAICYA; SATA 44

Stockton, Frank R. .... **TCLC 47**
See also Stockton, Francis Richard
See also DLB 42, 74; SATA 32

Stoddard, Charles
See Kuttner, Henry

Stoker, Abraham 1847-1912
See Stoker, Bram
See also CA 105; SATA 29

Stoker, Bram .... **TCLC 8**
See also Stoker, Abraham
See also CDBLB 1890-1914; DLB 36, 70;
WLC

Stolz, Mary (Slattery) 1920- .... **CLC 12**
See also AAYA 8; AITN 1; CA 5-8R;
CANR 13; MAICYA; SAAS 3;
SATA 10, 70, 71

Stone, Irving 1903-1989........... **CLC 7**
See also AITN 1; CA 1-4R; 129; CAAS 3;
CANR 1, 23; MTCW; SATA 3; SATO 64

Stone, Robert (Anthony)
1937- .... **CLC 5, 23, 42**
See also CA 85-88; CANR 23; MTCW

Stone, Zachary
  See Follett, Ken(neth Martin)

Stoppard, Tom
  1937- ... **CLC 1, 3, 4, 5, 8, 15, 29, 34, 63**
  See also CA 81-84; CANR 39;
  CDBLB 1960 to Present; DLB 13;
  DLBY 85; MTCW; WLC

Storey, David (Malcolm)
  1933- .... **CLC 2, 4, 5, 8**
  See also CA 81-84; CANR 36; DLB 13, 14;
  MTCW

Storm, Hyemeyohsts 1935- .... **CLC 3**
  See also CA 81-84

Storm, (Hans) Theodor (Woldsen)
  1817-1888 .... **NCLC 1**

Storni, Alfonsina 1892-1938 .... **TCLC 5**
  See also CA 104; 131; HW

Stout, Rex (Todhunter) 1886-1975 ... **CLC 3**
  See also AITN 2; CA 61-64

Stow, (Julian) Randolph 1935- .. **CLC 23, 48**
  See also CA 13-16R; CANR 33; MTCW

Stowe, Harriet (Elizabeth) Beecher
  1811-1896 .... **NCLC 3**
  See also CDALB 1865-1917; DLB 1, 12, 42,
  74; MAICYA; WLC; YABC 1

Strachey, (Giles) Lytton
  1880-1932 .... **TCLC 12**
  See also CA 110

Strand, Mark 1934- ...... **CLC 6, 18, 41, 71**
  See also CA 21-24R; DLB 5; SATA 41

Straub, Peter (Francis) 1943- .... **CLC 28**
  See also BEST 89:1; CA 85-88; CANR 28;
  DLBY 84; MTCW

Strauss, Botho 1944- .... **CLC 22**

Streatfeild, (Mary) Noel
  1895(?)-1986 .... **CLC 21**
  See also CA 81-84; 120; CANR 31;
  CLR 17; MAICYA; SATA 20, 48

Stribling, T(homas) S(igismund)
  1881-1965 .... **CLC 23**
  See also CA 107; DLB 9

Strindberg, (Johan) August
  1849-1912 .... **TCLC 1, 8, 21, 47**
  See also CA 104; 135; WLC

Stringer, Arthur 1874-1950 ...... **TCLC 37**
  See also DLB 92

Stringer, David
  See Roberts, Keith (John Kingston)

Strugatskii, Arkadii (Natanovich)
  1925-1991 .... **CLC 27**
  See also CA 106; 135

Strugatskii, Boris (Natanovich)
  1933- .... **CLC 27**
  See also CA 106

Strummer, Joe 1953(?)- .... **CLC 30**
  See also The Clash

Stuart, Don A.
  See Campbell, John W(ood Jr.)

Stuart, Ian
  See MacLean, Alistair (Stuart)

Stuart, Jesse (Hilton)
  1906-1984 .... **CLC 1, 8, 11, 14, 34**
  See also CA 5-8R; 112; CANR 31; DLB 9,
  48, 102; DLBY 84; SATA 2, 36

Sturgeon, Theodore (Hamilton)
  1918-1985 .... **CLC 22, 39**
  See also Queen, Ellery
  See also CA 81-84; 116; CANR 32; DLB 8;
  DLBY 85; MTCW

Styron, William
  1925- .... **CLC 1, 3, 5, 11, 15, 60**
  See also BEST 90:4; CA 5-8R; CANR 6, 33;
  CDALB 1968-1988; DLB 2; DLBY 80;
  MTCW

Suarez Lynch, B.
  See Borges, Jorge Luis

Suarez Lynch, B.
  See Bioy Casares, Adolfo; Borges, Jorge
  Luis

Su Chien 1884-1918
  See Su Man-shu
  See also CA 123

Sudermann, Hermann 1857-1928 .. **TCLC 15**
  See also CA 107; DLB 118

Sue, Eugene 1804-1857 .... **NCLC 1**
  See also DLB 119

Sueskind, Patrick 1949- .... **CLC 44**

Sukenick, Ronald 1932- ..... **CLC 3, 4, 6, 48**
  See also CA 25-28R; CAAS 8; CANR 32;
  DLBY 81

Suknaski, Andrew 1942- .... **CLC 19**
  See also CA 101; DLB 53

Sullivan, Vernon
  See Vian, Boris

Sully Prudhomme 1839-1907 ...... **TCLC 31**

Su Man-shu .... **TCLC 24**
  See also Su Chien

Summerforest, Ivy B.
  See Kirkup, James

Summers, Andrew James 1942- ..... **CLC 26**
  See also The Police

Summers, Andy
  See Summers, Andrew James

Summers, Hollis (Spurgeon Jr.)
  1916- .... **CLC 10**
  See also CA 5-8R; CANR 3; DLB 6

Summers, (Alphonsus Joseph-Mary Augustus)
  Montague 1880-1948 .... **TCLC 16**
  See also CA 118

Sumner, Gordon Matthew 1951-.... **CLC 26**
  See also The Police

Surtees, Robert Smith
  1803-1864 .... **NCLC 14**
  See also DLB 21

Susann, Jacqueline 1921-1974....... **CLC 3**
  See also AITN 1; CA 65-68; 53-56; MTCW

Suskind, Patrick
  See Sueskind, Patrick

Sutcliff, Rosemary 1920- .... **CLC 26**
  See also CA 5-8R; CANR 37; CLR 1;
  MAICYA; SATA 6, 44

Sutro, Alfred 1863-1933.......... **TCLC 6**
  See also CA 105; DLB 10

Sutton, Henry
  See Slavitt, David R.

Svevo, Italo .... **TCLC 2, 35**
  See also Schmitz, Aron Hector

Swados, Elizabeth 1951- .... **CLC 12**
  See also CA 97-100

Swados, Harvey 1920-1972 .... **CLC 5**
  See also CA 5-8R; 37-40R; CANR 6;
  DLB 2

Swan, Gladys 1934- .... **CLC 69**
  See also CA 101; CANR 17, 39

Swarthout, Glendon (Fred) 1918- ... **CLC 35**
  See also CA 1-4R; CANR 1; SATA 26

Sweet, Sarah C.
  See Jewett, (Theodora) Sarah Orne

Swenson, May 1919-1989..... **CLC 4, 14, 61**
  See also CA 5-8R; 130; CANR 36; DLB 5;
  MTCW; SATA 15

Swift, Augustus
  See Lovecraft, H(oward) P(hillips)

Swift, Graham 1949- .... **CLC 41**
  See also CA 117; 122

Swift, Jonathan 1667-1745.......... **LC 1**
  See also CDBLB 1660-1789; DLB 39, 95,
  101; SATA 19; WLC

Swinburne, Algernon Charles
  1837-1909 .... **TCLC 8, 36**
  See also CA 105; CDBLB 1832-1890;
  DLB 35, 57; WLC

Swinfen, Ann .... **CLC 34**

Swinnerton, Frank Arthur
  1884-1982 .... **CLC 31**
  See also CA 108; DLB 34

Swithen, John
  See King, Stephen (Edwin)

Sylvia
  See Ashton-Warner, Sylvia (Constance)

Symmes, Robert Edward
  See Duncan, Robert (Edward)

Symonds, John Addington
  1840-1893 .... **NCLC 34**
  See also DLB 57

Symons, Arthur 1865-1945 .... **TCLC 11**
  See also CA 107; DLB 19, 57

Symons, Julian (Gustave)
  1912- .... **CLC 2, 14, 32**
  See also CA 49-52; CAAS 3; CANR 3, 33;
  DLB 87; MTCW

Synge, (Edmund) J(ohn) M(illington)
  1871-1909 .... **TCLC 6, 37; DC 2**
  See also CA 104; CDBLB 1890-1914;
  DLB 10, 19

Syruc, J.
  See Milosz, Czeslaw

Szirtes, George 1948- .... **CLC 46**
  See also CA 109; CANR 27

Tabori, George 1914- .... **CLC 19**
  See also CA 49-52; CANR 4

Tagore, Rabindranath 1861-1941.... **TCLC 3**
  See also CA 104; 120; MTCW

Taine, Hippolyte Adolphe
  1828-1893 .... **NCLC 15**

Talese, Gay 1932-................ **CLC 37**
  See also AITN 1; CA 1-4R; CANR 9;
  MTCW

Tallent, Elizabeth (Ann) 1954- ..... **CLC 45**
  See also CA 117

Thurber, James (Grover)
1894-1961 ...... **CLC 5, 11, 25; SSC 1**
See also CA 73-76; CANR 17, 39;
CDALB 1929-1941; DLB 4, 11, 22, 102;
MAICYA; MTCW; SATA 13

Thurman, Wallace (Henry)
1902-1934 .... **TCLC 6**
See also BLC 3; BW; CA 104; 124; DLB 51

Ticheburn, Cheviot
See Ainsworth, William Harrison

Tieck, (Johann) Ludwig
1773-1853 .... **NCLC 5**
See also DLB 90

Tiger, Derry
See Ellison, Harlan

Tilghman, Christopher 1948(?)-..... **CLC 65**

Tillinghast, Richard (Williford)
1940- .... **CLC 29**
See also CA 29-32R; CANR 26

Timrod, Henry 1828-1867 .... **NCLC 25**
See also DLB 3

Tindall, Gillian 1938-.............. **CLC 7**
See also CA 21-24R; CANR 11

Tiptree, James Jr............... **CLC 48, 50**
See also Sheldon, Alice Hastings Bradley
See also DLB 8

Titmarsh, Michael Angelo
See Thackeray, William Makepeace

**Tocqueville, Alexis (Charles Henri Maurice
Clerel Comte)** 1805-1859..... **NCLC 7**

Tolkien, J(ohn) R(onald) R(euel)
1892-1973 .... **CLC 1, 2, 3, 8, 12, 38**
See also AITN 1; CA 17-18; 45-48;
CANR 36; CAP 2; CDBLB 1914-1945;
DLB 15; MAICYA; MTCW; SATA 2,
24, 32; WLC

Toller, Ernst 1893-1939 .... **TCLC 10**
See also CA 107

Tolson, M. B.
See Tolson, Melvin B(eaunorus)

Tolson, Melvin B(eaunorus)
1898(?)-1966 .... **CLC 36**
See also BLC 3; BW; CA 124; 89-92;
DLB 48, 76

Tolstoi, Aleksei Nikolaevich
See Tolstoy, Alexey Nikolaevich

Tolstoy, Alexey Nikolaevich
1882-1945 .... **TCLC 18**
See also CA 107

Tolstoy, Count Leo
See Tolstoy, Leo (Nikolaevich)

Tolstoy, Leo (Nikolaevich)
1828-1910 ..... **TCLC 4, 11, 17, 28, 44;
SSC 9**
See also CA 104; 123; SATA 26; WLC

Tomasi di Lampedusa, Giuseppe 1896-1957
See Lampedusa, Giuseppe (Tomasi) di
See also CA 111

Tomlin, Lily.................... **CLC 17**
See also Tomlin, Mary Jean

Tomlin, Mary Jean 1939(?)-
See Tomlin, Lily
See also CA 117

Tomlinson, (Alfred) Charles
1927- .... **CLC 2, 4, 6, 13, 45**
See also CA 5-8R; CANR 33; DLB 40

Tonson, Jacob
See Bennett, (Enoch) Arnold

Toole, John Kennedy
1937-1969 .... **CLC 19, 64**
See also CA 104; DLBY 81

Toomer, Jean
1894-1967 ..... **CLC 1, 4, 13, 22; SSC 1**
See also BLC 3; BW; CA 85-88;
CDALB 1917-1929; DLB 45, 51; MTCW

Torley, Luke
See Blish, James (Benjamin)

Tornimparte, Alessandra
See Ginzburg, Natalia

Torre, Raoul della
See Mencken, H(enry) L(ouis)

Torrey, E(dwin) Fuller 1937-....... **CLC 34**
See also CA 119

Torsvan, Ben Traven
See Traven, B.

Torsvan, Benno Traven
See Traven, B.

Torsvan, Berick Traven
See Traven, B.

Torsvan, Berwick Traven
See Traven, B.

Torsvan, Bruno Traven
See Traven, B.

Torsvan, Traven
See Traven, B.

Tournier, Michel (Edouard)
1924- .... **CLC 6, 23, 36**
See also CA 49-52; CANR 3, 36; DLB 83;
MTCW; SATA 23

Tournimparte, Alessandra
See Ginzburg, Natalia

Towers, Ivar
See Kornbluth, C(yril) M.

Townsend, Sue 1946- .... **CLC 61**
See also CA 119; 127; MTCW; SATA 48,
55

Townshend, Peter (Dennis Blandford)
1945- .... **CLC 17, 42**
See also CA 107

Tozzi, Federigo 1883-1920........ **TCLC 31**

Traill, Catharine Parr
1802-1899 .... **NCLC 31**
See also DLB 99

Trakl, Georg 1887-1914.......... **TCLC 5**
See also CA 104

Transtroemer, Tomas (Goesta)
1931- .... **CLC 52, 65**
See also CA 117; 129

Transtromer, Tomas Gosta
See Transtroemer, Tomas (Goesta)

Traven, B. (?)-1969............. **CLC 8, 11**
See also CA 19-20; 25-28R; CAP 2; DLB 9,
56; MTCW

Treitel, Jonathan 1959- .... **CLC 70**

Tremain, Rose 1943-.............. **CLC 42**
See also CA 97-100; DLB 14

Tremblay, Michel 1942-.......... **CLC 29**
See also CA 116; 128; DLB 60; MTCW

Trevanian (a pseudonym) 1930(?)-... **CLC 29**
See also CA 108

Trevor, Glen
See Hilton, James

Trevor, William
1928- .... **CLC 7, 9, 14, 25, 71**
See also Cox, William Trevor
See also DLB 14

Trifonov, Yuri (Valentinovich)
1925-1981 .... **CLC 45**
See also CA 126; 103; MTCW

Trilling, Lionel 1905-1975 .... **CLC 9, 11, 24**
See also CA 9-12R; 61-64; CANR 10;
DLB 28, 63; MTCW

Trimball, W. H.
See Mencken, H(enry) L(ouis)

Tristan
See Gomez de la Serna, Ramon

Tristram
See Housman, A(lfred) E(dward)

Trogdon, William (Lewis) 1939-
See Heat-Moon, William Least
See also CA 115; 119

Trollope, Anthony 1815-1882 .. **NCLC 6, 33**
See also CDBLB 1832-1890; DLB 21, 57;
SATA 22; WLC

Trollope, Frances 1779-1863 ..... **NCLC 30**
See also DLB 21

Trotsky, Leon 1879-1940........ **TCLC 22**
See also CA 118

Trotter (Cockburn), Catharine
1679-1749 .... **LC 8**
See also DLB 84

Trout, Kilgore
See Farmer, Philip Jose

Trow, George W. S. 1943-........ **CLC 52**
See also CA 126

Troyat, Henri 1911-.............. **CLC 23**
See also CA 45-48; CANR 2, 33; MTCW

Trudeau, G(arretson) B(eekman) 1948-
See Trudeau, Garry B.
See also CA 81-84; CANR 31; SATA 35

Trudeau, Garry B.................. **CLC 12**
See also Trudeau, G(arretson) B(eekman)
See also AITN 2

Truffaut, Francois 1932-1984...... **CLC 20**
See also CA 81-84; 113; CANR 34

Trumbo, Dalton 1905-1976 .... **CLC 19**
See also CA 21-24R; 69-72; CANR 10;
DLB 26

Trumbull, John 1750-1831....... **NCLC 30**
See also DLB 31

Trundlett, Helen B.
See Eliot, T(homas) S(tearns)

Tryon, Thomas 1926-1991 .... **CLC 3, 11**
See also AITN 1; CA 29-32R; 135;
CANR 32; MTCW

Tryon, Tom
See Tryon, Thomas

Ts'ao Hsueh-ch'in 1715(?)-1763....... **LC 1**

Wallace, Irving 1916-1990 . . . . . . **CLC 7, 13**
See also AITN 1; CA 1-4R; 132; CAAS 1;
CANR 1, 27; MTCW

Wallant, Edward Lewis
1926-1962 . . . . **CLC 5, 10**
See also CA 1-4R; CANR 22; DLB 2, 28;
MTCW

Walpole, Horace 1717-1797 . . . . **LC 2**
See also DLB 39, 104

Walpole, Hugh (Seymour)
1884-1941 . . . . **TCLC 5**
See also CA 104; DLB 34

Walser, Martin 1927- . . . . **CLC 27**
See also CA 57-60; CANR 8; DLB 75

Walser, Robert 1878-1956 . . . . **TCLC 18**
See also CA 118; DLB 66

Walsh, Jill Paton . . . . **CLC 35**
See also Paton Walsh, Gillian
See also CLR 2; SAAS 3

Walter, William Christian
See Andersen, Hans Christian

Wambaugh, Joseph (Aloysius Jr.)
1937- . . . . **CLC 3, 18**
See also AITN 1; BEST 89:3; CA 33-36R;
DLB 6; DLBY 83; MTCW

Ward, Arthur Henry Sarsfield 1883-1959
See Rohmer, Sax
See also CA 108

Ward, Douglas Turner 1930- . . . . **CLC 19**
See also BW; CA 81-84; CANR 27; DLB 7,
38

Warhol, Andy 1928(?)-1987 . . . . **CLC 20**
See also BEST 89:4; CA 89-92; 121;
CANR 34

Warner, Francis (Robert le Plastrier)
1937- . . . . **CLC 14**
See also CA 53-56; CANR 11

Warner, Marina 1946- . . . . **CLC 59**
See also CA 65-68; CANR 21

Warner, Rex (Ernest) 1905-1986 . . . . **CLC 45**
See also CA 89-92; 119; DLB 15

Warner, Susan (Bogert)
1819-1885 . . . . **NCLC 31**
See also DLB 3, 42

Warner, Sylvia (Constance) Ashton
See Ashton-Warner, Sylvia (Constance)

Warner, Sylvia Townsend
1893-1978 . . . . **CLC 7, 19**
See also CA 61-64; 77-80; CANR 16;
DLB 34; MTCW

Warren, Mercy Otis 1728-1814 . . . **NCLC 13**
See also DLB 31

Warren, Robert Penn
1905-1989 . . . **CLC 1, 4, 6, 8, 10, 13, 18,
39, 53, 59; SSC 4**
See also AITN 1; CA 13-16R; 129;
CANR 10; CDALB 1968-1988; DLB 2,
48; DLBY 80, 89; MTCW; SATA 46, 63;
WLC

Warshofsky, Isaac
See Singer, Isaac Bashevis

Warton, Thomas 1728-1790 . . . . **LC 15**
See also DLB 104, 109

Waruk, Kona
See Harris, (Theodore) Wilson

Warung, Price 1855-1911 . . . . **TCLC 45**

Warwick, Jarvis
See Garner, Hugh

Washington, Alex
See Harris, Mark

Washington, Booker T(aliaferro)
1856-1915 . . . . **TCLC 10**
See also BLC 3; BW; CA 114; 125;
SATA 28

Wassermann, (Karl) Jakob
1873-1934 . . . . **TCLC 6**
See also CA 104; DLB 66

Wasserstein, Wendy 1950- . . . . . **CLC 32, 59**
See also CA 121; 129; CABS 3

Waterhouse, Keith (Spencer)
1929- . . . . **CLC 47**
See also CA 5-8R; CANR 38; DLB 13, 15;
MTCW

Waters, Roger 1944- . . . . **CLC 35**
See also Pink Floyd

Watkins, Frances Ellen
See Harper, Frances Ellen Watkins

Watkins, Gerrold
See Malzberg, Barry N(athaniel)

Watkins, Paul 1964- . . . . **CLC 55**
See also CA 132

Watkins, Vernon Phillips
1906-1967 . . . . **CLC 43**
See also CA 9-10; 25-28R; CAP 1; DLB 20

Watson, Irving S.
See Mencken, H(enry) L(ouis)

Watson, John H.
See Farmer, Philip Jose

Watson, Richard F.
See Silverberg, Robert

Waugh, Auberon (Alexander) 1939- . . **CLC 7**
See also CA 45-48; CANR 6, 22; DLB 14

Waugh, Evelyn (Arthur St. John)
1903-1966 . . . **CLC 1, 3, 8, 13, 19, 27, 44**
See also CA 85-88; 25-28R; CANR 22;
CDBLB 1914-1945; DLB 15; MTCW;
WLC

Waugh, Harriet 1944- . . . . **CLC 6**
See also CA 85-88; CANR 22

Ways, C. R.
See Blount, Roy (Alton) Jr.

Waystaff, Simon
See Swift, Jonathan

Webb, (Martha) Beatrice (Potter)
1858-1943 . . . . **TCLC 22**
See also Potter, Beatrice
See also CA 117

Webb, Charles (Richard) 1939- . . . . . . **CLC 7**
See also CA 25-28R

Webb, James H(enry) Jr. 1946- . . . . **CLC 22**
See also CA 81-84

Webb, Mary (Gladys Meredith)
1881-1927 . . . . **TCLC 24**
See also CA 123; DLB 34

Webb, Mrs. Sidney
See Webb, (Martha) Beatrice (Potter)

Webb, Phyllis 1927- . . . . **CLC 18**
See also CA 104; CANR 23; DLB 53

Webb, Sidney (James)
1859-1947 . . . . **TCLC 22**
See also CA 117

Webber, Andrew Lloyd . . . . **CLC 21**
See also Lloyd Webber, Andrew

Weber, Lenora Mattingly
1895-1971 . . . . **CLC 12**
See also CA 19-20; 29-32R; CAP 1;
SATA 2, 26

Webster, John 1579(?)-1634(?) . . . . **DC 2**
See also CDBLB Before 1660; DLB 58;
WLC

Webster, Noah 1758-1843 . . . . **NCLC 30**

Wedekind, (Benjamin) Frank(lin)
1864-1918 . . . . **TCLC 7**
See also CA 104; DLB 118

Weidman, Jerome 1913- . . . . **CLC 7**
See also AITN 2; CA 1-4R; CANR 1;
DLB 28

Weil, Simone (Adolphine)
1909-1943 . . . . **TCLC 23**
See also CA 117

Weinstein, Nathan
See West, Nathanael

Weinstein, Nathan von Wallenstein
See West, Nathanael

Weir, Peter (Lindsay) 1944- . . . . **CLC 20**
See also CA 113; 123

Weiss, Peter (Ulrich)
1916-1982 . . . . **CLC 3, 15, 51**
See also CA 45-48; 106; CANR 3; DLB 69

Weiss, Theodore (Russell)
1916- . . . . **CLC 3, 8, 14**
See also CA 9-12R; CAAS 2; DLB 5

Welch, (Maurice) Denton
1915-1948 . . . . **TCLC 22**
See also CA 121

Welch, James 1940- . . . . **CLC 6, 14, 52**
See also CA 85-88

Weldon, Fay
1933(?)- . . . . **CLC 6, 9, 11, 19, 36, 59**
See also CA 21-24R; CANR 16;
CDBLB 1960 to Present; DLB 14;
MTCW

Wellek, Rene 1903- . . . . **CLC 28**
See also CA 5-8R; CAAS 7; CANR 8;
DLB 63

Weller, Michael 1942- . . . . **CLC 10, 53**
See also CA 85-88

Weller, Paul 1958- . . . . **CLC 26**

Wellershoff, Dieter 1925- . . . . **CLC 46**
See also CA 89-92; CANR 16, 37

Welles, (George) Orson
1915-1985 . . . . **CLC 20**
See also CA 93-96; 117

Wellman, Mac 1945- . . . . **CLC 65**

Wellman, Manly Wade 1903-1986 . . **CLC 49**
See also CA 1-4R; 118; CANR 6, 16;
SATA 6, 47

Wells, Carolyn 1869(?)-1942 . . . . . . **TCLC 35**
See also CA 113; DLB 11

Woodruff, Robert W.
See Mencken, H(enry) L(ouis)

Woolf, (Adeline) Virginia
1882-1941 . . . **TCLC 1, 5, 20, 43; SSC 7**
See also CA 104; 130; CDBLB 1914-1945;
DLB 36, 100; MTCW; WLC

Woollcott, Alexander (Humphreys)
1887-1943 . . . . **TCLC 5**
See also CA 105; DLB 29

Wordsworth, Dorothy
1771-1855 . . . . **NCLC 25**
See also DLB 107

Wordsworth, William
1770-1850 . . . . **NCLC 12, 38; PC 4**
See also CDBLB 1789-1832; DLB 93, 107;
WLC

Wouk, Herman 1915- . . . . **CLC 1, 9, 38**
See also CA 5-8R; CANR 6, 33; DLBY 82;
MTCW

Wright, Charles (Penzel Jr.)
1935- . . . . **CLC 6, 13, 28**
See also CA 29-32R; CAAS 7; CANR 23,
36; DLBY 82; MTCW

Wright, Charles Stevenson 1932- . . . **CLC 49**
See also BLC 3; BW; CA 9-12R; CANR 26;
DLB 33

Wright, Jack R.
See Harris, Mark

Wright, James (Arlington)
1927-1980 . . . . **CLC 3, 5, 10, 28**
See also AITN 2; CA 49-52; 97-100;
CANR 4, 34; DLB 5; MTCW

Wright, Judith (Arandell)
1915- . . . . **CLC 11, 53**
See also CA 13-16R; CANR 31; MTCW;
SATA 14

Wright, L(aurali) R. . . . . **CLC 44**
See also CA 138

Wright, Richard B(ruce) 1937- . . . . . . **CLC 6**
See also CA 85-88; DLB 53

Wright, Richard (Nathaniel)
1908-1960 . . . **CLC 1, 3, 4, 9, 14, 21, 48,
74; SSC 2**
See also AAYA 5; BLC 3; BW; CA 108;
CDALB 1929-1941; DLB 76, 102;
DLBD 2; MTCW; WLC

Wright, Rick 1945- . . . . **CLC 35**
See also Pink Floyd

Wright, Rowland
See Wells, Carolyn

Wright, Stephen 1946- . . . . **CLC 33**

Wright, Willard Huntington 1888-1939
See Van Dine, S. S.
See also CA 115

Wright, William 1930- . . . . **CLC 44**
See also CA 53-56; CANR 7, 23

Wu Ch'eng-en 1500(?)-1582(?) . . . . **LC 7**

Wu Ching-tzu 1701-1754 . . . . **LC 2**

Wurlitzer, Rudolph 1938(?)- . . . **CLC 2, 4, 15**
See also CA 85-88

Wycherley, William 1641-1715 . . . . **LC 8, 21**
See also CDBLB 1660-1789; DLB 80

Wylie, Elinor (Morton Hoyt)
1885-1928 . . . . **TCLC 8**
See also CA 105; DLB 9, 45

Wylie, Philip (Gordon) 1902-1971. . . **CLC 43**
See also CA 21-22; 33-36R; CAP 2; DLB 9

Wyndham, John
See Harris, John (Wyndham Parkes Lucas)
Beynon

Wyss, Johann David Von
1743-1818 . . . . **NCLC 10**
See also MAICYA; SATA 27, 29

Yakumo Koizumi
See Hearn, (Patricio) Lafcadio (Tessima
Carlos)

Yanez, Jose Donoso
See Donoso (Yanez), Jose

Yanovsky, Basile S.
See Yanovsky, V(assily) S(emenovich)

Yanovsky, V(assily) S(emenovich)
1906-1989 . . . . **CLC 2, 18**
See also CA 97-100; 129

Yates, Richard 1926- . . . . **CLC 7, 8, 23**
See also CA 5-8R; CANR 10; DLB 2;
DLBY 81

Yeats, W. B.
See Yeats, William Butler

Yeats, William Butler
1865-1939 . . . . **TCLC 1, 11, 18, 31**
See also CA 104; 127; CDBLB 1890-1914;
DLB 10, 19, 98; MTCW; WLC

Yehoshua, Abraham B. 1936- . . . **CLC 13, 31**
See also CA 33-36R

Yep, Laurence Michael 1948- . . . . . . **CLC 35**
See also AAYA 5; CA 49-52; CANR 1;
CLR 3, 17; DLB 52; MAICYA; SATA 7,
69

Yerby, Frank G(arvin)
1916-1991 . . . . **CLC 1, 7, 22**
See also BLC 3; BW; CA 9-12R; 136;
CANR 16; DLB 76; MTCW

Yesenin, Sergei Alexandrovich
See Esenin, Sergei (Alexandrovich)

Yevtushenko, Yevgeny (Alexandrovich)
1933- . . . . **CLC 1, 3, 13, 26, 51**
See also CA 81-84; CANR 33; MTCW

Yezierska, Anzia 1885(?)-1970 . . . . . **CLC 46**
See also CA 126; 89-92; DLB 28; MTCW

Yglesias, Helen 1915- . . . . **CLC 7, 22**
See also CA 37-40R; CANR 15; MTCW

Yokomitsu Riichi 1898-1947 . . . . . . **TCLC 47**

York, Jeremy
See Creasey, John

York, Simon
See Heinlein, Robert A(nson)

Yorke, Henry Vincent 1905-1974 . . . **CLC 13**
See also Green, Henry
See also CA 85-88; 49-52

Young, Al(bert James) 1939- . . . . **CLC 19**
See also BLC 3; BW; CA 29-32R;
CANR 26; DLB 33

Young, Andrew (John) 1885-1971 . . . . **CLC 5**
See also CA 5-8R; CANR 7, 29

Young, Collier
See Bloch, Robert (Albert)

Young, Edward 1683-1765 . . . . **LC 3**
See also DLB 95

Young, Neil 1945- . . . . **CLC 17**
See also CA 110

Yourcenar, Marguerite
1903-1987 . . . . **CLC 19, 38, 50**
See also CA 69-72; CANR 23; DLB 72;
DLBY 88; MTCW

Yurick, Sol 1925- . . . . **CLC 6**
See also CA 13-16R; CANR 25

Zamiatin, Yevgenii
See Zamyatin, Evgeny Ivanovich

Zamyatin, Evgeny Ivanovich
1884-1937 . . . . **TCLC 8, 37**
See also CA 105

Zangwill, Israel 1864-1926. . . . . . . **TCLC 16**
See also CA 109; DLB 10

Zappa, Francis Vincent Jr. 1940-
See Zappa, Frank
See also CA 108

Zappa, Frank . . . . **CLC 17**
See also Zappa, Francis Vincent Jr.

Zaturenska, Marya 1902-1982. . . . **CLC 6, 11**
See also CA 13-16R; 105; CANR 22

Zelazny, Roger (Joseph) 1937- . . . . . **CLC 21**
See also AAYA 7; CA 21-24R; CANR 26;
DLB 8; MTCW; SATA 39, 57

Zhdanov, Andrei A(lexandrovich)
1896-1948 . . . . **TCLC 18**
See also CA 117

Zhukovsky, Vasily 1783-1852 . . . . **NCLC 35**

Ziegenhagen, Eric . . . . **CLC 55**

Zimmer, Jill Schary
See Robinson, Jill

Zimmerman, Robert
See Dylan, Bob

Zindel, Paul 1936- . . . . **CLC 6, 26**
See also AAYA 2; CA 73-76; CANR 31;
CLR 3; DLB 7, 52; MAICYA; MTCW;
SATA 16, 58

Zinov'Ev, A. A.
See Zinoviev, Alexander (Aleksandrovich)

Zinoviev, Alexander (Aleksandrovich)
1922- . . . . **CLC 19**
See also CA 116; 133; CAAS 10

Zoilus
See Lovecraft, H(oward) P(hillips)

Zola, Emile 1840-1902 . . . **TCLC 1, 6, 21, 41**
See also CA 104; WLC

Zoline, Pamela 1941- . . . . **CLC 62**

Zorrilla y Moral, Jose 1817-1893 . . **NCLC 6**

Zoshchenko, Mikhail (Mikhailovich)
1895-1958 . . . . **TCLC 15**
See also CA 115

Zuckmayer, Carl 1896-1977 . . . . **CLC 18**
See also CA 69-72; DLB 56

Zuk, Georges
See Skelton, Robin

Zukofsky, Louis
1904-1978 . . . . **CLC 1, 2, 4, 7, 11, 18**
See also CA 9-12R; 77-80; CANR 39;
DLB 5; MTCW

Zweig, Paul 1935-1984 . . . . **CLC 34, 42**
See also CA 85-88; 113

Zweig, Stefan   1881-1942 . . . . **TCLC 17**
  See also CA 112; DLB 81, 118

Literary Criticism Series
Cumulative Topic Index

This index lists all topic entries in the Gale Literary Criticism Series *Classical and Medieval Literature Criticism, Contemporary Literary Criticism, Literature Criticism from 1400 to 1800, Nineteenth-Century Literature Criticism,* and *Twentieth-Century Literary Criticism.*

CMLC Cumulative Nationality Index

CMLC Cumulative Title Index

515

CMLC Cumulative Critic Index

Zeydel, Edwin H.
  Gottfried von Strassburg **10**:258
  Wolfram von Eschenbach **5**:307

Zhirmunsky, Victor
  Book of Dede Korkut **8**:96

Zimmer, Heinrich
  Arabian Nights **2**:32
  *Sir Gawain and the Green
    Knight* **2**:187

Zweig, Stefan
  Cicero, Marcus Tullius **3**:225

Critic Index